C000174979

A HANDBOOK FOR TRAVELLERS IN INDIA, PAKISTAN, NEPAL, BANGLADESH AND SRI LANKA (CEYLON)

"India and the Golden Chersonese
And utmost Indian Isle Taprobane,
Dusk faces with white silken turbans wreathed."

—MILTON, *Par. Reg.*, iv. 74-76

Contributors to this edition of the *Handbook* include
Mildred Archer and W. G. Archer on art
Penelope Chetwode on Khajuraho
Elizabeth von Fürer Haimendorf on Nepal
J. D. A. Stainton on Nepalese flora

A HANDBOOK FOR TRAVELLERS IN INDIA, PAKISTAN, NEPAL, BANGLADESH AND SRI LANKA (CEYLON)

TWENTY-SECOND EDITION

Edited by

Professor L. F. Rushbrook Williams

LONDON

JOHN MURRAY, ALBEMARLE STREET

1982

THE FOLLOWING ABBREVIATIONS ARE USED IN THIS BOOK

a-c	Air-conditioned.	*m.*	Mile.
A.H.	Year of Hijra (the Hegira).	*m.g.*	Metre gauge.
b.g.	Broad gauge.	*n.g.*	Narrow gauge.
Cants.	Cantonments.	*n.p.*	"naye paise"—new decimal currency.
C.H.	Circuit House.	*N.W.F.*	North-West Frontier.
C. of S.	Church of Scotland.	*p.*	Page.
D.B.	Dak Bungalow.	*P.W.D.*	Public Works Dept.
D.B.K.	With cook.	*pop.*	Population.
D.F.O.	Divisional Forest Officer.	*R.*	Refreshment Room.
dt.	District.	*R.C.*	Roman Catholic.
E.I.Company	East India Company.	*R.H.*	Rest House.
ft.	Feet.	*R.R.*	Retiring Rooms.
G.H.	Guest House.	*Rs.*	Rupees.
I.A.C.	Indian Airlines.	*ry.*	Railway.
I.B.	Inspection Bungalow.	*stn.*	Station.
in.	Inch.	*s.m.*	Station-master.
H.	Hotel.	*T.B.*	Tourist Bungalow.
Jn.	Junction.	*T.L.*	Travellers' Lodge.
		yds.	Yards.

* This sign indicates a centre for excursions, with accommodation.

First published 1975
Reprinted 1978, 1982

Printed in Great Britain
by CLARK CONSTABLE LTD., Hopetoun Street
Printers to the University of Edinburgh
and published by JOHN MURRAY (PUBLISHERS) LTD
ISBN 0 7195 2828 3

PREFACE TO THE TWENTY-SECOND EDITION

THE *Handbook for Travellers in India* was originally published by Mr John Murray in three volumes for the Bombay, Madras and Bengal Presidencies. The first of these parts appeared in 1859, the Bengal volume not until 1882. The fourth volume dealing with the Punjab and North-West India was added in 1883. They were prepared by Captain E. B. Eastwick, M.P., who made long visits to India in the fifties, sixties and seventies of the 19th century in order to collect the material for them on the spot.

These volumes were revised and brought up to date on several occasions, and in 1892 the *Handbook* was issued in a single volume. The description of Sri Lanka (Ceylon) was written by Sir Arthur Gordon (afterwards Lord Stanmore); and the whole *Handbook* passed through the hands of Sir George W. Forrest, then Keeper of Records to the Government of India. A second edition of the consolidated *Handbook* was published in 1894.

The third edition was issued in 1898, the general revision being undertaken by Mr Norwood Young. The next, the fourth edition, which was a reprint of the third, brought up to date, was prepared in 1901 by Dr J. Burgess, C.I.E. The fifth was a thorough revision, undertaken by Mr Herbert C. Fanshawe, C.S.I., in 1904; and in that the Ceylon part was revised by Mr C. G. Ryan. The sixth, which was a reprint of the fifth, brought up to date, was also undertaken by Mr Fanshawe in 1907. The seventh in 1908 was the work of the same editor, and was mainly a reprint of the fifth. The sections on Burma and Ceylon were finally revised with the assistance of Mr G. E. Marindin and Mr C. G. Ryan.

The next general revision was made in the eighth edition of 1911 by Mr Fanshawe. By 1913 another edition was called for, and a complete revision in the ninth was made by Mr Charles E. Buckland, C.I.E. The tenth edition of 1919, which was likewise a general revision, was also prepared by Mr Buckland; but it suffered from the disabilities arising from the First World War. In 1920 a reprint of the 1919 edition was issued, with some necessary changes. The revision for the eleventh (1924) and the twelfth (1926) editions was undertaken by Sir John G. Cumming. The thirteenth edition, published in 1929, and the fourteenth, in 1933, were supervised by Sir Evan Cotton. The fifteenth and sixteenth editions were the work of Colonel Sir Gordon Hearn, one time Chief Engineer, Indian State Railways.

The seventeenth and eighteenth editions, the work of Sir Arthur C. Lothian, were extensively re-shaped both to take account of post-War changes and to divide the Directory from the Index for greater ease of reference. The general pattern thus set was followed by Professor Rushbrook Williams in planning the nineteenth, the twentieth, and the twenty-first, editions. The conditions to be encountered by travellers in the countries covered by the *Handbook* now change so rapidly that the task of noting new developments and revising earlier statements becomes ever more extensive. This present twenty-second edition which covers the overland route, Package Tours and notes the greatly increased official encouragement of the tourist industry, will, it is hoped, be found serviceable by the traveller of today. The sections dealing with *Hints to Travellers*, with *Motoring*, and with *Art* have been completely rewritten. So many tourists now visit Nepal, and so few go to Burma, that the former country replaces the latter in this edition of the *Handbook*. The emergence of East Pakistan into the independent People's Republic of Bangladesh has also been noted.

References in the text assume a knowledge not always possessed by the tourist. A section of the Introductory Information has accordingly been allotted to an historical outline. The Index, still distinct from the Directory, supplements this outline. The Directory gives the latest information available as to accommodation and hotels but it is advisable to check this locally, as the situation in this respect alters quickly, and it can scarcely be hoped that the Editor has been able to keep pace with all the changes involved. India, Pakistan and Sri Lanka (Ceylon) have Tourist Bureaux which are invaluable to the traveller. Full use should be made of them. In India, many State Governments maintain local Bureaux which supplement the offices set up by the Central Government. Against the smaller places are shown the principal objects of interest in the vicinity, not only as a guide in planning tours but also because air and motor transport have brought most of them within easy reach. Folding maps are placed near the end of the relevant text in order to facilitate reference. The book should also be useful as a Gazetteer. The map in the pocket is new, and the other maps and plans have been revised where possible. Population figures are estimates based on the latest Census Reports.

The spelling followed has been, nearly always, that used by the Indian Survey Department, but takes account of modifications introduced since 1947. This system makes exceptions in favour of the older, though irregular, spelling of certain well-known places. The spelling of the Survey Department, Sri Lanka, has been followed.

The routes shown in this book cover all the places likely to be of interest to tourists, and should constitute an adequate framework for the eventual programme. Any one of the well-known Agencies will place experience at the disposal of the tourist and work out tours in detail. Most of them use this book.

This latest edition owes much to the assistance received from the official representatives in London of the countries concerned, from their Tourist Bureaux and from the Motoring Associations. The Editor is also indebted to many friends—among whom he would like to make special mention of Mr Günter Köpf and Mr John Keay—for information regarding areas with which they have special acquaintance and to numerous correspondents who have supplied corrections and modifications to the text of earlier Editions.

To all these he would like to render his grateful thanks.

John Murray desires to associate himself with the Editor in according his best thanks to all who have lent their assistance.

It is impossible, when conditions in the East are changing so rapidly, to ensure freedom from error in a book containing such a multiplicity of detail. The Publisher therefore hopes that the indulgent traveller will kindly point out any inaccuracies with a view to their correction on the first opportunity. Communications may be addressed to John Murray, 50 Albemarle Street, London, W1X 4BD.

CONTENTS

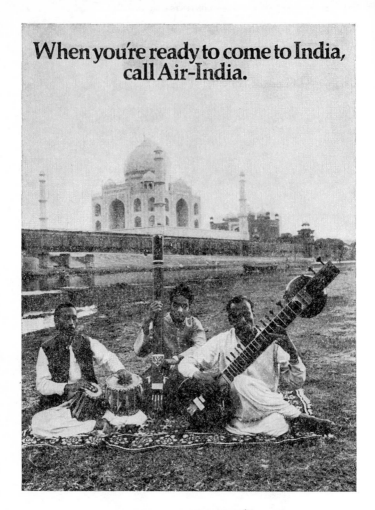

INTRODUCTORY INFORMATION

SEASON FOR VISIT

The best season for a visit to the plains of India, Pakistan, Nepal and Bangladesh lies between 15th November and the end of March; but the Indian Government Tourist Bureau now offers attractive "hot weather" tours, mainly covering hill stations, from May onward at concession rates. In October and April the heat is apt to be severe. Up to 15th October and after 10th April the weather may be trying—much more so than in July, August and September, when rain cools the atmosphere. In Sri Lanka, August and September are agreeable months during the S.W. monsoon period, while December, January and February are pleasant when the N.E. monsoon is blowing in the Bay of Bengal.

The historic P. & O. mail and passenger services between Britain and India have ceased; but cruise liners call at Karachi, Bombay, Calcutta and Colombo, which are also served by American President Lines, British India Steam Navigation Co., Eastern Shipping Corporation, Lloyd Triestino, Messageries Maritimes and Scindia Steam Navigation Co. Most travellers now arrive by air, while for the adventurous the overland route from Europe via Turkey (see page 12) holds many attractions.

TOURIST CARDS, VISAS, ETC.

The countries covered in this book encourage tourism; but citizens of countries outside the Commonwealth require visas for India, Pakistan, Bangladesh and Sri Lanka if they stay more than three weeks. For certain areas noted in the text special permits are necessary. All visitors to Nepal require a visa obtainable at the Royal Nepalese Embassies in Delhi and other capitals. Bangladesh demands visas from *everyone* except Indians.

British tourists intending to visit India are advised to obtain Tourist Cards from the India Tourist Office, 21 New Bond Street, London. For Pakistan, the Press Attachés of the Missions will be helpful. In Pakistan, the Director of Tourism, Karachi; and in Sri Lanka, the Government Tourist Bureau, Colombo, readily supply advice and information. The services of a reliable Travel Agency are invaluable. The Agency can advise about package tours (see page 4) at concession rates—designed to meet the needs of a wide variety of travellers; it can also supply essential information about passports, visas, and about the certificates of vaccination against smallpox, cholera, typhoid, and yellow fever on which the Health authorities of many countries now insist.

LANGUAGE

English is officially recognised, widely used and understood in large towns and centres of tourist attraction. But a few words of Hindi or Urdu are very useful in India and Pakistan.

LOCAL CURRENCIES

In India, Pakistan, Nepal and Sri Lanka the unit is the rupee, divided into 16 annas and 100 paisa, except in Sri Lanka, where it consists of 100 cents. In Bangladesh the unit is called the *taka*—equivalent to the rupee.

In Spring 1981 the exchange rates were as under

India	Rs. 18.10	(per £1)	8.18 (US$)
Pakistan	21.55	,,	9.87 ,,
Bangladesh	Takas 34.95	,,	15.88 ,,
Nepal	26.40	,,	12.00 ,,
Sri Lanka	38.62	,,	17.55 ,,

It is important to keep bank receipts when money is changed as they may be asked for when reconverting rupees into foreign currency on departure.

EXPENSES

By Western standards both accommodation and travel on the subcontinent are reasonable. Even in the major cities (where many luxury hotels with international standards and tariffs have recently been constructed) it is still possible to find comfortable accommodation at 60 to 100 rupees per night for double room with breakfast. In the larger cities inexpensive accommodation is available in Y.M.C.A.s and Y.W.C.A.s: while many tourist centres have Youth Hostels, where accommodation is spartan but cheap. Travel Agencies and Tourist Bureaux should be consulted. Outside the main cities there is a vast network of tourist Rest Houses, Travellers Lodges and Dak Bungalows (see p. 6). Prices vary from 10 to 100 rupees per night for a single room, depending on the status and furnishing of the place. Many are comfortable and delightfully situated. Tourist Bureaux should be contacted about reservations and conditions.

Food is generally cheap. Dinner for one in a good restaurant in a major city can be had for 25 or 40 rupees. Spirits, even beer, on the other hand, are comparatively expensive—imported liquor even more so.

Internal air travel costs about 80 n.p. (naye paise) per mile and distances are great. Visitors have to buy air tickets in foreign currency, but a $375 ticket can be bought which allows flying anywhere for 15 days. First-class air-conditioned travel on the railways—extremely luxurious—costs a little less than air travel. Ordinary first-class rail tickets cost about 30 n.p. per mile and second-class about 7 n.p. per mile. Buses are also cheap, 10-15 n.p. per mile. On longer routes some are fitted with air-conditioning and reclining seats.

Taxi charges vary considerably, depending on the type of journey. In the cities they are usually metered, but for longer journeys it is best to agree a lump sum or a per-mile rate of about 1.50 rupees per mile. Many local Tourist Bureaux operate a few cars with fixed charges for visiting places of local interest. Most of the larger cities have their own distinctive forms of "popular" transport —motor rickshaws in Delhi, Bangalore, Karachi and Lahore; horse-drawn landaus in Bombay; hand-pulled rickshaws in Calcutta, etc.—all of which are cheap.

ELECTRIC CURRENT

This is usually 220 A.C. 50 cycles; but some places are still on D.C. Travellers should enquire before using electric shavers, etc.

MOTORING

Cars, buses, jeeps and Land Rovers are now found everywhere, since within the last few years roads in India, Pakistan, Nepal, Bangladesh and Sri Lanka have greatly improved. The National Highways of India and Pakistan now link all important places: few large rivers lack road bridges. The main Oil Companies maintain chains of shops supplying oil and petrol: local mechanics in rural areas are clever at extemporising emergency repairs, but full servicing facilities are seldom available outside the large towns, where the principal manufacturers of British, German, French, Japanese and American cars maintain their own agencies.

The Automobile Association Offices are very helpful in advising motorists about routes, service stations, spare parts and the like. The offices are to be found in Bombay, New Delhi, Allahabad, Calcutta, Madras and Bangalore for India: in Karachi and Lahore for Pakistan: and in Colombo for Sri Lanka. Addresses and telephone numbers are available in Hotels and in local Tourist Bureaux. For touring in Pakistan, local advice is readily obtainable from the bureaux in Peshawar, Rawalpindi, Murree, Quetta, Swat and Gilgit.

Road maps are obtainable from the A.A. offices, from the Shell Company in large towns and from the Tourist Bureaux. Some of the "official" maps, which are not always up to date, may need checking with local information.

The import of cars is strictly controlled, but facilities are granted to tourists bringing their own vehicles which they will later take out. To enjoy these facilities, careful documentation is essential—a Tourist Agency or A.A. offices in the tourist's own country should be consulted.

Touring by car is best done in the cold weather, and even then difficulties may be encountered away from main roads. Advice from A.A. offices is available particularly about tyre pressures, simple un-ditching equipment, precautions against glare and heat, food supplies *en route*, and the like. Sunglasses of the Polaroid type and salt tablets to be taken after long exposure to the sun are advisable, as is a good eye lotion—roads are often dusty.

WINTERING IN PAKISTAN, NEPAL AND N. INDIA

Warm overcoats are essential for nights, early mornings and on drives before the sun rises or after it sets. While the midday is always warm, sometimes hot, the evening dews may be so heavy as to wet an overcoat. Also, the cold of the nights and mornings is often very sharp, so that the secret of dressing is to begin the day in things that can be thrown off as the heat increases, and can be resumed as the cold returns. Sleeveless pullovers are therefore very useful adjuncts. In some places in the north in the winter months the temperature will fall between 40° or 50° within the two hours on either side of sunset, and the risks of serious chills are very great. It has often been said with truth that more illness is contracted in South Asia from local chills than from the heat. Real home winter clothing and an anorak or a rough sheepskin coat which can be purchased locally may be needed if it is intended to visit the mountainous regions of the Himalayas and Karakorams. On the hills of the North-West Frontier Province, icy winds from the Hindu Kush are formidable.

IN THE SOUTH—S. INDIA, ALSO BANGLADESH AND SRI LANKA

Throughout the South,[1] and at most times in Karachi, Dacca, Bombay and Calcutta, tropical clothing is required. Clothes which do not have to be ironed are the most practical. It is advisable to buy them in England as non-iron material is difficult to find in India.

A traveller in Sri Lanka and Bangladesh will seldom require any but the lightest of clothing, except in the mountains, where the temperature becomes

[1] This may be taken as applying to all places S. of Hyderabad (A.P.), including Bangladesh and Sri Lanka but excluding the higher plateau of Mysore, and the various hill-stations.

cooler as he ascends. At Kandy a light overcoat, and at Nuwara Eliya warm wraps and underclothing are necessary.

Arrangements for washing clothes, usually charged by the piece, can be made at most halting-places.

Tourists going into camp, or visiting game reserves—of which there are wonderful examples in India, Pakistan, Nepal, Bangladesh and Sri Lanka—(see p. 68) should avoid bright-coloured clothing in favour of something like khaki drill.

Protection against the sun is essential, but the old-fashioned topi or sun hat has been replaced by a felt hat and glare glasses of the Polaroid type and of proper optical quality. After long exposure to the sun it is now usual to drink plenty of water with salt tablets, obtainable from chemists.

BEDDING

For nights spent in ordinary Dak Bungalows—not Travellers' Lodges or Rest Houses—a sleeping-bag with a cotton lining is useful but no longer essential for travellers who adopt the modern practice of using the internal airline services to get from tourist-centre to tourist-centre, and then making day-excursions by car. For train journeys by night, pillows and bedding are provided only on luxury expresses but can be hired at some of the main Railway Stations.

PACKAGE TOURS

Package Tours, planned and paid for in advance in the tourist's own country, are being used more and more widely by those taking a short holiday in the regions covered by this *Handbook*. At the time of writing (1977-78) some typical examples of these tours and of their cost are as under:

> A 16-day escorted tour of India (Delhi, Agra, Jaipur, Udaipur, Bombay) is available in London at costs ranging from £786 with standard hotel accommodation and from £856 in superior hotels.
>
> A 20-day escorted tour in the Himalayas (Delhi, Agra, Chandigarh, Simla, Katrain, Kulu Valley, Alhilal, Dharamsala, Jammu, Srinagar) costs about £930.
>
> A 16-day tour of southern India (Bombay, Bangalore, Mysore, Madurai, Tiruchirapalli, Madras, Manchipuram, Covelong) can be had from £878.
>
> A longer 21-day tour including Sri Lanka as well (Anuradhapura, Sigiriya, Kandy, Colombo) costs from about £1100 upwards.
>
> Specialised tours are also available covering places of notable archaeological or architectural interest.

Details of these and many other package tours can be had from Messrs Thos. Cook & Son and other Travel Agents. The Government of India Tourist Office supplies a brochure giving details of tours covering India by all the principal operators.

INDEPENDENT TOURING

Travellers who have more time to spend than a Package Tour permits, or who prefer to plan their own journeys, will find Messrs Thos. Cook & Son, and other well-known Agents, as well as the Government Tourist Bureaux located in many large towns and in the foyers of hotels, very helpful in suggesting routes, checking timings, arranging plane, railway and hotel bookings and giving up-to-date advice, while their descriptions of important places and of sites of tourist interest will enable the traveller to select exactly what he wants to see.

DOMESTIC AIR SERVICES

N.B. As routes are sometimes changed, these services should be checked with a Travel Agency.

The following places in India and outside are at present accessible by regular air-services of I.A.C.: Agartala, Agra, Ahmedabad, Allahabad, Amritsar, Aurangabad, Bagdogra, Bangalore, Belgaum, Bhavnagar, Bhopal, Bhubaneshwar, Bhuj, Bombay, Calcutta, Chandigarh, Cochin, Coimbatore, Dabolim (Goa), Delhi, Dibrugarh, Dimapur, Gauhati, Gorakhpur, Gwalior, Hyderabad, Imphal, Indore, Jabalpur, Jaipur, Jammu, Jamnagar, Jodhpur, Jorhat, Kanpur, Kathmandu, Keshod, Khajuraho, Leh, Lilabari, Lucknow, Madras, Madurai, Male, Mangalore, Nagpur, Patna, Porbandar, Port Blair, Pune, Raipur, Rajkot, Ranchi, Silchar, Srinagar, Tezpur, Tiruchirapalli, Tirupati, Trivandrum, Udaipur, Vadodara, Varanasi, Vijayawada, Vishakhapatnam.

In *Pakistan*, the domestic services of P.I.A. link up the following places by frequent flights: Chitral, Dehra Ismail Khan, Gilgit, Gwadar, Hyderabad, Jiwani, Karachi, Lahore, Lyallpur, Mohenjodaro, Multan, Nawabshah, Panjgur, Pasni, Peshawar, Quetta, Rawalpindi, Sui, Sukkur.

In *Bangladesh*, Chittagong, Cox's Bazar, Dacca, Dinajpur, Ishurdi, Jessore, Lalmanirhat, Shamshernagar and Sylhet have airports, and domestic air services are being gradually restored.

When using any of these air services it is most important to book in advance and then to confirm the reservation in person at the city office of the airline.

RAILWAYS

The first railway in India was opened between Bombay and Thana as early as 1853. India now possesses one of the world's largest rail networks with a high reputation for safety and punctuality if not for speed. The trains are very popular and travelling on them provides a unique insight into the local way of life.

The system is divided into seven zones each publishing its own timetable. Alternatively there is Newman's Indian Bradshaw which gives details of trains and air services for the whole system. On most main lines the track is broad gauge (5 ft. 6 in.) allowing for roomy carriages with corridors. Metre gauge still predominates in the old Princely States and narrow gauge (2 ft. or 2 ft. 6 in.) on the mountain railways.

In view of the long distances nearly all compartments have seats designed to convert to bunks for the night. No extra charge is made for a berth. Most passengers bring their own bedding (bed-roll or sleeping-bag), but it can sometimes be hired at major stations. Only in first-class air-conditioned coaches is bedding free of charge. For any journey which involves a night on the train advance booking is essential and journey tickets are only issued on evidence of a reservation ticket. Buying tickets can be a tiresome business; an Agency or hotel employee willing to handle it is a great asset. An *Indrail Pass* has been introduced which allows unlimited travel on all trains. It is by far the most economical way of covering long distances. Full details can be obtained at the Government of India Tourist Office or at the Rail Tourist Guide in Bombay, Delhi, Calcutta and Madras.

Although many long-distance trains now have restaurant cars, meals whether from the train or station restaurants are usually ordered at the beginning of the journey and delivered to your compartment. European as well as Indian food is available on most services.

There are a few wholly air-conditioned expresses like the Delhi-Calcutta

"Rajdhani" with air-conditioned sleeper and chair accommodation, and the Karachi-Lahore-Rawalpindi service in Pakistan. Air-conditioned coaches are attached to a few other mainline services, but throughout the winter months ordinary first class will be found comfortable if not luxurious. Four- and two-berth (coupé) compartments are normal either with a corridor or with their own private lavatory. Sometimes there is also a shower. A considerable quantity of luggage can be stowed in the compartments but care should be taken to discourage pilferage by closing all shutters at night. Station porters, distinguished by their armbands and red turbans, are trustworthy and should be paid 1 to 1·5 rupees per load. Railway officials are generally helpful and always speak some English.

These general remarks also apply broadly to Pakistan and Bangladesh, which are served by their own railway systems. Travelling conditions in Pakistan are similar to those in India; while in Bangladesh railway communications cover smaller distances through a more densely-populated terrain.

DAK BUNGALOWS AND GOVERNMENT REST HOUSES

The Governments of India, Pakistan, Nepal, Bangladesh and Sri Lanka maintain rest houses in almost all the places which their officials, and those who travel on official business, are required to visit. In addition, various Services of the respective Governments—Public Works, Forest, Irrigation—maintain their own special rest houses, generally called Inspection Bungalows.

All fall into certain grades—Dak Bungalows, Inspection Bungalows, Circuit Houses. But the point which the traveller must remember is that they are intended for Government Officials, who always have the first call upon them. Circuit Houses, in particular, are primarily for the use of high officials like judges or ministers on tour; the ordinary traveller can only stay in them by special favour, and even then his reservation may be cancelled at the last moment to fall in with official needs. Inspection Bungalows of the P.W.D., Forest, Irrigation and other Services are also only available to the traveller by special permission; but this can often be arranged if application is made in good time to the appropriate Office (address from Tourist Bureau), or apply to local Collector. Many of these Inspection Bungalows are situated in beautiful and remote spots; they, along with the Circuit Houses, are well furnished and well maintained, with a cook and other servants. The charges are moderate and fixed; notices of what has to be paid are displayed.

This is also true of the simplest form of accommodation—the Dak Bungalows, which are very numerous, and very cheap to stay in. The accommodation is limited to a few rooms, each with a bathroom. There is a central sitting-room where meals can be served by the man in charge, if he is given notice in good time. Bedding is not as a rule provided. Residence is generally limited to 24 hours, but can be extended if the accommodation is not wanted by new arrivals. Some of the Dak Bungalows have fallen out of use now that road communications between large towns and outlying areas have improved; and in planning a tour off the beaten track, the traveller should find out from the nearest Tourist Bureau whether particular Dak Bungalows are still in operation, and should arrange for notice of his arrival to be sent ahead.

The ordinary tourist, however, finds himself less and less dependent upon this type of accommodation when he keeps to what are now the well-organised circuits of principal attractions. In India, Pakistan, Nepal, Bangladesh and Sri Lanka; special provision for his needs exists in the shape of Travellers' Lodges, Tourist Bungalows and Tourist Rest Houses now found in increasing numbers; and the visitor is urged to make frequent and systematic use of the services of the various Tourist Bureaux and Information Centres in finding out the location of these Lodges, their charges (which are moderate, but higher than those of Dak Bungalows) and in booking accommodation.

THE FOOD OF THE COUNTRY

Countries covered in this *Handbook* can produce a high standard of cooking, although the food may appear strange to the traveller. The climates affect the flavour of meat, fowl, game, eggs and fish; so that cooked in the European way the results may be disappointing. But with the seasoning characteristic of local cooking they are excellent. Fish is generally good: the Pomfret of Bombay and the Prawns and Mango Fish of Calcutta as well as the Smoked Hilsa of Dacca are renowned. They are sent long distances in refrigerated containers. Fresh river fish is generally best cooked in the local way. Quail, snipe, teal, duck, partridge and sand grouse often appear on the menu in the cold weather.

Many localities in India, Pakistan, Nepal, Bangladesh and Sri Lanka have their own specialities, about which Tourist Centres and Hotels will provide information. The India Tourist Development Corporation publishes an excellent brochure: *India: A Gourmet's Paradise,* to be obtained from Information Centres and Travel Agents.

Food can be roughly "zoned" as follows. In the Northern parts of India, Pakistan and also in Nepal, there is a strong tradition of Mughal cooking—pilaus and roasts, rich and sumptuous. This is also true of Rajasthan. In the East, West Bengal and Bangladesh, as well as in Sri Lanka, fish cooking is famous, rivalled only in the West by Maharashtra and Gujarat. As travellers go South and West, they will find a very strong vegetarian tradition: food tends to be more liquid in form and much hotter.

The traveller would be wise to take certain sensible precautions against digestive upsets and to carry with him such remedies as his own doctor may suggest. Antibiotics are widely used, but can be obtained locally only on prescription and are expensive, so that it is wise to bring a supply. In many modern hotels, notices indicate that the tap water is drinkable; but many people prefer the bottled waters of proprietary brands which are readily available. Off the beaten track unboiled water should be avoided; tea, which involves boiling the water used, is safer; but tinned or bottled milk should be carried.

PROHIBITION

"Hard" drinks are not easy to obtain in India, Bangladesh and Pakistan outside hotels. Prohibition is a matter for State Governments, whose regulations differ. It is strict in Gujarat and Mount Abu. Pakistan is mostly "dry"—in the sense that alcoholic drinks are unobtainable rather than prohibited—outside the larger towns.

Foreigners enjoy certain exemptions, of which details can be obtained from the Tourist Offices. The most usual system is a liquor permit, entitling the holder to a monthly quota. In Pakistan, the signature of a simple form indicating that the Tourist is a non-Muslim usually suffices, and even this is often not required. In all the countries covered in this *Handbook*, imported spirits and wines are very expensive; but distilleries exist to supply local needs, and their products—rum, gin and beers—are palatable. Locally produced whiskies will not appeal to travelling Scots.

HEALTH

There is no need to expect illness. It is best to avoid heavy beer or spirits until after sundown. Maintenance of good general health will normally combat indispositions, but heavy colds, sore throats and flu are apt to occur and it is therefore wise to carry antidotes. The necessity of using warm overcoats or pullovers early or late in the day has been mentioned. Malaria is still a problem in the Subcontinent and ideas on prevention have changed recently (1980) and may change again. Check with the Information Department at the Ross Institute of Tropical Medicine, Keppel St., London WC1. West of longitude 80° and in Sri Lanka, Paludrine is satisfactory. Eastwards, it is necessary to use two drugs together, Maloprim and Nivaquine. Avoidance of fatigue is necessary upon the occurrence of any indisposition, and only light food should be taken until it passes away. There are excellent doctors in every large town; and most hotels have a medical man at call. The Ross Institute publish a useful little book: *The Preservation of Personal Health in Warm Climates.*

SHOOTING

The import of firearms and cartridges requires a licence; but there are concessions for tourists, of which Travel Agencies can supply details. An Arms Possession Licence, which can be obtained from the appropriate Diplomatic Mission in the tourist's own country, will be needed.

In India, because of the alarming depletion of big game by poaching, poisoning and by the commercial exploitation of forest resources, hunting is very strictly controlled. In many States, the shooting of tigers and panthers is entirely forbidden except for the destruction of man-eaters and cattle-killers by the appropriate District Officials. To avoid disappointment, tourists who are looking for big-game shooting should enquire from the Official Tourist Bureaux about the availability of forest blocks and should put themselves in the hands of one of the reputable Sporting Agencies whom the Bureaux can recommend. The Agency will arrange for the necessary permits, which specify how many animals, and of which kinds, may be shot. The same Agency can also arrange—with much less trouble—small game shooting, which is still good, although no longer to be found almost everywhere. There are Game Protection Societies in India, and many beautiful Nature Reserves. Certain species are carefully protected.

Conditions in Pakistan are somewhat easier: small-game shooting is easily obtained, and in Provinces such as Sind is very good. Some species, like the Lesser Bustard, are protected: a local Sporting Agency will advise. In the mountainous areas, snow leopard, ibex, markhor, bear and other big game are still common; but licences to shoot them are required. Here too, certain species are protected. In Bangladesh, tigers are still found in the Sunderbans, but, as in India, are protected.

FISHING

The subcontinent is something like an angler's paradise.

In the rivers and lakes of India, Bangladesh and Pakistan, fishing is very good, particularly for trout and mahseer. So much so, indeed, that Package Tours specially arranged for anglers are laid on by some Agents. The trout fishing in Kashmir is world famous: advance booking for beats is advisable through the Director of Fisheries at the Tourist Centre in Srinagar. It is also excellent in Himachal Pradesh, in the Nilgiris, in Swat and in the Kaghan Valley (Pakistan). The mahseer is a fighting fish for which special tackle is required. It is widely distributed in the rivers of India, Pakistan and Nepal. Fishing Permits, obtainable locally, are necessary everywhere, but are inexpensive.

CAMPING AND TREKKING

Many of the more remote places in the plains of India and Pakistan which are of interest to tourists have been brought within range by car, jeep, and bus, so that it is no longer necessary to "go into camp" to reach them. But to sportsmen botanists, ornithologists, as well as to all who love mountain scenery, camping, far from being superseded by improved communications, still affords an experience which cannot be achieved by any other method. The Himalayas, the Karakoram, Hindu Kush and other ranges afford some of the grandest scenery in the world, enriched by a wealth of animal and bird life to be found nowhere else.

Travel Agencies arrange Package Tours which provide facilities for exploring these areas either by pony or on foot; and in India, Pakistan and Nepal, Tourist Bureaux can recommend local operators who will lay on longer and more extended trips than Package Tours provide. The season is short—less than six months as a rule, before the weather closes down; and early booking is essential. It is usual for local operators to quote fixed charges per week which cover tents, sleeping-bags, mules or ponies, porters and food, and they also give expert advice on the selection of routes, clothes, medical supplies and so forth.

They do not as a rule supply binoculars, fishing rods, guns or climbing gear; the visitor should bring these with him.

It should be noted that some of the most picturesque places in India and Pakistan cannot be reached without special permits to enter the area in which they lie; so that in planning a camping or trekking holiday careful enquiry should be made from Travel Agents and Tourist Bureaux as to whether permits are necessary and if so, how they can be obtained. Current restrictions, operative at the time this *Handbook* was compiled, are noted under the particulars given of individual areas.

PHOTOGRAPHY

Personal cameras and 25 film rolls enter India free; similar concessions for tourists in the other countries. Although the bright sun and gay colouring to be seen in many places seem to encourage the amateur photographer, the results are often disappointing. Without relatively expensive equipment, successful picture-taking is not easy. Actinic conditions favour an ultra-violet filter, with a factor 4 yellow for sky values. For architectural work with a tripod, a Linhof or Nikon, with rising front is desirable; but Pentax and Rollei also give good results. A single-lens reflex like Canon FT is easy to use, with its automatic controls. Light-meters and lens hoods are *musts*. Electronic or flash equipment is essential for interiors. For black and white, a fine grain slow speed panchromatic film about ASA 40 is good; for colour a film like Kodachrome 25 about ASA 25 works well. Film should be processed quickly after exposure. There is a Kodak processing laboratory at Bombay. It is wise to arrange for a trial film to be processed at an early stage of the trip, for readings on the exposure meter often need a correction-factor which only experience can determine. A haze filter is essential. Haze does not register on the exposure meter and most films are ruined by under-exposure. If films are brought back to Europe, controlled development should be arranged to ensure correct colour values or to compensate for under-exposure. Photography of anything of strategic importance (bridges, harbour facilities, airports) is forbidden.

ARTS AND CRAFTS[1]

One of the great attractions offered to the traveller in India, Pakistan, Nepal, Bangladesh and Sri Lanka is the abundance of hand-made metal work, enamel,

[1] See *Arts and Crafts of India and Ceylon* by A. K. Coomaraswamy

carving, jewellery, embroidery, rugs, carpets, silk and cotton fabrics of ancient traditional design. In former times the finest examples of all these—examples now rarely encountered outside museums and private collections—were produced, regardless of labour and cost, under the patronage of the ruling families of the now-vanished Princely States. This kind of patronage has vanished, and with it the kind of articles it produced. But although it has now been largely superseded by a mass-market, in which cheapness is the key to success, articles of quality are still produced because of the willingness of the prosperous middle-class to buy beautiful objects of traditional design. The best glazed pottery is made in the W. Punjab (blue and white) and in Sind (of turquoise blue) under a transparent glaze, the usual ornament being a conventional flower pattern. A fine coal-black pottery is produced in many parts of India. The Madurai (p. 545) pottery deserves mention for elegance of form and richness of colour. Gwalior pottery too, is charming.

Central and Local Governments in all these countries encourage cottage and traditional industries and maintain workshops, as well as emporia where products of good quality can be purchased. The Kashmir State Emporium in Bombay is an example: the goods are not cheap, but their quality is good and their design authentic. Tourist Bureaux will supply particulars of similar shops in their localities, while a visit to the bazaars of any large city will show craftsmen of many kinds producing articles in common use.

The Punjab has long produced gold and silver work, and especially parcel-gilt surahis or water vessels of elegant shape and delicate tracery. Kashmir, Kutch, Lucknow, Bombay, Dacca and Cuttack (filigree) all produce gold and silver ware, while Tanjore (Thanjavur) makes silver work on brass and copper. The Kutch hammered repoussé work shows Dutch *motifs*. The embossed silver work of Tamil Nadu, with Dravidian figures in high relief, is called Swami ware. Bidri work of silver and gold inlaid on iron has been revived at the Government Industrial School at Bidar (p. 453). Domestic utensils in brass and copper (Hindus using the former and Muslims the latter) are made in many places. The copper bazar at Bombay is celebrated. Moradabad (p. 368) produces brass and lacquered ware, Benares (Varanasi) and Jaipur mythological images and costume figures. Burdwan (p. 137) and Midnapore (p. 412) fabricate kansa, which is bell metal. Nagpur, Ahmedabad, Nasik, Poona and Murshidabad are noted for brass and copper ware, which in Kashmir and at Peshawar has Persian features. Nepalese brass work includes lamps, incense-burners and bells.

In the older type of Jaipur enamelling—the best in India—the colours are placed in depressions hollowed out of the metal and are made to adhere by fire. Jaipur is particularly famous for a fiery red (pigeon's blood). Other centres for this are Moradabad and Varanasi. For enamel on gold Delhi may be mentioned; on silver Lahore, Kangra and Multan, several places in Sind, Bhuj in Kutch and Kashmir; on copper the Punjab and Kashmir. Glass was known in India at the time of the Mahabharata, and bangles are made all over the country in enormous numbers. Ganges water flasks come from Sawansa in Partabgarh District. Alwar produces engraved gold and silver plate and book-binding.

In jewellery pieces exhibiting a variety of brilliant colours are produced by the free use of small chips of gems, otherwise valueless and are widely worn. Delhi and Colombo, like Calcutta and Lahore are internationally famous for precious stones. Purchasers of gems should insist on detailed receipts, as there are Customs regulations to deter the unauthorised export of jewellery to evade Exchange controls. Jaipur is one of the great centres of the trade in gems of the less valuable sort. Gold jewellery may well have spread from the South where the Mysore mines are worked to-day. Silver filigree work is an art of very ancient origin, and at Cuttack. Dacca and in Sri Lanka usually has a leaf design.

Silver fish, flexible-jointed, are made in the Monghyr District (p. 391). Each article of Bhutan jewellery is a work of art. Enamelled pieces come from places already named and from Hyderabad in the Deccan. The old Delhi work in cut and gem-encrusted jade is highly prized. Modern examples can still be bought. The pietra dura inlaid work of Agra is supposed to have been introduced by Austin of Bordeaux.

The black wood-carving of Bombay, in large pieces, and of Ahmadabad, in more portable objects, is in a style derived from the Portuguese. Kashmir also produces an endless variety of fine woodwork as does Hyderabad (Andhra Pradesh). Sandalwood may be enriched with marquetry (all the way down the West Coast and in Mysore), or ebony (at Nagina and Bijnor) or ivory (at Delhi, Benares, Vizagapatam and Amritsar). Ivory carving is carried on in Delhi, in Sylhet (fans), at Ratlam (bracelets) and Vizagapatam (boxes, with stag's horn interposed). The Trivandrum School of Arts makes a speciality of ivory carving. White marble figures of gods and animals are carved all over Rajasthan, where this stone is found, and at Fatehpur-Sikri models are made in soapstone. Models in clay of fruit and figures are made at Lucknow, Poona, Krishnagar and in the Punjab. Artistic leather work has been taken up as an industry in W. Bengal and West Pakistan.

Weaving was first perfected in India, but embroidery came in with the Muslims. The Greek name for cotton fabric, sindon, is etymologically the same as India (Sind). The word chintz is derived from the Hindu chhinta (variegated), while calico is derived from the place of its production, Calicut (p. 527). Dacca muslin (the name is derived from Mosul) had names which suggests its airiness. Indian and Pakistan mills now produce cotton cloths in great variety and Ahmedabad is famous, like Bombay and Calcutta, for the hand-woven cloth (Khadi) popularised as national wear by Mr Gandhi. Pure silk fabrics are made at Lahore, Agra, Benares, Hyderabad (A.P.) and Tanjore. Gold and silver brocaded silks (kincobs from the word kimkhwab, connected with the Chinese kin, gold) are luxury articles: Benares makes the best. Surat produces printed silks, worn by Parsi ladies with charming effect. Bahawalpur (p. 563) is noted for damasked silks. The industry is reviving in Bengal and elsewhere. Gold and silver wire is drawn out with great skill, two rupees worth of silver drawing out to 800 yards. The best embroidery comes from the North, much tinsel being used but without a tinselly appearance. In the West, Kutch produces fabrics attractively inset with tiny mirrors. The shawls of Kashmir, made from the finest wool of the Himalayan goat, are famous all over the world: there is a large export trade in the soft wool from which they are woven. Puttoo is a coarse woollen cloth made in the North of India and Pakistan, in lengths for suitings, rough or smooth. The Rampur chadar is a shawl, made at Amritsar and Ludhiana, of Rampur (Kangra) wool (pashmina).

In the carpets, made in places like Mirzapur, Amritsar, Lahore and Kashmir, the intrinsic difference between Eastern and Western decorative art is shown in the flowing classical "line of beauty" and in the "tree of life" borrowed from Iran. Both India and Pakistan produce pleasing modern carpets, the chemical dyes of which, however, are inferior to the older vegetable dyes still used in luxury articles. Intending purchasers of these carpets, as well as of the carpets which come from Iran and Afghanistan on caravans, should consult an expert. Tourist Information Bureaux will help the traveller to obtain sound advice. Good carpets are expensive, especially old ones in good condition. "Bargains" are suspect: hence the need for expert appraisal before purchase. Cotton rugs can be obtained by special order, but the dhurry or shatranji striped floor-covering is common all over India and Pakistan, and has the advantage of immunity from insects. Central Asia carpets come in by caravan and are best purchased near the point of entry, Peshawar or Quetta, but many go through to other places. A common design includes the filpai, the elephant's foot. The jai-nimaz rug represents a slab in a mosque floor.

CURIOS

Antique pieces can still be found, but it is best to go to a reputable dealer—Tourist Information Bureaux can advise here—unless one is possessed of expert knowledge, or has a friend who can supply it. Special caution should be exercised in the purchase of Oriental paintings and porcelain, for imitations are widely produced which can easily deceive the unwary. The export of certain types of antiquities, such as stone carvings and ancient bronzes, is forbidden; the Information Bureaux should be consulted on this point.

2. AIR ROUTES TO THE EAST

India, Pakistan, Nepal, Bangladesh and Sri Lanka (Ceylon) possess international airports which are served by some two dozen of the principal airlines of the world. In addition, India, Pakistan, Nepal and Sri Lanka have their own airlines, and Bangladesh has started its own.

Travel Agencies, and individual airline offices, will provide full details of routes and fares, as well as of charter flights, laid on either by airlines themselves or by the Governments of particular countries. Such flights often save as much as 50 per cent. of the standard fares.

It is worth while to enquire about details of accommodation, for the aircraft of the largest networks do not always provide as much individual accommodation, especially for tourist passengers, as the aircraft of some of the smaller lines. There is little to choose between them in the way of safety, excellence of meals and courtesy of service, since competition for passenger traffic runs high.

Air travel is not cheap, even by charter flight, but is quick, convenient and all expenses are included in the price of the ticket. The main disadvantage from the point of view of those travelling to the countries mentioned in this *Handbook* is that the limitation on the free weight of baggage may make it difficult to carry all the clothing needed to cope with wide varieties of climatic conditions. But suitcases can be sent by air freight at far cheaper rates than the charges for excess weight over the free allowance, and they will arrive three to four days after the passenger. Visitors may import goods of up to Rs. 500 value. There is the usual tobacco and alcohol allowance although some states require a liquor consumption permit.

Photography is forbidden at many of the airports *en route*; and even transit passengers are often required to show passports and vaccination certificates when they disembark from the aircraft during halts for refuelling.

3. OVERLAND TRAVEL TO THE EAST[1]

(Consult *The Road To India*, J. Prendergast, Murray 1977 for full details.) The main European routes converge on Istanbul, from which point there are excellent road maps issued by the National Tourist Organisations of Turkey, Iran and Pakistan in cooperation showing the trunk road from Istanbul to Ankara and Tehran, and thence via Isfahan, Kerman and Zahedan to the

[1] At the time of going to press (1981) the unsettled situation in Iran and Afghanistan makes this impractical.

Pakistan frontier at Qila Safed via Quetta to Karachi or to Lahore and the Indian frontier (The R.C.D. highway). Hotels, Motels, Restaurants, Petrol Stations, Service Stations, Post and Telegraph facilities, Tourist Information points, Camping Sites and Rest Houses are plainly indicated. Secondary roads are also shown. This route, however, is not as well maintained as the alternative, somewhat shorter, route from Tehran to the Pakistan-Indian border via Kandahar and Kabul and the Khybar Pass to Peshawar and Lahore, which misses some of the very interesting places in Iran which the more southerly route takes in. These places from Istanbul eastwards to the frontiers of Pakistan and Afghanistan can be studied in the separate pamphlets and local maps issued by the Tourist Organisations of the respective countries. There are regular bus services, usually once a week, running from Brussels, Munich, and other European cities to Istanbul, Ankara and Tehran, of which a Travel Agency can provide details of fares and routes. Such bus services provide the cheapest way of going to India, Pakistan and Nepal from Europe, and are increasingly popular with students of limited resources and with people who have a taste for adventure. The journey calls for some fortitude as well as physical stamina, as a wide variety of climatic conditions, food and the like are encountered. There are internal bus services in Iran between all the principal cities, and the same thing holds good for Afghanistan, Pakistan and India.

It is essential for all travellers, whether by bus or by private car, to inform themselves of the currency, customs, health, passport and visa regulations in force along the frontiers. These differ from country to country; the essential documentation should be carefully checked before the journey begins. It is also prudent to ascertain in advance any restrictions which may be imposed on the use of cameras as well as the availability of currency exchange facilities.

Travellers using their own cars should not fail to seek advice from the A.A. or the R.A.C., if they are starting from Britain, about current road conditions, regulations governing the entry and exit of cars for each country that has to be traversed, and for advice about spares to be carried. The A.A. publishes an excellent leaflet (OS 110) covering routes through Iran and Afghanistan to Pakistan, India and Sri Lanka. Other useful leaflets deal with motoring in Iran and Afghanistan, India and Pakistan, and the Middle East.

Tourist buses, calling at major places of interest, take about eight or nine weeks to reach Kathmandu in Nepal from London. A typical fare for the journey is about £125, to which should be added about £2·50 per day for food, drinks and simple accommodation. There are more economical journeys, planned for students and young people, in which the daily expenditure can be reduced to about £1·70. Usually the bus crew consists of a courier as well as a driver; stages are planned so far as possible to avoid undue fatigue. The Travel Agency as a rule issues, along with the ticket, advice about visa and passport requirements, vaccinations, climate and clothing, currency facilities and the like.

For British travellers using their own cars, there are a number of alternative routes from the Channel Ports to Istanbul; the A.A. or the R.A.C. will provide particulars of the best one to follow at any particular juncture, along with notes on halting places, petrol and service facilities.

The shortest is Calais-Munich (596 m.) Munich-Belgrade (621 m.) Belgrade-Salonika (444 m.) and Salonika-Istanbul (462 m.) It may be quicker sometimes to take the Belgrade-Sofia (260 m.) and Sofia-Istanbul (381 m.) road.

The Turkish frontier is crossed at **Edirne,** where there are hotel, motel, post and telegraph, petrol and service facilities.

From Edirne the Trunk route runs via **Corlu** (restaurant, petrol, servicing) 78 m. to **Istanbul** (144 m.) where motorists will find all necessary facilities, both for servicing and for accommodation. The Government Tourist Bureau publishes a guidebook for all the main sites of local beauty and of tourist interest. From Istanbul the road runs via **Izmit** (59 m.), **Sapanca Lake** (68 m.), **Adapazani** (84 m.) and **Duce** (128 m.). In all four places there are petrol and servicing facilities, while in **Bolu** (157 m.) there is also a motel, as well as a Tourist Information Centre. At **Ankara** (277 m.) capital of the Turkish Republic, there are all the facilities of a major city for the accommodation and assistance of motorists. There is an airport and a Tourist Information Centre. From Ankara, the route passes **Kirikale** (49 m.), **Cerikli** (78 m.), to **Sivas** (278 m.) which is bypassed and then **Zara** (45 m.), **Erzincan** (156 m.) and **Erzerum** (276 m.). In Erzerum, petrol, servicing, an Information Bureau and accommodation are to be found.

There is an alternative route going north-east from Cerikli through **Sungurlu** (113 m. from Ankara), **Corum** (159 m.) and **Merzifon** (199 m.) to **Samsun** (368 m.), all facilities. From Samsun the road skirts the Black Sea via **Unye** (55 m.), **Ordu** (104 m.), **Giresun** (133 m.) to **Trabzon** (227 m.). There are hotels, restaurants, petrol pumps and service facilities at the three places mentioned, while at Trabzon there are to be found all the amenities of a large city, as well as a camping site and an Information Bureau. The road then goes south-east from the coast to join the main route between Erzincan and Erzerum.

From Erzerum, the road runs through **Agri** [Karakose] (117 m.) **Dogubeyazit** (177 m.) to **Gurbulak** (199 m.) on the Iranian frontier. There is a hotel at Agri, and a restaurant at Dogubeyazit. Petrol is available at all three places.

At **Bazargan,** the first Iranian town encountered, there is a Tourist Information Bureau; but the nearest petrol pump is at **Makoo,** 13 m. further on, where there is also a motel. At **Marand** (109 m.) there are a rest house, petrol and servicing facilities. At **Tabriz** (153 m.), with its airport, there are full facilities of every kind for the motorist, including an Information Centre. From Tabriz the road runs through **Mianeh** (116 m.), **Zandjan** (202 m.), **Ghazvin** (312 m.) and **Karadj** (378 m.), all of which have petrol, accommodation in hotels and rest houses and servicing facilities, to the capital **Tehran** (406 m.), where all facilities are to be found and there is an Information Centre.

From Tehran onwards to Pakistan and India there is a choice of routes. The northern runs from Tehran to **Mashad** (574 m.) and thence into Afghanistan via Kandahar to **Kabul** (953 m.) and via Jallalabad and the Khybar Pass to Peshawar and India. The southern runs from Tehran to Isfahan and thence via Yazd, Kerman, Bam, and Zahidan across the Pakistan frontier to Quetta in Baluchistan. The road is very bad in places and is subject to flooding. The stages on the southern route are as follows:

Tehran to **Saveh** (85 m.)—hotel, restaurant, petrol and servicing; **Delidjan** (132 m.) with similar facilities; **Isfahan** (279 m.)—one of the loveliest cities in Iran—with an airport, full tourist facilities and Information Centre and a camping site. Isfahan to **Naein** (90 m.) then to **Ardakan** (166 m.) and **Yazd** (204 m.). All three places have hotels and petrol and service facilities and Yazd has an airport. Yazd to **Rafsandjan** with a hotel, petrol and servicing facilities (161 m.) and thence to **Kerman** (240 m.). Kerman has a hotel, an Information Centre, petrol and servicing facilities and an airport. From Kerman the road runs through **Bam,** with a hotel and petrol supplies (128 m.) to **Zahedan** (336 m.), which has an airport, Information Centre, a hotel, petrol and service facilities. **Mirdjaveh** (398 m.) is the last important place in Iran before the Pakistan frontier is crossed at **Qilasafed.**

Inside Pakistan there is a restaurant and a service station at **Nok Kundi** (78 m.) **Quetta** (394 m.) has an airport, hotels, a motel, Tourist Information Centre and full facilities (see *Handbook*).

From Quetta there is a choice of routes. The "R.C.D." highway runs directly south to Karachi; but travellers making for the Indian frontier near Lahore on their way to Nepal can go from Quetta to Ziarat and thence to **Multan,** where a trunk road will take them via **Sahiwal** to **Lahore.** Sahiwal has petrol and servicing facilities and a rest house; Multan has an airport, a hotel, a rest house and petrol and servicing facilities.

Details of these routes should be ascertained from the Tourist Information Centre at Quetta.

Returning to Tehran in Iran, some particulars of the northern route via Afghanistan are as under:

Tehran to **Mashad** is 607 m. or 971 km., the road running via **Gorgan** (247 m.), **Shah Pasand** (45 m.), **Bojnurd** (145 m.) and **Quchan Ghoochan.** Mashad is a large and important pilgrimage centre, with rest houses, petrol and other facilities.

The next stage, Mashad to **Herat** is 234 m. or 376 km. by an excellent road. At **Tayyebat** (144 m.) is the last Iranian customs post; 5 m. further comes the Afghan frontier, and at 158 m. at **Islam Qila** is the customs post with rest house and other facilities. Herat is a large city and has the usual facilities. Before entering it there is a toll-barrier.

From Herat to **Kandahar** is 350 m. or 536 km. along an excellent road, with several toll-barriers; the receipts given must be shown at the end of each stage. At 125 m. there is a service area with a hotel and petrol; petrol is also available at **Dilaram** (203 m) and at **Girishk** (279 m.). At 336 m., 14 m. outside Kandahar, there is another toll-barrier. At Kandahar, a road runs into Pakistan, via **Chaman, Qila Abdullah, Bostan** to **Quetta.** (80 m.). No servicing until Quetta.

From Kandahar, with its modern extensions, hotel, petrol and other facilities, there is a modern highway (again punctuated by toll-barriers) covering the 318 m. (512 km.) to **Kabul.** Petrol is available at Kalat-i-Ghilzai (85 m.) and at **Mukur** (159 m.) where there is a rest house. At **Ghazni** (227 m.) there is a rest house and petrol. After passing the final toll-barrier at 306 m., Kabul is entered after a further 12 m. Here are to be found up-to-date hotels, rest houses, petrol and all other facilities expected in a capital city.

The distance from Kabul to **Peshawar** is 190 m. (305 km.). There is a toll-post at **Sarobi** (50 m.). At **Jalalabad** (97 m.) there are consulates of Pakistan and India and tourist facilities. At **Dakka** (146 m.) is the last Afghan customs post; Pakistan is entered at **Torkham** (155 m.) and motorists drive on the *left* of the road. The route runs through the Khyber Pass via **Landi Kotal** and **Jamrud** to Peshawar. The Pass is closed at night. From Peshawar, with hotels and full tourist facilities, the Grand Trunk Road runs via **Rawalpindi** (101 m.), **Jhelum** (174 m.) to **Lahore** (274 m.) and thence 12 m. to the Pakistan-Indian frontier at Wagah/Attari. Enquiries should be made at Lahore about the hours when the border is open. Sometimes there are considerable delays.

From the Indian frontier, the National Highway runs via Amritsar (pp. 355-358), Delhi (pp. 317-344), Agra (pp. 299-311), Lucknow (pp. 381-389) and Varanasi (pp. 155-168). Thence to Raxaul (p. 392), the last Indian town on the frontier with Nepal, and after passing the customs, by the highway to Katmandu.

4. THE PRE-1947 FOUNDATIONS OF INDIA, PAKISTAN AND BANGLADESH

Before 1947, in which year British rule came to an end, all three countries were part of the British Indian Empire. But the British *raj* was a comparatively short episode in the subcontinent's long history, and the foundations upon which each country has built its national life had been slowly laid in the course of many centuries.

Thus their religions, their cultures, their history and their systems of government lend themselves to common treatment up to the time when they became independent.

THE MUSLIMS

The Muslims form the majority community in Pakistan and Bangladesh, and are an important minority community in India.

Muhammad ("the praised", from *hamd*, praise) was born at Mecca (Makka) on the 29th August A.D. 570 in the Koreish (Quraish) ruling tribe. His father, Abdulla, was a merchant, son of Abdul Muttalib, the patriarch of the House of Hashim; his mother's name was Amina. His father died before his birth, his mother when he was barely five years old. He remained three years in the charge of his grandfather, and on the latter's death passed to the care of his uncle, Abu Talib. When twenty-five years old he became manager or agent to a rich widow named Khadija, who, although fifteen years his senior, offered him marriage. By her he had sons, who all died in infancy, and four daughters, of whom three survived, the youngest, Fatima, being married to Ali, the son of Abu Talib; from her are descended the nobility of Islam, the Saiyids and Sharifs, who wear green turbans.

At the age of forty Muhammad announced he had received the first divine communication in the solitude of the mountain Hira, near Mecca, where the call came to him, and the angel Gabriel commanded him to preach the new religion. The Meccans persecuted him and his followers for his preachings; his wife and uncle died; and he became poverty-stricken. Threatened with death, Muhammad, accompanied by Abu Bakr, left Mecca on the 16th July 622. Escaping from the Koreish, they reached the rival city, Yathreb, some 270 m. to the N., where he was accepted as a Prophet. The city was henceforth called the City of the Prophet—Medinat-un-Nabi, or, shortly, Medina. The Meccans pursued him and the Medinists with hostility, and he repelled their attacks. In the year 630, he with 10,000 men, conquered Mecca. Returning to Medina, he died on the 8th of June 632, and was there buried.

Islam is generally held to mean submission to God; some describe it as "striving after righteousness". A Muslim, or Mussalman, is one who professes Islam. In its dogmatical form it is Iman (faith), in its practical Din (religion). The fundamental principle is, "There is no God but God; and Muhammad is the Prophet of God (Lá illáha illá 'lláh Muhammad Rasulu 'lláh)". This is the *Kalima*, or creed, which is to be recited. There are also four principal duties: (1) Daily prayers (which should be said five times a day—at daybreak, noon, afternoon, sunset, nightfall); (2) the giving of alms; (3) the fast of Ramazan (from dawn to sunset for a month, from the appearance of the new moon); (4) a pilgrimage (Hajj, Hajji), once in a lifetime, to the ancient shrine of the Ka'aba, at Mecca. In the Koran (which embodies the teachings and precepts of Muhammad, and is believed to have been sent down by God to the seventh or lowest heaven and then revealed from time to time to Muhammad by the angel Gabriel), a holy war or *jihad* in defence of Islam is enjoined on believers.

Muslim subjects of a government, under which the practices of the religion of Islam are freely permitted, are bound to obey the government. They believe in resurrection, heaven, and hell, but the meaning of the description of a future existence as given in the Koran is much disputed. On the one hand large masses of Muslims accept the statements of the Koran as to the sensuous delights of Paradise in their literal sense; on the other hand, they are regarded as word-paintings used in a figurative sense. In hell all who deny the unity of God will be tortured eternally. The idea of the exclusion of women from Paradise is at variance with the whole tenor of the Koran.

Muhammad enjoined ablution of the hands, mouth and nose before eating or praying. The Koran forbids the use of wine, including all inebriating liquors and any intoxicants. It forbids also the eating of the flesh of swine; and no animal is lawful food unless it be slaughtered by cutting the throat. Usury and games of chance are prohibited, and the laws against idolatry are very stringent.

A Muslim is allowed to marry one, two, three, or four wives, provided he can treat all with equity; if not, he is limited to one. In modern times, however, whether for economic reasons or because of the advancement of women, the general rule is to have only one wife, and the old practice is falling into disuse. Divorce is easy, consisting merely of the threefold repetition of the words "Thou art divorced" in front of witnesses but the wife's dowry must be returned to her. Amongst the orthodox it is considered wrong for a man to look upon the face of any woman except a near relative.

There is no priesthood in Islam; every man is his own priest and pleads for forgiveness and mercy. It recognises no distinction of race or colour among its followers. Hope and fear, reward and punishment, with a belief in predestination, form the system of faith. It is contrary to strict orthodoxy to make any figure or representation of anything living. The Muslim always attaches great importance to old mosques, and will not consent to demolition, even if they have long been disused. His name is selected from the ninety-nine attributes of Allah. Difference between two divisions arises out of the question of the title to the spiritual and temporal headship of Islam. The Sunnis advocate the principle of election, and recognise Abu Bakr, Omar, and Othman as the first three Khalifas (Khalifa, Caliph = Viceregent), and Ali as the fourth; the Shias adhere to apostolical descent by appointment and succession, and regard Ali as the first Khalifa. The Ismailis form a third and separate sect whose spiritual head is H.H. the Aga Khan, lineal descendant of the Old Man of the Mountains. In India the great majority of Muslims are Sunnis. These are again divided into four principal "persuasions"—the Hanafi, Shafei, Maliki and Hanbali—after their founders. Shiaism is the State religion of Iran. In the 16th century Sultan Salim, the great Osmanli conqueror, obtained the Caliphate from the last Caliph at Cairo; the Osmanli rulers of Turkey were recognised as spiritual head, *Shaikh-ul-Islam*, by the bulk of the Sunnis in India and elsewhere. In November 1922 the Grand National Assembly at Ankara declared that the office of Sultan had ceased to exist, and in March 1924 abolished the Caliphate.

Muslim architects, scholars, historians, poets and musicians have contributed greatly to Western culture. Painters have produced miniatures and illuminated manuscripts. Muslim medicine has made notable contributions to the healing art.

Among Muslim eras, the Hijra takes its name from the "departure" of Muhammad from Mecca, commencing with the date of Friday, the 16th of July A.D. 622, ordered by the Khalifa Omar to be used. The year consists of twelve lunar months, alternately of 30 or 29 days, totalling 354 days in all.

The year, therefore, is 11 days short of the solar year. Every 30 years the month Zil Hijja is adjusted. To correlate the Hijra year with the Christian year, express the former in years and decimals of a year, multiply by ·970225, add 621·54, and the total will correspond exactly to the Christian year.

During the month of Ramazan the Muslim goes without food or water from sunrise to sunset.

The Tarikh Ilahi or Era of Akbar, and the Fasli or Harvest Era begin from the commencement of Akbar's reign on Friday, the 5th of Rabi us-sani, 963 A.H. = 19th of February A.D. 1556.

MUSLIM FESTIVALS

Bakar Id, *Id-ud-uz-ha*, or *uzzoha*, or *Id-i-kurban* (sacrifice), is held on the 10th of Zil Hijja in memory of Abraham's offering of Ishmael, which is the version of the Koran. Camels, cows, sheep, goats, kids, or lambs are sacrificed.

Muharram (The Sacred[1]) is a period of mourning (the Shias fast on some of the days) in remembrance of the death of Husain, the son of Ali by Fatima, the daughter of Muhammad. Hasan, eldest son of Ali, was poisoned at the instigation of the future Khalif Yezid in 49 A.H., and Husain was murdered at Karbala on the 10th of Muharram, 61 A.H. = 9th October A.D. 680. The fast begins on the 1st of Muharram and lasts ten days. Muslims of the Shia persuasion assemble in the Taziya Khana, or house of mourning. On the night of the 7th an image of Burak, the magical horse on which Muhammad is popularly related to have ascended to heaven, is carried in procession, as on the 10th are Tabuts[2] or Taziyas (biers). These are thrown into the sea, or other water, and in the absence of water are buried in the earth. The mourners move in a circle, beating their breasts with cries of "Ya Hasan! Ya Husain!" or "Ya Ali!"

Akhiri-Chahar Shamba, held on the last Wednesday of Safar, when Muhammad recovered a little in his last illness and bathed for the last time. It is proper to write out seven blessings, wash off the ink and drink it, as also to bathe and repeat prayers.

Bárah Wafát, held on the 12th of Rabi ul awal in memory of Muhammad's death, 11 A.H.

Shab-i-barát (night of allotment), held on the 16th of Sh'aban, when it is supposed that human deeds are measured and their meeds allotted: only observed in India; celebrated with fireworks. The Koran ought to be read all night, a sermon is preached, and the next day a fast should be observed.

Rámazán,[3] the month of fasting of the Muhammadans. The night of the 27th is called Lailat-ul-Kadr, "night of power", because the Koran came down from heaven on that night.

'Id-ul-fitr (also called Id-us-sadaqah or Feast of Alms), the festival when the fast of the Ramazan ends after the new moon has been seen. The evening is spent in rejoicings.

THE HINDUS

The Hindus are by far the largest community in India and are a small but influential element in the populations of Pakistan and Bangladesh.

Such words as Vedism, Brahmanism and Hinduism are not recognised by the Hindu orthodoxy. They do not connote religion in the sense of a system of worship, etc., which would lead to heaven or give man his desires through the medium of a deity.

The first form of the Hindu "religion" was Vedism, the worship of Nature, as represented in the songs and prayers collectively called Veda, and in which the chief gods were the triad, Indra (rain), Agni (fire) and Surya (sun). Then followed Brahmanism, which introduced the idea of a universal spirit, or essence, which permeated everything, men, gods and the visible world being merely its manifestations. Prose works, called Brahmanas, were added to the Vedas, to explain the sacrifices and the duties of the Brahmins, or priests. The oldest of these may have been written about 1000 to 1200 B.C.

1 The name is derived from the corresponding old Arabic month, in which it was unholy to wage war.

2 The shape of this is intended to simulate the tomb of Ali at Karbala.

3 The name is derived from ramaz, burning, this month being the middle summer month in the first Muhammadan year.

The code of Manu (A.D. 100-300) specified the rules of domestic conduct and ceremony. It divided Hindus into four *Varnas* (lit. "colours")—first, the Brahmins; second, the warriors, called Kshatriyas; and third, the agriculturists and traders, called Vaisyas. (All these, being of Aryan descent, were honoured by the name "twice born".) Fourth were the Sudras, or non-Aryan tribes. Thus a Hindu was born a Hindu, neither baptized into nor converted to Hinduism.

By the time this code was formed racial distinction between the Aryans and non-Aryans ceased, and the Sudras included all persons who were not born in the twice-born status. The Sudras were not allowed to be present at the great national sacrifices or at the feasts. The priests asserted that they, the Brahmins, came from the mouth of Brahma; the Rajputs, or Kshatriyas, from his arms; the Vaisyas from his thighs; and the Sudras from his feet. Each trade in time came to have a separate caste; and the priests insisted on the *varna*-duties, because they held that social order was dependent thereon. In the 1941 Census, however, many professed Hindus were unable to name their castes.

A brief account of Hindu mythology is given below in order to assist in the identification of temple sculptures. There is one impersonal and spiritual Being which pervades everything—one God, called Brahm. His three personal manifestations are as *Brahma*, the Creator; *Vishnu*, the Preserver; and *Siva*, the Destroyer and Reproducer. *Brahma*, the Creator, is generally represented with four heads and four arms, in which he holds a portion of the Veda, a spoon for lustral observations, a rosary, and a vessel of lustral water (see Plate 1). *Sarasvati*, the wife of Brahma, rides on a peacock, and has a musical instrument, the "vina", in her arms (see Plate 1). She is the goddess of music, speech, hte arts and literature.

Vishnu holds a quoit in one hand, a conch shell in another, and sometimes a mace or club in another, and a lotus flower in a fourth (see Plate 1). A common picture shows him with his wife, Lakshmi, sitting on Shesh, the snake (eternity), with Brahma on a lotus springing from his navel (see Plate 2). He is said to have come down to the earth nine times, and is expected a tenth time. These nine incarnations (*avatara*) were in the form of—(1) a fish (*Matsya*); (2) a tortoise (*Kurma*); (3) a boar (*Varaha*); (4) a man lion (*Narsingh*); (5) a dwarf (*Vamana*); (6) *Rama with the axe* (*Parasu rama*); (7) *Rama*, the hero of the epic poem, the *Ramayana*; (8) *Krishna*; and (9) *Buddha*.

Rama carries a bow and arrow (see Plate 1). He is revered throughout India as the model of a son, a brother, and a husband. When friends meet it is common for them to salute each other by uttering Rama's name twice, thus "Ram Ram". His name is frequently given to children, or is usually invoked at funerals and in the hour of death. His ally, *Hanuman* (p. 22), is represented under a monkey form (see Plate 1). He is the model of a faithful, devoted servant, and often appears at the gates of forts.

Krishna's great popularity is associated with the rise of Vaishnavism. The story is told in the *Mahabharata*, the *Bhagavata Purana* and in Jayadeva's great poem *Gita Govinda*. His life among the cowherds of Vrindaban, and his love for the milkmaid Radha, are celebrated in poetry, painting and sculpture. As a boy he vanquished the serpent Kaliya by trampling upon his head. He lifted the mountain-ridge of Gobardhan (p. 296) on his finger to shelter the herdsmen's wives from the wrath of Indra, the Vedic rain-god. He had countless wives and sons, and is represented as dark blue in complexion. Sometimes he is represented as standing on a snake, with his left hand holding its body and a lotus in his right (see Plate 2); and sometimes he is playing the flute.

The adoption of Buddha as one of the incarnations aimed at a compromise with Buddhism. This led in India to the reabsorption of Buddhism into the general Hindu culture.

Devotion to Vishnu is directed principally to his human incarnations of

Rama and Krishna. His descents upon earth were for the delivery of men from the threefold miseries of life—viz. (1) from lust, anger, avarice, and their evil consequences; (2) from beasts, snakes, and wicked men; (3) from demons. Vishnu has power to elevate his worshippers to eternal bliss in his own heaven.

Vishnu's wife, *Lakshmi*, the goddess of wealth and beauty, sprang from the froth of ocean when churned by gods and demons (see Plate 1). An image of her is often to be found in the houses of shopkeepers. She is worshipped during the Diwali festival.

Siva is also called Mahadeo, the great god, and his wife, who is known by several names and in several characters, as Parvati, the goddess of beauty (see Plate 1); Durga, or Kali, the terrible (see Plate 1), etc., is also called Devi *the* goddess (see Plate 1). The commonest of these is *Kali*, who requires to be propitiated by sacrifices. Siva holds in his four hands a trident, an antelope, a noose for binding his enemies, and a kind of drum, and wears a tiger's skin about the loins. He is a less human and more mystical god than Vishnu, and is worshipped in the form of a symbol, the *lingam*, or a bull (*Nandi*, the Joyous). As destroyer, Siva haunts cemeteries and burning-grounds, but his terrible qualities are now more especially associated with his wife, Kali. He is the impersonation of the reproductive power of nature, the word Siva meaning "blessed" or "auspicious". He is also the typical ascetic and self-mortifier; and as a learned philosopher he is the chief god of the priests.

Siva has two sons—Ganesh, or Ganpati, and Kartikkeya. *Ganesh* has a fat body and an elephant's head (see Plate 1). He is invoked at the beginning of many Indian books as a bringer of success, and also because he is the god of learning. *Kartikkeya* is the god of war, the leader of the hosts of good demons (see Plate 1). In the south of India he is called Skanda or Subrahmanya.

There are very few (some say only three) temples dedicated to Brahma. Hindus are (with few exceptions) Vaishnavite or Saivite. It is reasoned that Vishnu the "Preserver" can destroy by ceasing to preserve, and can also create. On plate 2 he is shown contemplating the creation of the world. Similarly Siva the "Destroyer" can preserve by refraining from destruction, and can create also. Therefore both are worshipped as possessing all the attributes of the Trinity.

The Hindu theory of metempsychosis or transmigration of souls arises from the belief that evil proceeds from antecedent evil, and that the penalty must be suffered in succeeding existences. The old-fashioned orthodox Hindu made offerings to the image of a god; he abstained from killing any animal; he gave money or gifts to the priests and strictly obeyed caste rules; and he was much concerned with questions of purity and pollution. Great care had to be taken not to eat food cooked by, nor take water from, a man of inferior caste. Travellers should not touch, therefore, any cooking or water-holding utensil belonging to a Hindu, nor let their shadows fall on strict Hindus when at meals, and they should not seek to approach any holy place if objection is made. Washing in any holy river, particularly the Ganges, and more especially at certain exceptionally sacred spots is of great efficacy in cleansing the soul of impurities. Hence pilgrimages are common. In practice, however, these restrictions or taboos are gradually being relaxed or ignored, as they are inconvenient under modern conditions. As regards marriage, the prohibition of inter-caste marriages is still generally observed, except amongst the Europeanised minority. A sacred thread of cotton is worn by the higher castes. The most revered of all animals is the cow. Garuda, a mythical being, half man, half bird, is the vehicle of Vishnu, the bull (Nandi) of Siva, the goose of Brahma, the elephant of Indra, the tiger of Durga, the buffalo of Yama, the rat of Ganesh, the ram of Agni, the peacock of Kartikkeya, and the parrot of Kama (the god of love).

The worship of idols is rejected by the Arya Samaj, a reformed body founded by Swami Dayanand (1827-53), which accepts the inspiration of the Vedas only. Another sect of Hindu reformers, the Brahmo Samaj, founded 1830 by Raja Ram Mohan Roy, rejects them as inspired scriptures, and is unitarian in its doctrine. But while the Arya Samaj commands a wide following, the influence exercised by the Brahmo Samaj (almost entirely confined to Bengal) has been out of all proportion to its numbers.

THE GREAT EPICS

The *Mahabharata* in its present form was compiled between 400 B.C. and A.D. 400, but recorded events which may be referred to about 1500 B.C. It celebrates the battle between the Pandava (Pandu) and Kaurava (Kuru) Princes. The former, five in number, named Yudhishthir, Bhima and Arjun sons of one mother, and Nakula and Sahadeva, sons of another, were the offspring of Pandu, ruler of Hastinapur, an ancient city on the Ganges, 60 m. N.W. of Delhi, who ceded the kingdom to his elder, but blind brother, Dhritarashtra. The Kauravas were the sons of Dhritarashtra, and compelled him to send their cousins into exile, during which the marriage of Draupadi, daughter of Drupada, King of the Panchalas, took place, and most of the adventures which led to their names being attached to so many places all over India. At the end of their exile the Pandavas received the Southern portion of the Hastinapur kingdom, and settled at Indraprastha, now Indrapat (p. 329). Having lost this share of their inheritance through gambling with their cousins, the Pandavas again went into exile for twelve years, after which they returned with an army and claimed five "pats", or small towns, of their former kingdom (Indrapat, Tilpat, Sonepat, Bhagpat and Panipat). Over this claim the great battle ensued, in which, after eighteen days, nearly all the Kauravas were killed. The account of the funeral ceremonies of the slain is almost Homeric. The five brothers then resumed their residence at Indrapat, and Yudhishthir celebrated the Aswamedha, or horse sacrifice, on the bank of the Jumna. A horse was let loose to wander as it pleased under guard for a year, and, if no other king could capture it, imperial rule was claimed and the horse was sacrificed. Finally the brethren and their wives retired to the Himalayas and sought to reach Mount Meru; but only the eldest brother survived to be admitted with his dog.

The *Ramayana*, ascribed to Valmiki, and probably compiled in the 5th or 6th century B.C., related the adventures of Rama, elder son of a King of Oudh, who was passed over in the succession in favour of the son of a younger wife, and banished by his father. Rama accordingly proceeded into exile with his wife Sita to the abode of the hermit Valmiki; and, although his half-brother proved loyal to him on his father's death, he refused to return to Oudh until the term of his banishment had expired. Before this Sita was carried off from their forest abode by Ravana, king of Lankā (Ceylon), inspired by his sister, whose love Rama had rejected. She was rescued from Lankā by Rama with the help of Hanuman, the monkey general, and proved her chastity by the ordeal of fire; but (according to a later tradition) was banished by her husband, and only after sixteen years in exile with Valmiki was finally reconciled to Rama, who is commonly known in India as Ram Chandra; his brother Lakshmana constantly appears in local legends and Ram Lila plays.

Ajodhya (p. 372), which ranks as one of the seven sacred Hindu shrines, is famous as the birthplace of Rama, and also as the scene of his cremation.

The Bhagavad Gita is a long exhortation by Krishna as charioteer of Arjuna on the duties of a soldier. It has been translated into many languages; and was made known to English readers as Sir E. Arnold's *Song Celestial*, but is better translated by Swami Prabhavananda and C. Isherwood in *Song of God* (London, 1947).

PLATE 1

Some Common Forms of Hindu Deities.

PLATE 2

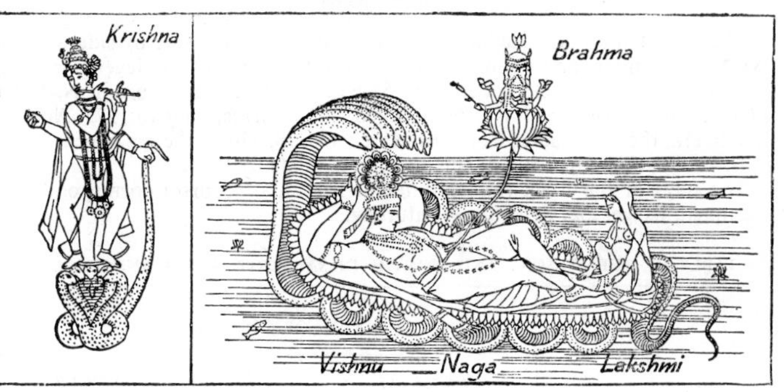

Sect Marks

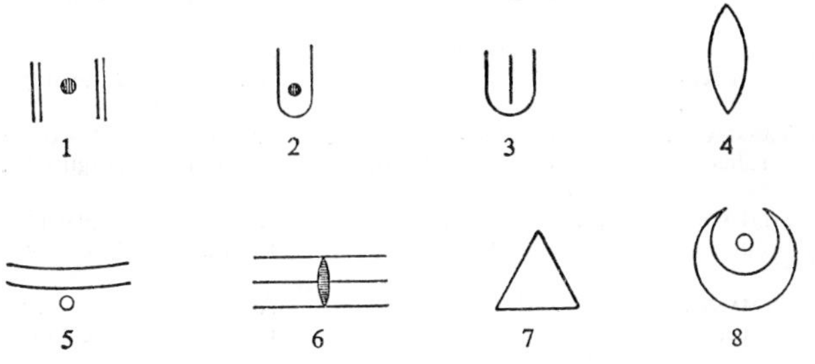

1, 2, 3, and 4, *Followers of Vishnu.*
5, 6, 7, and 8, *Followers of Siva.*

Buddha

HINDU ERAS

The chief Hindu era, the Samvat, is now used officially side by side with the Western calendar, and commenced from the first year of the legendary King Vikramaditya, on the 23rd February 57 B.C. It is in ordinary use in N. India. The Vikramajit year, as it is usually called, 2032, corresponds to 1975. Another Hindu era, the Saka, dates from 3rd March A.D. 78. This is the era in general use in S. India. The year 1897 of this era corresponds to 1975.

The days of the week (under different names, of course) correspond with European usage, e.g. Sanichar = Saturday.

TABLE OF THE SEASONS AND MONTHS IN SANSKRIT, HINDI AND ENGLISH

	Names of Months		
	Sanskrit	Hindi	English
1. Vasanta . . spring	Chaitra (Aries) Vaishakha	Chait Baisakh	March-April April-May
2. Grishma . . hot season	Jyeshtha (Gemini) Aushadha	Jeth Asarh	May-June June-July
3. Varsha . . rains	Sravana (Leo) Bhadra (Virgo)	Sawan Bhadon	July-August August-Sept
4. Sharada . . autumn	Ashwina Kartika	Asvin Kartik	Sept-Oct Oct-Nov
5. Hemanta . . winter	Margasirsha Pausha	Aghan Pús	Nov-Dec Dec-Jan
6. Shishira . . cold season	Magha Phalguna (Pisces)	Magh Phagun	Jan-Feb Feb March

HINDU FESTIVALS

The great secular national festival of present-day India is Republic Day (26th January), which is celebrated throughout the country by processions and feasting. The parade in New Delhi is particularly impressive, and is followed by popular festivities, attracting many foreign visitors. Other holidays are Independence Day (15th August), Gandhi's birthday (2nd October), Good Friday and Christmas Day.

The main Hindu *religious* festivals are these: (for Muslim and Buddhist festivals see p. 18 and p. 32).

Makar Sankranti.—On the 1st of the Month Magh (about 12th January) the sun enters the sign Capricorn or Makar. From this day till the arrival of the sun at its extreme N. altitude the period is called Uttarayana, and from that time till he returns to Makar is Dakshinayana, the former period being lucky and the latter unlucky. At this festival the Hindus bathe and rub themselves with sesamum oil. They also invite Brahmans and give them pots full of sesamum seed. They wear new clothes with ornaments and distribute sesamum seed mixed with sugar. This festival is also called *Pongal.*

Vasant Panchami is on the 5th day of the light half of Magh and is a festival in honour of vasanta or spring. Students lay writing materials and books at the feet of the goddess Saraswati.

Sivarat, the night of Siva, is held about the middle or end of February, when Siva is worshipped with flowers during the whole night.

Holi.—A saturnalia at the vernal equinox, celebrated with the squirting or throwing of red or yellow powder.

Janam Ashtami, held on the 8th of the dark half of Sawan, when Krishna is said to have been born at Gokul (p. 295). At night Hindus bathe and worship an image of Krishna, adorning it with *tulsi* or *basil*.

Ganesh Chaturthi, held on the 4th of Bhadon, in honour of Ganesh, an image of the god being worshipped and Brahmins entertained. The Hindus are prohibited from looking at the moon on this day, and, if by accident they should see it, they get their neighbours to abuse them in order to remove the curse.

Dasahara (*Dasahra*, or ten days, commonly Dussehra), held on the 10th of Asvin, in honour of Durga, or Devi, the wife of Siva, who on this day slew the buffalo-headed demon Mahishasur. On this day Rama marched against Ravana, and for this reason the Mahrattas and the Thugs chose it for setting out on their expeditions. This is an auspicious day for sending children to school. The nine preceding days are called Navaratra, when Brahmins are paid to recite hymns to Durga. The Durga Puja holiday is the principal holiday of the year in Bengal and the Dasahara is celebrated with great ceremony in Mysore, early in October.

Diwali, "feast of lamps", held on the new moon of Kartik, in honour of Lakshmi, the goddess of prosperity, when merchants and bankers count their wealth and worship it. It is said that Vishnu killed a giant on that day, and the women went to meet him with lighted lamps. In memory of this, lighted lamps of humble earthenware or blazing electric bulbs, according to means, are displayed from all houses, and are set afloat in rivers and in the sea, and auguries are drawn from them according as they remain lit or are extinguished.

There are also many famous local festivals, which are noted under the localities in which they occur. These include the car-procession of Jagannath at Puri, the immersion of images in the sea at Bombay; the snake-boat races in Kerala. Details and dates can be obtained from Tourist Information Centres.

THE SIKHS

The Sikhs[1] are a reformed sect of Hindus, followers of a teacher named Nanak, born near Lahore in 1469, who taught the worship of God as Truth—hence the Sikh form of greeting *Sat Shri Akal*. They are not a race, but a brotherhood. The word Sikh means a "disciple" of the Guru or teacher. Nanak's teaching was a reformation of Hinduism combined with various foreign elements. All the Gurus inveighed against caste; Guru Govind finally abolished it, established the religion (1699) on a political and military basis, promulgated as the depository of the principles and doctrines of the Sikh religion the Granth, or holy book, which is now the principal object of the Sikh devotions, and firmly established the Khálsa, as the Sikh brotherhood is called. (Khálsa is from the Arabic *Khális*, which means pure, and was chosen by the Guru to indicate the purity of his faith.)

In the middle of the 18th century the Sikhs, who had been gradually rising into power, struggled with the Afghans for supremacy in the Punjab and finally won it. In 1764, they fought a long and doubtful battle with the Afghan Ahmad Shah Durani in the vicinity of Amritsar, and on his retirement they took Lahore, which soon became the centre of their power, Amritsar being

[1] Pronounced like "seeks": but, more correctly, "sicks".

the religious centre. The government was at first in the hands of a number of *misls*, or confederacies, which were gradually absorbed by Ranjit Singh of the Sukarchakia Misl, who finally became Maharaja and the head of the Sikhs. In 1799 he obtained Lahore from the Afghan ruler, and in 1802 Amritsar. He occupied Ludhiana in 1806, and in 1809 made the Treaty of Amritsar by which British protectorates were advanced to the Sutlej. By 1820 he was paramount in the Punjab, and in 1823 drove the Afghans to the hills beyond Peshawar. In 1838 he assisted the British in the First Afghan War.

Ranjit Singh died in 1839, and his son Kharak Singh and his grandson Nau Nihal Singh died in November the next year, the latter from injuries received in passing a gateway as he was returning from the funeral of his father. Maharaja Sher Singh became ruler of Lahore, and was murdered in September 1843 by the Sindhanwalia Sirdars, who also killed the Prime Minister, Raja Dhian Singh, of Jammu; and upon this Dhalip Singh, a putative son of Maharaja Ranjit Singh, succeeded. His mother, Rani Jindan, attempted to rule through Hira Singh, son of Dhian Singh, Jawahir Singh, her brother, and Lal Singh, her lover, but the first two in turn were murdered, and the real power in the State rested with the army and with Raja Gulab Singh, of Jammu. To relieve themselves of their embarrassments with the army, the Rani and her counsellors encouraged a war with the British, against whom various causes of complaint were alleged, and finally, the army breaking away from all control, crossed the Sutlej at Hariki early in December 1845. Upon this followed the First Sikh War, which was ended by the battle of Sobraon on 10th February 1846 (p. 364) the Jullundur Doab being annexed. The first Treaty of Lahore (8th March 1846) and the Treaty of Amritsar (16th March 1846) resulted in Kashmir and other territories being transferred to Gulab Singh, upon his undertaking to pay a war indemnity. Administration was placed by the second Treaty of Lahore (16th December 1846) under a council of regency on behalf of the minor Maharaja Dhalip Singh, subject to the advice of the Resident in Lahore, first Sir Henry Lawrence and then Sir Frederick Currie. Matters were progressing as well as could be expected when the incident of Multan (p. 564) occurred on 20th April 1848, upon which the Sikh soldiery and people rose in support of their national cause. Serious operations against them were not undertaken till December, when, after indecisive skirmishes at Ramnager and Sadulpur (22nd November and 3rd December 1848), the battle of Chilianwala (p. 586) was fought on 13th January 1849, and the victory of Gujrat was won on 21st February. On 21st March 1849 the Punjab was formally annexed to British India. In 1857 Sikhs fought on the British side, and afterwards provided some of the finest fighting men in the Army. They have an honoured place in the new India, where they occupy leading positions as generals, Air Force commanders, industrialists, engineers, and doctors. Their farmers are among the most progressive and prosperous agriculturalists in the subcontinent.

The following is a chronological table of the Sikh Gurus:

	BORN	GURU
1. Nanak, founder of the Sikh sect	1469	till he died, 1538
2. Angad	1504	1538-1552
3. Amar Das	1509	1552-1574
4. Ram Das, builder of the original lake-temple at Amritsar (1577)	1534	1574-1581
5. Arjan Mal, compiler of the Adi Granth (1604)	1563	1581-1606
6. Har Govind, first warlike leader	1595	1606-1645
7. Har Rai, his grandson	1630	1645-1661
8. Har Krishna, died at Delhi	1656	1661-1664

9. Tegh Bahadur, put to death by Aurangzeb .	1622	1664-1675
10. Govind Singh remodelled the Sikh Government; assassinated at Nander . .	1666	1675-1708

Guru Govind refused to name a successor. He said: "He who wishes to behold the Guru, let him search the Granth."

The Sikhs are known now either as Malwai (which comprises those S. and E. of the Sutlej and Beas) or Manjha (lying N. and W. of these, in the Bari Doab between the Sutlej and the Ravi). After the 1947 Partition the former Sikh States of Patiala, Jind, Nabha, Kapurthala and Faridkot were joined together in a union of which the then Maharaja of Patiala became Prince-President. This was abolished in 1956. In 1967 the Punjab was divided between the Hindi-speaking and Punjabi-speaking populations, the new State of Haryana being created for the former. A Sikh is not necessarily born of that religion, but is baptised into it when of adult age, and in consequence some of the sons of Sikhs fall back into the Hindu religion by simply not taking *khandidipahal*, the portion of the Sikhs. These are called Sahijdhari, and are not baptised at all. They do not consider it necessary to wear the habiliments of the Sikhs.

Orthodox Sikhs are distinguished by the five *kakkars*—uncut hair (*kesh*), short drawers (*kachh*), iron bangle (*kara*), wooden comb (*kanga*) round which the hair is rolled, and iron-handled knife (*kirpan*). A quoit is worn on the turban by Akhalis who are formidable zealots.

The Sikh religion prohibits idolatry, hypocrisy, caste exclusiveness, the cremation of widows on their deceased husbands' funeral pyre, the seclusion of women, tobacco-smoking, infanticide, slander, pilgrimages to the sacred rivers and tanks of the Hindus; it bids its followers to *avoid*—but does not formally prohibit intoxicants—and it inculcates loyalty, gratitude for all favours received, philanthropy, justice, impartiality, truth, honesty, and all the moral and domestic virtues known to the model citizens of any country.

THE RAJPUTS

Although the Rajputs are predominantly Hindus—there is a small section who are Muslims—they have a claim to separate notice as one of the historic races of India.

Their annals are a mine of romance and chivalry, and they were fortunate in their chronicler, Colonel James Tod, according to whom: "There is not a petty State in Rajasthan which has not had its Thermopylae, and scarcely a city which has not produced its Leonidas". There are two important Rajput areas outside Rajasthan—Madhya Pradesh, and the Hill Tracts of Himachal Pradesh and Jammu.

Of the former units which now constitute the State of Rajasthan, Jaisalmer, Jodhpur (or Marwar), and Bikaner form a group on the west and north. Alwar lies likewise to the north. In the east and south-east are Jaipur, Bharatpur, Dholpur, Karauli, Bundi, Kotah and Jhalawar. Those in the south are Partabgarh, Banswara, Dungarpur, and Udaipur or Mewar, with Sirohi on the south-west.

The former British province of Ajmer-Merwara occupied the centre, and was surrounded by the former State of Kishangarh, the chiefships of Shahpura and Lawa, and parts of the former Muslim State of Tonk. With the exception of Tonk, and of Bharatpur and Dholpur, whose family are Jats, the ex-Rulers are all Rajputs. The ruling families of the majority of the former States in Kathiawar and Gujarat are also Rajputs. The Jadeja clan is represented in Kutch (the head), Morvi, Gondal and Nawanagar. Other clans are the Gohels (Bhavnagar and Palitana), the Jethwas (Porbandar) and the Jhalas.

Udaipur (Mewar), Jodhpur (Marwar), Jaipur and Bundi are the four original great States of Rajasthan. Descent from the Sun is claimed by the Maharana of Udaipur, who is head of the Sesodia clan, and holds pride of place among Rajputs. He shared with the Maharawal of Jaisalmer, who is the chief of the Lunar Rajputs, the distinction of belonging to a dynasty which, through eight centuries of foreign domination, held the lands won by its founder until the Ruling Princes disappeared. Round the fortress of Chitor cling legends of a tragic past. Three times Chitor suffered the horrors of sack. Time after time, when all hope was lost, the fatal *johar* was commanded. The women committed their bodies to the flames, and the men, arrayed in bridal robes of saffron, sallied out and died fighting. The last conqueror of Chitor was Akbar in 1567. Thirty thousand of her inhabitants fell on that day: and the tragedy is still remembered by every Rajput.

Even when, compelled to make a virtue of necessity and give their daughters in marriage to the Mughals, as in the case of the Rathor princes of Jodhpur, the personality of the Rajput was not submerged. Some of the most celebrated Emperors, such as Jahangir, Shah Jahan, and Aurangzeb, were the sons of Rajput princesses.[1] The most brilliant conquests of Akbar, Jahangir and Aurangzeb were made by their Rajput generals.

The Maharaja of Jaipur is the head of the Kachhwaha Chauhans. The beautiful ruined city of Amber was their original capital, but Jaipur founded by the famous astronomer-Prince Jai Singh (1699-1744) is now the capital of the modern Indian State of Rajasthan. No lesser place in history has been won by Maharaja Man Singh (1592-1615), who conquered Arakan, Orissa, and Assam, and held in succession the governorships of Bengal and Bihar, the Deccan and Kabul, where he died.

The Maharao Raja of Bundi is the chief of the Hara Chauhan sept, who, like the Kachhwahas, are *agnikula*, or "children of the fire-pit" on Mount Abu. Bundi lies off the beaten track, but readers of Kipling's *From Sea to Sea* will not need to be told that it is one of the places most worth seeing in the whole of India, an old walled town untouched by modernity. The former durbar dress of the nobles was most picturesque, distinguished by a wide pleated skirt. The neighbouring State of Kotah separated from Bundi in 1572. From 1771 to 1824 the reins of authority in Kotah were in the hands of the Regent Zalim Singh, the blind Machiavelli of Rajputana, who survived successfully the many dangers of these troubled years, and managed to get the administration of the State vested in perpetuity in himself, his heirs, and successors. This arrangement subsequently proved unworkable, and after a time a portion of the Kotah State was broken off to form the separate State of Jhalawar for Zalim Singh's descendants. When India became independent, the Princely States were merged into the Union. As a condition of their renunciation of Sovereign powers, the former Rulers were guaranteed both pensions based upon their ancient revenues and also certain personal privileges. These legacies of past greatness, although guaranteed by articles in the Indian Constitution, were gradually eroded, and finally brought to an end by amendments of the Constitution effected by Mrs Indira Gandhi's government in 1971.

THE PARSIS

The Parsis, formerly inhabitants of Iran, are followers of Zoroaster (probably 589-539 B.C.), and form a numerous and influential portion of the population of Surat and Bombay. Their chronology dates from 10th June A.D. 632.

[1] Aurangzeb, in spite of his orthodoxy, also married a Rajput princess. Of the twelve Mughal Rulers who succeeded Akbar, six had Hindu mothers.

When the Sassanide Empire was destroyed by the Muslims in A.D. 651 the Zoroastrians were persecuted, and some of them fled (*c.* 717) to India—first to Diu, in Kathiawar, then to Sanjan, about 25 m. S. of Damao, where the ruler of Gujarat became their protector, and for some hundreds of years they lived there and in the neighbourhood in peace and quiet, finally making Navsari their headquarters. In the 16th century they suffered considerably from Muslim persecution until the time of the British occupation. The sacred fire, which Zoroaster is said to have brought from heaven, is kept burning in consecrated spots, and temples are built over subterranean fires. The priests tend the fires on the altars, chanting hymns and burning incense. They do not worship the sun or fire, as is often commonly supposed. "God, according to Parsi faith, is the emblem of glory, refulgence, and light, and in this view a Parsi while engaged in prayer is directed to stand before the fire, or to direct his face towards the sun, as the most proper symbols of the Almighty." There are fire-temples in Bombay for public worship. The Dasturs are their high priests. A partially successful attempt was made in 1852 to restore the creed of Zoroaster, the Zend Avesta, corrupted by Hindu practices, to its original purity. In order not to pollute the elements, which they adore, the Parsis neither burn nor bury their dead, but expose their corpses to be devoured by birds (see "Towers of Silence",[1] Bombay, p. 104). They have been quick to adopt Western ideas, while in many respects maintaining scrupulously their own manners and customs. This has been noticeable in the matter of education, especially women's education; and this, coupled with social freedom, has given Parsi ladies in the past an advantage. The Parsis were the first Indians to take up cricket. They largely follow commercial pursuits, in which they are most enterprising and successful. Their charity is well known, and is not restricted to their own community.

THE "BACKWARD CLASSES" AND TRIBAL PEOPLES

The former "Untouchables" or "Harijans", must be distinguished from tribes living in special areas for whom the Central and certain State Governments have a special responsibility. These tribes include the Nagas of Nagaland, the Apa Tanis, Daflas and other groups in such areas as Meghalaya, Mizoram and Arunachal Pradesh: the Gonds in Madhya Pradesh, the Santals in Bihar, the Todas in the Nilgiris, and others. The Government of India has done much for their welfare: the official policy (to be seen at work in such areas as Mizoram and Meghalaya) is to preserve tribal institutions so far as is compatible with general progress, political and economic, and to control the pace of change.

The "Backward Classes", properly so-called, permeate every part of India. They may include aborigines who were conquered by Aryan invaders of ancient India, and were condemned to such work as the leather trade and scavenging. The leather worker, indeed, despises the scavenger, but the scavenger is a necessity and is not always badly off, especially if employed by the well-to-do, whose surplus food he can enjoy. Many among these classes might in a Western country take high places in a community, and rumour attributes considerable means to some. In the South, where they may be cultivators, their presence within a range of forty yards was formerly regarded as a pollution to a high-caste Hindu. They were denied access to temples, until Mr Gandhi's crusade, to schools, wells and even burning ghats, but a determined effort has been made in the new Indian constitution to remove these disabilities by making their enforcement a penal offence. The community was fortunate in having their most distinguished representative, Dr Ambedkar, Law Member of

[1] The vernacular name of these structures is Dokhma.

the Indian Government when the new constitution was framed. But the process of embodying them in the Hindu fold as equal members will take time, in spite of the best efforts of the Government.

BUDDHISM AND THE BUDDHISTS

Outside Ladakh, Sikkim, Darjeeling district, and Chittagong, only in Nepal and Sri Lanka will the visitor to the countries dealt with in this *Handbook* find Buddhism very prominent. Tibet, of course, is Buddhist, in spite of the ruthless atheism enforced by Communist China and the exile of the Dalai Lama. The great Buddhist contribution to the cultural heritage of the sub-continent is brought home to the traveller by the magnificent monuments of Buddhist art and architecture at such places as Ajanta and Ellora, Bodh Gaya, Kasia (Kushinagar), Kausambhi, Lumbini, Nalanda, Rajgor, Saheth-Maheth, Sanchi, Sankasya, Sarnath and Vaisali, which are described in this *Handbook*. The Pali Text Society is doing much for the elucidation of Buddhism by publishing original Pali works and some translations. Buddhism is too vast a subject to be treated exhaustively in a few pages, but some account of the origin of the religion is required.

Siddhartha Gautama, afterwards called Buddha (the Enlightened), or Sakyamuni, the sage of the Sakyas, belonged to the Kshatriya or warrior caste, and was the son of Suddhodana, ruler of the Sakya clan, settled around Kapilavastu, in the Nepalese Tarai, N. of the Basti district of Uttar Pradesh. The Mahabodhi Society of India accepts the year 624 B.C. for his birth at the Lumbini garden, the modern Rummindei, near Kapilavastu, and 544 B.C. as the year of his death.

The story of his life contained in the sacred literature of the Buddhists is undoubtedly based on truth, though enveloped in a mass of legend. The sacred literature means the Pali Canon called the "Three Pitakas" (or Baskets), besides subsequent commentaries. It contains the alleged genuine sayings of the Buddha and the moral and religious principles of Buddhism. Among the works in the Canon are the Sutras (or Suttas), the dialogues, the Dhammapada, the Jatakas, the Buddhist psychology, etc., Pali (the "Text") was a literary version of an Aryan dialect, later than the Vedas, earlier than classical Sanskrit. It had ceased to be a vernacular, but was the religious literature of Sri Lanka, Thailand and Burma, written on talipot palm-leaves (say 595 B.C.).

At the age of twenty-nine Gautama made "the great renunciation" of the world and its pleasures. Much troubled by the spectacle of human suffering —age, disease and death—and impressed by the sight of a peaceful saint, he decided to leave his happy home, his loved wife, and his lately born child, and surrender himself to the search for mental peace. Cutting off his long hair and changing his princely raiment, Gautama left the palace suddenly and secretly in ragged garments. As a disciple of two celebrated Brahman sages, he strove to content himself with their teaching and severe self-mortification; the strict austerities he practised produced no peace of mind or divine enlightenment—only great bodily weakness and a conviction of their inutility. So he abandoned penances, and sat in meditation under the Bo-tree, the "tree of knowledge", at Bodh Gaya, where he was tempted by Mara, the personification of carnal desire, to return to the world; but he resisted, and became the Buddha—the Enlightened.

At Varanasi (Benares), he preached his first sermon on "The Foundation of the Kingdom of Righteousness" (Dharmachakra Prawartana) commemorated by the Dhamek Stupa at Sarnath, and devoted his life to teaching. In the kingdom of Magadha (now Bihar). where he travelled he was received with great reverence and hospitality by all classes. Sometimes the King, or another wealthy donor, would build a residence for the Teacher. His disciples formed, under rules framed by the Master, the community of mendicants (Bhikshus) from which the great monastic organisation, called the *Sangha,* was developed. Places such as Lumbini and Bodh Gaya and his temporary residences became sacred spots. At nearly eighty he died at Kusinagara, modern Kasia, in Gorakhpur District. The cremation of his body was conducted with pomp, as for a King, and his ashes were divided, as precious relics, among the chief peoples to whom he had preached. Some of these have been discovered at Peshawar (p. 598) and at Piprâwá (p. 393). At his death Buddhism was the reformed religion of a sect, prevalent within the limited area of his preaching; it was maintained by the organisation of the *Sangha* until the day of its expansion dawned.

Only a summary of the philosophical doctrines of Buddhism can be attempted here. But some knowledge of its character as a religion is essential for an understanding of a great period of ancient India.

In the Buddhist religion the personality of the Buddha is predominant. No Supreme God is admitted in the system. The Buddha, as the teacher of the truth, and therefore the guide and saviour, is the central object of faith and devotion. By his doctrine the work of salvation is limited to human agency—that is, the human mind can achieve omniscience, and human nature arrive at absolute perfection; its purpose is to lead men to a higher life. Human and animal happiness are its avowed object as a practical religion. It has a kindly spirit, and a central tenet is to keep to the "middle path" between worldliness and asceticism. Buddha, it is believed, taught that all life is suffering; that suffering arises from indulgence in desires, especially the longing for continuity of life; and that the only hope of relief lies in the suppression of sensual passions and every attachment, in Nirvana, the highest bliss—meaning, not the extinction or negation of being, but the extinction, the absence, of passionate desire, the goal by which union with the perfect good is obtained. Ignorance, delusion and anger also are fundamental evils and hindrances that must be completely destroyed by intense and continuous mental discipline. Each man must depend on himself and his own efforts towards intellectual and spiritual clearness. Each man must purify his life, grasp the law of causes, perceive the sorrow of existence, the impermanence of all states, and cease to believe in any "soul" apart from the elements which make up the individual and are dissolved at his death. Rewards and punishments, strictly speaking, do not come into the creed, but the inexorable working of cause and effect proceeds without a break, and thus good and evil done in one life bear fruit in the next. The connection between the lives is not the transmigration of a soul but the *Karma* (action), the force that passes on and causes the newly assembled elements of existence to form a new being living on earth or in one of the heavens or hells according to the acts and intentions of a former life, for those constitute the individual's *Karma.* A man's object should be to hear somewhere, at some time, the teaching of a Buddha and become enlightened by meditation and introspection, so as to earn a cessation of the cycle of lives through which he would otherwise be destined to pass, and thus finally to reach Nirvana, the sinless, calm state of mind in which there is no renewed individual existence. Thus the final death, with no new life to follow—as there is no soul which continues to exist after death—is a result of Nirvana, but it is not Nirvana. All men are capable of attaining Nirvana, without distinction of caste, and neither sacrifices nor bodily mortifications are of any avail. To attain salvation by obtaining freedom from delusions, the Buddhist must follow the eightfold path and pass through four stages of higher and higher saintliness. This, the Noble Path, is the very core of Buddhism, by which alone the Buddhist can reach *Arhat,* the state of salvation, the state of a man made perfect. The

Buddha himself is believed to have passed through a great number of existences in the course of the preparation for his final mission. The legends of these lives of Gautama are the famous *jataka* tales which have formed the subjects of many ancient sculptures, paintings and literary works of Buddhist countries.

The principal virtues inculcated by Buddhism are charity, compassion, truthfulness, chastity, respect for the *Sangha*, and self-restraint in regard to all the ambitions, pleasures and attachments of life. The stricter code—the ten precepts—is binding on the religious order: only the first five precepts are binding on the laity. They are practical rules forbidding (1) the destruction of life in any form, (2) theft, (3) unchastity, (4) lying, (5) indulgence in intoxicating drinks, (6) eating at forbidden hours, (7) frequenting performances, (8) use of unguents and ornaments, (9) use of a large or ornamented couch, (10) accepting money.

The Buddhist ideal is lofty, and has done much for Oriental civilisation wherever it has prevailed. In practice the religion has been adapted to the needs of believers of many races, and prominence was given from early times to almsgiving and acts of piety, such as the building of shrines and monasteries. Faith in, adoration of, and meditation on, the Buddha are of great efficacy. Gautama is said to have been preceded by three "Dhyani" Buddhas, and a future Buddha, Maitreya, is looked for. The more austere Hinayana ideas of *arhatship* (saintliness) and *Nirvana* (cessation of sorrow by destruction of craving) developed into the glowing conceptions of Mahayana Buddhists, multiplying Buddhas and Bodhisattvas (predestined Buddhas), and carrying the notion of *Nirvana* far beyond *arhatship*. The Tashi Lama of Tibet is believed to be the manifestation of Gautama, the Dalai Lama of a Bodhisattva.

Buddha is generally represented in one of three attitudes—he sits cross-legged, either with both hands raised in the preaching posture, or with his hands in contact in an attitude of profound meditation, or with one hand pointing to the earth (see Plate 2 on p. 23).

BUDDHIST FESTIVALS

The New Year Festival corresponds to the Makar Sankranti of the Hindus (see p. 24).

The last birth of Gautama is celebrated at the end of April by the worship of his images, followed by processions. In Sri Lanka the legendary coming of the Buddha to the island is celebrated by a festival in March of April, when the pilgrims visit either his footprint on Adam's Peak or the sacred Bo-tree at Anuradhapura.

In 1956 the 2,500th anniversary of Buddha's birth, enlightenment, and death was celebrated throughout India by an international symposium to which Buddhist scholars from all over the world were invited.

THE JAINS

The founder was Vardhamāna, commonly known by his title of Mahavira, and designated Nataputta by the rival order of Buddhists. Mahavira was born probably about 599 B.C. to Raja Siddhartha, head of the Nata clan of Kshatriyas, settled at Vaisali (the modern Basarh), about 27 m. N. of Patna. His mother was Trisala, a King's daughter. At thirty he adopted a spiritual career and became a monk of the Parsvanatha order. After twelve years his divine mission was recognised; he was entitled Mahavira (Great Hero) and acknowledged to be a Jina (spiritual conqueror), from which the system Jainism and sect Jain are derived. In the Jain hierarchy Parsvanatha was Mahavira's immediate predecessor; from him the sacred hill Parasnath, in the Hazaribagh district, has its name. Mahavira taught his religious system and organised asceticism for thirty years, chiefly in Bihar, in the same area as Gautama Buddha, without conflicting. He died probably in 527 B.C. at Pawa, in the Patna district. (These are the traditional dates: *The Cambridge History of India*, vol. 1, p. 697, gives 540-468 B.C.)

Jainism is a monastic organisation—not strictly a religion. The Jains acknowledged caste, and the Brahmins as priests; their monastic order included four classes—monks, nuns (Svetambaras only), lay-brothers, and lay-sisters. Through this lay element Jainism survived in its monastic settlements and lay communities when Buddhism disappeared. The Svetambaras collected and preserved their sacred books in a Council at Pataliputra, the modern Patna, about 310 B.C.; a subsequent Council at Valabhi, in Gujarat, made a revised edition. In A.D. 70 or 82 a schism took place between the Svetambaras (white-clad or yellow-robed) and Digambaras (sky-clad or naked).

The chronicling spirit is strong in the Jains, who maintain lists of the succession of teachers. Ancient Jain stupas and inscriptions have been discovered. The object being to obtain liberation from the bonds of transmigration, the only remedy lies in an abnegation of the world. Thus is their attainment of Nirvana (liberation from any further re-birth) to be obtained in life, not after death, by the principles of Right Faith, Right Cognition, Right Conduct. Right Faith is absolute reliance on their founder as *the* Tirthankara, or path-maker, to Nirvana. There were twenty-four Tirthankaras, from the first, Adinath, to the last three, Neminath, Parsvanatha and Mahavira. Each is known by a symbol (see p. 236). Right Cognition means the correct understanding of the Jain theory of the world, which assigns a soul to every individual person or thing. Right Conduct is summed up in five great vows, which include their regard for the minutest creatures of animal life as possessing souls. Priests therefore wear gauze respirators to prevent involuntary inhalation of insects.

Only monks can attain Nirvana; nuns cannot, nor can lay adherents for whom the vows are relaxed. Jainism has developed by the introduction of a religious cult into their essentially atheistic system. The building of temples and other religious features are excrescences on the pure Jain system, due to the admission of the lay element. The Jains chiefly reside in the trade centres of W. India and Rajasthan. Many of the wealthy Marwaris in Calcutta are Jains from Bikaner, Marwar or Jaipur. Their most famous shrines are at the hill of Parasnath (p. 131), Satrunjaya, and Girnar, in Kathiawar (p. 278), Pawa Puri in Bihar, Mount Abu (p. 255), and Ranakpur (p. 215). They maintain pinjrapols, or hospitals, for all decrepit animals. They are very charitable.

CHRISTIANITY

The oldest established Christians in India are the Syrian Christians of Travancore and Cochin, probably the result of Nestorian missionary activity in the 6th century, although they claim apostolic origin from St Thomas. Next to them come the Roman Catholics of Goa[1] and the other former Portuguese possessions, where wholesale proselytising was carried on in the 16th century. Protestant Christian Missions[2] have been active in India for the last century and a half, and their labours have also not been without fruit. The Christian population was estimated at 14 million in 1974.

The Anglican Church was disestablished by the India Church Act and

[1] St Francisco de Xavier (1506-52) began missionary work in India in 1542 at Goa, and among the Paravas, the pearl-fishermen. His course lay through Travancore, Sri Lanka, Mailapur, Malacca, the Malay Archipelago, India and Malacca again, Japan, Goa, Singapore; he died on the Chinese coast of Kwangtung, and was eventually buried at Goa.

[2] The first Protestant missionaries were the Lutherans at Tranquebar in 1706, the Baptists at Serampore in 1793, and the Anglican Church in 1813.

Measure (1927). On the 27th September 1947 the Anglican, Methodist, Congregationalist, Presbyterian and Dutch Reformed Churches of South India joined in one Church of South India with its metropolitan see in Madras. Later, the Church of North India was established along similar lines. The Roman Catholics are the most numerous body, served by Jesuit Fathers (who are often learned men of scientific interests) and by other orders with a considerable hierarchy. The Salvation Army has worked mainly in Kerala, and in the Punjab, where its efforts at the uplift of those formerly regarded as "Criminal Tribes" have been very successful.

Most of the Indian Christians have come from the Backward Castes and from aboriginal races. The movement towards Christianity among these classes has been largely due to social causes; and two results have been the education of their children and their uplift from degradation. The main centres of this work have been (1) in *Northern India*—the Chenab Colony in the Punjab, Madhya Pradesh, Bihar, and the Khasi Hills in Assam; and (2) in *Southern India*—the Telugu Country in the north of the Tamil Nadu State, the Tinnevelly district and Kerala in the south.

In the case of the higher grades of Indian society, the number of Indian Christians is comparatively small; but these have exercised a much greater influence over the educated classes of the community than their number would suggest. At the same time the study of Christian teaching has had a reflex action on the higher classes, and the value of the work done in the Mission colleges and schools has been immense; but Christianity in the East is not now reliant on Western influence. The philanthropic ideals of Christianity have also been manifested on a large scale through medical missions, whose hospitals and dispensaries have had an important influence. Mission schools have done much pioneer work, especially in the field of female education.

5. ART

It would be difficult in a short summary to deal separately with the art of India and that of Pakistan, since, prior to the Muslim period, what is now Pakistan had no Islamic art or architecture and, during the Muslim period, much of what is now India was affected by Muslim culture. In what follows, the terms "India" and "Indian" accordingly refer to the undivided subcontinent and have no present political significance. It should be noted that Hindu, Buddhist and Jain sculptures are closely connected with religious edifices and that, apart from abstract or floral decoration on buildings, there is, strictly speaking, no Islamic sculpture. So far as art is concerned, it is in the sphere of Indian miniature paintings rather than in that of sculpture that major Muslim influences are apparent. For further information, Sections 6 and 7 as well as individual entries under routes should be consulted.

SCULPTURE

Until the end of the 19th century, Indian sculpture was almost totally ignored by the West. "Before the rise of Expressionism in Germany and France," Heinrich Zimmer has said, "the appreciation of practically all Indian works was rendered impossible for Europeans, both by the conventional classicistic ideals that prevented the understanding of even baroque painting, sculpture and architecture, and by a squint-eyed Protestant-Puritan outlook on life, which simply stood piously aghast at the wild display of the sensual and demonic offered in the Indian revelation." More perhaps than any other country, Western or Eastern, India has regarded the human body as inherently noble and has vividly expressed this belief in sculpture. It is true that a general repudiation of the senses is implied in many sublime examples, but a basic delight in love and physical well-being accounts, in other cases, for "a radiance and unity of form", which in Sir William Rothenstein's words, "has never been better expressed". "I doubt", he adds, "whether anything lovelier has been made by the hand of man than the Indian medieval temples." If to this assessment is added the Indian sculptor's mastery of technique, his rhythmical approach to composition, command of elegant naturalism on the one hand and of expressive distortion on the other, above all his supreme ability to express in stone such different qualities as emotional intensity, erotic poise, ecstatic exaltation and philosophic calm, it is evident how much was lost in the West by former neglect.

The earliest large-scale Indian sculpture to survive was made between the 3rd century B.C. and the 2nd century A.D. and reflected the place of religion in early Indian life. As in ancient and medieval Europe, early India was peopled by male and female nature spirits associated with rocks, hills, trees and streams. An earth goddess of abundance was revered and fertility in crops and men were attributed to her favours. Nature spirits (*yakshas* and *yakshis*) were visualised as male and female figures and in order to promote welfare stone sculptures of them were sometimes erected under trees and offerings made of fruit and flowers. Early figures from Parkham (Mathura Museum) and Besnagar (Indian Museum, Calcutta) have a tough bucolic presence while a third figure, the Didarganj *chauri*-bearer (Patna Museum) has a polished smoothness, sumptuous elegance and an open-eyed charm which superbly epitomises early Indian ideals of feminine beauty. Her exact role and identity have been disputed but it is as a *yakshi* (a female nature spirit) of regal authority that she should most probably be regarded.

It was into this world that the Buddha and his previous incarnations had been born and while his purpose was to demonstrate that ultimate extinction (release from the cycle of birth and rebirth) could be achieved by the elimination of passionate cravings, it was in terms of life as it was that Buddhist pilgrimage centres were devised. At Sanchi and Bharhut in Central India, Sarnath near Benares, and at Nagarjunikonda, Jaggayyapeta and Amaravati in South India, *stupas* or mounds containing relics of Buddhist teachers or disciples were surrounded by carved railing-pillars pierced by four entrances. At Sanchi, the "first" or Great Stupa, was further embellished by four huge gateways heavily sculpted with figures of elephants, *yakshas* and *yakshis*. The purpose of this sculpture was didactic—to illustrate, as in the medallions on the railing-pillars, incidents in the lives of the Buddha; propitiatory, as in the frank depiction of nature spirits redolent of fertile charms; protective, as in the insertion at the entrances of large guardian figures and great lions; and finally magical by the association with the site of symbols of fertility (elephants symbolic of clouds, rain and royalty or lotus plants symbolic of water, vegetation and crops). One further function must be stressed. Despite the strict boycott of art and luxury imposed on Buddhist monks, lay Buddhists expressed their veneration by multiplying sculptures as a form of adornment. To Buddhist monks all was vanity; to lay Buddhists art was merit. The resulting plethora of carving, ranging in style from the placid gravity of the *yaksha* and *yakshi* figures at Bharhut (Indian Museum, Calcutta), the bounding gusto of narrative scenes at both Bharhut and Sanchi, the frank parading of feminine charm at Sanchi (*in situ*) to the suave mannerism of figures at Amaravati (Madras Museum; British Museum, London) indicates the great breadth of the early Indian achievement. At Mathura in Uttar Pradesh, a relic mound to a disciple of Mahavira, founder of Jainism and parallel as a teacher to the Buddha, included the same type of exuberant *yakshi* figures, their characters as spirits being indicated by the dwarfs and water creatures on which they stand or by the branches which they clutch.

In addition to relic mounds, Buddhist and Jain communities also availed of a second major type of structure. For many centuries caves had been regarded as an appropriate haunt for ascetics and, perhaps on account of their obvious resemblance to the womb, as a means of achieving profound levels of insight. To enter this twilight realm, it could be argued, was tantamount to "returning to the womb". In later free-standing shrines, the term "womb" was even applied to the sanctum. The Buddhist and Jain innovation was to construct artificial cave temples (*chaityas*) and cave assembly halls (*viharas*) by cutting them out of the living rock. As in the case of *stupas*, entrances to these structures required special protection and at two of the greatest Buddhist sites, Karli and Kanheri in the Bombay area, male and female couples (*mithunas*) depicted as either standing together, embracing, holding bunches of flowers or even dancing, confronted the pilgrim with lively demonstrations of exuberant joy. Although at one time mistakenly regarded as donor figures, their robust and glamorous physiques had almost certainly a different purpose, to distract baleful spirit-marauders, to imbue the site with lush fertility and promote the welfare of the local community. Congeries of Buddhist cave temples were carved from the rock at other sites (see in particular Ajanta) and at Ellora, Jain and Buddhist caves were constructed in close proximity.

Before the 2nd century A.D. neither the Buddha nor the Jain Mahavira were shown in human form but were represented by symbols. Gradually, however, the two teachers were deified as Saviours and sculpture glorified their physical presence. Under the Central Asian Kushan dynasty of Northern India (2nd and 3rd centuries A.D.), images of the Buddha, notable for their rarified serenity and air of bland compassion, were carved at Mathura, and at approximately the same time a second style, also depicting the Buddha in human form, arose in North-west India in the ancient province of Gandhara on the trade routes to and from the former Roman Empire. Here sculptures of the Buddha and his attendants, the Bodhisattvas (or Buddhas-to-be), are tinged with the mannered idealism of provincial Greco-Roman art and are at times reminiscent of statues of Apollo. In sculptures made for Buddhist monasteries and shrines in Gandhara, the grouping of the figures, their gestures and the treatment of the drapery owe much to Greco-Roman influence.

Under the Guptas (4th to 6th centuries), a dynasty of Northern India controlling an empire almost as large as that of the Mauryas (4th to 2nd centuries B.C.), Buddhist and Jain communities expanded their interest in sculpture, the Gupta ideal of sensuous refinement imbuing many figures with exalted nobility (Ajanta Caves; Sarnath Museum). At the same time Brahmanical Hinduism began to emerge as a potent rival. Figures of the Hindu gods, especially Vishnu and Siva with their consorts Lakshmi and Parvati, were rendered in quasi-human terms and were endowed with equal grace and majesty. From the 7th century onwards Buddhism and its world of nature-spirits was gradually superseded and although under the Senas and Palas of Bengal (8th to 12th centuries) suave and shining figures of the Buddha in black chlorite stone were still produced, by 1200 Buddhism in India was extinct.

By contrast Brahmanical Hinduism quickly spread and by the 7th century had become the dominant Indian religion. During a transition period (6th to 8th centuries) the Buddhist practice of excavating caves was at times adopted for Hindu ends. At Badami three Brahmanical caves containing sculptures of Vishnu and Siva with attending beauties were made in the 6th century. At Ellora, seventeen Brahmanical caves were added in the 7th and 8th centuries to the existing twelve Buddhist and five Jain ones; and at Elephanta, an island off Bombay, cave temples to Siva were excavated in the 8th century, one of them including perhaps the greatest achievement of Indian sculpture, a huge three-headed figure of Siva expressive of his might, tenderness and serene beneficence. A second Buddhist practice of carving the living rock was also adopted at Ellora and Mahabalipuram. At Ellora it resulted in an astonishing *tour de force*, the Kailasa temple (7th century), a great structure hewn from the hill-side and seething with turbulent figures, while in South India at Mahabalipuram (7th century) large boulders were covered with scenes from Hindu mythology and in seven cases were cut into free-standing temples.

This recourse to Buddhist conventions was a transient experiment and for the most part Hindu temples from the 6th century onwards were conceived as free-standing structures built in the open and comprising a porch or gateway, a tower and an inner shrine. Within the shrine was a statue or emblem of the god —normally either Vishnu or Siva—the latter often represented by the male organ (*lingam*) set in the female organ (*yoni*). On the outside of the tower or within the porch, sculptures of celestial beauties (*surasundaris*), dancing girls (*apsarases*) and musicians (*gandharvas*) were incorporated as adjuncts to the court of a heavenly king. Other gods were also portrayed in close association. The supernatural nature of all these characters, whether regarded as visiting royalty or as palace attendants, was often shown by the inclusion at their feet of midget figures. In contrast to the early period, male and female couples (*mithunas*) were at times shown in actual intercourse—the union of man with woman being regarded in later Hindu thought as the nearest analogy to the state of blissful extinction in godhead which was the goal of Indian living.

To accompany these new conceptions markedly different styles of sculpture evolved in different parts of India. In Karnataka (Mysore) under the Hoysala dynasties (11th to 14th centuries) gods with their attendant dancers and musicians festooned with jewellery were treated with baroque exuberance and florid majesty. In Orissa at Bhubaneswar (10th to 12th centuries) panels of vegetative scrolls were interspersed with lithe celestial figures, their sumptuous forms reinterpreting traditional ideals. At Konarak, also in Orissa, a temple to Surya, the Sun God, was erected in the form of a giant chariot. It was covered with erotic sculptures depicting with rough vigour a variety of sexual postures, possibly in celebration of a fertility festival. The squat figures and over-large heads are symptomatic of its later date, the 13th century. In Central India and Rajasthan under the Chandellas hosts of temples were erected, covered in some cases with figures of loving couples, heavenly beauties, deities and rearing lions. A prime centre was Khajuraho (11th century) where elongated figures were represented with a flowing linear rhythm and with innocent radiance. In Rajasthan at Mount Abu (10th to 13th centuries) a series of Jain temples modelled on Hindu practice were covered with lace-like marble fantasies. Finally in the south, from the 11th century onwards (long after Muslim invasions had curtailed temple-building and sculpture in the Deccan and the north) massive temples with giant tower-gateways testified to the lasting vigour of the Indian sculptor at sites such as Madura(i), Thanjavur (Tanjore), Srirangam, and Kanchipuram (Conjeeveram).

Besides sculpture in stone, images in copper and bronze ranging from styles of primitive distortion to those of sleek refinement and relaxed grace have been characteristic of most periods.

PAINTING

In the sphere of painting India is renowned for the scope of its large murals and for its long tradition of painting in miniature. From the earliest period onwards walls of palaces and temples were painted with scenes drawn from Buddhist, Jain and Hindu mythology, courtly love poetry, legends and traditions. In some cases sculpture also was coloured. As in Europe the great majority of these murals have disappeared but at Ajanta murals in Caves 1 and 2 (6th century A.D.) survive on a big enough scale to give an overwhelming impression of sensuous magnificence.

A second type of painting—miniatures—is more accessible. Like those in European mediaeval manuscripts these pictures were small—rarely more than 12 by 8 inches. They were executed in gouache on a prepared ground and burnished to produce a smooth enamel-like surface. The earliest miniatures to have survived (11th to 12th centuries) are associated with Eastern India where Buddhist palm-leaf texts were provided with auspicious illustrations in a style of supple naturalism. The exquisitely modelled deities depicted are reminiscent of figures in the Ajanta murals. The arrival of Muslim invaders from the north extinguished this painting and with the decline of Buddhism, the tradition came to an end. Painting persisted, however, in Western and Central India and in Rajasthan where the rich merchant community of the Jains sponsored copies of their distinctive religious texts on palm-leaf and later from the 14th century onwards on paper. In contrast to the style of Eastern India, Jain painting is marked by strong reds, blues and golds, wiry angularity, hieratic distortions, flat geometric shapes and the strange convention of three-quarter view faces with one of the eyes protruding.

As a result of the Muslim invasions, Persian artists and manuscripts reached India and in the 15th and early 16th centuries new styles arose at a number of small Muslim courts. These styles, known as Sultanate, were an adaptation to Indian conditions of local styles of Persian painting. At Jaunpur in Eastern India and Mandu in Central India, Muslim rulers commissioned illustrated secular texts, including the Bustan of Sadi and a book of cookery. The Jain style was also modified to include the illustration of Indian love-poetry. It was out of these experiments that Rajput painting in Central India and Rajasthan was to develop in the 16th century.

Side by side with these developments (16th century) new styles arose in the Sultanate kingdoms of the Deccan—Ahmadnagar, Bijapur and Golconda. In Ahmadnagar, painting combined influences from the Hindu empire of Vijayanagar in South India (which had had a tradition of wall-painting) with Muslim idioms drawn from Central Indian painting. In Bijapur and Golconda styles of dignified opulence evolved from the blending of Persian conventions with European influences from the Portuguese settlement at Goa.

In the second half of the 16th century the Mughals, a Muslim dynasty from Turkistan, established themselves at Delhi and gradually built up a vast empire. Akbar (1556-1605), the third Mughal emperor, was the first to feel firmly established and from the late fifteen-sixties painting flourished under his patronage. Studios were set up under the supervision of two Persian artists, Mir Sayyid Ali and Abdus Samad, and many Indian artists were enrolled. The finest materials were provided and the emperor himself commissioned many projects, especially histories of the Mughal house. He also ordered illustrations to religious texts. At the same time Western Renaissance and mannerist influences filtered into India through the agency of Christian missionaries and Portuguese embassies. As a result a new style of fluent naturalism developed in which bounding line and brilliant colour captured dramatic situations with lively skill. Under Jahangir (1605-27) the style further developed to include sensitive portrait studies. As a result of the emperor's personal interest in natural history, studies of birds, animals and plants were also added. The reign of Shah Jahan (1628-57), which is renowned for its rich marble architecture, jades, jewellery and metal work, saw a wealth of elaborate miniatures, especially portrait studies and scenes of court life. From the end of the 17th century, as the Mughal empire slowly waned, royal patronage diminished and the quality of the court art declined. Nevertheless, painting continued until the 19th century not only in Delhi but also in provincial centres such as Patna, Murshidabad, Fyzabad, Lucknow and Farrukhabad, where the Mughal viceroys or great landlords patronised painting. Most of these paintings were intended to be looked at individually. Often they were set in elaborate mounts and bound together into albums.

While the Mughals were establishing their empire in Northern India in the late 16th century, painting had continued under the Muslim dynasties in Central India and under the Rajput rulers of Rajasthan. Here the symbolic colours of western Indian painting and the old expressionistic distortions were preserved and applied to a whole new range of subject-matter. The romantic situations present in Sanskrit love-poetry were illustrated as well as the great Hindu religious texts relating the stories of Rama and Krishna. The rise of Vaishnavism in which the romance of Krishna with Radha was celebrated and devoted love was regarded as a means to salvation led to many paintings on Krishna themes. Musical subjects as well as poems about the seasons were also depicted. The former, known as *Ragamalas* or "Garlands of music", are unique to Indian painting. Musical modes were symbolised by princes with their consorts and sons. So popular did this subject become that it spread to Muslim society. Brilliant colour, stark compositions and angular gestures gave this early type of painting in Rajasthan and Central India vigour and sophistication.

By the end of the 17th century Mughal influence had spread and in states such as Marwar, Bikaner and Kishangarh the old style was softened by Mughal elements. Portraits on horseback became popular and in these pictures Rajput chivalry was seemingly embodied. At Kishangarh the career of Raja Sawant Singh, an ardent Vaishnava and himself a poet, sparked off a style of visionary elegance, and in Kotah, paintings of the jungle had naïve charm.

As in Rajasthan, miniature painting also flourished at the numerous Rajput courts in the Punjab Hills of Northern India, almost every state having its own traditional style. While portraits were often made, favourite topics were *Ragamalas* as well as romantic love-poetry. As in Rajasthan, the cult of Vaishnavism was a potent influence and texts such as the *Bhagavata Purana*, the *Gita Govinda* and the *Bihari Sat Sai*, describing Krishna's romance with Radha and his life among the cowherds of Brindaban, were illustrated. In certain states, such as Basohli, Mankot and Kulu, styles of fierce distortion using vivid hot colours were prevalent in the 17th and early 18th centuries. Later styles at Guler, Kangra and Garhwal were marked by soft languorous forms and delicate colouring and provided one of the most romantic and idyllic interpretations of Indian poetry and religion.

With the growth of British power in the 19th century Mughal patronage came to an end and with the gradual undermining of the feudal power and riches of the Rajput nobility, Rajput painting both in Rajasthan and the Punjab Hills also declined. As Western values became fashionable amongst wealthy or educated Indians, so traditional painting lost its appeal. Many of the artists who had formerly worked for Indian patrons moved to the large British settlements and painted subjects which had an appeal for the British community such as pictures of costume, occupations, festivals, methods of transport, flowers, birds and animals. The style which emerged and which persisted for a century is known as "Company Painting".

In Bengal throughout the 19th century a form of popular water-colour painting was patronised by pilgrims to the Kalighat temple near Calcutta.

In the second half of the 19th and early 20th centuries attempts were made through art-schools to revive traditional Indian painting but, in spite of the efforts of enthusiasts such as E. B. Havell and the neo-Bengal school, had little success. Today Indian artists belong to the international tradition though their Indian roots are still apparent. Twentieth-century Indian painters who have made distinctive and original contributions include the poet Rabrindranath Tagore, Amrita Sher-Gil, Jamini Roy, M. F. Hussain, Satish Gujral, Avinash Chandra and F. N. Souza.

BOOKS

For a general account of Indian sculpture and painting see Sherman E. Lee, *A History of Far Eastern Art* (Thames & Hudson, London, 1964) and Sir Leigh Ashton (ed.), *The Art of India and Pakistan* (Faber, London, 1950); and for histories of Indian art, chiefly sculpture, see Benjamin Rowland, *The Art and Architecture of India* (Penguin Books, London, 3rd ed., 1967), H. Zimmer (ed. J. Campbell), *The Art of Indian Asia* (Pantheon, New York, 1955), Stella Kramrisch, *The Art of India* (Phaidon, London, 1954), A. K. Coomaraswamy, *History of Indian and Indonesian Art* (paperback, Dover publications, New York, 1965) and *Concise History of Indian Art* (Craven, Thames & Hudson, London, 1976).

For other books on sculpture significant mainly for the range and high quality of their illustrations, see Raymond Burnier, *Hindu Medieval Sculpture* (La Palme, Paris, 1950), Louis Frédéric, *Indian Temples and Sculpture* (Thames & Hudson, London, 1959), Ajit Mookerjee, *Art of India* (Oxford Book & Stationery Company, Calcutta, New Delhi, 1952) and Pierre Rambach & Vitold de Golish, *The Golden Age of Indian Art* (Thames & Hudson, London, 1955).

For individual monographs on sculpture dealing with particular styles or periods see L. Bachhofer, *Early Indian Sculpture* (New York, 1929), D. Barrett, *Sculptures from Amaravati* (British Museum, London, 1954) and Madeleine Hallard, *The Gandhara Style and the Evolution of Buddhist Art* (Thames & Hudson, London, 1968).

For general accounts of Indian painting see W. G. Archer, *Indian Painting* (Iris colour books, Batsford, London, 1956) and *Indian Miniatures* (New York Graphic Society, Greenwich & Studio, London, 1960), P. S. Rawson, *Indian Painting* (Pierre Tisné, Paris; Universe Books, New York, 1961), D. Barrett and B. Gray, *Painting of India* (Skira, Zwemmer, London; World Publishing Co., Cleveland, 1963) and J. K. Galbraith and M. S. Randhawa, *Indian Painting* (Houghton Mifflin, Boston; Hamish Hamilton, London, 1968).

For books and monographs dealing with painting in particular areas or periods see, for murals, Madanjeet Singh, *The Cave Paintings of Ajanta* (Thames & Hudson, London, 1965), and S. Sivaramamurti, *South Indian Painting* (National Museum, New Delhi, 1968); and for miniatures, Percy Brown, *Indian Painting under the Mughals* (Clarendon Press, Oxford, 1924), Karl Khandalavala and Moti Chandra, *New Documents of Indian Painting* (Prince of Wales Museum, Bombay, 1969) and W. G. Archer, *Indian Paintings from the Punjab Hills* (Sotheby Park Bernet, London, New York; Oxford University Press, Delhi, 1973).

The following books and monographs on miniature painting are either parts of a publisher's series or are issued by particular institutions:

Faber Gallery of Oriental Art, Faber, London: W. G. Archer, *Kangra Painting* (1952), *Garhwal Painting* (1954), *Central Indian Painting* (1958); D. Barrett, *Painting of the Deccan* (1958); J. V. S. Wilkinson, *Mughal Painting* (1948).

Victoria and Albert Museum monographs, H.M.S.O., London: W. G. Archer, *Indian Painting in Bundi and Kotah* (1958), *Paintings of the Sikhs* (1966) and *Kalighat Paintings* (1971).

Asia Society, 112 East 64th Street, New York: Sherman E. Lee, *Rajput Painting* (1960), S. C. Welch, *The Art of Mughal India* (1963), S. C. Welch and M. C. Beach, *Gods, Thrones and Peacocks* (1965).

Lalit Kala Akademi, Rabindra Bhavan, Janpath, New Delhi: Moti Chandra,

Mewar Painting (1957), Pramod Chandra, *Bundi Painting* (1959), Karl Khandalavala and Eric Dickinson, *Kishangarh Painting* (1959).

National Museum of India, New Delhi: M. S. Randhawa, *Kangra Paintings of the Bhagavata Purana* (1960), *Kangra Paintings on Love* (1962), *Kangra Paintings of the Gita Govinda* (1963).

Publications Division, Government of India, Old Secretariat, New Delhi-8: M. S. Randhawa, *Kangra Valley Painting* (1954), *Basohli Painting* (1959).

For the relations between Indian painting and poetry, see W. G. Archer, *The Loves of Krishna* (Allen & Unwin, London, 1957; paperback, Grove Press, New York, 1964) and Deben Bhattacharya and W. G. Archer, *Love Songs of Vidyapati* (Allen & Unwin, London, 1963; paperback, Grove Press, New York, 1970).

For Tantric Art, a secretive product chiefly of Eastern India, see Ajit Mookerjee, *Tantric Art* (Kumar Gallery, New Delhi, New York, 1967) and P. S. Rawson, *The Art of Tantra* (Thames & Hudson, London, 1973).

For primitive Indian sculpture and painting see W. G. Archer, *The Vertical Man* (Allen & Unwin, London, 1947), Ajit Mookerjee, *Folk Toys of India* and *Indian Primitive Art* (Oxford Book & Stationery Company, Calcutta, New Delhi, 1956, 1959), Verrier Elwin, *The Tribal Art of Middle India* (Oxford University Press, London, 1951) and Mildred Archer, *Indian Miniatures and Folk Paintings* and *Indian Paintings from Court, Town and Village* (Arts Council of Great Britain, London, 1967, 1970).

For modern Indian art see W. G. Archer, *India and Modern Art* (Allen & Unwin, London, 1959) and P. R. Ramchandra Rao, *Contemporary Indian Art* (Moosaram Bagh, Hyderabad-36, India, 1969).

For Company Painting see Mildred Archer, *Company Drawings in the India Office Library* (H.M.S.O., London, 1972) and with W. G. Archer, *Indian Painting for the British* (Oxford University Press, London, 1955).

MUSEUMS

Apart from the sites and monuments referred to above, Indian sculpture can be studied in the following museums: in India, the National Museum of India, New Delhi, the Indian Museum, Calcutta, the Allahabad, Baroda, Lucknow, Madras, Mathura (Muttra) and Patna Museums, the Prince of Wales Museum of Western India, Bombay, the Museum and Art Gallery, Chandigarh, and in the Archaeological Museums at Sarnath (Varanasi) and Gwalior. One of the most important collections, easily overlooked, is at Bharat Kala Bhavan (Indian Art Museum), Hindu University Varanasi (Benares). Due to its late creation, after Independence, and the reluctance of State museums to part with important pieces, the National Museum of India, New Delhi, is not so well endowed with sculpture as is the Indian Museum, Calcutta, which despite the replacement of Calcutta by New Delhi as the capital of India, has retained its former "national collection". The finest collections of Gandhara sculpture are at the Museum and Art Gallery, Chandigarh; at the Taxila Museum and at the Lahore Museum. The largest collection of South Indian bronzes is in the Madras Museum.

Of Indian miniature paintings the finest collections in India are at the National Museum of India, New Delhi, Bharat Kala Bhavan (Hindu University), Benares, the Museum and Art Gallery, Chandigarh, Jaipur State Museum, Rampur State Library, Salar Jang Museum, Hyderabad, the Prince of Wales Museum of Western India, Bombay and the N. C. Metita Collection at Sanskar Kendra, Ahmadabad. In Pakistan, the Lahore Museum has an important collection of Rajput paintings from the Punjab Hills.

Outside India the following museums have important collections of both

Indian sculpture and paintings: in London, the Victoria and Albert Museum (Indian Section), the British Museum (Department of Oriental Antiquities); in Paris, the Musée Guimet; and in America, the Cleveland Art Museum, Ohio, the Museum of Fine Arts, Boston, the Los Angeles County Museum of Art and the Metropolitan Museum, New York.

The collections at the following museums are significant mainly for sculpture: in America, the Philadelphia Museum of Art, the De Young Museum, San Francisco, the Seattle Art Museum and the Nelson-Atkins Gallery of Art, Kansas City (bronzes).

The collections of the following institutions are significant mainly for paintings: in London, the British Library (Department of Oriental Manuscripts—distinct from the Department of Oriental Antiquities, British Museum) and the India Office Library; in Oxford, the Bodleian Library; in Dublin, the Chester Beatty Library; and in America, the Walters Art Gallery, Baltimore, the Freer Gallery of Art, Washington, and the Fogg Art Museum, Harvard, Cambridge.

The largest collection of Company Paintings is at the India Office Library, London, and of Kalighat and Sikh paintings at the Victoria and Albert Museum, London.

Paintings of India in oils and water-colours by British artists are well represented in the Victoria Memorial Hall, Calcutta.

All museums, galleries and libraries normally have on public display only a small part of their collections; the remainder being kept in reserve collections available to the public on application to the curatorial staff. In India and Pakistan, museums are often closed on Mondays and Fridays.

6. HISTORY AND ARCHITECTURE, Part I

ANCIENT INDIA

Indians, Pakistanis and Bangladeshis take great pride in their ancient civilisation. In this sketch, designed to link up for the benefit of visitor or the ordinary resident what may be familiar to the scholar, it is impossible to examine at any length the painstaking research which has contributed to the present state of knowledge. The Archaeological Departments of India and Pakistan have done much good work. Their discoveries, and the wealth of ancient monuments now rescued from decay, have been summarised for the information of the traveller in numerous well-illustrated brochures available at the Official Tourist Information Offices. Reference should also be made to section 5 on Art, p. 34 *seq.*, above.

The principal sites of historical and archaeological interest are described in this *Handbook* under the appropriate localities.

A brief chronological framework may help the traveller to form some idea of the immense time-sequence of ancient Indian civilisation.

The story begins with the most ancient "Chalcolithic" sites at Harappa, Mohenjodaro and elsewhere, places to which approximate dates prior to 2000 B.C. have been assigned. The "Indus Civilisation" was of high order, with amenities superior to those of many modern Asian towns of equal size. This civilisation has been discovered in the Ambala District near Rupar (p. 355), Maski near Raichur (p. 438), at Maheshwar in the Narbada Valley, and Lothal near Ahmedabad. At Taxila also (p. 591) the earliest of the three cities was first occupied before 2000 B.C. This so-called Indus Valley civilisation was first disclosed by Sir John Marshall. More recently the archaeologists of Pakistan and India have greatly added to existing knowledge of it.

The settlement in North India of the "Aryans" whose social development became Hinduism, took place between 2000 and 900 B.C.

KEY DATES

1200-1000 B.C. Matrix of the Rigveda.
518 B.C. N.W. India added to Persian Empire.
500 „ Extension by Bimbisara of Magadha Kingdom.
326 „ Alexander the Great enters N.W. India.
321 „ Mauryan Empire, Chandragupta (Sandrakottos); conquers Punjab, -317.
262 „ Conversion of Asoka (273-232) to Buddhism.
202 „ Andhras in Upper Godavari Valley.
184 „ Sunga dynasty at Avanti (Ujjain), -70.
170 „ Sirkap (Taxila) built by Eucratides (Bactria).
80 „ Sakas (Scythians) take Taxila.
70 „ Andhras in Malwa and Bundelkhand—to A.D. 80.
58 „ Sakas occupy Punjab; Vikrama era of Azes.
44 „ Parthians in Punjab.
62 A.D. Kushans take Taxila (Sirkap).
78 (or 125) A.D. (Saka era) Kanishka founds Sirsukh (Taxila).
225 A.D. End of Kushan Empire.
319 „ Era of Chandragupta II (Imperial Guptas, -455).
430 „ "Little" Kushans, followed by "White Huns", 450.
455 „ Later Guptas, -606.
510 „ Mihiragula (Hun) in Punjab, Gujarat and Malwa, -534.
550 „ Chalukyas (Badami), -753.
606 „ Harsha (Thanesar), -647; capital Kanauj.
629 „ Hiuen Tsang in India, -645.
711 „ Muslim invasion of Sind from Arabia.
753 „ Rashtrakutas conquer Chalukyas, -972.
788 „ Shankar Acharya (Sringeri, Dwarka, Badrinath, Puri).
850 „ Rise and decline of the Chola Empire, -1279.
973 „ (Second) Chalukyas conquer Rashtrakutas, -1190.
1190 „ Hoysalas in Mysore (Halebid), -1326.

EARLY EMPIRES

The earliest "Aryan" colonies were in the Punjab and in the valleys of the Jumna and the Ganges. When the work ascribed to Manu assumed its present shape, the whole space between the Himalayas and the Vindhya range north of the Narbada river was acknowledged to be Aryan territory. The Dravidian South has remained mainly aboriginal, but has been absorbed into the Hindu pale. Indraprastha (Indrapat, p. 329, now on the edge of the new capital at Delhi, is a traditional site) was founded about 1500 B.C. Karnal and Thanesar (p. 347) are supposed to be equally ancient. Muttra was founded before 600 B.C., Valabhipur (p. 275) and Ajodhya (p. 372) are other very important ancient cities.

The Punjab and Sind formed part of the "Indian Province" of the Persian Empire of Darius (521-486 B.C.). The boundary probably ran up the Indus from its mouth, then along the Sutlej, and then along the Beas (Hyphasis). The province is said to have been rich at that time, but became arid until restored to prosperity by British irrigation canals. Darius probably visited this outlying satrapy about 518 B.C. At Bhita, near Allahabad (p. 126), a cross-section of the remains covers a period from long before 321 B.C.

The kingdom of Magadha, which developed into the Mauryan Empire (321-184 B.C.), was started by Saisunaga in the Bareilly District. It was expanded about 550 B.C. by the addition of Monghyr and Bhagalpur by Bimbisara (582-554 B.C.) with a capital at Rajagriha (p. 136). His successor, Chandragupta, added Benares, Oudh and Northern Bihar, probably also Orissa on the east coast. When Alexander the Great came to India to consolidate his hold on the Persian Empire in 326 B.C., the King of Taxila met him in the Kabul river valley. Alexander himself crossed the mountains north of the river and proceeded to Aornos, a place identified (although the identification is now disputed) by Sir Aurel Stein some twenty miles north of the confluence of the Kabul river with the Indus, which Alexander crossed at Hund. A second division traversed the Khyber Pass, or one of the other passes close by, into the Peshawar vale. Resistance was met on the Jhelum river where Alexander defeated Porus (Paurava) near the battlefield of Chilianwala (p. 586). At the Beas River (Hyphasis) his troops refused to proceed farther, perhaps because here they had reached the boundary of the Persian Empire. He proceeded down the Sutlej and the Indus, which then may have taken a course nearer the hills by the Manchhar Lake (p. 566), since Jacobabad (p. 569) is now below the bed of the Indus. Sending his fleet along the shores of the Persian Gulf, he marched to Kandahar by the Bolan Pass (p. 570), a journey of great hardship, as British armies in 1838 and 1878 could testify.

The Mauryan Chandragupta became stronger. A successor to Alexander, Seleucus Nikator, about 305 B.C., desisted from attack and made a treaty handing over the "Indian Province" (Kandahar, Kabul and parts of Baluchistan). He sent an envoy to the court of Chandragupta at Patna, then above the confluence of the Son and the Ganges. The Memoirs of this envoy, Megasthenes recorded the shifting of the beds of the great rivers, and the primitive nature of the dwellings, only those on high ground being made of materials more substantial than "wattle and daub". The country then must have been well wooded. In modern times, for lack of afforestation, the melting of the Himalayan snows and the monsoon rains used to cause the rivers to overflow the wide beds in which they meander during the cold season. Rivers are now held to their courses at the great railway bridges, and new reclamation projects protect land and villages.

Chandragupta's empire extended to the Narbada river on the south. On his abdication Bindusara (297-274 B.C.) subdued the Deccan, probably up to the Krishna river. Asoka succeeded, and the extent of his influence is shown by an edict at Jonnagiri (Yaraguda) in the Kurnool District, and another at Siddapura, in the Chitaldrug District of Mysore (p. 485); beyond (much later) were Dravidian kingdoms, Cheras, at Karur (p. 520), Pallavas, Cholas, and Pandyas. Traditionally Srinagar (p. 605) was founded by him, and he is supposed to have visited Sravana Belgola (p. 488) in Mysore.

BUDDHIST INDIA

In 262 B.C. Asoka was converted to Buddhism. Now began the fashioning of stupas and pillars, and the decoration of caves by carving which was carried on by Buddhists, Jains and Hindus. Brahmanism was latent but became generally accepted about A.D. 700, and Jainism was practised as an undercurrent. Asoka sent missions into Sri Lanka (Ceylon), China and to the West, even to Epirus, but outside India Buddhism was widely accepted only in the East. Chinese pilgrims came to visit India, for example Hiuen Tsang in A.D. 629-645, and have recorded interesting if sometimes perplexing place-names and other details. According to Sri Lanka tradition a successful Buddhist mission there was headed by Asoka's brother.

About this time, it may be supposed, the simplest houses consisted of bamboo screens interwoven with palm or other branches and possibly plastered with mud or, as in many parts of India to-day, of mud in mass or sun-dried mud bricks. No kiln-burnt bricks have been found which can be dated before 400 B.C. except in the phenomenon of the "Indus Civilisation". Concrete floors, made of potsherds and lime, were used before 700 B.C. and lime mortar in Kashmir about 250 B.C., but both were rare. Roofs were flat or curved, if bamboos were used, the upper ends being lashed together and the lower ends tied and backed by the walls. Framed timber followed. Posts were set, as they still may be, in jars of earthenware to protect them from white ants. This developed in stone in the Gupta age after A.D. 319, and the "pot and foliage" base was produced in carvings. About 400 B.C. burnt brick, for which the sandy silt of the Ganges is well adapted, came into use, as at Bhita (p. 126). This brick was laid in mud, the floors were of brick and plaster, ceilings were timbered, covered with reeds and a layer of mud plastered on the top, or if pitched (or curved) were tiled with finials of terra-cotta as illustrated by Cunningham (*Stupa of Bharhut*, Pl. XXVI, 7). Brick in mud pillars made columns necessarily thicker than wooden pillars.

Dressed stone appears first in the time of Asoka, in the *lats* or stone pillars which he caused to be erected and in a monolithic rail at Sarnath (p. 165). These display a mastery over material rarely afterwards equalled by Indian masons, and not surpassed even in the marble work of the Parthenon. Every sanctified Buddhist locality was marked by the erection of a small brick *stupa* (mound), which, if it contained relics of the Buddha, was called a *dagoba*. Such relics were contained in a casket just below the summit of the dagoba, called a *tee* (hti). The tee, at first a few stones in the form of a swastika, developed into a square or mushroom-shaped umbrella which, multiplied in tiers, became a spire in pagodas. The older memorial pillars were called *stambha* (or *lat*, if carved out of one stone) bearing emblems—such as lions or wheels (following "the path"). Sometimes the pillars became pedestals for lamps, or for vehicles of the Hindu gods. Stupas of Asoka's time are at Sanchi (p. 217) and Sarnath (p. 165). Two examples of his pillars are at Delhi (pp. 328 and 329), but the Iron Pillar (p. 336) is not one. The Barabar Caves near Gaya (p. 129) belong to this period. Otherwise the monuments consist of the rock edicts in Brahmi found over a wider area of India than any subsequently controlled by one ruler (except, possibly, Muhammad ibn Tughlaq and certainly Aurangzeb) before the British obtained paramountcy in 1849 over the Sikhs.

After Asoka's death, in 232 B.C., the Mauryan Empire weakened, and the dynasty came to an end in 184 B.C. with the slaying of Brihadratha by Pushyamitra, founder of the Sunga dynasty and previously Viceroy of Ujjain. The dynasty lasted until 78 B.C. and gradually lost territory. The Greek successors of Alexander in Bactria warred between themselves, but in 206 B.C. Antiochus III received the submission of the Punjab, and about 170 B.C. the city of Sirkap at Taxila was founded. In 155 B.C. Menander had a capital at Sialkot (p. 585) and raided as far as Rupar on the Sutlej and to Karnal (p. 346) on the Jumna, 100 m. beyond the old Persian boundary. He is said to have advanced as far as Patna, but was recalled by trouble in Bactria. Before this, about 201 B.C. (when Scipio Africanus took Carthage), the Andhras (Telugus), occupying the east coast from the Godavari to the Krishna rivers, had extended their sway along the Godavari Valley north-westwards until the second king, Krishna, reached Nasik. They established a capital at Paithan (p. 153). Through this place ran a road from the west coast, leading through Bhilsa (p. 221) to Patna, with a branch from Bhilsa to Saheth Maheth (p. 372). About 90 B.C. there were three powers—the Greeks, the Sungas and the Andhras—who extended down to the Krishna river. The Besnagar pillar (p. 221) was erected by an envoy from the Greek king at Taxila about 90 B.C., the fourteenth year of Bhagabhadra, last but one of the Sungas, whose dynasty ended in 70 B.C. After this the Andhras extended northwards and occupied Ujjain and possibly Patna, and to them some of the monuments at Sanchi (p. 217) may be attributed.

There were other smaller independent kingdoms. In 169 B.C. a king, Kharavela of Kalinga on the Mahanadi river, recorded his independence in an inscription in the Hatigumpha cave (p. 415) near Bhubaneshwar. In Sunga times Muttra was the capital of the Curacenas and Chitorgarh (p. 209) was in their territory. There were Panchalas in the Bareilly district, and always there were Dravidians south of the Krishna river.

The Greeks in Gandhara, from Kandahar to the North-West Punjab, did not outlast the Sungas. Sakas (Scythians) had been pressed from Central Asia through Afghanistan and Baluchistan into Sind. About 75 B.C. they made their way northwards and conquered the Punjab, spreading down to Mathura (Muttra), which passed under their rule after 50 B.C. Later they occupied Taxila and Peshawar (p. 598). Their rule in the North-West lasted until after A.D. 380, and some rulers of Western India were known as Satraps (i.e. Viceroys of the Saka Monarchy) from A.D. 119-388.

The period of the Sungas (184-70 B.C.) and following centuries produced highly decorative work in stone. The important *dagobas* were enlarged and cased in stone. Thieves in search of the treasure caskets have destroyed the tees. The earliest caves, possibly the work of the Andhras, are not far from Bombay at Karli, Bhaja and Bedsa (p. 429), but at Ajanta (p. 138) some are contemporary, and others continue a succession until about A.D. 650, when Buddhism declined and Brahmanism took its place. At Ellora (p. 146) the Buddhist series commenced later and continued later than at Ajanta, while Jain and Brahman caves are found. At Nasik (p. 115) the Buddhist series may be dated 200-100 B.C. The caves at Kanheri (p. 109) near Bombay may have been made by exiled Buddhists between A.D. 200 to 950 or later.

In the earlier caves the few slender stone pillars were copied from timber, as were the timber walls, roofs and gateways in every detail down to the nail heads. Timber was still used, as at Karli, in addition to stone. In the later caves pillars are heavy, being copied from brick in mud. Temples were called *chaityas*, and assembly halls *viharas* (see plans at pp. 148 and 430 and for further details see under *Sculpture* above). Examples of both of these are near Bhilsa (p. 221), but generally are to be found in caves cut out of hard basalt or trap rock, as at Ellora. In spite of the labour necessary without modern explosives, Fergusson estimated in his *History of Indian and Eastern Architecture*, often quoted in this *Handbook*, that the cost was only one-tenth of that involved by quarrying, transporting, carving and erection in a building. In some caves external cutting and carving were confined to the entrances. Characteristic details of early Buddhist (Hinayana—"Lesser Vehicle") sculpture are emblems —the wheels, trident, and swastika, or a pair of footprints—with patterns representing rails and horse-shoe windows, simple topes and sacred Bodhi (pipal) trees.

The development in the use of stone in sacred monuments during the Sunga or (later) Andhra period is particularly well illustrated by the railings of Bharhut (now in the Calcutta Museum, p. 176), Bodh Gaya (p. 130), and the gateways of Sanchi (placed at the cardinal points of the compass), in that order. The development from timber models took quite a short space of time.

Foreign influences in Indian architecture (according to some authorities) received a fresh stimulus under the Sakas (after 75 B.C.), and later under the Parthians and Kushans, when a Hellenistic school, known as Gandhāran, became established, about A.D. 200, on the North-West Frontier and was devoted to the service of Buddhism. The masonry at Sirkap (p. 591) has a diaper pattern, layers of small stones or bricks filling interstices between massive blocks. Arches, pointed or rounded, were constructed by horizontal corbelling. The Corinthian capital and the undulating garland are common motifs.

The Mahayana ("Greater Vehicle" doctrine), representing the figure of Buddha, outgrew the Hinayana (Lesser Vehicle), using symbols only. At Ajanta (p. 138) the paintings describe the *jatakas* or birth stories and other incidents of the life of the Buddha. They date from A.D. 150. The Mahayana formulated a pantheon, with Boddhisatvas, demons, and imagery of all sorts. This had much in common with the latent Brahmanism, and merged into the modern Hinduism. The tide of Hellenistic art affected the Mathura school and may have reached its high-water mark of progress at Amaravati (p. 427), near Vijayawada on the Krishna river. At Kanchipuram (Conjeeveram) (p. 509) the Hinayana form lasted until after A.D. 400.

The rule of the Sakas in Northern India gave place to that of the Kushans, possibly from A.D. 45 to 225, but the dates are most perplexing. Two great kings of this dynasty were Kanishka and his successor Huvishka. Saka or Parthian Satraps still ruled under them in Kathiawar and in Malwa (A.D. 200-388). In the Ganges basin a kingdom was formed in Magadha and Oudh by Chandragupta II (the first was the Mauryan), who founded the dynasty of the Imperial Guptas and reigned A.D. 319-30, with a capital again at Patna. Samadragupta (330-75) extended the kingdom to Assam, made an expedition into Orissa and along the coast to Kanchipuram, and acquired the Deccan, Malwa and Bundelkland. Vikramaditya Chandragupta III (375-413) consolidating these gains, added Kathiawar, Gujarat, and the Mahratta country. His capitals were at Ajodhya (p. 372) and Kaushambi (p. 125), and he held India north of the Krishna river, except that portion north of a line from Sukkur in Sind to Delhi and Ambala. In the time of Kamaragupta (413-53) there was much literary activity; the famous dramatist Kalidasa flourished. Towards the end of his reign Skandagupta (455-80) had to repel invaders, the "White Huns", who had in 455 driven out the Gandharans into Kashmir and Gilgit. One of these, Mihiragula, occupied Sangala (Sialkot, p. 585) and the Rechna Doab between the Chenab and Ravi rivers. It is supposed that these Huns were absorbed into the "soldier caste", by Brahmanism, but if so, the chivalrous Rajputs have never in history displayed the unpleasant characteristics attributed to Huns traditionally.

Under the early or Imperial Guptas, settled conditions revived the work of the guilds of painters at Ajanta and sculptors at Sanchi, the vitality of plastic decoration being now restrained and more refined. Examples are to be found in cave temples at Ajanta and Ellora, in the Dhamek stupa at Sarnath (p. 165), and in flat-roofed temples at Deogarh (p. 222), although the flat roof itself is not a distinctive feature of the period. The treatment of mouldings and of other decorative features must be the true indication. The later Guptas reigned from 455 until 606. There was a gradual revival of orthodox Hinduism during this period, and both Jainism and Buddhism had to yield it pride of place.

For the principal Buddhist shrines and pilgrimage-places in India see pp. 30-31 above.

HINDU INDIA

In A.D. 606 Harsha succeeded to the kingdom of Thanesar (p. 347), made Kanauj his capital, and extended his dominions to the Ganges delta, including Nepal, with the Narbada river as his southern boundary with the Chalukyans, attacking without success Pulikesin in 620. In 643 Hiuen Tsang, the Chinese pilgrim, was present at a disputation where Harsha honoured equally Brahmins, Buddhists and Jains. Harsha died in 647, but a kingdom of Kanauj lasted, after many dynasties had risen and fallen elsewhere, up to the time of the Muslim conquest in 1192.

Meanwhile the Jain religion persisted unobtrusively, and Jain caves exist side by side with those of other religions. The temples at Mount Abu (p. 255) and elsewhere, including those rearranged as mosques at Ajmer and Delhi, have distinctive features in the deep-carved brackets of the capitals to the pillars, subdividing the covered area, and horizontal domes, thus avoiding the thrust of the radiating arch. Hardly any two ceilings to the small squares between the pillars have the same design, while elaborate carved pendants hang from the larger horizontal domes in the Mount Abu temples, sometimes carved from two large blocks of marble made to fit. The two towers of Fame and of Victory at Chitorgarh (p. 211) are examples of Jain work. All those buildings mentioned belong to the period of what may be termed Rajput rule. The Jains built temples in clusters.

The earliest Brahmanical temples, probably built of wood, have disappeared. The structural stone temple was a development of the stupa. An image of Buddha on the front might be covered by a porch, then moved into the interior, and the tee became a spire, surmounted by a copper-gilt Kalas, too great a temptation to the plunderer. The Hindu temple displays a small flag. Stone temples date from the time of the Pallavas or of the Chalukyans.

The first Chalukyan kingdom arose about 550. By the time of Pulikesin (609-42) it lay south of a line from Ellora to Orissa, north of the Krishna river and west of the Tungabhadra, which rises in the north of Mysore. It is possible that the Chalukyans at times ruled farther north. Fergusson gave the name of *Chalukyan* architecture to a mixture of northern and southern styles, combining elegance of outline with elaboration of detail in animal friezes. It acquired distinctive traits, a polygonal (or later star-shaped) instead of a square plan, a high carved plinth, following the outline of the temple, and a low pyramidal roof, in horizontal layers, instead of the high *sikhara* or spire with vertical lines. The style emanated perhaps at Aiholi (p. 476) and Pattadakal close by Badami (once the capital of the Western Chalukyas) where there are caves also (A.D. 550-80); temples at Somnathpur (p. 491) and Halebid (Dorasamudra), were built by the Hoysala Ballalas in A.D. 1000-1300 in a perfect style, covered with sculpture. In the north-east corner of the Eastern Chalukyan kingdom some temples of Bhubaneswar (p. 416) are dated from 500 onwards, and the Black Pagoda at Konarak (p. 422) may have been built about 1200. In the north-west corner the temple of Kailasa at Ellora(p. 149), excavated out of hard trap rock externally as well as internally, is attributed to a Rashtrakutan king at Nasik, Dantidurga (725-55), a western successor to the Chalukyans. He is supposed to have adopted the style of a Papnath temple at Pattadakal. One authority places the Rashtrakuta dynasty between 753 and 972, when it was succeeded by a second Chalukyan dynasty until 1190. Yadavas at Deogiri and Hoysalas at Halebid (p. 487) followed.

Shankar Acharya (A.D. 788-820), who founded the Sringeri Math in Mysore, gave Hinduism a great impetus. Temples in the *Dravidian* style are well represented and accessible at Hampi (p. 478) and along the Railway from Madras to Rameswaram (p. 552). The oldest may date from A.D. 1050. A square (often twin) shrine is covered by a pyramidal storeyed tower (*vimana*), and a porch (*mandapam*), sometimes multiple, covers the approach; but the principal features are high oblong *gopurams* or pyramids over the gateways, near the cardinal points, leading to the quadrangular enclosures and courts which may have cloistered corridors. At Thanjavur (Tanjore, p. 537) one *gopuram* is 216 feet high. Some of the carvings in these temples are erotic, symbolising in Hindu eyes the sanctity of the creative force.

There are rock-cut temples at Mahabalipuram (p. 515) south of Madras,

A.D. 150-800, and at Kanchipuram (Conjeeveram) (p. 509) the work of Pallava kings, one of whom was contemporary with and fought with Pulikesin of Chalukya. Afterwards the Cholas at Tanjore and Pandyan kings (at Madurai, p. 545) were great builders from 950 onwards. In 1023 Rajendra Chola raided into Bengal. Wars stopped building.

The *Indo-Aryan* style, so named by Fergusson, prevailed north of the Tapti and Mahanadi rivers, and includes some of the temples at Bhubaneswar (p. 416) which date after 950 and show development in the same way as Muslim architecture evolved at Delhi. Another large and well-preserved group is at Khajuraho (p. 227), some temples being Jain, in a variety of this style. A curvilinear steeple divided into vertical bands above a square sanctuary may have developed from the bamboo spire of primitive times. In palaces the style is seen at Gwalior (p. 231), Udaipur (p. 212), Amber (p. 269) and Dig (p. 296), and it still persists in modern buildings.

7. HISTORY AND ARCHITECTURE, Part II

KEY DATES

622 (16th July). Muhammad flees from Mecca, A.H. era.
711. Invasion of Sind by Arabs.
725. Occupation of Gujarat.
1001. Mahmud of Ghazni raids India, -1026.
1192. Shahab (or Muiz-) ud din of Ghor defeats Prithvi Raj.
1195. Qutb-ud-din Aibak takes Anhilwara in Gujarat.
1310. Malik Kafur raids Southern India.
1323. Muhammad ibn Tughlaq takes Warangal and proceeds South.
1336. Vijayanagar kingdom founded.
1347. Bahmani kingdom in Deccan.
1398. Timur invades and takes Delhi, retires.
1424. End of Hindu kingdom of Warangal.
1489. Bahmani kingdom split into five.
1509-30. Krishnaraja of Vijayanagar.
1526. Babur—soldier, statesman, diarist—defeats the Delhi Sultan, Ibrahim Lodi, at Panipat, and becomes the founder of the Mughal Empire.
1527. Babur defeated the Rajput confederacy at Khanua.
1556-1605. Akbar—Scholar, Administrator, Inventor.
1565. Deccan Muslims defeat Hindus of Vijayanagar at "Talikota".
1599. Akbar's son takes Ahmadnagar City.
1605-27. Jahangir—Diarist, Naturalist, Art Patron.
1627-58. Shah Jahan—Builder of the Taj Mahal.
1639. Raja of Chandragiri grants Madras to English.
1658. Aurangzeb deposes his father Shah Jahan.
1687. Aurangzeb conquers Golconda.
1698. Capture of Gingee and Carnatic.
1707. Death of Aurangzeb.

THE MUSLIM STRUGGLE FOR SUPREMACY

The rise of Islam as a world power began after the death of Muhammad when a wave of conquest rolled west from Arabia through Egypt and along the northern shore of Africa, crossing into Spain in A.D. 711. In the same year piratical attacks from Sind on Arabian ships provoked reprisals, and Muhammad bin Kasim sailed up the Indus to Aror (p. 562) and Multan, the Muslims retaining their hold on Sind and the Punjab to the borders of Kashmir. In 1001 Mahmud of Ghazni took Peshawar and started raids into India almost yearly, notably to Kangra in 1008, Muttra in 1017, and Somnath (p. 284) in 1024: one of his lieutenants took Varanasi (Benares) in 1033, after Mahmud's death. Masud, his successor, conquered the Punjab in 1036, but in 1038 Seljuk Turks took Ghazni and, although the Punjab was held by descendants of Masud, raids ceased.

In 1176 Shahab-ud-din of Ghor took Sind, and in 1178 attempted, but failed, to take Gujarat. In 1179 he took Peshawar, and in 1181 built a fortress at Sialkot (p. 585) deposing the last descendant of Masud. In 1191 he advanced to Bhatinda, and at Taraori, north of Karnal, fought unsuccessfully against Prithvi Raj of Delhi, by far the strongest ruler in India. In 1192 he defeated Prithvi Raj and took Ajmer (p. 263) but not Delhi, which his general, Qutb-ud-din Aibak, took in 1193, after taking Varanasi. Kanauj (p. 378) fell to him in the following year, Anilwara (p. 255) in the next year. By 1202 the dominion had been extended to Gaur (p. 398) and Nadia (p. 394) in Bengal. In 1206 Shahab-ud-din, commonly known as Muhammad of Ghor, was killed and Qutb-ud-din assumed the title of Sultan, with Delhi as his capital. Here (p. 317) the development of Indo-Saracenic architecture can best be studied in tombs, mosques and palaces, showing the adoption of the dome and radiating (no longer horizontal) arch, and culminating in the Palace buildings in the Fort. Fatehpur Sikri (p. 311) and Agra (p. 299) fill in the gaps in the Mughal period.

Extension towards the south was begun under Ala-ud-din Khilji by an expedition in 1297 into Gujarat (p. 247). His general, Malik Kafur, went much farther, took Warangal (p. 464) in 1309, and Halebid (p. 487) in the following year, after which he went down to the coast, some say to Cape Comorin or Rameswaram (p. 552), but his occupation of the south was not effective. The terrible Muhammad ibn Tughlaq (1325-51) advanced in 1323 from Cambay into the south, took Devagiri and Anagundi (p. 478), but restored it to the Hindus, and also Warangal (p. 464) east of Hyderabad. In order to centralise his administration, in 1338 he ordered a wholesale emigration of the inhabitants of Delhi to Devagiri (Daulatabad, p. 143) and did the same in 1340, but famine in the Deccan made him order their return. In 1326 Halebid had been destroyed, but the Hindus of Warangal, Anagundi, and the Hoysala Bellalas combined, and in 1336 the kingdom of Vijayanagar (p. 477) was founded. In 1378 a remnant of the Muslims, still in Madurai, was conquered.

Muslim occupation of the Deccan was now effective, although not for long subject to Delhi. The Bahmani kingdom arose at Daulatabad and moved to Gulbarga (p. 437) in 1347. Firoz Shah of Delhi did not interfere and his successors became too weak to do so, especially after the devastating raid of Timur into northern India in 1398. Bahmani rule extended from the Kistna river north into Berar and Ahmadnagar and west to Bijapur, but Warangal had been retaken by the Hindus in 1345, who kept it until 1424. In 1470 the Bahmani captured Rajamundry beyond the Godavari, but not permanently. For more than two centuries Vijayanagar led a Hindu confederacy of the south in far too great strength to be conquered. There were at least twenty-eight clashes between Muslims and Hindus, usually in the triangle formed by the Tungabhadra and Kistna rivers, especially round Raichur and Mudgal, and Adoni, south of the Tungabhadra. At times the Hindu Raja had to pay tribute, but his wealth was enormous. His territory extended, at one time or another, from Rajamundry (p. 425) along the Carnatic to Tiruchirapalli (Trichinopoly) (p. 540), and Tinnevelly (p. 550) up along the west coast to Goa, where later the Portuguese did a great trade in horses with him. His Muslim adversaries became weakened by the splitting up of the Bahmani kingdom in and after 1489 into five dynasties: Berar (Imad), Ahmadnagar (Nizam), Bijapur (Adil), Golconda (Qutb) and Bidar

(Barid), to which place the Bahmani king had moved his capital in 1428 from Gulbarga, calling it Ahmadabad after himself. In 1520 the Hindu Raja occupied Bijapur. At last there were attempts at combination against Rama Raya (1535-1565) and four Muslim Rulers combined to defeat and kill him at the battle of Talikota (so called, for the field lies many miles away, at a bend of the Tungabhadra). Into this battle the Hindu is related to have put three-quarters of a million men, with 2000 elephants, his opponents having half that number of men with 600 guns. Fantastic as these figures may seem, it must be remembered that armies consisted of *levees en masse* and most men were then accustomed to the use of arms. These the Vijayanagar Raja could supply, for his territory was very rich, especially in diamonds. Aurangzeb, as Viceroy of the Deccan, was able to collect a huge army to usurp the throne and depose his father in 1658.

The Muslim coalition lasted long enough for a thorough sack of Vijayanagar, but little conquest farther south was then attempted. Adoni fell into Bijapur hands in 1572, and Rajamundry to Golconda in the same year, with further additions almost down to Nellore in the Carnatic in 1579. In 1593 Bijapur took Srirangapatnam (Seringapatam), but trouble at home caused a withdrawal. In Mysore, Bolacharama Wadiyar, Viceroy of Vijayanagar, refused tribute after the battle of Talikota, and became independent. Kanthariva Narasimha (1638-1659) and Doddadevaraya (1659-72) extended the borders and consolidated the State. Chikkadevaraya (1672-1704) fought many battles and patronised many bards. He acquired Bangalore from Vyankoji the Mahratta, organised the administration, established a postal service, constructed irrigation works, and formed a friendship with Aurangzeb, who conferred on him the title of Jagat Deva Raja and presented the ivory throne (p. 495). Chikka Krishnaraja Wadiyar (1734-66) fell under the sway of intriguers, and in 1761 Haidar Ali, a soldier of fortune, became master of Mysore. Tipu, his son, lost the State in 1799 and it was taken under British administration. The handing back of this very rich State by the British Government in 1881 to the original Ruling Family after nearly fifty years of administration, ushered in a period of rapid development under a succession of able rulers until it was merged into the Indian Union in 1947-48.

In 1602 the Nayakkas became independent in Madura(i) and Tanjore, while the States of Gersoppa (p. 486) and Bhatkal also broke away, but the descendant of the Vijayanagar Raja at Chandragiri (p. 440) was able to confirm a grant of land to the English at Madras in 1639. In 1647 Golconda captured the surrounding territory and renewed the grant. In 1687 Aurangzeb captured Golconda and the Carnatic came into the Mughal Empire. This marked the ultimate southern boundary of Mughal conquest.

The extension of the Mughal Empire into the Deccan can hardly be termed a Muslim conquest, although Akbar (1556-1605) had to subdue the Rajputs at Ajmer and Chitorgarh (1567) before he could absorb Gujarat, Ahmadnagar and Berar, all Muslim kingdoms. Aurangzeb, an orthodox Sunni, swept away the Shiah Muslim kingdoms, Bijapur and Golconda, and took Gingee (p. 532) from the Mahrattas in 1698. His death in 1707 saw the beginning of the end of Muslim rule.

This rule and, in particular, the Mughal period of it, endowed India and Pakistan with some of their most famous and beautiful buildings, which even today rank among the leading tourist attractions. They are to be seen at their finest in Delhi, Agra, Lahore and in many of the cities of the old "Deccan" region. The early Mughal Emperors were men of wide and cultivated interests, notable patrons of painting, letters and architecture. Babur, first of the line, wrote *Memoirs* in Turki (later translated into Persian and many other languages) which rank among the world's great autobiographies. Humayun, his son, Akbar, Jahangir and Shah Jahan—and even the puritanical Aurangzeb—were in the same cultural tradition. No other country in their age could claim Rulers of equal calibre as soldiers, statesmen, and lovers of the liberal arts, of which indeed several of them were notable exponents.

MAHRATTA RULE

Sivaji, the Mahratta leader (1627-80), has become the hero of all Hindus and, in particular, of those in Maharashtra, where his memory is deeply revered. There is a magnificant modern statue to his memory near the Gateway of India (Bombay). His grandfather, Malaji Bhonsla, in 1599 received a grant of land at Poona from the Ahmadnagar Sultan (p. 436). Almost immediately the territory was transferred to Bijapur by arrangement with Akbar. Sivaji rebelled in 1646. The Mahrattas had plenty of war experience in the armies of Bijapur and Ahmadnagar. They emerged as the main rivals of the British for the control of India.

Key-Dates of the Mahratta Supremacy

1646. Sivaji (1627-80) makes war on Bijapur.
1677. Sivaji captured Gingee.
1689. Shahu (grandson) prisoner to 1707.
1713. Balaji Vishvanath, appointed Peshwa, by Shahu.
1719. Mahomed Shah of Delhi grants "Chauth" in Deccan.
1749. Death of Shahu.
1750. Balaji Baji Rao, Peshwa, assumes power.
1761. Third Battle of Panipat, Ahmad Shah Abdali (Durani) defeats Mahrattas.
1761. Fourth Peshwa, Madho Rao, -1772.
1771. Shah Alam at Delhi after twelve years.
1775. Raghava Rao, Peshwa (expelled), signs Treaty of Surat.
1776. Treaty of Purandhar, with British.
1779. Convention of Wargaum with British (Bombay).
1782. Treaty of Salbai, negotiated by Scindia.
1795. Last Peshwa Baji Rao II (son of Raghava).
1802. Battle of Poona, Holkar defeats Peshwa and Scindia.
Treaty of Bassein, between fugitive Peshwa and British.
1803. Mahratta War; Wellesley in South; Lake takes Delhi.
1817. Pindari War and Third Mahratta War.
1818. Peshwa deposed and sent to Bithur.

In 1656 Sivaji took the fort of Pratapgad and proceeded to capture other forts in Maharashatra, making his capital at Raigarh. In 1664 he plundered Surat in Mughal territory. Mastered by them in 1666 he went to Agra, but escaped back to the Deccan. In 1673 he took Satara and raided also Golconda. In 1674 his brother Vyankoji took Tanjore in the far S. (p. 537). In 1677 Sivaji marched right across India (the Muslims on his flank consenting), taking Kurnool, Vellore and Gingee (p. 532) near Madras. He died in 1680. The cult of Sivaji became a leading feature of the Nationalist movement in Western India, especially at Poona. His exploits are still recited by the *gondhali* or wandering minstrels to rapt village audiences, and lose nothing in the telling. It is the great merit of Sivaji in Hindu eyes that he challenged the Brahmin monopoly and showed that a Hindu revival was possible in which all classes could unite on the basis of a common patriotism against the Muslim conqueror.

His son Sambhaji was captured, blinded, and executed by Aurangzeb, and his grandson Shahu, released in 1707, had none of the hardy Mahratta qualities. He appointed a Konkan Brahmin named Balaji Vaishvanath, as his Peshwa or Prime Minister (1713-20), who by his ability became the real head of the

Mahratta Empire, and in whose family the office of Peshwa came to be hereditary. In 1705 the Mahrattas invaded Gujarat and exacted tribute there from 1723 onwards. In 1718 Balaji Peshwa sent a force to intervene in affairs at Delhi, and in 1720 his troops took part in a Mughal expedition against Asaf Jah, the Nizam ul Mulk, Subadar of the Deccan since 1713. The Mughal Court returned from Agra to Delhi. The Peshwa then obtained from Mahomed Shah, for the grandson of Sivaji, the right to the "Chauth" or one-fourth of the revenues in return for the feudal service of supplying troops. In 1732, under the second Peshwa, Baji Rao I (1721-40), Malhar Rao Holkar seized Malwa, which was ceded to the Mahrattas under Balaji Baji Rao (1740-61), and in his time Janoji, son of Raghoji Bhonsla, the Chief of Nagpur and a leading Mahratta feudatory, invaded Bihar and Bengal, obtained the cession of Orissa, and of the chauth of Bengal from the Murshidabad Viceroy, Alivardi Khan. This alarmed the British and led to the construction of the Mahratta Ditch round Calcutta in 1743, although there were no means of garrisoning such a large perimeter.

In 1739 Nadir Shah, the Persian, had dealt the Mughal empire a heavy blow by sacking Delhi, and the Mahratta power became stronger and stronger until it received a severe set-back at the battle of Panipat in 1761 from Ahmad Shah Abdali or Durrani (p. 345). The Bhao, or generalissimo and cousin of the Peshwa, was missing, Scindia nearly lost his life, the Peshwa's son was killed, and the life of the Peshwa himself is believed to have been terminated by grief.

Ranged in order from left to right at this time were four great chiefs: the Gaekwar at Songhad in Gujarat, Holkar in Malwa, Scindia in Gwalior, and the Bhonsla Raja in Nagpur. None of them was a Brahmin. Sivaji himself was a *kunbi*, or cultivator, although a pundit from Benares drew up a pedigree of his descent from the Sun in order to justify, in Mahratta Brahmin eyes, the coronation of a Sudra. But although of relatively low caste, these Chiefs had the same military virtues as were later shown by Mahrattas in the World Wars, and they would have been formidable antagonists had they consented to combine permanently. Ahalya Bai (p. 203) kept her Indore dominions quiet from 1765-95. Against the Nizam and Haidar Ali of Mysore, the Peshwa directed operations through generals who never made themselves independent.

The fourth Peshwa, Madho Rao (1761-72), checked the rising power of Haidar Ali of Mysore. He reinforced the Malwa Chiefs in 1769, recovered Gwalior, and reoccupied Delhi. In 1771, when Shah Alam (who had succeeded in 1759) decided, against the advice of Warren Hastings, to return to Delhi, he was met by a vakil of Scindia with a message that he must acquiesce in the grant of the chauth and place himself under his master's protection. This was not always effective, for in 1788 a Rohilla, Ghulam Qadir, obtained temporary possession of Delhi, and blinded Shah Alam. In 1772 the Mughal Emperor made over to the Mahrattas the revenues of the two districts of Kora and Allahabad (p. 123) and the East India Company ceased payment of their dues, so that their most formidable opponents should not benefit. Scindia, however, had resources which enabled him to build up a powerful French-trained army. Shah Alam was not relieved from his tutelage until 1803.

The next Peshwa, Madho Rao Narayan (1774-95), succeeded as an infant, and was under the control of his minister Nana Farnavis, who was able to keep the Chiefs in some sort of combination until his death in 1800. The succession of this Peshwa was disputed by his uncle, Peshwa Raghava Rao, and he sought the help of the British in Bombay. The results are described later.

The last Peshwa ruled nominally from 1795 to 1818. In 1802 Jaswant Rao Holkar defeated him and Daulat Rao Scindia in the battle of Poona (p. 432), and the Peshwa sought British aid, signing the Treaty of Bassein. In consequence Colonel Arthur Wellesley advanced from Harihar (p. 485) in Mysore into Mahratta territory and restored him in 1803, defeating the recalcitrant

Scindia and the Bhonsla Raja, while Lake advanced from Kanpur (Cawnpore), ceded by Oudh in 1801, and took Delhi, relieving Shah Alam of Mahratta tutelage. Berar, west of the Wardha river, was ceded and given to the Nizam. Gujarat and Orissa also were ceded to the British, who had occupied these provinces. Otherwise the Mahratta Chiefs were treated lightly. Another war occurred over a great round-up of raiding Pindaris in Central India in 1817; for the Peshwa (in spite of a new treaty) and Indore took their part. The Peshwa was defeated at Kirkee, deposed and sent on a pension to Bithur, where he died in 1853. The Nana Sahib of 1857 notoriety was his adopted son. Thus the Bombay Presidency was extended at last above the Western Ghats. The Bhonsla Raja, Appa Sahib, was defeated at Sitabaldi (p. 195) and deposed. The Indore army, at Mehidpur on the Sipra river, sustained defeat and Khandesh was surrendered. Scindia had been detached by a treaty. Until the Nagpur Raja died childless in 1853, and the Central Provinces (now part of Madhya Pradesh) were formed, no other Mahratta territory was acquired by the British.

THE EUROPEAN IMPACT

The Portuguese were set on the road to India by Prince Henry the Navigator (1394-1460), a grandson of John of Gaunt. He founded a navigation school at Sagres, near Cape St Vincent, in 1429. Explorers crept down the West Coast of Africa to the Congo river in 1484, and in 1486 Bartolomeo Diaz discovered the Cape of Good Hope. Settlements were made on the East African coast. In 1498 Vasco da Gama arrived at Calicut (p. 527) but returned to Lisbon. In 1505 Almeyda arrived as first Viceroy at Cochin (p. 525) with a large armament, and d'Albuquerque, succeeding him, captured Goa (p. 449) in 1510.

The English came much later as traders only, although their ships had to carry guns against pirates. The Charter of the London Company was granted by Queen Elizabeth on 31st December 1600. First a factory was founded at Bantam in Java, and Armagaum (p. 501) on the Coromandel coast was a branch, founded in 1625. There were other agencies along the coast, but Madras was not occupied until 1639, under a grant of a Naik of Vijayanagar confirmed by the Raja in 1645, reconfirmed by Golconda in 1647, and by the Nawab of Arcot in 1763. Madras also was a branch of Bantam, until it became a "Presidency", under a governor or president with a council, in 1683. Trade was carried on under concessions obtained from local rulers, or from officials of the Mughal Emperor.

On the west coast Surat (p. 241) was opened to English traders by a firman of Jahangir in 1612, and on this coast also there were many posts, separate or shared with French and Dutch traders. The marriage of Charles II with Catherine of Braganza in 1661 brought from her brother the first acquisition of territory, Bombay Island, which had been obtained from the King of Gujarat by the Portuguese in 1534. It was occupied in 1665 and handed over by King Charles to the Company in 1668 (p. 88). The Western Presidency was moved there from Surat in 1687, but in 1689 the Mughals besieged it until satisfied by a fine in 1690.

In Bengal the Portuguese had founded Hooghly in 1537, but the English factory here was not started until 1651, again by concession. The Dutch had been at Chinsura (p. 190) since 1645. In 1690 the English moved to Calcutta (p. 169), and it was fortified by consent of the Nawab of Bengal. This post remained under Madras until 1699 when it was recognised as a Presidency. Villages round Calcutta were acquired with the Nawab's consent in 1696. These early settlements were all therefore established peacefully, and not by force of arms.

The French, with whom business was a secondary consideration in the limited hinterland of Madras, showed the English (or British after the Union of 1707) the benefits that might accrue from taking part in politics and war. The French settled Pondicherry (p. 533) in 1672, lost it to the Dutch, but got it back. The War of the Austrian Succession (1740-48), in which the British took part in 1744, gave rise to hostilities in India.

KEY DATES

1498. Vasco da Gama arrives at Calicut.
1510. d'Albuquerque captures Goa.
1600. Charter of Queen Elizabeth to London Company.
1611. Factory established at Masulipatam.
1612. English traders in Surat.
1640. Madras occupied. (Presidency, 1683.)
1665. Bombay transferred by Portuguese to English; to London Company 1668. (Presidency, 1687.)
1672. French settle Pondicherry.
1690. English reoccupy Calcutta. (Presidency, 1699.)
1746. Madras surrenders to Labourdonnais. Dupleix takes over. (Restored in 1749 after Treaty of Aix-la-Chapelle, 1748.)
1750. War, British and French, in India only.
1751. Clive at Arcot (to England 1753, returns 1755).
1756. Calcutta taken by Suraj-ud-daulah; "Black Hole" incident.
1757. Clive recovers Calcutta; Battle of Plassey.
1764. Battle of Buxar; firman from Shah Alam, 1765.
1767. First Mysore War.
1772. Warren Hastings, President in Bengal (Gov.-General, 1774-85).
1778. General Goddard's march across India. Mahratta War to 1783.
1780. Second Mysore War with Haidar Ali and Tipu, -1784.
1788. Trial of Hastings, acquitted 1795.
1790-92. Third Mysore War with Tipu, Treaty of Srirangapatnam (Seringapatam).
1798-99. Fourth Mysore War. Tipu killed at Srirangapatnam.
1803. War with Mahrattas. Lake takes Delhi.
1809. British territory advanced to Sutlej by Treaty of Amritsar.
1843. Sind occupied by British.
1849. Occupation of the Punjab by British after Second Sikh War.

GROWTH OF BRITISH RULE

Labourdonnais, Governor of Mauritius, arrived before Madras in 1746, and the citizens, who had a fort but no means of defending it, could only submit to a ransom, with which Labourdonnais sailed away, to spend years in the Bastille. Dupleix, Governor of Pondicherry, occupied Fort St George, but it was restored in 1749 after the Treaty of Aix-la-Chapelle (1748). Paradis, with 400 men, had defeated the Nawab of Arcot, who advanced to take the place, and thus showed how Europeans could fight.

The next war with the French in India began in 1750, while Britain and France were at peace. It arose over questions of succession to the offices of Subahdar of the Deccan (Asaf Jah died in 1748 aged 75) and Nawab of the Carnatic, both supporting rival claimants. Madras had had a breathing space, and had raised some European troops and sepoys. The term European is correct, for the men were enlisted from many sources, and indeed at the time of the Sepoy Rebellion in 1857 there were many Germans in the "European

Fusiliers". The diversion made by Clive against Arcot (p. 498), with a very small force, not only was brilliant strategy, drawing away much larger forces from Tiruchirapalli (Trichinopoly) but also established the prestige of British-led troops. The British Government complained to the French king about Dupleix, who was recalled to France (1754) to die in poverty in 1764. His greatness is recorded by a statue at Pondicherry, at Chandernagore and by one at Landrecies, his birthplace.

In 1756 the Seven Years War commenced and the French sent out to Pondicherry in 1758, Count de Lally de Tollendal, a hero of Fontenoy, with his own regiment and the Regiment de Lorraine. He took Fort St David in 1758 but failed to take Madras (1758-59), and after being defeated by Eyre Coote at Wandiwash in 1760 (p. 531) had to surrender Pondicherry in 1761. He was sent to England, but decided to return on parole to France, where he was thrown into the Bastille and executed in 1766. By the Treaty of Paris the successions to Hyderabad and Arcot were settled, but the British were not relieved of apprehension about French influence until 1803, for the Nizam had a French contingent (1750 to 1799) and De Boigne (recommended by Warren Hastings) built up with French officers a formidable army for Scindia between 1782 and 1796, and on his retirement his task was taken over by Perron.

Some English troops had been sent to Bombay in 1665. In 1754 the first King's regiment (39th Foot), commanded by Adlercron, arrived at Fort St David, and other regiments followed. Madras now had military as well as commercial aims. In 1756 Calcutta was lost owing to the enmity of Suraj-ud-daulah, Nawab of Bengal, who had succeeded in 1755 aged 20. Captain Clive, who had gone out on the *Stretham* in 1755 as Deputy Governor of Fort St David, sailed from Madras, taking two months on the voyage. He treated with the Nawab while he collected or raised and trained a few more troops. He captured Chandernagore, depriving the Nawab of French support, and won the battle of Plassey (p. 394) in his thirty-second year. This good turn from Madras was repaid by Warren Hastings in 1780. Clive returned to England, but was sent out in 1765 to remedy abuses among servants of the Company. In 1764 Hector Munro had won the battle of Buxar—more important than Plassey—(p. 132), defeating the King of Delhi, Shah Alam and the Wazir of Oudh, supporting Mir Kasim, Nawab of Bengal. Clive got at Allahabad (p. 123) a royal firman (1765) making the Company Diwan of Bengal, Bihar and Orissa, receiving the revenues and being responsible for the defence, and another for the Northern Circars, taken from the French in 1759 by Col. Forde (p. 425). Clive left India in 1767, and was refused a pension by the Company. In 1773 an inquiry was made into his administration and he was honourably acquitted, the Commons voting that he "had rendered great and praiseworthy services to his country".

Warren Hastings became President of Bengal in 1772. He had arrived in India (1750) as a clerk, at the age of 18, and became Resident at the court of the Nawab of Bengal, then at Murshidabad, in 1757. He thus obtained a good knowledge of the methods of Indian rulers. He became a member of the Bengal Council in 1761, returned to England in 1765 and was unemployed until 1769, when he was reappointed by the Company as second member of the Madras Council before being transferred again to Bengal as President of Fort William. In 1774 he was appointed Governor-General in Bengal, under the Act of 1773, with a Council which had authority over other Presidencies in relations with Indian Rulers. A great deal of controversy has raged over the acts of his administration, for some of which his Council was responsible. Many have formed opinions based on the sonorous but biased prose of Lord Macaulay, and are apt to accept his accuracy, because he was a Member of the Bengal Council (1834-38). Light was thrown on these transactions by the publication in 1907 of *Selections from the Letters, Dispatches and other State Papers preserved in the Foreign Department of the Government of India, 1772-85*. The editor, Sir George Forrest, Director of Records, Government of India, said in his Introduction: "The time has come when the rash and indiscriminate judgments passed on Hastings and his work should be carefully revised". These Selections show in which actions the Council prevailed. Hastings was impeached, and his trial by the Lords lasted from 1788 to 1795, when he was acquitted (by the twenty-nine peers who had lasted out) of all the charges, reduced by that time from twenty-two to four. Most modern historians, however, take the view that the proceedings were an off-shoot of the bitter party politics of the time, and a grave injustice to one of the greatest Englishmen who ever served his country abroad. The justice of the execution of Nand Kumar in 1775 has been questioned, but, although his arrest on the charge of forgery of a deed took place two months after he brought charges against Warren Hastings, there is no reason to suppose that Hastings inspired the charge, because preliminary proceedings had been taken earlier. Nand Kumar wa found guilty by a Full Bench of the new Supreme Court. Under Statute of George II (1729), forgery was at that time a capital offence; two years later, in 1777, the Rev. Dr Dodd was hanged for forgery in England.

The policy of Warren Hastings was to maintain friendly relations with the Mahratta Chiefs and the other principal powers, the Nizam of Hyderabad, and Haidar Ali of Mysore, and also to keep them to their boundaries. As a buffer in the north-west, he supported the Nawab Wazir of Oudh to the utmost. The Company's Bengal army had grown from 1500 Europeans and nineteen battalions of sepoys in 1765, formed into three brigades—at Monghyr, Allahabad and Bankipore—each including a European battalion and a troop of Indian cavalry, one company of artillery, and seven sepoy battalions. By 1781 there were three regiments of cavalry, three European battalions, and forty-four battalions of sepoys, besides militia and bodyguards of local dignitaries. There was also a French detachment, taken into service after the capture of Chandernagore and Pondicherry. The army was not used for aggression, although it had to support the other two Presidencies in consequence of embarrassing mistakes of policy, and part was lent on payment, which was always hard to collect, to the Nawab of Oudh in 1772 and 1774, for the Rohilla War and afterwards.

In 1775 Bombay made a treaty (of Surat) with the fugitive Raghunath Rao, the uncle of the Peshwa, an infant, to obtain Salsette and Bassein, but the Minister Nana Farnavis, at the head of one faction, opposed it. The Bengal Council also disapproved, and Colonel Upton was sent across India from Kalpi, a two months' march of 948 miles, to conclude the Treaty of Purandhar in 1776. He remained there a whole year and then marched to the Coromandel Coast, reaching Calcutta on 1st July 1777.

The treaty with Raghunath was annulled and further assistance to him was refused, while Bassein (p. 111) was not taken; Broach and twelve lakhs were to be given to the Company. Bombay and Raghunath were indignant. Then followed further hostilities between Bombay and the Mahrattas. In support of Bombay Hastings sent a force of one cavalry regiment, six sepoy battalions and an artillery train across India under Colonel Goddard (succeeding Colonel Leslie, who died). Starting from Kalpi, the force reached Burhanpur (p. 119) early in 1779. There Goddard, now General and Plenipotentiary, learnt of the defeat of the Bombay force, and the Convention of Wargaum (p. 431), so he turned along the Tapti valley to Surat, took Dabhoi (p. 244) from the Peshwa, detaching the Gaikwar, took Ahmedabad, and at the end of 1780 Bassein, covered by Colonel Hartley. Early in 1781 Goddard forced the Bhor Ghat

(p. 429), but had to retreat. Hastings used diplomacy, made a treaty with Scindia in 1781, and this was followed by the Treaty of Salbai, ratified at Poona, in 1782, which gave peace for twenty years.

In 1778 the revolt of the American colonies was supported by France, and Pondicherry was taken by Hector Munro. Madras proceeded to send a force to take Mahé (p. 528) in 1779, although warned that Haidar Ali of Mysore would disapprove; he did and made a treaty with the Mahrattas. He attacked Madras, and the disaster of Pollilur (p. 513) followed (1780). Hastings appealed to Sir Eyre Coote, who had arrived as Commander-in-Chief, Bengal, the previous year, to take command, and he sailed with 600 Europeans only, making the passage in the short time of twenty-four days. A force of five sepoy battalions had to be sent by land, the Raja of Berar having been induced by Hastings to permit their transit. They did not join Sir Eyre Coote until August 1781, by which time Haidar had been defeated at Porto Novo (p. 534). In 1782 Haidar died, but Tipu disregarded his father's advice to make peace. A French naval expedition under Suffren arrived in 1782, but its effect was countered by a British fleet under Hughes after several indecisive engagements. As news of an armistice in Europe was received before all the French troops were disembarked, the Marquis de Bussy, their commander, withdrew French aid from Tipu, but the war went on until 1784, when the Treaty of Mangalore was framed. Thus, when Hastings resigned in 1785 there was peace, of which Scindia took advantage to occupy Delhi in 1786.

Lord Cornwallis made an alliance with the Nizam and the Mahrattas against Tipu who had attacked Travancore. His territory was invaded in 1790 from Tiruchirapalli (Trichinopoly) and Malabar by the British, and by their allies from the north, without much success until the Governor-General himself took command, and fresh forces made Tipu accept the Treaty of Seringapatam (Srirangapatnam) (1792) losing much territory, including Coorg (p. 496). The invasion of Egypt by Napoleon Bonaparte in 1798 caused Lord Mornington to renew war with Tipu, who unwisely had sent a mission to Mauritius. This time the invasion was made from Vellore (p. 497) and again from Malabar; the "God-given" province of Mysore was conquered by the storming of Srirangapatnam, Tipu dying in the assault. Mysore was then restored to a descendant of the former Hindu Ruler, supported by a British force under Colonel Arthur Wellesley.

After the second Mahratta War ended Jaswant Rao Holkar became active in 1804. He started raiding in Rajputana and Central India, and then, defeating a force commanded by Colonel Monson (p. 290), marched on Delhi, which was defended with difficulty (p. 327). His capital was taken by a Bombay force in August and Lake now moved from Kanpur (Cawnpore) a force, before which Holkar retired to Dig, assisted by the Raja of Bharatpur, who lost this fortress (1804). Bharatpur withstood four assaults in 1805, before a treaty was made with the Raja. Holkar wandered to the west, but in September moved north from Ajmer, and at the end of the year a Treaty of Rajpur Ghat on the Beas ended this adventure, and hostilities with the Mahrattas, until 1817. Lake was anxious to make British a strip of territory west of the Jumna, but could not persuade the Governor-General (Barlow), and left India in 1807.

The results of the Pindari War, the annexation of Sind (1844), the Sikh Wars, the Burmese Wars, and the Nepal War, all against aggressive action, added some territory, but very large areas remained in the possession of their Rulers. Oudh was annexed (1856) on account of maladministration, and the Central Provinces (1853) because the line of Mahratta Rulers died out. After 1862, however, the right of adoption by Rulers was recognised.

In 1857 a serious attempt was made to destroy British rule by the instrument which had enabled that rule to be established. Forty-seven battalions of the Bengal Army mutinied, twenty were disarmed, and only seven (one a Gurkha battalion) remained staunch. The Mutiny did not receive any support from the greater Ruling Princes, showing that the treaties made with them had not been interpreted to their disadvantage. Also the Amir of Afghanistan observed his obligations.

On the British side, the Punjab, with some assistance from Sind, provided the besiegers (at times the besieged) at Delhi. To reinforce the besieged at Lucknow, and later to carry out the final relief, troops from Madras, a China expeditionary force, and a large army sent out round the Cape from England, all contributed. The relief would have been more difficult if a force of Bombay troops, under Sir Hugh Rose, had not made a remarkable advance northward through Saugor and Jhansi (p. 223) to Kalpi, and relieved the Commander-in-Chief, Sir Colin Campbell, from a "pain in the neck, due to looking over his shoulder". Further reference to these operations is made in the descriptions of Delhi, Lucknow, Jhansi, Kanpur (Cawnpore) and elsewhere.

Various causes have been assigned for the outbreak, all of which may have played some part, but it is difficult even now to decide what was the major precipitant. Probably as good an explanation as any was that given by an Indian: "A wind blew and we all ran before it". Modern Indian historians sometimes refer to the revolt as a War of Independence.

S. N. Sen's *Eighteen Fifty Seven*, published May 1957 by the Government of India in the centenary year of the revolt provides a well-balanced and authoritative account of the tragedy, which sets the "nationalist" element in the rising in its due proportions as being in the main a hankering after the restoration of older régimes which the British had displaced—a kind of reaction against change and progress.

CONSTITUTIONAL BACKGROUND OF BRITISH RULE

The Charter to a syndicate of London merchants granted by Queen Elizabeth was renewed on several occasions. In 1698 a rival Company was authorised by Act of Parliament, but after a troubled period of co-existence, the two Companies were merged in 1709. In 1767 an Act restricted dividends to a maximum of 10 per cent. In July 1773 a Regulating Act (Lord North) was passed to come into force on 1st August 1774. A Governor-General was appointed in the Bengal Presidency, with a Council, and with some authority over the Madras and Bombay Presidencies as regards their political relations. A Supreme Court was set up (Sir Elijah Impey, C.J.) and arrived in Calcutta in October 1774. Another great change came in 1784, when Pitt's India Act established a Board of Control. This consisted of six Privy Councillors, including the Chancellor of the Exchequer and one Secretary of State. It was anticipated that 1833 would see the end of the Company's agency to govern, but the British Government was not yet prepared to take over. As a result of the Mutiny on 1st November 1858 Lord Canning announced the transfer, under the Act of that year, of the Government from the intermediary East India Company direct to the Crown, Queen Victoria issued a Proclamation, which placed Indians on an equality with British subjects, and their association with the higher administration began.

In 1861 an Indian Councils Act enabled the Governor-General (now also Viceroy) to nominate six to twelve Indians and Europeans as additional members of his Council for the purpose of making laws and regulations. Similar powers were given in Bombay and Madras, while Councils were formed later in Bengal (1862), the United Provinces (1886) and the Punjab (1897). In 1885 the (unofficial) Indian National Congress was founded.

In 1892 another Councils Act applied a form of election to the Governor-General's Legislative Council and also to Provincial Councils, then increased in numbers. They were enabled to discuss the "Budgets" but not to vote supply. The capital of India was transferred from Calcutta to Delhi in 1912.

BRITISH "COLONIAL" ARCHITECTURE

The new capital, designed by Sir Edwin Lutyens and Sir Herbert Baker, forms the most impressive of the many architectural legacies of British rule. The entire layout, with its avenues, vistas and rotundas; its magnificent buildings for official use, and its pleasing provision for private residences and staff accommodation make it a worthy home for the Central Government of Independent India. Moreover, the planners made provision for flexible expansion in the sites provided for further building—a provision of which the Indian Government has taken full advantage. In addition, British rule has left many legacies of Georgian and Victorian building, some copied from famous British houses such as Kedleston, others in an Indo-Saracenic style intended to harmonise with the traditions of Mughal architecture.

Critics did not fail to point out that the plans for the construction of the latest of the many cities which successive dynasties had erected in and around Delhi coincided with events pointing irrevocably to the gradual ending of the *Raj* which was building it.

RELAXATION OF BRITISH CONTROL

The system of representation without responsibility in the Advisory Legislative Councils did not go far enough for Indian leaders like G. K. Gokhale (1866-1915), who declared, "We march round the fortress of bureaucracy, seeking entrance but finding none". An entrance was given by another Councils Act of 1909, embodying the Morley-Minto Reforms. Two Indians were appointed to the Council of the Secretary of State, another as Law Member to the Executive Council of the Governor-General, while others were appointed to the Executive Councils in Madras and Bombay. Election was introduced for all Councils with non-official majorities in Provincial Councils. The All-India Muslim League had been formed in 1906 and Lord Minto had promised separate representation for Muslims, a step much criticised by Hindu opinion, as tending to perpetuate a rift in natural cohesion. It was still considered, however, that training in administrative practice could be given best through Municipal and similar Boards, and stage by stage District Officers ceased to be *ex-officio* presidents of such bodies.

Indian support during the First World War led to a declaration in Parliament in 1917 that the policy of H.M. Government was that of the increasing association of Indians in every branch of the administration, leading to "Responsible government in British India as an integral part of the British Empire".

In the Provincial governments a system of "Dyarchy" was applied, certain subjects being "reserved" to the Governor-in-Council (including Indian members), others being "transferred" to Indian Ministers elected to the Legislative Councils, and appointed by the Governor, but not necessarily selected from the party having a majority in the Chamber.

These reforms did not satisfy Indian aspirations to self-government, and a powerful movement, of which Mahatma Gandhi became leader, continued to press for Indian control of Indian affairs. Gandhi's unique personality, and his insistence on non-violence, gained him an international reputation and brought much support for the Indian nationalist movement from the outside world.

The Act of 1919 provided for a full inquiry not later than ten years after its passing. In the winter of 1927 Sir John Simon was designated to preside over the Commission appointed for the purpose of making this inquiry. Indians had agitated for membership of the Commission, but this was not possible, as it was a Statutory Commission confined to Members of the two Houses of Parliament, and not a Royal Commission. The Congress Party and some other sections of Indian opinion decided not to co-operate in any way. The members of the Commission toured extensively round India, and presented their report in 1930. This was followed by Round Table Conferences, meant to find the greatest common measure of agreement, in 1931 and the two following years. In 1931 Gandhi attended as sole representative of Congress. The British Government formulated proposals in a White Paper in March 1933, and this was considered by a Joint Select Parliamentary Committee, which reported late in 1934. A Government of India Bill was drafted, providing for Provincial Autonomy as a first stage, and for Federation of British Provinces and Indian States later. The Act received the Royal Assent in August 1935. Part II, the first stage, came into force on 1st April 1937.

Federation required the "accession" of a sufficient number of the rulers of Indian States, but this had not been achieved when the outbreak of the Second World War compelled its postponement. The Executive Council was increased to fourteen members.

All the seats in the Viceroy's Executive Council, except that of Commander-in-Chief, were transferred to Indian leaders. An "Interim Government" was formed in 1946, and by Convention, decisions of Council by majority vote, a system which had been abandoned ever since the Act of 1786, were resumed.

Meanwhile a strong movement, led by M. A. Jinnah, had grown up among the Muslim community to secure the creation of a Muslim National House when British rule came to an end (see Pakistan, p. 554, below).

INDIAN INDEPENDENCE ACT

Rear-Admiral Viscount (now Admiral of the Fleet, Earl) Mountbatten of Burma, K.G., assumed the office of Viceroy and Governor-General on 24th March 1947, and succeeded in ending the political impasse resulting from the conflicting aims of Congress and the Muslim League by securing agreement to the partition of India into two Dominions. India (mainly Hindu) and Pakistan (mainly Muslim) with capitals at Delhi and Karachi, came into being as independent sovereign countries on 15th August 1947. In 1971 the eastern wing of Pakistan became independent under the title of the People's Republic of Bangladesh.

8. ADMINISTRATIVE STRUCTURE OF INDIA, PAKISTAN AND BANGLADESH

BASES OF ADMINISTRATION IN INDIA, PAKISTAN AND BANGLADESH

Since all three countries have been for long periods of their history parts of a single Empire, their administrations are derived from a common source. The basic unit is the village, each with its own officials—headman, watchman and members of the village council. In all three countries, these councils now exercise wider powers than under the British, and form part of larger groupings with local government functions of the kind familiar in the West. These groupings function in tahsils or subdivisions; a number of these form a district. Each district has a headquarters, which is the seat of the District Officer, termed either Collector, District Magistrate or Deputy Commissioner, exercising executive and magisterial powers as the principal representative of government in his area; in India he is generally a member of the Indian Administrative Service, in Pakistan of the Civil Service of Pakistan, and in Bangladesh of the Bangladesh Administrative Service. He wins his place in his Service in open competition conducted by the Civil Service Commissions of each country, and the process of selection is rigorous—rightly so, because he is the backbone of the whole administration and represents the Government in the eyes of millions of ordinary people.

At his headquarters there are a number of other officials; the Superintendent of Police; the District and Sessions Judge; the Principal Medical Officer; the Public Works Engineers; the Development Officers, and specialists in Forestry, Irrigation, Agriculture and so forth, each of whom heads a chain of subordinates throughout the area. The Head of the District, who is responsible for revenue collection, has his own representatives—subdivisional officers and so forth —who are generally members of a State, rather than a National, Service. Consistent efforts have been made by all three countries to devolve powers from official to non-official agencies, to associate ordinary people with the task of government, and to inculcate initiative and self-help in dealing with local problems.

In Pakistan, in certain (but not all) States in India, but not in Bangladesh, the Districts are grouped into Divisions, presided over by a very senior officer entitled Commissioner, whose functions are directive and co-ordinating, rather than executive. Where he exists, he is the main link between his area and the Secretariat which each State maintains in the State Capital; in States where there is no Commissioner, the Secretariat corresponds with the District Officers. Each State has its own judicial machinery (of which the District and Sessions Judge is a member) under the direction of its own High Court, except that some of the smaller States maintain a single High Court in common. In each State Secretariat, often housed in fine modern buildings in the State Capital (examples: Bombay and Chandigarh) are numerous Departments of Government, each with a Secretary or senior official who is responsible to a Minister who is a member of the Government, appointed by a Chief Minister who leads the majority party in the Legislature which is elected by adult suffrage. At the head of the whole administrative structure is the State Governor, appointed by the President of the Nation. Normally he acts on the advice of his Ministers, but in certain instances he is given special responsibilities by the President—for example, the protection of tribal peoples and backward classes.

THE LAND AND THE PEOPLE

Until comparatively recent times, land in every part of the subcontinent was looked on as the demesne of the ruler, who made grants of it as he pleased and lived upon the revenues he exacted—whether in cash, kind or military service— leaving the grantees to recoup themselves from the actual cultivators. Some land he kept in his own hands. The Mughals regulated the system and fixed the proportion of the crop which the cultivator had to hand over. Later, the collection of the revenue was farmed out to intermediaries who, when the central Government was weak, set themselves up as independent magnates. When the British came, the Company at first continued the system, but made experiments in regulating it, as when Lord Cornwallis introduced the Permanent Settlement, turning the revenue collectors of Bengal into landlords in the hope that they would, for the sake of self-interest, improve agricultural conditions. This failed to work well, and by degrees the British *raj* introduced a plan of periodically-fixed "settlements", sometimes with the actual cultivators, sometimes with the landlords, the land being classified by productivity. This work employed a great many officials, working full-time to keep the records up to date.

When the British left, the new independent Governments showed themselves anxious to improve the lot of the cultivator, and embarked upon radical measures of agrarian reform of a kind which no foreign Government could have safely undertaken. Intermediaries were removed; the authorities dealt direct with the cultivator, who was encouraged to purchase his land on easy terms. There was a strict limitation on the size of holdings, the object being to make land available to the landless. Much land was acquired by compulsory purchase; a strong movement was set on foot by Vinobha Bhave to encourage gifts of surplus land by individuals and even whole communities to the landless. Community Development, village self-help, and the encouragement of cottage industries are now all playing their part in improving agricultural conditions, but progress towards the goal of the Welfare State is slow, not only because of the immense number of people involved, but also because of the great population increase which threatens to offset the improvements as they are made.

Of recent years the "Green Revolution" resulting from the use of new seed-strains, the introduction of simple but practicable agricultural machinery, and the spread of electric power have greatly increased agricultural productivity in all three countries, which, with the exception of Bangladesh—which relies for its prosperity on a single cash crop, jute—are steadily becoming more self-sufficient in the production of food grains. At the same time, all three countries are making great efforts to cope with the "population explosion" and the longer expectation of life (resulting from improvements in public hygiene) by the encouragement of family planning. The aim is to stabilise the population at a figure which will enable the Welfare State to be achieved.

Even though all three countries have made great progress in the field of both light and heavy industry—the principal installations and organisational groupings are noted in the *Handbook* under the appropriate localities—agriculture still remains the pillar of their national finances. For this reason, irrigation projects are of great importance, as the main safeguard against periodic failures of the monsoon—vagaries which once caused the finances of the subcontinent to be described as "a gamble in rain".

IRRIGATION AND HYDRO-ELECTRIC SCHEMES

The tapping of the great rivers, fed by melting snow and rain, and the storage of water in places where the monsoon never fails completely, guarantees local security and stability of out-turn. The British laid out Rs. 146½ crores in works which irrigate 50,000 sq.m., with an estimated crop value of Rs. 91 crores a year, and the successor Governments are no whit behind in making every effort to develop the irrigation system. Not all the works are individually productive, that is, earn a sufficient rate of interest on capital outlay, but, taking all together, the return has been remunerative.

The conservation of water is an old practice, exemplified by tanks in Udaipur, Hyderabad and Bundelkhand. In Southern India there are many tanks in chains down a watercourse, most of them with earthen dams, very liable to burst if the N.E. monsoon drops water into a tank already full. One bursting tank carries away the next dam, and so on down the chain. Many of the old reservoirs have been improved and are utilised for modern needs.

Innumerable wells draw water from the subsoil but irrigate only 5 per cent. of the cropped area. In modern times, motor-driven pumps have been installed and they are particularly valuable to lower the subsoil water level in tracts where saltpetre (*reh*) may be drawn to the surface by evaporation. Along the Runn of Kutch reservoir water becomes very salt.

The "father" of canal irrigation (the builder of the Grand Anikuts, p. 544, is unknown) was Firoz Shah Tughlaq (1351-93) who built a canal from the Jumna to Hissar. It was extended to Delhi by Ali Mardan Khan about 1640. The repair of this Western Jumna canal was the first British irrigation scheme in 1817-20. It had an outfall near Okhla, on the Jumna below Delhi. The Eastern Jumna Canal (1830) from the same "head" also tails into the Jumna opposite Delhi.

The Ganges Canal extends from Hardwar down to Kanpur, and seven falls produce electricity, operate tube wells, and light towns on the "grid" system. The *doab* down to Allahabad is irrigated from another head at Narora (p. 369). The densely populated region north of the Ganges is irrigated from numerous tributaries. The Sarda canal was opened in 1928.

The annexation of the Punjab in 1849 found the country in a very bad condition. In 1851-59 the Bari *doab* (Ravi-Sutlej) Canal was followed by the Sirhind Canal in the Sutlej-Jumna *doab*. A Lower Chenab Canal (1892-1900) irrigates the Rechna *doab* between the Chenab and the Ravi. The Jhelum Canal irrigates the Lyallpur District, where lands, previously waste, were settled by families whose heads had given good public service, but large transfers have followed Partition. Such enterprises as the Triple Canals scheme which enables an enormous area to be watered in Bahawalpur and Bikaner, on the fringe of the Great Indian Desert, led to a long dispute between India and Pakistan over the sharing of the Indus Basin waters which was finally resolved only in 1960.

In Sind, the waters of the Indus have for many years enabled crops to be grown by irrigation canals; in fact a great deal of inundation has to be prevented by levees, which require careful watching in case of a diversion of the river from its course. The Great Barrage at Sukkur (p. 568) was built (1923-32), and in addition to the benefit to lands on the west bank, has irrigated a very large area on the east bank, where canals operated formerly at high water only. In the N.-W. Frontier Province the Kabul river was tapped, and the waters of the Swat in tribal territory were taken through the Benton tunnel into the Kabul river valley, generating electricity on the way. Since 1947 the Pakistan Government has been actively engaged in developing its irrigation and hydro-electric resources. The Great Barrage at Sukkur has been supplemented by a barrage on the Lower Indus at Kotri, named after the late Governor-General, Ghulam Mahommed, while a new barrage, named after M. A. Jinnah, has been constructed at Kalabagh to feed water to the Thal Development project in W. Punjab, which has brought no less than 1½ million acres under cultivation. Other large mixed-purpose schemes have been undertaken, notably at Warsak near Peshawar, at Mianwali, Mangla, and Taunsa on the Indus. Bangladesh has inherited a magnificent dam project on the Karnaphali River, which provides electricity for a wide area and helps to keep the harbour of Chittagong free from silt.

The Indian Government also has taken up similar work with energy. The great Bhakra-Nangal project[1] in the E. Punjab and the Uhl River hydro-electric scheme are complete. In Bihar, West Bengal, and Orissa, the Son, Midnapore and Mahanadi canals, the Mayurakshi R. V. project, and the Damodar Valley Scheme, controlled by a public authority on the lines of the Tennessee Valley Authority; and the Kosi River Scheme, represent notable recent developments.

In Andhra Pradesh, the Mettur hydro-electric dam in the Salem district (p. 518) and the Krishnaraja Sagar in Karnataka (p. 495) have been con-

[1] Well worth a visit. The 740 foot high dam is the tallest of its kind in the world. The artificial lake is magnificent and the views impressive. There are good rail and bus connections with Delhi. There are rest houses for visitors. Passports must be shown.

structed, while the Cauvery Power Works also utilise the water to generate electricity. A great dam has been constructed on the Tungabhadra near Bellary.

Along the Western Ghats in Maharashtra water is conserved, not only for the Tata Hydro-Electric Company (p. 105) but also for the water supply of Poona and for the Nira canal system (p. 441), to mention one only. In the southern extension of these ghats the Periyar dam (1887-96) turns water flowing normally west into the plains of Madura. These Indian irrigation works challenge comparison with any in the world. Without them the population could have faced periodical disaster.

FORESTS

Throughout the centuries, the subcontinent, once very rich in forests, suffered severe losses through denudation and lack of care. Indiscriminate grazing, especially by goats, and reckless felling for fuel produced adverse effects on soil conservation and even climate. Under the British, scientific forestry along European lines was practised on a larger scale than almost anywhere else. By the time the British left, there were a quarter of a million square miles of forest under the control of the Forest Department; and the succession States have been able to expand forest industries very considerably. Scientific exploitation for timber, newsprint, and other kinds of paper adds to the wealth of India, Pakistan and Bangladesh—the last possesses in the Chandragona Mill on the Karnaphuli River one of the largest and most up-to-date paper mills in Asia, with a growing export trade. All three countries have magnificent tracts of forest, as have Nepal and Sri Lanka (Ceylon). Not all these tracts are covered with marketable timber; some of them are scrub jungle on which grazing and firewood cutting is permitted.

The scientific expansion of forest industries is reducing the area of "wild" forest, with a consequent reduction in the numbers of the fauna inhabiting it. This is one of the reasons why the wild life conservation movement is important for all the countries covered in this *Handbook*, since certain of the species which once flourished in India, Pakistan, Bangladesh, Nepal and Sri Lanka (Ceylon) are now threatened with extinction because of the reduction of the area in which they must find their food. All five countries now control shooting very strictly, and certain species are rigorously protected; while numerous Game Reserves and National Parks have been established (as is noted in the text of this book) to ensure that forest fauna can continue to live in certain areas unmolested by the development of forest resources in the national interest.

THE CENSUS

The (first in 1871) Indian Census at intervals of ten years is a gigantic undertaking, but the organisation makes it less difficult than might be expected, and the error in numbers is calculated to be less than one in a thousand. Classification is not so accurate, for various reasons, some of them usual elsewhere. Preparations commence with the appointment of a Census Commissioner, usually selected from officials experienced in land-settlement work, or interested in civil conditions. Two famous former Commissioners were Sir Denzil Ibbetson and Sir Herbert Risley. Assistants in the Provinces, and the District officials co-operate, but the cost would be enormous without the help of an army of voluntary enumerators.

The 1921 Census showed an increase of only four millions, largely due to an epidemic of influenza in 1918, which caused approximately six million deaths in a few months; but that of 1941 showed an increase of some fifty millions; and by 1971 the population of India alone was 547,367,000. This startling rate of increase, which threatens, in spite of birth control drives, to outpace the increase in the food-producing capacity of the country, constitutes perhaps India's gravest problem. The 1961 Census showed the population of the new India as 439,235,000 and of Pakistan as 93,720,000, of which the then East Pakistan accounted for 50,840,000. Census figures for Pakistan and Bangladesh are not so up to date; but it is estimated that there are some 65,000,000 in Pakistan and upwards of 70,000,000 in Bangladesh. Thus the population of the whole subcontinent cannot be less than about 682,000,000.

Almost 86 per cent. of the population of Pakistan and Bangladesh is Muslim, but the overwhelming majority of the population of India is Hindu. There are nevertheless some 14,000,000 Christians in India (of whom nearly two-thirds are Roman Catholics), and approximately the same number of Sikhs.

Density of population is a difficult matter to assess. The most densely populated areas are Kerala and Bengal, with considerably over one person to the acre, closely followed by Bihar and the U.P. Calcutta, with Howrah and its suburbs, holds more than 7,000,000 persons, including a shifting population in the mills and the docks which swells the provincial density. The 5,900,000 people living in Bombay City may be considerably reduced in the harvesting season. Figures for other cities are given in the text.

While there is a great deal of illiteracy, the figures have much improved in the last forty years. The languages spoken, exclusive of dialects, some of which are purely local, number 225. Hindustani is the *lingua franca* over the greater part of Northern and Central India. In its Urdu form (i.e. written in Persian characters and with a largely Arabic and Persian vocabularly) it prevails in the Delhi and Lucknow areas, and wherever Muslim influence was predominant. In its Hindi form (i.e. written in Devanagari characters and with a largely Sanskritised vocabularly) it is current in the rest of Northern and Central India, and has now been declared the official language of India. In the South, English is still to a great extent the actual lingua franca. The names Bengali and Punjabi, Marathi and Konkani, indicate the areas in which they are generally spoken. Oriya is the language of Orissa, Pukhtu (guttural), or Pushtu (sibilant) on the N.W. Frontier and Baluchistan. Telugu, Tamil, Kanarese, or Malayali are spoken in Madras and S. India. Only thirteen principal languages have been mentioned in this account.

POSTS, TELEGRAPHS AND TELEPHONES

All the countries covered in this *Handbook* are linked to each other and to the outside world by a modern system of communications through postal services, cables and wireless. Internally, each country has airmail and railway delivery of letters, through central and local post offices. These perform savings-bank and other functions as in Western countries. The development of wireless has made long-distance telephone calls easy and practical; while in every large city the local telephone service expands year by year. Motor mail-vans are not only used for postal deliveries within the cities; they now penetrate to rural areas which not so long ago could only be reached by runner. These runners, carrying a spear hung with bells to warn off wild animals, now only operate in very remote areas where roads are still primitive. There is a surcharge for the internal airmail service. Unfortunately the reliability of the Indian postal service is far from perfect and duplicates of important letters should be sent by different posts. It is important that stamps should be seen to be cancelled.

BROADCASTING

There has of recent years been a great development of radio services in the East. In addition to the general service in Hindi and regional languages and domestic news services in English, All-India Radio maintains short-wave broadcasts to Europe in English and French, as well as Burmese, Chinese and Indonesian services on wave-lengths between 16 and 50 metres. Programmes are published in the principal newspapers. There are transmitting stations at Calcutta, Bombay, Poona, Tiruchirapalli (Trichinopoly), Madras and Lucknow, in addition to the Central Broadcasting Station in Delhi.

In the Pakistan of a few years ago there were only three low-powered medium-wave transmitting stations at Lahore, Peshawar and Dacca, with no interlinking arrangements. Now with the erection of the Central Broadcasting Station at Karachi equipped with high-powered short-wave transmitters, services have all been integrated, and five external services are now maintained as well as the internal. Medium-wave stations are located at Rawalpindi and Peshawar, and in Bangladesh at Chittagong. Dacca and Rajshahi, while others are under consideration. These operate on short-waves between 16 and 90 meters, and medium-waves between 206 and 477 metres. An "All-Wave" receiver should operate between 16 and 550 metres. Sri Lanka (Ceylon) has its own central broadcasting stations operating in English, as well as in the language of the country.

Television services, at present confined to the larger cities, operate in India, Bangladesh and Pakistan, but their audience is still small in comparison to that relying on the broadcasting network.

THE PRESERVATION OF MONUMENTS

The Governments of India, Pakistan, Bangladesh and Sri Lanka (Ceylon) take great pride in their national monuments, of which all have a great wealth. They have expanded and enlarged the Archaeological Departments bequeathed by the British, and have cleaned and beautified many of the sites visited by tourists in addition to carrying out extensive excavations to trace the relics of ancient civilisations. New discoveries have added much to knowledge; the leaflets and brochures which the Departments publish, which can be obtained either on the sites themselves, or from Tourist Information Centres, are of great interest. All these countries possess excellent archaeological museums; the most important are noticed in the Directory under the places where they are situated.

It was not until 1878 that the British Government awoke to the condition into which the national monuments were sinking, and the Viceroy, Lord Lytton, pressed for the appointment of a Curator of Ancient Monuments. The post was sanctioned and held until 1884 by Major Cole, who did much towards the repair of ancient structures, notably those in the Gwalior Fort and at Sanchi. Later, Lord Curzon greatly encouraged both the care of ancient monuments and archaeological exploration. The active co-operation of the rulers of Indian States was secured. Some of them, like the then Nizam of Hyderabad, set up excellently efficient Departments of their own.

Under the direction of Sir John Marshall (1902-31) and his successors the more important groups of monuments, besides others throughout India and Burma, were overhauled and put into repair. On the "beaten track" the Taj Mahal at Agra, the Fort, the tomb of Itimād ud daula, the Chini ka Rauza and Akbar's tomb at Sikandra were renovated and the surroundings cleared. At Delhi the Palace in the Fort, the tomb of Humayun and very many other buildings received attention. At Lahore the Fort, the mosque of Dai Anga and the tomb of Jahangir at Shahdara were conserved. To these Muslim monuments may be added those at Mandu and Dhar in M.P., at Ahmedabad in Gujarat and Bijapur in Maharashtra, at Gaur and Pandua in Bengal, and at Rohtasgarh in Bihar.

Among Buddhist and Hindu monuments may be mentioned the topes at

Sanchi and Sarnath, the temples of Khajuraho in Bundelkhand and of Bhubaneshwar in Orissa, the city of Vijayanagar, the temples of Kanchipuram (Conjeeveram) and Belur (Vellore) in Tamil Nadu.

Not content with the conservation of visible remains, the Department undertook excavations to uncover remains which had been buried for centuries. At Taxila in the Punjab, Bhita and Sarnath near Benares, Harappa and Mohenjodaro in the Indus valley, and other excavations at Rupar and Maski (in the Raichur district) and at Maheshwar extended knowledge of the "chalcolithic" period. Since India and Pakistan became independent, as already noted, both Governments have taken up enthusiastically the task of preserving their respective national heritages. Excellent pamphlets and brochures are now available from Tourist Bureaux which explain what is being done.

Notes on some of the most important museums in India and Pakistan will be found under Section 5 of this Introduction as well as in the description of the localities where each museum is situated.

WILD LIFE SANCTUARIES AND NATIONAL PARKS

The Tourist Information Departments of the various countries will supply details of the facilities available for visitors and the range of animals to be seen at particular Sanctuaries, both of which are summarised in the text under the appropriate localities. The following are among the Sanctuaries and National Parks of the greatest interest to the ordinary visitor.

India:

Anamalai (Tamil Nadu); Bandipur (Karnataka); Chandarprabha (U.P.); Corbett National Park (U.P.); Keoladeo Ghana Bird Sanctuary (near Bharatpur); Gir Forest (Gujarat); Kanha (M.P.); Kaziranga (Assam); Manas (Assam); Mudumalai (Karnataka); Periyar (Kerala); Ranganthittoo Bird Sanctuary (Karnataka); Ranthambhor near Chitorgarh; Sariska (Rajasthan); Shivpuri (U.P.); Wynaad (Kerala).

Pakistan:

Changamanga; Hazar Ganji; Khebaki Jheel; Kalan Kahar; Lai Sukara; Nammal Jheel; Nara; Rakh Mirjal; Ucchali Jheel.

Bangladesh:

Kassalong Forests; Pablakhali.

Sri Lanka (*Ceylon*):

Gal Oya; Kumana; Lahugale; Mihintale; Ruhuna; Wilpattu; Wirawila Tissa.

9. GLOSSARY OF THE PRINCIPAL VERNACULAR TERMS USED IN THIS BOOK[1]

(A) signifies Arabic; (H) Hindûstání or Hindí; (K) Kanarese; (Mal) Malayálam; (M) Mahrátti; (My) Malay; (P) Persian; (S) Sanskrit; (Sin) Sinhalese; (Tel) Telugu; (Tur) Turkish; (T) Tamil.

AIL (Isle), (H) The low earthen ridge round fields in rice-growing areas.

AMÍR (Ameer), (A) commander, a title of Princes and nobles, as the Amirs of Sind, and formerly of Afghanistan.

[1] See p. 630 for a glossary of the principal vernacular terms used in Nepal.

ÁNÁ (Anna), (H) the 16th part of a rupee (now superseded in India and Pakistan by the new decimal coinage ("*naye paise*")).

ANIKUT, (T) weir, dam (*annai kutta*).

ANJUMAN, (P) assemblage, society, institute.

ĀRĀMA, (S and Sin) a pleasure-garden or park.

BABÚL, (H) a thorny mimosa (the *Acacia arabica* tree), in N. India named the Kíkar.

BAHÁDUR, (P) brave, chivalrous, a title of honour.

BANA, (Sin) reading of the sacred books in public.

BAND (correctly bándh), (H) an embankment or dyke—commonly Bund.

BANDAR, (P) a port or harbour.

BANYAN-TREE, the Indian fig-tree (*Ficus Indica*, or *Ficus Bengalensis*, L.) which has aerial roots.

BÁOLÍ, (H) a rectangular well with steps and galleries.

BÁRADARÍ, (H) (twelve doors), a summer-house; a mansion.

BÁZÁR, (P) a market or market-place; a street of shops.

BEGAM (Begum), (Tur) a lady of rank; in Pakistan a courtesy title for married ladies.

BEL, (H) a fruit-tree (*Aegle marmelos*).

BHATTÁ (Bhátá or Batta), (H) allowance given on field service or to public servants on duty at a distance from headquarters.

BUNGALOW (bangalá), (H) a house of one storey with verandahs; often designed like a tent.

CASTE, class; sect; corruption of the Portuguese *casta* or race.

CATAMARAN, (T) *kaṭṭu*, "to bind", *maram*, "a tree", a log-raft on which the boatmen of Madras paddle through the surf.

CHABÚTRÁ, (H) a raised platform, usually of stone or brick; terrace.

CHADAR (Chádar), (H) sheet worn by men and women.

CHAITYA, (S) a Buddhist chapel or church; primarily a heap or tumulus; also a place of sacrifice or religious worship; any building of the nature of a religious monument (Fergusson, *Ind. Arch.*).

CHAKRA, (S) a wheel; the wheel of the Buddhist law.

CHAR, an alluvial formation, as an island in a river.

CHAUKIDAR (Chokidar), (H) a watchman, by day or night.

CHAURÍ, (H) a fly-whisk; a mark of rank.

CHÁWADI, (Tel) a rest house for Indian travellers, English corruption *Choultry*.

CHHATRÍ (Chhattar), (H) umbrella; insignia of rank; a monumental structure or pavilion erected in honour of a person of rank.

CHÍTAL, (H) the spotted deer (*Axis maculatus*), gregarious, and formerly common but now protected in many parts of India and Pakistan.

CHUNAM, (T) an English corruption of (H) *chúná*, lime, a plaster or mortar (sometimes made of powdered shells) of a remarkable whiteness and brilliance.

COMPOUND, an enclosure, perhaps a corruption of the Malay word *Kampong*.

CRORE (Karor), (H) 100 lakhs or 10 million.

DAGOBA, a Sinhalese word from Pali *dhatugabbha* and Sanskrit *dhatugarbha* = relic-receptacle; strictly a *stupa* containing relics of Buddha.

DÁK, (H) post, relay of horses; dak bungalow (or Musáfar Khana), a staging or rest house for official travellers.

DÁKGÁRI, (H) stage-coach, for one or two travellers; mail train.

DARBÁR (Durbar), (P) a royal court; an audience or levee; a hall.

DARGÁH, shrine; place of burial of a Muslim saint.

DARWÁZA, (P) gateway, door.

DEODÁR, the *Cedrus deodara* of the Himalaya: from *deva-daru*, the "wood of the gods".

DHARMSÁLÁ, (H and M) (*dharma*, "justice", "piety", and *sálá*, "a hall"), a place of accommodation for travellers and pilgrims.

DHOLI, (H) *Dhooli* (properly *dolī*), a swinging cot or litter suspended from a pole carried by bearers.

DHOTI, (H) a loin-cloth or lower garment.

DÍWÁN, (P) a royal court, a minister, especially the chief financial minister.

DÍWÁN-I-AM, DÍWÁN-I-KHÁS, (P) hall of public, private, audience.

DOÁB, the country between two rivers.

DWÁRPÁL, (H) a door-keeper, commonly sculptured at sides of door in Buddhist shrines and Hindu temples.

EKKA, (H) a pony-cart.

FAKÍR, (A) a religious Muslim who has taken a vow of poverty; a poor man; also inaccurately applied to Hindu devotees and ascetics.

FARMÁN, (P) a royal order or grant.

GADDÍ, (H) seat; royal seat; throne of a Hindu Prince.

GAON, (H) village.

GARUDA, a fabulous bird; the vehicle of Vishnu.

GHARÁ, (H) an earthen water-pot or jar.

GHARI, (H) a carriage (Tikka, for hire).

GHÁT (Ghaut), (S) *ghaṭṭa*, a landing-place, steps on a river-side; a mountain pass; a range of hills.

GIRI, (S) hill, rock.

GIRJA (Port), church: from Portuguese *igreja*.

GOPURAM, (H) the pyramidal gateway of a Dravidian temple.

GOSAIN, (H) Hindu monk or devotee.

GUMBAZ, (P) a cupola; a dome.

GURU, (H) a spiritual adviser.

HAJI, (P) a Muslim who has performed the pilgrimage (*haj*) to Mecca.

HAMMÁL, (A) a bearer of a *palkí*; in Bombay, an orderly or house-bearer.

HAMMAM, (P) bath.

HARÍM (harem), (P) a sanctuary; ladies' apartments.

HAUZ, (A) cistern, tank, reservoir.

HAVILDÁR, (H) one holding an office of trust; an officer in Indian Infantry corresponding to a sergeant; also Havildár Major.

HUḲḲA (Hooka), (A) Indian or Pakistani tobacco-pipe.

HUZÚR, (A) the royal presence; a respectful term applied to high officials.

IDGÁH, (P) an open enclosure on the W. of a town where the Id prayers are offered.

IMÁMBÁRA, (P) a building to which the Shias carry the *tazias* or biers in the *muharram*, often the tomb of the founder.

ISHWAR, or ISWAR, (S) God, Lord, title of a Hindu deity.

JÁGÍR, (P) a tenure by which the public revenues of an estate or district were granted during pleasure or for life to a jagirdar, with powers to collect, and to administer the general affairs of the estate. Land reform has abolished this system.

JAMADÁR, (A) an Indian officer next to a Súbadár, and corresponding to lieutenant.

JHATKA, (H) covered pony-cart in S. India.

JHÍL, (H) pool, lake, swamp.

JOGI, (S) a Hindu devotee, as Fakir is a Muslim. Also known as *Swamy*.

JOHAR (Jauhar) (H) sacrifice or immolation practised by Rajput women to avoid capture.

KABR, (A) a tomb (Muslim); Kabristan, cemetery.

KACHAHRÍ, (H) commonly Cutcherry, a court or office for public business.

KADI. Homespun cloth, popularised as national wear among Hindus by Mahatma Gandhi.

KALIMA, (A) (in full, Kalimat-ul-shahadat, the word of testimony) the Muslim declaration of faith.

KANDA, (Sin) mountain.

KANKAR, (H) nodular or block limestone, with which roads in N. India are often metalled.

KARBALA, (A) designation of cemetery or place where *tazias* are buried, derived from the city on the Euphrates where Husain, son of Ali, the 4th Imam, is buried.

KHÁN, (A) a Muslim title of respectability answering to "Esquire".

KHÁNSÁMÁ, (P) literally "master of the household gear" = butler, or house-steward. In Upper India it is the title of the chief table-servant and provider, generally a Muslim. In N. India and Kashmir, it means the cook. In Tamil Nadu and S. India, this title is not used; "butler" is general, and he is seldom a Muslim.

KHIDMATGÁR, (A, P) the "service-doer", always applied to a Muslim waiter at table.

KIBLA, (A) a niche in the wall to which Muslims look when praying, i.e. in the direction of the Ka'ba at Mecca.

ḲILA, ḲILADAR, (P) fort, commandant of fort.

KIMKHWÁB (Kincob), (P, H) gold brocade.

KOTHÍ, (H) residence, house, mansion.

KOTWÁL, KOTWÁLÍ, (P) police officer, police station.

KULAM, (T) tank: see Teppa Kulam.

ḲULÍ (Cooly), (T and Tur) a labourer; porter at railway stations and elsewhere.

KUND, (S) a pit, hollow, pool, well, small tank.

LÁKH (Lac), (S) the number 100,000. By customary use "a lakh" means "a lakh *of rupees*" (= about £5500 while the Indian Rupee stands at Rs. 18 to the £).

LĀT, (H) a stone monolithic pillar = *stambha*, common to all styles of Indian architecture.

LINGAM (Linga), (S) symbol of Siva as the God of reproduction; phallus.

MAIDÁN, (P) plain, open space, field of battle.

MAKBARA, (P from *Kabr*) grave of a saint.

MAMLATDÁR, subordinate revenue collector.

MAN (Maund), (H) a weight, varying in different parts of India. Now largely superseded by metric weight.

MANDAPAM, (S) a pillared pavilion or porch in front of a temple; also Mantapam, Mahamandapam, etc.

MASJID, (A) mosque (place of prostration, *sijda*). Jámi Masjid, congregational mosque, used on Fridays.

MASNAD, (P) cushion, throne of a Muslim Ruler.

MASULA, (T) a boat sewed together, used for crossing the surf on the Madras side.

MATH, (H) Hindu monastery, of which a Mahanth is Abbot.

MAULVI, (A) one who can read and write Arabic.

MELÁ, (H) a fair.

MIHRÁB, (A) an arch; the recess in the wall of a mosque on the side nearest Mecca, to which Muslims turn at prayer—usually termed Kibla.

MIMBAR, (A) the pulpit in a mosque; the preacher stands on the middle step of the three while delivering his sermon.

MONSOON, (A) a corruption of the (A) *mausim*, "a season"; applied to seasonal rains during the S.W. monsoon, from June to September, or N.E. on the Coromandel Coast later.

MUEZZIN, (A) one who calls Muslims to prayer from the minaret (Azan).
MUFASSAL (often written Mofussil), separate, detailed, particular: commonly meaning "the interior of the country", as distinguished from the towns.
MUNSHÍ (Moonshi), (A) a writer; a secretary; a teacher of languages.
NÁIK, (S) corresponding to a corporal in Indian Infantry; an ancient Hindu title of a governor.
NANDI, (S) bull; vehicle of Siva, often carved in kneeling attitude facing Saivite temples.
NAUBAT KHÁNA, NAKKÁR KHÁNA, (A) the chamber over a gateway, where a band was once stationed for ceremonial music.
NÁUTCH (Nach), (S) a dance; an exhibition of dancing-girls.
NAWÁB (for nuwwāb), (A) this word means lit. "deputies", being the honorific plural of *ná'ib*, "a deputy". A Muslim title.
NIZÁM, (A) lit. arrangement; an administrator; a title of the Prince whose former capital was Hyderábád, in the Deccan.
NULLA, (H) properly Nálá, water-course, or depression.
PAGODA (origin obscure), a temple in S. India; also a coin formerly in use = 3½ rupees, called by Indians *hún*, but deriving the former name from its showing a temple on one face.
PALANKEEN (Palanquin), (H) an Anglican corruption of the word *pálkí*, a means of conveyance, of the shape of a long box with sliding sides, in which persons were once carried for long distances on men's shoulders.
PÁLEGÁR (Polygar), (T, Tel) a shareholder; a landed proprietor or petty chief. A title of persons in the South corresponding to zamindars in other parts of India.
PÁN, (S) the leaf of the betel creeper. Pan-supari is areca nut finely sliced, rolled in betel leaf with a little shell-lime and sometimes tobacco for chewing. It is immensely popular as a digestive and mild stimulant.
PANDIT, a Brahman, proficient in Sanskrit.
PARDA, (P, H) a curtain, especially one that screens women; *pardanashin* = one sitting behind a curtain—i.e. secluded.
PARGANA, a sub-district: see Tahsíl.
PATEL, (S) the headman of a village, invested with some magisterial and revenue functions.
PEEPUL (Pípal), (S, H) a great fig-tree (*Ficus religiosa*), or Bodhi tree.
PEON, from the Portuguese *peao*, Spanish *peon*, "footman".
PESHWÁ, (P) the Brahman Prime Ministers of the Rájás of Sátárá, who afterwards became hereditary Chiefs of the Mahrátta nation.
PHINS, (T) the Toda name for the stone circles on the Nílgiri Hills.
PICE, (H) a corruption of the word *paisá* (money).
PILIMAGÉ, (Sin) image-house.
PINDÁRI, (Pendhara) (M) organised bodies of raiders and bandits.
PINJRAPOL, (H) (*pinjra*, a cage) an animal hospital, generally maintained by the Jains; animal infirmary.
PINKAMA, (Sin) merit-act; entertainment.
PÍR, (P) old; a Muslim saint.
PIRIVEN, (Sin) series of monks' cells.
PRÁKÁRA, a great corridor between a temple and the surrounding wall.
PURA, (S and Sin) (PURAM, T) a town, or city.
RAI SAHIB or BAHADUR: RAO SAHIB or BAHADUR, Indian titles of rank.
RÁJÁ, MAHARAJA, MAHARAJA DHIRAJA, MAHARAO, (S) a Hindu King or Prince.
RANÍ, (S) the wife of a Rájá; a Queen or Princess; also used as a courtesy title for married ladies.
RATH, (S) a chariot formerly, now refers to bullock carts, or cars used for Hindu gods on ceremonial occasions.

RATHS or RÁTHAS, the name given to rock-cut monolithic Dravidian temples at Mahalbalipuram, near Madras.
RISÁLDÁR, (A) a captain of a troop of cavalry.
RISÁLDÁR MAJOR, the senior cavalry officer.
ROZA (Rauza), (A) a tomb in an enclosure, originally the garden at Medina adjoining the chamber (hujra) in which Muhammad was buried.
RYOT, (A) a corruption of the (A) word *ra'iyyat*, a subject, a peasant.
ṢADR (Sadar, Sudder), (A) top, chief, principal.
ṢADR 'ADÁLAT, (A) formerly the Chief Court of Justice in India.
SÁHIB, (A) lord; a title applied to any gentleman in India.
SAIYID, (A) a descendant from the daughter of Muhammad.
SAMÁDH, (H) cenotaph of a Hindu; also self-immolation.
SANDAL, (A and S) the fragrant wood of the *Santalum album*, L.
SANGAM, (S) junction of two or more rivers—commonly a sacred place of pilgrimage.
SANGHÁRÁMA, a group of apartments for a community of monks, a monastery.
SARÁÍ, (P) a rest house for travellers; a caravanserai.
SÁRÍ, (H) a robe worn by Hindu women.
SATÍ (Suttee), (S) a chaste wife, especially one burnt with her deceased husband; the ceremony of burning of such a wife.
SHÁH, (P) a King.
SHAIKH, (A) old, respected; a class or rank of Muslims.
SHANKH, (S) a conch shell, large specimens of which are blown as horns by the Hindús during religious ceremonies.
SHIKÁR; SHIKÁRÍ, (P) game, shooting; gamekeeper or hunter.
SHOLA, (T) a patch of jungle; a wooded dell or copse.
SIKRA (Sikhara), (S) spire or finial of Hindu temple; pyramidal; many-storied; always surmounting the cell of the image.
SINHÁSAN, (S) a lion-seat (*singh*, lion) Hindu throne.
SIPÁHÍ (Sepoy), (H) an Indian soldier, one of a *sipáh* or army.
STAMBHA = LĀT (q.v.).
STUPA (or TOPE), a relic-shrine; a mound or monument containing relics; or a tower commemorative of an event or sacred spot (Fergusson).
SÚBADÁR, (A) Governor of a Province; an infantry officer corresponding to a captain.
SÚBADÁR MAJOR, the senior officer in Infantry.
TAHSÍL, (P) a division of a Zilla, equivalent to Taluk, etc.
TAHSÍLDÁR, (P) a sub-collector of revenue, who may also be a magistrate.
TAIKHANA, (P *tah-khana*, lower house) underground room for retreat in summer (P *sardáb*).
TÁJ, (P) a crown.
TAKA. Unit of currency in Bangladesh: equivalent to the rupee.
TALE, (Sin) a tank.
T'ALUK, (A) or more properly *ta'alluk*, a tract, or subdivision of a district.
TANK, a reservoir, an artificial pond or lake, made by excavation or by damming (a word of both Indian and European origin).
TAPPÁL, (H) in Bombay the post; and in Tamil Nadu a relay of horses.
TATTÍ, (M) matting; a mat-shade.
TEPPA KULAM (*South India*), a tank surrounded by steps, with usually a temple in the centre, to which the deity is rowed on a raft.
THÁNÁ, a police-station; THÁNADÁR, the officer in charge of it.
TIFFIN, luncheon, a word of hybrid and uncertain origin.
TÍRTHA, (S) a ford; a bathing-place, especially one to which religious pilgrimages are made.
TIRTHÁNKÁR, (S) Jain saint.

Tongá, (H) a low-seated two-wheeled vehicle drawn by a pony.
Trimurti, the three-faced bust of Siva in the characters of the Hindu Trinity.
Tripulia, (H) a gateway, or approach with three arches.
Tughrá, (A) an ornamental character of writing, used for royal signatures and titles; other styles are Nashki and Nastaliq.
Tulsi, (S) the *Ocimum sanctum*, the sacred Basil plant, venerated by the Hindus.
Váhana, (S) the vehicle of a Hindu god.
Vihára, (S) a Buddhist monastery, or an apartment or hall in a monastery or cave: in Sri Lanka, a Buddhist temple; a meeting-hall of monks.
Vila, (Sin), Vilei, (T) a pond.
Vimána, (S) the principal part, the actual temple itself: has a pyramidal roof, and contains the cell for the image or emblem of the Hindu god.
Wapi or Vapi, (S and Pali) a tank.
Wazír, (A) a prime minister.
Wewa, (Sin) a tank.
Zamíndár, (P) a landed proprietor, a landlord.
Zanana, (P) women's quarters—commonly Zenana.
Ziárat, (A) pilgrimage, and hence a burial-place, a place of Muslim pilgrimage.
Zila (Zilla), (A) a portion, division, or district; hence, the area or tract constituting the jurisdiction of the District Officer—i.e. a Magistrate and Collector, or a Deputy Commissioner.

PRONUNCIATION OF INDIAN, PAKISTANI AND BENGALI WORDS

Consonants are pronounced as in English. *Ch* should be sounded as in "church", and *dh* and *th* as in "woodhouse" and "boathook". In Western India ḍ as written is in certain circumstances pronounced almost like *r*; e.g. Manmaḍ (Manmar), Anhilwaḍa (Anhilwara), Mahanwaḍa (Mahanwara), and such proper names as Ghorpaḍe (Ghorpuré).

Vowels are ordinarily pronounced as in Italian: thus, *pul*, *Mir*, *Mūl* and *nou* have their English equivalents in "bull", "peer", "pool", and "now". *Ai* has the vowel sound as in "mine", *ou* (Oudh) as in "proud". A long *ā* is pronounced as in "father", e.g. Rām, Māhārājā; and a short *ă* like *u* in "but", e.g. Akbar (Ukbar), parda (purda), except in Bengal, where it is given an *o* sound, e.g. Bangaon = Bongong. The accent is distributed almost equally on each syllable.

ETYMOLOGY OF SOME PLACE-NAMES IN INDIA AND PAKISTAN

Meanings of some of the more common component parts of place-names, other than those mentioned in the Glossary, p. 68; and for certain Sri Lanka place-names, see p. 742.

ÁBÁD, (P) peopled.
ÁSRAMA, (S) hermitage.
ACHALAM, (T) hill.
ARU, (T) river.
BÁGH, BAGHÍCHA, (P) garden.
BAN, (H) grove.
BÁṚÍ, BÁTÍ, (H) house.
CHERUVA, (Tel) tank.
COTE, COTTA, COTTE, COTTAH. See KOT.
DIGHÍ, (H) tank.
DHÁRO, (Sindi) river.
DIH, (P) village.
DONGAR, (M) hill.
DRUG, DURGA, (T, Tel) fort.
ERI, (T) tank.
GANJ, (H) mart.
GÁCHÍ, (H) grove.
GAṚH, (H) fort.
GHAR, (H) house, habitation.
GIRI, (S) hill.
GÓTH, (Sindi) village.
GRÁM, GRÁMAM, GÁON, (H) village.
GUDDI, (K) hill.
GUHÁ, (S) cave.
GUNTA, (Tel) tank.
HÁṬ, (H) market.
IŚVARA, (S) lord.
KADU, (T) forest.
KERE, (K) tank.
KHÁL, (H) channel.
KHAṆD, (S) portion.
KHIND, (M) pass.
KHET, (H) (KSHETRA, (S)) field.
KHEṬ, (S) small town.
KILO, (Sindi) fort.
KOVIL, (T) temple.
KOṬ (S), KOTA (Tel), KOTTAI (T), KOTTE (K), fort.
KOTAL, (P) kol or pass.
KUPPAM, (T) hamlet.
MAHÁL, (H; from A mahall) quarter.
MALAI, (T) hill or range.
MANDALAM, (T) tract of country.
MANDI, (H) market.
MANE, (K) habitation.
MANGALAM, (S) happiness.
NÁD, (T) tract of country.
NADÍ, (H) river.
NAGAR (S), NAGARAM, town.
PAHÁR, (H) PAHÁD, (Sindi) hill.
PALAIYAM (T), PALEM (Tel), petty kingdom.
PALLI (T), PALLE (Tel), village.
PÁṚÁ, PÁṚÍ, (H) quarter of a town.
PATI, (S) lord.
PATÁM, PATAN, PATANA, PATNA, PATTANAM, (S), etc., town or city.
PET, PETA (Tel), PETTAI, (T) quarter of a town.
QILA, (A) fort.
SHAHAR, (P) city.
SOT, (H) spring or stream.
STHÁNA, (S), STHAN, STHAL, STHALI, THÁN, TÁN, place.
TALÁO, (P) pond.
TOTA, (Tel), TOTTAM, (T) garden.
UR, (T), URU, (Tel) village.
VARAM, (T) village.
VANA, (Tel), VANAM, (T) grove.

10. PLACES OF SPECIAL INTEREST OR RELIGIOUS IMPORTANCE IN INDIA, PAKISTAN AND BANGLADESH

A selection of the places of interest most likely to appeal to the tourist is given below. Kashmir on both sides of the truce line is of course *hors concours* for natural scenery. Visitors from India can travel to the world-famous Vale of Kashmir and the beauty spots surrounding it: visitors from Pakistan can travel to the equally beautiful Kaghan Valley, to Hill States like Swat and Chitral and to Gilgit for the remote and romantic lands of Hunza and Nagar. It should be noted that Tourist Cards are required by those who travel to Gilgit and surrounding areas (see Kashmir, Part 2, p. 609). For visits to Hunza and Nagar there are special regulations and passes must be applied for to the Kashmir Division of the Pakistan Ministry of Home Affairs in Islamabad.

India

Abu.
Agra.
Ahmedabad.
Ajanta.
Allahabad.
Amber.
Amritsar.
Aurangabad.
Badami.
Benares (Varanasi).
Bhubaneswar.
Bidar.
Bijapur.
Bikaner.
Bombay.
Bundi.
Calcutta.
Chandigarh.
Chitorgarh.
Cochin.
Darjeeling.
Delhi.
Ellora.
Fatehpur-Sikri.
Goa.
Gwalior.
Hyderabad.
Jaipur.
Jaisalmer.
Jodhpur.
Kodaikanal.
Khajuraho.
Lucknow.
Madras.
Manali (Kulu).
Madurai.
Mandu.
Mathura (Muttra).
Mysore.
Ootacamund.
Poona.
Ranikhet.
Sanchi.
Sarnath.
Shillong.
Simla.
Srinagar.
Thanjavur (Tanjore).
Tiruchirapalli (Trichinopoly).
Trivandrum.
Udaipur.
Varanasi (Benares).
Vijayanagar (Hampi).

Pakistan

Chitral.
Dir.
Gilgit.
Harappa.
Islamabad (New Capital).
Kaghan Valley.
Karachi.
Khyber.
Lahore.
Mangla.
Mardan.
Mohenjodaro.
Multan.
Murree.
Muzaffarabad.
Nagar.
Peshawar.
Quetta.
Rawalpindi.
Skardu.
Swat.
Taxila.

Bangladesh

Chittagong.
Cox's Bazar.
Dacca.
Kaptai.
Mainamati.
Paharpur.
Sundarbans.
Sylhet.

PLACES OF RELIGIOUS IMPORTANCE

Ajmer.
Ajodhya.
Allahabad.
Amritsar.
Badrinath.
Benares (Varanasi).
Bhubaneshwar.
Brindaban.
Buddh Gaya.
Cape Comorin.
Chidambaram.
Dwarka.
Girnar.
Hardwar.
Kanchipuram.
Kusinagar.
Nalanda.
Nasik.
Nathdwara.
Palitana.
Parasnath.
Puri.
Pushkar.
Rameswaram.
Sarnath.
Varanasi (Benares).

For Buddhist sites, the Indian Tourist Development Corporation booklets *Buddhist Shrines* and *In the Footsteps of the Buddha* are useful guides for the tourist.

11. RAILWAY ROUTES IN INDIA, PAKISTAN, BANGLADESH, AND SRI LANKA, WITH THE STATES TRAVERSED

Heavy Type indicates places which are described *en route.*

INDIA

PAKISTAN

12. SUGGESTIONS FOR BACKGROUND READING

The best compact one-volume book for the historical background is Vincent A. Smith, *Oxford History of India* (3rd edition, ed. Percival Spear, 1958). This will help the traveller to understand what he sees as will the large book by A. L. Basham, *The Wonder that was India* (Sidgwick & Jackson, 1954; Fontana paperback, 1971). Both these books suggest further reading on special subjects.

Also useful are the Penguin *History of India* (1970 in two vols. Vol. 1 to 1526 by Romila Thapar and vol. 2 1526 to Independence and beyond by Percival Spear); Philip Woodruff, *The Men Who Ruled India* (Cape paperback, 2 vols.);

Rushbrook Williams, *The State of Pakistan* (revised edition, 1966); Bamber Gascoigne, *The Great Moghuls* (Cape, 1972); John Keay, *Into India* (John Murray, 1973, paperback 1975), John Prendergast, *The Road to India* (John Murray, 1977); Philip Mason, *A Matter of Honour: An Account of the Indian Army* (Penguin, 1977).

13. LIST OF MAPS AND PLANS

THE REPUBLIC OF INDIA

Area: 1,261,816 square miles
Population (1976): 606,200,000
President: Sanjiva Reddy
Prime Minister: Mrs Indira Gandhi

Prior to 1947, travellers passing through the country traversed hundreds of miles of territory which did not form part of British India, but was ruled by Indian Princes. The Princely States varied in size from great areas like Hyderabad and Kashmir, which were larger than many European countries, to tiny holdings of less than 1 square mile. All these Princely States have been amalgamated into the Indian Republic since 1947-1948. At that time the Rulers were given compensation for the surrender of their sovereignty in the shape of annual grants (the "Privy Purses") proportionate to their former revenues and were allowed certain personal privileges and dignities, all of which were enshrined in articles of the Indian Constitution. By 1970, however, the special position occupied by the former Rulers was regarded by the Government as anomalous; and in 1971 the Constitution was amended in such a way as to abolish their titles, their privileges and their Privy Purses. Thus all the citizens of India are now equal before the law, and the writ of the Government of India runs through the length and breadth of the land.

When the independent Government of India came to power, it found the existing boundaries of Provinces and Princely States, which were largely based upon historical accident, both illogical and unwieldy. After careful examination, the whole country was divided anew, mainly in accordance with local cultural and linguistic unities. All the new units, with the exception of certain special areas, are called States. The whole may be listed as follows:

State	*Population*	*Capital*
Andhra Pradesh	43,000,000	Hyderabad
Assam	14,000,000	Dispur
Bihar	56,000,000	Patna
Gujarat	26,000,000	Gandhinagar
Haryana	9,000,000	Chandigarh
Himachal Pradesh	3,000,000	Simla
Jammu & Kashmir[1]	4,000,000	Srinagar
Karnataka (formerly Mysore)	29,000,000	Bangalore
Kerala	21,000,000	Trivandrum
Madhya Pradesh	41,000,000	Bhopal
Maharashtra	50,000,000	Bombay
Manipur	1,000,000	Imphal
Meghalaya	1,000,000	Shillong
Mizoram	329,000	Aijal
Mysore		*see* Karnataka
Nagaland	515,000	Kohima
Orissa	21,000,000	Bhubaneshwar
Punjab	13,000,000	Chandigarh

[1] The state of Jammu and Kashmir is divided by a truce line. The figure given is for the population on the Indian side of the line.

Rajasthan	25,000,000	Jaipur
Sikkim	208,000	Gangtok
Tamil Nadu	41,000,000	Madras
Tripura	1,500,000	Agartala
Uttar Pradesh	88,000,000	Lucknow
West Bengal	44,000,000	Calcutta

In addition, the following Union Territories and Special Areas exist:

Andaman & Nicobar Islands	115,000	Port Blair
Arunachal Pradesh	444,000	Shillong
Delhi	4,000,000	Delhi
Goa, Daman & Diu	857,000	Panjim
Laccadive, Minicoy & Amindivi Islands	31,000	Kavaratti
Pondicherry	471,000	Pondicherry

During the quarter of a century of independent existence, the Republic of India, as it has been since 1950, has developed into a strong and prosperous State. At first, it remained a Dominion within the Commonwealth and Lord Mountbatten was invited to stay on as first Governor-General. In 1948 he retired, his place being taken by Mr Rajagopalachari. Meanwhile the government of the country was carried on by Jawaharlal Nehru as Prime Minister, while the elected Constituent Assembly was framing a new constitution. The nation suffered a grievous blow in January 1948 through the assassination of Mr Gandhi, "the father of the country" by a Hindu reactionary. But his doctrines, of truth-seeking and of non-violent resistance to evil, continued to inspire many millions of Indians.

The new constitution was finally adopted in 1950. The framers sought inspiration from many previous models, and eventually adopted a system based on that of Westminster—a dual-cameral legislature to which a Cabinet chosen from the political party with an elected majority in the Lower House (Lok Sabha) is responsible. There is universal adult suffrage—the biggest Parliamentary electorate in the world. Individual freedoms are guaranteed; the State is religiously impartial and undertakes to protect minorities. Although the constitution is republican in form, India decided to remain within the Commonwealth. Dr Rajendra Prasad was elected the first President under the new constitution, and Jawaharlal Nehru, heading the Congress Party which had a large majority in the Constituent Assembly, continued as Prime Minister. In the elections of 1952 he was returned to power. Under his leadership, India played a prominent part in international affairs, and became the acknowledged spokesman on Asian matters in the United Nations, while pursuing a policy of non-alignment between the Communist and the non-Communist power *blocs*. With Pakistan, India's relations were strained, and feelings in both countries rose high from time to time over such matters as the division of the Indus Basin waters and the situation in Kashmir.

Jawaharlal Nehru attached great importance to economic development; the Planning Commission which he set up became one of the most influential organs of the administration. Great progress was made in the establishment of both light and heavy industry and good use was made of the economic assistance received from the U.S.A., the Soviet Union, and from many Western European countries. Successive Five-Year Plans co-ordinated the ends to be achieved with the means available; substantial progress was achieved in raising the Gross National Product, the *per capita* income, and the level of literacy. The General Election of 1957 confirmed the Congress Party in power at the centre, but with reduced majorities in several States, where there was impatience that political independence had not immediately produced an economic millennium.

The country as a whole, and Jawaharlal Nehru in particular, sustained a severe shock when hostilities with China broke out in 1962, as the course of events seemed to cast doubts upon the wisdom of non-alignment—as hitherto practised—in foreign affairs. But the nation rallied well in response to the "emergency". Jawaharlal Nehru died in 1964, mourned by the country which he had done so much to build up. His successor, Lal Bahadur Shastri, successfully steered India through the difficulties resulting from the outbreak of war with Pakistan. His sudden death in January 1966, immediately after the conclusion of peace with Pakistan in a conference held under Soviet auspices at Tashkent, was deeply regretted; he was succeeded as Prime Minister by Mrs Indira Gandhi, Jawaharlal's daughter. Her early days were difficult; the Congress Party split, and the section which she led was defeated in 1967 in many States and retained only a bare majority at the Centre. But the strength of her leadership gradually made itself felt; her programme of warring on poverty and nationalising important institutions such as banking and insurance appealed to the masses of the electorate; and in a short-term election in 1971 she decisively defeated her political opponents and was returned to power with an authority hardly inferior to that which her Father had exercised even in his greatest days. This position was still further strengthened by military successes against Pakistan forces operating in East Bengal and her sponsorship of the emergence of Bangladesh as an independent nation; and in 1972 the party she led repeated in the State elections its triumph at the Centre in the preceding year. However, her later conviction by the Indian Courts of electoral malpractices, led her to suspend the Constitution and many opposition leaders and journalists were imprisoned. Free elections were eventually held in 1977 in which Mrs Gandhi and her party were heavily defeated. Since then the situation has gone a full circle and Mrs Gandhi came back into power early in 1980.

1.—BOMBAY AND THE ENVIRONS

(*Maps face pages* 92, 105 *and* 117)

Changes in Street Names

Coluba Causeway	now called	Shahid Bhagatsingh Road
Marine Lines	,,	Sir Dinshah Mulla Road
Marine Drive	,,	Netaji Subash Road
Queens Road	,,	Maharshi Karve Road
Flora Fountain	,,	Hutatma Chowk
Bazar Gate Street	,,	Perin Nariman Street
Hornby Road	,,	Dr Dadabhai Naoroji Road
Ballard Road	,,	Shoorji Vallabhdas Marg
Cruikshank Road	,,	Mahapalika Marg
Carnac Road	,,	Lokmanya Tilak Marg
Parel Road	,,	Dr Babasaheb Ambedkar Road
Princess Street	,,	Samaldas Gandhi Marg
Dongari Street	,,	Shayda Marg
Lamington Road (N)	,,	Dr Anandrao Nair Road
Lamington Road (S)	,,	Dr Dadasaheb Bhadkamkar Marg
Jacob's Circle	,,	Sant Gadge Maharaj Chowk
Bellasis Road	,,	Jehangir Boman Behram Marg
Grant Road	,,	Maulana Shaukat Ali Road
Byculla Station Road	,,	Ganesh Hari Parundekar Marg
Victoria Garden (Parel) Road	,,	Sir Jamsedji Jijibhoy Road
Nepean Sea Road	,,	Laxmibai Jagmohandas Marg
Clerk Road	,,	Keshavrao Khadye Marg
Warden Road	,,	Bhulabhai Desai ("B.D.") Road

Note.—The former names are still widely used and well understood by taxi-drivers and the like.

Hotels.—Bombay has more than 30 hotels which can be recommended to visitors, many of them Government approved. Travel Agencies have full particulars of prices, accommodation and location. Advance booking is essential in the main tourist season.

History.[1]—There is little doubt that the W. coast of India had trade relations with the Assyrian, Persian and Roman empires; but the direct connection of modern Europe with it dates only from the arrival of the Portuguese in 1498. Albuquerque conquered Goa in 1510, and Sultan Bahadur Shah, of Gujarat, in 1534 ceded Bassein, Salsette and Bombay to the Portuguese. In 1626 the Portuguese buildings in Bombay were raided and destroyed by a combined English and Dutch force. In 1661 Bombay was ceded to England as part of the dowry of Catherine of Braganza, but owing to disputes with the Portuguese Viceroy, the actual possession of it was not transferred

[1] An excellent summary of the history of Bombay is in *Oxford History of India* (1958). For advice about current literature, and for brochures specially prepared for tourists, recourse should be had to the Government of India Tourist Office, 123 M. Karve Road, Churchgate (Tel. 293144). It is also represented in many Hotels. *The Times of India Year Book* should be consulted for the latest statistics and business addresses. The population in 1971 was 5·9 million.

till 1665, and on the 23rd September 1668 it was made over to the East India Company by King Charles II to be held at an annual rent of £10 in gold "as of the manor of East Greenwhich, in the county of Kent, in free and common soccage". This was paid until 1730. One of the terms of the transfer was that the English should support the Portuguese in India against the Dutch, who were rapidly supplanting them everywhere.

The name was supposed to be a corruption of the Portuguese Bom Bahia, or Fair Bay. But the vernacular name *Mumbai* (see f.n., p. 102) suggests that it was originally called after the Koli goddess Mumbai, a form of Amba Bhawani, or Parvati, the consort of Siva.

At the time of the transfer from the Portuguese, Bombay consisted of seven islands, separated at high tide by the sea, which at low tide left a wilderness of malarious mud-flats. Dense coconut plantations covered it, and the inhabitants were chiefly fishermen and toddy-drawers; respectable Hindus and Parsis shunned it on account of Portuguese intolerance. Its unhealthiness was notorious: 17th-century travellers speak of it as "a charnel-house" and mention a contemporary proverb, "two monsoons are the life of a man". The gradual transformation in drainage and reclamation of this pestilential swamp into the great city of to-day, which proudly styles itself *Urbs prima in Indis*, has been the work of many hands, but the chief credit is due to Gerald Aungier, the real founder of Bombay, President, 1669-1677, who, by his policy of toleration, induced the Parsis, Banias and other merchants to settle under the protection of the British flag. The Parsis first came to Bombay in 1670.

In 1665, when attacked by the Dutch, Bombay Castle mounted 4 brass guns, and in 1674, 120 pieces of ordnance, and had a garrison of 300 English, 400 Portuguese and 500 militia. In 1687 the Presidency was finally transferred from Surat (p. 241) to Bombay. The first four Governors held Bombay for the Crown. After the transfer to the East India Company, except for occasional visits and during three years (1672-1675) of the rule of Gerald Aungier, the Governors of Bombay spent almost the whole of their time at Surat, of which factory they were Presidents. During their time Bombay was administered by an officer styled Deputy-Governor; this title fell into disuse between 1720 and 1738.

In 1708 it became the trading headquarters of the Company on the W. coast, Surat being no longer a safe place. Before 1720 the town, outside the castle, contained a population of 50,000, and was enclosed by a wall built by Governor Boone (1715-22). It already possessed a mint; a bank was founded shortly afterwards, and the port flourished considerably from the encouragement given to the China trade. In 1755 Bombay was made the refitting base for the Navy during the cyclone season on the E. coast, and came into prominence in connection with the suppression, in 1756, of the Angria corsairs, who haunted the coast S. of Bombay, a position which was confirmed by the results of the struggle of the Company with the Mahrattas, who in 1739 had taken Bassein and Salsette from the Portuguese.

On the Portuguese preparing to recover Salsette (1774), the island was seized by the Company and retained after the Peace of 1776. Although surrendered by the Convention (Armistice) of Vadgaon (Wargaon) (1779), the fulfilment of this was avoided by the arrival of General Goddard with troops from Bengal. After Bassein had been captured in 1780, these acquisitions remained with the British by the Treaty of Salbai, confirmed 1783.

From that time the development of the port and city proceeded steadily apace. The city was visited by General Wellesley (the future Duke of Wellington) in 1804, and to him was due the first road practicable for artillery up the Bhor Ghat and to Poona. It seems certain that it must have been visited by Lord Nelson while a midshipman in 1775, as the *Seahorse*, on which he made his first cruise, was in the Persian Gulf and at Bombay in that year.[1]

The framework of administration of the Presidency and its Capital was shaped by Mountstuart Elphinstone in 1819-27. The Bishopric was established in 1835, the Chamber of Commerce in 1836, and the Bombay Bank (which is now merged in the State Bank of India) in 1840; the University was created in 1857, and the Legislative Council in 1862; the Municipal Authority, formed in 1872, was converted into a Corporation in 1888. The Port Trust was constituted in 1873, and the Bombay City Improvement Trust in 1898. The mail service with England was undertaken by the P. & O. Company in 1852; the G.I.P. Railway, which had been opened as far as Thana in 1853, was extended up the Ghats in 1863, and in the same year the Bombay Baroda and Central India Railway, part of which had been opened in 1860, was extended to Ahmedabad.

The four most remarkable developments since 1850 have been (1) the reclamation of land; (2) the construction of docks (p. 95); (3) the development of cotton mills (the first founded in 1853); and (4) the erection of a splendid series of public buildings, many due, as will be seen below, to the munificent charity of private persons. The constructive stage may be said to have begun during the Governorship of Sir Bartle Frere (1862-67), when the American Civil War poured immense wealth into Bombay in connection with the export of cotton, and over-speculation was followed by a severe financial collapse. At this date the old fort walls were at last removed.

The castle guarding the harbour front yet stands, and fragments of Fort George, which stood at the Northern end of this front, survive in the grounds of St George's Hospital. On the S. side the defences followed the line of Rampart Row from the Apollo Gate to the S.W. corner, and then that of Esplanade Road, passing the Church Gate and D. Naoroji Road, to the N.W. corner and the Bazar Gate, whence they turned E. to Fort George. Outside the W. defences was a fine esplanade, and in the centre of the fort was the green on the site of which Horniman Circle now stands.

Steady progress in civic amenities stems from the activities of the Corporation and its Improvement Committee. It has been greatly stimulated since 1960, when Bombay became capital of the new State of Maharashtra. Notable building activity impresses the visitor: even so population-growth poses an insistent problem. It rose from 150,000 in 1800 to 4,152,000 in the 1961 census and 5,968,000 in 1971. The approximate proportions are Hindus 60 per cent., Muslims 17 per cent., Indian Christians 5 per cent. and Jains 2 per cent.

The Corporation, under a Municipal Commissioner, has over a hundred members, almost all elected. Inside the Corporation, which is a deliberative body, are four statutory committees: (1) the Standing Committee consisting of sixteen members elected by the Corporation, which is practically the Finance Committee of the Corporation; (2) the Education Committee consisting of sixteen members, twelve elected by the Corporation from its own body and four, of whom two must be women, from outside; (3) the Improvements Committee of sixteen members, all elected by the Corporation; and (4) the Bombay Electric Supply and Transport Committee consisting of nine members, one of whom is Chairman of the Standing Committee and the

[1] In Lord Nelson's original letter of thanks to the East India Company for the gift of £10,000 voted to him after the Battle of the Nile (dated 3rd July 1797, and written on board the *Foudroyant* at Naples), he says, "Having *in my younger days* served in the East Indies, I am no stranger to the munificence of the Honble. Company". This letter may be seen in the Library of the India Office. It is reproduced in Douglas's *Bombay and W. India.*

others from persons of suitable experiences who may, or may not, be members of the corporation.

There are a number of other *ad hoc* Consultative Committees to whom the corporation can refer any matter for consideration and report. The Municipal Commissioner appointed by Government exercises supreme executive authority in all municipal matters excepting primary education, in respect of which the entire executive authority is vested in the Education Committee.

The Central Government (Posts and Telegraphs) now controls the Telephone Service.

A City Improvement Trust was created by a special Statute in 1898 for the purpose of improving the sanitation of the city and developing new residential areas. A Development Directorate was also created by the Government of Bombay in 1920, with the object of providing for the development of the City of Bombay and of relieving congestion and overcrowding. The programme originally planned was as follows: (*a*) The provision of 50,000 one-roomed tenements for the working classes; (*b*) reclamation of 1145 acres in Back Bay and of 132 acres in the harbour, on the W. and E. of Colaba Point, by pumping silt across a narrow neck; (*c*) the development of South Salsette, partly for residential and partly for industrial purposes; (*d*) the provision of other industrial areas at greater distances; (*e*) the improvement of communications to the suburban areas; and (*f*) the improvement of the supply and transport of building materials. The "Back Bay Scheme" did not achieve a financial success at first, but has since proved of great value to Bombay.

The adoption of these great proposals for the improvement of the material conditions of the City of Bombay was mainly due to the energy of the late Lord Lloyd, when Governor of Bombay.

The work of improvement and development is now looked after by the Improvements Committee of the Corporation.

The **Island of Bombay** is situated in lat. 18° 53′ 45″, long. 72° 52′. It was originally a group of islands separated from the mainland and from one another by very narrow channels, the principal islands being Bassein, Dharave (Dravi), Salsette, Trombay (in which the hill called the Neat's Tongue, 1000 ft. high, is a conspicuous mark), Bombay and Elephanta.

The southernmost of these islands was Colaba (p. 96), so called from the Koli fishermen who inhabited it. On the W. extremity, between Colaba on the S. and the bold and striking promontory of Malabar Hill or Walkeswar (p. 103), now the fashionable residential quarter, on the N., lies the shallow basin, about 3 m. broad, known as Back Bay. On the E. side, between the island and the mainland, is Bombay Harbour, a fine expanse of water, 5 to 9 m. broad. In the narrow neck of land between Back Bay and the Harbour is the old site of the Fort, the nucleus of the city. Farther N. are the bazars and mill quarters; beyond these again the suburbs.

Bombay Island is 11½ m. long from the S. extremity of Colaba to Sion Causeway, over which the Central Railway passes to the island of Salsette, and from 3 to 4 m. broad in that portion which lies to the N. of the Esplanade. The area is 22·48 sq. m.

Climate.—Bombay is neither very hot in summer nor cold in winter. The coolest month is usually February. The periods just before and after the S.W. monsoon (May to June and October) are hot and humid, and the torrential rains of July, August and September, though cooling, are inconvenient for sight-seeing. Malabar Hill is usually several degrees cooler than the Fort, and healthier. The average rainfall is 70·30 in.

Bombay Harbour.—The panorama which confronts the traveller, as he enters Bombay from the sea, has been compared to the Bay of Naples. To the W. the shore is crowded with buildings. To the N. and E. are numerous islands, and on the mainland hills rising to an altitude of from 1000 to 2000 ft. Note particularly Bawa Malang, otherwise called Mallangarh, on the top of which is an enormous mass of rock with perpendicular sides, crowned with a fort, now in ruins.

The East India Company had a marine (1612) which continued as the Indian Navy until 1863. Bombay was made the headquarters of the Royal Indian Marine in 1892, and of the Royal Indian Navy in 1934. It is the present headquarters of the new Indian Navy.

Santa Cruz Airport is now reserved for internal flights only and a new international airport has been opened on the far side of Santa Cruz. The latter is about ten miles from the centre of Bombay. Airline bus or taxi takes about an hour to the airports. There is a good modern hotel (Sun 'n Sand) at **Juhu** ten minutes away, also a Holiday Inn. There is a second Airport at Juhu, at which the Flying Club is based.

Ballard Pier, where travellers by sea land, is only a few minutes' drive from the principal hotels. It is named after General Ballard, chairman of its Port Trust (1872-79).

Customs and other Formalities.—Travellers are given forms on the ship or the aircraft which must be completed for presentation to the Health, Immigration, Passport and Customs authorities. *Bona fide* tourists can bring in free articles for personal use, including two cameras, 24 roll films, five firearms for sport and 200 cartridges. Details should be checked with Thos. Cook & Son or other travel agents, who, on request, will send a representative to meet the traveller on arrival. It should be noted that the importation of alcoholic liquor is forbidden. Beer is available: for other liquor a permit is needed. The tourist who has not brought a liquor permit with him (p. 7) can obtain one locally at the cost of a little trouble and delay.

Communications

Visitors wishing to leave the beaten track must make their own arrangements. Help is not available from tourist agencies. If comfort and time-saving outweigh the slight extra expense, advantage can be taken of the rapid speed of air-communications to visit all the important centres, and to plan from each centre a series of excursions by road or rail. Alternatively, Bombay is linked by rail with all these same centres; and the main expresses are equipped with restaurant cars and air-conditioning at extra cost. A combination of air and rail travel, with local excursions, will enable the visitor to see more of the country in four weeks than travellers in earlier times could see in four months—and this with the minimum fatigue and discomfort.

For touring by car *see* pp. 109, 112.

General Description of Bombay and its Suburbs.—The visitor who halts in Bombay should visit Malabar Hill, the Zoo, the Prince of Wales Museum, the Jehangir Art Gallery and the Old Fort behind the Town Hall. The Aarey Milk Colony, 20 miles north, with the nearby National Park, is a favourite place for excursions.

The road from the Ballard Pier, after leaving the Grand Hotel on the right and passing the Custom House, skirts the Ballard estate of the Port Trust, reclaimed by spoil from the docks, and enters the circuit of the Old Fort of Bombay just above the ancient Castle. From this point Mint Road leads N. to the Victoria Terminus and onwards to the more central part of the city—Marine Street and Apollo Street lead S. to Rampart Row (along the S.E. side of the Port), and the open space W. of the Apollo Bunder—and Vir Nariman Road (Church Gate Street) leads W. to Mahatma Gandhi Road, which follows the landward line of the former defences, and to the Back Bay on the Western side of the Island. Vir Nariman Road leads to the **Brabourne Stadium.**

Along the shore there is free access to Back Bay and Netaji Subash Road (Marine Drive), the railway, which formerly ran to Colaba, having been removed beyond Vir Nariman Station. Along Mayo Road, which runs parallel to it, is the range of Public Offices. S. of the open space, near which all the principal hotels are situated, extends the promontory of Colaba.

Northwards, along Back Bay, Netaji Subash Road leads to Malabar Hill, which bends round the N.W. side of the bay, and is continued to the N. by Cumballa Hill. E. of the two hills lies the main bazar area, with the quarters of Byculla and Mazagon along the N. side of it. In Parel, N. of Byculla, is the principal location of the Bombay Mills; in Mazagon are the P. & O. Docks, below which, and E. of the main city, lie the Prince's, Victoria and Alexandra Docks. On the N.W. side of the Fort are a number of places of business, though some are still inside the Old Fort.

PUBLIC OFFICES

The impressive Government buildings already mentioned succeed one another in the following order: from S. to N., the Prince of Wales Museum and the College of Science in Mahatma Gandhi Road; then come in Mayo Road the old Government Secretariat, the University Hall, Library and Clock Tower, the High Court, the Public Works' Secretariat and the Telegraph Office.

Mayo Road

The old **Bombay Government Secretariat** (1874) is 470 ft. long, with two wings. The style is Venetian Gothic, after the designs of Colonel Wilkins. The carving is by Indian artists. The staircase is lighted by the great window, 90 ft. high, over which rises the tower to 170 ft. At the entrance are the arms of Sir Bartle Frere (1862-67), who was Governor when the plans were formulated for erecting public buildings, and to whom Bombay owes many of its improvements. A magnificent new Secretariat, in modern style well adapted to the climate, has been erected on Netaji Subash Road (Marine Drive) in a commanding position.

University Hall (1874).—This ornate building, in the French Decorated style of the 15th century, is 104 ft. long, 44 ft. broad and 63 ft. high to the apex of the groined ceiling, with an apse separated from the Hall by a grand arch, and a gallery, 8 ft. broad, round three sides. The painted-glass windows have an excellent effect. The Hall is called after Sir Cowasjee Jehangir Readymoney, who contributed towards the cost of erection. A statue by Woolner of Sir Cowasjee stands in the University Gardens. The University was founded in 1857.

The **University Library and Clock Tower,** like the Hall, were designed by Sir Gilbert Scott in the style of 14th-century Gothic. The Library is a long, low room, adorned with carving, and the great **Rajabai Tower** on the W. side forms part of it, and is from its height (260 ft.) the most conspicuous building in Bombay. It was built at the expense of Mr Premchand Raichand, in memory of his mother, Rajabai. The Tower is divided into an octagonal lantern spire, with figures in niches at the angles. There are twenty-four figures in all upon the tower, representing the castes of W. India. There is an opening in the centre of each floor, so that one can look up 115 ft. to the ceiling of the Dial Room. The fourth floor contains the great clock. Under the dials outside are four small galleries, with stone balustrades. From the top of the tower there is a fine view of Bombay. On the E. are the harbour, fringed with islands, Mody Bay and the Fort; and to the

W. are Malabar Hill and Back Bay; and to the S. Colaba Point.

The **High Court** was established as Supreme Court in 1823 and became a High Court in 1861. This immense building, 554 ft. long, with a tower 175 ft. high, was opened in 1879. The style is Early English. The principal entrance is under a large arched porch in the W. façade on either side of which is an octagon tower 120 ft. high, with pinnacles of white Porbandar stone, and surmounted by statues of Justice and Mercy. The main staircase is on the E. side, and is approached by a noble groined corridor in Porbandar stone, which runs through the building. The offices of the High Court are on the first and third floors. The Appellate and Original Courts are on the first and second floors. The Criminal Court is in the centre of the building, above the main corridor, and has a carved teak gallery for the public running round three sides. The ceiling is of dark polished teak in panels, with a carved centrepiece. The floor is Italian mosaic. A number of portraits of past Chief Justices and Judges hang in the different Courts.

Next to the High Court and separated from the old Post Office by Vir Nariman Road, a broad road which leads E. to Horniman Circle and W. to the Church Gate Station of the Western Railway, is the **Public Works' Secretariat,** with a façade 288 ft. long, the central part having five storeys. The Railway Inspection, Irrigation and other Engineering Departments are accommodated in this building.

On the S. side of the arm of the road leading to the W. are the **Statues** of three former Governors of Bombay, Sir Richard Temple (1877-80), Lord Reay (1885-90), and Lord Sandhurst (1895-1900). Opposite, on the corner site formed by Marine Lines and Queen's Road, is the office of the Western Railway, which has a façade 280 ft. long and a tower 160 ft. high.

The **Old General Post Office,** which was absorbed into the Telegraph Office, is opposite the Public Works' Secretariat in Vir Nariman Road. It has three floors, and is 236 ft. long, with wings on the N. side. Part of it is used as a Post Office for the Fort area. The present **General Post Office** (p. 98), a large building crowned by a dome, is near the Victoria Terminus Station.

The **Telegraph Office,** which is now in the old Post Office, is built in Romanesque style and has a façade 182 ft. long. The facing of it and of the Post Office is of coursed rubble stone from Kurla, in Salsette, and the columns are of blue basalt.

VIR NARIMAN ROAD (CHURCH GATE STREET)

From Hutatma Chowk (the Flora Fountain erected in honour of Sir Bartle Frere), following Vir Nariman Road into the area of the Fort, Horniman Circle, occupying the site of the old Green, is reached. In Mahatma Gandhi Road, running S. from the fountain, and in D. Naoroji Road, running N. (together marking the western limits of the Fort), are the principal shops and places of business.

The **Bombay Club** used to have its buildings here, but it moved some years ago to the junction of Netaji Subash Road (Marine Drive) and B. D. Road.

On the N. side of Vir Nariman Road, in Bazar Gate Street, are the headquarters of the Chamber of Commerce, and on the S. side is the **Cathedral of St Thomas.** This was begun by Gerald Aungier in 1672, but was not formally opened until 1718. In 1816 it was consecrated by Bishop Middleton of Calcutta, who had created an Archdeaconry of Bombay in 1814. Upon the installation, in February 1836, of the first Bishop of Bombay, it became the Cathedral of the Diocese, and the low belfry was converted into a high tower. It is simple in plan, and a mixture of the classical and Gothic in style. The chancel, added 1865, is a modern example of Early English.

A monument by Bacon to Jonathan Duncan (1811), Governor for sixteen years, represents him receiving the blessings of young Hindus with reference to his successful efforts in suppressing infanticide in certain districts near Benares, and afterwards in Kathiawar, through the zealous and able agency of Colonel Walker. Another beautiful monument by Bacon, in the form of a medallion on the E. wall, commemorates Katharine Kirkpatrick (1760), whose son, Major General William Kirkpatrick (Resident at Hyderabad in 1797), was the grandfather of Sir Richard and Sir John Strachey. There are also monuments to Captain G. N. Hardinge, R.N., who died in 1808 in a brilliant engagement, when he took the famous French cruiser *Piémontaise*; Colonel Burr, who commanded at the battle of Kirkee (5th November 1817); Colonel John Campbell, defender of Mangalore against Tipu in 1784; Commodore John Watson, mortally wounded at the siege of Thana in 1774; John Carnac (1800). who had served with Clive in Bengal, and his wife Eliza Rivett (1780), whose portrait, by Reynolds, is in the Wallace Collection in London; Admiral Maitland (1839), who received Napoleon on board the *Bellerophon*; and Major Eldred Pottinger, distinguished in the defence of Herat (November 1837 to September 1838). Bishop Carr's effigy in marble is in the S. transept. One of the chalices was the gift of Gerald Aungier in 1675; another was presented in 1632 by the "Greenland merchants of the City of York". The fountain in front of the Cathedral was erected by Sir Cowasjee Jehangir Readymoney.

Horniman (Elphinstone) Circle

Horniman Circle (Bombay Green) has on the E. side the Town Hall; in the middle is a well-kept garden with marble statues by Bacon of Marquess Cornwallis and Marquess Wellesley. From the centre of the S. side, Bank Street leads to the **State Bank of India,** formerly the Bank of Bombay.

The **Town Hall,** designed by Colonel T. Cowper, was opened in 1833, and the cost was partly raised by lotteries. The building has a colonnade in front, and the façade is 260 ft. long. The pillars in front, and the external character of the edifice, are Doric; the interior is Corinthian. On the ground floor are some of the weightier curiosities of the Royal Asiatic Society. In the upper storey is the Grand Assembly Room, 100 ft. square, for public meetings and balls; the Assembly Room and Public Reading Room of the Bombay Branch of the Royal Asiatic Society; and the Library of this Society, founded in 1804 by Sir James Mackintosh when Recorder of Bombay (1804-11), containing about 100,000 volumes. The place of honour in the Grand Assembly Room is occupied by a statue of the distinguished Governor, the Hon. Mountstuart Elphinstone (1819-27), executed by Chantrey, as were also those of Sir J. Malcolm (Governor 1827-30), and Sir C. Forbes (1774-1849), a famous Bombay merchant. At the head of the staircase, on one side, is a statue, by Foley, of Lord Elphinstone, the Governor in 1857, and on the other side is a statue, by Woolner, of Sir Bartle Frere, an excellent likeness. Between the circular flights of stairs is Marochetti's statue of Sir Jamsetjee Jeejeebhoy.

The former Levée Rooms of the Governor and the Commander-in-Chief, and the Council Room, are no longer used. In the Library of the Asiatic Society, instituted for the investigation and encouragement of Oriental Arts, Sciences and Literature, are busts of Sir James Rivett-Carnac

(Governor 1838-41) by Chantrey, and Sir J. Mackintosh. The Geographical Room contains portraits of Sir Alexander Burnes (who was murdered at Kabul in November 1841) and the two first Presidents of the Bombay Geographical Society—Sir John Malcolm and Captain Daniel Ross, a distinguished hydrographer who was for many years (until 1849) Marine Attendant at Bombay. The collection of maps is an extremely fine one. The Geographical Society was merged into the Asiatic Society in 1873.

The **Mint** is close to the Town Hall, but farther back, having a tank in front of it. It is a plain building, with an Ionic portico, designed by Major J. Hawkins and completed in 1829. Authority was granted to the Company by the Crown to establish a mint so early as 1674. The old Portuguese Quinta (Manor House) was close by. Pherozeshah Mehta Road runs due E. and W. through the former Gunbow Street from Hornby Road to a point almost opposite the Mint.

N. of the Mint, at the E. end of the Ballard Road, which leads to the Ballard Pier (p. 91), are the imposing **Offices of the Port Trust** (p. 101). At the junction of the W. end of Ballard Road with Frere Road, leading to the N. past St George's General Hospital, is the Ruttonjee Mooljee Fountain.

Immediately behind the Town Hall are the remains of the **Castle** of the Old Fort, now used as an Arsenal. Only the walls facing the harbour and a portion of the wall to the N. now remain. There is a flagstaff here from which signals are made to ships, and also a clock tower, where a time signal-ball, connected with the **Observatory** at Colaba, falls at 1 p.m.

The old **Custom House** (Mandvi, built 1720) contains the Collector's office S. of the Town Hall. The new Custom House is near the Ballard Pier.

The **Government Dockyard,** constructed for the country trade in 1736 by Lavji Nasarvanji Wadia, a Parsi from Surat (d. 1774), and extended 1803-10, has a sea-face of nearly 700 yds. King Edward VII, as Prince of Wales, landed here in 1875. There are five graving-docks, three of which together make one large dock 648 ft. long, the other two graving-docks making a single dock 582 ft. long. There are also four building-slips opposite the Apollo Pier and on the S.E. side of the enclosure. Bombay is the only place where the rise of the tide is sufficient to permit docks on a large scale. The highest spring tides reach to 17 ft., but the usual height is 14 ft. In the dockyard four generations of Wadias built a number of British men-of-war, but shipbuilding started in 1717 on the shore. A floating dock was launched at Colaba in 1946.

From the Dockyard, Marine Street leads into Apollo Street and past the old Great Western Hotel (now a block of offices and formerly the High Court building). In an old ice-house here Wenham Lake ice from Massachusetts used to be stored. On the left, here, is the fine building which served as the Royal Alfred Sailors' Home.[1] The sculpture in the gable, representing Neptune with nymphs and sea-horses, was executed by Mr Bolton of Cheltenham. The Home, which is now too far from the Docks to serve its original purpose, was taken over (1928) by the Government, and a **Council Chamber** for the Bombay Legislature has been built at the back. Opposite is the Prince of Wales Museum of Western India. A bronze statue of King George V (the gift of Sir Sassoon J. David) flanks the Museum on this side, while that of King Edward VII (p. 96) flanks the site on the other side.

The **Wellington Fountain,** erected in 1865 to commemorate the visits of the Duke to Bombay in 1801 and 1804,

[1] The building occupies part of the site of the old cemetery at Mendhams Point. This was closed in 1760 in order that a clear field of fire from the Fort might be secured, and the tombstones were razed to the ground.

stands opposite the Sailors' Home at the junction of the Esplanade and Apollo Bunder Road. The latter road leads S.E. from the Wellington Fountain to the Apollo Bunder Pier, originally known as the Wellington Pier, passing between the old premises of the Royal Bombay Yacht Club (now a Naval Officers' centre) and its present home on the right.

Situated on the **Apollo Bunder,** the former landing-place for passengers, is the **Gateway of India** erected to commemorate the landing of King George V and Queen Mary in December 1911. An iron shed, with a curved roof, after the style of a Mongol tent, formerly provided shelter while waiting on the Bunder. This shed was removed and a temporary pavilion and hall erected in white plaster for the reception. It was suggested by Lord Sydenham, then Governor of Bombay, that a permanent pavilion should be erected to commemorate the event, to form a sea gateway to India and provide a reception hall for all important occasions. The scheme was carried out by his successor, Lord Willingdon. The gateway consists of a central hall with great archways forming the entrance, while side halls provide seating accommodation for 600. The design (by Mr G. Wittet) is Indian in character, based on the work of the 16th century in Gujarat. The stone is yellow basalt obtained near Bombay, but the pierced stonework in the arches of the side halls is from Gwalior. The three halls are roofed with domes.

A fine equestrian statue of Shivaji the Great was erected in 1961, soon after the new Maharashtra State came into existence.

Colaba

Near the head of the Colaba Causeway, running S.W. from the fountain, are the headquarters of the Y.M.C.A., and farther S. is the Taj Mahal Hotel (1903) on the seashore. At the corner of the causeway and the adjacent Wodehouse Road, is the Hotel Majestic, and just beyond are the new Roman Catholic Church of the Holy Name and the official residence of the Roman Catholic Archbishop of Bombay. The Methodist Church is located nearby. The Causeway leads past the old Cotton Green (now removed to Sewri) and the Sassoon Dock, the first wet dock made in India, to the entrance end of the promontory of **Colaba,** formerly a separate island, with the Observatory.

St John's Church, a memorial of the First Afghan War, and consecrated in 1858, consists of nave and aisles 138 ft. long, with a chancel 50 ft. long, and a tower and spire 198 ft. high, conspicuous for some distance at sea.

At the extremity of the promontory are the Old Lighthouse (1771), and an old European Cemetery. The present lighthouse (1874) is on Prongs Island, ½ m. S. of Colaba Point, with which it is connected by a ridge of rock exposed at low tides; it is 150 ft. high, and the light which flashes every 10 sec. is visible 18 m. off at sea. Another lighthouse on Khanderi Island marks the N. entrance to the harbour. This island and the adjoining island of Andheri, which are about 7 m. S. of the entrance, are known to mariners as Hendry Kendry, and were occupied by pirates up to 1756.

The Fort Area

Returning to the Wellington Fountain, the Mahatma Gandhi Road along the W. side of the open ground leads past a fine block of buildings, consisting of the Science Institute, the Elphinstone College, and the Sassoon Institute. Opposite is the equestrian statue of King Edward VII as Prince of Wales, by Sir Edgar Boehm, presented to the city by Sir A. Sassoon, and the new Art Gallery presented to the City by Sir Cowasjee Jehangir, Bart.

The **Prince of Wales Museum** of Western India (10.00-18.00. Entry

75p. Free Tuesdays. Closed Mondays)—This fine building, the foundation-stone of which was laid by King George V, then Prince of Wales, in 1905, on the occasion of his first visit to India, occupies an island site at the Southern end of Mahatma Gandhi Road. The scheme consists of three units, arranged round three sides of a quadrangle, the central block (1914) and one wing (1937) being completed. The style of the structure is based on the Indian work of the 15th and 16th centuries in the Presidency, and the materials used are the blue and yellow basalt found in the vicinity of Bombay.

Its contents comprise Art, Archaeology and Natural History. A section devoted to Forestry has been added, and a small local Geological collection of Rocks, Minerals and Fossils is also exhibited.

Art Section.—This consists principally of the Sir Ratan Tata bequest of pictures, a splendid collection of Oriental arms, a varied and unique exhibit of jade, beautiful examples of china, Indian brass, silver, Indian and Persian draperies and *objets d'art.* Other pictures were presented by the late Sir Dorab Tata. Among Sir Ratan Tata's pictures are many most interesting examples of the Dutch, British, French and Italian Schools, and works by such masters as Cuyp, Lawrence, Romney, Gainsborough, Troyon, Poussin and Titian. Sir Dorab Tata's gift includes representative works of the late Italian Schools and a few good modern French and British pictures. There is also a collection of Indian paintings (Mughal and Rajput) and an extremely interesting collection of relics of the Satara Rajas, both purchased from Mr P. V. Mavji in 1914.

Archaeological Section.—This contains three main divisions, the Brahmanical Section; Jain, Prehistoric and Foreign antiquities; and Buddhist Section. In the first category are some large bas-reliefs discovered at Dharwar and attributed to the 5th or 6th century A.D.; a bust of Siva from the Elephanta Caves (p. 106), numerous other interesting sculptures of Siva, some images and bas-reliefs of Brahma, a magnificent image of Vishnu (from Elephanta), and a miscellaneous collection of articles used in Brahmanical worship. The prehistoric antiquities are mostly from Madras, and comprise paleolithic and neolithic implements; also pottery, including examples of necropolitan pottery utilised for coffins. A number of interesting bas-reliefs come from Mesopotamia and some good Jain sculptures are on permanent loan from the Bombay Branch of the Royal Asiatic Society. In the Buddhist Section are portions of the Stupa of Amaravati, some terra-cotta figures of Buddhas and Bodhisattvas, fragments and images of Buddhas (Gandhara School) and very interesting bas-reliefs (of the same school) representing subjects from the Jataka stories.

Natural History Section.—The exhibits (in the new wing) are specimens from the collections of the Bombay Natural History Society (started 1883 and still existing). These include examples of all the Indian ruminants and carnivora; Other sections deal with reptiles, birds, fishes and insects. The Birds' Section contains, besides many beautiful specimens, a collection of drawings by Gronwold.

Forest Section.—This includes specimens of timbers grown in the Bombay Presidency.

Adjacent is the **Jehangir Art Gallery** (1952), where exhibitions are held.

Mahatma Gandhi Road

The **Institute of Science.**—This important group of buildings owes its inception to Lord Sydenham when Governor of Bombay (1907-13), who laid the foundation-stone in 1911, and to the generosity of Sir Jacob Sassoon, Sir Cowasjee Jehangir, Sir Currimbhoy Ebrahim and Sir Vasanji Tricumji Mulji, who furnished contributions for the erection of the various units. The scheme includes a College of Science occupying a three-storey block fronting Mayo Road, a science library, a public hall at the corner of Mayo Road and Mahatma Gandhi Road, and a block of examination schools facing Mahatma Gandhi Road. The building, which is Renaissance in character, is constructed of yellow basalt stone, obtained from quarries in the vicinity of Bombay. The architect was Mr G. Wittet.

The **Elphinstone College,** removed from Byculla in 1890 (p. 101), occupies a large building in the Romanesque Transition style. The main hall is called after Sir Cowasjee Jehangir in recognition of his large contribution for the purpose of building the original institution. The Elphinstone Institution was founded as a memorial to the Hon. Mountstuart Elphinstone, the Governor of Bombay. In 1856 it was divided into a High School (see p. 99), and this College for the higher education of Indians. Sir Alexander Grant, Bart., was Principal of the College in 1862, and distinguished scholars, such as Sir Ramkrishna Bhandarkar, the great Orientalist, have filled Professorships. In the library is a fine portrait of Elphinstone by Sir T. Lawrence.

The **State Record Office** occupies most of both wings. Amongst the records are preserved the oldest documents relating to the E.I. Company (the letter-books of the Surat Factory go back as far as 1630), and many other priceless historical papers, including the letter from General Wellesley announcing the victory at Assaye.

The **Mechanics' or Sassoon Institute** was founded originally in 1847, but refounded and renamed by David Sassoon and his son Sir Albert in 1870. Lectures are delivered and prize medals awarded. In the entrance-hall is a statue of Mr David Sassoon, by Woolner. There is also a good library.

D. Naoroji Road

From here Mahatma Gandhi Road leads across Vir Nariman Road to D. Naoroji Road. On the W. side of the entrance to D. Naoroji Road are the Oriental and other buildings, while a little back in Outram Road is the Cathedral High School for boys. On the right is the **Jamsetjee Jeejeebhoy Institute,** founded in 1849 by Sir Jamsetjee Jeejeebhoy and his wife, Lady Avabai. The Government of India are the trustees. The income is divided into 400 shares, of which 180 go for the Boys' and Girls' Schools in Bombay, 70 for those in Surat, and 150 for charities for the poor. Farther N. are the Terminus and Offices of the Central Railway and the Municipal Offices on the W. Between them, on a circular garden plot, is a statue by Brock of the late Sir Dinshaw Petit, first Baronet.

The remodelled **Victoria Terminus** in D. Naoroji Road contains a Railway Information Bureau. It was opened on 27th March 1929, and contains, as well as refreshment rooms, bed- and dressing-rooms and bathrooms. The former station, which adjoins, is now reserved for suburban traffic. The offices were completed in 1888, in an imposing building, with a large central dome.

S. is the **General Post Office,** which occupies the block in Frere Road between Fort Street and St George's Road. It was erected under the supervision of Mr G. Wittet, and was designed by Mr J. Begg in the Bijapur style of architecture (p. 465). E. of the railway station is **St George's Hospital.**

The **Municipal Buildings** were designed by Mr F. W. Stevens, and were opened in 1893. The Oriental feeling introduced into the Gothic architecture has a pleasing effect. The tower, 255 ft. high and surmounted by a masonry dome, can be seen from all parts of Bombay. The central gable terminates in a statue 13 ft. high, representing *Urbs prima in Indis*. The grand staircase is also crowned by an imposing dome. Immediately in front of the building is a statue by Derwent Wood of the late Sir Pherozeshah Mehta, who took a prominent part in the civic life of Bombay and in Indian politics.

From opposite these buildings Wardby Road leads S.W. to the Queen's Statue, passing the Capital Theatre, the Scots Kirk, the Lady Ratan Tata Palace, the Masonic Hall and the Alexandra School for Girls, founded by Mr Maneckjee Cursetjee, to the E. of it, and the open space of the Maidan or General Parade Ground and the Bombay Gymkhana Club on the W. At the corner of the Maidan, opposite the Municipal Buildings, is a statue of the late Mr Jamshedji Tata, flanked by allegorical figures.

From the Victoria Railway Station, D. Naoroji Road continues N. up to the Crawford Market and the main Indian residential quarters, passing on the left the *Times of India* Office, the Anjuman-i-Islam (Islamia) School and the School of Art; while from the station to the N.W. runs Cruikshank Road in front of the Municipal Offices, and past the Police Courts, the Allbless and Cama Hospitals, St Xavier's College and the Elphinstone High School. On Carnac Road, which joins these two roads and forms the third side of a triangle with them, are the St Xavier's High School and the Gokaldas Tejpal General Hospital. Paltan Road, which runs behind the Crawford Market and is so called from the former Barracks, forms the commencement of Mahomed Ali Road, which crosses Carnac Road and penetrates through the densely populated bazars in a slight curve until it joins Parel Road at its junction with Sardar Patel Road. Under the name of Kingsway, Parel Road continues past the King's Circle as far as Sion (11 m.).

The **Anjuman-i-Islam School** in D. Naoroji Road was erected in 1893 with the co-operation of Government, which gave the site and a money grant. The building was designed by Mr James Willcocks, and its erection marks an epoch in the history of the Muslim community.

The **Sir Jamsetjee Jeejeebhoy School of Art,** was first opened for pupils in 1857. In 1877 the present building was erected. Excellent drawings and designs are made here, as well as work in silver and copper, and decorative carving in wood and stone. The buildings in Western India owe their mural paintings to students of this institution. The School has become particularly distinguished in recent years; many artists who studied here are now internationally known. It may be recalled that Rudyard Kipling was born in Bombay, while his father, J. Lockwood Kipling, was Principal of the School.

The **Gokaldas Tejpal Hospital** (in Carnac Road), for Indians, can contain 200 patients. It owes its origin to gifts made by Mr Gokaldas Tejpal and by Mr Rustomjee Jamsetjee Jeejeebhoy.

St Xavier's College in Cruikshank Road, and **St Xavier's High School** in Carnac Road, founded in 1867, are now separate institutions, both under the Jesuit fathers. The College, which is affiliated to the University, and has 800 students, includes a highly equipped science department. The High School is a massive building, with a high octagonal tower.

Opposite the High School is the **Court of Small Causes.** Nearby was formerly the Robert Money School, founded in 1838, but now removed to Girgaon and under the management of the C.M.S.

The **Elphinstone High School,** at the junction of Carnac and Cruikshank Roads, is the Government public school of Bombay, and retained possession of the original buildings on this site when the *College Department* was separated to form the Elphinstone College. In front of it is a fine flight of steps.

The object of this school is to teach up to the standard of the University entrance examination, at fees within the reach of the middle-class people of Bombay and the districts. It has classes for the study of English, Marathi, Gujarati, Sanskrit, Latin and Persian. The building, which is

452 ft. long, was designed by Mr G. T. Molecey. Sir A. Sassoon contributed 1½ lakhs of rupees towards it.

The **Pestonji Kama Hospital,** for *Women* and *Children,* in Cruikshank Road, is a Gothic building. It owes its existence to gifts by Mr Pestonjee Hormusjee Kama, as the **Allbless Obstetric Hospital** beyond it does to the munificence of Mr Bomanjee Eduljee Allbless. Both are under the Dufferin Fund and the sole management of lady doctors. Further E., and adjoining the Municipal Offices, are the Esplanade Police Courts, erected in 1884-88.

The **Crawford Market,** which is situated at the junction of D. Naoroji Road and Carnac Road, was founded by Mr Arthur Crawford, C.S., Municipal Commissioner from 1865 to 1871. It consists of a Central Hall, in which is a drinking-fountain given by Sir Cowasjee Jehangir, surmounted by a Clock Tower, 128 ft. high. To the right is a wing, 150 ft. by 100 ft., in which are fruit and flowers, and on the left is another wing, 350 ft. by 100 ft., for vegetables, etc. The whole is covered with a double iron roof. Over the entrance gate are bas-reliefs executed by J. Lockwood Kipling, by whom the fountain was also designed. The ground is paved with flagstones from Caithness. There are many kinds of plantains or bananas; the finest are short, thick and yellow. The best oranges are those from Nagpur, and the best grapes are from Aurangabad. The mangoes arrive in May; the bulk of them come from orchards in the Konkan and from Goa.[1] The Alfonzo is the best variety. The Pomelo, the *Citrus decumana,* is particularly fine in Bombay. The *Fish Market* is at the end of the *Mutton Market.* The oysters are of moderate size and well flavoured. The *Palla* fish, generally about 2 ft. long, the salmon of India, is excellent, but has many troublesome bones. The best fish of all is the pomflet, or pomfret, a flat fish. The *Bombil,* called by the English *Bommelo* and *Bombay Duck,* is a glutinous fish, used with curry when salted and dried. On the S. side is the *Poultry Market,* where game also may be purchased.

Starting a little N.W. of the market, and extending to near the Marine Lines Station, is Princess Street, named after, and in 1905 opened by, Queen Mary (then Princess of Wales). This was the first arterial thoroughfare opened by the City Improvement Trust. Another main one, Sardar Patel Road, runs from the head of the Back Bay to Dongri Street, and through Naoroji Hill to the Docks. Another Trust road, Lamington Road, runs from Queen's Road to Jacob's Circle, and passes between the site of the former **Byculla Club** and the main entrance of the **Central Station** of the Western Railway.

The principal commercial **Docks** of Bombay lie to the E. of the market. The **Victoria Dock** (1885-88) covers 25 acres, and has an entrance 80 ft. in width. **Prince's Dock,** lying N. of this and connected with it, was commenced during the Prince of Wales's visit in 1875-76 and completed 1879. Remains of a submerged forest were found at a depth of about 10 ft. The dock extends over 30 acres, and is capable of containing twenty ocean steamers. It has a tidal observatory. In April 1944 a munition ship blew up and caused extensive havoc.

N.W. is the **Merewether Dry Dock** (1891), and a street of warehouses and offices, round which the Harbour Mission works. South of the Victoria Dock is the **Alexandra Dock,** of which the foundation-stone was laid by King George V (then Prince of Wales) on 13th November 1905. It extends S. of the Ballard Pier, and encloses an area of 49·52 acres. The depth of water in it is 37 ft., and the Hughes Dry Dock is 1000 ft. long and has an entrance 100 ft. wide.

All these docks were excavated on the estate known as the **Elphinstone** and **Mody Bay Reclamations,** which have taken in from the sea 483 acres

[1] It was the failure of supplies of Mazagon mangoes which specially annoyed the Wazir Fazl-ud-din in *Lala Rookh.*

and have raised and improved 157 acres, transforming the Eastern foreshore of the island from a mud swamp. A greater reclamation lies between Mazagon and Sewri, containing a grain depot as well as depots for coal, and the Cotton Green was moved from Colaba to Sewri in 1925.

The Trustees' Docks are connected with the two main line railways which feed Bombay, and by the Port Trust Railway, the point of junction being at Wadala, about 6 m. N. of the Alexandra Dock.

The **Port Trust** is composed of twenty-five members under an official Chairman, eleven nominated by Government, and the remainder elected by various special bodies. All the main business interests are represented. The principal articles of trade are: Imports—cotton, piece-goods, metals, machinery, silk manufactures, railway plant, kerosene oil, sugar and timber; and Exports—coal, cotton, grain, oil, seeds, tea, hides, raw wool piece-goods, twist, yarns and manganese ore.

The **Dockyards** (1845) **of the P. & O. Company** and **B.I.S.N. Company** are worked by the Mazagon Docks Company in the suburb of Mazagon. The Ritchie Dry Dock is 495 ft. long and capable of receiving vessels of deep draught. Close by is the Electrical Power Station at Parel (p. 103), which lights the city.

CITY

The visitor can plunge at once into the more Indian part of the city by stepping across Carnac Road at the Crawford Market and entering Abdul Rahman Street (which is a prolongation of D. Naoroji Road). The Muslim quarter extends along the Parel Road as far as Byculla. The Parsis are to be found chiefly in Dhobitalao, the district between Kalbadevi Road and Queen's Road.

In the **City** proper the streets and bazars are narrow and tortuous. Some of the houses are in the wooden architectural style of Gujarat. Their fronts are covered with carving, and some have projecting storeys supported upon elaborately sculptured corbels. Here and there are mosques and Hindu temples gaudily painted. The streets teem with life. Sir Edwin Arnold wrote of them: "A tide of Asiatic humanity ebbs and flows up and down the Bhendi bazar, and through the chief mercantile thoroughfares. Nowhere could be seen a play of livelier hues, a busier and brighter city life. Besides the endless crowds of Hindu, Gujarati and Mahratta people coming and going between rows of grotesquely painted houses and temples, there are to be studied here specimens of every race and nation of the East." It is said that the triangle formed by Kalbadevi Road, Sheikh Memon Street and Carnac Road contains an epitome of the Indian peninsula and much of its wealth.

There are nearly 3000 jewellers of the different Indian nationalities in Bombay, who find constant and lucrative employment. One of the most active industries is the manufacture of brass and copper pots and other utensils. The black woodcarving is famous, as is the sandalwood and other carving; the term "Bombay Boxes" includes sandalwood carving as well as inlay work. Tortoise-shell carving is a specialty, also lacquered turnery. Gold and silver thread is manufactured and used for lace, and Bombay embroidery is much prized.

The once-famous **Byculla Club,** a residential Club with extensive grounds founded in 1833, was situated in Bellasis Road, but closed down in 1946. The **Arab Stables** have moved to the Mahalakshmi Race-course. Bellasis Road leads to the Central Station (Western Ry.).

The **Nal Bazar,** in Sardar Patel Road, in the N.W. quarter of the city, supplies a large part of Bombay, and is generally immensely crowded.

A little S. of the Nal Bazar is the **Pinjrapol,** or Infirmary for Sick and Aged Animals, a curious institution, covering several acres, and maintained here, as elsewhere in India, by the Jain community. This is in the quarter called **Bhuleshwar,** "Lord of the Pure-minded"; and the temple of the deity, a form of Siva, is within the enclosure. To the S.W. is the **Roman Catholic Church** of **Nossa Senhora da Esperanza**[1]: and to the S.E. is the **Mombadevi Tank** and Temple, from which the name of Bombay is believed to be derived.[2] The **Copper Bazar** is opposite the Tank. S. of the Tank in Princess Street is the **Jami Masjid,** and E. of this is Abdur Rahman Street, continued N. by Parel Road.

Dr Babasaheb Ambedkar (Parel) Road

Near the cross-roads with Maulana Shaukat Ali (Grant) Road, from the W., is the **Jamsetjee Jeejeebhoy Hospital,** erected in 1845 at the joint expense of that gentleman and the E.I. Company. In the hall is a bronze statue of Sir Jamsetjee Jeejeebhoy, a copy of one in the Town Hall. Attached to it are a Hospital for Incurables, the Bai Motlabai Wadia Obstetric Hospital, and the Dinshaw Maneckjee Petit Hospital for women and children, erected in 1889 and 1890.

Adjoining the Hospital is the **Grant Medical College,** established in 1845 in memory of Sir Robert Grant, Governor of Bombay (1835-38). The Museum is full of curious things. The grounds cover 2 acres, and are made instructive by planting in them all kinds of useful trees and shrubs.

The Northbrook Gardens, in Grant Road, close by, were laid out in 1874.

A little to the S.E. of the J. J. Hospital lies the old **Jail** (now a remand home for boys). N. from the Hospital, Parel Road leads past Christ Church and the Byculla Station to the old Victoria Technical Institute and the Victoria and Albert Museum, and finally to the old Government House at Parel. The Victoria Jubilee Technical Institute which used to occupy the building opposite the Victoria Gardens, vacated in 1890 by the Elphinstone College, has since been transferred to a new building near Matunga.

The **Victoria and Albert Museum** (10.30-17.30 daily except Mondays. Entrance 5p. Reserved for ladies and children, Wednesdays) stands in the Victoria Gardens. Until 1857 the collection (1848), including prints, maps, photographs, etc., illustrating the history of Bombay, was kept in the Fort Barracks, but, on Sir G. Birdwood being appointed Curator by Lord Elphinstone, he raised a subscription for building this Museum. Sir B. Frere laid the first stone in 1862, and Government completed the building in 1871. The Clock Tower in front of it was erected by Sir Albert Sassoon, who also presented the statue of the Prince Consort, by Noble. The **Victoria Gardens** have an area of 34 acres. To the right of the S. entrance to them is the stone elephant which gave the island of Elephanta its name; and on the E. side of them are Zoological Gardens.

Parel Road continues from here past the Veterinary College, built on a site given by Sir Dinshaw Maneckjee Petit, to the **Old Government House.** The building occupies the site of the Hindu temple of Parali Vaijnath, from which the locality takes its name. In 1673 the Jesuits had a church and convent here; the latter was taken over in 1719 by Governor Boone, who used it as a country house. The first Governor who lived here permanently was William Hornby, between 1771 and 1780; and the right and left wings were added by Mountstuart Elphinstone (1819-27). In 1885 Lady Fergusson, the wife of the then Governor, died here of cholera, and

[1] The original church, which was built in 1596, stood on the Esplanade and was demolished in 1760, when the present church was built in Kalbadevi at the expense of the Government.

[2] Momba (Mumba) itself is possibly a corruption of Maha Amma (Amba), Great Mother, a goddess of the Kolis, and probably the tutelary deity of Bombay. The temple and tank originally stood on part of the site of the Victoria Terminus, and were demolished in 1737, when the fortifications of the old town were enlarged. The present temple and tank are said to date from 1753.

the place remained vacant until 1897, when it was utilised as a plague hospital. Two years later, W. M. Haffkine opened a Plague Research Laboratory in the building. This became the Bombay Bacteriological Laboratory in 1906, and it has been known as the **Haffkine Institute** since 1925. Under this name it is used as a laboratory for Bacterial Research, the study of Tropical Medicine and the preparation of plague vaccine. A Rabies Institute also is established here. The public rooms were in the centre facing the W. The drawing-room or ballroom, above the dining-room, occupied the place of the old Portuguese chapel. In addition to these two Institutes, a fine range of buildings has been erected in the grounds and in the immediate neighbourhood. The King Edward Memorial Hospital, the Sunder Das Medical School, the Wadia Maternity Home and the Wadia Hospital for Children form one of the largest and most complete medical treatment centres in the East. Nearby also, on Hospital Avenue, is the Tata Memorial Cancer Hospital and Research Institute.

There are large railway workshops at Parel; and spinning-mills as well as at Tardeo and Warli. The Receiving Station of the Tata Hydro-Electric Works is at Parel (p. 105).

The Franciscan Church of Nossa Senhora da Gloria in Parel was the headquarters of the Padroado (Portuguese) section of the R.C. community until an agreement effected with the Vatican in 1928.

The **European Cemetery,** at Sewri, E. of Parel, until 1867 a Botanical Garden, is a sheltered spot under Flagstaff Hill.

MALABAR HILL

The drive round the Back Bay to **Malabar Hill,** 180 ft. high, by Netaji Subash Road (2 m. long, 140 ft. wide) and Malabar Hill Road, is extremely beautiful and interesting. Beyond the Marine Lines Station are an enclosed burning-place of the Hindus, a Muslim burying-ground and the Girgaon English and Scottish cemeteries (now disused). Opposite, on the ocean side of the railway line, is the aquarium. Further on, in Chowpatty (Chaupati), is the **Wilson College** (named after Rev. Dr J. Wilson, F.R.S., Oriental scholar and Scottish missionary), for the education of young men. Near Chowpatty Beach at 19 Laburnum Road is Mani Bhavan, where Gandhi spent much of his time while in Bombay, now a museum.

At about 3 m. from the Fort the road begins to ascend a spur of Malabar Hill. Near the top, on the left, are the entrance gates to the drive through the grounds (private) of **Government House at Malabar Point,** now styled Raj Bhawan, with a pleasant view of the city across Back Bay. Below, at the extreme point, there used to be a battery. Not far off to the N. a large ship, the *Diamond,* was wrecked, and eighty passengers were drowned. Sir Evan Nepean (1812-19) was the first Governor to reside at Malabar Point. In 1819-20 Mr Elphinstone added a public breakfast-room and a detached sleeping-bungalow on a small scale. In 1828 Sir John Malcolm gave up the Government House in the Fort and considerably enlarged the residence at Malabar Point. Since 1885, when Parel was abandoned, it has been the official headquarters of the Governor.

Close by is the picturesque temple of **Walkeswar,** the "Sand Lord", built *c.* 1000. Throngs of Hindus will be met coming from it, their foreheads newly coloured with the sectarian mark. Rama, on his way from Ajodhya (Oudh) to Lankā (p. 21) to recover his bride Sita, carried off by Ravana, halted here for the night. Lakshman provided his brother Rama with a Lingam from Benares every night. This night he failed to arrive in time, and Rama made for himself a Lingam of the sand at the spot. On the arrival of the Portuguese in after ages, this Lingam sprang into the sea from horror of the barbarians. There is a small but very picturesque tank here, adorned with flights of steps, surrounded by Brahmans' houses and shrines. When Rama thirsted here, he shot an arrow into the earth, and forthwith appeared the *Vanatirtha*, "Arrow-Tank".

In the centre of the Hill, about 180 ft. above the sea, are the grounds of the Ladies' Gymkhana, and beyond them the Pherozeshah Mehta Gardens, called the **Hanging Gardens.** Kamala Nehru Park affords lovely views of Back Bay, of the buildings rising on the farther side of it, and of the harbour and islands and mountains beyond.

The drive continues (below) along the seashore by the Hornby Vellard[1] to Warli, and through the beautiful Mahim woods of coconut and other palm-trees.

The **Parsi Dharmsala,** in the Gamdevi Road, intended for poor Persian Parsis, is passed on the approach to the Towers of Silence from the S. A similar dharmsala close by was erected by Sir Cowasjee Jehangir, in memory of his grandfather in 1812.

The **Babulnath Temple,** on the S.E. part of Malabar Hill, is near the steps leading to the Towers of Silence. It is not an ancient building; the spire and pillared hall and terrace were completed in 1900: but it is a prominent landmark and figures in all views of "Bombay from Malabar Hill".

Between the gardens is All Saints' Church, and beyond them and N. of the head of the curve of the bay are the **Five Parsi Towers of Silence,** where the Parsis dispose of their dead. Sir Jamsetjee Jeejeebhoy, at his own expense, made the road which leads to the Towers on the N. side, and gave 100,000 sq. yd. of land on the N. and E. sides of the Towers. Within the gateway of an outer enclosure a flight of eighty steps mounts up to a gateway in an inner wall. Special permission is required for visitors to proceed beyond this point.

Exposure of corpses to birds of prey originates from the veneration the Parsis pay to the elements. Fire is too highly regarded to incur pollution from the dead. Water is almost equally respected, and so is earth; hence this singular mode of disposal has been devised. There is, however another reason. Zartasht (Zoroaster) taught that rich and poor must meet in death. The surroundings of the Towers are arranged to foster calm meditation. Under the shade of fine trees, relatives of the deceased can sit and meditate; and the view to the W. and S. over the waters, and to the E. and N. over the harbour and the distant mountains beyond, is enchanting. Even the cypresses, as the Parsis themselves say, tapering upwards, point the way to heaven. At the S.E. foot of the hill is an **Almshouse** for indigent Parsis of both sexes, erected by the sons of the late Fardonjee Sorabjee Parekh.

Laxmibai Jagmohandas Marg (Nepean Sea Road)

The drive from Malabar Point, and thence along the Nepean Sea Road to **Breach Candy,**[1] is pleasant in the evening, but the views which formerly marked it are shut off from the road by buildings. On these hills are situated some of the finest houses in Bombay, surrounded by small but bright gardens. Evan Nepean was Governor from 1812 to 1819.

On Cumballa Hill is the Bomanji Dinshaw Petit Hospital for Parsis. At the N. end of Breach Candy are the **Mahalakshmi Temples,** the oldest in

[1] The Hornby Vellard (Portuguese *Vallado*, fence) or Warli Causeway was constructed early in the 18th century between Mahalakshmi and Warli to shut out the sea, which at high tide made the central portion of the island a swamp.

[1] Various derivations and meanings of this name have been put forward. Possibly it means "the beach at the mouth of the hollow or pass—that is to say, the hollow between Cumballa ridge on the north and the Malabar ridge on the south". Candy = khind or pass.

Bombay, dedicated to three goddesses, images of whom were found in the sea. Just beyond the Temples is the Tomb of Haji Ali on an island connected to the mainland by a causeway which is submerged at high tide.

Along Clerk Road is the **Race-course,** where races are held in cold weather on Wednesdays and Saturdays, under the management of the Western India Turf Club. It has been considerably enlarged, and a new Park has been opened close by. Here also is situated the **Willingdon Sports Club,** founded by Lord Willingdon (Governor of Bombay, 1913-18) as a meeting-place for Indians and Europeans, with its Golf-course, Polo ground and Tennis courts.

The **Tata Hydro-Electric Works.**—Bombay is supplied with electric power and current from the Receiving Station of the Tata Hydro-Electric Works, which is at Parel. This scheme, which was inaugurated by Sir Dorab Tata, impounds the monsoon rainfall (often 500 in.) on the Ghats at Lonavla (p. 429), in three lakes formed at Shirawta, Walwan and Lonavla, with intercommunicating duct lines, forebay, etc. The dams of these three lakes are approximately 90, 70 and 34 ft. in height, with areas of 3000, 1700 and 720 acres respectively, all at 2000 ft. above sea-level. The foundation-stone of the first dam, which impounds the Lonavla Lake, was laid by the then Governor, Sir George Clarke, on 8th February 1911. The ducts lead the water to a forebay near the Duke's Nose, where it enters the Pipe Line, to take a plungs of 1740 ft. down to the Generating Station at Khopoli. The power generated is conveyed 42 m. to the Parel mission cables, crossing several navigable creeks on lofty steel towers.

RAILWAY STATIONS

The two principal railway stations in Bombay are the **Victoria Terminus,** the headquarters of the old Great Indian Peninsular Railway, now the Central Railway, and the **Central Station,** headquarters of the old Bombay Baroda and Central India Railway, now the Western Railway, of which mention has already been made (p. 98). The Harbour Branch (1925) runs from the Victoria Terminus to Kurla, 10 m., where it connects with the main line of the Central Ry. The three lines are electrified, and also the main lines to Poona and Igatpuri (p. 98).

ROUND THE ISLAND OF SALSETTE[1]

The beach at Juhu (10 m. from the city) provides splendid bathing. There are excellent Hotels. Even nearer is Pali Hill, with a nine-hole golf-course. Farther afield the monsoon jungles of the Lake District of Vehar and Pawai attract the naturalist, the Caves of Kanheri, Jogeswar, and Borivli (p. 109) draw pilgrims, and the old-world charm of the early Portuguese church of Bhayndar and the parochial village life of the "island" of Dharavi (road *via* Bhayndar) reveal an unsuspected element in modern Indian life.

A good motor road encircles the whole island of Salsette (distance about 50 m.). Bombay is left by way of Parel Road and its continuation, Kingsway. This leads *via* Causeway Sion (1805) to Thana, between which place and Ghorbunder (D.B.) the Ulhas river breaks through the magnificent gorge of Gaumukh (the Cow's Mouth), the road closely following it. Bombay is re-entered by Bandra and the Mahim Causeway. The trip, about 75 m. in all from the Apollo Bunder, can be done comfortably in a day, but lunch should be carried. A shorter round trip through the Lake District (distance about 45 m.) takes a road which skirts Lake Pawai.

EXCURSIONS IN THE VICINITY OF BOMBAY

I. In the Harbour and by Sea

1. Elephanta.
2. Chaul.
3. Down the Coast.

[1] See map facing p. 117.

II. Along the Western Railway or by Car

III. Along the Central Railway or by Car

I. In the Harbour and by Sea

(1) Indian mythology is well ex- Emplified at **Elephanta** [Restaurant and Retiring Room], a small island about 6 m. from the Fort of Bombay, to which launches run frequently from Apollo Bunder.[1] The Indian Tourist Office may be consulted about timings. A bunder-boat may be hired, but the length of the passage will depend on wind and tide. A cheap and convenient way of making the trip is to go by the Harbour Ferry from Apollo Bunder. It usually starts at 7.30 and is back by 12.15 the same morning, giving ample time to see the **caves,** which are reached by a walk of 1 m. from the old landing-place in the S.W. of the island. The boat will pass close to Butcher's Island, which is 3 m. nearly due E. from Mazagon Dock. The view in this part of the harbour is fine. To the N. is the hill known as the Neat's Tongue, on Trombay Island, which is 1000 ft. above sea-level. The highest point of Elephanta is 568 ft. To the S. is the hill above Karanja, called Dronagiri—a mass of rock thrown down by Hanuman on his flight to Ceylon.

Elephanta is called by Indians *Gharapuri*. The caves, which date from A.D. 450-750, are called *Lenen* (Lena), a word used throughout India and Ceylon for these excavations. The island consists of two long hills, with a narrow valley between them. About 250 yd. to the right of the old landing-place, at the S. end of the island on the rise of one of the hills, and not far from the ruins of an ancient city, was a mass of rock cut into the shape of an elephant, from which the place derives its European name. In September 1814 its head and neck dropped off, and in 1864 the remainder was removed to the Victoria Gardens, where it was re-erected in 1912.

The modern landing-place, N.W. of the island, consists of a rather slippery pier of separated concrete blocks. The caves are distant about ¼ m., and about 250 ft. above the sea, and are approached by easy steps constructed in 1853 by an Indian merchant. There is a custodian's bungalow at the entrance, where a fee is paid. The rules should be studied. The date of the excavation of the Seven Caves is now placed about the middle of the 8th century.

The Great Cave faces the N., and is open also E. and W. (cruciform). The steps have lions on each side. The main hall had two wide colonnades of six columns and two centre collonnades of four columns, the recesses on the N. and S. sides consisting of two aisles separated by two columns, the outer aisle being much shorter than the inner; the length of the central hall from the pillars at each end is 130 ft., and the breadth from the wall of the S. recess to the pillars on the outer side of the N. recess is just the same. Of the twenty-six columns, eight have fallen by seepage of water. The columns present variety of shape and ornament, they have a square shaft rising about half-way up to a fluted neck, and a capital of the shape of a squeezed cushion, bound in the middle; the height of the columns varies from 15 ft. to 17 ft.

The *Lingam Shrine*, at the W. end of the hall, stands 4 ft. above the floor of the cave. It is 19½ ft. square, with four doors facing cardinal points. At the outside of each entrance are two large figures representing *dwarapals* or door-keepers, who lean on

[1] Except during the monsoon. The Government Tourist Office can supply a *Guide to Elephanta* or a shorter brochure.

dwarfs. The Lingam, a cylindrical stone 3 ft. high, the emblem of Siva, is worshipped on great occasions by crowds of devotees.

On entering the Great Cave a striking feature is the colossal *Three-headed Bust*, or *Trimurti*, in the S. wall facing the N. entrance. It is 19 ft. in height, and the faces are between 4 and 5 ft. long. It is the representation of Siva, who is the leading character in all the groups of the cave. The front face is Siva in the character of Brahma, the creator; the E. face (spectator's left) is Siva in the character of Rudra, the destroyer; and the W. face (spectator's right) is considered to be Siva in the character of Vishnu, the preserver, holding a lotus flower in his hand. On either side of the recess is a pilaster each carved on the front with a gigantic dwarapal.

The *Arddhanariswar*, or *androgynous Divinity*, in the first compartment to the E. of the central figure (spectator's left), represents Siva. It is 16 ft. 9 in. high. The right half of the figure is intended to be that of a male, and the left that of a female, and thus represents Siva as uniting the two sexes in his one person. The bull on which two of the hands of the figure lean, known as his *vahana*, or vehicle, is called Nandi, a constant attendant on Siva. Brahma, on his lotus throne, supported by five swans, and with his four faces, is exhibited on the right of the figure. On the left, Vishnu is seen riding on what is now a headless Garuda, a winged creature, half man, half eagle. Above and in the background are found a number of inferior gods and sages of the Hindus, among them Indra, the Rain-god, mounted on an elephant.

In the W. (right) compartment of the *Trimurti* are two gigantic figures of *Siva* and *Parvati*, the former 16 ft. high, the latter 12 ft. 4 in. Siva has a high cap, on which is a crescent over each temple. From the top of it rises a cup or shell, on which is a three-headed female figure, with broken arms, representing the Ganga proper, the Jumna and Saraswati, which three streams are supposed to unite at Prayag, near Allahabad, the sacred meeting-place of the three plaited locks, and form the Ganges. According to a Hindu legend, the Ganges flowed from the hair of Siva. The god is standing, and has four arms, of which the outer left rests on the head of a dwarf with curly or matted hair. In the dwarf's right hand is a cobra, in his left a *chauri* (fly-whisk); from his neck hangs a necklace, with a tortoise ornament. On Siva's right are Brahma, on his lotus seat, borne by five swans, with four hands, bearing the lotus, roll of the Vedas, and butter-dish, and Indra on his elephant.

The *Marriage of Siva and Parvati* is a sculptured group (greatly damaged) in the S. wall of the W. aisle. The position of Parvati on the right of Siva shows that she is newly wed; for to stand on the right of her husband, and to eat with him, are privileges rarely permitted to a Hindu wife, save on her wedding-day. In the corner, at the right of Parvati, is Brahma, known by his three visible faces, sitting and reading, as the priest of the gods, the sacred texts suited to the marriage ceremony. Above, on Siva's left, is Vishnu. Among the attendants on the right of Parvati is one bearing a water-pot for the ceremony. This is probably Chandra, the moon-god. Behind the bashful goddess is a male figure, probably her father, Himalaya, who is pushing her forward.

Opposite this, in the N.W. (near the door), is a relief of *Kapalabhrit* or *Bhairava*, with skull and cobra on head and rosary of skulls round neck; two of his eight hands are devoted to the slaughter of a human being, and a third holds up a body for slaughter. At the W. end of the N. aisle, by which the cave is entered, is a relief of *Siva performing the Tandava dance* (world-shaking); on his left is Parvati, and above a perfect Ganesh. Opposite this, at the E. end of the aisle, is a representation of *Siva* as *Lakulisa*, which much resembles Buddha. The figure has the remains of two arms, which appear to have rested in its lap. It is seated on a lotus, the stalk of which is supported by two figures below. In the aisle behind the E. entrance again are two reliefs on the N. and S. ends. The first of these represents *Ravana, the demon king of Lanka*, or Ceylon, attempting to remove Kailas, the heavenly hill of Siva, to his own kingdom, in order that he may have his tutelary deity always with him, for Ravana was ever a worshipper of Siva. Ravana has ten heads and twenty arms, and is with his back to the spectator. Siva is seen in Kailas, with Parvati on his right, and votaries and Rishis in the background. The legend runs that Ravana shook Kailas so much that Parvati was alarmed, whereupon Siva pressed down the hill with one of his toes on the head of Ravana, who remained immovable for 10,000 years.

The second relief opposite this shows *Siva and Parvati* seated together, with groups of male and female inferior divinities showering down flowers from above. The rock is cut into various shapes to represent the peaks of Kailas, Siva's heaven. Behind Siva and Parvati is a female figure carrying a child on her hip, from which it was supposed that the sculpture represents the birth of Skanda, the war-god; the later view is that the scene represents Parvati in a temper.

Beyond the main hall on the E. side is the *East Wing*, consisting of an open court 55 ft. wide, in the centre of which was a circular platform, probably for a Nandi. On the S. side of the court is a temple on a high terrace, reached by steps with lions at the top of them. The portico of the temple has a chamber at each end, that on the W. end with figures of Siva, Vishnu and Brahma, and of the seven great goddesses or divine mothers (p. 22). The shrine of the temple measures 14 ft. by 16 ft., and has an altar and Lingam inside it. The *West Wing* of the cave has also an open court with a large cistern on the S. side, and on the W. side a small open chapel with a Lingam in it.

Round the hill, a little to the S., are two other excavations fronting the E. These are also Lingam shrines, with *dwarapals* sculptured outside, marred by disintegration of the rock.

(2) **Chaul.**—A group of ancient Portuguese and Moorish forts at the mouth of a creek just outside the harbour. The steamer sails every day in the fair season (October-May), and the stopping-place is called Revdanda. One night out is sufficient, but better two. On the S. side of the creek there is a former Janjira State Bungalow, for which leave has to be asked from the District Magistrate; but it is scantily furnished; food and bedding must be taken. It is possible to camp out in a tent, if preferred, on the summit of Korlai hill, a lovely fort, with a panoramic view. On the N. side of the creek is the old Portuguese city-fort of Chaul, similar but second to Bassein, with its walls and groups of churches in ruins overgrown by a dense grove of palms. Chaul was taken by the Portuguese in 1522 and made subordinate to Bassein, but was lost to the Mahrattas in 1739. On the overthrow of the Peshwa Baji Rao in 1818, it passed with the surrounding country to the British. There are still a number of monuments inside the Portuguese fortifications—the only remains of the famous city. Ralph Fitch mentions the "great trade" of Chaul in 1584, and Pyrard de Laval describes it about 1663 as differing from Bassein and Daman "in being extremely rich and abounding in valuable goods". The village of Korlai contains the Church of Our Lady of Mount Carmel (excellent wooden bas-reliefs) and a Christian population of fishermen, who retain the old Portuguese customs.

(3) **Down the Coast.**—Steamers of the Bombay Steam Navigation Company ("Shepherd Company"), regularly sail from the Alexandra Dock for Panjim (Nova Goa), carrying the mails, and calling at Ratnagiri and

Vijayadrug, an old Angria stronghold, taken by Vice-Admiral Watson and Clive in 1756 on their way to the Coromandel coast (daily service also to Vijayadrug). Since the former Portuguese possessions of which Goa was the capital became part of India in March 1962, communications with Bombay have become easier; and the sea-trip is a pleasant alternative to the railway journey described on p. 78. There is first-class saloon accommodation for eight passengers. (See Route 24, p. 78.) A service of steamers twice weekly serves Mangalore (p. 530), leaving Bombay on Tuesdays and Fridays at 13.30 and arriving at Mangalore on Thursdays and Mondays. (Return: Depart Saturdays and Tuesdays, 08.00 Arrive Bombay, Mondays and Thursdays.) These timings should be verified locally, as many changes are being made. The steamers call *en route* at Vengurla, Mormugão and Karwar.

The Scindia Steam Navigation Company run three services a week to ports down the coast.

II. Along the Western Railway or by Car

(1) **Bandra** (station 7 m. from Bombay (Central) opposite Mahim) has a large commuter-population. The cathedral-like chapel of *Mount Mary* has been rebuilt. **Juhu** (second airport; flying club) lies 3 m. from Bandra with a modern hotel (*Sun 'n Sand*). Beyond Santa Cruz airport is the Aarey Milk Colony a model institution in beautiful surroundings which attracts many visitors as does the Gandhi Memorial at Borivli nearby.

From Andheri station, 2 m. W., is the seaside village of Vesava, used as a holiday resort for Bombay. There are only private bungalows. The aerodrome lies ½ m. W. A day's trip should include a sea bathe and a visit across the creek to Aldeamar Fort, first a Portuguese then a Mahratta stronghold.

(2) The **Jogesvari Cave** lies not far from Andheri Station (11 m.) on the Western Railway, and can be reached by car. Dr Burgess attributed this Brahman cave to the second half of the 8th century A.D. Like the Elephanta Cave, it has extensive wings to the central hall, which has a shrine 24 ft. square in the middle, with four doors and a large Lingam. The veranda (S. side) is 120 ft. long, and has ten columns (seven replaced) of Elephanta pattern, while twenty such pillars form a square in the hall.

Electric torches are a "must" both to see the interiors and to avoid any snakes sheltering.

(3) **Cave Temples of Kanheri** (*Kennery*).—These caves are all excavated in the face of a single hill in the centre of the island of Salsette. Train to **Borivli** station, 19 m. from Bombay (good waiting-room); the caves are about 12 m. away in a National Park (Krishnagiri Upavan). Buses run from the station on Sundays and holidays only. Cottages for picnickers are available at the caves from the Superintendent.

There are one hundred and nine Buddhist caves, but only two or three are of interest. It is possible that the greater part of them were executed by a colony of Buddhists, "who may have taken refuge here after being expelled from the continent, and who tried to reproduce the lost Karli in their insular retreat". They date from the end of the 2nd century A.D. to about the middle of the 9th, or possibly a little later. The great *Chaitya* is one of the earliest here; those on each side may be two centuries later: the latest is probably the unfinished one, which is the first the traveller approaches by the Borivli route, and which dates about the 9th or 10th century A.D., or is even still more recent. However this may be, it is certain that, to quote Bishop Heber, "the beautiful situation of these caves, their elaborate carving, and their marked connection with Buddha and his religion, render them every way remarkable".

Most of the surrounding hills are

covered with jungle, but the one in which the caves are is nearly bare, its summit being formed by one large rounded mass of compact rock, under which a softer stratum has been denuded by the rains, forming natural caves, which, slightly improved by art, were appropriated as cells. The path runs in a N. direction up to the ravine, lying E. and W., round which the caves are excavated on six ledges in the mountain side connected by flights of steps. Shortly before the end of the ravine is reached, a steep ascent leads up to a platform facing W., where the Great Chaitya Cave (No. 3) is situated, and whence steps lead down to the ravine.

Cave No. 3, entered through a forecourt and a veranda, probably dates from the 6th century. It is 86 ft. long and 40 ft. wide, and has a colonnade of thirty-four pillars, which encircles the dagoba, standing 16 ft. high, at the back. A number of the pillars have bases and capitals carved with elephants, dagobas, trees, worship of sacred feet, etc. At the ends of the great veranda are two later figures of Buddha, 21 ft. high, and over the door is the great arched window, which forms one of the principal characteristics of these structures. In front of the veranda are two pillars, and on the screen of the back wall are Buddhist carvings. In the forecourt are two attached pillars, on which are four lions and three squat figures. On the left of the court is a round cell with a dagoba, and on the right, at the end of a long excavation (No. 2), are three ruined dagobas, with a Buddhist litany (p. 31) on the rock round them.

At a distance of 150 yd. up the ravine, N.W. of the Chaitya Cave, is the Darbar of the Maharaja Cave (No. 10), which was a dharmsala, or chapter-house, and not an ordinary vihara. It is 73 ft. by 32 ft. in size, and has two stone benches running down its longer axis and some cells on the left and back walls. The veranda, which is approached by three flights of steps, has eight columns along the front of it.

No. 14, farther up the same (left) side of the ravine, has some traces of painting, and No. 21 has columns of the Elephanta type, a Buddhist litany, and a figure of Padmapani, crowned by ten cobra-heads, in a recess on the right of the porch.

Above No. 10 is No. 35, a vihara 40 ft. by 45 ft., with benches round it, and four octagonal columns in the veranda; on the walls are reliefs of Buddha seated upon a lotus, of a disciple spreading his cloak for him to walk upon, and of another litany.

N.W. from these and from the front of No. 56 is a fine view of the sea; in No. 66 are some fine sculptures and another litany. Some 400 yd. to the S., and beyond the Chaitya Cave, is a terrace with monuments over the ashes of Buddhist monks. The many cisterns and small tanks round the caves and the flights of steps connecting them are remarkable.

(4) **Montpezir Caves** (*Mandapeshwar*).—Western Railway to **Borivli** station, 19 m., thence 1 m. by road. At the caves are a ruined Portuguese church and Franciscan monastery with a cross close by. Round the N.E. corner of the church are three Brahman caves hewn out of the rock, dating from the 8th century. The cave on the E. is 5 ft. 8 in. by 21 ft. Adjoining this cave to the W. is a stone basin for water, of which there is a good supply, said never to fail, and this may be one reason why the Portuguese have built here. The next cave is 27 ft. 3 in. by 14 ft. 9 in. In the W. wall is a group of 25 Gana (celestial dwarfs), figures very much mutilated, and a four-armed Siva. In the corner of the outside wall is half a teak door of the church, with two saints carved on it.

The third (W.) cave was a vihara (monastery) in which ten or twelve hermits lived, but was converted into a R.C. chapel. In the N. part of the E. wall, upside down, is the stone originally over the entrance door, inscribed with the date 1555. The interior measurement of the *mandapam*, or hall, is 51 ft. by 21 ft.

The conversion into a church was effected by the building of a wall in front of it and by screening off the Saivite sculptures or covering them with plaster. This is one of the very few instances of the transformation of a Brahmanical cave-shrine into a Christian place of worship. The King of Portugal, John III (1521-57) diverted to the church (which was dedicated to N. D. de la Misericordia) the revenues of the temple, and also built the monastery.

S., on a hill, is a round tower (40 ft. high), which the priest calls a Calvarium, surmounted by a statue of Jesus Christ. An Orphanage has been built close by, and the old church has been restored. There is a good view from the top over the plain.

(5) **Bhayndar** station, 25 m. from Bombay, is on the S. edge of the Bassein creek, which divides Salsette from the mainland. The railway here crosses the river by a very long bridge (Route 10). On the right, and for some miles up the stream, the scenery is most beautiful—the Kamandrug Hills and Ghorbunder, with the quiet water between them, forming a charming tropical landscape.

(6) **Bassein** (Vasai) was a Portuguese city from 1534 to 1739. Its walls are intact, and contain many ruined churches and palaces. It is reached by a road, 7 m. from Bassein Road station. A visit can be made in one day. The Government Tourist Office should be consulted about facilities for food and shelter, including permission to use the D.B. (if it is free) as well as the services of a guide.

The churches belonged to Franciscans, Dominicans, Jesuits and Augustinians, and the *Matriz*, or mother church of St Joseph, was called the Cathedral. The survey should be completed by a walk round the seaward side of the walls.

The first notice of Bassein is in 1532, when the Portuguese ravaged the neighbourhood. In 1534 they took Damao,[1] which they held until December 1961; and obliged Sultan Bahadur Shah of Gujarat, weakened by the Emperor Humayun, to cede Bassein in perpetuity. "For more than 200 years Bassein remained in the hands of the Portuguese, and during this time it rose to such prosperity that the city came to be called the Court of the North, and its nobles were proverbial for their wealth and magnificence. With plentiful supplies of both timber and stone, Bassein was adorned by many noble buildings, including a cathedral, five convents, thirteen churches, and an asylum for orphans. The dwellings of the Hidalgos, or aristocracy, who alone were allowed to live within the city walls, are described (1675) as "stately buildings" (Hunter). Fryer wrote of the town in 1675: "Here were stately dwellings graced with covered balconies and large windows, two storeys high, with panes of oyster-shell, which is the usual glazing amongst them (the Portuguese) in India, or else latticed".

On the 17th February 1739 the Mahratta Chimnaji Appa invested Bassein, and the town surrendered on the 16th of May after a most desperate resistance, in which the commandant, Silveira de Menezes, was killed and 800 of the garrison were killed and wounded, the Mahrattas' loss being upwards of 5000. They held it until 1780, when General Goddard arrived with very powerful artillery, and one battery of twenty mortars, which shortly after opened at a range of 500 yd. and did great execution. The place surrendered on the 11th December, on which day Colonel Hartley, with a covering force, defeated a Mahratta relieving party, and killed its distinguished General, Ramchandra Ganesh. Bassein was, however, restored to the Mahrattas by the Treaty of Salbai, 1783.

The Treaty of Bassein with the fugitive Peshwa Baji Rao II was signed on 31st December 1802.

The Fort, on the Bassein creek, a little away from the sea, is now entered from the N.

[1] The poet Camoens distinguished himself on this occasion.

The Old Town contains the ruins of the Cathedral of St Joseph and churches built by early Roman Catholic missionaries. Several inscriptions remain, the earliest dated 1536. Among the ruins are the Church of St Anthony, the Jesuits' church and convents.

3½ m. N.W. from Bassein Road station is **Sopāra,** which is now an insignificant place, but which, up to the beginning of the 14th century, was the principal port of the Konkan. It has been identified by some writers with Solomon's Ophir, on the ground that "Ophir" appears as "Sophir" in the Septuagint version of the Bible. Some support of the theory may be found in the fact that the place is also locally known as "Opara". One of the Rock Edicts of Asoka was found here, but is now lost.

III. Along the Central Railway or by Car

(1) The **Vehar Lake** can be reached by car from Kurla station (10 m.) on the Central Railway, and is close to Bhandup station (17 m.) on the same line. But the most convenient method of approach is by motor from Bombay, either by Sion Causeway and Kurla, or by Mahim Causeway and Andheri. The lake covers 1400 acres, and measures 2 m. by 1¼ m.; it was made (1856-59) by Mr Conybeare, C.E., by damming up the Garpur river. It can supply 8,000,000 gallons of water a day. The embankment is 30 ft. broad and 30 ft. above the water. The water is 75 ft. deep, of which 50 ft. are available for the supply of Bombay and 25 ft. are kept for *settling*. There are many crocodiles in the lake: fish life is not very abundant in consequence. The former Golf Club at Sewri moved in 1940 to Chembur, situated in pleasant surroundings near Kurla, 11 miles by road from the Bombay G.P.O. *Pawai Lake*, lying below Vehar, was formed by the Municipality in 1890. Its water is now used to supplement the main supply.

The *Tulsi Lake*, which lies 2 m. to the N., was completed in 1879, and water is carried thence to the top of Malabar Hill; 2 m. N. again are the Kanheri Caves.

(2) **Mumbra** (station 25 m. from Bombay on the Central Railway line to Kalyan) is a favourite week-end resort. The Mumbra Creek is a fine stretch of water, and the background of wooded hills completes a charming picture. The scenery on the Vihas river between Mumbra and Bassein Creek has been compared to the Rhine from Mainz to Cologne.

(3) The **Tansa Water Supply** (Central Railway to Atgaon station, 59 m., D.B.).—The increase in the population led the Corporation to construct a reservoir (planned 1872) on the Tansa river, about 55 m. N.E. of Bombay, which was formally opened by Lord Lansdowne in 1892. The Dam, which encloses the valley of the Tansa river, completed 1891, is of a uniform height of 118 ft., and is 2 m. long, 103 ft. thick at the base, and 24 ft. at the top, where a flagged road runs along it. The lake, originally 8 sq. m. in area, has been twice enlarged, and huge mains, 6 ft. in diameter, have been laid down.

The hot wells of Vajrabai, or Vajreshwari, 12 m. N. of Bhiwandi (Bundy) near the bed of the Tansa river in the village of Wadowli (Vadavli), were very popular in the 18th century. James Forbes in his *Oriental Memoirs* describes them as consisting of a small cistern with water at a temperature of 120°F. Except that it contained no iron, the water tasted like that of Bath. With the discovery of Mahabaleshwar (p. 442) in 1826-29, the wells ceased to be so famous but are much visited by Bombay people. (Buses from Bassein Road or Thana.)

(4) The **Thal and Bhor Ghats.**—These inclines pass through some of the prettiest scenery in all India. Those who do not travel by railway trains in daylight should make a point of visiting them separately.

The **Thal Ghats** can be seen by a

trip to Igatpuri (85 m.) (Route 2, p. 115); it is possible to return the same day after taking refreshment at Igatpuri station.

The **Bhor Ghats,** passed on the route to Poona (Route 23, p. 429), are even finer than the Thal Ghats, and should not be missed. At **Khandala*,** 78 m. from Bombay (bus and train), scenery and climate are enjoyable, especially in September. A visit to the Karli Cave can be combined with a trip to Khandala; but this is best reached from Lonavla (see below).

There are excellent metalled roads up both Ghats, and motor-cars find no difficulty in making the ascents. The main road to the Bhor Ghat (1830) goes from Thana by way of Mumbra Creek and Panvel (43 m.) to Khopoli (65 m. from Bombay) and Khandala (71 m.). There are a few hairpin bends, but the majority of the turnings are on the right. For the Thal Ghat the best route is to proceed about 8 m. from Mumbra along the road to Panvel and then to take the Kalyan road (which turns off to the left) to Bhiwandi (6 m. from Kalyan). Here the main road to Igatpuri and Masik is met.

(5) **Matheran,** by rail to Neral station (Central Railway), 54 m. from Bombay, thence by pony or steam tramway, 13 m. (see Route 23, p. 428). Fine views of Bombay.

(6) **Karli Cave,** reached from Lonavla station (R.), 80 m., or by road (168 m.) from Bombay (see Route 23).

(7) **Poona** by the Deccan Queen, Poona Express and other trains, 119 m. from Bombay (see Route 23, p. 432). The former Mahratta capital.

ROUTE 2

BOMBAY TO CALCUTTA by **Kalyan, Nasik, Manmad, Jalgaon** (Caves of Ajanta), **Bhusawal, Khandwa, Itarsi, Piparya** (for **Pachmarhi**), **Jabalpur** (for the **Marble Rocks**), **Katni, Manikpur, Allahabad, Moghul-sarai** (for Benares), and thence to **Asansol** and **Howrah** *via* (*a*) Grand Chord, by **Gaya** (Buddh Gaya) and **Parasnath,** and (*b*) main line by **Arrah** and **Patna.**

Rail 1349 m. to Calcutta. Electrified for 276 m as far as Bhusawal.

For continuation to N. India, see Route 9.

Fares[1]—Luggage—free, 120 lb., 60 lb. and 30 lb.; halve those figures to obtain seers, the Indian standard of weight. Surcharge for air-conditioned coaches. The 85 m. between Bombay and Igatpuri should be passed in daylight.

On leaving Bombay, between Sion and Kurla, the railway passes on a causeway from the island of Bombay to the larger island of Salsette. There are four tracks as far as Kalyan.

10 m. **Kurla** station. Close by (right) are cotton-mills, the first started. The Vehar Lake can be visited from here. The first electric railway in India was opened from bombay to Kurla, for suburban traffic, in 1925.

17 m. **Bhandup** station for the N. shore of the Vehar Lake.

21 m. **Thana** (pop. 170,000 in 1971) station (D.B., and a *dharmsaal* for Indians). The railway to this point was the first opened in India (1853). An early Portuguese settlement, com-

[1] The railway time-tables should be consulted. Thos. Cook & Son issue sixty-day tickets allowing break of journey at any station *en route*.

manding the most frequented route from the mainland to the island of Salsette. Marco Polo (1298) wrote: "Tana is a great kingdom, lying towards the West. . . . There is much traffic here, and many ships and merchants frequent the place." In 1320 four Christian companions of Friar Odoricus suffered martyrdom here. Friar Jordanus narrates that he baptised about ninety persons ten days' journey from Thana, besides thirty-five who were baptised between Thana and Sopāra.

The country round Thana was highly cultivated, and was studded with mansions of the Portuguese, when, in 1739, it was wrested from them by the Mahrattas. In 1774 the Portuguese sent a formidable armament from Europe with the avowed object of recovering their lost possessions. The Government of Bombay determined to anticipate their enterprise, and to seize the island for the English. A force was prepared under General Robert Gordon, and Thana was taken after a siege of three days. On 6th March 1775 the Pretender Peshwa Raghoba, by the Treaty of Surat, ceded the island of Salsette in perpetuity. Although this treaty was annulled next year by the Treaty of Purandhar, the possession of Salsette was confirmed.

In 1816 Trimbakji Danglia, Minister of Baji Rao II, the last Peshwa, effected his escape from the fort of Thana, though guarded by a strong body of European soldiers, only to be recaptured in 1818. The difficulties of this escape were greatly exaggerated; it was compared to that of Sivaji from the power of Aurangzeb. The principal agent in this exploit was a Mahratta syce who was in the service of one of the British officers of the garrison, and who, passing and re-passing Trimbakji's cell, sang the information he wished to convey in a careless manner, which disarmed suspicion.

The **English Church** was consecrated by Bishop Heber on 10th July 1825. In the 16th century the Silk Industry here employed about six thousand persons. It is now believed to be confined to one family.

34 m. **Kalyan** Junction (R.). Here the line to Madras through Poona and Raichur branches off S.E. (Route 26). This is a very ancient town. In 1780, the Mahrattas having cut off the supplies from Bombay and Salsette, the Government of Bombay determined to occupy the Konkan opposite Thana as far as the Ghats. Accordingly several posts were seized, and Kalyan amongst them; and here Captain Richard Campbell was placed with a garrison. Nana Farnavis forthwith assembled a large force to recover Kalyan, on which he set a high value, and attacked an English advanced post at the Ghats, and killed or made prisoners the whole detachment. He then compelled Ensign Fyfe, the only surviving officer, to write to Captain Campbell that, unless he surrendered, he would put all the prisoners, twenty-six in number, to death, storm Kalyan, and put all the garrison to the sword. To this Campbell replied that "the Nana was welcome to the town if he could take it". After a spirited defence he was relieved by Colonel Hartley, on the 24th May, just as the Mahrattas were about to storm. The remains of buildings round Kalyan are very extensive; and Fryer, who visited the place in 1673, "gazed with astonishment on ruins of stately fabrics, and many traces of departed magnificence".

Between Kalyan and Igatpuri the railway (completed 1865) ascends from the Konkan to the Deccan plateau by the mountain pass known as the **Thal Ghat.**

50 m. **Vasind,** alt. 178 ft. The incline up the Thal Ghat commences. Most beautiful in September with masses of wild flowers: the country below the Ghats is inundated, and the Ghats themselves are all cascades and torrents.

59 m. **Atgaon** station, for Tansa Lake (p. 112).

75 m. **Kasara** station (R.), 970 ft.

above the sea. Here the steeper ascent of the Ghat begins. In 9 m. the line (opened 1865) ascends 1050 ft. higher from Kasara to Igatpuri. There are ten tunnels of an aggregate length of 2281 yd., five viaducts and eleven bridges.

At 79½ m. was the reversing station, now avoided by a realignment. The Ehegaon Viaduct is 182 ft. above the valley. The ascent terminates at 85 m., **Igatpuri** D.B. (R.).

Igatpuri, properly Wigatpura, "the town of difficulties", so-called on account of the precipitous road, is a sanatorium, 1900 ft. above the sea, and summer resort of people from Bombay. Half a mile from the station a picturesque lake supplies Igatpuri and Kasara with excellent water. The line to Manmad was opened in 1861, the rails having been carted up the Thal Ghat before the work there was finished. To the S. can be seen the peak of Kalsubai (5427 ft.), the highest mountain in the State, and Sivaji's hill-forts of Alang, Bitangad, Aundha and Arr.

91 m. Ghoti. The Wilson dam (270 ft. high) is 21 m. S. (Permits to visit from Hydraulic Engineer, Bombay Corporation.) The Darna river dam, an important irrigation work finished in 1912, is 2 m. from Asvali station (101 m.).

113 m. **Deolali** station. During both world wars this served as a transit camp for troops arriving from or proceeding to Europe. It is also a hill-resort much patronised by Parsis and others from Bombay.

117 m. **Nasik** Road station* D.B. The town, the *Nasika* of Ptolemy, 2000 ft. above sea-level, lies 5 m. N.W. of the station. A tramway and taxi-cabs convey passengers. The Security Printing Press (1925), the Currency Note Press (1928) and a Police Training College are large establishments. The Western India Golf-course at Nasik is a favourite resort for the residents of Bombay. There is accommodation at the Club-house for bachelors and also for married couples. Visitors belonging to recognised clubs are eligible for temporary membership. The climate is equable and pleasant. There is a motor ramp at the railway station.

Nasik (pop. 176,000 in 1971) is a very holy place of the Hindus, owing to its position on the banks of the sacred River Godavari (the Ganges of the Deccan) about 19 m. from its source at Trimbak, and may be called the Western Benares. The sanctity of the river was revealed by Rama to the Rishi Gautama.[1] The Godavari and the Ganges are said to issue from the same source by an underground passage.

Many hundreds of families of Brahman priests reside here. Hindus of rank on visiting it leave a record of their visit with their Upadhya, or "family priest", for each noble family has such a priest at each celebrated place of pilgrimage. In this record are entered the names of the visitor's ancestors, and thus the pedigree of every Hindu chief is to be found in the keeping of these Upadhyas. Even Sir Jang Bahadur (1816-77), the *de facto* ruler of Nepal, had his Upadhya at Nasik. One of the Baroda family owed his succession to this, for when, in 1874, the Gaekwar, Malhar Rao, was deposed, and an heir sought for, the family Upadhya at Nasik supplied proofs of the young prince's legitimate descent from Pratap Rao, brother of Damaji II, the third Gaikwar.

At Nasik the river, here 80 yd. broad, is lined on either side with flights of steps, and dotted with temples and shrines, and the view along the banks when hundreds of men and women are bathing is extremely picturesque. The part of the town which stands on the right bank of the river is built upon three hills, and is divided into the **New Town** N. and the **Old Town** S. The quarter on the left bank, where are the chief objects of interest, is called *Panchavati*. The manufacture of brass and copper

[1] A Kumbh Mela (p. 125) is held here every twelfth year.

ware, especially of idols, caskets, boxes, chains, lamps, etc., flourishes here. Specimens of the beautiful old work may occasionally be found in the "old" copper bazar.

The temples of Nasik, though picturesque, have no striking architectural features. The **Sundar Narayan Temple** stands at the head of the Ghats on the W. side of the city, close to the Sati gate and ground, and is a miracle of art. A marble tablet over the E. doorway records that it was built in 1756 by one of Holkar's Sardars. The cost of the temple and the flight of 68 steps which lead to the river is said to have been about 10 lakhs. Once a year, on the Kartik full moon (November-December), the temple and steps are brilliantly lighted. Below the temple may be seen the temples of *Balaji* and of the *White Rama*, and the *Memorial*, erected to the Raja of Kapurthala, who died in 1870, near Aden, on his way to Europe. The river is then crossed by the Victoria Bridge, completed in 1897.

Half a mile to the W., on the Panchavati side, is a fine house of the Rastia family. From here a walk a few hundred yards up a lane leads to five very old and lofty banyan trees (*Ficus Indica*). Under the largest is a small building which marks the entrance to the **Sita Gupha,** or Sita's Cave. The cave was Sita's hiding-place, and it was from here that Ravana, disguised as a religious mendicant, carried her away to Lanka (Ceylon). Near the cave is the great temple dedicated to **Kala Rama,** or "Black Rama". It stands in an oblong stone enclosure, with ninety-six arches. To the W., up stream, and just before reaching the river side, is the oldest temple in the place, **Kapaleswar,** "God of the Skull", a name of Siva. The ascent to it is by fifty stone steps. It is said to be six hundred years old, but there is no Nandi bull in front. Opposite to it the river foams and rushes in a rocky bed. Rama is said to have passed his long banishment at Nasik. **Rama Kund** is the place where the god is said to have bathed; hence it is specially sacred, and ashes of the dead are taken there to be washed away. Down the stream, are three temples erected by Ahalya Bai of Indore (p. 53). One is a large square building, with a stone foundation and brick superstructure, dedicated to Rama; N. of it is a long dharmsala. About 200 ft. down the stream is **Naru Sankar's** temple, with an elaborately carved portico and a large stone enclosure; this is the last of the temples at the water's edge on the Panchavati side.

At the E. end of the city on the S. bank is the hill of **Sunar 'Ali,** and another called **Junagarh,** or Old Fort, on which is a square building in which Aurangzeb's chief officials used to reside. They command fine views over the city. W. of these are the **Jami Masjid** and the **Sarkar Wada,** an old palace of the Peshwas (Chief Ministers), at present used for Government offices. Its beautiful carved woodwork has been removed; but there are other fine examples in the town.

Sharanpur ($1\frac{1}{2}$ m.) once the seat of the mission founded by the Church Missionary Society in 1835, in the Junawadi part of Nasik, and removed here by Mr W. S. Price in 1855. Connected with this mission was an African Asylum for youths rescued from slavery, and from here Livingstone's *Nasik boys* were drawn. It was closed in 1875, and the boys were taken to the E. coast of Africa. A new church was built in 1898.

5 m. to the S.W. of Nasik, on the Bombay road, is a group of twenty-three Buddhist (Hinayana) Caves, called **Pandu Lena,** dating from the 1st century B.C. to the 2nd century A.D., and some of which were altered in the 6th or 7th century A.D. They are on the easternmost of the three conical peaks which form the extremity of the Trimbak range. The caves include three large viharas or halls, and one fine chaitya or chapel, and are excavated at the back of a terrace 350 ft. above the level of the

plain. The path to the caves,[1] which are numbered from W. to E., reaches the terrace about the middle of them.

Nos. 3, 10 and 18 are the most interesting. No. 3 is a large vihara, measuring 41 ft. by 46 ft. and having a stone bench and eighteen cells round the sides and end walls. In the veranda, behind a decorated screen rail, are six octagonal pillars, each carrying four elephants, or bullocks or horses, on their capitals; and above these is a frieze of rail pattern, with a band of animals at the bottom of it. The sculptured door leading into the cave resembles the gateways of the Sanchi tope (p. 217); over it are the three Buddhist symbols of the Bodhi tree (p. 131), the dagoba or tope, and the chakra or wheel of the law, and on each side of it is a guardian dwarpal. In the centre of the end wall of the cave is a large relief of a dagoba. The details of this cave and of No. 10 are almost identical, but the latter is of much earlier date; the carved screens and rail patterns in both of them are specially noticeable.

The vihara No. 10 measures 43 ft. by 45 ft.; it dates from shortly after the Karli Cave (p. 429), and the carving in it is much more graceful and pleasing than that in the copy of it, No. 3.

No. 18 is the Chaitya Cave, oldest and nearly contemporary with the Karli Cave. The front, which is decorated with Buddhist railings, dagobas, serpents and chaitya windows, is extremely effective; the elaborate carving in the head of the doorway under the great window, which is finished with a representation of wooden beams, simulates the wooden framework with which such windows were once fitted. The interior measures 39 ft. by 22½ ft. by 23¾ ft., and is divided by two rows of five plain octagonal columns into a nave and two aisles; at the end of the nave five more columns run round the back of a dagoba 6¼ ft. high and 5½ ft. diameter.

No. 20 is the third largest vihara, measuring from 37½ ft. to 44 ft. across and 61 ft. deep. The veranda is carried by four octagonal columns, with bell-shaped capitals. On either side of the hall are eight cells, and in the end wall are three cells and an antechamber, from which two more cells open; all three walls are faced by a low bench. The antechamber to the shrine has two carved columns; the door of the latter is flanked by two gigantic dwarpals. Inside it is a colossal seated image of Buddha, 10 ft. high, attended by two *chauri*-bearers.

The other caves, which have not been described, contain little of interest, or have been damaged. There are cisterns on the terrace, which affords beautiful views of the country round Nasik.

On the road to **Trimbak** from Nasik (18 m. W. by road) are several stone-faced wells, and at Prayag Tirth, on the right of the road, is a beautiful tank lined with stone, with two small pagodas built by Ahalya Bai of Indore. Near Anjaneri two conical hills, about 900 ft. high, face each other on either side of the road. From these the hills run in fantastic shapes to Trimbak, where they form a gigantic crescent from 1210 to 1500 ft. high. Below this mountain wall, which has near the top a scarp of about 100 ft., is the small town deriving its name from *Tri*, "three" and *Ambak*, "eye", "the three-eyed" being a name of Siva. The **Fort** stands 1800 ft. above the town, and 4248 ft. above the sea.

The **Temple of Trimbakeswar,** E. of the town, not far from where the Nasik road enters, was built by Balaji Baji Rao, third Peshwa (1740-1761). It stands in a stone enclosure, which has no corridor, but a portico, which is the music gallery, and is 40 ft. high. The ascent is by steps

[1] The account of these caves is taken mainly from the monumental work on the *Cave Temples of India*, by Fergusson and Burgess, published in 1880 but still not superseded. Those who are specially interested in the subject will find the original work indispensable.

outside, and non-Hindus are permitted to mount in order to look into the interior of the temple, which none but Hindus may enter. A flight of six hundred and ninety steps up a hill at the back of Trimbak leads to the sacred source of the River Godaveri, where "the water trickles drop by drop from the lips of a carven image shrouded by a canopy of stone" into a tank below. This is the sacred bathing-place of pilgrims, and is called the Kusháwari. The Sinhast festival lasts for 13 months once every 12 years. Bathing is said to cleanse from the worst sins. At the S. end is a temple to Siva.

147 m. **Lasalgaon,** Chandravati, overhung by a fine hill-fort, alt. 3994 ft., commanding a pass into Khandesh, is 14 m. N. by a good road. The Holkar family of Indore were hereditary castellans of the fort, which was taken by the British in 1804, and again in 1818.

156 m. *Summit* station, on the watershed of the Tapti basin flowing into the Arabian Sea and the Godavari flowing into the Bay of Bengal.

162 m. **Manmad** (Manmar) Junction, D.B. (R.), for the Dhond and Manmad chord line between the N.E. and S.E. branches of the Central Ry. The Godavari Valley branch (1900) of the former Hyderabad State Ry. (metre-gauge) runs from here to Daulatabad and Aurangabad (for the Caves of Ellora) and to Secunderabad (Route 4). About 4 m. S. are the Ankai Tankai Forts, now in ruins, and seven Buddhist caves of some interest. Between the caves and the station rises a curious hill called Ram Gulni ("one finger" hill), surmounted by a natural obelisk of trap rock 80 or 90 ft. high.

204 m. **Chalisgaon** Junction, headquarters of the West Khandesh District, acquired from Holkar by the Treaty of Mahidpur in 1818. At 7 m. is a bridge over the Girna river, on a branch (35 m.) at **Dhulia** (pop. in 1971 137,000) (D.B.), which is connected by a motor service with Nardana (District Bungalow) on the Tapti Valley railway, 20 m. N. along the Agra road. The Tapti is crossed at Savalda by a bridge (1932). 110 m. from Dhulia, on the same road, is Kalghat (Inspection Bungalow), on the Narbada, which is crossed by a road-bridge 2269 ft. long (toll).

232 m. **Pachora** Junction. N.G. branch to Pahur (25 m. for Ajanta Caves) and Jamner (35 m.).

261 m. **Jalgaon** (pop. in 1971 106,000) Junction for Ajanta Caves (Route 3). Headquarters of the East Khandesh District, also acquired from Holkar in 1818. The railway to this point was opened in 1862. Formerly the haunt of aboriginal hill-tribes and wild tribes, it has become a prosperous and fertile cotton-growing district, with cotton-gins and presses, and cotton-spinning mills. But in the hills that enclose it on the N., E. and S. tigers and leopards were once plentiful, along with sambhar and spotted deer. There are several advanced educational institutions in the city. A civil Hospital was erected by public subscription in memory of King Edward VII. Connected with it is a District Nursing Association, with a capital, publicly subscribed, of Rs. 80,000, to supply nurses to this hospital and to district dispensaries.

From Jalgaon a branch (1900) runs to Amalner and joins the Tapti Valley railway (p. 243). At 3 m. is a bridge over the Girna river.

Amalner Junction, 35 m. W. from Jalgaon. Terminus of the Tapti Valley railway from Surat (160 m.). Amalner has a High School and an Institute of Philosophy, also a cotton-mill: an important commercial centre.

276 m. **Bhusawal** Junction (R.). (Insp. Bung. available with permission of the Asst.-Collector, E. Khandesh, Jalgaon; no servants or supplies.) An important railway colony and Junction for the Nagpur Branch (Route 7).

A through carriage is run daily from Bhusawal to Surat, *via* Jalgaon and Amalner (on the Tapti Valley railway, see above) in connection with the Howrah-Bombay mail *via* Nagpur.

N. of Bhusawal the railway (1866) passes between the Satpura and Vindhya ranges on the W. and the Mahadeo Hills on the E.; these ranges constitute the geographical divisions between Hindustan (N. India) and the Deccan or South-country.

279 m. the **Tapti Bridge,** 2556 ft. long (1872). The first bridge built was abandoned in consequence of the inferior nature of the stone of which it was constructed. The Tapti drains Berar and the Satpura range. There is a causeway for road traffic down-stream.

310 m. **Burhanpur** (pop. 105,000 in 1971) station (3 m. to town) on the Tapti river road to Amraoti. There is a very fine D.B. in the Imad Shahi Palace, part of which has been restored. Burhanpur has been a place of much importance, and was fortified by the first Asaf Jah in 1731. The neighbourhood contains several Muslim ruins and a curious aqueduct still in use. In the town are two handsome mosques—the Jami Masjid and the Bibi Masjid. The *Badshahi Kila*—a ruined citadel and palace—is on a bluff overlooking the Tapti river. The Mughal water-works were constructed for the most part between 1618 and 1650.

Founded in 1400 by Nasir Khan of the Farrukhi Dynasty of Khandesh, the city was annexed to the Mughal Empire by Akbar in 1596. It was the capital of the Deccan province of the Empire when in 1614 Sir Thomas Roe, ambassador from James I to "The Great Mogul", passed through, and paid his respects to the Viceroy Prince Parviz, son of Jahangir, and it was near here at Zainabad that Shah Jahan's wife, the "Lady of the Taj", died in 1629 (see p. 301). In 1635 the seat of government was transferred to Aurangabad (p. 151), but between 1720 and 1728 it was the headquarters of the Nizam Asaf Jah. It was occupied by the British under General Wellesley on 16th October 1803, given back to Scindia the next year, but was transferred again to the British in 1860.

The principal handicraft is the production of silk cloths embroidered with gold and silver lace, in the same manner as described by Tavernier in 1658. It is also the centre of a gold and silver wire industry, the drawing of which can be seen by arrangement. Vines planted by Aurangzeb still produce grapes.

322 m. from Bombay is **Chandni** station, 7 m. from **Asirgarh** (R.H.), conspicuous from the railway, standing at an elevation of 2300 ft. above sea-level. Visitors should make prior arrangements through a Government Tourist Office for food and accomodation. The ascent is long, and involves a climb of well over 1000 ft. The fortifications and gateways are in a good state of preservation. The walls were breached (W. and E.) and the fort captured on 21st October 1803 by Colonel Stevenson, and again taken on 9th April 1819 by Generals Doveton and Malcolm. It was formerly an important fort, being on the main line of communication between the West and the centre of India. Until 1904 it was garrisoned, but the barracks were later dismantled, and some interesting cannon were removed to Nagpur. At certain seasons the fortifications are beset by wild bees, which are very dangerous if disturbed by voice or movement.

339 m. **Dongargaon,** watershed of the Tapti and Narbada basins.

353 m. **Khandwa** Junction station, D.B. (R.). A civil station (Ratagarh on a ridge N.E.), the headquarters of the District of Nimar in Madhya Pradesh, the former Central Provinces, Khandwa was created a municipality in 1867. From here the metre-gauge system of the Western Railway runs N. to Mhow, Indore, and through Western Malwa to Ajmer, and thence to Agra, a favourite route. (See Routes 8 and 10.) A new metre-gauge line also joins the Manmad-Secunderabad line (Route 4) at Purna making

it the only connection between the northern and southern metre-gauge systems. The town is supplied with water from Mohghat reservoir (4 miles). Khandwa is a place of considerable antiquity, traditionally surrounded by the Khandava forest of the Mahabharata. Four kunds or small tanks, with stone embankments, have been constructed round the town in the direction of the four points of the compass. On the bank of each tank is a temple, but only one of them is in use. The Padma (Lotus) Kund has an inscription of 1132. One of the temples at Rameswar has the appearance of a cave.

417 m. **Harda** station, D.B. good. An important mart for the export of grain, cotton and seeds. Here the railway enters the great wheatfield of the Narbada Valley, which extends to Jabalpur. A good road, starting from Harda, leads to Indore, crossing the Narbada river at Handia (Fort).

464 m. **Itarsi** Junction, D.B. (R.). The Central Ry. broad-gauge line to Delhi (Route 9) runs N. *via* Bhopal (p. 216), Bina (junction for Katni, p. 222), Jhansi (branch 137 m. to Kanpur), Gwalior (p. 231) and Agra (p. 299). A branch to Nagpur (186 m.) from Itarsi runs S. through Betul, opened for through traffic in 1924 (p. 194). From Amla Junction (81 m.) a b.g. branch goes E. (54 m.) to join the n.g. system at Parasia through the Chhindwara coalfield.

The Betul District is cool but formerly malarious: the elevation varies from 1500 to 2200 ft. In the E. and S. the Mahadeo hills are higher, the Khamla plateau in the S.W. corner being 3787 ft. above sea-level. The open tract lies in the centre of the District, and grows wheat as its chief crop; surrounding this tract the country is very broken and clad with forest. The Tapti, Narbada and Wardha rivers have sources at the top of the plateau, and find their way to the plains below through rocky valleys, often of great beauty. The heavy forest in the outlying portions of the district still provides some big-game shootings, though it is hard to reach, owing to the broken character of the country. The small-game shooting is poor. Thirty-six per cent. of the population of the District are aboriginals.

Betul, 67 m. from Itarsi (D.B.), is connected with Ellichpur, Chhindwara, Itarsi and Nagpur by metalled roads. Along all these roads there are good rest houses, or inspection bungalows, 8 or 10 m. apart, but they are in charge of *chaukidars* only, and visitors must arrange to bring their own supplies with them. The only complete D.Bs. are at Shahpur (on the Itarsi road), at Multai (on the Nagpur road) and at headquarters.

The district is well worth a visit, if only for its scenery; the steep sections, where the railway enters and leaves the plateau, afford a most pleasant prospect, especially at the end of the rains or in the early cold weather.

505 m. from Bombay on the line to Jabalpur, **Piparya** station. There is a comfortable D.B. close to the station. A good road leads in 32 m. S. to **Pachmarhi**, the hill-station of Madhya Pradesh. The station is 3500 ft. above sea-level. There is a D.B. at Singanama (19 m.); the ascent from here, which is 12 m. long, is very pretty. Some big-game shooting in the forests below the station may still be had by special arrangement with the Forest Department. Motor-cars are available at Piparya (Pachmarhi Motor Service Company), and single seats in cars, mail bus and motor-lorries; time about three hours. There is a Pachmarhi Hotel (a converted D.B.) close to the Club, and boarding-houses. The scenery is very fine, and there are numerous roads and drives leading to view-points such as the Bee Falls.

A visitor would do well to take his own car. Accommodation is strictly limited. The local *Pachmarhi Guide* may be consulted.

On the S. edge of the Pachmarhi plateau is **Chauragarh**, a square-headed bluff which rises to 4385 ft.

in the Mahadeo Hills. It is reached through a ravine past the Cave of Mahadeo, where a spring flows from beneath an archway 300 ft. within the hill. The place is thronged in February and March by pilgrims, who usually take the S.E. route from Chhindwara.

Between 590 m. **Bikrampur** and 597 m. **Bhitoni** the railway crosses the Narbada river. The first bridge, which was built in 1863-65, was washed away by heavy floods on 21st September 1926: and the present bridge was opened for traffic in June 1928. It consists of six spans of 169 ft. from centre to centre of the steel trestle piers, and two spans of 40 ft. also on steel trestles at either end. The whole of the steel, amounting to about 2800 tons, was supplied from Messrs Tata's works at Tatanagar (p. 200).

616 m. **JABALPUR** (Jubbulpore) (pop. 533,000 in 1971), 733 m. from Calcutta by Allahabad route (R.). An important civil and military station, established 1819. A n.g. railway runs to Nainpur Junction (whence there are branch lines running W. to Seoni and Chhindwara and E. to Mandla), 69 m. S. of Jubbulpore, and 73 m. farther on to Gondia Junction, on the old Bengal-Nagpur line (p. 196). The town is about a mile from the railway station and divided from the cantonment on the S. by the railway. The Great North Road from Nagpur to Mirzapur has been diverted to a submersible bridge at Tilwaraghat, 4 m. lower down the Nerbudda from the old ferry. This bridge is 1222 ft. long, with six main arches of reinforced concrete and 98 ft. clear span, completed in 1932. The Gandhi and Nehru memorials are near the N. end of the bridge. The n.g. railway bridge (p. 195) is nearly 3 m. above the ferry.

Jabalpur (1318 ft.) ranks as the second city in Madhya Pradesh. Water is plentiful near the surface, and the climate is comparatively cool. The town and station are well laid out and well cared for. The Victoria Town Hall has a statue of Gandhi. There are Protestant and Roman Catholic Churches, six High Schools and three colleges, Training College and Robertson College (founded at Saugor in 1836, and transferred here in 1873), and the Hitkarni College in the city. It was formerly an important military centre, and the British Government located their great gun-carriage factory there, 1 m. N.E. of the railway station. Close to the railway station is a well-furnished *dharmsala*, named after the late Raja Gokuldass, whose statue is placed in front of the building. The Rani Durgavati Museum is worth a visit.

During the British administration of India few incidents carry more dramatic interest than the suppression of the **Thags** (*Thugs*), a fraternity devoted to the murder of human beings by strangulation. The principal agent in hunting down these criminals was Colonel Sleeman,[1] appointed 1829, and it was at Jabalpur that a number of Thag informers and their families were formerly confined, and the once-famous "School of Industry" was established in 1836 by Captain Low. Originally there were 2500 of these people in confinement here. The "School" was closed in 1889, and is now used as a Reformatory School for boys and as an Industrial School, where carpentry and other crafts are taught.

The **Marble Rocks**, known to Indians as Bhera Ghat, are 13 m. from Jabalpur. About 4½ m. to the W. is a remarkable ancient fortress of the Gond Kings, known as the Madan Mahal, which is perched on the summit of a huge granite boulder. At 9½ m. a branch road turns to the rocks. On the high ground above the lower end of the right side of the gorge are two small D.Bs., and 100 yd. beyond the bungalow is a flight of

[1] Colonel Sir W. Sleeman's *Rambles and Recollections of an Indian Official* and *Diaries of a Journey in Oudh* lately reprinted by Cambridge University Press are among the most fascinating books ever written on India. Meadows Taylor's *Confessions of a Thug* is the finest of all his writings although he took no part in Sleeman's work.

107 stone steps which leads to the *Madanpur Temple* (Chausath Yogini), surrounded by a circular stone enclosure. All round it are figures of the sixty-four Joginis, much mutilated. Three-quarters of a mile beyond the temple hill the Narbada may be reached above the gorge at the point where its waters plunge down the Dhuandhar or Smoke Cascade into the cauldron at the upper end of the Marble Rocks. In a recess below the bungalow is the embarkation place for a trip by boat up the gorge. Two men to row and one to steer are required. The white cliffs of magnesian limestone are only 90 ft. to 105 ft. high, but the effect of the gleaming faces and rifts is extremely picturesque, especially under moonlight; the water is said to be 150 ft. deep in places. Near the entrance to the gorge, which is about 1 m. long, is a spot named the "Monkey's Leap". Farther on, to the right, is an inscription cut by order of Madho Rao Peshwa (1761-72), and near the end of the gorge are some curiously shaped rocks called the *Hathi ka paon*, or Elephant's Foot. The gorge is closed by a cascade waterfall over a barrier of rocks. There are usually large nests of wild bees on the rocks, and care must be taken not to shout, smoke, or shoot. Near the landing-place is a memorial of a young engineer officer who was drowned in seeking to escape the attack of infuriated bees.

640 m. from Bombay, **Sihora Road** station.

At **Bahuriband** (17 m. N.W.) is a Jain statue 12 ft. high. This place is believed to be the Tholobana of Ptolemy. Many ruins of temples are found here. A Sati pillar, dated 1298, may also be seen.

At **Rupnath,** 3 m. from Bahuriband and about 19 m. from Sihora Road railway station, there is a rock edict of the Emperor Asoka, engraved about 232 B.C. It is the oldest of the known inscriptions, and the only one of its kind in Madhya Pradesh.

673 m. **Katni** Junction for the loop (210 m.) from Itarsi (p. 120), *via* Bhopal (p. 216), Bina and Saugor (p. 222); branch S.E. to the coal-fields at *Umaria*, 36 m., and thence to Bilaspur (197 m.) (p. 198). Katni, near the source of the Son river, is famous for the manufacture of lime and cement and the preparation of stone slabs.

At **Bilahri,** 8 m. S.W. of Murwara, which adjoins Katni Junction, images and sculptured stones are scattered all about the village and built into the houses, but few temples now remain. A small fort was partly destroyed during the rising of 1857.

At **Bargaon** (6 m. from Salaiya station, 33 m. from Katni, on the Katni-Bina line) is a temple dating from the 5th or 6th century A.D. Several other ruins—Brahmanical and Jain—are about a mile to the W.; on the banks of the Katni river are more remains. The stones are beautifully carved.

734 m. **Satna** station (R. and Govt. D.B., *Hotel Park*). When in the former Rewa State, Satna was the headquarters of the Baghelkhand Political Agency. A good motor road runs E., connecting to the Great Deccan Road (21 m.), whence **Rewa** (31 m., altitude 1042 ft.) can be reached.

To the W. is a motor road which passes through Panna, Khajuraho (p. 227), Chhatarpur, Nowgong and Jhansi. The scenery in the Kain Valley is striking. Near Satna were found the remains of the Bharhut stupa (180 B.C.), removed to the Calcutta Museum in 1876. At Bandhogarh, S. of Rewa, 23 important inscriptions (A.D. 200-400) close a gap in Indian history.

782 m. **Manikpur** Junction station. From this place a branch of the Central Railway, formerly the Indian Midland Railway, runs W. (1889) to Jhansi, 181 m. (p. 223).

840 m. **Naini** Junction (R.). Close by is the **Jail,** one of the largest in India; there are also a Leper Mission and Asylum here. The former East

Indian Railway reached here in 1864. 2 m. farther the line crosses the Jumna by a bridge (14 spans of 205 ft. and 3 of 30 ft., opened 1865), and enters

844 m. **ALLAHABAD*** (alt. 312 ft.), 512 m. from Calcutta, one of the largest towns in Uttar Pradesh (pop. 513,000 in 1971), railway centre; Bamrauli Airport; seat of a famous University and a High Court (established 1866). It is situated on the left bank of the Jumna, on the wedge of land between it and the Ganges.

The Fort stands near the junction of the two rivers. The Civil Station, Cantonments, and City stretch W. and N.W. 6 m. from this point. The present Fort and City were built by Akbar in 1583, but the Aryans inhabited a very ancient city here called Prayag, which the Hindus now call Prag (place of sacrifice). It is a very sacred place with them, as they believe that Brahma performed a Horse Sacrifice here, in memory of his recovering the four Vedas. The merit of almsgiving to Brahmans is enhanced a thousandfold if the gift is made at Prayag.

In A.D. 643 Hiuen Tsang, the Chinese pilgrim, visited and described the town. It was first conquered by the Muslims in 1194, under Shahab-ud-din-Ghori. It received the name of Allahabad in 1584, and was made the capital of a Province. At the end of Akbar's reign Prince Salim, afterwards the Emperor Jahangir, governed it and lived in the Fort. Jahangir's eldest son, Khusru, rebelled against him, but was defeated in 1606 and put under the custody of his brother Khurram, afterwards the Emperor Shah Jahan. Khusru died in 1622, and the *Khusru Bagh* (see below) contains his mausoleum. In 1739 Allahabad was taken by the Mahrattas, under Raghoji Bhonsla, who held it till 1750, when it was sacked by the Pathans of Farrukhabad under Nawab Ahmad Khan. Clive met the Emperor Shah Alam here in 1765 and concluded a treaty by which the diwani (revenue-collection) of Bengal, Bihar and Orissa was granted to the E.I. Company.[1] In November 1801 it was ceded by Saadat Ali Khan, Nawab Wazir of Oudh, to the British.

Allahabad was the headquarters of the Government of the N.W. Provinces from 1834 to 1835, when the Lieut.-Governor moved to Agra. In 1858, Lord Canning's famous Durbar was held here, after the suppression of the Mutiny, when Queen Victoria's memorable Proclamation of 1st November, announcing the transfer of the government of India from the E.I. Company to the Crown, was read. It then again became the seat of the N.W.P. administration. In 1902 the N.W. Provinces and Oudh were amalgamated as the United Provinces of Agra and Oudh under a Lieut.-Governor, who was replaced in 1920 by a Governor. They are now termed Uttar Pradesh, with the capital at Lucknow. The first Indian National Congress was held in Allahabad in 1885, Allan Hume, I.C.S., presiding.

The **Khusru Bagh,** close to the railway station on the S. side, is entered by an old archway, nearly 60 ft. high and 46 ft. deep, overgrown with creepers. Within the garden are three square mausolea. That (domed) to the E. is the tomb of Prince Khusru, son of Jahangir. W. of it is the grave of a sister of his, and W. again that of his mother, a Rajput lady. They are shaded by some fine tamarind trees. The interior of the mausoleum of Khusru is ornamented with many Persian couplets, and with paintings of trees and flowers, which are now faded. The cenotaph of white marble is on a raised platform, without inscription. To the right and left two of Khusru's sons are buried. All three monuments have been put into a thorough state of conservation. E. of the gardens lie the main bazars.

[1] A picture commemorating this historic event may be seen in the Victoria Memorial Hall at Calcutta (p. 178).

On the N. side of the railway lie the **Civil Lines,** an old European quarter, laid out amongst a network of wide avenues. Just to the N. of Alfred Park is the Municipal Museum, established in 1931. The museum contains a remarkable collection of great archaeological value from Bhita. The terracotta collection, in particular, is unique.

The museum also houses a collection of a Russian, Prof. Nicholas Roerich's original paintings, and in another, the paintings of Prof. Asit Kumar Haldar. The coin cabinet of the museum is notable for ancient Indian coins. There is a lovely Children's Park just opposite the Municipal Museum.

The **High Court** and **All Saints' Cathedral,** in the 13th-century Gothic style, 225 ft. long by 40 ft. broad, built of red and white stone, are N. of the railway station. The throne is a memorial of Bishop Johnson of Calcutta and Metropolitan of India (1876-98). Depredators have removed a fine organ. St Joseph's, the **Roman Catholic Cathedral,** in the Italian style, with the Bishop's Palace, a Convent and Boys' and Girls' Schools, finely laid out, are W. of the Alfred Park, and near by is the **Club.** There is also the Macpherson Park in Cantonments. Anand Bhawan, formerly the home of the Nehru family, is now a museum devoted to the life of Nehru.

In the Alfred Park is the **Thornhill** and **Mayne Memorial,** with a fine Public Library. It commemorates two former Commissioners of the Allahabad division. A marble figure of Queen Victoria, seated under a canopy, was removed from the Park in 1957. Beyond the park is the Circuit House, with pictures belonging to Begum Samru from Sardhana; and to the N. of the Alfred Park is the **Muir College,** in the Saracenic style, with a tower 200 ft. high. Close by, to the W., is the *Mayo Memorial Hall,* with a tower 180 ft. high. The University (now residential) was founded in 1887.

Holy Trinity Church is opposite the University Buildings, near Prayag railway station. It contains a tablet in memory of those who perished in the Mutiny; another commemorates four officers of the Buffs who were killed or died during the Gwalior campaign of 1843.

8 m. W. is the important **Bamrauli** Aerodrome.

Canning Road and Fort Road lead to the Fort, built by Akbar in 1583; it looks impressive from the river. The principal gateway is capped with a dome and has a wide vault underneath it. The walls are from 20 ft. to 25 ft. high; below them is a moat which can be filled with water.

Asoka's Pillar.—In front of the gateway inside the Fort is the Asoka Pillar, which rises 35 ft. above ground. Of stone, highly polished, it is of much interest. It was probably brought here from Kaushambi (p. 125) by Firoz Shah Tughlaq, but some say by Akbar. It was found lying on the ground in the Fort in 1837, and was then re-erected. On it are inscribed the famous Edicts of Asoka (issued about 242 B.C.); a later record of the victories (about A.D. 340) of Samudragupta (*c.* A.D. 326-375) and an inscription by Jahangir (1605-27), to commemorate his accession. There are also minor inscriptions, beginning almost from the Christian era. According to James Prinsep (p. 177), who deciphered this and other Asoka inscriptions in 1838, the pillar was lying on the ground when some of the inscriptions were cut. Check with the Local Military Authority whether access to this and to the **Zenana building** of the old Palace, enclosed by the Arsenal, is possible. "A square hall, supported by eight rows of columns, eight in each row, thus making in all sixty-four, surrounded by a deep veranda of double columns, with groups of four at the angles, all surmounted by bracket capitals of the most elegant and richest design, and altogether as fine in style and as rich in ornament as anything in India."[1] Attached to the Fort is a powerful Wireless Installation.

The **Akshai Vata or undying banyan.**—Hiuen Tsang, the Chinese pilgrim (A.D. 629-45), who visited *Prayag* 643, gives a circumstantial description of the undecaying tree. In the midst of the city, he says, stood a Brahmanical temple, to which the presentation of a single piece of money procured as much merit as that of a thousand pieces elsewhere. Before the principal room of the temple was a tree surrounded by the bones of pilgrims who had sacrificed their lives there.

The tree is situated under the wall of the Palace, and is reached through a small door in the E. wall of the Fort. Close by is a deep octagonal well flanked by two vaulted octagonal chambers. A few steps lead to a dark underground passage, which goes 35 ft. straight to the E., then S. 30 ft. to the tree. As no tree could live in such a situation, the stump is no doubt renewed from time to time. Some images are ranged along the passage. In the centre of the place is a Lingam of Siva, over which water is poured by pilgrims. General Cunningham, in his *Ancient Geography of India,* gives an interesting sketch of the probable changes in the locality, and concludes: "I think there can be little doubt that the famous tree here described is the well-known Akshai Bat or undecaying banyan tree, which is still an object of worship in Allahabad".

The ramparts at the N.E. side of the Fort afford a view of Tribeni Ghat, the **Confluence of the Ganges** which is 1½ m. broad, flowing from the N., with the **Jumna,** ½ m. broad, flowing from the W., and the mythical Saraswati. The shallower and more rapid Ganges is of a muddy colour, the Jumna is bluer with a deeper bed. The **Magh Mela,** a religious fair of great antiquity, is held at Tribeni every year, between 15th January and 15th February, when thousands of pilgrims flock to Allahabad to bathe at the junction of the sacred rivers: and every twelfth year the festival is known as the **Kumbh Mela.** Kumbh Melas are held in succession every three years at Hardwar (p. 365), Allahabad, Nasik (p. 115), and Ujjain (p. 207). At one of them, early in February 1954 at Allahabad, some 350 people were killed and 1000 injured by a stampede towards the water. The auspicious day is known as the Amáwas.

W. of the Fort is the Minto Park, with the memorial (1910) of the Royal Proclamation of the assumption of the rule of India by the British Crown It consists of a stone *lat* (pillar), which used to have medallions of Queen Victoria, King Edward VII, and King George V, surmounted by four lions bearing the Imperial coronet. A King George V Memorial was unveiled in 1939. Farther W. upstream of the railway bridge over the Jumna is the Ewing Christian College of the American Presbyterian Mission.

The Akbar **Band** runs N.E. from the Fort to Daraganj. Here the railway line to Benares crosses the Ganges by the Izat bridge of 40 spans of 150 ft. each, to Jhusi. N. of the old Cantonment the railway to Jaunpur (p. 373), Fyzabad, and Lucknow crosses the Ganges by the Curzon Bridge (15 spans of 200 ft.).

There are roadways on the Jumna and Curzon railway bridges, by which motors can pass. The Izat bridge has no roadway, but a new road bridge now replaces the old pontoon one.

The following routes run from Allahabad: (1) To Benares, 78 m., and 45 m. on to Ghazipur; (2) to Jaunpur, 57 m., Fyzabad, 99 m. and Lucknow, 141 m.

Kaushambi can be identified with the ruins existing at Kosam, 38 m. from Allahabad up the River Jumna in the Allahabad District. It can now be reached by bus. A place of great

[1] *History of Indian and Eastern Architecture,* by J. Fergusson, J. Burgess and R. P. Speirs, 2, 298.

antiquity, it is commonly known from the Pali Canon as a Buddhist town and the Capital of King Udaya, a contemporary of Buddha, who flourished in the 6th century B.C. and was a direct descendant of the Pandavas. References to the city of Kaushambi are to be found in the Epics and in the Puranas.

Near the village of Kosam are remains of the high bastions and the earthen ramparts of an immense fortress with a circuit of a little over 4 m. The ground inside the fort, which is now cultivated, is thickly strewn with old brickbats, the remains of the ancient city of Kaushambi. The chief object of archaeological interest inside the ruined fort is a highly polished Asoka pillar with its top broken and capital missing. As it stands now it measures nearly 23 ft. Unfortunately no inscription of Asoka is to be found on it, although it contains a number of inscriptions ranging from the age of the Guptas to the present day.

Pabhosa. About 2 m. W. of Kosam is the Pabhosa Rock, which contains important rock inscriptions. Even today Pabhosa is a place of pilgrimage for the Jains.

Bhita is 11 m. by road S.W. of Allahabad, and on the opposite side of the Jumna. Excavations, conducted by Sir J. H. Marshall, while Director-General of Archaeology, showed that Bhita was the site of a settlement from prehistoric ages, and that it was a fortified city from the Mauryan (321-184 B.C.) down to the Gupta (A.D. 320-455) period, when it appears to have been given over to jungle tribes who were still in the neolithic state of culture.

Arrow-heads of iron, and numerous sling or catapult balls of stone, marble and earthenware have been found within the walls, the balls ranging in dates from the 7th or 8th century B.C. to the later Gupta period (A.D. 455-606). Nearly all the interior of the fort so far excavated is occupied by bazars and houses of considerable size divided up into well-defined blocks by roads and narrow alleys.

The latest buildings, of the later Gupta period, are characterised by the smallness of their rooms and the poorness of their construction. Below these come structures of the early Gupta or still earlier Kushana (A.D. 45-225) period, which are largely constructed out of the remains of earlier structures, which, forming the third stratum, belong to times preceding the Kushana dynasty; while the fourth and the lowest series of houses belongs to the period of the Mauryas.

Floors of well-made concrete and of burnt clay occur in the lower strata, which must go back at least some seven hundred or eight hundred years B.C., and associated with them are well-made vessels of grey and red pottery (frequently covered with a black metallic glaze), terra-cotta figurines, roof finials, and the like. Thus, even in those early ages, the culture represented here was considerably advanced.

Among the antiquities (in the Museum) the most noteworthy are: seals of ivory, bronze and stone, and clay impressions, which furnish the names of the householders and of the places and people with whom they were in correspondence; coins of the Kushan Emperors of the North, of the Andhras of the South, and of the kingdoms of Avanti, Kausambi and Ajodhya; terra-cotta statues and figurines, well-finished in colour, which portray in detail the costumes of the time; copper and earthenware vessels of manifold shapes and various fabrics; goldsmiths' utensils; toilet boxes of steatite and marble, personal ornaments of many kinds; to which may be added also a number of celts and stone implements belonging to jungle tribes who occupied the deserted site.

Garhwa is the name given to a walled enclosure surrounding a group of temples, in a depression among low hills. It is 5 m. from Shankargarh, the headquarters of the Raja of Bara, which is at 26 m. from Allahabad on the Jabalpur road. About 2 m. of this road just preceding Garhwa is not motorable. There are images of Brahma, Vishnu and Shiva, as well as those of the ten incarnations of Vishnu in the Hindu mythology. The ruins of the big temple in the centre are supported by 16 stone pillars with beautiful carvings on them. Several inscriptions here indicate that most of these buildings were built in the days of Chandra Gupta II, but there are also inscriptions to indicate that this place was famous even before the 1st century B.C.

On the west of the ruins of the fort is a big tank about 600 ft. long, known as Garhwa Tal.

Jhusi is on the Benares Road immediately across the Ganges from Allahabad. It was the capital of Chandravanshi kings of ancient days and is mentioned as Pratishthanpur in the sacred books of the Hindus. It was an important town even in the days of the Gupta dynasty (A.D. 320-445), and there is still a big well, known as Samudra Koopa, believed to have been constructed by the famous King Samudra Gupta. In 1830 an inscription on a copper plate was found here (now at Calcutta). South of Samudra Koopa is the tomb of a Muslim saint Sheikh Taqui. It was built in 1384, and a fair is still held there every year.

Main Line

At 856 m. the Tons river is crossed by a bridge 1194 ft. long (1864).

892 m. from Bombay, 458 m. from Calcutta, **Mirzapur** (pop. along with Vindachal 105,000 in 1971) station (D.B. and P.W. Insp. Bung.). Before the opening of the old East Indian Railway it was the largest mart on the Ganges for grain and cotton; it is still a commercial centre of importance. There are excellent sandstone quarries near, on which Government levies a royalty. Mirzapur is noted for its brass industry and for its hand-made woollen carpets and rugs, dyed with traditional vegetable dyes, which are permanent. Shellac is prepared from stick-lac at eighty factories and large quantities of Bengal silk are absorbed for distribution in Upper India. There is a handsome river front, with ghats and temples, containing some beautiful carvings. The Civil Station is to the N.E. of the city. 6 m. from the town is the deserted Cantonment of Tara where there is a fine waterfall of 60 ft. caused by the descent of a rivulet from the plateaux of the Vindhya range.

A National Highway runs from Nagpur to Allahabad *via* Mirzapur and Rewa. At Vindhachal station, 4 m. W. of Mirzapur, is a Kali temple which used to be a rendezvous of the Thugs.

438 m. from Calcutta, **Chunar** has an old Fort on a hill (400 ft. high and 2 m. from station), commanding the Ganges. The Emperor Humayun (1530-56) took it in 1537, but Sher Shah Sur, the Afghan, recaptured it shortly after, and strengthened himself against Humayun. It was recovered by Akbar in 1575, and remained with the Mughals till 1750, when it passed into the hands of the Nawab Wazir of Oudh. The British stormed it after the battle of Buxar in 1764. To this fort Warren Hastings retreated from Benares in 1781, after Raja Chait Singh's rebellion. The tomb of Iftikhar Khan, a Governor in Jahangir's reign, is here. There is a stonework screen round the mausoleum of Shah Kasim Suleimani, which stands in a durgah, or walled enclosure. Up to 1860, Chunar was the station of the European "invalids" who had enlisted for 21 years, or for life. Heber mentions meeting one of them in 1824 "who had fought with Clive". After that it became a residence of Anglo-Indian pensioners and then a Reformatory for boys. There is an Inspection Bungalow in the Fort under the control of the Executive Engineer, Allahabad.

418 m. from Calcutta, **Moghul Sarai** Junction (R.) for **Benares Cantonment** station, 10 m. distant (Route 5), across

the Ganges, crossed by the Dufferin Bridge (p. 163).

(a) *By Grand Chord from Moghul-Sarai to Asansol* via *Gaya, Parasnath (for Parasnath Mountain) and Sitarampur.*

From Moghul Sarai the Bombay mail train to Calcutta follows the Grand Chord route through Gaya to Asansol (opened 1906).

The Karamnasa river is crossed (see p. 132).

386 m. from Calcutta and 32 from Moghul Sarai, **Bhabua Road** (Inspn. Bung.); 10 m. to the S. is Bhabua (Inspn. Bung.) and 5 m. to the S.W. of Bhabua is the ancient Hindu temple of Mundeswari, on the summit of a hill 600 ft. above sea-level; an inscription dates it to A.D. 635. 8 m. S. of Bhabua are immense earthwork fortifications. They enclosed in a valley an ancient town, the only remains of which are broken bricks covering an area of about 2 sq. m.; the foundations of the houses are still below the soil. 6 m. to the W. of Bhabua is **Chainpur**, once an extensive town. There is a fort built by Raja Salivahan, whose descendants reside now at Bhagwanpur, 6 m. S. of Bhabua. The fort is now a famous place of pilgrimage, owing to a Brahman priest having done "dharna" or fasted till he died in protest against an injustice. A short distance to the W. is the mausoleum of Bakhtiyar Khan, a noble of the time of Sher Shah; it is similar to those in Sasaram, standing in an enclosed courtyard. Scattered over all this part of the country are the remains of old forts, attributed to the Savars or Suiris, an aboriginal people. They consist of high mounds of earth, on which used to be situated the house of the local chief, the whole being surrounded by a deep moat. 15 m. N.W. of Bhabua Road station is **Baidyanath** (popularly, Baijnath), containing traces of early and mediaeval Brahmanical buildings. It is believed to have been the centre of the Savar kingdom.

372 m. from Calcutta, **Kudra** (D.B.). 16 m. to the S. is the hill-fort of Shergarh, on a small plateau about 800 ft. in height. It was fortified by Sher Shah, and a palace, still in a fair state of preservation, was built on the summit. 8 m. farther S. into the hills are the caves of Gupteswar, several hundred feet in length.

356 m. **Sasaram** Junction (D.B.), The name Sahasram (Sahasra Arjunpura) is said to be derived from Arjuna, a chief with a thousand arms, cut off by Parasu Rama. A view can be had from the train of the reddish stone mausoleum of Sher Khan Sur (*d.* 1545), the Afghan ejector of Humayun, on a terrace approached by a bridge in a tank 1000 ft. square. The height from the floor to the apex of the dome is 101 ft., the total height above the water being over 150 ft.; the dome has a span of 72 ft. In the town is the mausoleum of his father, Hasan Sur Khan, killed at Kalinjar; in an enclosed courtyard, and about a mile to the N.W. is the tomb of his son, Salim Shah, which was intended to be larger than his father's, but was never completed; it also stands in a tank. In a small cave just below the summit of a hill rising above the town is an Asoka inscription dating back to 232 B.C. A n.g. railway (61 m.) runs from Sasaram to Arrah (p. 133) and connects the Grand Chord with the main line.

345 m. from Calcutta, **Dehri** (D.B.). Here the River Son is spanned by a girder bridge (opened in 1900), with 93 spans of 100 ft. each, the total length being 10,052 ft. Above the bridge the Grand Trunk Road crosses the river, and higher up are the headworks of the Son Canals, consisting of a dam 2½ m. long, with main canals on either side, also generating electricity for tube wells. The Grand Trunk Road crosses the Son by a new road bridge at Barun (2 Inspn. Bungs.). A n.g. railway runs from Dehri up the river to Rohtas station, 24 m., overlooking which is the ancient hill-fort of **Rohtas** (Inspn. Bung.) occupying a plateau 4 m. by 5 m. and 1500 ft. above sea-level.

The fort was impregnable, being surrounded for the greater part by sheer precipices 500 ft. to 1000 ft. in height, with the few comparatively vulnerable points protected by strong defensive works consisting of double and triple lines of ramparts and bastions. It is of very ancient origin and was taken from its Hindu ruler by Sher Khan Sur in 1539 by means of a stratagem. Man Singh strengthened the fortifications in 1607: but it was surrendered to Capt. Goddard in 1764 without a fight. A Mughal Palace in an excellent state of preservation is entered from the W. through a great courtyard. The ascent should be made in the cool of the evening, but care should be taken to arrive at the D.B. on the plateau at the top before sunset (drinking-water and provisions should be taken).

342 m. **Son East Bank** station. A line runs to Daltonganj, extended as the Central India Coalfields Railway in December 1928 to Barkakana, where it meets the b.g. line from Kharagpur *via* Muri Junction, 36 m. by n.g. railway from Ranchi, the former summer headquarters of the Bihar Government (Route 7).

292 m. from Calcutta, **Gaya** (D.B. about 1 m.; R. room at station) a city of 179,000 inhabitants in 1971, nearly all Hindus. A motor service runs between Gaya and Ranchi *via* Hazaribagh. There is an aerodrome on the Indian Airlines route.

The district of Gaya, which was included within the ancient kingdom of Magadha, contains many places of great sanctity. The name Gaya is said to have been the name of an Asura, or heavenly being, so holy that all who saw or touched him were admitted to heaven. The rocky hills abound in remains, sculptures, images and sites of the religion of Buddha, many diverted to Hindu worship.

The **Barábar** Caves (the "Marabar" Caves of E. M. Forster's *Passage to India*), 16 m. north of Gaya, and 6 to 8 m. E. of Bela railway station, on the Patna-Gaya line are very old (264 and 225 B.C.) and dark. Two of the caves have tablets recording their dedication by Asoka himself to the Ajivakas, a sect of Brahman ascetics devoted to Narayan, a form of Vishnu.

Gaya is visited by two or three hundred thousand Hindu pilgrims yearly. From all parts of India they come to pray to preserve their ancestors from torment by a recognised tour of pilgrimage of which Gaya is the centre. There is a lengthy legend to the effect that Vishnu promised that the rock on which the old town now stands should be known as *Gaya-kshetra*, and that whoever offered funeral cakes (*pindas*) and performed the *sradh* ceremonies there should be translated with their ancestors to the heaven of Brahma. The pilgrim, before leaving his home, must walk five times round his native village, calling upon the souls of his ancestors to accompany him on his journey. There are forty-five places within an area of 35 sq. m. at which pilgrims should offer funeral cakes, but they usually visit only seven and often only three of the forty-five. Arrived at Gaya, they are forthwith placed in charge of a special Brahman guide, and have to bathe in the sacred streams of the Phalgu and the Pūnpūn. *Pindas* are offered on Ramsila hill, which adjoins the town on the N. and also on Pretsila, the Hill of Ghosts (541 ft. high), 5 m. N.W.

The centre of the pilgrimage is the **Vishnupad Temple** in the old portion of the town, approachable only on foot, owing to the extreme narrowness of the streets. As it is not easy to find, previous intimation should be sent to one of the leading Gayawals (the hereditary priests of the temple), who will, as a rule, most courteously supply a guide. Visitors must remove their shoes if they wish to enter the inner temple.

The present temple, built about the year 1787 by Ahalya Bai, ruler of Indore (p. 53), is a solid structure of grey granite; the main building is a *mandapa* or open hall, 58 ft. square, supported on eight rows of pillars in two storeys, and covered in the centre by a dome. The sanctum has an octagonal tower, 100 ft. high, with a pyramidal roof, which culminates in a single pinnacle surmounted by a large gilded flag.

Within the sanctum is an octagonal basin, 4 ft. in diameter, inserted into the pavement and plated with silver, which surrounds the impress on the rock of the god's foot. The **Vishnupad** (*Footmark of Vishnu*) is about 16 in. long, and 6 in. broad. Flowers and other offerings are made to it. Immediately in front hangs a bell presented by Ranjang Pande, minister of the Raja of Nepal (1838-43), and at the entrance to the sanctum is a second bell bearing an inscription in English: "A gift to the Bishnupad by Mr Francis Gillanders, Gya, 15th January 1790". Gillanders was the Government Collector of the Pilgrim Tax, and died in 1821: his grave is in the old cemetery at the foot of Ramsila Hill.

S. of the temple, almost touching it, is a pillared hall or porch, with the pillars let into the solid rock, where the pilgrims assemble before making the round of holy places. In a small shrine on the way to the temple, is the figure of an elephant plucking flowers and fruit, which can be dated to the beginning of the Christian era.

N. of the Vishnupad is a temple with a statue of the Sun God: his seven horses driven by Arjun are on the pedestal. It stands to the W. of the Surajkund Tank.

Half a mile to the S.W., immediately under the Brahmajuni Hill, is the *Akshai Vata* (cf. p. 125) or undying banyan tree, at which the pilgrims make their final offerings to the Gayawals and conclude their pilgrimage.

The so-called Gaya black stone is carved into ornaments, bowls and figures of gods and animals. A popular type of bowl shows Basudeva carrying the infant Krishna in his arms; when the bowl is filled slowly, the water runs away without wetting the feet of Krishna.

(Bodh) **Buddh Gaya** (taxis and bus service from Gaya: G. of I. Tourist Board Travellers' Lodge, P.W. Inspn. Bung., State Rest house, Tourist Information Centre) is 7 m. S. of Gaya. There is a good metalled road leading up to it. The **Temple,** of great antiquity, is closely connected with events of the life of Buddha. The shrine is now administered by a friary of Hindu Saivite sannyasis, established at the end of the 16th century. The building, which in its main features represents the structure seen by Hiuen Tsang in A.D. 635, consists of a main tower, 180 ft. high, in the form of a truncated pyramid, with a finial springing from a platform, at the corners of which are four similar smaller towers.

The entrance is on the E., and on the altar at the W. wall of the sanctum is a large gilded image of Buddha, which is worshipped by the community as an incarnation of Vishnu. The original figure of Buddha, which, according to Hiuen Tsang, was of perfumed paste, was destroyed centuries ago. The Temple is built over an earlier temple erected by Asoka.

Much of the stone railing, once believed to be associated with Asoka, but now known to be of Sunga date, has been restored. It has four bars of stone, supported by pillars at intervals of 8 ft. The top rail is ornamented with carvings of fish-tailed women inserting their arms into the mouths of Makaras—that is, mythical crocodiles with large ears like those of elephants and long hind legs. Below this top bar are three others, also of stone, ornamented with carvings of lotus flowers. The pillars are adorned with carvings of various groups—such as a woman and child, a man with a woman who has the head of a horse, centaurs, and so on. Twenty-three of the pillars were found by Lord Curzon in the Hindu Mahant's residence, where they were serving as supports to an interior arcade, and were restored at his instance. Many of the pillars are now in the archaeological museum near the site. Casts have been put in their place.

The plinth of the temple is 26½ ft. high, and at the top is a space 13 ft.

broad, which allowed a passage round the tower. At each corner of the platform was a small temple, and outside the rail (erected during the Sunga period, 184-72 B.C.) were many subordinate temples. Adjoining the N. side of the Temple is a long wall bearing 19 lotus pillars, marking the spot where Buddha paced up and down for seven days wondering whether he should reveal his knowledge to the world. A few yards to the W. of the W. wall of the temple is the famous pipal tree, known as the Bodhi tree, under which the Buddha received enlightenment. Under the tree is a red sandstone slab, the Vajrasan or diamond throne, which is reputed to be the centre of the universe. Round the temple in the sunken courtyard are ranged a number of *stupas*—votive offerings by Buddhist pilgrims.

A Burmese inscription records a restoration in 1306-1309. In 1877 permission was granted for a further restoration; but Raja Rajendralal Mitra, who was deputed by the Local Government to inspect their work, stated that "the Burmese carried on demolitions and excavations which in a manner swept away most of the old landmarks". As a result of this investigation, a third restoration was undertaken by the Government, and completed in 1884. The model used was a presentation in stone of the temple as it existed in mediaeval times.

To the N.W. is a small but very ancient temple, in which is a figure of Buddha standing. The doorway is finely carved. A remarkably beautiful image of Buddha, brought from Japan, is now accommodated in a lovely modern Japanese temple, the ceiling of which is covered with fine paintings of birds and botanical subjects. There are also large Thai and Tibetan temples in their national styles.

At 290 m. from Calcutta the Phalgud river is crossed.

At 251 m. **Gujhandi** is the watershed of the Ganges and Barakar river basins.

245 m. **Kodarma** is noted for its mica mines. It has a motor service (42 m.) to Hazaribagh.

215 m. **Hazaribagh Road** (D.B.). There is a motor service to Hazaribagh town (42 m.) and (58 m. farther on) Ranchi (p. 201). Hazaribagh can also be reached in 2 hours by a motor service from Sarak on the Gomoh-Daltonganj line.

Hazaribagh* (2013 ft. above sea-level, with a peak of 2817 ft.) does not mean 1000 tigers or gardens, but takes its name from Hazari, residence of the Zamindars of Ramgarh from 1772. Hazaribagh National Park is a favourite resort, with sambhar, spotted deer, nilghai, and other fauna, and a great variety of bird life. There is a Tourist Lodge and a canteen, and a Forest Rest House (apply to Divisional Forest Officer, Hazaribagh). The district was formed in 1834 out of the "conquered provinces" of Ramgarh. During the last war, Hazaribagh became a centre for the training of Chinese forces. St Columba's College and Zenana Hospital are under the University of Ranchi. From Hazaribagh the tourist can visit the great **Damodar Valley Project Area,** with impressive dams and power plants.

198 m. **Parasnath** station, for **Parasnath Mountain,** 13 m. N.E. along a motor road to Madhuban at the foot and to the R.H. (poorly serviced) at the top. To the summit of the mountain the distance is 5½ m.; the journey, which occupies 2¾ hr., is made on foot or by chair and bearers.

The mountain can be reached from Nimiaghat station (193 m. from Calcutta). There is a D.B. on the Grand Trunk Road, close to the foot of the mountain, 1 m. from Nimiaghat and about 3 m. from Parasnath. The khansamah can send supplies up the mountain. Information should be given beforehand to the sub-Inspector of Dumri Police Station for bearers. **Dumri** (D.B. with two servants), which is 203 m. from Calcutta by the Grand Trunk Road, is 2 m. from the railway. The Howrah-Dehra Dun expresses stop at Parasnath at night.

The journey can be broken at Dhanbad, where there is a refreshment room.

This far-famed place of pilgrimage is 4479 ft. above sea-level (temple spire 4569 ft.) and is the Eastern metropolis of Jain worship. According to tradition, Parasnath, who was the 23rd Tirthankar (deified saint) of the Jains, was born at Benares, lived 100 years, and was buried on this mountain. The temples are of no great antiquity.

At Madhuban, 1230 ft., are the local headquarters of the Digambara and Swetambara sects of Jains. The most prominent Jains met with in Bengal are the Marwaris, whose home is in Rajputana.

The ascent of the mountain is up a pathway worn by the feet of innumerable pilgrims from all parts of India. Ten thousand still visit the place annually. The path leads through woods with large clumps of bamboo over slatey rocks of gneiss, much inclined and sloping away from the mountain. The view from a ridge 500 ft. above the village is superb. Ascending higher, the path traverses a thick forest of *sal* (*Shorea robusta*), and other trees spanned with cables of *bauhinia* stems. At 3000 ft. the vegetation becomes more luxuriant, and the conical hills of the white ants disappear. At 3500 ft. the vegetation again changes, the trees becoming gnarled and scattered. The traveller emerges from the forest at the foot of a great ridge of rocky peaks, stretching E. and W. for 3 or 4 m.

On the saddle of the crest (4230 ft.) is a small temple, one of the many which occupy prominences on the ridge, with a beautiful view. To the N. are ranges of low wooded hills, and the Barakar and Adjai rivers. To the S. is a flatter country, with lower ranges and the Damodar river.

The twenty-four Jain temples commemorate the attainment of Nirvana (the cessation of individual existence) by the twenty-four deified saints recognised by the Jains. The principal temple is below the saddle in a hollow facing the S., surrounded by groves of plantain and *Ficus indica*. It contains little but the sculptured feet of Parasnath and some marble cross-legged figures of Buddha, with crisp hair, and the Brahmanical cord.

The railway crosses the Damodar river (cf. p. 131) to, 187 m. from Calcutta, **Gomon,** junction for the line to (46 m.) Adra; (97 m.) Bankura; (142 m.) Midnapur; and (150 m.) Kharagpur Junction (Route 7, p. 411).

169 m. from Calcutta, **Dhanbad,** (pop. 433,000 in 1971), junction for Bhojudih on the Adra-Khargpur line (see above) and (31 m.) the Jherria coalfield (p. 137). A School of Mines was opened here as early as 1926.

143 m. **Barakar,** headquarters of the Bengal Steel and Iron Co., is on the Barakar river (bridge 1850 ft. long). The iron ore, a high-grade haematite, is obtained from the Pansira and Buda quarries in the Singhbhum district.

141 m. **Kulti,** another important industrial centre.

138 m. from Calcutta, **Sitarampur,** junction of the Grand Chord and the main line of the former East Indian Railway. Thence to Howrah (p. 187).

(b) *By the main line from Moghulsarai to Asansol,* via *Arrah, Dinapur, Patna and Mokameh.*

The Punjab mail (from Delhi) takes the old route (1862) from Moghul Sarai to Asansol.[1] Passing Dildarnagar, 434 m. from Calcutta (branch, 11 m.) to Tari Ghat, on the opposite side of the Ganges to Ghazipur (p. 393) the line, before reaching Chausa (418 m. from Calcutta), crosses the Karamnasa river ("destroyer of merit"), which divides Uttar Pradesh from Bihar (road bridge also). The water of this river, if it wets the feet of returning pilgrims washes away the merit gained by bathing in the Ganges at Varanasi.

411 m. from Calcutta, **Buxar**

[1] On the journey from Bombay to Calcutta the Mail train travels over the Grand Chord (see p. 128).

station (D.B.), famous for the great victory won on 23rd October 1764 by Major Hector Munro of H.M. 89th Highlanders against Shah Alam, the Nawab Wazir of Oudh, Shuja-ud-daula, and the ex-Nawab of Bengal, Mir Kasim—a battle of a much more serious nature than Plassey—which secured the English in Bengal. The resistance offered to Munro was of the most stubborn character, and a threatened defeat was turned into an unexpected victory at the eleventh hour. The losses of both parties were severe; 816 were killed and wounded on the British side, the enemy lost 165 guns, and their whole camp. The King, Shah Alam, then surrendered himself to British protection. Buxar is also of interest as a place of pilgrimage. The great Rama (the hero of the *Ramayana*) is said to have crossed the Ganges here on his way to Mithila (Darbhanga District) to marry Sita, and to have killed a huge demoness named Tarka.

391 m. **Raghunathpur**; about 3 m. from the station is a temple of Siva, near which a very large cattle fair is held every year.

369 m. from Calcutta, **Arrah** Junction (D.B.) in Shahabad District. Special interest for English visitors centres round the defence of the "little house at Arrah" against the mutinous sepoys of Dinapore, threatening Havelock's advance on Kanpur in 1857. It was held for a week during the hot weather by twelve Englishmen, supported by fifty Rattray's Sikhs, against a body of two thousand mutineers and a large mob, before being relieved by Major Vincent Eyre.[1] The house, now in the compound of the Judge, declared an historical monument by Lord Curzon, is in shape nearly a square, and has two storeys, with a veranda on three sides, supported by arches, which the besieged filled up with sandbags. The lower storey, which is little over 10 ft. high, was held by the Sikh soldiers.

[1] Sir George Trevelyan gave an account of the defence in his *Interludes in Verse and Prose.*

Arrah is on a branch of the *Son Canals,* the great irrigation work of South Bihar, designed by Lt.-Col. C. H. Dickens, R.E.

A n.g. railway from Arrah to Sasaram connects the Main line with the Grand Chord line.

360 m. **Koilwar.** The line crosses the Son river by a bridge of 28 spans of 150 ft. (opened in 1862). There is a roadway for motors under the up-track. At Maner, on the road to Dinapore, there is a perfect Muslim shrine (D.B. on the shore of a lake).

344 m. from Calcutta, **Dinapore** station; 6 m. to Dinapore Cantonment (D.B.), which is about 15 m. E. of the Son.

338 m. from Calcutta, Patna Junction* (R., 3 H., C.H., D.B., 12 rooms, close to the railway station), for **Patna New City** and **Bankipore.** New Patna, which stretches for 2 m. W. of Bankipore, is the headquarters of the Government of Bihar. The capital is well laid out. The airport at Patna is on the I.A.C. route from Delhi to Calcutta. Motorists travelling from Delhi, Agra and Varanasi to Nepal pass through Patna but are not advised to take the ferry crossing there. It is better to go *via* Bakhtiyarpur-Mokameh - Barauni - Samastipur - Muzaffarpur-Matihari to Raxaul on the Nepal frontier. This is 100 m. longer, but the road is new and good. (Note: a new road bridge across the Ganges at Patna which should alleviate these difficulties should be open by 1981).

Old Bankipore forms the western extremity of **Patna City** (station 6 m. E., 490,000 inhabitants in 1971), which covers 10 sq. m. and with its suburbs extends 9 m. along the S. bank of the Ganges. Round the Bankipore Maidan, a wide open space containing a race-course and golf-links, are large houses. The Protestant Church (Christ Church) dates from 1857. Near the river-bank to the N. are the Collectorate, Judge's Court, Bihar National College, Medical College and Hospital, Patna College (1837), Science and Training Colleges, Uni-

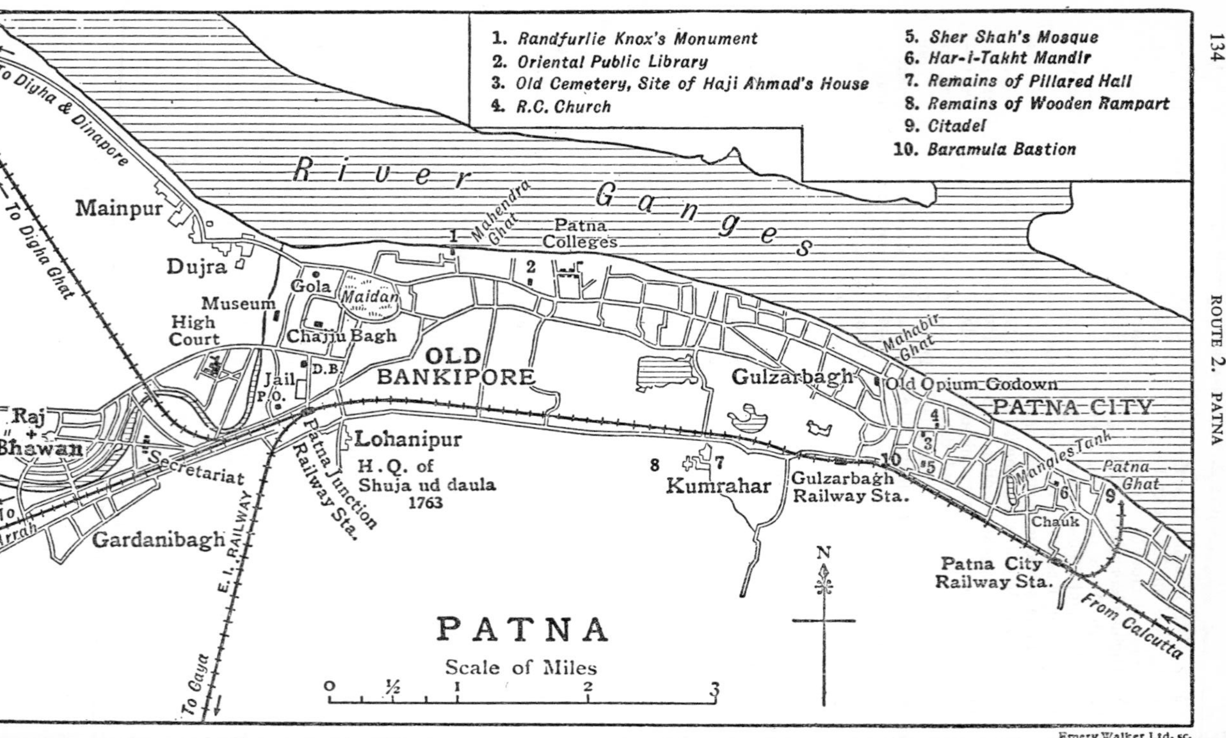
1. Randfurlie Knox's Monument
2. Oriental Public Library
3. Old Cemetery, Site of Haji Ahmad's House
4. R.C. Church
5. Sher Shah's Mosque
6. Har-i-Takht Mandir
7. Remains of Pillared Hall
8. Remains of Wooden Rampart
9. Citadel
10. Baramula Bastion
To Digha & Dinapore
To Digha Ghat
River Ganges
Mainpur
Mahendra Ghat
Patna Colleges
Dujra
Gola
Maidan
Museum
High Court
Chajju Bagh
OLD BANKIPORE
D.B.
Jail
P.O.
Mahabir Ghat
Gulzarbagh
Old Opium Godown
PATNA CITY
Raj Bhawan
Lohanipur
H.Q. of Shuja ud daula 1763
Secretariat
Patna Junction Railway Sta.
Kumrahar
Gulzarbagh Railway Sta.
Mangles Tank
Patna Ghat
Chauk
To Arrah
Gardanibagh
E. I. RAILWAY
N
Patna City Railway Sta.
From Calcutta
PATNA
Scale of Miles
0 ½ 1 2 3
To Gaya
Emery Walker Ltd. sc.

versity Senate House, Law College, the Bihar College of Engineering and the Khuda Bakhsh Oriental Library.

In the compound of the Judge's Court is a tall obelisk erected in memory of "the truly gallant Randfurlie Knox", who raised the siege of Patna by Shah Alam in 1760, after a memorable march of thirteen days from Burdwan, and died in 1764, after Major Andrews had restored order in the city.

The **Oriental Library,** founded in 1900 by Maulavi Khuda Bakhsh Khan Bahadur, is famous throughout the world for its collection of rare Arabic and Persian MSS and Mughal and Rajput painting; it possesses the only volumes saved from the sack of the Moorish University of Cordova.

The Golghar, at the W. corner of the Maidan, like a huge beehive, was built by John Garstin for a granary in 1786 "for the perpetual prevention of famine in these Provinces", but it has been used only occasionally. It is 426 ft. round at the base, built of brick, with walls 12 ft. 2 in. in thickness, the interior diameter being 109 ft. It is about 90 ft. high, and might contain 137,000 tons. Inside there is a most wonderful echo; the best place to hear it is in the middle of the building. As a whispering gallery there is perhaps no better building in the world. The faintest whisper at one end is heard most distinctly at the other. The ascent to the top is by steps outside. Sir Jang Bahadur of Nepal once rode a pony up the steps to the top.

The **Patna Museum,** near the Civil Court buildings, is famous for its Yaksi from Dadarganj (3rd century B.C.) and Kurkihar bronzes (11th-9th century B.C.)

3 m. E. of the Patna College is **Gulzarbagh** (station on the main line between Patna Junction and Patna City stations), the quarter in which the Opium Factory and storehouses were situated. Patna formed, with Ghazipur, the two agencies by which the Government monopoly of Bihar and Bengal opium used to be worked. This opium has been famous from time almost immemorial. The old opium godowns, which are on the river-bank and are surrounded by a high wall, are now occupied by the Government Press and a map-drawing office. They stand on the site of the old English Factory outside the W. wall. The Dutch Factory, at Choupar mentioned by Tavernier (1666), was ceded to the British in 1824.

On high ground ¾ m. W. is the Duchess of Teck Hospital (built 1893-1895), maintained by the Zenana Bible and Medical Mission and staffed by lady doctors and nurses.

E. of Gulzarbagh, on the main road, is the west gate of **Patna City** proper or Azimabad, as it is locally called, from the name conferred upon it in 1704 after the then Subadar, Prince Azim-us-Shan. Near the Chauk is the **Har Mandir Takht** or Sikh temple, built by Ranjit Singh, which marks the birthplace (1660) of the tenth Guru Govind Singh. In the temple, which forms one of the four sacred places of the Sikhs, are shown the Guru's cradle and shoes. A small Sikh community which is settled here, is strictly orthodox.

Half a mile W. is the old **Cemetery,** in a corner of which, by the City Dispensary, is an obelisk erected over the well in which the bodies were thrown of the sixty British captives[1] murdered at the instigation of Mir Kasim by Samru (p. 352) on 6th and 11th October 1763—a massacre avenged by storm by Major Adams, H.M. 84th Foot, a month later. The Dispensary is believed to cover part of the site of the house in which this took place. Opposite the cemetery is the **Roman Catholic Church** of the Blessed Virgin Mary, which was built in 1775; there are a number of old tombs in the graveyard.

[1] One of these, H. Lushington, aged only 26, who had already escaped from the Black Hole, slew three of his murderers before he was overpowered. A monument to his memory may be seen in the old Parish Church at Eastbourne.

Close by is a tank with a garden round it, known as Mangal Talao or the tank of pleasure, but in reality a corruption of the name of Mr Ross Mangles, V.C., the Collector, who had it excavated in 1875. S. of the main road is the Shikarpur quarter, with a mosque built by the Afghan Emperor Sher Shah (1540-45). The Citadel was in the N.E. corner.

The ancient city of Pataliputra (the Palibothra of the Greeks) lies buried from Patna city to Dinapore. It was the capital of Chandragupta (321-297 B.C.), Bindusara (297-274 B.C.), and Asoka (274-237 B.C.), and extended 10 m. along the river and 2 m. inland to the old bed of the Son. Excavations in the hamlet of Kumrahar, S. of the city, have disclosed the remains of a large pillared hall, which resembles the throne-room of Darius at Persepolis; and at Bulandi Bagh, ¼ m. W. of Kumrahar, a wooden structure has been found which is thought to be a wooden rampart mentioned by Megasthenes. To the N.W. of this site is Bhikna Pahari, an artificial mound about 40 ft. high which has been identified with the hermitage built by Asoka for his brother Mahendra, the apostle of Sri Lanka.

On the Patna-Gaya railway line is 7 m. **Punpun** station, on the banks of the river of that name. The waters are supposed to wash away sins: and pilgrims halt here to bathe on their way to Gaya (p. 129).

310 m. from Calcutta, **Bakhtiyarpur** Junction. There is a railway to Bihar Sharif and Rajgir Kund (33 m.). 6 m. S.W. of Bihar is the village of Bargaon (museum, R.H., I.B.) the site of the great **Nalanda** monastery—a most important ruin once populated by 10,000 monks and founded by Kumar Gupta (A.D. 427). Hiuen Tsang, the Chinese pilgrim (A.D. 629-645) resided here for five years. Burmese, Japanese, and Jains have rest houses. For further details consult the booklet published by the Archaeological Survey obtainable at the Nalanda Tourist Information Centre. The Rajgir hills are filled with Buddhist and Jain caves and remains. A hermitage of the Buddha is at Gridhra Kuta. **Rajgir,** the ancient Rajagriha (R.H., C.H., I.B., Youth Hostel)—Bus services from Patna, Gaya, and Nalanda: details from Information Centre Rajgir. Buddhist and Jain sites. A great tourist attraction, it was the capital of Bimbisara (p. 44).

The main stupa had corner towers and a Buddha image outside. The hot springs are mentioned in Buddhist sutras. On a cylindrical Motiyar Math are indications of snake worship. In a Satapain Hall mentioned by both Chinese pilgrims a synod was held on the death of Buddha.

283 m. from Calcutta, **Mokameh** Junction (R.). Line to the N. for Mokameh Ghat and Tirhut (p. 392). To the E. a loop-line (opened 1862) leaves the main line at (262 m.) **Lakhisarai** (Kiul) Junction (the bridge is 1458 ft. long), and runs along the banks of the Ganges *via* **Jamalpur** (branch to Monghyr), Bhagalpur, **Sahibganj,** and **Tinpahar** (see Route 19, p. 390) to **Khana** (see below), where it rejoins the main line.

201 m. from Calcutta, **Jasidih** Junction; branch (4 m.) to Baidyanathdham (Deogarh), whence motor service to Dumka, 41 m., also from Dumka to Rampur Hat, 39 m., on loop-line. Deogarh is a famous place of pilgrimage.

183 m. from Calcutta, **Madhupur** Junction (R.) for Giridih and the coalfield. Bengalis treat the upland country at Simultala, Jasidih, Deogarh and Madhupur on this route as a sanatorium.

138 m. from Calcutta, **Sitarampur,** junction with the Grand Chord line from Moghul Sarai (p. 127).

(c) *Asansol to Calcutta* (*Howrah*).

132 m. from Calcutta is **Asansol** (pop. 157,000 in 1971) (D.B.) Junction station (R.), with the coalfields line of the former Bengal-Nagpur railway (Route 7), and on the Grand Trunk

Road. In the vicinity are the iron and steel works built with British help at Durgapur (pop. 207,000 in 1971), and the locomotive factory and colony at Chittaranjan. Buses from Asansol to *Maithon* and *Panchet* the Damodar Valley Authority's biggest dams. (Pop. of Darg-Bilainagar 245,000 in 1971).

121 m. from Calcutta is **Raniganj** station (D.B.) on the E. edge of the great coalfields of Bengal and Bihar, which stretch out 384 m. to the W., and extend under the bed of the Damodar. The place was formerly the property of the Maharajadhiraj of Burdwan. The railway reached this point in 1855, and it was still the rail-head in 1857.

That coal existed here was known as early as 1800: "The coal of Bengal is all derived from the rocks of the Gondwana system, and is of the Permian age, or rather younger than the coal of England". The area of the Raniganj field is not less than 500 sq. m. Until 1905 it produced the largest outturn, but has since fallen behind the Jherria field, about 20 m. W. of the Raniganj field, which possesses many thick seams at shallow depths. These two fields, with the Giridih field, 30 m. N.W. of the Raniganj field, and the Bokaro-Ramgarh and Daltonganj areas, 10-30 m. W. of the Jherria field, account for 90 per cent. of the coal raised in India. The Parbelia colliery in the Raniganj field is 1500 ft. deep. The Raniganj and Jherria coals are liable to spontaneous combustion, and the mines to flooding in the rains. At Raniganj are Burn & Co.'s Potteries and the Bengal Paper Mills.

75 m. from Calcutta is **Khana** Junction for the loop-line (original main line) from Mokameh.

67 m. from Calcutta is **Burdwan** (pop. 144,000 in 1971) station (R.), D.B., headquarters of a District assigned to the British in 1761, and residence of the Maharajadhiraj of Burdwan, the descendant of a Punjab Kshatri, who settled at Burdwan soon after the place had been conquered by Prince Khurram, later the Emperor Shah Jahan, in 1624. Until the recent agrarian legislation, the head of the Burdwan family was the leading landholder in Bengal. Thara is a fine Palace. Permission to view the extensive gardens and the collection of pictures, which includes a striking portrait by Chinnery, two historical paintings by Tilly Kettle, and several Indian landscapes by Daniell, can be obtained on application to the Superintendent.

The "Star of India Arch", at the entrance to the town, was erected in commemoration of Lord Curzon's visit during his Viceroyalty. A bridge over the Damodar river connects with the Grand Trunk Road.

38 m. from Calcutta, **Pandua,** now only a small village, formerly the seat of a Hindu Raja and fortified by a wall and trench, 5 m. in circumference, of which traces are still to be seen. A five-storeyed tower, 120 ft. high, obviously built in imitation of the Kutb Minar at Delhi, with a court-house at its foot, is said to commemorate a victory of the Muslims over the Hindus in 1340. The mosque has 27 domes still upstanding, out of the original 63.

25 m. from Calcutta is **Bandel,** junction for the line to Naihati by the Jubilee Bridge (p. 190).

On the Barharwa-Bandel branch (distances given from Bandel, the junction) is

26 m. **Kalna.** A residence of the Maharajadhiraj of Burdwan, and formerly the port of Burdwan, on the River Bhagirathi or Upper Hooghly. Inspection Bungalow.

65 m. from Bandel, **Katwa.** At the junction of the Bhagirathi and Adjai rivers. Inspection Bungalow. There is a n.g. railway 32 m. to Burdwan.

Main Line

23 m. from Calcutta, **Hooghly.** The railway to this point was the first section of the old East Indian Ry, opened in 1854. 21 m. from

Calcutta, **Chandernagore** and 13 m. from Calcutta, **Serampore** (p. 187) stations. 6 m. from Calcutta, **Bally** station. From Bally Ghat to Dakhineswar, the Willingdon double-track bridge with roadway, built across the Hooghly river at a cost of 3 crores, connects to the Docks.

1349 m. from Bombay by the Grand Chord Route is **Howrah, Calcutta terminus,** on the west bank of the Hooghly river. (Route 6.)

ROUTE 3

CAVES OF AJANTA

The Ajanta caves are beyond question one of the most remarkable sights in India. Sir John Marshall, ex-Director-General of Archaeology, placed them, with the stupas of Sanchi (p. 217), amongst the noblest memorials of Buddhism in the country.

The most convenient way of visiting the caves of Ajanta and Ellora is to take the daily air service from Bombay to Aurangabad (see p. 151), a journey of some 80 minutes, and to make both excursions from there. For those who prefer rail travel, Jalgaon (p. 118), 261 m. from Bombay and 15 m. from Bhusawal, by the Central Ry. is the nearest main-line railway station for the Ajanta Caves. Jalgaon is 34 m. by road from Fardapur, and the Caves are 3 m. S.W. of Fardapur. From Aurangabad there are conducted bus excursions both to Ajanta and Ellora. Aurangabad has a Government-approved Hotel (The Aurangabad) and three other more modest hotels in Western style. At Jalgaon there are a Tourist Reception Centre (Nehru Chowk), Traveller's Bungalow, Holiday Camp, and some R.H. and I.Bs.

The caves can also be visited by car from Bhusawal and from Manmad Junction (Route 4). There is a regular bus service from Jalgaon Ry. Sn. to the caves, and the trip there and back can be done in one day. Cars can be ordered to meet at Pahur, and there is a service of motor omnibuses. Permission must be obtained from the Collector of East Khandesh, Jalgaon, to occupy the D.Bs., but a stay is not necessary. There are two D.B.s, a Travellers' Bungalow and a State R.H. (reservations from Executive Engineer B.C. Dept.) at Fardapur and a Holiday Camp (reservations from

Regional Tourist Officer). Catering is arranged at a daily rate all the year round.

The route from Aurangabad passes through the old town of **Ajanta** (5 m. S. of the caves), which is surrounded by a strong wall and a deep moat, completed in 1727 by the first Nizam. Ajanta Town is the place where Sir Arthur Wellesley halted after the battle of Assaye (23rd September 1803). A fine view can be had from the roof of the *baradari*, which was utilised as a hospital for the wounded.

From Aurangabad as a base (Route 4) the caves can also be seen in one day, another day being devoted to the Ellora Caves. The Ajanta Caves are 66 m. from Aurangabad, and the Ellora 27 m. At Ajanta there are Forest R.H., I.B. and Restaurant-cum-Retiring Rooms (Reservations from the Manager).

The **Caves of Ajanta,** unlike the majority of Buddhist caves, are excavated in amygdaloid trap rock in the scarped side of a deep ravine in the Indhyari hills, a crescent facing S.E. A stream (Waghora) flows down the ravine and ends abruptly in a series of seven waterfalls (Sat Kund), of which the last makes a leap of 70 or 80 ft. The view of the curved front of the caves, from the inner entrance to the ravine, is extremely picturesque.

The chapels and monasteries, discovered in 1819, date from about 200 B.C. to before the expulsion of Buddhism from India, i.e. about A.D. 650. They were visited by Hiuen Tsang about A.D. 640. They are therefore entirely Buddhist.

Historically, the twenty-nine caves are divisible into two main groups. Near the centre of the crescent are the five earliest (Hinayana, p. 32), Nos, 13, 12, 10, 9 and 8 in point of age probably of the 2nd and 1st centuries B.C. The second group in order of age is made up of Nos. 11 (possibly an intrusion or modifiedl ater), 14, 15, 16, 17, 18, 19 and 20; the last probably dating A.D. 580. Nos. 6 and 7 may have preceded 19 and 20. Nos. 1 to 5 on the E., and Nos. 21 to 29 on the W. of the crescent, may be referred approximately to the period between A.D. 500 and 650. Nos. 9, 10, 19 and 26 are chaityas or chapels, and the rest are vihara halls or monasteries. On a short visit Nos. 1, 10, 17, 26 will be found representative.

The Ajanta caves were discovered by British tiger-hunters. In 1849 copying began after the caves were systematically cleared and an attempt made to preserve the flaking frescoes with shellac. The first copies perished in a fire. Further copying commenced and during the 1920s much of the old shellac was removed and the frescoes treated afresh. Systematic copying began again in the 1950s and the frescoes have recently been undergoing special investigations into how to free them of the earlier preservative which has hazed, and to determine the causes of their deterioration. At the same time, new frescoes have been exposed by modern methods. For a while, access to some of the caves has been limited.

The following description of the caves commences from the E. of the crescent:

No. 1 Mahayana, (p. 32) is a splendidly decorated vihara (assembly hall). dating from about A.D. 500. In the front is a veranda borne by six columns, once preceded by a porch borne by two. Outside the veranda are three excavations on each wing, and inside is one at each end. The hall, which measures nearly 64 ft. square, is borne by twenty columns enclosing a central space, and has five cells on either side. At the back an ante-chapel with two columns, flanked by two cells on either side, leads to a large shrine. All along the front of the cave is a sculptured architrave with spirited representations of elephants, hunting scenes, and groups of figures. On the W. chapel are representations of the scenes of sickness, old age and death, which led Buddha to renounce the world. In the upper part of the frieze are geese under a band of lions' heads. Three doors and two windows open into the hall from the veranda, the centre door being elaborately carved, as are the columns of the back row in the hall and the sides of the other rows which face inwards. These carvings deserve detailed notice, being among the richest and most ornate known. In the shrine is a colossal statue of Buddha, supported on either hand by Indra, Vedic deity of Rain. At the sides of the doorway are statues of the goddesses of the Ganges and Jumna above, and of two snake-hooded guardians at the bottom.

The whole of the cave was once covered with paintings. In the four corners of the ceiling are interesting panels which represent groups of foreigners—perhaps Persians. On the front wall is represented the reception of an embassy in Persian dress by a Raja in his palace, supposed to be the Chalukya Pulakesin II in A.D. 625-26, from Khusru II. On the back wall to the E. of the antechamber is a mountain scene, and between the doors of the two cells are a Naga Raja and his wife in conversation with another personage, while high up on the wall is a snake-charming scene; farther on is another scene of a Naga Raja and ladies; and between the second and third cell doors, on the E. wall, is a scene of elephants and soldiers. On the back wall of the antechamber to the shrine is a painting of the Temptation of Buddha by Mara, such as is represented in the bas-relief in cave No. 26. The best are those of the Boddhisatva Padmapani holding a lotus, and of a "black princess", on the back wall of the cave near the openings of the antechamber. Note, on a pillar, four deer in different positions with one head.

No. 2 is a vihara hall, 48 ft. square, supported by twelve pillars, with five cells on either side and one chapel room at each side of the antechamber and shrine. There are also two chapel rooms at each end of the veranda, the front of which is carried by four pillars with flower-shaped capitals; the roof of the veranda projects 7 ft. to the front of the columns. Access is given by a finely decorated door, and two windows give light to side aisles formed by the columns in the hall, which are richly carved. At the end of these aisles are two chapel rooms, that on the E. side with the figures of a king and a queen holding a child, with small figures of sporting children below them; and that on the W. side with two large male figures. A richly carved doorway leads to the shrine; in front of the seated figure in it are kneeling worshippers. Traces of painting exist in this cave on the roofs of the veranda and the hall and its aisles, and in the shrine and the two side chapels. The scenes on the E. wall of the hall represent a royal procession with elephants, horses and armed retainers, and a sailing boat laden with jars, "*Vidhura-pandita jataka*". On the wall on the left is a painting of the Birth of the Buddha.

No. 3 has only a veranda.

No. 4 is the largest of all the viharas, measuring 89 ft. square, and supported by twenty-eight pillars. It is surrounded by cells as usual, and has a large shrine, approached by an antechamber at the back. The veranda was carried by eight octagonal columns, and has three doors and two windows in the back wall leading to the hall, the centre door being decorated with elaborate carvings. Between it and the right window is a sculptured relief of the Buddhist Litany, in which two figures are represented in each compartment as fleeing to Buddha from danger, from fire, snakes and wild beasts.

No. 5 has been commenced only, but has a handsome door at the back of the veranda.

No. 6 is the only cave here with two storeys. The lower stage, of which the front has fallen, measures roughly 54 ft. square. It was borne by sixteen plain octagonal columns in four rows, but only seven of these now stand. They are connected above by beams carved on the ceiling. On each side and at the back are cells, and in the middle of the last an ante-chamber with Elephanta-like columns leads to the shrine containing a seated figure of Buddha. The stair from this storey leads to the veranda of the upper storey, once carried by four columns, with chapels outside it and rooms at the end of it. The hall measures rather less than that of the lower storey, and is carried by twelve columns arranged round a central space. There are cells all round this hall also, and a shrine with a front chamber in the back wall. Some frescoes (discovered 1935) over the doors of the cells should not be missed.

The other (**No. 7**), a vihara of unusual design, has no hall; the veranda, preceded by two porches borne by columns of the Elephanta type, leads directly to four cells and to the ante-chamber to the shrine; both the last are profusely decorated with sculpture. The Buddha has his legs crossed, and his right hand raised to bless.

The Hinayana group commences with **No. 8,** a small vihara, now used as a dynamo shed for lighting the other caves—entry prohibited.

The Chaitya Cave, **No. 9,** which is dated about 100 B.C., is 45 ft. deep, 22¾ ft. wide, and 23 ft. high. In dimensions and in the decoration of its façade, except (later) figures of Buddha on either side of the entrance, it much resembles the Nasik Chaitya Cave (p. 117), although rather older. Fourteen plain octagonal pillars on each side separate the nave and aisles, and eleven more continue the colonnade round the dagoba at the end of the cave. The vaulted roof once carried wooden ribs; in front of it is the great horseshoe window, 11½ ft. high, with a terrace and rail in front of it, and a second terrace over the porch, with a guardian *dwarapala* at either end. The dagoba is 11 ft. high to the top of its capital; this is in the form of a relic-box, and probably once bore a wooden umbrella. Remains of paintings are still visible on the left and back walls.

No. 10 is a (Hinayana) Chaitya dated 150 B.C., measuring 95 ft. by 41 ft. by 36 ft., and was also once fitted with wooden ribs, the roofs of the aisles having ribs carved in the stone. Its façade has fallen. An inscription in characters of the 2nd century B.C. records its presentation by a pious donor. The dagoba resembles that in No. 9, and, as in that cave, there are remains of paintings. The costumes depicted in these resemble those on the S. gateway of the Great Stupa at Sanchi. The Chadanta Jataka illustrated in three panels shows aboriginal Nagas. Probably the oldest painting is the picture on the left wall of a king and queen and princess with women attendants watching the worship of the sacred Bodhi-tree.

No. 11, contemporary with No. 10, appears to have been remodelled, being a mixture of both styles. The roof of the veranda is painted with birds and flowers. The hall measures 37 ft. by 28 ft. by 10 ft., and is carried by four primitive columns. There is a bench along the right side. There are three cells on the left side, and two cells and a shrine in the end wall; in the shrine is a free-cut statue of seated Buddha, with a fine kneeling figure in front of it.

No. 12 is a vihara measuring 36 ft. square, with four cells on each of the three inner sides. Over their doors the upper wall is ornamented with a horseshoe type of canopy.

No. 13 is a small hall, 16½ ft. by 13½ ft. by 7 ft., with seven cells, each with a stone couch.

This completes the group of Hinayana caves.

Cave **No. 14,** a vihara, is unfinished; it is reached above No. 13.

No. 15 has a hall 34 ft. square without columns preceded by a veranda (note the conventional birds over the door) and with six cells on each side; in the back wall are two cells and a shrine. The image of Buddha is carved out of the solid rock.

No. 16 has a veranda 65 ft. long and nearly 11 ft. wide, borne by six plain octagonal pillars; from the front of it steps descend to a chamber with a representation of a Naga Raja. A good view of the ravine can be obtained. Three doors and two windows open from the veranda into the hall, which is nearly 66 ft. square, and has twenty octagonal pillars, the roof of the front aisle being carved to simulate beams. On each side are six cells. The shrine, which is entered direct from the hall, and has side aisles separated off by two columns, contains in the centre a huge statue of Buddha in the teaching attitude. On the left wall of the hall is a beautiful painting of a dying princess, and others represent Buddha with a beggar's bowl, and teaching in a vihara. On the right wall, left of the door of the first cell, are the remains of a representation of Prince Siddhartha drawing the bow.

No. 17, called Cave of the Carpenter, is very similar in size and arrangement to No. 16, but has an antechamber to the shrine. Over the central door to the hall is a row of painted Buddhas. There is one side door and three windows. Between the veranda and No. 16 is a fine cistern. In front of the figure of Buddha in the shrine stand two figures, one with a mendicant's bowl, "Visvantra jataka". On the left of the door of the shrine is a painting of the return of Buddha after his enlightenment, and his reception by his wife and son. On the back wall of the E. half is a painting of three females and a male figure flying through the air. On the W. portion of the back wall is a picture with scenes of a court of justice, and hunting, and others in which a lioness plays the principal part, "Sutasoma jataka". On the right wall is a scene supposed to represent the landing of Vijaya in Sri Lanka, and another of female demons devouring victims.

No. 18 may be omitted.

No. 19 is the third Chaitya Cave, measuring 46 ft. by 24 ft. by 24 ft. high. It is profusely decorated throughout. Most of the court has fallen; but the porch at the back of the court under the great arched window still stands, and, like the whole façade, is covered with elaborate ornament. Five pillars on each side of the nave separate the aisles from it, and five more run round the dagoba. Outside the first two pillars of each colonnade is another, thus completing an aisle passage all round the cave. The columns have square bases and rounded shafts with bands of carving and bracket capitals richly decorated. Above the columns on the wall under the curved roof were painted multiple figures of Buddha, divided by floral arabesques. The front of the tall dagoba bears a figure of Buddha, and a triple umbrella reaches to the roof. Outside the cave to the W. is a relief of a Naga Raja, with a seven-headed cobra hood, and his wife with a single hood.

No. 20 has a veranda, of which the roof is carved in imitation of rafters, and a hall 28 ft. by 25 ft.; the antechamber here projects into the hall.

The rest of the caves, from 21 to 29, complete the group of the later (A.D. 600-650) Mahayana caves, and lie considerably farther W. Of these, the only ones calling for attention are Nos. 21, 24 and 26.

The veranda of **21,** which has fallen, had at each end a chapel with two pillars in front, with the earliest representation (as Dr Burgess believed) of the leaf falling over the corners of the capitals. The jewel or necklace pattern on the frieze above is characteristic of the work of the 7th century. The hall measures 51 ft. square, and has twelve columns; the image in the shrine is attended by huge *chauri* bearers.

No. 24, the largest vihara but never completed, shows how these caves were excavated by means of long galleries, which were broken into one another; the carving which exists is very elaborate.

No. 26, the fourth Chaitya cave, is 68 ft. deep, 36 ft. wide and 31 ft. high. The veranda, borne by four columns, here also opened on to a court with sculptures on the sides of it, one on the east side representing the Buddhist Litany again. Over the veranda was a broad balcony in front of the great window, 9 ft. high; on each side of this are various sculptured reliefs of Buddha. A colonnade of twenty-six pillars forms the aisles, and runs round the cylindrical dagoba at the back of the cave. The frieze above the colonnade is richly sculptured, and the roof is decorated with stone ribs. The walls of the aisles are also profusely decorated with sculpture; on the left wall, near the door from the veranda, is a colossal image of the dead Buddha, about to enter Nirvana, and farther down the wall is the relief of the temptation of Buddha by Mara. The dagoba has representations of Buddha all round it, and is over 20 ft. high.

For the Ellora Caves *see* under Route 4, p. 146.

ROUTE 4

Manmad to Daulatabad, the Caves of ELLORA, Aurangabad, Jalna, and Secunderabad.

Manmad (Manmar), 162 m. from Bombay.—The metre-gauge (Godavery Valley) section of the former Nizam's State Railway, has its terminus here (opened 1900): connection with the Dhond-Manmad Chord of the Central Ry. There are waiting and refreshment rooms at the station.

63 m. from Manmad is **Daulatabad,** the former Deogiri. The railway passes near the S. side of the 13th-century fortress, built on a huge isolated conical rock of granite, 800 ft. high and 2250 ft. above sea-level, with a perpendicular scarp of from 80 ft. to 120 ft. all round. A fine view of three sides of it can be had from the train.

On the E. side of the Fort were two outer lines of defence, and beyond these stood the walled city, now in ruins, and crossed from S. to N. by the road to Rauza and Ellora. On the left of the road stands the entrance to the outer line of defence, consisting of a hornwork with three gateways inside it, protected by a bastion 50 ft. high. Beyond the gate are (*r*) a Hindu temple with a lamp tower 13 ft. high; and (*l*) a small shrine of the Pir-i-kuds. On the latter side a little farther on are a large masonry tank, now dry, and a mosque converted by Mubarik Khilji (1310-21) out of a Jain temple, which has also served as a Hindu place of worship. Opposite these the Chand Minar or Pillar of Victory, a minaret of Persian form, rises 100 ft.; it bears the date 1435. The inner line of defence is passed by another triple gate like that in the outer line, the wooden doors in both cases being spiked to prevent battering by elephants; and a steep flight of steps leads onwards to a third gate, giving access to a platform on the edge of the ditch, 40 ft. wide. On the right here is the *Chini Mahal*, with encaustic decoration, in which Abul Hasan Tana Shah, the last King of Golconda, spent thirteen years of imprisonment; close by on a bastion is a gun 21 ft. 10 in. long, called the Kila Shikan, or Fort Breaker. The moat is crossed by a narrow stone bridge, at the end of which the road ascends to the Balakot by rock-cut chambers and passages, and emerges into the air 50 ft. higher up. The opening was formerly covered with an iron shutter, 20 ft. long and 1 in. thick, made in ribs (part of it is gone), which in case of siege was heated red hot. To provide ventilation for the fire a large hole has been tunnelled through the rock.

Passing a gateway and the shrine of the Fakir Sukh Sultan, the path leads to a Baradari, or pavilion, from which there is a fine view. It is believed to have been the residence of the Yadava Rani of Deogiri, and was a favourite resort of the Emperor Shah Jahan in 1636. The pavilion has a wide veranda, with a precipice of over 100 ft. in front, and a view to Aurangabad on the E. and to Rauza on the N.

One hundred steps must be climbed to reach the citadel itself, on a platform 160 ft. by 120 ft. At the W. corner is a one-gun battery, 60 ft. by 30 ft. The gun is 19 ft. 6 in. long, with a bore of 7 in. On a bastion is another large gun, on which is a Gujarati inscription, saying that the funds for its construction were provided by certain Banias, and also a Persian inscription, naming the gun "Creator of Storms". Tavernier wrote that the gun on the highest platform was raised to its place under the directions of a European artilleryman in the service of the Great Mughal, who was promised leave to return to his native land if he succeeded.

Deogiri was the capital of the Yadava dynasty after the fall of the Western Chalukyas. In the year 1293 Ala-ud-din, afterwards King of Delhi, took the city. The citadel still held out, and he finally raised the siege on receiving a ransom of 15,000 lb. of pure gold, 175 lb. of pearls, 50 lb. of diamonds, and 25,000 lb. of silver. Twenty-five years later (1318) the Yadava Rajas were exterminated by Qutb-ud-din Mubarak Shah. In 1338 Muhammad Shah Tuglaq removed the inhabitants of Delhi here, and changed the name to Daulatabad; but his attempt to establish his capital in the Deccan ended in complete failure. Seventeen years later the exiles were permitted to return to Delhi. Shah Jahan took it in 1636 from the last Nizam Shahi King.

Daulatabad is the nearest station to the caves of Ellora, but as previously mentioned (p. 138) the trip is best made from Aurangabad, where there are Western-style Hotels. Permission to stay at the State Guest House at Rauza (Khuldabad) must be obtained from the Executive Engineer B. & C. Dept. Aurangabad. No permission is necessary to visit the Fort. There is a Local Fund Bungalow at Khuldabad. Field-glasses should be taken—fine views.

DAULATABAD

The road from Daulatabad to Rauza (8 m.) ascends the Pipal Ghat, paved by one of Aurangzeb's courtiers, as recorded on two pillars about half-way up the hill.

Rauza or **Khuldabad** ("The Heavenly Abode") is a walled town, 2000 ft. above the sea, and is 2 m. from the caves of Ellora. It is the *Karbala* (holy shrine) of the Deccan Muslims, and the burial-place of the Emperor Aurangzeb; of Asaf Jah, the founder of the Hyderabad dynasty, who died in 1748 at Burhanpur (p. 119); of Malik Ambar, the powerful Abyssinian Minister of the last Nizam Shahi King; and of certain minor celebrities.

Rauza once contained a considerable population, and is surrounded by a high stone wall (built by Aurangzeb) with battlements and loopholes.

Old and ruinous mosques and tombs abound in every direction on each side of the road.

Midway between the N. and S. gates of the city is the **grave of Aurangzeb** in the Dargah of Saiyad Zain-ud-din, on the right side of the road. An ascent of 30 yd. leads to a domed porch and gateway. In the centre of the S. side is an exquisite little Nakkar Khana, or music gallery from which ceremonial music was played. The W. side is occupied by a large mosque, the roof of which is supported on scalloped arches. Facing the N. end of the mosque is a small open gateway leading into an inner courtyard, in the S.E. angle of which is the door of Aurangzeb's tomb. Above the door is a semi-circular screen of marble.

The grave is on a marble platform, and is open to sun and rain, as it should be according to orthodox Muslim ideas. Aurangzeb, who was a man of austere piety, is said before his death to have desired that his sepulchre should be poor and unpretentious, in accordance with the tenets of the Koran, and to have expressly "desired in his will that his funeral expenses should be defrayed from the proceeds of caps which he had quilted and sold, an amount that did not exceed Rs. 10; and that the proceeds of the sale of his copies of the Koran, Rs. 805, should be distributed to the poor". The late Nizam erected a marble screen around the tomb.

Fifteen or twenty paces to the E. of Aurangzeb's tomb is a small quadrangular enclosure of marble, within which are three graves, the one on the right being that of the daughter of Saiyad Zain-ud-din, the Muhammadan saint buried close by; the next, that of Azam Shah, Aurangzeb's third son, attached to which is a small marble headstone carved with floral devices; and the one beyond, the grave of Azam Shah's wife. The whole is surrounded by a plain screen of white marble. Between these tombs and that of Aurangzeb is the mausoleum of Saiyad Zain-ud-din, on the E. side of which are inscribed a number of verses from the Koran and the date of the Saiyad's death, 1370. This tomb, however, was erected many years after that period by one of his disciples. The doors of the shrine are inlaid with silver plates of some thickness; the steps below it are embellished with a number of curiously cut and polished stones, said to have been brought here from time to time by Fakirs and other religious devotees of the shrine. A little distance to the rear of this tomb is a small room built in an angle of the courtyard wall, which is said to contain a robe of the Prophet Muhammad. It is carefully preserved under lock and key, and is only exhibited to the gaze of the faithful once a year—on the 12th Rabi-ul-awwal.

Opposite this Dargah, on the left side of the road, is that of Hazrat Saiyad Burhan-ud-din, a saint who died at Rauza in 1344, with the grave of Nizam-ul-mulk Asaf Jah, the first of the Nizams of Hyderabad. The entrance is through a large quadrangle, having open-fronted buildings on all sides and a Nakkar Khana (music gallery) at the E. end. The W. end is used as a school for instruction in the Koran. A door at this end gives access to an inner courtyard in which are a number of graves. Facing the entrance are the tombs of Asaf Jah and his son Nasir Jang, surrounded by a lattice screen of red sandstone, and that of Hazrat Saiyad Burhan-ud-din.

He was the successor of Muntajib-ud-din, sent by Nizam-ud-din-Aulia (p. 332) from Upper India with 700 disciples a few years before the first invasion of the Deccan by Ala-ud-din (1294), and was himself succeeded by Zain-ud-din. Deposited within the shrine are some hairs of the Prophet's beard, which are said to increase yearly in number. The shrine, however, boasts of a still more unique treasure. On the pavement to the S. of the building, small lumps of silver are shown. These are supposed to be the remains of trees of solid silver, which grew miraculously after the saint's death and were broken up and sold for the maintenance of the shrine. Subsequently, a small jagir was allotted to the disciples of the Saiyad, and since that time only a few buds of silver appear at night. The doors of the shrine are covered with plates of white and yellow metal wrought into designs of trees and flowers.

THE CAVES OF ELLORA

are 19 m. from Aurangabad* (bus service). A motor road to the entrance was constructed in 1925.

This group of **Cave Temples** in the Deccan trap rock comprises twelve Mahayana Buddhist, seventeen Brahman, and five Jain works. The road down the Ellora Ghat passes the S. side of the Kailasa Temple, and divides the caves into two groups, twenty to the left and fourteen to the right of it. The Buddhist caves lie at the S. end and the Jain caves at the N. end of the hill, facing W. and nearly 1½ m. long, the Brahman caves and Kailasa being situated between the two groups.

The caves are numbered S. to N., and as they face W. are best seen in the afternoon. Not all the caves are important, the most noteworthy being 10 and 12 (Buddhist), 14, 15 and 16 (Brahman), and 33 (Jain).

A guide provided by the Regional Tourist Office attends visitors. Besides the D.B., which is available for the use of visitors, there is a State guest-house (p. 139). Explanatory booklets, postcards and photographs can be purchased.

"Architecturally," wrote Fergusson,[1] "the Ellora caves differ from those of Ajanta, in consequence of their being excavated in the sloping sides of a hill and not in a nearly perpendicular cliff. From this formation of the ground almost all the caves at Ellora have courtyards in front of them. Frequently also an outer wall of rock with an entrance through it is left standing." They are mentioned by Masudi, the Arab geographer of the 10th century, as a celebrated place of pilgrimage; and Thévenot, who visited them about 1667, has left an interesting description.

Buddhist Caves.—These are to the S. of the Ghat road, beyond three Brahman caves. The farthest group at the S. end is named the Dherwara or Outcastes' quarter, dating from A.D. 350 to 550.

No. 1 is a vihara (assembly hall), measuring 41½ ft. by 42¼ ft., and having eight cells round it. **No. 2,** which was a hall for worship, is approached by a flight of steps, and is reached through a veranda carved with figures and having large *dwarapalas* (guardians) at the door of the cave, which is flanked by a window on either side. The interior, 48 ft. square, flat-roofed, has a lateral gallery on each side; the roof is supported by twelve columns arranged in a square, with high bases and cushion capitals, and the two galleries have four pillars in front of them—all richly decorated. A shrine, with huge *dwarapalas* and a seated Buddha 11 ft. high in the centre of it with two standing Buddhas on either hand, occupies the middle of the back wall, and on each side of the shrine is a double cell elaborately carved. **No. 3** was a vihara, measuring 46 ft. square, and having twelve cells round it; the twelve columns which support it have a drooping leaf or ear over their circular necks. In the N. end of the veranda is a chapel with a Buddha seated on a lotus supported by snake-hooded figures, and on the right of this is a pictorial litany. **No. 4** is a much-raised vihara, now measuring 35 ft. by 39 ft. deep. At the inner end is a cross aisle, beyond which a shrine, with a statue of Buddha under the Bo-Tree, and two cells were excavated; the columns are similar to those in No. 2. **No. 5,** known as the Maharwada, and formerly as the Dherwara cave, is again reached by steps. It is the largest single-storeyed

[1] *Indian Architecture.*

vihara cave here, measuring 58½ ft. by 117 ft. deep. The roof is carried by two rows of ten columns, similar to those in No. 2, with two more between them at each end, and two stone benches run down the cave parallel to the range of pillars. On either side of the cave is a recess with two pillars and a number of cells, and at the end is a shrine. From its arrangement it appears that this cave was a hall of assembly or refectory. **No. 6,** to the N. of No. 5, is reached through a lower hall with three cells on the E. side; it measures 26½ ft. by 43 ft., and has an antechamber and shrine at the back of it, the former richly carved, and the latter containing a large seated Buddha. The figure on a stone at the foot of the goddess Saraswati on the S. wall of the antechamber deserves notice. Beyond it is yet a third hall, measuring 27 ft. by 29 ft., with three cells on the E. and N. sides. **No. 9** lies in the N.W. angle beyond the third hall, and is reached from the central hall of No. 6; it has a well-carved façade. **No. 7,** to which the stairs in the first hall of No. 6 lead, is a large vihara, 51½ ft. by 43½ ft., supported by four columns only. **No. 8** is entered from this, and is a hall measuring 28 ft. by 25 ft., with three cells on the N. side, a shrine with a passage round it, and a seated image of Buddha in it, and a smaller hall on the W. side. On the face of the rock by this is a group of the child Buddha with his mother and father.

No. 10 is the only chaitya or chapel cave of the group, and lies some way to the N. It is known as the Viswakarma or Carpenter's Cave, and is not earlier than A.D. 700. In front of it is a large court, which is reached by steps, and from which a second flight of steps leads to the veranda. The galleries round the court are borne by elegant pillars, and at the foot of each of these was a fine stone lion facing outwards. At the back of the side galleries are two chapels elaborately carved, and at the ends of the back gallery or veranda are two chapels and two cells. The fine railed terrace above the veranda is reached by a flight of steps in the N. gallery. The façade is surmounted by a bold projecting cornice cut in the rock, and the great horseshoe window is here divided into lights. The interior measures 86 ft. by 43 ft. by 34 ft., and the nave and aisles, which run round the dagoba, are separated by twenty-eight columns. The dagoba is 27 ft. high, and has a colossal seated Buddha in the front of it. The roof is carved in imitation of ribs, and the projecting wall under it and the above columns is carved with two rows of panels, the upper with Buddha and the lower with ganas or dwarfs.

The Do Thal[1] cave (**No. 11**) was discovered in 1876 to have three storeys; it also is preceded by a court. The lowest storey consists of a veranda only, with a shrine and two cells at the back of it. The middle storey has eight pillars in front and five chapels or cells, of which only the three richly carved ones in the middle are completed. The centre chapel is a small hall with two pillars and a statue of Buddha.

The Tin Thal[2] cave (**No. 12**) dates probably from about A.D. 700. This again has a fine forecourt, but in this instance without side galleries. Steps lead from the court into a great hall, 115 ft. by 43 ft., with three rows of columns; beyond this a second hall, 42 ft. by 35 ft., borne by six columns, extends up to the shrine, with a seated statue of Buddha on either wall. The shrine contains a colossal seated Buddha and a number of other figures. On the walls of the front hall a relief of Buddha with attendants and *chauri* bearers is repeated in many places.

Steps at the S.W. corner of the front hall lead to the middle storey. borne by two rows of eight pillars, The shrine is elaborately carved, and two fine *dwarapalas* guard the door. The topmost floor is carried by five rows of eight columns, the hall

[1] Do Thal = Two storeys.
[2] Tin Thal = Three storeys.

measuring 115 ft. by 70 ft. Along both side walls are large figures of Buddha seated on a throne, and on the back wall are the seven human Buddhas, seated under trees at the one side and under umbrellas at the other. The antechamber, which is very large and has two pillars, is sculptured all round with large figures; in the shrine is a very large squat Buddha. The sculptures are almost Brahmanical.

Brahman Caves.—50 yd. N. of the Tin Thal cave begins the group of sixteen Brahmanical caves, or seventeen including the Temple of Kailasa. The first of these is a plain room only; next comes the Ravan ka khai,[1] and then the Das Avatára, between which and the Kailasa temple there is a footpath. All these were probably constructed in the 7th and early part of the 8th centuries A.D., the temple being the latest in date.

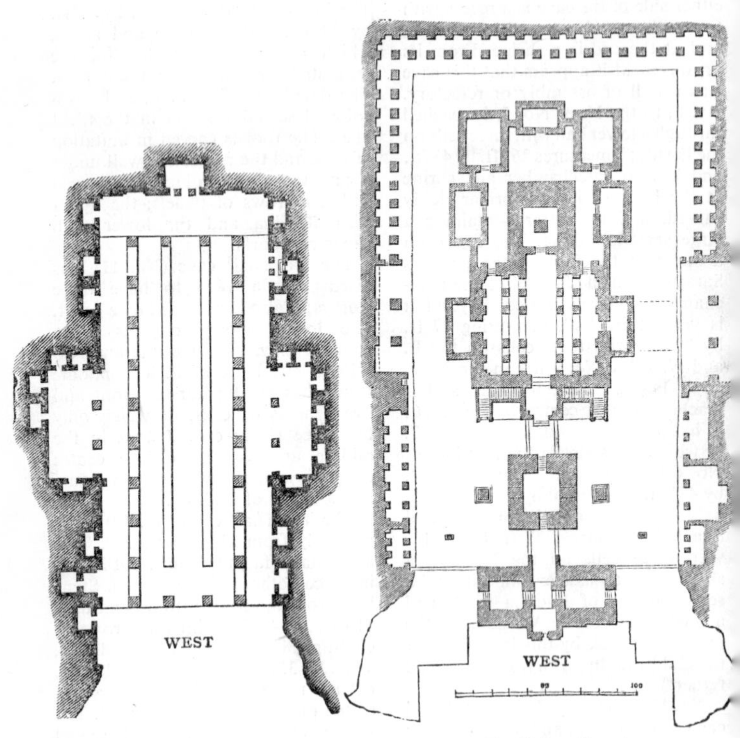

The Maharwada or Dherwara Cave. The Kailasa Temple.

The **Ravan ka khai (No. 14)** presents a different arrangement from any Buddhist cave. At the entrance were four columns making a front aisle; behind, twelve columns enclose the central space of the hall; and beyond these is a shrine standing free at the end of the hall. The pillared portion measures nearly 55 ft. square, and the depth of the cave to the back

[1] Ravan ka khai = Excavation of Ravana.

wall behind the shrine chapel is 85 ft. The S. wall bears Saiva sculptures of the slaughter of the buffalo demon, Siva and Parvati playing chess, and Siva dancing the tandava (a dance of exultation at his victory over the demon Mahisa), Ravana shaking Kailasa, and Bhairava;[1] while the N. wall has Vaishnava representations of Durga, Lakshmi, wife of Vishnu, the Varahani, or boar incarnation of Vishnu, a four-armed Vishnu, and Vishnu seated with Lakshmi. Inside the shrine is an altar and a broken figure of Durga: in the passage outside it on the S. side is a group of three skeleton demon gods, Ganesh and the seven great goddesses, each with a child, and her cognisance below—viz., Chamundi[2] and owl, Indráni and elephant, Varahani and boar, Lakshmi and Garuda eagle, Kaumari and peacock, Maheswári and buffalo, Bráhmi and *hans* or goose.

The **Dás Avatara**[3] cave (**No. 15**) is reached by a considerable flight of steps at the end of a large court hewn in the rock, which in this instance has a chapel in the middle of it and smaller shrines and cisterns round it; inside the chapel are four columns on a platform which has a huge modern stone image of a bull (nandi) on it. The cave has two storeys, of which the lower is carried by two rows of eight plain pillars, two more standing between four cells in the back wall. Above the lintel of the doorway is an unfinished inscription mentioning the visit of a Rashtrakuta Ruler. From the N.W. corner of the cave a staircase leads first to a landing with eleven reliefs of Hindu gods, beginning with Ganesh and ending with Durga, and then to the upper storey, which measures 95 ft. by 109 ft. deep, and is supported by seven rows of six columns, those in the front row being richly carved. The sculptured scenes on the walls are mainly similar to those in the preceding cave; among other noticeable scenes are Bhairava with a necklace of skulls and the marriage of Siva and Parvati on the N. wall; Siva springing from a lingam; Lakshmi with elephants pouring water over her on the back wall; and Vishnu, resting on the five-hooded serpent, and incarnated as a dwarf and as Narsingh (man-lion), on the S. wall. In the shrine, behind an antechamber with two columns, was a lingam or emblem of Siva.[1]

The **Kailasa Temple,** dedicated to Siva, (**No. 16**) is the noblest Hindu memorial of ancient India. It is attributed to a Rashtrakuta King Dantidurga (A.D. 725-755), and is carved out of the black volcanic rock of the hillside. Some 200,000 tons must have been excavated. The back wall of the pit is over 100 ft. high, and the court itself is 276 ft. long and 154 ft. broad. A rock screen, pierced by a fine entrance passage, stands on the W. side; near it are two gigantic stone elephants. Between the screen and the temple, and connected with both, is a nandi (bull) shrine, 26 ft. square and two storeys high, with a stone flagstaff on either side; and beyond this is the temple, measuring 164 ft. from front to back and 109 ft. from outside to outside of the side porches, and rising 96 ft. above the floor of the court. It consists of three parts—a porch (in the ceiling of which are

[1] See p. 107.

[2] The name of this goddess, a specially ferocious form of Durga, is derived from the two giants Chanda and Munda, whom she slew. She wore an elephant hide and a necklace of corpses, and used to rejoice in human sacrifices. See play of Malati and Madhava in Wilson's *Theatre of the Hindus*.

[3] **Dás Avatara = Ten Incarnations.**

[1] A Thug affirmed to Col. Meadows Taylor that the caves at Ellora contained all the mysteries of his profession, and that every particular of the murderous methods of Thagi (Thuggee) was depicted on the walls, from the marking down of the victim to the burial of the body in a hidden grave. For an account of the proceedings of this hereditary guild of assassins who justified their strangling of human beings as a sacrifice to the goddess Kali (Bhowani, Durga), Meadows Taylor's *Confessions of a Thug* (Oxford Univ. Press) should be read. Active operations against this criminal fraternity were begun by Sir William Sleeman and others in 1829, but it was not until 1861 that most of the gangs were dispersed. See *The Deceivers* by John Masters, 1952. cf. p. 121 (*supra*).

traces of painting), a central hall measuring 57 ft. by 55 ft., and borne by sixteen massive square columns arranged in four groups of four each, with broad aisles between, from W. to E. and from N. to S., and a dark shrine, 15 ft. square inside, with the Ganges and Jumna as guardians at the door. A passage leads all round the shrine and to five chapels placed at the sides and back of it; these illustrate the shape of the cells on the terraces of structural Buddhist viharas. The solid plinth of the temple is carved with a splendid series of immense elephants and monsters projected from the wall, and forms quite one of the finest remains of antiquity in the whole of India. At the sides of the bridge connecting the porch and *Nandi* chapel, and of the staircases leading to the former, are large sculptures and reliefs, the latter representing scenes from the *Ramayana*. On the S. side of the court opposite the porch is a rock-cut gallery, borne by two columns, with statues of the seven great goddesses with children on their laps and Ganesh. E. of this is a plain cave, 55 ft. by 34 ft., borne by four pillars, and with a veranda, also with two columns. There is also an upper storey to this cave, once connected with the temple by a flying bridge, under which, on the temple wall, is a relief of Ravana shaking Kailasa. From this point the E. half of the court round to the N. side porch of the temple is encircled by a corridor cut in the overhanging rock, with twelve large compartments of sculpture on the S. side, nineteen on the E., and twelve again on the N., representing various Saiva and Vaishnava scenes.

W. is another plain corridor, under the large Lankeswar cave. This cave is 108 ft. by 60 ft., exclusive of a nandi chapel in front of it, and is reached by a dark winding staircase from yet a fifth corridor W. of the fourth. The cave is borne by sixteen pillars arranged in fours as in the Kailasa temple. In the N.W. corner of the court is a small cave shrine with two pillars in the front decorated with representations of the three river goddesses of the Ganges, Jumna and Saraswati; and above this is a small unfinished excavation.

A footpath near the N. side of Kailasa leads up to the plateau past a cave with a Trimurti, or Triad figure of Siva, in it (p. 107). Farther N. are four unimportant Brahman caves, beyond which the **Rameswara** cave (**No. 21**) is reached. This is a Saiva temple, once with a porch in front of it. The next important cave is known as the **Nilkantha** (**No. 22**); it has a small ruined chapel in the forecourt, from which thirteen steps lead into the cave, measuring 70 ft. by 44 ft. In the shrine is a lingam. The **Khumbarwada** cave (**No. 25**), 95 ft. by 27 ft., including the smaller hall at the back, has a figure of the sun god in his seven-horse chariot in the vestibule to the shrine. The next temple is a large hall with several chapels, measuring 112 ft. by 67 ft. The path now reaches a fine ravine, over the scarped head of which a waterfall descends after rain. On the S. side of this is the Vaishnava, Milkmaid's or **Gopi** cave (**No. 27**), and on the N. side the cave (**No. 29**) named **Sita-ki-Naháni** (or bath). The inner hall measures 53 ft. by 22 ft. No. 29 will remind every one of the great cave at Elephanta, of much the same period, A.D. 650-725. It consists of a principal hall, facing nearly W., with a recess on the S. side opening on to the ravine, and a larger recess of irregular shape on the N. side. The central hall measures 149 ft. in depth and 95 ft. in breadth, including the two side aisles, which lead to the recesses. The steps to this are guarded by two lions, and in front of them is a circular platform for a *Nandi*. In the veranda and front aisles of the cave are carved reliefs much as at Elephanta. The shrine is a small square room, approached by four doors as in that cave, and contains a lingam. From the S. recess steps descend to the ravine, of which a charming view is obtained at this point. The N.

recess is also reached by steps guarded by lions; a small low cave exists at the E. end of this, and from the S.W. corner of the recess a passage has been broken into an excavation with six pillars; there is usually water in this wing, which prevents close examination, but keeps it cool.

Jain Caves.—The five Jain caves, dating from the 8th to the 13th century, lie beyond the Brahman caves, the first being the **Chhota Kailasa (No. 31),** some way up the face of the hill. This temple is in a pit measuring 130 ft. by 80 ft. It was copied from the great Kailasa temple, and left incomplete.

The **Indra Sabha (No. 32),** believed to be the earliest of the group, is entered through a rock screen facing S., in front of which, to the E., is a temple with nude statues of Parasnath, Gomata Swami with creepers round his limbs, and the last Tirthankar, Mahavira. In the S.E. corner of the court is a large elephant, and opposite it was a monolithic column, in front of a cave with six columns, containing reliefs of the same three Tirthankars. In the centre of the front of the court is a chapel with a quadruple image of a Jain saint; at the back of the court is an incomplete hall. Over this, reached by a staircase in the veranda, is a second hall with wings to the front of it, each with a small temple borne by four columns. The hall, measuring 55 ft. by 65 ft., is supported by twelve pillars, in the centre of which was once an image; the walls all round are divided into compartments filled with Jain saints, and the shrine has a statue of Mahavira. The figures at the ends of the veranda are noteworthy, also the cornice round the shrine and a door.

The **Jagannath Sabha,** portion of No. 33, is also a two-storied cave with a court in front. On the W. wing of this is a small hall, and at the side of the main cave is a small chapel. The cave is supported by four columns in front and by four more inside; the sculptures in it are in an unusually perfect condition. The outside staircase to the upper storey leads to another hall, 57 ft. by 45 ft., the ceiling of which was once painted in concentric circles, and the walls of which are sculptured with figures of Mahavira and Parasnath. This cave connects internally with the Indra Sabha, and also with another to the W. of it. On the top of the hill in which the Jain caves are excavated is a rock-hewn statue of Parasnath 16 ft. high, protected by a structural building raised over it some 200 years ago.

In the village of Ellora there is one of the ancient Jyotri Linga temples called Ghusrinesa which was restored by Ahalya Bai of Indore after Muslim destruction.

71 m. **Aurangabad***; Hotel: (pop. 150,000 in 1971) airport, an important town historically, was first called Khadke, and was founded in 1610 by Malik Ambar, the Abyssinian slave who became the famous minister of the King of Ahmadnagar.

The *Panchakki*, or water-mill, the shrine of Baba Shah Muzaffar, a Sufi of the *Chishti* sect (p. 265) and spiritual preceptor of Aurangzeb, is situated on the right of the road from the Cantonment to the Begampura bridge, and on the very edge of the Kham, the river of Aurangabad. In the garden is a brimming tank of clear water, full of *Kohl* fish up to 3 ft. long.

This overflows into a lower one, and that again into a narrow conduit. Beyond the first tank and the ornamental garden is a second and much larger tank. It is entirely supported on vaults, with two rows of massive pillars. Below is a noble hall, reached by steep steps, down to the level of the river. On the right of the second tank is a fine mosque, the roof of which is supported by four rows of massive pillars. In two of the rows the pillars are of teak, and in two of masonry. At the S.W. corner of this mosque, in a little garden, is the diminutive Tomb of the saint, of beautiful light-coloured marble.

¼ m. N. from the *Pan Chakki* is the *Mecca Gate* of the city and the *Mecca*

Bridge, which are probably early 17th century. The top of the parapet of the gateway is 42 ft. above the road. Flanking towers are surmounted by domes. Inside the gate there is a black stone mosque built by Malik Ambar. In the centre is a niche with the Divine Name and "Victory is near". Above that is the *Kalima* and some verses of the Koran written in difficult Tughra. Close by is a recess with a bell-shaped ornament. This is perhaps the oldest mosque in the city.

The **Government Art College** is 2 m. to the N.E. of the Cantonment, and in or near the *Kila Arh* or citadel, built by Aurangzeb. This spot, the site of gentlemen's houses in the reign of Aurangzeb, not long ago was entirely covered with cactus and jungle, the haunt of hyenas and other animals. Sir Salar Jang, the Nizam's Minister, had the site cleared, and numerous reservoirs, fountains and other works of interest were discovered. Their ancient magnificence can be imagined. Only one archway of Aurangzeb's citadel remains, but here fifty-three great Princes, such as the Maharajas of Jaipur and Jodhpur, attended the court of the Emperor with thousands of armed retainers, and Aurangabad was then the Delhi of the South. As soon as Aurangzeb died the Princes departed, and Aurangabad sank at once into comparative insignificance.

The Jami Masjid is in a grove. One immense *Ficus Indica* (banyan) stands close to the road, and shades some 300 ft. of it. The Mosque and minarets are low, but the façade is rendered striking by an ornamental band of carving 2 ft. broad along the whole front. Over the central niche are the *Kalima* and inscriptions in Tughra writing, as in Malik Ambar's Mosque. A net (not seen anywhere else) covers the entire façade, so that no birds or bats can enter. Malik Ambar built half and Aurangzeb the other half.

1 m. N.W. of the town is the Bibi-ka-Muqbara—the **Mausoleum** of **Rabi'a Daurani,**[1] wife of Aurangzeb. The great door at the gateway is plated with brass, and along the edge is written, "This door of the noble mausoleum was made in 1089 A.H., when Ataullah was chief architect, by Haibat Rai". Near the inscription there is an infinitesimally small figure, said to be a bird, indistinctly carved. The curious roof of the gateway of the mausoleum should be observed. In the garden is a long narrow basin of water, in which fountains used to play, and on either side of the water is a walk and ornamental wall.

The building is a replica of the Taj Mahal at Agra. In the wall of the mausoleum is a small door, only 6 ft. high, plated with brass, where a second "bird" is pointed out on the edge close to the upper central knob. The carving of the flowers on this door is curious, and that of the dragons particularly so. Those who wish to enter the tomb are expected to take off their shoes. The cenotaph is enclosed in an octagonal screen of white marble lattice-work exquisitely carved, and stands on a raised marble platform.[2] The place for the slab is empty, and nothing but earth appears. This is much approved by Muslims, as showing humility. In the gallery above the tomb is a marble door exquisitely carved. The former Government of the Nizam went to great expense in restoring this mausoleum.

Below the right corner of the platform a second tomb is said to contain the remains of Rabi'a Daurani's nurse. There is no inscription. To the W. of the mausoleum is a mosque of brick faced with cement (*chunam*) of a dazzling whiteness. The pavement is covered with patterns of prayer-carpets. The *mimbar*, or pulpit, is of marble.

The **Caves of Aurangabad** in the Deccan trap, are near Rabi'a Dau-

[1] By some writers the lady is said to have been a daughter of the Emperor, which is a mistake. The gravestone is nameless.

[2] Tavernier mentions this tomb in his travels, and states that he met carts coming down from N. India with white marble for it.

rani's mausoleum. A road goes to the foot of the hill, wherein the caves are excavated in two groups, facing S. and E. The nine Buddhist caves (Mahayana except No. 4, which is Hinayana) date from the 7th century; there are five in the W. group, and four in another lying ¾ m. E. Nos. 2 and 7 may be inspected. The sculptures and arrangements of these caves show a distinct approximation to the Brahman caves of Ellora. **No. 1,** at the W. end of the first group, is a vihara, a good deal higher up than the other four. Only the porch and veranda (76½ ft. by 9 ft.) were completed, and the former has been crushed by a fall.

No. 2 was intended to be a Chaitya (*c.* A.D. 650). At the back of the veranda, 21½ ft. by 13 ft., is an aisle, and behind this is a shrine with a passage all round it; at the sides of the shrine door are two tall figures standing on a lotus flower and *naga* figures, and inside is a seated figure of Buddha, 9 ft. high, in the teaching attitude. Many figures are on the walls of the shrine and the passages.

No. 3 is a vihara hall, 41½ ft. by 42½ ft., with twelve columns splendidly decorated as in the later caves at Ajanta; there is a decorated recess also, and on each side two cells. In the front corners of the shrine are a number of life-sized worshipping figures with garlands and elaborate head-dresses.

No. 4 is a chaitya, much ruined, which dates probably from the 2nd century.

Of **No. 5** only the shrine remains, now dedicated to the Jain Parasnath.

No. 6, first of the E. caves, is much higher up the hill face than the other three caves in that group. The hall was supported by four columns, and the antechamber of the shrine by two more; in the side walls are four cells, and in the back wall two. The shrine has a passage round it, and a smaller Buddha with smaller worshippers in front. There are traces of painting.

No. 7 has a veranda with four columns and a chapel at either end and a hall 38 ft. by 28 ft., in the centre of which the shrine has been placed, while three cells have been excavated in each side wall, and two chapels with sculptures in the back wall. To the left of the entrance to the hall is one of the best representations of the Buddhist Litany (p. 140); to the right is a figure of Manjusri, patron of the Mahayana sect. The front of the shrine has three large female figures on either side; on the left of the figure of Buddha in the shrine is the representation of a dance and of female musicians.

No. 8 is an unfinished vihara hall. In its present condition it consists of a hall, 22 ft. by 20 ft., with 2 cells on its left side and a smaller hall on its right side.

No. 9 is also higher up in the cliff. On the W. wall is a sculpture of the dead Buddha 16 ft. long.

28 m. S. of Aurangabad by road is **Paithan,** one of the oldest cities in the Deccan, on the N. bank of the Godavari. Mention is made of its inhabitants in the 14th Edict of Asoka. It was visited by Greek traders 300-200 B.C. and was an Andhra capital *c.* A.D. 150. Excavations have disclosed six layers of remains, the lowest dating before 2000 B.C.

110 m. from Manmad is **Jalna** (D.B.), which was from 1827 to 1903 an infantry cantonment (put into service again during the 1939-45 war). There is a motor service to Malkapur (p. 193) *via* Buldana. Jalna was the place of exile of Abul Fazl, the author of the *Ain-i-Akbari*; and Aurangzeb when Viceroy of the Deccan, also lived here. The fort contains a well with underground chambers. From Jalna the battlefield of **Assaye,** 30 m. distant, may be visited. Several old forts are passed *en route*, and the two fortified villages of Pipalgaon and Warur on opposite sides of the Kaitna river, which showed General Wellesley where the ford was. A view of the field of battle, fought on 23rd September 1803, is obtained from the tower of the fort of Assaye,

on the bank of the Juah, between which and the Kaitna the Mahratta army was drawn up. The forces of Scindia and of the Bhonsla Raja of Nagpur consisted of 16,000 infantry and 20,000 cavalry, and the British force of 4500 men all told; the killed and wounded on the British side were 1600. N. of it the British dead were buried.

A memorial plaque to the officers and men of the Highland Light Infantry who fell in the battle has been erected in the low wall surrounding the site.

M.G. Branch

181 m. Parbhani Junction for Purli Vaijnath connecting there with a broad-guage line to Vikarabad (p. 453) *via* Bidar.

187 m. **Pingli.** From this station the old cantonment of Mominabad (Amba) can be reached (42 m.). Near by are some ruined cave temples, both Brahman and Jain.

199 m. **Purna** (R.). Junction for a branch line to **Hingoli** (50 m.) which was an artillery cantonment from 1819 to 1903. Some of the graves in the British cemetery date back to 1829. Hingoli was a centre of the Thugs, and is mentioned by Meadows Taylor in his *Confessions of a Thug*. About 9 m. from **Chondi** station (21 m.) on this line (good road) is the Jaganath Saivite temple, founded by Shanker Acharya, at **Aundha**; a splendid example of mediaeval Hindu architecture, closely resembling the temple at Halebid (p. 487). The carving on the hornblende base is very fine.

Main Line

218 m. **Nander.** An important centre for motor-bus services N. to Hingoli and S.W. to Latur (86 m.) (p. 437). About 1 m. from the station is a Sikh gurdwara, which contains the tomb of Guru Govind, last of the ten Gurus (p. 27), assassinated near Nander in 1708. Europeans are permitted to enter the temple and sit on a special carpet. A training college for young Sikhs is maintained here.

269 m. Near Basar the Godavari river bridge, 1392 ft. long (1900).

294 m. **Dichpalli.** The Vishnu temple on a hill near the station is an example of the mediaeval Hindu style, with wonderful stone carving.

386 m. from **Manmad** is **Secunderabad** (p. 462).

ROUTE 5

BENARES AND SARNATH

BENARES,* now called VARANASI, headquarters of a division and district in Uttar Pradesh (pop. 582,000 in 1971). Seat of Benares Hindu University (G. of India Tourist Office (The Mall); U.P. Govt. Tourist Office (Parade Mothi); Official Guide Services and Conducted Tours available. H. Clark's. Tourist Corporation Motel) is situated on the left bank of the River Ganges, which flows here from S. to N. and then N.E. It is connected by convenient air services (I.A.C.) from Babarpur Airport to Delhi, Calcutta, Agra, Lucknow and Allahabad. Travellers by rail alight at the Cantonment station.

The Ganges forms a crescent along the city; and a fine view of the long line of bathing-ghats and temples can be enjoyed by the visitor, who makes his entrance across the Dufferin Bridge (p. 163) by way of Moghulsarai Junction (10 m.). The view is apt to be misty in the afternoon, especially in the cold weather.

Originally and now again Vārānasi, and commonly called Kashi by the Hindus, who add the suffix Ji as a mark of respect, the city has been the religious capital of India from beyond historical times. It is mentioned in both the *Mahabharata* and *Ramayana*. Although known in the 18th century as Muhammadabad, the name did not endure. The derivation of the name *Vārānasi* is from the names of the two streams Vāruna (modern Barna), a river of some size on the N. and W. of the city, and Asi on the S., a mere *nulla*. Once the Asi was well away from the city.

Benares is one of the Seven Sacred Cities of the Hindus,[1] and is the great northern centre of the worship of Siva. The annual number of pilgrims who visit it is about a million, while the number of Brahmins residing in the place is over 30,000. Every pilgrim, besides visiting the holy spots in the city, must make the circuit of the **Panch Kosi** road, unmetalled, outside the city, round the sacred territory of Benares, commencing at the Manikarnika Ghat, proceeding by the Asi Ghat, and returning by the Barna Ghat (see p. 163). The route, which is 36¼ m. in length and the pilgrimage of which occupies six days, is attractively lined by fine trees and small shrines. The end of each stage is marked by a picturesque village, with numbers of temples and small *dharmsalas*. Benares is said to combine the virtues of all other places of pilgrimage. Any one of whatever creed, and however great his misdeeds, dying within the compass of the Panch Kosi road, is transported straight to heaven. This belief leads many people to end their days at Benares. Its peculiar sanctity is derived from the "ten-horse sacrifice", referred to under Dasaswamedh Ghat (p. 159).

The site of Benares has often changed, and the city is claimed to be the oldest in the world. The Chinese traveller Fa-Hian visited it in A.D. 399 and Hiuen Tsang in A.D. 629-645, when he mentions about 100 Siva temples with 10,000 votaries. In past ages it has been a city of sanctity and learning, the home of philosophers and grammarians. It was a most important place six centuries before the Christian era, for Sakyamuni (Buddha), who was born about 624 B.C. and died in 544 B.C., came to it from Gaya to establish his religion. Many important writers of the Hindus are first heard of here.

It was raided (1033) by a lieutenant of Mahmud of Ghanzi. We learn

[1] The other six are Hardwar, Ujjain, Mathura (Muttra), Ajodhya, Dwarka (in Kathiawar) and Kanchipuram (Conjeeveram) (in S. India).

from Hasan Nizami's history that in 1194 Jaichand, Raja of Benares, "whose army was countless as the sand", was defeated and killed by Qutb-ud-din Ghori; Ala-ud-din Khilji, Sultan of Delhi (1294-1316) destroyed temples and built mosques on their sites. From that date the city was governed by the Muslims, so that hardly one building in Benares dates before the time of Akbar (1556-1605), and few are older than the second half of the 18th century.

The city was ceded by the Nawab Wazir of Oudh to the British in 1775. Raja Chait Singh, as Zamindar of Benares, continued to farm the revenue. In 1779 two battalions from Dinapore enforced payment of a special contribution on account of trouble with the Mahrattas. Warren Hastings in 1780 called on the Raja to furnish a cavalry contingent for the same reason. When Chait Singh evaded compliance, Hastings in August 1781 went to Benares and placed him under house-arrest. The small guard from Major Popham's escorting regiment was overwhelmed by Chait Singh's retainers, being without ammunition. Hastings went to Chunar. He ordered down reinforcements from Cawnpore and Chait Singh retired to the service of Scindia at Gwalior and died in 1810. The E.I. Co. assumed the administration; and with the appointment in 1787 of Jonathan Duncan (p. 159) as Resident, a regular settlement of the revenue was taken in hand.

In 1857, like most other military establishments in Upper India, the garrison mutinied, but the Raja remained loyal.

Benares is famous for ornamental **Brasswork** which is met with all over the world, but genuine old pieces are difficult to procure. Small idols and other images in brass and other materials are made in great quantities in the narrow lanes around the Golden Temple. The *Thatheri* or *Pital* (*Brass*) *Bazar*, which is about 1 m. from the Cantonment railway station, is well worth a visit. White metal (phūl) is likewise largely used for domestic articles. The charming lacquered toys are famous. **Shawls, silks** and **embroideries** may also be purchased. The weaving of brocades (Kamkhwabs or Kincobs) is an old Benares speciality: its origin cannot be traced. Mughal Emperors, especially Akbar, encouraged the industry, sending brocades as presents to European monarchs. The industry has been revived. Hindu custom allows the use of silk —considered pure for ceremonial purposes—and brocades for all kinds of wearing apparel, upholstery and furniture. In brocade work *Kalabatun* (gold thread) is as essential as silk in the weaving. The loom employed is elaborate, and modern machinery is now found: the process is complex, because very elaborate patterns are often produced. The workmen display skill in the arrangement of forms and colours with the subdued elegance characteristic of Indian decorative art. Several firms sell silks, brocades and kincobs.

The banks of the River Ganges are bordered by Ghats,[1] or flights of stone steps, descending to the water from the most famous buildings in the city; the visitor can view them from a boat.

For those who are pressed for time, it will be sufficient to see the Durga (Monkey) Temple, and to proceed thence to the riverside for the Observatory and the Ghats as far as the Panchganga Ghat, disembarking there to see the Golden Temple. This involves an interesting walk of ¾ m. through narrow picturesque streets.

Unfortunately a number of the ancient temples in Benares are now closed to foreigners. Americans and others may be reminded of the amusing chapters 53-56, about Benares, in Mark Twain's *More Tramps Abroad.*

The River Ganges and the Indian city are nearly 3 m. from the

Cantonment, N. of the railway line and N.W. of the city. Near the *Hotels* is **St Mary's Church**, with old tombs removed from the old city cemetery

[1] A map faces p. 164.

in Chaitganj. N. of these, on the opposite side of the River Barna, which is crossed by a stone bridge, is the **Civil Station** of Sikarul (Secrole); here are the Courts, the State Bank of India, and a number of residences. Beyond the Civil Courts is a house known as **Hastings House**; a sun-dial of Chunar stone on the edge of the road outside the garden was, according to the inscription upon it, erected by Lieut. James Ewart in 1784, by order of Warren Hastings. From this quarter a road leads to Sarnath.

Recrossing the bridge and proceeding by Raja Bazar Street, the visitor will find the Nandeswar Kothi, the Post Office, the old Mint House, and Queen's College.

The **Nandeswar Kothi** belongs to the Maharajas of Benares, where they entertain distinguished visitors—King George V and Queen Mary as Prince and Princess of Wales stayed here in 1906. Here Mr Samuel Davis,[1] Judge and Magistrate of Benares, was attacked by the followers of Wazir Ali (the deposed Nawab of Oudh) who had just killed Mr Cherry, the British Resident, in the building now occupied by the Collector's Court, on the 14th January 1799. Mr Davis sent his wife and two children on to the roof, and, with a running footman's pike, placed himself at the top of the staircase leading to it, which he successfully defended until he was rescued by the arrival of a regiment of cavalry from the old Cantonment 10 m. away on the Sultanpur road. A tablet was affixed by Lord Curzon to the wall of the house.

Opposite, the **Old Mint House** belongs also to the Maharaja: another of Lord Curzon's tablets records that it was built as a Mint in 1820-21 from the designs of James Prinsep, the celebrated antiquarian, who resided here as Mint Master until the abolition of the Benares Mint in 1830.[1] In 1926 the interior was remodelled, and steps lead up to a banqueting hall and drawing-room. The lower floors are now used as a guest house.

From the Nandeswar Tank the Grand Trunk Road (from Calcutta) skirts the N. of the city. At $1\frac{1}{2}$ m. along it the **Bakariya Kund,** on the right side of the road, is a tank teeming with Muslim monuments and mosques converted from Hindu buildings, and built of their materials; close to it is a shrine, known as the Battis Khamba, or Thirty-two Pillars, now a Muslim tomb.

The **Lat Bhairon,** in the loop made by the railway lines, is now represented by the stump of a massive pillar, painted red, which stands in a small enclosure in an open *idgah* (Muslim place of worship on festival days). It was pulled down in 1809 during a serious riot, and was broken to pieces. It is probably a Buddhist relic, and may possibly be one of the Lats erected by the Emperor Asoka.

The **Ganj-i-shahid Mosque,** not easy to find, behind some broken-down steps, on the S. side of the open space in front of the Kashi railway station, was erected as a memorial of the Muslims who fell in the early captures of Benares. It is another instance of the conversion of an old temple, supposed to be Buddhist, to the uses of the Muslim faith.

Near the Kashi station also is the **Arhai Kangura Mosque,** which probably dates from the early period of Muslim conquest. The pillars have clearly been taken from some older temple. Its name (*arhai*, two and a half, *Kangura,* dome) is belied by the single dome. There is a Hindu inscription of 1190. Antiquities excavated from the old citadel are in the Saraswati Bhawan museum.

The drive may be continued to Ramnagar (p. 165).

S. of Pensioners' Lane the **Pisach Mochan Tank** is connected with

[1] Davis was an accomplished amateur artist, and a collection of his water-colours is on view at the Victoria Memorial Hall, Calcutta (p. 178).

[1] Visitors should obtain a look in some public library at *Benares Illustrated,* a series of beautiful lithographs after drawings by James Prinsep, published at Calcutta in 1831.

Bhairon. On the platform of one of the surrounding temples is the head of the *pisach* (goblin or demon) from whom Bhairon delivered the city (*mochan*, deliverance).

The **Hindu College and School,** S. of the Allahabad Road, is in the Kamachcha quarter. It was started in 1899 under the auspices of Mrs Annie Besant, and had for its object the combination of religious and moral education with mental and athletic development for Hindu youths. The College is now used as a high school.

Raja Bazar Road continues as Bagh Road past the **Queen's College,** which was erected by Major Kittoe, of the Bengal Engineers, in 1847-52, a handsome building in the Gothic style. On the N. side is an ancient monolith, 31½ ft. high, found near Ghazipur. On the obelisk there is an inscription (which has not been deciphered) and an English record of its removal. To the N.E., adjoining the College grounds, is the Saraswati Bhawan, containing a famous collection of Sanskrit MSS. The Sanskrit department of the College is renowned for its *pandits*. A tablet in the S.E. corridor inside the main entrance to the College records the foundation in 1791 of the original Sanskrit College by Jonathan Duncan, who was resident at Benares from 1787 to 1795 and Governor of Bombay from 1795 until his death there in 1811.

At the Bagh the road turns S. and then forks. One branch, Chaitganj Road, the main motor approach to the river, passes the old Chaitganj cemetery and the *Victoria Park*, and leads to the Dasaswamedh Ghat (p. 160).

To the S. is the Central Hindu College and the **Vizianagram Palace,** and close to this on the W. are several Jain Temples. This is the reputed birthplace of Parasnath, the famous Jain Saint.

THE DURGA, OR "MONKEY" TEMPLE

Most of the principal temples are in the centre of the city and are described later. But, as the visitor makes his way S. to the University buildings, he will pass one shrine which figures prominently in every book on Benares,

The **Durga Temple,** miscalled the Monkey Temple by Europeans from the numbers of monkeys which inhabit the large trees near it, is about three-fifths of a mile S. of the Vizianagram Palace. It is stained red with ochre, and stands in a quadrangle surrounded by high walls. In front of the principal entrance is the band room, where musicians beat a large drum three times a day. The central portion is supported by twelve curiously carved pillars on a platform raised 4 ft. from the ground. Through the doors, plated with brass, the image of the goddess may be seen; in the porch are two bells. One of these bells has a curious history. Round the rim is engraved the following inscription in Urdu characters: "Mister Willim Jems Garant sahib Bahadur Kalaktar shahr Banaras mah Asarh Fasli 1215". William James Grant, who was Collector of Benares in 1808 (which corresponds with the Fasli year 1215), was out on the river with his wife and children when they were caught in a whirlpool off Garhwa Ghat, which is near the Maharaja's palace at Ramnagar (p. 165). The boatmen invoked the aid of the goddess Durga and brought the boat to shore with the greatest difficulty, whereupon the Collector presented the bell as a thank-offering. The temple and the fine tank adjoining (Durga Kund) were constructed by Rani Bhawani of Natore in Bengal in the 18th century. As Durga is the terrific form of Siva's wife, and is said to delight in destruction, bloody sacrifices of goats are offered to her here.

Next to the temple is the white marble tomb and shrine of Swami Bhaskarananda. Although entirely modern, it is one of the most beautiful buildings in Benares and commemorates an impressive personality. Just S. of the temple is the modern Tulsi Manas Mandir with a series of illustrations of the Ramayana.

Farther S. the **Benares Hindu University** should be visited. The buildings, which cover an area of 2 sq. m., are some distance from the river-bank, and are almost opposite the Ramnagar Fort on the other side of the Ganges (p. 165). The foundation-stone was laid by Lord Hardinge in 1916, and the University moved into the buildings in 1921. Pandit Madan Mohan Malaviya (1862-1946) a leader of the Hindu Mahasabha, was Vice-Chancellor for many years. The various Departments form the diameter of a semicircle; behind them are hostels and extensive playgrounds; the residences for the staff are on the circumference. There are important collections of Indian sculpture and miniature paintings at the University's Bharat Kala Bhavan. Closed Sunday.

Down the fork of Chaitganj Road, running E., the road runs through the city to pass the Zenana Mission, the Ishwari Memorial Hospital (built by the late Maharaja H.H. Parbhu Narain Singh, Bahadur, in memory of his father), and the King Edward VII **General Hospital** (Shiva Prasad Gupta Hospital). Adjoining the Hospital is the **Garden of Madho Das,** now in the possession of the Radha Swami sect, where Warren Hastings was encamped on 16th August 1781, when he gave orders to arrest Raja Chait Singh (see p. 156). At a later date (1787-95) the house was occupied by the Resident, Jonathan Duncan (p. 156). At the Municipal Gardens will be found the Town Hall (built by the Maharaja of Vizianagram, a Madras landholder, who died here in 1845), and the Kotwali, or central police station, which looks like a fort. A road runs S. to the Golden Temple (p. 161). The Machodri garden (Gokul Chand Park) is on the Rajghat Road, with temples nearby.

THE RIVER FRONT

From the Durga Temple, connected with the Asi Ghat by a very narrow road, the visitor may embark either at the upper end of the Ghats from the Asi Ghat, or more conveniently from the central **Dasaswamedh** or **Man Mandir Ghat** (1½ m.), and be rowed slowly past them. In the following account the Ghats are given in succession from the S., proceeding downstream.

The **Asi Ghat** is one of the five special places of pilgrimage in Benares. These are known as the **Panchtirath,** and the pilgrim should bathe in them successively on the same day; proceeding from Asi to Dasaswamedh and the Barnasangam (beyond the Dufferin Bridge) and then retracing his steps to Panchganga and Manikarnika. The channel of the Asi is about 10 ft. broad. The steps at the Ghat are a good deal broken. Boats are available to cross from Nagwa Ghat (the next on the S.) to Ramnagar, the palace of the Maharaja of Benares.

The next, **Lala Misr Ghat,** belongs to the Maharaja of Rewa. At the N. end of the **Tulsi Ghat,** which follows, huge masses of masonry have fallen, and lie on the river's edge; this Ghat is named after Gosain Tulsi Das, author of the famous version in Hindi of the *Ramayana*, who died at Benares in 1623. He is said to have lived in the corner building at the N. of the Ghat, while writing the latter part of the epic (which contains 12,800 lines), and also to have composed there the *Rama-dataka*, one of his minor poems, in a single night. His shoes and pillow (takya) and a piece of wood on which he is supposed to have crossed the Ganges are preserved, but are not, as a rule, shown to visitors.

The **Janki Ghat** is new; at the top are four Siva temples with gilded pinnacles, and behind them is the fine Lularik well. At the foot of the Ghat is the pumping station of the Benares Water Works. The **Bachhraj Ghat** belongs to the Jains, who have built three temples on the bank of the river.

Next comes the **Sivala (Shiwala) Ghat,** where the fort in which Chait Singh resided stood. It is a handsome building, and appears as fresh as when first constructed. From a window in the face Chait Singh made his escape when fleeing from arrest in 1781. It is now called the Kali Mahal, after the goddess Kali, and was repurchased by the Maharaja of Benares. The Sivala Ghat is one of the finest of all the Ghats. Part of it is assigned to the religious ascetics called Gosains.

The next, **Dandi Ghat,** devoted to the staff-bearing ascetics called Dandi Panths, is very fine.

Hanuman Ghat is generally crowded; at the top of it is a temple of the Monkey God.

The **Smashan** (or **Masan**) **Ghat** is used as a subsidiary cremation ground. It is also known by the name of **Raja Harish Chandra,** a favourite hero of Hindu drama, who gave up his kingdom, and selling his wife and child into slavery, became himself the slave for a year of the *chandal,* or outcaste, whose duty it was to attend to the burnings at this very Ghat.

Passing the **Lali Ghat,** the temple just above **Kedar Ghat** is the popular shrine of the Bengalis, who inhabit this quarter of the city and also of the Tilanga pilgrims (from S. India). Kedar is a name of Siva, but it also signifies a mountain, and especially a part of the Himalayan mountains, of which Siva is the lord, hence called Kedarnath. His temple is spacious, and the centre is supposed to be the place where Kedarnath dwells; the interior can be seen from the doorway. At the four corners are Sivalas, with cupolas. There are two brass figures, hidden by a cloth, which is removed on payment of a fee. The walls and pillars are painted red or white. There are also two large black figures, which represent *dwarapals,* or janitors; each has four hands holding a trident, a flower, a club, and the fourth empty to push away intruders. Half-way down the Ghat is a pool cut in the steps called the Gauri Kund, or "well of Gauri", Siva's wife, the waters of which are considered to possess healing properties; on the steps of the Ghat are many lingam emblems of Siva.

The **Mansarowar Ghat** (built by Raja Man Singh of Amber) leads to a tank, round which are sixty shrines, now very dilapidated. Mansarowar is a lake in Tibetan territory, just across the borders of India, at the foot of the Kailash mountain, where the god Siva is believed to have had his abode, and very near the source of the Ganges. Near the tank is a stone 4½ ft. high and 15¼ ft. in periphery, which is said to grow daily to the extent of a sesamum seed. In a street to the E. of the tank are figures of Balkrishna, or the Infant Krishna, and Chatarbhuj or Vishnu.

At the **Chauki Ghat,** under a pipal, are idols and figures of snakes. In a street close by, called Kewal, is a figure of Durga with ten arms.

The **Someswar Ghat** is so called from the adjacent temple of the moon (*Soma* = "moon", and *Iswar* = "lord"). Every kind of disease is supposed to be healed. Close by is an alley, in which is the shrine of Barahin Devi, a female Aesculapius, who is worshipped in the morning and is supposed to cure swollen hands and feet. The head of the **Narad Ghat,** named after a famous Rishi, winds up under two fine pipal trees.

At **Raja Ghat** the stairs ascend into a large house, or *sarai,* built for Brahmins by Amrit Rao, adopted son of the deposed Peshwa, Raghunath Rao. The **Chausathi Ghat** is old. The **Rana Ghat,** built by the Maharana of Udaipur, is not much frequented.

The **Munshi Ghat,** most picturesque, was built by Munshi Shri Dhar, Diwan of the Raja of Nagpur, and now belongs to the Maharaja of Darbhanga (p. 392). **Ahalya Bai's Ghat** between this and the Dasaswamedh Ghat was built by the wise Mahratta princess who governed Indore from 1767 to 1795 (p. 203). Both the ghat and the building which surmounts it are striking.

The **Dasaswamedh Ghat** is one of the five celebrated places of pilgrimage in Benares, the other four being the junctions (sangam) of the Asi and Barna with the Ganges, and the Manikarnika and Panchganga Ghats. It is specially thronged during eclipses. Here Brahma is said to have offered in sacrifice (*medh*) ten (*das*) horses (*aswa*), and to have made the place equal in merit to Allahabad. The road to this Ghat from the W. was formerly the only approach to the river between the two extreme ends of the town, until the Municipality opened up another but much less important road at the Masan (Smashan) Ghat (see above), called the Harish Chandra Road.

At the S. end of the Ghat, which should be visited on foot, is a low white-washed shrine of Sitala, the goddess of smallpox, and of the presiding deity of the Ghat, figured under a brass lingam. Farther on at the Ghat are life-size stone figures in niches of the Ganges, Saraswati, and Jumna rivers, and of Vishnu, the Trimurti or Trinity, and the Narsingh or lion-man incarnation of Vishnu, which are passed on the way to the

Man Mandir Ghat (and **Observatory**) are much admired by some experts. The greater part, however, was restored at the end of the 19th century, with inferior brick and plaster,[1] but one portion of the original work remains. High up, on the extreme N.E. corner, is an exquisite stone balcony which is one of the gems of Benares. A good view can be had from the river, but a better one from the Ghat, standing N.E. of it. This lofty building gives a fine appearance to the Ghat and commands a beautiful view of the river. It was erected by Raja Man Singh of Ambèr (p. 266) about the year 1600.

The Observatory was added in 1710 by Raja Sawai Jai Singh, the founder of Jaipur, who erected four others—at Delhi, Muttra, Ujjain and Jaipur. On entering the Observatory, the first instrument seen is the Bhittiyantra, or "mural quadrant". It is a wall 11 ft. high and 9 ft. 1¼ in. broad, in the plane of the meridian; by this are ascertained the sun's altitude and zenith distance, and its greatest declination, and hence the latitude. Then come two large circles, one of stone and the other of cement, and a stone square, used, perhaps, for ascertaining the shadow of the gnomon and the degrees of azimuth.

The Samratyantra is a wall which is 36 ft. long and 4½ ft. broad, and is set in the plane of the meridian. One end is 6 ft. 4¼ in. high, and the other 22 ft. 3½ in., and it slopes gradually up so as to point to the North Pole. By this, the distance from the meridian, the declination of any planet or star and of the sun, and the right ascension of a star, are calculated. There are also a double mural quadrant, an equinoctial circle of stone, and another Samratyantra. Close by is the Chakrayantra, between two walls, used for finding the declination of a planet or star; and near it a Digamsayantra, to find the degrees of azimuth of a planet or star. The instruments are fully described in a leaflet obtainable at the Observatory.[1]

The **Mir Ghat** (used by Muslims) leads up to the Dharm Kup, or Sacred Well, and the Lalita Ghat to the **Nepalese Temple**; picturesque. The erotic carvings are notorious but possess religious significance for the Nepalese whose Hinduism is strongly tainted with tantric Vajrayana Buddhism. This temple is remarkable for its double roof such as those on Chinese temples.

The famous **Golden Temple** is some way from the river, located between this Ghat and the **Jalsain Ghat,** or Burning Ghat, which is crowned by a mass of temples and spires. Numbers of cremations are usually in progress on the spot, and many sati stones will be noticed all round it; it is naturally regarded by the Hindus as one of the most holy places in the

[1] An oil-painting by Thomas Daniell, now in Calcutta (p. 173), shows the original river front.

[1] See also *A Guide to the Old Observatories at Delhi, Jaipur, Ujjain and Benares,* by G. R. Kaye (Calcutta, 1920).

whole of Benares. The name is derived from Vishnu in his manifestation of Jalsai, "the sleeper on the ocean".

The **Manikarnika Ghat** is considered the most sacred of all the Ghats, and in November is visited by multitudes of pilgrims. Just above the flight of steps, which are enclosed by piers running out into the river, is the Manikarnika Well, or pool, and between it and the steps is the temple of Tarkeswar. The well has its name from *Mani*, "a jewel", and *Karna*, "the ear". Parvati, the wife of Mahadeo, is said to have dropped her earring, and Mahadeo in searching for it, dug a large hole with his trident. This became the tank, and the god's sweat filled it with water. During an eclipse of the sun it is visited by great numbers of pilgrims. The well, or, more properly, tank, is 35 ft. square, and stone steps lead down to the water. Offerings of the Bel tree flowers, milk, sandalwood and sweetmeats are thrown into it. Between the well and the Ghat is the Charanpaduka, a round slab projecting slightly from the pavement, on which stands a pedestal of stone; on its marble top are two imprints, said to have been made by the feet of Vishnu. The privilege of being burnt at the Charanpaduka, instead of the usual burning Ghat, is confined to a few families, and is much prized. At the second flight of steps of this Ghat is a temple to Siddha Vinayak, or Ganesh. The idol has three eyes, is painted red, and has a silver scalp and an elephant's trunk covered with a bib. At the feet of the image is the figure of a rat, which is the vahana, or "vehicle", of Ganesh. Overhanging the Ghat is the red-domed temple of the Raja of Amethi (an Oudh landowner), which is one of the best from an artistic point of view.

The **Dattatreya Ghat** is called after the great Brahmin saint and teacher, in whom parts of the three great Hindu deities, Brahma, Vishnu and Siva, were said to have been incarnated. His *paduka*, or footprint, is shown in a small temple on the Ghat.

Scindia's Ghat was intended to have been one of the grandest of the whole front, but, owing to the great weight of the superstructures, the foundations sank and it has had to be reconstructed. It was built about 1830 by Baiza Bai, widow of Daulat Rao Scindia.

Passing two Ghats, the **Bhosla,** miscalled the Ghosla, **Ghat,** was built by the **Nagpur** Raja more than one hundred years ago, and is very massive. The next Ghat was built by Baji Rao II, the last of the Peshwas. The **Ram Ghat,** which comes next again, was built by the Raja of Jaipur.

The next large Ghat is the **Panchganga Ghat,** beneath which five rivers, Ganges, Jumna, Saraswati, Kirana and Dhutpapa are supposed to meet; it was built by Raja Man Singh of Ambèr. Above it rises the **smaller mosque of Aurangzeb** called the **"Minarets"** or Alamgir mosque. These were taken down and restored under the direction of James Prinsep (p. 182) as the foundations were giving way. The mosque occupies the site of a temple to Vishnu under the name of Bindu Madhav, which is described by Tavernier in 1666, and this is the probable reason for the local name (Madho Rai ki Masjid). The view from the top of the minarets, which rise nearly 150 ft. above the platform of the mosque, is extremely fine, and it is quite worth while to ascend to the roof of the building. The two *stupas* at Sarnath can be seen from here, and the Mirzapur Hills to the W. From the river the view of the mosque is impressive.

Four unimportant Ghats lie between this and the second Sitala or Raj Mandil Ghat, below which is the **Gai Ghat,** so called from the stone figure of a cow.

The **Trilochan Ghat,** the next reached, has two turrets in the river, and the water between them possesses a special sanctity. Pilgrims bathe in the Ganges at this Ghat, and then proceed to the Panchganga and there bathe again. At the head of the Ghat is a temple of Trilochan, or the Three-

Eyed, another form of Siva. From the **Prahlad Ghat,** the last masonry Ghat, a view is obtained of the whole river front. Farther down the stream is the site of the old Raj Ghat ferry, replaced by the railway and road bridge; also by a pontoon bridge, except in the rains. These bridges are near the **Raj Ghat**: the *Barna Sangam*, or junction of the Ganges and Barna, is ¾ m. downstream.

The **Malaviya (Dufferin) Bridge** is 3518 ft. in length (seven spans of 333 ft.) and carries the Grand Trunk Road. Raj Ghat Fort dated from antiquity and is now dismantled. There are clusters of temples at the confluence with the Barna. Within the area of the Fort and in the S. corner of the plateau is the **Tomb of Lal Khan,** a minister of a former Raja of Benares, with coloured tiles and mosaics, described by Mr Havell as one of the few original Muslim buildings in Benares with any pretensions to architectural beauty.

TEMPLES AND MOSQUES

The **Golden Temple** is dedicated to Biseswar (Sanskrit Visvesvara), or Siva, as the Lord of the Universe. Shoes will have to be removed. It is reached by leaving the Chauk (the centre of the city close to the Town Hall) by a gateway on the E. and turning sharply to the right into Kachouri Gali, a typical Benares lane, full of shops.

The temple, dating about 1750, surrounded by narrow streets, is in a roofed quadrangle, above which rises the tower. At each corner is a dome, and at the S.E. a Sivala over the sanctuary. The gate has finely wrought brass doors. From the upper rooms the interior may be seen. The music gallery was built at the expense of Warren Hastings.

The curvilinear[1] tower (left) is that of Mahadeo's temple; next to it is a gilt dome, and on the right is the gilt tower (51 ft. high) of Biseswar's temple. The three are in a row in the centre of the quadrangle. Two of them are covered with gold plates, over plates of copper which cover the stones. The expense of gilding was defrayed by Maharaja Ranjit Singh, of Lahore. Between Biseswar and Mahadeo temples hang nine bells from a carved stone framework. One of these, and the most elegant, was presented by the Maharaja of Nepal. The temple of Mahadeo was built by Ahalya Bai, Princess of Indore (p. 203). Outside the enclosure is the Court of Mahadeo, where on a platform are a number of lingams, and many small idols are built into the wall. They are thought to have belonged to the old temple of Biseswar, which stood N.W. of the present one, and of which the remains are still to be seen at the back of the mosque which Aurangzeb built on them.

In the quadrangle between the mosque and the Temple of Biseswar is the famous **Gyan Kup,** or Gyan Bapi, "Well of Knowledge", where, according to Hindu tradition, the emblem of Siva took refuge when the original temple was destroyed, and still remains. The well is protected by a high stone screen, and covered by a stone canopy, and the worshippers, an eager and excited crowd, by whom the quadrangle is always thronged, are no longer permitted to cast offerings of flowers, etc., into it. A draught of its sacred water is held to induce the highest spiritual illumination. The roof and colonnade of the quadrangle were built about 1830 by Baiza Bai, widow of Daulat Rao Scindia of Gwalior. On one side of the colonnade is a Nandi bull, 7 ft. high. On another side is an iron railing, within which is a shrine of white marble and one of white stone, and a carved stone support, from which hangs a bell. Around are many richly carved small temples, particularly one to the S. of Biseswar; the gateways of the courtyard are

[1] These towers are called *Sikharas*. The curvilinear *Sikhara* is most common in the eastern Deccan. It derives from the elementary forest shrines made by tying together a clump of bamboo.

similarly carved, and small gilded spires add to the picturesqueness.

The **great Mosque of Aurangzeb** lies to the N.W. side of the Gyan Kup. The two octagonal minarets are 232 ft. above the Ganges. The Hindus claim the courtyard between it and the temple wall, and in consequence it is entered from the side. The zealot Emperor Aurangzeb (1658-1707) is accused of destroying the most ancient and sacred Siva temple of Biseswar, but it only dated from 1600. During the period of three and a half centuries since the mosque was built not a stone has been loosened. A good number of the faithful assemble here on Fridays. The beautiful columns in the front of the mosque belonged to the destroyed temple, of which further remains may be seen at the back.

Just outside the Golden Temple is the **Shrine of Sanichar,** or Sani, the planet Saturn or its regent. The black image is worshipped to ward off misfortune. A garland hangs from either ear, and a canopy is spread above.

Beyond is the **Temple of Annapurna,** a goddess whose name is compounded of *Anna*, "food", and *Purna*, "who is filled". She is supposed to have express orders from Biseswar to feed the inhabitants of Benares, and in front of this temple are always a number of beggars who are chiefly women. It was built about 1725 by the Peshwa of that date, Baji Rao I. There are four shrines in this temple dedicated to the Sun, Ganesh, Gaurisankar and the monkey-god Hanuman. Between the Temple of Annapurna and that of Sakhi Vinayak is a curious **Figure of Ganesh,** squatting on a platform raised a little above the path. This image is red, with silver hands, feet, ears and elephant's trunk. Next is the temple of **Sakhi Vinayak,** the witnessing deity, built in 1770 by a Mahratta, whose name is not recorded. Here pilgrims after finishing the Panch Kosi circuit round Benares get a certificate of having done so. S. of the temple to Sani is that of **Shukareswar** (*Shukar* being the planet Venus), where prayers are made for handsome sons.

The narrow streets and lanes which connect the Ghats with one another, and the parts of the city lying more remote from the river front, will be found exceedingly interesting; but they cannot be described as clean or sweet smelling, and they must be traversed on foot. This mass of narrow streets, overhung by lofty houses, is known as the "Pakku Mahals" and is one of the most characteristic features of Benares. It comprises the whole of the city nearest the river, but is of varying depth and covers altogether several square miles. Almost every corner of the Pukka Mahals is picturesque. The effect of the closely crowded houses can be seen from the minarets of the *smaller mosque* of Aurangzeb above the Panchganga Ghat.

Near the Town Hall the **Temple of Bhaironath** is in a lane at some little distance from the back of the Post Office. It was built by the ex-Peshwa Baji Rao II in 1825. The image in the temple is considered to be the Kotwal, or superintendent of the city, who rides about on a ghostly dog. There is an image of a dog close to the idol, and the confectioners near sell images of dogs, made of sugar, which are offered to it. A Brahmin waves a fan of peacock's feathers over visitors to dust off the evil spirits, and they in return must drop offerings into the coconut shell he holds. The idol is of stone, with a face of silver and four hands. The Dandpan temple close to this contains the staff of Bhairon, a stone shaft 4½ ft. high, and the famous Kal Kup, or Well of Fate, into which the sunlight falls from a hole in the wall above. If the face of the onlooker is not reflected, death comes to him within a year.

The **Gopal Mandir** lies off a narrow lane behind the Kotwali and close to the Dandpan and Kal Kup. In the garden of the temple is a small house or hut in which Tulsi Das (p. 159) is said to have composed his *Binaya Patrika*, a poem which some authorities, Indian and British, consider to be superior to the *Ramayana*. A tablet was affixed to the wall by Lord Curzon. The Kameswar temple of the God of Love lies to the N.E. of Bhaironath and near the Machodri garden (Gokul Chand Park). It is of the 12th century and quite interesting.

The Bharat Mata Temple, about 1 m. S. of the Cantonment Station, has a very large and excellent marble relief map of all of Hindustan.

The dingy **Briddhkal** temple, which lies N.E. from the Municipal Garden, is one of the oldest in the city, and originally had twelve courts, of which seven remain. It contains a well and a small tank renowned for the healing of diseases. The name *Briddhkal* means "the fate of old age"; and the temple is said to have been built by an aged and infirm Raja whom Mahadeva restored to youth and health.

The palace and fort of the Maharaja of Benares at **Ramnagar,** on the right bank, afford a splendid view of the river front, and of the Banaras Hindu University on the opposite side. There is a temple of some interest. The late Maharaja Sir Aditya Narayan Singh (d. 1939) belonged to the family of Raja Balwant Singh, father of Raja Chait Singh. The State was created in 1911, when the late Maharaja was granted the powers of a Ruling Chief in his domains, which extended over an area of 875 sq. m. Previously the title was personal, obtained from the Mughal King in 1738. In 1949 the State was merged in Uttar Pradesh.

SARNATH

Sarnath[1] (conducted tours, bus services and taxis from Benares: Birla Rest House: International Guest House—no catering), the site where Buddha preached his first sermon, is some 4 m. N. of Benares, not far from the high road to Ghazipur, which is left at the third milestone. Shortly after turning to the left two towers are seen—the Chaukhandi, on a hill: the other the Dhamekh[2] *stupa*. Sarnath can also be reached by rail from Benares Cantonment station and can well be combined with a visit to Jaunpur.

Rules for observance by visitors should be studied.

Sarnath was known as the "Deer Park", and is prominent in one of the Jataka, or Birth-stories of the Buddha. In his lifetime his five early attendants retired there for meditation after forsaking their master; there Buddha first made known his doctrines to the world. Buddhists have always revered the spot where he sat and preached as holy ground. The Chinese travellers —Fa-Hian, at the beginning of the 5th century; Hiuen Tsang, about A.D. 640—visited the site. The former mentioned two monasteries as existing in the Deer Park, and four memorial topes, which he saw. The latter, Hiuen Tsang, described more fully the whole *sangharama* (monastery) as he saw it. He mentioned 1500 priests in the convent, a *vihara* 200 ft. high, a figure of Buddha represented as "turning the wheel of the Law"—i.e. preaching—Asoka's stone *stupa*, a stone pillar 70 ft. high, three lakes, other monuments, and the most magnificent *stupa* of all, 300 ft. high. Sarnath was probably destroyed when Qutb-ud-din, Shahab-ud-din Ghori's General, devastated Benares in 1194, but in any case after the overthrow of Buddhism in India *c.* A.D. 800 Sarnath was completely deserted.

The *stupa* locally known as the Dhamekh Tower (a little to N.E. of a modern Jain temple) consists "of a stone plinth 93 ft. in diameter and solidly built, the stones being clamped together with iron, to the height of 43 ft. Above that it is in brickwork, rising to a height of 104 ft. above the terrace of the temple, and 143 ft., including its foundations. Externally the lower part is relieved by eight projecting faces, each 21 ft. 6 in. wide

[1] Guide books to the Ruins and to the Archaeological museum can be obtained from the Tourist Information Offices.

[2] Dhamekh is a corruption of Dharmeksha, the pondering of the Law.

and 15 ft. apart. In each is a small niche, intended, apparently, to contain an image, and below them, encircling the monument, is a band of sculptured ornament of the most exquisite beauty. The central part of this band consists of geometric patterns of great intricacy, but combined with singular skill, while above and below are rich floral arabesques, the whole being peculiarly characteristic of the art of the Imperial Guptas. The carvings round the niches and in the projections have been left unfinished, and judging by the absence of any fragments either in stone or brick or plaster around the *stupa*, it seems not improbable that the upper part of the tower was never completed."[1]

In his examination of the Dhamekh Tower General Sir A. Cunningham found, buried in the brickwork, an inscribed stone with the Buddhist formula "Ye dharmma hetuprabhava", etc., said to be in characters of the 7th century, a record held by the latest opinion to be contemporary with the last rebuilding of the *stupa*. It is believed that a smaller first *stupa* on this spot was afterwards built over and enlarged to the present dimensions.

Some 500 ft. to the W. of the Dhamekh Tower there was another, called the Dharmarajika *stupa* or Jagat Singh *stupa* (from the name of a Diwan of a Raja of Benares, who had it dug for bricks), now a mere shell; the innermost existing ring has a diameter of over 44 ft. On the discovery of this *stupa* in 1794, Sarnath became a hunting-ground for treasure seekers, and cartloads are said to have been carried away.

A conspicuous structure is to be seen some 20 yd. due N. of the Jagat Singh *stupa*, named the "Main Shrine", which both "served as a shrine and formed the centre of numerous smaller memorials built round it. It is a rectangular building measuring 95 ft. by 90 ft., with doubly recessed corners, and still standing to a height of some 18 ft. It is built partly of stone, partly of brick, and much of the stone has been taken from earlier structures, notably of the Gupta period. From the thickness of the original walls and the additions subsequently made to them in the interior of the building, it is evident that they were intended to support a massive and probably lofty superstructure." A small *stupa* in the S. chapel of the Main Shrine is surrounded by a stone railing cut entire from one single block of stone, and the chiselling and polishing of the stone have been executed with a skill which it would be impossible to surpass. Two inscriptions noticed on it are not earlier than the 3rd or 4th century A.D., but its workmanship connects it with the epoch of the Emperor Asoka (274-237 B.C.). The Main Shrine continued in use to the 11th century A.D. Round it was a concrete pavement, 40 ft. square, covered with numerous chapels, *stupas* and monuments of brick, plaster and stone, ranging from the Kushana period (A.D. 45-225) to the destruction by the Muslims.

Most of the area excavated under the pavement is occupied by a large rectangular chamber or court measuring 48 ft. by 28 ft., with a variety of other structures adjoining it. This chamber was surrounded on three sides by a railing of Mauryan date (321-184 B.C.), built into the brickwork of the walls. The position of all the columns and cross-bars is clearly marked by indentations in the brickwork. The excavations have been extended some distance on every side of the Main Shrine, disclosing numerous small chapels and *stupas*, separate and in groups, some in perfect preservation, and yielding numbers of sculptures from the relic chambers. The Northern—called the Monastery —Area has already revealed parts of four monasteries, three being of the 3rd, the largest of the 11th or 12th century A.D.

To the W. of the Main Shrine is the broken shaft of the Asoka sandstone

[1] Memorandum by the Director-General of Archaeology in India.

column. The capital is in the Sarnath Museum. The portion still standing measures 16 ft. 8 in. in height, with a diameter of 2 ft. 6 in. at the bottom. The whole height, including the capital, appears to have been about 50 ft. The capital, "which measures 7 ft. high, is of the Persepolitan bell-shaped type, surmounted by four magnificent lions sitting back to back with a wheel between them—symbolising the law of the Buddha, which was first promulgated at Sarnath." This wheel and the lions have been adopted as the symbol of the Indian Union, and shown on the President's flag. Beneath the lions is a drum ornamented with four animals in relief—viz., a lion, an elephant, a bull, and a horse—separated from each other by four wheels. The four crowning lions and the reliefs below are wonderfully vigorous and true to nature. That the column was set up by Asoka is evident from the presence of an edict on the portion still *in situ*. This edict enjoins that whatsoever monk or nun creates schisms in the *sangha* should be made to put on white clothes and reside outside the convent. "His Sacred Majesty further urges that his order should also be made known to the lay-members. The superintendents of the sacred law should also familiarise themselves with the edict, and make it known in their own circles and elsewhere."

On the summit of a large *stupa* about half a mile to the S. of the Dhamekh Tower on a mound known locally as the Chaukhandi or "square" mound, is an octagonal brick tower, erected by the Emperor Akbar in 1588 to commemorate a visit of his father, Humayun, to the spot. An inscription in Arabic characters on a stone slab above the doorway contains the following record: "As Humayun, king of the Seven Climes, now residing in paradise, deigned to come and sit here one day, thereby increasing the splendour of the sun, so Akbar, his son and humble servant, resolved to build on this spot a lofty tower reaching to the blue sky. It was in the year 996 A.H. that this beautiful building was erected." It is believed that the whole *sangharama* at Sarnath, as elsewhere, was surrounded by a massive circuit wall, 9 ft. thick.

The sculptures brought to light at Sarnath "divide themselves naturally into four groups—the first comprising those of the Mauryan epoch, the second those of the Kushana epoch, the third belonging to the age of the Imperial Guptas, and the fourth including all later examples. The chief examples of Mauryan work are the Asoka column and capital, the railing in the Main Shrine, portions of another railing, and two separate capitals. The Kushana group is represented mainly by two colossal pieces of carving, one a Boddhisattwa statue standing 9½ ft. high, the other a gigantic umbrella measuring 10 ft. across, and adorned on its under surface with designs of animals, religious symbols, and geometric patterns." These carvings are now in the Museum.

The significant building age was that of the Imperial Guptas (A.D. 320-455); during which there was an important and far-reaching school of sculpture. The Gupta origin of the Dhamekh *stupa* is now no longer doubted; its decoration is reproduced in several of the Gupta sculptures unearthed. This Gupta style exhibits many semi-classical affinities, due to the influence exerted on it by Mauryan, and still more by Gandhara, art. Its pervading spirit, however, and the decorative "motifs" which peculiarly distinguish it, are essentially and indisputably Indian. Of these motifs the most characteristic are floral arabesques treated with superb grace and boldness, and often enriched by the addition of human figures clinging in supple attitudes among the foliage. Geometric designs, too, of an intricate but never bewildering nature, play an important role in the schemes of decoration; while motifs borrowed from jewellery are perhaps more conspicuous in this than in any other school of Indian Art. No less characteristic is the treatment of human figures, which are free from the exaggerated development that makes some Indian sculpture alien to Western eyes.

Among the Gupta sculptures are two bas-reliefs of special interest—one in eight panels, referring to the eight chief places of Buddha's life, while the other depicts events thereof. Inscriptions, on statues, images and seals help to fix dates and the name of the monastery where Buddha's first sermon was delivered—namely, **Dharmachakrapravarttana vihara** or, in short, **Dharmachakra**. The difficulty is to identify the buildings as they now are with those mentioned by the Chinese travellers. Two, the Monastery No. 1 and the Main Shrine, are later than the date of Hiuen Tsang.

The sculptures and carvings found have been distributed between the Indian Museum, Calcutta and the **Museum** at Sarnath (1908), designed like a Buddhist monastery. Exhibits were rearranged in 1929. There is a good catalogue with a useful introduction.

One of the things that a visitor must now see is the temple built by the Maha Bodhi Society of India, Japan and Ceylon, known as the Mula Gandhakuti Vihara. The chief feature is a series of interior frescoes executed by a Japanese artist. The frescoes depict scenes from the life of Lord Buddha. In the temple is one of the relics from the Main Shrine, and one from Nagarjunakonda (p. 483). Outside is an Aswatha tree transplanted from Ceylon, where a seed of the original tree of Buddh Gaya was planted in about 300 B.C.

ROUTE 6.—CALCUTTA CITY AND ENVIRONS

(*Maps* face *pages* 172 *and* 187)

INDEX

Changes in Street Names on Map

Cornwallis Street	now called	Bidhan Sarani
Machuabazar Street	,,	(Madan Mohan Street and Keshab Sen Street)
Harrison Road	,,	Mahatma Gandhi Road
Mirzapore Street	,,	Suryya Sen Street
Lower Chitpur Road	,,	Rabindra Sarani

Bowbazar Street	now called	Bepin Behary Ganguly
Wellington Street	,,	Nirmal Chunder Street
Wellesley Street	,,	Rafi Ahmed Kidwai Road
Lower Circular Road	,,	Acharya Jagadish Bose Road
Chowringhi Road	,,	J. L. Nehru Road
Theatre Road	,,	Shakespeare Sarani
Lansdowne Road	,,	Sarat Bose Road
Ballyganj Store Road	,,	Gurusaday Road
Buckland Road	,,	Bankim Ch. Road

History.—Calcutta, now the capital of West Bengal,[1] is younger than Madras or Bombay. Hooghly, at which a factory had been established in 1642, was abandoned in 1686 for three villages on the present site, Sutanati, Kalikata and Govindpur. Job Charnock was the leader of the merchants. Driven down the river, they returned in 1687. In the former India Office Library are eleven volumes of "Bengal Consultations" (July 1690 to 1706); in the first of these may be read, in the words of Charnock himself, how the English reoccupied Sutanati, which had been abandoned for Madras in 1688, for the third time in 1690. Permission to rent the three villages was given in 1698 by Azim-us-Shan, grandson of the Emperor Aurangzeb. Until December 1699, Bengal was subordinate to Fort St George (Madras), and the first Governor of Fort William for the New Company was Sir Charles Eyre, Charnock's son-in-law.

In 1696 Sir John Goldsborough laid out the lines of a fort (on the W. side of what is now Dalhousie Square) in the Kalikata village area and to which the name of Fort William was given in honour of the reigning King. Queen Mary having died the year before.

Calcutta continued to flourish, owing to its favourable position at the gate of the principal waterways of N. India, until 1756, when it was attacked and taken by the Nawab of Murshidabad, Suraj-ud-daula. Most of the British, including the Governor, fled down the river in ships to Falta; the others became the victims of the historical tragedy of the Black Hole (20th-21st June). In December Colonel Clive arrived with troops from Madras and ships under Admiral Watson. Calcutta was retaken by them on 2nd January 1757; the Nawab's position was attacked on 4th February, and his forces were withdrawn from near the town.

After negotiation the Nawab promised to restore the trading privileges of the Company and return the property. The Seven Years War, between the French and British, was anticipated by the capture of Chandernagore (23rd March). Encouraged by the French in his service and by hints of support from the Mahratta Chief of Nagpur, Suraj-ud-daula ultimately refused to accept an exclusive alliance with the British, and this led to the Battle of Plassey, on 23rd June 1757, and Suraj-ud-daula's death.

Mir Jafir, who now became Nawab with the help of Clive, gave the English the zemindari of the 24 Parganas, as well as a free gift of the town. Heavy compensation was paid to the Company and its servants, and with part of the compensation money

[1] Tourist Centres (see Directory) have brochures available. Many of the best books on Calcutta are still the old ones, often reprinted. Busteed's *Echoes from Old Calcutta* (Thacker, Calcutta, 3rd edn., 1897) contains much information about the place at the end of the 18th century. Another excellent book on the same period is the *Memoirs* of William Hickey (Hutchinson). Blechynden's *Calcutta, Past and Present* (Thacker, 1905), Firminger's *Guide to Calcutta* (Thacker), and Cotton's *Calcutta, Old and New* (specially recommended; Newman, Calcutta), are also full of interest. See also *Calcutta* by Geoffrey Moorehouse (Penguin, 1975).

Govindpur was cleared of its inhabitants.

The foundations of the present Fort William were laid in 1758. The building was completed about 1781 at a cost of two million sterling, half a million of which was spent to protect the west face from the erosion of the river. The area in which no buildings were allowed, lest they should overlook the Fort, became the Maidan; and the European quarter, which was located between Canning Street and Hastings Street, began to extend southwards along Chowringhi. In 1774 Warren Hastings, President in Bengal two years previously, was made the first Governor-General of Fort William in Bengal, with authority over Bombay and Madras in political relations, and the Supreme Court of Judicature was established. The old Cathedral of St John was built between 1783 and 1787, and the Bishopric of Calcutta was created in 1813, the first Bishop being Thomas Middleton, and the second (1823), Reginald Heber. The "great apartments" of the present magnificent Government House were opened on the 4th May 1802; the Town Hall was completed in 1813, and the old Mint in Strand Road between 1824 and 1830, while the Botanical Gardens at Sibpur, on the right bank of the Hooghly, were laid out as early as 1786.

In 1854 Calcutta passed with the rest of Bengal under the direct control of a Lieutenant-Governor, a form of government which continued until 1911, when Bengal was restored to her former rank as a Presidency with a Governor. In 1857 the University was established. In 1862 the Legislative Council of the Lieutenant-Governor was created, and in 1865-76 the municipal government of Calcutta was in the hands of Justices of Peace. The Chamber of Commerce dates from 1834, and the Port Trust Commission from 1870.

The transfer of the capital from Calcutta to Delhi, and the creation of a Presidency of Bengal were announced by George V at Delhi on 12th December 1911, but this scarcely affected Calcutta's pre-eminence as a business centre. In 1947, with the coming of partition, Calcutta lost a large part of its commercial hinterland, but it substantially withstood the shock, and is still the home of a large Indian and European business community. The climate is pleasant in spite of the humidity during the cold-weather months (November to February). On alluvial soil at least 1250 ft. thick, it is the headquarters of the Government of West Bengal.

Numerically, Calcutta is, next to London, the largest city in the Commonwealth. In 1971 the population of the city and suburbs, including Howrah, was over 7 millions. A great increase took place since the 1951 census, not entirely due to natural causes, as the urban population has been artificially swollen by the influx of refugees consequent on the upset caused by Partition. The area has also been enlarged. Early in the last century the population was about 200,000, and in 1850, 400,000. The first census was taken in 1872.

The **Port** of Calcutta is still one of the leading ports in the East, though a change of current in the Ganges many years ago has been causing very bad silting in the Hooghly in recent decades. The silt, instead of adding to the size of the Delta has been settling higher up, the salinity of the Hooghly has considerably increased and the tidal bore comes every three days now. No ship of 10,000 tons or more can now get near Calcutta and a lot of traffic is being diverted to other ports. (See also p. 191.) The silting should be helped once the **Farakka Barrage** 160 m. to the north has been completed. This could divert fresh water into the Hooghly from the Ganges, but Bangladesh has separate interests in the Barrage Scheme which may present difficulties.

The site of Calcutta on the left bank of the Hooghly was originally selected for maritime trade. The Hooghly carries to the sea the large volume of exports brought to Calcutta by the railways and river steamers; and by it enters the large volume of imports for an extensive hinterland. The port proper extends from Konnagar, 9½ m. N. to Budge Budge (a subsidiary port dealing with petroleum), 13 m. S.; but the jurisdiction of the Conservators of the port approaches extends from Kalna, 60 m. N., at the head of tidal action, down to the Eastern Channel Light Vessel, 126 m. S., where the pilot vessel awaits ocean steamers.

The navigation of the river between Calcutta and the sea is rendered difficult by shifting shoals and sandbanks: these necessitate the maintenance of large suction dredgers, an elaborate and scientific system of survey, and the service of skilled pilots.

Until the separation of East Pakistan from West Bengal in 1947, Calcutta enjoyed a practical monopoly of Jute exports, and still has a large trade; other important commodities are shellac, tea and coal. The imports consist chiefly of cotton goods, oils and petrol, and miscellaneous goods of European manufacture, together with sugar from Java and rice and timber from Burma, but trade with Burma may take long before it revives to its former level.

A passenger-steamer service, initiated by the Port Trust in 1907, has a fleet of vessels, which ply up and down the river from daylight to dark.

There are numerous moorings in the stream, thirteen riverside jetties and the Kidderpore Docks with thirty berths. The King George's Dock at Garden Reach (p. 181) provides for the largest vessels that can navigate the Hooghly. See p. 191 for the Haldia port project.

The Port is administered by a body called the Calcutta Port Commissioners, consisting of a salaried Chairman and Deputy Chairman, certain nominated and a number of elected Commissioners, representing business interests and the railways.

There are many large factories and mills in and around Calcutta. The major industry is in jute, Calcutta manufacturing most of the hessians and gunny bags in use in the world. The mills attract large numbers of labourers.

The civic administration is vested in the Corporation (1899), remodelled by an Act of the local Legislature, which came into force in April 1924, and again in 1939. At the head of the Corporation are a Mayor and Deputy Mayor, who are elected for one year by the Councillors. The Corporation appoints, in addition to officers to whom particular duties are assigned, a Chief Executive Officer, to whom it delegates certain powers, duties or functions, under the Act.

The further improvement and expansion of Calcutta was, by an Act of 1911 (amended in 1931), entrusted to a Board and a Chairman. The **Improvement Trust** opened up congested areas, laid out or widened streets and provided open spaces. It began by running a 100-ft. road from S. to N., now called Chittaranjan Avenue, through the congested north of Calcutta some 3 m. in length, with another at right angles to it, and widening Russa Road almost the same length from the S.E. corner of the Maidan S. to Tollygunge, the Diamond Harbour Road leading out to the S.W. It carried out a number of smaller schemes in the city, rebuilt all the bridges over the canals and Tolly's Nullah, and laid out the Lansdowne Road area, before embarking on the development of the Dhakuria area towards the S.E. Another remarkable transformation was effected in the area of Park Circus N. of Ballygunge and Entally, and the Trust has had for some years a development scheme in Manicktola and Ultadanga between the Circular Canal and the Salt Lakes. The Trust's authority covers Howrah.

In spite of the Improvement Trust's efforts, the overall situation in Calcutta has become critical. The relentless pressure of an increasingly immigrant population (p. 171) on the public utilities and housing, has produced a situation which the City can no longer solve for itself. In 1961 the Calcutta Metropolitan Planning Organisation was founded, financed by money from Central Government funds, West Bengal funds, and the Ford Foundation. In 1966 it produced a Basic Development Plan admirable in its flexibility. To date, however, little of the Plan has become a reality. There is now talk of Calcutta being given top priority by a large consortium of international relief agencies.

Arrival in Calcutta

The traveller by air arrives at Dum Dum (p. 186) airport: new Hotel: 7 m. from Calcutta, and drives in I.A.C. bus or by taxi along the new Super Highway, reaching the centre of Calcutta *via* Chittaranjan Avenue. The railway traveller arrives at **Howrah,** on the right bank of the River Hooghly. The river is crossed by a cantilever bridge (1500 ft.) which was opened in 1943, replacing the former **Pontoon Bridge,** constructed by Sir Bradford Leslie in 1874.

The old bridge was capable of being opened for river traffic and when it happened Howrah and Calcutta were completely cut off from one another. Even in the daytime the congestion on the narrow roadway meant that it would often take half an hour to cross the bridge in any sort of vehicle. There was a long-drawn-out controversy whether the erection of a permanent bridge on piers would cause silting up in the Port of Calcutta. Other rivers in the Bengal Delta are liable to change their courses in a most arbitrary manner. The stretch of the Hooghly on which Calcutta stands is contained within more or less permanent banks, but shoals and deep channels within the bed are liable to move as a result of obstructions. Finally it was decided not to risk placing even two piers in the river to carry a bridge, and the new Howrah Bridge was built on the cantilever principal with a single span. To obtain this span the steel work has to rise to a remarkable height; so that the structure, which compares with that of the Sydney Bridge, dwarfs Howrah railway station and all the buildings on either side of the river except the new Government Secretariat in Strand Road, 13 stories and 196 feet high, and the new Central Telephone Exchange in Dalhousie Square.

On the E. side of the bridge the **Strand Road** runs from N. to S. along the left bank of the river, the European residential quarter lying to the S.E. past the Esplanade. Direct access to **Sealdah Station,** the terminus of the railway lines running to Northern and Eastern Bengal and Assam, is afforded by the **Harrison Road,** which runs from the bridge W. to E. through the heart of the purely Indian quarter.

Strand Road is congested with traffic from the jetties. Harrison Road was in the same state until recently a 100-ft. wide road was driven by the Improvement Trust in a wide curve from the N.E. corner of Dalhousie Square to the Bridge approaches.

The Maidan and Quarters East and South

The centre of Calcutta is the famous **Maidan** (plain, parade-ground), bounded on the W. side by the Hooghly river and the Strand Road, and on the E. side by Chowringhi Road; it is nearly 2 m. long, and is ¾ m. broad at its head, and 1¼ m. broad at the S. end, Tolly's Nullah. Government House, the residence of the Governor, faces it on the N., while Belvedere, where the Lieutenant-Governors of Bengal used to live, and which is now occupied by the National Library, is south of Tolly's Nullah. In the centre of the W. side is Fort William, and on the E. side are hotels, various shops, the sites of former Clubs, the Indian Museum and the Cathedral; in the N.W. corner are the Eden Gardens, and on the S., from W. to E., are the Race-course, the Military Station Hospital, the Presidency General Hospital, the Victoria Memorial and the Calcutta Club. The Red Road, once the fashionable evening resort, runs down the centre of the Maidan from N. to S., and joins Queen's Way, leading to the Victoria Memorial. The broad gravelled walk on the W. of the Red Road is called Secretary's Walk, and dates back to the year 1820.

The **Eden Gardens**, for which Calcutta is indebted to the sisters of Lord Auckland (hence the Indian name, Lady Baghan), are beautifully laid out, and at one time were the principal evening gathering-place of Calcutta society. In them is the old ground of the Calcutta Cricket Club, and on the side of the miniature lake, a Burmese Pagoda brought from Prome (1856). A recent development has been the Calcutta Stadium.

The Chandpal Ghat used to be the official landing-place of the Governor-General and his Councillors, the Commander-in-Chief, and the Judges of the Supreme Court. Here the first members of the Supreme Council sent from England, and Sir Elijah Impey and the Judges of the Supreme Court, landed in October 1774. The practice continued for seventy years.

From Chandpal Ghat, Esplanade Road leads E., passing the High Court, the Town Hall and Government House, and ending at Chowringhi Place, from which Chowringhi Road leads S. along the E. side of the Maidan, and Central Avenue leads to the N. of the city. To the E. of Bentinck Street lies the Chinese quarter with a Chinese temple; but the visitor who wants to see it should ask his hotel or a tourist agency for a suitable guide.

The Supreme Court was converted to a High Court in 1861.

The **High Court,** designed by Walter Grenville after the Staadhaus at Ypres, with a tower 180 ft. high, was erected in 1872. A view over the city can be had from the corner turrets. An extension, connected by an over-bridge, contains the Sessions Court. The Chief Justice's Court is in the S.W. corner. The Courts of Original Jurisdiction are at the S.E. corner. In the E. face is the Bar Library. The Attorneys' Library is in the E. corner.

The buildings contain many portraits and statues of former Judicial dignitaries.

The records of the Court include the trial of Nuncomar by Sir Elijah Impey with three other judges and a jury (on loan to the Victoria Memorial Collection).

The **Town Hall,** standing W. of Government House, was completed, as an inscription in English and Urdu on the S. façade records, "under the Government of Lord Minto in the year of Christ 1813". Its construction was determined upon by the inhabitants of Calcutta as early as 1804: and the cost was met by a lottery, which was announced in the following year "under the patronage and sanction" of Lord Wellesley, who was then Governor-General. The style is Doric, with a fine flight of steps leading to a portico on the S.

A **Council House,** to accommodate the Bengal Legislature, enlarged to two Houses, stands to the S. of the Town Hall.

Government House, now renamed Raj Bhawan, the official residence of the Governor of Bengal, is situated in a fine enclosure of 6 acres, at the end of the Maidan.

Its construction was begun in 1799 under Marquess Wellesley (the architect being Captain Charles Wyatt of the Bengal Engineers), and finished in 1802, the design being an adaptation of that of Kedleston Hall, Derbyshire, built by Adam (1759-70). The *Dining Room* is of white chunam, with a floor of veined white marble. The *Throne-room* is so called from its containing the Throne of Tipu Sultan. Above the dining-room and the adjoining rooms is a splended ballroom. The floor is of polished teak, and the ceilings are beautifully panelled. The crystal chandeliers were bought in 1801 at the sale of General Claude Martin's effects at Lucknow (p. 386).

On the S. of Government House is the Cenotaph erected to the memory of citizens of Calcutta of British descent wno fell in the First World War.

At Chowringhi Square is the *Statesman* newspaper office, also a mosque erected by Prince Ghulam Muhammad, son of Tipu Sultan, in gratitude to God, and in commemoration of the Honourable Court of Directors granting him the arrears of his stipend in 1840.

N. of the Maidan are the Curzon Gardens, with the tramway terminus on the E. The Shadid Minar on the S. is a column 152 ft. high. Foreigners wishing to climb the tower must first obtain a permit from Police HQ, Lal Bazar. From the galleries a fine view over Calcutta is obtained.

At the head of Chowringhi Road are the premises of the Y.M.C.A and the Grand Hotel, and farther along is the Indian Museum. In front of the Museum on the Maidan side is the Monohar Das Tank (excavated at the cost of a Benares banker in 1793), and farther to the N. at a junction of roads, Thorneycroft's statue of Lord Mayo (Viceroy, 1869; assassinated 1872).

At the junction of Surendranath Banerji Road and Corporation Street, the Municipal offices contain a Council Chamber fashioned after the Chamber of Deputies in Paris. The Sir Stuart Hogg Market, and a number of cinemas are in this quarter. Beyond, on Wellesley Street (which with Wellington, College and Cornwallis Streets forms a second great thoroughfare from S. to N.), stands the Calcutta Madrasa, a Muslim College founded by Warren Hastings in 1780. Close by in Wellesley Square is the Scottish Church.

The **Indian Museum** (1875), 300 ft. long (known to Indians as the Jadu Garh, or house of magic), stands at the corner of Chowringhi and Sudder Street. The entrance is from Chowringhi Road by a pillared vestibule. It houses the best collection of exhabits in India, and a visitor can form a good idea of India's culture and scientific background by going round the galleries.

On the ground floor a quadrangle has a colonnade in Italian style and surrounds an open turfed space. The N. side of the colonnade is occupied by *Geological Galleries* (the Mineral and Meteorite Galleries), the E. side by a *Zoological Gallery* (the Invertebrate Gallery) and the S. side by *Archaeological Galleries* (the Gupta, Asoka and Inscription Galleries).

Another Archaeological Gallery (that of the *Bharhut Stupa*) runs from the vestibule on the right, and a Geological Gallery (that of the *Siwalik Fossils*) to the left. The Bharhut Stupa Gallery leads to the *Indo-Scythian Gallery*, which has another extensive gallery on its S., also devoted to archaeology, and the exhibits from the pre-historic period of the Indus Valley civilisation are displayed here. The N.E. corner room in the ground floor of the main building is the *Insect Gallery*, which leads by a bridge to the first storey of the Sudder Street Block, in which is the *Ethnographical Gallery*. There is also a collection of Russian relics.

The Sudder Street block houses also a library, herbarium, laboratory and offices of the Industrial and Botanical Sections.

In the centre of the landing on the first floor stands a marble statue of Empress Victoria. Behind it is the entrance to the *Library of the Zoological Survey of India*. N. and S. from the library extend galleries in which *Zoological Collections* are stored for purposes of research. (Admission obtainable through the Director, Zoological Survey of India.) On the N. side is a gallery containing *Fossils*; in the N.E. corner room is the *Small Mammal Gallery*, from which a bridge extends to the *Industrial Gallery* in the second storey of the Sudder Street Block. The *Large Mammal Gallery* occupies the E. side, and contains an albino tiger. At the S. end are the *Bird and Reptile* and the *Fish Galleries*.

On the first floor of the New Wing allotted to the *Art Section* and entered from the Fish Gallery is the *Artware Court*, where collections are shown of textiles, metal and woodwork, ceramics, etc.

The second floor extends along the whole length of the W. side of the Main Building and the New Wing. There is a large public lecture-hall on this floor, the rest of which is devoted to laboratories of the Zoological and Anthropological Section, and offices. The Picture Gallery of the Art Section is at the S. end.

The E. block (three floors) houses the library of the Geological Survey of India, the exhibits of the Section being shown in four galleries in the Main Buildings. Complete Catalogues of the various Sections are obtainable.

To the south of the entrance vestibule, in the Bharhut Gallery, have been reconstructed parts of the great railing round the stupa of Bharhut in Baghelkhand, with original stones brought from the site. These stones bear bas-reliefs that illustrate scenes from the pre-births (jatakas) and the last birth of Gautama Buddha, with labels in ancient characters. There are also some carved stones of the old railing round the Bodhi tree at Bodh-Gaya, casts of friezes in the ancient caves of Orissa, and casts of some of the ancient bas-reliefs of Sanchi. These sculptures date from the 2nd to the 1st century B.C.

In the room to the south of the Bharhut Gallery are displayed Graeco-Buddhist sculptures from Gandhara (N.W. India), a few dating from the 1st century A.D. To the E. of the Gandhara room in the Gupta Gallery are exhibited sculptures from the stupa of Amaravati (destroyed, but its appearance can be judged from a bas relief), from Sarnath of the Gupta period and later mediaeval sculptures from Bihar, Bengal, Orissa, Southern India, Java and Cambodia. In the room E. of the Gupta Gallery are displayed Sanskrit, Arabic and Persian inscriptions.

On the ground floor of the New Wing, to the S. of the Gandhara Room, in the New Hall are miscellaneous antiquities. On the walls of the southern balcony of the New Hall are displayed casts of the edicts of Asoka. Adjoining the balcony is the strong room, with an extensive and magnificent collection of Indian coins. Architectural pieces are exhibited in the eastern veranda of the main quadrangle and additional specimens of later mediaeval Buddhist and Brahmanic sculptures from Bihar and Orissa in the southern veranda.

The Siwalik Fossil Remains (ground floor) include the Hyaenarctos or Hyaena-Bear; the Amphicyon, a dog-like animal as large as the Polar bear; the Machairodus or Sabre-tooth tiger, whose canine teeth were 7 in. long; also the Siwalik cat, which was at least as large as a tiger. There is the skeleton of an elephant 11 ft. high. Amongst Siwalik birds are the shank-bone and the breast-bone of a wading-bird as big as an ostrich (Megaloscelornis) and these bones are the only ones belonging to this species existing in the world. The Museum is particularly rich in fossil remains of the elephant, hippopotamus, rhinoceros, giraffe and pig, and contains interesting remains of Siwalik apes. The remains of the Crocodilus crassidens are those of an extinct species of enormous dimensions. There is also a specimen of the Siwalik Colossochelys, a gigantic tortoise of astonishing size. Whereas the species and many of the genera of the Siwalik Mammals and Birds are entirely different from those now inhabiting the earth, all the genera of the Reptiles have living representatives in India. The Collection of the Fossil Vertebrata of the Siwaliks is the most complete and comprehensive in the world.

The upper Palaeontological Gallery contains remains of the Invertebrates and Plants from the stratified rocks of the Indian sub-continent, which range from the Cambrian to the Tertiary period, and also large collections of fossils from foreign countries. Amongst the Indian specimens the following are worthy of special attention: the magnificent collection of Gondwana plants, the fossils from the Productus Limestone of the Salt Range, the South Indian cretaceous and the various fossiliferous rocks of the Himalayas and Burma.

In the Geological Section, the collection of zoolites, and that of meteorites, of which over 400 falls are represented, are among the finest in the world. In the adjoining galleries there are exhibits of various types of Indian flora.

At the corner of Chowringhi and Kyd Street are situated the newly acquired premises of the Geological Survey of India. Just beyond, at the corner of Park Street, is the **Royal Asiatic Society of Bengal** in a building now partly demolished. This institution was established in 1784 as the Asiatic Society by Sir William Jones, and led to the foundation of the Royal Asiatic Society in London by H. T. Colebrooke. Visitors can be elected members. The *Asiatick Researches* (the k was dropped in 1825) began to be issued in 1788, and continued to be published until 1839. The *Journal* began in 1832, under the auspices of Professor H. H. Wilson and James Prinsep, who added the words, "of Bengal", and first deciphered the Brahmi rock and pillar inscriptions of King Asoka. From 1832 to 1839 both publications were issued. The library contains over 15,000 volumes, and there is a large collection of valuable coins, copper plates, pictures and busts. The bulk of the Arabic and Persian MSS. formed part of Tipu Sultan's Library: and there are also MSS. in Sanskrit, Burmese, Nepalese and Tibetan. The pictures include portraits of Warren Hastings, by Tilly Kettle, and of Sir William Jones as a boy, by Sir Joshua Reynolds.

In Middleton Row, turning off Park Street, are **St Thomas's Roman Catholic Church,** commenced in 1841, and the Convent of Our Lady of Loretto (once the residence of Sir Elijah Impey).

Near the E. end of Park Street, on the right, is **St Xavier's College,** with a fine science laboratory and astronomical observatory. Both sides of Park Street are fringed by old Cemeteries in which are the tombs of many notable Anglo-Indians, and have now been turned into Gardens of Remembrance.

In front of the W. end of Park Street, facing the Maidan, there was an equestrian statue of Sir James Outram (by J. H. Foley); the statues of various Commanders-in-Chief and Viceroys used also to adorn both sides of the Red Road. Some of these, however, have now been moved elsewhere.

Chowringhi Road, the old residential quarter *par excellence* of Calcutta society,[1] continues S., past the partly demolished Bengal Club (founded 1825, and occupying the site on which Lord Macaulay once lived), to St Paul's Cathedral.

The Saturday Club (1872), which has the largest membership amongst European Clubs, stands to the E. at the corner of Theatre Road and Wood Street.

At the extreme S.E. of the Maidan is **St Paul's Cathedral,** which was designed by Major W. N. Forbes, Bengal Engineers, commenced in 1839, and opened in 1847; it is 240 ft. long and 80 ft. broad, and the spire was 200 ft. high. In the vestry of the Cathedral is a large folio MS. volume entitled "History of the erection of St Paul's Cathedral", which contains a plan of the Cathedral at p. 265. Over the porch is a library, left to the public by Bishop Daniel Wilson, with an excellent bust of him. The great west window, designed by Sir E. Burne-Jones, was erected in 1880 by the Government of India as a memorial to Lord Mayo. The original East window was given by the Dean and Chapter of Windsor, to whom it was presented as a gift by George III for St George's Chapel. One S. window is a memorial to Bishop Milman

[1] It was from the spacious houses in Chowringhi that Calcutta obtained its name of "The City of Palaces".

(1867-76). In the centre of the transept is a statue of Heber, the second Bishop (1823-26), by Chantrey.

On the left side of the vestibule is a black marble tablet to sixteen officers of the Bengal Engineers, who fell during the Indian Mutiny in the years 1857-58. It is ornamented with a relief representing the blowing up of the Kashmir Gate, Delhi, by Lieutenants Salkeld and Home (p. 321). There follow many other memorial tablets and monuments. The organ is one of the finest ever made by Messrs Willis. The steeple was rebuilt on the design of Bell Harry Tower at Canterbury and dedicated 1938.

Adjoining the Cathedral to the S. is the Academy of Fine Arts with a number of galleries exhibiting paintings, old prints, fine carpets, etc. Exhibitions by local artists are held regularly. Further S. is the Rabindra Sadan, a modern theatre erected by the Govt.

Ashutosh Mukharji Road leads through Bhowanipur to the suburb of **Tollygunge** (4 m. from Government House). This is the old "pilgrim's path" to Kalighat. The European community frequents the Tollygunge Gymkhana Club and the Royal Calcutta Golf Club (started 1829). Ruins of the palaces once occupied by the eleven sons of Tippoo Sultan are in this suburb.

Until the 1930's suburban Calcutta extended no farther, but since the Partition of India in 1947 a large number of Hindu refugees from Eastern Bengal, then part of Pakistan, settled in this area, and temporary huts extend along both sides of Gharia Hat Road. An interesting short circular trip by motor may be made out to Tollygunge, round by Gharia Hat, and back through Jodhpur and beside the Dhakuria Lakes.

On the Lower Circular Road, running E. and leading to **Ballygunge,** are Bishop Middleton's College (1823) and the Martinière Schools (1833). The Lower Circular Road turns N., and in the cemetery (1840) at the corner of Park Street (on the right-hand side) are buried Sir Wm. Macnaghten, murdered in Kabul in 1841; James Wilson, the financial expert; Sir John Woodburn, and many other distinguished Anglo-Indians. Cemeteries in Park Street date from 1767 and 1796 (on the W. side).

Kalighat, celebrated as the site of a temple in honour of the goddess Kali, the wife of Siva, lies about 1½ m. S. of the Cathedral, by a long detour, on the bank of Tolly's Nullah, an old bed of the Ganges cleared out by Major Tolly in 1775.

The place, after which Calcutta is named, derives sanctity from the legend that when the corpse of Siva's wife was cut in pieces by order of the gods, and chopped up by the quoit (*sudarsan chakra*) of Vishnu, one of her fingers fell on this spot. The original temple is supposed to have been built 350 years ago. A member of the Sàbarna Chaudhury family of Barisal, who owned estates in this part, rebuilt the temple *c.* 1809, and allotted 194 acres of land for its maintenance. A man of the name of Chandibar was the first priest appointed to manage the affairs of the temple. His descendants have taken the title of Haldar, and are proprietors. The principal religious festival of the year is on the second day of the Durgapuja, in October.

The **Victoria Memorial** must be visited (main entrance from Queens Way). It dominates southern Calcutta. To Lord Curzon its conception is due, to show a collection illustrative of Indian history and especially of that of the Victorian era. The funds were voluntarily subscribed by the Princes and Peoples of India. The architect was Sir William Emerson, and King George V, when Prince of Wales, laid the foundation-stone on the 4th January 1906. The late Duke of Windsor, as Prince of Wales, on the 28th December 1921, opened the building. The design is chiefly Renaissance with traces of Saracenic influence. The facing is polished marble from Makrana in Jodhpur. The groups of statuary over the entrance porches and figures surrounding the dome were designed and executed in Italy.

The figure of Victory, standing 16 ft. high and weighing 3 tons, surmounts the dome, and revolves upon its base, a sphere 2 ft. in diameter. From the ground-level to the base of the figure is 182 ft. The dimensions of the hall itself at the corner towers are 339 ft. by 228 ft.

The entrance is on the N. past a bronze statue of Queen Victoria by Sir George Frampton, R.A., which is flanked by two tanks; the surroundings of the statue and the gates were designed by V. Esch. On either side of the bridge on which the statue stands and also on either side of the portico are finely executed bronze reliefs by Sir W. Goscombe John, R.A. In the entrance hall, the visitor will find bronze busts of King Edward VII and of Queen Alexandra and marble statues of King George V (Mackennal) and of Queen Mary (Frampton). The busts, which are by Sydney March, were presented by King George V, and the statues were presented by H.H. The Aga Khan. The antique clock is a fine specimen by Whitehurst of Derby (F.R.S., 1713-88).

To the right, in the Royal Gallery, is a collection of paintings representing events in the life of Queen Victoria, the gift of King Edward VII. Queen Victoria's piano and writing-desk occupy the centre of the room, while on the south wall hangs Verestchagin's masterpiece, depicting the State entry of King Edward VII, when Prince of Wales, into Jaipur in 1876. This exhibit, which was presented by the Maharaja of Jaipur, should on no account be missed.

To the left of the entrance hall in the portrait gallery a collection of Persian books will be of interest to the antiquarian, and among the pictures on the walls will be found portraits of Holwell (by Reynolds); of Lord Clive (after Dance, R.A.); of the King of Oude and the Nawab of Arcot, both presented by King George V; of Dwarka Nath Tagore (1795-1846), a Bengal notable whose enlightenment was in advance of his time; of Sir Henry Rawlinson (1810-94), and of Lord Lake (1744-1808). A portrait by Reynolds of Major-General Stringer Lawrence (1697-1775), the "Father of the Indian Army", was bequeathed by Lord Curzon. The statues in the corners are of Lord Wellesley and of Lord Dalhousie; and between them has been placed Flaxman's statue of the Marquess of Hastings (Lord Moira).

Passing through the Queen's vestibule into the Queen's Hall under the dome, one sees the dignified statue of Queen Victoria at the age when she ascended the throne (the work of Sir Thomas Brock, R.A.); this gives the keynote to the whole edifice. On the marble panels in the recesses of the walls are engraved in several languages proclamations to the people of India by Queen Victoria, while the mural paintings encircling the gallery (by Frank Salisbury) illustrate the principal events of her lifetime. These will be better seen across the hall from the gallery itself.

The bronze doors on the two sides of the Queen's Hall are fine examples of modern workmanship, and beyond them on the terraces are groups of marble statuary, with Lord Cornwallis, by John Bacon, junior, as the central figure of the one (on the east) and Warren Hastings, by Sir Richard Westmacott, as the central figure of the other (on the west).

Continuing through the building we come to the Prince's Hall. The marble statue of Lord Clive, by Tweed, a replica of the one in bronze which stands outside the India Office in London, and two French guns captured at the Battle of Plassey, together with a number of busts of distinguished men, are the principal objects on view.

On the left is the Darbar Hall. The First World War enforced economy, but the consequent change from marble to Chunar stone enhances the general effect. On either side of the entrance are hung framed colours of the famous Bengal European Fusiliers which fought in every battle in Upper India from Plassey until the storming of Delhi in 1857. The art exhibits comprise Miss Eden's water-colour sketches, Atkinson's mutiny drawings, Daniell's Twelve views of Calcutta in 1786-88, miniatures on ivory, engravings, and a fine collection of Oriental paintings. Philatelists can examine the fine stamp collection.

At the end of the Darbar Hall is the historic black stone *masnad*, or throne, of the Nawabs Nazim of Bengal, Bihar and Orissa, 6 ft. in diameter and 18 in. high; the whole, including the four pedestals, has been hewn out of one block. The Persian inscription cut round the edge records that it was made at Monghyr in the year 1052 of the Hegira (1641). It belongs, therefore, to the time of Sultan Shujah (second son of the Emperor Shah Jahan), who was Subadar of Bengal from 1639 to 1647, and must originally have been kept at Rajmahal (p. 390), whence it followed the Nawabs to Dacca and Murshidabad (p. 395). It was upon this throne (which was presented in 1904 by the Nawab Bahadur of Murshidabad) that Clive installed Mir Jafir after the Battle of Plassey (1757), and saluted him as lawful Nawab; and in 1765 he sat upon it side by side with the then Nawab Nazim and proclaimed the assumption of the Dewani (civil administration) by the E.I. Company.

Across the Prince's Hall is one of the Picture Galleries, containing pictures and engravings of Indian scenery by Thomas Daniell (1749-1840, R.A.), and his nephew William (1769-1837, R.A.). Among these is a collection of aquatints presented by Queen Mary. Other paintings include portraits of Sir Elijah Impey by Tilly Kettle (a variant of the one at the High Court), Abu Taleb Khan by Northcote, Rudyard Kipling by Burne-Jones, and of Burke and Macaulay. "The Embassy of Hyder Beck", the "Tiger Hunt near Chandernagore", and "Claude Martin and his Friends", by Zoffany, are in a room beyond. In the room between is the Lyell collection of Indian landscapes by the Daniells (presented in 1932), among them being a beautiful view of the Taj Mahal at Agra.

In the Picture Gallery on the first floor a collection of paintings includes a portrait of Warren Hastings and his wife in a group, a very fine one of Mrs Hastings (both by Zoffany), and two portraits of the great Governor-General in his old age, one by Lemuel Abbott, one attributed to Hoppner. The centre room contains a large collection of engravings, while in the "Calcutta" room at the end will be found a comprehensive series of prints of old Calcutta and a model of Fort William. Two fine oil-paintings by Thomas Daniell represent Old Court House Street in 1786 and the river front opposite the old Fort William. Among the historic documents in the annexe is the original indictment of Nuncomar for forgery of a bond, which is also on view in original (see High Court).

A magnificent view of the Maidan can be had from the balcony over the main entrance. The southern entrance is formed by a lofty arch surmounted by an equestrian statue of King Edward VII, by Sir Bertram Mackennal, R.A. A second statue of Lord Curzon is by F. W. Pomeroy, R.A. To the east of the Memorial building in the garden is the marble statue of Sir Andrew Fraser, recently moved there from Dalhousie Square.

The Memorial is open on Sundays and week-days (excluding Mondays) from 10 a.m. to 5 p.m. There is a charge of 30p, which admits to the whole building. Children are half-price. On Mondays the building is closed.

On the Lower Circular Road, S. of Victoria Memorial, is the **Presidency General Hospital** (1768), formerly intended for Europeans, but now open to all and made into a Medical College and teaching hospital. In its place the European business community has established a well-found clinic of its own. The Military Headquarters, Calcutta Sub Area, conspicuous by its pillared frontage, was (1773) the Court House of the Sadar Diwani Adalat, the chief provincial Court of Appeal, which ceased to exist on the establishment of the High Court in 1862.

Alipur

The Alipur Road, crossing Tolly's Nullah by the Zeerut bridge, leads to the **Zoological Gardens,** inaugurated on 1st January 1876 by King Edward VII (then Prince of Wales). They comprise an area of 40 acres attractively laid out, and a large collection of animals in houses. The Reptile House usually contains a King Cobra. Special attention should be given to the southern extensions, where birds, deer and cattle are grouped under natural conditions. In an island enclosure, in the centre of the gardens, about 100 yd. along the broad pathway from the main entrance, gibbons and orang-outangs may be seen in practically a wild state as well as a large colony of fruit bats. On the S. side of the gardens is the Alipur Observatory, of the Meteorological Department, on whose predictions the attacks on Mount Everest depend.

Belvedere House, transferred (1912) from the Lieutenant-Governors of Bengal, and subsequently used by the Viceroy on the occasions of his visits to Calcutta, is now the home of the **National Library,** the largest in India with more than 1 m. books. At a spot W. of the entrance of Belvedere, on the Alipur Road, was fought, on 17th August 1780, the duel between Warren Hastings and Philip Francis, in which the latter was wounded. S. of Belvedere are the **Agri-Horticultural Gardens** (1872), managed by a Society which was founded in 1820. Off Judge's Court Road stands Warren Hastings' private residence, known as "Hastings House". It was used for a time as a Guest House for Indian Princes, and subsequently as the headquarters of the Eastern States Agency. Alipur is a large residential suburb and headquarters of the 24 Parganas (Clive's jagir).

The **Race-course** (1 m. 5 furlongs) under the Royal Calcutta Turf Club, is perhaps the finest in the East. The Christmas race meeting is one of the principal social events of the winter season in Calcutta. Besides the public stands, there is a members' stand, admission to which can only be secured upon an introduction by a member of the Club. The bridge S.W. of the Race-course, across Tolly's Nullah, leads to Watgunge, so called after Colonel Henry Watson (Francis' second in the duel with Hastings), who in 1780 established wet and dry docks here. The docks were afterwards owned by the two East Indian sons of Colonel Kyd, who is supposed to have given his name to the adjoining Dockyard. Between 1781 and 1821 ships were built at these Docks, and in 1818 the *Hastings*, a 74-gun ship, was launched there. In **Kidderpore** is St Stephen's Church, and close by was the Military Orphan Asylum, in the mansion of Hastings' colleague, Richard Barwell.

The last bridge across Tolly's Nullah (Govindpur Creek), Hastings Bridge, leads past the Government Dockyard and the Kidderpore Docks (1892) with 28 berths, to **Garden Reach,** once known for its palatial suburban residences, and the home of the last King of Oudh, Wajid Ali, who was deposed in 1854, and survived his deposition by more than thirty years. On the way are passed the offices of the Bengal-Nagpur railway. The **King George's Dock,** which was opened by Lord Irwin, on 28th December 1928, covers a water area of 190 acres, with a depth of 36 ft. Alongside the entrance lock (700 ft. by 90 ft.) are two graving docks.

At the W. extremity of Garden Reach was the fort of Aligarh, and opposite to it, on the other bank of the river, the fort of Tanna, both of which were taken by Clive in the recapture of Calcutta in 1756-57.

On the Strand Road is Cooly Bazar,

near the site of which Nuncomar was hanged for the offence of forgery on 5th August 1775, near a boundary mark of Govindpur.

In front of St George's Gate of Fort William (S.W. corner) is a statue of Lord Napier of Magdala opposite **Prinsep's Ghat,** now some distance inland since the reclamation of the foreshore, which is marked by a pavilion of stone, supported by pillars, and inscribed "James Prinsep" in memory of the great Oriental scholar. King George V landed here in 1912. A second bridge is being built across the Hooghly at Prinseps Ghat. A short distance S. stands the memorial to the Indian Lascars of Bengal and Assam who lost their lives in the First World War through enemy action. Farther N., and opposite the Water Gate of the Fort, is the Gwalior Monument, erected by Lord Ellenborough in 1844, in memory of the officers and men who fell at Maharajpur and Panniar in 1843, and designed by Colonel W. H. Goodwyn, Bengal Engineers. It is of brick faced with Jaipur marble surmounted by a metal cupola made from guns taken from the enemy. In the centre the names are engraved on a sarcophagus.

The first **Fort William** received its name from William III. The site was changed in 1757, from that now occupied by the Post Office, to the river-bank farther S., where Clive commenced a new fortress, which was finished in 1781 and has never been attacked. It is an irregular octagon, enclosing an area of 2 sq. m., of which five sides look landward and three on the river, and is surrounded by a fosse 30 ft. deep and 50 ft. broad, which can be filled from the river. There are six gates—Chowringhi, Plassey, Calcutta, Water Gate, St George's and Treasury Gate. There is also a sally port between Water and St George's Gates. Inside the Chowringhi Gate (S.E.), past the one time Governor's residence, is the Fort Church of St Peter (1828), in the centre. Over the Treasury Gate are rooms once the residence of the Commander-in-Chief. The *Arsenal* is worth a visit, for which the permission of the officer commanding the Fort (residence, Chowringhi Gate), is necessary. Many of the guns were captured in the Sikh Wars.

Around Government House

This part was developed about 1775. To the N. of Government House are three streets, Old Court House on the E., Wellesley Place in the centre, and Council House Street on the W. These lead to **Dalhousie Square,**[1] with a garden and tank in the middle. In Wellesley Place is the **Central Telegraph Office** (on the E. side).

From Council House Street Hastings Street leads towards the river on the line of the Khal Kata Creek, which ran by Wellington Square and Creek Row to Beliaghata and the Salt Lakes, forming the N. boundary of Govindpur.

The **Church of St John,** first a Chapel, became the Cathedral in 1815. In the N. veranda is the Tomb of Lady Canning, brought from Barrackpore Park, where it was originally erected over the grave in 1861. Outside the Church, to the N. of the W. entrance, is a domed pavilion about 50 ft. high, with twelve pillars. The inscription bears the names of fourteen officers who fell in 1794 during the Second Rohilla War. A silver plaque in the church placed by the 2nd Dorset Regiment records the presence of men of the 39th Foot at Plassey.

The church, which was opened in 1787, is designed on the lines of St Stephen's Church, Walbrook, London. The main entrance, which was at the E. end, has been blocked up, although the original portico and ramp for the use of palanquins has been retained. Access to the building is obtained through an iron gate in Council House Street.

The South aisle has on the left a picture of the Last Supper (once the

[1] This was formerly known as the Lal Bagh, and the tank (1712) is still known to the populace as the Lal (red) Dighi.

altar-piece), painted and presented to the church by Johann Zoffany (1733-1810), in which the Apostles are all portraits of contemporary inhabitants of Calcutta. In the E. end of the nave is the grave of Bishop Middleton, first Bishop of Calcutta (d. 1822), and among the many fine memorials are those of Colonel James Achilles Kirkpatrick, Resident at Hyderabad from 1798 to 1805, John Adam (officiating Governor-General, 1823), and others.

In the N.W. corner of the graveyard is the large octagonal mausoleum of Job Charnock, the founder of Calcutta, 24th August 1690, who died on 10th January 1692 according to the Latin inscription. In this has been placed the slab which covered the grave of Surgeon William Hamilton, who in 1717, having cured the Emperor Farrukhsiyar, obtained for the E.I. Company the right of importing their goods free of duty, and other great privileges. (Persian inscriptions.)

A few yards to the S. is the tomb of Admiral Charles Watson, who, with Clive, retook Calcutta (d. 16th August 1757). A dome covers the grave of "Begum" Johnson, the grandmother of a British Prime Minister, the first Earl of Liverpool (1812 to 1827). She was taken prisoner by Suraj-ud-Daula in 1756 and died in Calcutta in 1812 at the age of eighty-seven. Lord Brabourne was buried here (1939).

At the junction of Council House Street and Hare Street is a building partly occupied by a Library and Reading Room attached to the Commercial Intelligence Department of the Government of India.

The Court of the Presidency Magistrate is beyond Hare Street, which passes the Small Cause Court, to the **Metcalfe Hall,** founded in honour of Sir Charles Metcalfe (later Lord Metcalfe) by public subscription, and built 1840-44. The design is copied from the portico of the Temple of the Winds at Athens.

On the Strand Road, N. of this, are the Sailors' and Seamen's Homes and the offices of the Port Trust, at the corner of Koila Ghat Street. Extending about ½ m. are Import jetties. Beyond the Cantilever bridge is the old Mint building, Doric in style, the portico being copied (half-size) from the Temple of Athena at Athens. The present Mint is situated at Mager Hat, South of Alipur.

Dalhousie Square

The site on the S. side of the Square until recently occupied by the Dalhousie Institute has now been taken over by the Department of Posts and Telegraphs, and the massive building built in its place is the Central Telephone Exchange.

On the W. side is the domed **General Post Office,** occupying part of the site of the Old Fort. It occupies an area of 103,100 sq. ft. The reinforced concrete dome at the S.E. corner is over 220 ft. high. The first **Fort William** lay between Koila Ghat Street, on the S., and Fairlie Place on the N. Its W. side was on the riverside. The W. and E. walls were 710 ft. long, the N. side measuring 340 ft. and the S. side 485 ft. After it was abandoned as a fort it was used as a Custom-house until the river moved away from the site. Part of the original arcades, which served as warehouses, may still be seen inside the yard of the Post Office. The Custom House (1819) was demolished (1938) to build the Reserve Bank. Where possible, the outlines of the Fort have been indicated by brass rails let into the ground.

At the N.E. corner of the Post Office is a tablet inside an arch, which indicates the actual site of the **Black Hole**[1] of 1756. The exact size of the

[1] The Black Hole was merely a guard-room of the Fort, and was a portion of a sleeping barrack in the S.E. corner of the Fort, enclosed from the rest of the building. The barrack was situated just to the N. of the S.E. bastion, and the Black Hole was therefore between the bastion and the barrack. Views of the Old Fort and of Holwell's monument are among Daniell's drawings of Calcutta (1786-92), and may be seen at the Victoria Memorial Hall.

room was 22 ft. by 14 ft., and its height was probably 16 ft. to 18 ft.; and into it, according to Holwell,[1] 146 human beings were forced on the night of 20th June, of whom 23 only survived next morning. The old obelisk, erected by the principal survivor, J. Z. Holwell, was removed in 1821. A memorial of the tragedy which stood at the road crossing at the N.W. corner of the Square was removed to St John's Churchyard after India became independent. Holwell, who was Governor in 1760, died in England at the age of eighty-seven in 1798.

On the N. side of Dalhousie Square are the long buildings of the West Bengal Secretariat, known as **Writers' Buildings** (1880). At the W. end St Anne's Church was built (1709-56).

E. of Writers' Buildings is St Andrew's Church opened in 1818, and called by Indians *Lal Girja* (Red Church).

E. of the square, in Mission Row (once Rope Walk), is the **Old Mission Church,** called the Purana Girja, or *Old Church,* in the vernacular. It was built by the celebrated missionary, Johann Zachariah Kiernander, who was born at Akstad, in Gothland, Sweden, in 1711, and educated at the Universities of Upsala and Halle. Being offered a post as missionary, he left England for India in 1740 and found his way to Calcutta in 1758. His second wife left jewels, and he founded a school. He called his church, which was consecrated in 1770, Beth Tephilla, "House of Prayer". When blind he was deceived into signing a bond which ruined him, and the church was seized by his creditors, but redeemed by Charles Grant (afterwards Chairman of the E.I. Company) for Rs. 10,000. Kiernander then went to Chinsura, and died in poverty at Calcutta in 1799. There is a window in the church presented by his grandson. and a curious engraving of him, with an inscription in German, hangs in the Vestry Room. There are many interesting tablets in this church.

Mission Row is one of the oldest streets in Calcutta. Tablets mark the houses once occupied by members of Warren Hastings' Council—Sir John Clavering and Colonel Monson.

N.W. of Dalhousie Square is the commercial quarter, in the former Clive Street, now styled Netaji Subhas Road. The principal buildings are Gillander House, the Chartered Bank, the National Bank of India, the Stock Exchange, and Messrs Martin & Company's buildings. The Hong-Kong and Shanghai Bank is on the site of Assembly Rooms, perhaps the "Lecture House" where Lord Metcalfe was born (1785). The Royal Exchange Building houses the Bengal Chamber of Commerce (1833). It stands on the site of a house once occupied by Clive and then by Philip Francis. The North-Eastern Railway Office is in Fairlie Place, and has a special counter for foreigners to make railway bookings. The Armenian Church of Holy Nazareth (reached from China Bazar Street) is the oldest place of Christian worship in Calcutta, built 1724 (tombstone in graveyard, 1630). When the Portuguese first came to Calcutta, the English granted them a piece of land in Portuguese Church Street, on which the friars of the order of St Augustine erected a chapel in 1700. Its successor, the **Roman Catholic Cathedral,** was built in 1797, and is dedicated to the Virgin Mary of the Rosary. N. of the Cathedral just off Rabindra Sarani is the house where the Indian poet Rabindranath Tagore was born and died, now a museum and cultural centre. Nearby on Muktaram Babu Street is the Marble Palace with an incongruous collection of European works of art (closed Monday and Thursday).

From the N.E. corner of Dalhousie Square, Lal Bazar (Police headquarters) and then Bow Bazar lead to **Sealdah** station, now the terminus of a division of the North-Eastern Ry., comprising the N. station (for

[1] The accuracy of Holwell account's has been disputed by Muslim authorities. See however Busteed's *Echoes from Old Calcutta.*

suburban trains), the Main station (for N. and E. Bengal), and the S. station, formerly Mutla station (for trains to Diamond Harbour, Budge Budge and Canning Town). The Railway Colony and Clem Browne Institute lie to the N. and the Campbell Hospital to the S. of the station.

College Street crosses Bow Bazar and leads, to the N., past the Eden, Ezra, and Medical College Hospitals, and the Medical College, to College Square, with the Bengali War Memorial for the First World War.

The Ezra Hospital is for Jews only. The **Medical College Hospital** was erected in 1853, and the **Eden** Hospital for women and children in 1882. Behind the Hospital is the **Medical College** (1834).

On the N. side of College Square is the **Sanskrit College,** which was founded by Warren Hastings in 1781: and on the W. side are the **Calcutta University** (1857), Hare School and the Presidency College. The University Senate House has been replaced by the new Centenary Building, part of which now contains the **Ashutosh Museum of Indian Art** (1937)—Bengal folk art and models. The Law College, and lecture halls adjoin. Close by is the **Hare School,** which is self-supporting. It was erected in 1817 out of the surplus fees of students. The **Presidency College** was developed in 1855 from the former Hindu College, founded in 1824. The Calcutta offices of the Mahabodhi Society face the E. side of College Square, and adjoin a large Buddhist international guest-house.

E. of Cornwallis Square and N. of the end of Beadon Street (abutting on Circular Road, which in its upper portion marks the line of the Mahratta Ditch, hastily dug in 1742, when these freebooters invaded Orissa and Bihar) is Halsi Bagan Road, so called from the gardens of the well-known Omichand (Amin Chand, d. 1758). He threatened to expose negotiations with Mir Jafir, but was tricked into silence by Clive. In a lane are the marble **Jain** temples in the garden known by the name of Badri Das. The temples are dedicated to the 10th Tirthankar, Sitalnath Ji, and the gardens form one of the prettiest spots in the whole of Calcutta.

The **Bose Research Institute,** 93 Upper Circular Road, founded by Sir Jagadis Chandra Bose, F.R.S. (d. 1937), adjoins the **University College of Science,** a fine four-storeyed building. The biological laboratories are at 35 Ballygunge Circular Road. At 243/1 is a Museum of Bengali relics.

The Botanical Gardens

The **Botanical Gardens,** Sibpur, on the W. bank of the river, opposite Garden Reach, were founded in 1786, on the suggestion of Colonel Kyd, who was appointed the first Superintendent. He died in 1793, and has had many eminent successors. The visitor may drive across the bridge and through Howrah, turning left over the East Indian Ry. by a bridge, or may take the ferry service from Chandpal or Takta Ghats to the Botanical Garden Ghat (if open), or may cross from Matia Bruz Ghat, ½ m. beyond Garden Reach. At Sibpur is the Engineering (Civil) College (1880), once the Bishop Middleton English College. The area of the gardens is 270 acres, with river frontage of a mile. At the N.W. corner is the Howrah Gate. From College Gate an avenue of Palmyra palms to the right, and one of mahogany trees to the left, lead to the centre and the memorial of Colonel Kyd, past the palm plantation, which is bordered by a canal crossed by picturesque bridges. From the memorial an avenue of palms leads S. to the Garden Ghat; and close by it are three conservatories. Leaving the above avenue to the left, the Great Banyan Tree[1]

[1] The name, according to Tavernier (1650), was given to this tree (which is the Hindustani *bar*) from the fact that the *baniyas* or Hindu traders at Gombroon (Ormuz) in the Persian Gulf built a little pagoda under one of them, which was the only tree that grew in the island.

(*Ficus indica*) covers ground 1251 ft. in circumference, and was over 88 ft. in height. The central column, damaged by fungus and a cyclone (1919), had to be eradicated in 1925, to preserve the radial parts, increased by pruning and grafting:

"The bended twigs take root and daughters grow
About the mother tree, a pillar'd shade,
High over-arched and echoing walks between."—MILTON, *Paradise Lost*.

On the left of an avenue near it is a monument to Roxburgh, with a Latin epitaph by Heber. Sir J. Hooker wrote in his Himalayan Journals that "the great Indian Herbarium, chiefly formed by the staff of the Botanical Gardens, under the direction of Dr Wallich, and distributed in 1829 to the principal museums of Europe, was the most valuable contribution of the kind ever made to science"; and added that "the origin of the tea-culture in the Himalayas and Assam was almost entirely the work of the Superintendent of the gardens at Calcutta and Saharanpur". The Superintendent has a house near the Herbarium (1883), containing some 40,000 species of dried plants. Attached is a Botanic Library.

Excursions in the Vicinity of Calcutta

(a) *Left bank of the river: By rail from Sealdah, the Calcutta terminus of the Bengal-Assam Rly.*

At **Dum Dum** Junction, 7 m. from Calcutta, is the Airport (with Hotel). Passengers are taken to Calcutta by bus or taxi. It was the headquarters of the Bengal Artillery from 1783 to 1853, when they were removed to Meerut; and their mess-house is known as the *Outram Institute*. A bust of Sir James Outram stands in the veranda. There is a monument to Colonel Thomas Deane Pearse, "Father of the Bengal Artillery" (d. 1769).

In the centre of the Barrack Square is a huge gun. Near this is a monument to the officers and men killed in the retreat from Kabul in 1841-42. The treaty which restored the British settlements after the recapture of Calcutta in 1757 was signed at Dum Dum. Clive had a house here; the Cantonment area is now derelict, but the old Garrison Church survives.

Dum Dum is connected to the W. bank by the Bally Railway Bridge. Tittagarh, an old Danish factory, is 13 m. distant from Calcutta.

The Barrackpore Road due N. from Calcutta is the best means of making an excursion from Calcutta in this direction by car. Going up Chittaranjan Avenue one forks to the right at the top and proceeds *via* Shambazar over a canal bridge and congested railway bridge on to the Barrackpore Trunk Road. N.E. from Shambazar is the Jessore Road which is a good motoring road through Dum Dum, past the Airport for 12 m. as far as Baraset, where by turning to the left one can get to Barrackpore and so make a round trip.

At 14 m. from Calcutta on the direct road is **Barrackpore.** The journey may also be made by train, or more pleasantly by river, if the use of a private launch can be obtained, as there is no public service by river. Passing up by river from Howrah Bridge one sees on either bank after leaving the city the great jute mills which are the industrial feature. Conspicuous on the E. bank at the N. end of the city is the Cossipore Generating Station of the Calcutta Electric Supply Company, the most up-to-date station in India with two tall white chimneys higher than any mill chimneys.

On the E. bank of the river at Barrackpore is situated the house that in the old days was the country residence of the Governor of Bengal. Now a Police Hospital, the once-beautiful park round it is covered with hutments.

300 yd. to the S. of the house, under a fine tamarind tree, is a polygonal enclosure, within which is a white marble monument to Lady Canning; it replaces that removed to St John's Church at Calcutta. The tomb of

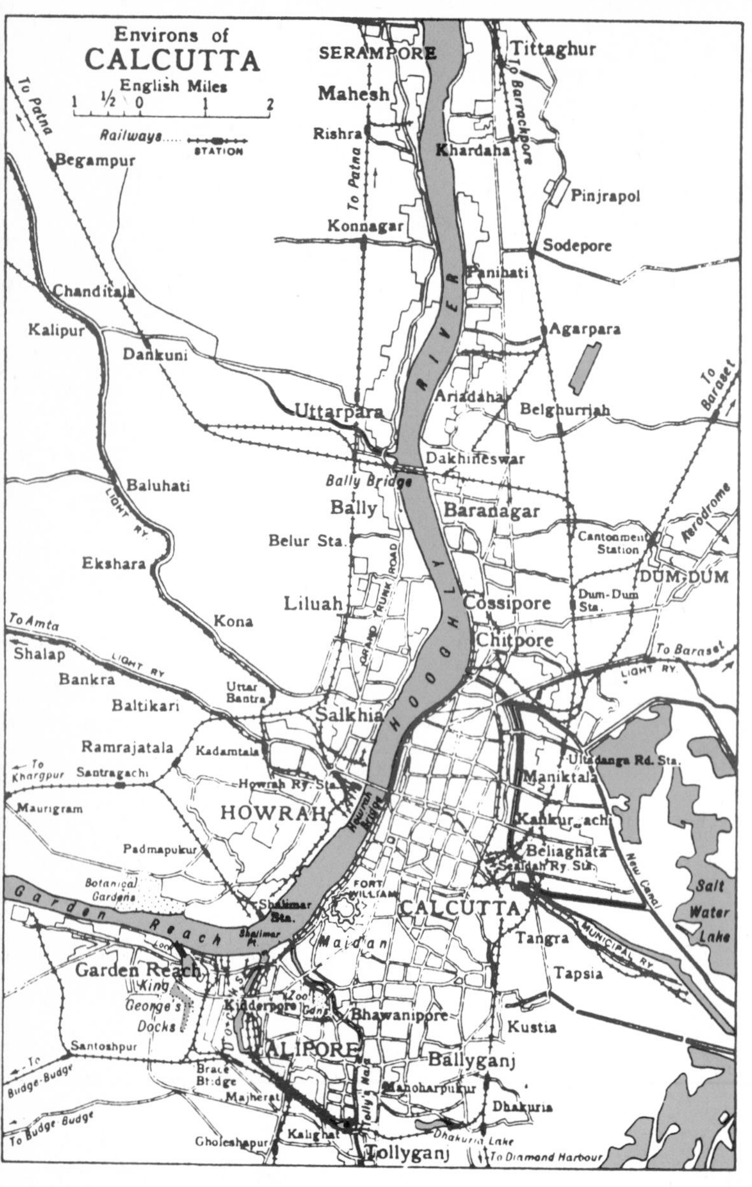

Environs of
CALCUTTA
English Miles
1 ½ 0 1 2
Railways.....
STATION
To Patna
Begampur
SERAMPORE
Tittaghur
Mahesh
To Barrackpore
Rishra
Khardaha
To Patna
Pinjrapol
Konnagar
Sodepore
Panihati
Chanditala
Kalipur
Agarpara
Dankuni
RIVER
To Baraset
Ariadaha
Uttarpara
Belghurriah
Dakhineswar
Bally Bridge
Baluhati
LIGHT RY.
Bally
Baranagar
Aerodrome
Cantonment Station
Belur Sta.
GRAND TRUNK ROAD
DUM DUM
Ekshara
Liluah
Cossipore
Dum-Dum Sta.
To Amta
Kona
Chitpore
Shalap
To Baraset
LIGHT RY
LIGHT RY.
Bankra
Uttar Bantra
Baltikari
Salkhia
HOOGHLY
Ramrajatala
Kadamtala
Ultadanga Rd. Sta.
To Khargpur
Santragachi
Howrah Ry. Sta.
Maniktala
Maurigram
HOWRAH
Howrah Bridge
Padmapukur
Beliaghata
Sealdah Ry. Sta.
New Canal
Botanical Gardens
FORT WILLIAM
Salt Water Lake
Garden Reach
Shalimar Sta.
CALCUTTA
Shalimar
Tangra
MUNICIPAL RY
Maidan
Garden Reach
Tapsia
King George's Docks
Kidderpore
Zoo
Bhawanipore
Kustia
Santoshpur
ALIPORE
To Budge-Budge
Brace Bridge
Ballyganj
Majherat
Tolly's Nala
Manoharpukur
Dhakuria
To Budge-Budge
Gholeshapur
Kalighat
Dhakuria Lake
Tollyganj
To Diamond Harbour

Sir John Herbert, Governor of Bengal (d. 1943), is in the grounds. A hall, built by the Earl of Minto in 1813, stands 100 yd. to the N. of the house within a colonnade of Corinthian pillars. Over the outside entrance is a black slab, inscribed: "To the Memory of the Brave". On the walls are four tablets, erected by different Governors-General to the memory of British soldiers who fell in Mauritius (Isle of France) and Java, 1810-11, and at Maharajpur and Panniar, 1843.

The original bungalow belonged to the Commander-in-Chief and was appropriated in 1801 by Lord Wellesley, who laid out the park and began to build a "country villa" which was enlarged by the Marquess of Hastings (1813-1823). The Governor now occupies the bungalow built for the Commander-in-Chief after 1801. There used to be a golf-course in the grounds to which the public were admitted, but during the last war the park was taken over and has since been occupied by the Military Police.

N. of the park is Barrackpore **Cantonment,** first used for the purpose in 1772, when the place received its name. In March 1857 a mutinous spirit first revealed itself amongst the sepoy troops at this station, but this was checked for the time being by the bravery of the officer commanding, General Hearsy, and the regiments concerned were later disarmed.

The **Race-course,** which was opened in January 1927, is the property of the Royal Calcutta Turf Club. It is 1½ m. from Barrackpore station by road; a branch railway runs direct to the back of the stands. The course is still the property of the Turf Club but is no longer used. During the war it was taken over for military purposes, together with a large area north of it which became the airfield serving air routes not only to the Assam and Burma fronts but the supply lines "over the Hump" to China. The airfield, no longer in civilian use, is now an Indian Air Force station.

There is a Small-arm Factory at Ichapur, 3 m. to the N. of Barrackpore; and at Cossipore ½ m. N. of the Circular Canal is a Gun and Shell Factory on the bank of the Hooghly.

Farther N. at Mulajore is the largest of the Calcutta Electric Supply Company's Generating Stations with 5 turbo-generators of 30,000 kilowatts each.

(b) *West bank of the river: By rail from Howrah, the Calcutta terminus of the former East Indian Ry.*

Howrah (population 740,622 in 1971) is on the right bank of the Hooghly. N.G. railways to Amta (28 m.) and to Sheakhala (20 m.). The Bhotbazar temple in Ghusri to the N. is an old Tibetan monastery, established by Warren Hastings in 1775, at the request of the Tashi Lama of Tibet. In 1720 there were docks and Armenian gardens.

The following places in the neighbourhood of Calcutta may be visited from Howrah by train, or by car along the congested Grand Trunk Road.

3 m. from Howrah station, **Lillooah,** with extensive Ry. carriage and wagon works, and locomotive sheds.

4 m. **Belur** is the home of the Ramakrishna Mission with a modern Temple. Across the river is Dakhineswar, where Ramakrishna served as a Temple priest. 6 m. **Bally** is a most orthodox and holy town. There is a fine library at the adjoining hamlet of Uttarpara, founded and maintained by the Mukherji family. The Vivekananda (once Willingdon) Bridge (seven spans of 350 ft.) over the Hooghly at Bally gives direct access to the Kidderpore Docks. In addition to a double rail-track it carries an 18-ft. roadway in both directions for vehicles and 8-ft. pathways.

11 m. **Rishra**; the site of an old chintz factory. Rishra House, which is close to the Hastings Jute Mills, was owned by Warren Hastings from 1780 to 1784.

13 m. **Serampore** station is on the

W. bank of the Hooghly, opposite Barrackpore. Serampore was formerly a Danish settlement, and was then called Fredericksnagore. The mansion of the Danish Governor is now the Subdivisional Officer's Court. In 1845 a treaty was made with the King of Denmark, by which all the Danish possessions in India—namely, Tranquebar, Fredericksnagore, and a small piece of ground at Balasore—were transferred to the E.I. Company for £125,000. The treaty confirmed the privileges conferred on Serampore College by the Royal Charter of the Danish King. Bankibazar, a settlement of the Dutch Ostend Company, closed 1743, was opposite.

Serampores' chief claim to notice arises from its having been from 1800 onwards the scene of the labours of Carey, Marshman, and Ward, the Baptist missionaries who did so much to promote education and Christian knowledge in Bengal. Serampore is now a centre of jute and cotton manufacture.

The old *Danish Church* (St Olaf's, 1805) is now Anglican. In it are tablets in memory of the three missionaries. Their tombs are in the Baptist cemetery, on the right hand of the Grand Trunk Road from the old railway station.

The *College*, founded in 1818 by the Serampore missionaries, on the banks of the river, commands a fine view across it over Barrackpore Park. The College has Faculties in Arts and Theology, and confers its own Divinity degrees. The Great Hall is 103 ft. long and 66 ft. broad. In it are portraits of Frederick VI of Denmark (who gave the College its Charter, empowering it to grant degrees in all the sciences) and of his Queen; of Dr Marshman, by Zoffany, and of King Christian of Denmark and his Queen. The last portrait does *not* represent Madame Grand, who afterwards married Talleyrand. The portrait of Carey by Robert Home, which was here at one time, is now in the National Portrait Gallery in London.

The Library contains first editions of Carey and Marshman's forty translations of the Bible, printed by Ward, curious Sanskrit, Tibetan and Pali manuscripts, and a Persian manuscript containing the lives of the Apostles, prepared by Jerome Xavier for Akbar or Jahangir.

In the College compound is the house in which Carey died (1834). In 1910 a large and handsome hostel was erected. The Government Weaving Institute was established in the year 1909 for the purpose of training Indian weavers in modern methods of weaving.

The fine mansion next to the chapel, which was the common centre of the Serampore brotherhood, with Carey's Park and botanic garden, is the property of the India Jute Company. Here, from 1835 to 1875, the weekly *Friend of India* was edited, and also the *Samachar Darpan*, the first vernacular newspaper in Bengal.

At Mahesh, some 2 m. from Serampore, there is a large and ancient temple dedicated to Jagannath. The car festival in July is the largest of its kind in India outside Puri.

14 m. from Calcutta, **Sheoraphuli,** junction for a branch line (22 m.) to **Tarakeswar.** The ancient temple of Siva here is believed to be the richest in Bengal. It is frequented by numerous pilgrims in February for the Sivaratri festival, when a three days' fair is held, and also in April for the Chait Sankranti, or **hookswinging** festival. Devotees are suspended by hooks through the fleshy muscles on either side of the spine. From Tarakeswar a good road runs to **Bishnupur,** ancient centre of Hindu architecture and music. The typical brick temples—Radha Govind, Radha Madhar, Madan Mohan, Jor Mandir, Jor Bangla and others are well worth visiting. For transport and accommodation consult Tourist Information Office, Calcutta.

21 m. **Chandernagore** station. The French settled here in 1673, and under Dupleix (1697-1764), of whom the place has a statue, a considerable trade arose during his superintendent-

ship (1730-41). In 1757 the Fort d'Orleans, bombarded by the Fleet, under Admiral Watson, surrendered, and the fortifications were demolished but in 1763 the town was restored to the French. In 1794 it was again given up to the British, and held till 1815, when it was again restored to the French. The railway station was just outside the French boundary.[1] A "Dutch Octagon" lay to the south, also a French Garden House occupied by Eyre Coote in 1779. Chandernagore was made over to India by the French Government in 1951 following a referendum by its inhabitants.

The buildings include the library and museum of the Institut de Chandernagore, formerly the Administrateur's residence (open 4-6 p.m., closed Thursday); a church built by Italian missionaries in 1726, and the Collège Dupleix, now a Higher English School.

Between Chinsura and Chandernagore is **Biderra,** where the British, under Colonel Forde, obtained a decisive victory over the Dutch on 25th November 1759. Forde was aware that his nation and the Dutch were at peace, and wrote to Clive for an Order in Council to fight. Clive was playing cards, and wrote in pencil: "DEAR FORDE,—Fight them immediately, and I will send you an Order in Council to-morrow".

At Goswami Ghat on the river between Chandernagore and Chinsura, a huge ruined temple is known to the neighbourhood as "Konē-Bo-yēr Mandir". At present there is no image in the temple; but formerly it was the temple of the Goddess Kali. According to tradition, it was erected by one Devi Sarkar upon the wish of his brother's wife, who was the "Konē-Boū", or the youngest bride, of the Sarkar family.

The three railway stations of **Chinsura** (23 m.), **Hooghly** (24 m.) and **Bandel** Junction (25 m.) are so close together that it will be found most convenient to alight at the last-named. The town of **Hooghly** is 2 m. from Hooghly station.

A Hooghly factory was founded by the Portuguese in 1537, when the royal port of Bengal, *Satgaon* (p. 190), began to be deserted owing to the silting-up of the Saraswati river. They commenced by building a fortress at Golaghat, close to the present Hooghly jail, some vestiges of which are still visible in the bed of the river. When Shah Jahan came to the throne complaints were made to him of the conduct of the Portuguese at Hooghly. The Emperor bore them a grudge, as they had refused to assist him against his father, and he sent a large force against the fort, which, after four and a half months' siege, in 1632, was stormed. Out of 300 Portuguese vessels only three escaped. The prisoners were sent to Agra, and forcibly converted to Islam. Hooghly was then made a royal port. The Portuguese returned to Hooghly in 1633. It was also the first settlement of the English in Lower Bengal. The E.I. Company established a factory there in 1651 under a *farman* from Sultan Shuja, Governor of Bengal and second son of Shah Jahan. This *farman* was granted, according to tradition, to Dr Boughton, who had cured a favourite daughter of the Emperor and asked for this reward. In 1669 the Company received permission to bring their ships to Hooghly to load, instead of transporting goods in lighters and then shipping them into the larger vessels. In 1686 a dispute took place between the English and Shaista Khan, Nawab of Bengal, and the Company sent a force to protect their Hooghly factories. It chanced that a few English soldiers were attacked by the Nawab's men in the bazars, and a street fight ensued. Colonel Nicholson on this bombarded the town, and 500 houses were burnt, including the Company's warehouses. Charnock, chief of the English factory, was obliged to fly to Sutanati, where the merchants returned from Madras in 1690.[1] In

[1] For the former French possessions in India, see p. 55.

[1] See p. 170.

1742 Hooghly was sacked by the Mahrattas, and in 1757 Clive took it by river.

The principal sight at Hooghly is the **Imambara,** built in 1836 by Karamat Ali (Superintendent 1837-76), the friend and companion of Arthur Conolly, who was murdered at Bokhara, at a cost of Rs. 300,000 from funds bequeathed by Muhammad Muhsin. The façade of the Imambara is 277 ft. by 36 ft.; and in its centre is a gateway flanked by two minarets, or towers, 114 ft. high. On either side of the door are inscriptions. Within is a quadrangle, 150 ft. by 80 ft., with rooms all round, and a fine hall paved with marble, having a pulpit with sides covered with plates of silver, and a verse of the Koran inscribed on each plate. The library was bequeathed by Karamat Ali, but a few books have since been added by other people. Among them are 787 MSS., including a fine folio Koran, in two volumes, given by Prince Ghulam Muhammad, grandson of Tipu Sultan. On the opposite side of the road from this Imambara is the old Imambara, built in 1776-77. In the W. corner lie the remains of Karamat Ali, and there is a white marble tablet placed against the wall, with an extract from the Koran, but no tomb.

Chinsura (Fort Gustavus, occupied 1653), 1 m. S. of Hooghly, was ceded by the Dutch to the British with £100,000 in exchange for Sumatra in 1825. The octagonal *Dutch Church* is said to have been built by the Governor in 1678. It is now a laboratory for teaching biology attached to the local college. The cemetery is 1 m. to the W. of the church; it contains many old tombs of former Dutch officials. The *Hooghly College* is to the S. of the church. It was established, as a tablet in the hall testifies, "through the munificence of the late Muhammad Muhsin" in 1836. The house, according to local tradition, was built by General Perron, who lived at Chinsura for a year after his surrender to Lake in 1803 (p. 377): it is a fine specimen of the Anglo-Indian domestic architecture of the period. Chinsura was once a frontier station of the E.I. Company, and contains large blocks of barracks and officer's quarters, now used as Government offices and residences. At Mahanad there is a temple with a sacred pool.

Between Chinsura and Chandernagore is Biderra, where the British, under Colonel Forde, gained a decisive victory over the Dutch in 1759.

Bandel, 1 m. N. of Hooghly. Junction of the former East Indian and Bengal-Assam Railways. The linking line, 5 m. long, crosses the river to Naihati (Route 20) by the great cantilever Jubilee bridge, 1213 ft. long (built in 1887 by Bradford Leslie). A Portuguese monastery and church were built at Bandel in 1599, and the keystone with the date was erected in the new one, which is of brick, and very solidly built. It is dedicated to Our Lady of the Rosary. There are fine cloisters on the S., and a priory, in which is a noble room called St Augustine's Hall. The church was founded by Augustinian friars, demolished by Shah Jahan in 1640, and rebuilt by John Gomez de Soto.

About 6 m. above Hooghly, at **Satgaon,** is a ruined mosque with a few tombs, remnants of the old capital. It was built by Saiyad Jamal-ud-din, son of Fakhr-ud-din, who, according to inscriptions in the mosque, came from Amel, a town on the Caspian. The river of Satgaon, up to Akbar's time, formed the N. frontier of Orissa, and Satgaon flourished while the Hooghly flowed by the town.

Down the Hooghly river from Calcutta to Sagar Island

The Bengal Pilot Service was inaugurated in 1667, when the pinnace *Diligence* of 60 tons with a crew was sent out. The Calcutta pilots occupy a high position. The Hooghly is a most dangerous and difficult river to navigate, as, apart from the chance of cyclones, which take place in any month except February, there is the normal danger of shoals, which are continually forming, and nothing but a daily experience of the river can enable a pilot to take a vessel up or down safely. The most dangerous shoal—called the **"James and Mary"** or Mukraputty—is 30 m. S. of Calcutta, just above the Rupnarain; but from the Damodar river to Hooghly Point, a distance of 6 m., the whole river is difficult. The s.s. *Sanctoria* foundered on the James and Mary Sand in 1919; but systematic dredging by three large dredgers has effected a marked improvement. The *Pathfinder* survey vessel replaced (1938) the *Industry* (1903). On this shoal the *Royal James and Mary* was wrecked in 1694. The name appears in a chart of 1711. The Hooghly used not to be navigated at night, and could only be ascended when the tide was high, but since 1915 it has been lighted in the Lower Reaches, that is, from Mud Point downwards, for a distance of 65 m., and now vessels, according to draught, can come up regardless of the state of the tide. The ordinary fall and rise of the tide is 11 ft. 8½ in. at Calcutta. A special feature of the rising tide is the bore, which attains a height of between 5 and 7 ft.; it very seldom does damage.

The view of the river, with ships at anchor along the Strand and down to Garden Reach, is very striking; the Maidan, the Esplanade, the Fort and the imposing buildings along Chowringhi present a most impressive picture. From between Garden Reach and the Botanical Gardens the vista to the N. is especially fine when the atmosphere is clear. The Victoria Memorial dome is seen straight ahead. The "Hooghly sunsets" are beautiful.

7 m. from Calcutta the last sight of the premier city of India is lost; 5 m. farther, **Budge Budge** (Baj Baj; railway to Calcutta, 17 m.) is passed on the left bank, with its petroleum depots; at a similar distance farther on **Ulubaria**, a small town, is passed on the right bank. Here the main road from Calcutta to the temple of Jagannath at Puri crosses the Hooghly, and here begins the Midnapore High-Level Canal. The river, which has hitherto followed a S.W. course, now turns due S. to Hooghly Point.

At 27 m., on the E. bank, a little above the mouth of the Damodar, is **Falta,** the site of an old Dutch factory and the place to which the British retreated on the capture of Calcutta by Suraj-ud-daula in 1756 and from which Clive advanced to the recapture of Calcutta.

The Damodar is navigable as far as Amta, which is 25 m. from its mouth, and quantities of coal are brought down from the Raniganj mines.

5 m. below Falta the Rupnarain river enters the Hooghly from the right bank nearly opposite Hooghly Point, and from here the river turns S.E. to Diamond Harbour, and then S. again.

At 12 m. up the Rupnarain river, on the W. bank, is **Tamluk,** a famous city, and port of the Buddhists, where the Chinese pilgrim Fa Hian embarked for Sri Lanka about A.D. 400. Hiuen Tsang about A.D. 645 speaks of it. It is now a long way from the ocean, but reached by the tide. A *Temple* here known by the name of Barga Bhima or Bhenna was originally a Buddhist temple. The shrine is surrounded by a curious triple wall. Motor services run from Tamluk to Panchkura (R.H.). Maisadal and Naraghat.

45 m. below the docks at Kidderpore a new port is being built at **Haldia**. When completed this will be able to handle ships of between 40,000 and 50,000 tons and get back some of the traffic which has been lost to other ports because of the silting higher up.

At 48 m. from Calcutta is **Diamond Harbour** (left)—30 m. by a metalled road—where the E.I. Company's ships used to anchor. There is an old fort and a Custom House here, and the officers board ships proceeding up the river. There is also a railway to Calcutta (37 m.), with frequent trains, but only cruising liners touch here. Launches run to Sagar Island.

At 50 m. there is the Gosada Co-operative Settlement, founded by the late Sir Daniel Hamilton in 1932.

At 56 m. (left) is the town of **Kalpi** (Culpee); road to Calcutta. Here the estuary of the Hooghly widens, and at 99 m., between Kedgeree and **Sagar Island,** it is 15 m. broad. At this island, where the Ganges is considered to join the sea, pilgrims gather from all parts of India, but principally from the Bengal districts, in the early part of January, the date of the great Bathing Festival, which lasts three days. The island was overwhelmed by a cyclone or tidal wave in 1864, when only 1500 out of 5600 inhabitants escaped. Fear of tidal waves caused the Docks to be retained at Calcutta, despite the disadvantage of dangerous navigation.

The sea is reached at 82 m., where there is a lighthouse of iron, 76 ft. high, commenced in 1808, on Middleton Point, at the S.W. end of Sagar Island; but pilotage continues 40 m. to the Sandheads.

ROUTE 7

BHUSAWAL to CALCUTTA (HOWRAH) by **Akola, Wardha** (for **Warora** and **Chanda**), **Nagpur, Kampti, Raipur, Bilaspur** and **Sini,** and from Sini to (*a*) **Purulia** and **Asansol,** and (*b*) **Ranchi** and **Kharagpur.**

This route from Bombay to Calcutta is 1223 m., or about 130 m. shorter than any other. Time, 37 hr. from Bombay. The scenery in parts of the line, notably at *Darekasa* and *Dongargarh* (p. 199), and *Saranda* (p. 198), is very fine.

The Route from Bombay as far as Bhusawal Junction (R.),

276 m. from Bombay, is described in Route 2.

Soon after leaving Bhusawal the traveller enters the districts of **Berar** (area 17,000 sq. m.), which continue almost all the way to Nagpur. They were restored to the Nizam after the Second Mahratta War of 1803, and assigned by his successor to the British by treaty in 1853, for the support of the Hyderabad Contingent Force. In December 1860, in recognition of the Nizam's services in the Mutiny of 1857,[1] a debt of 50 lakhs was cancelled, the districts of Dharaseo (now known as Osmanabad) and the Raichur Doab were restored, and the Hindu State of Shorapur[2] (administered by Meadows Taylor from 1841 to 1853) was ceded to him. By an arrangement in 1902, made by Lord Curzon with the Nizam, Osman Ali Khan, involving a fixed payment of 25 lakhs yearly to the Hyderabad State,

[1] The Nizam, Nasir-ud-daula, died in May 1857, but his successor, Afzal-ud-daula, carried on his policy.

[2] Its ruler had joined the 1857 Mutiny and was dispossessed.

in consequence of further arrears of payment, the permanent administration of the Berar districts by the Central Government was secured, and they were added to the Government of the Central Provinces. The Hyderabad Contingent Force was subsequently incorporated in the Indian Army without further obligation on the Nizam. In March 1926 the Viceroy (Lord Reading) and the Secretary of State (Lord Birkenhead) decided against the reopening of the settlement of 1902. In connection with the Government of India Act of 1935 a further agreement was concluded with the Nizam in respect of Berar whereby his suzerainty over Berar was acknowledged, his heir-apparent being styled the Prince of Berar. It has, however, now been made an integral part of India as a result of the changes consequent on India gaining its independence in 1947.

The Berar districts form one of the richest and most extensive cotton-fields in India. The soil is black loam overlying basalt. The districts of Berar are Akola, Amraoti, Buldana, and Yeotmal. The railway to Nagpur was opened in 1867. There are many railway branches and light railways.

308 m. **Malkapur.** Motors available to Jalna (Railway Station) *via* Buldana (D.B.), alt. 2119 ft., 28 m. S. from Malkapur. "The coolest and most pleasant headquarter station in Berar."

333 m. **Jalamb** Junction (D.B.) for a branch 8 m. S. to *Khamgaon* (D.B.) station, where there is an important cotton and grain mart. About 50 m. S. from Khamgaon (motors available) is the town *Mehkar*, and 15 m. S. of Mehkar is a curious soda lake called *Lonar*, formed in the crater of an extinct volcano. The salt is used for washing and dyeing purposes, and is exported in considerable quantities.

363 m. from Bombay, **Akola** (D.B.K.) station, alt. 953 ft., is the headquarters of a district, and one of the principal centres of the cotton and grain trade in Berar (pop. 168,000 in 1971).

A road from Akola runs S. to Basim (D.B.) and to Hingoli (p. 154) 73 m.

Another road runs N. to Akot (28 m.), whence Narnala Fort is about 15 m.—the last 5 m. impassable for motors. Another fort at Balapur, 13 m. W. of Akola. Balapur was the headquarters of the Imperial Army in the Deccan in the time of Akbar.

386 m. **Murtazapur,** junction for the n.g. railway, 48 m. N. to Ellichpur. Anjangaon (32 m.) is on the watershed of the Tapti and Wardha basins. Another n.g. railway 70 m. S.E. to **Yeotmal** (headquarters of district). **Ellichpur** was the administrative capital of Berar until 1853. The deserted Cantonment here was garrisoned by Hyderabad Contingent Infantry until 1903. There is a group of Jain temples at Muktagiri, 7 or 8 m. N. of Ellichpur, on the Betul road, in a valley.

Also N. of Ellichpur is the hill fort of **Gawilgarh,** a stronghold, the Governor of which founded the independent kingdom of Berar (Imad Shahi dynasty) in 1484. It was absorbed by Ahmadnagar in 1574. This fortress of the Mahratta Raja of Berar was taken by Colonel Arthur Wellesley on 15th December 1803 in the Second Mahratta War. The ramparts were demolished in 1858. It is situated S.E. of

Chikalda, which is a small sanatorium, dating from 1839, on a plateau in the Satpura hills, about 3819 ft. above sea-level, 5 m. long by ¾ m. broad. Motors (all classes) from Amraoti (62 m.) and from Ellichpur station (30 m.).

413 m. **Badnera** Junction (waiting-room, D.B.K.); branch 6 m. N. to **Amraoti** station (waiting-room, D.B.K., near railway station). Amraoti is the headquarters of the Commissioner of the Berar Division. There is a cotton market here.

453 m. **Pulgaon** Junction. N.G. railway to Arvi, 22 m. (D.B.K.) on the Wardha river and 36 m. from Wardha.

472 m. from Bombay, **Wardha** (R.), now an important industrial and commercial centre, is the junction for

the broad-gauge line (opened 1876) to *Warora* (83 m.), and the Balharshah Colliery in the Chanda District and on the shortest route to Madras. There are a D.B., a Sarai, a Town Hall, Church, Circuit House; also a Medical Mission of the Church of Scotland. The late Rao Bahadur Bachraj's temple of Lakshminarayan is richly carved and decorated. The town was once Gandhi's home. The Centre of Science for Villages (Magan Sangrahalaya) is a museum promoting the type of village economy advocated by Gandhi. In Sevagram the original huts of his ashram have been preserved and are open to the public. At Mahadev Bhawan beside Sevagram's hospital is a photo exhibit covering the main events of Gandhi's life.

45 m. **Warora** station (D.B.), in the Chanda District and a considerable cotton mart.

74 m. **Chanda,** the headquarters of the Chanda District (D.B. and Circuit House), is surrounded by remains of the city of Bhadravati, visited by Hiuen Tsang, the Chinese pilgrim. The town is surrounded by a continuous wall of cut stone 5½ m. in circuit with four gates, ornamented with Gond crests. The civil station lies to the N. There are extensive forest preserves in the neighbourhood.

Tombs of the Gond kings, and the temples of Achaleswar, Maha Kali, and Murlidhar, are all worth a visit. The tomb of Bir Shah (d. 1672) is of carved white stone, and the oldest is that of Ballal Shah (1207-42). At *Lalpeth,* in the town, a large space is covered with monolith figures of gigantic size, which appear to have been prepared for some great temple never erected.

Chanda Fort is connected with Nagpur by a n.g. railway, Chanda Fort-Itwari (Nagpur), 135 m., through Naghbir. Chanda is 125 m. by road from Nagpur and 129 m. from Sironcha.

83 m. from Wardha, **Balharshah** (Ballarpur), a coal-mining centre (1906) with the Ballarpur, Ghusgus, Sasti and Rajura collieries. There is iron ore nearby but not worked. The fort was founded by the Gond king, Khandkia Ballal Shah (1437-62), and underground passages are believed to run to Chanda Fort. There is a teak depot at Allapilli.

A broad-guage line (1928) runs from Balharshah to Kazipet, providing a new direct route (shorter by 200 m. than the route *via* Manmad) from Madras to Delhi.

520 m. from Bombay on the main line is **Nagpur,*** capital of the former Central Provinces, now in Maharashtra and also linked by I.A.C. services to Calcutta, Delhi, Bombay and Madras.

The district of Nagpur itself has an area of 3840 sq. m. Among the inhabitants are many aborigines known as Gonds. Of these the hill-tribes have black skins, flat noses and thick lips. A cloth round the waist is their chief garment. The religious belief varies from village to village. Nearly all worship the cholera and the smallpox deities, and there are traces of serpent worship.

The ancient history of this region is very obscure. In the 5th century A.D. a race of foreigners, *Yavanas,* ruled from the Satpura plateau, and between the 10th and 13th centuries Rajputs of the Lunar race governed the country round Jabalpur, while the Paramaras (Ponwars) of Malwa ruled S. of the Satpuras. The Chanda dynasty of Gonds reigned probably as early as the 10th or 11th century, and the Haihayas of Chattisgarh were of more ancient date. In 1398 there were local Rulers at Kherla, on the Satpura plateau, of whom Ferishta says: "They possessed all the hills of Gondwana". In 1467 they were conquered by Muhammad Bahmani (1463-82). The Gonds again rose to power in the next century; but in 1740 Raghuji Bhonsla conquered the country. At Sitabaldi, on the 26th and 27th of November 1817, the Mahratta troops of the Bhonsla Raja, Appa Sahib, attacked the Resident, Mr (afterwards Sir Richard) Jenkins, and the few troops he had been able to assemble. The Mahrattas for a time got possession of one of the two eminences of the Sitabaldi hill. The British were at length victorious, but the disbandment of the Bhonsla's army was only obtained after a second battle. Appa Sahib escaped, and died in exile. A child was raised to the throne under the title of Raghoji III, and on his death, in 1853 without issue or collateral heirs, the country was annexed by the British. In 1861 it was, with the Saugor and Narbada territories (which had been taken over in 1818) formed into the Central Provinces by Lord Canning.

Nagpur (pop. 866,000 in 1971) is bounded on the S. by the River Nag, from which it takes its name. The municipality includes the suburb and civil station of *Sitabaldi*. In the centre, W. of the railway station, is Sitabaldi hill, crowned by a fort (built in 1818, and possessing many antique specimens of arms), which commands a fine view, and is a landmark for miles round. W. of Sitabaldi hill is the civil station, in which are the Secretariat, in modified Renaissance style; the Courts; the Legislative Council Chamber (enlarged); the Science College and University (1923); the Victoria Memorial Technical Institute; the English Church which has been enlarged into a Cathedral (Diocese 1902); a Roman Catholic Cathedral and school; Mission of the Church of Scotland; two hospitals for men and women; and a fine Mahratta church; also the High Court building. N. are the Police Lines and the Sadr Bazar, and the suburb of Takli, once the headquarters of the Nagpur Irregular Force. Government House, now renamed Raj Bhawan, is on Takli hill; under the British régime the Governor used to go to Pachmarhi (p. 120) for the hot weather.

Sitabaldi is the suburb S. of the hill of that name, N.E. of which is the railway station; beyond, to the E., is the Jumá Talao, a large tank, and the Empress Mills, opened in 1877; and still farther E. is the city, hidden in foliage. Three great roads lead from the civil station through the city—one on the N. and one on the S. bank of the tank; the third, and most northerly of the three, crosses the railway by a bridge to the N. of the station. Besides the Jumá Talao, there are two other fine tanks, the Ambajheri and Telinkheri (200 acres), W. of the city. The Ambajheri Tank, built by the Bhonsla Rajas, was in 1873 brought into use as a reservoir. The city's water supply was greatly increased by the opening, in 1911, of the Gorewara reservoir, about 4 m. to the N.W. of the civil station. It has a dam 2350 ft. long. The chief gardens are the Kasturchand Park, the Maharaj Bagh, near Sitabaldi, the Tulsi Bagh, inside the city, and the Paldi, Shakardara, Sonagaon, and Telinkheri gardens in the suburbs.

Nagpur is famous for its delicious oranges, quantities of which are exported. There are large cotton-mills. There is also a small but rich Museum maintained by Government grant.

The *Bhonsla Palace*, in the city, built of black basalt, was burned down in 1864, and only the Nakkar Khana, or Music Gallery, remains. Near it are the Hislop College (Missionary) and the Town Hall. The Morris College (Government), formerly in this neighbourhood, is now in the old Residency building, at the foot of the western slope of Sitabaldi hill.

The *Cenotaphs of the Bhonsla Rajas* are in the Shukrawari quarter, to the S. of the city.

The old Great Indian Peninsula Ry. terminated at Nagpur, and from this point E. to Calcutta (703 m.) the lines belonged to the Bengal-Nagpur Ry. A n.g. line runs 92 m. N. to Chhindwara (p. 197), and another, 139 m. S. to Chanda Fort, on the branch line from Wardha (p. 193).

529 m. **Kampti** (D.B.K.), a large town and once a military Cantonment (1821), on the right bank of the

Kanhan river, which is spanned by a handsome stone bridge and close by is the railway bridge. The Anglican church was built in 1833, and there is a Roman Catholic establishment of the Order of St Francis de Sales, with a church and convent. There are five mosques and a number of Hindu temples.

Beyond Kampti, and 25 m. N.E. of Nagpur, from which it is easily accessible by road or rail, is **Ramtek.** The town runs in a straggling line along the foot of a well-wooded hill sacred to Rama, from whom it takes name. The hill is crowned by a citadel with a double line of defences, and within the citadel, at the western end of the summit, stands a group of temples, which are the object of pilgrimages from all parts of India. The inner line of defences was built after 1740 by Raghoji I, the first Bhonsla ruler of Nagpur, but the citadel itself is much older, and the temples are shown by inscriptions to be at least 600 years old. The principal temples are those of Rama, and Sita, his wife. Below the eastern end of the hill, in a picturesque valley, lies the village of Ambala, with a small tank surrounded by shrines, erected by individual devotees. From Ambala a flight of steps rises to the summit of Ramtak Hill. A good road runs E. (3 m.) to Khindsi irrigation reservoir, like a Scottish loch, with a capacity of 4059 million c. ft.

559 m. **Bhandara Road** station is about 7 m. from Bhandara, the district headquarters, which is close to the Wainganga river. There are a rest house and a Club. Bhandara is on the main road from Nagpur to Raipur. A branch road runs to the railway station; motor transport is available.

At 573 m., beyond Tumsar Road station, is the Wainganga river, with a bridge 1450 ft. long (1887).

601 m. **Gondia** Junction (D.B.K.). A n.g. line runs from here N. *via* Balaghat to Nainpur Junction, 73 m., and Jabalpur (p. 121), 141 m., crossing the Narbada river at 132 m.

Another n.g. loop runs S. to Naghbir (82 m.), in Chanda District, whence one branch goes to Nagpur (70 m.) and another to Chanda (69 m.) crossing the Wainganga river at 66 m., bridge 2602 ft. long.

There is a good rest house and waiting and refreshment rooms at the station, where stores are obtainable. From Gondia a road runs S. to Arjuni (28 m.) on the Great Eastern Road from Nagpur to Raipur and the districts beyond. The forests in the neighbourhood of Arjuni (R.H.) offer attractions to the sportsman (licence necessary).

At **Nainpur** Junction, 73 m. (D.B.K.), the Mandla District is entered. From Nainpur a branch line runs N.E. for 26 m. to Mandla Fort (D.B.), the headquarters of the district. The railway station is on the opposite side of the River Narbada to the town. The road bridge is 2300 ft. long.

Mandla (supposed to have been named Mahishmati) is of interest as the capital of the Garha-Mandla Gond (Nishad in old Sanskrit documents) Rajas. The dynasty was of Dravidian origin, founded by Eklavya, who killed the last Haihaya king, of which dynasty there was a copper-plate grant in A.D. 123. Driven from the rich plains of Jabalpur and Saugor about 1564 by the Mughals, the Rajas re-established themselves first at Ramnagar, a riverside village 10 m. from Mandla, and afterwards at Mandla. Hirde Shah, who reigned in the middle of the 17th century, built himself a palace at Ramnagar, now in ruins. It is three-storeyed, built for strength alone, and commands a magnificent view of the River Narbada, which flows at the foot. A Sanskrit inscription (1667) gives the names of the Gond kings. Mandla fort was built a few years later by a succeeding Raja, Narendra Shah; on three sides it is surrounded by the Narbada, and on the fourth by a deep ditch. A bastioned wall once encircled it, but Mandla masons have robbed the old battlements piecemeal of their stones, and the site of the fort is now a luxuriant tropical jungle. The foundations of the wall, however, are still visible, and a few of the larger towers have survived.

The District is rich in forests, which once teemed with game. Tiger, panther, bison, sambhar, barasingha and chital may be found in the **Kanha National Park** 48 m. from Mandla and 108 m. from Jabalpur (p. 121) (good roads). There are rest houses at Kanha and Kristi and watch towers at selected viewpoints. Elephants are available for visitors. Details and reservations from Divisional Forest Officer, E. Mandla Division, Mandla. A visit should be made to the Siva temple of Bhoromdeo situated on a lake 50 m. S. of Kanha and reached by a track leading west after Chilpi on the Karwardha Road.

The River Narbada, which rises a mile or two outside the eastern border of the District, forms in the neighbourhood of Mandla a deep 10-m. reach, nearly half a mile broad. Its banks are studded with temples and ghats, for the water hereabout is of peculiar sanctity, and bathing in the sacred stream is popularly supposed to wash away all sins. The only temple of antiquarian interest is at Kukarramath, built by Jains about the 10th century. It is situated 9 m. from Dindori and 73 m. from Mandla. Local superstition supposes that a cobra with red eyes circles the neck of the image every night and spreads his hood over Mahadeo's head.

From Nainpur, in the Mandla District, a narrow-gauge branch line runs W. to Chhindwara *via* **Seoni,** a distance of 88 m. By this line **Chhindwara** is 157 m. from Jabalpur and 161 m. from Gondia. Chhindwara is also 78 m. by road, or 92 m. by the narrow-gauge railway, N. of Nagpur. This railway continues to the Chhindwara coalfield at Khirsadoh (branch to Parasia) and Barkuhi.

The Central Railway broad-gauge line from Nagpur to Itarsi passes through the S.W. corner of the Chhindwara District. A branch runs from Amla, in the Betul District, to Parasia (54 m.) through the Chhindwara coalfield. The chief collieries are Damua, Lower Ghorewari, Datla and Junnordeo. Pench (2700 ft.) (D.B.) is 1½ m. from Parasia.

Five metalled roads radiate from Chhindwara to (1) Nagpur, (2) Seoni, (3) Narsinghpur, (4) Matkuli on the Piparia-Pachmarhi Road, and (5) Multai on the Nagpur-Betul-Itarsi Road.

Deogarh, 10 m. W. from the Nagpur Road and railway at Umra Nala (on the Nagpur line) has a small fort, which was the headquarters of the Gond Raja, Bakht Buland (*c.* 1700). The buildings cover the hill. The Chhindwara coalfield is the most important in this part of India. Chicoli at mile 41 of the Nagpur-Betal Road, has a banyan tree covering about 2 acres. The D.B. at Tamia, 35 m. N. on the Matkuli Road, has a fine view of the Pachmarhi hills. An hour's run by motor E. of Tamia along the Chindi Road brings one within a short walk of the edge of the Patalkot. This is a wild valley, 1500 ft. deep and 3 m. wide, with numerous precipices.

14 m. from Gondia on the main route from Bhusawal to Calcutta is 615 m. **Amgaon** station (R.).

At Amgaon the **Chattisgarh** "36 Forts" country is entered and continues to Raigarh. The old name for this region was Maha Koshala. The natives of this country still regard themselves as a separate people: the *Chattisgarhias*. Except in the hilly portion, the population consider themselves of Haiheya descent but they are undoubtedly part Gond, though entirely Hindu in religion. The Rajas of Ratanpur (p. 198) ruled originally over their thirty-six forts, each the chief place of a District; but about A.D. 750 the kingdom was divided into two, and a separate Raja ruled in Raipur. Kalyan Sahi, who ruled between 1536 and 1573, made his submission to Akbar at Delhi, and this prudent conduct resulted in the Haihaya rulers retaining their country until the Mahratta invasion in 1740.

The tract is in the shape of a vast amphitheatre opening to the S. on the plains of Raipur, but on every other side surrounded by tiers of hills. It is a great grain-producing country, irrigated from the Mahanadi river. There is considerable forest land. Application may be made to the Forest Authorities if a shooting permit is required.

From 624 m. **Salekasa** the line passes through hills and heavy bamboo jungles. At 631 m. **Darekasa** is on the watershed of the Narbada and Mahandi river basins, a pass with a tunnel at the summit. Next comes, 647 m. from Bombay, **Dongargarh** (R., Hotel), an engine-changing station, with a considerable railway settlement. There is a guest-house in the town. The ruins of a fort are on the N.E. face of a detached hill, some 4 m. in circuit. There are tanks for water supply, but no buildings.

708 m. from Bombay, **Raipur** (pop. 205,000 in 1971) Junction (alt. 995 ft.). n.g. railway to Abhanpur Junction and Dhamtari (35 m.). The chief town of a District of the same name, and the headquarters of the Commissioner of *Chattisgarh*. Of the *Fort*, built by Raja Bhubaneswar Singh in 1460, no trace now remains except isolated mounds. The *Burha Tank*, on the S., the same age as the Fort, covered nearly 1 sq. m. The public gardens are on its E. shore. There is a Raipur Museum. The *Maharajbandh Tank* was constructed by a revenue farmer in the times of the Mahrattas, and close to it is the temple of Ramchandra (locally known as the Dudhadhari temple), built in 1775 by Bhimbaji Bhonsla. In the centre of the town is the *Kankali Tank*, constructed of stone throughout, at the close of the 17th century. About 2 m. to the S. is the former Rajkumar College, for the education of the sons and relatives of notables of Bihar, Orissa, and the surrounding country.

From Raipur a broad-gauge railway, crossing the Mahanadi river at 26 m. by a bridge 2624 ft. long, runs 290 m. through wild and picturesque country to Vizianagram Junction (p. 428), on the Coromandel coast. At 133 m. the bridge over the Tel river is 2158 ft. long.

777 m. **Bilaspur** (pop. 130,000 in 1971) Junction (R.) (alt. 885 ft.). Big game in the N. and Central parts of Bilaspur District.

A branch-line runs N.W. through a mountainous district and the coalfields of **Umaria** to 198 m. **Katni** Junction (p. 122). This branch passes at *Pendra Road* station the **Amarkantak** plateau (3500 ft.), where the Narbada, the Son and Mahanadi rivers have their sources. There are several temples and a "Kund" or reservoir enclosing the Narbada spring. The plateau is frequented by the "tirth bàsis" and other pilgrims. The scenery between Khodri, S. of Pendra, and Khongsara is notable.

About 15 m. N.E. of Bilaspur is the precipitous *hill of Dalha*, 2600 ft. high, rising sheer out of the plain.

15 m. N. of Bilaspur is **Ratanpur,** the old capital of the formerly self-contained kingdom of *Chattisgarh, or the Thirty-six Forts*, comprising the Districts of Raipur, Drug (in which is the Iron and Steel plant at **Bhilai,** a State enterprise built with Soviet help) and Bilaspur. The town lies in a hollow surrounded by hills. It ceased to be the capital in 1818, but the crumbling arches of the old fort, the broken walls of the ancient palace, and the half-filled-up moat which surrounded the city, recall its former condition. The Brahmins of Ratanpur are still the leaders of their class all over Chattisgarh. The numerous small temples in the vicinity are scattered over an area of 15 sq. m. A Siva temple with an unusual oval hall decorated with rishis, stands on the lakeside at Pali, 13 m. N.E. of Ratanpur. There are at Ratanpur many fine mango groves, with numerous tanks and temples scattered

amidst their shade. Great blocks of masonry of uniform shape commemorate distinguished satis (*suttees*). The most prominent of these is near the old fort, where a large building records that there in the middle of the 17th century twenty ranis of Raja Lakshman Sahi devoutly fulfilled the duty of self-immolation.

802 m. **Naila** station. At Janjgir, 1½ m. S., stands a magnificent Chedi style temple of 11th century dedicated to Vishnu, its porch decorated with superb figures of Rama, Sita and Lachsman. The temple is protected as an ancient monument.

809 m. **Champa** station the Hasdo river is crossed. The stream cuts the coalfields of **Korba** some 20 m. N. of the railway.

At 844 m. the Mand river is crossed.

859 m. **Raigarh**, capital of a former State of that name, now absorbed in Madhya Pradesh.

890 m. **Belpahar** station, after leaving which the **Ib** river (boundary of Orissa), which flows S. into the Mahanadi river, is crossed.

903 m. **Jharsuguda** Junction station. There is a P.W.D. Inspection Bungalow, which may be available to travellers if not occupied by local officers. Flint implements have been found.

A branch line runs to **Sambalpur** (alt. 484 ft.; D.B. and Circuit House, available for travellers). Near here diamonds of considerable value have been procured. They are said to be found in the bed of the Mahanadi upstream from the town. Nearest (10 m.) town to **Hirakud** Dam (4th largest in world). Airstrip: impressive control project for Mahanadi R. Lake with boats for hire. The project supplies power to a large new industrial complex, of which the Hindustan Steel Plant at **Rourkela** (125 m.) (pop. 172,000 in 1971) with modern well-landscaped township is a leading feature. (For accommodation apply Public Relations Officer.) I.A.C. Service from Calcutta *via* Jamshedpur (116).

From Jharsuguda the railway takes a N.E. course, and continuing through a well-inhabited plain country to

916 m. **Bagdehi** station, where it enters the hills, in which it continues until the plains of Bengal are reached.

936 m. **Garpos** station. Hereabouts the forests are very dense, and in the rainy season are the favourite resort of wild elephants.

Between 958 m. **Kalunga** and Panposh the Brahmani river is crossed: the bridge is 1506 ft. long (1891). The local people work in the limestone quarries and manganese mines of the former Gangpur State. The view upstream is very grand when the river is in flood, at the confluence with the Sankh river.

991 m. **Manharpur** station. Here the railway enters the **Saranda** forests, which contain some of the finest sal trees (*Shorea robusta*) in India. The line winds round hills, passing close under them on both sides. The summit of the range is reached through a heavy cutting leading into a tunnel. Traffic in ironstone, limestone, timber and sabai grass for paper manufacture has expanded. The inhabitants of these wilds are nearly all aboriginal Hos or Mundas. A light railway runs from Manharpur to the vast iron-ore deposits of Saranda, which are mined by the Bengal Iron Company.

1029 m. **Chakradharpur** station (D.B.K.), a large railway settlement and engine-changing station. The town is also increasing in size and importance, as it is a centre for the timber trade. There is a D.B. with a khansama near the railway station. The main road connecting Patna with Cuttack runs through Chakradharpur. Starting from Chakradharpur a very pleasant motor trip can be made to Ranchi (72 m.) and thence to Hazaribagh, Gaya and Patna. The road to Ranchi is metalled and bridged throughout, and rising about 1500 ft. between the 64th and 40th m. runs through very picturesque forest scenery. From Chakradharpur also it is possible to motor to Jaipur Road on the Madras branch of the Eastern Ry. The road passes through Chaibasa (16 m.), the headquarters of the district, and is metalled and bridged as far as the Baitarani river (52 m.), which forms the boundary between the district of Singhbhum and the former State of Keonjhar. The Baitarani river is bridged, and thence there is a good gravelled road passing through Keonjhar to Jajpur.

Chaibasa (alt. 754 ft.), headquarters of Singhbhum district, is situated about 16 m. to the S.E. A service of motor-omnibuses (S. 1½ hr.) connects it with Chakradharpur. It is also reached by rail (12 m.) from Amda (see below). Accommodation at the D.B. where there is a khansama. The country round Chaibasa is inhabited by the aboriginal race of Hos or Larka Kols. Palaeolithic finds in the neighbourhood.

1042 m. **Raj Kharsawan** Junction (Amda). A branch line runs through Chaibasa (12 m.) to Gua (65 m.) in the S. of the district where a very large and rich haematite deposit is being worked. There are also manganese and chromite deposits near Chaibasa.

1051 m. **Sini** Junction: a branch line runs N.E. to Asansol, while the main direct line runs E. to **Kharagpur** and **Howrah.**

Sini Junction to Asansol

On the line from Sini Junction to Asansol are the following stations:

17 m. from Sini, **Chandil** station. Before this place is reached the hills close in on the line. Dalma hill, 3060 ft. above sea-level, is visible 12 m. E. Labour for the tea-cultivation in Upper Assam and Cachar used to be recruited from this tract, but the development of local cultivation of lac has reduced the supply. After crossing the Cossye river

31 m. from Sini, **Barahabhum** station, for Balarampur, where there are several shellac factories.

50 m. **Purulia** station. Headquarters of the Manbhum district, through which the traveller has been passing for many miles.

From here a n.g. line runs to Kotshila Junction (22 m.). The Kotshila-Muri-Ranchi line has been converted to broad-gauge. From Kotshila a new b.g. line goes to Gomoh (Route 2). From Ranchi a n.g. line goes to Lohardaga (see below). At 67 m. is the Subarnarekha river.

75 m. **Adra** Junction (R.). Here the Kharagpur-Bankura-Gomoh railway diverges from the main line. 16 m. from Gomoh the Damodar river is crossed. At Mohuda, 14 m. from Gomoh, a branch runs to Barkakana (see below); the railway colliery at **Bokaro**, near Bermo station on this line, is a quarry with 80 ft. of solid coal-face and an estimated content of 70 million tons. Bokaro, with its great steel plant, has become an impressive modern "Steel City" with a population (1971) of more than 108,000. From Bankura, 33 m. S.W. from Adra, a n.g. railway runs 60 m. E. to Rainagar, on the bank of the Damodar river.

101 m. from Sini **Asansol** Junction station (D.B. and Inspection Bungalow). About 6 m. before Asansol is reached the River Damodar is crossed on a bridge 2364 ft. long. For the section Asansol to Calcutta, a distance of 132 m., see Route 2 (p. 77).

Sini Junction to Ranchi and Kharagpur

On the main direct line from Sini Junction to Kharagpur the first station of importance after crossing the Kharkai river is

1068 m. from Bombay, **Tatanagar,** for the great industrial centre of **Jamshedpur,** where the parent company of Tata's Iron and Steel Works is now the centre of a ring of industries, covering tin-plates, agricultural implements, jute machinery, enamel ware, locomotive parts, chemicals, etc. Pop. 465,000 in 1971 and growing rapidly. At night there is a blaze of light. Air connections with Calcutta.

From Tatanagar a branch runs (95 m.) to **Barkakana,** a few miles W.

of Ramgarh in the Damodar valley; and thence to **Daltonganj** (p. 129), and Son East Bank. Ramgarh was a P.O.W. Camp during the last war, and also a training centre for Chinese forces (Stilwell's).

At **Muri** (59 m. from Tatanagar on the Barkakana branch) is the site of the Canadian-sponsored Indian Aluminium Factory and the junction with the lines from Purulia and Gomoh (see above) to Ranchi and Lohardaga. The journey (262 m.) from Howrah to Ranchi by this route (*via* Kharagpur, Tatanagar and Muri) takes 12 hr. daily from Howrah).

Ranchi* (2138 ft., pop. 256,000 in 1971) used to be the summer capital of the Government of Bihar from May to October, and still is the headquarters of the Commissioner of the Chota-Nagpur Division.[1] It is also the headquarters of Hindustan Steel and of the Heavy Engineering Corporation and there is a large industrial suburb. Air connections with Calcutta. The climate in the hot weather has little advantage over the plains, but in the rains and cold weather it is excellent. There are hotels and boarding-houses. The Railway Hotel is comfortable: guests may play on the golf courses. Taxis can be obtained, and there are several garages. The Club will admit accredited visitors as temporary members. There are two golf-courses, one good, the other indifferent; both belong to the Club. The Sunday services at the Protestant and R.C. churches are largely attended by the Christian Kols, and are interesting.

The motorist will find an admirable centre for excursions in Ranchi, also excellent metalled roads, with bridges, connect with Hazaribagh (58 m.), from which place (42 m.) Hazaribagh Road station on the Grand Chord Line (p. 77) can be reached, Purulia (96 m.), Chaibasa (88 m.) and Lohardaga (46 m.), the terminus of the n.g. line from Purulia and the old district headquarters. The last-named road continues (96 m.) to **Netarhat**, "The Queen of Chota-Nagpur" (3700 ft.), with wonderful views. There are Forest, Revenue and Public Health I.Bs. and a Youth Hostel. Reservations to be fixed in Ranchi. The Daltonganj road branches off from the Lohardaga road at Kuru (35 m.) and is suitable for motors throughout the year. Public motor-lorries run to Hazaribagh, Gaya, Chaibasa and Lohardaga; arrangements can be made for first-class passengers. In addition to the places mentioned, the following are accessible by motor-car: Jamshedpur, Giridih, Dhanbad and Calcutta, and also Jajpur Road station (for Cuttack) on the main line from Calcutta to Madras (Route 22).

At Kanke, 5 m. from Ranchi, is a Mental Hospital, the largest of its kind in India. A Lac Research Institute, investigating lac, the great local industry, has been established at Namkam (4 m. from Ranchi), where there are Bishop Westcott schools for boys and girls. At Itki (14 m. from Ranchi on the railway to Lohardaga) there is a tuberculosis sanatorium. There is a fine waterfall at Hundru, 28 m. from Ranchi; the first 14 m. of the road are metalled and the remainder gravelled. There are waterfalls at Jonah and Bhera, temples at Jagannathpur (5 m.) and Rajroppa. The Ichadag sanatorium bungalow is 23 m. from the railway station. McCluskieganj (1935) is an Anglo-Indian colony.

From Tatanagar, the main line crosses the Subarnarekha river just before reaching,

1084 m. from Bombay and 139 m. from Howrah, **Galudih.** Near lie several copper mines. On the railway there are large copper works with mill, refinery and by-product recovery plant. Extensive deposits of copper sulphide exist in the hills running S.

1151 m. from Bombay and 72 m. from Howrah, **Kharagpur** (p. 411) junction for the main line to Madras (Route 22), and 1223 m. from Bombay, **Howrah,** the Calcutta railway terminus.

[1] For this interesting part of India Bradley Birt's *Chota-Nagpur* (John Murray) may be consulted.

ROUTE 8

KHANDWA to AJMER by **Mortakka** (for **Omkarji**), **Mhow** (for **Mandu** and the **Caves of Bagh**), **Indore, Ujjain, Ratlam, Nimach, Chitorgarh** (for UDAIPUR) and **Nasirabad.**

Khandwa, Mandu, the Bagh Caves and surrounding country can be conveniently visited from Indore, which is connected with Bombay and Delhi by air services.

353 m. from Bombay on the main line to Calcutta (Route 2) is **Khandwa** (p. 119), the starting-point of the metre-gauge section of the Western Ry. which passes through Ratlam to Ajmer, and connects there with the metre-gauge mail route to Jaipur and Delhi (Route 10).

34 m. from Khandwa is Sanawad, where there is a D.B.

38 m. from Khandwa, near **Mortakka** station (Omkareshwar Road station), the Narbada river is crossed by a railway bridge and a road causeway. The river was formerly the boundary between the Deccan and Hindustan. The neighbourhood was formerly famous for large game.

A road (motor service) leads 6 m. E. to **Mandhata,** more properly called **Omkarji,** which can be visited from Mhow. The trip will easily occupy a whole day.

In the Puranas the place is called Omkar Kshetra. *The Great Temple of Omkar* is situated on the island of Mandhata, in the Narbada. It is said that the hill was originally called Baidurya Mani Parvat, but its name was changed to Mandhata as a boon from Siva to Raja Mandhatri, the seventeenth monarch of the Solar Race, who performed a great sacrifice here to Siva.

The island is about 1½ m. long and the area is five-sixths of a square mile, and a deep ravine cuts it from N. to S. At the N. the ground slopes gently, but terminates at the S. and E. in precipices 500 ft. high. At this point the S. bank of the Narbada is equally steep, and between the cliffs the river is exceedingly deep and full of crocodiles and large fish. The village is built partly on the S. bank of the river and partly on the island. It is most picturesque, the rows of temples, houses and shops standing on terraces with the Raja's palace overhanging the rest.

The river is at present crossed by private ferry, although a new concrete bridge is nearing completion. The rocks on both sides are of a greenish hue, very boldly stratified, with remains of fortifications erected by ancient Rajas. It is said that the Temple of Omkar and that of Amreswar, or Manileshwar, on the S. bank of the river, are two of the twelve great Sivite temples which existed in India when Mahmud of Ghazni destroyed Somnath in 1024. When the Peshwa Baji Rao II desired to repair the temple it could not be found, as the banks were overgrown. So a new one was built, with a group of smaller ones. Afterwards part of it was found, and a former Raja of Mandhata built a temple over it; but the sanctity and name of Manileshwar have been appropriated by the Peshwa's temple.

The Raja of Mandhata, who is hereditary custodian of the temples, is a Bhilala (of mixed Rajput and Bhil descent), and claims to be the direct descendant of the Chauhan Bharat Singh, who took Mandhata from Nathu Bhil in 1165. The old temples have been damaged by Muslims; every dome has been overturned and every figure mutilated. The gateways are finely carved.

The oldest temple is on the *Birkhala rocks* at the E. end, where devotees used to cast themselves over the cliffs from Puranic times up till the year 1824. The junction of the Kavari with the Narbada was also favoured for this meritorious self-sacrifice, according to the Puranas. The temple consists of a courtyard, with a veranda and colonnades supported by massive pillars boldly carved. On the hill are the ruins of a very fine *Temple to Siddha Nath*, which stood on a plinth 10 ft. high. Round the plinth was a frieze of elephants 5 ft. high, carved in relief on slabs of yellow sandstone; all but two are mutilated. The temple is classified as an Ancient Monument.

In front of the *Temple to Gauri Somnath*, on the hill at the W. is an immense Nandi carved in a green stone, and 100 yd. farther is a pillar 20 ft. long. On the island itself all the temples are Sivite, but on the N. bank of the Narbada are some old temples to Vishnu, now in ruins, and a group of Jain Temples, called Sidhvar Kut. On the S. bank is a temple of Brahma, without a figure. Where the river bifurcates are some ruined gateways, and a temple of Varah, on which are twenty-four figures of Vishnu well carved in green stone. In the middle is a large figure of the boar Avatar. On an image of Siva in the same building is the date 1346. Farther down the bank, in the ravine, is a prostrate female figure (wrongly called Ravana, really Chamundi), 18½ ft. long, with ten arms holding clubs and skulls. On its chest is a scorpion, signifying the pangs of hunger, and at its right side a rat, and one foot rests on a prostrate human figure.

The bed of the ravine is covered with huge basalt blocks slightly carved. The *Jain Temples* stand on an eminence a little back from the river. The largest is on a plinth of basalt 5 ft. high. The E. wall is still complete. On each side of the doorway is a figure with Saivite and Jain emblems curiously intermixed.

Gandpad, the guru of Shankaracharya, lived here, and Nanak the Sikh guru paid a visit. It is said that a demon Hedamb haunted the place. In the Skand Purana Kavar performed a sacrifice at the confluence with the Kavari.

There is a fair at the Shivaratri festival (Feb.-March), and another in November at the Kantik Pirmina. According to a prophecy the sanctity of the Ganges expired in 1899 and was transferred to the Narbada.

41 m. from Kandwa is **Barwaha** station (D.B.), the seat of a palace of the Maharaja Holkar (no admission). A metalled road runs from here (44 m. W.) to **Maheshwar** (D.B.), until 1738 the capital of the Holkars, in Nimàr District, on the banks of the Narbada, where is the magnificent **Chhattri** of Ahalya Bai (d. 1795), widow of the son of Malhar Rao Holkar. Sir John Malcolm said: "She sat every day for a considerable period in open darbar transacting business. Her first principle of government appears to have been moderate assessment and an almost sacred respect for the native rights. . . . She heard every complaint in person, and although she continually referred causes to courts of equity and arbitration and to her Ministers for settlement, she was always accessible. . . . Her charitable foundations extend all over India, from the Himalayas to Cape Comorin, and from Somnath to the Temple of Jagannath." She had the courage to watch her daughter become *sati*, after vainly seeking to dissuade her.

Opposite Maheshwar is a prehistoric site, Navdateli, of a post-Indus culture. The inhabitants were neolithic farmers. It was destroyed c. 200 B.C.

58 m. from Khandwa is **Choral** station. From this point the ascent of the Vindhya Range commences on a grade of 1 in 40 and continues almost into Mhow. The scenery is striking. On approaching

71 m. **Patalpani** station, the waterfall of that name is passed.

74 m. **Mhow*** station (R.), D.B. (alt. 1926 ft. above sea-level) on the watershed of the Narbada and Chambal basins. British troops were stationed here under the Treaty of Mandasor of 1818 with Malhar Rao Holkar II, and it is still an important cantonment. Mhow is a centre for many excursions.

From Mhow an expedition of 55 m. may be made S.W. to the ruined city of **Mandu,** capital of the Muslim kingdom of Malwa. This was once in Dhar, a former Mahratta State, founded by Anand Rao Puar I, to whom it was assigned by the Peshwa Baji Rao I (1734).

The best route to Mandu is by motor through the town of Dhar (33 m.), D.B. An alternative route of 58 m. is *via* **Manpur** (13 m. from Mhow), which is 12 m. from Gujri (Inspection Bungalow) on the Agra-Bombay road; it has the advantage of beautiful scenery. A third route (78 m.) is from Ratlam (p. 161) along a good metalled road. Motors can pass right into the old fort and, except in the rains, as far as the palace of Baz Bahadur. There are R.Hs. and a Travellers' Lodge at Mandu in which visitors can stay. Apply Executive Engineer P.W.D., Dhar. There are bus connections with Bhopel, Mhow, Ujjain, and Dhar.

It is possible to see all the main buildings and return to Mhow the same day. On arriving at Mandu it is most convenient to drive right through the ruins to the farthest point close by the pavilion of Rupmati, then work back to the Barnes Kothi, a rest house situated near the centre of the ruins. Between the months of June and November the locality is unhealthy.

Dhar, once capital of Malwa, founded by Raja Bhoj from Ujjain, contains several half-ruined mosques. Bhojashala is a large stone mosque with ancient Sanskrit inscriptions. The tomb of the muslim saint Kamal Maula adjoins. Dhar has a well-preserved fort with good views from the ramparts. Outside the N. wall of the Lat Masjid at Dhar (1405) lies a lat, or pillar of wrought iron, thought to have been originally a pillar of victory. **Jahangir** in his diary stated that Bahadur Shah of Gujarat ordered it to be removed, but in this process it fell and broke in two: the smaller part, 13 ft. long, has disappeared; the larger part, 22 ft. long, remains *in situ*, partly buried in the ground.

Dilawar Khan Ghori, appointed Governor (1387), assumed the title of Sultan (1400) and moved to Mandu.

Mandu (1944 ft.), originally 37 m. in circumference and 20 sq. m. in area, now occupies 8 sq. m. of ground, extending along the crest of the Vindhyas; and is separated from the tableland, with which it is on a level, by a deep valley crossed by a causeway, above the southern side of which the battlemented walls and gates of the old city rise. The perimeter follows a contour serrated by ravines. Mandu rose in the 11th century but was conquered by the Khiljis of Delhi in 1304. It became independent in 1401 as capital of Malwa and so remained until annexed by the Mughals under Akbar.

The jungle has been cleared from all the ruins of interest, the chief being the *Jami Masjid* (1454), less ruined than any of the others, and claimed to be the finest and largest specimen of Afghan architecture extant in India. The courtyard is 90 yd. square and is surrounded by a double colonnade. The mosque proper consists of five aisles of seventeen bays. To the W. of the mosque a second enclosure contains the fine white marble tomb of Alif Khan Hoshang Shah Ghori (1406-35). Facing the eastern entrance to the mosque are remains of the mausoleum of Muhammad the Great, and at its N.W. angle is the lower part of a circular tower of victory, formerly seven storeys high.

Between it and the great arched gateway in the northern wall of the city are a number of ruined palaces and courts, including the **Jahaz Mahal,** or Ship Palace, which takes its name from the lakes between which it stands. It was staffed entirely by women, and consists mainly of three great halls, with a beautiful little bath at the N. end: there is a fine view over the city from its roof. Close by is the **Hindola** ("Swing"—from its sloping walls) **Mahal,** a hall of fine massive proportions. Farther

W. are the **Champa Baori**, a well with subterranean retreats for hot weather, and the remains of some baths.

2 m. S.E. is the *Palace of Baz Bahadur*, the last Sultan of Malwa (1555), and on rising ground nearby stands the pavilion of Rupmati, his lovely Hindu mistress. From here there is a splendid view southwards across the Narbada valley, 1000 ft. below.

S.W., near the inner citadel of Songarh, is a quaint ravine with temples and a small tank, specially mentioned in the memoirs of the Emperor Jahangir. These buildings are still very striking on account of their massive proportions.

The fortifications were constructed by Hoshang Shah Ghori, in whose time the city attained its greatest splendour. In 1526 Mandugarh was taken by Bahadur Shah, ruler of Gujarat, and annexed to his dominions, of which it remained part until their conquest by Akbar in 1567. Sir Thomas Roe, the Ambassador of James I of England, entered Mandu in the train of Jahangir, part of the triumphal procession of the Great Mughal being 500 elephants. He complains of the lions which then infested the country and killed one of his baggage ponies. The Rulers of Mandu and Chitor were at feud with each other for many years.

The **Caves of Bagh** lie 30 m. W. of Mandu and are connected by good roads with Bombay, Ujjain and Indore.[1] Motor service (87 m.) to the caves, through Dhar and Sardarpur, a former British Cantonment (travellers' bungalows at convenient stages); there is a small rest house near them and also a comfortable State Inspection Bungalow in the village of Bagh (5 m.) in charge of a P.W.D. Overseer. It would be as well to consult the representative of the Archaeological Dept. at Gwalior as to arrangements. The village of Bagh is situated on the Bagh river, in a valley 800 ft. above sea-level on the S. slope of the Vindhya range. To the S. at the foot of a hill is the Baghesvari temple, which has been reconstructed from portions of a 12th-century building.

[1] Latest reports (1981) are that in spite of restoration work the caves are in very bad condition owing to smoke, water and crumbling.

The caves[1] E. of the village were originally more numerous, but some are blocked by their fallen roofs. They are known locally as the *Panch Pandu* or *Pandava Gupha*, the Buddhist figures in the second cave being wrongly supposed to represent the five Pandava brothers. The excavations are in the face of a sandstone hill and occupy a frontage of 700 yd. They are manifestly Mahayana, dating A.D. 400-700. All are *viharas*, or assembly halls; a small chamber at the back forms a *chaitya* or chapel, and the cells are at the sides. Cave No. 1 at the extreme N.E. of the cliff, is probably the earliest, with a dagoba. Cave No. 2 (the Gossain's Cave) is the most complete of the series, although the paintings have been obliterated by smoke and bats. It is approached by a steep flight of steps. There are eighteen cells round the cave. Two groups of well-executed figures stand on the sides of the ante-chamber, representing a Buddha and two attendants. Two *dwarapalas*, or guardians, are placed on either side of the entrance to the sanctum. This is the only cave in which there are stone figures.

No. 3 (*Hathikhana*, or Elephants' Stable) contains paintings of the Buddha with kneeling worshippers (their race not identified) on the walls of the chamber on the N.E. side of the hall, which is fronted by a pillared vestibule. Between this cave and the next are 200 yd. of solid rock.

Cave No. 4, which has a common portico with No. 5, is the most magnificent of the series, and is known as the Rang Mahal or Painted Hall. The portico is covered with paintings

[1] See *The Bagh Caves*, a comprehensive account, with illustrations of the paintings, published by the Royal India Society in 1927: also *My Pilgrimage to Ajanta and Bagh*, by Makal Chandra De (1925).

of kings, priests, horsemen, elephant riders, dancers and attendants. Copies are in the Archaeological Museum at Gwalior and also at the British Museum. A colossal figure, a King or Yaksharaja, is seated in a recess 13 ft. high outside the portico.

Cave No. 5 would appear from its shape to have been a lecture-hall (*shala*) or refectory. Cave No. 6 was evidently purely residential: it is entered by a small ante-chamber from No. 5. In 1910 signs of frescoes were visible in Cave No. 7, which is 45 ft. away from No. 6, but it has now collapsed. Caves 8 and 9 are also blocked up. 2 m. N.E. of the caves is the half-ruined shrine of a 12th-century Hindu temple of Siva.

87 m. from Khandwa **Indore** (Hotel, D.B.K., R.H., C.H.), airfield, with daily services from Bombay, Delhi and Bhopal, alt. 1805 ft., headquarters under British rule of the Central India Agency, and capital of the former Indore State. On National Highway between Bombay and Delhi. The principal chiefs of the House of Holkar have been Malhar Rao (d. 1766), the founder (1733); Ahalya Bai (1767-95) widow of his son Khande Rao; Tukoji (1795-97), her general; Jaswant Rao (d. 1811); Malhar Rao II (d. 1833); Tukoji Rao II (1852-86); and Shivaji Rao (abdicated 1893).

Indore (population 572,000 in 1971), built by Ahalya Bai, stands on the banks of the rivers Sarasvati and Khan. It was destroyed in 1801, but recovered.

The *Rajwada*, with many-storeyed gateway, faces the chief square. On the N. of it and separated from it by a street is the *New Palace*, now a hospital. On the S. side of the square is the *Anna Chhatra* (alms-house), where food is daily distributed to the poor.

In the streets are some good timber houses, with deep recessed verandas, and carved corbels and pillars. To the W. of the Old Palace is the *Sarafa Street* of the Marwari money-lenders, and close by are the *Haldi Bazar* and the *Aditvar* or Sunday Street, where a market is held on Sundays. On Sunday Street is the Seth Hukamchand Temple (Kanch Mandir), a mirrored Jain temple.

On the W. bank of the Khan, near the bridge, is a statue of Sir Robert Hamilton (1802-87), who was A.G.G. in the years preceding the Mutiny. On the riverside are numerous Chhattris erected to the memory of members of the Holkar family.

In the *Chhattri Bagh*, an oblong enclosure surrounded by a battlemented wall, are the cenotaph of Malhar Rao Holkar I, richly ornamented with sculpture in low relief; a smaller one of Ahalya Bai (see p. 203), and one to her son Male Rao Holkar (d. 1766): this is a twelve-sided building on a rectangular plinth also delicately ornamented with low relief sculpture. A similar walled enclosure a few hundred yards farther down the Sarasvati river contains the Chhattri of Maharaja Hari Rao Holkar IV (d. 1843).

Of modern buildings in the town the principal are the *King Edward Hall*, opened 17th November 1905, by King George V (then Prince of Wales), whose visit is commemorated by the new *Courts of Justice*; the *M.R. Tukoji Rao Hospital*; and the *City High School*. There are also some flourishing cotton-mills. The *Institute of Plant Industry* is famous as a nursery of scientists.

S.W. of the town is the *Lal Bagh* palace (the principal residence of the Maharaja), standing on the banks of the Sarasvati, amongst well-wooded gardens and grounds. 1 m. from this palace is the State guest-house, *Manik Bagh*; and 1 m. farther (S. of the town) is *Holkar College*. There is a Museum in the Nara Ratna Mandir.

Adjoining the town, on the E., is the old **Residency** Bazar area, which originally was assigned by treaty, but was retroceded in 1931. This contained the houses of the Resident for Central India (formerly styled Agent to the Governor-General) and his staff; quarters of the Malwa Bhil Corps; the *Post Office*; the *Anglican* and *R.C. Churches*; the *Presbyterian Church of Canada*; the *King Edward Memorial Hospital*, a training school for members of the subordinate medical services, with 160 students; the *Daly College*; and a beautiful *Park* and *Garden* through which flows the River Khan.

Daly College, which was instituted for the education of Indian princes and nobles, is a fine marble building with a large hall and contains a series of portraits of Indian princes by Herbert Olivier.

About 3 m. to the S.W. of Indore is the palace of *Shirpur*, near which there used to be a large Blackbuck preserve, and 1 m. beyond is Sukhnewás, a pleasure palace.

In 1857 some of the Indore troops rose and attacked the Residency, and also the Cantonment of Mhow on 1st July. The A.G.G., Colonel Durand, who had arrived at Indore only on 14th May, and the Europeans with him, were compelled, after a fight, to retire to Sehore and Hoshangabad. The Maharaja (Tukoji Rao Holkar II), aged only 15, gave assistance and refused to surrender a number of Christians to whom he had given sanctuary in the palace. Captain Hungerford, with the Maharaja's help, drove the mutineers off from Mhow and remained there until a Bombay force arrived on 14th December.

112 m. from Khandwa is **Fatehabad** Junction (R.), where Aurangzeb defeated Jaswant Singh of Jodhpur (1658) on his march to usurp rule. From here a short branch line of 15 m. runs to

Ujjain (pop. 209,000 in 1971), (R.R., C.H., D.B.), 23 m. N.W. from Dewas,[1] on the Agra-Bombay road, and 42 m. S.S.W. from Agar, a former Cantonment of the Central India Horse. Junction for the Central Ry. broad-gauge line (114 m.) from Bhopal, and its prolongation (24 m.) to Nagda, where it meets the Western Ry. main line from Bombay to Delhi. Taxis, tongas and cycle-rickshaws available.

This famous city (the Greek Οζήνη), one of the seven sacred cities of the Hindus (p. 76), is situated on the right bank of the River Sipra, which, rising in the Vindhyas, falls into the Chambal. The principal bathing festival is the Kumbh Mela; celebrated triennially at Hardwar (p. 365), Allahabad (p. 123), Nasik (p. 115) and Ujjain, it is held here every twelfth year. The old name of Avanti, by which it was formerly known, was also applied to the Malwa country, of which it was once the capital. It stands in N. lat. 23° 11′ 10″, the first meridian of Hindu geographers. It is said to have been the seat of the viceroyalty of Asoka during the reign of his father at Pataliputra, now Patna, about 275 B.C. It is, however, best known as the capital of the legendary Vikramaditya (Valour's sun), long believed to be the founder of the Samvat era. He was fabled to have driven out the Scythians, and to have reigned over almost all N. India, and at his court were said to have flourished the Nine Gems of Hindu literature—viz. Dhanvantari, Kshapanaka, Amarasinha, Shanku, Vetalabhatta, Ghata-karpara, Kalidasa (of world celebrity), Vararuchi and Varaha-mihira.

The Paramara king Bhoja (1010-1060) removed the capital to Dhar. Altamish of Delhi captured Ujjain in 1235 and destroyed a famous temple of Mahakal (restored in the eighteenth century). The whole province of Malwa was conquered by Ala-ud-din Khilji, who reigned at Delhi 1295-1317. In 1387 the Muslim Governor, Dilawar Khan Ghori, declared himself independent and moved to Mandu. In 1531 Malwa was conquered by Bahadur Shah, King of Gujarat, and in 1562 by Akbar. In 1658 the decisive battle between Aurangzeb and Murad and their elder brother Dara was fought near this city. In 1732 the Mahrattas

[1] There were two Maharajas of Dewas, called Senior and Junior. Both were Mahrattas (Puars) of the same caste as the Maharaja of Dhar (p. 204) and the Rajput Paramaras.

conquered Malwa, and Ujjain was awarded to Ranoji Rao Scindia to support his troops, remaining the capital of Scindia until 1810, when Daulat Rao Scindia removed to Gwalior.

In 1792 Tukaji Holkar took Ujjain from Madhava Rao Scindia, and burned part of it.

Ancient Ujjain lay to the N. on high ground known as *gadh* (fort), along the right bank of the River Sipra. At the Vaishya Tekre (4 m. N.E.) a large stupa has been unearthed, cremated bones and skeletons found, with coins dating A.D. 100-300. The *nagara* (town) and *vana* (forest) have exchanged places, for the modern city stands on the Mahakalavara (grove of Mahakal). The change probably occurred about 1300. The modern city was once surrounded by a stone wall. Near the palace of Maharaja Scindia is an ancient gateway (known as the Chaubis Khamba Ghaj), said to have been part of the enclosure of the Mahakal temple. To the W. of this are the picturesque ghats and temples on the river; and outside the city to the S.W. are the remains of the old Hindu **Observatory**, erected, while Governor of Malwa (1728-34), by Maharaja Jai Singh II of Jaipur (p. 266). 5 m. to the N. of the town is a restored Water Palace (Kaliadah) of the Sultans of Mandu on an island in the Sipra river. It was formerly used by the Maharajas of Gwalior when they visited Ujjain.

161 m. **Ratlam** (pop. 118,000 in 1971) Junction (R. good; D.B.K.) of the Western Ry., B.G. line from Bombay (*via* Baroda, Godhra, Nagda, Kotah, Bharatpur and Muttra) to Delhi (mail route), and of the (metre-gauge) section of the Western Ry. from Ajmer to Indore, Mhow and Khandwa Junction. Ahmadabad, 153 m., can be reached by a branch line (1894), from Godhra to Anand, and Ujjain and Bhopal by a branch (1896) from Nagda. Ratlam was the capital of the former State of that name.

The State was granted by Shah Jahan to Ratan Singh, great-grandson of Udai Singh, Maharaja of Jodhpur. Ratan Singh was killed at the battle of Fatehabad, near Ujjain (1658), in which Jaswant Rao Rathor, with 30,000 Rajputs, fought the combined armies of Aurangzeb and Murad. His outstanding valour is recorded in Tod's *Rajasthan*. The Maharaja's Ranjit Bilas palace is within the walls. There is a Chauk or square built by Munshi Shahamat Ali. Beyond this is the Chandni Chauk of the bankers, which leads to the Tripulia Gate, and the Amrit Sagar tank. A road connects with Mhow, 78 m.; Dhar, 56 m.; Mandu, 78 m.; and Indore (*via* Mhow), 92 m. Inspection Bungalows, with glass, crockery and cutlery, are situated at intervals of about 10 m.; one of these, at Sardarpur, formed part of an old "water-palace". D.Bs. (with khansamas) are at Dhar, Mhow and Indore.

181 m. **Jaora,** the capital of a former Muslim State, created by the Treaty of Mandasor (1818) confirming grants of land to Ghafur Khan, brother-in-law of Amir Khan, by the Indore government. The late Ruler, Lt.-Col. H. H. Nawab Sir Muhammad Iftikhar Ali Khan Bahadur, K.C.I.E., used to run a pack of hounds. The palace is called Machhi Bhawan.

213 m. **Mandasor** (Mandsaur) station (D.B.), in the former Gwalior State, on the Mhow-Nimach road, 133 m. from Mhow and 30 m. from Nimach, where, in 1818, after a defeat at Mahidpur, a treaty was made between the British and young Malhar Rao Holkar II. Severe fighting occurred here in 1857 between the rebels and a brigade of British troops moving from Mhow to relieve Nimach. The place was originally known as Dashapura, "the township of the ten hamlets", supposed to have been built by Dasarastra, son of Rama.

Discoveries were made by the Archaeological Dept. of the former Gwalior State. In a field at Sondni, about 2 m. S.E. of the fort, are preserved two monolithic sandstone pillars, over 45 ft. high, with lion and bell capitals and bearing inscriptions reciting the glories of Yasodharman, King of Malwa, who defeated Mihiragula, the Hun leader, about A.D. 528; also of Naravarman (A.D. 404) and of Banduvarman (A.D. 437-73), now at Gwalior; two images of Ganas (attendants on Siva) of the same period, and found in the same field. A remarkably fine statue of Siva stands in a temple in the town. In the Fort there is a carved pillar of a temple gateway. Both are admirable specimens of the Gupta period (6th century A.D.).

243 m. **Nimach** (Neemuch) station (R.; D.B.); in an outlying portion of the former Gwalior State, was for long a British Cantonment. It was also the headquarters of the Malwa Opium Agency and of the Crown Representative's Police. The Cantonment Club occupied the house built by General Ochterlony, the first British Resident in Rajputana and Malwa. The country around was formerly a famous tiger-shooting area. To the E. are Rampura (32 m.) and Bhanpura (52 m.; chhattri of Jaswant Rao Holkar).

At Khor, 15 m. N.W. by a good road, are ruined temples of which a Nautoran (nine arches) is of interest.

278 m. from Khandwa is **Chitorgarh** Junction (R.R., D.B., I.B.) (alt. 1338 ft.) (branch to Udaipur, 69 m.). The **Fort**[1] crowning the rocky ridge, running N. to S. on the E. of the line, is about 3 m. distant (2 m. to the foot; 1 m. ascent). No permission is necessary, but it is desirable to inform the Tourist Assistant, Government Sarai, who can arrange a guide and to inform the Assistant Engineer P.W.D. if accommodation is required. There are regular bus services, as well as taxis from Udaipur which has I.A.S. connections with Bombay and Delhi.

History.—**Chitor** was taken (or founded) about A.D. 728 by Bappu Rawal. According to legend Bappu was reared by Bhils and, in token of this at the installation of the Udaipur Ruler, a Bhil applies to his forehead blood from a cut finger. The history of Chitor is written in the annals of Rajputana. Three times her defenders preferred death to surrender. The "crime of the sack of Chitor" was long an expression of recrimination among Rajputs.

The first siege was in 1303, when Ala-ud-din Khilji, the Pathan King of Delhi, appeared to claim the beautiful Padmini, wife of the Rana's uncle, Bhim Singh. By a ruse Bhim Singh, who had been taken prisoner, was released, and the attack defeated. But Ala-ud-din returned; and when he was about to prove successful in spite of the sacrifice of eleven princes, each made Rana for a day, all the Rajput women marched in procession to an underground cave, Padmini entering last, and were there immolated by fire. The famous *jauhar* having been thus performed, Bhim Singh and his clansmen arrayed themselves in bridal robes of saffron and sallied forth. Hamir recovered the Fort in 1313.

The second siege, by Bahadur Shah, Sultan of Gujarat, came in 1535. The Rajputs put up a stout resistance; the Queen-Mother, Jawahir Bai, a Rathor princess, headed a sally, in which she was slain. At last nothing remained but to put the last hope of the Sesodias, the infant Udai Singh, in a place of safety, and to die fighting. As Chitor can only be defended by royalty, the crown of Mewar was placed on the head of Bagh Singh, the prince of Deolia.[1] The *jauhar* was again commanded, and thirteen thousand Rajput women gave themselves to the flames. The gates were then thrown open, and the Deolia chief, at the head of his saffron-clad warriors, rushed on his fate. Every clan lost its chief; and over 32,000 Rajputs were slain.

Chitor was for the third time

[1] For a striking account of this wonderful Fort, see *The Naulakha* and *Letters of Marque*, both by Rudyard Kipling.

[1] The Princely family of Pertabgarh is descended from Bagh Singh.

sacked in 1567, but although Akbar triumphed, the honour rested with the Rajputs, and particularly with two vassals of Mewar, Jaimal, the Rathor Thakur of Bednor, and Patta (Fatha), the Sesodia Rawat of Kelwa.[1] The Maharana Udai Singh (1541-72) had left when Akbar sat down before it; and when the Salumbar chief[2] fell at his post, the "Sun Gate", the command devolved upon his fellow-clansman Patta. His mother bade him put on the saffron robe, and both she and his bride died fighting by his side. Jaimal took the lead when the Sesodia fell, but was killed by a shot fired by Akbar himself. For the third time in the history of Chitor, the *jauhar* was performed, and few, if any, of the 8000 Rajputs who passed through the opened gates survived to "stain the yellow mantle". Again all the clans lost their chiefs: nine Ranis and five princesses perished in the flames; and 1700 of the immediate kin of the Maharana sealed their duty to their country with their lives. The names of Jaimal and Patta are still household words in Mewar, and their deeds are the subject of many Rajput ballads. Chitor was then lost to the Maharana, and he transferred his capital to Udaipur, but Chitor was restored in 1616.

The Fort.—The abrupt rocky hill, crowned by the magnificent Fort, rises 500 ft. above the surrounding country, though its great length of 3½ m. makes it look lower than it really is. The whole of the summit is covered with ruins. In the Fort itself there is a village, and a large palace was built by Maharana Sir Fateh Singh (d. 1930), now a museum.

The Fort was in existence when it was taken by Bappu Rawal from the Mori Rajputs, its previous owners. Up to the year 1568 the city was situated within the Fort. The modern town of Chitor, known as Talaiti or Lower Town, lies at the foot of the hill, surrounded by a wall. The principal entrance to the Fort is on the W. Guides are easily found.

The Gambheri river below is crossed by an old bridge of grey limestone, with ten arches, of pointed shape, except the sixth from the W. bank, which is semicircular. The gateways and towers which existed at either end of the bridge have now disappeared.

An ascent 1 m. long, with two zigzags, is defended at intervals on the W. by seven magnificent gateways, large enough to contain guard-rooms and even fine halls. They are the Pádal Pol, the rebuilt Bhairon or Tuta (Broken) Pol, the Hanuman Pol, the Ganesh Pol, the Jorla Pol, the Lakshman Pol, and the Main Gate, or Ram Pol. The gate on the E. is the Suraj Pol, or Sun Gate. At the N. extremity is another gate, the Lokhota Bari, and near the S. extremity is a small aperture in the wall through which traitors and criminals were thrown out.

Immediately outside the Pádal Pol, on the left, is a stone marking the spot where Bagh Singh, the chief of Deolia, was killed during the siege of Chitor by Bahadur Shah, of Gujarat, in 1535.

Between the "Broken" and the Hanuman gates there are on the right two chhattris marking the spots where Jaimal of Bednor and his clansman, Kalla, were killed in Akbar's siege in 1568. Kalla carried his wounded chief down to have a last stroke at the enemy, and both died fighting. Another chhattri further up the hill indicates the place where Patta (or Fatha) of Kelwa fell.

Facing the Ram Pol or main gate is a pillared hall, used as a guard-house, and apparently of ancient

[1] The descendants of Jaimal and Patta are still among the nobles of Mewar, who form a numerous and respected body. The territories of the Mewar Omraos and Rawats comprised more than half the former State, and they sat in darbar above the heir-apparent. For this reason the heir-apparent never appeared when they were present.

[2] The Salumbar chief had the hereditary right to lead the van in the battle, and to command the Suraj Pol gate of the fortress when besieged. On all old grants the sign of the Salumbar lance precedes the Udaipur monogram.

construction. From the top of this hall, on which there are two four-pillared chhattris, a fine view of the plain is obtained.

The Ram Pol is crowned by a Hindu horizontal arch, in which the upper courses of either side are corbelled out till they nearly meet, and are then connected by an overlying slab. This is the construction of all the gateways on the ascent, except the Jorla. In one, the Lakshman, the lower angles of the projecting courses are sloped off, giving the whole the outline of a regular pointed arch. Inside the gate, on each side, is a hall, supported on square-shaped and slightly tapering antique pillars.

The principal objects of interest in the old city are the Towers known as the *Kirtti Stambh*, or Tower of Fame, and the *Jaya Stambh*, or Tower of Victory. The Tower of Fame, which is much the older, is near the E. rampart and is reached by a broad road turning to the left inside the Ram Pol, and passing the Kukerswar Kund and Palace of Ratna Singh, or by a path proceeding directly to the E. Fergusson thus described it: "One of the most interesting Jaina monuments of the age (the first or great age of Jaina architecture, which extended down to about the year 1300, or perhaps a little after that) is the Tower formerly known as Sri Allata's (who ruled A.D. 953-972). It is a singularly elegant specimen of its class, about 75 ft. in height, and adorned with sculptures and mouldings from the base to the summit. An inscription once existed lying near its base which is said to have given its date as A.D. 895, though the slab has now been lost. This, however, is much too early a date for the style of the structure. . . . The tower most probably belongs to the 12th century, and, it is said, was dedicated to Adinath, the first of the Jain Tirthankars, and nude figures of them are repeated some hundreds of times on the face of the tower, distinguishing it as a Digambara monument. The temple in the foreground, S. side, is of a more modern date, being put together, partly, of fragments of older buildings, which have disappeared."

The tower consists of seven storeys with an internal narrow and cramped staircase; the roof of the open top storey, which rests on pillars, was much damaged by lightning, but has been well restored. Fragments of an inscribed stone are on the ground under a tree just N. of the tower.

S. of the Tower of Fame the 13th-century temple of Nilkantha Mahadeo is passed on the right, and the **Suraj Pol,** or Sun Gate, and its tanks on the left. Beyond is a striking 15th-century temple—Adhbuthnath—with huge *trimurthi.* A mile farther on is the Raj Tila or State hill, the south end of which is an extensive deer park. The broad road passes round this and returns N. by the Mori Tank, but walkers will probably cross from the E. gate (the Suraj Pol) across the Chaugan to the palace of Rana Bhim Singh and his **Rani Padmini**—a large building overlooking a tank. In the tank itself, is Padmini's island retreat, from which Akbar carried off the bronze gates now in the fort at Agra (p. 306). The oldest temple (Kalika Mata) in the Fort, incorporating an 8th century sun temple, is near.

Of the Jaya Stambh, or **Tower of Victory,** Fergusson wrote: "A revival of Jaina architecture took place in the 15th century, especially under the reign of Kumbha, one of the most powerful of the kings of the Mewar dynasty, whose private capital was Chitor. His reign extended from 1428 to 1468, and it is to him that we owe the other of the two towers that still adorn the brow of Chitor. . . . This one was erected to commemorate his victory over Mahmud Khilji, of Malwa, in the year 1440. It is therefore in Indian phraseology a *Kirtti* or *Jaya Stambha,* or Pillar of Victory, like that of Trajan at Rome, but in infinitely better taste as an architectural object than the Roman example, though in sculpture it may be inferior. . . . It stands on a basement 47 ft. square and 10 ft. high, being nine storeys in height, each of which is distinctly marked on the exterior. A stair in the interior communicates with each, and leads to the two upper storeys, which are open, and more ornamental than those below. It is 30 ft. wide at the base, and 122 ft. in height, the whole being covered with architectural ornaments and sculptures of Hindu divinities to such an extent as to leave no plain parts, while at the same time this mass of decoration is kept so subdued that it in no way interferes either with the outline or the general effect of the pillar." The old dome was injured by lightning, and a new one was substituted by Maharana Sarup Singh (1842-61). The stair is much wider and easier than that in the Jain tower (the small Kirtti Stambh), and in the inside are carvings of Hindu deities with the names below. In the top storey are two of the original four slabs with long inscriptions. The tower took ten years to build—from 1458 to 1468. On the road at the corner of the lower platform is a square pillar recording a *sati* in 1468.

S.W. of the Tower of Victory is the **Mahasati,** a small wooded terrace, which was the place of cremation of the Ranas before the move to Udaipur. Here there are many *sati* stones, recording the self-immolation of the widows of the princes and nobles. Below, on a low terrace, are the Gaumukh springs and reservoir. The springs issue from the cliff at places carved with a cow's mouth—hence the name. Near by is the opening of a cave where Rani Padmini and the Rajput ladies are said to have performed the *jauhar*. To the S.W. is an ancient temple, restored by Rana Mukalji, beside which is a huge carved head of Vishnu.

To the N. of the Tower of Victory rises the **Temple of Vriji,** built by Rana Kumbha about 1450—a massive building with a *Sikhara* (or tower) of unusually large proportions (see Fergusson, *Indian Architecture*, 2, 151). Hard by is a similar temple, built by his wife, the famous Mira Bai, of which the chief peculiarity is that the procession path round the cell is an open colonnade with four small pavilions at the corners. Between the Tower and the Ram Pol are the Nau Katha Magazine and Nau Lakha Bhandar, or Treasury, and on the wall connecting these is a small and very beautiful Jain temple. Near this is the **Palace of Rana Kumbha,** in a ruinous condition. The road now traverses the old Moti Bazar to the Western Gate, and completes the circuit.

8 m. N. of Chitorgarh is Nagari, the ruined temples at which are described by Prof. D. R. Bhandarkar, in No. 4 of Memoirs, Arch. Survey of India (Calcutta, 1920).

A branch line, 69 m., runs from Chitorgarh to Udaipur. At Mavli Junction (45 m.) there is a branch running down the Aravalli scarp to Marwar Junction (94 m. p. 258). The views along this line are very picturesque and it affords a convenient route for taking in Udaipur, and Ajmer or Jodhpur in one circular journey.

About 2 m. before reaching Udaipur, the Arh river is crossed, with the town of that name on its banks (p. 214). This stream collects the whole drainage of the Girwa. An immense masonry embankment, made by Maharana Udai Singh, forms the Udai Sagar Lake ($2\frac{1}{2}$ m. by $1\frac{1}{4}$ m.), the surplus waters from which, escaping, form the Birach river, which flows past Chitorgarh.

UDAIPUR (Airport) (pop. 162,000 in 1971) (1893 ft. above sea-level), "City of Sunrise", can also be reached by I.A.C. service from Delhi, Ahmedabad and Bombay. The princely family, which is Sesodia[1] Rajput by caste, is descended from Rama, the deified King of Ajodhia, by one of whose descendants, Kanak Sen, the

[1] The original four great States of Rajputana were Udaipur (Sesodia), Jodhpur (Rathor), Jaipurn (Kachhwaha) and Bundi (Hara Chauha).

ruling family was founded about A.D. 144. The Maharana of Udaipur is the highest in rank and dignity amongst the Hindu Princes, head of the "Solar" Rajputs, the sun in splendour being emblazoned on his standard.

Udaipur was founded as his new capital by Maharana Udai Singh after the third sack of Chitor in 1567.

There are four good hotels—Alka, Lake Palace, Lakhshmi Vilas Palace, and State—a Circuit House and a Tourist Bungalow and Travellers' Lodge. Three full days, or more, can be well spent here.

The *City* is surrounded by a bastioned wall, which, towards the S., encloses large gardens. The W. side is bounded by the beautiful Pichola lake, and the N. and E. sides by a moat supplied from the lake, while on the S. the fortified hill of Eklinggarh rises steep and wooded. The principal gateways are the Hathi Pol or "Elephant Gate", to the N.; the Kishan Gate, to the S.; the Suraj Pol, or "Gate of the Sun", on the E.; the Delhi Gate, on the N.E., and the Chand Pol, or "Moon Gate", on the W., opening on to the bridge across the N. end of the lake.

The former Residency, with a lovely garden, is well worth a visit. Nearby is the Bhartiya Lok Kala Mandal with a folk museum specializing in traditional puppetry. To the W. of the city is the Sajjangarh hill, 1100 ft. above the Fateh Sagar lake, with beautiful views of the lake from it. The Sajjangarh Palace is on the hill.

The main street of the city leads from the Hathi Pol (Elephant Gate) to the Maharana's palace, passing a clock tower and the Lansdowne Hospital. The Jagannath or Jagdish temple (built *c.* 1640) is approached by a flight of steps, with an elephant on each side at the top. The temple is a good example of the Indo-Aryan style. The tower is ornamented by bold figured friezes and other architectural decoration. In front of the temple is a shrine with a brazen image of a Garuda. The City Palace (most of it can be seen for a Rs. 2 ticket) is an "imposing pile of granite and marble, of quadrangular shape, rising at least 100 ft. from the ground, and flanked with octagonal towers, crowned with cupolas. Although built at various periods, uniformity of design has been well preserved; nor is there in the E. a more striking structure. It stands upon the very crest of a ridge, running parallel to, but considerably elevated above, the margin of the lake. The terrace, which is at the E. and chief front of the palace, extends throughout its length, and is supported by a triple row of arches, from the declivity of the ridge. The height of this arcaded wall is full 50 ft., and although all is hollow beneath, yet so admirably is it constructed that an entire range of stables is built on the extreme verge of the terrace. From this terrace the city and the valley lie before the spectator, whose vision is bounded only by the distant hills; while from the summit of the palace nothing obstructs the view over lake and mountain."[1]

The entrance to the palace is through the Bari Pol (1600), or Great Gate, containing the Royal drums, and by the inner Tripolia (1725); between the two gates are eight carved arches or torans, under which various Maharanas have been weighed in the past against gold and silver, afterwards distributed in largesse. Beyond the Tripolia the Ganesh Deori gate leads S. to the fine old court known as the Rai Angan or Royal courtyard (1571), adjoined on the E. side by the Jewel Room, and from this the visitor will be conducted over a number of palace enclosures—all picturesque, and some beautifully decorated. Of these the Chhoti Chitra Shali has brilliant mosaics of peacocks, the Manak (Ruby) Mahal is filled with figures of glass and porcelain, the Moti (Pearl) Mahal is decor-

[1] *Handbook of Mewar*, by Mehta Fateh Lal, son of a Prime Minister of the Mewar State, also *Mewar History*, a guide to Udaipur, by Dev Nath Purohit.

ated with mirrors, and the Chini ki Chitra Mahal (1711-34) has beautiful ornamentation of inlaid mirror work and fine tiles of Dutch and Chinese make; the Bari Mahal, or Amar Vilas (1699-1711), has a charming garden in the centre of it. On the W. side the Tripolia are the Karan Vilas (1620-28) and Khush Mahal buildings, while southwards lies the Shambhu Niwas Palace, to which Maharana Fateh Singh added another residence, the Shiv Niwas.

The Pichola lake (2½ m. by 1½ m.) on the W. is reached through beautiful gardens S. of the palaces, named the Sajjan Niwas, but commonly called the Gulab Bagh; the Victoria Hall Library is now located here. From these a road runs past the Dudh Talai down the E. side of the lake to the Khas Odi, built by Maharana Sir Sajjan Singh (1874-84) at its southern end for use as a shooting-box. The feeding at this place of the wild pigs every evening is an interesting sight. Beautiful as the lake is when seen from the palace and other points, the view of it near the S. end, with the marble-capped islands in the foreground and the lofty palace and city in the distance, is one of still greater loveliness.

The southern island, named the Jagmandar, is chiefly notable for the Gul Mahal, a domed pavilion built by Karan Singh (1621-28)—most of the other buildings date from the 18th century. On it Prince Khurram, later Shah Jahan, lived when in revolt against his father, the Emperor Jahangir, and refugee European ladies and children from Nimach (p. 208) were protected during the 1857 Mutiny by Maharana Sarup Singh.

N. is the Jagniwas Palace island (1740), with the older Dilaram and Bari Mahal palaces, in beautiful gardens. The Lake Palace Hotel is now the main feature of the island and trips for non-residents go from Bansi Ghat just S. of the City Palace. Beyond the island to the W. are two small structures in the lake.

Visitors who wish to go on the lake should embark at the Sarup Sagar Ghat, near the Mission House at the N. end of the chain of lakes (the Sarup Sagar, the Rang Sagar and the Pichola); a gratuity to the boatman at the end is customary. Visitors can land and be shown over the two islands, and can go to Odi Khas, and by previous arrangement can return by car. A view of the city from the bridge below the Gangour Ghat is also specially effective. This bridge is reached by way of the lanes to the W. of the main street; also by using a boat.

On the bank of the Pichola lake, N. of and adjoining the Shambhu Niwas, is the Minto Hall, of which the foundation-stone was laid during Lord Minto's Viceroyalty, to serve as a Darbar hall. N. of the lake and connected with it by a canal is the Fateh Sagar constructed by Maharana Fateh Singh. The foundation-stone of the embankment was laid by the Duke of Connaught in 1889. It can be reached by the road going W. from the hotel, which winds among the hills and along two sides of the lake, and then crosses the dam. On the *band* a new guest-house has been built to accommodate distinguished visitors. It commands a delightful view. Underneath the dam is the *Sahelion-ki-bari*, or Garden of the Maids of Honour, well laid out. On the way back, the former *Residency* is passed. A visit should be paid to the *Central Jail*, to see the carpet-weaving.

2 m. S. of the hotel are remains of the ancient city called Arh, or Ahar. The Chhattris or cenotaphs of the Maharanas, in the Jain style, on high plinths, stand in the Mahasati or royal place of cremation, which is enclosed by a wall and is adorned by many fine trees. The most remarkable are those of *Sangram Singh II* (1734), a large and beautiful structure, and of Amar Singh (1621), grandson of Udai Singh. The Amar Museum adjoining the chhattris has exhibits dating back to 2000 B.C. Near the village of Arh there are

ruined temples of an older town.

14 m. N. of Udaipur in a ravine is the **Eklinji Lake** with a white marble temple sacred to the family deity of the Maharana. Near this, at Nagda, are two Hindu temples, called the Sas-bahu, or mother and daughter-in-law.

At **Delwada,** 19 m. N. of Udaipur, is a large palace (closed) and several Jain temples.

The **Nathdwara Temple** (32 m. N. of Udaipur) contains an image that was at Muttra in 1495, and was brought here by Rana Raj Singh in 1691. It should be seen if possible.

The Great Lake of **Kankroli,** or Rajnagar, called the Rajsamund, is 44 m. N. of Udaipur. The Nauchoki Bund is of massive masonry, in many places 40 ft. high, and is 1115 ft. long with pavilions and arches, or torans, all of marble and exquisitely carved. It was erected in 1660 by Rana Raj Singh, who defeated Aurangzeb on many occasions. On the S.E. side of the lake is the town of Kankroli, with a beautiful temple.

About 50 m. N. of Udaipur is the remarkable Jain temple of **Ranakpur,** thought by some to be even finer than those of Mount Abu. Built, according to an inscription, in 1439, it is dedicated to Adinath whose four-sided image stands in the inner temple. Some eighty domes are supported by hundreds of pillars.

The **Jaisamand Lake,** made by Rana Jai Singh at the end of the 17th century, is about 32 m. S.E. of Udaipur; it measures about 9 m. by 5 m. The dam is 1000 feet long and 98 ft high. The drive to, and the scenery round, the lake is most picturesque.

379 m. from Khandwa is **Nasirabad** station (D.B., 1 m.), the military Cantonment for Ajmer, from which it can be visited by frequent trains, or by a picturesque road (14 m.). The station was laid out in 1818 by Sir David Ochterlony.

Deoli, on the Banas river, the former Cantonment of the Deoli Regiment and of the Mina Corps, is situated 57 m. S.E. of Nasirabad. It was used at one time as an internment camp for terrorist détenus, and during the Second World War as a Prisoner of War Camp. Raj Mahal lies a few miles to the N., where the Banas river enters the hills. The scenery around is very striking.

Bundi (pop. 34,200 in 1971) founded 1342, capital of the former state of that name is 30 m. S.E. of Deoli on a picturesque road. Although neither very large nor very wealthy, the State ranked high in the hierarchy of Rajput Dynasties. The family belongs to the Hara Chauhan clan of Rajputs, which is one of the four Agnikula created by Vishnu at the fire-pit at Gaumukh on Mount Abu (p. 255). The title of Maharao was conferred by the Udaipur Ruler.

The palace, by a lake with islets on which are temples, was commenced *c.* 1600. Approached by a steep ramp, it has rooms decorated with fine mural paintings. To enter the fort and palaces of Bundi special permission must be obtained from the Maharaja, tel. no. 1, Bundi.

There is a comfortable Circuit House (apply to Collector, Bundi), Ranjit Niwas G.H., P.W.D.D.B. (apply Asst. Engineer Bundi), and a couple of days can be well spent in exploring the beauties of this quaint, old, and so far unspoiled, Rajput town. The jungles around formerly contained many tiger, and the Mej river is full of crocodiles. Readers of Kipling's *From Sea to Sea* may remember his delightful description of his sojourn in Bundi. There is a beautiful circular drive to Phool Sagar, taking in Kishar Bagh (cenotaphs of Rulers) and the lovely Jait Sagar.

24 m. from Bundi, linked by a good road, lies Kotah, capital of the former state of that name (see p. 290). Regular bus service between Kotah and Bundi. Kotah is now often spelled Kota.

393 m. from Khandwa is **Ajmer** Junction station, whence the metre-gauge mail route to Delhi proceeds *via* Jaipur and Rewari (Route 10, p. 263).

ROUTE 9

ITARSI JUNCTION to JHANSI by **Bhopal, Sanchi,** and **Bina** (line S.E. to **Saugor**), and from Jhansi to
(1) **Kalpi** and Kanpur;
(2) **Orchha, Barwa-Sagar, Harpalpur** (for **Nowgong** and **Khajuraho**), **Banda** and Manikpur;
(3) **Datia,** GWALIOR, **Dholpur** and Agra, Muttra and **Delhi.**

Bhopal (and Sanchi), as well as Gwalior, are accessible by air from Bombay and Delhi (I.A.S.).

Itarsi Junction station, 464 m. from Bombay on the Central Ry. (see p. 120). The "Punjab Mail" train from Bombay branches off here and proceeds *via* Jhansi and Gwalior to Agra, 24 hr., and to Delhi, Amritsar or Simla.

12 m. **Hoshangabad** station (476 m. from Bombay), C.H., D.B.K. (1 m.), named after Hoshang Ghori of Mandu (p. 204), built as a defence against the Gonds. The railway crosses the Narbada on a bridge 2306 ft. long. About 4 m. N. of the Narbada river the well-wooded picturesque ascent of the Vindhya Hills commences, and at the top, Barkhera station (492 m.), the line runs on the tableland of Malwa.

521 m. from Bombay **Bhopal*** Junction (R.) D.B., Bairagarh Airport. The town (alt. 1622 ft., pop. 392,000 in 1971) stands on the N. bank of a lake, 4½ m. long and 1½ m. broad, and is enclosed by a wall. Another lake, 2 m. long, is close by. There is a small Hotel (*Pagoda*) and State guest-house, at which travellers who have the necessary introductions may be permitted to stay. It was formerly the capital of the State of Bhopal, and has now been made capital of the reconstituted Madhya Pradesh. **Sanchi** (28 m.) can be conveniently visited from Bhopal.

The dynasty was founded by Dost Muhammad, an Afghan chief in the service of Aurangzeb, who, appointed governor of Bhairsia (1690), took advantage of the troubles that followed the Emperor's death in 1707 to establish independence. He died 1723, leaving a Muslim island State in Malwa. In 1778, when General Goddard made his famous march across India, Bhopal was the only State which showed itself friendly. In 1809, when Colonel Barry Close commanded another expedition in the neighbourhood, the Nawab of Bhopal applied to be received under British protection, but did not succeed. The Nawab then obtained assistance from the Pindaris in the gallant struggle he maintained to defend himself against Daulat Rao Scindia and Raghoji Bhonsla of Nagpur, in the course of which his capital underwent a severe siege for nine months.

In 1817 the British Government intervened and formed an alliance with the Nawab, who was, in 1818, guaranteed his possessions by treaty, on his furnishing a force, for whose maintenance certain districts in Malwa were assigned. Islamnagar, 5 m. N., was then restored. The Nawab was soon afterwards killed by a pistol accidentally discharged by a child. His nephew, a boy, was declared his successor, and betrothed to his infant daughter, but the Nawab's widow, Kudsia Begam, refused consent (1837), and the declared heir resigned his claim to the throne and to the hand of the Nawab's daughter, Sikandar Begam, in favour of his brother Jahangir Muhammad. After long dissensions Jahangir Muhammad was installed as Nawab in 1837, through the mediation of the British. He died in 1844, when his infant daughter, Shah Jahan, was recognised as his successor, and Sikandar Begam, his widow, was made regent. After the Mutiny of 1857 Sikandar Begam was made the actual ruler, Shah Jahan becoming heir-apparent. Sikandar Begam died in 1868. Shah Jahan Begam ruled till 1901, and was succeeded by Nawab Sultan Jahan Begam, who abdicated in 1926 in favour of her only surviving son, Nawab Hamidullah Khan, internationally famous as a polo-player, sportsman, and administrator, who died in 1960.

The Birla Museum has an excellent collection of Hindu sculpture, and there is a fine view of the lake from the adjoining temple.

The *Palace of the Nawab* is a large and imposing building, with sheer walls down to the lake. The walls of Fatehgarh on the S. afford a view of the lake. The *Jami Masjid* was built by Kudsia Begam, and the *Moti Masjid*, resembling the Mosque in the Delhi Palace, by Sikandar Begam. The *Mint* and *Arsenal*, and the *Gardens* of the Kudsia and Sikander Begams also deserve a visit.

The *Taj-ul-masjid*, commenced by Shah Jahan Begam, is the largest mosque in India; the armoury in Fatehgarh, the *Chauk* in the centre of the city, the Lady Lansdowne Hospital, and the club for *parda* ladies which was established by the Sultan Jahan Begam, the Alexandra High School for boys in the Be-nazir palace, the most picturesque building in Bhopal, and the Sultania Girls' School in the Taj Mahal palace may also be seen.

The town waterworks were built by Kudsia Begam. Excellent sailing yachts and rowing-boats are kept on both lakes. A drive to the Simla Kothi will well repay those who have time for it. The shooting (big and small game) round Bhopal has deteriorated.

A branch line (broad-gauge), opened 1895, runs from Bhopal (114 m.) to Ujjain (p. 207). 24 m. from Bhopal on this line is **Sehore** (alt. 1818 ft.), formerly headquarters (1820) of the British Political Agent, and a cantonment.

Main Line

549 m. from Bombay is **Sanchi.**[1]

[1] The best guide is still *Monuments of Sanchi* (3 vols., 1938), by Sir John Marshall; but an interesting brochure is available in Tourist Bureaux.

Most conveniently visited by car or bus from Bhopal. There is now a new and excellent Travellers' Lodge—one of the chain managed by the Tourism Development Corporation—at Sanchi, as well as C.H., R.R., R.H. Information Centre at Museum.

The monuments at Sanchi constitute the largest of several groups of Buddhist monuments situated near the ancient city of Vidisa, capital of the Sunga King Agnimitra, at the junction of the Besh and Betwa rivers (near the modern Bhilsa, which is the next station on the line), and often referred to as the "Bhilsa Topes". "Tope" is derived from *thupa*, the Prakrit form of *stupa*. In contrast with other famous centres of Buddhism, Sanchi had no connection with the life or acts of the Buddha; nevertheless its buildings are perfect examples of Buddhist architecture. Perhaps it was the interest taken in the spot by the great Emperor Asoka, who was to Buddhism what Constantine the Great was to Christianity, that accounts for the splendour of these structures. For one of the queens of Asoka, Devi by name, came from Vidisa; and it was on the hill of Sanchi, then known as Chetiyagiri, that a monastery is said to have been built for his son (or brother) Mahendra, the apostle of Sri Lanka. The earliest buildings date from the time of Asoka, who is commemorated here more than anywhere else in India, and are contemporary with caves at Ajanta. The site was found by a military officer in 1818 after the Pindari War in Malwa. In 1822 a zealous district officer made an excavation in the Great Stupa and found relics which were lost. In 1851 General (Sir) Alexander Cunningham made a record, and in 1883 the Archaeological Department filled the breach and did other work of restoration.

The majority of the monuments were excavated (1912-19) by Sir John Marshall on behalf of the then Bhopal Darbar, and much has been done to preserve their fabrics. The plateau on the hilltop, about A.D. 1100, was enclosed by a circuit wall of solid stone construction. The buildings on this plateau divide themselves naturally into four classes: firstly, the *stupas*, or *pagodas*, which were erected either to enshrine the relics of the Buddha or of one of his saints, or to commemorate some specially holy spot; secondly, the memorial pillars set up by the Emperor Asoka or by other devotees in later ages; thirdly, the chapels or *chaitya* and shrines; and fourthly, monasteries or convents in which the monks and nuns lived. Small objects are in a Museum (1919).

The description will follow an itinerary from the R.H. on the N.W. through the enclosure wall to the West gate of the Great Stupa, then to the South gate and some structures on the S., then to the East gate and buildings on the E., then to Stupa 3, the North gate, and back by Stupa 2 to the R.H. A guide is available.

West Gateway

The carved gateways or *toranas* at the cardinal points are of similar design—the work of stone-masons inspired by carpenters—and have survived in remarkable preservation for nearly 2000 years. The best preserved is the northern one. Each gateway was composed of two square pillars surmounted by capitals, which in their turn supported a superstructure of three architraves with spirals carved at the ends, one above the other. The capitals were adorned with standing dwarfs or with the forefronts of lions or elephants set back to back in the Persepolitan fashion; also, acting as supports to the projecting ends of the lowest architrave were Carytid figures (see photograph on back of jacket). Other images were disposed among the architraves, while crowning and dominating all was the sacred wheel (broken), flanked on either side by attendants and *triratna* emblems.

Pillars and superstructure were elaborately enriched with bas-reliefs illustrative of the *jataka* legends or scenes from the life of the Buddha and episodes in the life of Asoka. Inscriptions carved on the gateways on the balustrades record the names of pious individuals or of guilds who contributed to their erection. Interpretation of the scenes has been rendered difficult by the practice, until the Mahayana period, of never portraying the Buddha in bodily form, but of indicating his presence by his footprints, or a throne, or the sacred tree associated with his enlightenment.

The West gateway (re-erected 1883) was the last to be put up. On the top lintel (front) are seven Buddhas, on the middle the Sermon at Sarnath, on the lowest Chaddanta Jataka with elephants (better done on the back of the South gateway). At the outer side of the right pillar is a grape-vine or Assyrian Tree of Life.

The **South Gateway** is the oldest (wrongly restored in 1883). The top lintel (front) shows the Birth of the Buddha, the middle a visit of Asoka to the Ramagriha Stupa, and, in the top panels of the inner face of the left pillar, Asoka is shown as at Buddh-Gaya.

The *stupas* on the sandstone hilltop number many scores, ranging in date from the 3rd century B.C. to the 12th century A.D., and varying in size from the Great Stupa to miniature votive *stupas* no more than a foot in height set up by the pious Buddhists as a work of merit which would help the donor a step nearer to his goal.

The **Great Stupa** or Tope, anciently called Chaitya giri, the Chapel Hill, is situated on a level platform about 350 ft. above the plain. Originally built of brick in Asoka's time, about half the present size, it was enclosed in stone (*c*. 150-100 B.C.) to form a dome, 42 ft. high and 106 ft. in diameter. A plinth 14 ft. high and 6 ft. wide, added but not bonded in, carries a terraced path, reached by steps on the S. side, used clockwise for the perambulation of the Tope. The Tope was crowned by an altar or pedestal surrounded by a rail, and an umbrella (*hti*). The berm was enclosed below at a distance of 9½ ft. from it by an outer railing slightly elliptical in shape, formed of pillars nearly 10 ft. high, carrying three bars of oval section, each 2 ft. 2 in. long, and separated by an interval of 3 in.; a rounded coping stone surmounts the whole. The gateways were erected *c.* 35 B.C. by the Andhras (see Chronology, p. 43). Facing each gateway, with its back to the wall of the plinth, is a large seated statue, probably representing the four last Buddhas. These were in place before A.D. 450.

The **Column** of Asoka (shattered) stood by the South gateway. It was 42 ft. high, and weighed about 40 tons. It was brought from Chunar near Benares, probably by water, up the Ganges, Jumna and Betwa rivers. On its broken stump is an edict written in the early Brahmi characters in which the Great Emperor exhorted the Buddhists to avoid schisms in their church. The three lions back to back on the capital (now in the Museum), with their swelling veins and tense muscular development, afford an example of what Greco-Persian art was achieving in India during the Maurya age and now form the State Emblem of the Indian Republic.

Of the shrines and monasteries the most noteworthy is the *chaitya* hall (Temple No. 18), which stands directly opposite the S. entrance of the Great Stupa, and is one of few structural edifices of this type. The classic-looking columns of the nave resemble the pillared aisles of Paestum or of Athens; and the rounded apse those of early Christian churches. The pillars and walls of this chapel date back no further than A.D. 650, and the sculptured jamb of the porch is more modern still by three or four centuries; but beneath the floor of the temple are the remains of three older chapels which, being constructed of wood, perished.

Another structure which recalls the classic temples of Greece, is a little shrine (No. 17) just E. of the one just described. It consists of a simple flat-roofed chamber with a pillared porch in front, characteristic of the age of India's "Renaissance" (*c.* A.D. 425). S. of this shrine is a lofty plinth supporting the stumps of numerous octagonal columns (Temple No. 40). Originally it was an apsidal *chaitya* hall, with a superstructure of wood, but the superstructure was burnt down about the beginning of the Christian era and the plinth was then enlarged and stone substituted for wood. Many of the columns bear *ex-voto* inscriptions in the early Brahmi characters.

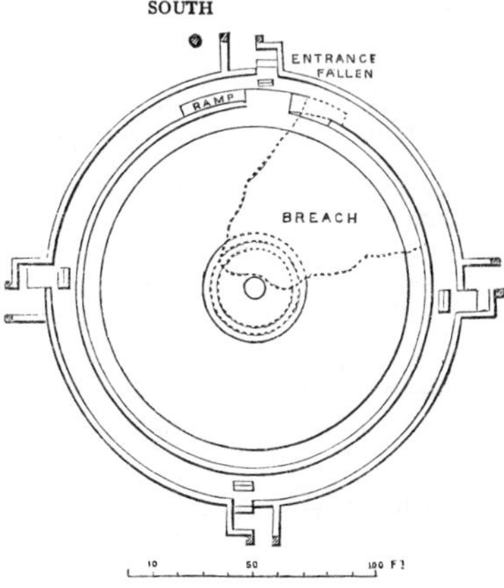

Great Stupa Plan (1851).

The reliefs on the **East Gateway**[1] are typical of the rest. On the right pillar are represented, in six panels, the six stages to Nirvana of the Buddhist Paradise. On the left, starting from the base, is Bimbisara, issuing from the city of Rajagriha on a visit to the Buddha, symbolised by a throne. In the three panels above

[1] Casts are in the Edinburgh Museum, and others were sent to European capitals at the request of Napoleon III, Emperor of the French.

is depicted one of the miracles by which Buddha converted the Brahman ascetic Kasyapa and his disciples. The Nairanjana river is shown in flood with Kasyapa and two of his disciples hastening in a boat to the rescue of Buddha. In the lower part of the picture, Buddha, represented again by his throne, appears walking on the face of the waters, and in the foreground the figures of Kasyapa and his disciples are repeated, now on dry ground and doing homage to the Master. The top two panels S. of the left pillar portray the temple at Budh-Gaya, built by Asoka, with the throne of Buddha within, and, spreading through its upper windows, the branches of the sacred tree. It is the illumination of Buddha.

On the inner side (top) Indra and Brahma visit the Buddha (an umbrella). The next below shows victory over a serpent (Naga).

The scenes on the lintels are still more elaborate. On the lowest we see, in the centre, the temple and tree of Buddh-Gaya; to the right, a royal retinue and a king and queen descending from an elephant, and afterwards worshipping at the tree. This is the ceremonial visit which Asoka and his queen Tishyarakshita paid to the Bodhi tree, for the purpose of watering and restoring it after an evil spell which the queen had cast upon it. The middle lintel is occupied with the scene of Buddha's departure from Kapilavastu (*Mahabhinishkramana*). To the left is the city with wall and moat, and issuing from its gate the horse Kanthaka, led by Chandaka his groom, who holds the umbrella symbolical of his Master's presence. In order to indicate progress, this group is repeated four times in succession towards the right, and then we see Chandaka and the horse sent back and the further journey indicated by footprints surmounted by the umbrella. In the topmost lintel are the seven last Buddhas, the first and last symbolised by thrones beneath their appropriate Bodhi trees, the rest by *stupas*.

The inner sides of the pillars and the whole back of the gateway are carved. At the top of the right pillar is Homage to Buddha, next, below, the Dream of Maya when conceiving him, and below again a miracle of levitation. The middle lintel shows the Illumination, and the back of the left pillar the heavens.

Of the fourth and last class of monuments on this site—namely the residence of monks and nuns—there are five examples, and they range in date from the 4th to the 11th century A.D. The earlier ones, which once occupied the eastern side of the plateau, were built of wood and have perished or been buried beneath the foundations of later structures. Those which have survived are all built more or less on the plan of the ordinary domestic house of ancient India, with a square open court in the centre and ranges of two-storeyed chambers on the four sides. The most interesting, as well as the most modern among them, is the one occupying the highest part of the plateau towards the E. Here are the remains of several courts, surrounded by monastic cells, and on the eastern side of what was evidently the principal court is a lofty shrine, containing an image of the Buddha seated beneath the Bodhi tree, when touching the earth with his right hand he called on her to bear witness for him against Mara, the Evil One. It might be thought that this shrine is not Buddhist at all but Hindu, for its style is precisely that of a Hindu temple of the late mediaeval period, were it not for the statue of the Buddha in the sanctum and some of the images in the niches round its outer walls. The reason for this is that by the 11th century Buddhism had come deeply under the influence of Hinduism, and this influence made itself manifest in many new doctrines and ideas, which it absorbed from the parent religion.

From the E. of the hill a view to the N. shows the surroundings of Bhilsa.

No. 3 Stupa (150-140 B.C.) stands about fifty yards to the N.E. of the Great Stupa and is of almost identical design but of smaller proportions, 50 ft. in diameter, 27 ft. high. The dome and railings have been reconstructed. There is one gate (*post* 70 B.C.). The surface was once coated with stucco; moulded in relief on this stucco were great garlands encircling the dome; gold and brilliant colours were used to pick out the decorations. In this stupa relics of two famous disciples of the Buddha—Sariputra and Mahamogalana—were discovered (1851) in a chamber set in the centre of the structure and on a level with the top of the terrace. It contained two stone boxes, each bearing a short inscription: on one the word *Sariputasa* "of Sariputra", and on the other *Mahamogalanasa* "of Mahamogalana"; and inside each of the boxes was a casket of steatite containing fragments of human bone and a variety of beads of pearl, garnet, lapis-lazuli, crystal and amethyst.

North Gateway. In this there are shown many episodes in the life-story of the Buddha in his last or previous incarnations. Stupa No. 2 (150-104 B.C.) stands on a ledge half-way down the western side of the hill. It was opened in 1822, and relics were found in 1851, when the dome was destroyed. There is no gateway, but the railing round the base (*c.* 70 B.C.) is almost intact and exhibits a variety of most interesting reliefs of the primitive Indian school, showing a remarkably crude treatment of living figures coupled with an extraordinary power of decorative design. Notice that horsemen are shown with stirrups, 500 years before these are recorded in any literature. The country for some distance round is studded with Buddhist remains, examined in 1851, but only at Sanchi are the remains abundant and well preserved.

Besides the group at Sanchi, there is at *Sonari*, 6 m. S.W., a group of eight topes, of which two are important structures in square courtyards, and in one of these numerous relics were found. At *Sadhara*, W. of Sanchi on the bank of the Bes river, is a tope 101 ft. in diameter, which yielded no relics, and one 24 ft. in diameter, in which were found relics of Sariputra and others like those found at Sanchi. At *Bhojpur* (Pipaliya) (7 m. S.E.) are thirty-seven topes, the largest 66 ft. in diameter, and in the next to it important relics were found. At *Andher*, 5 m. S.E. of Bhojpur, is a group of three small but very interesting topes, well preserved.

555 m. **Bhilsa** station (alt. 1407 ft.), on the Betwa river, 16 m. N. of Sanchi. An old gun in the fort, 19½ ft. in length, with a bore of 10 in., is said to have been made by order of the Emperor Jahangir. Bhilsa is a place of Hindu pilgrimage to the temples in the bed of the Betwa river. The Bijaimandal Mosque was built from old Hindu temple remains (Vijaya Mandir). Bhilsa (Bhailas Vasman) superseded Vidisa. At *Besnagar* (part of an ancient city, Vidisa, whence came Asoka's wife, extending from the junction of the Betwa and Bes rivers as far S.W. as Udayagiri Hill and S.E. to the Lohanggi Rock, citadel of Bhilsa) is a monolithic pillar, locally known as Khamb Baba, of the date of 90 B.C. The inscription records that it was erected as an Eagle banner (Garudadhavaja) in honour of the god Vasudeva (Vishnu) by Heliodoros, a Greek ambassador of the Indo-Greek King Antialkidas of Taxila (p. 591) at the court of Bhaghadra, King of Vidisa. At the bottom of a nearby tree are *steel* wedges. At Udayagiri (4 m. W.) are caves in sandstone with sculptures and inscriptions of the Gupta period (A.D. 320-606), with a colossal image of the Varaha Avatara (Boar incarnation). Two inscriptions refer to Chandragupta Vikramaditya (A.D. 380-414), and a third to Kumaragupta (A.D. 414-455). At Gyaraspur (24 m. N.E. on the Saugor road) there are remains of mediaeval temples with carvings. The Athakhamba are pillars of a temple (A.D. 982). At Bajramath are three adjoining shrines,

the centre one of Surya the Sun, the southern of Vishnu, the northern of Siva. The Maladevi Hindu temple has been converted to Jain use. There are stupas also.

579 m. from Bombay, **Basoda** station. Road to **Sironj** (30 m. N.W. across the Betwa), stronghold of Amir Khan, and a great centre of the Thugs.

585 m. from Bombay is **Bareth** station. 4 m. E. by metalled road in the village of Udayapur is a magnificent temple of Siva known as Udayeswar or Nilkhanteswar, built by Udayaditya a Paramara (1059). The carving on every part of this Indo-Aryan temple is exceptionally fine. Sher Khan's mosque (1488) and the Shahi Masjid are Muslim.

605 m. from Bombay is **Bina** Junction (R.). 8 m. from Bina, at Eran, are some Jain and Buddhist ruins, including two monolithic pillars.

Bina-Kotah Branch Line

From Bina a line runs N.W. to 74 m. Guna, 147 m. Baran, and 188 m. Kotah, where it joins the shorter route between Bombay and Delhi, now part of the Western Ry.

Bina-Katni Branch Line

47 m. from Bina Junction on a branch line (165 m. running S.E. to Katni Junction (p. 122) is **Saugor** (pop. 154,000 in 1971, D.B.), ceded 1818, 1732 ft. above sea-level, on the borders of a fine lake (*Sagar*), nearly 1 m. broad, from which it derives its name. The lake is said to be an ancient Banjara work, but the present city dates only from the end of the 17th century, and owes its rise to a Bundela Raja Udaussa, descendant of Nihal Singh of Jhalaun. He built a small fort on the site of the present structure in 1660, and founded a village called Parkota, now a quarter of the modern town. Saugor town is well built, with wide streets. The large bathing-ghats on the banks of the lake, for the most part surrounded with Hindu temples, add much to its appearance.

The existing *Fort* at Saugor, completed by the Mahrattas about 1780, stands on a height N.W. of the lake, commanding the whole of the city and surrounding country, and consists of twenty round towers, varying from 20 ft. to 40 ft. in height, connected by thick curtain walls. It encloses a space of 6 acres, and was a prison for Thugs (1829). A Police Training School in the Fort, was opened here in 1906, and an Equitation School in 1910. The local College has now been made into a University.

24 m. W. of Saugor, on the road to Bhilsa, is **Rahatgarh Fort,** taken by Sir Hugh Rose in February 1858 from the Nawab of Garhi Amastani. He marched 10 m. on to Barodia Naunagar where he defeated the Raja of Banpur. Having relieved Saugor he marched to Garakota and defeated the Raja of Shahgarh. Returning to Saugor he marched towards Jhansi.

95 m. on this line is **Damoh** (D.B.K.) headquarters of a district.

Main Line

Proceeding N. by the main line from Bina Junction, 636 m. from Bombay is **Jakhlaun** station. Unmetalled road, 12 m. to **Deogarh.** On a bluff overlooking the Betwa are the remains of temples dating back to early Gupta times. On one, panels show Vishnu reclining on Ananda (Plate 2).

646 m. from Bombay is **Lalitpur** station (D.B.), in the Jhansi District.

21 m. W. of Lalitpur is **Chanderi,** which was a place of considerable importance under the Sultans of Mandu. The road for the first 13 m., as far as Rajghat (Causeway) on the Betwa river, is motorable from November to June (R.H. on left bank of river). Between Rajghat and Chanderi the road is metalled; there is rather a steep ascent for about 1½ m. near Chanderi. The road continues S. (24 m.) to Mungaoli station

20 m. from Bina Junction, on the Bina-Kotah branch line. Chanderi is connected also with the Agra-Bombay road *via* Esagarh (D.B.), which is 14 m. S.E. of Shivpuri. D.Bs. at Chanderi and Mungaoli (travellers must make their own arrangements about food).

Chanderi is situated on a bay of hills, overlooking the valley of the Betwa. The old Hindu town, 8 m. N. of the modern town, is hidden in thick jungle. The ruins of a few Jain temples of about the 10th century A.D. contain some fine sculpture. The modern town is widely known for its muslins and gold brocades.

At the height of its prosperity, it seems to have covered an extensive area: for there are numerous remains of palaces, sarais, wells, mosques and tombs, in the Mandu variety of the Pathan style of architecture. The hill fort overlooks the town. The Koshak Mahal at Fatehabad, a Muslim palace, is a ruin, but is maintained as an archaeological monument. There are some rock-cut Jain statues in the Khandar hill. Three palaces on the outskirts, built by the Bundela Rajas, have been repaired and are used as shooting-boxes. (A guide to Chanderi, published by the Archaeological Dept., can be obtained at the D.B.)

671 m. **Talbahat** station. There is an Inspection House. A picturesque town with a fine old fort overlooking a large piece of artificial water covering more than 1 sq. m. The water is retained by damming the streams that flow through a rocky barrier about 800 ft. high.

At 676 m. the Betwa river is crossed.

702 m. from Bombay is **Jhansi*** Junction (R., D.B.), an important railway centre. The main line runs N. to Gwalior, 61 m., Agra, 133 m., and Delhi, 255 m., one branch N.E. to Kanpur, 137 m., and Lucknow, 181 m., and another E. through Banda 119 m., to Manikpur Junction (p. 122), 181 m., where it connects with the Bombay-Calcutta mail route, *via* Jabalpur.

By road Jhansi to Saugor (D.B.) is 122 m., a good motoring road. The Betwa river is crossed at 24 m. from Jhansi by a new bridge. Jhansi to Banda is 122 m., *via* Nowgong 65 m. (ferry over the Betwa, 8 m. from Jhansi). Jhansi to Shivpuri or Sipri (W.) is 61 m. by a metalled road. Shivpuri (p. 238) used to be the summer headquarters of the Gwalior State administration. 12 m. short of Shivpuri is **Surivaya,** a ruined fortress enclosing a Hindu monastery. Three Hindu temples with fine carvings and a *baoli*[1] are to be seen here; all are of the 10th century A.D. Jhansi to Gwalior is 61 m., to Dholpur 103 m., to Agra 138 m.

Jhansi (alt. 848 ft.; pop. 198,000 in 1971) is notable for its fort, which the British Government ceded in 1858 to and got back in 1886 from Maharaj Scindia in exchange for Gwalior; and places of interest—Datia (p. 231), Orchha and Barwa-Sagar (p. 225)—can be reached from it.

The area called **Bundelkhand,** in which Jhansi was situated, was for ages turbulent and difficult to manage. At one time the Orchha State extended from the Jumna to the Narbada and from the Chambal on the W. to the Tons (p. 127) on the E. Bir Singh Deo of Orchha (1605-27) built the fort of Jhansi, 8 m. to the N. of his capital, which is situated on an island in the Betwa river. He incurred the heavy displeasure of Akbar by the murder of Abul Fazl, the Emperor's favourite Minister and historian, at the instigation of Prince Salim, afterwards the Emperor Jahangir. A force was sent in 1602; the country was ravaged and devastated, but Bir Singh himself contrived to escape. On the accession of his patron, Salim, in 1605, he rose into great favour; but when, in 1627, Shah Jahan mounted the throne, Bir Singh revolted unsucessfully, being defeated by Aurangzeb (then only 13 years of age). He never regained his

[1] A deep ornamented well with steps down to it.

former power and independence. During the troubled times which succeeded, Orchha was sometimes in the hands of the Muslims and sometimes under Bundela Chiefs.

In 1732 Chhatarsal, a Bundela Chief, who had acquired possession of most of Eastern Bundelkhand, called in the Mahrattas, who were then invading the Central Provinces under their Peshwa Baji Rao I. On Chhatarsal's death in 1734 the Peshwa was rewarded by a bequest of one-third of his dominions. This he left to an illegitimate son, Ghamsha Bahadur, on whose behalf the next Peshwa found a pretext for attacking the Orchha State and annexing it amongst other territories. Their General founded the city of Jhansi, and peopled it with the inhabitants of Orchha.

Jhansi remained under the rule of the Peshwas until 1803, when certain rights passed to the E.I. Company. Under British protection, successive Rajas ruled until their incompetence ruined the State, and when the dynasty died out on the death of Gangadhar Rao, in 1853, their territories lapsed to the British Government. Although a pension of £6000 a year was granted to the childless widow of the late Raja Rao, Lakshmi Bai, she considered herself aggrieved, both because she was not allowed to adopt an heir, and also because the slaughter of cattle was permitted in the Jhansi territory. The events of 1857, accordingly, found Jhansi ripe for rebellion. On the 5th of June a few men of the 12th Bengal Infantry seized the fort, containing the treasure and magazine. Many European officers were shot and the remainder capitulated a few days after, but were massacred with their families, in spite of a promise of protection sworn on the Koran and Ganges water.

The Rani tried to seize the supreme authority, but quarrels arose amongst the rebels, and a small British force under Sir Hugh Rose succeeded in retaking the town the following year. This was a memorable feat of arms as the campaign took place during the fierce hot weather and the troops had no protection from the sun.

The fort has since been modernised. The views from the top and from the road round the ramparts are very extensive.

The old civil station (**Jhansi Nauabad**) attached to Jhansi before 1861 remains the headquarters of the district.

(1) *Jhansi* to *Kanpur* (138 m.) and *Lucknow* (183 m.) direct by Central Ry. (broad-gauge).

Between Jhansi and Kanpur the country used to abound in black buck. Numerous old fortified villages are seen from the railway train. Jhansi to Kanpur *via* Hamirpur is 197 m. by road.

14 m. from Jhansi is **Paricha,** the head works of the Betwa Canal 71 m. long, irrigating Hamirpur and Jalaun districts. A masonry dam (1885) holds up the water of the Betwa river. A second dam was constructed in 1908 at Dhukwan, 20 m. farther up the river. There is a metalled road to Dhukwan from Jhansi (22 m.). At both places there are bungalows. Permission may be obtained from the Executive Engineer (Irrigation), Jhansi.

56 m. Ait Junction for a short branch line to Kunch (9 m.).

69 m. is **Orai** station (R., D.B.K., food available). The headquarters of the Jalaun district.

92 m. from Jhansi is **Kalpi** station (R.H. 1 m. distant. Permission to occupy it must be obtained from the Executive Engineer, P.W.D., Orai). The town is situated amongst deep ravines on the right bank of the Jumna, which is here crossed by a girder bridge of ten spans of 263 ft. (1888), with a roadway (1934). The piers are about 60 ft. in height, built on wells sunk 100 ft. below low water level.

Tradition says that the town was founded by Basdeo or Vasudeva, who ruled at Kanauj from A.D. 330 to 400. During the Mughal period Kalpi played a large part in the annals of this part of India. It was the birthplace of Mahesh Das, afterwards famous as Raja Birbal, the minister of Akbar. After the Mahrattas came to Bundelkhand (1732), the headquarters of the Government were at Kalpi. At the time of the British occupation of Bundelkhand, in 1803, Nana Gobind Rao, Subahdar ot Jalaun, seized the town. The British besieged it in December of that year, and, after a few hours' resistance, it surrendered. After a certain amount of change and exchange of territory, it finally became a British possession in 1806. During the Mutiny Sir Hugh Rose fought and won an important battle here against a large force under the Rani of Jhansi and Tantia Topi.

Kalpi manufactures a gold-flecked paper used by wealthy people for correspondence. The western outskirts of the town contain a large number of ruins, notably a tomb of the Lodi period called the 84 *Domes*, and twelve other handsome mausolea. In the heart of the town is a curious monument, a big cylindrical tower on which is sculptured a huge figure of Ravana. It was erected in 1895 by a lawyer of Kalpi, who imagined himself to be an incarnation of this mythological personage.

138 m. from Jhansi is Kanpur Junction (p. 379), and 45 m. farther on is Lucknow Junction (Route 18).

(2) *Jhansi* to *Manikpur*, 181 m., by Central Ry., broad-gauge branch.

7 m. S. from Jhansi is **Orchha** station, at the old capital of the former Orchha State, now only a village. It is built on the N.W. bank of the Betwa. There is an imposing fortress, connected by a masonry bridge with the rest of the town, containing int he S.W. corner of the city, within the walls,t he magnificent 17th-century palace of Bir Singh Deo (p. 223), and a palace built for the Emperor Jahangir but never used. The Chhattri of Bir Singh Deo is also fine. The name Bundela is derived from Vindhyela, and the Orchha family, Kshatriyas of the Surya Vansh, are the recognised head of the Bundelas.

Tikamgarh, the later capital, founded by Maharaja Vikramajit, in the S.W. corner of the State, is about 60 m. S. from Orchha, with which it is connected by road; also with Lalitpur railway station on the W. and Mau-Ranipur railway station on N.E. by metalled roads, 36 m. and 42 m. respectively. The earlier name was Tehri, the present name is derived from an appellation of Krishna, Ranchor Tikam.

14 m. from Jhansi is **Barwa-Sagar** station (D.B.). The town is picturesquely situated at the foot of a rocky ridge on the shore of the Barwa-Sagar lake, an artificial sheet of water formed by a masonry embankment ¾ m. in length, constructed by Udoi Singh, Raja of Orchha, between 1705-37, and containing two craggy, wooded islets. Below, a tract of land, extending over 4 m., is thickly planted with mango and other trees, many of great age and enormous size. N.W. of the town rises a fine old castle, also built by Udoi Singh, but now uninhabited. 3 m. W. stand the remains of an old Chandel temple, built of solid blocks of stone, carved with the figures of Hindu gods, much defaced.

40 m. **Mau-Ranipur** station (D.B. ½ m., and Inspection House), next to Jhansi the principal commercial town of Jhansi district. Its buildings are in the style peculiar to Bundelkhand, with deep eaves between the first and second storeys and hanging balconies. Trees and temples ornament the town, the principal being that of the Jains, with two solid spires and several cupolas. An old brick-built fort and bastions adjoins the bazar, and contains the public offices.

53 m. from Jhansi is **Harpalpur** station (R.), for **Nowgong** (D.B. and C.H.), a former Cantonment, 19 m. distant. There is also an Inspec-

tion Bungalow for military officers. Nowgong was at one time a large military station. The Kitchener College (1930) has a statue of the Field Marshal. It is now used for training N.C.Os.

About 3 m. from Nowgong on the Chhatarpur road lies the village of Mau, situated between two picturesque lakes, Jagatsagar and Dubela Tal. On the far side of the latter are the Cenotaphs of Chhatarsal and his wife.

Motor-bus service, Harpalpur-Nowgong-Chhatarpur.

67 m. **Bela Tal** station for **Jaitpur,** formerly the capital of a State, which was resumed by Lord Dalhousie in 1849 on the death of the last Raja without issue. It is situated on the W. of a large tank, called Bela Tal, said to have been built by Bala Varma, a Chandel ruler (A.D. 514-63); it has a circumference of nearly 9 m. Two irrigation canals are run from it. A tank of about the same size, called the Majhgawan Tank, was excavated in 1914 some 6 m. S. of Bela Tal, and serves to irrigate the S.W. part of Kulpahar pargana. On the W. edge of Bela Tal runs a chain of several low hills; a fort is built on the top and along the slopes. The town of Jaitpur, originally founded by Jait Reshi (A.D. 525), and fort are ascribed to Jagatraj, second son of the famous Chhatarsal. There is a temple called the Dhamsa. The canal bungalow at Jaitpur is not available, but another can be occupied by permission from the Collector of Hamirpur.

86 m. from Jhansi is **Mahoba,** the nearest station for Khajuraho. (District Board and Survey Bungalows can be used with permission of the Collector of Hamirpur.)

Mahoba is believed to have existed under different names in all the successive cycles through which the world has passed. Its name in the present evil age, Kala-Yug, Mahoba, is said to be derived from a great sacrifice (Mahot-Sava) performed by its reputed founder, Chandra Varma, a Chandel Raja, about A.D. 800. The town stands on the edge of Madan Sagar lake, named after the great Chief Madana Brahma (1015-70). There are three distinct portions of the town: the old fort, N. of a low hill; the inner fort, on the top of the hill; and the Dariba, or "pan" bazar, on the S.

Architectural antiquities of the Chandel period abound throughout the neighbourhood. The Ram Kund marks the place where Chandra Varma, founder of the dynasty, died; a reservoir into which the waters of all holy streams unite. The fort, in ruins, commands a view over the hills and lakes. The temple of Mania Deva, partially renovated, has in front of its entrance a stone pillar, inscribed to Madana Brahma, the "Dewal dip", and another, "Alha ki Gilli", the staff of Alha, is near Madan Sagar. Alha was a hero in songs of Rajput bards. Farther along the *dargah* of Pir Mubarak Shah is built entirely of Hindu materials. Of the lakes, confined by magnificent masonry dams, two have greatly silted up, but the Kirat Sagar, built by Kirat Brahma (1070-1115), and Madan Sagar (1030) still remain deep and clear sheets of water. The shores of the lakes and the islands in their midst are thickly covered with ruined temples, monstrous figures carved out of the solid rock, Jain and Buddhist sculptures and other early remains, while on the hills above stand the summer-houses of the early Rajas, and shrines overhang the edge. Relics of Jain temples and Buddhist inscriptions also occur. Muslim monuments include the tomb of Jalhan Khan, constructed from the fragments of a Saivite temple, and a mosque, also built of Chandel materials. There are broken Jain statues, and Buddhist statues are found. On a hill adjoining the S.E. bank of Madan Sagar there are twenty-four rock-hewn images of the "Tirthankaras", dated Sambat 1206 (A.D. 1149). (See *Six Sculptures from Mahoba,* No. 8, Memoirs. Arch. Surv. of India, 1921, by K. N.

Dikshit.)

Roads from Nowgong and Chhatarpur uniting at Kaimaha, where there is a picturesquely situated D.B. on the Urmal river, skirt Mahoba and continue to Banda.

Khajuraho was one of the capitals of the Chandel Rajput kings during the 10th to the 12th centuries A.D. Over fifty temples were built, twenty-two of which are still standing. They form one of the most important groups in India. There is a rest house, Travellers' Lodge (bedding provided), C.H., Hotel (Chandella), Motel, and Tourist Bungalows. It is situated about 60 m. S.E. from Harpalpur *via* Nowgong (D.B., R.H. for Lake Dubela, Palace, Museum) and Chhatarpur (D.B.K.) and about 36 m. from Mahoba. During the tourist season there is a daily flight from Delhi to the airstrip at *Khajuraho*. Motor transport available from Harpalpur. Good road from Varanasi *via* Rewa and Panna.

The temples, which are of local sandstone (with three exceptions), are not built within the customary walled enclosure but stand on high stone terraces (*Adhisthana*). The architecture is in the *Nagara* style of northern India (formerly called Indo-Aryan) and in this region the characteristic curvilinear towers (*Sikharas*) have clusters of lesser turrets (*Uru-sringas*) of varying heights clinging to them, suggestive of rising mountain peaks converging round a great central peak.

The sculpture at Khajuraho is world famous and blends so perfectly with the architecture that each building appears to have been conceived by a single master mind. Round the giant plinths there are friezes of horsemen and martial elephants and scenes of feasting and carnal pleasure. Round the exterior walls of the temples there are two, sometimes three, superimposed rows of figures in high relief of gods, goddesses, kings and heroes, courtesans and heavenly nymphs (*Apsarases*) including the embracing couples (*Mithuna*) which have given rise to the supposition that tantric practices, in which ritual sex played an important part, were influential in Khajuraho during mediaeval times. In the recessed angles of the buildings and sometimes free-standing on the terraces are innumerable carvings of rampant lions (*Sardulas*) which symbolise heroism and ferocity.

The basic interior plan of the larger temples consists of an open portico (*Ardha Mandapa*) which may be single or double, leading into the great hall (*Maha Mandapa*) which is supported on four pillars and has lateral transepts. The hall leads into the vestibule (*Antarala*) beyond which is the enclosed cella (*Garbha Griha*) containing the free-standing cult image. Round the sides and back of the cella runs the ambulatory (*Pradakshina*), with a second pair of lateral transepts (in the smaller shrines the latter, together with the ambulatory, are omitted). The interior carving is as lavish as that on the exterior of the buildings with ceilings consisting of corbelled cupolas exquisitely carved in lace-like patterns, elaborate pillars with bracket capitals, the finest being in the form of celestial nymphs (*Apsarases*), and rows of figure sculpture round the outside of the cella when the plan includes an ambulatory.

The temples are scattered over an area of some eight square miles and stand in three separate groups, the most important being the **Western Group,** which today is surrounded by a well-laid-out park enclosed in a ring fence (gate in village street, open from sunrise to sunset. Small fee). Opposite the entrance gate to the west is the Vaishnavite temple of **Lakshmana** (*c.* A.D. 930-50)[1] which Dr Krishna Deva in his invaluable guide to Khajuraho (published by the Archaeological Survey of India in 1971 and usually available on the site) states is the best preserved of the evolved

[1] All the dates given here are taken from Dr Krishna Deva's Guide. See also Krishna Deva: *The Temples of Khajuraho in Central India* (Ancient India Series No. 15, 1959).

temples of Khajuraho and the only one which has its four subsidiary shrines (at the four corners of the platform) still standing. The shrine to the S.W. has an interesting small panel on its eastern face showing a master architect sitting at his drawing board and surrounded by apprentices. On the base of the temple proper there is a striking elephant frieze and on the walls above it there are two parallel bands of figure sculpture in the typical Khajuraho style. The building is entered through a double looped arch springing from the jaws of two flanking crocodiles (*Makara Torana*). The delicately carved cusped corbelled cupolas of the two succeeding porticos should not be missed. The interior of the main hall has a number of the beautiful bracket capitals in the form of *Apsarases* (heavenly nymphs) for which Indian art is justly famous. The sanctuary door is elaborately carved with various forms of Vishnu and his consort and the object of worship within is a four-armed statue of *Vaikuntha* (Vishnu with three heads: that of a boar to the left, a man in the centre and a lion to the right).

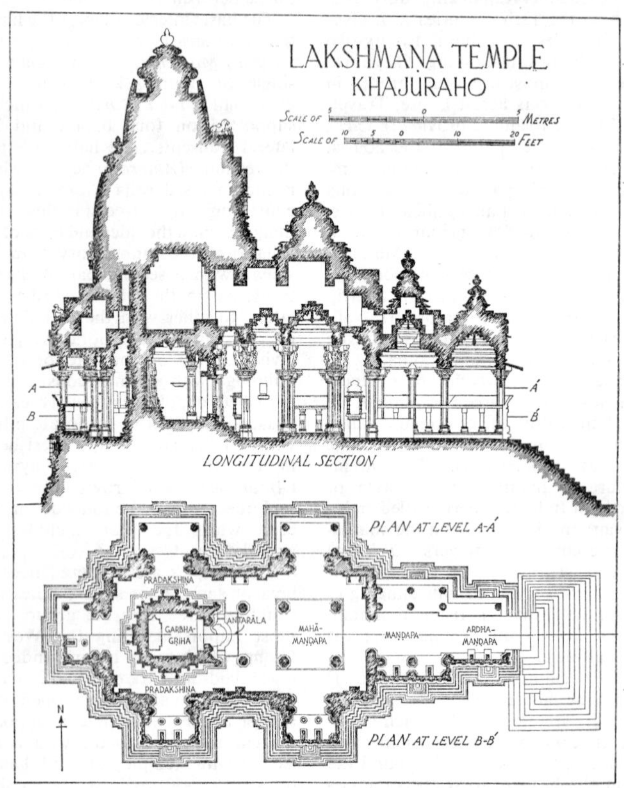

Before leaving the temple a walk should be taken round the exterior of its great plinth which is notable for its lively friezes of battle, hunting and domestic scenes, including a curious one to the south which depicts various forms of bestiality.

Some 200 yards to the N.W. of the Lakshmana, three temples stand on a single platform, the first being the Shaivite temple of **Khandariya Mahadeva**, the largest, and in the opinion of many, the most perfect of all the temples at Khajuraho (*c.* 1025-1050). Dr Krishna Deva writes: "All mark it as the most evolved and finished achievement of the central Indian building style and one of the sublimest creations of Indian architecture". The sikhara with its clusters of gently bulging turrets clinging to the great central tower is a poem of rhythmic beauty and round the exterior walls there are three parallel bands of figure sculpture carved almost in the round.

Beside the Khandariya stands a small ruined shrine and beneath its open portico sits a large and furious *sardula*, from which it may be deduced that this was once a Devi temple. Beyond it, and still on the same vast platform is the temple of **Jagadambi** (*c.* 1000-1025), Vaishnavite but later given over to Devi worship as is shown by the statue of Parvati now standing in the cella. The standard of sculpture decorating this temple both inside and out is as high as any that Khajuraho has to show and is particularly noteworthy for the sensitive treatment of its rapturous erotic couples (*mithuna*).

About a hundred yards to the north of Jagadambi and only slightly later in date, stands the temple of **Chitragupta,** the only one at Khajuraho dedicated to Surya, the ancient Aryan sun god. There is a fine statue in the cella, in which he is shown standing in his chariot drawn by seven horses.

The Shaivite **Visvanatha** temple beside the road some 200 yds. to the N.E. of the Chitragupta has an inscription stating that it was built in the year 1002 by the Chandella King Dhanga. It is a fine example of the fully developed temple plan of the period with two of its original four subsidiary shrines still standing. On the same terrace there is an open pavilion sheltering a colossal image of Nandi, the sacred bull of Shiva.

Just inside the ring fence, there is an open shrine standing on a high plinth containing a huge monolithic image of the boar, Varaha, the fourth avatar of Vishnu. In front of it stands one of the earliest temples in the area and the only ancient shrine still in worship, the **Matangesvara** (*c.* 900-925). There is little decorative carving and no mandapa but the large corbelled cupola of the spacious cella is structurally remarkable and beneath it stands a huge highly polished lingam 2·5 metres high and 1·1 metres in diameter.

Also included in the western group but involving a cross-country walk of a mile or so from the buildings listed above are two of the oldest temples of archaeological interest only: the **Chaunsath-Yogini** (about a quarter of a mile to the S.W. of the Shiva-sagar tank) and the **Lalguan-Mahadeva** temple (*c.* 900) three-quarters of a mile west of the Chaunsath-Yogini.

The **Eastern Group.** The most pleasant way to visit this and the southern group is by cycle rickshaw (strike a bargain at the hotel before setting out), as not all the temples can be approached by car and the rickshaw wala knows all the paths, which are intricate and lead in and out of the villages. The eastern group will take about three hours to see at leisure and the southern group from one to one and a half hours.

Proceeding north up the main street of modern Khajuraho a cart track strikes off to the east and on the far bank of a silted up tank stands the little ruined **Brahma** temple (*c.* 900), originally Vaishnavite as shown by the small image of Vishnu on Garuda carved on the lintel of the cella doorway. The cella roof is in the form of a stepped pyramid. The **Vamana** temple (*c.* 1050-75) stands out in the fields a few hundred yards to the N.E. of the above with a simple curvilinear sikhara and pyramidal-roofed mandapa, both more akin to the Orissan than to the Khajuraho style. Round the exterior of the cella walls there is a double band of excellent figure sculpture and the cella contains a statue of the third, dwarf avatar of Vishnu as Vamana.

The **Javari** (*c.* 1075-1100) lies about 200 yds. south of the above and is one of the most perfect of the smaller temples of Khajuraho, compact and harmonious in outline with superb decorative carving and figure sculpture both inside and out. To reach the next shrine it is necessary to wind one's way through the old village of Khajuraho to the south of which stands the **Ghantai** temple (late 10th century) beside a cart track. It is in a ruinous condition but is worth inspecting for the delicate chain and bell (*Ghanta*) designs which decorate its tall pillars, a Hindu motif which became prominent in early Mughal architecture.

500 yds. to the S.E. is a group of Jain temples surrounded by a modern whitewashed wall. This can be reached direct by metalled road from any of the hotels or guest houses and should be visited by car by those who have not the time to see the outlying temples. The **Santinatha** is largely modern but encloses several ancient shrines with some good panels of sculpture here and there. The chief object of worship in the central shrine is a tall highly polished statue of Adinatha, one of the Jain Tirthankaras (teachers). It is 4·5 metres high. The **Parsvanatha** (*c.* 950-970) is the largest of the Jain temples, and with its wealth of decorative and figure sculpture both inside and out is indistinguishable from its Hindu counterparts. Notice particularly the exquisite portico ceiling with two intertwined nymphs hanging from the central pendant. The **Adinathata** (late 11th century) lies a little to the north of the above and although on the small side it has three bands of wonderful figure sculpture on the exterior depicting all the usual Hindu gods and goddesses and dancing girls, and only the cult image in the cella proves that the dedication is Jain.

The **Southern Group.** Nearly a mile to the south of the **Ghantai** temple (see above) stands the **Duladeo** (early to middle 12th century) with a fine clustered sikhara but rather stereotyped bands of figure sculpture. It is the latest of all Khajuraho temples. The **Chaturbhuja** (*c.* 1100) is 1 m. south of Khajuraho village and can only be reached by car along a bullock cart track, in dry weather. It is a small Shaivite temple containing a beautiful image of Shiva as Dakshinamurti.

The **Archaeological Museum** stands back from the southern end of the main street of modern Khajuraho. It contains many statues and fragments of interest from the locality and should be visited by those with time to spare.

113 m. **Khairada** Junction (road from Jhansi); the branch line (79 m.) through Hamirpur Road to Kanpur is now disused. At 116 m. the Ken river is crossed.

119 m. from Jhansi is **Banda** station (R., D.B.) (alt. 419 ft.). It stands on an undulating plain, 1 m. E. of the right bank of the Ken river.

The modern town derived its importance from the residence of the Nawab of Banda, descended from Shamsher Bahadur, a Mahratta General at Panipat in 1761. The Nawab was removed in 1858 for his share in the Mutiny. His mosque is E. of the town. There are five Jain temples, and an old temple of Shri Shankar (approach motorable). The two characteristics of Banda District are its liability to agricultural calamity and its trade in the cutting and polishing of precious stones, especially agates obtained from the Ken riverbed.

35 m. S. of Banda on the last spur of the Vindhya mountains looking N. over the Gangetic plains, is the famous hill fort of **Kalinjar,** besieged by Mahmud of Ghazni (1021), the place where Sher Shah accidentally met his death (1545): taken by

Martindell (1812). It contains many temples and antiquities. some dating back to the 12th century. On the highest point there is a fine monument to Andrew Wauchope, of Niddrie, Midlothian, the first British Commissioner of Bundelkhand. It is accessible *via* Naraini (22 m. from Banda) by a fair-weather unmetalled road. Ajaigarh, captured in 1809 by Martindell, is connected to Naraini by a metalled road (8 m.). There are rest houses at both places and at Naraini (13 m. from Kalinjar). Raja Ajai was a descendant of Chhatarsal.

157 m. from Jhansi is **Chatrakot** station, a celebrated place of pilgrimage where Sita, Rama and Lakshman are said to have lived after their exile from Ajudhia. Special facilities for Hindus.

162 m. from Jhansi is **Karwi Tarahwan,** in 1805 a Cantonment, and later residence of the ex-Peshwa's relative, Amrit Rao, who lived in state, and built several beautiful temples and wells. Numerous traders from the Deccan were thus attracted to Karwi. There is a fine temple and tank known as the Ganesh Bagh, built by Vinayak Rao, son of Amrit Rao, in 1837.

181 m. from Jhansi and 883 m. from Bombay is **Manikpur** Junction (p. 122), on the Central Ry. main line from Bombay to Calcutta, *via* Jabalpur (Route 2).

(3) *Jhansi* to *Agra,* 133 m., and *Delhi,* 255 m., via *Datia*, *Gwalior* and *Dholpur*, by the Central Ry.

718 m. from Bombay on the Central Ry. main line to Delhi is **Datia,** capital of the former Datia State (912 sq. m.). Datia stands on a rocky height surrounded by a stone wall. The Maharaja's residence stands within the town. To the W. of the town, on a hill within the walls, is the Govind Palace of Bir Singh Deo, (now tenanted only by bats), which Sir Edwin Lutyens considered one of the most interesting buildings architecturally in the whole of India.

725 m. **Sonagir** station. 2 m. off and visible from the railway are eighty Jain temples of modern date, forming an extremely picturesque group, well worth a visit.

763 m. from Bombay is **GWALIOR*** (pop. 406,700 in 1971), 194 m. from Delhi (R., D.B., C.H., Hotels), once capital of the former Gwalior State. Gwalior was one of the largest of the Indian States, area 26,397 sq. m., and has had some very progressive Rulers. Of the Scindia family the most remarkable have been Ranoji, the founder (d. 1750), Mahdaji (d. 1794), his grand-nephew Daulat Rao (d. 1827), Jayaji Rao (1843-86), and Maharaja Mahhav Rao (1886-1925).

Gwalior is famous for its ancient fort, and gigantic rock sculptures.[1] At *Morar*, a few miles E. of the fort, a garrison of British troops was stationed from 1858 to 1886, when the fort, with Morar, was made over to the Maharaja in exchange for Jhansi.

The railway station is about $1\frac{1}{2}$ m. from Lashkar, the new town. The Hotel Gujri Mahal is in High Court Lane; the Usha Kiran Palace Hotel is in Lashkar. Gwalior is on the National Highway (Bombay-Delhi). Air connections with Bombay and Delhi.

History

An inscription in Gwalior Fort records that a temple of the Sun was erected on the hill in the reign of Mihiragula (p. 43), son of the Hun adventurer Toramana. Two other inscriptions show that Gwalior was included in the kingdom of Kanauj under the Gurjara Pratihara, King Mihira Bhoja, who ruled over a great part of N. India about A.D. 900. After A.D. 950, Vajradaman of the Kachhapagata or Kachhwaha dynasty, captured Gwalior from the Pratiharas of Kanauj. The Kachhwahas ruled over Gwalior for nearly 200 years. They are the Pal Kings of the bards. Gwalior, according to bardic chronicles, not strictly

[1] Described on p. 233.

historical, was founded by Suraj Sen, a Kachhwaha Chief, who was a leper, and coming when hunting to the Gopagiri Hill, on which the fort stands, received a drink of water from the hermit Gwalipa, which cured him. He received a new name, Suhan Pal, from the hermit, with a promise that his descendants should reign as long as they were called Pal. Eighty-three reigned accordingly; but Tej Karan, having discarded the name of Pal, lost his kingdom. To this dynasty seven Parihara Princes succeeded, who ruled, with a short break, for 103 years—till Gwalior was taken by Altamish in the 21st year of the reign of Sarang Deo.

The capture of Gwalior by Altamish was commemorated in an inscription placed over the gate of the Arwahi, and the Emperor Babur states that he saw it, and the date was 630 A.H. = A.D. 1232. In 1398, after the invasion of Timur, the Tomar Chief, Bir Singh Deo, declared himself independent, and founded the Tomar dynasty.

Early in the 15th century the Gwalior Chiefs paid tribute to Khizr Khan of Delhi, and in 1424 Gwalior, being besieged by Hoshang Shah of Malwa, was delivered by Mubarak Shah of Delhi. In 1425 Dongar Singh commenced the great rock sculptures at Gwalior, and his son Kirti Singh, 1454, completed them. In 1465 Husain Shah, the Sharqi king of Jaunpur, besieged Gwalior, and obliged it to pay tribute. Man Singh (1486-1516) acknowledged the supremacy of Bahlol Lodi and of Sikandar Lodi of Delhi; the latter in 1505 marched against Gwalior, but fell into an ambuscade, and was repelled. In 1516 he made great preparations at Agra for the conquest of Gwalior, but died. Ibrahim Lodi sent an army of 30,000 horse, 300 elephants, and other troops, against Gwalior, and a few days after they reached that place Man Singh died.

He was the greatest of the Gwalior Tomars, and constructed many useful works, amongst others the great tank to the N.W. of Gwalior, called the *Moti Jhil*, now silted up. His palace in the fort is the noblest specimen of Hindu domestic architecture in N. India. After Man Singh's death his son Vikramaditya sustained the siege for a year, but at last surrendered, and was sent to Agra, where he became the friend of Ibrahim, and died fighting at his side against Babur at Panipat in 1526.

Babur sent Rahimdad with an army to Gwalior, which he took by a stratagem, suggested by the Saint Muhammad Ghaus. In 1542 Abul-Kasim, Governor for Humayun, surrendered his fortress to Sher Shah. In 1545 Salim, son of Sher, brought his treasure from Chunar, and in 1553 died. Ram Sah, grandson of Man Singh, tried to seize Gwalior, but, in a great battle for three days with Akbar's troops, was defeated, and the fortress remained in the hands of the Mughals until the Mahrattas took it in 1754.

In 1761, after the battle of Panipat, Gwalior was taken by Bhim Singh, the Jat Rana of Gohad[1] (25 m. N.E.), who lost it again in 1769, but it was captured from the Mahrattas by Captain Popham in 1780, and restored to the Rana. Madhadji Rao Scindia[2] recaptured it in 1784. Colonel White took the fortress in 1804, but it was retroceded to Scindia by treaty in 1805. In 1843 there was a mutiny, and after the battles of Maharajpur and Panniar, it was virtually resumed until restored to Jayaji Rao.

During the 1857 Mutiny Maharaja Jayaji Rao Scindia had, besides 10,000 troops of his own, a Contingent under British officers of two regiments of Irregular Cavalry—1158 men of all ranks—seven regiments of Infantry—aggregating 6412 men—and 26 guns, with 748 Artillerymen. The Maharaja and his Minister,

[1] The late Maharaj Rana of Dholpur (p. 238), was a descendant.

[2] This Prince was wounded at the Battle of Panipat (p. 52), where one of his brothers was killed. Two more brothers fell in other engagements.

Sir Dinkar Rao, remained staunch, but the Contingent mutinied on Sunday, 14th June.

In May and June 1858 there was much fighting in and around Gwalior between the mutineers commanded by Tantia Topi and the Rani of Jhansi and the British under Sir Hugh Rose, as a result of which the rebels were eventually driven out of Gwalior, and the fort was regained. The Rani of Jhansi, who was wearing a man's dress, was found amongst the slain.

The **Old City** lies along the N.E. and N. ends of the rock. Flanking the city to the N. stands a curious old Pathan archway, the remains of a tomb. Outside the gate of the fort is the **Jami Masjid,** with its gilt pinnacled domes and lofty minarets. Sir W. Sleeman says (*Rambles*, I, 347): "It is a very beautiful mosque, with one end built by Mutamad Khan, in 1661, of the white sandstone of the rock above it".

On the eastern outskirt of the city is the noble tomb of **Muhammad Ghaus,** a saint venerated in the time of Babur and Akbar. It is of stone, and is one of the best specimens of Muslim architecture of the early Mughal period, built by Gwalior masons. It is a square of 100 ft., with hexagonal towers at the four corners, attached at the angles to form an octagon. The tomb is a hall 43 ft. square, with the angles cut off by pointed arches, from which springs a lofty Pathan dome. The walls are 5½ ft. thick, and are surrounded by a lofty veranda, with square bays in the centre of each side, closed by double lattice screens. These are protected from the weather by double eaves (*chajja*), long stone slabs resting on brackets. The dome was once covered with blue-glazed tiles.

The **Tomb of Tansen,** the famous musician, is a small pavilion 22 ft. square, supported on pillars round the tombstone, close to the S.W. corner of the large tomb. The tamarind tree near the grave is much visited by singers, as the chewing of the leaves is alleged to impart a wonderful sweetness to the voice. Tansen was one of "The Nine Gems" of Akbar's Court.

The Fort[1].—The *main entrance* to the fort is on the N.E. Flights of broad steps, alternating with pieces of paved level road, have been removed, and there is now a continuous road. Permission is no longer required to visit the Fort area and the Man Singh Palace; but the other Palaces are not usually open to visitors.

"The great fortress of Gwalior", said General Cunningham, "is situated on a precipitous, flat-topped, and isolated hill of sandstone", which rises 300 ft. above the town at the N. end, but only 274 ft. at the upper gate of the principal entrance. The hill is long and narrow; its extreme length from N. to S. is 1¾ m., while its breadth varies from 600 ft. to 2800 ft. The walls are from 30 ft. to 35 ft. high, and the rock immediately below them is steeply but irregularly scarped all round the hill.

The view from the fort is varied and extensive, but, except during the rainy season, when the hills are green, the general appearance of the country is brown and arid. To the N., on a clear day, may be seen the gigantic temple of Suhania, about 30 m. distant, and still farther in the same direction the red hills of Dholpur. To the W., and within gunshot, lies the long, flat-topped sandstone hill of Hanuman, with a basaltic peak at the N. end and a whitewashed temple on its slope, whence the hill has its name. Beyond, as far as the eye can reach, nothing is seen but range after range of low sandstone hills. The conical peak of the Raipur hill towers over the lower ranges in the S., and to the E. the level plains, dotted with villages, lengthen till they pass out of sight. On the plain below lies the Old City of Gwalior, encircling the

[1] *Gwalior Fort Album*, published by the Archaeological Department. Sold at the Archaeological Museum. Brochure from Regional Tourist Office.

N.E. end of the fortress, and to the S., upwards of 1 m. distant, is the New City of *Lashkar*.

The entrance is protected by six successive **Gates** which, beginning from below, are:

The *Alamgiri* Gate, built by Mu'-tamad Khan, Governor of Gwalior, in 1660, and called after Aurangzeb, whose title as Emperor was Alamgir. It is quite plain, and the inscription is obliterated. Inside is a small court-yard and an open hall in which the Muslim Governors sat to dispense justice.

The *Badalgarh*, or Hindola Gate, so called from the outwork Badalgarh, which was named after Badal Singh, the uncle of Man Singh. This gate is also called Hindola, from *hindol*, "a swing", which existed outside. It is a fine specimen of Hindu archi-tecture, contemporary with the Gujari Palace. An inscription on an iron plate which recorded its restoration by the Governor Saiyad 'Alam in 1648 no longer exists.

Close under the rock to the right is the stately **Gujari Palace,** built by Man Singh for his favourite Gujari wife, Mriganaya, *c.* 1500. It measures 300 ft. by 230 ft., and is two storeys high. It is built of hewn stone, and was once a very fine building. The **Archaeological Museum** contains Brahman and Jain sculptures, inscriptions,[1] and miniature paintings. There is a fine set of copies of nine frescoes in the Caves of Bagh (p. 205). The Museum[2] is closed on Mondays.

The *Bhairon*, or Bansur Gate, which has been removed, was the work of one of the earliest Kachhwaha Rajas. It was called Bansur, from *bansur*, "archer" — literally a "bamboo-splitter"—from the guard of bow-men which had the charge of it.

The *Ganesh* Gate was built by Dongar Singh, who ruled 1424 to 1454. Outside is a small outwork called *Kabutar Khana*, or "pigeon-house", in which is a tank called Nur Sagar, 60 ft. by 39 ft. and 25 ft. deep. Here, too, is a Hindu temple sacred to the hermit *Gwalipa*, from whom the fort got its name. It is a small, square, open pavilion, with a cupola on four pillars. There is also a small mosque with a chronogram giving a date corresponding to 1664.

Before reaching the *Lakshman* Gate is a temple hewn out of the solid rock and called *Chatarbhujmandir*, "shrine of the four-armed", sacred to Vishnu, inside which, on the left, is a long inscription, dated Sambat 933 = A.D. 876. It is 12 ft. square, with a portico in front 10 ft. by 9 ft., supported by four pillars. There is a tank here, and opposite to it the tomb of Taj Nizam, a noble of the Court of Ibrahim Lodi, who was killed in assaulting this gate in 1518. An awkward flight of steps leads to the *North-eastern group* of Jain Statues in a cliff (p. 237). The sculptures are small, and unaccom-panied by inscriptions, and are, therefore, unimportant; some of the caves are large. Farther S., on the face of the rock, are carvings of Maha-deva and his consort and about fifty lingams. A colossal figure, 15½ ft. high, of Siva slaying the demon Gaja, who had assumed the body of an elephant, which is seen as a canopy at the top, is one of the oldest sculptures in Gwalior.

The *Hathiya Paur*, or Elephant Gate, was built by Man Singh, and forms part of his palace. Here was the carving of an elephant, which Babur and Abul-Fazl praised. Inside the Hathiya Paur, and under the S. end of the Palace of Man Singh, was the *Hawa* Gate (now removed); a cool draught of air justified the name.

Turning to the right on reaching the level of the fort, the five palaces under which the ascent has passed may be first visited. The first of these is the **Man Singh Palace** (1486-1516, repaired in 1881), also called the *Chit Mandir*, or Painted Palace, as

[1] Gwalior is rich in buried monuments; and excellent work was done by the State Archaeological Department in the direction of excavation and preservation, notably at Mandasor (p. 208), Chanderi (p. 222) and Bagh (p. 205).

[2] See *A Guide to the Archaeological Museum at Gwalior.*

"the walls are covered with a profusion of coloured tiles—bands of mosaic candelabra, Brahmani ducks, elephants and peacocks—enamelled blue, green and gold, giving to this massive wall an unsurpassed charm and elegance. The tiles of the great windowless S. wall possess a brightness and delicacy of tint unblemished by the four centuries which they have weathered. Nowhere do I remember any architectural design capable of imparting similar lightness to a simple massive wall" (Rousselet).[1] The palace excited the admiration of Babur (1527). It is two storeys high, with two storeys of underground apartments, now made uninhabitable by bats. Intended as cool apartments in the summer, they were used by the Mughals as a State prison. The last Sultan of Ahmednagar died here (1600), and Aurangzeb confined his brother Murad in 1659 until he died in 1661. The E. face is 300 ft. long and 100 ft. high, and has five massive round towers, surmounted by open-domed cupolas, and connected at top by a battlement of singularly beautiful open lattice-work. The S. face is 160 ft. long and 60 ft. high, with three round towers connected by a battlement of lattice-work. The N. and W. sides are somewhat ruined. The rooms are arranged round two courts—small, but with singularly beautiful decoration.

The *Vikramaditya Palace* (1516), between the Man and Karan Palaces, is connected with them by narrow galleries.

The **Karan Palace** should be called the Kirti Mandir. It is long and narrow, and of two storeys. It has one room 43 ft. by 28 ft., with a roof supported by two rows of pillars. There are smaller rooms on either side, and bathrooms below, with some fine plaster-work on the domed ceilings. Close by to the S. is a hall (1516) 36 ft. square, with a roof in the form of a Hindu dome, supported on eight carved ribs, of which four spring from the side pillars and four from the angles of the building. Internally the top of the dome is a flat square formed by the intersection of the ribs. The roof is flat, and once had a pavilion on it.

The **Muslim Jahangiri** and **Shah Jahan Palaces** at the N. end of the fort are of rubble plastered quite plain.

A little to the N.W. of them is the Johar tank, so called from the immolation of Rajput women, just before the fortress was taken by Altamish in 1232. On the W. wall slightly to the S., and just above the Dhonda Gate, are the ruins of the buildings known as the Nauchauki or Nine Cells, also used as a State prison in the time of the Mughal Emperors. The narrow, steep staircases leading to the dungeons can still be traversed.

On a salient on the eastern verge of the rock, and a furlong to the S. of Man Singh's Palace, are the two **Sasbahu** temples, and from the walls nearby a fine view is obtained of the eastern cliff of the fortress. The word Sas-bahu means "mother-in-law and daughter-in-law", two similar objects standing side by side. The larger temple is 100 ft. long by 63 ft. broad. An inscription in Sanskrit in the porch records that it was commenced by Raja Padmapala, of the Kachhwaha dynasty, and completed in 1093 by Raja Mahi Pal, his brother. The entrance is to the N., and the shrine to the S. The temple is now 70 ft. high, but the spire (*sikhara*) has disappeared, and it may have been 100 ft. high. It stands on a richly carved plinth. There are figures of Vishnu over the main entrances. The central hall is 31 ft. square. It is crowded with four massive pillars to aid in bearing the enormous weight of its great pyramidal roof.

The smaller temple is cruciform, and is open on all four sides. The body is 23 ft. square, supported on twelve pillars. The plinth is 6 ft. high, and is decorated like that of the great temple. The pillars are round, with octagonal bases and bracketed

[1] *India and its Native Princes*, by Louis Rousselet.

capitals. The lower parts of the shafts in both temples are ornamented with groups of female dancers. They are fine specimens of the ornate style of mediaeval Hindu architecture.

From this point it is necessary to cross again to the W. side, where the Teli-ka-mandir stands, passing the Suraj Kund tank *en route*. This tank is 350 ft. by 180 ft., and is believed to be the oldest reservoir in the fort.

Caves. S.-E. Group.		Sculptures.			
No.	Front depth and height.	Names.	Position.	Height.	Symbol.
	Feet			Feet	
1	23 × 21 × 27	—	—	30	—
2	10 × 10 × 10	—	—	—	—
3	15 × 12 × 17	Adinath	Standing	7	Bull
		4 others	—	—	—
4	15 × 14 × 16	Adinath	—	14	Wheel
		Nemnath	—	—	Shell
5	—	Adinath	—	—	Bull
6	26 × 12 × 16	Supadma	Sitting	15	Lotus
7	15 × 10 × 20	—	Standing	20	—
8	21 × 10 × 20	Adinath	Sitting	6	—
9	16 × 7 × 28	Male Figure	Standing	21	—
10	10 × 7 × 15	Female	Lying	—	—
		Chandra Prabha	Standing	12	—
		2 others	—	12	—
11	12 × 8 × 25	Chandra Prabha	Sitting	21	Crescent
12	31 × 10 × 25	Sambhunath	—	21	Horse
13	40 × 10 × 25	Nemnath	Standing	21	Shell
		Sambhunath	Sitting	—	Horse
		Mahavira	Standing	—	Lion
14	26 × 16 × 32	Adinath	Sitting	29	Bull
15	26 × 16 × 33	Adinath	Sitting	28	—
16	24 × 22 × 34	—	—	30	—
17	80 × 8 × 30	Kantanath	Standing	26	Goat
		Shantanath	Sitting	26	Antelope
		Adinath	Sitting	26	Wheel
		And 4 others	—	26	—
18	15 × 10 × 30	—	Standing	26	—
19	16 × 10 × 30	—	—	26	—
20	12 × 8 × 20	Adinath	—	8	Wheel
21	27 × 35 × 15	—	—	—	—

The **Teli-ka-mandir**[1] (probable date, 9th century; restored 1881-83) is 60 ft. square, with a portico projecting 11 ft. on the E. side. The sides slope upwards to 80 ft., where the building ends in a horizontal ridge 30 ft. long. It is the loftiest building in Gwalior. The doorway is 35 ft. high, and has a figure of Garuda over the centre. It was originally a Vishnavite temple, but since the 15th century it has been Saivite. The name appears to be a corruption of *Telangana*, and from the Dravidian style of the spire, it has been thought that the architect was a Telangana, or Teluga. The whole is covered with sculptures. The gateway in front of it was formed out of fragments found in the fort during restoration work in 1881-83.

There are two tanks close to the cliff of the western Arwahi ravine, the Ek Khamba tank on the N. with a pillar in it, and the Chamar, close to which is the point, still called Faringhi Pahar, of Captain Popham's escalade in 1780.

At the S. point of the fort are interesting tanks (Dhobi Talao, Rani Talao, Chedi Talao) with a view of Lashkar. The military buildings in the S. portion of the Fort are now used for a residential school, conducted on the lines of an English Public School.

[1] "Oilman's Temple", see Fergusson's *Indian Architecture*, 2, 139.

Returning from the S., past the Gangola tank, the route may be pursued past the Suraj Kund to the gate which forms the entrance to the Arwahi ravine, on the farther side of which is the Mansarowar tank. The S. end of the ravine is closed by a wall with a double gate, near which are the wells which supply the fort with drinking water; and on either side of it, from the bottom of the steep descent from the N. gate, are the Jain statues of the Arwahi group.

"These **Rock Sculptures** of Gwalior", wrote General Cunningham, "are unique in Northern India, as well for their number as for their gigantic size. They are all excavated in the steep cliff immediately below the walls of the fortress, and are most of them easily accessible. There are small caves and niches in almost every place where the face of the rock is tolerably smooth and steep, but the more prominent excavations may be divided into five principal groups, which I will designate according to their positions, as 1st, the Arwahi group; 2nd, the South-western group; 3rd, the North-western group; 4th, the North-eastern group; 5th, the South-eastern group. Of these the first and the last, which are by far the most considerable both in number and size, are the only sculptures that have attracted travellers." Most of them were mutilated by order of the Emperor Babur, 1527, only seventy years after they were made. Babur himself records the fact in his Memoirs: "*I directed these idols to be destroyed*". The statues, however, were only mutilated, and the broken heads have since been replaced by the Jains with coloured stucco.

The *Arwahi group* consists of twenty-two principal figures, which are accompanied by six inscriptions, dated Sambat 1497, 1510 = A.D. 1440 and 1453, during the sway of the Tomara Rajas. The chief statues are: No. 17 a colossal figure of Adinath, the first Jain pontiff, who is known by the symbol of a bull on the pedestal. This has a long inscription, dated 1440, in the reign of Dongar Singh. The largest figure, the colossus, No. 20, is 57 ft. high, six and a half times the length of the foot, which is just 9 ft. The extreme W. figure of this group, No. 22, is a seated colossus upwards of 30 ft. high, of Nemnath, twenty-second Jain pontiff, known by a shell on the pedestal.

"The *South-western group*, just outside the Arwahi wall, consists of five principal Jain figures. No. 2 is a sleeping female 8 ft. long, lying on her side, with her head to the S. and face to the W. No. 3 is a seated group of a male and female with a child, who are Siddhartha and Trisala, the reputed father and mother of the infant Mahavira, the last of the twenty-four Jain pontiffs. The sleeping female also is probably intended for Trisala." S. of this group is the Gargaj Gate (closed). A car should be ordered to the ravine exit, for the Jain sculptures on the S.E. face are more than a mile from this point, by a road to Lashkar, and round to the last group.

The *South-eastern group* is the most important group of colossal statues which occupy the whole face of the cliff for upwards of ½ m. They are all of date 1468-73, and are the latest of such works in India. In many cases a screen-wall has been left in front of the shelves as at Ellora. The table (p. 236) gives details of each statue.

The *North-western group* is best visited by passing round the N. side of the city; the figures, however, are insignificant.

The New City, or **Lashkar** (Usha Kiran Palace H.).—After Daulat Rao Scindia obtained possession of Gwalior in 1809, he pitched his camp to the S. of the fort, and the populated area still retains the name of Lashkar, or The Camp. The *Sarafa*, or Merchants' Quarter, is the Chandni Chauk of Gwalior. In the *Phul Bagh* are the *Jai Bilas* and *Moti Mahal Palaces*. Much of the Jai Bilas Palace has now been opened as a museum, although the Maharaja still lives there. There is a fine collection of Victorian, Indian and Chinese furniture and paintings, as well as weapons and trophies. Among the curiosities are: a silver model electric train running the length of a 40 ft. dining table, and carrying decanters and cigar boxes: two of the world's largest chandeliers, said to weigh 3 tons each and carrying 500 electric candles: a carpet claimed to be the largest in Asia: and furniture constructed of solid glass. In the centre of Lashkar is the Jayaji Chauk and the *Barah*, or *Old Palace*. The King George Park close by contains a Hindu temple, a Muslim mosque, a Sikh *gurdwara*, a Theosophical lodge and a statue of Maharani Sankhyaraja Sahiba (d. 1919); also another Museum (1910).

The water supply comes from Tigra reservoir, 9 m. W., on the Sank river.

The later buildings worthy of a visit are the *Dufferin Sarai*, the *Jinsi Building*, the *Jayaji Rao Memorial Hospital*, and the *Victoria College*, *Maharaja Jayaji Rao's Cenotaph*, the *General Post Office*, the *Theatre Hall*, and the *Market*. The New Race-course, on the road connecting Lashkar and Morar, is used by the Gwalior Sports Association for All-India and other matches. The old race-course was N.W. of Morar.

The Madho Sagar Lake was for some time a flying-boat base.

Lashkar presents a scene of the utmost animation at the Dasehra festival (in October) procession to the State temple at the Gurki, also when the Muharram procession is held on the ninth day of the period of mourning annually observed by Shiah Muslims, in remembrance of the murder of Hosain at Kerbela in A.D. 680. In this a State Taziya is carried.

From Gwalior two light railways run: one N.E. to Bhind (53 m.), and the second W. by S. to Sabalgarh and Sheopur (124 m.).

Shivpuri or **Sipri** (C.H., formerly the summer headquarters of the Gwalior administration), lies on a plateau, 1300 ft. above sea-level, on the Agra-Bombay road; 73 m. from Gwalior, by road. This runs through a National Park, containing tiger, panther, deer and other big game—sometimes to be seen on the road. Near Sakhya Sagar (lake) are the handsome mausoleums of Maharani Sakhya and Maharaja Madho Rao. Metalled roads run N. to Gwalior (74 m.), S. to Guna (61 m.), and E. to Jhansi (81 m.). The old and historic town of **Narwar** (Nalapura) can be reached by motor, 26 m. to the N. The fort has a perimeter of 5 m. and is 500 ft. above the plain, with old guns. A Jait Khamba has inscriptions of Tomara Rajas.

About 7 m. S. of Dholpur there is a bridge over the Chambal, 2714 ft. long, built of the famous red sandstone of Dholpur, a ridge of which, from 560 ft. to 1074 ft. above sea-level, runs for 60 m. through the territory, and has many quarries. The river is bordered by a labyrinth of ravines, some of which are 90 ft. deep and extend to a distance of 4 m. from the river-banks. The floods of the river are very remarkable. The highest recorded flood above summer level rose no less than 97 ft. Higher up the river, in what was Kotah state, a great hydro-electric scheme is under way.

804 m. **Dholpur** (R.) is the chief town of the former Jat State of that name.

It was created in 1805, when the Governor-General (George Barlow) gave the last Jat Rana of Gohad (a State founded in 1505), three of Scindia's districts N. of the Chambal, and transferred Gwalior and Gohad to Scindia. In 1658 Aurangzeb defeated his elder brother Dara Shikoh at Ran-ka-chabutra, 3 m. E. of Dholpur, and in 1707 Aurangzeb's sons, Azam and Mu'azzam, contending for the crown, fought a great battle at the village of Bareta, near Dholpur, the former being killed and the latter becoming Emperor, with the title of Bahadur Shah. The palace of Dholpur is built of red sandstone. The High School is housed in a building originally built as a mausoleum of Sadik Muhammad (d. 1597), a general of Akbar. A n.g. railway runs from Dholpur to Bari, 20 m., and to Tantpur (37 m.).

Among other subjects of archaeological interest in Dholpur State are: (1) Shergarh fort, which is supposed to have been built some 3000 years ago by Raja Maldeo. It was repaired and rebuilt by several Rajas in the later generations. In 1540 Sher Shah, of the Sur dynasty, who drove Humayun out of India, restored it and gave it its present name of Shergarh. It was last used by Maharaja Rana Kirat Singh in the early part of the 19th century; but is crumbling away. (2) The fort of Bari, which was built by the Ghori King Firoz Shah in 1286. It is now used as headquarters of the Bari Tahsil. (3) Khanpur Mahal, which is situated some 3 m. to the S. of Bari, and consists of a long and picturesque series of pavilions, the principal of which are enclosed by a wall. The Mahal was built for the Emperor Shah Jahan by Safi Khan Aziz Khan, a local Mansabdar. The palace was never occupied and gradually fell into ruin. Some of the pavilions, however, have been repaired. Below, on Talshahi lake, duck shoots used to be held by the former rulers. (4) Mach Kund, a famous old tank, is surrounded by temples both ancient and modern, the older falling to pieces. It is regarded as a sacred place, and its name is traced back to a Raja Mach, twenty-fourth of the Surajbansi, who reigned nine generations before the birth of Sri Ramchandra. (5) Ram Sagar. This is an extensive irrigation tank constructed by Maharaj Rana Ram Singh (1901-11) to supply water to the surrounding villages in Tahsil Bari. Around Ram Sagar is a sanctuary in which tigers and other wild animals may be seen moving about quite regardless of man.

835 m. from Bombay, **Agra Cantonment** station where travellers by this route alight for the hotels (Route 13). The Central Ry. runs through the Raja-ki-Mandi station (where there is a branch to Agra city) to

868 m. **Muttra** Junction (p. 290), passing **Sikandra** (p. 310). From Muttra the line continues as in Route 12 to

957 m. **DELHI** Main Station (Route 14).

ROUTE 10

BOMBAY to DELHI by **Surat, Broach, Miyagam** (for Dabhoi), **Baroda** and **Ahmedabad,** by broad-gauge; thence by metre-gauge of the Western Ry. to Delhi (849 m.) by **Mehsana, Palanpur, Abu Road (for Mt Abu), Marwar** Junction **(for Luni** Junction, branch line to Hyderabad, Sind and Karachi), **Jodhpur Merta Road** (for **Bikaner**), **Ajmer, Phalera** Junction, JAIPUR, **Bandikui** Junction, **Alwar, Rewari,** and **Gurgaon.**

For air-travellers, there are frequent services from Bombay to Delhi. The flight can be broken for sightseeing at Ahmedabad, Udaipur and Jodhpur.

Both the "Saurashtra Mail" (Route 11) and the "Gujarat Mail", start from the Central station of Bombay and run over the broad-gauge line of the former B.B. and C.I. Ry. This railway was opened from Bulsar to Ahmedabad in 1860-63 and was brought into Grant Road in 1864, being extended to Church Gate in 1870. From Ahmedabad the journey to Delhi is continued over the metre-gauge line *via* Marwar Junction, to Ajmer, Jaipur, Bandikui, Alwar and Rewari. Total distance to Delhi 845 m.

At Marwar Junction the former Jodhpur State railways branch off, and passengers for Karachi and Sind used formerly to proceed this way, but since partition the railway has been interrupted at the Pakistan frontier, and the mail train now stops at Barmer.

6 m. **Mahim** station, where the railway crosses a causeway connecting the island of Bombay with the island of Salsette. There was a Portuguese fort here. The Mahim causeway was constructed (1864) largely at the expense of the first Lady Jamsetjee Jeejeebhoy.

At 29 m. the railway crosses the Bassein creeks; the S. bridge is 4313 ft. long (1864) and the N. 1611 ft.

44 m. the Vaiturni river (near Virar) crossed again at 45 m.

105 m. **Daman Road** (now called **Vapi)** station (P.W.D.B.) (permit from Executive Engineer, Surat). *Daman* (Damão) is a little over 148 sq. m. in area, and consists of three separate portions, Damão, Dadra, and Nagar Haveli. It was seized by the Portuguese in 1531, and finally was ceded by Bahadur Shah of Gujarat in 1559 in return for an alliance. The Indian Government after pressing for its rendition for several years, occupied it in 1961. The town (of historic interest) is situated on the Damão Ganga river, with a bad bar and a roadstead, but in the days of small ships had a very considerable trade. In the main fort, Damão Grande (once a Diocese), on the left bank, are ruins of monasteries and two churches and also the houses of the former Governor and the public offices. The smaller fort of St Jerome, opposite, is more modern. At Damão Paquena (7½ m.) on this bank is a Customs Inspection Bungalow, permit from Assistant Commissioner, Salt, at Surat.

111 m. **Udvada** station. Remarkable as containing the oldest Parsi sacred fire in India. It is said to have been originally brought from Persia by the Parsis, and first kindled at Diu in A.D. 700. The Fire-temple is modern.

At 118 m. is the Par river.

121 m. **Bulsar** station. Near it is the village of Tithal, on the seacoast, where many inhabitants of Gujarat resort in the hot season. There are fine sands. Motor service from Bulsar E. to Dharampur (18 m.); Wilson Hills (34 m.), height 2300 ft.; also to Nasik (95 m.).

At 126 m. is the Auranga river.

145 m. **Navsari** station. The headquarters, from the earliest days, of the Parsi community. Here the Zoroastrian Priesthood receive their initiation and confirmation. There are sanatoria for Parsis at Maradi and Umreth.

At 150 m. is the Poorna river, and at 156 m. the Mindhola river.

163 m. **Surat** station (pop. 1971, 471,000; R., D.B., 2 m.). The name is connected with Saurashtra, or Sorath, a term applied to the neighbouring districts of Gujarat and Kathiawar, which occurs in the *Mahabharata* and the *Periplus*, and which has now been revived by independent India. It is variously interpreted as meaning the "good land" or "the land of the Suras". Surat had a large trade in 1600, and even in 1796, after some decline, held 800,000 people, the port being much frequented by European traders.

Situated on the River Tapti, it is surrounded on the land side by a wall about 5½ m. in circuit, with twelve gates. Except the main street, running from the station road to the castle, the streets in Surat are narrow and tortuous, and some of them still bear marks of the great fire in 1837, which raged for nearly two days. Again in 1889 a fire broke out, which raged over twelve hours and destroyed much of the city. Besides fires, Surat has suffered severely from floods.

About the 12th century the Parsis, who were driven from Persia 500 years before and had settled in *Sanjan*, 70 m. S. of Surat, found their way here. In 1512 the Portuguese sacked the then open town. On the 26th February 1573 it surrendered to Akbar after a siege of one month and seventeen days. Under the Mughals, as the "Gateway of Mecca", it became a port of primary importance for trade and pilgrim traffic; and the Banyas of Surat grew fabulously wealthy. The English began to trade, and in 1612 the Mughal Emperor sent a *farman* authorising an English envoy to reside at his court, and opening to English subjects the trade at Surat.[1] In 1615 Captain Downton, with four ships, mounting eighty guns, defeated the Portuguese fleet, consisting of four galleons, three other large ships, and sixty smaller vessels, mounting in all 134 guns. This victory off Swally at "Bloody Point" was decisive in establishing British superiority over the Portuguese.

Dutch trade commenced in 1616, and for some years competed successfully with the English there. The French Factory was not founded till 1668, when the agents of the French E.I. Company (1664) settled at Surat. On the 5th January of the same year the prosperity of Surat received a severe blow from Sivaji, the founder of the Mahratta Empire, who with 4000 horse surprised the city, and plundered it for six days. The defenders of the English Factory, under Sir George Oxenden, President 1663-1669, defied him and recommended Sivaji to "save the labour of his servants running to and fro on messages, and come himself with all his army", and in the end werel eft unassailed. Their courageous defiance so pleased Aurangzeb that he sent Oxenden a robe of honour, and granted the English a reduction in customs. The walls of Surat up to this time were of mud, but they were now ordered to be built of brick.

In 1687 the Presidency of the English Factory was transferred to Bombay from Surat. In 1698 the E.I. Company became faced with an English rival as the New London Company obtained a Charter, and on the 19th of January 1700 Sir Nicholas Waite, President for the New Company, arrived at Surat. A struggle between the Companies continued till 1708, when they were united. This marked a new era for the English at Surat, then the greatest emporium of W. India. A dock was built (1720), and in 1723 there were two British shipyards. In 1735 an Indiaman was launched.

In 1759 the Nawab of Surat, provoked by misgovernment and oppression of the Company's officers, started a conflict. The townspeople welcomed the arrival of British forces, whose

[1] There is an excellent account (with illustrations) of the Surat factory in *British Beginnings in Western India*, by H. G. Rawlinson (Oxford, 1920).

attack from Athwa resulted in the complete defeat of the Nawab's troops. He then signed a treaty by which the castle and fleet were made over to the British for a yearly stipend of Rs. 200,000. This arrangement was confirmed by the Emperor at Delhi, and the British authority was firmly established in Surat, which was definitely taken over in 1800. In 1842 the last titular Nawab died without a direct heir, and the flag of Delhi was removed from the castle.

The **Castle** stands at the point where the Tapti bridge abuts on the banks of the river. It was erected by Khudawand Khan about 1546, and is a brick building with walls about 8 ft. thick, much modernised. There is a good view of the city and river from the S.W. bastion. Over the E. gateway is an inscription, and adjoining it is the well-kept *Victoria Garden*, of 8 acres.

The European factories are all near I.P. Mission High School. The remains of the original *English Factory* are near the way to the Kataragam Gate, close to the river, on the N. side of the city. It is doubtful whether, in spite of the tablet to that effect, the house occupies the actual site. Near it is the *Portuguese Factory*, where some records are still kept. A wooden cross marks the site of the church. Close to this are the vacant sites of the *French Lodge* (abandoned in 1723 for Mahé) and the *Persian Factory*. The Dutch Factory was outside. There is a fine view of the town from the *Clock Tower*.

The **English Cemetery,** N. of the city, on the Broach road, should be visited. To the right on entering, is the massive mausoleum of Sir George Oxenden, President of Surat and Bombay, who died on 14th July 1669, and his brother Christopher (d. 1659). The structure is composed of two tombs. The first, a domed building with four pinnacles at the corners, was erected over the grave of Christopher, and a Latin inscription in the old English character, written by his brother, was placed inside on a small marble slab. On the death of Sir George, it was enclosed in another building, similar in style, but two-storeyed, and surmounted by a dome which resembles an open cross. In the upper compartment is a large marble tablet bearing an inscription. Close by is another tomb, supposed to be that of Gerald Aungier (d. 30th June 1677), Oxenden's successor; it remained for years without an inscription, but now bears a tablet. Out of 400 tombs, ranging in date from 1646 to the middle of the 19th century, over seventy are in memory of children under the age of five.

The adjoining **Dutch Cemetery** contains huge monuments. The most striking is that of "His High Nobility" Baron Adriaan van Reede (d. 15th December 1691), "Commissary for India of the United Netherlands East India Company, representing in that capacity the Assembly of the Noble Lords of the Seventeen", who was the author of the *Hortus Malabaricus* and the collector of valuable books and curiosities which he sent to Holland. The tomb consists of a double cupola of immense dimensions with a gallery above and below, supported on handsome columns. It was formerly decorated with frescoes, escutcheons and passages from Scripture, and its windows were filled with wood-carving. A bill is extant charging the Dutch Company with Rs. 6000 for mere repairs. It will be noticed that in the inscription, which is in Dutch, "Cochim" and "Souratte" are engraved in capital letters and "bombai" in small ones. Near the Dutch cemetery is the Armenian cemetery, with many well-carved stones, having inscriptions in the Armenian language. All the cemeteries are kept in good order at the expense of Government.

The chief **Mosques** of Surat are:

1. Khwaja Diwan Sahib's Mosque built about 1530. He is said to have come to Surat from Bokhara, and to have lived to the age of 116. 2. The Nau Saïyid Mosque, "Mosque of the Nine Saïyids", on the W. bank of

the Gopi Lake. 3. The Saïyid Idrus Mosque, in Saïyadpura, with a minaret, one of the most conspicuous objects in Surat; it was built in 1639 in honour of the ancestor of the present Kazi of Surat. 4. The Mirza Sami Mosque, built in 1540 by Khudawand Khan, who constructed the castle.

The **Tombs of the Bohras** deserve a visit. There are two chief **Parsi fire-temples,** built in 1823. The Hindu sect of the Wallabhacharis has three temples. The **Swami Narayan** temple, with three white domes, is visible all over the city. In the two old temples in the Ambaji ward the shrines are 15 ft. underground, a sign of Muslim persecution. The **Shravaks,** or Jains, have forty-seven temples, some 200 years old. There are several *Cotton Mills* in Surat. Gold and silver wire and spangle manufacture and brocade work are important industries; while carved sandalwood and inlaid work are still manufactured to some extent. Silk weaving is the chief "home industry".

Beyond the Hope Bridge (3 m.) is *Rander*, built on the site of a very ancient Hindu city (200 B.C.), destroyed by the Muslims in 1225. The Jami Masjid stands on the site of the principal Jain temple. In the façade the bases of the Jain columns are still visible, and the doorstep is reputed to be a great idol placed head downwards. In another mosque are the wooden columns and domes belonging to a Jain temple, the only wooden remains of the kind in India.

Besides the three cemeteries in the city, there was another place of interment for Europeans at **Swally** (Suvali) the old seaport of Surat, about 12 m. W., outside the mouth of the Tapti. Here, according to his friend Edward Terry, chaplain to Sir Thomas Roe's embassy to the court of Jahangir, was the grave of Thomas Coryat, the "English Fakir" and author of "Coryat's Crudities", who tramped on foot from London to India, limiting his expenses to twopence a day, which he procured by begging. From the Mughal Court at Ajmer (p. 263) he walked to Surat, where he arrived desperately ill with dysentery and died in December 1617. All trace of his grave has disappeared, although local tradition identifies it with a monument in the Muslim style at Rajgari, a village near Swally. At Jajira, not far from Swally, is a lighthouse on the N. bank of the Tapti, near the mouth of the river; and adjoining it is a tomb with a high dome which bears no inscription but is known as Vaux's Tomb. Vaux was Deputy-Governor of Bombay and was drowned with his wife in 1697 by the upsetting of their boat on the river.

Near Swally is the little seaside village of **Dumas,** the residence of the Nawabs of Sachin, who, like their relatives, the Nawabs of Janjira (44 m. below Bombay on the coast), were descended from the Sidi (Abyssinian) admirals of the coast.

The Tapti Valley Ry. (opened 1900) runs from Surat to Amalner (147 m. through Nandurbar; continued by the Central Ry., 35 m., to Jalgaon (p. 118).

After leaving Surat the *Tapti* or *Tapi river* is crossed by railway and road bridges.

From (194 m.) *Ankleswar* Junction a branch runs (41 m.) N.E. to *Rajpipla* capital of the former Rajpipla State whose late Ruler was well known in English racing circles.

Close to Broach the *Narbada* or *Narmanda* river is passed by the Silver Jubilee bridge (1935), consisting of 16 spans of 280 ft. (no roadway).

200 m. **Broach** (*Bharoch*) (pop. 92,000 in 1971) Junction (R., D.B.) is a place of extreme antiquity. The author of the *Periplus*, c. A.D. 210, mentions Broach under the name of Barugaza. It was then ruled by a feudatory Gurhara Prince, and subsequently fell under the rule of the Solankis, in the 10th century. It is mentioned by Varamihira, a Hindu astronomer (6th century). The Muslims had appeared in the 8th century from Sind, and ruled Broach from 1297 to 1772.

In 1613 it was visited by Aldworth and Withington, English merchants; and in 1614 a house was hired for a factory. The Dutch set up a factory in 1617. The Nawab did not meet obligations, and on the 14th of November 1772 British troops stormed the place with the loss of their commander, Brigadier David Wedderburn, whose tomb is at the N.W. corner of the fort, in the grounds of the Civil Hospital. It was made over in 1783 to Madhava Rao Scindia; but on the 29th of August 1803 Broach was again taken by the British and annexed.

The city covers a strip of land 2½ m. long and ¾ m. broad, hence by its inhabitants it is called Jibh, or "the tongue". The *Fort* stands on a hill more than 100 ft. above the river, and a massive stone wall lines the river-bank for about 1 m. The streets of the city are narrow and some of them steep. The Jami Masjid, lying at the E. foot of the fort, is an old Jain temple. In an old mansion complex in the S.W. corner of the fort there is a mosque dated 1037 A.D. At the W. end of the city is the spacious 'Idgah, or the Muslim place of worship on the 'Id festivals. At the place called "Krusi", is the Rothfeld Garden, on the high bank of the river.

The Dutch tombs are 2 m. W. of the fort, and some 100 yd. off the road, left. Two of them are from 16 ft. to 20 ft. high. Opposite the Dutch tombs are five *Towers of Silence*, one of them about 15 ft. high. The second tower is still in use.

On the N.W. side of the city, at a distance of 1 m., is the tomb of Bawa Rahan, and a mosque situated on an isolated high hillock.

Outside the E. gate, on the river bank, is the *Temple of Bhrigu Rishi*, from whom the town got the name of Bhrigukachba, contracted into Bharoch. The Parsi surname of Bharucha denotes a man of Broach.

10 m. to the E. of Broach is the celebrated place of Hindu pilgrimage, **Suklatirth,** on the N. or right bank of the Narbada. Here a legendary Chanakya, King of Ujjain, was purified of his sins, having arrived by sailing down the Narbada in a boat with black sails, which turned white on his reaching Suklatirth. Here, too, Chandragupta and his Minister Chanakya, were cleansed from the guilt of murdering his predecessor, and here Chamund, king of Anhilwara, in the eleventh century, ended his life as a penitent. There are three sacred waters—the Kavi, the Hunkareswar, and the Shukal; at the second is a temple with an image of Vishnu.

Opposite Mangleswar, 1 m. upstream from Suklatirth, is an island, in which was a famous *Banyan Tree*, called the *Kabir wad*, or "the fig-tree of Kabir", from whose toothpick it is said to have originated. Forbes, who visited Broach 1776-83, and was the first Collector (1803), says, in his *Oriental Memoirs* (I, p. 26), that it enclosed a space within its principal stems 2000 ft. in circumference. It had 350 large and 3000 small trunks, and had been known to shelter 7000 men. Bishop Heber, in April 1825, wrote that, though much had been washed away, enough remained to make it one of the most noble groves in the world. A small temple marks the spot where the original trunk grew.

225 m. **Miyagam** Junction for a system of narrow-gauge railways (2′ 6″) radiating from Dabhoi.

Dabhoi Junction (Bus service from Baroda; by train from Pratapnagar Station, Baroda), 20 m. E. from Miyagam, is a town of the former Baroda State, birthplace of the Gujarat style of Hindu architecture. The fort is said to have been built by the Vaghela king of Patan or Anhilwara (p. 255), Jayasimha Siddharaja Chapotkaha or Chavana, in the 13th century. There are four gates.

On the *Baroda Gate*, 31 ft. high, with pilasters on either side, the carvings represent the incarnation of Vishnu, and nymphs sporting with makras or crocodiles. Near this are colonnades in the fort walls affording shelter to the garrison. The S., or

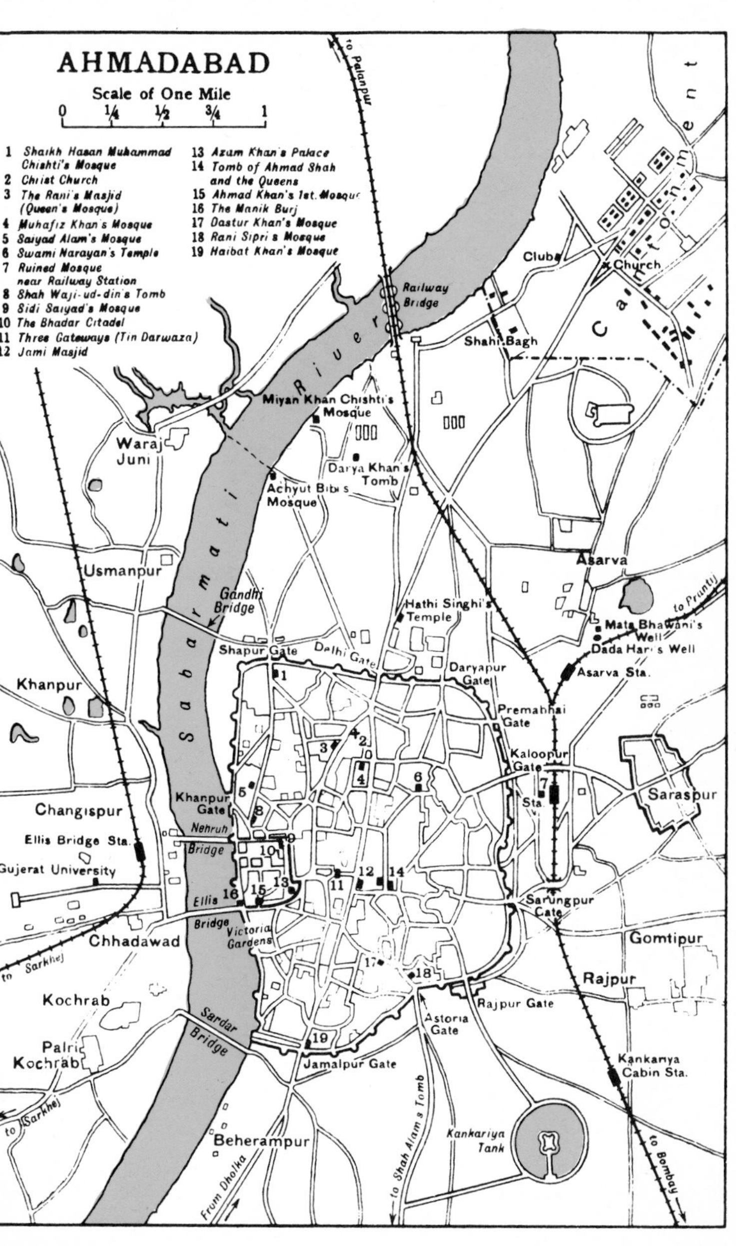
AHMADABAD
Scale of One Mile
0 1/4 1/2 3/4 1
1 Shaikh Hasan Muhammad Chishti's Mosque
2 Christ Church
3 The Rani's Masjid (Queen's Mosque)
4 Muhafiz Khan's Mosque
5 Saiyad Alam's Mosque
6 Swami Narayan's Temple
7 Ruined Mosque near Railway Station
8 Shah Waji-ud-din's Tomb
9 Sidi Saiyad's Mosque
10 The Bhadar Citadel
11 Three Gateways (Tin Darwaza)
12 Jami Masjid
13 Azam Khan's Palace
14 Tomb of Ahmad Shah and the Queens
15 Ahmad Khan's 1st Mosque
16 The Manik Burj
17 Dastur Khan's Mosque
18 Rani Sipri's Mosque
19 Haibat Khan's Mosque
to Palanpur
Cantonment
Club
Church
Railway Bridge
Shahi Bagh
Sabarmati River
Miyan Khan Chishti's Mosque
Waraj Juni
Darya Khan's Tomb
Achyut Bibi's Mosque
Usmanpur
Asarva
Gandhi Bridge
Hathi Singhi's Temple
to Pranti
Mata Bhawani's Well
Dada Hari's Well
Shapur Gate
Delhi Gate
Daryapur Gate
Asarva Sta.
Khanpur
Premabhai Gate
Kaloopur Gate
Sta.
Saraspur
Khanpur Gate
Changispur
Nehruh Bridge
Ellis Bridge Sta.
Gujerat University
Ellis Bridge
Sarungpur Gate
Victoria Gardens
Chhadawad
Gomtipur
to Sarkhej
Rajpur
Kochrab
Rajpur Gate
Astoria Gate
Sardar Bridge
Palri Kochrab
Jamalpur Gate
Kankarya Cabin Sta.
to Sarkhej
Beherampur
to Shah Alam's Tomb
Kankariya Tank
to Bombay
From Dholka

Nandod, Gate is 29 ft. high and 16 ft. 4 in. wide. Trees have grown in the walls and fractured them with their thick roots. The Hira Gate, on the E., is the subject of many local legends. About 10 ft. up, in the N. face of the centre, a man and woman are carved, 4 ft. high, standing with a tree between them, like representations of Adam and Eve. To the left is the figure of a devil. High in the centre face is an elephant, under which the builder of the gate is said to have been interred. Outside is the Vaijanartha shrine. On the N. side of the town is the former palace. On this side there is the Mori Gate. On the left, looking out from inside the tower, is the temple of Mata Kali, a wondrous example of carving, which is now rather worn by the weather.

From Dabhoi Junction a branch railway runs 10 m. S. to **Chandod** station, a celebrated place of Hindu pilgrimage, owing to its situation at the confluence of the *Narbada* and the *Or*. Thousands flock there every full moon.

Another line runs from Dabhoi 23 m. E. to Bodeli, and to Chota Udaipur (46 m.), the capital of the former State of that name (not to be confused with the great Rajput State of Udaipur or Mewar). Other lines go W. from Dabhoi to Baroda and Jambusar, and N. to Timba Road.

244 m. from Bombay is **BARODA**, I.A.C. flights from Bombay and Delhi (R.R., R.H., D.B., Hotels), formerly the Gaekwar's capital. The State covered an area of 8164 sq. m., but in 1948 was absorbed into the Indian Union. Now called Vadodara.

W. of the railway station are situated the residences of many high officials, and a combined State Guest-House and Hotel. E. of the station is the city (pop. 467,000 in 1971), with a Museum and Picture Gallery (1894) in the Victoria Diamond Jubilee Institute, the *Baroda General Hospital*, the *State offices* and *Library*, the Juna Kot, etc. Baroda College has now the status of a University. The Vishvamitri river flows between the railway station and the city, and is spanned by four stone bridges. The city is intersected at right angles by wide thoroughfares, which meet in a market-place, where there is a square Muslim pavilion, a clock tower, and the old Nazar Bagh Palace (1721) with a Shish (mirror) Mahal. One gold and one silver gun of the State were kept in the L.F. Battery. The gold gun contained 280 lb. weight of solid gold, and was drawn by splendid milk-white bullocks stabled hard by. The **Lakshmi Vilas Palace** (now closed) is built in the Indo-Saracenic style of architecture. S. of the Palace, within its grounds, is the Maharaja Fatesingh Museum with a collection of European art.

N. of the city are the former British *Cantonment* and *Residency*. The *Anglican Church* was consecrated by Bishop Heber in 1825, and in 1838 was almost entirely rebuilt. There is a good public garden with a zoological collection on the banks of the river, between the Cantonment and the city.

Baroda is supplied with water from the artificial *Ajwa Lake*, 12 m. distant, completed in 1890. Bus service. The air-field (1937) is at Harsi. Free education has been compulsory since 1904.

The palace of **Makarpura** is 4 m. S. of the city.

The *Naulakhi Well*, 50 yd. N. of Lakshmi Vilas Palace, is a fine structure of the Boali class. The *Baolis*, in Gujarat, are large wells. According to Mr A. Forbes, in his work on Gujarat, the *Ras Mala*: "Some are large circular wells containing galleried apartments; others are more properly described as *waos*, or *baolis*. The *wao* is a large edifice, of a picturesque and stately, as well as peculiar, character. Above the level of the ground a row of four or five open pavilions, at regular distances from each other, is alone visible; the roofs are supported on columns, and are, in the structures of the Hindu times, pyramidal in form. The entrance to the *wao* is by one of the end pavilions; thence a flight of steps descends to a landing immediately under the second dome, which is now seen to be supported by two rows of columns, one over the other. A second flight of steps continues the descent to a similar landing under the third pavilion, where the screen is found to be three storeys in height. In this manner the descent continues stage by stage, the number of the columns increasing at each pavilion, until the level of the water is at last reached. The last flight of steps conducts to the most adorned portion of the *wao*, an octagonal structure, in this position necessarily several storeys high, with a gallery at each storey, and covered by a dome. The structure, which is sometimes 80 yd. in length, invariably terminates in a circular well." Another fine *baoli* may be seen at Adalaj near Ahmedabad (p. 254).

The broad-gauge line of the Western Ry., the route from Bombay to Delhi (865 m.), turns N.E. to Champaner Road, 267 m.; Ratlam, 404 m.; Nagda, 434 m.; Kotah, 570 m. and Muttra, 771 m., where it connects with the Central Ry. (Route 12). An excursion to Champaner and Pavagadh and another to Dabhoi can be made.

The main broad-gauge to Ahmedabad continues to

259 m. Mahi river, bridge 1748 ft. long.

266 m. from Bombay, **Anand** Junction, known for its creamery.

(*a*) A branch line runs N.E. to **Godhra,** 49 m. (p. 289).

At 19 m. (D.B.) **Dakor** station, there are a large lake, and a temple with an image much venerated by the Hindus, with a pilgrimage in October and November.

About 20 m. N. of **Dakor** is the walled town of Kapadvanj (below).

Midway between the two places are the hot springs of **Lasundra,** the highest temperature being 115°. The water is slightly sulphurous, and is efficacious in skin diseases.

At 33 m. is the Mahi river bridge, 1920 ft. long.

(*b*) Another line runs S.W. 14 m. to the town of **Petlad,** and 33 m. to **Cambay,** capital of a former Muslim State.

This port for Ahmedabad is of great antiquity, described by the Arab traveller Masudi in A.D. 913 as standing on the shores of a deep bay surrounded by towns, villages, farms, cultivated fields, trees and gardens. It was governed by the kings of Anhilwara (the modern Patan) up to 1400. Muslim writers then called it the "first city in Hind". The beauty and wealth of the country led to its invasion by Ala-ud-din in 1304, when the city was plundered and its temples destroyed.

Cambay reached the height of its glory about 1600. The Muslim Kings of Gujarat (1485-1535) are often known as "Kings of Cambay". In the second canto of *Hudibras* (1674) mention is made of the "Prince of Cambay", whose "daily food is asp and basilisk and toad". In 1583 letters carried by Fitch, Leedes and Newberry from Queen Elizabeth, were addressed to Akbar, as king of Cambay. The Portuguese and Dutch had already established factories here; in 1613, when the English appeared, it was still a flourishing city, and, although declining as Surat increased in importance, the factory continued to 1722. It was plundered more than once by the Mahrattas. The silting up of the harbour completed its decline; but oil and natural gas, recently discovered may give it a new prosperity.

Cambay was formerly a stronghold of the Jains, and still possesses some of their MSS., second only to those at Patan. The *Jami Masjid* (1325), built with fragments of Jain and Hindu temples, contains the tomb of Imrar Ahmed Kajarani. The Nawab's *Kothi* (residence) was the old English factory.

The town is celebrated for the manufacture of agate, cornelian and onyx ornaments.

The main line continues from Anand to

277 m. **Nadiad** Junction. A branch line (metre-gauge) runs N. to Kapad-

vanj, 28 m. (D.B.), noted for its glass, soap and leather jars for *ghi*. Nadiad (pop. 108,000 in 1971) is the most important town in the Kaira district.

288 m. **Mehmadabad** and **Kaira** Road station. Mehmadabad was founded by Mahmud Bigara, Sultan of Gujarat, in 1479. There is a fine tomb 1½ m. E. of the town, built in 1484 in honour of Mubarak Saïyid, a Minister of Mahmud. A double veranda and screens of tracery give a subdued light. Mahmud Bigara also constructed the *Bhamara Baoli* (well), which is passed on the way to the tomb. It has two stone arches, on which it was said the king's swing was hung. It is 74 ft. long by 24 ft. broad, is entered by four winding stairs, and has eight underground chambers.

Kaira, 7 m. (public conveyances), is said to date from 1400 B.C. Chalukya copperplate grants show that the city was in existence in the 5th century. The chief industry is printing cloth for saris and other garments. In the centre of the town is the Court House, a building with pillars of a Greek order. Near it is a Jain temple, with beautiful dark wood carving. Kaira was formerly of importance, being on the main route from Cambay to N. India, and the boundary of British possessions. It was at one period a military Cantonment of the Gaikwar's troops, but proved unhealthy. The large church was consecrated by Bishop Heber in 1822, and had a beautiful bell, since removed to St Paul's Church, Poona.

Game formerly abounded: the Nilgai, antelope and Indian gazelle being common as were the Sarus, a tall grey crane with a crimson head; wild-fowl, Macqueen's bustard and florican, partridges and quails, sandgrouse, plovers and bitterns and green pigeon. Shooting them is now forbidden throughout Gujarat. The mahseer is found in the Mahi, Vatrak, Meshwa, and Sabarmati rivers, and affords excellent sport.

At 292 m. is the Vatrak river.

306 m. **Ahmadabad** (strictly correct spelling, but usually spelt **Ahmedabad**) Airport (alt. 180 ft.), (R.R., C.H., Hotels, Sightseeing Tours, Tourist Information Centre) is now connected with Bombay and Delhi *via* Udaipur, Jodhpur and Jaipur by frequent flights of I.A.C. It is the principal city of the State of Gujarat, interesting in itself, an excellent centre for sight-seeing, and the mother of the new administrative capital, *Gandhinagar* about 12 m. N. with its impressive buildings styled by Le Corbusier and others.

The famous old city[1] (pop. 1,588,000 in 1971) covers 2 sq. m. on the left bank of the Sabarmati river, across which Gandhi's *ashram* (small museum: handicraft and spinning wheel factories) attracts modern pilgrims. No one should pass this ancient capital, the stronghold of the Northern Jains, without visiting the Jami Masjid, the *Tombs of the Queens* and the Rani Sipri Mosque. The museum in Sanskar Kendra, a building designed by Le Corbusier, has a very fine collection of miniatures.

Ahmedabad, once the greatest city in Western India, is said to have been from 1573 to 1700 the "handsomest town in Hindustan, perhaps in the world". It was founded in 1411 by Sultan Ahmad I, second King of Gujarat, who made Asaval, the old Hindu town, now included in the S. part of the city, his capital. It passed through two periods of greatness, two of decay, and one of revival; it recovered under the Mughals; from 1709 to 1779 it dwindled with them; and it has again increased. It is now a main centre of the cotton trade and manufacture.

Prior to its association with Gandhi's social work, Ahmedabad was rarely visited by tourists; but the fame of this work has attracted many who are now beginning to discover the charm of this ancient city. Although Jahangir is said to have called it Gardabad (the city of Dust) it certainly ranks high amongst the cities of India for the beauty and

[1] Map faces p. 244.

extent of its architectural remains.[1] Its architecture is an interesting and striking example of the combination of Hindu and Saracenic forms. The Jain feeding-places for birds, called "parabdis" which at the first glance look like pigeon-houses, may be seen in many of the streets, and are a peculiar feature. Many of the houses in the streets have fronts beautifully ornamented with wood-carving.

The old parts of the city are divided into quarters wholly separated off from one another and named "pols". The buildings should be seen in the following order:

The Jami Masjid and Tombs of Ahmad Shah and his wives (12 and 14)[2]; the Rani Sipri Tomb and Mosque (18); Dastur Khan's Mosque (17); the Bhadar (10); Shaikh Hasan's Mosque (1); the Rani (or Queen's) Mosque in Mirzapur (3); Muhafiz Khan's Mosque (4).

With half a morning to spare, the visitor should take a car to Sarkhej, across the river to the S.W. giving himself about two hours for the trip. A second afternoon can be devoted to the Kankariya Tank and Shah Alam, S. of the city, and perhaps the modern Jain Temple of Hathisingh, outside the Delhi Gate. Recent extensions to the city may make a guide useful.

Near the railway station are handsome lofty minarets and an arched central gateway, which are all that remain of a mosque (7) which was destroyed when the Mughal commander, Jawad Mard Khan, surrendered Ahmedabad to the Mahrattas in 1753.

The **Jami Masjid** (12), or *Friday mosque*, stands near the centre of the city, on the S. side of the main street (Manik Chauk), a little E. of the Three Gateways. It was built by Sultan Ahmad I (Ahmad Shah) in 1424. The mosque is entered from the N. by a flight of steps. On the S. is another porch leading into the street, and on the E. is the enclosure, in which is the tomb of the founder. The court is surrounded by a cloister. To the W. is the mosque proper. On the threshold of the main arch, embedded in the pavement, lies a black slab brought from Chintaman's Temple, which according to Sir T. Hope, is a Jain idol turned upside down for the faithful to tread on; and touching it on the E. is a white marble crescent, where the Imam stands to lead the prayers.

In the right-hand corner on entering is a gallery, probably used by the members of the Sultan's family. The roof, supported by 260 columns, has fifteen cupolas, with galleries round the three in front. The centre cupola is larger and much higher. The two "shaking" minarets lost half their height in the earthquake of 16th June 1819 and were finally demolished by a tremor in 1957. On the marble slab above the centre of the three *kiblas*, or prayer-niches, are these words in Arabic: "This high and far-stretching mosque was raised by the slave who trusts in the mercy of God, the compassionate, the alone-to-be-worshipped". The Koran says: "Truly mosques belong to God, worship no one else with him". "The slave who trusts in God, the Aider, Nasir-ud-dunya, wa-ud-din Abu'l Fath Ahmad Shah, son of Muhammad Shah, son of Sultan Muzaffar".

Through the E. gate is the **Tomb of Ahmad Shah** (14) (repaired 1587). He was the first King of Gujarat. This domed building has a portico to the S. with eighteen pillars. The windows are of perforated stonework. The central chamber is 36 ft. square. It is paved with marble of different colours. The centre cenotaph is that of Ahmad Shah, the one to the W. is that of his son, Muhammad Shah, and that on the E. is that of his grandson, Kutb Shah, died, respectively, 1441, 1451, and 1459.

50 yd. to the E., across the street, are the **Tombs of the Queens of Ahmad**

[1] The amplest details of the architecture of Ahmedabad will be found in a volume of the *Archaeol. Survey of N. India*, by Dr Burgess.

[2] These numbers in brackets refer to the numbers on the accompanying plan.

Shah (14), Rani Ka Hujra. The houses quite shut out the façade of the mausoleum, which is raised on a platform. In the façade are thirteen highly ornamented carved recesses. Inside is a rectangular court, with a corridor running round it. In the centre are eight large cenotaphs and several small ones. The centre tombstone is made of black stone or marble, inlaid with white, and is finely carved. This building is much out of repair.

Rani Sipri's Mosque and **Tomb** (18) are almost the most beautiful monuments in Ahmedabad. Rani Asni, by whom the mosque and tomb were really built, was one of the wives of Mahmud Bigara, and they were completed in 1514. "They are the first of a series of buildings more delicately ornate than any that preceded."[1] The mosque has two minarets, about 50 ft. high, having four compartments tapering up to the top. The roof is supported by a row of six coupled pillars with single ones behind. The rauza, or tomb, is 36 ft. square, with screens and no arches.

Dastur Khan's Mosque (17), built in 1486 by one of Mahmud Bigara's Ministers. The open stone screenwork that shuts in the cloister round the courtyard is very fine. In the gateway the marks of shot may be seen. A few yards to the E. of Dastur Khan's Mosque is *Asa Bhil's Mound*, the site of the fort of the Bhil Chief, from whom an earlier town of Asaval had its name.

A little to the N.E. of the Jamalpur Gate is **Haibat Khan's Mosque** (19), adapting Hindu elements. Haibat Khan was one of the noblemen of Ahmad Shah's court. The mosque is very plain. The front wall is pierced by three small pointed arches some distance apart. The minarets are small and without ornament, and rise like chimneys from the roof. The central dome, of Hindu workmanship and of great beauty, is slightly raised above the others. The pillars, taken from different temples, display every variety of rich ornament. Except for the form of its dome, the outer porch would suit a Hindu temple.

[1] Sir T. Hope's *Ahmadabad.*

The **Tin Darwaza**, or **Three Gateways** (11), built by Sultan Ahmad I. is of stone richly carved. It crosses the main street a little to the N. of the Jami Masjid. This gateway led into the outer court of the Bhadar, known as the Royal Square, and was surrounded in 1638 by two rows of palm trees and tamarinds (J. A. de Mandelslo's *Voyages*, 1669, p. 76). Facing the Bhadar Gate is a municipal garden. To the W. is the Hemabhai Institute, with a good library and newspapers and periodicals. W. of this Institute—reached by leaving the main road—is the Government Telegraph Office. Near it is the **Mosque of Malik Sha'ban,** with an inscription which records that it was built in the reign of Qutb-ud-din of Gujarat by Sha'ban, son of 'Imad-ul-mulk, in 856 A.H. = A.D. 1452.

The **Bhadar** (10), an ancient enclosure or citadel, built by Ahmad Shah, 1411, and named after the goddess Bhadra, a propitious form of Kali, is occupied by public offices. In the E. face is the **Palace,** built by **Azam Khan** (13), the 23rd Viceroy (1635-42), who was called Udai, "the white ant", from his love of building. It is now the Post-Office. S. of the palace are the Civil Court buildings. Over the gate is a Persian chronogram giving the date 1636. The N. entrance to the Bhadar, under an archway 18 ft. high, opens into a regular octagonal hall of great elegance, containing in the upper storey an arched gallery, having in front a low wall of open-cut stone, and each gallery surmounted by a cupola. Underneath this hall is a fine vaulted chamber, entered by a flight of steps at each side, with a reservoir and fountain in the middle. Close to the Jail is a temple to Bhadra Kali Muta.

At the N.E. corner **Sidi Saïyid's Mosque** (9) forms part of the wall. He was a slave of Ahmad Shah I. Two of its windows are filled with delicate stone tracery of tree-stems and branches beautifully wrought. Fergusson, who gives an illustration of one of the windows, says in his *Indian Architecture*, 2, 236-37: "It would be difficult to excel the skill with which the vegetable forms are conventionalised just to the extent required for the purpose. The equal spacing also of the subject by the three ordinary trees and four palms takes it out of the category of direct imitation of nature, and renders it sufficiently structural for its situation; but perhaps the greatest skill is shown in the even manner in which the pattern is spread over the whole surface. There are some exquisite specimens of tracery in precious marbles at Agra and Delhi, but none quite equal to this."

In the S.W. corner of Bhadar is **Ahmad Shah's Mosque** (15), built by him in 1414, being perhaps the oldest here. It is said to have been used as the King's private chapel. The façade is almost bare of ornament. The two minarets are evidently unfinished. The *mimbar*, or pulpit, is adorned with what look like laurel leaves. The architecture shows the first attempts at building a Muslim edifice in what had been a Hindu city. The pillars still bear Hindu figures and emblems. The N. porch, leading into the latticed ladies' gallery, is Hindu throughout, and may be part of a temple *in situ*. To the left, on advancing towards the mosque, formerly stood the Ganj-i-Shahid, or quarter of Martyrs, where the Muslims killed in the storming of the town were buried.

W. of this mosque is the **Manik Burj** (16), or Ruby Bastion, built round the foundation-stone of the city. There is a small round tomb in the yard near the Collector's office, which is said to be that of Ibrahim Kuli Khan, a Persian warrior.

Shah Wajih-ud-din's Tomb (8), built by Saiyad Murtaza Khan Bokhari, 11th Viceroy, 1606-1609, is a very beautiful monument.

Saïyid Alam's Mosque (5), was built about 1420 by Abubakr Husaini. The inner details are as rich as Hindu art could make them.

The **Mosque, Tomb** and **College of Shuja'at Khan**, Deputy Viceroy. It stands 400 yd. N.E. of the Lal Gate of the Bhadar, near G.P.O. It has two slender minarets, and is divided by piers into five bays. Over the kibla are written the creed and date = 1695. The walls, up to 6 ft., are lined with marble. The tomb is of brick, with a marble floor, much damaged. It is called both the Marble and the Ivory Mosque.

The **Rani Masjid (Queen's Mosque)** (3) *in Mirzapur* a few yards to the S. of the D.B. (now the "Grand Hotel"), built probably in Sultan Ahmad I's reign. There are two minarets, unfinished or partly destroyed by an earthquake (1819), now only 33 ft. high. The roof has three domes, and is supported by thirty-six pillars, the taller of which raise the domes to provide light without glare.

N.E. of the mosque is the rauza or tomb (restored). Under the dome are two cenotaphs of white marble; the central one is the tomb of Rupvati (1430-40), a Princess of Dhar. It is in good preservation, while that on the W. side is much injured, both are ornamented with the chain and censer, a Hindu device. Fergusson gives a plan of this mosque, and says: "The lower part of the minaret is of pure Hindu architecture. We can follow the progress of the development of this form from the first rude attempt in the Jami Masjid through all its stages to the exquisite patterns of the Queen's Mosque at Mirzapur."

The **Mosque of Shaikh Hasan Muhammad Chishti**, *in Shahpur* (1), is in the N.W. angle of the city, not far from the Sabarmati, 1565. The minarets are unfinished. "The tracery in the niches of their bases is perhaps superior to any other in the city." On the S. or left side of the central arch is a Persian quatrain. This chronogram gives the date 1566.

East of the Rani's Masjid is the **Mosque of Muhafiz Khan** (4), built in 1465 by Jamal-ud-din Muhafiz Khan, Governor of the city in 1471 under Mahmud Bigara. According to Sir T. Hope, "its details are exquisite", and the minarets of the mosque and those of Rani Sipri "surpass those of Cairo in beauty".

S.E. of this mosque is the modern **Swami Narayan's Temple** (6), finished in 1850. It has an octagonal dome, supported on twelve pillars, and is a fine building with exquisite wood carvings. Close to it in the Panjrapol area and opposite the Polytechnic is a Jain Asylum for Animals.

The enclosure is surrounded by sheds, where many animals are lodged. There is also a room where travellers are put up free on condition that they allow the various insects to feed on them. Close to the S. are nine tombs, each 18 ft. 3 in. long, called the **Nau Gaz Pir,** "the Nine Yard Saints".

In addition to its reputation as a centre for textiles, Ahmedabad has long been celebrated for its Handicraftsmen—goldsmiths, jewellers, etc., who carry the *chopped* form of jewellery (the finest archaic jewellery in India) to perfection; copper and brass-workers, as instanced particularly in the graceful and delicate brass-screens and *pandans* (betel-boxes): carpenters, famous for their carving in *shisham*, or blackwood, of which fine specimens are to be found here; stonemasons, lacquer-workers, carvers in ivory—also for the manufacture of "Bombay boxes"; mock ornaments for idols; leather shields; cotton cloth; calico-printing, gold-figured silks (mentioned by Fryer in 1674), and gold and silver tissues; kimkhwab (*kinkab*), or brocades, the noblest produced in India; gold and silver lace and thread, and all manner of tinsel ornaments.

Its industrial importance is shown by the fact that "the Nagar-Seth", or Lord Mayor, of Ahmedabad is the titular head of all the Guilds, and one of the highest personages in the city.

ENVIRONS.—An excursion may be made to **Lothal** (50 m.)—see also p. 274 for Ry. connections—where excavations have revealed a former seaport of the Indus Valley Civilization period. This is of particular interest to Indian archaeologists, since the most famous sites of this civilisation, Mohenjodaro (477) and Harappa (476) are in Pakistan. All the characteristic features—neat brick-work, scientific drainage, hand tools, seals—are also found at Lothal. For 12 m. round Ahmedabad the country is full of interesting ruins; but only the principal can be mentioned. Just outside the Delhi Gate, on the N., is the **Hathi Singh Temple,** built (1848) partly of white marble surmounted by fifty-three domes and pointed sikaras. The dimensions are of the first order; its style pure Jain. In its sculptures may be seen representations of the twenty-four holy men, or Tirthankars, and hundreds of other images, all similar, but each labelled on the base with the emblem of some distinct Jain. The entrance is from a court-yard surrounded by a corridor, and then ascending a portico richly carved and supported by pillars between two towers. The inner porch has two storeys and a special form of roof. The temple consists of an outer and an inner chamber, both paved with coloured marbles, chiefly from Makrana, in Marwar: in the interior is the image of Dharmnath, represented as a beautiful youth, with a sparkling tiara of imitation diamonds.

N.W. is the ruined Tomb of **Darya Khan,** 1453, Chief Minister of Mahmud Bigara. The dome is 9 ft. thick, and the largest in Gujarat. Near this is a hostel, for students of the R.C. High School, built by the late Sirdar Sir Chinubhai M. Ranchhodlal.

Near by is the **Chhota** (small) **Shahi Bagh,** where it is said the ladies of the royal harem lived. Across the railway line is the **Shahi Bagh,** a fine garden-house, now used as an official residence. A subterranean passage is said to communicate between the two places. The building was erected in 1622 by Shah Jahan, when Viceroy of Ahmedabad, to give work to the poor during a season of scarcity. In the 17th century this was the great resort for the people of the city. The Shahi Bagh is close to the railway bridge over the Sabarmati.

½ m. S.W. of the Shahi Bagh is **Miyan Khan Chishti's Mosque,** built in 1465 by Malik Maksud Wazir; and ½ m. more to the S.W. is **Achyut Bibi's Mosque,** built in 1469 by 'Imadu'l Mulk, one of Mahmud Bigara's ministers, for his wife Bibi Achyut Kuki, whose tomb is close by. There were seven minarets here, all of which were thrown down in the earthquake of 1819.

At Asarva, about ½ m. N.E. of the Daryapur Gate, and close to the Asarva railway station, are the **Baolis,** or **Wells of Dada Hari** and **Mata Bhawani.** The real name of Dada (1435) is said locally to have been Halim, "mild", but he was called Dada Hari because he was the husband of the Dai, or wet-nurse of one of the Sultans. A portico, supported by twelve pillars, gives entrance to three tiers of finely constructed galleries below ground, which lead to the octagonal well, with inscriptions in Sanskrit and Arabic. A second well has pillars round it and a fence wall. Beyond this is a circular well for irrigation. A very narrow staircase leads to the level ground, where by the side of the well are two stone kiosks. About 50 yd. to the W. is Dada Hari's Mosque, one of the best decorated buildings at Ahmedabad, though no marble is employed. The stone is of a dull reddish-grey colour. The bases of the two minarets are richly carved; the tops were thrown down by the earthquake of 1819. To the N. is the Rauza of Dada Hari, or Halim. The N. door is exquisitely carved, but the inside is quite plain.

Mata Bhawani.—This well is about 100 yd. N. of Dada Hari's, but is much older, and perhaps of the time of Kayna Solanki (1063-93), a Chalukhyan ruler when Ahmedabad was called Karanavati. The descent to the water from the platform is by fifty-two steps and pillared galleries, as at Dada Hari baoli.

Most of the houses in the Madhavpura suburb are warehouses, and it is the great business quarter. Saraspur, E. of the railway station, is a distinct walled town, the largest of the suburbs. In this suburb is the Jain **Temple of Chintaman,** built 1638, restored 1868 by Shantidas, a rich merchant. Aurangzeb, while Viceroy, changed it into a mosque. The Jains petitioned the Emperor Shah Jahan, who ordered his son to restore the temple, but in 1666 Thévenot speaks of it as still a mosque.

¾ m. S.E. of the Rajpur Gate is the Hauz-i-Qutb, generally called the **Kankariya Lake,** or Pebble Lake. This is a polygon of thirty-four sides, each side 190 ft. long, the whole being more than 1 m. round. The area is 72 acres. It was constructed by Sultan Qutb-ud-din in 1451, and was then surrounded by many tiers of cut-stone steps, with six sloping approaches, flanked by cupolas and an exquisitely carved water-sluice. In the centre was an island, with a garden called Nagina, or the Gem, and a pavilion called Ghattamandal. On the E. bank of the lake are some Dutch and Armenian tombs, Saracenic in style, with domes and pillars a good deal ruined. The dates range from 1641 to 1689.

The expedition may be continued to **Batwa,** which is almost 5 m. due S. of the Rajpur Gate. Here Burhan-ud-din Qutb-ul-Alam, the grandson of a famous saint buried at Uch on the Sutlej, is interred. He came to the court of Sultan Ahmad I, settled at Batwa, and died there in 1452. The mausoleum, built by Sultan Mahmud Bigara, resembles the buildings at Sarkhej, but the aisles are arched and vaulted, and the dome is raised by a second tier of arches. Much has fallen, the pillars not resisting the thrust. Adjoining it are a mosque and tank. In this tomb there is a small log, which (it is said) one night struck the saint's foot. On his calling out and asking whether it was a piece of iron, stone or wood, the log at once began to contain all these materials. Many have tried to discover its real substance.

The tomb of **Shah Alam,** the son of the saint buried at **Batwa,** is 2 m. S.E. of the city on the Batwa road. Before reaching the tomb the road passes under two plain gateways, and then through one with a Nakkar Khana (music gallery) above the archway, and so into a vast court. To the W. is the mosque. The Rauza is to the E., and is protected by metal lattices; Shah Alam was a spiritual guide of Mahmud Bigara, and died in 1475. To the S. is an assembly hall, built by Muzaffar III (1561-72), and partly destroyed by the British under General Goddard in 1780 to furnish materials for the siege.

The tomb is attributed to Taj Khan Nariali, one of Mahmud's courtiers. Early in the 17th century Asaf Khan (p. 301), brother of the Empress Nur Jahan, adorned the dome with gold and precious stones, now gone. The floor is inlaid with black and white marble, and doors are of open brass-work, and the frame in which they are set, as well as the space between the door-frame and the two stone pillars to the right and left, are of pure white marble, beautifully carved and pierced. The tomb itself is enclosed by an inner wall of pierced stone. The outer wall in the N. is of stone trellis-work of the most varied design, and here Shaikh Kabir, renowned for his learning, who died in 1618, is buried.

The mosque, built by Muhammad Salih Badakhshi, has three large and eighteen small domes. The minarets of seven storeys, handsomely carved and about 90 ft. high, were much damaged by the earthquake of 1819, but have been repaired. To the S. of the mosque is a tomb like that of the chief mausoleum, where the family of Shah Alam are buried. Outside the wall to the W. is a reservoir built by the wife of Taj Khan Nariali, now known as Chandola tank, which has been greatly improved by the Public Works Department.

Sarkhej is 6 m. S.W. on the railway line to Dholka (p. 274). The road crosses the Sabarmati river (the channel of which is about ½ m. broad, but the water in the dry weather is only 2 ft. deep) on a massive iron bridge of fourteen spans, called the Ellis Bridge. On the E. bank is the Victoria Garden, with a marble seated statue of Queen Victoria by G. A. Mhatre. The river-bed is dotted with enclosures for the cultivation of melons, potatoes and other vegetables and the running water is lined with gaily dressed women washing their clothes. The remains of an old bridge will be seen to the S. of the Ellis Bridge; both the road and the old railway bridges were carried away by a great flood in 1875. Near the bridge the city wall is from 40 ft. to 60 ft. high. Near the W. end of the Bridge is the Gujarat University. Close by, is the fine building of the Science Institute, built by the late Sirdar Sir C. M. Ranchhodlal.

At 2¾ m. is the massive brick **Mausoleum of Azam and Mu'azzam,** built probably in 1457. These brothers are said to have been the architects of Sarkhej, and to have come from Khorasan. The immense structure which contains their tombs is raised on a platform.

Just before reaching Sarkhej there are two brick towers about 30 ft. high, the bases of which, close to the ground, have been so dug away that it seems a miracle they do not fall.

Then the road passes under two arches, leading into the courtyard of Sarkhej. To the left on entering is the fine mausoleum of **Mahmud Bigarha**[1] and his sons, and connected with it by a beautiful portico another equally magnificent tomb on the border of the tank for his Queen Rajabai. To the right is the **Tomb of the Saint** Shaikh Ahmad Khatri Ganj Bakhsh,

[1] Reigned 1459-1511. Bigarha means either "with horn-like moustaches" *or* "two forts"—from his capture of Champaner and Junagadh.

called also Maghrabi. Ganj Bakhsh lived at Anhilwara, and was the spiritual guide of Sultan Ahmad I, and a renowned Muslim saint; he retired to Sarkhej, and died there in 1445 at the age of 111. The tomb has a great central dome and many smaller ones. Over the central door of the tomb is a Persian quatrain. It gives the date 1473. The shrine inside is octagonal, surrounded by finely worked brass lattice-screens. The pavement is of coloured marbles, and the dome inside richly gilt; from it hangs a long silver chain, which once reached to the ground. The vast adjoining **Mosque** is of an elegant simplicity; it has ten cupolas, supported on eighteen rows of pillars. The whole of these buildings, according to Fergusson, "are constructed without a single arch; all the pillars have the usual bracket capitals of the Hindus, and all the domes are on the horizontal principle". S. of the saint's tomb is that of his disciple Shaikh Salah-ud-din.

Mahmud Bigarha excavated the great tank of 17½ acres, surrounded it by flights of stone steps, constructed a richly decorated supply sluice, and built at its S.W. corner a splendid palace and harem, which have been repaired by the Archaeological Department.

The Sarkhej buildings have the special interest of being almost purely Hindu, with only the faintest trace of the Saracenic style. A little S. of the lake is the tomb of Baba Ali Sher, a saint even more venerated than Ganj Bakhsh. Close by are the remains of Mirza Khan Khanan's Garden of Victory, laid out in 1584 after his defeat of Muzaffar III, the last Ahmedabad Sultan. Sarkhej was so famous for indigo that in 1620 the Dutch established a factory there. None is grown now.

8 m. N. of Ahmedabad is the beautiful and celebrated *wao vasli* (p. 245), or well of **Adalaj**. There is a model of it in the Bodleian Library at Oxford.

From Ahmedabad main station a line branches off to the N.E. to Khed-Brahma through **Parantij** (41 m.) and Himatnagar (55 m.), the capital of the former Idar State, conquered by sons of Abhi Singh (Subadar of Gujarat, 1731). The famous Sir Pertab Singh, who was three times Regent of Jodhpur (p. 259), was Maharaja of Idar from 1901 to 1911, when he abdicated.

Leaving Ahmedabad, the railway crosses the Sabarmati river quite close to the Shahi Bagh on a bridge which carries the rails for both gauges and a footway.

From Ahmedabad to Delhi by the Western Ry. metre-gauge line.

This railway was opened in 1881.

At 310 m. **Sabarmati** Junction the metre-gauge runs to Delhi, whilst the broad-gauge turns W. for Viramgam and Kathiawar (Route 11). There is also a branch line to the S.W. passing Sarkhej (above) to Dholka (39 m.) and Dhanduka (77 m.) Junction for Botad. The Dholka mosques are beautiful.

322 m. **Kalol** Junction: branch lines 30 m. N.E. to Vijapur, and 17 m. N.W. to Bhoyani Road.

349 m. **Mehsana** Junction. About 18 m. from Mehsana by bus or car is the early 11th-century temple of **Modhera,** dedicated to the Sun God. Rich carvings and a fine tank. Images in the Persian style suggest the cult of Mithras. This is the junction for three branch lines constructed by the Gaekwar of Baroda. They are: (1) a line passing through Kheralu to Taranga Hill, 35 m. N.E.; (2) a line through **Patan,** the historic capital of Gujarat, to Kakosi Metrana Road, 50 m. N.W.; (3) a chord line to **Viramgam** (p. 273), 41 m. S.W., which connects the Rajputana and Kathiawar metre-gauge systems.

On these branch lines two places only need be noticed.

Vadnagar, 21 m. N.E. on the line to Taranga Hill. This place, the site of Anandpura, is stated to have been conquered by a Rajput Prince from Ajodhya (p. 372) in A.D. 145. There are some interesting ruins, including a very fine Kirtti Stambha gateway, and the Temple of Hatkeswar Mahadeo is worth a visit. It is now the religious capital of the Nagar Brahmins, a most influential class of men in Gujarat and Kathiawar. In former years it was the chartered refuge ot a class of robbers known as Dhinoj Brahmans.

Patan, 25 m. N.W. of Mehsana on the site of the ancient **Anhilwara,** capital (A.D. 746) of the Hindu kings of Gujarat, which was taken by Mahmud of Ghazni on his way to attack the temple of Somnath in 1024. It was taken again by Almas Beg or Alaf Khan, brother of Ala-ud-din Khilji, in 1306. The site has been a quarry, but it is still famous for its libraries of Jain MSS, and there are 108 Jain temples.

On the main line is,

362 m. **Unjha** station. Unjha is the headquarters of the Kadwakanbis, a caste of agriculturists with peculiar marriage customs. Marriages among them take place but once in eleven years, when every girl over forty days old must be married on one or other of the days fixed. Should no husband be found, a proxy bridegroom is sometimes set up and married to a number of girls, who immediately enter a state of nominal widowhood until an eligible suitor presents himself when a second marriage takes place.

370 m. **Sidhpur** station, on the Sarasvati river. The place dates back to A.D. 950, and contains the ruins of Rudra Mahaya Temple. It was wrecked by Ala-ud-din Khilji in 1297. The stones are gigantic and the carving superb, but very little of it remains. A row of small temples has been converted into a mosque. Modern temples are very numerous. Mehsana, a division of the former Baroda State, in which Sidhpur is situated, is the only part of Western India in which poppies are allowed to be grown and opium manufactured.

389 m. **Palanpur** Junction (R., D.B.). The chief town of the former Muslim State of that name, now merged in Gujarat State. The line to Deesa has been extended to Gandhidham with a further extension to the new port of **Kandla** (p. 273), whose development has been given the highest priority by the Indian Government, as it is essential to give W. India a substitute port for Karachi. **Deesa** was formerly a British military Cantonment, but was given up in 1928.

425 m. **Abu Road** station (R., D.B.), a railway colony. Mount Abu looks down on it from the N.W.

A few miles away in the former Danta State is the famous temple of **Ambaji**, a great Hindu pilgrimage resort. Abu Road is now connected through Sirohi and Erinpura with the Rajputana road system, and motorable routes exist through Danta and Palanpur to Dungarpur, Udaipur and Idar.

The excursion up Mount Abu is one of the most interesting in India on account of the Jain temples. The ascent to it, 17 m., is by bus or motor. Rooms may be booked at the Palace, Jaipur, or Lake House Hotels, or at the Government D.B. (4 rooms), Tourist Bungalow, Circuit H. (by permission), or Government Cottages. Though of the same formation as the Aravalli range, which runs up to Delhi, Abu is detached by a valley about 15 m. wide. The plateau at the top is about 14 m. by 4 m., and varies in height from 3500 ft. to 5600 ft.

Abu* (3822 ft. above sea-level) was used as the headquarters of the Resident for Rajputana until 1947, and also as a sanatorium for troops. It was at one time in Bombay State and when that State split into Maharashtra and Gujarat, it fell to the latter. As Rajasthan needed it as a Hill Station, Gujarat gave it up on condition that prohibition was maintained there. So Abu is now "dry" and liquor permits must be obtained from the Tourist Office. The climate is cool in winter. (T.B.)

Abu is remarkable for the number and variety of its birds and for the flowering trees in its jungles. In the rains there are numerous orchids, and mushrooms are found in quantity.

In Abu are the former Residency (now occupied by the Governor of Rajasthan), and many private houses on the margin of the *Nakki Talao*—a most charming piece of artificial water studded with islands, and overhung by a curious rock that looks like a gigantic toad about to spring into the water. Many of the Rulers from the surrounding parts of India had houses there. Honoria Lawrence (d. 1854), wife of Sir Henry Lawrence, is buried in the cemetery. The surface of Abu is very hilly, with few and narrow motor roads. Ponies can be hired. The views over the plains from various points, such as the Crags, are exceedingly fine. The most accessible is called *Sunset Point*, S.W. of the lake. There was til recelntly a Lawrence School for the children of British soldiers, now a Police Training School, as well as an R.C. High School conducted by the Irish Lay Brothers, and a branch of the Ajmer Convent. At the Rajputana Club tennis, racquets, squash, badminton and cricket are available, and there is a sporting golf-course about a mile distant, but polo is no longer played.

The old Agency Office is now occupied by the Railway Survey Office.

The **Dilwara Temples**,[1] one of the great attractions of Abu, are reached by a good road (1½ m.). No official pass is now needed by visitors, but leather articles must be left outside. Open noon until 6 p.m.

The temples are very beautiful, containing the finest marble-carving in India: they find a fitting framework in their nest of mango-trees, with hills surrounding them on all sides.

"The more modern of the two temples is usually ascribed to the same brothers, Tejapala and Vastupala, whose names are associated with the triple temple at Girnar; the inscriptions, however, ascribe the erection and endowment to Tejapala alone. This was consecrated in 1230 and for minute delicacy of carving and beauty of detail stands almost unrivalled." (Note the lotus pendentive in the mandapam—closed hall.) It is dedicated to Neminath, the 22nd Tirthankar.

"The other, built by Vimala, a minister or governor under Bhimadeva in the year 1031, is simpler and bolder, though still as elaborate as good taste would allow in any purely architectural object. Being one of the oldest as well as one of the most complete examples known of a Jain temple."

"The principal object here, as elsewhere, is a cell lighted only from the door, containing a cross-legged seated figure of the Jina to whom the temple is dedicated—in this instance Rishabhanath, or Adinath. The cell terminates upwards in a sikhara, or pyramidal roof, which in these Abu temples, however, are too low to be properly designated spires. To this, as in almost all instances, is attached a mandapam, or closed hall, and in front of this a portico, in this instance composed of forty-eight free-standing pillars; and the whole is enclosed in an oblong courtyard, 128 ft. by 75 ft. inside, surrounded by a double colonnade of smaller pillars, forming porticoes to a range of cells, as usual fifty-two in number, with some extra chapels at the S.W. corner; these enclose it on all sides exactly as they do in Buddhist viharas. In this case, however, each cell, instead of being the residence of a monk, is occupied by one of those cross-legged images of Jinas which belong alike to Buddhism and Jainism. In other religions there may be a great number of separate chapels attached to one building, but in no other would fifty-two be found, as in this example, each containing an image of a Tirthankar, and all so nearly identical as to be almost undistinguishable. With the

[1] See *Mount Abu*, by Om Prakash Gupta, 1941, and brochures available at Rajasthan Tourist Information Centre (opposite bus stand).

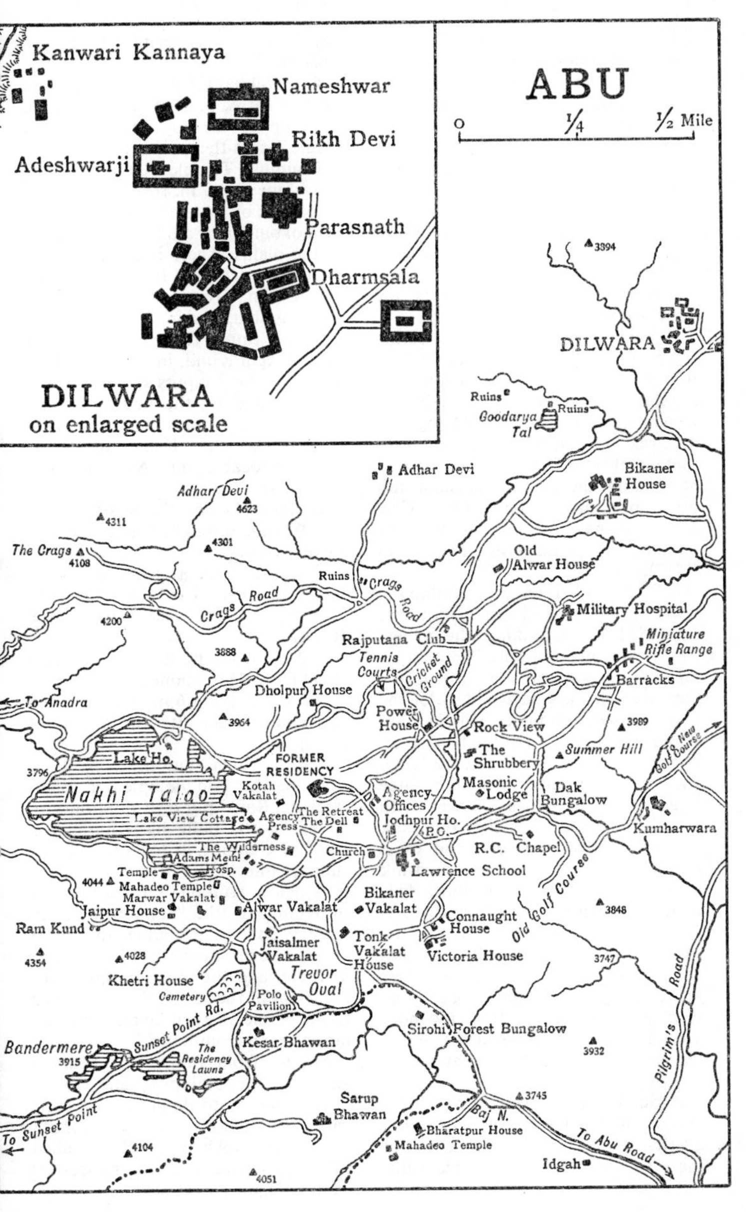

ABU
0
1/4
1/2 Mile
DILWARA
on enlarged scale
Kanwari Kannaya
Nameshwar
Rikh Devi
Adeshwarji
Parasnath
Dharmsala
DILWARA
Ruins
Goodarya Tal
Ruins
Adhar Devi
Bikaner House
Adhar Devi
4623
4311
The Crags
4108
4301
Old Alwar House
Ruins
Crags Road
Crags Road
Military Hospital
4200
Rajputana Club
Miniature Rifle Range
3888
Tennis Courts
Cricket Ground
Barracks
To Anadra
Dholpur House
Power House
3964
Rock View
3989
To New Golf Course
Lake Ho.
FORMER RESIDENCY
The Shrubbery
Summer Hill
3796
Nakhi Talao
Kotah Vakalat
Masonic Lodge
Dak Bungalow
Agency Offices
Lake View Cottage
Agency Press
The Retreat
The Dell
Jodhpur Ho.
P.O.
Kumharwara
The Wilderness
Church
R.C. Chapel
Adams Mem! Hosp.
Temple
Lawrence School
4044
Mahadeo Temple
Old Golf Course
Marwar Vakalat
Bikaner Vakalat
3848
Jaipur House
Alwar Vakalat
Connaught House
Ram Kund
Tonk Vakalat House
Jaisalmer Vakalat
Victoria House
4354
4028
3747
Trevor Oval
Khetri House
Cemetery
Polo Pavilion
Sunset Point Rd.
Sirohi Forest Bungalow
Pilgrim's Road
Bandermere
3915
The Residency Lawns
Kesar Bhawan
3932
Sarup Bhawan
3745
To Sunset Point
Baj N.
Bharatpur House
Mahadeo Temple
To Abu Road
4104
Idgah
4051

Jains it seems to be thought the most important point that the Jinas, or saints, are honoured by the number of their images, and that each principal image should be provided with a separate abode. The long beams, stretching from pillar to pillar, supporting the dome, are relieved by curious angular struts of white marble, which, springing from the lower capital, seem to support the middle of the beam" (Fergusson).

One mile above Dilwara is the Trevor tank.

Achalgarh is reached by following the road past Dilwara for about 4 m. to the village of Uriao (There is a regular bus service from Abu to Achalgarh.) There is a small bungalow at Uria and permission to occupy it may be obtained from the Magistrate at Abu, but there is no khansama and no supplies are available. From Uria a road turns right 1 m. to the first temple of Achalesvar Mahadeva (1412).

S.E. are other temples containing a toe of Siva and a brass Nandi (one Jain, 1513) overlooking the valley. The view is magnificent. These buildings can be seen on the right during the ascent from Abu Road. S. of the first temple is a tank, Manda Kini Kund (*c.* A.D. 900). On the bank is an image of Adi Pal, the Paramara King, with his bow, and near him three large stone buffaloes pierced with arrows. The legend is that this tank was once filled with *ghi*, and these buffaloes came every night to drink it up—till they were all shot. This figure is superior in style and treatment to most; and the same may be said of the statues in other temples around the Hill. Owing to their wonderfully picturesque situation, the Achalgarh temples are, to many, more attractive than the renowned Dilwara temples, though not comparable in size or finish.

Around Mount Abu in the plain and on the hillside are other temples, all charmingly situated; but a visit to these should not be attempted without a guide or person who knows the country intimately, as it is very easy to get lost.

Guru Sikhar (5646 ft.) is the highest peak of Mt Abu. There is now a road right up to the top. A small Siva shrine marks the summit.

Gaumukh Temple, 500 ft. down the S.E. slope and 3 m. from the church, is reached by a path behind the High School buildings, along the main road to the plains. There is a brass figure (facing the temple). Images of Rama and Krishna are on either side of the sage Vasishta, who in Vedic anthology was their tutor. This place is famous for the Agni Kund, in which the four tribes of the Rajputs claim to have been created by the gods, in order to counteract the arrogance and tyranny of the Kshatryas. (Tod wrongly located this Agni Kund at Achalgarh.)

Gautama lies on the S. side of the hill, W. of Gaumukh; 5 m. from Abu. Lovely view.

Rishi Krishna, at the foot of the hill, S.E. side, 14 m. from the Civil Station, is easily visited from Abu Road.

472 m. from Bombay is **Erinpura Road** for the abandoned Cantonment of Erinpura, lying 6 m. W. (so called by Captain Irving after the land of his birth).

483 m. **Falna** station. 25 m. E. is the marble Jain temple of **Sadri** (really at Ranakpur or Rampura, 5 m. S. of Sadri), built by Kumbha, a Rana of Udaipur, in 1440, in a ravine running into the western slope of the hills below Kumbha's favourite fort of Kumbhalgarh. "It is still nearly perfect and is probably the most complicated and extensive Jain temple in India, and the most complete for the ritual of the sect." It is now open to the public and can be reached by a tarmac road from Sadri.

524 m. from Bombay is **Marwar** Junction for Jodhpur, and for a line running E. to Phulad, connecting with the Udaipur railway (p. 212). A tongue of Ajmer territory called Merwara separates Udaipur (Mewar) from Jodhpur (Marwar).

Marwar Junction to the Frontier of Pakistan

From Marwar Junction the Jodhpur railway branches N.W. (opened 1884) to (44 m.) **Luni** Junction, from which it formerly continued W. for 309 m. through desolate country to Hyderabad (Sind), but since partition through traffic to Pakistan has been stopped, and it is not at present possible to get farther by rail than Munabao (183 m.). The Luni river is crossed by a bridge, 1295 ft. long. Balotra (50 m.) is the junction for the salt-works at Pachbadra (10 m.).

110 m. from Luni Junction is **Barmar,** station for **Jaisalmer** (98 m.), capital of the Bhati Rajputs of the "Lunar" dynasty, founded by Jaisal, in 1156. It is famous for buildings constructed of yellow-brown stone, for its handsome Jain temples (open mornings only) and the Fort. The desert track from Barmer, though very bad, is practicable for motors. Jaisalmer can also be reached by rail from Jodhpur by a new metre-gauge line via Pokaran, or by the new asphalt road following the same route. It can also be reached by car *via* Bap from Bikaner. It is well worth a visit, as some of the buildings are beautiful, and it is one of the remotest places in India. The view of the fort in the distance is very striking. (T.B. on opposite side of city from station.)

9 m. away at Ludwara some Jain temples, destroyed by the Ghaznavids and Ghoris, are being restored.

Marwar Junction to Jodhpur and Merta Road

64 m. from Marwar Junction is **JODHPUR** (alt. 771 ft.) (pop. 318,000 in 1971), once capital of the famous State of that name. Rajasthan State Hotel, C.H., R.R., D.B.K., T.B. Tourist Information Bureaux at T.B. There is an extensive and well-equipped airfield, a training-centre for the Indian Air Force. Close by is an Indian Air Force Mess, once a State Hotel.

Jodhpur, otherwise Marwar, the "Land of Death",[1] covered 35,000 sq. m., and was founded from Kanauj, after the defeat of the Rathors there in 1211. The city was built by Rao Jodha in 1459 as a new seat of his government. The wall was built by Maldeo (1532-73).

From Rao Jodha are descended, not only the Jodhpur Maharaja's family, but the princes of Bikaner, Kishangarh, Idar, Ratlam, Jhabua, Sailana and Sitamau. Rao Udai Singh (d. 1581) received the title of Raja from Akbar, and his son, Sawai Raja Sur Singh (d. 1595), conquered Gujarat and part of the Deccan for Akbar. Maharaja Jaswant Singh (d. 1678) commanded the armies of Shah Jahan and Dara Shikoh against the forces of Princes Aurangzeb and Murad in 1658, and died in Kabul, commanding the Imperial Forces there. His son, Maharaja Ajit Singh (d. 1731), drove the Mughals out of Ajmer, and Maharaja Abhai Singh (d. 1750) took Ahmadabad.

The State came into treaty relations with the British in 1818, and was merged into the Indian Union in 1947. Maharaja Sir Umaid Singh, who died in 1947, took a great interest in flying, and was responsible for the development of Jodhpur as one of the premier air centres in the East.

The famous Sir Pertab Singh, who died in 1922, was a member of the Jodhpur ruling family, and acted both as Chief Minister and Regent. He was also for a time Maharaja of Idar.

The city (pop. 318,000 in 1971), S. of a range of sandstone hills running E. and W., is surrounded by a strong wall nearly 6 m. in extent, with seven gates, each bearing the name of the town to which it leads. Some of the houses and temples in the city are of stone richly carved. Amongst the most important buildings are the Temple in the Dhan Mandi (grain market), and the Talaiti Mahal, an old palace now used as the Jaswant Female Hospital.

The **Fort** (no permit necessary)

[1] This derivation is disputed.

stands up boldly. The rock is on every side scarped, but especially at the S. end, where the palace is built on the edge of a perpendicular cliff at least 120 ft. high. There is a notable collection of antique cannon on the ramparts. A modern road winds to a massive Gateway of Victory. Here is the first of seven barriers thrown across the zigzag ascent, having immense portals with separate guards at each. On the wall of the last (Loha Gate) are handprints of fifteen widows of the Maharajas, who performed *sati* (six of them widows of Man Singh (1843)).

At the top of the rock are the highly interesting Old Palaces. There are courtyards within courtyards, all solidly built and surrounded by lattice windows of the most delicate and beautiful designs. There is a very nice small armoury and two painted durbar rooms are shown. At the far end of the ridge, past a row of old cannons, is an old temple to Devi. The view from the palace windows shows the town nestling under the huge rock. The cenotaph to the N. was erected to the memory of Maharaja Sir Sardar Singh. There was formerly great scarcity of water in the fort, and the women had daily to walk all the way to Mandor (see p. 261) to fetch it, but now it is brought up to the top of the fort in pipes. There is a well in the fort 450 ft. deep.

The principal **Tanks** are: the Padam Sagar Tank, in the N.W. part of the city, excavated out of the rock, but of small size; in the same quarter is the Rani Sagar, at the foot of the W. entrance into the fort, with which it is connected by outworks; the *Gulab Sagar*, to the E., is handsomely built of stone, and is capacious, with a smaller one adjoining it; outside the city 1 m. W. is a lake called Akherajji ka Talao, which is a fine sheet, resembling a natural lake. The Kailana Tank, close to the last-named is the largest of all, with a capacity of 191 million cu. ft. of water. The Umaidsagar Lake to the W. of the city supplies the water-works. This has been supplemented by the construction of the Takht Sagar, to which water is led by gravity and pumping from a point in the Aravallis beyond Pali, some 70 m. away.

Farther N. is the old Residency, a fortified mansion among the hills. 3m. N. of the city is the Balsamand Tank, with a palace on the embankment and a beautifully laid-out garden (1936).

Pig-sticking, tennis and polo were the chief sports available at Jodhpur, which has been the training-ground of some of the most outstanding Indian polo players. There is also a somewhat inferior golf-course.

S.E. of the city are the Raikabagh Palace, where the late Maharaja Sir Umaid Singh[1] used to reside, and the new palace on Chhitar Hill, which he caused to be constructed, now turned into an hotel. The Ratanada Palace, 2 m. farther S., is kept for military use. Near Raikabagh are the Jubilee Buildings, containing the Chief Court and administrative offices. 5 m. to the S.W. is Chopasni, a high school for the education of the sons of nobles and Rajputs.

There are two fine hospitals, the "Windham" for men (named after Colonel Windham, a former Chief Minister), and the "Umaid" for women.

The **Willingdon Gardens** and fine stone houses of officials have now replaced a barren tract that formerly bounded the city on the S. side. The Sardar Museum (1909) is comprehensive. There is also a Zoo, and a good library.

At about 1½ m. outside the N.E. angle of the city is a small walled town of 800 houses, called the **Mahamandir**, or "great temple". The roof of the temple is supported by 100 pillars, and the interior is richly decorated. This town is defended by a stone wall, with a few bastions.

[1] He was succeeded in 1947 by his eldest son, Hanwant Singh, who died as the result of an air crash after only a few years on the gădi.

Mandor.—This was the capital of Marwar before the foundation of Jodhpur. It is situated about 5 m. to the N. of Jodhpur. To the right are some of the *Chhattris*, or cenotaphs of the former rulers, erected on the spots where the funeral pyres consumed their remains. Some are fine, massive buildings, that dedicated to Ajit Singh (d. 1731) being the largest and finest. These "proud monuments", as Colonel Tod calls them,[1] are built of "a close-grained free-stone of a dark brown or red tint, with sufficient hardness to allow the sculptor to indulge his fancy. The style of architecture here is mixed, partaking both of the Saivite and the Buddhist, but the details are decidedly Jain, more especially the columns."

On the left of the road is a pantheon called the Shrine of the 300 million gods, containing a row of gigantic painted figures of divinities and heroes. At the end of the long building where these figures are arranged is a curious fresco of a sea-piece. Near this is the stone palace of *Abhai Singh*, who succeeded Ajit Singh. The rocky plateau, site of the ancient city, is covered with heaps of debris, in the midst of which is a large ruined temple. Farther on is a group of *Chhattris* of the relations of the ancient Chiefs. Beyond are the Panch Kund, or five small tanks, recessed naturally in the rock.

A new railway and road link Jodhpur with **Jaisalmer** (see p. 259).

Osian, 41 m. from Jodhpur on the Jaisalmer line, has a group of ancient Jain temples. The town is inhabited by hundreds of peacocks.

64 m. from Jodhpur and 128 m. from Marwar Junction is **Merta Road** Junction for Bikaner and Bhatinda. **Merta**, a fortified Marwar town, is 9 m. S.E. and connected by a branch. Only gateways remain. Near this town was fought a decisive battle on the 11th September 1790, between the disciplined battalions of Mahdaji Rao Scindia, under the famous Benoit de Boigne,[1] and the forces of the Maharajas of Jodhpur and Jaipur. The Rajputs fought with desperate valour: "It is impossible", wrote de Boigne, "to describe the feats of bravery performed by the forlorn hope of the enemy, the *jard Kapra wallahs*" (men in yellow raiment, the garb of doom); but, in spite of their repeated charges, they were totally defeated. Close to the station is an enclosed Jain monastery of great sanctity.

[1] For full details see Tod's *Rajasthan*, ii, 835 (Oxford edition, 1920).

Merta Road to Bikaner
(Opened 1891)

35 m. from Merta Road is **Nagaur.** The crenellated wall, houses and groups of temples make an agreeable break in the monotonous desert.

At 59 m. is **Chilo,** where the old Bikaner railway commences.

107 m. from Merta Road is **Bikaner** (Rajasthan State Hotel, C.H., D.B.K., alt. 760 ft.), the capital of the former Bikaner State. The city (pop. 188,000 in 1971) was founded in 1488 by Rao Bikaji, son of Rao Jodhaji of Jodhpur (d. 1495), a Rajput of the famous Rathor clan, from whom the present house of Bikaner is descended.

A former Maharaja, Sir Ganga Singh, who succeeded in 1887 and died in 1943, was perhaps the best known in Europe of all the Indian princes. He was at the Imperial War Conferences in 1917 and 1919 as a representative of India, a member of the War Cabinet and a British Empire delegate at the Peace Conference. His son, Sir Sadul Singh, who followed, died in 1950, and was succeeded by the present Maharaja Karni Singh.

The State, now part of the Rajasthan Union, had an area of about 23,000 sq. m., consisting largely of desert, and water is only found at a depth of 150 ft. to 300 ft. The population is chiefly agricultural, and a fine breed of sheep, much valued for their wool, is produced. The Bikaner camels are well known, and the

[1] See the first half of S. Bidwell's *Swords For Hire* (Murray, 1971).

Camel Corps (Ganga Rissala) distinguished itself in China, commanded by Maharaja Ganga Singh in 1900, and in Somaliland in 1903-4. It was also sent to Egypt during the First World War. In the city itself and in the large towns reside numbers of wealthy Marwari merchants, the "Lombards" of India.

The city is situated on an elevation, and has an imposing appearance, being surrounded by a battlemented wall, and possessing many fine buildings. It is the fifth largest city in Rajasthan. The stone carving with which many of the houses are faced is unique.

The *Fort*, containing the old palaces, lying to the N.E. of the city, was begun by Raja Rai Singh (1571-1611), one of Akbar's distinguished generals. It is 1078 yd. in circuit, and the view from outside is picturesque in the extreme. The palace buildings are the work of successive rulers. Among the finest are the Chaubara, erected by Raja Rai Singh; the Phul Mahal, the Chandra Mahal, the Gaj Mandir, and the Kachcheri—all built by Maharaja Gaj Singh (1746-87); and specially the Anup Mahal, dating from the time of Maharaja Surat Singh (1788-1828), the Chetar Mahal and Chini Burj of Maharaja Dungar Singh (1872-87), and the beautiful audience hall, called the Ganga Niwas, built by the late Maharaja, of finely carved red sandstone.

The Fort also contains a fine library of Sanskrit and Persian books, and a valuable armoury, which includes the Order of the Fish and Alam Ambali (golden howdah), presented by Mughal Emperors, also the Nakli and Khasa State Palanquins.

No permit is now required for visiting the palaces.

Facing the Fort is the Public Park. Of modern buildings in the suburbs, the Dungar Memorial College, the Walter Nobles' School, the King Edward Memorial Road, and the temples completed by former Rulers may be specially marked. Outside the city the principal buildings are the latest Palace, Lalgarh, of carved red sandstone, designed by the late Sir Swinton Jacob, the Sardar and Ganga Golden Jubilee Clubs, the Public Offices, and an excellent modern hospital. Sadul Singh, when heir-apparent, constructed a charming garden-house and garden on waste land outside the city not far from the golf-course. Gajner Palace, on a lake famous for its Imperial sand-grouse shoots, is 19 m. S.W.

5 m. to the E. of the city is Devikund, where the *Chhattris* (cenotaphs) of the rulers of Bikaner are situated.

Other objects of interest are *Bandasar*, a Jain temple in the S.W. corner of the city, and dating from before its foundation; a *well*, 450 ft. deep, near the Fort, now pumped by electrical power; and *Nagrechiji*, 2 m. S., containing an eighteen-armed image, a relic of Kanauj.

A visit should also be paid to the carpet and other manufactories at the Central Jail, for which Bikaner is famous.

The Bikaner Gang Canal, a portion of the Sutlej Valley Irrigation Project, was commenced in 1925, and opened in October 1927. It irrigates 1100 sq. m. From the headworks at Ferozepore to the gates at Shivpur, a distance of 84 m., both the bed and the sides of the canal are lined with concrete. The experiment was the first of the kind to be made in India.

Bikaner is connected with Bhatinda (201 m. N.); also with Hissar (181 m. N.E.), and *via* Ratangarh, Sadulpur and Loharu with Rewari.

From Merta Road Junction the Jodhpur railway continues N.E. to **Degana**, 155 m. from Marwar Junction, whence there is a branch *via* Sujangarh to Ratangarh (connection with the Bikaner railway), continuing to Hissar (p. 363).

201 m. from Marwar Junction is **Kuchaman Road**, junction of the former Jodhpur and B.B. and C.I. railway lines. The railway carries on thence 20 m. to Phulera, the junction with the main metre-gauge line of the Western Ry.

Between Kuchaman Road and Phulera is the *Sambhar Lake*, on the border of the former Jaipur and Jodhpur States. The surrounding country is arid and sterile, being composed of rocks abounding in salt. The lake is 21 m. long from E. to W. after the rains, when the average breadth is 5 m. from N. to S., but the depth, 1 m. from the shore, is only 2½ ft. The water dries up from October to June, and leaves about an inch of salt in the enclosures. From the 17th century the salt was worked by the Jaipur and Jodhpur Governments conjointly till 1870, when the British Government took leases from both States. The works under the Government of India Salt Department are on the E. and N. edges of the lake.

Excavations at Malisar (4 m.) have disclosed three layers of buildings, the middle layer of Kushan and Gupta periods, with baked bricks, the top dating about A.D. 800. The pottery is unique, and a coin of Huvishka has been found. A tank of burnt clay resembles others found at Taxila, Ur and in Egypt.

Marwar Junction to Ajmer, Jaipur, Alwar, Rewari and Delhi

The main metre-gauge line of the Western Ry. to Delhi proceeds from Marwar Junction (p. 259) towards Ajmer. After leaving

Haripur station (D.B.), 557 m. from Bombay, there is a rocky ascent, which continues until close to

Beawar station (D.B.), 578 m. from Bombay, in Ajmer-Merwara, a long narrow tract skirting the Aravalli Hills between the former States of Mewar and Marwar. There is a shrine here over the tomb of Colonel C. G. Dixon, who was Superintendent of Merwara from 1836 to 1848, and commanded the Merwara Battalion, which he raised (1825), until his death in June 1857. On the shrine, which is an object of worship by the Mers (cp. Kipling's story, *The Tomb of his Ancestors*), there used to be a glass case containing a richly embroidered silk dress, which had come from Paris for the Colonel's Indian wife (see *The India We Served*, by Sir W. Lawrence, p. 38).

611 m. from Bombay **AJMER** Junction, alt. 1593 ft. (C.H., D.B.K., R.R., I.B., Tourist B., Restaurants). Near the station there are also one or two Indian-style hotels. A line runs S. to *Khandwa* (see Route 8).

Ajmer[1] (pop. 262,000 in 1971), ceded by Daulat Rao Scindia (1818), was the capital of the former Chief Commissioner's province of Ajmer-Merwara, now absorbed in Rajasthan.

The city is situated in a basin at the foot of Taragarh Hill (2855 ft. above the sea). It is surrounded by a stone wall with five gateways. According to tradition, Ajmer was founded by Ajaipal, one of the Chauhan Kings.[2] It was sacked in 1024 by Mahmud of Ghazni, on his way to Kathiawar, and again by Muhammad Ghori in 1193. After the invasion of Timur in 1398 it was seized by Rana Kumbha of Mewar. The Muslim rulers of Malwa held it from 1470 to 1531, when it passed into the possession of Maldeo, the Rathor chief of Marwar. It was annexed in 1556 by Akbar, who was fully aware of its strategic importance and made it a royal residence.

Jahangir and Shah Jahan spent much time at Ajmer. An account of the city has been given by Sir Thomas Roe, the ambassador of James I, who was received in audience here by Jahangir[3] with "courtly condescension" on 16th January 1616, and went with him to Ujjain (p. 207) in the following year. While Roe was on his way to Ajmer, he was met by "the famous unwearied walker, Tho. Coryatt, who on foote had passed

[1] See *Ajmer*, by Har Bilas Sarda (Fine Art Printing Press, Ajmer, 1941).

[2] The date of Ajaipal is placed about 1100 by Dr Bühler. Ana, the son of Ajaipal, who built the Ana Sagar embankment, is shown by an inscription found at Chitor to have been living in 1150.

[3] A picture by Sir W. Rothenstein, commemorating the audience, forms one of the frescoes in St Stephen's Hall, Westminster.

most of Europe and Asya and was now in India, beeing but the beginning of his travells". Coryatt had spent £2, 10s. on the journey from Jerusalem to Ajmer: he died at Surat (p. 241) in December 1617.[1]

In 1720 Ajit Singh Rathor, son of Raja Jaswant Singh of Marwar, seized the city, which was recovered by Muhammad Shah, and made over by him in 1731 to Abhai Singh, the son of Ajit, as Viceroy on his behalf. In 1750 Abhai Singh's son Ram Singh, called in the Mahrattas, under Jai Appa Scindia, who seized and held it until 1787, when the Rathors recovered Ajmer, but after their defeat at Merta in 1790 the Rathors had to surrender it again to Scindia. On the 25th of June 1818 Daulat Rao Scindia handed it over by treaty to the British Government.

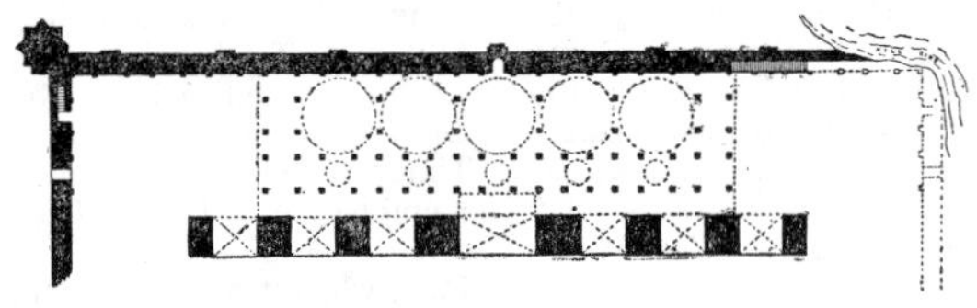

The Arhai-din-ka-jhonpra Mosque at Ajmer.

Ajmer is the headquarters of about 1800 m. of the metre-gauge section of the Western Ry. Near the railway station are extensive workshops employing many thousands of the local inhabitants.

The old **Residency**, now a C.H., with a beautiful view, especially in the morning and evening, is on a hill overlooking the artificial lake called the **Ana Sagar,** constructed by Raja Anaji (1135-50) and lying N. of the city and railway station. It dams the water of the River Luni, which flows into the Rann of Kutch. The Emperor Shah Jahan erected a noble range of marble pavilions on the embankment, which were restored by direction of Lord Curzon (1899). The walk along the *bund*, or embankment (which is public) is very delightful. To the W. is the broad expanse of the lake, and to the E., under the *bund*, is the *Public Garden.* As the Ana Sagar is liable to dry up after two or three years of scanty rainfall the city obtains its water-supply from the *Foy Sagar*, 3 m. higher up the valley, but a new source of supply is being developed. As shooting is prohibited on Ana Sagar, it is the home of many species of wild fowl, including on occasion the flamingo and sea eagle.

Akbar's Palace is inside the city, near the E. wall. The entrance gate is very fine. It was once an arsenal, and then used as a *tahsil* building. The central pavilion has been repaired, and is now used as the local Museum.

The mosque, called the **Arhai-din-ka-jhonpra,** or "The Hut of Two and a half Days", is just outside the S.W. city gate, beyond the Dargah. The name is derived from a tradition that it was built supernaturally in two and a half days. Originally a Jain College, built in 1153, it was damaged by Muhammad Ghori, who took Ajmer in 1192, and turned into a mosque by building a massive screen or façade of seven arches in front of the many pillared hall. This work was done by Qutb-ud-din in about 1200. The rows of slender pillars are probably *in situ.* Their ornamentation is very complex, no two being alike. The mosque is ruined, and only part of the screen of arches (200 ft. long), and part of the Jain hall behind them, now remain, the other three sides of the enclosure having disappeared. The

[1] See p. 243 (*supra*), also *Roe's Journal* Oxford University Press).

work was repaired in 1875-78 and 1900-03, and is a Protected Monument.

The mosque was once very much larger than the one at the Qutb near Delhi, the measurements of the exterior being 172 ft. by 264 ft., and of the interior quadrangle 200 ft. by 175 ft. The mosque proper measures 259 ft. by 57 ft., and has ten domes in the roof borne by 124 columns. The screen in front of it is a work well deserving attention; it is the glory of the mosque, and consists of seven "horizontal" arches like those with which Altamsh adorned the courtyard of the Qutb. In the centre the screen rises to a height of 56 ft., and at the corners above this arch rise two short minarets with Tughra inscriptions. Nothing can exceed the taste with which the Kufic and Tughra inscriptions are interwoven with the more purely architectural decorations and the constructive lines of the design.

The bridle-path to **Taragarh** (Star-Fort) passes this mosque, and reaches the summit in 2 m. The view from the top is very fine; but the ascent is somewhat trying, and had better be made in the early morning. There is also an interesting graveyard of Muslim martyrs, who fell in the assault on the fort.

The **Dargah,** in the S.W. of the city, is a most revered Muslim shrine. It was commenced by Altamsh and completed by Humayun. It derives its sanctity from being the burial-place of Khwaja Muin-ud-din Chishti (1142-1256), who was called Aftab-i-Mulk-i-Hind, the Sun of the Realm of India. He came to Ajmer in 1166. He was the son of Khwaja Usman, and was called Chishti from a quarter in the city of Sanjar in Persia. Of this family of saints and courtiers, Farid-ud-din is buried at Pakpattan, in the Punjab; Nizam-ud-din, Kutb-ud-din, and Nasir-ud-din near Delhi; Shaik Salim at Fatehpur-Sikri near Agra; and Banda Nawaz (1321-1422) at Gulbarga in the Deccan (p. 438).

The memory of the Ajmer Chishti was held in particular respect by the great Akbar, who was accustomed to pay a yearly visit to his shrine. Several of these pilgrimages were made on foot from Agra and other places. The road from Fatehpur-Sikri to Ajmer was so much used by Akbar that he caused "Kos Minars" (masonry columns answering to our milestones) to be erected along the route every 2 m. Several of these minars can still be seen from the railway.

Visitors are expected to remove their shoes before entering the Dargah. Passing through a lofty gateway, a courtyard is entered, in which are two very large iron cauldrons. Rich Muslims on their first visit to Ajmer pay for a feast of rice, ghi, sugar, almonds, raisins and spices, to be cooked in one of these, the contents being ladled out and finally scrambled for by various families connected with the shrine, who live near the Dargah in a quarter known as Inderkot, and have a right to perform the ceremony called "looting the pot", which they do forcibly.

On the right is a mosque built by Akbar, with drums and candlesticks taken in 1576 from the army of Daud Khan Sultan of Bengal, and presented to the mosque by Akbar. Farther on in an inner court is a white marble mosque, 100 ft. long, and with eleven arches to the front, built by Shah Jahan; a Persian inscription runs along the whole front under the eaves. In the centre of the second court is the *Tomb* of the saint, a square building of white marble surmounted by a dome. It has two entrances, one of which is spanned by a silver arch. As at Fatehpur Sikri, the doors of the shrine are covered with votive horse-shoes, nailed there by horse-dealers to commemorate successful deals. Several doors in the precincts of the Dargah are plated with silver.

On the hillside high above the Dargah is the Mazar, or tomb of Bibi Hafiz Jamal, daughter of the saint, and W. of it, close by her tomb, is that of Chimni Begam, daughter of

Shah Jahan. These can now be approached by non-Muslims (leave a small bakshish). There are some very fine trees in the enclosure.

At the S. end of the Dargah enclosure is the Jhaira, a deep tank partly cut out of the rock, and lined by steep flights of irregular steps.

S.E. of the city is the **Mayo College,** opened in 1875 for the education of the sons of Rajput Princes and nobles, but now no longer confined to these classes. The central building is of white marble; in front of it is a statue of Lord Mayo. The subsidiary buildings have been erected by various States as hostels. The park round the buildings comprises 200 acres. Many of the former Ruling Princes owed at least their early education to this institution. It was also a great nursery of polo talent.

The sacred lake of **Pushkar** (Tourist B., bus service from Ajmer) lies about 7 m. W. of Ajmer.

The road skirts the W. shore of the Ana Sagar, and at 3 m. passes the village of Nausar, in a gap in the hills which divide the Ana Sagar and the Pushkar valleys. This striking pass through the hills is 1 m. long. Pushkar, the most sacred lake in India, lies in a narrow valley overshadowed by fine rocky hills, and is said to be of miraculous origin. In the 5th century, according to Fa Hien, it was one of the most frequented objects of pilgrimage, and is still visited during the great *mela* (fair) of October and November by about 100,000 pilgrims. On this occasion is also held a great fair for horses, camels and bullocks, at which the unusual spectacle of camels racing and jumping may be seen.

Although the ancient temples were destroyed by Aurangzeb, the five modern buildings, with their ghats on the margin of the lake, are highly picturesque. The temple to Brahma, at the farther end of the lake, is regarded as a peculiarly holy shrine, from the fact that it marks the spot where the incarnation of Brahma took place. It is usually said to be the only one in India. Over the gateway is the figure of the *hans*, or "goose", of Brahma.

20 m. E. of Ajmer is the battlefield of Lakhairi (1792), where De Boigne just managed to defeat Tukoji Holkar.

654 m. from Bombay is **Naraina** station, headquarters of the Dadupanthi sect of reformers. Their religion, ethics, and teaching are embodied in a mass of poetry written by one Dadu and his disciples. A division of the sect is composed of military monks (Nagas), who used to be employed in the irregular forces of the Jaipur State.

660 m. from Bombay is **Phulera** Junction.

A direct chord line (metre-gauge), 133 m. long, runs N.E. to Rewari (p. 271); to the W. a branch runs to Kuchaman Road (p. 262) and thence to Degana, Merta Road (for Bikaner), Jodhpur and Marwar Junction. The mail train runs by the old main line.

695 m. from Bombay is **JAIPUR,*** more easily reached by I.A.C. from Ahmedabad and Delhi by air (pop. 613,000 in 1971; alt. 1414 ft.); with six good hotels (C.H., R.R., Youth Hostels, Tourist B., Tourist Information Office in Rajasthan State H.). The palaces at *Jaipur* and *Ambèr*, are open to the public on payment of small entrance fees. Ambèr is the ancient capital and was founded in A.D. 928. Jaipur is the residence of the Maharaja (head of the Kachhwaha clan of Rajputs) and the headquarters of Rajasthan State. The former Jaipur State covered an area of 15,600 sq. m.

Jaipur has had some notable rulers with a strong tradition of public service dating from Mughal times, supplying trusted statesmen, soldiers and administrators. Maharaja Sir Madho Singh II (1880-1922) founded the Indian Peoples' Famine Fund. The late Ruler, Maharaja Sir Man Singh[1] (born in 1911, d. 1970), was

[1] Lieut.-General H.H. Maharaja Sir Man Singh Bahadur, G.C.S.I., G.C.I.E.

Rajpramukh of the new-formed Rajasthan Union, in 1948. He was later appointed Ambassador at Madrid.

In 1556 Raja Bhar Mal was presented at Akbar's court and gave him his daughter Mariam-zamani in marriage; she was the mother of Jahangir. Bhar Mal's grandson was the celebrated Raja Man Singh (d. 1615) whose name and fame are so closely associated with Akbar. Jaipur derives its name from the famous Maharaja Jai Singh II (1699-1744), who founded it in 1728. This Chief supported the son of Prince Azam Shah in the struggle for the Empire on the death of Aurangzeb, and drove the Mughals out of Jaipur. The first treaty with the British was concluded in 1818 by Maharaja Jagat Singh.

The town is surrounded on the N. and E. by rugged hills, crowned with forts. That at the end of the ridge overhanging the city on the N.W. is the Nahargarh, or "Tiger fort". The face of the ridge is scarped and inaccessible on the S. or city side, while on the N. it slopes towards Ambèr.

A crenellated wall, with seven gateways, encloses the city, which is the capital of one of the most prosperous tracts of Rajputana, and is a very busy and important commercial town, with large banks and other trading establishments. It is a centre of Indian manufactures, jewellery, tie-dyed cloths and muslins. The enamel-work is notably excellent. The crowded streets and bazars are most lively. The jewellers' bazar is near the Sanganer Gate on the S. The city is remarkable for the width and regularity of its main streets. It is laid out in rectangular blocks, and is divided by cross streets into six equal portions. The main streets are 111 ft. wide, and are paved. The procession at the Vasam Panchami festival (February) should be seen, also the Tij festival at the commencement of the Rains.

The old **City Palace,** with its beautiful gardens and pleasure-grounds, ½ m. long, adorned with fountains, fine trees, and flowering shrubs, occupies the centre of Jaipur, covering one-seventh of its area. The whole is surrounded by a high embattled wall, built by Jai Singh II, but many of the buildings included in it are of a later date. The Chandra Mahal, which forms the centre of the great palace, is a lofty and striking building, seven storeys high, looking over the gardens. On the top storey there is a magnificent view over the centre city. Close by, to the right, on the ground floor, is the Diwan-i-Khas, or private hall of audience, built partly of white marble, also a Clock Tower and Armoury. Ram Bagh, the modern palace of the Maharaja is now a hotel 2 m. out.

E. of the Chandra Mahal is the famous Jantra (Yantra Mantra), or **Observatory,** the largest of the five built by the celebrated patron of astronomy, Jai Singh II; the others are at Benares, Delhi and Ujjain (the Muttra one has disappeared). It is a courtyard full of curious masonry instruments designed at his instance. It was constructed between 1718-34, and was restored by Mahdo Singh II of Jaipur through the agency of the late Lieutenant A. Garret, R.E., and Pandit Chandradhar Guleri, who published a monograph upon it.

The principal instruments are, first on the W., the two circular Ram Yantras for reading altitudes and azimuths, with twelve horizontal sectors of stone radiating from a round vertical rod; then E. of these, the twelve Rashivalayas for determining celestial latitudes and longitudes; and next, the great Samrat Yantra, or gnomon, 90 ft. high, situated between two graduated quadrants, with sextants in a chamber outside them. The gnomon's shadow thrown by the sun touches the W. quadrant at 6 a.m., gradually descends this at the rate of 13 ft. per hour till noon, and finally ascends the E. quadrant. To the N. of this is a Dakhshina Bhitti Yantra, or meridional wall, near which is a large raised platform known as Jai Singh's seat, and near it are two brass circles, one of which is a map of the celestial sphere. Between these and the Ram Yantras are a number of other instruments, known as the Kranti Yantra, the Kapali, and the Chakra Yantra, the last being a graduated brass circle corresponding to the modern equatorial.

S.W. of the Observatory, and adjoining the Tripolia (Three Arches) Gate, are the Palace **Stables,** round courtyards; and beyond, towards the E., is the Hawa Mahal, or **Hall of the Winds,** of five storeys, built by Sawai Pratap Singh in 1799, overlooking one of the chief streets.

Near the Tripolia Gate rises the Iswari Minar Swarga Sul, the "Minaret piercing heaven", built by Raja Iswari Singh (1744-51) to overlook the city.

The **Public Garden,** outside the city wall to the S., 36 acres in extent, laid out by Dr de Fabeck, contains a zoo. In the centre is the **Albert Hall,** designed and built by the late Sir Swinton Jacob. It contains a large Darbar Hall and a Museum (1887), with collections of modern works of art and industry, and also of antiquities, from every part of India. There is a fine view from the top.

The **Mayo Hospital,** with a clock tower, lies just outside the gardens. About half a mile distant on the Tonk Road is another hospital named after Lady Willingdon.

Before it joined the Indian Union, Jaipur, as a result of the interest taken by the Ruler, had exceptionally well-equipped State Forces, consisting of a Guards battalion, two battalions of infantry and a cavalry regiment, some of which have since been incorporated in the Indian Army.

The **Transport Gardens,** now commonly called the Naya Ghat, were laid out in 1896 by the then Commandant of the Corps in the bed of the Amnisha Nulla adjoining the Transport lines, and are more than 2 m. in length.

The **Church** is near the hotels and on the way to the railway station, a little to the W. of the road. There is also a R.C. church at Ghat Darwaza.

At the **School of Art,** a handsome modern building, are first-rate technical and industrial classes for teaching and reviving various branches of local artistic industry—such as metal and enamel-work, embroidery, weaving, etc.

The **Maharaja's College.**— The College, founded in 1844 and maintained entirely by the Darbar, was moved outside the city in 1930, into a large building, and is a free institution. It is now the central institution of the Rajasthan University.

The **Maharaja's Public Library.**— This was founded by Maharaja Sir Ram Singh in 1866 for the educated public. It contains English, Sanskrit, Hindi, Persian, Arabic, Urdu, and other books. The very valuable Razm-Namah contains 160 miniatures.

The *Chhattris*, or cenotaphs of the Maharajas, at Gethur are just outside the N.E. city wall. They are in well-planted gardens, the trees of which are full of solemn-looking grey-headed monkeys. The first seen on entering is the Chhattri of Maharaja Jai Singh II—the finest of all. It is a dome of the purest white marble, supported on twenty beautifully carved pillars rising from a substantial square platform, and profusely ornamented with scenes from Hindu mythology. S.E. of Jai Singh's *Chhattri* is that of his second son, Mahdo Singh I (1774-79), a dome rising from the octagon on arches reversed. The only ornaments are carved peacocks. W. of this *Chhattri* is that of Pertab Singh, his son (1779-1803), completed by Maharaja Sir Ram Singh (1835-80). It is of white marble brought from Alwar.

The water which supplies Jaipur comes from waterworks at Ramgarh lake, about 11 m. N. of the city.

An expedition for the sake of the *view* may be made 1½ m. from the E. or Surya Gate, to the Shrine of the Sun God at *Galta*—350 ft. above the plain, on the summit of a range of hills about 1½ m. to the E. of Jaipur.

Behind the temple is a deep gorge

filled with temples and sacred tanks shadowed by rugged crags; a paved causeway leads through the ravine.

There is also a pleasant drive to a similar gorge along the Agra Road, 2 m. E. through the deserted Purana Ghat which is well worth a visit.

The excursion to **Ambèr**[1] (5 m. from the city gate and 7 m. from the hotels), the capital of Jaipur till 1728, will occupy a whole morning. A motor road extends all the way.

On the left of the road a line of fortified hills is passed; these culminate in the great Fort, 400 ft. above the old palace, connected with it and built for its defence. The picturesque situation of Ambèr at the mouth of a rocky mountain gorge in which nestles a pretty lake, has attracted the admiration of all travellers, including Jacquemont and Heber. Founded by the primeval Minas, it was flourishing in A.D. 967. In 1037 it was taken by the Rajputs, who held it till a move was made to Jaipur.

The **Old Palace** at Ambèr, begun by Man Singh I (1600),[2] and completed by Jai Singh I, lies low on the slope of the hill, picturesquely rooted on its rocky base and reflected in the lake below. The interior arrangements are excellent. The suites of rooms afford striking vistas from the windows.

Entered by a fine staircase from a great courtyard is the Diwan-i-Am, with a double row of columns supporting a massive entablature, above which are latticed galleries. Its magnificence attracted the envy of Jahangir, and the Mirza Raja,[3] to save his great work from destruction, covered it with stucco. To the right of the Diwan-i-Am steps is a small ancient temple of Kali (Mateswari) which the Maharaja must visit when he is installed.

On a higher terrace are the Maharaja's apartments, entered by a splendid gateway covered with mosaics and sculptures, erected by Jai Singh I, over which is the Sohag Mandir—a small pavilion with beautiful latticed windows. Through this are further marvels—a green and cool garden with fountains, surrounded by palaces, brilliant with mosaics and marbles. That on the left is the Jai Mandir, or Hall of Victory, adorned by panels of alabaster, some of which are inlaid, and others are adorned with flowers in alto-relievo, "the roof glittering with the mirrored and spangled work for which Jaipur is renowned". Near the Jai Mandir a narrow passage leads down to the bathing-rooms, all of pale creamy marble. Above is the Jas Mandir, "which literally glows with bright and tender colours and exquisite inlaid work, and looks through arches of carved alabaster and clusters of slender columns upon the sleeping lake and the silent mountains".

At the N.E. angle is a balcony, whence there is a fine view over the town of Ambèr and the plain beyond to the hill which overlooks Ramgarh. Some *Chhattris* outside the wall are those of Chieftains who died before Jai Singh II. In the palace to the right is a chamber, on the right wall of which are views of Ujjain, and on the left views of Benares and Muttra. The room opposite the Jai Mandir is called the Sukh Niwas, "Hall of Pleasure". In the centre is an opening for a stream to flow into the channel which runs through the hall. The doors are of sandalwood inlaid with ivory.

A steep path leads down to the Khizri Gate, beyond which, it leads to one of the forts, Kantalgarh. At the bottom of this path is the Jagat Shiromani Temple to Thakurji, or Vishnu. It is white and beautifully carved, and just outside the door is a lovely square pavilion exquisitely carved with figures representing Krishna sporting with the Gopi milkmaids.

Ambèr formerly contained many fine temples, but most are now in ruins. On a Temple of the Sun is an inscription (A.D. 955).

[1] Locally pronounced Ambair.

[2] Man Singh was the nephew of Raja Bhagwan Das, the friend of Akbar.

[3] Raja Jai Singh I (d. 1668) was known by this title.

Sanganer (Jain Temples), about 8 m. to the S. of Jaipur, may be reached by a drive past the Residency and the Moti Doongri, an old building on a small hill which the Maharaja has made into his private residence, converting his former palace of Ram Bagh into a hotel (p. 267).

The road into the town is through two ruined Tripolias, or triple gateways of three storeys, about 66 ft. high. The second storey has an open stone veranda, supported by four pillars on either side of the archway. On the right ascending the street is a small temple sacred to Kalyanji, or Krishna, the door of which is handsomely carved. Opposite is a temple to Sitaram, with a pillar, 6 ft. high, of white Makrana marble, called a Kirtti Khambh. On the four sides are Brahma, with four faces; Vishnu, cross-legged, holding the lotus; Siva, holding a cobra in his right hand and a trident in his left, with Parvati beside him, and Ganesh.

Higher up, on the left, are the ruins of the *Old Palace*. N. by E. from this is the Sanganer Jain Temple, with three courts, and finely carved marble work.

At Lalsot, 40 m. S., Jaipur and Jodhpur together defeated De Boigne, the general of Scindia, in 1787.

52 m. from Jaipur on the Alwar Road, at Bairat, is a Jain temple (1587), a Buddhist monastery, and circular temple, with an edict of Asoka. Coins of Greek and Indo-Greek kings were found (1940).

The former Jaipur State Ry., now part of the Western Ry., runs from Siwai Madhopur (where it connects with the main Western Ry. broad-gauge line to Delhi) to Jaipur, 83 m., and then continues N. through Reengus (junction with the Phulera-Rewari line) to Sikar, 147 m., junction for Fatehpur, and then to Jhunjhunu, 187 m., linking up at Loharu (225 m.) with the cross-country line from Bikanir to Rewari and Delhi.

751 m. from Bombay is **Bandikui** Junction (R.). Railway workshops, and a colony of railway employees. The line for Agra branches off E. (see Route 12).

788 m. from Bombay, **ALWAR** (pop. 100,000 in 1971) is the capital of the former State of that name, founded in 1771 by Rao Pratap Singhji of Macheri (d. 1791), who threw off allegiance to Jaipur. The town is on rising ground, dominated by the Fort, which crowns a conical rock and is backed by a range of hills. It is connected by motor road both with Delhi and Jaipur. The Alwar Maharajas were Naruka Rajputs of the Kachhwaha clan, of which the Maharaja of Jaipur was the head.

There is a C.H. with Western and Indian food (beds and linen provided), P.W.D.R.H. opposite Ry. Station, Rajasthan State House at **Siliserh** (6 m.) and Tourist R.H. at **Sariska** (15 m.).

Palaces.—There are several palaces in the capital. The Vinai Vilas Palace is named after Maharao Raja Vinai Singhji (1815-57), and is now the Rajrisai College. The city palace is at the very end of the city and consists of a group of buildings partly detached, and built in a variety of styles, separated from the base of the mountain by a picturesque tank (Sagar). The handsome Shish-Mahal (Mirror room) overlooks the tank.

This palace contains a Museum (closed Friday) and an excellently kept Library rich in Oriental manuscripts. Eminent Sanskrit and Persian scholars from Western countries visit this library to take copies of ancient manuscripts. A matchless *Gulistan*, which cost about £10,000 to produce, is beautifully illustrated with miniature paintings. It was finished in 1848 by the order of Maharoa Raja Vinai Singhjil. Another beautiful book is the *Dah Pand*, written in 1864.

The Armoury contains a splendid collection of sabres and other weapons finely wrought and finished and studded with jewels; also of handsome swords with hilts of gold. Dozens of these swords are from Persia, while many of them were made at Alwar, in imitation of the Ispahan steel. The arms of Maharao Raja Vinai Singhji could only be used by a man of great stature.

On the W. of the Sagar are temples and shrines with Bengali roofs; and raised upon the centre of a platform on the S. is the cenotaph of Maharao Raja Bakhtawar Singhji (1781-1815). The plinth is made of red sandstone and the cenotaph itself of beautiful marble with Bengali arches. Visitors entering must take off their shoes. Hundreds of pigeons fly about and stately peacocks strut about the stone pavements.

In the city, just right of the main palace entrance, is the house of the Elephant carriage. It was built by Maharao Raja Vinai Singhji. It is a car two storeys high, and can carry fifty persons, drawn by four elephants.

The Company Bagh (Garden).—This is a public park on the outskirts of the town. In the centre is summer-house, with fountains and beautiful ferns. There is also a small menagerie.

There is little to see at the *Fort*, except the view from this great height of the city below and the surrounding country interspersed with lakes. The old ascent is steep, and is paved with slippery stones. At a point about 150 ft. up, the steepest part begins. It is called Hathi Mora, "the Elephant's turn", because they could not go further; a motor road now runs right up to the top of the hill. Behind the fort, at a distance of 1 m., is the *Chhattri* of Maharao Raja Pratap Singhji (d. 1791), the Founder of the State, and alongside it is a small monument of his Maharani who became *sati*.

The tomb of Fateh Jang, a Minister of Shah Jahan, near the station, on the Bharatpur road, is a conspicuous object with an immense dome, and bears the date, in Nagri, 1647. In the interior there is plaster-work in relief, with flat surface patterns and rectangular mouldings.

2 m. to the S. is the Artillery Ground and Top Khana, "Artillery Arsenal".

Alwar and its outskirts are supplied with water from Siliserh, a lake full of crocodiles, 6 m. S.W. of the city. A masonry dam, about ½ m. long, and 4 m. from the Moti Doongri hill, has been constructed, at a cost of Rs. 8 lakhs to impound water from the Ruparel river. The water stored by this masonry dam, amounting to some 1100 millions of cu. ft., forms a splendid reservoir, covering an area over 4 sq. m. It is known by the name of "Jey Samand Lake", named after a late Maharaja, and used to be ornamented with beautiful Chhattris (domed pavilions).

At **Sariska** (15 m.) is a Wild Life Sanctuary, with tigers, panthers, pythons and many species of deer. Arrangements on application to Game Warden. There is a charge for photography. There is a T.B.

20 m. E. of Alwar, and adjoining the Mewati hills, is the battlefield of **Laswari,** where General Lake annihilated the last brigades of Daulat Rao Scindia's French-trained army on 1st November 1803. This great British soldier, within a space of two months, and with a force never exceeding 8000 men, crushed 31 battalions of Scindia's troops in four pitched battles, and captured 426 guns. He took two fortresses (Aligarh and Agra), and entered the capital of India (Delhi) as deliverer of the Mughal Emperor.

794 m. from Bombay and 52 m. from Delhi is **Rewari** Junction (R., D.B. and Hindu-Muslim Hotel). Rewari was founded in A.D. 1000 by Raja Rawat. There are the ruins of a still older town E. of the modern walls. The Rajas of Rewari were partially independent, even under the Mughals. Near the town they built the mud fort of Gokalgarh, which was once very strong. They coined their own currency, called Gokal Sikka. Rewari is a place of considerable trade, particularly in iron and brass. The Town Hall is handsome, as are the Jain Temples and Tej Singh's Tank, close to the town.

From Rewari a metre-gauge line,

187 m., runs N.W. to Hissar and Bhatinda Junction (see Route 15), and another runs, *via* Loharu, to Sadulpur, where it joins the line from Hissar to Ratangarh and Bikanir.

On the chord line between Rewari and Phulera (pp. 262, 266), 32 m. S.W. of Rewari lies **Narnaul,** made over to the Patiala State for loyal services in 1857.

On the main line,

826 m. from Bombay, is situated **Gurgaon,** the headquarters of the South-Eastern District of the Punjab. Two metalled roads E. to Delhi; one road 15 m. S. to Sohna, thence bifurcating S.E. to Palwal (p. 298) and S. to Alwar. **Sohna** is remarkable for a hot-spring, situated in the town which is close to hills, some crowned with the walls and bastions of an unfinished fort. The water of this spring is strongly impregnated with sulphuric acid, which, however, evaporates very rapidly. The spring is covered with a domed building and surrounded by small open bathing tanks. The water is considered of great value for purposes of rheumatism, gout, and skin diseases.

845 m. from Bombay is **DELHI** Central station* (Route 14).

ROUTE 11

From AHMEDABAD by **Viramgam, Kharaghoda, Wadhwan, Palitana, Bhavnagar, Junagadh, Girnar, Somnath, Porbandar, Rajkot, Jamnagar** and **Dwarka.**

The peninsula of **Kathiawar** is believed to have been an island in remote times. It has an approximate area of 20,332 sq. m., and once consisted of a mass of 222 States, large and small, plus the once-Portuguese island of Diu, and portions of the district of Ahmedabad and of the former Baroda State. The States were amalgamated in 1948 to form a Union, named Saurashtra after the ancient classical appellation for Kathiawar. Kutch, virtually an island, was made a separate Chief Commissioner's province because of its strategic situation on the Pakistan frontier. In 1956, by the States Reorganisation Act, all these States were merged in Bombay State; since 1959, they are part of Gujarat. Kutch was the largest of the former Western India States and had an area of 7616 sq. m., exclusive of the Rann of Kutch, which covers an area of about 9000 sq. m. The Maharaos are head of the Jadeja Rajput clan; the present Prince, Madansinhji, reached ambassadorial rank in the Indian Diplomatic service. Kutch is cut off from the mainland by the Rann on the N. and E., the Gulf of Kutch on the S., and the Arabian Sea on the W.; but is easily accessible by air from Bombay, and steamers run about twice a week to **Mandvi** the chief port on the S. from which there is a road to the old capital, **Bhuj** (airfield). The State is noted for some ancient palaces and for the work of its silversmiths and enamellers. A new major port for ocean-going steamers has been constructed at **Kandla** on a site first developed by Maharao Khangarji III; and is linked by rail and road to Deesa (p. 255) and Ahmedabad: an airport (services from Bombay) is used by Kandla and the adjacent new township of **Gandhidam,** set up by the Maharaos of Kutch for refugees from Sind in 1947. At Surkotada, about 100 m. N.E. of Bhuj, an important stronghold of the Harappan period has been excavated. There are massive fortifications and an elaborate gateway—the first time such structures of this period have been found in India.

Peculiar to Kathiawar are long lines of *palias*, or memorial stones, on which men are usually represented as riding on very large horses, whilst women have wheels below them to indicate that they used a carriage. A woman's arm and hand indicate a monument to a *sati* lady.

Formerly, there was much game, big and small, in Kathiawar: but with the relaxation of the game laws [once strictly enforced by the local ruling Princes] which followed the absorption of their territories into independent India, panthers have become rare, and even partridges and quail take a good deal of finding. The Indian lion, once widely dispersed in Kathiawar, is now found only in the Gir, a wild tract of forest S.E. of Junagadh where it is strictly preserved. It is the only Asian species; its mane is often smaller than that of the African lion (see also p. 283).

The Saurashtra Mail leaves Bombay (Central) daily, and proceeds on the broad-gauge to

Ahmedabad (p. 247), 306 m., from Bombay. From 4 m., *Sabarmati* Junction on the N. bank of the river, the metre-gauge continues N. to Delhi and Agra. The broad-gauge (opened 1871) turns W., and passing through a well-cultivated country, reaches

346 m. **Viramgam** Junction—a walled town. The Mansar Tank dates from 1100. It is shaped like a shell, and surrounded by a flight of stone steps; round the tops of the steps runs a row of small temples, in the sides of which there are holes, through which it is said a rope used to pass, enabling a worshipper to ring the bells in all the temples at once. Black buck, sand-grouse and all manner of water-fowl, once abundant, are now greatly depleted.

From Viramgam a broad-gauge line runs N.W., passing at 18 m. Patri (D.B.), a small walled town with a citadel; and, at 23 m. reaches **Kharaghoda,** where there are very extensive salt-pans on the edge of the **Little Rann of Kutch.**[1]

In the dry season the **Rann** presents the appearance of a hard, smooth bed of dried mud; camels can traverse it at any place. There is absolutely no vegetation except on some small islands which rise above the level of the salt inundation: there are herds of wild asses (rarely seen), which feed on the lands near its shores at night, and retreat far into the desert in the daytime. With the commencement of the S.W. monsoon in May the salt water of the Gulf of Kutch invades the Rann, and later in the season the rivers from Rajasthan pour fresh water into it. The Rann then becomes very dangerous; entire armies have perished in it in ancient times. The sea is now encroaching rapidly on the Rann at its junction with the Gulf of Kutch. The centre of the Rann is slightly higher than the borders, and dries first. The railway has many sidings extending into the Rann, to facilitate the collection of salt. The salt is evaporated by the heat of the sun from brine brought up in buckets from depths of 15 ft. to 30 ft. From the air, the views over the Rann are very striking, and the island-character of Kutch is plain to the observer. Wonderful mirages are seen in the Rann, and in the winter season the flights of flamingoes—which nest there—and other birds are extraordinarily large. There are sand-grouse and Imperial grouse and many wild-fowl.

[1] The Great Rann separates Kutch (India) from Sind (Pakistan).

The Saurashtra Mail proceeds from Viramgam by metre-gauge to the junction at Wadhwan, now called Surendranagar (D.B.), 386 m. from Bombay.

To the N. runs the Dhrangadhra railway, and to the S. the Bhavnagar railway, which connects at Dhola Junction (see p. 254) with the Gondal-Porbandar railway, which opens up a large tract of country in S. Kathiawar.

To the W. the Morvi railway runs to Rajkot; thence the Jamnagar railway runs to Jamnagar and Dwarka (p. 288), terminus of the Kathiawar mail route, and the Jetalsar Rajkot railway to Jetalsar, where it crosses the Gondal-Porbandar line. The Junagadh railway runs from Jetalsar to Verával *via* Junagadh, and from Junagadh to Visavadar. All the railways in Saurashtra are on the metre-gauge, and have been made branches of the Western Ry. system instead of being independently managed as formerly.

At the Talukdari School in the former Wadhwan civil station, the sons of *Girassias,* or Rajput landowners, were educated when their parents were unable to afford the cost of sending them to the College at Rajkot. About 20 m. E. of Wadhwan is the **Nul Sarovar** Bird Sanctuary, where a great variety of birds can be seen, including flamingoes and pelicans during the winter.

Dhrangadhra, on the line running from Surendranagar to Halwad, is the capital of the former Dhrangadhra State. Industries are the Shri Shakti Alkali works and weaving fabrics with silver and gold thread.

Proceeding S. from Surendranagar by the Bhavnagar line, the river is crossed close to the station.

4 m. **Wadhwan (Surendranagar) City** station (R., D.B.; alt. 404 ft.). Towards the centre, on the N. wall, is the ancient temple of **Ranik Devi.** She was a beautiful girl, born in the Junagadh territory when Sidh Raja was reigning at Patan Anhilwara, and was betrothed to him. But Rao Khengar, who then ruled Junagadh, carried her off and married her, which caused a feud between him and Sidh Raja, whose troops marched to Junagadh. Khengar was betrayed by two of his kinsmen, and was slain by Sidh Raja and his fortress taken. The conqueror wanted to marry Ranik Devi, but she performed *sati,* and Sidh Raja raised this temple to her memory. It bears marks of extreme old age, the stone being much worn; all but the tower is gone. Inside is the effigy in relief of Ranik Devi, and a smaller one with a representation of the goddess Ambaji. N. of this temple, and close to the city wall, is a *sati* stone dated 1519. Near the Lakhupol Gate is a well with steps, ascribed to one Madhava, who lived in 1294.

The Palace in the centre of the town has four storeys, and is 72 ft. high. It stands in a court facing the entrance, on the right of which is a building called the Mandwa, where assemblies take place at marriages. There is also a Palace called the Balchandra Vilas, built by a former Ruler.

17 m. **Limbdi** station—chief town of the former Limbdi State: with a handsome Palace. The title of the Chiefs of both Wadhwan and Limbdi was Thakor Saheb, and both are Jhala Rajputs. Limbdi town manufactures ivory bangles and brass-plated boxes. Education is free.

20 m. S.E. Rangpur is a chalcolithic site.

47 m. **Botad** Junction. Frontier of the former Bhavnagar State. Branches to (1) **Jasdan,** capital of the former State of that name, and (2) Dhanduka Junction for Dholka and (30 m. by road) Dholera port. On the line to Dholka is **Lothal,** the Harappan site mentioned on p. 251. But this is best visited by road from Ahmedabad.

74 m. from Wadhwan is **Dholka** Junction (R.). From here the Gondal-Porbandar railway runs W. to Dhasa, Jetalsar, Dhoraji and Porbandar; a branch line goes S. to (23 m.) Sava Kundla, and (72 m.) Mahuva, on the Gulf of Cambay, with a junction at Dungar to Port Albert Victor.

Two excursions can be made if the visitor continues E. to Bhavnagar by the main line.

87 m. from Surendranagar Junction on this line is **Songadh** for the ancient city of **Valabhipur,** which is nearly identical with the modern town of Vala, 12 m. N. by road, capital of a State.

Valabhipur, once the capital of all this part of India, was perhaps as old as Rome (573 B.C.). The Vallabhi dynasty, founded by a general of the Gupta kings, reigned from A.D. 480-790, as shown by copper-plate grants. Hiuen Tsang visited it (A.D. 639). Old foundations, terra-cotta, coins (apparently Andhra), copper plates, mud seals, beads, stone bulls, and household images have been found. Specimens have been placed in the Museum. The ruins cover a large area.

Resuming the railway route from Songadh to Bhavnagar, the traveller passes, 91 m. from Surendranagar, **Sihor** station (D.B.), junction for Palitana, 17 m. Sihor was at one time the capital of the Bhavnagar branch of Gohel Rajputs. The town, 1½ m. S. of the railway, has interesting Hindu temples. The name is a corruption of "Singhpur", "the lion's city"; a still more ancient name is "Saraswatpur". It is famous for copper and brass work, snuff and plaster (chunam). Near the S. wall is situated Brahma Kund, the water of which possesses special virtue. Farther up the River Gautami lie the Gautam Kund and Gautameswar Mahadev.

Palitana (bus services from Ahmedabad), G. H., 18 m. by rail from Sihor station, is much enriched by pilgrims during their visit to the Holy Mountain of Satrunjaya and its famous Jain temples. The State was founded by Shahji, a Gohel Rajput, of the same clan as the Maharaja of Bhavnagar. Its princes have been cultured and enlightened rulers. There is a State Paddock, where horse-breeding from pure Kathi stock is carried on.

The distance from Palitana to the foot of **Satrunjaya,** or the **Holy Mountain,** 1977 ft. above sea-level, is 1½ m. There is a motor road to the foot: many steps to the top.

The Satrunjaya Hill is truly a city of the gods, with 863 temples; there is nothing else within the gates; there is a cleanliness about every square, passage, porch and hall. The silence, too, is striking. The top of the hill consists of two ridges, each about 350 yd. long, with a valley between. Each of these ridges, and the two large enclosures that fill the valley, are surrounded by massive battlemented walls fitted for defence. The buildings on both ridges, again, are divided into 9 separate enclosures called *tuks,* generally containing one principal temple with varying numbers of smaller ones. Each of these enclosures is protected by strong gates and walls, and all gates are carefully closed at sundown. The area enclosed on the top is small enough for any one of ordinary activity to see all over it in a two hours' visit. There is one gate leading into the enclosure, but there are nineteen inner gates, leading to the nineteen chief temples. Adjoining the temple of Shri Adeshwara is the Muslim shrine of Anjar Pir where childless women offer miniature cradles. There is a rich jewel collection, to be seen by permission of the Hill Inspector. Not far from the *Ram-pol* ("pol" means gate) is a resting-place used by persons of distinction, with a tolerable room surrounded by open arches.

Fergusson wrote: "All the peculiarities of Jain architecture are found in a more marked degree at Satrunjaya than at almost any other known place, and, fortunately for the student of the style, extending over a considerable period of time. Some of the temples may be as old as the 11th century, but the Muslim invaders of the 14th and 15th centuries made sad havoc of all the older shrines, and we have only fragments of a few of them. In the latter half of the 16th century, however, the Jains obtained tolerance and security, and forthwith began to rebuild their old fanes. From 1500 they are spread pretty evenly over all the intervening time down to the present century."

On reaching the summit of the mountain, a panorama presents itself from the top of the walls. To the E. the prospect extends to the Gulf of Cambay near Gogha and Bhavnagar; to the N. it is bounded by the granite range of Sihor and the Chamardi peak; to the N.W. and W. the plain extends as far as the eye can reach. From W. to E., like a silver ribbon across the foreground to the S., winds the Satrunjaya river, which the eye follows until it is lost between the Talaja and Khokara Hills in the S.W.

104 m. from Surendranagar the terminus **Bhavnagar,** C.H., R.R., Guest H., Western India A.A. District Rep. (pop. 226,000 in 1971) founded 1723, stands on a tidal creek from the Gulf of Cambay. It is easily accessible from Bombay by air, with a harbour for shipping of light draught, and an extensive trade, as one of the principal markets for cotton in Kathiawar. There are no interesting ruins, but abundance of very handsome modern buildings on Indian models, water-works, reservoirs and gardens, Gaurishanker Lake is a beautiful picnic spot, and at the port will be seen modern mechanical improvements.

The Maharajas are Gohel Rajput by caste. The Barton Museum (1895) contains arms, armour and coins. Childrens' Museum and Gandhi Museum in the same building.

Bus connections with Ahmedabad, Rajkot, Palitana, Baroda, Junagadh, Jamnagar and Somnath. Rail travellers return to Dhola and change for places in W.

Jetalsar Junction (R.), 153 m. from Surendranagar. Here the line branches to Verával for Somnath; to Porbandar (p. 286); and to Rajkot, Wankaner and Wadhwan (pp. 274, 288).

(1) *Jetalsar to Junagadh and Verával*

17 m. from Jetalsar is **Junagadh** station (C.H., Tourist G.H., R.R., I B., airport at Keshod 29 m. I.A.S. from Bombay), former capital and residence of the Nawab. On partition, the Muslim Ruler joined Pakistan, but as the great majority of his subjects were Hindus, the Indian Government intervened, the State was incorporated in the Union, and the former Rulers live in Pakistan.

From Junagadh branch lines run to Visavadar and Prachi Road. There is also a line W. *via* Bantva between Shapur (a station between Junagadh and Verával) and Saradiya for Kutiana. The Bantva Taluka is owned by Babi Musalmans of the same clan as the Nawabs of Junagadh and Radhanpur.

Situated under the Girnar and Datar Hills, **Junagadh** was first ruled by Chavda Rajputs with a capital at Vamansthali (now Vanthali), but they transferred the capital to Junagadh in A.D. 875.

The fortifications of the present town were all built by the Muslims after the capture of the place by Sultan Mahmud Bigarha, of Gujarat, about 1472. He changed the name to Mustafabad and placed it under a Fouzdar. The last Fouzdar, Sherkhan Babi, became independent in 1748 and took the title of Nawab Bahadur Khan from his brother, the founder of his family, an Afghan, in the reign of Shah Jahan. The Nawab's Old Palace, containing the Rasaul Khanji Museum (1925), has the Haveli and Darbar Kacheri Hall opposite. In front of the Darbar is a circle of shops with the Aina Mahal on the E.

Entering the Reay Gate from the station we come to the Orphanage and Law Courts; opposite the last is the makbara, or mausoleum, of the Nawabs, adjoining the public mosque. At four cross-roads lies the old Makbara, a highly finished building.

Entering the Makbara enclosure by the N. gate the tomb of Nawab Bahadur Khan II (d. 1840) is in front on the left, next to it the tomb of Nawab Hamid Khan II (d. 1851) and on its left that of Laddibu Bibi. Beside these is the tomb of Nawab Mahabat Khan I (d. 1774) in Saracenic style, and finely carved. The tombs of Bibi Najobibi and her notorious servant, Chaitibu, are to be found at Bara Saiyad in another quarter of the town. The tomb of Vizir Sahib Baha-ud-din Bhar has minarets with spiral stairs outside.

Outside the town lies the new suburb. The Art College, which contains a fine hall, was designed and built by a local architect in 1900. Both in and outside the walls many improvements have been carried out during recent years. The various gardens, Moti Bagh, Sardar Bagh, Lal Bagh, the new Diagonal Garden and the Sakar Bagh are a great feature of the place. The Zoological Collection, including Gir lions successfully bred in captivity, is housed in Sakar Bagh, 1 m. to the N. of the State Paddock, where the famous Kathi breed of horses can be inspected. Sakar Bagh also houses a fine museum.

The soft sandstone which everywhere underlies Junagadh was formed apparently in very shallow water, showing on all sides complicated lines of stratification. The facility with which the stone is worked may be one reason why it has been largely excavated into cave-dwellings in Buddhist times.

The **Caves.**—In the N. part of the town enclosure, on the way to Dharagadh Gate, is the group of caves called the Khapra Khodia. These caves appear to have been a monastery, and bear the cognisance of the then ruling race—a winged griffin or lion. They seem to have been two or three storeys high. They are excavated in good building stone, and the modern quarrymen have been allowed to encroach and injure them, but they have recently been cleaned out and built up with supporting masonry. The most interesting caves of all (which are now protected by an iron gate) are in the Uparkot (p. 277) about 50 yd. N. of the great mosque. They consist of two storeys, the lower chambers being 11 ft. high. The upper storey is made up of a tank surrounded by a corridor, and of a room 36 ft. by 28 ft., supported by six columns, beyond which is a small kitchen. From here a winding staircase leads to the lower storey, measuring 39 ft. by 31 ft., with broad recesses all round it, and over them a frieze of chaitya windows. Of the columns, Dr Burgess says: "Few bases could be found anywhere to excel in beauty of design and richness of carving, those of the six principal pillars".

Inside the Wagheswari Gate are the caves known by the name of Bawa Piara—a comparatively modern Hindu ascetic who is said to have resided in them. These caves which date from about the time of Asoka (272-231 B.C.), are among the very oldest in all India, and are nearly all small and plain. They are situated in the scarp of a circular detached mass of rock, and face S. and E., a third line to the N., also facing S., being excavated on a higher level than the S. line. Facing E., a number of caves were dug round a central space.

The **Uparkot,** on the E. side of the city, now practically deserted, was the citadel of the old Hindu Princes, and is probably the spot from whence Junagadh derives its name. The Uparkot is a most interesting old fort. The parapets on the E., where the place is commanded by higher ground, have been raised at least three times to give cover against the increasingly long range of projectiles. Here were quartered the lieutenants of the great Asoka, and later of the Gupta Kings. The entrance is beyond the town in the W. wall, and consists of three gateways, one inside the other. Only small cars can go inside. The fort walls here are from 60 to 70 ft. high, forming a massive cluster of buildings. The inner gateway, a beautiful specimen of the Hindu Toran, has been topped by Muslim work. The approach is cut through the solid rock. On the ramparts above the gate is an inscription of Mandalika V, dated 1450.

About 150 yd. to the left, through a grove of *sitaphul* (custard apples), may be seen a cannon known as the Lilam Top, of bell-metal, 17 ft. long, 4 ft. 6 in. round at the muzzle, and 6 ft. 6 in. at the breech, with a bore of 9½ in. This gun was brought from Diu, where it was left by the Turks. There is an Arabic inscription at the muzzle, which may be translated: "The order to make this cannon, to be used in the service of the Almighty, was given by the Sultan of Arabia and Persia, Sultan Sulaiman, son of Salim Khan. May his triumph be glorified, to punish the enemies of the State and of the Faith, in the capital of Egypt, 1531." At the breech is inscribed: "The work of Muhammad, the son of Hamza." Another large cannon called Chudanal, also from Diu, in the S. portion of the fort, is 12 ft. 8 in. long, 5 ft. in circumference at the muzzle, and 5 ft. 7 in. at the breech, on which is inscribed: "The work of Ali, son of Jarza". Near this is the **Jami Masjid,** evidently constructed from the materials of a Hindu temple by Mahmud Bigarha. The mosque is ruined.

The **Tomb of Nuri Shah,** close to the mosque, is ornamented with fluted cupolas, and a most peculiar carving over the door. There are two **Wells** in the Uparkot—the Adi Chadi, said to have been built in ancient times and named after slave girls of the Chudasama rulers, is approached by a long flight of steps (the sides of the descent show the most remarkable overlappings and changes of bed in the strata); and the Naughan, cut to a great depth in the soft rock, and with a wonderful circular staircase.

There is a fine dharmsala belonging to the goldsmiths near the Wagheswari Gate.

Girnar.—This mountain is the great feature of Junagadh, and the Jain temples upon it are ancient. It is 3666 ft. high, and is one of the most remarkable mountains in India. From the city of Junagadh only the top of it can be seen, as it has in front of it lower hills, of which Jogniya, or Laso Pawadi, 2527 ft., Lakhshman Takri, Bensla, 2290 ft. high, and Datar, 2279 ft. high, are the principal. Girnar, which was anciently called Raivata, or Ujjayanta, is sacred amongst the Jains to Neminath, the 22nd Tirthankar, and was, doubtless a place of pilgrimage before the days of Asoka (272-231 B.C.).

The traveller, in order to reach Girnar, passes through the Wagheswari Gate, which is close to the Uparkot. At about 200 yd. from the gate, to the right of the road, is the Temple of Wagheswari, which is joined to the road by a causeway about 150 yd. long. In front of it is a modern temple, three storeys high, flat-roofed. About a furlong beyond this is a stone bridge, and just beyond it, on the right, is the famous **Asoka Stone,** a round boulder of granite, measuring roughly 20 ft. by 30 ft., and inscribed on three sides. The inscriptions proved on examination to be (1) fourteen Edicts of Asoka (250 B.C.) in Deva Nagari characters, (2) Rudradaman's (A.D. 150) in Sanskrit, and (3) Skandagupta's (A.D. 454).[1] Nearly identical inscriptions of Asoka have been found elsewhere.

On leaving the Asoka Stone the route crosses the bridge over the Sonarekha river, a fine sheet of water, then passes temples, at first on the left bank of the river and then on the right, where Jogis go about entirely naked, to the largest temple dedicated to **Damodar,** a name of Krishna, from Dam, a rope, because by tradition his mother in vain attempted to confine him with a rope when a child. The reservoir at this place is accounted very sacred. The path is now through a wooded valley, with some fine Indian fig-trees. Near a cluster of them is an old shrine called **Bhavanath,** a name of Siva, and round it are a number of large monkeys, who come on being called. Persons who are not active climbers can proceed up the hill in a *doli,* a seat swung from two poles carried by four men.

A long ridge from the W. culminates in a scarped rock, on the top of

[1] See *Baroda Arch. Dept. Memorial,* by Hirananda Sastri.

GIRNAR

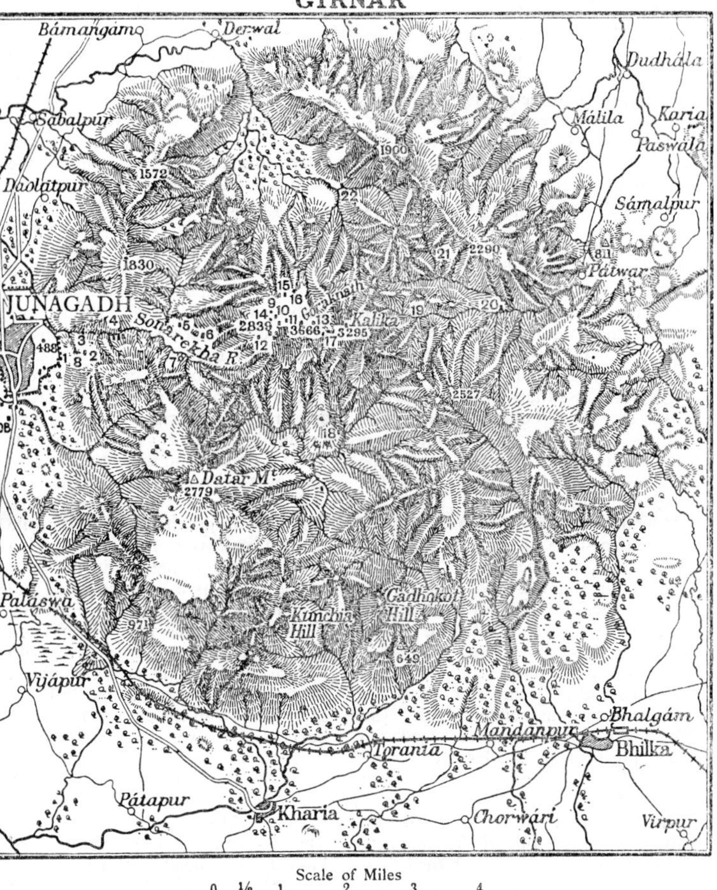

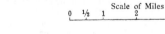

Scale of Miles
0 ½ 1 2 3 4

1. Wagheshwari Gate.
2. Asoka's Stone.
3. Bridge.
4. Temple of Damodar.
5. ,, ,, Savanath.
6. ,, ,, Bhavanath.
7. Chadá-ni-wao Well.
8. Wagheshwari Temple.
9. Bhairo-Japa.
10. Gaomukhi Temple.
11. Amba Devi Temple.
12. Máliparab Kund.
13. Datátraya.
14. Háthi pagla Kund.
15. Sesáwan Temple.
16. Hanmandhára Kund and Temple.
17. Kamandal Temple.
18. Sakri ámbli.
19. Malbela.
20. Suraj Kund.
21. Sarkharia.
22. Bawaha Madhi.

which are the temples. Close to the old shrine is a well called the Chadani-wao. The paved way begins just beyond this, and is now continuous from the foot of the hill up the precipice and over the three peaks. The way is paved with dressed granite blocks, with parapets and easy steps. The first R.H., Chodiaparaba, is reached 480 ft. above the plain, and the second halting-place, at Dholi-deri, 1000 ft. above the plain. From here the ascent becomes more difficult, winding under the face of the precipice to the third R.H., 1400 ft. up. So far there is nothing very trying to any one with an ordinarily steady brain. But from this point the path turns to the right along the edge of a precipice, although it is never less than 1 metre wide and in very good condition. The *doli* almost grazes the scarp, which rises perpendicularly 200 ft. above the traveller. On the right is seen the mountain of Datar, with a Muslim Mosque on top. At about 1500 ft. there is a stone dharmsala, and from this there is a fine view of the rock called the Bhairav-Japa, "the terrific leap", because devotees used to cast themselves from its top, falling 1000 ft. or more.

At 2370 ft. above Junagadh the gate of the enclosure known as the **Deva Kota,** associated with Rao Khengar I of Kutch, is reached. On entering the gate the large enclosure of the temples is on the left, while to the right is the old granite temple of Rao Bhojraj of Kutch, and farther on the much larger one of Vastupala (p. 281). Built into the wall on the left of the entrance is an inscription in Sanskrit. Some sixteen Jain temples here form a sort of fort on the ledge at the top of the great cliff, but still 600 ft. below the summit. The largest temple, of Neminath (see plan below) stands in a quadrangular court 195 ft. by 130 ft. It consists of two halls (with two *mandapams*), and a shrine, with multiple conical spires, which contains a large black image of Neminath, the 22nd Tirthankar, with massive gold ornaments and jewels. Round the shrine is a colonnade, with many images in white marble. Between the outer and inner halls are two shrines. The outer hall has two small raised platforms paved with slabs of yellow stone, covered with representations of feet in pairs, which represent the 2452 feet of the first disciples. On the W. of this is a porch overhanging the perpendicular scarp. On two of the pillars of the mandapam are inscriptions dated 1275, 1281 and 1278—dates of restoration, when Dr Burgess says it was covered with a coating of chunam, and "adorned with coats of whitewash" within. The enclosure is nearly surrounded inside by 70 cells, each enshrining a marble image, with a covered passage in front of them lighted by a perforated stone screen. The principal entrance was originally on the E. side of the court; but it is closed, and the entrance from the court in Deva Kota is used.

A passage leads into a low, dark temple, with granite pillars. Opposite the entrance is a recess containing two large black images; in the back of the recess is a lion rampant, and over it a crocodile in bas-relief. Behind these figures is a room from which is a descent into a cave, with a large white marble image, an object of veneration by the Jains. It has a slight hollow in the shoulder, said to be caused by water dropping from the ear, whence it was called Amijhera, "nectar drop". In the N. porch are inscriptions which state that in Samwat 1215 (= A.D. 1159) certain Thakurs completed the shrine, and built the Temple of Ambika.

Of three temples to the left, that on the S. side contains a colossal image of Rishabha Deva, the 1st Tirthankar, exactly like that at Satrunjaya, called Bhim-Padam. On the throne of this image is a slab of yellow stone carved in 1442, with figures of the 24 Tirthankars. Opposite this temple is a modern one to Panchabai. W. of it is a large temple called Merakvasi, sacred to Parasnath. N. again of this is another temple of Parasnath, which contains a large white marble image canopied by a cobra, whence it is called Sheshphani, an arrangement not infrequently found in the S., but rare in the N. It bears a date = 1803. The last temple

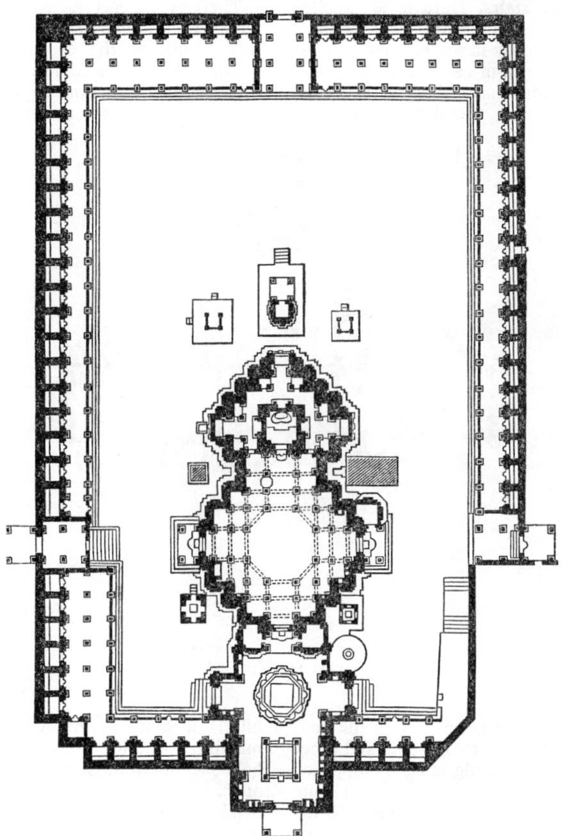

Temple of Neminath, Girnar.

to the N. is **Kumarapala's,** which has a long open portico on the W., restored in 1824 by Hansraja Jetha. These temples are along the W. face of the hill, and are all enclosed. Outside, to the N., is the Bhima Kunda, a tank 70 ft. by 50 ft., in which Hindus bathe.

Behind the temple of Neminath is the triple one erected by the brothers **Tejapala** and **Vastupala** (built 1177). The plan is that of three temples joined together. The middle shrine has an image of Mallinath, the 19th Tirthankar; the side ones are masses representing mountains, Maru and Parusnath. N. is the temple of **Samprati Raja,** date 1158. Samprati is said to have ruled at Ujjain in the end of the 3rd century B.C., and to have been the son of Kunala, Asoka's third son. E. of this, and 200 ft. above the Jain temples, is the Gaumukha Shrine, near a plentiful spring of water. From it the crest of the mountain (3330 ft.) is reached by a steep flight of stairs. Here is an ancient temple of Amba Mata, which is much resorted to by newly-married couples of the Brahmin caste. The bride and bridegroom have their clothes tied together, and, attended by their male and female relations, adore the goddess and present coco-nuts and other offerings. This pilgrimage is supposed to procure for the couple a long continuance of wedded bliss. To the E., not far off, are the three rocky spires of the Gorakhnath, the Neminath or Gúrúdattáraya, and the Kalika peaks.

S.E. of the Kalwa Gate of Junagadh is the **Shrine of Jamal Shah,** or **Datar.** After passing under a low arch near the city the house of the Mujawir, or attendant of the shrine, is seen in front. To the right is a stone platform surrounding an unusually fine mango-tree, with a tank just beyond, and the shrine of Datar, a building 30 ft. high with a fluted cone at top. Here it is necessary for a visitor to take off his shoes.

There is a **Leper Asylum** near the Datar Temple for 100 lepers of both sexes, built at the expense of the Wazir Sahib Baha-ud-din. Above it, 4 m. in S.E. direction, is the Datar Peak (2779 ft.). On the summit of the hill is a small shrine, which commands a beautiful view. The hill is held sacred by Muslims and Hindus alike, and is supposed to have a beneficial effect on lepers, who repair to it in considerable numbers.

Temple of Tejapala and Vastupala, Girnar.

67 m. from **Jetalsar** is **Verával*** station (R.R., C.H.). The railway terminus is on the W., close to the walls, and about ½ m. from the landing-place.

This is a very ancient seaport, and probably owes its existence to its more celebrated neighbour *Patan Somnath.* It rose into notice during the time of the Gujarat Sultans, and in their reigns became, until superseded by Surat, the principal port of embarkation for Muslim pilgrims to Mecca. It is still a flourishing seaport. (T.B.)

In the Temple Harsad Mate a celebrated inscription (1264) records that a mosque was endowed in that year, and bears dates in four different eras. It was from this inscription that it was discovered that the Valabhi era commenced in A.D. 319 and the Sri Singh era from A.D. 1113.

The River Devka, N. of Verával, joins the sea at Dani Barn. The Polo. The anchorages at Verával and Pátan are so bad that it is hard to account for the undoubted fact that from the earliest times they carried on a trade with the Red Sea, Persian Gulf and African coast. The place is renowned in Hindu mythology. Here the Jadavas slew each other, and here Krishna, the late legends of whom are connected with Kathiawar as the earlier ones are with Muttra (p. 291), was shot by the Bhil, Jara. In the **Gir Forest**, inland from Pátan, is the only area in India where the Asian

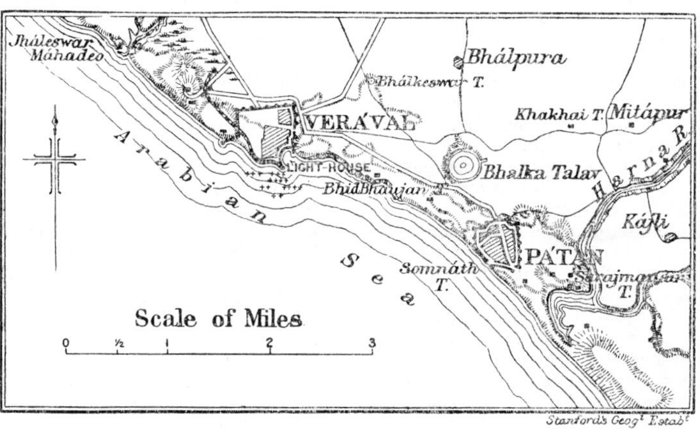

Verával and Pátan.

Jhálesvar Temple, about 2 m. N.W. from the town, at the mouth on the right bank, is of great antiquity. Half-way to it, on the sand dunes is the C.H. erected by the former Junagadh State. On the S.W. face of Verával there is a modern sea-wall and a stone pier. Harbour works have been constructed with a breakwater and foreshore pier. A railway connects Verával to Una Delvada (59 m.). A large Custom House has been built on the sea face, and near it is a dock estate, on reclaimed land.

On the seashore, nearly 3 m. to the S.E., is **Pátan Somnath** (R.H., Guest H.), also known as Prabhas Pátan, or Deva Pátan, the Semenat of Marco lion is found. (R.S. Sasangir: Forest R.H., I.B. Reservations from Conservator of Forest Junagadh.) Conducted tours to show the lions leave from Keshod airport and Junagadh (Rs. 10 per head, charge for photography). The lion population is estimated at about 150. There are also leopards, nilghai, blackbuck, gazelles and four-horned antelopes; but the extension of grazing by domestic animals threatens the future of wild life. Mahmud of Ghazni conquered Pátan in 1025, and it appears that he left behind a Muslim Governor. Subsequently the Hindus recovered their power, but it was again cast down by Alaf Khan (brother of Ala-ud-din Khilji), who invaded Somnath in 1297, when the coast belt or Nagher kingdom was conquered. From this date Muslim supremacy prevailed throughout the belt, and from the reign of Muhammad Tughlaq governors were regularly appointed. Through the gallantry and statesmanship of Diwan Amarji, it was conquered in 1770 by the Nawab of Junagadh.

Proceeding from Verával to Pátan, to the right is a vast burial-ground. with thousands of tombs, and *palias*. The Junagadh, or W. Gate, by which Pátan is entered, is a triple gate of Hindu architecture. The central part of the first division of the gateway is very ancient, and has a carving of two elephants on either side pouring water over Lakshmi, whose figure is almost obliterated.

After passing the second gate the W. wall of a mosque of the time of Mahmud is seen on the left. There is no inscription, but its antiquity is undoubted. After passing the third portal of the Junagadh Gate there are four stones on the right hand, of which two have Gujarati, and two Sanskrit inscriptions. Driving on straight through the bazar, which is very narrow, and has quaint old houses on either side, the *Jami Masjid* is reached. The entrance is by a porch, which has been a mandir in front of a Hindu temple. The most interesting part of this very ancient building is that in each of the four corners is a carving of two human figures with the Bo-Tree between them. A low door in the W. side of the porch leads into the court of the mosque, which was deserted for twenty-five years, and inhabited by Muslim fishermen, who dried their fish in it, but is now used again.

To reach the **Old Temple of Somnath** take the new broad access road which skirts the outside of the E. wall of Pátan. The structure is close to the sea. Fergusson considers that it was probably Jain and never large, but that the dome of its porch, which measures 33 ft. across, is as large as any of its age and type. Muslims record an image in it, not a lingam. It was, no doubt, surrounded by an enclosure. The temple has been completely restored through the efforts of the late Sardar Vallabhai Patel, whose statue stands outside the main entrance. There are three entrances to the porch, and a corridor round the central octagonal space, which was covered by the great dome. There are four smaller domes. The dome in the centre is supported by eight pillars and eight arches. The pillar on the right hand, looking from the E., next but one before reaching the adytum, has an inscription of which the date only, Samwat 1697 = A.D. 1640, is legible. The walls on the N., S. and W. side have each two handsomely carved niches, in which there have been idols.

The temple is said to have been first built of gold by Somraj (the Moon-god), then of silver by Ravana, then of wood by Krishna, and then of stone by Bhimdeva. It was destroyed in 1024 by Mahmud of Ghazni and restored by Kumarpal of Anhilpatan in 1169. In 1297 Alaf Khan Khalji (p. 283), destroyed it and again it was rebuilt by Mahipaldev of Wanthi in 1325. After Muzafir Khan's destruction in 1394 it was soon afterwards restored, but in 1706 Aurangzeb ordered its destruction.

The celebrated expedition of Sultan Mahmud of Ghazni to Somnath took place in 1024. He marched with such rapidity, by way of Gujarat, that the Hindu Rajas were unable to collect their forces for its defence, and after a sharp fight for two days, he conquered both the city and the temple. Immense spoil was found in the temple, and after a short stay Mahmud returned to Ghazni, taking with him the famous "Gates of Somnath". Sir Henry Elliot records that 10,000 populated villages were held by the temple as an endowment, and that 300 musicians and 500 dancing-girls were attached to it. There were also in the time of Mahmud of Ghazni

300 barbers to shave the heads of the pilgrims.

The **confluence of the Three rivers,** or *Tribeni,* to the E. of the town, has been a sacred spot from times of remote antiquity. It was near this that, according to tradition, Krishna, sleeping under a deer-skin, was accidentally shot by a Bhil named Jara and killed. The road to it passes through the E. gate, called the *Nana,* or "small gate", also the *Sangam,* or

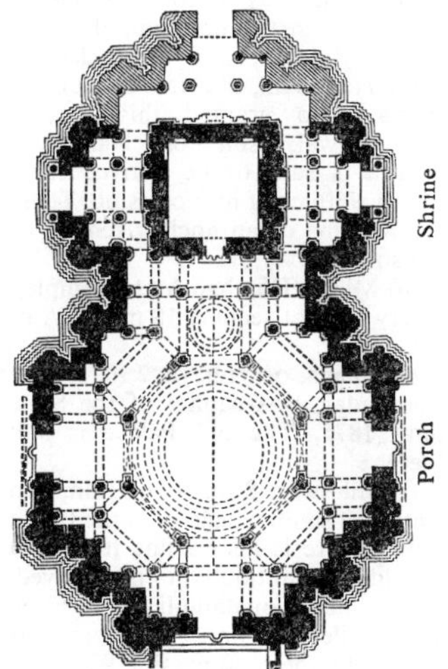

Plan of Temple of Somnath, by Dr J. Burgess.

"confluence gate". It has pilasters on either side, and on the capitals figures are represented issuing out of the mouths of Makaras, fabulous crocodiles which in Hindu mythology are the emblems of the God of Love. About ¼ m. outside the gate is a pool on the right hand, called the Kund, and a small building on the left, called the Adi Tirth, and next to these is a temple and the Tirth of Tribeni, where people are always bathing. The stream here is from 100 yd. to 200 yd. broad, and runs into the sea. N. of this, about 200 yd. off, is the **Suraj Mandir,** or Temple of the Sun, half broken down by Mahmud, standing on high ground and wondrously old and curious. Over the door of the adytum are groups of figures, with a tree between each two. Inside the adytum is a round red mark for the sun, not ancient; and below is a figure of a goddess, also coloured red. On the W. and S. outer walls are masses of carving much worn. At the bottom there is a frieze of *Keshari* lions—that is, lions with elephants' trunks. This temple is probably of the same age as that of Somnath. About 250 yd. to the W. is a vast tomb, quite plain; and below, in a sort of quarry, is a subterranean temple, which is called Ahdi Shah's. The same name is given to a mosque with six cupolas to the N., which has been a Hindu temple. 200 yd. to the N.W., inside the Nana Gate, is a temple built by Ahalya Bai of Indore to replace the ancient Somnath. Below it is another, reached by descending twenty-two steps. The dome of this subterranean building is supported by sixteen pillars. The temple itself is 13 ft. square.

Returning towards Verával, about ½ m. outside the Junagadh Gate, is the vast burial ground again. Its temple, the **Mai Puri,** was dedicated to the Sun. The carving of this building is exquisite. In the centre of the building is an enclosure 6 ft. square, in which Mai Puri, "the Perfect Mother", is buried. A legend states that she brought about the siege of Somnath by Mahmud. The temple (or mosque, as the Muslims have made it) contains a mass of old Hindu carving mutilated. On a pillar to the W. is an inscription, weathered and illegible. Not far from the Mai Puri is the tomb of Silah Shah. To the S.E., about 50 yd., is the tomb of Mangroli Shah, which has been restored. Two inscriptions on marble slabs in the W. wall give dates 699 A.H. (= A.D. 1299) and 1003 A.H. Before reaching the shrine the visitor passes through the porch of an ancient Hindu temple.

Near this spot is the Bhid Bhaujan Pagoda on the shore, locally known as Bhidiyo—very old, perhaps of the

14th century. It is 60 ft. high, and forms a good landmark.

Occasional coasting steamers call at Verával, and the journey can be made by sea to Bombay or to Porbandar or Kutch.

The island of **Diu** (7 m. long from E. to W., and 2 m. at its broadest point from N. to S.) is separated from the S. extremity of the Kathiawar peninsula by a narrow channel. Diu town and fort (constructed in 1536 by the Portuguese) stand at the E. of the island. Diu, when Portuguese, was subordinate to Goa (p. 449). It was attacked in 1545 by the Egyptians from Suez, but they were beaten off. Its history has been uneventful since 1670, when it was raided by Arabs from Muskat. It was once a port for export of Malwa opium. The village of Goghla, on the mainland opposite, and the fort of Simbur on a blunt peninsula about half a mile out to sea, were also Portuguese.

The Indian Government occupied it in 1961. The entrance from the mainland is 6½ m. W. on the road from the town of Una.

(2) *Jetalsar to Porbandar*

(Porbandar Ry.)

9 m. **Dhoraji,** an important commercial town. Tramway communication to the town.

78 m. from Jetalsar is **Porbandar** (Guest H., airport, I.A.S.), capital of the former Jethwa Rajput State of that name, area 642 sq. m., now part of Gujarat. It is a stopping-place on the Bombay-Bhuj Air Line.

Adatiana stone is much used at Bombay. In spite of heavy competition, commerce is considerable, including, besides traffic with the Konkan and Malabar coast, a brisk trade with the Persian Gulf, Arabia, and the E. coast of Africa. Silk of good quality and cotton cloth are manufactured.

Mahatma Gandhi was born (1869) a subject of the State. His birthplace—Kirti Mandir—has a shikhara 79 ft. high marking his age at his death.

The town is identified with Sudâmapuri, mentioned in the *Bhagavadgita*. Nearby is an old temple of Sudâma. A goods branch along the shore to the creek W. of the town terminates in a wharf. Porbandar is easily reached by air.

The places of interest in the neighbourhood are:

(*a*) Srinagar, 7 m. N.W. of Porbandar, said by Bardic Chronicles to have been the first capital of the Jethwa Rajputs, who claim descent from Hanuman, the faithful ally of Rama, who granted this site to Makardhwaj, son of Hanuman. Jethwa is said to be derived from Jethiji, 95th chief in succession. There are remains of an ancient temple of the sun.

(*b*) Miani (Harshad Mata Temple), a very ancient seaport 18 m. N.W. of Porbandar.

(*c*) Chaya, or Vhhaya, 2 m. S.E. of Porbandar, was capital of the State until 1875. The old Palace is still there.

(*d*) Bileswar, 8 m. N. of Ranawao station, a small village E. of the Barda Hills. There is here a fine temple of considerable antiquity, well preserved.

(*e*) Ghumli, or Bhumli, about 12 m. N. of Bileswar, or 24 m. from Porbandar by the road passing W. of the Barda Hills, was the second capital of the Jethwa Rajputs. It lies in a gorge; the ruins are of the 11th or 12th century. After the sack of Ghumli the Jethwas retired to Ranpur, and, some time afterwards, were driven to Chaya (above). They acquired Porbandar and Navi from the Mughals. The chief remains are the Lakhota, Ganesh Dehra, Rampol, Jeta Wao, the temples near the Son Kansari Tank, and some ruins on the summit of Abapura Hill. It is about 4 m. S. of Bhanwar, a fort belonging to Nawanagar.

40 m. S.E. from Porbandar is **Madhavapur,** where Krishna is said to have been married. There is a temple dedicated to him.

(3) *Jetalsar to Rajkot, Wankaner, and Wadhwan*

(Gondal Ry.)

23 m. **Gondal** (Guest House, D.B.), capital of the former Gondal State. A former Maharaja, Sir Bhagwatsinhji Sagramji, G.C.S.I., G.C.I.E., Rajput of the Jadeja clan, had a remarkable career. He received full powers in 1884, after completing his education at Edinburgh, where he took the degrees of M.D. and F.R.C.P. He was also a D.C.L. of Oxford and LL.D. of Edinburgh. Owing, moreover, to his financial foresight, the State was free from taxes, customs duties and octroi. He died in 1946.

The founder, Kumbhoji I, son of Meramanji I of Sardhar, received Ardoi in 1634 and expanded his possessions. Sagramji I, his successor, obtained Gondal from the Subahdar of Junagadh in return for help against Kusbatis, Muslim marauders. The capital was moved here in 1653. Gondal has always been notable for the vigour of its public works. It has a College for the sons of Girassias (Rajput landholders) who cannot afford the Rajkumar College at Rajkot. The town also contains the Bai Sahib Asylum, the Bhagwatsinhji Orphanage, a Girls' High School, and waterworks for irrigation and water supply.

47 m. **Rajkot** (pop. 300,000 in 1971) station (C.H., D.B.K.; alt. 404 ft.; airfield). Rajkot, where I.A.C. planes call, was formerly the capital of a small Jadeja Rajput State, whose Ruler, the Thakor Sahib, belongs to the clan which is headed by the Maharaos of Kutch. It was also, until 1947, the headquarters of the British Resident for the Western India States, who lived in a small civil enclave rented from the Thakor. The former home of Gandhi is now a school. In recent years there has been a great development of small-scale industry in the city and surrounding areas.

The most important public work in Rajkot is the Kaisar-i-Hind Bridge over the Aji River, built by R. B. Booth, at the expense of the late Maharaja of Bhavnagar.

The Rajkumar *College* for the education of the young nobles of Kathiawar, Gujarat, and other localities, was founded in 1870 by Colonel R. H. Keatinge, V.C. It is now a Public School run on more traditional lines, and has become one of the foremost and best in the whole of Western India. The buildings are impressive; there is a fine quadrangle and excellent sports grounds.

The Alfred High School was opened in January 1875. It was built at the expense of the Nawab of Junagadh. Here Gandhi received his secondary education; his statue stands outside the school.

In the former Civil Station are the Jubilee Gardens, containing the Memorial Institute. It comprises (1) the Lang Library; (2) the Connaught Hall, which is used for public meetings and official Darbars; and (2) the Watson Museum (1888) (daily except Sat. and Sun.)—a collection of antiquities, products, and manufactures of Kathiawar. The Connaught Hall contains portraits of the leading Chiefs of Kathiawar.

N.E. of Rajkot there are (1) the Victoria Jubilee Waterworks, for the Civil Station; and (2) the Lalpuri Irrigation Works, for the Rajkot city, with irrigation canals.

The Saurashtra Mail of the Western Ry. continues from Rajkot to (51 m.) Jamnagar, which is on the I.A.C. route from Bombay and served by daily planes.

Jamnagar, (pop. 214,000 in 1971) (Lal Bungalow, G.H., Hotel (Indian Style) Ashoka). Important I.A.F. Station: capital of the former Jadeja Rajput State of Nawanagar, of which the famous cricketer, Jam Ranjitsinhji, was ruler from 1907 to 1933. His successor, the late Jam Sahib, was for many years in the Indian Army and in 1948 became Rajpramukh (Prince President) of Saurashtra until this unit was abolished and its area absorbed first into Bombay (1956) and then into Gujarat (1960). Marble is found in the

Kandorna and Bhanvad Mahals, copper in the Khambhalia Mahal. There is also a pearl fishery lying off the S. shore of the Kutch Gulf. The Jamnagar dyers are well known, and the town is famous for silken and gold embroidery. The Kotha Bastion and Lakhota (fort in middle of lake: Museum) are sights, and the City Palace. Jam Ranjitsinhji's gift to the State of a solarium for radiant heat treatment is unique in western India. Bedi port has considerable local trade, and sea-connections with Kutch. Balachari is a seaside resort with a golf-course.

Beyond Jamnagar, the temples at **Dwarka** ("door") and **Bait** ("island"), R.H., in the extreme N.W. of Kathiawar, are in the district of **Okhamandal,** which in 1817 became part of the territory of the State of Baroda. They are very sacred to Hindus. Dwarka was the capital of Krishna, who founded it after his flight from Mathura (p. 291), when attacked by Jarasandha the King of Magadha. It ranks as one of the Great Seven places of pilgrimage, with Benares, Muttra, Hardwar, Ajudhia (in Oudh), Ujjain, and Conjeeveram (in S. India). The temple of Dwarkanath (a title of Krishna) is believed to have been raised in a single night (open only to Hindus). A *Math* (monastery) one of the four founded by Shankarachaya is also at Dwarka.

Bait island is associated with Vishnu, who is said to have destroyed a demon named Sankhasun here, and to have turned the demon's wife, Tulsi, into the basil plant, which is so called. The temple is dedicated to Satiya Bhimaji, consort of Krishna.

The original possessors of Okhamandal were a war-like tribe of Rajputs, called "Wakhars", who were notorious pirates. Though reduced (1820) by the British Government, they still remained unruly, and the British Government retained special control over them until 1932.

The return journey to Ahmedabad is made from Rajkot, whence a metre-gauge line runs N.E. to **Wankaner** junction (26 m.). This is the capital of the former Jhala Rajput State of the same name (417 sq. m.). The country around rises into hills W. and S. The Palace stands on a hill. By arrangement, visitors can stay as guests of the Maharana either in the Palace or in Oasis House, an annexe about a mile N. There are fine game trophies and a family museum in the Palace, while the annexe has an indoor swimming pool.

From Wankaner there is a branch (16 m.) N. to **Morvi,** the capital of the former State of that name (822 sq. m.). Originally a Jethwa Rajput State, it was conquered by the Muslim King of Gujarat, Sultan Mahmud Bigarha (p. 253), who granted it to Khengarji I, founder of the present Kutch Dynasty. There is a launch-service between Naulakhi, the port of Morvi, and Kandla in Kutch.

The main line runs E. to (47 m.) Wadhwan and (88 m.) Viramgam (see p. 273). A chord line runs (41 m.) to Mehsana (see p. 254) for Ajmer and Delhi.

ROUTE 12

BARODA by Western Ry. (broad-gauge), to **Champaner Road** (for **Champaner** and **Pavagadh**), **Bayana** (junction for Agra), **Bharatpur,** MUTTRA, and thence to DELHI.

The Western Ry. "Frontier Mail" from Bombay turns E. on the broad-gauge chord, opened 1903, from **Baroda** (p. 245, Route 10), to

267 m. from Bombay, **Champaner Road** station. N.G. railway (31 m.) to the Pani Mines. The fortified hill of Pavagadh, at the foot of which lies the ruined city of **Champaner,** stands out from the plain of Gujarat and is visible for many miles. The hill is about 1 m. from the Pavagadh station on the N.G. railway. The summit is about 2700 ft above sea-level and the ascent may be made on foot (2 hr.) or in dhoolies. It is an all-day trip, best made by car from Baroda. D.B. at Halol station (7 m. from Champaner Road), 5 m. off; there is no arrangement for travellers to stop the night at Pavagadh.

Champaner was the ancient fortress city of local Rajput kings. After many vicissitudes it was taken, in 1484, by Mahmud Bigarha, of Ahmedabad, who made it his capital, and renamed it Muhamadabad. In 1535 it was besieged by the Emperor Humayun, father of Akbar, who, with a small party which he led in person, scaled the precipices of the fort by the aid of iron spikes driven into the rock, and opened the gate to admit his army. There are remains of many mosques, tombs, and tanks in the lower city; and in the forest for miles around, the ruins of massive wells, minarets, and palaces testify to the former greatness of Champaner.[1]

[1] For the architecture of Champaner, the best account is still Burgess's *Mohammedan Architecture of Gujarat* (1896).

The Jami Masjid has been restored by the Archaeological Department, and has eleven domes. The Borah Masjid is also well worth a visit. The height and strength of the part of the city wall which remains standing give an idea of the importance of the city.

In the ascent of **Pavagadh** there are interesting ruins at the Medi and Medi Talao. Other ruins are the Buria Durwaza, the Champavati or Champa Ranina Mahal, which is a sort of summer-house in three storeys abutting on the hill, the fortifications near the Machhi Haveli, which is half-way up, and the gate and fortifications higher up. There is a temple of Bhawani on the summit, which is surmounted by a shrine of Sadan Shah, a Muslim saint. This shrine is built on the spire of the Hindu temple, the top of which has been removed to make room for it—a curious arrangement, which is supposed to represent the triumph of Muslim conquerors over the Rajput Chiefs.

289 m. from Bombay **Godhra,** headquarters of the Panch Mahals district of Bombay. A n.g. railway, 26 m., runs to Lunawada, chief town of a former State. A b.g. branch, 49 m., connects with Anand on the main line between Baroda and Ahmedabad (Route 10, p. 240).

334 m. **Dohad,** in a pass through the hills, contains the tomb of Mahmud II, Khilji of Mandu, executed (1526) by Bahadur Shah of Gujarat.

384 m. Mahi river, bridge 1100 ft. long.

404 m. **Ratlam** (D.B.K.), capital of the former State of that name (p. 208). Junction for the metre-gauge line from Khandwa to Ajmer (Route 8).

429 m. Chambal river.

430 m. **Nagda.** Branch line (broad-gauge) of the Central Ry. to Ujjain and Bhopal (Route 9).

From Nagda the main line of the Western Ry. turns N. and runs to 518 m. **Sri Chatrapur,** 17 m. from **Jhalra Patan.** Both these towns are in the former State of Jhalawar, created out of the parent State of Kotah in 1838 to make a separate raj for the descendants of the blind Zalim Singh, the famous regent of Kotah, in return for the extinction of their hereditary right to control the administration. It is now part of the State of Rajasthan. Baroli, N.W., and the Dhamnar caves, S.W., may be visited.

At 540 m. **Darah,** the line passes through the famous Mukand Dwara Pass, from which, in the summer of 1804 Colonel Monson made his disastrous retreat of over 200 m. to Agra before Jaswant Rao Holkar; the scenery here is striking; the railway is on a curved viaduct.

570 m. Kotah Junction. **Kotah** (pop. 213,000 in 1971) (alt. 824 ft.) (R.R., C.H., Hotel Navranj) is the capital of the former Kotah State, separated from Bundi (p. 215) in 1572. The former ruling family were Rajputs of the Hara sept of the Chauhan clan.

Kotah is situated on the east bank of the Chambal just below a striking stretch of the river enclosed in a deep gorge, which is well worth exploring by boat; the fine old palace, now a museum, and cenotaphs lie S. of it. The new palace is called the Umed Bhawan. There is a fine General Hospital in the city; also a Hospital for Women. Other public buildings of interest are the Crosthwaite Institute, situated in the Public Gardens; the Herbert High School; the Curzon Wyllie Memorial, and the Girls' School. The lake above the gardens should be seen. There is a Game Sanctuary at Dara.

Near Kotah on the Chambal there is an atomic power plant, an impressive modern barrage and a hydro-electric power-station.

A mile or two from Kotah on the W. bank of the river there is a tank full of more or less tame crocodiles which come on call to be fed. **Bundi** (p. 215) is only 24 m. off on a good motoring road, but the Irish bridge across the Chambal is often submerged in the rains. When this occurs, traffic uses the road across the top of the Kotah Barrage.

A branch (broad-gauge) of the Central Ry. runs from Kotah, 188 m., to Bina Junction (p. 222), through (114 m.) **Goona,** a Cantonment of the Central India Horse until 1924. The last lion in Central India was shot here (1874).

575 m. the railway crosses the Chambal river again, on a bridge 1652 ft. long (1909).

N. of Kotah the main line of the Central Ry. passes, 637 m., Sawai Madhupur, from which a metre-gauge line branches N.W. to Sanganer (p. 270). Nawai (41 m.) on this line is the station for **Tonk,** across the Banas river. Round Tonk the scenery is very picturesque. Amirgarh Fort was built by Amir Khan.

Near Sawai Madhupur is a game sanctuary formerly belonging to Jaipur where there are many tigers, and not far off is the famous hill-fort of Ranthambhor, reachable on foot or by pony. There is another ancient fort at Kundhar, near the junction of the Banas and Chambal, where excellent mahseer fishing is to be had.

704 m., Hindaun, in the Jaipur, was once a place of importance, but was devastated by the Mahrattas.

724 m. from Bombay **Bayana** (Biana) on the bank of the Gambhir River, once a famous city, near which Babur defeated the Sanga Rana (Sangram Singh) of Chitorgarh on 16th March 1527, after sustaining a severe check from this Prince in the previous month; it was from Babur's victory that Sikri received the name of Fatehpur. The Rana, who was the bravest Hindu warrior of his day, refused to return as a defeated Chief to Chitor. Bayana, in Bharatpur State, was first invaded by Muhammad Ghori in 1196. Shortly afterwards it passed back into the hands of the Hindus, but was reconquered by Altamsh in 1235. It was visited by Akbar in 1601, and the mother of Jahangir planted a garden there, a fine gateway of which still exists. Muslim buildings are numerous.

Broad-gauge branch, 47 m., to

Fatehpur Sikri and **Agra Fort** station (Route 13).

750 m. from Bombay is **Bharatpur** Junction (D.B., outside Muttra Gate). A metre-gauge line of the Western Ry. from Bandikui Junction to Agra Fort meets the main broad-gauge line to Delhi here. Bharatpur, or Bhurtpore, is the capital of a former Jat State. The Maharaja's palace is at Golbagh, about 1 m. outside the city.

The family is descended from a Jat Zamindar, Churaman, who harassed the rear of Aurangzeb's army during his expedition to the Deccan in 1681. He was succeeded by his brother, and (1720) by his nephew, the famous Suraj Mal, who fixed his capital at Bharatpur (1733), and subsequently (1761) drove out the Mahratta Governor from Agra, which he made his own residence. He was killed in 1763, and in 1765 the Jats were repelled before Delhi and driven out of Agra in 1770. In 1782 Scindia seized Bharatpur and its territory; but he restored fourteen districts, and when he fell into difficulties (1787) formed an alliance with Ranjit Singh (who ruled between 1763 and 1805). The Jats, however, were defeated by Ghulam Kadir at Fatehpur-Sikri, and were driven back on Bharatpur, but being reinforced at the end of the same year, 1788, they raised the blockade of Agra, and Scindia recovered it. In 1803 the British Government concluded a treaty with Ranjit Singh, who joined General Lake at Agra with 5000 horse, and received territory in return. Upon Ranjit Singh supporting Jaswant Rao Holkar, in 1804, Bharatpur was besieged by General Lake, but after four unsuccessful assaults on the fort the Chief made overtures for peace, which was ratified on the 4th of May 1805.

On a dispute about the succession, Bharatpur was besieged by General Lord Combermere, and on the 18th of January 1826, after a siege of three weeks, the place was stormed. The treasure taken amounted to 48 lakhs of rupees. The fortress was then dismantled.

The **Walled City** of Bharatpur is an irregular oblong, lying N.E. and S.W. The **Inner Fort** (museum), surrounded by a ditch and a lofty mud wall, is contained in the N.E. half of the outer fort. Three Palaces run right across the centre of the inner fort from E. to W., that to the E. being the Raja's Palace. Next is an old Palace built by Badan Singh. To the W. is a Palace generally styled the Kamra.

There are only two gates to the inner fort—the Chauburj Gate on the S., and the Assaldati on the N. The fine bastion at the N.W. corner of the inner fort is called the Jowahar Burj, and is worth ascending for the view. N. of the Kamra Palace are the Court of Justice and the Jewel Office. On the road between the Chauburj Gate of the inner fort and the Anah Gate of the outer fort are the Gangaka Mandir and the Laksmanji Temple.

There is a chhattri erected by a former Maharaja in the Victoria Park Gardens in memory of General Sir James Willcocks, who died here in December 1926. A great marsh, the **Ghana**, 2 m. N.W. of the city, was famous for the annual duck-shooting, very strictly preserved. Enormous bags were secured. But Ghana is now a Bird Sanctuary, with a motel for visitors—new and good. Ninety-five species of migratory birds can be seen in winter. There is a Forest R.H. at Shanti Kutir. Tourist Information Bureau in Agra Road supplies details of reservations and guided excursions.

771 m. from Bombay by the Western Ry. broad-gauge route is **MUTTRA** (or Mathura) (pop. 140,000 in 1971) on the W. bank of the Jumna. The city lies to the N. of the municipal area. S. of this comes the Cantonment and to the S. of the Cantonment and interlaced with it are the Civil Lines.

Outside the city proper the other places of interest are the Headquarters Hospital, erected mainly at the cost of Goswami Sri Gobardhan Lalji, the high priest of the Nathwara temple in Udaipur, in memory of his pilgrimage to Muttra in 1912; the

Victoria Memorial; the Dampier Park and the Curzon Museum. All these places lie on the Grand Trunk Road between the city and Cantonments.

In **Cantonments** are situated the D.B. (small and of an indifferent character) and the three churches, two Protestant and one Roman Catholic. The Anglican Church contains a few interesting tablets; the Roman Catholic Church was constructed by Mr Growse (a collector, and author of the *Mathura Gazetteer*) in an attempt to combine features of both Western and Oriental architecture. The cemetery, which is just behind the D.B., contains monuments to the memory of officers, who fell at the Battle of Dig in 1804.

Railways.—Muttra is served by three railway lines. The main Central Ry. line from Bombay, 868 m., through Jhansi, Gwalior, and Agra Cant. to Delhi; the Western Ry. broad-gauge from Bombay, 771 m., *via* Nagda, and metre-gauge, 259 m. from Agra Fort *via* Achnera to Kanpur. This connects with the Northern Ry. system at Hathras Road Junction, 30 m. from Muttra. All three lines converge at the junction station, situated about 2 m. from Cantonments and the city, and equipped with ample waiting-room accommodation and refreshment rooms. The small Cantonment station (metre-gauge), about half-way between the city and Civil Lines, is used mainly by passengers proceeding to or arriving from the E. There is a small waiting-room. Masani station (formerly the City station) is on a branch metre-gauge line from Muttra to Brindaban, and is mainly used by pilgrims travelling between these two places.

Roads.—The Cantonments and Civil Lines are well laid out with the usual broad roads and avenues of trees. In the city the roads are extremely narrow.

Motorists proceeding from Agra to Delhi or Brindaban who do not wish to pass through the city, should take the diversion-road which leaves the Grand Trunk Road just S. of the quarterguard in Cantonments, and, skirting the city, rejoins it outside the Shahganj Gate near the Masani station. From Muttra there radiate metalled roads to Delhi (98 m.); to Brindaban (6 m.); to Bharatpur (25 m.); to Dig (24 m.); to Agra (35 m.); to Hathras (25 m.). The road to Hathras crosses the Jumna on the Western Ry. metre-gauge bridge. About 2 m. E. of the railway bridge another metalled road branches off leading to Gokul, Mahaban, Baldeo and thence to Sadabad and the Etah district.

The **Government Museum of Archaeology** in Dampier Park (daily except Mondays: no fee), which was opened in January 1933, contains a collection of Mauryan, Sunga, Kushan, Jain and Brahman objects found in the Muttra district. Among the sculptures are the Bacchanalian group of Pali Khera, remarkable for its pronounced classical inspiration, and the exquisitely carved standing Buddha image of the 5th century A.D., which was unearthed on the site of the Buddhist monastery founded by King Huvishka, now occupied by the Collector's court-house.

Among later acquisitions are the colossal statue from the village of Parkham, which belongs to the 2nd century B.C., and is one of the oldest detached images found in Indian soil; and the image of a Nága, or serpent god, of the reign of Huvishka (A.D. 162-182), obtained from the village of Chhargaon. Two pillars are worthy of notice. An inscription upon one of them, engraved in the Gupta year 61 (A.D. 380-381) during the reign of Chandragupta III, gives the earliest date upon which he has been proved to have been on the throne. On the other, the inscription supplies the earliest date (the year 28 = A.D. 107) yet known of the reign of the Kushan King Huvishka who was apparently then ruling conjointly with his brother Vasishka, while their father, the great Kanishka, was campaigning beyond the mountains. There is also a sacrificial post (*Yupa*) erected by a Brahman in the reign of Vasishka (year 24). Of Kanishka there is a life-size statue, which shows the King's costume and weapons. The head has been lost. Together with this, two other images were found, one of colossal size, which also must represent Princes of the Kushan dynasty.

Sport.—Black buck, chinkara and small game were common but have now been depleted: there is still excellent pig-sticking in the bed of the Jumna.

History.—The site is of great antiquity, and has been inhabited from at least 600 B.C. The earliest town appears to have been farther back from the river towards the modern village of Maholi, but in the course of centuries the city has gradually moved nearer the Jumna, which may have altered its course. Muttra is referred to by Ptolemy as Μόδουρα ἡ τῶν Θεῶν (Modoura of the Gods) and was a great Buddhist stronghold in the Buddhist period.

Fa Hian (A.D. 401-410) found there 20 Buddhist monasteries with 3000 monks: but when Hiuen Tsang visited the place in A.D. 634, the number had declined to 2000. Buddhism had disappeared when Mahmud of Ghazni came to Muttra in A.D. 1017. He pillaged and burned the city, and carried off five golden idols, whose eyes were of rubies, worth 50,000 dinars = £25,000. A sixth idol of gold weighed 1120 lb., and was decorated with a sapphire weighing 300 Mishkals, or 3½ lb. There were also 100 idols of silver, each of which loaded a camel, weighing, say, 400 lb. apiece. The idols together were worth not less than £3,000,000. The Brahman temple of Kesava Deo was built on the site where the great Buddhist monastery, Yasa Vihara, stood. Muttra was attacked by Sikandar Lodi in 1500, and great harm was done to the shrines and temples.

The Fort, Badulgarh, rebuilt in Akbar's time, was in the centre, but only the substructure remains. In his tolerant reign and that of his son Jahangir, Muttra again began to flourish, but the present city dates from the time of Abd-un-Nabi—one of Aurangzeb's Governors (1660-68). He was killed in a local revolt, which Aurangzeb utilised as a pretext for demolishing all the chief temples in the town, including the Kesava Deo temple.

With the break-up of the Mughal Empire, a time of trouble ensued. Lying on the high roads between Delhi and Agra, Muttra became the cockpit of the fighting that took place between the later Mughals, the Jats and Mahrattas. It was the favourite residence of Madhava Rao Scindia.

The district and city of Muttra came into the possession of the British as the result of Lord Lake's famous campaign, 1803-05. Since then, its history has been uneventful save for the operations undertaken in 1825 against Bharatpur and a brief upset during the 1857 mutiny.

Religious Associations.—The abiding interest of Muttra lies in its religious associations. Not only the town itself but the greater part of the district, known as Braja Mandal, or Brij, commands the reverence and respect of Hindus. It is studded with places of pilgrimage, connected with the Krishna legend, and is visited throughout the year by devout crowds of pilgrims. In the rainy season, large bands, under the guidance of their religious leaders, perambulate the district, performing the "Banjatra", or "pilgrimage of the groves" (of which there are 12 main and 24 subsidiary), and acting the main scenes in the life of Krishna at the localities connected by legend with them.

The chief places of pilgrimage are Muttra city itself, Brindaban, Mahaban with Gokul, Baldeo, Gobardhan and Radha Kund, and Barsana.

Muttra City. The city is entered by the Holi Gate, built by the Municipality. The finely carved stonework façades of the better class of houses are well worthy of inspection.

In the centre of the town, on an

isolated site, rises the **Jami Masjid,** built by Abd-un-nabi, once covered with encaustic tiles; its court is 14 ft. above the level of the street. On either side of the façade of the gateway are Persian lines. The chronogram gives the date 1660-61. Over the façade of the mosque proper are the 99 names of God. At the sides are two pavilions roofed in the Hindu manner. There are four minarets, which are 132 ft. high. About ¼ m. beyond is the **Katra,** which is an enclosure like that of a sarai, 804 ft. long by 653 ft. broad. Upon a terrace 30 ft. high stands a great red stone mosque, built by Aurangzeb, and used as an **Idgah,** and the most conspicuous object in a distant view of Muttra. This mosque was raised on the ruins of the Kesava Deo Temple, which was destroyed by Aurangzeb, and which, shortly before its destruction, was seen by the travellers Bernier, Tavernier, and Manucci. The foundations of the temple used to be traceable at the back of the mosque. The Brahmanical temple of Kesava Deo was built on the ruins of a large Buddhist monastery, which, as appears from inscriptions found here, dated back to the Kushan period, and still existed in the days of the Gupta Emperors. The earliest Buddhist inscriptions found here may be assigned to the beginning of the Christian era, and one of the latest contains the genealogy of the Gupta dynasty, down to Samudra-Gupta (A.D. 330-375). A Buddha image, extracted by General Cunningham from a well in 1862, and now preserved in the Lucknow Museum, mentions the *Yasá-vihara.* The inscription is dated in the Gupta year 230 (A.D. 549-550).

At the back of the Katra is a modern temple to Kesava, built by Bir Singh Deo of Orchha, and close by is the **Potara-Kund,** a tank in which Krishna's baby linen was washed. This tank is faced with red sandstone, and has flights of stone steps down to the water. There is also a very steep ramp for horses and cattle.

The **River** and **Ghats.**—The Jumna in winter is about 300 yd. broad. A paved street runs the whole way along it, with bathing ghats, descending to the water, and ornamental chabutras, or platforms, and small pavilions.

The *Arati* ceremony, or worship of the sacred river, takes place about dusk at the **Vishant Ghat,** when cows, monkeys and turtles are fed. The most convenient way of seeing the ceremony is to take a boat.

80 yd. N. of the bridge is the fine **House** of the **Guru Parshotamdas.** Then comes another named after a Gujarati merchant, **Ballamdas.** N. again is a slender quadrangular tower of red sandstone, 55 ft. high, known as the **Sati Burj.** The upper part is said to have been destroyed by Aurangzeb, and the plastered dome is modern. It was built (after 1574) to commemorate the *sati* of a wife of Raja Bhar Mal, of Ambèr, by her son, Bhagwan Das (p. 269). The traveller now descends several steps to the Visvant Ghat, a little N. of the Sati Burj, and so to a sort of square, where Rajas were weighed against gold. There is a small white marble arch here close to the river. Beyond this is a ghat built by Maharaja Jai Singh, of Jaipur, and the enormous house and temple of the late Seth Lakshman Das. The observatory of Jai Singh (p. 267) has gone.

Excursions

Mahaban (bus service) is about 6 m. S.E. of Muttra, on the left bank of the Jumna, and is reached by a good road across the railway bridge. It is a very ancient town and place of pilgrimage, and in the year A.D. 1017 shared the fate of Muttra, and was sacked by Mahmud of Ghazni. The Hindu Raja is said to have solemnly slain his wife and children and then committed suicide. In 1234 Mahaban is mentioned as one of the gathering places of the army sent by Shams-ud-din

Altamsh against Kalinjar in Bundelkhand. It is also mentioned in his diary by Babur in 1526.

The surrounding country, although now bare of woods, appears to have been once literally *Mahaban*, "a great forest". Even as late as 1634, the Emperor Shah Jahan held a hunt here, and killed four tigers. This ancient woodland country fringing the sacred Jumna is the scene of very early religious legends. In Sanskrit literature it is closely associated with **Gokul** (temple of Gokulnath), about a mile off, overhanging the Jumna. Indeed, the scenes of the youthful adventures of Krishna, actually shown at Mahaban, about a mile from the river are ascribed in the Puranas to Gokul. Gokul seems to have been originally the common name for the whole, although it is now restricted to what must have been a waterside suburb.

The ruins of Mahaban, a hill of brick and mud covering about 30 acres are on the site of an old fort built by Rana Katira of Mewar. The architectural remains combine Buddhist and Hindu forms. Mahaban is celebrated as the place where in his infancy Krishna was brought by his nurse and exchanged with the newly-born daughter of Jasoda, wife of Nanda, to save him from death, at the hands of Krishna's uncle, the giant Kans. This recalls the story of Herod.

The so-called **Palace of Nanda,** foster-father of the changeling Krishna, consists of a covered court, re-erected by Muslims in the time of Aurangzeb as a mosque, and is divided into 4 aisles by 5 rows of 16 pillars, 80 in all, from which it takes its popular name of Assi Khamba, or the "Eighty Pillars". Many of the capitals are curiously carved with grotesque heads and squat figures. Four of them are supposed to represent by their sculptures the four ages of the world. The pillar known as the Satya Yug, or "Golden Age", is covered with rich and beautiful carving; that known as the Treta Yug, or "Second Age" of the world, is adorned with almost equal profusion. The Dwapar Yug, or "Third Age", is more scantily carved; while the Kali Yug, or present "Iron Age" of the world, is represented by a crude unsculptured pillar.

In the Palace of Nanda are laid the scenes of Krishna's infancy. His cradle, a rough structure covered with red calico and tinsel, still stands in the pillared hall, while a blue-black image of the sacred child looks out from under a canopy against the wall. The churn in which Krishna's foster-mother made butter for the household is shown, and consists of a long bamboo sticking out of a carved stone. A spot in the wall is pointed out as the place where the sportive milkmaids hid Krishna's flute. One pillar is said to have been polished by his foster-mother's hand, as she leant against it when churning, and others have been equally polished by the hands of generations of pilgrims. From the top of the roof there is a view over mounds of ruins, with the Jumna beyond, at intervals.

Mahaban is a popular place of Hindu pilgrimage. Thousands of Vishnu worshippers, with yellow-stained clothes, yearly visit the scenes of the infancy of the child-god. The anniversary of Krishna's birth is celebrated during several days in the month of Bhadon (August).

The river-side village of **Gokul,** about a mile from Mahaban, where Vishnu first appeared as Krishna, is approached by a lofty and beautiful flight of steps (ghat) from the river. For more than three centuries it has been the headquarters of the Valabhacharya sect, or Gokulastha Gusains, whose founder started the cult of Krishna at Brindaban. Pilgrims come chiefly from Gujarat and Bombay yearly, and have built numerous temples.

Some 5 m. from Mahaban, on the same road, lies another famous place of pilgrimage, **Baldeva,** known more familiarly as "Dauji". The town derives its celebrity from the famous temple of Baladeva, Krishna's elder brother. Hard by the temple is a brick-built tank over 80 yd. square, called the "Khirsagar", or "sea of milk". Here, it is said, Gusain Gokul Nath was warned in a vision that a god lay concealed. Immediately a search was made, and the statue of Baladeva was revealed to the assembled multitudes.

16 m. to the W. of Muttra, on the Dig road, is the famous pilgrimage centre of **Gobardhan.** This town lies astride a low narrow range of hills called the "Giriraj (Girraj) Pahar", which Krishna is fabled to have held aloft on the tip of his finger for seven days and seven nights to cover the people of Braj from the floods poured down upon them by Indra. The houses cluster round the margin of a very large irregularly shaped masonry tank, called the "Manasi (Mansi) Ganga", which, as the name denotes, is supposed to have been called into existence by the operation of the Divine will. Close to the Manasi Ganga is the famous temple of Harideva (Hardeo-ji) erected during the reign of Akbar by Raja Bhagwan Das of Ambèr. It is an edifice 135 ft. long by 35 ft. in width, and both in plan and design is singularly like those early Romanesque Churches constantly met with in the South of France, belonging to the 11th and 12th centuries. On the opposite side of the Manasi Ganga are two stately cenotaphs, or *chhattris*, to the memory of Ranjit Singh and Balwant Singh, Rajas of Bharatpur. In that which commemorates Ranjit Singh, who died in 1805, the exploits of the British Army under Lord Lake during the unsuccessful assaults on Bharatpur, figure conspicuously in the paintings on the ceilings of the pavilions.

From Gobardhan a metalled road runs N. to **Radha Kund**, distant about 3 m.—another famous place of pilgrimage. On the way between the two places is a cenotaph, erected in honour of Raja Suraj Mal, the founder of the late ruling family of Bharatpur, who was killed in 1763, at Shahdara, on the Hindun river, by a detachment of Mughals, while hunting. There are several poor paintings, in one of which Suraj Mal is shown with several French officers round him. Behind the cenotaph is an extensive garden, and in front is an artificial lake called Kusum Sarovar.

Radha Kund consists of a small town clustering round two lakes, called respectively Krishna Kund and Radha Kund, after Krishna and his favourite consort. The lakes are faced on all sides with stone ghats and only parted from each other by a broad terrace of the same material. They were constructed in 1817. The holiness of the place is derived from a tradition that Krishna bathed to remove the pollution he had incurred in slaying the demon bull Arishta.

Some 15 m. from Gobardhan and some 10 m. by road from Kosi, on the Grand Trunk Road, lies another famous place of pilgrimage, **Barsana.** This, according to Hindus, was the home of Krishna's favourite "milkmaid" Radha. The town is built at the foot and on the slope of a small chain of hills. It was destroyed by the Mughal troops of Najaf Khan in 1773, after defeating the Jats of Bharatpur. The four prominent peaks of the hills are regarded as emblematic of the four-faced divinity of Brahma, and are crowned with different buildings, mostly dedicated to deities or personages prominent in the Krishna legend. The fine buildings, nearly all now in a ruinous condition, were the work of Rup Rám Katára and Mohan Rám Lavania. Conspicuous among them is the tank and pavilion, known as Bhanokhar, with pavilions supported on a series of vaulted colonnades opening on to the water.

For 3 m. before reaching Dig, 23 m. W. of Muttra, the road forms a sort of causeway above a very low, flat country, which was once a morass and formed the principal defence of the fortress.

At **Dig** (or Deeg) the chief object of interest is the splendid **Palace,** or rather group of palaces, built by

Suraj Mal of Bharatpur. Fergusson (*Ind. Arch.*, 2, 179) says of it: "The glory of Dig consists in the cornices, which are generally double, a peculiarity not seen elsewhere, and which for extent of shadow and richness of detail surpass any similar ornaments in India, either in ancient or modern buildings. The lower cornice is the usual sloping entablature almost universal in such buildings.... The upper cornice, which was horizontal, is peculiar to Dig, and seems designed to furnish an extension of the flat roof which in Eastern Palaces is usually considered the best apartment of the house." The palace enclosure is 475 ft. by 350 ft., and has two pavilions on each side and one at each end. Several of these are figured in vol. 2, p. 82 of the *Rambles* of Sir William Sleeman. The chief pavilions are the **Gopal Bhawan** (1763), flanked by two smaller pavilions and faced by an arch for a swing and two marble thrones, which stands E. of the fine unlined Tank; the **Nand Bhawan,** N.E. of this, a fine hall, 150 ft. by 80 ft. by 20 ft.; the **Suraj Bhawan** and the **Hardeo Bhawan,** S.; and the **Kishan Bhawan,** E. again of these. The Suraj Bhawan is built of white marble and mosaic work; the other halls are of cream-coloured sandstone. All are highly decorated, and between them are charming gardens surrounding a small tank.

Beyond the gardens is the large **Rup Sagar Lake** and beyond it the N. gate of the fort. This has twelve bastions and a ditch 50 ft. broad. The walls are very massive and lofty. There are seventy-two bastions in all; and on the N.W. bastion, about 80 ft. high, is a very long cannon.

Dig is celebrated for the battle fought on the 13th November 1804, in which General Frazer defeated Jaswant Rao Holkar's army, which took shelter in the Fort of Dig. On the 1st December following General Lake joined the army before this place, and immediately commenced siege operations. On the night of the 23rd his troops captured an eminence which commanded the city. The enemy then evacuated Dig on the following day and the fort on the succeeding night, and fled to Bharatpur.

6 m. from Muttra is **Brindaban** (Jaipuria Bhawan R.H., no reservation possible) (properly Vrindaban, meaning a forest of basil plants), to which Krishna removed from Gokul.

Buddhism never meant much for Brindaban; indeed the most ancient temples, five in number, date only from the 16th century. It is, however, famous as the place where Krishna sported with the Gopis (milkmaids), and stole their clothes when they were bathing. The Jumna originally bounded the town to the N. and E. The river has shifted its course, leaving the ghats high and dry.

Near the entrance to the town, on the left, is a large **Red Temple,** dating from 1590, sacred to Gobind Deo (the Divine Cowherd, i.e. Krishna), now a protected monument. "It is one of the most interesting and elegant temples in India, and the only one, perhaps, from which a European architect might borrow a few hints. The temple consists of a cruciform porch. The *antarala*, or inner mandap, of the original temple was afterwards apparently converted into a shrine, and is perfect internally, and used for worship, but the sikhara is gone, having been destroyed along with the sanctuary, after which the *antarala* was made into a shrine. Though not large, its dimensions are respectable, the porch measuring 117 ft. E. and W. by 105 ft. N. and S., and is covered by a true vault, built with radiating arches—the only instance, except one (the temple of Hardeoji at Gobardhan), known to exist in a Hindu temple in the N. of India. On each side of the original shrines are two side chapels. Over the four arms of the cross the vault is plain, and of 23½ ft. span, but in the centre it expands to 35 ft., and is quite equal in design to the best Gothic vaulting known. It is the external design of this temple, however, which is the most remarkable. The angles are accentuated with singular force and decision, and the openings, which are more than sufficient for that climate, are picturesquely arranged and pleasingly divided. It is, however, the combination of vertical with horizontal lines, covering the whole surface, that forms the great merit of the design" (Fergusson).

At the back of the Red Temple on the W. are, at two corners, two other temples which resemble each other. There is a new temple adjoining this to the W., built by a Bengali. It has a finely carved door.

E. is a modern temple, built by two Seths in the Dravidian style. Europeans are not allowed to enter the inner court, but above the W. gate is a terrace which commands a view. The temple consists of a vast enclosing wall, with three gopurams, like those of S. India, which are 80 ft. to 90 ft. high, while the gates are about 55 ft. It is dedicated to Sri Ranga, a name of Vishnu; and figures of Garuda, the man-bird of Vishnu, are very conspicuous. In the great court are two white marble pavilions, one E. and W. of the tank, and a stone pavilion with a flat roof, supported by sixteen pillars, opposite the E. gopuram.

The **Temple of Gopi Nath,** which is probably the earliest of the series, was built by Rasulji, who distinguished himself under Akbar. It is in a ruinous condition. Its special feature is an arcade of three bracket arches.

The **Temple of Jugal Kishor** is at the lower end of the town, near the Kesi Ghat. It is said to have been built by Neo-Karan, a Chauhan Chief, in A.D. 1027. The choir has pierced tracery in the head of the arch, and above it a representation of Krishna supporting the Hill of Gobardhan. The **Temple of Radha Ballabh,** of which the shrine was demolished by Aurangzeb, is a picturesque ruin.

The **Madan Mohan Temple** stands above a ghat on an arm of the river. Under two fine trees, a *Ficus indica* and a *Nauclea orientalis*, is a pavilion, in which many cobras' heads are represented. Siva is said to have struck Devi with a stick here, when she jumped off this ghat, and made it a place for curing snake-bites. On the ghat is a Saligram (a species of Ammonite worshipped as a type of Vishnu), with two footprints 2¼ in. long. This temple is 65 ft. high, and is in the shape of a cone.

The Muttra district is highly irrigated. On the W. of the Jumna, the Agra Canal has head-works at Okhla, near Delhi. On the E. of the Jumna the water is provided by a branch of the Upper Ganges Canal.

Main Line

From Muttra Junction to Delhi Main station (90 m.) the line runs close to the Grand Trunk Road, marked by Kos minars and sarais of old kings. The country used to be wooded and the haunt of robbers, but the Agra Canal brought cultivation.

920 m., *via* the main line, **Palwal,** in the Gurgaon District, 37 m. S. of Delhi. The Pandits identify it as the Apelava of the *Mahabharata*, part of the Pandava kingdom of Indraprastha, and tradition associates with the same period the high mound of the old site of Aharwan, a village a few miles to the S.W. It is said to have lain in a state of decay for a long period, and then to have been restored by Vikramaditya some 1900 years ago. The oldest part covers a high mound formed by accumulated debris of many centuries. During the Mughal times it was without a history, but on the downfall of the Empire it was given with surrounding territory in *jagir* to General De Boigne, and, after the conquest by General Lake, to Murtaza Khan of Delhi for a few years, after which it came under direct British rule. The town carries on trade in cotton, and has a R.H. about 3 furlongs from the railway station.

934 m. **Ballabgarh,** 21 m. S. of Delhi on the Muttra road: built on

symmetrical chess-board lines. The old Raja's palace is picturesque. Permission to occupy the R.Hs. in Gurgaon Dt. must be obtained from the District Board, Gurgaon.

945 m. **Tughlakabad**; on the outskirts of New Delhi. The line passes through the ruins of old places S. of Delhi (p. 317), the Kutb Minar, 7 m. to the W., being in full sight.

949 m. **Okhla,** for the head-works of the Agra Canal (1874).

952 m. **Hazrat Nizam-ud-din.** The line beyond was diverted for the new capital in 1920.

956 m. **New Delhi** (p. 340).

957 m. **DELHI** Central station. From Delhi the "Frontier Mail" of the Western Ry. now has its terminus at Amritsar.

ROUTE 13

AGRA AND FATEHPUR-SIKRI

(*Plan faces p.* 309)

AGRA.* Hotels: Agra; Clark's Shiraz; Grand; Lauries; Mughal; Holiday Inn. Tourist B. The majority of visitors now reach Agra either by air from Calcutta or Delhi, or else by car from Delhi, Gwalior or Muttra. The railway communications from all these places are, however, quite good and the Taj Express, to and from New Delhi daily, is outstanding. (Route 9.)

Two bridges across the river Jumna carry both the railway track and vehicular and foot traffic: the Strachey Bridge, and the Jumna Bridge. The latter connects with the Fort station; the former goes to the City station. A third road bridge has been built to the north of these carrying the Agra by-pass, the E. bank section of which lies immediately S. of the Rambagh Gardens.

Agra, headquarters of a Division and a District, in size and importance the third city in Uttar Pradesh has a pop. of 637,000 (1971), and stands on the W. bank of the Jumna, 534 ft. above sea-level.

Roads lead to (1) **Gwalior,** 77 m. and Jhansi, 136 m.; (2) Bharatpur, 33 m.; (3) Muttra, 36 m., and Delhi, 125 m.; (4) Aligarh, 50 m.; (5) Mainpuri, 68 m.

Though a week might be spent in visiting the sights in and around Agra (Tourist Information Office: 191 The Mall), much can be seen in a shorter time, and the following itinerary may be of service:

1st Day, *Morning.*—Fort and Palace. *Afternoon.*—Drive to the Taj Mahal (Travellers' Restaurant).

2nd Day, *Morning.*—Drive to Sikandra. *Afternoon.*—To Jami Masjid, Itimad-ud-Daula, and Chini ka Rauza, on the E. bank of the Jumna.

Half a day should be enough for the excursion to Fatehpur-Sikri (23 m.).

The modern city comprises the

Cantonment on the S., the Civil Station on the N.W., and the Fort on the N.E., with the bazars resting in the centre of the triangle. The Jumna flows past the city in a direction from N. to S., but below the Fort it turns on a great elbow, and in consequence the Taj is nearly due E. of the S. end of the Fort. It is desirable to visit the Agra Fort before Delhi, as otherwise it is difficult to understand the exact relation of the now isolated buildings of the Delhi palace.

The hotels are situated at the S. of the old city in and about the angle where the Cantonment boundary narrows on the W. Near them are the Post Office, banks, and club, the last at the W. end of the Mall, a very fine broad avenue, which leads E. to the Taj Road and the MacDonnell Park, laid out between the Taj and the Fort. S. of the telegraph office are fine public gardens. N. of the hotels, and on the W. of the city, situated on the Drummond Road (Mahatma Gandhi Road), are the District Courts, the Agra and St John's Colleges. To the E. of these and on the N. of the city, are the R.C. Cathedral, College and Convent, and 1 m. to the N. are the Court of the District Judge and the R.C. Cemetery. The road to Sikandra, which is the main road to Muttra, runs N.W., and that to Fatehpur-Sikri S.W. through the suburb of Shahganj.

The chief **Articles of Local Manufacture** are gold and silver embroidery, carving in soapstone, and imitation of the old inlay work (*pietra dura*) on white marble. Agra is famous also for its carpets. There is a flourishing boot and shoe industry.

History.—Nothing definite is known of Agra before the Muslim conquest. Sikandar Lodi seized it from the rebellious Muslim Governor of Bayana, and made it his capital in 1501. Sikandar Lodi died at Agra in 1517, but was buried at Delhi; he built the Baradari Palace, near Sikandra, which suburb received its name from him. Babur claimed to have employed eighty stone-masons daily, and is said to have had a garden-palace on the E. bank of the Jumna, nearly opposite the Taj. There is a mosque near the spot, with an inscription, which shows that it was built by Babur's son, Humayun, in 1530.

The Emperor Akbar resided at Agra in the early years of his reign. His capital was at Fatehpur-Sikri from about 1570 to 1585. After a period at Lahore, he returned to Agra in 1599, where he died in 1605. The only buildings that can now be attributed to him with certainty are the walls and the buildings in the S.E. corner of the Fort. Jahangir left Agra for Kashmir in 1618, and never returned. Shah Jahan resided at Agra from 1632 to 1637, and re-named the city Akbarabad after his grandfather, but the new title did not endure. He built much of the Fort and constructed the principal buildings of the palace and the Taj. Between 1638 and 1650 he caused the palace at Delhi and the Jami Masjid to be erected, and he doubtless intended to remove the capital to that place. Before this was finally done he was deposed by his son Aurangzeb in 1658, but lived as a State prisoner seven years longer at Agra. Aurangzeb removed the seat of Government permanently to Delhi.

In 1761 Agra was taken by Suraj Mal of Bharatpur, leader of the Jats, who did much damage. In 1770 the Mahrattas captured it from the Jats, who recovered it, but were themselves expelled by Najaf Khan, General of Shah Alam, in 1773. When Muhammad Beg was Governor, Agra was besieged and taken (1785) by Mahdaji Scindia and the Mahrattas held it till it was taken by General Lake, 17th October 1803, Colonel Hessing, who commanded, surrendering after a brief bombardment. Agra was also the centre of much fighting during the Mutiny[1] of 1857.

[1] A vivid picture of the state of affairs in Agra during this period is given in M. Thornhill's *Personal Adventures and Experiences of a Magistrate in the Indian Mutiny*. See also Lord Roberts' *Forty-one Years in India*.

The seat of government of the N.W. Provinces was at Agra from 1835 until 1859, when it was transferred to Allahabad. After 1902 the N.W. Provinces and Oudh (which were placed under one Lieutenant-Governor in 1877) were known as the United Provinces of Agra and Oudh. Since independence they have been renamed Uttar Pradesh.

The **Taj Mahal** (Travellers' Restaurant nearby) should be seen at different times of the day. The best perhaps is late in the afternoon, but it should be seen by moonlight also. It was commenced in 1040 A.H., or A.D. 1630, by the Emperor Shah Jahan as a tomb for his favourite queen, Arjumand Banu, entitled Mumtaz-i-Mahal, the "Elect of the Palace", whence the name Taj Mahal is derived. She was the daughter of Asaf Khan, brother of Nurjahan, the famous empress-wife of Jahangir. Their father was Mirza Ghiyas Beg, a Persian, who came from Teheran to seek his fortune in India, and rose to power under the title of I'timad-ud-daula (see p. 309). Mumtaz-i-Mahal married Shah Jahan in 1615, had by him fourteen children, and died in child-bed of the last in 1629, at Burhanpur, in the Deccan (p. 119). Her body was brought to Agra, and first laid in the garden. The Taj took twenty-two years (1630-52) to build, according to Tavernier, who records that he saw both its commencement and completion, and that the scaffolding used was constructed of brick. Two silver doors at the entrance were taken away and melted by Suraj Mal and his Jats. Austin of Bordeaux, a silversmith in the Emperor's service, probably took part in the decoration, especially in the metal work of the doors and golden screen which originally enclosed the cenotaph.[1]

Before reaching the Taj the Government Circuit House may be seen on the left. The surroundings of the Taj enclosure have been restored and both the tomb and the Fatehpuri mosque of red sandstone flanking the approach from the Fort are prominent.

The approach is by the *Taj Ganj Gate*, which opens into an outer court 880 ft. long and 440 ft. wide. Inside the court are two tombs raised on an upper storey in the S.W. and S.E. corners; and in the N.W. and N.E. corners are two enclosures. On the right is a gate which leads into the quarter S. of the Taj, where are portions of the original serai erected by Shah Jahan.

On the left is the **Great Gateway** of the garden, built 1648, of red sandstone, inlaid with ornaments and inscriptions from the Koran in white marble, and surmounted by twenty-six white marble *chhattris*.

The Taj garden is laid out in formal style, the whole to the S. of the platform of the Taj being divided by two main causeways into four portions, which are again subdivided into four. The principal vista is along a red sandstone watercourse, set between rows of cypresses, formerly peaches, and interrupted in the middle by a marble platform. The Taj rises at the end, and is mirrored in the watercourse. Endless beautiful views can be enjoyed from seats in the gardens. Along the S. wall on either side of the great gate is an extremely fine pillared gallery of red sandstone. The beauty of the Taj is perhaps most perfect immediately after sunset, or under the moonlight; but every change of light seems to lend new graces to it, and the view at sunrise is magnificent. Those who linger for evening or night effects must take precautions against a chill.

[1] According to Fray Sebastian Manrique of the Society of Jesus, who visited Agra in 1640, the designer of the Taj was a Venetian jeweller of the name of Geronimo Veroneo, who died at Lahore in that year and is buried in the old R.C. cemetery at Agra. The ultimate authority for the statement is Father Josef da Castro, another Jesuit, who was Veroneo's executor, and died at Agra in 1646. Mr Havell, however, discredits the story (*XIXth Century*, June 1903). Dr Chaghtai considers that Shah Jahan himself designed it, inspired, perhaps, by the Tomb of Humayun at Delhi.

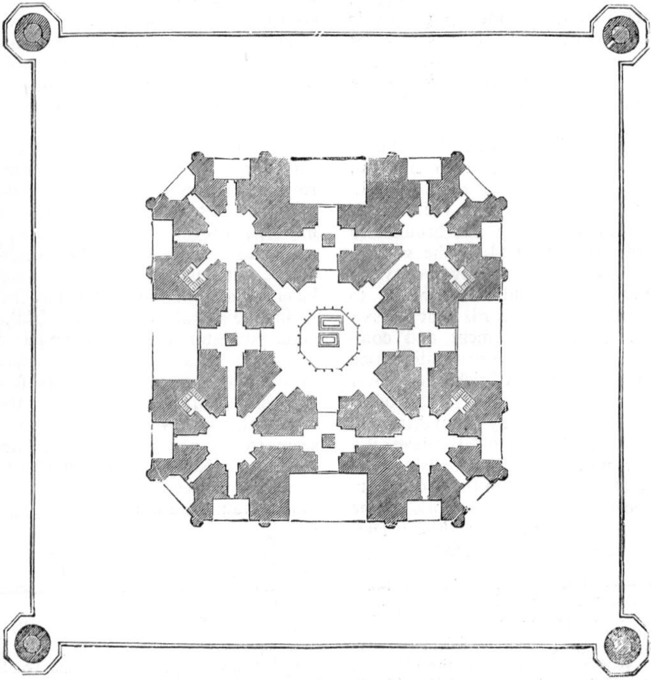

The central marble platform on which the tomb stands is 22 ft. high and 313 ft. square. At each corner is a minaret of white marble picked out by black lines, 137 ft. high. The tomb itself measures 186 ft. on each side, the corners being bevelled off and recessed into a bay. On either side of each angle corner is another small bay, and in the centre of each side is a deeply recessed bay 63 ft. high. The height of the walls and parapet over them is 108 ft.; at each corner above them rise smaller marble domes, and in the centre soars the great central dome, which rises to a height of 187 ft., the metal pinnacle making a total of 243 ft.

All the spandrels, as well as the angles and important details, are inlaid with semi-precious stones. These are combined in wreaths, scrolls and frets, as exquisite in design as beautiful in colour, and convey a high idea of the taste and skill of the Indian architects of the age.

The delicately sculptured ornamentation, in low relief, is in its way as beautiful as the *pietra dura* work itself. The letters of the inscription over the central bay are graduated in size to appear equal from below.

In the centre of the tomb is an octagonal chamber surrounded by other rooms. From each corner room spiral stairs lead to the roof. Each side of the central room measures 24 ft. The inner dome rises 80 ft. above the pavement, and is 58 ft. in diameter. Under the centre of the dome, enclosed by a trellis-work screen of white marble—it probably dates from the reign of Aurangzeb—are the tombs of Mumtaz-i-Mahal (in the centre) and of Shah Jahan (shaped like a pen-box). "These, however, as is usual in Indian sepulchres, are not the true tombs—the bodies rest in a vault, level with the surface of the ground, beneath plainer tombstones, placed exactly below those in the hall above." Over the two tombs hangs a fine Cairene lamp, the graceful gift of Lord Curzon. The inscriptions on them are "The resplendent grave of Arjumand Banu Begam, called Mumtaz-i-Mahal, died in 1040 A.H." (A.D. 1629); and "The illustrious sepulchre of His Most Exalted Majesty, dignified as Razwan (the guardian of Paradise) having his abode in Paradise and his dwelling in the starry heaven, inhabitant of the region of bliss, the second lord of the Kiran (the conjunction of Jupiter and Venus, during which he was born) Shah Jahan the King valiant. He travelled from this transitory world to the world of eternity on the night of the 28th of the month of Rajab 1076 A.H." (A.D. 1666). The Queen's Tomb bears the 99 names of Allah. "The light to the central apartment", says Fergusson, "is admitted only through double screens of white marble trellis-work of the most exquisite design, one on the outer and one on the inner face of the walls. In our climate this would produce nearly complete darkness; but in India, and in a building wholly composed oı white marble, this was required to temper the glare that otherwise would have been intolerable. As it is, no words can express the chastened beauty of that central chamber, seen in the soft gloom of the subdued light that reaches it through the distant and half-closed openings that surround it.[1] There is a most wonderful echo in the dome."

Much expenditure has been incurred during recent years in repairing the dome and other parts of the structure.

On a lower level at either side of the mausoleum are two fine buildings of red sandstone, a mosque on the W., and an assembly hall, its *jawab* (answer) or complement on the E. On the pavement in front of the hall, which bears the unusual decoration of flowers, is a representation of the finial of the Taj. The Taj was intended to be seen balanced between these two buildings.

[1] The light in the interior has become inadequate since the marble grilles were fitted with glass to keep out birds.

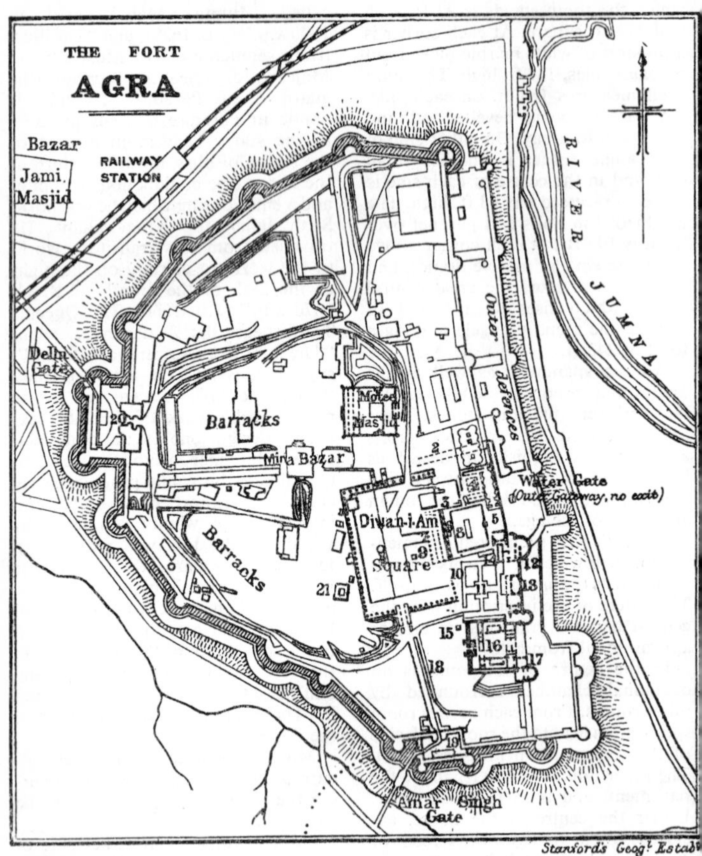

1. Northern Tower.
2. Descent to Water Gate.
3. Nagina Masjid and ladies' private Bazar.
4. Small Courts and ruins of Baths.
5. Open Terrace with Diwan-i-Khas on South side.
6. Recess where the Emperor's Throne stood.
7. Diwan-i-Am (Hall of Public Audience).
8. Machchi Bhawan.
9. Mr Colvin's Grave.
10. Mina Mosque.
11. The Anguri Bagh (Grape Garden).
12. Saman Burj (Octagon Tower). At North angle is an outlet by secret passage.
13. Khas Mahal.
14. Shish Mahal (Mirror Palace).
15. Well.
16. Palace of Jahangir (or Akbar).
17. Tower. At the base is an entrance to a a secret passage.
18. Incline from Amar Singh's Gate.
19. Court of Amar Singh's Gate.
20. Elephant Gate.
21. Kiosk of Salimgarh.

By crossing the river in the ferry-boat, which will be found at the end of the road which runs outside the W. wall from the entrance to the outer court, this beautiful view can be obtained. An immense construction on the W. will be remarked, resembling a well, with a well-run by which water was once raised from the river to supply the fountains. From the farther side various paths lead to the E. end of the Jumna Bridge, if it is desired to return by that route.

The **Fort.**—Many magnificent Mughal buildings are situated within the Fort, which has a circuit of over a mile. Visitors do not now need a pass to enter by the only ingress, the Amar Singh Gate. The walls and flanking defences are of red sandstone, and present an imposing appearance, being nearly 70 ft. high; the finest portion of them is along the N. side and to the S. of the N.E. bastion. The ditch is 30 ft. wide and 35 ft. deep. The Water Gate on the E. is closed, also the Delhi Gate on the W. to which the visitor should walk. Outside the Delhi Gate, and connecting with the Jami Masjid, was the Tripulia court, removed after 1857; in it was the Nakkar Khana, music gallery. Inside the Delhi Gate, the inner archway bearing a date of 1600, a somewhat steep slope between red sandstone walls will be found to lead to another gateway called the *Hathi Pol*, or "Elephant Gate". The archway is flanked by two octagonal towers of red sandstone, relieved with designs in white marble. The domed interior of the gateway, with a raised platform for the guard on either side, is very striking. Inside the Hathi Pol one road sweeps to the left and turns to the front of the Moti Masjid and the N. gate of the court in front of the Diwan-i-am, while another connects with the Amar Singh Gate and the S. gate of the court of the Diwani-i-Am. The first should be followed. At the summit a palace building was destroyed after 1857. (This area inside the Delhi Gate is closed, 1980.)

The **Moti Masjid**, the "Pearl Mosque" (1646-53), was built by Shah Jahan on ground sloping from W. to E., and the fine entrance gateway of red sandstone makes a trihedral projection from the centre of the E. face; it is approached by a double staircase. The exterior is faced with slabs of red sandstone, the interior built of marble—white, blue and grey veined. In the centre there is a marble tank, 37 ft. 7 in. square, for

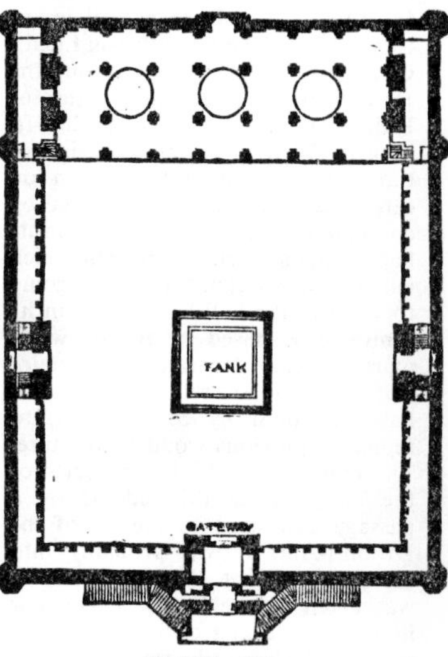

Moti Masjid.

ablutions, S.E. of which there stands an ancient sun-dial, consisting of an octagonal marble pillar, 4 ft. high, with no gnomon, but simply two crossed lines and an arc. A marble cloister runs round the E., N. and S. sides of the court, which measures 234 ft. and 183 ft., interrupted by archways, of which those in the N. and S. sides are closed.

The mosque proper (149 ft. by 56 ft.) consists of three aisles of seven bays opening on to the courtyard, surmounted by three domes. On the E. face over the front row of supporting pillars, there is an inscription running the whole length, the letters being of black marble inlaid into the white. The inscription records that the mosque was built by Shah Jahan and likens it to a precious pearl. Narrow steps lead to the roof of the mosque, from which there is a fine view.

Beyond the cross road to the Mina bazar, now demolished, on the right and the descent to the Water Gate on the left is the entrance to the court of the Diwan-i-Am, with colonnades. In front of the Darbar Hall is the tomb of Mr Colvin, the British Lieut.-Governor who died there during the 1857 Mutiny. The **Diwan-i-Am,** or Hall of Public Audience, is 208 ft. long by 76 ft. deep, and consists of three aisles of nine bays open on three sides. The roof is supported by columns of red sandstone. Along its back walls are grilles, through which ladies could watch what was going forward in the hall below, and in its centre is a raised alcove of white marble, richly decorated with *pietra dura* work and low reliefs. The present hall was built by Shah Jahan, to replace a previous wooden structure. The entrance to the inner courts of the Palace from this side is by a passage and steps to the N. of the Diwan-i-Am; it was probably into these courts that William Hawkins was taken by the Emperor Jahangir in 1609.[1] The first enclosure entered is the **Machchi Bhawan,** or "Fish Square", which formerly possessed a large tank. A two-storeyed cloister runs all round it, except on the side which fronts the Jumna, where the upper storey gives place to an open terrace. In the N. side are two bronze gates (kept closed) taken by Akbar from Chitorgarh (p. 209), and at the N.W. corner is a beautiful little three-domed mosque of white marble, called the **Nagina Masjid,** or "Gem Mosque". This was the private mosque of the royal ladies of the court, and was built by Shah Jahan. Beneath, in a small courtyard, was a bazar where merchants used to display their goods to the ladies of the court. On the terrace on the riverside is a black throne with a white seat opposite it. The throne has a long fissure, which is said to have appeared when the throne was usurped by the Jat Chief of Bharatpur in 1761. A reddish stain in one spot is alleged to be blood. An inscription runs round the four sides, stating that "when Salim became heir to the crown his name was changed to Jahangir, and for the light of his justice he was called Nur-ud-din. His sword cut his enemies' heads into two halves like the Gemini." The date given is 1011 A.H. = A.D. 1603. Beneath this terrace is a wide enclosure within the outer walls, where contests between elephants and tigers took place. On the N. of the terrace is the site of a hall of inlaid marble and of various rooms of the Bath, or **Hammam.**

On the S. is the **Diwan-i-Khas,** or Hall of Private Audience, consisting of an open colonnade in front and an enclosed room at the back, and measuring 65 ft. by 34 ft. by 22 ft. high. The carving is exquisite, and the flowers inlaid on the white marble with red cornelian and other valuable stones are introduced with better, because more sparing, effect than in the Diwan-i-Khas of Delhi. The date of the building is 1046 A.H. = A.D. 1637 derived from the chronogram Sa'adat Sarai wa Humayun Asas, the Abode of Joy and Auspicious Home. A staircase leads from the Diwan-i-Khas to the **Saman Burj,** a few steps on the right conducting to the tiny **Mina Masjid,** or private mosque of the Emperor, probably the smallest mosque in existence. The proper name of the Saman Burj is Musamman, or Octagon, but it is generally known by a corruption of its name as the Jessamine (Yâsmin) Burj; the chief

1 "Perceiving I had the Turkish tongue, which himselfe well understood, hee commanded me to follow him into his chamber of presence (*diwan-i-khas*), being then risen from that place of open audience" (*diwan-i-am*). See the account as reproduced in Sir William Foster's *Early Travels in India* (Clarendon Press, 1921, P. 81).

Sultana lived in the beautiful pavilion, with a fountain and retiring-room over the river. The lovely marble lattice-work seems to have been broken by cannon-shot in some places. Part of the marble pavement in front of it is made to represent a Pachisi board.[1]

Opposite the Saman Burj, but usually entered from the next court, is the **Shish Mahal,** literally "Mirror Palace". It consists of two dark chambers furnished with fountains and an artificial cascade arranged to fall over lighted lamps. The walls and ceilings are decorated with pounded talc and with innumerable small pieces of mirror glass.

Above the buildings at this spot, and approached by steps above the Mina Masjid, are the remains of reservoirs and water-ducts and arrangements for the raising of water from below. From the roof a fine view is also obtained of the courts, on either side of it, of the Moti Masjid and the Taj, of which many views are obtained along the river from the terrace of the Machchi Bhawan to the Palace of Akbar.

The **Anguri Bagh** or "Grape Garden", now entered, is a square of 280 ft., now planted with grass. In the centre of the E. side is a lovely hall called the **Khas Mahal,** the gilding and colouring of which were in part restored in 1895. In front are small tanks and fountains. The Khas Mahal undoubtedly formed the model upon which the Diwan-i-Khas at Delhi was built; it measures 70 ft. by 40 ft. Under the platform are subterranean apartments for use in the summer, from which passages continue behind the fort wall.

On either hand, also facing the river, are the **Golden Pavilions,** so called from their curved roofs being covered with gilded plates of copper. In them are bedrooms for ladies, with holes in the wall 14 in. deep, into which they used to slip their jewels. These holes are so narrow that only a woman's hand could draw out the contents.

In the S.E. corner of the Anguri Bagh three rooms, beautifully decorated in fresco, were the private apartments of Shah Jahan. In the room nearest the river, an octagonal pavilion and very beautiful, according to tradition, Shah Jahan died in 1666, gazing upon the Taj. To the W. of the rooms is another in which stand the spurious Gates of Somnath (p. 284), 12 ft. high and finely carved; they are of deodar, not sandal-wood, and of a later and corrupt, though well recognised, Muslim design. There is a Kufic inscription running round them, in which the name of Sabuktagin has been read. They were captured by General Nott at Ghazni, and brought in 1842 to India at the desire of Ranjit Singh.

The **Jahangiri Mahal,** of red sandstone, 249 ft. by 260 ft., was built probably by Akbar, and stands in the S.E. part of the fort, between the palace of Shah Jahan and the Bangali bastion. The principal façade on the W. is decorated with bright tiles in the upper portion, and is pierced in the centre by an entrance gateway. This leads through a vestibule into a domed hall, 18 ft. square, the ceiling of which is elaborately carved, and from which a corridor leads into the central court, which is 72 ft. square, The general atmosphere and design of this court is predominantly Hindu, but the minute and exquisite surface carving is Saracenic.

"On the N. side of the court is a grand open pillared hall, 62 ft. long and 37 ft. broad. The pillars support bracket capitals richly carved and ornamented with pendants. The front brackets support broad sloping eaves of thin stone slabs. But the stone roof or ceiling of this pillared hall is the most remarkable feature about it. It is supported most curiously by stone

[1] The game of *Pachisi* is not in the least like chess, to which it is often compared. It is played by four players, who each have four pieces. The moves are regulated, as in backgammon, by the throwing of dice The board consists of four rectangles, of which each is made up of three rows of eight squares.

cross-beams, which are ornamented with the quaint device of a great serpent or dragon carved on them lengthways. A covered passage or corridor runs round the top of this hall, from which one can look down into it. The other pillared hall on the opposite or S. side of the grand court is somewhat less in size."

From the grand court a large chamber to the E. leads to a recessed portico in the centre of a quadrangle which faces the river, supported by two lofty pillars and two half pillars of the more slender and graceful Saracenic kind. Some of the chambers are lined with stucco, which has been painted, and has lasted better than the stonework. The palace ends on the side facing the river, with a screen wall and two corner bastions, each surmounted by an ornamental tower with a domed cupola. There are many vaulted chambers underneath the palace, used during the summer.

The **Akbari Mahal** lies to the S. of the so-called Jahangiri Mahal. From the eastern rooms, opened up by the Archaeological Department (little else remains), a view of the Taj and river is obtainable. The principal feature of these buildings was the large central courtyard, some 140 ft. square. The western façade of the building stretched southwards to a point near the S. outer wall of the Fort, terminating in a *burj*, or tower, probably similar in design to the southern *burj* of the Jahangiri Mahal. A small portion of the façade near the southern *burj* of the Jahangiri Mahal shows a similarity in design to the façade of the Jahangiri Mahal. The foundations were all disclosed by excavation, and the plan of the palace is now outlined by shrubberies. The two small courtyards in front of the Akbari Mahal were probably constructed about 1800.

In the space in front of the Jahangiri Mahal is the *Hauz* of Jahangir, an enormous monolithic cistern of light-coloured porphyry, externally nearly 5 ft. high, and internally 4 ft. deep and 8 ft. in diameter at top; and at the N.W. corner is the head of the descent to the Amar Singh Gate, so called from the elder brother of Maharaja Jaswant Singh of Jodhpur, who was disinherited by his father for his turbulence, and was killed there in 1644 with all his followers after a fatal brawl in the Diwan-i-Am, Shah Jahan being present. The S.W. bastion was battered by General Lake in 1803 so successfully that the Mahratta garrison at once surrendered.

Before descending, the little Early Mughal Pavilion, situated on high ground outside the S.W. corner of the Diwan-i-Am court, should be visited. It is an ornamental structure apparently, contemporary with the Jahangiri Mahal, but ascribed by some writers to Salim Shah (1545-55).

Outside the Amar Singh Gate is the half-buried figure of a horse in red sandstone, and to the S.W. are old cemeteries. Nearby is the N. end of the MacDonnell Park in which stood a memorial of Queen Victoria, by Thorneycroft.

West of City

On Drummond Road (Mahatma Gandhi Road) is the **Agra University**. This owes its origin to Maharaja Daulat Rao Scindia, who in 1796 gave certain villages in the districts of Muttra and Aligarh to a learned Brahmin for the twofold purpose of keeping up a Sanskrit School and of supplying the wants of pilgrims visiting the shrines around Muttra. In 1818 the original grantee left his lands in trust to the E. India Co., who devoted part of the proceeds to the establishment of this college, opened 1823. It is managed by a board of trustees and forms part of Agra University (1927). N. of the Agra College the grounds on each side of the Drummond Road belong to St John's College, founded by the Church Missionary Society and now a Christian College within the University. It carries out Rural

Reconstruction Services in villages W. of Agra. The buildings were designed by Sir Swinton Jacob, and contain a library and a very large hall. Adjoining the College are large schools for Christian boys and girls. Extending eastwards from the Drummond Road towards the Fort are the Dufferin Hospitals, Medical Schools and Sarojini Naidu Hospital. The Medical School, founded in 1854, affords teaching only. Situated in the western outskirts of the city is the Kalan Masjid of the Early Mughal period.

Close by also on Nuri Gate Road is the Lady Lyall Hospital.

The Muttra Road leads to the **Roman Catholic Cathedral, Convent** and **Schools,** dedicated to the Virgin Mary, the first with a tower about 150 ft. high; also St Peter and St Paul's College. The Mission was founded in the time of Akbar, and has long been celebrated for its school.

The earliest tombs of Christians are in the R.C. cemetery at Lashkarpur, which lies ¾ m. to the N. The most ancient epitaphs are in the Armenian character. Among the tombs are those of Colonel John Hessing, in Scindia's service (d. 1803), a miniature of the Taj in red sandstone, John Mildenhall (d. 1614), the self-styled envoy of Queen Elizabeth (the earliest known European tomb in northern India), and the notorious Samru, Walter Reinhardt (d. 1778).

At the end of Church Road is the Kandahari Bagh (Bharatpur House), where Shah Jahan's first Persian wife was buried, and N. of it again the Seth's Garden, once containing the graves of Faizi and Abul Fazl (p. 316) and their sister, Ladli Begam.

In the Protestant cemetery, close to St Paul's Church, are the tombstones of three English factors, Ofley (1627), Drake (1637) and Purchas (1651). The Cantonment (Havelock Memorial) Church was rebuilt in 1873 on the site of a Baptist Church.

1½ m. N.W. of the Civil Courts is **Dayal Bagh,** a settlement (1915) of the Radha Swami Sect, founded by Sir Anand Sarup, where interesting co-operative experiments in education and social and religious life are being made by a community. It is also possible to watch work in progress on an exquisitely ornamented marble temple.

The **Jami Masjid** faces the Delhi Gate of the Fort, close to the Fort railway station, and a good view of it is obtained from the footbridge to the station. It stands upon a raised platform 11 ft. high, reached by flights of steps on the S. and E. sides. The mosque proper measures 130 ft. by 100 ft., and is divided into five compartments, each of which opens on the courtyard by an archway. The inscription over the main archway sets forth that the mosque was constructed by the Emperor Shah Jahan in 1648 in the name of his daughter, Jahanara, who afterwards shared her father's captivity (p. 300). Three great full-bottomed domes without necks, built of red sandstone, have zig-zag bands of white marble circling round them.

East of the Jumna

The **Tomb of I'timad-ud-daula** lies about 250 yd. to the N. from the E. end of the Jumna railway bridge, which carries vehicular and foot traffic. The mausoleum was built by the Empress Nur Jahan for her father, Mirza Ghiyas Beg, a Persian, who was grandfather of the lady of the Taj. The tomb stands on a platform 4 ft. high measuring 150 ft. each way, and is itself 69 ft. square. At each corner is an octagonal tower 40 ft. high, and on the terrace of the roof is a pavilion 25 ft. square; and the design of the mausoleum seems to have served for that of the Emperor Jahangir also, built by Nur Jahan at Shahdara, near Lahore (p. 583). The centre room below, 22 ft. square, contains the two tombs of I'timad-ud-daula and his wife, made of yellow coloured marble; the side rooms round it display paintings of flower vases, fruits, etc., which were also reproduced in the Shahdara mausoleum. The marble lattice-work of the passages admitting light to the interior is extremely fine. The pavilion on the terrace has a curved Bengali roof and broad sloping eaves, and contains two marble cenotaphs corresponding to those below. The whole of the exterior and much of the interior is of white marble with inlay work, the earliest of its particular character known in India (1628), though its prototype will be seen in the spandrels, etc., of the South Gateway of Akbar's Tomb at Sikandra (1614).

Half a mile N. of this is the **Chini ka Rauza,** or china tomb. The Persian influence will be noticed. It is the burial-place of Afzal Khan, who was in the service of Jahangir and Shah Jahan. He died at Lahore in 1639, and was buried at Agra in the tomb he had erected during his own lifetime. It has one great dome resting on an octagonal base. In the centre of the octagonal domed chamber, much ruined, are two tombs of brick, which have replaced marble cenotaphs. The outside is decorated with enamelled plaster work, such as was also used on Mughal buildings at Lahore; the flower patterns of many of the panels are very effective.

Farther up the east bank of the river again is the Rambagh, where the Emperor Bābur is said to have been buried pending the erection of his mausoleum at Kabul, with a terrace on the riverside.

The mausoleum of the **Emperor Akbar** at **Sikandra** (so named from Sikandar Lodi, who reigned 1488-1517) is at 5½ m. along the Muttra Road. The Delhi Gate, built in Shah Jahan's time, stands across the road. There are two *Kos minars*, or milestones, and several tombs on the way. On the left side of the road, about 4 m. from Agra, and nearly opposite the lofty arched gateway of an ancient building called the Kachi ki sarai, there is a sculptured horse, said to have been erected in memory of a favourite horse of Akbar's, which died near this spot. At ½ m. farther on, a little back from the road on the E. side, is a tank of red sandstone, with ornamental octagonal towers, called Guru ka Tal. On the S. side are three flights of steps, and E. of them is a long and broad water-channel. ½ m. beyond the mausoleum of Akbar is a red sandstone two-storeyed building, the ground floor of which contains forty chambers. Each corner of the building is surmounted by an octagonal *chhattri*. It is the Baradari of Sikandar Lodi, built 1495, and tomb of Mariam uz Zamani, a Hindu, wife of the Emperor Akbar, and whom tradition has converted (on no real grounds) into a Christian. In 1838 the building was handed over to the Church Missionary Society for the accommodation of famine orphans. A church and school were built, and the tomb was converted into a printing press. In 1912 it was purchased by the Government and is now a protected monument. The carved sandstone facing has sustained some damage.

A fine gateway leads to the great garden enclosure in which the mausoleum of the Emperor Akbar is situated: on either side of it in flanking walls are boldly pierced sandstone grilles. It is of red sandstone, inlaid with white marble in various polygonal patterns, very massive, and with a splendid scroll of Tughra writing, a foot broad, adorning it. On the top of the gateway, at each corner, rises a marble-faced minaret of three storeys; cupolas destroyed by the Jats have been restored. The gate should be ascended to view the mausoleum.

A broad paved causeway leads to the mausoleum, a pyramidal building 74 ft. high, of four storeys, three of which are of red sandstone, the fourth of white marble. The lowest storey, 30 ft. high, measures 320 ft. each way, and the top storeys 157 ft. A massive cloister runs round the lowest storey, broken in the centre of the façade by a lofty archway, the portion on the S. forming the entrance to the tomb chamber. The vaulted ceiling of the vestibule was elaborately frescoed in gold and blue, and a section of this has been restored. The Surah-i-mulk (chapter of the Koran) runs under the cornice in a scroll 1 ft. broad. A gentle descent leads to the dark chamber. On the S. façade, on either side of the main arch, some bays of the cloister are screened off, and contain tombs with inscriptions in beautiful characters. In a niche in the side of the room, farthest from the entrance, is an alabaster tablet inscribed with the 99 divine names.

Narrow staircases lead to the platforms and terraces above. The top storey is surrounded by a beautiful cloister of white marble, carved on the outer side into lattice-work in squares of 2 ft., every square of a different pattern. In the centre, in a triple-domed pavilion, is the splendid white monolith cenotaph of the Emperor, engraved with the 99 glorious names of Allah, exactly over the place where his body rested in the vaulted chamber below. On the N. side of the cenotaph is inscribed the motto of the sect he founded, "Allahu Akbar", "God is great"; and on the S. side, "Jalla Jalalahu", "May His glory shine". To the N. of it, at the distance of 4 ft., is a handsome white marble pillar 2½ ft. high, which according to tradition, was once covered with gold and contained the Koh-i-nur.[1] The gateway recesses in N., E. and W. walls of the garden are decorated with marble mosaics.

FATEHPUR-SIKRI. C. H. Travellers' B. Taxis and Tourist Buses with guides (apply Govt. Tourist Office, The Mall, Agra) are available. Tourist Buses meet the Taj Express at Agra Cantonment Station. The road (which is the one used by Akbar himself) is shady, but the drive is apt to be dusty. There is also a railway station (27 m.) on the Western Ry. broad-gauge chord line from Agra Fort station to Bayana (Route 12).

The road runs through the suburb of Shahganj, at the entrance to which the ruins of a mosque, with an inscription recording that it was built in 1621, mark the site of the old Ajmer Gate. Farther on is a Muslim cemetery, with a tomb said to be that of Mirza Hindal, son of Babur, father of Akbar's chief wife. At the foot of the tomb is a monolith 7 ft. high, with the date 1570. The road, like that to Sikandra, is marked by *Kos minars*, or milestones, 20 ft. in height, at distances of 2 m., continued to Ajmer.

The royal, long-deserted city of *Fatehpur-Sikri*, standing on a low sandstone ridge, was the creation of Akbar (1569), who experimented in Hindu and Persian styles. Perfectly preserved, it is a unique specimen of a city in the exact condition in which it was occupied by the Great Mughal and his court. The alleged reason for its construction was the presence on the spot of the Chishti Saint, Shaikh Salim, who foretold the birth of Akbar's son Salim (Jahangir); and the reasons for its desertion were the difficulty of obtaining good water, and unhealthy surroundings.

The city, which was nearly 7 m. in circumference, was surrounded on three sides by a wall pierced by eight gateways; on the N.W. side was a large artificial lake, now dry, which measured some 20 m. round the banks.

The buildings seem irregular, but the whole was carefully planned. The position of the Khwabgah, Akbar's personal suite, commands the *Daftar Khana*, Record Office, and the whole of the principal buildings, and from it he could reach, without being observed, the "Jodh Bai" Palace, Miriam's House, Birbal's House, the Panch Mahal, the Turkish Sultana's House, and the Ibadat Khana (Diwan-i-Khas).

The visitor enters by the Agra gate at the N.E. corner, takes the right-hand road at the fork (the road to

[1] The diamond of this name probably did not come into the Mughal possession till the reign of Shah Jahan. See Appendix to Ball's *Tavernier*.

Bayana (p. 290) is on his left), and drives past a large quadrangle with a ruined cloister. The road then passes beneath the Naubat Khana, from the upper rooms of which musicians played as the procession entered. Farther (left) are the remains of the **Treasury,** and opposite it what is known traditionally as the **Mint.** Near the Mint a new Travellers' Rest House has been built. There is also a large C.H. for official use.

The road enters the court of the **Diwan-i-Am,** measuring some 366 ft. from N. to S. by 181 ft. from E. to W., and surrounded by a flat-roofed cloister. On the W. side is the Audience Hall, with a deep veranda in front, and an isolated space for the Emperor between two pierced stone screens of fine geometric design. The room behind has a peculiar roof, which was painted.

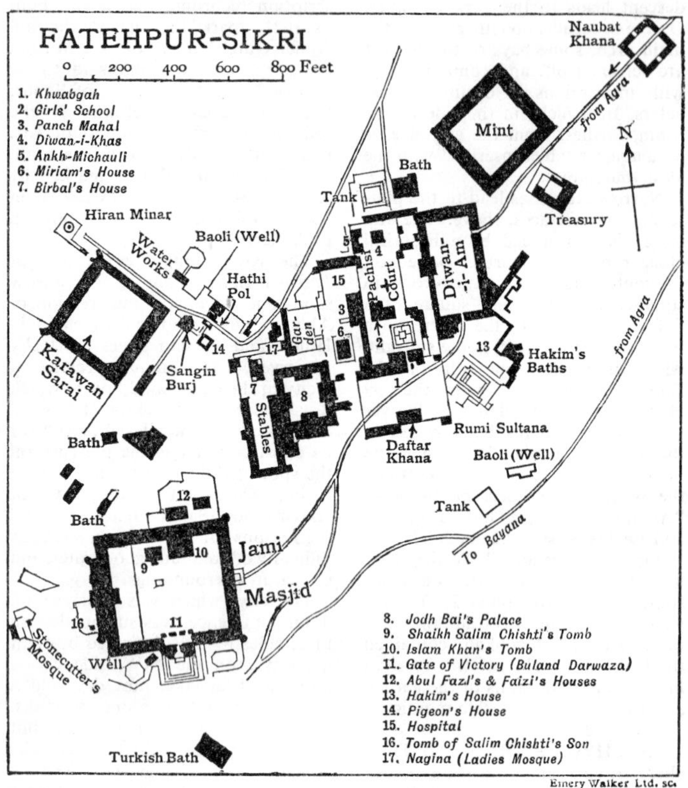

The road leaves the courtyard on the S. to the **Daftar Khana,** or Record Office. At the back is a staircase leading to the roof, from which there is a good view of the city. The inner stone partition wall is modern.

On the right of the road is the back of the **Khwabgah,** or Sleeping Apartment, literally "House of Dreams"

Written on the internal walls over the architraves of the doors are some Persian complimentary verses (much defaced). Below is a room, and at the E. end of it a platform, supported by two fine red sandstone shafts, beautifully carved. According to tradition a Hindu priest lived here.

The area to the N. was the **Khas Mahal** with, at the S.E. corner, the **Rumi Sultana,** or **"Turkish Queen's" House,** which many consider the most interesting apartment of all. As it now stands it consists of only one small chamber, 15 ft. by 15 ft., but every square inch is carved. Inside is a most elaborate dado about 4 ft. high, consisting of eight sculptured panels representing forest views, animal life, etc. Above, the wall takes the form of a stone lattice screen, the divisions of which were used as shelves. Much of the carving is curiously like Chinese work, and reminds one of what Abul Fazl says of the local red sandstone: "Clever workmen chisel it so skilfully as no turner could do with wood, and their works vie with the picture-books of Mani" (a legendary Persian painter).

The **Girls' School** is a small, plain building, carried on square stone piers. Upon the paving-stones of the open space in front is the Pachisi board,[1] with the Emperor's stone seat in the centre, in the form of a cross laid out in coloured pavement. It is said that the game was played with slave girls as pieces.

Just to the W. of this is the **Panch Mahal,** a building of five storeys, borne by open colonnades, each tier being stepped back from that below, till nothing but a small kiosk remains on top. It was probably erected for the ladies of the court as a pleasure resort, as the sides were originally enclosed with stone screens. The first floor is remarkable on account of the variety of the fifty-six columns which support the storey above, no two being alike in design. While many shafts are similar, the caps vary; at the angles of one are elephants' heads with interlaced trunks; on another is a man gathering fruit. At the N.W. angle is a group of four columns, which should be examined. From the top floor there is a splendid view.

At the N. of the quadrangle is the so-called **Diwan-i-Khas,** or hall of private audience: it is generally known as the **Ibadat Khana,** or worship house (completed in 1575), although the identification has been disputed. From the outside it appears to be two storeys high, but on entering it is found to consist of one only, with a central octagonal pillar crowned by a circular corbelled capital, radiating from which to the four corners of the building are four stone causeways enclosed by open trellis stone balustrades (restored). Tradition says that in the centre of this capital the Emperor sat, whilst friends disputed around; and the corners were occupied by the four Ministers. The shaft is beautifully carved, and deserves careful study. On the E. and W. sides are stone staircases communicating with the roof. The open screen-work in the windows is modern.

A little W. is the **Ankh Michauli,** where the Emperor is said to have played hide-and-seek with the ladies of the court; but it was most likely used for records. It consists of three large, lofty rooms, surrounded by narrow passages. The ceilings of two of the rooms are curved, but the third is flat, and supported on struts ornamented with grotesque carving. In front of the S.E. corner is a small canopied structure said to have been used by an astrologer, who may have been a Hindu Guru, or "teacher". The *torana* brackets are essentially Hindu in character: otherwise the original design is typically early Mughal. The under side of the dome was painted. Adjoining these buildings to the W. is the Hospital, with some of the stone partitions forming the wards still extant. The ceilings are of solid slabs of stone, carved on the exterior to represent tiles.

[1] There is a similar board in the Saman Burj in Agra Fort (p. 306).

Outside, to the W. of the Khas Mahal enclosure, is the **House of Miriam,** daughter of Raja Bhar Mal of Jaipur, Mariam uz Zamani, mother of Prince Salim, afterwards the Emperor Jahangir. One defaced fresco, in which the wings of angels are distinctly visible, has been thought to suggest the Annunciation. At one time the whole house was painted inside and out. The original name Sonahri Makan, or "Golden House", was given it on account of the profuse gilding of the walls.

N.W. is Miriam's Garden, and at the S.E. angle her bath, with a large column in the centre. On the W. side is the Ladies' **Mosque,** or **Nagina,** with the remains of a small Turkish bath. At the S. end of the garden is a small fish tank.

To the N.W. a road leads to the **Hathi Pol** (Elephant Gate) on the N. of the city. Over the W. archway, 20 ft. from the ground, are two life-sized elephants much mutilated—perhaps by Aurangzeb. On the left of the gateway are the so-called **Pigeon House**—possibly intended for a magazine—and the **Sangin Burj,** a groined bastion or keep.

Down the old stone-paved road on the left is the **Karawan Sarai** (caravanserai), a large court 272 ft. by 246 ft., surrounded by the merchants' hostels. Formerly the S.E. side was three storeys high. At the N. end, beyond the Sarai, stands the **Hiran Minar** ("Deer Minaret"), a circular tower some 70 ft. high, studded with protruding elephants' tusks of stone. Tradition says that it is erected over the grave of Akbar's favourite elephant, and that from the lantern in the top the Emperor shot driven antelope and other game. The land to the N. and W. was a large lake in Akbar's time, sometimes flooded even now.

On the left of the road returning to the Hathi Pol is a very fine stone well surrounded by rooms and staircases, which formed a part of the waterworks. The water was lifted from this level by a series of Persian wheels and a system of reservoirs to the arched gate on the N.W. corner of Birbal's House, and thence distributed throughout the palace.

The House of **Birbal** stands to the S.W. of Miriam's Garden, near the N.W. corner of the Jodh Bai Palace. It is said to have been built by Raja Birbal for his daughter, who, however, was not one of the wives of Akbar. It is a two-storeyed building of red sandstone standing on a raised platform, and consists of four rooms 15 ft. square, and two entrance porches on the ground floor and two above with small terraces in front of them, enclosed originally by stone screens, forming a ladies' promenade. Over the upper rooms are flat-ribbed cupolas, carried on octagonal drums, and supported on richly ornamented corbel brackets stretching across the angles of the rooms; and the stone-panelled walls and niches are covered with intricate patterns. The ceilings of the lower rooms are supported on a fine and unique frieze, and the whole of the interior—pilasters, recesses, walls, and cusp-arched doorways—are elaborately and beautifully carved with geometrical patterns. The exterior walls are almost as profusely ornamented. No wood has been used in the construction of this extraordinary building, to which the words of Victor Hugo have been applied: "If it were not the most minute of palaces, it was the most gigantic of jewel-cases". Raja Birbal was celebrated for his wit and learning, and was the only Hindu of eminence who embraced the new religion of Akbar, whose favourite courtier he was. He was no soldier, and perished with the whole of the army he was commanding in the Yusafzai country to the N.E. of Peshawar in 1586.

S. of Birbal's house are the **Stables** for 102 horses and nearly as many camels. In some of the mangers stone rings for the horses' halters still remain, and on the N.W. side one of the old doors. The camel stables are lighted by openings in the roof. To the S.E. is the **Palace of Jodh Bai,** wife of Jahangir, but more likely used by Akbar's chief wife, Sultana Rakiya, who was also his first cousin. The entrance is on the E. from the open space in front of the Record Office. It is a quadrangular building 232 ft. by 215 ft. The courtyard within has reception rooms on the N., S., and W. sides, connected by a flat-roofed corridor partly closed by stone walls. The room on the W. is more ornate than the others, and in the rear wall is a fireplace. There are chambers above, and those on the N. and S. sides rise to two storeys; they are gable-roofed and ornamented with blue enamelled tiling, recalling the Man Mandir Palace of Gwalior (p. 235). At the angles the chambers are surmounted by cupolas, originally painted. Overlooking Miriam's garden is a small projecting room, the walls of which are entirely composed of beautiful stone lattice work.

The **Dargah Mosque** lies S.W. of the Jodh Bai Palace. The E. gate, called the Badshahi, or "royal" gate, opens into the quadrangle, which measures 433 ft. by 366 ft. To the right is the Tomb, or Dargah, of Shaikh Salim Chishti, a descendant of the Pir Shakkar Ganj, who is buried at Pakpattan (see pp. 565 and 311). It is surrounded by marble geometrical lattice-work screens, the outer entrance doors also being of marble. The canopy over the tomb of the saint is inlaid with mother-of-pearl, no longer adorned with ostrich eggs over it. On the cenotaph is written the date of the saint's death (1571) and the date of the completion of the building (1580), "May God hallow his tombs!—the beloved helper of the sect and its saint, Shaikh Salim, whose miraculous gifts and propinquity to the Divine Being are celebrated, and by whom the lamp of the family of Chishti is illuminated. Be not double-sighted, looking to the transitory self, as well as to the everlasting Deity. The year of his decease is known throughout the world." The brackets which support the dripstone or eaves of the tomb are copies of those in the mosque of the stone-cutters (below). Childless women, both Hindu and Muslim, resort to the tomb and pray the saint to intercede in their favour. On the N. of the quadrangle is also the tomb of Islam Khan, surmounted with a cupola; he was the grandson of the saint and Governor of Bengal.

The **Mosque** proper, on the W., is said to be a copy of the one at Mecca. It is about 70 ft. high, and very beautiful. It consists of three interior square chambers surrounded by rows of lofty pillars of Hindu type. At the N. and S. ends are screened aisles. Outside a door at the back of the mosque, in an enclosure on the right, is an infant's tomb, said to be that of the saint's son, whose life was sacrificed at the age of six months in order that Akbar's son (Jahangir) might live when born.

In the S. wall the **Gate of Victory Buland Darwaza** ("high gate"), towers to the height of 176 ft. The grandeur of this great height is increased by a great flight of steps on the outside.[1] In the archway is an inscription on the left hand going out, which says that the "King of Kings, Shadow of God, Jalal-ud-din Muhammad Akbar the Emperor, on his return from conquering the kingdoms of the S. and Khandesh, formerly called Dhandesh, came to Fatehpur in the 46th year of his reign (corresponding to 1601), and proceeded from thence to Agra". On the opposite side is inscribed: "Isa (Jesus), on whom be peace, said: 'The world is a bridge, pass over it, but build no house on it. He who hopes for an hour may hope for eternity. The world endures but an hour, spend it in devotion. The rest is unseen.'" The doors of this great gateway are studded with iron horseshoes, affixed by the owners, who implore the prayers of the saint for their recovery. A **Mela**, or fair, commences on the 20th of *Ramazan*, the anniversary of the saint's death, and

[1] The gate and shrine are specially noticed by the traveller William Finch, who visited Fatehpur-Sikri in 1610.

lasts for eight days. In front of the steps are some Turkish baths. Local divers leap into the pool to amuse tourists.

W. of the Dargah, and outside the quadrangle, is the old **Mosque of the stone-cutters,** where Shaikh Salim lived in a cave covered by a room. (None but Muslims may enter.) In a portico on the right the saint taught his disciples. The stone-cutters are said to have built it for him before the foundation of Akbar's city.

Outside the N. wall of the Dargah are the houses of the brothers **Abul Fazl** and **Faizi,** the favourites of Akbar and followers of his new religion. Faizi was appointed poet-laureate in 1588 and died in 1595. Abul Fazl, the "King's Jonathan", was murdered in August 1602, on his way to Agra from the Deccan, by Raja Bir Singh Deo of Orchha, at the instigation of Salim (Jahangir). N.E. of the Record Office to the right of the road back to the Diwan-i-Am, is the **Hakim's,** or doctor's house, and a very large and fine **Hammam,** the walls and ceilings of which are richly ornamented with stamped plaster-work.

S. of these, and adjoining the Bayana-Agra road, is a spacious and interesting **Baoli,** from which the baths and this part of the city were supplied. Leading to a well at one end is a broad staircase enclosed on each side by rooms. Around the well are chambers for Persian wheels.

ROUTE 14.—DELHI

(*Map faces p.* 340)

INDEX

Changes in Street Names on Map

Roberts Road	now called	Murti Marg
Clive Road	,,	Tyagraja Marg
King Edward Road	,,	M. Azad Road
Queen Victoria Road	,,	Dr Rajendra Prasad Road
Raisina Road	,,	Feroze Shah Road
Curzon Road	,,	Kasturba Gandhi Road
Havelock Road	,,	Kali Bari Marg
Reading Road	,,	Mandir Marg
Circular Road	,,	Jawahar Lal Nehru Road
Over Bridge Road	,,	Desh Bandhu Gupta Road
Elgin Road	,,	Nethaji Subhash Marg
Wazirabad Road	,,	Timapur Road
York Road	,,	Motilal Nehru Marg
Queen Mary's Av.	,,	Pt. Pant Marg

DELHI—(alt. 709 ft.; pop. in 1971, 3,629,000), the old Mughal capital, was by the Imperial Proclamation on the 12th December 1911, on the occasion of the Coronation Durbar, once more re-established as capital by King George V and has continued to be the capital of the Indian Republic. There are many hotels of every grade as well as Y.M.C.A. and Y.W.C.A. and other Tourist Hostels. An international airport at Palam, shared by the Indian Air Force, now links Delhi to the world's capitals as well as to almost every important city in the Republic. All the principal airlines have offices in Delhi and there are numerous Travel and Shikar Agents. A detailed description of New Delhi is given on p. 340. et seq.

Delhi is famous for its jewellers, silversmiths and embroiderers, and many artistic products of other parts of India will be found in its shops. Assam, Bengal, Bihar, Delhi Territory, Karnataka, Kashmir, Kerala, M.P., Orissa, Punjab, Rajasthan, U.P. and other States maintain their own handicraft shops and their Tourist organizations are also represented. The A.A. of Upper India (14 Connaught Place) will advise motorists. The Central railway station (with five retiring rooms) lies in Queen's Road on the N. side of the city; the Queen's Gardens separate it from the Chandni Chauk, which forms a street running E. and W. from the Fort and Palace, on the Jumna, to the Fatehpuri Mosque, near the Lahore Gate. Facing the S.W. angle of the Fort is the great Jami Masjid. In the N. wall of the city are the Kashmir and Mori Gates; at the N.W. corner was the Kabul Gate (removed); next the Lahore Gate (removed); at the S.W. corner the Ajmer, on the S. the Turkoman and Delhi Gates. Outside the N. wall lies the civil station, bounded on the E. by the river and on the W. by the Ridge, beyond which the Cantonment lay in 1857. S. of the walled city, which should properly be known by the name of Delhi-Shahjahanabad, the ruins of old cities and fortresses stretch for 12 m. to the S.—first Firozabad, then Indrapat, with the tomb of the Emperor Humayun and the Shrine of Nizam-ud-din Aulia beyond it; then, at a considerable interval farther to the S.W., the ruins of the defences of Siri, Jahanpanah, and the Fort of Rai Pithora, in the citadel of which are situated the Qutb Mosque and Minar; 11 m. from Delhi, and 5 m. E. of the Qutb, the remains of Tughlaqabad and the fortress round it.

The Tourist Office (22 Janpath) will help plan sightseeing tours. For those who can spare only three days the following itinerary may be of use (map, facing p. 340):

1st Morning.—Fort and Palace, Jami Masjid, Kalan Masjid, Jain Temple and Chandni Chauk.

Afternoon.—Visit sights N. of the city.

2nd Morning.—Firozabad, Indrapat and New Delhi.

Afternoon.—Drive by the Mausoleum of Ghazi-ud-din to Jai Singh's Observatory and Safdar Jang's Tomb in New Delhi, by the tomb of Nizam-ud-din Aulia to that of Humayun, and so back past Indrapat.

3rd Day.—Drive to the Qutb (stopping *en route* to see the tank of Hauz Khas). Proceed to Tughlaqabad, and return by the Muttra Road to Delhi.

The Architecture of Delhi

The buildings in and round Delhi may be conveniently classified as follows, according to their dates and styles. The so-called early Pathan style is really Turki, but the old nomenclature is generally followed:

(1) Early Pathan, 1193-1320

The Qutb Mosque and Minar—the tomb of Altamsh; the Alai Darwaza (p. 337) and the Khizri or Jamaat Khana Mosque at Nizam-ud-din (p. 332).

At first, adoption and adaptation of Hindu materials and style to Saracenic motifs and requirements; then, developments of elaborate and beautiful decorative features from Hindu prototypes, with true arches and domes, rising from pendentives.

(2) Middle Pathan, 1320-1414

Earlier style.—Tughlaqabad and tomb of Tughlaq Shah (p. 339).

Later and severer style.—Kalan Masjid of Delhi (p. 326); mosque of Kotla Firoz Shah (p. 329); Qadam Sharif (p. 327); ruined buildings on the Ridge (p. 328); Hauz Khas tomb (p. 335); mosques of Nizam-ud-din, Begampur and Khirki (pp. 322, 335 and 339).

First, buildings of local stone, or of red sandstone with sloping walls, marble dressings being sparingly used; then buildings with sloping walls of stone and mortar plastered all over, and domes borne by rough columns of simple rectangular stones; mosques generally built on high raised platforms.

(3) Later Pathan, 1414-1556

Tombs of Saiyad and Lodi Kings (p. 334); Purana Qila and Mosque (p. 329); Jamali Mosque (p. 329); tomb and mosque of Isa Khan (p. 332).

Buildings usually with fine domes, and decorated with coloured marbles and tiles, and in some cases inside with fine plaster ornamentation.

(4) Mughal, 1556-1660

Earlier.—Tomb of Humayun (p. 331); tomb of Azam Khan (p. 334).

Middle Period.—Fort and Palace of Delhi (p. 323); Jami Masjid, Delhi (p. 325); Fatehpuri Masjid, Delhi (p. 327).

Later decadent style.—Zinat-ul-Masjid Mosque (p. 325); Moti Masjid at Mahrauli (p.338); Sonehri Masjids in Chandni Chauk (p. 326) and of Javed Khan (p. 325); mosque tomb and college of Ghazi-ud-din Khan (p. 326); tomb of Safdar Jang (p. 334).

Buildings at first of red sandstone, with marble dressings; restrained decoration. In the middle period, white marble increasingly used; decoration more free; domes assume bulbous form, and lofty minarets prominent. In the late Mughal style, tendency to over-elaboration with florid decoration. Buildings are in the charge of a Supdt. Arch. Survey.

History.[1]—Though the country round Delhi is connected with the early history of India, as recorded in the *Mahabharata*, little is known

[1] Those interested in the history and archaeology of Delhi will find details in *The Seven Cities of Delhi*, by Sir Gordon Hearn, and in brochures available from the Government Tourist Office.

prior to the Muslim conquest in 1193. According to tradition, a city called Indraprastha was founded by a king called Yudhishthir, and the fort of Indrapat, also called Purana Kila, or "Old Fort", stands, perhaps, on the site, although excavations have revealed nothing which can be identified as ancient. The extensive ruins lying S. of modern Delhi, and covering an area of about 45 sq. m., are the remains of many forts or cities. The oldest are the Hindu forts of Lal Kot, built by Anang Pal Tomar in 1052, and of Rai Pithora Prithvi Raja Chauhan, built about 1180. These two forts, the two Asoka pillars, and the iron pillar at the Qutb are the only remains of the Hindu period, with the exception of the Suraj Khund, a sunken amphitheatre, and the Arangpur *bund*, 2½ m. S.W. of of Adilabad.

The earliest Muslim cities were Siri, built by 'Ala-ud-din in 1304; Tughlaqabad, built by Tughlaq Shah in 1321; and Jahanpanah, enclosed by Muhammad Tughlaq, about 1325. Subsequently Firozabad was constructed by the Emperor Firoz Shah Tughlaq, and the Purana Qila was founded and built by Humayun and Sher Shah. This new Delhi was not favoured by the Emperors Akbar and Jahangir, and the walled city dates from the commencement of the fort by Shah Jahan in 1639, whence it was called Shahjahanabad.

Delhi has been often captured. It was sacked by Timur, the Mughal, in 1398; also by Nadir Shah, the Persian, in 1739. On the 10th March 1739 the small Persian garrison was attacked. On the 11th he gave his troops, who had been summoned from the encampment outside the city, orders for a general massacre. From sunrise till 12 o'clock Delhi presented a scene of appalling carnage. The Mughal Emperor Muhammad Shah then interceded for the people. Nadir Shah replied, "The Emperor of India must never ask in vain", and commanded the massacre should cease. A vast multitude of persons had, however, perished, and Nadir Shah carried with him from Delhi the famous Peacock Throne (since broken up), and the Koh-i-nur diamond. It was sacked also by the Afghan, Ahmad Shah Durani, three times between 1757 and 1761. In 1771 the Mahratta Chief, Madhav Rao Scindia, captured Delhi, and the Mahrattas held it off and on till September 1803, when General Lake defeated Scindia's General, Louis Bourquien, gaining possession of Delhi and of the family and person of the King Shah Alam. In October 1804, Delhi was besieged by the Mahratta, Jaswant Rao Holkar, but was successfully defended by Colonel William Burn (p. 327). From that time to 1857 the old capital of India remained in the possession of the British, although the descendants of the Mughal were allowed to retain their outward royal dignities. The last King, Bahadur Shah, succeeded in 1837, and was about eighty years old when the Mutiny broke out. With his death at Rangoon, in 1862, the Mughal dynasty ended.

Delhi Territory

Ever since 1911, a separate administrative area has been marked out to contain Delhi and its surroundings. The area of the Delhi Territory, which (like the District of Columbia) is immediately under the authority of the Central Government, is 578 sq. m.

The Mutiny, 1857

The principal events of the great mutiny of the Bengal army in 1857 centred originally round Delhi.

These are of interest mainly to readers of British birth, and a detailed description necessary to do them justice would unbalance a book designed for readers of all nationalities. Below therefore they are given only in the briefest outline. Those who wish for fuller information may refer to books like S. N. Sen's *Eighteen Fifty Seven* (Govt. of India, 1957) or

Michael Edwardes' *Red Year* Hamish Hamilton, London 1973, also p. 6).

On the 10th May 1857 a mutiny broke out in the Cantonment of Meerut, 42 m. N.W. of Delhi. The Mutineers departed that same day for Delhi and succeeded in inducing the sepoy battalions there to join them. There were no British troops in Delhi, and the Civil officials who had taken refuge in the Fort were murdered. Every vestige of British power disappeared and the King assumed authority. Measures were taken at once by General Anson, the Commander-in-Chief, to collect troops from the Punjab, from Ambala and from Meerut, and a force under the command of Major-General Sir Henry Barnard,[1] after defeating a large army of rebels at Badli-ki-Sarai (6 m. N. of Delhi) on the 8th June, gained possession of the Ridge overlooking Delhi from the N. After many vicissitudes owing to enemy attacks and sickness, the small British force, which never exceeded 6600, carried Delhi by storm between the 13th and 20th September 1857, the hero of the assault being Brigadier-General Nicholson, who was mortally wounded at the moment of victory. He was buried in the Kashmir Gate cemetery.

Delhi and its Surroundings

For the convenience of sightseeing, Delhi and the adjoining country may be divided as follows:

(1) The city, including the old Arsenal, the Fort and Palace, the Jami Masjid and Kalan Masjid, and the Chandni Chauk.

(2) The tract lying N. of the city walls, in which the principal incidents of the Siege of Delhi and the Imperial Assemblages took place.

(3) The tract lying immediately S. of the city, and including the ruins of Firozabad, the Purana Qila, the Mausolea of the Emperor Humayun and Nawab Safdar Jang, and Nizam-ud-din Aulia, the Saiyad and Lodi tombs, and Jai Singh's Observatory in new Delhi.

(4) The tract lying still farther S., including the tomb of the Emperor Firoz Shah at Hauz Khas, Siri, Jahanpanah, Qila Rai Pithora, the citadel of Lal Kot, with the Qutb Minar and Mosque, Surajkhund and Tughlaqabad, 5 m. to the E. of these.

(5) The buildings of the new capital, included in (3).

(1) The City

The **Kashmir Gate** was the scene of some desperate fighting during the Mutiny, and on its outer face is a memorial tablet to Lieutenant Salkeld and the other heroes who fell there.

Inside the Gate is **St James' Church,** built by Colonel Skinner, C.B. (d. 1841), whose residence stood on the opposite side of the clear space here; in the churchyard are the graves of the Skinner family and of Mr William Fraser, murdered in 1835, and of Sir T. Metcalfe. Inside the church are a number of memorial tablets.

St Stephen's College, formerly run by the Cambridge Mission but now by the Church of North India, has been transferred from this area to a site N. of the Ridge near the University. On the left is the High School building, a portion of which was formerly the library of Prince Dara Shikoh. The road now divides into two branches with a long grass plot in the centre. At one end of the latter is the granite memorial of the officers of the Telegraph Department who fell in 1857.

Farther along the same plot stand the gateways of the old **Magazine.** Over the central gate is a memorial to Lieutenant Willoughby and the eight heroic men who shared in its defence during the Mutiny; in the S.E. corner at the back are the steps by which the survivors escaped. The road now passes the old cemetery (closed 1855) on the left; and beyond the arch of

[1] Succeeded on his death, in July, by Brigadier-General Archdale Wilson.

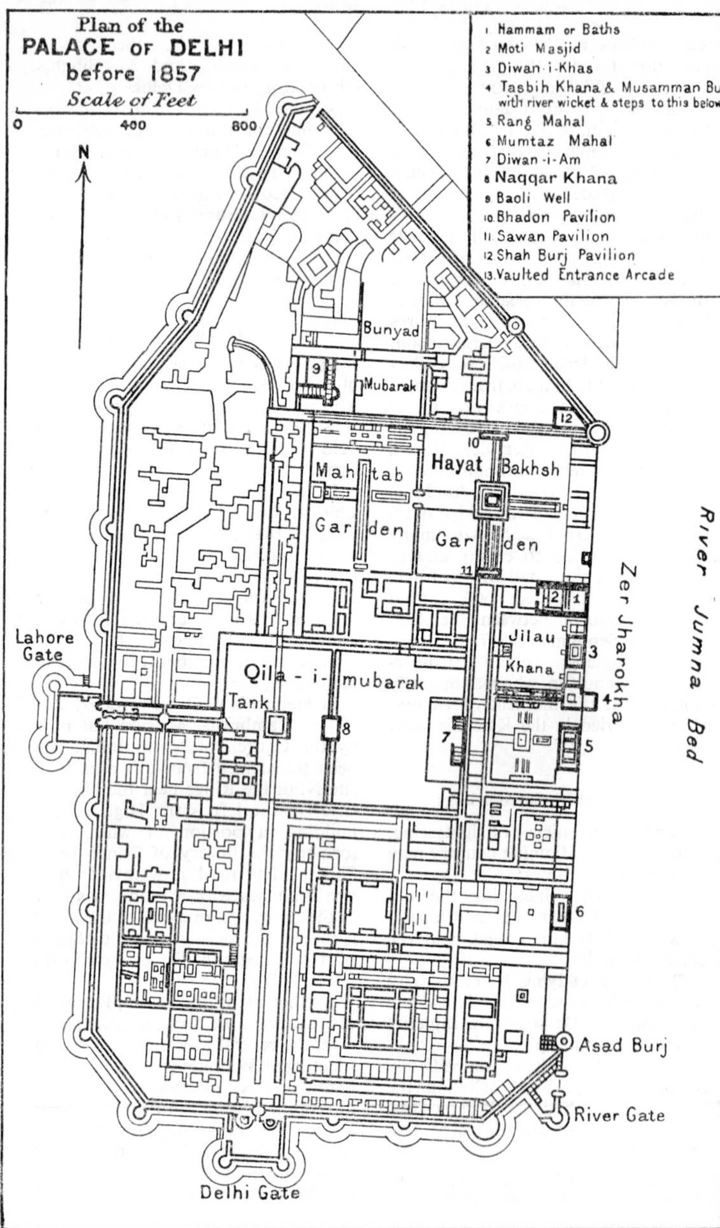
Plan of the
PALACE OF DELHI
before 1857
Scale of Feet
0
400
800
N
1. Hammam or Baths
2 Moti Masjid
3 Diwan-i-Khas
4 Tasbih Khana & Musamman Bu
with river wicket & steps to this below
5. Rang Mahal
6 Mumtaz Mahal
7 Diwan-i-Am
8 Naqqar Khana
9. Baoli Well
10. Bhadon Pavilion
11. Sawan Pavilion
12 Shah Burj Pavilion
13. Vaulted Entrance Arcade
Bunyad
Mubarak
Mahtab
Garden
Hayat Bakhsh
Garden
Jilau
Khana
Qila-i-mubarak
Tank
Lahore
Gate
Zer Jharokha
River Jumna Bed
Asad Burj
River Gate
Delhi Gate

the railway bridge the main thoroughfare (side roads branch from here to the railway station on the right, and to the ghats and the Jumna bridge on the left) ascends the slope in front to the **Mughal Fort and Palace,** built by the Emperor Shah Jahan between 1639-48. Visitors are recommended not to miss the **Son-et-Lumière** exhibitions, lasting an hour, arranged at the Red Fort by the Indian Tourist Development Corporation. Particulars from the Tourist Information Bureau.

There are two fine gates to the Fort, as at Agra. The one in the centre of the W. side at the E. end of the Chandni Chauk is called the Lahore Gate; and the other, at the S.W. corner, the Delhi Gate, leads to Old Delhi. A good view of the magnificent red sandstone wall (whence the name Lal Kila or Red Fort) is obtained by walking along the ditch to the N.W. corner, where the two bridges between the Fort and the Salimgarh may be seen, also the traditional site of the Dasaswamedh and Nigambodh ghats, where the Imperial Horse sacrifice was performed by Yudhishthir (Introd., p. 21), and the sacred Vedas were recovered from the bottom of the ocean.

Entering the forework, erected by the Emperor Aurangzeb, in front of the **Lahore Gate,** and passing under the archway, the visitor will find himself under a vaulted arcade (see plan of Fort and Palace). From the octagon in the centre of it a gateway to the left conducts to the steps leading up to the rooms (now private quarters) over the Gate, the scene of a ghastly episode during the Mutiny. The vaulted arcade ends in the centre of the outer court, which measured 540 ft. by 360 ft., of which the side arcades and central tank have been removed.

In the E. wall was the now isolated **Naubat** or **Nakkar Khana,** the band gallery measuring 100 ft. by 80 ft.; and here everyone except Princes of the royal blood was required to dismount. The carving of the flowers on the red sandstone dado of the gateway is unusually good. The inner main court to which this gateway led was 540 ft. broad and 420 ft. deep, and was also surrounded by arcade galleries, where the great feudatories used to mount guard. This space has been cleared (1903-12) of military structures, the courtyard being now represented by a lawn, and the arcades by shrubberies, maintained by Government.

On the farther side is the Hall of Public Audience, the **Diwan-i-Am** (100 ft. by 60 ft.). The proportions of this hall, with its columns and engrailed arches, are extremely good. The whole was originally covered with ivory polished chunam. At the back in the raised recess was the throne of the Emperor. Below it is the marble seat of the Wazir, and around it above are twelve inlaid panels executed by Austin of Bordeaux, including that of the artist as Orpheus, recovered by Lord Curzon from the S. Kensington Museum. The hall was thoroughly restored by the efforts of Lord Curzon; and a Florentine, Sr. Menegatti, renewed (1909) the inlay work of the throne recess and the plaques of the arch to the W. side of the throne. Bernier gives a full account of the splendid appearance of the hall in the time of Aurangzeb.

A gate on the N. side of the hall led to the innermost court of the palace, and to the **Diwan-i-Khas,** or Hall of Private Audience, in which the peacock throne used to stand. Tavernier records a minute description of the glories of this throne, carried off (1739) by Nadir Shah.[1] The following description is from Mr Beresford's *Guide to Delhi*: "It was so called from its having the figures of two peacocks standing behind it, their tails being expanded,

[1] The peacock throne is no longer in existence. It was broken up when Nadir Shah was murdered in North-east Persia in 1747, and such fragments as survived were inserted in a seat or throne which may still be seen in the museum of the royal palace at Tehran.

and the whole so inlaid with sapphires, rubies, emeralds, pearls and other precious stones of appropriate colours as to represent life. The throne itself was 6 ft. long by 4 ft. broad; it stood on six massive feet, which, with the body, were of solid gold, inlaid with rubies, emeralds and diamonds. It was surmounted by a canopy of gold, supported by twelve pillars, all richly emblazoned with costly gems, and a fringe of pearls ornamented the borders of the canopy. Between the two peacocks stood the figure of a parrot, said to have been carved out of a single emerald."

The general effect has been spoilt by the removal of the marble pavement in front of it and of the arcaded court which once enclosed it like the Khas Mahal at Agra (p. 307). It measures 90 ft. by 67 ft., and is built wholly of white marble, the dado of the interior walls and piers being inlaid with precious stones; the ceiling, which was once of silver, removed by the Mahrattas (1760), has been restored in wood, supported by iron girders above. At either end of the hall over the two outer arches, is the famous Persian inscription:

"Agar Fardaus bar ru-i-zamin ast
Hamin ast wa hamin ast wa hamin ast."

"If there is a Paradise on the face of the earth,
It is here, oh! it is here, oh! it is here."

The Diwan-i-Am has many historical connections—the presence of Nadir Shah the Persian, and Ahmad Shah the Afghan, the thanksgiving service of the Delhi Field Force on the 27th September 1857, and the trial of the last King of Delhi in January and March 1858. The Diwan-i-Khas has seen the blinding (1788) of King Shah Alam by the brutal Ghulam Kadir, and the reception of General Lake after the Battle of Delhi in 1803.

N. of the Diwan-i-Khas, connected by a shallow water channel, which also passed through the Royal Apartments, are the **Royal Baths.** These consist of three large rooms, the flooring inlaid with *pietra dura* work, and crowned with domes. They were lighted by windows of coloured glass in the roof. In the centre of each room is a fountain, and in the wall of one of them a reservoir of marble.

Opposite to them, to the W., is the **Moti Masjid,** or the "Pearl Mosque", of white and grey-veined marble. A bronze door covered with designs in low relief leads to the courtyard, 40 ft. by 35 ft. The mosque proper has three arches, and is divided into two aisles. The walls are decorated with low reliefs. It was built in 1659 by Aurangzeb: originally the domes were covered with gilded copper plates.

To the N. of these buildings lies the **Hayat Bakhsh,** or Life-giving garden-court, 200 ft. square, with the Shah Burj pavilion in the N.E. corner and the Bhadon and Sawan Pavilions on the N. and S. sides. Beyond these the road to the N. leads to the Salimgarh, built by Salim Shah in 1546. W. of the above garden was another called the Mahtab (moon) Bagh, and near what was the N.W. corner of it is a picturesque baoli or tank.

The **Royal Private Apartments** consist of three sets of rooms and of a tower called the Musamman (octagonal) Burj, projecting over the river. In the open central bay is an alabaster panel with a representation of the heavens round the Scales of Justice, Mizan-i-adl (shown on the President's flag), and in others will be found beautiful decorations and pierced grilles. Two of the smaller rooms contain articles representative of those in daily use by Mughal Emperors. S. of these apartments is the **Rang Mahal,** or Painted Palace, the residence of the Chief Sultana; the marble water channel (see below) runs through this also.

Farther S. is the **Mumtaz Mahal,** the Delhi Museum of Archaeology,[1]

[1] The Archaeological Survey of India published a Guide to the Delhi Fort buildings many years ago. Copies can be obtained, together with smaller guidebooks, from the Tourist Information Office.

formed (1868) as a Municipal **Museum,** moved to the Naubat Khana (1909), and here in 1911. It contains Mutiny relics, views and plans of Delhi in former times, and a collection of Mughal miniature portraits.

The S.E. bastion is the Lion Tower. On the S.W. is the **Delhi Gate.** Near it, on the right, the King of Delhi was imprisoned after September 1857. Between the inner and outer gates used to stand two large stone elephants replaced at the expense of Lord Curzon. Beyond the Southern glacis of the Fort, on which a cross marks the site of an old cemetery, lay the old Cantonment of Dariaganj. The Dariaganj area is bounded on the W. by the Faiz Bazar leading to the Delhi Gate, of the city; near the Khairati Gate N.E. is the **Zinat-ul-Masjid Mosque,** built by a daughter of Aurangzeb in 1707.

From the Delhi Gate of the Fort the Khas Bazar once led to the **Jami Masjid,** and on the open space stood private palaces. In the southern portion of this open space and E. of the Jami Masjid is Edward Park. S. is the Victoria Memorial Hospital for women, and to the W. the Dufferin Municipal Hospital. In front of the Delhi Gate is the graceful **Sonehri Masjid** of Javed Khan, built in 1751.

The Jami Masjid

Fergusson wrote of the **Jami Masjid** as follows: "The Jami Masjid at Delhi, begun in 1644, but not finally completed till 1658, is not unlike the Moti Masjid in the Agra Fort in plan, though built on a very much larger scale, and adorned with two noble minarets, which are wanting in the Agra example; while from the somewhat capricious admixture of red sandstone with white marble it is far from possessing the same elegance and purity of effect. It is, however, one of the few mosques, either in India or elsewhere, that is designed to produce a pleasing effect externally. It is raised on a lofty basement, and its three gateways, combined with the four angle towers and the frontispiece and domes of the mosque itself, make up a design where all the parts are pleasingly subordinated to one another, but at the same time produce a whole of great variety and elegance. The mosque itself is 201 ft. in length by 120 ft., and is flanked by two minars 130 ft. high, formed in alternate vertical stripes of sandstone and white marble, and crowned by light marble pavilions."

The three gateways are approached by broad flights of steps. The great doors of the main gateway on the E. which used to be opened only for the Mughal Emperor, are massive and overlaid with brass arabesques half an inch thick. Visitors entering any part of the floor space of the mosque are required to wear overshoes of canvas (provided).

Inside is a quadrangle, 325 ft. square, in the centre of which are a marble basin and fountain. Round three sides of the quadrangle runs an open sandstone cloister, 15 ft. wide, with pillars of the same material. The inscription on the front of the mosque gives the date in Arabic as 1658, the year in which Aurangzeb deposed his father, Shah Jahan; it is found in the two words "Ya Hadi", "O Guide", on the centre panel. The three white marble domes are relieved by thin vertical lines of black marble. The two minarets are reached from the S. gate over the roof of the arcade. At the N.E. corner of the court is a pavilion in which are placed relics of the Prophet Muhammad. The view of the Fort walls from the galleries on the E. side of the court is very fine; also that of the back wall from the W. On the E. side is the tomb of a Muslim leader, Maulana Shaukat Ali (1873-1938).

From the Jami Masjid the Chaura Bazar leads S.W. to the Qazi Hauz and the Lal Kuan Bazar, which extends up to the Fatehpuri Masjid. S. from the Qazi Hauz one main street runs past the Kalan Masjid to the Turkman Gate, and another W. to the Ajmer Gate. The **Kalan** (Great)

Masjid, popularly known as the Kali (Black) Masjid, once included within the limits of Firozabad, was built by Firoz Shah in 1386. The outside consists of two storeys, of which the lower, forming a kind of plinth, is 28 ft. high, the total height to the top of the battlements being 66 ft. The walls, which are very thick, have in the upper storey openings, with red stone screens, much mutilated; the arcades are supported by square columns of stone. There is a stern look about this sombre building, the plan of which Bishop Heber says, "is exactly that of the original Arabian mosques—a square court surrounded by a cloister, and roofed with many small domes of the plainest and most solid construction".

E. of the mosque, beside Turkman Gate, is the tomb of Turkman Shah, styled the "Sun of Devotees". He died in 638 A.H. = A.D. 1240, in the time of Muizz-ud-din Bahram Shah.

A little to the N. of this saint's grave, in the Bulbuli Khana, is the tomb of **Sultan Raziya,** daughter of the Emperor Altamsh, and the only Muslim Empress of India, who ruled from 1236 to 1240; she was killed in flight from a battle in which she sought to recover her throne. The mausoleum at the **Ajmer Gate,** enclosed in a modern horn-work (1805), was constructed by **Ghazi-ud-din Khan,** who was interred there in 1710. He was the father of the first Asaf Jah of Hyderabad, whose son, Ghazi-ud-din (d. 1752), is buried here, and whose grandson, Ghazi-ud-din (Imad-ul-Mulk), played a prominent part in the decline of the Mughal empire. In addition to the graves standing in a small enclosure surrounded by panels of pale-coloured sandstone, some pierced and some carved with flowers, there are a mosque and a college, occupied by the Anglo-Arabic School.

Close to the Jami Masjid, on the N.W. side, is a **Jain Temple,** approached by narrow streets. It stands upon a high, walled platform, gained by narrow steps, and consists of a small marble court surrounded by a stucco colonnade, in front of the temple proper, which is surmounted by an oblong dome. Within, the ceiling and walls are richly gilded, and are supported by two rows of small marble columns. In the centre of the temple is a pyramidal platform in three tiers, upon which rests the small figure of a Jain saint, seated beneath an elaborate ivory canopy. Fergusson draws particular attention to the exquisite device in the porch of filling in the back of the struts which support the architrave beneath the dome with foliated tracery.

To the N. the **Dariba** leads to the Kotwali in the **Chandni Chauk.** The portion of this famous street between this point and the Fort was called the Urdu, or Camp.[1] On the N. side a large residence, which formerly belonged to the Begam Samru, is now occupied by the Bank of India. W. of the Dariba the Flower Market and the Jewellers' Market have been absorbed into the Chandni Chauk proper. Houses built both across and down it were removed, and the channel from the W. Jumna Canal, built by Ali Mardan Khan to supply the Palace, was covered over. Opposite the S.E. gate of the Queen's Gardens is the **Kotwali.**

W. of the open space is the **Sonehri Masjid** of Roshan-ud-daula, on the platform of which Nadir Shah watched while the inhabitants were being massacred. On the left-hand side of the Kotwali is the Sisganj Gurdwara, a sacred place of the Sikhs, erected to mark the traditional site of the martyrdom of their *guru* Tegh Bahadur, by order of Aurangzeb. Farther down, on the same side of the Chandni Chauk, is the **Khuni Darwaza,** or Gate of Blood, where the massacre by Nadir Shah is said to have been stayed.

Opposite the Kotwali, on the site of the **Karawan Sarai,** built by **Jahan-**

[1] The mixed language which grew up in the royal residence (*urdu-i-muhalla*, the sublime camp) was called *zaban-i-urdu*, the camp language, and became gradually known as Urdu.

ara Begam, daughter of the Emperor Shah Jahan, and held by Bernier to be one of the wonders of Delhi, the Northbrook Clock Tower was situated which collapsed in 1951. Between the Municipal Buildings and the main railway station are the Begam or Queen's Gardens, with a cricket ground, much frequented both by travellers by the railway and by townspeople. In the gardens is situated the Public Library, erected in memory of Lord Hardinge.

The Chandni Chauk ends at the **Fatehpuri Mosque** constructed by Fatehpuri Begam, one of the wives of Shah Jahan, in 1650; it is built of red sandstone, and is surmounted by a single dome. On the S. side of the mosque a street leads to the Lal Kuan Bazar, and on the N. side another leads to the **Lahore Gate** and the smaller Sarhandi Mosque, erected by another wife of Shah Jahan, in front of it. Beyond are the quarters of Paharganj and Kishanganj (p. 329).

On the crest of the Ridge is the **Idgah** (of Firozabad) and at the foot of the Ridge is the picturesque enclosure of the **Qadam Sharif,** or Sacred Foot, in which Prince Fateh Khan, eldest son of the Emperor Firoz Shah, was buried in 1373. The name is derived from the imprint of a foot of the Prophet Muhammad carved on a small slab preserved under water on the tomb.

A road from the Fatehpuri Masjid past the W. end of the Queen's Gardens and the Cambridge Mission Church leads to Queen's Road which skirts the N. side of the gardens to the Kabul Gate. On the left side of the road, in a large house which once belonged to Nawab Safdar Jang, the Cambridge Mission used to be located. (its functions now taken over by the Church of North India). Besides the College and School, there is a large womens' Hospital at Tis Hazari, below the S. point of the Ridge. Farther on, just before arriving at the site of the **Kabul Gate,** a piece of the old wall has been left to mark the spot where **Brigadier-General Nicholson** was mortally wounded on 14th September 1857. The gate and main portion of the wall were demolished to make way for the Burn Bastion Road and the railway in 1904. Outside the gate is the Karol Bagh (1917).

(2) Tract lying N. of the City

The Dufferin Bridge, crossing the railway from Queen's Road, leads to the Mori Gate and the old Civil Station. The **Mori** or **Shah Bastion,** 200 yd. to the W. of the gate, affords a fine view of the S. end of the Ridge and of the N. wall front to the Kashmir Gate.

The walls of Delhi were built by Shah Jahan, but the towers were enlarged into bastions by the British about 1809, after the attack on the city by Jaswant Rao Holkar in October 1804. The repulse of 70,000 Mahrattas, with 130 guns, by Colonel Burn, with two and a half battalions of sepoys, was a most notable feat of arms, almost forgotten, like the Battle of Delhi in 1803 (p. 320). On the right, just outside the Kashmir Gate, is the **Qudsia Garden,** and on the left the Nicholson Garden, named after Brig.-General Nicholson. He is buried in the cemetery N. of it. The grave bears the brief, soldierly inscription:

The Grave of
Brigadier-General JOHN NICHOLSON,
Who led the assault of Delhi but fell
In the hour of victory
Mortally wounded,
And died 23rd of September 1857,
Aged 35 years.

About a mile farther on, after passing Maiden's Hotel on the right, the traveller comes to a high mound where Timur's Camp was sited. A little farther on are the temporary Secretariat buildings, which are now occupied by Government Offices. The old Legislative Council Hall, in the centre of the block, serves as a Convocation Hall for the Delhi University, which was established by statute in 1922 as a teaching and residential University. Three Colleges—St Stephen's (moved here in 1940), Hindu and Ramjas—are affiliated.

The road now proceeds N. for ¾ m., and then turns W. by the "Khyber Pass" through the Ridge, the northernmost outcrop of the Aravallis, the Ridge Road to the left leading to the **Flagstaff Tower,** to which another steeper road leads direct from the S. From the roof a complete view is obtained of the whole encampment of the British besieging force. S.E. of the Ridge, the pale dome of St James' Church marking the site of the Kashmir Gate, and the square roof of a factory that of the Mori Bastion. The large house to the W. from the Flagstaff Tower, built at the time of the Coronation Darbar in 1903 for the Viceroy, and used until 1931 as Viceregal Lodge, is now the University Offices. A pleasant walk may be taken through the University Campus in which "bells of arms" for keeping the muskets can still be seen and which the Najafgarh Canal bounds on the farther side. The area on both sides of the canal (in reality a drainage cut from swamps at Najafgarh) was used for the main Civil Camps in 1903, and at the Coronation Darbar of 1911. Near the drainage cut is **Rajpur Cemetery,** where General Sir H. Barnard and the brave men who fell before Delhi lie buried.[1] There is a memorial cross of grey Aberdeen granite. Some 2 m. to the N. side of the road is the Plain of Barwari, on which the Imperial Assemblage of 1st January 1877 and the Coronation Darbars of 1st January 1903 and 12th December 1911 were held, and presented scenes of splendour. The earthwork of the amphitheatre erected in 1911 has been maintained, and the site of the thrones occupied by their Imperial Majesties marked by a granite column. A railway was made to Kingsway, where there is now a Hospital for Tuberculosis.

4 m. down the Karnal road is the field of the Battle of Badli-ki-sarai, fought on 8th June 1857 (p. 321). A memorial to the 75th Foot is in Sarai Pipal Thala village area. A mile to the W. of the old Mughal Sarai, of which only the two main gateways now remain, are the ruins of the Shalimar Gardens of the Emperor Shah Jahan, the scene of the coronation of his usurping son, Aurangzeb.

Returning to the **Flagstaff Tower,** and proceeding S. down the Ridge, an ancient building, probably a tomb, of the time of Firoz Shah, now known as the **Chauburji Mosque,** is reached in half a mile. This formed the left of the British position on the Ridge, and round it traces of the breastworks may be seen. The dark building that rises ½ m. farther S. is the so-called **Observatory,** most probably a portion of Firoz Shah's *Kushak-i-Shikar*, or hunting-lodge, known generally as the Pir Ghalib.

Hindu Rao's House, now a Hospital, the key of the position on the Ridge, was held by Major Reid with his Gurkhas,[1] supported by the 60th Rifles and the Guides. From the N. side of this, on the edge of the reservoir of the Delhi Waterworks, a fine view is obtained of the slope from the Mori Gate up to the right of the British position. At the bottom of the slope, on the W. side, is a fine *baoli* (tank), which belonged to the Hunting Palace of Firoz Shah. At the bottom of the baoli an old underground passage leads through the Ridge.

Within the grounds of the Hunting Palace was erected the pillar or **Lat of Asoka,** 250 yd. S. of Hindu Rao's House. It was broken by an explosion early in the 18th century and lay on

[1] This walk can be prolonged by 4 m. by walking N. through the old Cantonment to the end of the Ridge and the tomb of Shah Alam situated near Wazirabad, on the bank of a nulla spanned by an old Pathan bridge.

[1] The 2nd King Edward's own Gurkha Rifles (The Sirmur Battalion) carry a bronze truncheon, surmounted by a crown in silver, supported by three Gurkha soldiers in bronze. On a ring of silver below the figures is the inscription: "Main Picquet, Hindu Rao's House, Delhi, 1857".

the ground for 150 years. It was originally at Meerut.

300 yd. S., the **Mutiny Memorial** occupies the site of the right batteries of the British position; on the panels round the base of the memorial are records of the troops who served before Delhi, of the various actions fought by them, of their losses, and the names of the officers who fell in them.

In the dip of the Ridge where the railway runs are the suburbs of Paharganj and Kishanganj, and farther to the W. **Sabzi Mandi** (Vegetable Market), through which the rebels often attacked the British position, and even their right rear at the General's Mound. W. of Sabzi Mandi are the **Roshanara Gardens,** created by the daughter of Shah Jahan, who lies buried here. She died in 1671—three years before her sister, Jahanara Begam (p. 334).

(3) Tract lying immediately to the S. of the City

A description of the portion of this tract which is covered by the New Capital is given separately from p. 340.

For the present purpose the tour will be made by starting on the E. side from the **Delhi Gate.** To the right on Circular Road, is the Irwin Hospital. Farther along, on Sikandra Road, to the right is the Lady Irwin College for women. A Pathan gate of decorated stonework, passed on the left, is known as the **Lal Darwaza,** or Red Gate, and was apparently the northern gate of the short-lived capital of Sher Shah (d. 1545), which probably was left incomplete. Then a road leads to the left to the **Kotla of Firoz Shah** (1351-1388), which formed the citadel of the city of Firozabad. North of the Kotla is Rajghat, where Gandhi was cremated. Opposite is the Gandhi National Museum. In the Kotla, on the top of a platform, rises the second **Lat of Asoka.** The pillar is 10 ft. 10 in. round where it leaves the platform, and the total height is 42 ft. 7 in., of which 4 ft. 1 in. are sunk in the masonry. At 10 ft. 1 in. from the base are some Nagri inscriptions, with the date in two of them of Samwat 1581 = A.D. 1524. These must have been inscribed after the removal of the pillar to Delhi. Above these Nagri inscriptions is the inscription, which contains the edicts of Asoka, the Mauryan King (Introd., p. 44). The characters, which are in Brahmi, the parent of the modern Devanagri and other allied alphabets, are very clearly written, but, when Firoz Shah assembled all the learned of his day to decipher the inscription, they were unable to do so. There is a second inscription, which records the victories of the Chauhan Prince Visaladeva, whose power extended from the Himalaya to the Vindhya. This record consists of two portions—the shorter one immediately above Asoka's edicts, and the longer immediately below them. Both are dated Samwat 1220 = A.D. 1163, and refer to the same Prince. There are minor inscriptions of little interest.

To the S. of the Lat is a **Mosque** now much ruined, but which must once have been imposing; it was surrounded by arcades and by a covered hall borne by plain stone columns. To the S. of it again are the spacious enclosures shut in by the very lofty walls which look so imposing from the Agra Road. The interior courtyards have been cleared of debris and grassed. A circular *baoli,* with two storeys of arches, is particularly worthy of notice. The ruins of **Firozabad** were extensively used for the cities of Sher Shah and of Shah Jahan, although scattered ruins show that its area must have been larger than that of the present city.

To the S. on the site of the old **Indrapat,** rise the lofty walls of the **Purana Qila,** with their graceful high gates, built by Sher Shah, with additions by Humayun. The S. gate, by which the Fort is most conveniently entered, is reached by a

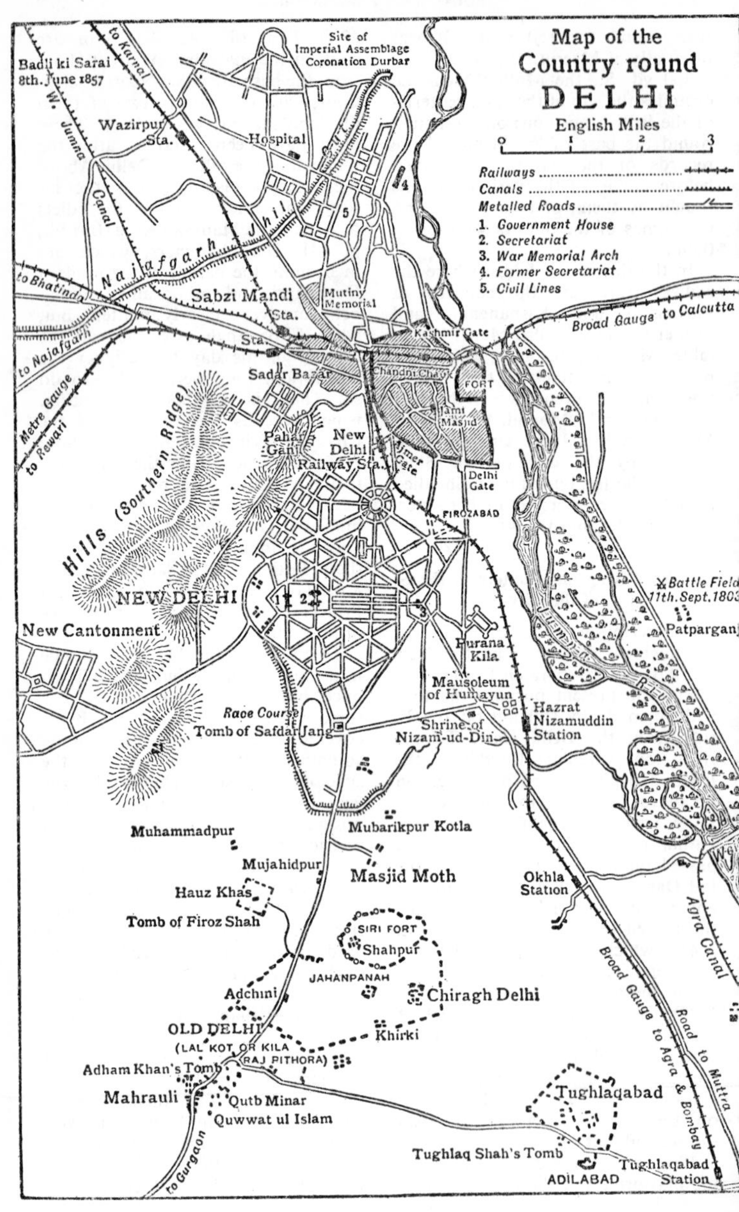
Map of the
Country round
DELHI
English Miles
0 1 2 3
Railways
Canals
Metalled Roads
1. Government House
2. Secretariat
3. War Memorial Arch
4. Former Secretariat
5. Civil Lines
Site of
Imperial Assemblage
Coronation Durbar
Badli ki Sarai
8th. June 1857
to Karnal
W. Jumna Canal
Wazirpur Sta.
Hospital
Najafgarh Jhil
to Bhatinda
Sabzi Mandi Sta.
Mutiny Memorial
Kashmir Gate
Broad Gauge to Calcutta
to Najafgarh
Sta.
Sadar Bazar
Chandni Chauk
FORT
Jami Masjid
Metre Gauge to Rewari
Hills (Southern Ridge)
Pahari Ganj
New Delhi Railway Sta.
Ajmer Gate
Delhi Gate
FIROZABAD
NEW DELHI
Battle Field 11th. Sept. 1803
Patparganj
New Cantonment
Purana Kila
Jumna River
Mausoleum of Humayun
Hazrat Nizamuddin Station
Race Course
Tomb of Safdar Jang
Shrine of Nizam-ud-Din
Muhammadpur
Mubarikpur Kotla
Mujahidpur
Masjid Moth
Okhla Station
Hauz Khas
Tomb of Firoz Shah
SIRI FORT
Shahpur
JAHANPANAH
Agra Canal
Adchini
Chiragh Delhi
OLD DELHI
(LAL KOT OR KILA RAJ PITHORA)
Khirki
Broad Gauge to Agra & Bombay
Road to Muttra
Adham Khan's Tomb
Mahrauli
Qutb Minar
Quwwat ul Islam
Tughlaqabad
to Gurgaon
Tughlaq Shah's Tomb
ADILABAD
Tughlaqabad Station

bridge across an old branch of the Jumna here; at the junction are the Khair-ul-manazil, a Madrasa and mosque built by the foster-mother of the Emperor Akbar. To the side of this is another gate similar to the Lal Darwaza, which formed the entrance of a large market. It is worth while to ascend the gate of the Purana Qila for the sake of the panorama. Paths lead to all the gates and round the double cloisters inside the walls. There is a *baoli* of great depth, with some underground baths near it. Adjoining the S. side of the Purana Qila is the Delhi Zoo (closed Friday).

A road from the gate leads to the **Mosque of Sher Shah**; the colour of the red sandstone, the brackets under the balconies, the floral carving round the arches and the pendentives of the dome of the interior are all worthy of special notice. There is a unique Persian inscription in Kufic in the mihrab. A little to the S. of the mosque is a red octagonal building, called the Sher Mandal, on the steps of which, on the 24th January 1556, the Emperor Humayun slipped while descending to offer the evening prayer, and received injuries of which he died three days later.

2 m. farther down the Delhi-Muttra Road,[1] at a tomb with a dome of green glaze, branch roads lead to the **Mausoleum of Humayun** on the E. and to the shrine of Nizam-ud-din Aulia on the W. From the Hazrat Nizam-ud-din station, on the Central Rly. line from Delhi Central to Agra and Bombay, a road runs past Humayun's Tomb to the Tomb of Safdar Jang (p. 334).

The road leads into a fore-court, on the right of which lies the entrance to an octagonal enclosure containing the mosque and tomb of Isa Khan, one of the best remains of the later Pathan period. It then enters the **Bu Halima Garden,** restored (1914) to its former purpose. Alighting at the Eastern Gate of the Bu Halima Garden, the visitor passes into a garden forecourt to Humayun's tomb enclosure. On the right of the forecourt is the gateway of the **Arab Sarai,** built by the widow of the Emperor Humayun. Immediately in front is the noble portal of the tomb enclosure. The gate takes the form of a deep, octagonally recessed bay—a treatment repeated in the central bay of the Mausoleum.

The tomb is 156 ft. long each way, and the height to the top of the dome is 125 ft. It stands upon a platform of red sandstone, and consists of a central octagon surmounted by a dome with octagon towers of unequal sides at the angles. "Its plan is that afterwards adopted at the Taj, but used here without the depth and poetry of that celebrated building. It is, however, a noble tomb, and anywhere else must be considered a wonder" (Fergusson). The red sandstone of the exterior is most artistically picked out in relief with white marble. The windows are recessed, and the lower openings are filled in with beautiful lattices of stone and marble. In the centre of each side of the main octagon is a porch 40 ft. high, with a pointed arch. From the S. porch a door leads to the central octagonal chamber, with a diameter of 48 ft., in which is the cenotaph of the King—it is of white marble, and quite plain, without any inscription. The actual grave chamber is in the basement, entered by a passage in the S. face of the platform. In the N.E. corner above is the tomb of his widow, Haji Begam, who built her husband's tomb. Steps lead from the side of the E. and W. bays, first up to a gallery round the upper portion of the central chamber, and then to the terrace round the neck of the great dome. The buildings on the terrace which once formed a small college, afford a splendid view of the country on all sides. Inside the garden of the mausoleum, which measures 13 acres, is a pretty tomb of red sandstone, with

[1] Left of the road will be seen a kos minar pillar or Mughal milestone. The kos of Akbar was a varying measure, averaging 2 m. 1000 yds.

some beautiful grilles; outside, at the S.E. corner, rises the blue dome of the tomb of Fahim Khan. Outside the N.E. corner of the garden is an interesting enclosure and mosque, said to have been the abode of Nizam-ud-din Aulia. At the tomb of Humayun Major Hodson received the surrender of Bahadur Shah, ex-King of Delhi, after the capture of the city. A few paces to the right are the tomb and mosque of **Isa Khan**; a visit should also be paid to the tomb of Khan-i-Khanan (despoiled by a Nawab of Oudh), and the old Barapala Bridge beyond it, over an old arm of the Jumna.

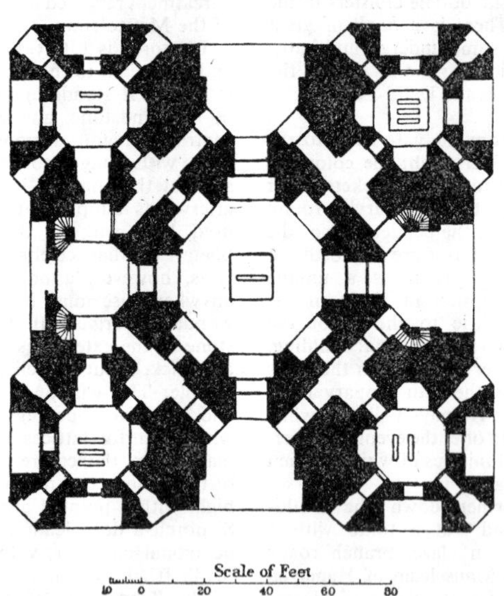

Plan of the Tomb of Humayun.

The tour may be broken here for a meal in New Delhi.

The **Dargah,** or **Shrine of Nizam-ud-din Aulia,** stands on the left side of the branch road to the W.[1] On the N. side are the Lal Mahal, or Red Palace, possibly of Ala-ud-din Khilji, and the Barah Khamba, or Twelve Columns; and on the S.E. side, in the village, a ruined mosque, with four arcaded courtyards, similar to that at Khirki (p. 339), and of the date of 1373.

The gateway leads to the tank, a special feature at Chishti Dargahs, and in this instance the traditional cause of the quarrel between King Ghiyas-ud-din Tughlak and the Saint, who died in 1325 aged 92. The story runs that the King requisitioned the workmen on the tank for labour on his fortress at Tughlaqabad, and that when the Saint arranged to carry on his work at night the King forbade the sale of oil to him. Thereupon the water of the tank miraculously served as oil and was duly cursed by the incensed King, in return for which the Saint cursed Tughlaqabad. Nizam-ud-din was concerned in the plot against the King, which resulted in his murder

1 See the comprehensive account in "A Guide to Nizam-ud-din," by Maulavi Zafar Hasan (No. 10 of *Memoirs, Arch. Survey of India*) and smaller books obtainable from the Tourist Information Office.

(1325); and the saying with which the Saint comforted his disciples when told that the King was returning to punish him, and, indeed, was only a few miles distant—"Dihli hanoz dur ast" ("Delhi is still far off")—is a proverb still in currency. The King was murdered *en route*.

On the left side a covered passage leads to an inner gate, and another beyond, which gives admittance to the court in which the **Tomb of the Saint** stands. This is built of white marble, and is 18 ft. square and surrounded by a broad veranda; there is very little of the original structure

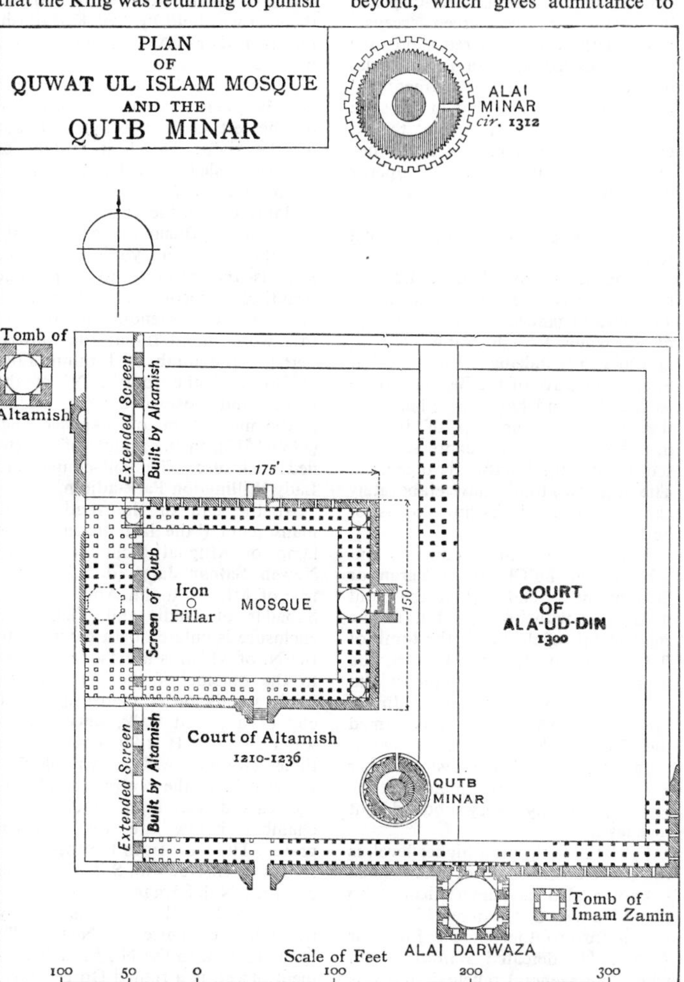

left. Round the covered grave is a low marble rail, and over it is a canopy inlaid with mother-of-pearl; in the walls are fine pierced screens.

W. of the tomb is a red sandstone mosque called the **Jamaat Khana,** with a large central compartment and two side bays, somewhat in the style of the Alai Darwaza; and at the N. end of the enclosure is a R.H. (not available) built by the Emperor Aurangzeb. The Jamaat Khana is a magnificent relic of the Khilji period, but it is obscured by surrounding tombs.

S. of the tomb of the Saint are, from W. to E., the grave enclosure of **Jahanara Begam,** sister of Aurangzeb; of **Muhammad Shah,** King 1719-48; and of **Prince Jahangir,** son of Akbar Shah. The grave of the Begam is open to the sky, and has grass planted in the hollow in the top of it; the inscribed headstone expresses the sentiment of this humble arrangement. The other two tombs have elaborately carved marble doors in screens of beautiful pierced marble.

Beyond the central court is another called the **Chabutra-i-Yaran,** or Seat of the Friends, where the Saint used to sit with his disciples. To the right in this enclosure is the tomb of the famous poet, **Amir Khusru,** the friend and disciple of the Saint, whom he survived about six months. In the inscription on the walls he is termed the Tuti-i-shakar maqâl, or sweet-tongued parrot. The grave chamber is surrounded by two pierced stone screens, and only a very subdued light reaches it.

E. of the tank, on a higher level, is the polychrome tomb of **Azam Khan** —known also as **Atgah Khan**—who saved Humayun at Kanauj (1540), and was a foster-father of the Emperor Akbar. He defeated Bairam Khan when that General rebelled, and was murdered at Agra on 16th May 1562 by Adham Khan (p. 338).

S.E. is the Hall known as the **Chausath Khamba,** or Sixty-four Pillars, which forms the family vault of the sons and brothers of Azam Khan, who were known as the Atgah Khail (or Gang), from the royal favours which were showered on them. It was built by Aziz Kokaltash, foster-brother of Akbar, and who died in 1625.

About 2 m. W. from the Dargah will be seen a domed mausoleum on the left (a mile away) and four on the right. The first is that of **Mubarak Shah,** murdered in 1433. Of those on the N. side, the octagonal building covers the grave of another Saiyad King, **Muhammad Shah** (1450), prototype of Humayun's tomb; the next is the gateway to a mosque beautifully decorated with plaster, and the most splendid specimen of this work in all India; the third is perhaps the tomb of Ibrahim Lodi (1526), and the fourth, N. of the village and close to a stone bridge, is the mausoleum of **Sikander Lodi** (1489-1517), in the middle of a fortified enclosure. The golf-course and Lady Willingdon Park adjoin.

At the end of the road is the mausoleum ("the last flicker of the lamp of Mughal architecture") of **Nawab Safdar Jang** (d. 1753), the title of Mirza Muqim Abul Mansur, Subadar of Oudh and Vizir. The enclosure is entered by a gateway, to the N. of which is a mosque opening to the outside of the garden. The tomb stands on a platform at the end of a paved walk, once with a water channel. It is 90 ft. square, of three storeys, with fawn-coloured stonework. In the central chamber is the carved cenotaph, and in the chamber below are two earthen graves. The view from the top of the roof is extensive. ½ m. S. is the Tomb of Mirza Najaf Khan (d. 1782).

The road to the N. runs directly through the centre of New Delhi (p. 340). 3 m. to the N., E. of Parliament Street, is a ruined Observatory, Jantar Mantar, erected, like those at Ujjain, Jaipur and Varanasi, by Maharaja Jai Singh II of Jaipur about 1725. The largest of the buildings is an immense equatorial dial, named by the Raja "Prince of Dials," the dimensions of the gnomon being as follows:

	ft.	in.
Length of hypotenuse .	118	5
„ base . .	104	0
„ perpendicular .	56	7

To the S. of the gnomon are two circular structures, with niches in the walls to enable the ascension and declension of the stars to be marked on them.

(4) The Extreme S. of the Surroundings of Delhi, including the Qutb (11 m. from Delhi) and Tughlaqabad (5 m. from the Qutb).

Immediately S. of the tomb of Safdar Jang is the field of battle upon which Timur utterly defeated Mahmud Shah Tughlaq and his Minister on 12th December 1398, and became master of Old Delhi. A mile farther S., on the left side of the road, is seen the dark wall of an Idgah, where Timur encamped the day after the battle. E. of this rise the walls of **Siri,** and to the S. of them a lofty platform known as the Badi Manzil, and the **Begampur Mosque** with many domes. This mosque has an extremely fine court, and was built by the Wazir Jahan Khan in the reign of Firoz Shah. Sockets of the Qasr-i-Hazar Satun (1000-pillared Hall) were found in 1933.

W. of the road, a large dome rising above trees indicates the **Mausoleum of Firoz Shah Tughlaq,** who died in 1389. It is built on the S.W. corner of **Hauz Khas,** constructed by Ala-ud-din Khilji, and is well deserving of a visit. A road has been made to this group of buildings. Here Timur first rested after his victory.

At the 9th milestone the road passes through the **Jahanpanah** defences, which were constructed to connect **Siri,** the new city of Ala-ud-din, with the older Delhi to the S. of it. The wall of this, originally the **Fort of Rai Pithora,** is crossed at the 10th mile, whence the northern wall of the citadel of **Lal Kot** can be seen. The remains of the walls of the citadel of Rai Pithora are marked out by beacons. In the middle of the E. side of the Lal Kot is the Qutb enclosure, and on the S. wall is the tomb of Adham Khan, foster-brother of the Emperor Akbar. Rai Pithora is the local name of Prithviraj, the gallant Chauhan Prince of Ajmer, grandson of both Anang Pal II, Tomar, and his conqueror Bisal Deo, Chauhan, who checked Shahab-ud-din Ghori near Thanesar in 1191, but was defeated and put to death the next year, the fortress falling in 1193.

The arrangement of the **Qutb Minar Enclosure,** now beautifully landscaped, well cared for, and with a pleasant Tourist Restaurant, is shown on the plan given on p. 333. The original **Quwwat ul Islam Mosque** was begun by Qutb-ud-din Aibak when Viceroy of Shahab-ud-din Ghori, after the capture of Delhi in 1193, as recorded by him in a Persian inscription over the inner archway of the E. entrance. It was seen by Ibn Batuta about 150 years after its erection, when he describes it as having no equal, either in beauty or extent, and was extolled by the poet Amir Khusru, who specially mentions the extension of Ala-ud-din. As originally designed, it was not large; but it is unrivalled for the graceful beauty of the flowered tracery which covers its walls. It occupies the site of Rai Pithora's Hindu Temple, now 5 ft. below ground level. Altamish in 1210-30 surrounded it by a larger cloistered court, in the S.E. corner of which stands the Qutb Minar, and added three arches N. and S. across the extensions; and in 1300 Ala-ud-din appended a further eastern court, entered by his great S. gateway, the Alai Darwaza, and designed a great addition, with a further extension of the screen on the N. side. Within this extended area he commenced to build the Alai Minar, which was to correspond with the Qutb Minar, but to be twice its size; the project died with him. Ruined piers of his screen still remain.

The entrance to the mosque is a

gateway in the centre of its E. wall. Steps ascending under this lead to the courtyard (942 ft. by 108 ft.), which is surrounded by cloisters formed of Hindu and Jain pillars placed one upon another. White pillars on the plan are missing.

The inscription over the E. gate states that the materials were obtained from the demolition of twenty-seven idolatrous temples, each of which had cost twenty lahks of diliwals, fifty diliwals being equal to one rupee. The domed pavilions in the angles of the colonnades may have come from Jain temple porches.

The famous Iron Pillar stands in front of the central opening to the mosque proper. The screen was erected by Qutb-ud-din. The central arch is 53 ft. high by 22 ft. wide.

The ornamentation, interspersed with texts from the Koran is evidently adapted directly from that on the old pillars of the cloister. Fragments of the roof of the mosque still remain, supported by old columns, and do not reach more than one-third of the height of the screen in front of it. When Delhi was captured by Timur, his troops massacred all the persons who had taken refuge in the mosque.

Restoration in 1912-16 indicated the various additions made to the original mosque.

The **Iron Pillar** is one of the most curious antiquities in India. It is a solid shaft of wrought iron, more than 16 in. in diameter and 23 ft. 8 in. in length. The height of the pillar above ground is 22 ft., but the smooth shaft is only 15 ft., the capital being 3½ ft. and the rough part below also 3½ ft.

"The Iron Pillar records its own history in a well-executed Gupta inscription of six lines of Sanskrit poetry. It was first studied by James Prinsep (*A.S.B. Journal*, 7, 630), and has been finally edited by Dr J. F. Fleet (*Gupta Inscriptions, Corpus Inscriptionum Indicarum*, vol. 3). It contains the posthumous eulogy of a king of the name of Chandra, who is said to have conquered the Vanga Country (i.e. Bengal), and, after having crossed the seven tributaries of the River Indus, to have vanquished the Váhlikas. In his memory the 'standard of the Lord Vishnu' was set up on the mountain called Vishnupada, 'the footprint of Vishnu'." From this it has been surmised that the Iron Pillar bore originally the effigy of the sun-bird Garuda, and stood in front of a Vishnu temple. It is also evident that the pillar does not now stand in its original position, as the locality cannot possibly be defined as a "a mountain". As the Gupta characters of the inscription belong to the Eastern variety, it is most likely that the pillar was brought to Delhi from Bihár, the ancient country of Magadha, which formed the nucleus of the Gupta empire. According to one theory, the King Chandra mentioned in the inscription is probably the Gupta Emperor Chandra-gupta Vikramáditya (who reigned A.D. 375-413). But Dr Vincent Smith held with Pandit Haraprasad Sastri that the Chandra of the Iron Pillar is Chandravarman, King of Pushkarana in Mewar, a contemporary of Samudra Gupta (A.D. 326-375). The name of Anang Pál also is inscribed on the shaft with the date Samwat 1109 = A.D. 1052. According to tradition, Anang Pál, the founder of the Tomar dynasty, erected the pillar. It rested on the head of a great snake until the Raja unwisely moved it to see if this were so—an act which cost the Tomars their kingdom. This tradition perhaps is based on the removal of the pillar to Delhi by Anang Pál. Four feet above the inscription is an indentation, said to have been made by a cannon-ball fired by the troops of the Bharatpur Raja. Tablets with the Sanskrit text of the inscription, together with translations in English, Hindi and Urdu, will be found in the northern cloister of the mosque.

Sir Robert Hadfield, F.R.S., to whom chippings of the Iron Pillar were sent for analysis, reported as follows:

"The material is an excellent type

of wrought iron, the sulphur being particularly low (0·006 per cent.), indicating that the fuel used in its manufacture and treatment must have been very pure (probably charcoal). The phosphorus is 0·114 per cent. There is no manganese present—a somewhat special point, as wrought iron usually contains manganese. The iron was ascertained by actual analysis, and not 'by difference'."

The **Qutb Minar**[1] looks what it is intended to be—a tower of victory. The lowest storey bears the name of Muhammad bin Sam (Shahabuddin), and of Qutb-ud-din Aibak, and the next three storeys contain that of Altamsh. At the entrance door is an inscription of Sikandar Lodi, with the date 1503. As seen at present, it is 238 ft. high, and rises in five storeys, with 27 flutings, broken by corbelled balconies and decorated with bands of inscription. The base diameter is 47 ft. 3 in. and that of the top about 9 ft. The three first storeys are of red sandstone with semi-circular and angular flutings; the two upper storeys are faced chiefly with white marble, and were almost entirely rebuilt by Firoz Shah Tughlaq in 1368, when he also added a cupola. On 1st August 1803 the pillar was injured by an earthquake and the cupola thrown down. It was restored in 1829, the battlements of the balconies being removed and replaced by the present balustrades. Notice should be taken of the honeycomb work beneath the brackets of the first-storey balconies, of which the "structure differs in no perceptible degree from that in the Alhambra". The lowest great band of text inscription is well seen from the top of the cloister of the mosque, or of the Alai Gate. A magnificent view is obtained from the summit, reached by 379 steps; but that from the first gallery 95 ft. above the ground, is nearly as good. At the summit is an aircraft beacon.

[1] The names of books and pamphlets describing the Qutb Minar in detail can be obtained from Tourist Information Offices.

The **Tomb of Altamsh** (Iltutmish, died in 1235) stands outside the N.W. corner of his extension of the mosque. It is of red sandstone. The main entrance is to the E., but there are also openings to the N. and S. The lower part of the interior is covered with beautiful Saracenic surface decoration, and is inscribed with finely written passages of the Koran; in the centre of the W. side is a Kibla of white marble discoloured with age. The tomb is in the centre, and stands on a high base; that the actual tomb is a cenotaph was proved by the discovery of a chamber beneath it (approached by a narrow flight of stairs) which apparently contains the real grave. General Cunningham notes that "there is good reason to believe that it was originally covered by an overlapping Hindu dome. A single stone of one of the overlapping circles, with Arabic letters on it, still remains."

The **Alai Darwaza,** 40 ft. to the S.E. from the Qutb Minar, is the S. entrance of the great or outer enclosure to the mosque. It was built of red sandstone richly ornamented with patterns in low relief, in 1310, by Ala-ud-din. Over three of the entrances are Arabic inscriptions, which gave Ala-ud-din's name and his well-known title of Sikandar Sani, the Second Alexander, with the date 710 A.H. (A.D. 1332). The building is a square with lofty doorways, with pointed horse-shoe arches on three sides and a rounded arch curiously decorated on the inner side. In each corner there are two windows, closed by massive screens of marble lattice-work. A considerable area of ground lying between the Qutb enclosure and the walls of the "Metcalfe Estate" enables the visitor to see the Alai Darwaza from the S. A few yards to the E. stands the richly carved building in which is the tomb of **Imam Zamin.** He came to Delhi in the reign of Sikandar Lodi, and died in 944 A.H. = A.D. 1537. The tomb is a small domed building, about 18 ft. square, of red sandstone, covered with chunam. There is an inscription in the Tughra character over the door.

The **Alai Minar** stands 150 ft. N. of the original Qutb enclosure. The inner tower and outer wall are of coarse rubble; the flutings in the exterior show the shape which the Minar would have assumed when faced with red sandstone. The total height as it now stands is 70 ft. above the plinth, or 87 ft. above the ground level. Had this pillar been finished it would have been about 500 ft. high. In the S.W. corner of the *outer* enclosure, corresponding with the tomb of Altamsh, is a group of ruined buildings. The ruin on the S. side is believed to have been the tomb of Ala-ud-din, and the grave in the centre room, brought to light in the course of excavation (1914), is said to be his: the buildings on the right are known as Ala-ud-din's College. Considerable conservation work was carried out in 1915 in connection with the Qutb group of buildings. The Government of India have made the entire enclosure an impressive showpiece.

To the S.E. of the Qutb Minar is a tomb of a brother of Adham Khan, once used as a country house by Sir T. Metcalfe, and 500 yd. beyond it is a mosque of the latest Pathan style, known as the **Jamali Mosque.** At the N.E. corner of it, in a separate enclosure, is the tomb of Shaikh Fazl-ullah, decorated with bright tiles. 200 yd. due E. of the mosque are the broken massive walls of the **Tomb of Balban** (1287), which formed a Dar-ul-Aman, or House of Refuge, in his lifetime.

To the W. of the Qutb enclosure, which is bounded by the road from Delhi to Mahrauli, a paved way leads to a well-known Hindu temple called the Jog Maya. 200 yd. farther S. the tomb of **Adham Khan** rises high on the S. wall of Lal Kot. Adham Khan, who was half-brother as well as foster-brother of Akbar, murdered Azam Khan, whose wife was also foster-mother to the Emperor, in the palace of Agra, and was thrown down from the terrace there by order of Akbar, who himself felled him with a blow of the fist. Adham Khan had previously driven Rupmati to suicide upon capturing Mandu (p. 204), while his mother put to death two of the Shahzadis for fear that they might complain to the Emperor. She is said to have died of a broken heart a few days after her son, and to have been buried here too. The style resembles that of the Middle Pathan period; it was probably rebuilt from the material of an earlier tomb.

A short distance to the S.E. of the tomb, across the road, is a large round well, into which men and boys used to dive. Nearby is the northern entrance of the **Dargah,** or shrine, of **Qutb-ud-din Bakhtiar Kaki**; the inner gateway and the ruined music-gallery gate on the right of the approach date from the time of Salim Shah. Close to a third gateway is the grave enclosure of the Nawabs of Jhajjar. In the small courtyard are a mosque and the tomb of Maulana Fakr-ud-din; on the right, and standing back from them, is a gate to another court and the main W. approach to the shrine. S. of this western court is an enclosure with a **Moti Masjid** of white marble, built by Bahadur Shah, eldest son of Aurangzeb, in 1709, and beyond it, in a separate court, are the simple graves of the Kings of Delhi Akbar Shah II (d. 1847), of the blind Shah Alam (d. 1806), and of Bahadur Shah I (d. 1712). The space between the last two was reserved for the last King of Delhi, but he died at Rangoon in 1862. From the eastern courtyard a passage, paved and lined with marble, and with a pierced marble screen on the right hand, leads past the **Grave of the Saint,** which stands in the open, protected by an awning above it; on the back wall of this enclosure, which may be entered only with uncovered feet, is some fine work of glazed tiles dating from the time of Aurangzeb. The Saint, who was born at Ush, in Turkestan, and perhaps came to Delhi before the Muslim conquest, died during the reign of Altamsh in 1235; his name, Kaki, is derived from the alleged miracle of his having been fed by heavenly food—*kâk* = cake. Outside the innermost shrine is the mosque where the Saint used to pray, and beyond it is a picturesque baoli (well). At the W. end of this is the grave of **Zabita Khan.** To the S. of these is a small court with the graves of the former ruling family of Loharu.

W. of the Dargah is a gateway known as the Mahal Sarai, and beyond it a mosque standing on a high platform built by Ahsanullah Khan, physician of the last King of Delhi. Turning S. along the main street of Mahrauli, the **Shamsi Hauz,** the great tank of Shams-ud-din Altamsh, will be reached on the right. It has a ruined pavilion in the centre like the Hauz Khas of Ala-ud-din. On the E. bank is a building of red sandstone called the Jaház, or Ship, Mahal and the **Aulia Masjid,** where, according to tradition, thanks were offered up on the capture of Delhi in 1193. On the opposite side of the road here is the picturesque Jhirna (Spring) garden, through which the overflow of the tank found its way past the tomb of Balban to Tughlaqabad. 3 m. W. is the underground tomb of a son of Altamsh.

The Fort of **Tughlaqabad** lies 5 m. to the E. of the Qutb. The road passes through the E. wall of **Kila Rai Pithora,** a mile farther on. The N.E. portion of this wall runs 1¼ m. N.E. to **Khirki,** where there is a most interesting covered mosque with four open courts, each 32 ft. square, built by Jahan Khan in 1380. About ¼ m. on the E. is a fine sluice of seven bays, apparently of the same date as the mosque, and ¾ m. N.E. again is the Dargah of Chiragh Delhi, the last great Delhi Saint, who died in 1356, and the Tomb of Bahlol Lodi (d. 1488).

Long before it is reached the Fort of Tughlaq Shah is seen rising high above the plain to the left of the road. General Cunningham writes that "it may be described with tolerable accuracy as a half-hexagon in shape, with three faces of rather more than ¾ m. in length, and a base of 1½ m., the whole circuit being only 1 furlong less than 4 m. It stands on a rocky height, and is built of massive blocks of stone, so large and heavy that they must have been quarried on the spot. The largest measured was 14 ft. in length by 2 ft. 2 in., and 1 ft. thick, and weighed rather more than 6 tons. The short faces to the W., N. and E. are protected by a deep ditch, and the long face to the S. by a large sheet of water, dry, except in the rainy season, which is held up by an embankment at the S.E. corner. On this side the rock is scarped, and above it the main walls rise to a mean height of 40 ft., with a parapet of 7 ft., behind which rises another wall of 15 ft., the whole height above the low ground being upwards of 90 ft." It had thirteen gates, and there are three inner gates to the citadel.

Opposite the causeway to the tomb an arched gateway leads into the fort at the point where the largest of the tanks in it was excavated. Beyond this, to the N.W. and N., are ruins of the palace and a mosque, and high above it, in the S.W. angle, is the citadel, which occupies about one-sixth of the area. It contains the ruins of an extensive palace, surmounted by an inner citadel, from which there is a splendid view. The ramparts are raised on a line of domed rooms, which rarely communicate with each other, and which formed the quarters of the garrison. One dark passage near the S.E. corner, below the inner citadel, leads to a small sallyport in the outer wall. The walls slope inwards, and the vast size, strength and visible solidity of the whole give to Tughlaqabad an air of stern and massive grandeur.

In the N. part of the fort below are the ruined walls of a Jami Masjid. The curse of the saint, Nizam-ud-din Aulia, upon Tughlaqabad was:

"Ya base Gujar
Ya rahe ujar."

(" May it be inhabited by Gujars
or may it remain desolate"),

and it contains small Gujar colonies in the midst of its desolation.

The Tomb of Tughlaq Shah (d. 1325) is outside the S. wall of Tughlaqabad, in the midst of an artificial lake, and surrounded by a pentagonal outwork, which is connected with the fort by a causeway 600 ft. long, supported on twenty-seven arches. Fergusson says (*Ind. Arch.*, 2, 215): "The sloping walls and almost Egyptian solidity of this mausoleum, combined with the bold and massive tower of the fortification that surround it, form a model of a warrior's tomb hardly to be rivalled anywhere". The outer walls have a slope of 2·333 in. per foot; at base they are 11½ ft. thick, and at top 4 ft. The exterior decoration of the tomb itself depends chiefly on contrast of colour, which is effected by the use of bands and borders of white marble inserted in the red sandstone. In plan it is a square, and three of its four sides have lofty archways, the space above the doorway being filled with a white marble lattice screen of bold pattern. It is surmounted by a white marble dome. In the S.W. corner of the enclosure is a small domed chamber with a number of graves.

"Inside the mausoleum there are three cenotaphs, which are said to be those of Tughlaq Shah, his Queen, and their son Juna Khan, who took the name of Muhammad when he ascended the throne." This King was, and is still, known as the Khuni Sultan, "the bloody King". Firoz Shah, his successor, bought acquittances from all those he had wronged, and put them in a chest at the head of his tomb, that he might present them on the Day of Judgment.

Opposite the S.W. corner of Tughlaqabad the embankment of the lake connects **Adilabad**; there is a sluice between it and the rocky ground at the N. end. Adilabad is said to have been built by Muhammad Tughlaq; there is a fine gate in the W. face. From the top there is a magnificent view of the fort and the Qutb Minar. A little farther to the E. is an isolated outwork called the Nai's (Barber's) Fort, which seems to have been a fortification of Tughlaqabad. 2½ m. farther on, and 8 m. from the Qutb, is **Badarpur** with an interesting Mughal Serai, on the road and railway from Delhi to Muttra. From Badarpur it is 7 m. to the mausoleum of Humayun and shrine of Nizam-ud-din. The boundary of the Delhi Territory is 1 m. S.

REFERENCES TO SKETCH PLAN

	No. in Plan.
Government Buildings.	
Legislative Buildings (Parliamentary Rotunda)	18
National Archives	13
Secretariat, North Block	20
Secretariat, South Block	21
Supreme Court Building	32
Residences.	
Rashtrapati Bhawan	24
Prime Minister's Residence	27
Members of Council	12
Churches.	
Anglican Cathedral of the Redemption	15
R.C. Cathedral	30
Wesleyan Church	29
Hospitals.	
Lady Hardinge College and Hospital for Women	1
Museum.	
National Museum	14
Memorials.	
All-India War Memorial	11
Imperial Service Cavalry Brigade War Memorial	26
Jaipur Commemorative Column	23
Open Spaces.	
Alexandra Place (Post Office)	5
York Place	16
Government Court (Raisina Hill)	19
Prince Edward Place	17
Nehru Park	2
Great Court	22
Moti Chauk	10
National Stadium	9
State Bank of India	7
Club	28
Jantar Mantar (Old Observatory)	8
Market Centre	4
Sikh Shrine	3
Police Lines	6
Bodyguard Lines	25
Y.M.C.A.	31

About 2 m. beyond Tughlaqabad on a good road there is a most interesting early Hindu structure of uncertain date called Suraj Khund, an amphitheatre like that of Dionysus at Athens. It is now a popular picnic place, although quite recently it was in the jungle.

(5) New Delhi

The new Capital of India is a conspicuous example of town-planning. At the time of the Delhi Darbar in December 1911, His Majesty the King-Emperor, George V, said: "It is my desire that the planning and designing of the public buildings to be erected be considered with the greatest deliberation and care so that the new creation may be in every way worthy of this ancient and beautiful city".

Work was immediately begun, but progress was suspended during the First World War, and the new city was not formally inaugurated until 15th February 1931. The general plan is pivoted on a line of origin which ties the new city with a great architectural feature of the old city. This is the straight line from the Raisina Hill, on which the Government Secretariat has been built, to the Jami Masjid (p. 325) in Old Delhi. At an angle of 60° from this alignment lies the main axis of the new city, which is oriented exactly E. and W. It centres at the E. end of the N.W. gate of the Purana Qila, or the old fort (Indrapat, p. 329), and is crossed at right angles by a N. and S. line, on which lies Janpath (once Queensway). Visitors should proceed from the New Delhi Railway Station near the Ajmer Gate (p. 326) and along Janpath to the point where it crosses the Rajpath.

This main avenue, originally called Kingsway, has a parkway width of 1175 ft. and is flanked by ornamental tanks. At the E. end are the Princes Place and the War Memorial. On both sides are the houses of Cabinet Ministers of the Government of India. On the N. side are the National Archives. S. of Rajpath is the National Museum, and adjoining it is the Archaeological Survey of India; within its compound is a building containing Sir Aurel Stein's Central Asian antiquities, with remarkable frescoes. Farther W. is Prince Edward Place, a spacious piazza, combining Buddhist, Muslim, and Hindu features.[1] The forecourt, which is provided with six fountains, covers an area of 26½ acres, and roads radiate from it in all directions. Through the centre runs the Processional Way, which commences at the All-India War Memorial and terminates at the wide steps, flanked by stone elephants, which lead to the Great Place (1100 ft. by 400 ft.) on Raisina Hill. On either side of the entrance to the Court are the Secretariat offices of the Government of India; these have been occupied since November 1926. The leading features on the E. front of each block are vaulted chambers enshrining the foundation-stones laid by Their Majesties on the 15th December 1911. In Committee Room A are paintings by modern Indian artists.

At the main entrances on to the Great Court, as though quartered on a shield, are the four **Dominion Columns** of red sandstone, presented by Canada, Australia, South Africa and New Zealand. Each column is 41 ft. in height, and on the summit of each is a gilded bronze model of a ship in full sail heading for the East. The coats of arms of the Dominions are carved on the base. In the centre of the Court is the Jaipur Commemorative Column, a gift of the late Maharaja of Jaipur. In the Great Place were once set statues of five Viceroys.

The former Viceroy's House, now **Rashtrapati Bhawan,** consists of a central block surmounted by a copper dome (177 ft. above the roadway) and four wings. Thirty-two broad steps lead to the protico and the main

[1] Compare the railing at the Sanchi Tope (p. 219).

entrance to the **Durbar Hall.** The Hall is in the form of a circular marble court, 75 ft. in diameter. Groups of yellow marble pillars support the dome. The main entrance commands a view of the Processional route along Central Vista and the massive War Memorial Arch in the distance. On the right of the Hall is the State Library. A drawing-room (38 ft. square) leads to the **Ball Room,** opposite the main entrance to which is a larger drawing-room (105 ft. long and 24 ft. wide). Next to this is the State Dining Room, panelled in dark wood. At one end of this room is a band gallery; at the other end two glass doors give access to the terrace. Marble staircases on either side of the Durbar Hall lead to the private apartments on the first floor. There are 54 bedrooms and accommodation for more than 20 guests. The woods used in the decoration are all Indian. At the back of the Palace is an Indian garden, a combination of Hindu and Mughal styles. On the radials of this are the quarters for the Government House staff and for the Private Secretary and Military Secretary.

To the north-east of the Raisina Hill on the line of origin already mentioned is the circular Parliamentary building. The main features of the design are the semi-circular chambers for the Legislatures, and the Central Library which is surmounted by a 90 ft. dome. Ample office accommodation and spacious lobbies are also provided for Government officials and members of the Legislatures. The road to the N.E. from the Parliamentary buildings, which is aligned on the Jami Masjid, is called Parliament Street, with All-India Radio Broadcasting House; and on the east is the old Observatory of Maharaja Jai Singh (p. 334).

The Rikabganj *gurdwara* (Sikh Shrine) at the corner of Church Road and Queen Mary's Avenue contains the *samadh* (tomb) of Tegh Bahadur the ninth *guru* of the Sikhs, who was put to death in 1675 by order of Aurangzeb at a spot in the Chandni Chauk (p. 326) known as the Sisganj *gurdwara*.

On the Lower Ridge (Reading) Road a communal (Birla) temple of Lakshmi Narayan, and a Buddhist Vihara adjoining were opened by Mr Gandhi (1939).

In Church Road is the Anglican Cathedral of the Redemption (consecrated on 15th February 1931, tower completed 1933). The altar was given by the Dean and Chapter of York in commemoration of the thirteenth centenary of York Minster; and the picture at the E. end was presented by Lord and Lady Irwin as a thanksgiving for escape from an attempt to blow up his train outside New Delhi in December 1929.

The northern portion of Janpath starts from the Station for State Entries. The road then to the S. passes through Indra Chauk (still called Connaught Place), an inner circle with a Circus round it, in which the Regal Theatre and cinemas are situated. From this Circus radiate several roads. Curzon Road gives a vista to the S.E. of Princes Place, in which is situated the War Memorial Arch. Parliament Street runs to the Parliamentary buildings to the S.W. The main road to the Cantonments also takes off here.

On Janpath are Telegraph and Telephone Offices, the Hostel for Members of the Legislatures, and the Imperial Hotel adjoining Western Court.

Janpath then proceeds to a circular space called Moti Chauk. The road next crosses Queen Victoria Road and traverses the Central Vista, past the National Archives; and crossing King Edward Road leads to York Place, an oval space, where diagonal roads, York Road and Akbar Road, intersect.

The residences built by the former Ruling Princes lie to the N. and S. of Princes Place, and along Curzon Road.

Three radial roads run N. from Princes Place, bearing the names of

Viceroys in whose times the Darbars of 1877, 1903 and 1911 were held. Shah Jahan Road is aligned on Safdar Jang's Tomb (p. 334) in the S.W., and Wellesley Road to the S.E. joins the Delhi-Muttra Road, and leads also to the Lodi Municipal golf-course.

The Government Offices at the E. end of the Raisina Hill are the meeting-place of Queen Mary's Avenue coming from Alexandra Place on the N. and of King George's Avenue coming from Gymkhana Club in the S. The Post Office is in Alexandra Place, and beyond to the N. is Market Road leading to the markets. In King George's Avenue are situated the British High Commissioner's House (the office is in Chanakyapuri), and a number of offices housing various departments of the Indian Defence Services.

Rashtrapati Bhawan is the meeting-place of the North Avenue and the South Avenue. North Avenue terminates in Cantonment Road. This road, starting to the S.W. from the shopping centre (Indra Chauk), reaches Alexandra Place, and, skirting the Rashtrapati Bhawan Estate as the Willingdon Crescent, proceeds to the Cantonment. On the west of the commencement of the Crescent is a public recreation space, Talkatora Park, on the site of an old Mughal garden, with grounds for football, hockey and tennis.

The Agricultural Research Institute, in 400 acres of grounds, lies west of the Upper Ridge Road approached by Linlithgow Avenue.

At the junction of South Avenue with Tinmurti Marg is the Imperial Service Cavalry Brigade War Memorial. Immediately opposite is the residence of the Republic's first Prime Minister, now the Nehru Memorial Museum. Farther south, beyond the Club and to the west of Safdar Jang's Tomb, is the Racecourse, in which are grounds for polo. South of this is the Safdar Jang (formerly Willingdon) Airport, the H.Q. of the Delhi Flying and Gliding Club.

The **All-India War Memorial** in Princes Park is an arch spanning the east end of the Central Vista, designed by Sir Edwin Lutyens, R.A. The Memorial is 138 ft. high and 90 ft. wide. The span of the arch is 30 ft. and the height from the ground to the crown of the arch is 75 ft. Over the arch on both sides is the word INDIA flanked by MCM. Immediately below on the left is XIV and on the right XIX. The upper portion is of white Dholpur stone and the lower of red Bharatpur stone. On the top of all is placed a great bowl, 11½ ft. in diameter. The Arch used to include a museum and commemorates more than 70,000 Indian soldiers who fell in defence of the Empire between 1914 and 1918; while 13,516 names engraved on the Arch and the fountains to right and left form a separate memorial to those who lost their lives in the N.W. Frontier operations of 1914-18 and the Afghan campaign of 1919. East of the Memorial is the National Stadium (1933) where a Horse Show used to be held annually. A Muslim grave in the vicinity is about 700 years old.

In Hardinge Avenue a number of foreign diplomats accredited to Delhi had houses for some time; but although some still reside there, the majority are now located in the new diplomatic enclave, appropriately named "Chanakyapuri"—after Chanakya, the great Mauryan diplomat.

The Lady Hardinge College and Hospital for Women, with a Child Welfare Centre, is on the west of Connaught Place. The Lady Irwin College for Women (1938) is in Sikandra Road. The Willingdon Hospital and Nursing Home serves the needs of the New Capital, and the Irwin Hospital (1936), S. of the Delhi Gate, is for the whole of Delhi.

The distance from the Railway Station to York Place is about 2½ m.; to the Parliamentary buildings about 1 m.; and to the Cantonments, beyond the Ridge on the W., over 5 m., while the distance from the War Memorial to Government House is about 1½ m.

The first of the chief engineers

engaged on the construction of the new capital was Sir Hugh Keeling (1912-25) and he was followed by Sir Alexander Rouse (1925-31). The architect of Government House was Sir Edwin Lutyens, who was also primarily responsible for the lay-out of the city, the Staff Quarters, Great Place and the Central Vista. The Secretariat, Parliamentary Buildings, and most of the residential bungalows were designed by Sir Herbert Baker. A new Supreme Court Building has been erected at the junction of Hardinge Avenue and the Delhi-Mathura Road.

Tourist Agencies will supply the details and tariffs of the various hotels in Old and New Delhi. Among the best hotels anywhere in the "International" Class are the Ashoka Hotel in New Delhi, which is Government-owned, and the Oberoi Inter-continental.

There is now a ring-road to the W. and to the E. of Delhi (not marked on maps on pp. 330 and facing p. 340.)

ROUTE 15

(*a*) DELHI to **Kasauli** (171 m.) and **SIMLA** (219 m.) by **Panipat, Thanesar, Ambala,** and **Kalka** (162 m.).

(*b*) DELHI to **PATHANKOT** (345 m.) by **Ghaziabad** Junction, **Meerut, Sardhana, Saharanpur, Ambala, Sirhind, Ludhiana, Jullundur,** and **Amritsar**; and from **Pathankot** (i) to **Jammu,** (ii) to **Kashmir,** (iii) to **Dalhousie,** the **Kangra Valley, Mandi** and **Kulu.**

(*c*) DELHI to **FEROZEPORE** (241 m.) by **Jakhal** and **Bhatinda.**

There are two routes from *Delhi to Ambala*, both broad-gauge:

(1) The Mail route from Calcutta, which proceeds along the W. bank of the Jumna, through *Panipat* and *Karnal*, to Ambala, 123 m., and thence to Kalka and Simla. This route was opened in 1891 as the Delhi, Umballa, Kalka Railway.

(2) The Mail route from Bombay, which follows the E. bank of the Jumna, crossing it twice, through *Ghaziabad*, *Meerut* and *Saharanpur* to Ambala, 162 m.

(*a*) Delhi to Kalka and Simla

Leaving the central station, the Delhi, Umballa, Kalka railway proceeds over a level plain to

9 m. **Bádli.** Before reaching this station the ruins of the Shalimar gardens may be seen on the left, and the battlefield of Badli-ki-sarai (pp. 321 and 328) on the right. Here the tract irrigated by the W. Jumna Canal is entered.

16 m. Boundary of the Haryana State.

27 m. **Sonepat,** an ancient place, and with Panipat (see below), Baghpat (lying E. on the Jumna), Indrapat

(p. 329) and Tilpat, one of the five estates or pats over which the traditional conflict of the *Mahabharata* took place about 1000 B.C. (Introd, p. 21). It was sacked (1035) by Musaud, son of Mahmūd of Ghazni.

55 m. **Panipat** Junction (D.B.K.). Branch, 44 m. W. to Jind Junction and another, 45 m. to Rohtak on the Delhi-Bhatinda line (p. 363). Large civil R.H. at Kabr, about 1 m., and a small P.W.D. bungalow, where travellers can stay after obtaining permission from the Deputy-Commissioner, but they have to make their own arrangements for food. The modern town stands near the old bank of the Jumna, upon a high mound consisting of the debris of earlier buildings.

The principal building of antiquity is the shrine of Abu Ali Kalandar, a celebrated saint. Legends about him show that he directed the Jumna to move back seven paces, as he had become stiff standing in the water, but in her hurry to obey she moved back seven miles. He gave a charm to the Panipat people which dispelled all the flies, but they grumbled at this, so he brought them back a thousandfold. His body is said to have been buried in three places—namely, at Karnal, Budha Khera and Panipat.

Panipat is famous as the place where three decisive battles have been fought; but scarcely any trace remains.

Here on the 21st April 1526, Bābur encountered Ibrahim Lodi, King of Delhi. On the night before the battle Bābur had sent 5000 men to make a night attack, but the attacking force did not reach the enemy's camp till dawn. The Mughal pickets reported that the Indians were advancing in battle array, but when they arrived at the Mughal lines they wavered before the Mughal musketry, and Bābur availed himself of their indecision to send his flanking parties to wheel round and charge them in the rear. Bābur's left wing was roughly handled, but he supported it by a strong detachment from the centre, and the Indians in the end were driven back. On the right, too, the battle was obstinately contested, but Bābur's artillery was the more effective, and at last the Indians fell into confusion. At noon they gave way in all directions. According to Mughal accounts, 15,000 Indians were left dead, and the pursuit continued as far as Agra. The body of Ibraham Lodi[1] was found the same afternoon amidst heaps of his soldiers, and was specially honoured by the victor. Bābur reached Delhi on the third day after the battle, and on the Friday following his name as King was read in the public prayers.

The **Second** great battle was fought on the 5th of November 1556, when the youthful Akbar, who had just succeeded his father, Humayun, and his General, Bahram Khan, defeated Himu, the General of Muhammad Shah Adil, nephew of Sher Shah Sur.[2] After a well-contested battle Himu was wounded in the eye by an arrow, taken prisoner, and put to death. This battle was decisive for the fate of the Pathan dynasty called the Sur, founded by Sher Shah, 1540-45, and finally re-established the fortunes of the House of Timur.

The **Third** battle took place on the 14th of January 1761, when the whole strength of the Mahrattas was crushed with terrible slaughter by Ahmad Shah Durani, the Afghan King. All the Mahratta Chieftains of note, Holkar, Scindia, the Gaekwar, the Peshwa's cousin and son, were present with their forces. The Mahratta army is said to have amounted to 15,000 infantry, 55,000 cavalry, 200 guns, and Pindaris and camp-followers numbering 200,000 men. The Afghan force consisted of 38,000 infantry, 42,000 cavalry, and 70 guns, besides numerous irregulars, and faced north.

The Mahrattas had been cut off

[1] The alleged grave of the King lies on the N.W. side of the city.

[2] Himu, who had driven Humayun's Governor out of Delhi, had the misfortune to lose his guns before the battle.

from Delhi for two months, and were compelled to fight by impending starvation. On the morning of the battle they marched out with the ends of their turbans loose, their heads and faces anointed with turmeric, in sign of despair. Seodasheo Rao, the Bhao, cousin of the Peshwa and Generalissimo, with Wiswas Rao, the Peshwa's eldest son, and Mulhar Rao Holkar, were opposite the Afghan Grand Wazir, Shah Wali Khan. The great standard of the Mahratta people, the *Bhagwa Jhanda*, floated in the Mahratta van, and there were three *Jaripatkas*, or Grand Ensigns, of the Peshwa in the field.

The Mahrattas made a tremendous charge full on the Afghan centre, and broke through heavy cavalry under the Wazir, which unwisely received them without advancing. The dust and confusion were so great that the combatants could only distinguish each other by their war-cries. The Wazir, who was in full armour, threw himself from his horse to rally his men, but most of them gave way; while Ibrahim Khan Gardi, trained by M. de Bussy, who commanded the Mahratta artillery and regular infantry, broke the Rohillas on the right wing of Ahmad Shah's army.

Ahmad Shah sent his personal guards to rally the fugitives, and ordered up his reserves to support the Wazir. In this protracted and close struggle the physical strength of the Afghans prevailed. A little after 2 p.m. Wiswas Rao was mortally wounded, and the Bhao, after sending a secret message to Holkar, charged into the thickest of the fight and disappeared. Holkar went off, and was followed by the Gaekwar. Madhava Rao Scindia was cut down and lamed for life by an Afghan horseman many miles away; he used to say that he constantly saw in his dreams his grim pursuer gaining on him, and finally leave him for dead.

The Mahrattas fled; thousands were cut down, and vast numbers were destroyed in the ditch of their entrenchment. The spot where the Bhao stood to watch the fight is now marked by a small monument, and is about 3 m. E. of Panipat.

66 m. **Gharaunda.** A small village on the Grand Trunk Road. To the W. of the village are the two handsome gateways of the old Mughal sarai. The Emperor Shah Jahan laid out a road from Delhi to Lahore, marking it at intervals of a kos with large masonry pillars shaped like acorns and called *kos minar*. At the various stages he erected large *sarais* for the benefit of travellers. Most of the kos minars still exist, but the only remains of the old sarais in the Karnal District are these two gates of Gharaunda. The Grand Trunk Road follows roughly the line of the old route.

76 m. **Karnal** station (D.B.K., comfortable; near Grand Trunk Road); also large Government Rest House (permit from Exec. Eng. Ambala), where no meals are supplied.

The town of Karnal is traditionally of great antiquity, having been founded by Raja Karna, champion of the Kauravas, in the great war of the *Mahabharata*. It was seized by the Raja of Jind about 1763, and wrested from him in 1797 by the Irish adventurer George Thomas. It was conferred by Lord Lake in 1803 upon Nawab Muhammad Khan, a Mandil Pathan. A British Cantonment existed here from 1811 until 1841, when it was abandoned (the church tower still remains) owing to the unhealthiness of the site, as the W. Jumna Canal intercepted the drainage and caused malarial fever. The canal was re-aligned in 1875. A wall 12 ft. high encloses the town. The Dairy Farm is now under the Agricultural Dept., for cattle breeding and agricultural instruction.

A large up-to-date hospital was erected in 1910-11 as a memorial to King Edward VII.

Karnal is the place where the Persian Kuli Khan, Nadir Shah, defeated the Mughal Emperor Muhammad Shah in 1739. The battle lasted two hours, 20,000 of the Indian soldiers were killed, and a much greater number taken prisoners. An immense treasure, a number of elephants, part of the artillery of the Emperor, and rich spoils of every description fell into Nadir Shah's hands. The Persian loss was small. The next day Muhammad Shah surrendered himself to his conqueror, who marched to Delhi (see p. 320).

97 m. **Kurukshetra** Junction (R.H. Dharamshalas). Branch of 54 m. W. *via* Kaithal to Narwana on the line to Bhatinda Junction (p. 363).

At 2 m. is **Thanesar** (D.B.), a famous place of Hindu pilgrimage and a very ancient town, sacked by Mahmūd of Ghazni (1011), near which Shahab-ud-din Ghori was defeated by and subsequently defeated Prithvi Raja in 1192. It was the capital of Harsha (A.D. 606-647) ruling the S.E. portion of the Punjab.

The Brahmsar or **Kurukshetra Tank,** 1 m. W. of Kurukshetra Junction, an oblong sheet of water 3546 ft. in length, is not only the centre of attraction to pilgrims but also the haunt of every kind of wild-fowl; shooting is prohibited. It is surrounded by temples, and flights of dilapidated steps lead down to the water on all sides. As many as 500,000 persons have been known to assemble here on the occasion of an eclipse of the sun, when it is believed that the waters of all other tanks visit this one here, so that he who bathes in it at the moment of eclipse obtains the additional merit of bathing in them all and washes away the sins of his ancestors also.

The area around, known to Hindus as Dharmakshetra, or the Holy Field, was the centre of Kurukshetra, the great plain of the *Mahabharata* battle of the Kauravas and Pandavas (Introd., p. 21). The plain (70 m. by 30 m.) extends W. to Pehowa and Kaithal, both sacred places. Kurukshetra is described in Sanskrit literature, and was named Brahmavarta, or land of divine sages, "fashioned by God and chosen by the Creator". On the Sarsuti, a mile N. of the town and a mile W. of the tank, and all round at various distances, are a number of sacred places and the new (1956) University.

The **Town** is about ¼ m. N. of the tank, and beyond it are extensive remains of the Muslim **Fort.** The chief building is the white-domed **Tomb of Shaikh Chilli Jalal** (d. 1582). It is an octagon of drab-white marble, lighted by trellis-work windows of fine design. It stands upon a small octagonal platform in the centre of a larger square one surrounded by cupolas. In the centre of the W. side is a small pavilion with deep caves, which also forms a tomb.

S.W. from here, within a stone's throw, is a small mosque of red sandstone (the **Lal Masjid**), supported on eight columns. The carving on the domes resembles that at Fatehpur-Sikri.

Between Thanesar and Ambala are passed the Sarsuti (ancient Saraswati), Markanda, and other torrents issuing from the Siwaliks, and above Ambala the Ghaggar or Drishadvati.

The strip of country included between the Sarsuti and the Ghaggar is "the Holy Land" of the Hindu faith, the first permanent home of the Aryans in India, and the spot in which their religion took shape. Hence the sanctity of the waters of the Sarsuti, to which worshippers flock from all parts of India.

31 m. **Kaithal** is the headquarters of the district. The town is situated on the banks of the Bidkiar lake or moat, with bathing-places and flights of steps. During the time of the earlier Muslim rulers it was a place of some importance. In 1767 it fell into the hands of the Sikh Chief Bhai Desu Singh, whose descendants, the Bhais of Kaithal, ranked among the most powerful of the Cis-Sutlej Chiefs. This territory came under protection in 1808, and lapsed to the British Government in 1843. The ruins of the old fort stand out prominently on the high bank of the lake.

123 m. from Delhi, **AMBALA** Cantonment. Ambala **City** and **Civil**

Station (pop. 102,000 in 1971) are 5 m. farther N.W. (alt. 900 ft.). The important Cantonments were formed in 1843; they cover 30 sq. m., and are laid out with good roads and fine trees.

The **Race-course** is on the E. Maidan; **Paget Park,** a favourite resort, is on the N. St Paul's Cathedral, once one of the finest in India, was bombed during the 1965 war and is now a ruin.

At 144 m. are the Ghaggar river and road bridges.

153 m. **Chandigarh,** capital of Punjab—temporarily shared by Haryana State (air services from Delhi), is a striking example of modern town planning which attracts many visitors. Conceived by Le Corbusier and Maxwell Fry, its design is marked by boldness in the adaptation of advanced styling to local climatic needs. A school of young Indian architects is growing up who are enthusiastic over the ideas it embodies. The population was 233,000 (1971). A park and a lake provide pleasant amenities. There is a fine Museum and Art Gallery with an extensive collection of Gandhara sculpture brought from the old Central Museum in Lahore. The imposing Secretariat, Assembly and High Court buildings are to the N. The shopping plaza in Sector 17 is one of the best in India. Visitors may stay in the Dak bungalow section of the Hotel Aroma, or in the private Mount View Hotel. Do not miss the great Bhakra Nanga Dam (65 m.). Bus services. G.Hs. The dam can also be visited from Amritsar (267 m.).

163 m. **Kalka** station (D.B., R.), the terminus of the broad-gauge railway, 2143 ft. above sea-level.

Thirteen miles S.E. of Kalka is the old Mughal Summerhouse of Pinjor, in picturesque gardens, now a public park, built by Fidai Khan, foster-brother of Aurangzeb and builder of the Badshahi Mosque in Lahore. The pavilions and water-courses and fountains are superb. Accommodation reservable through Tourist Bureau.

The n.g. mountain railway (1903) from Kalka to Simla, 60 m., follows the line of the old Tonga Road most of the way; it passes round the W. and N. sides of the Jutogh Hill, and reaches Simla on the N. side, the track being carried to the station on the S. face of the Ridge by a tunnel. The gradient of nearly half the line is 1 in 33; the curve-radius is 120 ft. only; there are three loops below Dharmpur and 103 tunnels.

Seats are booked through the Station-Master, Kalka. Only hand-luggage can be taken into the carriages. Rail motors with fixed timings also run during the season; no heavy luggage allowed. It is wise to put on warmer clothing at Barogh whenever the upward journey is made in the summer. Some people suffer from rail sickness and may prefer to motor by road; it is cheaper and quicker.

21 m. **Dharmpur** (D.B. good) in the former Patiala State, 4900 ft. There is a Tuberculosis hospital here. Station for Kasauli (which can also be reached from Kalka, 16 m., by the old Simla road, now a bridle-path), Sanawar and Sabathu. A good and well-graded road goes up below Sanawar to

9 m. **Kasauli** (22 m. from Kalka by motor service). Spectacular views overlooking the Kalka Valley, and 6322 ft. above sea-level. Favourite holiday resort for trekking, small game shooting and fishing. Cantonment. Tourist Information Bureau. At Kasauli is the Central Research Institute preparing vaccines and sera against typhoid, cholera, smallpox and antidotes for snake bite and rabies. Visitors allowed on Tuesdays.

The bridle-road continues on through *Kakarhatti*, *Sairi*, and *Jutogh* (see below) to Simla (41 m.).

3 m. off, across a dip, the road rises to **Sanawar**, which, however, is not quite so high as Kasauli. One of the Lawrence Military Schools (started 1841 and so named after their founder Sir Henry Lawrence) was located here, the others being at Abu, Murree and Ootacamund. There is also a Tuberculosis Sanatorium.

From Dharmpur another road leads N. 10 m. to **Sabathu** (1816) between the old tonga and bridle-roads. The next station,

24 m. **Kumarhatti** (5200 ft.), serves the Cantonment of **Dagshai.** The railway now passes under the Barogh Ridge (the road goes over the top 900 ft. higher) by a tunnel of 3756 ft., and at Barogh station (5020 ft.) clothes may be changed.

The line runs high above the fine valley of the Giri, famous for its mahsir fishing, to

29 m. **Solon** (H. and D.B.), 4900 ft.; College of Agriculture.

37 m. **Kandaghat,** the level has fallen to 4698 ft.: station for the Patiala summer headquarters, Chail. The line then turns N. and ascends the slopes high above Sabathu until it reaches a level run round to

53 m. **Tara Devi,** passing under the bold cliffs of that peak. It then winds round the W. and N. slopes of Jutogh Hill, the Tonga Road rising 1500 ft. up the S. face, through fine woods of pines and rhododendrons, and reaches

56 m. **Jutogh.** Curving round the N. side of the hill the railway passes Summer Hill, and by a tunnel to Simla, 60 m. on S. of the Ridge. ½ m. farther E. is the terminus for goods traffic.

SIMLA, Capital of Himachal Pradesh, bears ineffaceable marks of its original creation by Britons seeking refuge from the heat of the plains. Against the background of the eternal snows, its skyline is incongruously dominated by a Gothic Church, a baronial castle and a Victorian country mansion. The town came into existence in 1819, after the Gurkha War, on the site of a village where a fakir used to give water to thirsty travellers. The climate commended itself to British officers on leave; houses grew up. In 1832 Lord William Bentinck, the Governor-General, spent the summer there. His example was quickly followed; and Simla soon became the recognised hot-weather headquarters of the Supreme Government of India. There are excellent hotels and "Holiday Homes." (pop. 55,300 in 1971)

After 1947, the summer exodus of officials from the plains ended. Until the new city in Chandigarh was completed, Simla served as the temporary capital of the east Punjab. Since 1966 it has been the capital of Himachal Pradesh, following the partition of the east Punjab into the two new States of Punjab and Haryana. To the districts of Simla, Kulu, Kangra Lahaul and Spiti were added the Punjab hill areas, thus doubling its size. For excursions by bus and car, apply Tourist Information Office, The Ridge.

The best view of Simla—a group of hills connected by long ridges, is from the top of Jakko (8048 ft.), with its old temple dedicated to Hanuman, the Monkey God, whose subjects abound on the site. Northward, the terrain is rather bleak, and ungracious. In the foreground is Elysium Hill, with the road leading along it through the Lakkar Bazaar, where rather indifferent wood carvings are on sale. Prominent on the Hill is Auckland House, a well-known girls' school on the site where Governor-General Lord Auckland once built his residence. Past the school lies Stirling Castle, now an orphanage for Tibetan children and a centre for the Tibetan exiles who have settled locally. The road then passes Snowdon, once the residence of the Commander in Chief, and now a modern hospital, and continues to Mashobra, Mahasu, and the villages of the interior, most of which are now connected by regular bus services with Simla.

South-east from Jakko is the long spur of Chota ("little") Simla, with a state guest house, Himachal Bhawan, once the residence of the Governor of the Punjab, then of the Governor of Himachal Pradesh, whose Secretariat occupies the massive building on the hillside below. Between the two runs the Mall, from which a road branches off to the villages of Kasumpti and Junga. On all sides of the Mall lie European style houses, with names like Strawberry Hill, Brockhurst, and the Grotto—an English oasis on the borders of Tibet. Below the Mall is Bishop Cotton School, founded in 1859, with its large chapel (some fine stained glass). From the Cart and Kasumpti roads many pleasant paths branch off in the direction of Tara Devi and Char Peak, fascinating to walkers.

From the southern base of Jakko stretches the Ridge, a favourite promenade with views of the northern mountains and—on a clear day—of the plains below. Here stands Christ Church (1857—Anglican) an imposing building now unfortunately painted yellow. Along the path beside the Church are the Y.M.C.A., Freemasons' Hall, and the former United Services Club, now partly offices and partly "holiday homes". Along the Ridge, past Gandhi's statue and the Library is the Town Hall, and the Post Office, where the Mall joins the Ridge—the "Scandal Point" of Kipling's Simla—is a statue of the Punjabi nationalist Lala Lajpat Rai.

Continuing eastwards, there is the Gaiety Theatre (1887) and many modern shops. Paths to the right lead down to the Lower Bazaar—well worth a visit for its panorama of Hill life. This part of the Mall eventually passes Clarke's Hotel on the way to Chota Simla. Westwards, the Mall passes many offices including H.Q. Western Command, next to which is the Roman Catholic Cathedral (1885). Further on is Gorton Castle, once the main Secretariat of the old Government of India and now the office of the Accountant-General of the Punjab Haryana and Himachal. A turning to the left leads to the Cart Road and the Railway Station. The next prominent building is the home (1921) of the Himachal Legislative Assembly. Then follow many private houses, with views to the north down on Annandale—the old race course, now an Army sports ground. A path right leads down to it and to the Glen, a favourite picnic place; further along is the Cecil Hotel (open May and June); on a hilltop above it is the Himachal State Museum. At length Observatory Hill is reached, on which stands the former Viceroyal Lodge (1888) now an Institute of Advanced Studies with a fine library. (Access obtainable on prior application to the Director.) Below Observatory Hill is Boileauganj; further west is Prospect Hill, with fine views over the plains.

Simla is a paradise for walkers. Two routes are specially worth while. First, from Christ Church through the Lakkar Bazaar, turning left in the middle, then past Auckland House to the foot of Stirling Castle where the lower right path circuits Elysium Hill and, bearing left, returns to the Cart Road (3½ miles). Second, from the Lakkar Bazaar take the right fork towards Sanjauli. Before the village a path on the hillside to the right leads to a walk round Jakko at a higher level. At Sanjauli turn right along Ladies' Mile, and, at the end, turn right again on a path which crosses the hill and emerges near Christ Church (5 miles).

Mashobra (5 miles) is a pleasant holiday place. Rest House at Carignano. Naldera (8 miles further) has a golf course. At Mahasu (8 miles) is Wildflower Hall, a Government-run hotel in pleasant surroundings. Kufri (8 miles) is now being developed as a ski-ing centre. For those who have time for a longer trek, the road to Kotgarh with its apple-orchards is worth exploration. The stages, with hotels and/or D.Bs. are:

Name of Stage	M.	Above Sea-level
Mahasu from Simla	8	8200 ft.
Fagu . . .	12	8200 „
Theog . . .	17	7700 „
Matiana . .	28	7720 „
Narkanda . .	39	9500 „
Kotgarh . .	49	6000 „

Three miles up the Sutlej Valley from Narkanda is Rampur, on a road which eventually leads to Shipki (212 miles) on the Tibet border. Since 1962, this has been closed to all but military traffic beyond Sarahan. The stages are:

	Miles
Simla to Kufri (P.W.D., R.H.) .	8
Kufri to Fagu (D.B.) . . .	4
Fagu to Theog (D.B.) . . .	5
Theog to Matiana (D.B.) . .	11
Matiana to Narkanda (D.B.) .	11
Narkanda to Kotgarh (D.B.) .	10
Kotgarh to Nirat (P.W.D., R.H.) .	10
Nirat to Rampur ,, .	13
Rampur to Gaora ,, .	7
Gaora to Sarahan ,, .	10

A beautiful excursion is the journey from Simla to Mussoorie (151 miles). These are the stages:

Simla to Mussoorie (151 m.)

	Miles	Ft.
Simla (7000 ft.) to Fagu (D.B.)	12	8200
Fagu to Sainj (B.) . . .	8	4400
Sainj to Kotkhai (B.) . .	13¼	5000
Kotkhai to Jubbal (R.H.) .	14	6000
Jubbal to Arakot (F.B.) . .	17	3650
Arakot to Tiuni (F.B.) . .	9	3900
Tiuni to Kathian (F.B.) { Road, / Path,	12 / 9	6600
Kathian to Mundali (F.B.) .	12	8200
Mundali to Deoban (F.B.) .	12	9000
Deoban to Chakrata (D.B.) . (to bungalow)	6	6900
Chakrata to Churani, or Chaurani Pani (D.B.) . .	9	7200
Churani Pani to Lakhwar (D.B.)	12	3700
Lakhwar to Mussoorie (p. 367)	15	6500

There are now bus services from Simla to Arakot and from Chakrata to Mussoorie. It is essential to book accommodation well in advance from offices of which the Tourist Office in Simla will give a list. In the Forest Bungalows there are generally beds and furniture for two persons only.

(*b*) Delhi to Amritsar *via* Ghaziabad

On leaving Delhi Central Station:

The line crosses the Jumna by a bridge of 12 spans of 293 ft., with a roadway beneath. 4 m. **Delhi-Shahdara.** 4½ m. S. of this and near Patparganj is the field of the Battle of Delhi, in which General Lake defeated the Mahrattas under M. Bourquien on 11th September 1803. An obelisk on the spot commemorates the officers who fell in the engagement.

N.G. ry., Shahdara, 92 m. N. to Saharanpur (p. 353).

13 m. **Ghaziabad** (pop. 128,000 in 1971) Junction. From this point the main line of the former East Indian Railway runs S.E. to Allahabad and Calcutta (Route 17), while another line runs E. to Moradabad (100 m.) (Route 16), crossing the Ganges canal and the Ganges at Garmukhtesar (59 m.).

42 m. from Delhi, **Meerut** city station. (By road, 42 m. to Delhi; 81 m. to Aligarh; 14 m. to Sardhana; 65 m. to Roorkee; 32 m. to Bagpat, on the Jumna.)

45 m. **Meerut** Cantonment (D.B.) (combined pop. in 1971, 367,000) was the scene of the outbreak of mutiny of the Bengal army (on Sunday, 10th May 1857).

The military station is very extensive, measuring 3½ m. from the railway on the W. to the police lines on the E., traversed by the **Mall,** and 3 m. from where the Bulandshahr Road, on the S., leaves the station, to the end of Church Street.

St John's Church, completed 1821, in the Italian style, was the first Church erected in the Upper Provinces of India. There are tablets in it to a great number of British officers who were killed in action or died in Upper India.

The large **Cemetery,** which lies to the N.W. of the Church, is divided into two parts—the new being marked by crosses and English tombs, the old by cupolas and pyramids. A pillar, 50 ft. high, was erected to Sir R. Rollo Gillespie, who subdued the mutiny at Vellore (p. 497) and fell in the Gurkha War. Sir D. Ochterlony, who joined the Bengal Army in 1777 and died in 1825, after 48 years' continuous residence in India, is also buried here.

The site of the old **Central Jail** (now abolished) is occupied by the Victoria Park. A 12-hole golf-course is 3 m. N.E. of Meerut on the Bijnor road.

Temples.—The Suraj Khund, commonly called by Europeans the "Monkey Tank", filled by water from the Ganges Canal, lies W. of Victoria Park. It was constructed by Jowahir Mal, a wealthy merchant, in 1714. There are numerous small temples, dharmsalas and *sati* pillars on its banks. The Baleswar Nath Temple is the oldest in the District, and dates from before the Muslim invasion. The Darga of Makhdum Shah Wilayat, standing near the Collector's office, is said to have been built by Shahab-ud-din Ghori. The Darga of Shah Pir is a fine structure of red sandstone, erected in 1628 by Nur Jahan, in memory of a pious fakir of that name. The Jami Masjid is said to have been built in 1019 by Hasan Mahdi, Wazir of Mahmud Ghaznavi, and was repaired by Humayun. The Makbara of Salar Masa-ud Ghazi is supposed to have been built by Kutb-ud-din Aibak in 1191. There are two large Imambaras —one near the Kamboli Gate and another in the Zabidi Mahalla—an 'Idgah on the Delhi Road, built in 1600, and a mosque built by Nawab Khairandesh Khan in the Saraiganj. Besides these there are 62 mosques and 60 temples of no particular interest.

Before reaching Sardhana the Ganges Canal, made by Sir Proby Cautley, is crossed. It is about 200 ft. wide here. At seven falls there are electric power stations.

52 m. **Daurala** station for **Sardhana** (D.B.), connected with Walter Reinhardt, an adventurer from Strasbourg, known as Samru, or Sombre, from his swarthy complexion, who became leader of a band of European deserters and sepoys. He joined one Gregory (Gurgin), an Armenian, who was high in the favour of Mir Kasim,[1] the Nawab of Bengal. After the fall of Monghyr (p. 391) he did his employer the base service of putting to death, on 6th October 1763, 60 English and 100 other prisoners, who had been collected at Patna (p. 133). He received a grant of the Pargana of Sardhana as an outpost against the Sikhs. He died at Agra in 1778.

His Begam, originally a Kashmir dancing-girl, was recognised as his widow, and succeeded to his domains. She married a French adventurer named Le Vaissoult (1792). The revolt which he had caused was quelled by the aid of the Irish adventurer, George Thomas. Sardhana came under British protection in 1805 and lapsed to the East India Company upon the Begam's death in 1836. From 1842 Sardhana was the chief seat in India of the ancient and long-descended Afghan Musavi (Ali Shah) family, who still own great property in the neighbourhood. Their royal titles, derived from Islamic international authorities, were not extinguished by the abolition of the Indian Princes' rights in 1971. Their Palace, and the mosque and tomb, in the ancient Imperial style, of the first resident Saiyid and Nawab of this line, may be visited on application to the Palace guard. Considerable restoration has been done by the present Head of the family, Idries Shah (H.S.H. The Saiyid Idries-el-Hashimi).

E. of the town is a modern English mansion, built 1834, and called the Palace, with a grand flight of steps at the entrance. It stands in a garden of 50 acres, and is commonly known as the **Kothi Dilkusha.** The house was sold in 1893 to the Roman Catholic Mission at Agra for use as a School and Orphanage. At Government House, Allahabad (p. 123), are portraits of the Begam in her old age (by W. Melville of Delhi); also pictures of the Begam presenting a chalice to the clergy at Sardhana and of General Allard, a French cavalry officer who fought at Waterloo and, entering the service of Ranjit Singh in 1822, died at Peshawar in 1839. Other pictures from the collection are in the Indian Institute at Oxford.

The **R.C. Cathedral,** built by the Begam Samru, is outside the town

[1] Mir Kasim died a beggar in Delhi, his last shawl being sold to defray his funeral expenses.

on the N. It stands in an enclosure surrounded by an ornamental wall. The cemetery, a protected monument, should be visited. By the side entrance, on the left, is the Begam's white marble monument, made at Rome. Close by is the **R.C. College,** once the Begam's own residence. It carries on the instruction of Indian priests, and was endowed by her.

79 m. Muzaffarnagar (D.B.K.).

111 m. from Delhi, *via* Ghaziabad, is **Saharanpur** Junction station (R., D.B.). Pop. 225,000 in 1971; alt. 797 ft.; a railway colony. From Saharanpur the Oudh-Tirhut section of the Northern Ry. runs S.E. to Lucknow and Benares (Route 16). Passengers change here for Dehra Dun and Mussoorie (*via* Lhaksar Junction) and also for Naini Tal (*via* Bareilly Junction and Kathgodam). Saharanpur is, by road, 42 m. from Dehra Dun, and 77 m. to Chakrata.

The town was founded in the reign of Muhammad Tughlaq about 1340, and named from Shah Haran Chishti, whose shrine is still much visited by Muslims and Hindus also. It was a favourite place of summer resort of the Mughal court. In the reign of Shah Jahan a royal hunting-seat, called Badshah Mahal, was built by Ali Mardan Khan, the projector of the **Eastern Jumna Canal,** never of much utility till the District came under British rule, when Sir P. Cautley (1802-1871) reconstructed it, and since then cultivation has spread on every side.

In 1814 Saharanpur was the base of Rollo Gillespie for the Gurkha War. There is an Anglican as well as an American Presbyterian Church, and a mission from that body. An old Rohilla fort, Ghansgarh, was built by Najib Khan Amir ul Amara, granted a jagir in 1757. A handsome modern mosque has been erected on the plan of the Jami Masjid at Delhi.

The **Government Botanical Gardens** (Company Bagh) attained their centenary in 1917. Many valuable plants have been acclimatised as well as many English vegetable seeds, which together with flower seeds are produced in large quantities for sale to the public. Fruit-trees are propagated and distributed throughout India, and the gardens contain a valuable collection of fruit trees. Near the E. gate is the fruit garden known as the Alsi Bagh. The Garden Superintendent's office is near the pot nursery. There are also a Hindu temple and wells in the gardens, and the S.E. gate leads to some *sati* monuments and *chhattris.*

At Nojli near Saharanpur, was a tower whence the **Trigonometrical Survey** of the Himalayas was extended north in 1835. There is a magnificent view of the snowy peaks to the N.

At 125 m., near Kalanaur, the Jumna river bridge has seven spans of 200 ft., and at 151 m. the Markanda river is crossed (rail and road bridge).

The railway then crosses the watershed of the Indus and Ganges rivers, 900 ft. above sea-level.

164 m. from Delhi, *via* Ghaziabad, and 123 m. *via* Panipat, is **Ambala** Cantonment station (p. 348), beyond which the Ghaggar river is crossed. The mileages below are given *via* Panipat.

141 m. **Rajpura** Junction (D.B.). From here a branch line runs S.W. 108 m., to Bhatinda, past Patiala, 16 m., and Nabha, 32 m., the chief towns of former States of the same names, which, with Jind, formed the three Phulkian States of the Malwai Sikhs, who lie S. of the Sutlej, the Manjha Sikhs occupying the Bari Doab across that river. All three States, when threatened by Ranjit Singh in 1806, sought British protection, which was afforded by the Treaty of Amritsar (1809). They rendered great assistance during the Mutiny of 1857, and received accessions of territory.

Patiala (pop. 151,000 in 1971) was the capital of the leading Sikh State and of the short-lived Pepsu[1] group of States but is now incorporated in

[1] The name given to the Patiala and E. Punjab States Union.

the reconstituted Punjab State. The Palaces of the Maharaja in the Baradari Gardens and at Moti Bagh, the Mohindar College, the Fort (Museum), the Temple of Mahakali and Rajeswari, and King Edward Memorial Hospital are the chief buildings. The Clinical Research Laboratory is an Anti-rabic Centre. There are fine cricket and polo grounds and a sports stadium.

Jind was the second of the Phulkian States. The town of that name is on the Delhi-Bhatinda-Ferozepore line (p. 363), but the capital of the state was Sangrur, on the Ludhiana-Jakhal Railway (p. 355). Its principal buildings are the Diwan Khana, the Baradari, the State Library and Victoria Golden Jubilee Hospital; also a D.B.

The third of the Phulkian States was **Nabha** (D.B.K.), whose chief town of that name is on the same branch line as Patiala.

From Nabha the line runs W. to Bhatinda (p. 363), and is crossed at Dhuri by the line from Ludhiana (see p. 355) to Jakhal.

156 m. from Delhi, *via* Panipat and Ambala, is **Sirhind** Junction. Sirhind once gave its name to a large tract embracing Ambala (now in Haryana) as well as Patiala, Jind and Nabha. In Cunningham's *Archaeological Survey* (ii. 205) a very interesting account of it will be found. Many Afghans of Shah Shuja's family while in exile and other Muslims of note are buried here. It is mentioned by Ferishta as the most Eastern possession of the Brahman Kings of Kabul. After the conquest by Mahmud of Ghazni it became the frontier town of the Muslims, whence its name of Sirhind, or Sar-i-hind, "Frontier of Hind". In 1191 it was taken by Shahab-ud-din Ghori, and besieged by Rai Pithora (Prithvi Raja) for thirteen months.

The fort (built by Sher Shah Sur) formed a quadrilateral with Bhatinda, Hanumangarh and Hissar. Humayun recovered India by defeating Sikander Shah here (1555). Between 1556 and 1707 Sirhind was one of the most flourishing cities of the Mughal Empire. Heaps of brick ruins surround the old city. In 1709 the city was plundered by the Sikh Chief Banda, who put the Mughal governor, Wazir Khan, to death in revenge for the murder of Guru Govind's mother and children. Banda was taken and executed in 1715. In revenge, in December 1763, Sirhind was taken and totally destroyed by the Sikhs.

The finest and oldest building is the **Tomb of Mir Miran.** This is of stone, and is surmounted by a large central dome on an octagonal base, with a smaller dome at each of the four corners on a square base, generally resembling tombs at Delhi. The dead walls are relieved by squares of blue enamelled tiles. This tomb is a specimen of the later Pathan architecture. The largest tomb is a plain brick building, attributed to Saiyid Khan Pathan, with a central dome of 40 ft. diameter. On another red brick building, attributed to *Khoja Khan*, the dome is 36 ft. in diameter outside. This building is probably of the 15th century. An octagonal **Tomb of Pirbandi Nakshwala** (or the painter), on open arches, is surmounted by the pear-shaped dome of the Mughal period. The body of the building is profusely covered with paintings of flowers, and the roof with glazed tiles, arranged so that the melonlike divisions of the dome are marked by dark blue lines, and the intervals are filled by coloured tiles laid herring-bone fashion, beginning with yellowish pale green at the top, and ending with dark green at the bottom. The only mosque worth mentioning is that of Sadan Kasai, to the N. of the present town. The centre space is covered by a dome 45 ft. in diameter. The Haveli or mansion of Salabat Beg, perhaps the largest specimen of domestic architecture of the Mughal Empire, consists of two great brick structures, 60 ft. square and about 80 ft. high, connected by high dead walls. The great *Sarai* of the Mughal Emperors is to the S.E. of the city. It was used as a public audience-hall by the Patiala authorities, and is called the Amkhas.

Beyond Sirhind at Doraha the railway crosses the **Great Sirhind Canal.** It takes off from the Sutlej at Rupar, and, passing through Ludhiana and Patiala, eventually irrigates the S. half of the Ferozepore District. At **Rupar,** which is the terminus of a branch line, 33 m. from Sirhind, Lord Wm. Bentinck had a famous meeting with Maharaja Rănjit Singh in October 1831, and which led to an alliance.

194 m. **Ludhiana** (pop. 1971, 401,000) (D.B.K.), headquarters of a District, on the S. bank of the Sutlej, 8 m. from the present bed of the river. It is a great grain market, and the chief centre in the State for hosiery and silk materials. The Fort lies to the N.W. of the city, and under it is a **Shrine of Piri-i-Dastgir,** or Abdul Kadir Gilani. The Fort is now occupied by the Government Hosiery Institute.

Ludhiana was founded (1480) by two Shahzadas of the Lodi family. In 1809, following the Treaty of Amritsar with Ranjit Singh, Colonel Ochterlony occupied it as Political Agent for the Cis-Sutlej States, and from 1834 to 1854 the town was a military station. Shah Shuja, expelled from Afghanistan, resided here 1816-1833 and again 1834-38. Three of the great battles of the **First Sikh War** were fought between Ludhiana and Ferozepore—viz. Mudki, Ferozeshah, and Aliwal. The first two are noticed at p. 364. **Aliwal** lies 16 m. W. of Ludhiana. In the battle here Sir Harry Smith defeated a body of Sikhs under Sirdar Ranjodh Singh. An *Obelisk* bears the inscription, "Aliwal, 26th January 1846", repeated in Persian and Gurmukhi.

The Christian Medical College and Hospital (500 beds) founded by Dr Edith Brown, with its international staff supported by 20 missionary societies in many countries, trains doctors, nurses health visitors and technicians, here. Ludhiana is an important junction on the Northern Ry. for the three lines—Main Line, Ludhiana - Ferozepore Cantonment (p. 364) (77 m.), and Ludhiana-Dhuri-Jakhal-Hissar (131 m.).

27 m. from Ludhiana on the Jakhal branch is **Maler Kotla,** the chief town of a former Muslim State.

49 m. on the same branch line is **Sangrur,** the chief town of the former Jind State (p. 354).

202 m. **Phillaur,** beyond the Sutlej, crossed by a bridge of 5133 ft., built for the railway, but now used for the Grand Trunk Road.

229 m. **Jullundur Cantonment** station (D.B.K.). Branch, 24 m., to Hoshiarpur, headquarters of a Division and District (1846). The city (station 3 m. N.) had a pop. in 1971 of 296,000. Anciently it was the capital of the kingdom of Jalandhar, or Trigarta, which, after the invasion of Mahmud of Ghazni, survived in the Hill State of Kangra (see p. 360). Hiuen Tsang, the Chinese pilgrim of the 7th century A.D., describes the town as 2 m. in circuit; now two ancient Tanks are all that are left of this. Under the Mughal Empire it formed the capital of the country between the Sutlej and the Biás. The modern city consists of a cluster of wards, each formerly surrounded by a wall. There is a fine *Sarai* built in 1857 by Shaikh Karam Bakhsh, a former Subadar.

12 m. from Jullundur City Junction, on a line which runs through Lohian Khas to Ferozepore Cantonment Junction (40 m.), is **Kapurthala,** the chief town of a former Sikh State, which can also be reached by road 15 m. N.W. from Jullundur City. Its Ruler was also one of the largest *talukdars* (landholders) in Oudh.

The Jalaukhana Palace is in the French Renaissance style. A sword of Jassa Singh, a legendary ancestor, is in the Treasury.

249 m. to 252 m. Between **Dhilwan** and **Biás,** the river Biás is crossed.

278 m. **AMRITSAR** is accessible by road, rail and air from Delhi. Air connections to Jammu, Srinagar

and Kabul. (Ariana Airlines.) Bus and Taxis to Bhakra Nangal Dam. A branch line goes N.E. 67 m. to Pathankot for Dalhousie, and Kashmir (see p. 359). Another branch line goes S. to Tarn Taran and Kasur (56 m.). A third runs N. to Narowal, 45 m. (for Sialkot, 84 m., and Jammu) and gives access to the Sikh shrines at Kartarpur and Dera Bāba Nānak (p. 358).

Amritsar, a city with a pop. 432,000 in 1971 is the religious capital of the Sikhs, founded in 1577 by Ram Das, 4th Guru of the Sikhs, upon a site granted by the Emperor Akbar around a sacred tank, from which the city takes its name, "Pool of Nectar". Ahmad Shah Durani destroyed it in 1761, blew up the temple, and defiled the shrines; it was rebuilt in 1764. After Ahmad Shah's retirement the city was divided amongst the various Sikh Chiefs, to each of whom was assigned a separate ward; but it gradually passed into the power of the Bhangi Misl, who remained supreme till 1802. In that year Ranjit Singh seized it, and roofed the great shrine with sheets of copper gilt; hence it was called the Golden Temple. He also built in 1805-09 on the S.W. the Fort of Govindgarh in order to overawe the pilgrims, and surrounded the city with a massive wall, the greater part of which has been demolished.

The manufactures for which Amritsar is most famous are those of Pashmina, silk, and carpets. (Pashmina is the name of any fabric made from the fine wool of a breed of goats found in and beyond the Himalayas.) Pashminas are either plain self-coloured cloths made in lengths, or woven into plain or embroidered shawls, some of which are known as Rampur chadars. There is a Government Weaving Factory. The manufacture of silk piece-goods, gold and silver thread, ribbon, spangles, etc., for embroidery, is still carried on. Ivory carving is practised, chiefly confined to combs, paper-knives, card-cases, and toys, and copper repoussé dishes are made. The materials for these manufactures are brought from all parts of Central Asia, and the merchants—Kashmiris, Afghans, Nepalese, Bokhariots, Baluchis, Persians, Turcomans, Tibetans, Yarkandis, and others—may be seen in their national and highly picturesque costumes. Besides raw materials they bring specimens of their own national manufactures and embroideries as Amritsar is also a depot for the Central Asian markets.

The city has twelve gates, of which the only old one is that on the N. facing the Rambagh. The direct road S. from the railway station to the Golden Temple in the centre passes two modern **Sarais** and several small mosques, and finally, through a deep archway in the centre of the municipal buildings, enters the **Kaisarbagh.** Opposite the statue is the Saragarhi Memorial erected by the Indian Army to the memory of the small detachment of Sikh soldiers who fell, in 1897, defending the fort of Saragarhi on the Samana Ridge, N.W.F., against overwhelming odds.[1]

At the entrance to the temple rises the **Clock Tower**, the upstairs rooms of which house the Central Sikh Museum. The road E. from the Clock Tower leads to the Jallianwala Bagh of unhappy memory. Martial law had been proclaimed in Amritsar in April 1919 because of an outbreak of rioting and murder, and all assemblies prohibited by proclamation. Nevertheless in spite of this a large crowd had assembled in the garden, and many casualties occurred when it was dispersed by armed force.

European visitors to the Golden temple remove shoes and are supplied with clean socks to wear over their own socks or stockings. The Sacred Tank is surrounded by a tessellated pavement of white marble 24 ft. broad, with ribs of black and brown, brought from Jaipur. It is a square of 510 ft. each way. The buildings around it are called **Bungahs,** and are the hostels of various persons and

[1] See p. 364.

village communities who come to worship. To the N.W. of the tank is the Akal Takht Sahib (*see below*), with a gilt dome. In the N.E. is the white bungah of the Chiefs of Patiala and Nabha, and beyond, to the E., are two pillars called the Ramgarhia Minars. A local guide by Sirdar Sundar Singh gives details. The Committee of management, under the Sikh Gurdwaras Act, employs an English-speaking guide who meets visitors at the Clock Tower. Rules to be observed are painted on a board near the main entrance—the Darshan (viewpoint) Darwaza. Beneath the arch is a Memorial of the part taken by the 35th Sikhs in the Chitral Expedition (1897). Here shoes must be discarded.

The **Golden Temple,** called by Sikhs and Hindus the Darbar Sahib, or the Harmandir, stands in the centre of the tank on a platform approached from the W. side by a white marble causeway 204 ft. long, flanked on either side by nine gilded lamps. Except for the lower part of the walls, which are of white marble, the whole of the building is encased in gilded copper, inscribed with verses from the Granth Sahib, written very clearly in the Punjabi character. It is entered by doorways on three sides, with doors plated with silver finely wrought. The walls are richly gilded and painted with representations of flowers, etc. On the E. side is seated the high priest, either reading from a copy of the Granth Sahib (the original is kept here) on an ottoman before him or waving a *chauri* over it, whilst pilgrims throw offerings into a sheet spread in the middle of the floor, and then taking their places around it, sit down and join in chanting verses of the sacred volume to the music of stringed instruments. On the roof is a small decorated Shish Mahal, or pavilion, with a curved roof in Chinese style. The brooms kept to sweep it out are made of peacocks' feathers.

Returning to the gateway, which has doors covered with massive silver plates, a staircase will be found to lead up to the **Treasury.** Permission to visit must be obtained from the President, Darbar Sahib Committee. This place has thirty-one pillars or poles of silver 9 ft. long and 4½ in. in diameter, and four large ones. In the chest are kept three gilt maces, a *panka,* two *chauris,* all with gilt handles, a canopy, weighing 10 lb. of pure gold, set with emeralds, rubies and diamonds, a pendant of gold, a coloured plan of the temple, and a magnificent diadem of diamonds with strings of pearl pendants, which used to be worn by Nau Nihal Singh, grandson of Ranjit Singh. There is also a sort of gilt arch 6 ft. high. All these are used when the Granth is carried in procession. On the W. side of the small square facing the gateway is the **Akal Takht,** with a gilt dome. This name is applied to the supreme religious council. This temple was built in the time of Arjun, the fifth Guru. A low staircase leads to a room with a projecting window. In the room is a gilt ark, and a sword is taken out and shown. It is a falchion 4 ft. long and widening towards the end, said to be the sword of Guru Hari Govind; a mace also is shown, which was wielded by one of the Gurus. In the ark are also the vessels for the initiation of new members into the Sikh brotherhood.

The **Temple Garden,** Guru ka Bagh, is on the S. side of the enclosure. It is 30 acres in extent, and contains a tank called Kaulsar and several small pavilions. Many of its fruit trees have now been cleared to make space for new buildings. At the S. end of the garden is the **Baba Atal Tower,** 131 ft. high. The lower room is richly painted with frescoes representing scenes from the life of Guru Nanak. A staircase leads up to seven galleries; there is then a wooden ladder which ascends to an eighth. This tower is dedicated to Atal Rai, the younger son of Guru Har Govind, who is said to have been reproved by his father for raising the snake-bitten child of a widow to life, on the ground that supernatural powers ought to be displayed in purity of doctrine and holiness of life, and not in miracles. Thereupon Atal Rai said that as a life was required and he had withheld one, he would yield up his own, and so lay down and died (1628).

Outside the Temple enclosure on the E. are the lofty plain **Ramgarhia Minars.** The one to the N. may be ascended. At the top there is a good view to the N.W. taking in a white temple to Siva at the extremity of the city, built by Sardar Tej Singh. To the N.E., at 1 m. off, **St Paul's Church** is seen peeping out among woods. Govindgarh Fort appears to the S.W.

The return journey may be made by the Rambagh Gate N. of the city. To the left is the mosque of Muhammad Jan, with three white domes and slender minarets. Farther to the N. is the 'Idgah; and close to it is the mosque of Khan Muhammad. In front of the gate, and just across the railway, are the pretty Rambagh **Public Gardens** which are about 40 acres in extent, enclosed by Ranjit Singh. In the centre is a pavilion in which Ranjit Singh used to stay, now a museum of old weapons (closed Wednesday). The aquarium is nearby.

The **Fort of Govindgarh** is a short distance to the S.W. of the city. It was completed by Ranjit Singh in 1809, the fortifications being traced by the French officers in his service. Such names as Ronde de l'Est may be seen on the walls.

There are Anglican (St Paul's) and Roman Catholic Churches in the Civil Station, and several missionary institutions. 2½ m. W. of Amritsar station, on the Grand Trunk Road, is the Khalsa College, which was founded in 1882. This is the National College for Sikhs and it is affiliated to the E. Punjab University in Arts and Science. It has a large staff, and accommodates about 700 students, some of whom are residents in the College hostels. The other educational institutions in the station are: the Medical College; the Government High School; the Muslim Anglo-Oriental High School; the Hindu Sabha High School; the Pandit Baij Nath High School; the Dayanand Anglo-Vedic High School; and the Government Clerical and Commercial School. There is a Government Hospital under the charge of a Civil Surgeon, a Dental College and Hospital and a Municipal Hospital as well as several dispensaries and health centres. The city is provided with a good water-supply with a sewage-disposal scheme. The Uhl River installation supplies electricity. The principal fairs held are at the Baisakhi festival in April, of Guru Arjun Singh in June, and at the Diwali festival in November. They gradually came to be utilised for the buying and selling of agricultural stock.

15 m. to the S. of Amritsar is **Tarn Taran** (D.B.), a place very holy to the Sikhs, through which a line runs to Patti (formerly to Kasur).

The **Temple** (Europeans are admitted) and **Tower** are situated on the E. side of a magnificent tank, filled with water from the Bari Doab Canal, made by Maharaja Rănjit Singh when he built the temple. The lower room of the temple has been handsomely painted with representations of trees, while the outside walls have paintings of gods and goddesses. The room has a corridor round it, on the S. side of which is the Granth, enveloped in silk wrappers, and fanned by an official with a *chauri*. The temple was the residence of the Guru Arjun, and is older than Amritsar; it has no writings on the walls. There is a small pavilion with open sides on the roof. The tank is said to possess miraculous powers to cure any lepers who can swim across it. At its N. corner is a tower built by Nau Nihal Singh. The neighbourhood is famous as the stronghold of the Manjha Sikhs, and a great recruiting-ground for the army.

34 m. N. of Amritsar on a branch line is the town of **Dera Bāba Nānak,** where the celebrated Sikh Guru, Bāba Nānak, lived and preached. The temple here is well worth a visit.

At 36 m. is the Ravi river.

The railway line from Amritsar to Lahore crosses the boundary of Pakistan. There is a daily train to and from the Wagah-Attari border from both Amritsar and Lahore, and also a regular bus service (9 a.m. to 5 p.m.).

Amritsar to Pathankot and Jammu for Kashmir, and for Dalhousie, the Kangra Valley, Mandi, and Kulu.

At Amritsar passengers for Jammu and Kashmir, and for Dalhousie, Chamba, Kangra, and Dharmsala take the Amritsar-Pathankot-Jammu branch line.

45 m. from Amritsar, on this branch **Gurdaspur** (D.B.K.), headquarters of a district.

16 m. W. from Gurdaspur, and connected by road, is **Kalanaur** (District Board R.H.), where is a monument to mark the place where Akbar was proclaimed Emperor. The Jhulna Mahal is an arched wall 40 ft. long and 10 ft. high which sways under a person sitting on it, like an elephant.

67 m. **Pathankot** junction (R., D.B., and R.H.). 8 m. to the N., on the high bank of the River Ravi, is the picturesque Shahpur Kandi Fort, dating back to the 16th century, with a R.H. in one of the old towers. The Rajas of Pathan often rebelled against the Mughal Emperors. Driven back in the hills, they settled at Nurpur, but still retained the clan name Pathanias. Pathankot has now become a thriving town, the hub of communications between India and Srinagar.

(i) *Route to Jammu and Kashmir.*

The railway between Sialkot and Jammu has been interrupted at the frontier since partition, but the Amritsar-Pathankot line has now been extended to Jammu. Direct trains from Delhi and Calcutta are run.

Jammu (D.B.K., C.H., Modern 50 room Motel. Tourist Reception Centre Vir Marg with modern sanitation, alt. 1127 ft.; pop. 155,000 in 1971, airport, daily connections with Delhi and Srinagar) is the capital of the Jammu and Kashmir State, and was formerly the winter headquarters of the Maharaja. G. of India Tourist Office, Ghulab Bhawan provides details of available facilities for excursions to numerous beauty-spots, pilgrimage centres and summer resorts.

The **Amar Mahal Museum,** to the N.E. of the city, is entered by a large irregular quadrangle, on the right side of which is a vast reception-room. The veranda of the small reception-room overlooks the Tawi River. The Dogra Art Gallery is in Gandhi Bhawan.

W. of the city is a temple covered with plates of copper-gilt. The Prince of Wales College commemorates a visit of George V in 1905, before he became King. Close by, to the E., is the old parade ground, with the hospital and college to the S.E. The Gumit Gateway gives access to the River Tawi by a flight of dressed stone steps. A road leads to the State R.H., in the S.E. corner of the city. 2 m. S. of this gate is a fine garden.

(ii) *Route to Dalhousie, the Kangra Valley, Mandi and Kulu.*

Kashmir hill stations are not the only ones accessible from Pathankot. Motor-cars and lorries proceed direct to **Dalhousie,** 52 m., or the journey can be broken at Dunera, 28 m., where there is a D.B. Motor service(s) also from Pathankot to Palampur, 78 m., for Kulu, *via* Guggal; and from Guggal to Dharmsala Cant.

A narrow-gauge railway, 102 m., whose construction involved some difficult work, runs through the Kangra Valley from Pathankot to Jagindarnagar. At 53 m. is the Dhundni tunnel, 250 ft. long; the pilgrim track between Kangra and Jawala Mukhi winds along the hillside here, about 200 ft. above the railway track. At 57 m. is the Daulatpur tunnel, 1000 ft. in length. At 59 m. is Kangra station, which is separated from the town (p. 360) by a gigantic cleft in the hills; and just beyond is the bridge over the Reond Khad river. Large *melas* are held at these places and also at Palampur (p. 361) and Dharmsala.

Dalhousie (D.B.K.), alt. 6678 ft., is a hill station and sanatorium, with a Cantonment at Bakloh (5500 ft.). From Dalhousie a visit may be paid to **Chamba** (D.B.), the chief town of a former Hill-Rajput State. The scenery is very fine, especially between Dalhousie and Chamba (20 m. distant across the Ravi), where the summer road passes at an average height of 8100 ft. for 6 m. through one of the most beautiful forests in the world. At 11 m. from Dalhousie, 9 m. from Chamba, is the "Marg", or green open space of the hamlet of Khajiar (6400 ft., D.B. and R.H.), a circle of green sward having a perimeter of 1 m., with a lake in the middle, in the midst of cedar forests, under the slopes of Dain Kund (9160 ft.), from the summit of which a semi-circle of snow-capped heights is to be seen. The lower or winter road is 21 m. (Chil, 12 m., and 9 m. to Chamba). Shooting occasionally available (permits from Forest Officer): there is excellent riding and trekking.

The former Chamba State, now in Himachal Pradesh, comprises the Upper Ravi and part of the Chenab Valley. It was under Sikh rule from 1810 to 1846. Chamba is a most Italian-looking town, on a plateau about 400 ft. above the river, with old temples, well worth seeing. An interesting collection of antiquities is on view in the Museum. Opposite the Museum are the Presbyterian Church and the Mission House of the Church of Scotland.

Chamba, being situated in the Ravi Valley, is very hot from June to August.

From Chamba roads branch off to Kashmir, to Pangi (over the Sach Pass) to Brahmaur, and on to Chamba Lahaul, and Kulu Lahaul. There are D.Bs. at Khajiar (closed for some months in the winter) and at Chamba. Travellers desiring information should apply to the Assistant-Commissioner, Dalhousie.

Dharmsala (D.B.K.), alt. 7185 ft., founded 1855, is reached (56 m.) by a motor road from Kangra. At Nurpur (ancient fort, with ruined temple), Kotla (29 m.), and Shahpur (40 m.), there are D.Bs. Thence the motor road leads to the upper station, which lies at an elevation of about 5500 ft. This is in the midst of fine forest trees, and overshadowed by the great rock wall or the Dhaula Dhar, which rises to 16,000 ft. Above this, at Dharmkot (about 7000 ft.), are the summer quarters of the American United Presbyterian Mission. There are many pleasant excursions as well as good riding, hunting and fishing. Particulars from Tourist Information Office. Above the upper station one of the main spurs of the **Himalayas** rises steeply to a height of 16,000 ft. to 17,000 ft. The great granite mountains appear almost to overhang the station, while the view S.E., S. and S.W., over the Kangra Valley and the Sewaliks and intervening foothills, is one of extreme beauty. Just below Dharmkot is McLeod Ganj where the Dalai Lama now resides. There is a new Buddhist monastery and many Tibetan guest houses and restaurants. Further down, at Forsyth Ganj, is the Church of Saint John in the Wilderness with its large monument to Lord Elgin who died at Dharmsala in 1863.

Kangra (D.B.K., alt. 2500 ft.), anciently known as Nagarkot or Bhawan, occupies a hill overlooking the Banganga torrent. The name Kangra properly belongs to the ancient Rajput fort, which crowns a precipitous rock, rising sheer above the Banganga, and dominates the whole surrounding valley. The **temple** of Devi Vajresri, on the N., and the fort were destroyed in the 1905 earthquake: the temple has been rebuilt. This temple is mentioned in Ferishta's account of the fourth invasion of India by Sultan Mahmud, in 1008, who sacked it, and again, in 1360, it was plundered by the Emperor Firoz Tughlaq. The headquarters of the District were removed from Kangra to Dharmsala in 1855.

28 m. E. of Kangra is **Palampur,** centre of the Kangra tea plantations. 9 m. E. again are the interesting temples of **Baijnath,** with two inscriptions in the Savada character, giving the date 1204, and a statue of the Jain Mahavira. By road, 21 m. S.E. of Kangra, is the famous temple of **Jwala-Mukhi,** picturesquely built up against a rocky cliff, from a cleft in which an inflammable gas issues. This is one of the most popular Hindu shrines in N. India, and the autumn fair is largely attended. The late Punjab Government purchased a large estate at Palampur for the purpose of establishing a health resort; March and April are the best months for the Kangra Valley.

There is a motor-road from the rail-head of the narrow-gauge railway at Jagindarnagar to **Māndi** (35 m.), capital of the former State of that name. There is a great Hydro-Electric installation in the Uhl river valley, dam 220 ft., tunnel 3 m. long, which supplies power to towns in N. India. The power station is at Jagindarnagar.

From Mandi a motor road runs into the Kulu valley, an important fruit-growing district, which is also served by I.A.C. air connection to **Sultanpur,** 44 m. from Māndi, now generally known as **Kulu** town. This is the principal place in the Kulu Valley, now a well-developed and popular tourist centre. May through June and September through October are the best months to visit the area. July and August, the monsoon months, are usually cloudy and unpredictable. The Dasahra festival in October is a great tourist attraction.

At Sultanpur is the temple of Raghunath (another name for Ram Chandra), which was built by Raja Jagat Singh of Kulu, who was a contemporary of Aurangzeb. On the occasion of the Dasahra festival (see p. 25) all the idols of the valley are brought to Sultanpur to do homage to Raghunath.

At Bajaura, 9 m. S. from Sultanpur, there is a stone temple, dedicated to Siva, with very fine carvings. Three niches in the outer wall contain bas-reliefs representing Ganesh, Vishnu, and Durga slaying the demons. On both sides of the entrance are figures of the river goddesses Ganga (the Ganges) and Yamuna (the Jumna) (see *Archaeological Survey Report* for 1909-10).

Manali, thanks to the recommendation of the late Jowaharlal Nehru, is now a tourist centre for the entire Kulu Valley, with excellent accommodation and bus services to Kulu Town, Naggar (Roerich Museum and superb situation), Katrain and Rohtang Pass (13,400 ft.) Snow-covered mountains surround the town. There are hot springs and an ancient temple at Vashisht, 1½ miles out of Manali. Two Tibetan gompas (monasteries) have recently been built at Manali.

The country holds bear (red and black), ibex, *burrhel, thar,* and *ghoral*; as well as leopards. To shoot big game, a licence must be procured from the Divisional Forest Officer, Kulu. The number of licences is strictly limited. A maximum of 1 bear and 1 ibex is allowed. The season runs from June to August but varies with the availability of game; often difficult to get labour and supplies; travellers and sportsmen should give ample notice of their visit to the Tourist Officer, Kulu, who can give them detailed information regarding supplies, prices, rates of coolie hire, etc. The Kulu Valley is famous for its fruit orchards, where the finest apples and pears are grown for export to the plains of India and as far as Aden, Ceylon and Burma. The Kulu streams have been stocked with trout. There is a hatchery at Patlikhul, and trout now breed in the Biás and its main tributary the Parbatti. Fishing is good. Licences for "beats" are issued by the Tourist Officers of Manali and Kulu, for Rs. 5 per day and Rs. 20 per week. Dry-fly fishing is, however, practically impossible during the rains, when the river is muddy.

Beyond the Rohtang Pass the road winds down into the **Lahaul Valley** with a turn-off to Spiti to the right. Since 1975 foreigners have been allowed to visit Lahaul without a permit but previous clearance is still required for Spiti which is closer to Tibet.

The Spiti valley is dry and barren and the population almost entirely Buddhists of Tibetan stock. The Lahauli people are about evenly divided between Buddhists and Hindus. Lahaul is only accessible from June to Sept. when there is a bus service from Manali. For the rest of the year the valley is completely cut off from the rest of India, the only link being a monthly helicopter bringing dak.

The valley is enclosed on all sides by snow-capped peaks and the open hillsides contrast sharply with the green forests of the Kulu valley. The villages are clusters of multi-storey, flat-roofed, clay-covered stone houses similar to those of Tibet. Potatoes are the main crop and numerous goats are kept.

There is a police check-point at Khaksar then the road continues down the riverside to Tandi where there is a divide, Udaipur to the left and Keylong to the right.

The entire interior of the Bhagputhi Devi Temple in Udaipur is covered with splendid woodcarvings with characters from the Ramayana and by the doorway there is a pair of unique Buddhist dwarapals. At Tirloknath, 2 m. before Udaipur high above on the opposite side of the river, is a Hindu temple occupied by Buddhist monks. There is a large Tibetan prayer wheel in a room to one side.

Keylong is a fair-sized town 5 m. from Tandi up the road to Leh in Ladakh. At present (1980) visitors cannot enter Kashmir from this side as the road passes through sensitive areas and there is no bus; however work is proceeding.

High on the hillsides surrounding Keylong are scattered seven Buddhist monasteries (gompas) where the authentic Tibetan ritual is preserved. The most famous is Kardang Monastery with thirty lamas and two chapels, one above the other. Stupas dot the landscape.

Kulu can be reached by air from Delhi and Chandigarh: there is an air strip 5 miles S. of the town. But flying conditions make the service liable to postponement or suspension. Cars for the road journey can be hired in Delhi and Chandigarh. There are bus services from Chandigarh and Pathankot (rail head). For a fuller picture—P. Chetwode: *Kulu* (John Murray, 1972).

(*c*) Delhi to Bhatinda and Ferozepore

44 m. **Rohtak** (pop. 124,000 in 1971) Junction (D.B.K.); headquarters of a District (1824), was a border town between the Sikh and Maratha powers and fell into the hands of various chieftains. Muslim turbans interwoven with golden and silver thread are made here. Branch line to Panipat Junction (p. 345).

79 m. from Delhi, **Jind,** junction for a branch, 44 m. to Panipat (p. 354).

100 m. **Narwana,** junction, 54 m. to Kurukshetra (p. 347).

124 m. **Jakhal,** junction for the broad-gauge line running, 131 m., from Hissar to Ludhiana (p. 355).

185 m. **Bhatinda** Junction (old name, Bikramgarh). Broad-gauge lines E. to Patiala, Rajpura and Ambala. Metre-gauge lines run S. to Bikaner and also to Hissar and Rewari (p. 271). There is a fort, Govindgarh, built by Sher Shah with walls 118 ft. high, seen from the railway, but the town contains only the shrine of Baha Ratan, a Muslim saint, who is said to have been a Hindu converted to Islam in the reign of Shahab-ud-din Ghori (*c.* 1200), and yet is believed to have lived in the days of the Prophet.

On the metre-gauge line, 187 m. S. to Rewari, are the following stations:

47 m. **Sirsa** station (D.B.K.), said to have been founded by Raja Saras about the middle of the sixth century. It was formerly well known as Sarasvati. The ruins of old Sirsa lie to the S.W. A great cattle fair is held here in August and September, at which 30,000 head of cattle are offered for sale. 98 m. **Hissar** station (R., D.B.), junction of three railway lines. A branch of the *W. Jumna Canal,* made by the Emperor Firoz Shah Tughlaq to irrigate his hunting-seat at this place, was restored by the British in 1826. The city and the fort on the W. side of it were founded in 1354 by this Emperor, who chose the locality as his hunting-ground. Lying on the main track from Multan to Delhi, it became a place of importance of which there are only buried remains now besides the old walls and gates. Within the limits of the original fort are the ruins of a Muslim building, the Gujari Mahal, constructed of Jain remains; and in the present citadel enclosure are the Emperor Firoz Shah's Lat and Mosque, and remains of an old palace. E. of the city is a fine stone building called the Jahaz, or Ship, from its shape. It was used as a workshop of the W. Jumna Canal, but is now a protected monument. A large cattle fair is held at Hissar twice a year. Haryana cattle are exported largely to Calcutta. S. and W. of the city there is a Government cattle-farm (*Bir*), with an estate of 60 sq. m. for pasturage. The *District of Hissar* borders on the arid tract of Rajputana, and the average rainfall being only 10 in., the country is subject to periodic famines. In 1939 the cattle were in danger of extinction. The *Ghaggar*, with scant verdure along its banks, winds through the N. of the district.

113 m. **Hansi** station (D.B.), on the W. Jumna Canal, founded in the eighth century by Anangpal Tomar, King of Delhi, and long the capital of ancient Haryana. There are ruins of an ancient citadel and some remains of gateways, and a high brick wall, with bastions and loopholes. In 1798 the famous sailor-adventurer, George Thomas,[1] fixed his headquarters at Hansi, but was driven out in 1802. In 1803 British rule was established. The famous Colonel Skinner, who

[1] See the second half of S. Bidwell's *Swords For Hire* (Murray, 1971).

raised the regiment known as Skinner's Horse, died here in 1841.

At **Tosham** (D.B.), 23 m. S.W., are some ancient inscriptions. They are cut in the rock half the way up the hill near a tank much visited by pilgrims who come from great distances to the yearly fair there. Tosham is about 9 m. from **Bawani** Khera railway station, which is 17 m. from

135 m. **Bhiwani** station (R.H.), formerly a great market for all North Rajputana. On the main line 211 m. from Delhi is Kot Kapura (R.), in the former Faridkot State, junction for a metre-gauge line, which runs 50 m. W. from Kot Kapura to **Fazilka** Junction. The town has a considerable trade in grain, and a fine market known as the "Bikram" Mandi.

219 m. from Delhi is **Faridkot** town (R.H.), chief town of the former Sikh State of that name. Chaudhri Kapura founded the Faridkot house in the middle of the 16th century, and his grandson, Sardar Hamir Sing, became independent a century later, having added considerably to the family possessions. Ranjit Singh took possession of the State in 1809, but agreed to relinquish it by the Treaty of Amritsar. For services rendered during the first Sikh war the Faridkot Ruler received the title of Raja and a grant of territory. The town, which lies 20 m. S. of Ferozepore, has a considerable trade in grain. The chief places of interest are—a fort built about 700 years ago by Raja Mokulsi, a Rajput, in the time of Bawa Farid-ud-din, a saint, who gave it his name, and the Davies Model Agricultural Farm and farmer's house. 239 m. from Delhi is **Ferozepore** Cantonment Junction (R., D.B.), lying midway between the Cantonment proper and the City. The fort is 1 m. W. of Cantonment station. It was rebuilt in 1858 and greatly strengthened in 1887. The railway passes between the City and the Fort; and the Grand Trunk Road between the Fort and the Cantonment.

The city was founded in the time of Firoz Shah of Delhi, 1351-1387. When it lapsed from the Sikhs to the British in 1835 it was in a declining state, but through the exertions of Sir Henry Lawrence and his successors it increased to its present importance as a market of raw produce, much of which is due to the Sirhind Canal, extended to the District in 1882, and the inundation canals along the Sutlej, inaugurated by Colonel Grey, in the years 1874-78. The main streets are wide and well paved, while a circular road which girdles the wall is lined by the gardens of wealthy residents.

A memorial was erected in 1933 to the Sikh garrison of Saragarhi on the Orakzai Samana range (p. 356), which fell to a man defending the post in 1897.

In the cemetery on the Grand Trunk Road to Ludhiana lie many distinguished soldiers, amongst them Major George Broadfoot, C.B., Governor-General's Agent, N.W. Frontier, General Sale, and General Dick.

The three great battlefields of the First Sikh War, fought by Sir Hugh Gough, can be visited from this point. Plain obelisks have been erected on each. **Mudki** (18th December 1845) lies 17 m. to the S.E.; **Ferozeshah** (21st and 22nd December), 11 m. E., and on the railway to Ludhiana and 8 m. from Mudki; and **Sobraon** (10th February 1846) 22 m. N.E. Mudki and Ferozeshah are accessible by motor to within 1½ m. and ½ m. respectively. To reach Sobraon requires a 5-m. ride across country from Mallanwala Khas station on the Jullundur line.

Until partition in 1947 the railway line to Kasur and Lahore crossed the Sutlej by the Kaisar-i-Hind bridge, but now the Sutlej is the boundary between Pakistan and India and Ferozepore is the terminus of the railway. Below Ferozepore on the Sutlej at Suleimanke (56 m.), Islam (138 m.), and Panjnad farther down still are the headworks of the various irrigation projects based on the river.

ROUTE 16

SAHARANPUR by the Oudh and Rohilkhand Section of the Northern Ry., through **Roorkee** to

(1) **Lhaksar** Junction for **Hardwar, Dehra Dun, Mussoorie, Landour** and **Chakrata**;

thence through **Moradabad** and **Rampur** to

(2) **Bareilly** Junction for **Kathgodam, Naini Tal, Almora,** and **Ranikhet**;

thence to LUCKNOW and on to **Benares** by (*a*) **Rae Bareli** and **Partabgarh** (mail route) and (*b*) **Fyzabad, Ajodhya, Jaunpur** and **Moghulsarai.**

Saharanpur Junction (see p. 353) is 50 m. from Ambala Cantonment (p. 347) and 111 m. from Delhi *via* Ghaziabad and Meerut (Route 15). Saharanpur is the junction for the Oudh and Rohilkhand section of the Northern Ry., which runs S.E. to Lucknow (322 m.) and thence by the North-Eastern Ry. (509 m.) to Benares and (520 m.) to Moghulsarai, where it connects with the main and Grand Chord lines to Calcutta (Route 2).

A motor service runs to Dehra Dun (p. 366) in 2½ hours.

22 m. from Saharanpur is **Roorkee** (*Rurki*) station (D.B.). It is 42 m. by road to Dehra Dun, 65 m. to Meerut, 32 m. to Muzaffarnagar, 19 m. to Hardwar. Roorkee stands on an artificial ridge of canal spoil overlooking the Solani river. Up to 1845 a mud-built village, it is now the headquarters of the Ganges Canal workshops, and the Corps of Engineers.

The Thomason Civil Engineering College, founded in 1847, in 1949 was given the status of a University, under the name of Roorkee University. The students are partly young officers of the Indian Engineers, partly civilians. It has large laboratories. The library has more than 30,000 volumes which are available to the public under certain restrictions.

30 m., bridge over the Solani river. An aqueduct carries the Ganges Canal.

33 m. **Lhaksar** Junction. A branch line from here (opened 1900) runs N. to **Hardwar** and Dehra Dun, giving access to the hill stations of Mussoorie, Landour and Chakrata.

(1) *Lhaksar Junction to Hardwar and Dehra Dun* (*for Mussoorie*)

17 m. from Lhaksar, **Hardwar** or Amarut station (D.B.; height above sea-level 1024 ft.) is situated on the right bank of the Ganges, at the southern base of the Siwalik range, at the mouth of a gorge. As the canal bank is closed by locked gates at intervals, the key should be obtained from the canal office. The Ganges here divides into several channels between large islands, many of which are above high flood-water. One of these channels commences about 2¼ m. above Hardwar, and flows by it, and by Mayapur and Kankhal, rejoining the parent stream.

The Ganges canal system commences at Hardwar, water being taken from between Mayapur and Kankhal on the west bank. The Bhimgoda headworks control the supply of water.

Hardwar is a town of great antiquity, and has borne many names. It was originally known as Kapila, or Gupila, from the sage Gupila, who passed a long period here in religious austerities at a spot still called Kapila Sthana.

The Chinese pilgrim Hiuen Tsang visited a city which he calls Mo-Yu-Lo, which General Cunningham identified with Mayapur, a little S. of the modern Hardwar.[1] Timur sacked the place in January 1399. The name Hardwar, "Door of Hari

[1] For the ancient history of Hardwar, see *Archaeol. Rep.*, 2, 231.

or Vishnu", probably does not date further back than 1400.

The great object of attraction is the temple of Daksheswara (see below) and the bathing ghat 2½ m. above. This ghat, which is known as Hari-ke-charan, has its name from the *charan* or footprint of Hari (Vishnu) impressed on a stone let into the upper wall, which is an object of great veneration at the annual gathering. Each pilgrim struggles to be first to plunge into the pool after the propitious moment has arrived, and stringent police regulations are required to prevent many fatalities. In 1819, Government built the present enlarged ghat of 60 steps 100 ft. wide. The cleansing from all sins is supposed to result from bathing in the Ganges here. The great assemblage of pilgrims takes place on the 1st of Baisakh (April-May), the day on which the Ganges is said to have first appeared, and when the Hindu solar year begins. Photography is strictly forbidden without a permit.

Every twelfth year, the planet Jupiter being in Aquarius and the sun entering Aries, a feast of peculiar sanctity occurs, called a Kumbh-mela. This festival is celebrated in turn in Allahabad (p. 125), Nasik (p. 115), or Ujjain (p. 207); at intervals of three years. Riots and bloody fights used to be common; in 1760, on the last day of bathing (10th April), the rival mobs of the Gosain and Bairagi sects had a battle, in which many perished. The Kumbh-melas now pass off quietly on the whole, although 500,000 may be present on the great bathing day; elaborate railway, lighting and sanitary arrangements are made.

Gangadwara is celebrated in the Puranas as the scene of Daksha's sacrifice, to which he neglected to invite Siva, the husband of his daughter Sati. Sati attended the sacrifice in spite of Siva's warning not to do so, and was so shocked at her father's disrespect that she went to the bank of the Ganges, and by her own splendour consumed her body. Enraged at Sati's death, Siva produced Vira-Bhadra, who cut off Daksha's head and threw it in the fire. Siva restored Daksha to life, but as his head had been consumed, replaced it with that of a goat or ram. The spot where Daksha is supposed to have prepared his sacrifice is now marked by the Temple of Daksheswara, a form of Siva. It is at the S. end of Kankhal, 2½ m. below the bathing ghat. Around the temple are several smaller ones of no interest.

There are three old temples at Hardwar—to Narayana-shila, to Maya-devi, and to Bhairava. The Temple of Narayana-shila is made of bricks, 9½ in. square and 2½ in. thick, and is plastered on the outside. The Temple of Maya-devi General Cunningham thought to be 10th or 11th century. Maya-devi is a three-headed and four-armed female in the act of killing a prostrate figure; in one hand is a discus, in another what resembles a human head, and in a third a trident. Close by is a squatting figure with eight arms, which must be Siva, and outside the temple is the bull Nandi. Outside the Temple of Sarvvanath is a statue of Buddha under the Bodh-tree accompanied by two standing and two flying figures. On the pedestal is a wheel, with a lion on either side. It is in the middle of the bazar. From Hardwar many pilgrims proceed to visit the shrine of **Kedarnath,** a name of Siva, and that of **Badrinath,** on the Tibetan border, far up in the Himalayas; also Rishi Kesh (14 m.); motors available. Rishi Kesh is 6 m. from Rishi Kesh station (15 m.) on a short branch line from Hardwar. The ghats and temples on the E. bank of the Ganges are accessible via a free launch service. The Lachman Jhula suspension bridge is further upstream. Rishi Kesh has many well-known centres for the study of yoga and meditation.

49 m. from Lhaksar **Dehra Dun** (pop. 199,000 in 1971) (or Doon) is the headquarters of the Dehra Dun District and the railhead for Mussoorie. By road Dehra Dun is 58 m. to Chakrata (D.B.), 14 m. to Mus-

soorie, 31 m. to Hardwar. At Kalsi, 32 m. from Dehra Dun, on the Chakrata Road, near the D.B., on the right bank of the Jumna, is the Kalsi stone, inscribed with an edict of Asoka.

Dehra is prettily situated in the midst of a mountain valley 2282 ft. above sea-level. It was founded by Guru Ram Rai (below). His temple is on the pattern of the mausoleum of the Emperor Jahangir at Shahdara. Research is carried on at a Forest Institute, an Agricultural Institute, and a Laboratory of the Archaeological Chemist. There are six Museums.

In March 1922 a public school, known as the Royal Indian Military College, was inaugurated for boys desirous of a military career. This was followed in December 1932 by the opening of the Indian Military Academy, which combines the functions of Woolwich and Sandhurst. Doon Court is a residence of the President. The place is also the headquarters of his Bodyguard. Dehra has a large community of pensioners. Lakshman Park is the residence of His Holiness Shri Mahant Lakshman Das.

In the earliest ages of Hindu legend Dehra Dun formed part of a region known as Kedarkhand, the abode of Siva, from whom also the Siwalik Hills are called. Here Rama and his brother are said to have done penance for killing Ravana, and the five Pandavas stopped on their way to the snowy range where they immolated themselves.

Authentic history begins in the 17th century, when Ram Rai was driven from the Punjab and the Sikh Guruship on account of doubts as to his legitimacy. In 1757 Najib-ud-daula, Governor of Saharanpur, occupied the Dun, but he died in 1770, when the country was swept by various invaders, last of all the Gurkhas. At the end of the Gurkha War, in 1815, the Treaty of Sagauli ceded the country to the British, who had easily occupied Dehra, and taken the strong hill fortress of Kalanga (5 m.) after a gallant defence, in which Sir Rollo Gillespie (p. 351) was killed. The approach to Mussoorie from Dehra is by way of Rajpur (7 m.), a large village (3000 ft.). The journey is made by motor-car or bus to a point about 2 m. from the Mussoorie Library. Road toll is payable. At Jharipani there is water and a bazar; and here, at an elevation of 5000 ft., the residential area begins.

4 m. **Mussoorie** (alt. 6570 ft., pop. 18,000 in 1971) is situated upon an outer range of the Himalayas, which lie to the N. of Dehra Dun. The hill rises in the form of a horseshoe gradually ascending to the centre, and enclosing in the hollow a number of ridges. Ridges also run down from the back of the hill to the valley in which flows a tributary of the Jumna; between the ridges N. and S. are deep, wooded gorges. The S. view from Mussoorie is over the valley ot the Dun and across the Siwalik Hills to the plains; the view towards the N. is bounded by the peaks of the snowy Chor range with the Bhandarpoonah peak. The hills towards the S., which are exposed to the prevailing winds, are nearly bare, To the N., however, not far below the ridge, trees are plentiful. They are principally oak, rhododendron and fir. In sheltered places apricots, apples, pears and cherries flourish, together with many English annual and perennial plants. Mussoorie is a very popular hot weather resort, with bungalows to hire and excellent hotels. There are many schools in Mussoorie, also the Wynberg Homes for the Anglo-Indian community, started in 1893.

Landour is a little to the E. of Mussoorie, connected with it by a narrow spur. The Hill is about 900 ft. above the average of the Mussoorie ridge. The houses and barracks are built upon the ascending slope of the spur and upon the precipitous slopes of the ridge.

There is a good road from Mussoorie (148 m.) to Simla *via* Chakrata, a hill station 7000 ft. above the sea, in the centre of the tract called Jaunsar Bawar (21 m.). There are forest R.Hs. at most halts, but food should be taken. The number of marches is twelve. The highest point crossed is the Patemalla Mountain (9368 ft.), 33 m. from Simla. Motor-cars can be hired for the journey from Dehra Dun to Chakrata (58 m.), but foreigners cannot go there at present without a permit from the Sub-Divisional Officer at Dehra Dun.

Main Line from Lhaksar Junction to Bareilly Junction

37 m. from Saharanpur is the Banganga bridge, and at 43 m. the Ganges bridge.

59 m. from Saharanpur, on the main line, is **Najibabad,** founded by Najib-ud-daula, a Rohilla chief, who was prominent in Delhi from 1761-70. His grandson was the infamous Ghulam Kadir (see p. 324). Branch to Bijnor (23 m.), and another to Kotdwara (15 m., D.B.), whence by road (26 m.) to the hill station (5828 ft.) of Lansdowne (D.B.), the former home of the Garwhal Rifles. Motor services by bus in 3 hours daily from Kotdwara.

73 m. **Nagina** station (D.B.), noted for its work in ebony. It is 19 m. by road from Bijnor. Taxis and ekkas are generally available. **Bijnor** (D.B.K.) is 3 m. from the Ganges. The Brahmanical threads (*janeo*) made here have acquired a general reputation.

120 m. from Saharanpur is **Moradabad** (pop. 272,000 in 1971) Junction (W. rooms; good D.B., 2 m.). Branch lines of the Northern Ry.: (*a*) 100 m. to Delhi, *via* Hapur (junction for Meerut, p. 351), and Ghaziabad, crossing the Ganges at Garhmuktesar, with temples of Mukandnath and Bahirav; (*b*) 28 m., on the old main line to Chandausi Junction for the line (61 m.) from Bareilly Junction to Aligarh Junction.

The former Rohilkhand and Kumaon Ry. runs (48 m.) to Ramnagar (junction at Kashipur for Lalkia on the Bareilly-Kathgodam branch of the same railway), also to Sambhal (below). The railway station lies to the S.E. of the city, which is on the right bank of the Ramganga river. To N.W. of the city is the civil station. The city is noted for its metal work, especially for inlaid work of brass and tin and bell foundries.

About ½ m. N. of the railway station is the *American Church*, and 1 m. from this church the Ramganga river is crossed by the railway and by a bridge of boats, except in the rainy season. To the W. is the Jami Masjid, dating from 1634, in the reign of Shah Jahān, after whose son, Murad Bukhsh, the place was named. N. are the ruins of the fort of Rustam Khan, a famous Mughal General, high in favour with Jahangir and Shah Jehan, who founded the city in 1625.

There is a road from Moradabad N.E. to Ranikhet and Almora with a branch between these two places to Naini Tal: but before taking it enquiry should be made about its condition. Another road runs 73 m. to Meerut. The mosque at **Sambhal** (22 m. S. by road) bears an inscription which states that it was built by the Emperor Bābur; but this is doubtful. It is claimed by the Hindus as a shrine of Vishnu; but it is a specimen of early Pathan architecture. Bābur's son Humayun, afterwards Emperor, was governor of the place, which was plundered by the Mahrattas under Tukaji Holkar in 1773.

On leaving Morādabad the Rāmganga river is crossed by a bridge (carrying the road also), and similarly the Kosi river is crossed at 135 m.

137 m. from Saharanpur, on a chord line, opened 1894, **Rampur** (pop. 161,000 in 1971) (D.B.K.), the capital of a former Rohilla State (see below, under Bareilly, for history), but since December 1949 the State has been merged in Uttar Pradesh. There is a fine Guest-house. The State **Library** is famous for its Oriental MSS.; it contains also a remarkable collection of portraits of the 16th to 18th cen-

turies, which includes one of François Bernier and a contemporary one of the Emperor Bābur. Among the principal treasures is a little volume of Turki verse with autograph notes by Bābur and Shah Jahan.

176 m. from Saharanpur is **Bareilly** Junction (R., D.B.) (pop. 326,000 in 1971; alt. 562 ft.). A metre-gauge line runs N. to (66 m.) Kathgodam, under Naini Tal (see p. 370). W. from Bareilly a branch line runs to Budaon and on across the Ganges to Kasganj (junction for the metre-gauge line from Kanpur to Muttra). A branch connects, *via* Chandausi, with Aligarh (p. 377), crossing the Ganges at Narora by a bridge 3040 ft. long. Below the bridge are the headworks of the Lower Ganges Canal, irrigating down to Allahabad.

By road Bareilly is 63 m. to Kathgodam, 47 m. to Shahjahanpur, 52 m. on to Sitapur, and 52 m. farther on to Lucknow; it is 33½ m. to Pilibhit, 128 m. to Muttra, 132 m. to Agra.

Bareilly is the capital of Rohilkhand. Two Afghan brothers, Shah Alam and Husain Khan, settled here in 1623. Ali Muhammad Khan, grandson of Shah Alam, united the Rohillas between 1707 and 1720, made Bareilly his headquarters, and his uncle Hafiz Rahmat Khan, who succeeded him, extended his power from Almora in the N. to Etawah in the S.W. On the death of Najib-ud-daula in 1772, the Rohillas provoked an invasion of the Mahrattas, and executed a promise to pay the Nawab Wazir of Oudh, who obtained British assistance in keeping the Mahrattas out. As the Rohillas, except Rahmat Khan, omitted to pay, the Rohilla War, 1773-74, ensued, in which the ruler of Oudh, again with the support of British troops, conquered Rohilkhand, Hafiz Rahmat being killed, the 23rd April 1774,[1] at Miranpur Katra, 15 m., on the line to Shahjahanpur. Faiz Ullah, son of Ali Muhammad Khan, was recognised by the Wazir as Chief of Rampur by a Treaty of Laldhang (1774), and from him the present Nawabs of Rampur are descended. Bareilly was ceded to the British by Saadatali Khan in 1801, to cancel a debt accruing by the loan of British troops.

Bareilly contains a mosque of Shaikh Ahmad Khandan with a Persian inscription (1284) of Balban, and another, the Mirzai, dating back to Shah Jahan. The splendid rows of Bamboos, from which it is commonly called Bans Bareilly, have practically all disappeared. In the churchyard of Christ Church is the tomb of Mr Thomason, Lieut.-Governor of the North-West Provinces, 1843-53, who founded the systems of land revenue and administration of N. India. At Aulah were palaces of the Rohillas. Bareilly has rosin, bobbin, catechu and match factories at Clutterbuckganj. The old industry of lacquered and gilt furniture has been replaced by woodwork and furniture making, which has received Government aid. The sugar industry expands rapidly. Cotton rope, newar, tents and durries are also made. There is one college of the first rank here and its history dates back a hundred years to the time when it started as a school. There are six high schools for boys, and a Government girl's high school, the first of its kind in the U.P.

[1] A narrative of the Rohilla War, may be read in Sir John Strachey's *Hastings and the Rohilla War* (Clarendon Press, 1892).

(2) *Bareilly Junction to Bhojeepura (for Sitapur) and Kathgodam (for Naini Tal).*

12 m. from Bareilly Junction is **Bhojeepura** Junction for Kathgodam (see below). The main line runs N.E. from here to 36 m. Pilibhit then turns S.E. to (115 m.) Lakhimpur, (144 m.) Sitapur, and (199 m.) Lucknow. At Mailani (78 m. from Bareilly) a branch crosses the Sarda River. A branch line runs from **Pilibhit** to, 38 m., Tanakpur on the Nepalese frontier. At Banbassa, 33 m. from Pilibhit, are the headworks of the Sarda Canal, built by Sir Bernard Darley. The Sarda joins the Gogra

25 m. upstream of the former junction at Rampur Mathra with the Sarju river. The canal irrigates the Gogra-Ganges Doab. A barrage of thirty-four bays, each of 50-ft. span, has been built across the river. 4000 m. of canal and distributing channels, will irrigate in a dry year over 2000 sq. m., of which one-fifth is under sugar-cane. The works took eight years to complete, and were opened on 11th December 1928.

Sitapur (D.B.) was once a military station. Good roads to Lucknow, Shahjahanpur and Lakhimpur (Kheri Dt.). The district has a large sugar industry with three model mills.

66 m. due N. of Bareilly, and 241 m. from Lucknow, is **Kathgodam** (R.) terminus. By road it is 63 m. from Bareilly to Kathgodam; and on to Naini Tal the distance is 22 m. Motor services from Kathgodam to Naini Tal, and thence to Ranikhet and Almora. At Pantnagar, with its Agricultural University, built with American help, there is an airport served by I.A.C. from Delhi thrice weekly during the season. (Buses to Naini Tal 44 m.)

The country is flat as far as Ranibagh (2 m.; D.B.). The road then ascends the valley of the Balaya, amidst picturesque scenery, with waterfalls flowing down deep ravines, to (12 m.) The Brewery. From here Naini Tal may be reached by a steep bridle-path, fit only for ponies or "dandies". About 1 m. below The Brewery, however, a motor-road takes off on the left, reaching Naini Tal (Talli Tal) in 10 m.

Naini Tal (D.B.); (pop. 25,700 in 1971) alt 6346 ft., founded 1841; the one-time summer residence of the U.P. is extremely picturesque, the lake forming a most striking feature The highest peaks are to the N.W. —China is 8568 ft. above sea-level, Deopatta, 7589 ft., and Alma, 7752 ft.

The Lake is nearly 1 m. long and 400 yd. broad, with an area of 120 ac. The flood-level is 6410 ft. above the sea. There are Sulphur Springs at the Talli Tal S. end. Both yachting and boating facilities are available.

The principal residences lie to the N.W. of the lake, close to the shore: the Capitol Cinema, and the Club about ½ m. farther (quarters for men). Polo, cricket, football and hockey are played on the "Flats".

Naini Tal still remembers an old catastrophe. In September 1880, after 33 in. of rain in two days, a landslip crushed part of the Victoria Hotel. The Assistant-Commissioner sent for the military to extricate the dead and wounded. At 1.30 p.m. the cliff overhanging the spot fell, burying at once the hotel, the soldiers, the assembly rooms and library. It was utterly impossible to extricate any of those entombed.

There is a pretty ride on the W. side of the lake, where the visitor may ascend to a considerable height. But the finest views will be obtained on the E. side—e.g. from Sher ka Danda (7886 ft.) or Larya Kanta (8140 ft.). An annual Kumaoni gala (July) commemorates former Chand rulers.

An excursion may also be made by a motorable road from Naini Tal to **Bhim Tal,** 12 m. (bungalow and fishing), to **Naukuchia Tal,** 2 or 3 m. from Bhim Tal (camping-ground and fishing), and to **Malwa Tal,** 10 m. from Bhim Tal over the hills, a very pretty lake (bungalow; fishing and shooting on a permit). There is also a motorable road to Ramgarh, a fruit-growing centre which goes on to Mukteshwar, where one gets a magnificent view of the Himalayas. From Bhim Tal it is possible to return direct to **Kathgodam** (9 m.) by a bridle-path. Another bridle-path leads (4 m.) to Bhawali, a growing resort, on the motor-road, 22 m. from Kathgodam.

There is a round route to **Ranikhet** and **Almora**: the direct route from Kathgodam is by Bhim Tal. There is a motor-road from Naini Tal *via* Ranikhet to Almora. The distances by motor-road are: Naini Tal N. to Ranikhet, 49 m.; Ranikhet E. to Almora, 29 m.; Ranikhet S.W. to

Ramnagar, 61 m. Between Ranikhet and Ramnagar lies an important game sanctuary, the **Corbett National Park,** named after a famous hunter and naturalist. His book *The Man-Eaters of Kumaon,* a most thrilling narrative of courage and insight into animal psychology, is still widely read. The Park has a very large tiger population, along with many species of deer, as well as buffaloes and elephants. There is a good rest house for tourists at Dhikala nearby: a second larger (50 beds) is being opened at Kinanauli.

At **Khairna,** on the Kosi river, is mahseer fishing, also gooral shooting, and there are leopards in the hills. From Khairna to Almora by the river is rough going.

Ranikhet (I.B., D.B.K., R.H.), with Chaubattia, a military hill station. Elevation 6000-7000 ft. The views of the Himalaya snows from this station are very grand. There are good hotels and an excellent club. Chaubattia, some 5 miles from Ranikhet, is famous for its fruits and research station, well worth visiting. Nanda Devi (25,645 ft.), 60 m. distant, has twin peaks.

Almora (Hotel; Tourist Home; D.B.) (pop. 21,000 in 1971) chief town of the District, 5400 ft. above sea-level. Almora, the old capital of Kumaon, was taken in the Gurkha War of 1815 and ceded by Nepal. There is a good walk up to the Kasar Devi temple with its excellent view. The Chowka river is the boundary with Nepal.

Almora to Pindari Glacier (13,000 ft.) (D.B. on the way, but no attendance. Eggs and vegetables usually obtainable.) Best time of year, May or early October. Bus from Almora to Kapkote; from here it is a 36 m. trek to the glacier.

Main Line from Bareilly Junction to Lucknow

At 203 m., **Miranpur Katra** (p. 369), a battlefield in 1774.

After crossing the Garra river at 220 m. Shahjahanpur Junction is reached. (D.B.K. in Cantonment.) Branch lines (1) N. to Pilibhit, 52 m., and (2) E. to Sitapur, 36 m. Motor-bus services to Pawayan, 17 m. N.E. Fatehgarh is 48 m., S.W., by road.

Shahjahanpur is the chief town of a District (pop. 144,000 in 1971). The principal local manufacture is sugar. The Rosa Sugar factory and rum distillery is situated on the Garra river, a few miles from the city. Excellent silk cloth is produced in the city. There is often some shooting to be had. Inquire locally for particulars and permits. At Shahabad (17 m. on the Lucknow road) a Treaty was signed, on 17th June 1772, which led to the Rohilla War.

260 m. **Hardoi** station (R., D.B.). Duck shooting is available in winter months in Hardoi District.

322 m. **LUCKNOW** Junction (R.) (Route 18). Branch, 45 m. to Kanpur (p. 379) on the main line from Delhi to Calcutta.

From Lucknow two lines run to Varanasi (Benares) the direct route (187 m.) by Rae Bareli and Pertabgarh; and the older and longer (209 m.), by Fyzabad, 80 m. from Lucknow, and Jaunpur, 165 m.

(a) *On the direct route.*

371 m. from Saharanpur, **Rae Bareli** (D.B.K.), junction for branches to Allahabad and to Unao, is the headquarters of an Oudh District (1856). The name comes from the once important tribe of Bhars. It contains an old fort of Ibrahim Sharqi of Jaunpur (1401-40).

430 m. from Saharanpur, **Partabgarh** (D.B.K.), headquarters of a district. Junction for a cross line from Fyzabad Junction through Sultanpur on the Gumti river to Allahabad Junction.

463 m. **Janghai,** junction with the branch line from Jaunpur (p. 373) to Allahabad.

(*b*) *By the longer route.*

18 m. from Lucknow is **Bara Banki** Junction (D.B.K.). The metre-gauge line from Lucknow (Aishbagh), which has been running alongside, here diverges to Chaukaghat on the Gogra. From Gonda Junction (D.B.K.) 31 m. beyond the Gogra, two branches turn N., one to (38 m.) **Bahraich,** Nanpara (branch for Katarnian Ghat, on the Gogra river), and a loop to **Balrampur** (D.B.), Uska Bazar (D.B.), and **Gorakhpur,** 136 m. (p. 393).

In **Bahraich** (D.B.K.) is the tomb shrine of Syad Salar Masud, nephew of the great Mahmud of Ghazni, who was killed here in 1033. The shrine is about a mile N. from the railway station and about 2 m. from the town.

Saheth-Maheth, on the borders of the Bahraich and Gonda Districts, marks the site of the ancient city of Sravasti and the famous Buddhist convent of the **Jetavana,** where the Buddha is said to have lived and preached for twenty-five years. The antiquities excavated are preserved in the Lucknow Museum. The place can best be visited by car from **Balrampur** (18 m. from Gonda), on the Rapti river and residence of the leading talukdar of Oudh.

80 m. from Lucknow is **Fyzabad** (pop. 109,000 in 1971) Junction (R., D.B.). Connection is made with Partabgarh by a branch line running through to Allahabad.

Fyzabad (old name Bungle) was once capital of Oudh, but the city has fallen into decay since the death, in 1816, of Bahu Begam (below).

The city is bounded to the N. by the Gogra river, which here divides into two streams, crossed by a bridge. The **Cantonment** lies to the N.W. of the Indian city, at the S.W. corner of which the railway to Benares passes.

The first Nawab of Oudh, Sa'ādat Khan (1724-39), seldom resided at Fyzabad; as also his successor, Safdar Jang (1739-53); but Shuja-ud-daula (1753-75), who succeeded, took up his permanent residence here. When defeated at Buxar (p. 133) in 1764 he fled to Fyzabad, and constructed "Fort Calcutta", with ramparts, 60 ft. thick, of rammed clay, over the Gogra. At his death, in 1775, his widow, the Bahu Begam, remained at Fyzabad, while Asaf-ud-daula, the next Nawab, removed to Lucknow.

The **Mausoleum of the Bahu Begam,** widow of Shuja-ud-daula, Nawab of Oudh, and mother of Asaf-ud-daula, is the finest mausoleum in Uttar Pradesh. The cenotaph is of marble, without inscription. The total height may be taken at 140 ft. The lady was one of the two Begams of Oudh whose alleged ill-treatment formed a subject of indictment of Warren Hastings on which Burke and Sheridan expended their oratory. Although Asaf-ud-daula, and the British officials acting with him, did put considerable pressure on the servants of the two Begams to compel them to disclose where the State money, retained by the ladies, was hid, the ladies themselves were untouched. They received their jagirs again in 1784, and wrote letters of condolence to Warren Hastings on his trial. Bahu Begam made large loans to the East India Company in 1814-1815, and offered to make it her heir.

The **Mausoleum of Shuja-ud-daula** (known as the Gulab Bari), 1½ m. away resembles the Begam's. On the ground floor there are three tombstones without inscription. The middle slab is that of Shuja-ud-daula. His mother's is to the W., and that of his father, Mansur Ali (removed to Delhi), to the E. In the W. side of the enclosure is a mosque at the N. end, with an Imambara on the S. The Civil Station, Cantonments and environs are well wooded.

In the **Guptar Park** is a good garden and Library. At the S. end is a temple where Rama is said to have disappeared. The word Gupt means disappearance.

By road Fyzabad is 79 m. to Gorakhpur, 29 m. to Gonda.

84 m. **Ajodhya** (Sanskrit *Ayodhya*) on the banks of the Gogra, is the place where the great Ram Chandra once reigned, and ranks as one of the

seven sacred Hindu shrines. The ancient city is said to have had a perimeter of 48 kos, or 96 m., and to have been the capital of Koshala, the country of the Solar race of Kings, of whom Manu was the first. A copper grant of Jai Chand, the last of the Kanauj Rathors, dated 1187, was discovered near Fyzabad. The Chinese traveller Hiuen Tsang found at Ajodhya twenty Buddhist monasteries with 3000 monks. According to him, the celebrated Toothbrush-tree of Buddha grew here. On entering Ajodhya the **Hanumangarhi Temple** will be found on the left. In the sanctum, the doors of which have silver frames, are images of Sita and Hanuman. The latter has a gleaming jewel of large size, which looks like a light-coloured sapphire. The temple is an oblong of about 200 ft. by 150 ft. The walls are 45 ft. high, and seem strong enough for a fortress; which justifies its name of Hanuman Garhi ("Hanuman's Fortress"). The town swarms with red monkeys. To the N.W. is the temple of **Kanak Bhawan,** or Sone Ka Garh, with images of Sita and Rama crowned with gold, whence the name "Palace of Gold", supposed to have belonged to Rama's stepmother, Maharani Kakai. The **Janam Sthan,** or place where Ram Chandra was born, is $\frac{1}{3}$ m. W. of the Hanuman Garhi; it is a plain masonry platform, just outside a temple, but within the outer enclosure on the left-hand side. The primeval temple perished, but was rebuilt, and was converted by Babur into a mosque. Europeans are expected to take off their shoes if they enter the inner gate, leading to the mosque, which is beyond a dividing wall and contains twelve black pillars taken from the old temple. On the pillar on the left of the door on entering may be seen the remains of a figure. In the corridor between the two enclosures is the Rasoi, the kitchen where Ram Chandra's food was cooked.

At about $\frac{1}{4}$ m. to the N. of the Barbari mosque is **Swarga Dwara,** or Ram Ghat, where Rama was cremated. S.W. is **Lakshman's Ghat,** where Lakshman, the half-brother of Rama, used to bathe. 1 m. to the S. of Hanuman Garhi is the Mani Parbat, and to its S. again are the Kuver Parbat and Sugriy Parbat, mounds of great antiquity. The **Mani Parbat** Hill is 65 ft. high, and is covered with broken bricks and blocks of masonry. The bricks are 11 in. square and 3 in. thick. At 46 ft. above the ground, on the W. side, are the remains of a curved wall faced with *kankar* blocks. General Cunningham supposed that the great monastery, described by Hiuen Tsang, is the **Sugriv Parbat,** which is 560 ft. long by 300 ft. broad, and that the Mani Parbat is the Stupa of Asoka, built on the spot where Buddha preached the law during his six years' residence at Saketa.

Ajodhya is now connected with Lakarmandi Ghat, across the Gogra, by a permanent bridge.

165 m. from Lucknow is **JAUNPUR City** (R., D.B.K.) on the Gumti river. There are two stations at Jaunpur, legacies from the old East Indian, and Bengal and North-Western Railways.: the Civil Lines, or Zafarabad station, is 4 m. farther on. Branch lines run: (1) 71 m. to Allahabad (junction at Janghai, 34 m. for the main line from Partabgarh to Benares); (2) (37 m.) to Aunrihar Junction and thence to **Ghazipur** (p. 393) and Bihar. By road Jaunpur is 36 m. from Varanasi (Benares), 57 m. from Allahabad, 46 m. from Mirzapur station. The town is celebrated for the manufacture of perfumes.

Jaunpur (pop. 76,000 in 1971) was named after Juna Khan, known as Muhammad bin Tughlaq (1325-51), by the founder Firoz Shah Tughlaq in 1360 (p. 335). It was the capital of an independent Muslim kingdom (the Sharqi, or Eastern, Dynasty) from 1397-1476, when it was captured by Sikandar Lodi of Delhi, but retained a partial independence until finally conquered by Akbar in 1559. Zafarabad is so called after a son of

Ghias-ud-Din Tughlaq. Vast Hindu temples and Buddhist monasteries stood at Jaunpur near the Gumti; there are any little tombs and shrines, in which the Muslims have used Hindu and Jain pillars. The architecture[1] is unique.

For a brief visit to Jaunpur, drive from Zafarabad over the stone bridge; then turn to the right, keeping the Fort on the right, until the Fort gate is reached. From the Fort can be seen the Atala and Jami Masjids to the N.W. and the bridge to the W. The Jhanjhari (Chachakpur) Masjid, which is on the E., is concealed by trees and is approached by a footpath from the city. Some way beyond the Jami Masjid is the Lal Darwaza Masjid, which is a replica on a smaller scale.

The massive stone **Akbari Bridge,** 654 ft. long, consists of fifteen spans, the middle group of four being larger than those at each end. It was designed by Afzal Ali, a Kabuli architect, at the expense of Munim Khan, Governor under Akbar, and formerly his guardian. It was commenced in 1564 and completed in 1568. The bridge has suffered frequently from floods, notably in 1773 and 1871. After 1887 the pavilions surmounting the piers were restored. Seven spans were damaged in the 1934 earthquake. At the S. end of the bridge is a stone **lion** somewhat larger than life, which was found in the fort. Under it is a young elephant, which it is supposed to have seized. From this point distances in the city and province were calculated.

The **Fort** (1360) of Firoz Shah, has an entrance gate, 47 ft. high, constructed by Munim Khan, and covered with *kashani hak*, a sort of blue and yellow enamelled bricks, of which beautiful portions remain. The inner gate has many stones of Hindu temples built into the walls, on some of which is carved a bell. 200 ft. from this gate is a low mosque, 130 ft. by 22 ft., divided into three sections by lateral walls, with a reservoir in front, and a remarkable lat, or *minar*, apparently unaltered since its erection. An inscription on the mosque records its erection in 1376 by Ibrahim Naib Barbak, brother of Firoz Shah Tughlaq. The river-face of the Fort is 300 ft. beyond this pillar, which is 150 ft. above the bed in height, and commands a view of the country and city. Before reaching it a round tower, called the magazine, will be noticed, with a *hammam*, or bath, on the left.

Some 400 yd. to the N. of the bridge, not far from the Town Hall, is the N. entrance of the **Atala Masjid,** completed 1408, on the site of an old Hindu temple dedicated to the goddess Atala Devi, which was destroyed in 1394, when Khwaja Kamal Khan, also called Khan-i-Jahan, a courtier of Firoz Shah Tughlaq, commenced to build the mosque from temple materials, the Sultan Ibrahim Sharqi (1401-40) completing the work. It has two-storied colonnades.

On the principal *mihrab* ("arch"), built of black marble, immediately in the centre of the main W. wall of the Masjid proper, in which the prayers are said, is a verse from the Koran, and above it the creed. The façade is 75 ft. high. In the large courtyard, paved with stones resembling the musallah, or praying carpet, is a well with fine citron-leaved Indian fig-tree (*Ficus venosa*). At the S.W. corner of the large square is a chamber screened by a lattice of stone, intended for the women. Leading from it to the roof is a staircase. Behind the propylon, screening the dome from the courtyard and surrounding three sides of the drum of the dome, is a chamber some 11 ft. high and 6 ft. wide. Munshi Haidar Husain of Jaunpur restored the façade in 1860.

½ m. N.W. of the Atala mosque, on a platform 20 ft. in height, is

[1] For the architecture of Jaunpur a volume published by Messrs Führer and Smith of the Archaeological Survey of India, entitled the *Sharki Architecture of Jaunpur* (Trübner), may be consulted, and Fergusson's *Indian Architecture*, 2, 222.

the **Jami Masjid,** mainly built by Sultan Hasan Sharqi (1452-78),[1] commenced by Shah Ibrahim 1438, and finished after 1478. Some attribute the completion to Ibrahim in 1448, as his family are said to lie in the cloistered court of a building adjoining the N. side of the Masjid.

At the S. gate an inscription (upside down) in Sanskrit (8th century) will be seen on one of the outer wedges of the exterior arch; another in Tughra characters over the top of the central *mihrab*; and a third in Arabic characters around the outer margin of the arch. The partments on the ground floor, and above are two zenana chambers, one on each side of the dome, with stone carved ceilings. On the E. side is an immense propylon 80 ft. high, divided by string courses into five storeys.

N. of the mosque is the burial-ground of the **Sharqi** Sultans, the walls of which approach the N. wall of the mosque within 30 ft. In the quadrangle is the tomb of one Ghulam Ali, with a fine Persian inscription. In the centre is the reputed tomb of Sultan Ibrahim Shah. The only inscription is on a round stone in the centre, which contains the Kalima. Next to

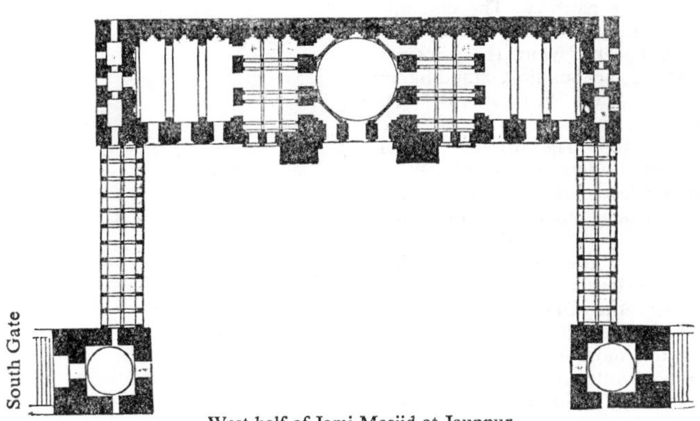

West half of Jami Masjid at Jaunpur.

E. side is in a dilapidated condition, and was probably damaged by Sikandar Lodi. The N. and S. entrance-gates were restored in 1860, and are surmounted by domes. In the cloisters and walls many stones from Hindu temples have been utilised. Its general arrangement resembles that of the Atala Mosque, although the cloisters here have three tiers, whilst those at the Atala have only two. The mosque (W. end) is very massive, almost fort-like in construction. It measures 59 ft. by 235 ft., including the thickness of the walls but not the bastions at the angles. It is divided into five com-

the supposed tomb of Ibrahim is said to be that of his grandson, Sultan Hasan Shah (1452-78).

Besides those already mentioned, six other mosques deserve visiting: (1) The Char ungli, **Mosque of Malik Khalis Mukhlis,** built on the site of a Hindu temple of Vijaya Chandra, which was broken down by Malik Khalis and Malik Mukhlis, governors under Sultan Ibrahim. (2) **Chachakpur Mosque,** called **Jhanjhari Masjid** on account of the "screen-like" appearance of its ornamentation, was a temple built by Jai Chandra, and converted by Ibrahim into a mosque. (3) To the W. of the city is the **Lal Darwaza Mosque,** so called in memory of the "high gate painted

[1] This King was conquered by Sultan Bahlol Lodi, of Delhi, but his son Barbak was allowed to remain in Jaunpur.

with vermilion" belonging to the palace erected close by at the same time by Bibi Raji, Queen of Sultan Mahmud (1440-52), and destroyed by Sikandar Lodi. This is the smallest of the Jaunpur mosques. The style of architecture is the same as that of the Jami and Atala Masjids, but the building throughout is on a less massive and much lighter scale. The date is uncertain, though probably the cloisters of the court were erected about 1447. On the N., S. and E. sides of the court are massive gate entrances. The cloisters are two bays deep, and the W. walls, as well as the cloisters, are panelled. The columns deserve study on account of their variety. The propylon, the principal feature of the building, standing in the centre of the W. façade, is 48 ft. 6 in. high, and is wider at the base than the top. The towers contain staircases leading to a mezzanine floor on each side of the dome. The principal mihrab is of black stone. On the top of the architrave is an Arabic inscription. (4) **Mosque of Nawab Muhsin Khan.** Sukh Mandil, who was the Diwan of Ali Kuli Khan-i-Zaman, had built a temple where this mosque stands. When Ali Kuli was killed the building came into the hands of Muhsin Khan, one of Akbar's governors in 1558, who destroyed the temple and built a mosque. (5) The **Mosque of Shah Kabir,** built by Baba Beg Jalair, Governor of Jaunpur in Akbar's reign, in 1567, in honour of the saint Shah Kabir. (6) The **Idgah Mosque,** built by Sultan Husain Sharqi (1452-78), and repaired in Akbar's reign by Munim Khan. Afterwards it fell into a ruinous state, and was deserted till restored in 1802.

The chief features of the Jaunpur mosques are the use of Jain materials, the two-storeyed arcades, the great gates, and the large central screen arches of the mosque proper, truncated pyramids, used as minarets as well as gateways.

169 m. Zafarabad Junction (for the Civil Lines of Jaunpur).

The mosque of Shaikh Barha, in Zafarabad, composed wholly of Jain materials, is older than any at Jaunpur.

187 m. from Lucknow by the Fyzabad loop is **Benares Cantonment** station (see Route 5).

520 m. **Moghul-sarai** Junction with the North-Eastern Ry. main line (see p. 127).

ROUTE 17

DELHI to ALLAHABAD by **Ghaziabad, Aligarh, Hathras** Junction, **Tundla** Junction, **Etawah** and KANPUR, and Kanpur to LUCKNOW.

From Delhi the main line of the former East Indian Ry., runs to

12 m. **Ghaziabad** Junction (see p. 351).

79 m. **ALIGARH** (pop. 254,000 in 1971) Junction (R., D.B., between the Civil Station and the city). A line from here runs N.E. to (61 m.) Chandausi and to (104 m.) Bareilly, crossing the Ganges (p. 369). Aligarh is 825 m. from Calcutta, 904 m. from Bombay; by road 81 m. to Meerut, 45 m. to Etah, 37 m. to Muttra (*via* Iglas), 35 m. to Anupshahr.

Aligarh, "the high fort", is the name of the fortress safe-guarding the town of Koil, which is of undoubtedly great antiquity. Buddhist remains have been found in excavating the eminence on which stood the citadel of Koil, which was in earliest times a noted Rajput stronghold. Qutb-ud-din Aibak marched from Delhi to Koil, "one of the most celebrated fortresses of Hind", in 1194. In 1252 Ghias-ud-din Balban was governor of Koil. He set up a great minaret, which bore an inscription with the name which he had before he ascended the throne "Baha-ud-din Shamsi", and the date 1253. In 1862 this minaret was pulled down.

Ibn Batuta mentions Koil in his account of his embassy from Delhi to China, 1342. He calls it a fine town surrounded by mango groves. In 1401-40 it became the scene of battles between the armies of Ibrahim Sharqi of Jaunpur and Delhi. An inscription in the fort of Koil records its construction during the reign of Ibrahim Lodi, 1524.

After the death of Aurangzeb (1707) Koil was considered by the Mahrattas, Jats, Afghans and Rohillas of great strategical importance as commanding a number of main roads, so that the Aligarh district became the battlefield of rival armies. In 1759 the Afghans, under Ahmad Shah Durani, drove out the Jats, and about 1776 Najaf Khan (who expelled the Jats from Agra in 1774) repaired the fort of Ramgarh and changed its name to Aligarh. In 1784 Maharaja Scindia captured Aligarh, in which he found treasure valued at a crore of rupees. In 1788 it was taken by Ghulam Kadir Khan (the Rohilla free-booter who blinded the Emperor Shah Alam in 1788), and retaken by Scindia, whose general, De Boigne, organised his army, receiving 32 parganas for their maintenance. In 1796 De Boigne was succeeded in command by Jean Perron, who, when the British declared war against Scindia in 1803, surrendered himself. Aligarh was then taken (29th August 1803) by a brilliant *coup de main* by General Lake.

The **Civil Station** of Aligarh lies N.E. of the city, across the railway. It includes the old Cantonment, which was abolished in 1869. It is well planted with trees, and has a large *maidan*, the old parade ground, known as Hardinge's ground in the centre. The principal thoroughfares are the Anupshahr Road, which runs past the W. side of the *maidan* and the road from the railway station which ultimately joins the Anupshahr Road beyond the College. On the left of the Anupshahr Road lie the District School, the Judges' Courts, a cemetery, Jail, and the District Office and Courts. Opposite the Judges' Courts a broad road runs between the Crosthwaite Hall, which is used for Municipal and District Board meetings, and the Clock Tower, in the Cadell Bagh. The Government of India Forms Press is at Aligarh. There are several metal works, especially lock works. The Lyall Library was founded by the Hindus of Aligarh in 1889, and is built in the modern Saracenic style. The old cemetery of 1802 lies towards the fort.

The object of chief interest is Aligarh University, which was founded in 1875 by the late Sir Saiyad Ahmad Khan, K.C.S.I., LL.D., as the Muslim Anglo-Oriental College. The buildings are on the plan of the Oxford and Cambridge Universities, and are surrounded by grounds of 1100 acres. It was raised to the status of the **Muslim University** in 1920 and became undenominational in 1948. There are five Institutions: the University proper, the Intermediate College, the Muslim University School and High School, and the Tibbia College. The control is in the hands of a University Court, an Executive Council and an Academic Council. Dr Zakir Husain Khan, a former President of India, was once Vice-Chancellor. Aligarh has a high reputation throughout the Muslim East, and many of its students come from far afield.

The Fort of Aligarh, 2 m. N. of the town, was built in 1524, and reconstructed by French engineers, as mentioned, and was further improved after its occupation by the British. It is surrounded by a ditch 18 ft. deep and from 80 ft. to 100 ft. wide. The main entrance is on the N. Perron's House, known as the Sahib Bagh, is ½ m. to the S. of the fort, and is the Medical Institution of the University. It has a square gateway in front, with an arched entrance and a guard-room above it. In the garden is a well with a Persian inscription. Another house belonged to the Chevalier du Drenec.

In the **City of Koil,** at the top of a long and rather steep slope, is the principal mosque, with three central domes, two side domes, and four minarets. It was built by Sabit Khan in 1728 during the reign of Muhammad Shah. The eminence on which it stands is called the Bala Kila, and in it have been discovered remains of Buddhist and Hindu temples, some of which have been placed in the compound of the Aligarh Institute, a scientific society founded before 1875.

S.E. of the great mosque is the Moti Masjid, or "Pearl Mosque". In the city is an historic tank, "Achal", surrounded by small Hindu temples and shrouded by magnificent trees swarming with monkeys. The Aligarh annual **Fair** (held early in February) usually offers special opportunity for witnessing the inner life of an Indian district.

97 m. **Hathras** Junction. The town is 6 m. from the station. The Fort was one of the strongest in Upper India until 1817, when it was captured by the British after a short siege, and dismantled.

The railway is crossed here by the metre-gauge Muttra-Kanpur line (Route 12). From Hathras Road Junction this proceeds *via* Kasganj (34 m.), junction for the line to Bareilly, Farrukhabad (101 m.), Fatehgarh (headquarters of the Farrukhabad district) (105 m.), and Kanauj (138 m.), to Kanpur (189 m.). From Farrukhabad by rail to *Pakhna* R.S. and then 7 m. to **Sankasya** (Buddhist site).

Kanauj, the famous northern capital, first of Tomar and then of Rathor Rajputs, was raided by Mahmud of Ghazni in 1018, and taken by Shahab-ud-din Ghori and Qutb-ud-din Aibak in 1194, whereupon the Rathors removed to Rajputana. The ruins of this great city are very scanty, but part of a mosque, "Sita's Kitchen", with Jain pillars, remains, and a tomb of Madan Shah in Makanpur. Humayun was defeated here by Sher Shah in 1540 and had to leave India.

127 m. **Tundla** Junction (R.). A line from here runs W. into *Agra*, distant 18 m. (Route 13). Visitors to Agra book to the Fort Station.

150 m. **Shikohabad** Junction for line to (66 m.) Farrukhabad Junction.

184 m. from Delhi is **Etawah** station (R., D.B. ½ m.), reached by the railway in 1861; by road it is 72½ m. from Agra, 61 m. to Fategarh, 66 m. to Gwalior (with State R.Hs. at

intervals), and 120 m. to Kanpur. Passenger buses run daily to and from Mainpuri, 33 m.

Etawah may have been founded by a Chauhan Chief, descended from the famous Prithviraj, King of Delhi (p. 335). The name is properly Itawa, and is popularly derived from *int*, "a brick". Both town and District were captured by Qutb-ud-din Aibak in 1193, but the Chauhans regained their power and held it till the reduction of Etawah in 1392 by Muhammad bin Firoz, who destroyed the old Hindu fort. Successive punitive expeditions followed till 1432, and then for a time Etawah passed into the hands of the Sharqi Sultans of Jaunpur, who built the extensive brick fort overlooking the Jumna. The rule of Delhi was restored in 1487 by Bahlol Lodi. Etawah rose to some importance under the Mughal Emperors, and then was held in succession by the Nawab of Farrukhabad, the Nawab Wazir of Oudh, the Rohillas and the Mahrattas. In 1774 it again came under the Oudh Nawab, but the headquarters were removed from Etawah to Kudar-kot, 23 m. E., and the fort was dismantled. The district was ceded to the East India Company in 1801.

The City stands picturesquely amongst a network of ravines on the N. bank of the Jumna, at a point where it bends sharply backwards on its own course. It is divided into two parts, a ravine from N.W. to S.E. separating the old city on the S. from the new. In the centre is Hume Ganj Square, named after Mr A. O. Hume, the "Father of the Indian National Congress", who was Collector here during the Mutiny. ½ m. to the N. lies the Civil Station. 1 m. W. of the city lies the Fisher Forest, an example of afforestation of ravine land.

The Jami Masjid, on high ground toward the Jumna, was built, possibly from old Hindu materials, by one of the Jaunpur kings. The screen, 47 ft. high, before the dome is similar to that of the Atala Masjid of Jaunpur (p. 374). The façade is 130 ft. long, but only 20 ft. wide.

The Bathing Ghats on the Jumna, below the ruined fort, are worth a visit. From them is seen the white spire of a modern Jain temple.

270 m. from Delhi is **KANPUR** (formerly known as **CAWNPORE**), 633 m. from Calcutta, 839 m. from Bombay; the railway reached here in 1859: by road Kanpur is 15 m. to Bithur, 49 m. to Lucknow, 70 m. to Orsi, 136 m. to Jhansi, 40 m. to Hamirpur, 134 m. to Etah, 48 m. to Fatehpur, 119 m. to Allahabad, 224 m. to Saugor *via* Hamirpur on the Jumna (boat bridge only). It is an important railway and industrial centre. It is also an airport. There are comfortable and convenient waiting-rooms.

The City (pop. 1,273,000 in 1971; alt. 404 ft.) is on the right bank of the Ganges; old Kanpur is 2 m. to the N.W. of the present city. The name means City of Kanh, or husband as applied to Krishna. Many textile, leather, sugar and other factories have been established here. Appropriately therefore it was made the headquarters of the Upper India Chamber of Commerce.

The city lies to the N.W. of the Cantonment; while the Civil Station and most of the mills and factories lie N.W. again of the city and near the river. The tail of the Ganges Canal separates the S.E. side of the city from the Sadr Bazar of the Cantonment, and the railway to Lucknow runs to the Ganges bridge below the outfall.

Kanpur will always have mournful associations for those of British birth, as it was the scene of General Wheeler's gallant but unsuccessful defence of a portion of the Cantonment during the 1857 Mutiny, and of the subsequent massacre. It is not proposed to describe these unhappy events here, but if the traveller wishes he is recommended to read Michael Edwarde's *Red Year* (Hamish Hamilton 1973) and John Harris

The *Indian Mutiny* (Hart Davis MacGibbon 1973)

The site of General Wheeler's *Entrenchment* is on the way to All Souls Church, which is about 1½ m. distant from the railway station. The line of the defences and the principal buildings inside them are indicated by pillars.

All Souls Church, built on the N.E. edge of the entrenchment, in Romanesque style, was consecrated in 1875. On the walls are fourteen memorial tablets giving the names of those who died in 1857. The beautiful marble memorial by Marochetti to the victims of the massacre has been removed to the Churchyard from its original site over the well in the Memorial Gardens; and the Memorial Gardens, renamed Company Bagh, have become a public park.

The **Sati Chaura,** where the massacre took place, is about ¾ m. N. by E. of the Church. A grassy road between high banks, lined with trees, leads down to the river. On the bank is a flourishing temple of Siva, of octagonal shape. Two narrow flights of steps lead from this temple to a broader flight. An inscription, "In Memoriam, 27th June 1857", used to recall the tragedy.

From the Sati Chaura Ghat ravine the road runs N. over the railway and the Ganges Canal to Phool Bagh. Here a colossal statue in bronze of the Queen-Empress Victoria has been removed; a fine building has been erected as a memorial of King Edward VII and is used for public functions and entertainments.

Company Bagh adjoins the Park. Close by is Christ Church, consecrated in 1840.

Bithur is 15 m. N., but the Non river (2 m. from Bithur) is passable only by a boat bridge in the dry season. At other times the railway or an aeroplane can be taken. At the Brahmavarta Ghat is shown the shoe of the horse which Brahma is said to have sacrificed after the creation of the world. A temple was built by the Mahrattas on a mound S. of the town, where Valmiki is said to have composed the original version in Sanskrit of the *Ramayana,* and where Sita, the consort of Rama, is said to have given birth to twin sons, Lava and Kusha, while in exile. His house is also shown. In early November is held a large festival. The Nana Sahib's Palace was destroyed after the battle of Bithur on 16th August 1857 because of the part he played in the Mutiny. There are still many Mahratta Brahmins in the town.

317 m. **Fatehpur** (D.B.K. near railway station and an Inspection Bungalow on the Grand Trunk Road); headquarters of the district of that name. Roads, to Kanpur, 48 m.; to Allahabad, 71 m.; N.E. to Rae Bareli; S.W. to Banda. Bus service as far as Lalauli, on bank of Jumna river, on the road to Banda; also a motor service to Kora (Jahanabad, 32 m.), an old town which in the days of Akbar and his successors formed part of the province of Allahabad. (*See below* under Kara.)

Four huge masonry pillars erected by Mr R. T. Tucker, the heroic judge of Fatehpur, who was killed, fighting to the last, in the 1857 Mutiny, stands on the Grand Trunk Road, to the W. of the town, close to the Inspection Bungalow. Two of these pillars bear inscriptions in Urdu and Hindi, giving the substance of the Ten Commandments. Similar Urdu and Hindi inscriptions on the other two pillars are quotations from St John's Gospel.

At **Khajuha** (21 m.) Aurangzeb in 1658 overthrew his brother Shuja. In honour of his victory he built a large *sarai,* enclosing 10 acres, and laid out the Badshahi Bagh, a walled garden covering 18 acres. One of the old garden pavilions, on high ground, is a protected monument.

354 m. **Sirathu** (in the Allahabad District), for **Kara** on the Ganges; the districts of Kora and Allahabad in the Ganges-Jumna doab, taken from the Nawab Wazir of Oudh by Clive in 1765 and given to Shah Alam until he left for Delhi in

1771, were often called "Corah and Currah".

Kora (Corah) is now in the Fatehpur district. There are still some interesting remains and ruins at Kara. It was here that Ala-ud-din Khilji basely murdered his uncle, the Emperor Jalal-ud-din, in 1296. On the opposite side of the Ganges is Manikpur, now a village in the Partabgarh district, where there are extensive remains of mosques and tombs dating from the reigns of Akbar, Jahangir and Shah Jahan.

391 m. **Allahabad** Junction (p. 123).

Kanpur to Lucknow

Kanpur is connected (45 m.) with Lucknow by parallel lines of railway; one broad-gauge and the other metre-gauge. As far as Ajgain (22 m.) the railway closely follows the road. There are some very fair snipe and duck jhils in Unao Dt.

The broad-gauge line passes N. of the Alambagh to the junction station at Lucknow, on the S. side of the old canal of Ghazi-ud-din-Haidar (Route 18).

ROUTE 18

Lucknow

LUCKNOW* became the Capital of the Nawab of Oudh in 1775 and is now the capital of Uttar Pradesh. Under the British régime it shared this with Allahabad. Since 1925, it has had its own Chief Court and gave its name to an Anglican bishopric (1893). Lucknow is the principal centre of Shia Muslims in India and there have been clashes with Sunnis. The city (alt. 391 ft.) with a pop. of 826,000 in 1971, stands on a bend of the River Gumti. Architecturally the buildings are of interest in the employment of brick, but are poor compared with those of Delhi or Agra—*Historic Lucknow*, by Sidney Hay, Pioneer Press (1940), and the Information Centre at Hazratganj, may be consulted.

Four broad-gauge and two metre-gauge lines run through Lucknow junction at Charbagh, S. of the city, which is the focus of the railway system of Oudh.

Lucknow is also an important road centre and airport, having connections with Bombay, Delhi and Calcutta. By road the distance to Fyzabad is 79 m., to Sitapur 52 m., to Kanpur 47 m., and to Rae Bareli 51 m.; to Hardoi (unmetalled) 67 m.

Topography[1].—To the left of the visitor, as he emerges north from the station, is La Touche Road, and to his right is Station Road; both of these lead into Abbott Road. (All-India Radio Studios.) Abbott Road proceeds E., near Government House, crossing Cantonment Road, Banks Road, and the end of Hazratganj, and then continues under the name

[1] Road names given here are the old ones and some have been changed. Visitors are advised to obtain a tourist map from the Information Centre.

of Outram Road to the Sikandarbagh and across the River Gumti, when it joins the Fyzabad Road at right angles near the Badshahbagh Clyde Road (in which is the Carlton Hotel), runs W. past the Moti Mahal and the Shah Najaf into the Strand Road.

The Kanpur Road which proceeds from the left of the junction station direct through the city to the Residency, passes through Aminabad, the modern business quarter, then N. past the Kaisarbagh and the Chief Court building (Pain Bagh) and skirts the E. side of the Residency, ending at the Strand Road.

Canning Street runs S. to N. from its junction with the Kanpur Road. This is one of the military roads which were cut through the heart of the city after 1857. Another military road, Victoria Street, also starts from the Medical College (Machhi Bhawan) and proceeds for about 3 m. in a S.W. direction.

Napier Street, the third military road, passes to the N. of the Chauk; this is the road to Hardoi and Shahjahanpur and the pilgrim route to Hardwar (Route 16, p. 365).

The Strand Road runs along the river bank from the Iron Bridge past the Residency and the Chhattar Manzil until it joins Clyde Road, which then runs S. to Wingfield Park. From the Baillie Guard Gate of the Residency Neill Road proceeds past the Kaisarbagh into Hazratganj, where the principal buildings of the Civil Station are, and continues, as Park Road and Bandaria Bagh Road, into the Cantonments and Dilkusha, leaving the Martinière and Major Hodson's tomb on the E.

Lastly, Havelock Road runs E. along the line of the Old Canal to the N. of the railway station. Most of the places of interest will be found on one or other of these roads. These cannot be seen properly in less than two and a half days.

Itinerary.—To those who are pressed for time, the following routes are suggested:

(1) Drive from Christ Church up Hazratganj: visit the Kaisarbagh quadrangle and the Museum in the Lal Baradari; then proceed along Neill Road to the Residency, passing the Chhattar Manzil palaces, which can be visited after the Residency, when driving down the Clyde Road to the Sikandarbagh. From here the starting-point can be reached down Outram Road past the King's Stables (Lawrence Terrace).

(2) Drive straight to the Residency and continue by the Strand Road; visit the Great Imambara, the Husainabad Imambara and the Jami Masjid. It is worth while, if there is time, to prolong the drive to the Musa Bagh, rather more than 2½ m. N.W. of Husainabad.

(3) Drive from the junction railway station S. to the Alambagh, and then proceed N.W. up Victoria Street until the Nadan Mahal Road is reached. Turn E. down this road and visit the Nadan Mahal and the tomb of Ibrahim Chishti. Then drive S.E. down Sri Ram Road, passing Aminabad Park, and crossing the Kanpur Road and La Touche Road, proceed down Hewett Road until it joins Abbott Road. Drive E. along Abbott Road until the junction with Hazratganj; then drive S. down Park Road past the Zoological Gardens to the Martinière and then to the Dilkusha.

Manufactures. — Lucknow has never been an industrial centre. The chief art products of the city are silverwork and clay models. An extensive trade is also carried on in copper and brass vessels and also in cotton fabrics. "Bidri" (silver damascening on gun-metal) work is a decaying art. The **School of Arts and Crafts,** which is located in buildings on the River Gumti, opposite the Chhattar Manzil, is reviving and developing art industries.

History

The original centre of the city is believed to be the high ground crowned by the Mosque of Aurangzeb (p. 388) on the right bank of the

River Gumti near the Hardinge Bridge. Here, on the spot known as Lakshman Tila, a family of Sheikhs from Bijnor, built a fort towards the end of the 13th century. Lucknow was then included in the dominions of the Sharqi Kings of Jaunpur (1394-1476) and acquired its present name. Its importance dates from the reign of Sher Shah of Delhi (1540-45). The traveller, De Laët, called it a *magnum emporium* in the days of Jahangir.

Modern Lucknow is largely the creation of the Nawabs of Oudh, afterwards known as the Kings of Oudh, a title accorded by the British in 1819. The first Nawab, Sa'ādat Khan Burhan-ul-mulk (1724-39), who was originally a Persian merchant, was made Governor of Oudh in 1732 and became Wazir (minister) of the Empire. His successor, Safdar Jang (1739-53) lived principally at Delhi and is buried there (p. 334). The third Nawab Wazir, his son Shuja-ud-daula (1753-75), who joined issue with the British at the battle of Buxar (p. 133), resided at Fyzabad, and is buried there. His son, Asaf-ud-daula, removed the capital to Lucknow, which under him grew into a great city; the fish insignia on so many of the royal buildings recall the Imperial Decoration (*mahi maratib*) granted by the King of Delhi to the Oudh Nawabs. Of those who followed, it must suffice to say that, with the exception of Sa'ādat Ali Khan, they were quite incompetent. Apart from the two tombs in the Kaisarbagh and the Jami Masjid, none of their buildings possesses any real architectural merits, though the hall of the great Imambara is a very grand room.

Asaf-ud-daula (1775-97). Built the Daulat Khana (on the banks of the river, of which only the Asafi Kothi remains), the great Imambara and its mosque, the Rumi Darwaza, Khurshid Manzil, the Banqueting Hall, which was the original Residency, and the garden pavilions at the Charbagh and Aishbagh. He was a friend of Warren Hastings, and during his tenure the Court was visited by such painters of European reputation as Zoffany, Ozias Humphry, and Thomas and William Daniell.

Sa'ādat Ali Khan (1798-1814), eldest brother of Asaf, was installed by Sir John Shore after the deposition of Wazir Ali (*see above*). Built the Moti Mahal and Dilkusha, the Throne Room (Lal Baradari), and the King's Stables; also the Terhi Kothi and the Baillie Guard, as a guard-room for the Resident, Major John Baillie.

Ghazi-ud-din Haidar (1814-27), inherited the fortune of Bahu Begam and became King of Oudh (1823). He built the Residency proper, the Kaisarbagh tombs, the Tomb at Shah Najaf, the Kadam Rasul and the Wilaiyati Bagh, and constructed the canal on the S. side of the city. He lent large sums to the East India Company in 1825-26.

Nasir-ud-din Haidar (1827-37). Built the Chhattar Manzils and the Tarawali Kothi.

Muhammad Ali Shah (1837-42). Built the Husainabad Imambara and Tank, the Sat Khanda, the Jami Masjid, and the Badshahbagh.

Amjad Ali Shah (1842-47). Built the Hazratganj Imambara, in which he is buried.

Wajid Ali Shah (1847-56). Built the Kaisarbagh Palaces (1850) and Sikandarbagh. In February 1856 he was deposed for incapacity and removed to Calcutta. General James Outram, Resident at the time, became First Chief Commissioner of Oudh. The ex-King lived thirty years in Calcutta, and there he died in 1887, aged sixty-eight. Portraits of most of the Kings of Oudh will be found in the Baradari in the Clock Tower gardens fronting the Husainabad Tank (p. 388).

Lucknow, as capital of the recently annexed Kingdom of Oudh at once became a major centre of the 1857 Mutiny, rivalling even Delhi itself in this respect. Providentially, unlike Kanpur, the siege had a happy ending, marred however by the death of the much loved Chief Commissioner, Sir Henry Lawrence. The small British garrison held out in the Residency for three months until relieved on the 25th September by a small force, under Sir Henry Havelock, but after that the combined force was invested again until the final relief of the garrison by Sir Colin Campbell on 17th November. Unfortunately, the heroic Havelock died of dysentery one week later.

The best books on the defence of the Lucknow Residency are perhaps Martin Gubbins' *Mutinies in Oudh* (1858), Lady Inglis' *Siege of Lucknow* (Osgood, 1893), Lieutenant-General McLeod Innes' *Lucknow and Oudh in the Mutiny* (Innes, 1895). Innes' book contains valuable views of the different posts in the Residency; and a number of photographs of the date of 1857-58 will be found in the first volume of Sir George Forrest's *History of the Indian Mutiny* (Blackwood, 1904). See also *Ordeal at Lucknow*, by Michael Joyce (John Murray, 1938), and *Historic Lucknow*, by Sidney Hay (Pioneer Press, 1940).

The best modern account is: Michael Edwardes *A Season in Hell* (Hamish Hamilton 1973).

The Residency

The **Residency** is entered on the E. side by Neill Road at the famous Baillie Guard Gate, named after Major John Baillie, Resident 1811-15; and the path then leads directly to the Residency between the Banqueting Hall on the right and Dr Fayrer's house on the left.

On the lawn in front of the Residency is a marble runic cross inscribed:

In memory of
MAJOR-GEN. SIR HENRY LAWRENCE,
K.C.B.,
And the brave men who fell
In defence of the Residency,
1857.

The **Residency Building** (built 1800) is almost ruined, but it is possible to ascend the staircase of one of the towers. Upon the other throughout the siege the British flag floated, and was flown, day and night, in tribute to the dead, until 15th August 1947.

The entrance to the Residency is on the W. by a modern portico. In a room on the ground floor, which has been fitted up as a **Museum**, is a model of the entrenched position as it was in July 1857. In 1857 the position was commanded by neighbouring houses (now completely swept away), so close that they were separated from the defences by narrow lanes and hastily improvised trenches and barricades. These houses were filled with sharp-shooters. Sir Henry Lawrence hardly expected to hold out without relief for more than fifteen days.

In the entrance hall of the Residency a marble tablet tells the story of those eighty-seven days. Lord Canning, it reminds us, expressed his admiration of the defence in the following words: "There does not stand recorded in the annals of war an achievement more truly heroic".

The **Cemetery** round the ruined **Church** lies to the E. of Innes' Post. Here rest the remains of Sir Henry Lawrence, Brigadier-General Neill, and 2000 men, women and children. General Neill's grave is on the S. side of Sir Henry Lawrence's, which is enclosed by an iron railing, and bears his own epitaph:

Here lies
HENRY LAWRENCE,
who tried to do his duty.
May the Lord have mercy on his soul
Born 28th of June 1806.
Died 4th of July 1857.

The Quarters S. and E. of the Residency

Beyond the Court of the District Judge, at some distance back on the left, are the **Terhi Kothi,** now the residence of the Chief Justice of the U.P. High Court, and the **Farhat**

Bakhsh ("Delight-giving") Palace. This name included also the Chhattar Manzil (1827-37), which constituted the ladies' apartments so long as the Farhat Bakhsh was the principal residence of the Oudh rulers—from Sa'ādat Ali Khan down to Wajid Ali Shah.

S.E. of the Jail was the **Painbagh** (now the High Court), E. of which projected the S. portion of the Chhattar Manzil enclosure, containing the small Chhattar Manzil, the Kasr-i-Sultan, or the Lal Baradari, and the Darshan Vilas.

Both the **Chhattar Manzils** are surmounted by an umbrella (*chhattar* or *chhattri*), whence their name. The larger is now the Central Drug Research Institute, and the smaller used as Government offices. Near this, opposite the Kaisarbagh, stood the marble memorial statue of the Queen-Empress Victoria under a canopy. The **Kasr-i-Sultan** was the throne-room in which the widow of Nasir-ud-din Haidar attempted to compel the Resident, Colonel Low, to place her son, born before the King married her, on the "masnad". Its other name, Lal Baradari, is due to the colour of the material, red sandstone, of which it is constructed.

N. of the former Telegraph Office is the **Sher Darwaza** gateway of the Dhooly Square, where General Neill was killed on 25th September 1857.

E. again, opposite the N.E. corner of the Kaisarbagh, was the **Hiran Khana,** or Deer House. Neill Road, which has been followed to the Sher Darwaza, now continues to Hazratganj past the N. front of the Kaisarbagh.

The fine stone tombs of Sa'ādat Ali and his wife in the **Kaisarbagh** were constructed by his son, Ghazi-ud-din Haidar; and the palace was built between the years 1848 and 1850 by Wajid Ali Shah. The building to the S. of the tombs now houses the archaeological section of the State Museum. It was erected to accommodate the Canning College (now at Badshahbagh, p. 387). The palace originally had one gate at the S.E. and two others on the N. and S., and its interior was divided into courts. The open square is still surrounded, except on the N. side, by double-storeyed buildings, made over to the Talukdars of Oudh. In the centre is a white-washed baradari, presented by the Maharaja of Balrampur, which was used as a hall for meetings of the Talukdars.

S.W. of this central baradari is the **Public Library,** erected by the Maharaja of Mahmudabad in memory of his father. The entrance from the E. and W. is made by the Lakhi Gateways, so called from the lakh of rupees which their erection cost. Outside the W. gateway is the **Kaisar Pasand,** which was built by Roshan-ud-Daula, the minister of Nasir-ud-din Haidar. On leaving the central courtyard by the E. gateway, Hazratbagh is entered: the Chaulakhi, the large pile on the right, was built by Wajid Ali's barber, and sold to him for four lakhs: hence the name.

In the Lal Baradari (the building between the Chhattar Manzil and the High Court) is the **State Museum**[1] (1863); the archaeological section is the most important. The large hall contains sculptures, the majority from Mathura (Muttra), which are partly Buddhist and partly Jain. The adjoining room is reserved for Brahmanical sculptures from different parts of the Province.[2] A special room has been set apart for the antiquities excavated on the site of Saheth-Maheth (p. 372), the ancient city of Srávasti, and the famous convent of the Jetavana. Some objects from Kasia (believed to be the ancient Kusinagara, where the Buddha entered Nirvána) are also exhibited separately. The epigraphical section contains numerous Sanskrit inscriptions both on stone slabs and on copper plates. The important coin collection is only shown

[1] Closed on Mondays.
[2] This section is now relocated. See first column of this page.

to visitors on application to the Curator. The Museum contains also a zoological section, which includes a good collection of stuffed birds. Part is in the Kaisarbagh.

Proceeding now by Clyde Road, the first building seen on the left is the **Moti Mahal,** once the Royal Library, with Martin's House[1] between it and Bruce's Bridge. It is situated on the bank of the Gumti. The three-storeyed gateway on the S. collapsed during the floods of 1923, and has been replaced by a fine Italian wrought-iron gate; the old walls are also gone, and a railing now surrounds the enclosure. The building itself is two-storeyed, of a blue colour, and surmounted by a gilt pinnacle. Originally it comprised also the Mubarak Manzil and the Shah Manzil, from which the King used to watch the fights between wild animals on the farther side of the river. The Moti Mahal was built by Sa'ādat Ali, and the other two by Ghazi-ud-din Haidar.

To the right of the road, on a high site, the base of which is still surrounded by defensive works, is the **Khurshid** ("Sun") **Manzil,** built by Sa'ādat Ali and named after his wife. It was used before the Mutiny as the Mess-house of the 32nd, and since 1876 has been occupied by the Girls' Martinière School. S. of it again is the **Tarawali Kothi,** or Observatory. This was built by Nasir-ud-din Haidar for his Astronomer-Royal, Colonel Wilcox.

500 yd. farther E. stand the Shah Najaf and Kadam Rasul, and nearly 1000 yd. on again lies the Sikandarbagh, round which desperate fighting took place in November 1857. **Shah Najaf** (named after the scene of the martyrdom of the Caliph Ali, 120 m. S.W. of Baghdad) is the domed tomb of Ghazi-ud-din Haidar Khan. One picture (copied by an Indian artist from Zoffany's famous picture) represents a cock-fight, at which the King of Oudh and General Claude Martin are present. The building is illuminated during the Muharram festival.

[1] Simon Nicolson Martin was Deputy-Commissioner of Lucknow in 1857.

The **Kadam Rasul** is a ruined building of red brick. The stone, with an imprint of the Prophet's foot which it contained, disappeared in 1857; it is approached by a path through the garden to the E. of Shah Najaf. Between the National Botanical Gardens and the **Sikandarbagh** a road leads to the bridge across the river. The gateway of the garden, which is 120 yd. square, still stands.

Just before the junction of Outram Road with Banks Road is the **Legislative Council Chamber** with the State coat of arms on the façade. To the S. of it is Raj Bhawan, formerly Banks' House, and originally the Hayat Bakhsh ("life-giving") Kothi. It dates from the time of Sa'ādat Ali. Outram Road now joins Havelock Road.

At the junction of Park and Abbott Roads is Christ Church. There are a number of interesting tablets on the walls. Those in memory of Sir James Outram and Sir H. Lawrence deserve particular attention. **Prince of Wales Zoological Gardens** is adorned with white marble pavilions and statues, and has a large pavilion in the centre, surrounded by 80 acres of grounds and and flower-gardens.

The Quarters S. of Prince of Wales Gardens connected with the Reliefs

The scenes of the operations of the second relief of Lucknow may now be completed by a visit to the Martinière, the Dilkusha, and the Alambagh, the advanced base of both of the reliefs. A road, striking off to the left from Park Road (which skirts the W. side of the Wingfield Park), leads through the Martinière Park. In one of two small grave enclosures near the gate will be found the grave of the famous Major Hodson of Hodson's Horse.

The **Martinière School** is housed in **Constantia,** the country residence of Maj.-Gen. Claude Martin (1735-

1800), who built it partially from designs of his own. It is an enormous structure, consisting of a central block and two semi-circular wings. The main building is five-storeyed and is bastioned, and loopholed. The basement storey is raised to a good height above the ground, and has extensive wings, but the superstructure has been styled "a whimsical pile". The strange array of statues on the roof led the Marquess of Hastings to pronounce that the idea was taken from a castle of pastry. Martin's tomb, restored in 1865, is in the E. crypt of the chapel; the plain sarcophagus was once guarded by a marble grenadier, with arms reversed, at each angle. To the E. of the building is a lake, in the centre of which rises a fluted masonry column 130 ft. in height. General Martin served as a soldier under Lally in the regiment of Lorraine. He, and some of his comrades, taken prisoner at Pondicherry (1761) formed a company of Chasseurs attached to the Company's Army, and rose to the rank of captain. In 1776 he entered the service of the Nawabs of Oudh, but Warren Hastings allowed him to retain his rank and to enjoy promotion. In 1783 he formed the acquaintance of De Boigne, and took part with him in cultivating indigo and lending money to the Nawab, by which he acquired a large fortune. Dying at the Farhat Bakhsh before the building was finished, he directed it should be completed out of the funds left to endow a school. This school, opened 1840, is for the education of Anglo-Indian children.[1] There are similar institutions endowed by Martin at Calcutta and Lyons, his birthplace.

The **Dilkusha**, or "Heart-expanding", was a villa built by Sa'ādat Ali Khan in the midst of an extensive deer-park. It stands S. of the Martinière, and is now a ruin. The grounds have been laid out as a flower-garden.

[1] "Kim", the hero of Kipling's well-known story, was sent to school at the Martinière.

There are some tombs of British officers in the adjoining ruins of the **Wilayati Bagh** (to the E. on the river-bank), which was originally a zenana garden made by Ghazi-ud-din Haidar in the European style; whence its name.

About 1½ m. S.E. of the Charbagh (junction railway station), on the Kanpur Road, is the **Alambagh,** with the grave and memorial of General Havelock. It is a walled enclosure 500 yd. square and was built by Wajid Ali. General Havelock's tomb is surmounted by an obelisk 30 ft. high, with an inscription.

Quarters N.W. of the Residency and across the Dumti

Across the bridge to the right is the **Badshahbagh,** from which the shell came which killed Sir Henry Lawrence. Of the three buildings of which it was composed, only the Red Baradari remains. The gateways also are still standing. It was given to the Raja of Kapurthala in 1858, and was purchased for the **Canning College** (1912). At Hassanganj, the Fyzabad road turns to the right and leads to the Kokrail Bridge and (3 m.) Ismailganj, 1½ m. in front of **Chinhat** (6½ m.). The main road to Sitapur proceeds N. to the old Cantonment of **Mariáon** (2½ m.).

1200 yd. N.W. of the Residency is the **Great Imambara** of Asaf-ud-daula, which is built on the W. slope of the **Machhi Bhawan**[1] enclosure. The fort was dismantled in 1877. The major portion of the site is occupied by **King George's Medical College** and **Hospital,** of which the foundation stone was laid on 26th December 1905. The building was completed in 1912. With the Canning College, also affiliated to Allahabad University until 1921, and the Isabella Thoburn College for women, the Medical Colleges form the **Lucknow University.**

[1] "Fish House", so named after the fish which Safdar Jang was permitted by imperial edict to use as his badge.

A stone bridge built by Asaf-ud-daula was replaced in 1912 by the **Hardinge Bridge**, and a road leads into the Sitapur Road past the **Karbala of Mohsin-ud-daula** and the unfinished Karbala, where his grandfather, Nasir-ud-din (d. 1837) is buried. Near the bridge, and on the right bank of the Gumti, is the so-called **Mosque of Aurangzeb**, built on the Lakshman Tila or Mound (p. 383). Between the Machhi Bhawan enclosure and the N. gate of the Chauk is **Victoria Park.**

The Great Imambara court contains a lofty mosque and two minarets on the W. side. The immense structure of the Imambara, at the head of steps on the S. side, was built by Asaf-ud-daula in 1784, partly as relief work in the terrible famine of that time, which swept over all N. India.

The great central hall, which contains his unpretentious tomb, is 163 ft. long, 53 ft. broad and 49 ft. high, and is one of the largest vaulted galleries in the world.[1] European gentlemen are requested to remove their hats in the hall. At the end of the roadway passing in front of the Imambara is the **Rumi Darwaza,** or Turkish Gate, built in imitation of the Sublime Porte.

Beyond this gate is the **Husainabad Imambara,** and opposite it, on the N. side of the road, a beautiful garden, with the Husainabad Clock Tower and Tank and the **Satkhanda,** or seven-storeyed tower. This Imambara, which was built by Muhammad Ali Shah, 1837, and contains the tombs of himself and his mother, consists of two large enclosures, one of which is at right angles to the other. It stands in a large quadrangle, which has a marble reservoir of water in the centre. One building is a mosque, the other purports to be a copy of the Taj. The hall contains the throne of the King, covered with beaten silver, and his wife's divan, with solid silver supports. Both the Imambaras, and also the Shah Najaf, are illuminated with thousands of oil lamps during the Muharram festival. The watch-tower, of which only four storeys out of seven were built, was commenced by Muhammad Ali Shah, but work ceased at his death. The octagonal tank is an extremely fine and picturesque work. On the N. side of it is a Baradari, now the offices of the Husainabad Trust, with portraits of most of the Kings of Oudh. The **Daulat Khana** was the palace of Asaf-ud-daula, and one house is known as the Asafi Kothi. The Clock Tower, to the W. of the tank, was built in 1881, and is 220 ft. high.

Farther to the W. the **Jami Masjid,** begun by Muhammad Ali Shah, and finished by his wife, has the usual three domes and two minarets, and stands on a high platform, approached by flights of steps. It is closed to non-Muslims. Rather more than 2 m. N.W. of Husainabad, and beyond the waterworks pumping station on the Gumti, is the **Musabagh.** The last ¾ m. to it must be accomplished on foot, on account of the brick walls which surround it.

Quarter W. of the Residency

To the W. of the Residency, and immediately to the S. of Victoria Park and the Medical College, is the N. gate (Gol Darwaza) of the **Chauk,** the principal street of the old city.

In the grounds of the Medical College is the **Shah Mina,** interesting on account of its importance in a popular cult. Sheikh Mina, whose proper name was Sheikh Muhammad, is the great saint of Lucknow, where he was born. It is said that the Sheikhs (p. 383) colonised Lucknow at his suggestion. The date of his death, according to an inscription on his tomb, was 884 A.H., but elsewhere his death is recorded as having taken place in 870 A.H. (A.D. 1465). The tomb is largely visited by persons in legal difficulties, who offer a piece

[1] Fergusson's *East. Arch.*, 2, 328-329.

of cloth; and on Thursday evenings the crowd is particularly great.

In the W. of the city is the **Dargah of Hazrat Abbas.** It is reached from the Jami Masjid by going E. along Napier Street and then, turning to the right, down Sarai Mali Khan Road, past the imambara of Ilmas Ali Khan (entrance about 100 yd. down on the right). The shrine of Hazrat Abbas is about ¾ m. farther on. A tank occupies the centre of the courtyard, which is surrounded with pillared porticoes. In the shrine is preserved the metal crest which is said to have surmounted the banner of a relative of the Caliph Ali who was killed in battle at Kerbela. The banners carried in the Muharram procession are brought to this building for consecration by touching the crest.

At the junction of Victoria Street and Aishbagh Road is the **King's Hospital,** originally in another building called the Dar-us-Shafa Kothi. The King's Poor House is close by. Both are supported from funds left for the purpose by King Muhammad Ali Shah (1837-42).

Before reaching the King's Hospital, a visit should be paid to a group of three buildings of the Mughal period, in a garden enclosure, on the Nadan Mahal Road, which connects Victoria Street with Canning Street.

The **Nadan Mahal** is the tomb of Sheikh Abdur Rahim Khan, the first Governor of Oudh under the Emperor Akbar. The building dates from about the year 1600 and is a good specimen of early Mughal architecture. The whole building, from the plinth to the parapet, was originally of Agra red sandstone. Its brackets are richly carved, and above the *chajja,* or projecting slab cornice, are traces of blue and yellow tile-work. The dome also was covered with tiles, which have almost entirely vanished. Within are two marble sarcophagi, both bearing the *kalamdan,* or "pen-box", placed on men's tombs only, thus disproving local tradition, which assigns the less elaborate tomb to the Sheikh's principal wife. In the centre is a headstone elaborately carved with inscriptions from the Koran.

A few yards to the E. of the Nadan Mahal is a pleasing little red sandstone pavilion, known as the Sola Khamba, from the sixteen pillars which support the roof; the brackets of the corner pillars are carved to resemble the head of an elephant. The pavilion contains five tombs, two of marble.

The **tomb of Ibrahim Chishti,** the father of Sheikh Abdur Rahim Khan, lies still farther eastward, now open to the Nadan Mahal Road. It is composed of *kankar* blocks, and was originally plastered and pointed. An inscription over the S. door gives the date of the death of Ibrahim Chishti as 1543.

Kanpur (45 m. by rail) may be visited during a stay in Lucknow (for route, see p. 380). If the traveller is going S. he will find much to interest him at **Jaunpur** (p. 373), which can be reached (165 m.) from Lucknow Junction by the Doon express. From Jaunpur the journey can be continued to **Varanasi** (Benares) Cantonment (Route 5) and **Moghulsarai** (p. 127).

ROUTE 19

(*a*) CALCUTTA (*Howrah*) by the North-Eastern Ry. loop-line to **Lakhisarai** and **Mokameh** by Nalhati Junction (for **Azimganj**), **Tinpahar Junction** (for **Rajmahal**), **Sahibganj**, **Bhagalpur** and **Jamalpur** (for **Monghyr**).

(*b*) **Mokameh** by North-Eastern Ry. metre-gauge line to **Tirhut** and **Kanpur** *via* **Gorakhpur**.

(*c*) CALCUTTA (*Sealdah*) by North-Eastern Ry. to **Plassey, Murshidabad** and **Lalgola Ghat.**

(*a*) **Calcutta** by North-Eastern Ry. loop-line to **Lakhisarai** and **Mokameh.**

Howrah (p. 173).

67 m. **Khana** Junction (p. 137). Here the loop-line branches off N. to

88 m. Adjai river.

91 m. **Bolpur** for Santiniketan (Vivabharati) University, founded (1901) by Sir Rabindranath Tagore (d. 1941), the famous national poet and educational pioneer.

137 m. **Nalhati** Junction. Branch to Azimganj City.

27 m. **Azimganj** Junction. The Bandel-Barharwa line on the W. bank of the Bhagirathi passes through here. Opposite Azimaganj City Station on the E. bank (no connection) is Jiaganj (D.B.). Azimganj is an important centre of the Jains. The Bhagirathi is here 700 ft. broad, and rises in the rains 25 ft., when the current runs 7 m. an hour.

188 m. from Calcutta, **Tinpahar** Junction station (R.H.).

A branch line runs N.E. to

7 m. **Rajmahal** station (D.B.K.) in the Santal Parganas. The town stands on the W., or right, bank of the Ganges. Here the visitor can see members of the aboriginal tribes of Santals and Mal Paharias.[1] The Santals supply labour in the coalfields.

Up to 1592 it was known as Agmahal, but when Raja Man Singh of Jaipur, Akbar's Rajput general, returned from the conquest of Orissa in 1592, he made it the seat of his Government, and changed its name to Rajmahal. In 1607 Islam Khan, Governor of Bengal, transferred the seat of Government to Dacca, but it was again brought to Rajmahal by Sultan Shuja in 1639. In 1707 Murshid Kuli Khan transferred the Government to Murshidabad, and Rajmahal fell into decay. In 1863 the Ganges shifted its channel, and Rajmahal was left 3 m. distant from the main stream. The river returned to Rajmahal in 1929.

Just beyond the railway station is the tomb of Miran, the son of Mir Jafir (p. 170), who put Suraj-ud-daula to death, and was killed by lightning in 1760.

N. of the station is the sub-Divisional Officer's Court (formerly the Mughal Governor's house). A little farther on are remains of a building called the Sangi Dalan ("Hall of Stone"). It is 100 ft. long from N. to S., and has three doors of black basalt in the centre. This is said to have been part of the palace of Sultan Shuja, son of Shah Jahan and Governor.

The Maina Tank is ¾ m. due W. of the Cutcherry. At its S. end is a massive brick building, with an Arabic inscription; and 100 yd. to the S. is the Maina Mosque. There is a tomb of a Maina Bibi.

The Hadaf is 4 m. to the N.W. The road at 1½ m. passes a solid brick building on the right hand, called the Tanksal, or Mint, with walls 5½ ft. thick. The Hadaf ruins are about 200 yd. off the road to the left. The entrance to the quadrangle is by the E. gateway, which is much injured. The mosque proper has a façade 200 ft. long, with seven arches, each

[1] Bradley Birt's *The Story of an Indian Upland*, although written nearly 70 years ago, is still very good reading.

22 ft. high. In the centre of the quadrangle is a reservoir, with steps down to the water. The buildings are surrounded by dense jungle, but the actual structures have been cleared.

From Tinpahar station the loop-line continues N. to

206 m. **Sakrigali** Junction, waiting-rooms, railway steamer for Manihari Ghat and Katihar, across the Ganges, on the North-Eastern (metre-gauge) Ry.

211 m. **Sahibganj,** a centre of trade (D.B.). The industries are the collection of *sabai* grass (for paper manufacture), flour mills and oil mills; there are stone quarries near. **Katihar** (530 m.) is the junction for the main line of the old Bengal and North-Western Ry. to Kanpur.

257 m. **Bhagalpur** Junction (D.B.K.) (pop. 172,000 in 1971) (old name Sujanganj), headquarters of a Bihar District, on the S. bank of the Ganges. There is a monument here to Augustus Clevland, who reclaimed the Santals from savagery and robbery.

A ferry connects a branch line to (23 m.) Thana Bihpur across the Ganges. Branch line also due S. (31 m.) to **Mandar Hill,** 700 ft. high. Vishnu is said to have cut off the head of Madhukaitab, a giant, and to have piled this hill over him. For a mile or two round its base old buildings are to be seen; also some stone figures. On the side is a spring, Akashganga (river of the sky), to which the only access is by a wooden ladder about 15 ft. high: on the left of the spring a colossal figure of Madhukaitab is traced on the rock. On an Asoka pillar the name of Magardhwaja Yogi is inscribed.

272 m. **Sultanganj**; famous for a Temple of Gaibinath, which is built on a rock in the middle of the Ganges, and is reached by boat.

282 m. **Jamalpur** Junction (R.) is a railway settlement built for the East Indian Ry. locomotive engineering workshops established here in 1862. They were damaged in the earthquake of 15th January 1934. A new railway colony has been built at Rampur, W. of the railway. Branch line to ($5\frac{1}{2}$ m.)

Monghyr (D.B.K.) (pop. 102,000 in 1971), on a promontory in the river. The Civil Station is inside an old Mughal fort, to which Mir Kasim moved (1762) from Murshidabad in order to be farther from Calcutta. The place was famous for the manufacture of arms and for ebony work. There is a large cigarette factory. Within the fort, towards its N.W. corner, on the edge of the spur, are several picturesque temples.

In the earthquake of January 1934 the town suffered severe loss of life and property, but recovery was rapid.

A ferry connects a branch line to Sahibpur Kamal, on the metre-gauge line of the North-Eastern Ry.; thence E. to Katihar, and W. to Barauni, for Chapra (p. 393).

3 m. to the E., on the hill called Pirpahar, stands a magnificent house, said to have been built by Mir Kasim's Armenian General, Gurghin Khan. A little to the S.E. of this are the sacred hot springs of Sitakund. Cleverly designed silver fishes are manufactured at Kharagpur (D.B.), 20 m. S.W. of Monghyr. Motor service available. This place has beautiful scenery.

254 m. **Lakhisarai** (Kiul Junction) for the main line (p. 127).

275 m. from Calcutta by loop-line, **Mokameh** Junction (D.B.K.) (p. 136). Branch to Mokameh Ghat.

(*b*) From **Mokameh** by the broad-gauge line to Barauni and Samastipur and thence by metre-gauge line of the North-Eastern Ry., to **Tirhut** and Kanpur, *via* **Gorakhpur.**

The broad-gauge line now crosses the Ganges by a new bridge near Mokameh. The Assam Mail uses this bridge and passengers change to the metre-gauge at Barauni Junction.

6 m. **Barauni** Junction. The main metre-gauge line from Kanpur runs E. to **Katihar** (112 m.), crossing the Kosi river (26 m. from Katihar) by a bridge 3172 ft. long. There are

branches to the river opposite Monghyr, Bhagalpur and Sahibganj.

The main line W. runs to Hajipur (54 m.), separated from Sonepur (57 m.) by the Gandak river, boundary of Oudh, and to Chapra (90 m.). **Sonepur** has a Fair in Oct.-Nov. Formerly, there were elephants for sale; and there used to be a large annual gathering here of planters from Tirhut. The fair commemorates a fight between Gajendra (lord of elephants) and a huge crocodile. The platform here is 2415 ft. long. For stations beyond Chapra on this line see p. 393.

A branch line runs from Sonepur to Palezaghat (8 m.), from which a steamer crosses to Mahendrughat for Patna Junction (p. 133).

The main line to Tirhut proceeds from Semaria Ghat to **Samastipur** (D.B.K., 38 m.), from which a loop runs *via* **Darbhanga** Junction (24 m. N.), crossing the Bagmati river at Dhang (80 m.).

Darbhanga (alt. 157 ft.) (pop. 132,000 in 1971) is the residence of the Maharajadhiraja, of Brahmin descent and formerly the leading landlord in this part of India. The title of Raja was granted to the family in 1710 by Ali Vardi Khan, of Maharaja in 1839, and of Maharajadhiraja in 1720. The Anandbagh Palace is a very fine building. The Government Offices are situated at Laheria-Sarai (good D.B.K.), which is 3 m. by rail from Darbhanga Junction. At Rajnagar there is a palace built by the late Maharajadhiraja, but damaged by the earthquake of 1934, with an epicentre to the N.E.

From Dharbhanga Junction a branch line runs 12 m. N.E. to Sakri Junction where it forks, one branch running due N. *via* Madhubani to Jaynagar on the Nepal frontier, and the other due E. *via* Jhanjharpur and Nirmali to the Kosi river.

From Samastipur the railway to Tirhut runs to **Muzaffarpur** (pop. 127,000 in 1971) Junction (D.B.K., 32 m. N.W.), headquarters of the Tirhut Division, and continues 50 m. to Motihari (D.B.), 63 m. to Sagauli, 77 m. to **Bettiah** (D.B.K.). A Capuchin Mission used to work in nearby Nepal (1707-67).

From Muzaffarpur there are buses and taxis to **Vaisali**, 23 m. (Tourist R.H., P.W.D.R.H., Youth Hostel), capital city of a 7th-century B.C. republic. Asoka Pillar: many temples tanks and stupas. Museum, Jain Research Institute. Tourist Office can supply Guide and conducted tours from Muzaffarpur R.S.

There is a road from Muzaffarpur *via* Motihari to Raxaul (for Kathmandu/Katmandu).

6 m. by road from Pusa Road station on the line between Samastipur and Muzaffarpur is **Pusa**, on the Gandak river. An Imperial Agricultural Research Institute (now removed to Delhi), was built on the initiative of Lord Curzon; Mr Phipps, an American gentleman, made a substantial donation towards its cost. The buildings were seriously damaged in 1934, and the Botanical Section now alone remains. The District abounds in old temples and places of historical interest, being identified with the ancient Hindu Kingdom of Mithila mentioned in Hindu mythological works.

From Sagauli a branch of 18 m. runs to Raxaul, the starting-point for **Katmandu** (alt. 4350 ft.), capital of Nepal, which once extended to the Sutlej river.

16 m. N. of Bettiah, at **Lauriya Nandangarh** is a Buddhist stone lat—crowned by a lion—of sandstone, 33 ft. high, with a capital nearly 7 ft. in length. Funeral mounds near this column are said to be the only indisputably Vedic monuments yet identified in India. There is another column at Araraj, 22 m. S.W. of Motihari station. Two other pillars (one of 45 ft.) are lying on the ground, at Rampurwa and at Basarh (Vaisali). All four were set up on the road from Pataliputra (Patna) to Nepal.

Main Line

From Sonepur station the main line goes W. to **Chapra** (D.B.K., old name Saran), 202 m. from Katihar, at the confluence of the Ganges and the Gogra, once an important river-mart, with Dutch and English factories: headquarters of the Saran district.

A branch runs N. to Captainganj Junction. Another branch crosses the Gogra river by the Inchcape bridge, 3819 ft. long, and runs *via* Ghazipur and Varanasi (Benares) Cantonment (Route 5) to Jhusi (near Allahabad).

79 m. from Chapra on this branch line is **Ghazipur** (D.B.K.). A mausoleum commemorates the death here on 5th October 1805 of Marquess Cornwallis, Governor-General. Ghazipur and Patna (p. 133) were the two opium agencies. The Patna agency was closed in 1911 and the cultivation of opium, now forbidden, was for some time continued by contract. From Aunrihar Junction (106 m. from Chapra), also on this line, a branch runs 37 m. N.W. to Jaunpur and another from Ballia *via* Phephna to **Azamgarh** (70 m.) and Shahganj (105 m.).

From Chapra the main line runs N.W. to (71 m.) Bhatni Junction for a branch to Varanasi (Benares) Cantonment, crossing the Gogra river by a bridge 3912 ft. long. Gogra means laughter.

The main line continues to **Gorakhpur** (pop. 230,000 in 1971) (112 m. from Chapra), named after a Hindu saint and damaged by earthquake in 1934. It is the centre for the recruitment of Gurkha soldiers; it has a College, and the headquarters of the North-Eastern Ry. D.B.K. (permission of Chairman, Dist. Bd., required); Inspection Bungalow (permission of Dist. Engr., required). Gorakhpur to Fyzabad, by road, 79 m.; Fyzabad to Gonda, 29 m.

A loop-line runs N. to (40 m.) **Uska Bazar** (whence there is a motor-road to Lumbini in Nepal), and to Gonda (p. 372).

The Tarai, N. of **Uska Bazar** (Basti Dt.), was certainly the locality of the birth of Buddha, and of many of the scenes connected with his life and death. What has been identified beyond all doubt are (1) a stupa raised over part of the relics of Buddha at **Piprâwá**; and (2) the Lumbini Garden, now called the **Rummin Dei** (in Nepal), where Buddha was born. The Lumbini Garden can be reached by train from Varanasi (Benares) or Lucknow to Nowgarh R.S. and thence by road. U.P. Govt. Roadways run bus and taxi services to the border from Nowgarh and Gorakhpur. The journey ends by rickshaw.

In the stupa here was found by Mr Peppé, owner of the estate, in January 1898, a relic-casket inscribed, "This relic shrine of the Divine Buddha is that of the Sákyas", who received one-eighth of the relics and erected a stupa over them near Kapilavastu. At the garden was discovered a lat of King Asoka, split down the middle, with an inscription that "here Buddha Sákyamuni was born". This column had been once surmounted by a horse, and Hiuen Tsang (A.D. 629-645) recorded that he saw at the birthplace a pillar which had been split by lightning, and which bore a horse. The bell-shaped capital of it has also been discovered, and in an adjoining temple a relief of the birth scene of Buddha, in which his mother, Maya-devi, stands erect holding the branch of a sal-tree, and the child stands on the ground at her right, a usual motive. Kapilavastu lay 10 m. to 15 m. W. of this garden, and the site is possibly marked by extensive ruins at Tauliya Kot (in Nepal), 9 m. N.W. of Piprâwá.

34 m. E. of Gorakhpur, is **Kasia** (connected with each of these places by bus and taxi services).

I m. W. of Kasia the extensive ruins of **Kushinagar** (Traveller's Lodge, R.H., Tourist H., I.B.; taxis from Gorakhpur) are traditionally the scene of the death and cremation of Buddha. These comprise six groups; the first consists of an isolated brick stupa some 50 ft. in height on the W. edge of the Ramabhar Tal, bearing the name of Devisthan or Ramabhar Bhawani: the second is a small mound of ruins to the S.W. of this stupa and a short distance to the N.E. of the village of Anrudhwa. The third is the Matha Kunwarka-kot, about a mile W. of the Ramabhar stupa, comprising a temple with a colossal recumbent image of the dying Buddha, a large stupa, several monasteries and other buildings. The fourth is a colossal statue of the seated Buddha, called Matha Kunwar, about 400 yd. S.W. from the kot, while the fifth consists of the remains of an enclosing wall and the last of a number of small earthen mounds and barrows, locally called Bhimawat, to the N. and E. of the kot.

Excavations show that the stupa and temple were the nucleus of a group of Buddhist buildings belonging to widely different periods, the later on the ruins of earlier monuments. Coins and inscribed objects prove that buildings may be dated to the Kushana and early Gupta periods. In the 5th or 6th century a portion of the buildings was destroyed in a fire, possibly due to an invasion of the Huns. Numerous clay seals inscribed "Convent of the Great Decease" have been found. The place is visited by Buddhist pilgrims.

9 m. from Gorakhpur the main line crosses the Rapti river and proceeds to Gonda (207 m. from Chapra). At 239 m. it crosses the Gogra river by the Elgin bridge, 3695 ft. long, and runs to 283 m., Lucknow (Aishbagh Junction) and, 328 m., Kanpur.

(*c*) **Calcutta** by North-Eastern Ry. to **Plassey** and **Murshidabad.**

Sealdah station (p. 184).

21 m. **Naihati** Junction for Bandel Junction on the East Indian Rly. (Route 2) across the Jubilee Bridge. At Mulajore is a Power Station of the Calcutta Electric Supply Corporation.

46 m. **Ranaghat,** junction for the main line to Siliguri and Darjeeling (Route 20). Branch to Santipur (12 m.), whence N.G. railway and Nabadwip Ghat to Krishnagar City.

Santipur was once famous for its fine muslins.

The Murshidabad branch runs to

62 m. **Krishnagar.** Headquarters of the Nadia Dt., and residence of the Maharaja Bahadur of Nadia.

Nabadwip (Nadia), by the n.g. railway from Krishnagar to Nabadwip Ghat, 8 m., or by the Bandel-Barharwa loop-line from Howrah, is a celebrated seat of Sanskrit learning, and is also a great place of pilgrimage, being known as the "Benares of Bengal". It was the birthplace of Chaitanya (1486-1527), the Hindu religious reformer.

93 m. from Calcutta, **Plassey** station. There is a good bungalow 3 m. from the railway station, close to the monuments on the battlefield; but travellers must make their own arrangements for meals and servants. There are no conveyances available.

The bungalow is in the charge of the Executive Engineer, Burdwan Division, Chinsura, Bengal; travellers should ascertain from him whether the bungalow will be vacant.

Plassey (Mira or Palasi, from the Palás-tree, *Butea frondosa*), is famous for Clive's victory in 1757. The position of the British forces is marked by a mound near the river-bank and the old monument, and has now been more fully indicated on the ground at the instance of Lord Curzon, who erected a second memorial.

The British force advanced from Chandernagore (p. 188) on 13th June, first to Katwa, and then across the Bhagirathi, between which and the Jalinghi Spill of the Ganges Plassey was situated, and advanced against Suraj-ud-daula's army at that place on the night of 22nd June. The battle opened the next day, 23rd, at 8 a.m., the French in the service of the Nawab facing the left of the British line, which touched the river, and the huge Indian forces of the Nawab forming a semicircle on the right front and right flank. About midday a heavy downpour of rain occurred, but the British guns, the powder having been protected, overpowered the advance made by the enemy a little later. The Indian forces then fell back to the entrenched camp; the Nawab was counselled by traitors to flee, and Mir Jafar separated himself.

Clive confirmed an order by Major Kilpatrick to advance, drove the French from their position, and afterwards took the entrenched camp, the enemy then offering but little resistance. The British casualties amounted to 28 killed and 50 wounded out of 3000—650 only of these being European—and the Nawab's force lost about 200. Captain Eyre Coote, who had been a strong supporter of the counsel to fight, which Clive ultimately adopted, distinguished himself greatly.[1]

Landmarks mentioned in accounts such as the Mango Tope, in which the British were entrenched, have mostly disappeared.

116 m. **Berhampore Court,** 7 m. below Murshidabad (D.B.). The Krishnanath College here is affiliated to the Calcutta University. As the factory house at Kasimbazar, where Warren Hastings resided, had been destroyed by Suraj-ud-daula, Berhampore was chosen as a site for a Cantonment in 1765.

In the cemetery here are buried George Thomas, the Irish sailor who became Raja of Hansi (p. 363), and the infant son of Mrs Sherwood, whose *Little Henry and His Bearer* was at one time a nursery classic.

118 m. **Kasimbazar.** This was the British trading-station previous to 1756. The English were settled here as far back as 1658, and Job Charnock, the founder of Calcutta (p. 170), was "Chief" in 1681. Of the factory nothing is visible except a mound containing a portion of the fortifications. In the old Residency cemetery, opposite the site of the factory, are buried the first wife of Warren Hastings and her daughter. She was the widow of Captain John Buchanan, a victim of the Black Hole, and died in 1759, while Hastings was Resident (1758-61). There is an old Dutch Cemetery lower down the river. Feringipur, the French factory, has been washed away. At Kasimbazar is the residence of the descendants of Hastings' famous dewan, Kantu Babu.

122 m. **Murshidabad** (pop. 16,000 m. 1971) (also on National Highway from Calcutta), once residence of the Nawab Nazims of Bengal, was called after the great Nawab Murshid Kuli Khan,[1] the original name being Maksudabad, whence the Muxadabad of old records. It was a prosperous place because it was on the line of trade from the interior of India to the European settlements on the Hooghly, down the Bhagirathi river.

Murshidabad was famous for carved ivory, embroideries, etc. But now these trades are confined to a few families of carvers at Jiaganj and Khagra. Fine silks are still made here.

The Bera (Raft) Festival is still celebrated here, in honour of Khwaja Khizr (the prophet Elias) on the night of the last Thursday of the Bengali month of Bhadra.

The old Palace of the Nawabs, which with the surrounding buildings, enclosed by a wall, goes by the name of the Nizamat Kila, is situated on the river-bank about the centre of the town, and is in the Italian style, somewhat resembling Government House at Calcutta. It was built in 1837, the architect being General Duncan Macleod (1780-1856) of the Bengal Engineers. It contains an imposing circular Darbar-room, a

[1] Clive took his title of Baron of Plassey in the Irish Peerage from the estate of Ballykilty in County Clare, which he purchased on his return from India, and which he renamed Plassey, after "the place where we gained our great victory in India, to which I owe all my good fortune". (Letter of 13th February 1761, to the Duke of Newcastle.)

[1] The well-known Subadars and Nawab Nazims of Bengal were Murshid Kuli Khan (known also as Jafir Khan, a converted Brahmin), died 1725; Shuja Khan, died 1728; Alivardi Khan, died 1756; Suraj-ud-daula; Mir Jafir and Mir Kasim. The famous Jain family of Murshidabad which bore the title of Jagat Seth, or World Trader, and played a prominent part in the affairs of India in the 18th century, resided at Mahimapur, 2 m. N. of Murshidabad.

Banqueting-room 290 ft. long, with a picture of the Burial of Sir John Moore, by Marshall, at the W. end, and many other handsome apartments. The Armoury is well worthy of a visit. In the Library are some very rare MSS.

In the same enclosure is the Imambara, built in 1847.

Just outside the city is the Katra, containing the tomb of Murshid Kuli Khan. It was constructed on the model of the Great Mosque at Mecca, with two minarets 70 ft. high, but is now in ruins.

Near this, and 60 yd. from the road, is the Great Gun, the sister gun to one at Dacca. It is 17½ ft. long, with a girth of 5 ft. at the breech and a calibre of 6 in. The gun was left on its gun-carriage and a *pipal* tree growing from a seedling beneath it now supports the gun entirely. The inscription is in Persian, with the date 1637.

2 m. S. of the city is the Moti Jhil, or "Pearl Lake". The Muradbagh Palace, on the bank of the lake, was seized by Siraj-ud-daula in 1756. Here Clive held the first English *puniya*, or collection of revenue, in 1765, sitting side by side with the Nawab Nazim, Najim-ud-daula. It was the home of Warren Hastings in 1761 and later on of Sir John Shore, who admired its "cooing doves, whistling blackbirds and purling streams". The pleasure garden is still known as the Company Bagh; but the only buildings which survive are the mosque of Shahamat Jang, the nephew and son-in-law of Alivardi Khan, and the ruins of the Baradari built by Mir Jafir after Plassey. In the Mubarak Manzil, the old Court House of the East India Company, a little to the E. of the Moti Jhil, there was kept the black stone throne of the Nawab Nazim upon which Clive installed Mir Jafir after the battle of Plassey. The throne has been removed to the Victoria Memorial Hall at Calcutta (p. 178) and its place taken by a plain stone slab. The lake contains a good many crocodiles.

The Khushbagh, or "Garden of Happiness", the old cemetery of the Nawabs, is opposite to the Moti Jhil on the right bank of the river. It consists of three walled enclosures. The entrance to the outer one, planted with flowers and shady trees, is from the E., close to where some ruined ghats stretch down to the deserted bed of the Bhagirathi. In the central enclosure are the tombs of the "good Nawab", Alivardi Khan, and his nephew and son-in-law Siraj-ud-daula. They are almost level with the ground, and are covered with embroideries. The third enclosure contains a tank and Musafir Khana (Travellers' House, not available). The Hira (diamond) Jhil, where the Mansurganj Palace stood, is near the Roshanbagh, also on the right bank of the river, opposite to the present palace.

The Nizamat College, or Nawab's Madrasa, which was formerly kept exclusively for the relatives of the Nawab (who live free of charge in a special boarding-house), has now been amalgamated with the Nawab's High School under the name of the "Nawab Bahadur's Institution".

The Cemetery of Jafraganj, about 1 m. to the N. of the palace, contains the graves of the later Nawabs Nazim who were appointed by the English. Opposite the gate is a handsome mosque.

The Jafraganj Deorhi was the residence of Mir Jafir before he became Nawab. In the women's quarters was held the last secret conference with Watts, the chief of the English factory, before the advance on Plassey. Siraj-ud-daula was killed here by Mir Jafir's son Miran.

The Murshidabad District is noted for its silk industry. The villagers rear the silkworm at home, and sell the cocoons to the spinners, who export the skeins. Silk cloth and handkerchiefs are woven here on hand-looms.

From Murshidabad the railway runs on to

145 m. **Lalgola Ghat,** on the Ganges (occasional steamer service to Raj-

mahal, p. 390). Railway steamer connection with Godagari Ghat across the river in Bangladesh, from which an M.G. line runs to Amnura Junction (14 m.), where it links up with the Eastern Bengal Ry. to Rajshahi and Ishurdi Junction.

ROUTE 20

CALCUTTA (*Sealdah*) by the North-Eastern Ry. to

(1) **New Jalpaiguri** via Malda (for Gaur and Pandua) and Kumedpur (for Katihar and Purnea).

(2) DARJEELING and SIKKIM

(3) **Gauhati** and **Shillong** *via* the **Duars.**

The quickest way to travel to Darjeeling and Shillong is by air (Bagdogra and Gauhati airports): but a new railway route in lieu of that *via* Ishurdi and Parbatipur, has been opened which skirts round Bangladesh.

NOTE: For some time, foreign travellers have needed special permits (details from Tourist Bureau) to visit Darjeeling, Kalimpong, Assam, Manipur, Nagaland and Kaziranga Wild Life Sanctuary. At least 2 weeks' notice should be allowed.

(1) From Calcutta to Jalpaiguri.

5 m. **Dumdum**: junction for Khulna.

63 m. **Burdwan** (p. 137).

95 m. **Bolpur**: station of Shanti Niketan, Sir Rabindranath Tagore's famous outdoor university (p. 390).

142 m. **Nalhati** Junction (p. 390).

187 m. **Barharwa Junction** A b.g. line goes from here to **Farakka** where a road-cum-rail bridge has been built on the Ganges. The line goes to **New Bongaigaon Junction** in Assam *via* **Malda Town, Old Malda, Kumedpur** and **New Jalpaiguri** which is the junction for the n.g. line to Darjeeling. From Kumedpur a branch b.g. line goes to **Katihar,** junction for the main Oudh-Tirhut line to Kanpur. Direct trains run from Calcutta and Delhi to New Jalpaiguri and New Bongaigaon.

Old Malda[1] lies at the confluence of the Kalindri with the Mahananda. It probably rose to prosperity as the port of the Muslim capital of **Pandua**. During the 18th century it was the seat of thriving cotton and silk manufactures, and the French and Dutch had factories here. The English factory was originally established in 1656 at Old Malda and was transferred in 1771 to English Bazar (Angrezabad). It was fortified with bastions, and the modern court-house and all the public buildings are within its walls.

English Bazar (now known as Malda Town) is on the right bank of the Mahananda, 4 m. below Old Malda. The local authorities, if advised from Tourist Bureau Calcutta, can arrange road and river transport and I.B. accommodation (*not* luxurious). From English Bazar to the N. of Gaur is about 4 m.; and to the Adina Mosque at Pandua about 13 m. The visit to either place will occupy a whole day.

Gaur and Pandua, successive capitals of Bengal, are in ruins, having been built of brick. They show the Bengali roof. The sites have been brought under the plough, and the dense jungles which sheltered tigers and leopards no longer exist.

Gaur was the metropolis of Bengal under its Hindu Kings. Its most ancient name was Lakhnauti, a corruption of Lakshmanawati. But the name of Gaur also is of great antiquity, and is found in the *Gauriya Brahmana*. Its known history begins with its conquest, about A.D. 1200, by Bakhtiyar Khilji, whose successors ruled for more than three centuries. A son of the Emperor Altamsh was Governor here, and the eldest son of Balban, Nasir-ud-din Bugra, became King of Bengal (1283-1325) and refused the throne of Delhi. He was succeeded by two sons and a grandson, and then, about 1338, Fakhr-ud-din rebelled and founded a dynasty of independent Afghan kings, made Pandua his capital, and robbed Gaur of building material. This accounts for the number of sculptured Hindu stones amongst the ruins of Pandua. Pandua was in its turn deserted about 1420.

Gaur, again the capital, was called Jannatabad ("Terrestrial Paradise"), a name which occurs in the *Ain-i-Akbari*. Humayan took it in 1537, but it was sacked by Sher Shah Sur in the same year and was absorbed into Akbar's empire in 1576. The city was entirely ruined by an outbreak of the plague in 1575. Contemporary narratives describe the place, in its prime, as extremely populous, containing the residence of the court and numerous seats of learning, and enjoying an immense trade.

The dimensions of the city proper, within the great continuous embankment, are 7½ m. from N. to S., and 1 m. to 2 m. broad. The W. side was washed by the Ganges, which flowed where the channel of the Little Bhagirathi now is. The E. side was protected by the Mahananda and by swamps. On the S. the Mahananda joined the Ganges, and left little space for an enemy to encamp. On the N. a fortification 6 m. long extends in an irregular curve from the old channel of the Bhagirathi at Sonatala to near the Mahananda at Bholahat. This rampart, in ruins, is 100 ft. wide at base.

In front lay the **Sagar Dighi**, 1600 yd. long by 800 yd. broad, dating from 1126. On the bank is the tomb of Makhdum Shaikh Akhi Siraj-ud-din and a small mosque, and S. of these is a ghat called Sa'adullapur, leading down to the sacred river. S. of this rampart was the N. suburb, between which and the city was another strong rampart and ditch. Towards the Mahananda the city rampart was double, and in most parts there have been two immense ditches, and in places three.

1 m. inside the city to the S., on the Baghirathi, was the Citadel, 1 m.

[1] Intending visitors to Malda and Gaur should make advance arrangements in Calcutta.

long from N. to S., and from 600 yd. to 800 yd. broad. The brick wall was very strong, with many flanking angles, and round bastions at the corner.

On the N. is the Dakhil Gate, built of small red bricks, and adorned with embossed bricks, which can still be seen on the towers at the four corners. The arch of the gateway is about 30 ft. high, and forms a corridor 112 ft. long.

In the S.E. corner was the palace, surrounded by a brick wall 66 ft. high and 8 ft. thick, with an ornamented cornice—hence called the Báis Gaji, "Twenty-two Yards Wall".

At the S.E. corner of the citadel are two mosques; the smaller Kădăm Răsul,[1] built by Nasrat Shah (1518-1532) in 937 A.H. (A.D. 1530), is kept in repair by the Indian Government. In connection with this mosque is preserved a stone, bearing what is reputed to be a footprint of the Prophet Muhammad. Near the Kădăm Răsul are the domed tomb of Fateh Khan and S.E. gateway of the citadel.

Half a mile N. outside the E. wall is a five-storeyed tower, known as Pir Asa Minar, which had a chamber with four windows at the top, to which access was gained by a winding stair. The correct name of this tower is Firoz Shah Minar, Pir Asa being a local corruption. It was probably erected by Husain Shah (1493-1519) in commemoration of his victories in Assam. Sir W. W. Hunter says: "For two-thirds of the height it is a polygon of twelve sides; above that circular until it attains the height of 84 ft. The door is at some distance from the present level of the ground: and altogether it looks more like an Irish or Pathan round tower than a *minar*." There is, or was, an inscription on this monument which ascribed its erection to Firoz Shah (1490).

Half a mile N.W. again of this, and above the N.E. corner of the citadel, is the Golden Mosque, or Baradari. It measures 168 ft. from N. to S., 76 ft. from E. to W., and is 20 ft. high. The entrance is by an arched gateway of stone 26 ft. in height and 6 ft. in breadth. The mosque originally consisted of four separate colonnades, arched and roofed over, and covered by handsome domes, in all 44 in number. Only one remains. Six minarets or columns of brown stone faced with black marble adorn the building; bands of hornblende about 12 in. in breadth embrace the column from the base to the capital, and are adorned with a profusion of flower work carved in marble. There was a raised platform at the N.W. corner of the mosque, probably for the use of ladies of the Court. The whole appearance of this building is strikingly grand, exhibiting the taste and munificence of the Prince who erected it—Nasrat Shah, 1526.

Half a mile E. of the Kadam Rasul, on the side of the main road, is the Tantipara Mosque, remarkable for the embossed brickwork on the front. It was probably built in 1475.

Half a mile S. again is the Lattan Mosque, also called the Painted Mosque, from the bricks being enamelled in green, yellow, blue and white, and arranged in bands.

Half a mile above it is the Piasbari Tank, with a small R.H. A tradition states that the water of this tank was formerly very impure and injurious to health, and that condemned prisoners were allowed only this water to drink.

In the S. wall of the city is a fine central gate, called the Kotwali Darwaza, which now marks the border with Bangladesh. S. from it, over the border, stretched an immense suburb called Firozpur. In it, 2 m. from the S. wall, is the Lesser Golden Mosque, the "gem of Gaur". It dates from about 1600. The carved stone panels in the front wall display very fine workmanship.

Pandua is 7 m. N.E. from Old Malda and begins at 11 m. from English Bazar. It was called by the Muslims Firozabad. The first inde-

[1] The only detailed account of the ruins at Gaur and Pandua is contained in Ravenshaw's *Gaur*.

pendent King of Bengal, Fakhr-ud-din, made it his capital (p. 398). A road paved with brick, from 12 ft. to 15 ft. wide, passes through Pandua, and almost all the monuments are on the borders of it. Near the middle is a bridge the abutments of which have evidently been brought from the Hindu temples at Gaur, as figures of men and animals are sculptured on them.

On approaching the ruins from the S., the first objects that attract attention are the 17th-century shrines of Makhdum Shah Jalal and Kutb 'Alam Shah, called the Chhe Hazári and Báis Hazári, or 6000 and 22,000, from the area allotted for their endowment. These are known locally as Chhoti Dargah and Bari Dargah. To the N. stands the small Golden Mosque. An Arabic inscription says that it was built by Makhdum Shaikh, son of Muhammad Al-Khalidi, in 1585. N. of this is a handsome building, called Eklakhi, as having cost a lakh. It is 80 ft. square, covered by one dome, and contains the remains of Ghias-ud-din (1389-1396), his wife, and his daughter-in-law.

2 m. beyond it is the tomb of Sikandar, father of Ghias-ud-din. It forms part of the great mosque, called the Adina Masjid, built about 1360 by Sikandar Shah, and shows traces of having been constructed out of Hindu and even Buddhistic remains, a "Buddhist railing", round the W. front. The Kibla (central hall) and Mimbar (pulpit) are gems of stone carving. It extends 500 ft. from N. to S., and 300 ft. from E. to W. This space is sub-divided by transverse brick walls and stone pillars into 127 squares, each covered by a dome. On the outside are many small windows, highly decorated with carved tiles disposed in arches. The mosque proper is composed of a central apartment and two wings. The first is 62 ft. high in the centre from the floor to the middle of the dome. To the N. of it is a ruined gallery known as the Takht Badshahi. The only other ruin of note in Pandua is the Satáisgarh, said to have been the King's Palace. It is situated opposite the Adina Mosque, in the midst of dense jungle. The remains of numerous cells, believed to be baths, may still be noticed.

The Katihar-Malda line now terminates at Singhabad (69 m.). Another M.G. line runs N. from Katihar to Purnea (17 m.) and Forbesganj (59 m.), terminating at Jogbani (67 m.) on the Nepal frontier.

From Jogbani there is a motorable road to Bhiratnagar in Eastern Nepal, near which a depôt for the British Brigade of Gurkhas has been set up.

Purnea (alt. 121 ft.) produces more than two-thirds of the jute crop in Bihar. It was invaded by Gurkhas in 1809, and badly damaged in the 1934 earthquake. The first flight over Mount Everest (29,028 ft.) was made from Purnea on 3rd April 1933.

(2) Darjeeling and Sikkim from Katihar or Jalpaiguri

From Katihar Junction the North-Eastern Ry. crosses the Mahananda river and then forks, one branch, which used to connect with Dinajpur and Parbatipur, now dead-ending at Radhikapur, just short of the Bangla Desh frontier. The other branch continues N. to

310 m. Kishanganj.

430 m. **Bagdogra**. Nearest airport to Darjeeling from Calcutta. Bus service and tourist cars from Bagdogra to Darjeeling 3½ hours. Bus service also to Siliguri.

443 m. **Siliguri** Junction (R., D.B.), by road to Gielkhola, 30 m., whence 11 m. E. *via* Tista Bridge (1940, 550 ft. long) to **Kalimpong** (3933 ft.), where are the St Andrew's Homes, established 1900 by Dr J. A. Graham for destitute children of European descent. The scenery along the route is magnificent. Kalimpong was formerly a market for wool brought on mules from Tibet. Buses, taxis and Land-Rovers to Kalimpong, from Siliguri and Bagdogra airport. There is an Arts and Crafts Centre, and an

Information Centre in Rishi Road above the Central Bank.

A motorable road runs from the Tista Bridge to (25 m.) **Gangtok,** the capital of Sikkim. Foreign visitors need permits to enter Sikkimese territory, obtainable from the Ministry of Home Affairs, New Delhi (6 photos, 2 application forms; advisable to quote an Indian referee; apply 3 months ahead).

Another road from the Coronation Tista Bridge runs to Bagrakot in the Duars.

A branch line runs 25 m. S.E. from Siliguri to Jalpaiguri (25 m.) and on to Haldibari (38 m.). This was formerly the main through route from Calcutta to Darjeeling, but is now a dead-end line.

Jalpaiguri (R., D.B.K., alt. 289 ft.). The Bengal Duars were ceded by Bhutan in 1863. The Duars Ry. now part of the North-Eastern Ry., runs through the district. There is a ferry over the Tista at Barnes Ghat near Jalpaiguri. There are many tea gardens in the district, and several reserved forests in which rhino, tiger and elephants are to be found.

Passengers for Kurseong and Darjeeling transfer at Siliguri to the Darjeeling-Himalayan Ry. (1879-81) on a gauge of 2 ft. The distance is 51 m., and the time occupied 5¾ hours. The maximum gradient is 1 in 20. There are two trains a day pulled by ancient steam engines. Motor-cars (quicker and cheaper) for the journey by road are available. A military road (1839) was improved in 1861.

Travellers are strongly advised to have extra warm clothing at hand, as the change of temperature is very great. Glare-glasses or goggles should be used against the dust, especially on the front seats of the open carriages, from which the best views are obtained. Only hand luggage can be taken into the carriages.

Siliguri was the base of the military expedition of 1904 into Tibet, Lhasa being 359 m. distant by the most direct route.

After crossing the Mahanadi river, at **Sukna** station, 7 m. from Siliguri, the cars begin to ascend. The turns are very sharp, and at each a fresh landscape is opened out. The sides of the mountain are clothed with lofty trees and masses of jungle, with tree-ferns at higher altitudes. At about 15 m. a spur projects from the mountain, and the line runs on the edge of a precipice of 1000 ft. The line makes a complete loop at Gayabari, above.

19½ m. **Tindharia** (R.), where railway workshops are situated, 2822 ft. above sea-level. At 25½ m. the line passes over the Pagla Jhora (mad water-course). The hillside at this point is continually sinking.

32 m. from Siliguri and 350 m. from Calcutta, **Kurseong** station (R., D.B.); there are tea-gardens here, and also several schools and colleges. Kurseong is 4864 ft. above sea-level. In damp weather leeches are numerous. The old Punkabari road crosses the line here, zigzags up the hill for nearly 2000 ft., and runs to Jor Bungalow, nearly parallel to the railway.

At 46 m. is Jor Bungalow, a collection of shops and huts on the narrow ridge or saddle which joins the Darjeeling spur to the Senchal Hill. Here the road to Kalimpong branches off; there are also roads to the Darjeeling Golf-course, near Tiger Hill, to the Darjeeling Waterworks, and to the Katapahar and Jalapahar Cantonments. At **Ghoom** station (47 m.) the main road to the Nepal frontier starts, and nearby the Auckland road to Darjeeling joins the railway. Ghoom station is the highest point on the railway, 7407 ft. About ½ m. from it, just above the road to the Nepal frontier, is the Buddhist monastery of the Yellow Sect, constructed by Lama Sherab Gyantso, near which is the interesting Buddhist burning-ghat. From Ghoom the train runs downhill to Darjeeling.

51 m. from Siliguri, **DARJEELING*** (place or town of the thunderbolt) (pop. 42,600 in 1971). Coolies

and jeep taxis to transfer passengers and luggage. There are good hotels. Foreigners need a permit to visit Darjeeling. Apply (allow 2 days) to Foreigners' Regional Registration Office in Calcutta. The nearest airport is Bagdogra (p. 400).

A ropeway for goods only runs to Biban Bari in the Little Rangit Valley, 4300 ft. below, with one span of 4680 ft. A second ropeway for passengers links North point near St Joseph's College to Barnesberg Station (5½ m.).

The beauty of its situation, upon a ridge (about 7146 ft. high) above the bed of the Great Rangit river, a tributary of the Tista, the mountain-side scattered over with villas and bungalows, and the colossal background of Himalayan giants towering above it, together with its moderate temperature, tend to make Darjeeling a most agreeable residence, and have rendered it the most important sanatorium of Bengal. Under British rule it was the summer headquarters of the Bengal Government.

From Darjeeling the highest **Mountain Peaks** in the world can be seen. Of these the loftiest is Mount Everest, 29,028 ft., visible from Tiger Hill, 8514 ft. (a 6-m. ride from Darjeeling) or from Jalapahar, though the distance is at least 120 m. Other peaks seen are Kinchinjanga (28,146 ft. high and 45 m. distant); to the W. of it, Kabru (24,002 ft.) and Jano (25,294 ft.); to the E. of it, Pandim, like a horn (22,010 ft.), with the "King's Minister", Narsingh (19,130 ft.), in front of it, and only 35 m. distant; and farther E. again the fine snowy peak of Siniolchu (22,620 ft.). Much of the surface of the highest peaks is too sheer for snow to lie.

The **Mountain Scenery**, in October to December and March to May, when unobscured, is unrivalled in grandeur, but often clouds veil the highest peaks for days together and there is no certainty of a view of Kinchinjanga. The eye looks across a vast chasm to the line of perpetual snow, about 17,000 ft. high, on the side of the stupendous Kinchinjanga. There is one special feature in the summit of Kinchinjanga, a wall of granite which appears to divide the summit into two portions. The effect is much more striking than if it were one great mass of snow. The grandeur of this scene is heightened by the colouring given to it by the rising and setting sun or by the moon.

The **District of Darjeeling** is divided into two portions—the N. is from 4000 ft. to 9000 ft. above the sea-level; the S., or Morang, consists of the foothills of the Himalayas and the plains to the District of Rangpur. Mountains which rise to between 12,000 ft. and 13,000 ft. divide it from Nepal. It was ceded by deed with the Raja of Sikkim in 1835. When Dr Campbell took charge, in 1839, there were only twenty families in the whole district; he remained Superintendent for twenty-two years, and established a convalescent depot at **Jalapahar,** the Military Cantonment S. of Darjeeling. Darjeeling is now a major centre for Tibetan resettlement: Tibetan refugees form a large proportion of the population. There is a Self Help centre, where their handicrafts can be purchased. Many small Tibetan restaurants have sprung up between the Clock Tower and the G.P.O.

About ½ m. beyond the Church are several schools and the Raj Bhawan (formerly Government House), beyond which lies a new park, The Shrubbery. Near the Secretariat is a Museum (1902) containing collections of butterflies, moths, wasps and ants. At Birch Hill is the Himalayan Mountaineering Institute, giving field training courses to Indians, run by Tenzing Norgay, the Everest hero, with a museum. There is a Zoological Park with Siberian tigers and Himalayan fauna.

The principal **Bazar** is in the centre of the town; on Saturdays and Sundays it is thronged by picturesque folk from all parts—Lepchas, Limbus, Bhutias, Tibetans, Nepalese, Paharis, Bengalis, Kashmiris and Marwaris.

The top of the ridge above the church known as **Observatory Hill,** is called by the Buddhists Dor-je-ling-gang, or the hill of the thunderbolt town. It was once crowned by a monastery, constructed by Lama Dor-je Legdenla. Buddhists and others offer prayers, ring bells, beat tom-toms, and make offerings. In the centre of the shrine are carved stones of Hindu-Buddhist deities, surrounded by bamboo poles, from which flutter paper of different colours, and cloth prayer-flags printed with the horses of wind and prayers for luck. Some way below the ridge on the E. side is an interesting Buddhist *Chorten*, or chaitya, and a Buddhist monastery of the Red Sect of a distinctly Tibetan type in the picturesque village of the Bhutia Basti. It is worthy of a visit, not only on account of the temple, but also to see the hill people who inhabit the small village. The Birch Hill Park for walks, picnics and views is a little over a mile from the railway station. The Victoria Falls are near Rosebank, the residence of the Maharajadhiraja of Burdwan.

The Botanical Gardens are immediately below the Eden Sanatorium, on its W. side. Besides trees, there are collections of ferns and orchids.

The chief industry of the Darjeeling District is the cultivation and manufacture of Tea (see also p. 401). The first tea-garden was opened in 1850.

There is little game in the neighbourhood of Darjeeling, but there is fishing in Teesta and Rangit Rivers. For the botanist, and the lover of the picturesque, there are endless excursions. There are 600 varieties of butterflies.

Darjeeling is lit from a hydro-electric power station at Sidrapong, 3000 ft. below on the W. side of the spur. The distance is about 5 m., and a tea-garden is passed through on the way.

At 1000 ft. below Darjeeling is a fine wooded spur called **Lebong** (on a motorable road), where English fruit-trees flourish and the tea-plant also succeeds admirably: the Race-Course, managed by the Gymkhana Club, is the highest in the world. Below is the village of Ging, surrounded by slopes cultivated principally with tea, also with rice, maize and millet. Above the Ging village there is a Buddhist monastery of the Zok-chen-pa Red Sect, a branch of the great Pami-ongchi monastery of Sikkim.

Excursions from Darjeeling

There are now motorable roads to many neighbouring beauty-spots and even Sikkim can be reached by jeep. Details can be obtained from the India Tourist Office, Darjeeling.

(1) With the aid of a pony, an interesting expedition may be made W. by **Tonglu** (Hunter's Farm) to **Phalluk La,** 49 m. in the direction of snows. Coolies, laden, should do 12 m. a day in the hills; the load is from 40 lb. to 60 lb.

The distances along the Singalila Ridge, boundary of Nepal, are to:

Jorpokri (7400 ft.), 13 m.
Tonglu (10,073 ft.), 10 m.
Sandakphu (11,929 ft.), 14 m.
Phalluk La (11,816 ft.), 12½ m.

The views are magnificent, especially from Sandakphu. There is a good D.B. at each of these places.

(2) Another excursion is to the **Suspension Bridge** over the Great **Rangit river** at Majhitar, to the N., and 6000 ft. below, which leads into Sikkim, the distance by the road being 11 m. The zones of vegetation are clearly marked, first by the oak, chestnut and magnolia, which grow from 10,000 ft. to 7000 ft.; secondly, below 6500 ft., by the *Alsophila gigantea*, or tree-fern (to be seen from the Himalayas to the Malayan Peninsula, in Java and Sri Lanka); thirdly, by the Calamus and Plectocomia palms (6500 ft. is the upper limit of palms in Sikkim); fourthly, by the wild plantain, which in a lower elevation is replaced by a larger kind.

At 6 m. from Darjeeling are the

Badamtam Tea-garden and a R.H.; at 2 m. below again, an excellent view may be had of the Suspension Bridge.

At 10 m. N.W. from Darjeeling is the junction of the **Rangit** with the **Rongnye.** The Rangit's chalky stream runs through a dense forest. The Rongnye, clear, almost black, comes tearing down from the top of Senchal, 7000 ft. above. Its roar is heard and its course is visible, but its channel is so deep that the stream itself is nowhere seen.

Farther down is the junction of the **Rangit** with the **Tista,** which is sea-green and muddy, while the Great Rangit is dark green and very clear. The Teesta is much the broader, deeper, and more rapid. Bathing is dangerous.

(3) **Senchal,** 8163 ft., is clearly seen from Jalapahar, and is about 6 m. S.E. It used to be a depot for European troops, but was abandoned on account of its climate and the effect on the troops. The water for Darjeeling is taken in pipes from the Senchal springs. From Tiger Hill above Senchal, **Mount Everest** may be seen. Senchal is comparatively easy of access (motorable road), and from Jalapahar the path along the ridge of the mountains may be seen. This path abounds in rare and beautiful plants, and traverses magnificent forests of oak, magnolia and rhododendron.

Nearly thirty varieties of fern may be gathered on this excursion in the autumn. Grasses are very rare in these woods, except the dwarf bamboo.

(4) **Kalimpong** (32 m.) can be reached by a pleasant ride through the forest from Darjeeling, by way of (14 m.) Lopchu, (4½ m.) Pashok, and (3 m.) Tista Bridge, from which point the remainder of the journey to (10½ m.) Kalimpong can be made by car (p. 400).

Sikkim

Sikkim, seized by the Gurkhas in 1810, was restored by the British in 1814 and merged into India in 1975.

Visitors to Sikkim are required to carry a pass (see p. 401). Applications must be made to the Ministry of Home Affairs, New Delhi. Extensions can be obtained from the Police Station in Gangtok.

The Capital of the State of Sikkim (Sukhim or "New-house"; in Tibetan, Den-jong, or "the rice country"), is **Gangtok** (5800 ft.), which has undergone rapid modernization since 1975 and lacks the weathered charm of Darjeeling. To the north is Raj Bhavan, the former Residency with a lovely garden and view. Above this is the new Tourist Lodge and nearby Enchen monastery. Some distance south along the ridge and much lower is the Namgyal Institute of Tibetology built in the traditional style, surrounded by an orchid sanctuary and beautiful woods.

There are, in Sikkim, only 528 villages and 38,194 occupied houses. The high mountains, as viewed from Darjeeling, have been described above (p. 402), but the lower hills also contain much beautiful scenery, and possess features of special value for all who are interested in the pursuit of botanical studies, butterflies, and some branches of zoology (reptiles, birds, mammals). "Sikkim[1] . . . is estimated to contain about 4000 species of flowering plants under 160 natural orders; also 250 ferns and their allies, of which eight are tree-ferns". It has also 660 recorded species of orchids, 20 of palms, and about 23 of bamboos. The flora and the trees vary according to the three zones—the subtropical from 700 ft. to 4000 ft. elevation, the temperate from 4000 ft. to 11,500 ft., the Alpine from 11,500 ft. to 18,000 ft. Butterflies are extremely abundant, distributed among about 600 species; the moths are estimated at 7000 species.

The 44 monasteries present objects of interest to students of religions. Lamaism, or Tibetan Buddhism (a mixture of orthodox Buddhism with a preponderating amount of mythology, mysticism and magic), is the State religion of Sikkim, professed by

[1] *Imperial Gazetteer*, 1, 166.

a large number of the inhabitants. The monks number about 1200. The principal monasteries are—(1) Sangachoiling; (2) Pamayangtse; (3) Tashiding; (4) Phodang, at Tumlong; (5) Rhumtek, 8 m. from Gangtok. Many *chortens* (cenotaphs in memory of Buddha or canonised saints) are met with, as well as *mendongs*, or low prayer-walls, faced with blocks bearing the mystic sentence *om mani padme hum* and other prayers, in addition to rough paintings of the deities.

The abnormal rainfall of Sikkim, ranging from 30 in. annually in the dry upper valleys, but reaching to 180 in. in some other parts, renders travelling arduous and disagreeable during the monsoon months. Travellers to the snow-mountains should choose May or October.

The main route into Sikkim is *via* Siliguri and the road alongside the course of the Tista river to Rongphu and up the course of the Rongnye river to Gangtok.

From Darjeeling, Sikkim can be entered by four routes—(*a*) to Phalluk La (already mentioned) and on to Chuwa Phangjang, thence northwards to Yampung, Dzongri and the snowline, or eastwards to Dentam and the Sangachoiling, Pamayangtse and Tashiding monasteries; (*b*) by the suspension bridge over the Rumman river, N. of Darjeeling, to Chakung, N. of and near to that river, and to the same monasteries; (*c*) by the suspension bridge at Majhitar, over the Great Rangit, to Namchi, Temi, Gangtok, and on to Tumlong; (*d*) by Pashoke and the Tista suspension bridge to Kalimpong, Rikyisum, Pedong, and Rhenak, where the road bifurcates, one leading N. to Pakyong and Gangtok, the other N.E. to Chumbi, in Tibet, *via* Sedonchen, Lingtam and the Jelep La Pass.

From Gangtok the track is continued northwards to Tung and Tsunthang, where it divides into the Lachen and Lachung valleys. The path up the Lachen leads to Thanggu, Gyaogong, and the Kongra La and Sebu La passes into Tibet; by the Lachung to the Ghora-la and Donkya-la.

No journey should be undertaken without previous communication with the Deputy Commissioner of Darjeeling. The bungalows are available only to persons provided with passes, issued by the Deputy-Commissioner of Darjeeling; or for certain bungalows, by the Executive Engineer, P.W.D., Darjeeling.

A separate pass must be obtained for each occupant, or for a party, for each bungalow, whether going or returning.

Pemayangtse Monastery in W. Sikkim can also be visited on the same permit issued for Gangtok.

Routes into Tibet

Since the Chinese occupation of Tibet permission to cross the frontier is no longer obtainable, but in case the frontier should be reopened, the route is indicated below. The best months for the journey are between May and September.

Kalimpong (p. 400) makes the best starting-point. The track goes N.E. past Pedong and Rhenak, to Rongli, Sedonchen and Gnatong (12,000 ft.). Between Gnatong and Champithang (in Tibet) the Jelep La is crossed (14,400 ft.); Chumbi is 11 m. from Champithang and Phari Jong (14,300 ft.) is 28 m. farther on. The route thence to Gyantse (13,200 ft., D.B.), once the seat of the Indian Trade Agent, crosses the Tang-la (15,200 ft.) and 42 m. beyond, the Kharola (16,500 ft.) and then the Khamba-la (16,800 ft.).

(3) Siliguri to Gauhati and Shillong.

To circumvent the intervening block of what is now Bangladesh, the Indian Government linked up Siliguri with Assam *via* the Duars. The route to Assam from Calcutta is given at the beginning of (1) on page 397, as far as Siliguri (New Jalpaiguri).

Thereafter it proceeds as below:

Siliguri, linked *via* **Bagrakote** to

30 m. **Mal** Junction (branch lines to Patgram and Metelli). Hasimara station is the closest to Phunsoling, entry point to Bhutan (Inner Line Permit and Bhutanese visa required for entry).

95 m. **Raj Bhat Khawa** Junction (branch line to Buxa Road and Jainti).

102 m. **Alipur Duars** Junction: on line to Cooch-Behar and Gitaldaha. From Alipur Duars a connection has been made with the Assam Valley line at Fakiragram.

145 m. **Fakiragram**: junction with line from Lalmanirhat *via* Golakganj and Gitaldaha. From Golakganj there is a branch line to **Dhubri** on the Brahmaputra, where there is an airport giving connection with Calcutta.

The scenery just above Dhubri is beautiful. On the right are the Garo Hills, and on the left, if the atmosphere is clear, the grand range of the Himalayas towers in the background, with the wooded Bhutan Hills in the middle distance: the snowy range shows to special advantage at sunrise. At **Goalpara** wild hill tribesmen may often be seen, who have come down from the mountains to trade.

New Bongaigaon: the broad gauge line from Calcutta and Delhi now terminates at New Bongaigaon and passengers must change there for metre-gauge coaches for Assam.

179 m. **Bijni**: a road junction.

192 m. **Sorbhog**: the overspill from Mymensingh district has settled in this locality.

196 m. **Barpeta Road.**

227 m. **Nalbari.**

237 m. **Rangiya**: junction for line to Balipara and Tezpur. The line crosses Brahmaputra R. on a road and rail bridge 3 m. below.

265 m. **Gauhati,** on the air-line from Calcutta, and thence 67 m. by car to

332 m. **Shillong,** the capital of Meghalaya (see p. 407).

ROUTE 21

ASSAM

Note—Special passes are necessary for visiting Assam and neighbouring States. They are obtainable (allow 2 days) from Assam House, Russell St., Calcutta. They normally cover specific routes and fixed durations of stay. The capital of Assam is now at Dispur near Gauhati.

Assam is surrounded by mountainous ranges on three sides—on the N. are the Himalayas, shutting off the table-lands of Bhutan and Tibet; on the N.E. is a series of hills which form a barrier between the Upper Brahmaputra Valley and the more or less independent Mongolian tribes who live W. of the boundary of China; on the E. and S.E. lie the hills which march with those forming the limits of the Republic of Burma and the State of Tripura; on the W. and S. it is cut off from the rest of India by Bangladesh on to which debouch the two valleys of the Brahmaputra and the Surma.

There is now an autonomous Hill State—**Meghalaya**—inside Assam, which includes much of the Khasi-Jaintia Hills. Meghalaya, along with **Manipur, Tripura,** and the Territories of **Arunachal Pradesh** (forming North East Frontier Administration) and **Mizoram** share a Governor and a High Court with Assam.

The valleys are separated by the Khasia Hills and the Garo range, which projects westward and causes a bend in the Brahmaputra. The physical features of the Province are full of variety. The valley of the Brahmaputra, otherwise known as the Assam valley, on the N. is an alluvial plain about 450 m. in length and 50 m. in average breadth, so that one never loses sight of the hills on either side.

There are four Wild Life Sanctuaries in Assam, and two Reserves. The Kaziranga Sanctuary (p. 409) is 130 m. from Gauhati, 180 m. from Shillong.

During the past century Assam has suffered from several very severe earthquakes, which have seriously changed the topography of the country.

The Tea Industry

Assam is the principal centre of the Indian tea industry, with 1100 gardens. China tea seed was introduced into India about 1848 by Mr Fortune, who was sent to China by the East India Company to collect seeds and plants. In 1823 indigenous plants had been discovered by Robert Bruce, Commander of a gunboat in the 1824 Burma War, and an agent of the last Ahom King. The tea was first sold in Mincing Lane on 10th January 1839.

The most convenient starting-point for describing the Assam routes is Gauhati, as it is the arrival station for most visitors to Assam, whether by air[1] from Calcutta, or by the roundabout railway route through the Duars, described on p. 405. Gauhati is also connected by road with the rest of India. The road runs from Barhi on the Grand Trunk Road to Bakhtiyarpur (p. 136), Mokameh, Barauni, Purnea, Dalkolha where the road from Calcutta joins it, Siliguri and Gauhati where the Assam Trunk Road between Goalpara and Dibrugarh has a junction (p. 409). There are buses and taxis between Gauhati and Shillong.

Air communications are of increasing importance and there are good local roads. There is an office of the Eastern India A.A. in Lamb Road, Gauhati.

Gauhati (Happy Lodge H., D.B.) (pop. 122,000 in 1971); once the capital of Koch Kings, then of the Ahom (Shan) Kings (1681-1826), now the headquarters of Kamrup District. It possesses a University (1948) and a Museum (1917). It is situated on the S. bank of the Brahmaputra, which here resembles a lake with wooded shores. In the middle of the river are the island and temple of Umananda, and on the N. bank, on a projecting ridge, is another temple, on the top of a hill approached by winding flights of steps. The celebrated temple of Kamakhya, on the Nilachal Hill, 2 m. below the town, is the resort of pilgrims from all parts of India. The magnificent views repay a visit. 110 m. from Gauhati and 25 m. from Barpeta Road R.S. is the **Manas** Wild Life Sanctuary in Kamrup District near the Bhutan frontier, famous for many varieties of animal and bird life. Tourist Information Office Gauhati should be consulted for facilities.

The road from Gauhati to Dibrugarh passes the new **Tourist Lodge** at **Kohara** (Kaziranga Wild Life Sanctuary—rhinoceros, elephants, tigers—one of the finest in India. See p. 409).

There is a daily motor service by a good road (63 m.) from Gauhati S. to Shillong. Motor owners should consult the Assam *Motor Manual for Shillong and Neighbourhood* (obtainable from A.A. of Eastern India, Calcutta).

The cars leave the railway stations at Pandu and Gauhati. Cars for luggage and servants accompany the first-class passenger cars, which make the 67 m. from Pandu to Shillong in 4 hours—only hand baggage allowed in passenger cars. The road from Gauhati runs S. through tropical forest, rolling grassy downs, and great pine-woods.

Shillong, (pop. 14,000 in 1971) now the capital of Meghalaya, and a military centre, has an altitude of 4900 ft. There are several good hotels, which help to make the place a most pleasant summer resort, the temperature at the height of the hot weather rarely reaching 80° F. The entire town was wrecked by an earthquake

[1] Tezpur, Jorhat, Mohanbari, Silchar, Imphal, and Agartala are also airports linked up by services from Calcutta.

in 1897; but it has been rebuilt amongst the pine-woods that clothe the hill. The surrounding country is not unlike the lowlands of Scotland; there is every facility for riding and driving. There is an excellent golf-course, and also a race-course on which there are races every Saturday.

The Khasis, who inhabit the Khasi and Jaintia Hills, speak a language of which the nearest affinities are as far distant as Cambodia and Annam; they are remarkable also from the fact that descent of property is traced through the female line, as on the Malabar coast (p. 552). Their dancing, which takes place at certain festivals, especially during the month of June, is seen at its best at the village of Nong Krem, about 13 m. from Shillong, and accessible by car.

Shillong is connected by motor roads with Sylhet (86 m.) and **Cherrapunji** (36 m. S., 4455 ft., D.B.K.), famous for the highest average annual rainfall in the world—426 in. In 1861 the extraordinary amount of 905 in., was recorded, of which 366 in. fell in July alone. A cemetery includes many graves of soldiers who committed suicide in the old barracks. A steep bridle-path leads in 10 m. to Therria, in the Surma Valley, and so to Sylhet. Motor services run from Shillong to Cherrapunji. As Sylhet is now in Bangladesh, there is a Customs barrier on this road.

From Pandughat (Gauhati) to Manipur and Dibrugarh by rail.

From Pandu the North-Eastern Ry. runs past Gauhati to (62 m.) **Chaparmukh** Junction, whence there is a line to (17 m.) **Nowgong** (D.B.), 74 m. from Gauhati. The line continues to Silghat (D.B.), opposite Tezpur, on the Brahmaputra, 103 m. from Gauhati. The method of transit for heavy packages is usually by steamer from Calcutta to Silghat, thence by road (32 m.) or train to Nowgong.

The Assam Trunk Road (Gauhati-Dibrugarh) is motorable all the year round. Roads generally are metalled and bridged.

From Chaparmukh the line proceeds to (118 m. from Gauhati) **Lumding** Junction, where it connects with the hill section from Badarpur Junction (p. 409), and so with Chittagong, the port of Bangladesh. From Lumding Junction the line runs E. to (33 m.) **Manipur Road** (Dimapur) station. There are carved monolithic remains in the old Kachari fort at Dimapur.

Manipur

From Manipur Road (Dimapur) the main road to Imphal, Manipur (134 m.) runs S. not far from the (abandoned) fort of **Samaguting** and **Kohima** (46 m.; alt. 4700 ft.; the limit of Japanese invasion). At Kohima there is a fine War Cemetery round the old D.C.'s bungalow where the Royal West Kents made their gallant stand. The road is metalled throughout, and motor lorries run between Manipur Road and Imphal. A lorry can be hired. Motor owners can make the trip comfortably in one day, providing there are no obstacles due to rain. The road ascends to 6700 ft., and then descends to the valley, the last 15 m. being level. The distance to Imphal is 134 m., and there are twelve well-furnished R.Hs. (no servants) at convenient distances. At Manipur Road there are a D.B. and small bazar and at Kohima (46 m.) supplies are also obtainable, but these are the only two places where anything can be procured.

Imphal (pop. 100,000 in 1971) (R.H., D.B.), the capital of the State of **Manipur** (daily air services from Calcutta), lies in a lovely valley, which is some 60 m. long and 30 m. wide, at a height of 2600 ft. above sea-level. The history begins in 1714, although tradition goes back for centuries before then. Burmese invasions were frequent, but the Treaty of Yandabo (1826) brought the State into India. It covers an area of approximately 8456 sq. m. It shares a Governor and a High Court with Assam and a group of other States and Territories (p. 406).

The scenery in the valley and on the roads leading to it is most beautiful. The valley is surrounded by hills, which rise from 2500 ft. to 5000 ft. above it. The whole drainage of the valley escapes at the southern end through a gorge in the hills only a few hundred yards wide. There are several large lakes, on which in the cold weather excellent duck shooting is obtainable. In the swamps round these lakes a species of Thamin is to be found, but only from March to May, when the swamps are at their driest.

The people of Manipur are very fond of games. Hockey and polo are played everywhere, and the religious dances of the Nagas, Kukis, etc., are most interesting spectacles. Sixty-oar boat-races used to be rowed on the palace moat.

For entry permits to Nagaland or Manipur foreigners must apply to the Ministry of Home Affairs, New Delhi, allowing at least 8 weeks for a reply. Application can also be made to Indian diplomatic missions abroad.

From Imphal a bridle-road, with R.Hs. (unfurnished and temporary) at every 13 m. or 14 m., leads *via* Bishenpur to (125 m.) Silchar and a motor road to Tamu and Sittaung on the River Chindwin (102 m.). A pass from the Police or local Political Officer is necessary, however, owing to the present unrest amongst the Nagas, for crossing what is termed the Inner Line, the limits of which can be ascertained locally.

From Manipur Road the line runs N. to Furkating, Jorhat, Titabar and Mariani (from Titabar and Mariani branches run to Jorhat and to Kokilamukh on the Brahmaputra), now the main ghat for Upper Assam. 60 m. from Jorhat, which is connected to Calcutta by a daily air service, is the **Kaziranga Game Sanctuary**. There are comfortable Tourist Bungalows at Kohora just outside the sanctuary, and R.Hs. at Arimora to the W. of it. [Apply to Forest Officer, Jorhat, or to a Tourist Agency for transport and accommodation.] There is a Tourist Information Officer on the spot who can arrange travel in the sanctuary by jeep or elephant (not expensive). The animals can be watched from towers inside the Sanctuary. The Great Indian Rhinoceros (one-horn), wild buffalo, bear, tiger, leopard and many species of deer are to be seen. There is also a remarkable variety of water birds.

325 m. from Pandu is **Tinsukia** (D.B.K.), whence one branch, dividing at Makum, runs N. to Talap (D.B.) and to Saikhoa ghat, on the River Luhit, through one of the best tea-garden areas. Another branch runs S. through Digboi to Margherita (D.B.), called after the Queen of Italy, where the main Assam coalfield is situated. 5 m. farther E. the line ends at Ledo, the starting-point of the Burma Road which is the nearest station for **Tikak**; where coal is dug out of the hillside. At **Digboi** are the oilfields and refineries of the Assam Oil Company.

From Tinsukia another branch (27 m.) connects with

Dibrugarh (D.B.K.), headquarters of the Lakhimpur District, with many tea estates in the country around.

From Dibrugarh the return to Calcutta can be made by air *via* the nearby Mohanbari airport, or by through coaches as far as Lucknow on the meter gauge line. Before 1947 there was an alternative route by taking train to Tinsukia and thence *via* Lumding and the hill section of the railway to Badarpur, Akhaura and Chandpur; but now the Bangladesh frontier intervenes between Badarpur and Karimganj, and the journey has become inconvenient because of the Customs barrier. The hill section referred to above is 115 m. long. Opened in 1904, it runs S. through the North Cachar Hills, which have a normal annual rainfall of 150 in. at the lower end of the line, and are subject to periodical earthquakes. In 1915 abandonment of the line, seriously damaged by slips, was

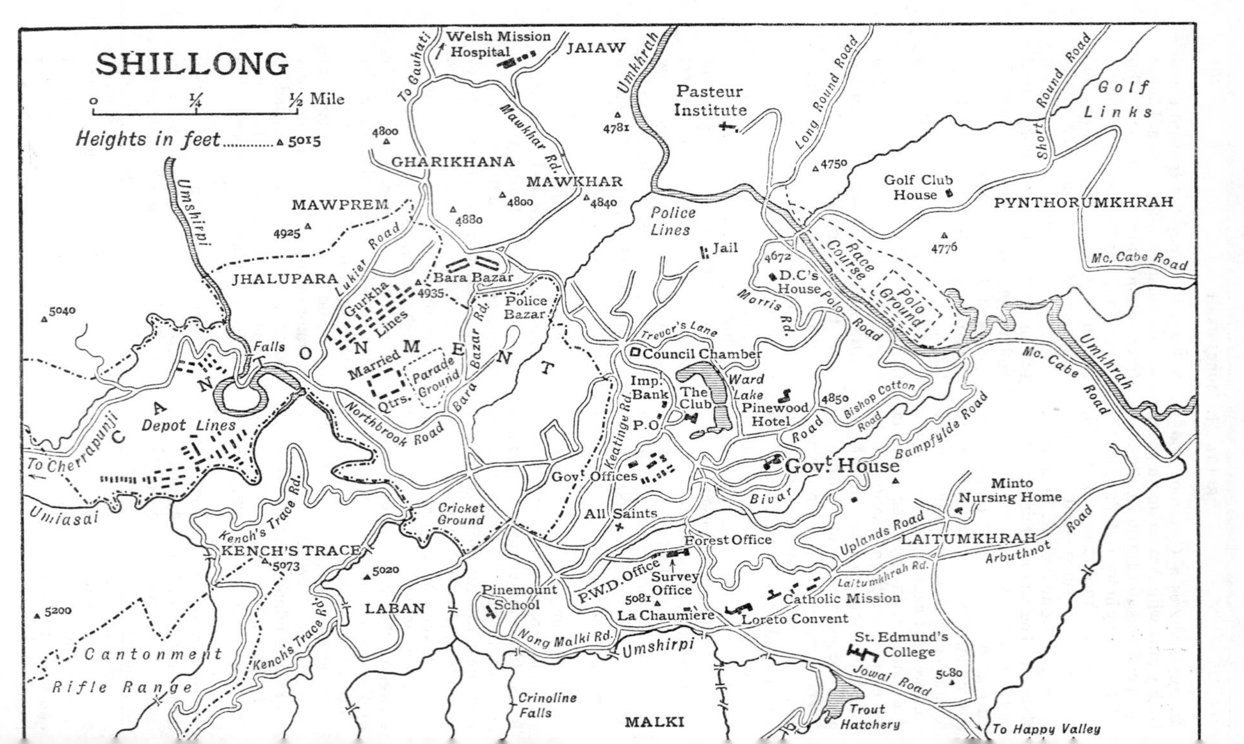

SHILLONG
0 1/4 1/2 Mile
Heights in feet............ 5015
Welsh Mission Hospital
To Gauhati
JAIAW
Umkhrah
Pasteur Institute
Long Round Road
Short Round Road
Golf Links
4800
GHARIKHANA
Mawkhar Rd.
4781
MAWKHAR
4750
Golf Club House
PYNTHORUMKHRAH
Umshirpi
MAWPREM
4800
4840
4880
4925
Police Lines
Jail
4776
Mc. Cabe Road
Lukier Road
JHALUPARA
Bara Bazar
4935
Gurkha Lines
4672
D.C.'s House
Race Course
Polo Ground
5040
Police Bazar
Marris Rd.
Polo Road
Falls
C A N T O N M E N T
Married Qtrs.
Parade Ground
Bara Bazar Rd.
Trevor's Lane
Council Chamber
Ward Lake
Mc. Cabe Road
Umkhrah
Depot Lines
Northbrook Road
Imp. Bank
The Club
Pinewood Hotel
4850
Bishop Cotton Road
P.O.
Keatinge Rd
Road
Bampfylde Road
To Cherrapunji
Gov.t Offices
Gov.t House
Bivar
Minto Nursing Home
Umiasai
Kench's Trace Rd.
Cricket Ground
All Saints
KENCH'S TRACE
5073
5020
Forest Office
Uplands Road
LAITUMKHRAH
Arbuthnot Road
P.W.D. Office
Survey Office
Laitumkhrah Rd.
Pinemount School
5081
Catholic Mission
5200
LABAN
La Chaumière
Loreto Convent
Nong Malki Rd.
Umshirpi
St. Edmund's College
Cantonment
Kench's Trace Rd.
Jowai Road
5080
Rifle Range
Crinoline Falls
MALKI
Trout Hatchery
To Happy Valley

considered. At Lumding the elevation is 456 ft., but the railway rises in two places to about 1850 ft., with descents to three rivers. The most important of these is the Dyong (62 m. from Lumding) crossed by a viaduct 109 ft. high, and here there is a loop round a spur of the Barial Range at Haflong.

Haflong, headquarters of the N. Cachar Hills subdivision is 3½ m. from **Lower Haflong** station; the elevation is 2300 ft.: there is an hotel, golf-course and lake.

From Haflong the former through-route of the old Bengal-Assam Ry. continues S., and after crossing the Barak river reaches Badarpur, the junction for the line between Silchar and Karimganj.

The railway line also continues 30 m. due S. to Hailakandi and Lala Ghat.

Silchar (D.B.K.), headquarters of the **Cachar** district, which was annexed by the British in 1830 and now forms part of Assam. There is a motor road to Shillong (86 m.) (interrupted, however, by a few miles of Bangladesh with resultant Customs formalities when driving through) and an airport with regular services to Calcutta. Excluding the hill subdivision, Cachar, along with part of the neighbouring Sylhet district, now in Bangladesh, constitutes the Surma Valley tea-growing area.

154 m. by road from Silchar is **Agartala,** capital of Tripura State (airport served from Calcutta). Foreigners need a permit to enter. There are Palaces and Temples and a Museum in the capital: the surrounding scenery is spectacular. An Information Centre assists tourists to see places of interest.

ROUTE 22

CALCUTTA to MADRAS by **Balasore, Cuttack, Bhubaneswar** (visit to **Udayagiri Caves**), PURI, (and the **Black Pagoda**), **Ganjam, Vizianagram, Waltair** for **Vishakhapatnam, Bezwada** and **Nellore.**

Distance 1032 m.; time occupied by mail train, 36 hours. Most travellers from Calcutta to Madras now use the quick and convenient air service (3½ hours): but the railway, like the motorists' National Highway, passes through many places of interest to tourists.

Howrah.—Calcutta (see p. 173).

5 m. **Santragachi** Junction for the Shalimar wagon ferry to the Docks.

20 m. **Ulubaria** (see p. 191), the former landing-place for Midnapur (by palanquin).

26 m. the **Damodar** river.

35 m. **Kola Ghat** (R.). Here the railway crosses the Rupnarain river, a large tidal river flowing into the Hooghly, near its junction with which is the famous James and Mary Shoal (p. 191).

Ghatal, an important trade centre, lies to the N. of the railway line. During the rains there is a daily steamer service from Calcutta; otherwise steamers proceed up to Ranichak, whence the journey is made by boats. Chief industries are the weaving of cotton and tussore silk cloths, the manufacture of bell-metal utensils, and of earthen pots.

72 m. **Kharagpur** (R., D.B.; pop. 161,000 in 1971) is the junction for the line to Nagpur (see Route 7). The main workshops of the Eastern Ry. are here. The railway settlement is self-contained and carefully laid out. There are High Schools, Girls' School and Technical Schools. In the Museum are Neolithic implements and copper-plate grants.

From Kharagpur there is also a branch, crossing the Cossye river to

(8 m.) **Midnapore** (D.B. ¾ m.), an old station of the East India Company, the revenue having been assigned by the Nawab of Bengal in 1760. This branch runs N.W. through Bankura to (105 m.) Adra junction between Sini and Asansol (p. 136). The road crosses by the Burge Bridge.

Cyclones and floods often cause damage during the monsoon.

Contai.—36 m. by road from Contai Road Railway Station (94 m.) The S.E. of the district is a maritime tract lying along the Bay of Bengal, submerged by a tidal wave in November 1942.

Kaukhali, or Cowcolly.—A village on the sea-coast 3 m. S.W. of Khajuri. A lighthouse was built here in 1810.

The District is full of Sal jungle, in which black bear and leopards are to be found. In winter snipe and duck can be shot.

118 m. the railway crosses the Subarnarekha river: there is also a road ferry.

133 m. **Rupsa** Junction; N.G. railway to Baripada and Talband (71 m.) in the former Mayurbhanj State, where iron ore is obtained. The Mayurbhanj Museum contains neolithic implements and copper plate grants. Another (1929) is at Khiching, the old capital, with temples.

138 m. a flood-opening 1785 ft. long.

144 m. **Balasore** (R., D.B. ½ m., furnished). Sea fish are sent to the Calcutta market. Mahseer may be caught in the Burabalang river. The Orissa Trunk Road runs through the place, and there are roads to Mayurbhanj and Nilgiri (unbridged).

The place, of which the correct name is Baleswar, was once of great commercial importance, and the Dutch, Danes, English and French had factories here. Pipli (Philip's City), in the District, is supposed to be the first spot at which, in 1634, the English East India Company established a factory in Bengal. It was a Portuguese stronghold and slave market. The Balasore factory was founded in 1642, in accordance with a grant issued by the Delhi Emperor. There are two old Dutch tombs, dated 1683, built like three-sided pyramids, about 20 ft. high, in a small enclosure near the town. The Dutch and Danish settlements were ceded by treaty in 1846. The Danish Settlement was in an area called Dinadardinga, on the Burabalang river.

There is a temple at Remina (6 m.) where pilgrims to Puri congregate. The god (Khirchora Gopinath), an incarnation of Krishna, is supposed to have settled here 800 years ago, but the temple is only about 100 years old, and the sculpture is crude.

183 m. **Bhadrak** (D.B.). From here the port Chandbali (D.B.) lies 31 m. S.E. by road; regular steamer service to and from Calcutta (Outram Ghat).

198 m. the Baitarani river is crossed. There is a road-bridge. The river in Hindu ideas is the first gate to Jagannath, and an off-shoot of the Ganges.

210 m. Jajpur Road (D.B.K.) for Jajpur, 18 m. E. (D.B.). The road crosses the Burah river; motor-bus service.

Jajpur,[1] (pop. 34,000 in 1971) capital of Orissa from about A.D. 500-950, was founded by Jajati Kesari (474-526), who celebrates the horse sacrifice at the Dasaswamedh Ghat on the Baitarani river. Here is the Navi Gaya (navel of a monster, Gaya Sur), where Hindu pilgrims offer rice cakes in expiation of the sins of their ancestors. The chief object is a pillar 32 ft. high, square, and composed of large plain blocks of stone. The shaft and capital are 26 ft. 7 in. high, and appear to be a monolith. The capital is carved to imitate lotus blossoms, and adorned below with lions' heads, from whose mouths depend strings of roses or beads. The capital once was crowned with a figure of the Garuda, or eagle-vehicle of Vishnu, said to have been hurled down by a Hindu renegade,

[1] There is an excellent little handbook of Cuttack, Jajpur, Bhubaneswar, Udayagiri, Puri, and Kanarak, by Mr Brown, formerly Judge of Cuttack.

Kala Pahad, in 1568; it is now in the temple of Narsingh, 1 m. S. of the temple of Jagannath at Puri. The finest temple is that of Trilochan, the Three-Eyed; others are dedicated to Akhandaleswar and Agneswar. Jajpur is also called Biraja Khetra, from the temple of Biraja (Shiva's wife). On the Binjharpur Road is a well-built ancient bridge. In the compound of the Subdivisional Magistrate are three monolithic statues of Indrani on her elephant. Varahi with the boar, and Chamundi represented as the Goddess of Famine; and seven other statues, each 6 ft. high, have been placed in a temple. Near the P.W.D. Bungalow is also the mosque of Nawab Abu Nasir Khan, built in 1681.

There is a bungalow at **Vyassorovar** (2 m. from Jajpur Road station). In a tank here King Duryodhan hid himself after defeat in the Kurukshetra battle. From this place there is a metalled road (not bridged throughout) *via* Keonjhar, Chaibasa (Singhbhum), Chakradharpur and Ranchi for motoring to Patna, the capital of the State of Bihar (p. 133).

The Nalatigiri hills contain Buddhist caves and inscriptions in Pali, and magnificent images of Buddha, dating A.D. 700-800. Motor-bus from Jagatpur Junction to Mahanga, 4 m. from the hill. P.W.D. R.H. on the Gobeeri river at the foot. A P.W.D. Bungalow is available at 2 m. from the hills.

217 m. near **Jenapur** is the Brahmani river, with a bridge 4640 ft. long. The scenery along the banks of this river and of the Mahanadi is beautiful, and if the visitor has a car, and time to spare, a motor tour *via* Cuttack, Talcher, Pal Lahara, Bonaigarh, Sambhalpur, Rampur, Baud, Nayagarh, and so back to Cuttack, is well worth doing, as this is an area of great natural beauty and is not over-populated. Some of the wilder aboriginal tribes live in this vicinity.

250 m. the Berupa river is crossed.

From 252 m. **Jagatpur** Junction a branch runs W. to Talcher (66 m.) and Angul is 14 m. W. again by motorbus from Meramendali, the previous station.

252 m. the Mahanadi river is crossed by a bridge 6912 ft. long.

254 m. **Cuttack*** (pop. 194,000 in 1971; R., D.B.K.) is situated at the apex of the delta of the Mahanadi river, which rises in the Raipur district of the Central Provinces, and has a length of 529 m. and a width of 7000 ft. above the narrow gorge of Naraj, 7 m. W. of the town of Cuttack, where it divides into two streams and encircles the city on the N. and E., and on the S. by its branch, called the Khatjuri. The river during the rains pours down a prodigious flood, and an important stone embankment has been erected on the spit of land on which the city stands.

Cuttack was the headquarters of the **Orissa** Government,[1] before the construction of the new capital at Bhubaneswar. The Secretariat and Legislative Council Chamber are at Chandawar. It was founded (p. 417) by Nripati (A.D. 920-935) of the Kesari, or Lion, dynasty. Its position as the key of the Orissa hill territory and the centre of the network of the Orissa canals gives it commercial importance. It is famed for its exquisitely delicate filigree work in gold and silver, as well as for Orissa *saris* and fabrics.

There are also a Circuit House and a Museum. The Ravenshaw College with imposing new buildings is affiliated to Patna University: there are also a Medical School and the Orissa School of Engineering. The Talcher coalfield at Ningundi is served by a railway from Jagatpur Junction, 2 m. N. of Cuttack. At Talcher the late Raja constructed a large walled-in sanctuary for wild animals.

The **Fort** (1 m. N.W.) is in ruins, and all that remains of it now is a fine gateway. It was built either by Ananga Bhim Deb (1189-1223) or Mukund Deb (1560-1568), last of the Ganga dynasty. The fort was taken by the British in 1803 from the

[1] Bus and Taxis from Bhubaneswar.

Bhonsle Raja of Nagpur. In the public gardens on the Taldanda Canal are a carved arch and other stones.

Near Cuttack are important weirs for regulating the flow of the rivers. Two of these, the Birupa and Mahanadi, may be seen in quitting the place. A road a little to the N. of the Taldanda Canal leads to the Jobra Ghat, where are the great P.W.D. workshops and the Mahanadi Weir, which is 6400 ft. long and 12½ ft. high. It was begun in 1863 and completed in 1869-70. The Birupa river leaves the Mahanadi on its right bank, and the weir there is 1980 ft. long and 9 ft. high. Of the four canals which form the Orissa Irrigation System, two take off from the Birupa Weir, and one with its branch from the Mahanadi Weir.

Kendrapara (D.B.), 38 m. E. of Cuttack, is connected by road 32 m. to Jagatpur railway station (motor-bus), and by motor-launch service on the canal to Cuttack. A place of pilgrimage for Hindus where Baldeb Jee, an incarnation of Vishnu, who killed the monster Kendra, is much revered. It is visited by up-country pilgrims, being known as Tulasi Khetra. There are four D.Bs. on the way.

Banki is situated at a distance of 28 m. to the W. of Cuttack. Two D.Bs. are on the way and a P.W.D. Bungalow is at Banki itself. It is an important centre of the Co-operative Credit movement in the Province. There is a temple of Charchi Kai, an incarnation of Durga, wife of Shiva. It is possible to motor from Cuttack to Banki at most seasons of the year, but the Khatjuri river has to be crossed.

256 m. the Khatjuri river bridge.

258 m. the Kuakhi river bridge.

About 6 m. N.W. of **Bhubaneswar**, 272 m. from Calcutta (see below p. 416), are the **Udayagiri Caves** which should be visited. Between 4 m. and 5 m. S.W. of Bhubaneswar is the Asoka rock at Dhauli (14 m., p. 419) near the Orissa Trunk Road S. of Chanka. From there one can drive to the Khandagiri R.H., where a couple of hours could be spent in examining the 63 caves, and then proceed to Bhubaneswar to visit the temples (4 hours).

The Udayagiri (Sunrise) Hill[1] is 110 ft. high, and the caves are at various levels. They date back to the Mauryan period. The first reached is the Chhota-Hathi Cave, from which a path to the right (E.) leads round to the Rani ka Naur and Ganesh Gumpha caves, and winds upward and backwards to below the Hathi Gumpha, where it is joined by the path which runs up steeply to the left from the Chhota-Hathi Cave past the Jaya Vijaya and Manchapuri caves.

The Chhota-Hathi has carvings on pilasters near the door, along the top of which runs a line of well-sculptured foliage with an elephant issuing from trees at the end of it.

The Rani ka Naur, or Queen's Palace (traditionally wife of Lalit Indru Kesari), faces E., and consists of two rows of cells, one above the other, shaded by pillared verandas, supporting the rock, with a courtyard, 49 ft. by 43 ft., cut out of the hillside; much has fallen.

The upper storey, which stands back, has eight entrances with sloping jambs, as at Barabar. At the N. end are two dwarapals, representing men in armour, with buskins and greaves, cut out of the solid rock in alto-relievo; these are probably figures of the Yavana warriors who conquered Orissa. At either end is a rock lion. The back wall of the veranda has an extensive series of tableaux, difficult to make out. First on the left are men carrying fruit, a group of elephants, and soldiers armed with swords—this is probably a scene from Ceylon. Then comes a scene, repeated at the Ganesh Gumpha (*below*), of a combat over a woman—and then one of the winged deer presenting itself to the King. The last scene which can be made out represents a love episode.

The lower storey also has eight low entrances from a colonnaded veranda

[1] 6 m. from Bhubaneswar, Taxis and Tourist cars.

44 ft. long, having a raised seat, or berm, along its whole inner line. It opened S. into an oblong chamber and N. into three rooms. Here also there is an extensive frieze; four fragments admit of description. The first represents a house, and a female figure looks out of each of the three doors, and one from the balcony, which is protected by a Buddhist rail. A similar rail runs in front of the lower storey, with a large tree by its side. In the second fragment a saint or priest holds a piece of cloth in his left hand and extends the right as in the act of blessing; one servant holds an umbrella, and another carries a sword. Next a devotee on his knees, and beyond two kneeling women bring offerings, one dusting the feet of a boy, who has one hand on her head. In the third fragment is a saddle-horse with three attendants, and the holy man with an umbrella held over him, and two attendants with swords. In the fourth fragment there is a group of six women, three carrying pitchers on their heads, and one kneeling and offering her pitcher to a figure, which is lost. On the right wing are scenes of a man and woman making offerings, and of a woman dancing to the accompaniment of four musicians.

The Ganesh Gumpha is almost due N. of the Rani ka Naur Cave, and much higher in the hill. It has only one storey, and consists of two compartments with a veranda in front. There are three pillars in the front of the veranda, square and massive, and two others have fallen. The pillars have brackets, with female figures carved on them. The flight of steps leading to the veranda has a crouching elephant on either side, each holding a lotus in his trunk. The veranda wall is ornamented with a series of eight tableaux in high relief. This frieze and that in the Rani ka Naur Cave represent the same story, but in this cave the figures are more classical and better drawn. The scenes include an escape on elephant back, dismounting from the elephant, and resting in the forest. The Buddhist trisula (trident) and shield are carved on this cave.

The Jaya Vijaya Cave, a double-storeyed one, has a frieze with three compartments, the base being formed of a line of Buddhist rails. In the central compartment is a Bo-Tree (p. 394). Beside the tree are two male figures, that on the left with folded hands, and that on the right holding a bit of cloth tied to the tree and a small branch. Near the men are two females bringing trays of offerings. The semi-circular bands of scroll-work over the doorways are different, and beyond them are two turbaned figures carrying trays of offerings.

The Manchapuri is a small two-storeyed cave, with the upper storey set back and a frieze of men and animals across the front of the lower storey, probably the prototype of the Rani ka Naur and Ganesh Gumpha.

75 yd. to the N.W. is the Hathi Gumpha, or "Elephant Cave", an extensive natural cave, improved by King Kharaveli of Kalinga (168-153 B.C.). It is perfectly plain, but has an inscription above it of 117 lines (translated by Prinsep), describing the King's career. To the left a boulder has been hollowed out into a cell 5 ft. square.

N. of the "Elephant Cave" is the Pavana Gumpha, or "Cave of Purification". About 75 ft. to the S.W. of the Pavana Gumpha is the Sarpa Gumpha, or "Serpent Cave", having on the top of the entrance a rude carving of the hood of a three-headed cobra. Under this is the door, through which a man can just crawl; the interior is a cube of 4 ft. Beside the door is an inscription translated by James Prinsep.

50 ft. to the N. is the very interesting Bagh Gumpha, or "Tiger Cave", cut externally into the shape of the upper part of a tiger's head, with the jaws at full gape. The eyes and nose of the monster are still well marked, but the teeth are now imperfectly discernible. The head at top, where it joins the hill, is 8 ft. 8 in. broad.

The gape is 9 ft. wide, and the entrance to the cell occupies the place of the gullet. To the right of the entrance is an inscription in the Asoka character. At the beginning of the inscription is a Buddhist monogram, and at the end a Swastika cross.

The Khandagiri Hill, close by, is 133 ft. high and faces E. It is thickly covered with trees. The path which leads to the top is steep, and at the height of about 50 ft. divides into two, one branch leading to the left, and to a range of Jain caves cut in the E. face of the hill (see below).

The path on the right leads to the Ananta Cave, which is a narrow Buddhist excavation, with four doorways and a veranda with pillars and pilasters with decorated sides. Instead of a capital, these have a projecting bracket, shaped like a woman. The lintel is heavy, and over it is a parapet supported on corbels. The frieze is in five compartments, and represents figures running with trays of offerings, athletes fighting with bulls and lions, and two lines of geese running with spread wings, each with a flower in its bill. In the semi-circular space under one of the arches is a nude female standing in a lotus-bush, and holding a lotus-stalk in either hand. Two elephants are throwing water over her with their trunks. This is a representation of Lakshmi, the first of the Hindu Pantheon to be revered by the Buddhists. In the other tympanum is a scene representing the worship of a Bo-Tree. In the centre of the back wall of the cave is a Buddha in bas-relief.

The remaining caves are Jain, perhaps converted from Buddhist. The left path leads to a modern gallery, and to the S. to a range of three openings. There is here a Sanskrit inscription of the 12th-century recording that the cave belonged to Acharya Kalachandra and his pupil Vellachandra. Next comes a range of caves facing the E., divided into two compartments by a partition in the middle. On the back wall is a row of seated Dhyani Buddhas and some new images of Jaina Deva. At the E. end is an altar of masonry, on which are ranged a number of Jain images. The second compartment is very similar. On the back wall is a row of Dhyani Buddhas 1 ft. high, and below, females seated on stools, some four-handed, others eight-handed, with one leg crossed and the other hanging. Under all are lions *couchant*.

From this to the top of the hill is a stiff climb, and the steps in one place are very steep. On the summit of the hill is a plateau and an 18th-century temple to Parasnath. From it is a magnificent panoramic view 15 m. all round. The groves of mango and jack trees are most beautiful. In front of the temple is a fine terrace, 50 ft. square, with a raised masonry seat all round. To the S.W. of the temple is a smooth terrace of 150 ft. diameter, gently sloping to the W., called the Deva Sabha. In the centre is a small square pillar, with a bas-relief of Buddha on each side, and round it four circles of chaityas. Three small boulders, set in a triangle and covered by a dolmen of sandstone, stand in the inner circle. E. of the Deva Sabha, at 100 yd., is a tank cut in the solid rock, called the Akash Ganga, or "Heavenly Ganges". Immediately below the tank is a cave where the remains of Rajah Lelat Indra Kesari (A.D. 617-657) are said to rest.

After visiting the Udayagini Caves, the traveller should proceed to **Bhubaneswar** (pop. 105,000 in 1971). —Capital of Orissa State. Airport with daily services from Calcutta and Visakhapatnam. Utkal University. There is an excellent Travellers Lodge (apply to Manager, Gautamnagar for reservations), a Tourist B., Circuit H., a Dt. Bd. Bungalow, and Guest House. It takes 3 to 4 hours to visit the temples in and around Bhubaneswar. There is a useful Archaeological Survey booklet. **Kanarak** (p. 422) with museum and Sun Temple can be visited by car or taxi. There are Travellers Lodge, Tourist B., P.W.D., D.B.

In Bhubaneswar itself an unfinished new city houses the Government Offices of the State of Orissa displaying broad avenues, residential areas and a modern Market, where the Tourist Information Centre is located. Excursions can be arranged to Chilka Lake (p. 423, 50 m.). I.B. at Balugan and Barkul. Houseboat (boats available). R.R. at Balugan. Tourist B. at Rambha. Wildfowl shooting, fishing. **Old Bhubaneswar** has a long history and once rivalled Varanasi in sanctity as a centre of Jainism.

The first mention of it in the Records of the Temple of Jagannath, dates from the reign of Yayati, A.D. 474-526, the first of the Kesaris, or Lion dynasty of Orissa. He expelled the Yavanas, thought by Stirling and Hunter to be the Buddhists who ruled Orissa for 150 years after a successful invasion about A.D. 300. His successors reigned at Jajpur until Nripati Kesari, in A.D. 920-935, founded Cuttack and made it his capital.

7000 shrines once encircled the sacred lake; now 500 remain in decay, exhibiting every phase of Orissian art. Two styles of architecture run side by side. The first is represented by the temples of Parashuramesvara and Muktesvara, the second by the Great Lingaraj Temple. They are not antagonistic but sister styles, and seem to have had different origins.

On a short visit the Great, Raj Rani, Mukhtesvara, and Parashuramesvara temples should be seen.

"The **Great Temple**[1] is", says Fergusson, "perhaps the finest example of a purely Hindu temple in India." None but Hindus may enter the enclosure, the high walls of which are 7 ft. thick and of large cut stones without mortar. From the top, however, of a platform outside the N. wall a view of the interior may be obtained. Besides the Great Temples and the halls of approach to it there are also many smaller temples in the enclosure, of which a plain one, 20 ft. high, is the oldest; at the N.E. corner is a pavilion, perhaps built for a music hall, but now containing an image of Parvati.

The Great Temple was built by Lelat Indra Kesari (A.D. 617-657), and consisted originally of only a vimana and porch; the Nath and Bhog mandirs (below) added between 1090 and 1104. The presiding deity is Tribhuvanesvara, "Lord of the Three Worlds", generally called Bhubaneswar. He is represented in the sanctuary by a block of granite 8 ft. in diameter, and rising 9 ft. above the floor, which is bathed daily with water, milk and *bhang*. There are three differently shaded portions, representing respectively Brahma, Vishnu and Maheswar (Siva). There are twenty-two *dhupas*, or ceremonies, daily, consisting in washing the teeth of the divinity, moving a lamp in front, dressing, feeding, etc.

"The **Great Tower** can be seen from outside the wall. It is 180 ft. high, and, though not so large, is decidedly finer in design than that at Tanjore. Every inch of the surface is covered with carving of the most elaborate kind; not only the divisions of the courses, the roll mouldings on the angles, or the breaks on the face of the tower but every individual stone in the tower has a pattern carved upon it." In the vertical sections seen from over the wall, "the sculpture is of a very high order and great beauty of design". The top of the spire is flat, and from the centre rises a cylindrical neck, supporting a ribbed dome over which is placed the Kalasha or "pinnacle". Twelve lions seated (Sardulas) support the dome, and over all is a broken trident. The shrine itself is called the Bara Dewal, and the original hall of approach to it, the Jagmohan. In front of the Jagmohan is the Bhog Mandir, or "Hall of Offerings", and E. of that the Nath Mandir, or "Dancing Hall".

Outside the enclosure are many small subterraneous temples. The jungle to the S. of the Great Tower,

1 *Indian Architecture*, 2, 99, where a plan and illustration of the Great Temple will be found.

to the extent of 20 acres, is said to be the site of Lelat Indra Kesari's Palace, and exhibits everywhere the remains of foundations and pavements.

N. of the temple is the tank called Vindusagar, "Ocean Drop", which is said to be filled with water from every sacred stream and tank in India and possesses in consequence, to a superlative degree, the power to wash away sin. In the centre is a Jal Mandir, or "Water Pavilion", consisting of several shrines. Here the god is brought to bathe one day in the year. In front of the central ghat of this tank there is a magnificent temple, with a porch, a more modern dancing-hall, and a Bhog Mandir. All but the last are lined with brick-red sandstone, elaborately sculptured. The temple is sacred to *Vasudev*, or Krishna, and *Ananta*, or Balaram, and no pilgrim is allowed to perform any religious ceremony in the town or to visit Bhubaneswar without paying for permission here. Along the E. side of the tank will be noticed several temples of the same shape as the Great Temple.

¼ m. E.N.E. of the Ananta Temple is one, about 40 ft. high, of Kotitirthesvara, "The lord of ten millions of sacred pools". It is evidently built of stones from some other edifice.

2 m. E. of this is the **Temple of Brahmesvara,** on a high terraced mound. It is most sumptuously carved, inside as well as out, and was erected at the end of the 9th century A.D. Close to its terrace on the W. side is a tank called Brahma Kunda. N.E. is an old ruined temple of basalt, to Bhaskaresvara, "Sun-god", and said to belong to the close of the 5th or the beginning of the 6th century.

At the N.E. corner of the Great Temple is a very handsome tank surrounded by a row of 108 small temples. About 900 yd. to the E. is a grove of mango-trees, called Siddharanya, "Grove of the perfect beings". Here many temples were built, of which more than twenty remain entire. Of these the most remarkable are Muktesvara, Kedaresvara, Siddhesvara and Parashuramesvara.

Muktesvara is the handsomest, though the smallest. It is 35 ft. high, and the porch 25 ft. high. The floral bands are better executed than in most of the temples; the bas-reliefs are sharp and impressive; the statuettes vigorous and full of action, with drapery well disposed; and the disposition of the whole is elegant and most effective. Among the subjects are a lady mounted on a rearing elephant and attacking an armed giant; a figure of Annapurna presenting alms to Siva; females, half-serpents, canopied under five or seven-headed cobras; lions mounted on elephants or fighting with lions; damsels dancing or playing on the *mridang*; an emaciated hermit giving lessons. The scroll-work, bosses and friezes are worthy of note. The chamber of the temple is 7 ft. square, but outside measures 18 ft. In front of the porch is a Torana 15 ft. high. It is supported on two columns of elaborate workmanship, unlike anything of the kind at Bhubaneswar. Over it are two reclining female figures. It is said that it is used for swinging the deity in the Dol Festival.

Kedaresvara.—Close by a tank behind this temple is the Kedaresvara Temple, and near it, against the outer wall of a small room, is a figure of Hanuman, the monkey-god, 8 ft. high, and one of Durga standing on a lion. Her statue is of chlorite, and has the finest female head to be seen in Bhubaneswar. The Kedaresvara Temple is 41 ft. high, and has an almost circular ground plan; it is probably older than the Great Temple, and possibly dates from the middle of the 6th century.

N.W. of Muktesvara is **Siddesvara,** which is very ancient, and was once the most sacred spot on this side of Bhubaneswar. It is 47 ft. high, and has a well-proportioned porch.

The **Parashuramesvara,** 200 yd. to the W. of the Muktesvara, is considered by Fergusson (*Ind. Arch.*,

2, 97) the oldest temple at Bhubaneswar. The ground plan is a square, the porch is oblong and covered with bas-reliefs representing processions of horses and elephants in the upper linear bands under the cornice, and scenes from the life of Rama in the lower. The roof is a sloping terrace, in the middle of which is a clerestory with sloping eaves which prevent the direct rays of the sun, or rain, from entering.

Beyond the Muktesvara and Parashuramesvara temples, is the **Temple of Raj Rani.** Fergusson (*Ind. Arch.*, 2, 103) says of it: "It is one of the gems of Orissan Art". It faces the E., and has a porch in front, both of dressed brick-red sandstone without mortar. The niches are filled with statues 3 ft. high, executed with great vigour and elegance. One pillar has three kneeling elephants and lions, with a Nagni or female Naga with her seven-headed snake hood. Over the door are represented the Navagraha, or "nine planets".

The famous **Dhauli** or Aswatama rock, on which is inscribed the best-preserved set of edicts of King Asoka in the official Magadha language, lies between 4 m. and 5 m. S.W. of Bhubaneswar. The rock is an isolated one on a plain in front of a low ridge; the face inscribed is 15 ft. by 10 ft., and above it are the remains of an elephant. The clearness of the 13 inscriptions (translated by James Prinsep in 1838), exposed to the sun and storms of twenty-two centuries, is wonderful.

283 m. **Khurda Road,** branch line to (27 m.) **Puri.** The great temple of Jagannath is seen soaring skywards long before Puri is reached.

310 m. from Calcutta **PURI,*** or Jagannathpur, (pop. 72,000 in 1971) one of the four principal pilgrimage cities of India; alt. 18 ft. The railway station is 1½ m. to the N. of the town and the Civil Station runs along the seashore. Information centres are located at Panth Niwas and Lion Gate, Jagannath Temple. Conducted Tours available. There is a good Railway Hotel. The Church is about 80 yd. from the Collector's office. Excellent bathing can be had.

The town of Puri is about 1½ m. in breadth from E. to W., and 3½ m. long from N. to S. It is of great antiquity, and was probably the Dantpura where the sacred relic of Buddha's tooth was preserved until it was finally transferred to Ceylon. The population during the great festivals increases enormously. The town covers an area of 1871 ac., including the Kshetra,[1] or "sacred precincts". It is a city of lodging-houses, and the streets are narrow, except the Baradand, or road for the Car of Jagannath, when he goes from his temple to his country-house in June or July. This road runs through the centre of the town N. and S., and is in places half a furlong wide.

The **Temple,** or Sri Mandir, is in the centre of the town and stands upon rising ground known as Nilgiri or "the Blue Hill". The endowments provide a large income which is augmented greatly by the offerings of pilgrims. There are more than 6000 male adults as priests, warders of the temple, and pilgrim guides, and, including the monastic establishments and the guides who roam through India to escort pilgrims, there are probably not less than 20,000 men, women and children dependent on Jagannath. The immediate attendants on the god are divided into thirty-six orders and ninety-seven classes. The administration is in the hands of a managing committee. At the head is the Raja of Puri, who in ecclesiastical matters represents the old rulers of Orissa. During the car festival, he fulfils the office of Sweeper to the God. There are distinct sets of servants to put the god to bed, to dress and bathe him, and a numerous band of nautch girls who sing before him.

The title **Jagannath** (Juggurnath) (Sanskrit = "Lord of the Universe")

[1] The whole country round is divided into kshetras, the Parvati round Jajpur, the Hara round Kanarak, the Padma (or lotus) round Bhubaneswar, and the Parushottama round Puri. Literature available from Tourist Information Centres.

is really a name of Krishna, worshipped as Vishnu; the immense popularity of the shrine is due to the doctrine preached that before the god all castes are equal. There are three images in the temple, representing Jagannath himself, his brother Balbhadra and his sister Subhadra. Jagannath and Balbhadra have "arms projecting horizontally forward from the ears", but the sister is "entirely devoid of even that approximation to the human form". A large diamond glitters on the head of Jagannath. Quaint representations of the images in a wooden shrine may be bought

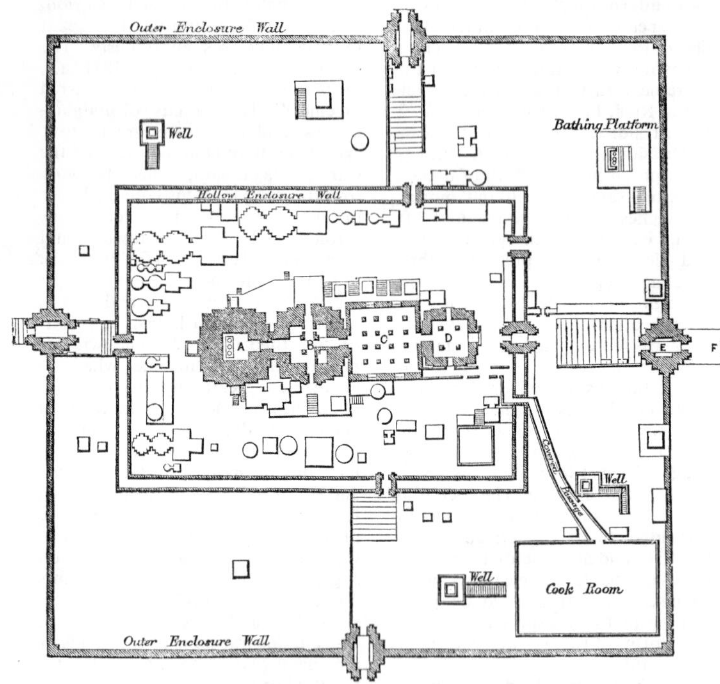

Plan of Temple of Jagannath. (Fergusson, *Ind. Arch.*, 2, 108.)

According to Babu Brij Kishore Ghose's *History of Puri*, the images are "bulky hideous wooden busts, fashioned in a curious resemblance of the human head, resting on a sort of pedestal. They are painted white, black and yellow respectively; their faces are exceedingly large and their bodies are decorated with a dress of different coloured cloth." in the bazar. *Bhog*, or *Prasad* is offered several times a day and afterwards sold to the pilgrims.

The three images are bathed at the Snan Jatra, and every June are drawn in procession at the Rathjatra, which commemorates the journey of Sri Krishna from Gokul to Mathura (p. 291). The car (rath) of Jagannath is 45 ft. high and 35 ft. square, and is supported on sixteen wheels of 7 ft. diameter and prancing horses in front; those of the brother and sister are smaller.[1] Precautions are taken to prevent accidents. Votaries have been known to throw themselves beneath the wheels; but the number has been greatly exaggerated, although mentioned by many travellers. A spread of cholera used to follow the dispersion of the pilgrims from Puri. Much has been done to improve the sanitation and water-supply.

The sacred enclosure is nearly a square, 652 ft. long and 630 ft. broad, within a stone wall about 20 ft. high, with a gateway in the centre of each side. The door stands open, but it is not possible for non-Hindus to see the temples, of which, besides the Great Pagoda, there are more than a hundred, thirteen of them being sacred to Siva and one to the Sun. The tower and temple frontage can be comfortably viewed from the roof of a lodging-house on the opposite side of the street—fee to servants of the house. The Mahant of Emar Math also gives facilities from the Raghunandan Library roof. The Library contains many palm leaf MSS and is a research centre for Orissa history. Open 8-11 a.m. and 3-5 p.m. except Sundays and holidays.

In front of the E. gate an exquisite Pillar (F),[2] brought from the Black Pagoda at Kanarak, stands on a platform of rough stones, and, reckoning to the top of the seated figure of the Garuda, or "eagle", which surmounts it, is 35 ft. high.

This gate (E) is known as the Lion Gate (Central Information Centre) from two large lions of the conventional form, with one paw raised, which stand one at either side of the entrance. Within is a second enclosure surrounded by a double wall, having an interval of 11 ft. between the walls, and within this again is the temple proper. The "Hall of Offerings", or Bhog Mandir (D), is said to have been brought from the Black Pagoda at Kanarak and re-erected by the Mahrattas in the 18th century. The Nat Mandir (C), or "dancing-hall", also of late date, is a square hall measuring 69 ft. by 67 ft. inside. The walls are plain, with only two figures of dwarpals, called Jaya and Vijaya, and a marble figure of Garuda 2 ft. high.

The Jagmohan (B), or "Hall of Audience", where the pilgrims view the images, is 73 ft. square and 120 ft. high. The Baradewal (A), or "Sanctuary", of the same area, where the images are, is surmounted by a conical "tower", or vimana, 192 ft. high, black with time and surmounted by the Wheel and Flag of Vishnu.

The temple was erected first by Yayati Kesari. The building of 1198 was a reconstruction by Raja Anang Bhim Deo, in expiation of the offence of having killed a Brahmin. The image of Jagannath is said to have appeared about A.D. 318. It was thoroughly repaired in 1922-23.

There is a street about 45 ft. broad all round the temple enclosure. Turning to the left from the Lion Gate (E) along this road, the visitor comes to the S. gate, where steps lead up to the entrance. The entrance itself is 15 ft. high, and is ornamented with many figures. Above are depicted scenes from the life of Krishna. The supports of the massive roof are of iron.

Rather more than a mile to the N. of the temple, and approached by the broad Baradand, is the famous **Garden House** (Gandicha Mandir), to which the Car of Jagannath is brought and stays for eight days during the festival, dragged by 4200 professionals, who come from the neighbouring districts, and live at Puri gratis. It is broken up yearly, when the timbers are made into sacred relics, and another is made of exactly the same pattern. The images are also treated in this way at intervals of 12 or 24 years.

[1] The Tooth Festival of Buddha in Japan and Ceylon is also celebrated with three cars. Hence the theory that the Puri images were originally Buddhist symbols diverted to Brahmanical worship.

[2] These letters refer to corresponding letters on the plan.

The Garden House is a temple within a garden enclosed with a wall. The principal gateway has a gabled roof, adorned with conventional lions. The gates to this temple are built upon the Hindu arch system, corbelled slabs supporting the roof, each projecting slightly over the one below. The temple is said to be very old; the interior, which strangers are permitted to enter, except during the Car Festival, is interesting as giving one an idea of the arrangement of the Great Temple. In one of the pillared halls kneels a Garuda on a column facing the shrine. On the side of the temple there is a plain raised seat 4 ft. high and 19 ft. long, made of chlorite, and this is called the Ratna Bedi, the throne on which the images are seated. On the walls are some fine carvings of horsemen, etc. Outside, over the door, are various figures of women, 2 ft. high, supporting the roof; also carvings of Brahma with four heads, worshipping Narayan; of Krishna playing to the Gopis, etc.

The legend is that King Indradyumna, King of Malwa, pitched his camp here when he discovered Puri, and set up an image of Narsingh, afterwards brought to the present temple. Here the Sacred Log from the White Island stranded, and here the Divine Carver made the images of Jagannath, etc., and here Indradyumna performed the horse sacrifice a hundred times over.

1 m. S.W., on the seashore S. of the Circuit House, is the Swarga Dwara, or "Door of Paradise", where, when all the ceremonies are finished, the pilgrims bathe in the surf and wash away their sins. There is a stump of a pillar 4 ft. high on the right hand, near a small temple. On this pillar offerings are placed, which are eaten by the crows. On the left is the Lahore Math or Monastery. Bathers will be seen, the surf rolling over them. Afterwards they make heaps of sand, resembling a temple, and stick small flag-poles into them.

N.W. of the city are the Chandan Tank, the Mitiani River, the Markhand Tank and Temple of Savitri. A Bridge built, according to Raja Rajendra Lal Mitra, in 1038-50, is 278 ft. long by 38 ft. broad, and has nineteen corbelled arches over the Atara Nala.[1]

20 m. N.E. from Puri is **Konarak** (Travellers' Lodge, Tourist B.), celebrated for its **Sun Temple**. The route *via* Pilpi on the Cuttack road is always open for cars and they can be driven right up to the temple gateway.

Clearance of debris in 1904 led to a high appreciation of the temple. Sir John Marshall, ex-D.G. of Archaeology, has recorded that there is no monument of Hinduism that is at once so stupendous and so perfectly proportioned as this temple. Stirling fixed the date in 1241; it may have been as early as the 9th century A.D. The spire was never completed. When Fergusson visited Konarak in 1837 a portion of the Great Tower was still standing, but had gone by 1869. The pagoda is called black in contrast to the white-washed pagoda at Puri, and both were landmarks. The shrine at the W. end of the temple has been cleared, and it is possible to appreciate the splendid carvings on it, including the wheels and horses, which indicate the fact that the temple was the chariot of the Sun-god. There are many carved figures of green chlorite on the walls, much of the decoration is erotic; inside is a beautifully carved throne, on which the idol once stood. The Jagmohan porch has a square base of 90 ft., and is built of red sandstone and laterite. The roof is covered with elaborate carvings. Fergusson says that there is no roof in India where the same play of light and shade is obtained. "On the floor it is about 40 ft. square, and the walls rise plain to about the same height. Here it begins to bracket inwards, till it contracts to about 20 ft., where it was ceiled with a flat stone roof, supported by wrought-*iron*

[1] See *Puri and its Environs*, by Robert Dunbar.

beams . . . blocks of short lengths, 3 in. or 4 in. square, built together, like bricks, and then covered with molten metal (*sic*, heated and welded into one long beam). The employment of these beams here is puzzling. They were not wanted for strength, as the building is sill firm after they have fallen and so expensive a false ceiling was not wanted architecturally to roof so plain a chamber. It seems to be only another instance of that profusion of labour which the Hindus loved to lavish on the temples of their gods" (*Ind. Arch.*, 2, 107).

The entrance of the Jagmohan is on the E., guarded by stone lions, with strongly marked manes and one paw lifted up, resting on the backs of elephants, which are smaller in size. The height of the entrance, built of chlorite, is 16½ ft.; the roof was supported by two rafters of iron and four of stone. Near the temple lie several massive iron bars, varying from 7 ft. to 36 ft. in length.[1] The interior of the hall has now been completely filled up in order to save the outer walls. As the E. door is guarded by lions, the N. door by elephants, and the S. by horses trampling down men, who from their tusk-like teeth, crisped hair, knives and shields, are intended for aborigines. The spirit with which the horses are carved, and also the device on one of the shields of two climbing lizards, should be noticed.

To the S. of the Jagmohan porch is a large banyan-tree, and a garden with a *math*, or devotee's residence. Over the E. entrance used to be a chlorite slab, on which the emblems of the days of the week, with the ascending and descending nodes, were carved. Some English antiquaries attempted to remove this in 1893 for the Museum at Calcutta, but, after dragging it 200 yd., gave up the attempt, though the Indian builders had conveyed it 80 m. across swamps and unbridged rivers to Kanarak. The carved back portion lies 200 yd. to the E. of the temple, and is 20 ft. 10 in. broad. It is disfigured with oil and red paint. The front part is now in the Archaeological museum in the temple enclosure.

The sea, about 2 m. off, is only visible by climbing on to the *débris* of the temple. Black buck (now preserved) are to be found between Puri and Kanarak.

[1] Other instances of the employment of large masses of iron occur at Dhar (p. 204) and at the Qutb Minar of Delhi (p. 337). These iron beams have probably something to do with the fable that there was once a lodestone in the tower of the temple, which used to draw passing ships on to the shore.

Main Line

327 m. from Calcutta is **Balugan.** There the railway line skirts the **Chilka Lake,** along which some of the scenery is of great beauty—to the W. are the jungle-clad hills of the Eastern Ghats, while the lake is dotted with islands on which, as on the mainland, game of all kinds abounds, and in the cold season has a surface crowded with wild-fowl. The lake is 45 m. long, averages 10 m. in width, is separated by a narrow stretch of sand from the sea, and is shallow; the water is brackish, and there is a very slight tide at the southern end, the sea running into it at Manikpatnam. Trade is carried on in flat-bottomed boats of peculiar structure with lateen sails of bamboo-matting. There is a P.W.D. Inspection Bungalow at Barkul, on the western shore of the lake. (Permission for occupation of the house from the Superintending Engineer, Cuttack.) This bungalow is connected by a good road, about 3 m. long, with Balugan railway station. From Barkul there is a good road (55 m.) to Gopalpur-on-Sea.

345 m. **Rambha,** picturesquely situated at the S. of the Chilka Lake. The large house on the margin of the lake was built by the egregious Mr Snodgrass[1] in 1792. At Jangada there is an Asokan rock edict.

[1] This was the gentleman who extorted a pension from the East India Company by sweeping a crossing in front of the India House in Leadenhall Street, London.

356 m. **Ganjam** station for Old Ganjam, situated on the Rushkuliya, and formerly the chief port and town of the District; in the early part of the 19th century it was ravaged by an epidemic of fever and abandoned in consequence. The ruined fort, commenced in 1768 by the first British Resident in Ganjam, recalls memories of former Residents and Chiefs in Councils established in 1760 for the Northern Circars here, at Masulipatam and Vizagapatam.

361 m. **Chatrapur** station, beautifully situated on high ground above the sea. D.B. at railway station, furnished.

375 m. **Berhampur** (pop. 117,000 in 1971; R., D.B.); Information Centre (District P.R.O.) for Gopalpur-on-Sea and tourist spots. Motors can be hired. Chief buildings are the Jubilee Hospital, Town Hall, Kalikot College. It was noted for its tussore silk cloths and gold-embroidered turbans. **Gopalpur-on-Sea** (hotels), the seaport of the District and a holiday resort is 9 m. by road; excellent bathing; good hotels and boarding-houses, I.Bs. and Youth Hostel. Details of excursions to Chilka Lake (pp. 417, 423), Phulbani (tribals), Taptapani (hot springs) from Information Centre, Berhampur. A motor-bus service (S) runs from Berhampur to Aska (25 m.), where there is a sugar-factory, and to Russellkonda (50 m.); also to Udayagiri (27 m. farther).

Rusellkonda (Russell's Hill) is the headquarters of the Maliah tracts, inhabited by Khonds, a primitive tribe which used to practise human sacrifice as a fertility rite. Between 1837 and 1854 more than 1500 of these "Meriahs" (as the victims were called) were rescued by British officers.

Mahendragiri (4923 ft.), the highest point of the Eastern Ghats in the Ganjam District, has on its top five unique structures built of massive stone. Three of these are temples of Kunti, dedicated to the god Siva, Yudhistira and Bhima. There is also a stone pillar on which are engraved the figure of a tiger, two fish, and an inscription. The Cholas of Tanjore, whose crest was the tiger, must have once extended their sway right up to Mahendragiri, and even further N. There is a private bungalow at the summit of the mountain, belonging to the Raja of Mandasa. There was once a proposal to lease the hill as a summer camp for the Government of Orissa.

437 m. **Naupada** Junction, N.G. line to (25 m.) Parlakimedi and Gunupur (56 m.).

466 m. **Chicacole Road** station (Srikakulam). Motor-bus service to **Chicacole** (8 m. by road; D.B., unfurnished), which contains a noble mosque built in 1641 by Sher Muhammad Khan, the first Faujdar under Golconda of the Chicacole Sirkar. It was formerly celebrated for its muslims. The port of Kalingapatam, a former centre of the Kalinga dynasty, is a pleasant seaside resort.

509 m. **Vizianagram** (pop 86,500 in 1971) Junction (R.), former headquarters of an extensive Zemindar estate once included in the Kalinga kingdom. The town, founded in 1712, adjoins the disused Cantonment. The fort (1 m. distant) is almost entirely occupied by the *Palace*, etc., of the Maharaja.

A Vizianagram and French force under de Bussy attacked Bobbili in January 1757, when, after putting the women to death, Raja Ranga Rao of Bobbili fell, sword in hand, in accordance with the old Rajput tradition. Not long after four of his old retainers murdered the Raja of Vizianagram. The tragedy is commemorated by an obelisk at Bobbili, erected in 1891.

A broad-gauge line, which runs N. to Bobbili and Parvatipuram (48 m.), was continued to Raipur in Madhya Pradesh (p. 198) in 1931. It traverses much wild and beautiful country.

From Vizianagram Buddhist remains at Ramatirtham, excavated by the Archaeological Department, can be visited. There is a good road up to the foot of the hill; but arrangements must be made for crossing the river. (The Tahsildar should be consulted.)

547 m. **Waltair** Junction, the meeting-place of the Eastern and Southern railways, from which a short branch line runs to Vishakhapatnam and Waltair. At Simhachalam, a temple on the hill is a very fine specimen of the Orissa style. The village is about 3 m. from Simhachalam railway station; about 10 m. from Waltair. The Raja of Vizianagram is the owner. The temple bears inscriptions on almost all the pillars and walls. These date from the 12th century. The great Vijayanagar king, Krishnaraya, who was ruling Southern India (1509-30) from Vijayanagar, is said to have conquered the Kalinga country and to have set up a pillar of victory at, or near, Simhachalam. This pillar has not been traced.

2 m. **Vishakhapatnam** (Vizagapatam) (pop. 362,000 in 1971) chief town of the district is a sea and airport on the route between Calcutta and Madras with air connection with Bombay *via* Hyderabad and Aurangabad. There are three good hotels. The **harbour,** formed by two almost parallel ridges jutting into the sea, is the only protected harbour on the Coromandel coast and is the main shipbuilding centre of India with a Caltex Oil Refinery. It now has a turning basin, ship-building yards, an oil refinery, it ranks as a major Port under the name of Gandhigram. It was in connection with this harbour that the broad-gauge line to Raipur was constructed. There are excellent road communications to Hyderabad, Madras and other centres. The ferry crossings have now all been replaced by bridges.

The British in Vishakhapatnam surrendered to de Bussy (25th June 1757). Colonel Forde landed in 1758, and drove the French from the Northern Circars, which the Nizam had allotted to them in 1753 for the support of de Bussy's force. The Andhra Research University is here, with a College of Arts. The suburb of Waltair to the N. of the town stands on elevated ground composed of red laterite rocks.

Waltair, "the Indian Brighton", has a T.B. sanatorium. The best hotels are now in Vishakhapatnam. The manufacture of *panjam* cloth and ornamental articles of ivory, buffalo-horn, and silver filigree work, are specialities of the district. In the district manganese ore occurs, of which large quantities are exported.

18 m. N.E. of **Vishakhapatnam** is **Bimlipatam,** a small port, where coasting steamers touch. There are several 17th-century tombs in the Dutch cemetery. One in the Flagstaff cemetery has a crest with two storks.

567 m. **Anakapalli**: at a distance of about 2 m. there are Buddhist remains, preserved as ancient monuments.

640 m. **Samalkot** station junction for (8 m.) **Cocanada Town** (Kakinada = "Crow Country") and (10 m.) **Cocanada (Kakinada) Port** (pop. 164,000 in 1971) connected with the Godavari river by navigable canals. Municipal R.H. at Cocanada. Ships lie in the Roads (Coringa Bay), which though shallow, are protected to the S. by a sandy promontory at the mouths of the Godavari. The jetties, wharves, and business houses are on the banks of a canal leading into the Roads. The branch railway formerly continued to Kotipalle on the Godavari.

671 m. **Rajamundry** (Rajamahendri) (pop. 188,000 in 1971, R.), seat of the Orissa Kings and of the Vengi Kings, is regarded by the Telugus as their chief town. It contains a museum and a provincial college. It was the headquarters of Bussy from 1754-57, during which he held possession of the Northern Circars. The Gorge, about 50 m. to the N.W., where the Godavari issues from the hills forms one of the most beautiful pieces of scenery in Southern India—a succession of Highland lochs in an Eastern setting. An excursion up river by launch or house-boat is well worth making. A few miles down the river from Rajamundry are the head-works of the magnificent Godavari Delta

Irrigation system, first designed by Sir Arthur Cotton (1852). The *anicut*, or dam, of masonry is 2¾ m. in length, with an earth bank another 1½ m. long. In the middle of it is a well-wooded island. Near the mouth of the river is the former French possession of **Yanaon.** A tidal wave flooded the delta when the volcano of Krakatoa blew up (1883).

674 m. **Godavari.** A railway bridge of 56 spans of 150 ft. (1900) crosses the river, and a road bridge.

727 m. **Ellore** station (R.). Formerly capital of one Northern Circar; now known only for its carpets. The Godavari and Kistna Canal systems join here.

The Kolair Lake lies to the E. Branch lines from Nidadavolu, a station on the main line, to Bhimavaram and Narasapur, from Bhimavaram to Gudivala on the Bezwada. Masulipatam line completely circumvents the lake.

764 m. **BEZWADA*** (now known as **Vijayawada**) (pop. 343,000 in 1971) Junction (R., R.R., D.B.), terminus of the railway from Warangal (Route 25). Metre-gauge line to Dronachellam and (279 m.) Guntakal Junction (Route 27). Airport served by I.A.C. from Calcutta and Hyderabad.

Bezwada (alt. 80 ft.) is a trading-place on the most frequented crossing of the Kistna river. It has now considerable importance, with several hotels and a modern suburb—Gandhinagar. A fort, erected here in 1760, has been dismantled. In making excavations for canals many remains were exposed, which show that the place was, in the Buddhist period, a considerable religious centre; and as such it was visited by Hiuen Tsang in A.D. 645. It is shut in on the W. by a granite ridge 600 ft. high, running N. and S., and ending in a scarp at the river.

At right angles to this ridge, and ½ m. from the stream, is a similar ridge sheltering the town on the N. Close to the E. end of this ridge is a sharp-pointed detached mass of gneiss, in which are Buddhistic caves and cells. On the S. side of the river, opposite to Vijayawada, is a hill similar to the W. ridge, of which it is a continuation. It is 450 ft. high, and from the town seems a perfect cone. On the S. side of the river, 1 m. to the W., is the Undavalli Cave-Temple (see below).

In the town are some old shrines with inscriptions from the 7th century downwards. At the **Victoria Jubilee Museum** (1890) there is a colossal figure of Buddha in black granite, which came from the hill to the E. of Bezwada. The river is here crossed by a great dam, or *anicut*, 3715 ft. long and 20 ft. above the bed level. From both ends canals take off and irrigate about 800,000 acres of land.

The telegraph line from Madras to Calcutta is carried across the Kistna river in a single span. The distance from support to support is 5000 ft., and the average height above the river bed is about 400 ft., but in midstream the lowest wire sinks to 66 ft. above the crest of the *anicut*.

Kondapalli (12 m. by road) is famous for its ancient craft of toy-making, sacred, human and animal figures of every kind. Craftsmen can be watched at work. (By rail, p. 465.)

Excursions from Vijayawada

(1) In order to reach **Undavalil** village it is necessary to cross the Kistna from Vijayawada by the railway or *anicut*, and go 1½ m. up the course of the river above and W. of Sitanagaram. There is a rock-temple of two storeys close to the village. In a recess facing N. is a five-storeyed Brahman excavation discovered (1797) by Colonel Mackenzie. The upper storeys are all set back, so that the façade represents the exterior of a structural building. The lowest storey across the whole front has three rows of seven pillars partially hewn out. The second originally had four compartments; at the back of one of these is a shrine cell with an altar, and in another is a relief of Vishnu and his wives. The façade on the front here

has a frieze of geese, and a cell at the left end one of elephants and lions. The third storey contains a hall 53 ft. by 36 ft., with a figure of Vishnu seated on the serpent Ananta, and of Narayana, 17 ft. long, resting on the great snake Shesha. The top storey consists of barrel roofs of the shape used in all Dravidian temples. The date of the excavation must be much the same as those of Mahabalipuram (Route 31).

(2) 40 m. by road *via* Guntur is **Amaravati*** (pop. 193,000 in 1971), on the right, or S., bank of the Kistna river, once the capital of the Andhra kingdom. It was the chief Southern centre of Mahayana Buddhism, and the site of a great stupa, larger than that at Sanchi (pp. 217-221); but scarcely anything remains. Portions of it are in the British, Calcutta and Madras Museums. The railings date A.D. 170, but the stupa, still older, was perhaps 100 ft. high with a base diameter of 172 ft. The Chinese traveller Hiuen Tsang visited the monastery adjoining. The sculptures and other finds in the Museum are of astonishing beauty.

A branch railway 50 m. long connects Vijayawada with **Masulipatam** (pop. 112,000 in 1971) (Machhlipatnam or "Fish Town"; D.B.), principal port of the Krishna District, one of the Northern Circars. It was taken by the Bahmani Kings (1476) from an Orissan Raja, and was a principal settlement, under Bantam, of the East Indian Company for trade on the E. coast, under a firman from Golconda. An agency was established here in 1611, after the failure of that at Pulicat, and a factory eleven years later; the Dutch and French also had factories here. There are Dutch tombs dating from 1624. In 1690 a firman of the Delhi Emperor confirmed the English privileges. In 1750 the French took it, and in 1753 the place was made over by the Nizam to de Bussy, but was carried by storm by Colonel Forde on the night of 7th April 1759. A Treaty with Salabat Jang, subadar of the Deccan, followed. The fort is now dismantled. The chintzes of Masulipatam were once famous.

Main Line

Immediately S. of Vijayawada the Kistna is crossed by a bridge, 3736 ft. long, 12 spans of 292 ft., carrying both gauges (roadway also).

784 m. **Tenali** Junction (R.); a branch (37 m.) passes through here from Repalle on the E. to Guntur Junction (p. 483).

850 m. **Ongole** (R.).

901 m. **Bitragunta** (R.).

923 m. Bridge over the Penner river to **Nellore** (pop. 133,000 in 1971; D.B.; alt. 57 ft.) on the right bank, a great Missionary centre. To the N.W. is the hill of Udayagiri, 3079 ft., with a fortress. Good snipe-shooting in the cold weather.

946 m. **Gudur** Junction (R.). Centre of the mica mining industry. Branch to (52 m.) Renigunta (p. 440) on the main line from Bombay to Madras (Route 23), and to Katpadi on the Madras-Bangalore line.

1010 m. **Ponneri.** 10 m. N.E. and 25 m. N. of Madras is **Pulicat** (Palaverkalu), the first Dutch Settlement in India. The fort, built in 1609, was named Castel Geldria, and a representation of it is carved on one of the tombs in the old cemetery, decorated with many coats of arms. On the opposite side of a long lake the hamlet of Coromandel is popularly supposed to have given its name to the whole of the E. coast. The word, however, is probably a corruption of Cholamandalam, "the realm of the Chola kings". English traders were so hampered here by the Dutch that they moved (1626) to Armagaon (40 m. N.) and then to Madras in 1639.

1021 m. **Ennur** (Ennore), a popular week-end resort from Madras, on a large backwater. Good boating and bathing.

1032 m. from Calcutta is **Madras** Central Station (Route 30).

Madras is now capital of the State of Tamil Nadu.

ROUTE 23

BOMBAY to MADRAS by Kalyan Junction, **Neral** (for **Matheran**), the **Bhor Ghat, Lonavla** (for the **Caves of Karli** and **Bhaja**), POONA, **Dhond** (for **Ahmadnagar**), **Sholapur, Hotgi** Junction, **Gulbarga, Wadi** Junction, **Raichur, Guntakal** Junction, **Renigunta** Junction (for **Tirupati**) and **Arkonam** Junction.

Rail 794 m. Mail train about 32 hours in transit. By air, the journey takes 2 hours 40 minutes.

The Madras mail of the Central Ry. leaves Victoria Terminus (Bombay) daily, and follows the same route as the Bombay-Calcutta mail (Route 2) as far as

34 m. from Bombay, **Kalyan** Junction. From Kalyan the Calcutta mail goes N.E. up the Thal Ghat, and the Madras mail ascends the **Bhor Ghat.** The section between Bombay and Poona has been electrified.

The country below the Ghats as far S. as N. Kanara is known as the Konkan—that above the Ghats from the Godavari (formerly from the Vindhya mountains) to the S. as the Deccan (Sanskrit, *dakshina*, "southern").

The first station on the Poona line, after leaving Kalyan, is

38 m. **Ambarnath,** "Immortal Lord", is a factory town. 1 m. E. is the Temple of Ambarnath, in a pretty valley. It is a specimen of genuine Hindu architecture, covered with beautiful designs, in which birds and the heads of the lion of the South are introduced. The roof of the hall is supported by four richly carved columns. The pediment of the doorway leading into the vimana (shrine) is ornamented with elephants and lions, and in the centre with figures of Siva. A curious belt of beautiful carving runs up each face of the vimana. An inscription inside the lintel of the N. door gives the date of the building of the temple as = A.D. 860.

54 m. **Neral** Junction (R.). For **Matheran** leave the rail here, and walk or ride up 8 m. in 1½ hours, or take the diesel train to Matheran, 13 m.

Matheran, "the wooded head", or "mother forest", is an outlier of the Sahyadri range, varying from 2300 ft. to 2600 ft. above the sea-level, and is an agreeable summer resort. Lord's Central Hotel caters for European visitors. The crown of the hill forms a narrow undulating table-land running N. and S., covered with small tree growth with spurs separated by ravines on all sides, with precipitous slopes everywhere, sometimes 1500 ft. high, the spurs terminating abruptly in bluffs called "points". Among the finest of these are Porcupine, Hart, and Monkey Points to the N.W., from which Bombay Harbour can be seen, Chauk Point, the S. extremity, where the old road of ascent emerges: and several points on the E. from which Khandala and the Ghats are visible. The finest of all is Panorama Point, to the N. of the bungalows. The distance is a little over 4 m. The road leads through a thick jungle of beautiful trees, and about ½ m. from Panorama Point comes to a point parallel with Porcupine Point, where a precipice descends abruptly 1000 ft. At 100 yd. from its termination the road goes quite round the brow of the peak, and affords an extremely beautiful panoramic view. To the left are Hart Point and Porcupine Point, at the N. and N.W. extremities of a promontory shaped like the head of a battle-axe. Between Matheran and Prabal the mountain sinks down abruptly to the plain. From Panorama Point the Bawa Malang Range, 10 m. long, with strange cylindrical or bottle-shaped peaks of columnar basalt, is visible some 15 m. to the N.

The extreme W. end is known as the "Cathedral Rocks". The huts of Neral village lie directly below, and beyond them is the curving line of the Central Ry. Bombay may be seen from this point on a clear day under the evening light.

62 m. **Karjat** Junction. A line runs S. (9 m.) to **Khopoli** on the Poona road, but is only used in the dry season.

The **Bhor Ghat** begins 1 m. from Karjat. The gradient is 1 in 37. The line first rises up the slope of the long spur which ends in the hill called Londgiri, which encloses the N. side of the Kampoli Valley, and at the height of 1000 ft. passes by a tunnel to another wooded valley on the N., which soon terminates in an extremely fine and beautifully wooded ravine. The old Reversing Station, 1350 ft. above the sea, was situated on an elevated spur, which afforded grand views of the ravine, but this has been superseded by the present realignment. A cement-lined tunnel, 3000 ft. long and 35 ft. in width, was driven, and a bridge carries the line over the ravine. The works were executed by the Tata Construction Company. From the reversing Station can be seen the curious sheer rock called "the Duke's Nose", and by the people Nāgphudi (the Cobra's Hood).

The hillsides form in the monsoon almost a continuous waterfall, surrounded by vivid green vegetation. The line now winds round to the E. side of the Khopoli Valley, and makes its way round the crest of the tableland to Khandala, which stands at the head of the ravine.

The Power Station of the Tata Hydro-Electric Works is in the Kampoli Valley, at the foot of a fall of some 1740 ft. by which water from three lakes, near Lonauli, descends in steel pipes, lying on the rocks at a steep angle. Here turbines generate a current at 5000 volts, transformed in the station to a pressure of 100,000 volts, which is conveyed by wires on pylons to Bombay, a distance of some 43 m. in a direct line.

78 m. **Khandala** (Hotels and Government Inspection Bungalow). This beautiful village is a favourite retreat for the inhabitants of Bombay in the summer months. It overlooks the great ravine. Above the head of the ravine, to the S., is the hill called the Duke's Nose, with a view over the Konkan. The ascent is by the S. shoulder, and is very steep. Khandala, with good hotels, is a convenient alternative to Lonavla for visits to Karli.

The Waterfall on the right side of the ravine, near its head, is very fine in the rains, the upper of the two falls into which it is divided having a clear leap of 300 ft.

80 m. **Lonavla** (Lonauli) station* at the top of the Ghat, 74 m. from Bombay by road (Hotels and R.). Here are the Railway School and Church, and a large railway colony. 2 m. S. is the Valvan Lake.

The great cave at Karli (7½ m.) and the caves of Bhaja (6½ m.) are accessible from Lonavla by car, which can go off the Poona Road at 68 m. S. to the Malavli station, ¾ m. distant from the caves of Bhaja, or N. to the base of the rocky ridge of the Karli cave. An Indian caretaker resides within ½ m. of the Bhaja cave. The ascent to the Karli cave is nearly 400 ft. by a good path, with a rather steep gradient; ponies and carrying-chairs are available at the foot of the ascent. Permission to take photographs using a tripod in these caves must be obtained from the Director of Archaeology, Aurangabad.

85 m. **Malavli** station (P.W.D. Inspection Bungalow, permit from Executive Engineer, Poona). The celebrated Hinayana cave is on a hill about 4 m. from the station.

The following is an abstract of Fergusson's description of it:[1] "The cave of **Karli** is certainly the largest, as well as the most complete, chaitya cave in India, and was excavated at a time when the style was in its greatest purity, and is fortunately the best preserved. Its interior dimen-

[1] *Rock-Cut Temples of India*, p. 27. See also *Indian Architecture*, 1, 142.

sions are 124 ft. 3 in. in total length, 81 ft. 3 in. length of nave. Its breadth from wall to wall is 45 ft. 6 in., while the width of the central aisle is 25 ft. 7 in. The height is only 46 ft. from the floor to the apex. The building resembles an early Christian church in its arrangements, while all the dimensions are similar to those of the choir of Norwich Cathedral." The nave is separated from the side aisles by fifteen columns with octagonal shafts on each side, of good design and workmanship. On the abacus which crowns the capital of each of these are two kneeling elephants, and on each elephant are two seated figures, generally a male and female, with their arms over each other's shoulders, but sometimes two female figures in the same attitude. The dagoba is plain and very similar to that in No. 10 cave at Ajanta,[1] but here a part of the wooden umbrella remains. The wooden ribs of the roof, too, remain nearly entire, proving beyond doubt that the roof is not a copy of a masonry arch; and the framed screen, filling up a portion of the great arch in front, like the centring of the arch of a bridge, remains. It consists of two plain octagonal columns with pilasters. Over these is a deep plain mass of wall, occupying the place of an entablature, and over this again a superstructure of four dwarf pillars. Except the lower piers, the whole of this was covered with wooden ornaments. The design appears to have consisted of a broad balcony in front of the plain wall, supported by bold wooden brackets from the two piers. This was the music gallery, or Nakkar Khana, which we still find existing in front of almost all Jain temples. There are no traces of painting in this cave, but the cave has been inhabited, and the smoke of cooking-fires has blackened the plaster. Its inhabitants were Saivites, and the cave was considered a temple dedicated to Siva, the dagoba performing the part of a gigantic lingam.

[1] pp. 138 seq.

The outer porch[1] is 52 ft. wide and 15 ft. deep. Originally the fronts of three elephants in each end wall supported a frieze ornamented with a rail pattern, but at both ends this has been cut away to introduce figures. Above was a thick quad-

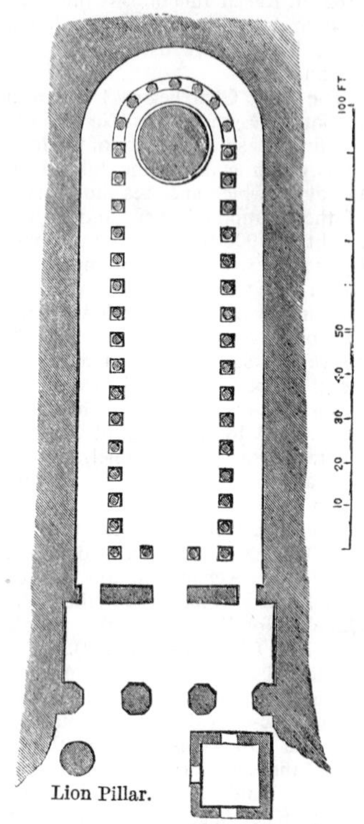

Cave at Karli.

rantal moulding, and then a rail with small façades of temples and pairs of figures.

"From the Sinhasthamba (lion pillar) on the left of the entrance Colonel Sykes copied an inscription, which Mr Prinsep deciphered in

[1] A modern temple to Ekviri, a title of Bhawani, the family goddess of Sivaji obscures the view of the arched doorway.

vol. 6 of the *Journal of the Asiatic Society*. It merely says: 'This lion-pillar is the gift of Ajmitra Ukass, the son of Saha Ravisabhoti'; the character, Mr Prinsep thinks, is of the 1st or 2nd century B.C.''

The principal viharas at Karli to the right of the entrance to the chaitya are three tiers in height. They are plain halls with cells, but without any internal colonnades, and the upper one alone possesses a veranda. The lower fronts have been swept away by great masses of rock which have rolled from above. To the left of the chaitya are some smaller viharas and cisterns.

The **Caves of Bhaja and Bedsa.**[1] —Bhaja is a village ¾ m. S. of Malavli railway station, and Bedsa is 5½ m. to the E. of Bhaja. The caves of Bhaja date from 200 B.C. There are eighteen excavations, of which the Chaitya No. 12 is the most interesting. It contains a dagoba, but no sculptures, and has its roof supported by twenty-seven sloping pillars. Outside there is a group executed in bas-relief, now much defaced, and marks show that a wooden front was once attached to the great arch. On both sides of the chaitya the hill has been excavated into the usual halls of instruction, with cells. A little way to the S. is a curious collection of fourteen dagobas, five of which are inside and the others outside a cave. On the first of the latter there is an inscription. The last cave to the S., some way beyond the others, is a vihara 16½ ft. by 17½ ft., decorated with excellent and interesting sculptures, including one of a prince on an elephant and another of a prince in his chariot, and three armed figures.

The caves at Bedsa lie 4 m. S.E. from Kamshet station beyond Malavli and date a little later than Bhaja. The plan of the chaitya resembles Karli, but is neither of so great extent nor so well executed, and appears more modern. It contains a dagoba; and its roof, which is ribbed and supported by twenty-six octagonal pillars 10 ft. high, seems to have been covered with paintings. There are four pillars about 25 ft. high in front, surmounted by a group of horses, bulls, and elephants, with a male and female rider upon them. These groups resemble those found on the Indo-Mithraic coins of the N. The hall of instruction has an apsidal end and a vaulted roof, and is situated close to the left of the chaitya.

[1] A full account of these places will be found in *Cave Temples of India*, pp. 223, 228.

96 m. **Vadgaon** (Wargaon) station (P.W.D. Inspection Bungalow, permit from Executive Engineer, Poona), celebrated for the stand of a British force under Lieutenant-Colonel Cockburn, on the 12th and 13th of January 1779, and for the conclusion of an armistice with the Mahrattas by General John Carnac of the Bombay Council, who was accompanying the force as a civilian. The Convention was, however, repudiated by Warren Hastings, and the war went on for four years.

116 m. **Kirkee** (now often written **Khidki**) is only 3¾ m., and better visited, from Poona. The plain S.E. of Government House, was the scene in November 1817 of a British victory over Baji Rao II, the last Peshwa.

Kirkee was the regimental centre of the Bombay Engineers.

On the road to Poona is Holkar's Bridge, over the Mula river. About 60 yd. S.W. of the S. end of the bridge is Holkar's Tomb, a temple to Mahadeo (Siva) in an oblong enclosure, erected in memory of Vithoji Rao Holkar, who was trampled to death by an elephant at Poona in 1802 (p. 434), and of his wife, who became a *sati*. On the right of the road is an old English cemetery. Beyond the Mula the road passes the Deccan College, and then come the Jamsetji Bund, the Fitzgerald Bridge, and the Bund Gardens, for all of which see below under Poona.

The former Government House, now the home of the new Poona University, is at Ganeshkhind, 1½ m. S.W. of Kirkee railway station. The name is derived from a small *khind*, or pass, between hills, about ¾ m. S.E. of the house, which resembles a modern French château, and has a tall, slim tower, 80 ft. high, from the top of which there is a fine view, including Kirkee and the Parbati Hill. The house contains a painting by Wales of the signing of the Treaty against Tipu Sultan in 1789, and portraits of the last Peshwa, Nana Phadnavis and Madhava Rao Scindia.

To the N. of Government House are the **Botanical Gardens.**

119 m. **POONA** (now mainly written **Pune**)* (Hotels), junction of the Central and Southern (M.G.) Rys. The Cantonment, which is on the Bombay, Belgaum, Colombo air-route is situated E. of the city, covering an area of 4¼ sq. m. within its limits. The Civil Lines lie N.W. of the Cantonment. Poona (lat. 18° 31′, long. 73° 51′; altitude 1905; pop. 853,000 in 1971) was, under the British régime, the headquarters of the Government of Bombay during the monsoon.

The first mention is in the Mahratta annals of 1599, when the parganahs of Poona and Supa (S.E.) were granted to Malaji Bhonsla (grandfather of Sivaji) by the King of Ahmadnagar. In 1750 it became the Mahratta capital under Balaji Baji Rao, the Brahman Peshwa, or chief minister (Pandit Pradhan), who deposed the descendants of Sivaji and imprisoned them in the Fort of Satara (p. 443). On 25th October 1802, Jaswant Rao Holkar defeated the combined armies of the Peshwa and Scindia, and captured all Scindia's guns, baggage and stores. By the Treaty of Bassein the Peshwa sought British help, and Poona was occupied by Wellesley in 1803. After the battle of Kirkee on the 17th November 1817, Poona surrendered to the British.

The city stands on the right of the Mutha river, before it joins the Mula. At its extreme S. limit is the Hill of Parbati, so called from a celebrated temple of the goddess Durga, or Parbati, on its summit (see p. 434). A few miles to the E. and S.E. are the hills which lead up to the still higher tableland towards Satara. The *Aqueduct*, now unused, was built by one of the Rastias, a family of great distinction amongst the Mahrattas. It starts from a well in the hillside near Khadakwasla, and supplied water to a reservoir at Sadashiv Peth. There are also extensive waterworks, constructed mainly through the liberality of Sir Jamsetjee Jeejeebhoy. On the road to the Bund Gardens, is the **Council Hall,** containing some pictures of interest, including those of Sir Bartle and Lady Frere, Lord Napier of Magdala, Sir Salar Jang of Hyderabad, Maharaja Khande Rao Gaekwar, and other notable men of Western India.

Opposite the Council Hall is the **Daftar** or **Record Room,** which contains priceless records of the Peshwas.

The Sassoon Hospitals, in the Gothic style, whose cost was borne by Sir Jacob Sassoon, are situated at the end of the Arsenal Road. There is a medical school for the training of sub-assistant surgeons attached to the hospitals. Fronting the main gate is the handsome **War Memorial,** erected by public subscription after the First World War in honour of "the Men of all classes and creeds, who went forth from this City and District of Poona to fight for the Empire in the Great War".

Opposite the hospitals are the Collector's Cutcherry and the Government Treasury. Close by is a large building in grey stone, erected in 1915, to accommodate the Government Offices. About 250 yd. S. of St Paul's Church is the *Jews' Synagogue*, a red brick building with a tower, 90 ft. high consecrated 29th September 1867. Mr David Sassoon's Tomb adjoins the synagogue, which was built by him. The mausoleum is 16 ft. square and 28 ft. high. S. of St Paul's Church is St Mary's Church, consecrated by Bishop Heber in 1825. The font, in the S.W. corner, is surrounded by stained-glass windows.

E. of St Mary's is the Race-course, about 1 m. long. Close also are the Gymnasium, St Andrew's Presbyterian Church, and the Masonic Lodge. To the E. of the Race-course are the celebrated **Empress Gardens,** containing grand specimens of tropical forest trees; and S. of these the handsome R.C. Cathedral dedicated to St Patrick. An Industrial Museum is in Ghole Road and one (1915) of Mahratta relics at 1321 Sadashiv Peth.

There are several mission establishments and schools in the city and suburbs.

The **Sangam** is the name given to the tongue of land at the confluence of the Mutha river, flowing from the S., with the Mula river, coming from the N.W.

The **Wellesley Bridge,** 482 ft. long and 28½ ft. broad, crosses the Mutha river to the Sangam promontory, close to its confluence with the Mula. This bridge, opened in 1875, takes the place of a wooden bridge erected to commemorate the victories of the Duke of Wellington in India.

On the left hand, after crossing the Wellesley Bridge, are the Judge's Court, the Poona Engineering College, and a long, low building (Sangamvadi), which stands on the site of the British Residency, burnt in 1817. At the E. end of Wellesley Bridge a path to the left leads to a garden containing temples. The first has a tower 40 ft. high. In the middle of the garden is a second temple. A third temple at the end of the garden was built by Holkar, who destroyed two other old temples to build it. All are dedicated to Mahadeo. At 300 yd. from the Engineering College is Mr Bomanjee Dinshaw Petit's house, called Garden Reach, built between 1862 and 1864. Permission to view is usually granted on application when the family is not in residence. The gardens are beautiful, and extend along the banks of the river. The ceiling of the drawing-room was beautifully decorated by Poona artists. In it is a full-length portrait of Mr David Sassoon.

After passing the Engineering College, a side road over the level crossing leads to Bhamburda. The main road continues to the former Government House, Ganeshkhind (p. 431). The Meteorological Observatory was opened in July 1928, when the Indian Meteorological Department was transferred here from Simla. On the right is the College of Agriculture. Its white dome forms a conspicuous landmark. On the return from Ganeshkhind the city is reached by a road passing the Fergusson College (1884), the Bhandarkar Oriental Institute, and the Women's College at Hingne.

From Garden Reach it is a pleasant drive of 1¾ m. *via* the Boat Club and Holkar's Bridge, to the Jamsetji Bund and the Fitzgerald Bridge. Across the bridge is Yeravda, where in the Aga Khan's Palace Mr Gandhi spent some time under house arrest. The Bund of stone dams the Mula river, and on the S. side of it are the **Bund Gardens,** of 6 acres. Opposite the Bund is Bund Hill, on which stands an ancient temple, and the Purna Kuti Palace, erected by the late Sir Vithaldas Thackersey. Here the British guns were mounted during the crossing of the Yeravda ford (17th November 1817, p. 432): and hence comes the alternative name of Picquet Hill. Above is the broad stream, 350 yd. wide, on which regattas take place, chiefly in February.

In E. Kirkee is the **Deccan College,** built of grey trap-stone, in the Gothic style. The **College,** which was removed to the present building in 1864, was originally the Poona Sanskrit College. The hall, 70 ft. long, used for the Library, contains portraits of former principals and professors, including Dr Wordsworth, a nephew of the poet, Sir Ram Krishna Bhandarkar and Prof. Kielhorn, the great Orientalists, Mr F.W. Bain, the author of *A Digit of the Moon*, and Sir Edwin Arnold; and also of the founder, Sir Jamsetjee

Jeejeebhoy, the first Parsi baronet. Another road leads N. to the Yeravda Golf-course and the Aga Khan's Palace.

The Khumbharves Dharan Causeway on the Mutha river at the approach from the Bombay Road is replaced by the Lloyd Bridge, which forms an impressive entrance to the heart of Poona city. The Law Courts are near the bridge. The streets of the **City** are wide, and some of the older houses are substantial and picturesque. It is divided into nineteen divisions, called *peths*, some of them named after the days of the week on which the market was held. The Sadashiv Peth is named after the general killed at Panipat (1761). Amongst the industries may be mentioned the making of gold and silver thread and wire for embroidery and for a simple kind of jewellery, the stringing of beads and berries for ornaments, and brass-work of all kinds.

The most convenient way of entering the city is by crossing the Lloyd Bridge. The road leads past the interesting Panchaleshwar Temple, of great antiquity, and the Sivaji Memorial Hall and Military School, whose foundation-stone was laid by the Prince of Wales in 1922. The equestrian **Statue of Sivaji** (in front of the Hall) is the work of Mr V. P. Karmokar, an Indian sculptor, and was cast in Bombay, is 31 ft. high and weighs 8½ tons. Poona owes this striking memorial of the Mahratta hero largely to a former Maharaja of Kolhapur (p. 446).

On the S. side of the Mutha is the magnificent gateway of the **Shanwar Wada** (Saturday Palace), which was built by Baji Rao, grandfather of the last Peshwa, and was burnt down in 1827. Only the walls remain. Excavations have disclosed the gardens of the palace with an elaborate system of irrigation. The spikes in the gate were placed to prevent the forcing of the doors by elephants. Remains of frescoes are also to be seen. Within are the Guard-house and Nakkar Khana (music gallery). Above the gateway is a small balcony. Here was the terrace from which, in 1795, the Peshwa, Madho Rao Narayan, fell, and died two days afterwards of his injuries, aged 21. Behind was the house of Nana Phadnavis, and W. is a temple of Onkareshwar. In front is a memorial to the Mahratta soldiers who fell in the First World War. A stone bridge leads to the village of Bhamburda and the Sangam, where tazias are thrown into the river on the last day of Muharrum.

Not far from the palace is a street in which, under the last Peshwa, offenders were executed by being trampled to death by elephants. One of the most memorable of these executions, on account of the princely rank of the sufferer, was that of Vithoji Holkar, brother of Jaswant Rao Holkar who, later in the year 1802, avenged him in the Battle of Poona (p. 432). Baji Rao II witnessed the scene from a window of his palace, where, on the morning of the 1st of April 1802, he took his seat with his favourite Balaji Kunjar. The Raja Kelkar Museum near Phule Market has a good collection housed in an old-style palace.

In the Budhwar, or "Wednesday", quarter of the city the visitor should on no account miss the delightful **Visram Bagh** Palace, with its beautiful pillars and courtyard, and its wooden porch. This almost perfect example of an old Mahratta palace has been used in turn as a Sanskrit College, a High School, and a Court. In Shukruwar (Friday) Peth the Scottish Mission has built a hospital, known as the N.M. Wadia Hospital.

The Environs

The **Parbati Hill**, with its temples, is situated S.W. of the town, about 3½ m. from the Poona railway station; the road to Sinhgarh leads to it past the Hirabagh, or "Diamond Garden". In a cemetery here is interred the celebrated African traveller, Sir

William Cornwallis Harris, Major in the Bombay Engineers, who died in 1848.[1] The Hirabagh had a lake and island and the villa of the Peshwas, mosque and temples. The lake has been drained for sanitary reasons, and the building is occupied by a social club. The Parbati temple was built by Peshwa Balaji Baji Rao in honour of the titular Raja at Satara. A long succession of steps and ramps leads up to the top of the hill and to the temples. At each corner of the first court are small shrines to Surya (the Sun), Vishnu, Kartikkeya (the Hindu Mars), and Durga; and in the centre is the principal temple dedicated to the goddess Durga or Parbati, the wife of Siva, so called from Parbat, "a mountain", as she is said to be the daughter of the Himalaya. In the temple is a silver image of Siva, with images of Parbati and Ganesh, of gold, seated on his knees. During the Diwali festival in October it is lighted up in a beautiful manner.

On the N.W. side of the enclosing wall is a Moorish-looking window, whence, it is said, Baji Rao watched the defeat of his troops at Kirkee. From the top of this wall, reached by narrow steps, there is an extensive view over Poona, Kirkee, and surrounding country, including Parbati Tank, to the E., and Parbati village, S. of the tank, over the Hirabagh to St Mary's Church and the Jews' Synagogue, far to the N.E.

S.W. is a ruined palace of the Peshwas, which was struck by lightning in 1817, the year of Baji Rao's overthrow by the British. A rupee may be given to the Brahman who shows the place, for the benefit of the temple and the numerous blind persons who frequent the hill.

At the foot of the hill is a square field, in the time of the Peshwas enclosed by high brick walls. At the end of the rains, about the time of the Dassara, gifts in money were presented to all Brahmans. In order to prevent the holy men from receiving more than their share, they were passed into this enclosure, at the gate of which stood a vast cauldron filled with red pigment. Each as he entered was marked with this, and nothing was given till all had gone in. They were then let out one by one, and the money was given to each. On one occasion the Peshwa is said to have lavished £60,000 in this manner. There are several other temples and shrines at the top of the hill.

About 6 m. from Poona is the Khondwa Leper Asylum, managed by the Mission to Lepers in India and the East. The asylum accommodates 200 lepers, and was opened in 1909.

Excursions from Poona

A road runs 73 m. N.E. to Ahmadnagar, continuing to Nasik, 132 m.

15 m. N.E. from Poona, along the Ahmadnagar road, is the battlefield of **Koregaon (Corygaum)**. Here a small force of Bombay sepoys, under Capt. Francis Staunton, kept a large Mahratta army, under the Peshwa himself, in check on 1st January 1818—one of the most notable achievements in the history of the former Bombay Army. A monument 70 ft. high (1821) stands in a square enclosure on the right bank of the River Bhima opposite the village.

43 m. from Poona is the deserted Cantonment of **Sirur** on the Ghod river. There are some interesting tombs in the cemetery. The D.B. is ½ m. farther on.

15 m. S.W. from Poona is **Sinhgarh** (the "Lion Fort")[1]. At 12 m. from Poona, is passed the Kharakwasla reservoir, Lake Fife, where excellent sailing and fishing can be had. The pretty bungalow may be occupied with the permission of the Executive Engineer, Poona Irrigation Division. The dam, 107 ft. high, spans the valley of the Mutha river, and was the first (1879) of the large dams built in the Deccan. The water feeds the

[1] He was the author of *Wild Sports in the West* and the *Highlands of Ethiopia.*

[1] See *Poona and its Battlefields*, by Col. L. W. Shakespear (Macmillan, 1916).

Mutha Right Bank Canal, and supplies drinking-water to Poona and Kirkee. The National War Academy is nearby.

The ascent to Sinhgarh in part is almost perpendicular. Being 4162 ft. above the sea, it is cool. There are several bungalows here occasionally occupied by summer visitors from Poona. The famous stronghold is intimately associated with the history of Sivaji. It was taken, during his rebellion against Bijapur (February 1670), by the renowned Tanaji Malusre. The Mahrattas scaled the precipice in the darkness and surprised the garrison, but Tanaji was killed at the head of his men. The fine gateway should be noticed; and the figure of a Mahratta warrior in a small shrine which marks the spot where Tanaji fell. There is also a monument to Tanaji's left hand, which he lost before he received his fatal wound. The story is popular in Mahratta history.

Purandhar is another hill fort to the S.E., about 17 m. as the crow flies, and 24 m. by road from Poona. The upper and lower forts are situated more than 300 ft. below the summit, which is 4560 ft. above sea-level, and are protected by a perpendicular scarp. A treaty was signed here on 1st March 1776, between the ministers of the Peshwa and Col. Upton, the envoy of Warren Hastings, who marched across Central India from Calcutta and back to the East Coast. It is still used as a sanatorium for summer visitors. There is a Dt. Bungalow for the use of officials on tour. Panthers are found in the hills, and deer and other game in the neighbourhood. The temple "Kedareswar" crowns the summit of the hill.

Poona to Madras

167 m. from Bombay on the main line to Madras is **Dhond** Junction (R.), with a railway colony. From this place the Dhond-Manmad Chord of the Central Ry. runs N. The only place of importance on this line is

51 m. **Ahmadnagar** station, usually called Nagar (R., D.B., Inspection Bungalow), founded in 1490 by Ahmad Nizam Shah Bahri, son of a Brahman of Vijayanagar, the first of the Nizam Shahi dynasty, which ended 1636. His territory was the only part of the W. coast to which the ravages of Portuguese piracy did not extend. They maintained a friendly intercourse for many years with Ahmadnagar. The power of this State extended over the greater part of Berar and the province of Aurangabad and some districts in Khandesh, Kalyan, and from Bankot to Bassein, in the Konkan. The fort, but not the whole kingdom, fell into Akbar's hands in 1599, after sustaining a siege under Chand Bibi (killed), widow of Ali Adil Shah, of Bijapur, the "Noble Queen" of Meadows Taylor's novel. It was taken from the Nizam by the Mahrattas in 1760. In 1797 the fort was made over by the last Peshwa to Daulat Rao Scindia, from whom it was taken by Sir Arthur Wellesley, afterwards Duke of Wellington, on 12th August 1803.

The fort is 2½ m. N.E. of the railway station. The D.B. is N.W. of it. The gate on the Poona Road is called the Máliváda Darwaza. The town (pop. 117,000 in 1971) is 3 m. from the railway. Firishta, the historian (1570-1611), lived here.

The Emperor Aurangzeb (Alamgir) died at Ahmadnagar on the 3rd March 1707, at the age of 97, and his embalmed body is said to have rested in the walled enclosure known as Alamgir's Dargah, near the Cantonment, prior to its removal to the mausoleum at Aurangabad (p. 151). To the E. of the tomb, which faces a mosque, is a white marble Darbar Hall (fine view from the roof). 2 m. S.E. of the town is the Pariabagh, or "fairy garden", an old palace of Burhan Nizam Shah (1508-53), completed 1583.

½ m. N.E. of the town is the mausoleum of Ahmad Nizam Shah with walls inscribed inside in Arabic gold letters. A canopy nearby covers the grave of an elephant which helped to capture (p. 478) Rama Raya of Vijayanagar at the battle of Talikot (1565). The Bagh Nizam is on the bank of the Sena river.

The tomb and mosque of Rumi Khan commemorate the Turkish caster of a great gun at Bijapur (p. 472).

The **Tomb of Salabat Khan,** commonly called that of **Chand Bibi,** is 6 m. to E., on a hill (alt. 3080 ft.). The building is octagonal and of three storeys. Below is the crypt, in which are two tombs. There is no inscription.

Main Line

184 m. from Bombay on the main line to Madras is **Diksal** station, 3 m. beyond which the Bhima river is crossed.

234 m. **Kurduwadi** Junction (R., D.B.). From here the Barsi Light Ry. leads N.E., through Barsi, to (86 m.) Latur, a great cotton and grain centre and S. to (32 m.) Pandharpur and (118 m.) Miraj, where it connects with the metre-gauge line of the Southern Ry. from Poona to Belgaum. At Ashti, 19 m. S., in a battle (Feb. 1818), Bapu Gokhale was killed and the Satara Raja released.

Pandharpur (D.B.), on the right bank of the Bhima river, with a very celebrated shrine (1228) to Vithoba, an incarnation of Vishnu. Immense crowds of pilgrims visit the temple particularly in July, at the Ekadashi Fair. A pilgrim tax is levied at the time of the three chief fairs, to provide for the sanitary safety of the town. On the Bhima river there are eleven ghats, or landing-places. In the centre of the town, on high ground, stands Vithoba's Temple, inscriptions on which show that portions of it were standing in the 14th century. There are numerous other temples in the river bed.

283 m. **Sholapur** station (D.B.K.; pop. 398,000 in 1971; alt. 1560 ft.) means "sixteen villages". The fort (S.W.), of Muslim construction, consists of a double line of lofty battlemented and towered walls, surrounded by a moat. In May 1818 Thomas Munro and General Pritzler marched against the remnant of Bajo Rao's infantry, attacked them under the walls of Sholapur, and routed them utterly. The fort, after a short siege, surrendered.

The city, which lies N.E. of the railway station, has grown greatly owing to the development of the cotton industry. There are several mills and many schools.

16 m. S. is Ashti, scene of General Sir Lionel Smith's defeat of Bapu Gokhale (*see above*).

4 m. N.W. of the city of Sholapur, on the Osmanabad road, is the **Ekrukh Tank** (1873), 6 m. in length, formed by an embankment of earth 7000 ft. long and 76 ft. high, across the Adhela river. Three canals from it irrigate the surrounding country. It also supplies the city with water.

43 m. N. is **Osmanabad,** or Dharashiv, in the former Hyderabad State. Groups of Jain and Vaishnava caves, which may be assigned to the period from A.D. 500 to A.D. 650, lie round the town. At **Tuljapur,** 28 m. from Sholapur and 14 m. from Osmanabad, is the temple of Tulja Bhawani (Durga), which is visited by Hindus from all parts of India. Meadows Taylor lived here and mentioned it in a novel, *Java*.

292 m. **Hotgi** Junction station (R.). From this point a branch line runs S. to **Bijapur** and Gadag Junction (see Route 26).

323 m. **Dudhni**; the last station in Maharashtra. The line here enters former Hyderabad territory, now included in the State of Karnataka.

353 m. **Gulbarga** (pop. 145,000 in 1971) station (D.B.). Gulbarga was the first capital of the Bahmani Kingdom of the Deccan (1347-1525), but was abandoned in favour of Bidar (p. 453) by Sultan Ahmad Shah in 1428. The Kingdom, founded at the close of the reign of Muhammad Tughlaq Shah (1325-51), by Hasan Zafar Khan, who took the name of Bahman, an early Persian King, dissolved into

the kingdoms of Bijapur, Golconda, Ahmadnagar, Bidar, and Berar. Bidar ended in 1609, and the last, Golconda, was taken by Aurangzeb in 1687. The Maidan stretches from the railway station to the city. The old fort in the background, black with age, and the numerous domes with which the plain is dotted, relieve the scene.

The outer walls and gateways and most of the old buildings of the **Fort** are in a very dilapidated condition. The Citadel, or Bala Hissar, has suffered least: it is a solid block of masonry. On the top of it is a curious old gun, 26 ft. long, and having twenty pairs of iron rings attached to it, by which it used probably to be slung or lifted. Close by, at the S. extremity of the inner fort wall, are the remains of an old Hindu temple. A plan is on sale.

In the old fort is the **Jami Masjid,** built in the reign of Firoz Shah Bahmani (1397-1432). There is a tradition that it was built by a Moorish architect from Cordova as a replica of the great cathedral mosque in that city. Visitors are expected to take off their shoes. It measures 216 ft. E. and W. and 176 ft. N. and S., and covers an area of 38,016 sq. ft. It is peculiar among the great mosques of India in that the whole area is completely covered over by a large dome over the mihrab, one at each corner and 75 smaller ones. The light is admitted through the side walls, pierced with great arches on all sides except the W.

The grand old **Tombs** in the Eastern quarter, huge fortress-like buildings, surmounted by domes 100 ft. high, are the burial-places of Bahmani Kings. They are roughly yet strongly built, but with the exception of some handsome stone tracery there are no exterior ornaments. The interiors are more elaborately finished. Some little distance from these tombs is the much venerated shrine or Dargah of Banda Nawaz, or Gisu Daraz (1321-1422), a saint of the Chishti family (see p. 265), who came to Gulbarga during the reign of Firoz Shah Tughlaq in 1413. The inner shrine is now accessible to all visitors.

The structure is said to have been erected in 1640 by a descendant during the reign of Mahmud 'Adil Shah. Ahmad Shah Wali, Firoz Shah's brother, made many valuable presents to the saint, gave him large *jagirs*, and built him a magnificent college close to the city. Some of his descendants still reside at his tomb. Close by are some buildings, consisting of a sarai of General Afzal Khan, mosque, and college (*Madrasa*) said to have been erected by Aurangzeb, who visited Gulbarga on several occasions. There is also a dome of polished ashlar masonry, built by Chand Bibi 'Adil Shahi as her tomb; but she was buried at Bijapur.

In the town is a cross-shaped bazar, 570 ft. by 60 ft., on pillars with sixty-one Hindu arches, with a block of buildings at either end.

370 m. **Shahabad** station (R.), known for its limestone quarries. Large quantities of the stone, and cement made from it, are exported.

376 m. **Wadi** Junction. From here the old Nizam's State Ry., now merged in the Central Ry., extended E. to Hyderabad and Bezwada (Route 25). Through carriage on the mail train.

427 m. **Krishna** station. Here the railway crosses the Kistna (= Krishna) river by a bridge of 36 spans, 3855 ft. long, into the Raichur Doab.

443 m. **Raichur** station (R.; alt. 1318 ft.).

In 1357 Raichur formed part of the dominions of the Bahmani Sultans. It was included in the Kingdom (Sirkar) of Bijapur, and was governed in 1478 by Khwaja Mahmud Gawan the justly-famed Minister. When Bijapur became independent in 1489, Raichur was its first capital.

The Fort is about 1½ m. from the railway station. The N. gate, flanked by towers, is best worth attention. There is a stone elephant, not quite the natural size, carved out of a boulder about 50 yd. outside the gate. On the inner wall a carving shows a stone beam 41½ ft. long being carted. At right angles to this gate is another called the Kasba Darwaza. Outside the latter is the door of a tunnel, out of which the garrison could come to close the gate. Near the W. gate (Sikandaria) is the old palace, with immensely thick walls.

The Citadel (1294; 290 ft. above the plain) should be seen for the sake of the view. The ascent commences from near the N. gate. No mortar is used in the walls. On the left is a row of cells belonging to the *dargah*, or shrine, and at the E. end, overhanging the precipice, is a stone pavilion. Near this, on the E., is a mosque 18 ft. high; and on the S. side is a place for a bell or gong 7 ft. high, with stone supports and a stone roof. The whole surface of the top is 70 ft. square.

Maski, reached *via* Lingsugur (56 m. W.), and then 17 m. S.E., is the site of a pre-Indus, neolithic culture.

461 m. The railway crosses the Tungabhadra river, and enters what is now Andhra Pradesh, by a bridge 4060 ft. long.

487 m. **Adoni** (Adwani—D.B.K.), is the principal cotton-mart in the Deccan. According to tradition, the town was founded 3000 years ago by Chandra Singh of Bidar. After the Battle of Talikota in 1565 the Sultan of Bijapur appointed Malik Rahman Khan, an Abyssinian, to govern it, which he did for thirty-nine years, and died there. His tomb on the Talibanda Hill is still an object of religious veneration. He was succeeded by his adopted son, Sidi Mas'aud Khan, who built the lower fort and the Jami Masjid. In 1690 Adoni was taken, after a desperate resistance, by one of Aurangzeb's Generals, and in 1740 fell to the first Asaf Jah.

Salabat Jang granted it (1757) in *jagir* to Basalat Jang, his younger brother, who endeavoured to form an independent State. He died in 1782 and was buried at Adoni, and a fine mosque and tomb were erected over his grave and that of his mother. In 1786 the citadel was captured by Tipu Sultan after one month's siege. He demolished the fortifications, and removed the guns and stores to Gooty. In 1792 it was restored to the Nizam and exchanged by him with the British in 1800 for other places. The citadel is built on five hills, two of which rise 800 ft. above the plain. Half-way up the rock is a fine tank containing good water, and never dry.

519 m. **Guntakal** Junction station (R.). From this junction the broad-gauge line continues S.E. to Madras. Metre-gauge lines run S. to Bangalore, N.E. to Guntur and (279 m.) Bezwada, and W. to Bellary, Hospet (for Vijayanagar), Gadag and (160 m.) Hubli (Route 27).

536 m. **Gooty** station (R.). Nearly 2 m. S. of the railway station is its famous hill fortress, first built between 1509 and 1530 on a precipitous mass of bare rock. The Fort, which is 989 ft. above the plain and 2171 ft. above sea-level, is approached by a long, winding, paved pathway, which leads to the summit. It was the stronghold of Murari Rao Ghorpade, who helped Clive at Arcot in 1751. It was taken by Hyder Ali in 1776, after a siege of nine months. Water having failed Ghorpade surrendered the fort and soon died.

At the foot is the English Cemetery, where rested until 1831 the body of Sir Thomas Munro, Governor of Madras, who died at Pattikonda, in Kurnool, on 6th June 1827. His remains now lie in St Mary's Church, Fort St George, Madras, but a cenotaph stands in this cemetery. There is a R.H. for Indians in the town, erected by Government to the memory of Sir Thomas Munro.

560 m. The Penner river is crossed.

566 m. **Tadpatri** station (R.). Bus service between Tadpatri and Anantapur. The town was founded during the time of the Vijayanagar Kings, about 1485, when the highly decorative temples of Rameswaraswami and Chintalarayaswami were built. They are about 2 m. from the railway

station. The one on the river-bank was never finished, but is the more imposing. Fergusson (*Ind. Arch.*, 1, 403, pictures on pp. 405-6) wrote: "The wonders of the place are two gopurams belonging to the second (the Rameswara), which is now a deserted temple on the banks of the (Penner) river. One of these was apparently quite finished."

581 m. The Chitravati river is crossed.

589 m. **Mangapatnam.** A serious accident occurred in 1902, when a bridge was washed away and the mail train ran into the gap.

632 m. from Bombay and 162 m. from Madras is **Cuddapah** (Kadapa) station (R.). The town (alt. 430 ft.) was formerly the capital of the Nawabs of Cuddapah. Situated between the Mahrattas, the Nizam and Mysore, they were gradually crushed and reabsorbed (1792) by the Hyderabad State. In 1800 the Cuddapah, Kurnool and Bellary Districts were ceded to the East India Company, and Thomas Munro was appointed the first Collector of all three. Places of interest, historical and archaeological, are few, the principal being Gandikota and Siddhavattam Forts (railway stations, Kondapuram, 17 m. from Tadpatri, and Vontimitta, 14 m. from Cuddapah, respectively). There are R.Hs. at both. The W. taluks are noted for their ground-nut and cotton crops; while in the Penner river-bed, near Cuddapah, are grown the melons for which the district is famous.

Jammalamadugu (R.H., 13 m. from Muddanuru station, 34 m. from Cuddapah) is a Mission centre. Owing to the many broad and unbridged streams in the district the roads are not suited to motor traffic. Persons travelling in the district must make their own arrangements for meals at R.Hs.

659 m. The Cheyair river is crossed by a bridge 3500 ft. long.

710 m. **Renigunta** (R.), junction with the metre-gauge branch of the Southern Ry., between Gudur (p. 427) and Katpadi Junction (183 m.) on the Madras-Bangalore line.

On the line from Renigunta S.E. to Katpadi, are

6 m. **Tirupati** East station (D.B.), celebrated for one of the most sacred **Hill Pagodas** (Sri Venkateswara Perumal) in S. India, now made into the Sri Venkateswara University; it stands at the top of the "holy hill" called Tirumala (part of the Seshachalam range) and is about 8 m. from the railway station. Frequent bus services run to the summit. There is a Tourist Bureau in the station which visitors should consult. Wooden and brass idols, toys, souvenirs, and incense sticks are a speciality of the lower town. There are several gopurams on the ascent visible from below. The antiquity of the temple is indisputable, but its origin is involved in obscurity. It is one of the richest in South India, having been endowed successively by Chola, Pandya, and Vijayanagar Rulers. The idol is an erect stone figure 7 ft. high, with four arms, representing Vishnu. In the temple at Tirumala are copper statues of the Vijayanagar Raja Krishnaraya and his two Ranis, and of Venkatapatiraya. No one but Hindus may enter the sacred area, but the Temple Trustees allow foreign visitors to stay on the hill where the shrines are situated subject to certain restrictions. The Seshachalam range is 2500 ft. high and quite bare, and has even peaks. On the seventh peak, Sri Venkataramanachellam, is the pagoda, surrounded by a broad belt of mango, tamarind, and sandal trees. In front of it is a Hall of 1000 Pillars. A picturesque stepped way leads from it to the temple gate, which is a fine one; admission to the temple is not granted. E. of the temple is the Swami Pushkarani tank, where pilgrims bathe before entering the shrine and many guest houses and bungalows set aside for pilgrims and visitors by the Temple Trustees.

14 m. **Chandragiri** station. The walled Fort is built on a large rounded mass of granite rising 600 ft. above

the valley. Below the hill is the *Palace* of the Vijayanagar Rajas. After the defeat of Talikota (1565) the capital was changed in 1600 to Chandragiri. But this was taken by the Golconda Ruler in 1646, occupied by the Nawab of Arcot in 1750, by Haidar Ali in 1782, and ceded by Tipu in 1792.

In the palace Sri Ranga Raya (1639) made to the East India Company the original grant of the land on which Fort St George (Madras) was built. It is most picturesquely situated in the fort, and at the back of it is a high, rocky hill. The best way to visit it is to drive from Renigunta.

32 m. **Pakala**; junction for a metre-gauge line to (142 m.) Dharmavaram, junction for the Guntakal-Bangalore line (Route 27, p. 477).

51 m. **Chittoor** (alt. 988 ft.; D.B.K. ¼ m. from station); 24 m. by road from Ranipet (Route 29). Haidar Ali died on 7th December 1782 at Narsingh Rayanapet, near Chittoor, where a monument marks the spot. A view may be had from Chase's Folly, one of the surrounding hills; a road, originally built by the Judge who gives his name to the hill, leads to the summit. There are some remarkable tombs in the old cemetery.

Main Line

From Renigunta station the main line continues S.E. to

751 m. **Arkonam** Junction (R.). Here the Southern Ry. branch to Jalarpet and Bangalore (Route 29) meets the Raichur N.W. line. A metre-gauge branch runs S. to Conjeeveram and Chingleput (Route 31).

768 m. is **Trivellore** (Tiruvallur) station, 30 m. by road from Madras. There is a large Vaishnava temple here of Viraraghava (see p. 536). 4 m. from the station is the site of the old fort of Tripasore, at one time the station for the East India Company's cadets, and afterwards for pensioners.

794 m. from Bombay is **Madras** Central station (Route 30).

ROUTE 24

POONA to GOA by **Wathar** (for **Mahabaleshwar**), **Satara, Miraj** Junction (for **Kolhapur**), **Belgaum, Londa** Junction, the **Braganza Ghat,** and **Marmagao.**

The traveller should note that there is an excellent system of Express Bus Services operating in the Western Ghats, covering such journeys as Bombay - Belgaum, Poona - Habli, Poona-Bangalore, etc.

The metre-gauge line of the Southern Ry. to (245 m.) Belgaum and (277 m.) Londa Junction, for Goa, branches off to the S. from the broad-gauge line of the Central Ry. to Madras (Route 23), 2 m. E. of **Poona** railway station (see p. 432).

48 m. **Nira** station. The Lloyd Dam at Bhatgarh, which is close to this station, forms the source of supply to the Nira canals system. Its length is 5333 ft., the area of the lake is 14½ sq. m., and the catchment area is 128 sq. m. The cost in 1928 was over 1¼ millions sterling. The reservoir completely submerges a former dam and Lake Whiting (1885). It feeds the old Nira Left Bank Canal and a new Right Bank Canal, each over 100 m. long and irrigating 4000 sq. m. Its value for the prevention of famine is incalculable. These irrigation schemes have been fully developed, and the estimated value of the crops raised in a single year has amounted to two and a half crores, about two millions sterling.

Passing through three hill ranges, the line next reaches

69 m. **Wathar** station (R.).

Passengers can alight here for **Mahabaleshwar,** the principal hill station of Bombay, about 40 m. distant by road to the W. It is a charming drive of about one hour, the first part through rolling country to

10 m. the **Shirgaon** Ghat.

21 m. **Wai** (D.B.) is situated on the left bank of the Krishna river, which is lined with pipal and mango-trees, and with handsome flights of stone bathing-ghats. Behind the city rise hills. One hill, 4 m. to the N.W., rises very abruptly, and has a hill fort on the top; it is called Pandavgad, according to the tradition that Wai is the Vairatnagar visited by the Pandavas (Introd., p. 21). The river is lined with handsome temples: the nearest to the D.B. is dedicated to Ganpati: the next to Mahadev: and one, at some distance, to Lakshmi. They form the great charm of this most picturesque spot. The *mandapam* or canopy, in front of Mahadev's temple, is very light, and a fine specimen of carving in stone.

Wai is a spot much famed in Hindu legend. Here, according to old tradition, the Pandavas spent part of their banishment and performed many great works (Introd., p. 21). On this account, and likewise because of its proximity to the source of the Krishna river, Wai is a place of great sanctity; and the Sanskrit school established here was once in much repute.

On leaving Wai the road begins a steep ascent to

28 m. **Panchgani,** containing several boarding-schools. From Panchgani the road descends a little for one-third of a mile; the country round is covered with low jungle and patches of cultivation. About 1 m. from Mahabaleshwar, a small lake made by the Raja of Satara is passed on the right; it winds and is about 810 yd. long, and not quite 200 yd. broad.

Mahabaleshwar,[1] the leading hill station of Bombay, was founded in 1828 by Sir John Malcolm, then Governor. There are two seasons—April and May and after the rains from October. From 1st October to 15th June mail motors run daily from Wathar to Mahabaleshwar; and direct from Poona to Mahabaleshwar (more convenient and very scenic route, 75 m.). There are four leading motor-service companies. There is also access by launch from Bombay to Dharamtar and thence by road (91 m.), or by road all the way. The climate is delightful from October to March. April and May are distinctly hot, with cool nights. In June mists prevail and torrential rains (from 150 in. to 400 in.) fall till the beginning of October. Christmas is a favourite season, and the climate usually dry and invigorating. The heavily wooded plateau has an abrupt descent to the E. of 2000 ft., and to the W. of from 3000 ft. to 4000 ft. In clear weather the sea can be seen, which is in a direct line only about 30 m. W. Orchids and lilies flower in April and May, and ferns and general vegetation are seen at their best in October, in which month butterflies abound.

There is a charmingly situated Club, open to non-members at a cost of Rs. 5.00 *plus* Rs. 1.50 per day, with residential quarters, and numerous furnished bungalows available on rent for the season. Frederick's Hotel is on the road from Panchgani, overlooking the golf-links and about 500 yd. E. of the Club; the Race View Hotel is on the Cassum Sajan Hill. Rooms should be booked well in advance during April and May.

There are excellent walks and rides. Golf, polo, tennis, etc., can be played and there is a library and reading-room at the Frere Hall, the N.E. half of the club building. Good vegetables are grown, and in the season strawberries can be had. Panthers were common, and tigers were occasionally found on the plateau; but the ordinary visitor is hardly likely to get any shooting. The plateau is very extensive. Its proximity to the sea makes the climate cool and equable. The

[1] See *Mahabaleshwar*, by D. B. Parasnis (Bombay, 1916).

view to the W., looking down upon the Konkan or narrow strip between the ghats and the sea, is very impressive.

The chief view-points and expeditions are Elphinstone Point and Arthur's Seat (overlooking the abrupt descent into the Konkan); Old Mahabaleshwar, with a very sacred temple, from which the Kistna is said to rise; Connaught Peak, with view of the Plateau; Lodwick Point (4067 ft.), with view of Pratapgad; Bombay Point, with perhaps the finest view of all; Kate's Point, on the road to Panchgani; the Falls of the Yenna into a lake 1000 ft. below, lie to E. and the Dhobi's Waterfall to W.

Former restrictions on cars have been abolished. For local transport, taxis and tongas are available. Cars are allowed on payment of Rs. 2.00 per day.

Pratapgad (Partabgarh) (D.B.) is a picturesque hill fort crowning a precipitous rock remarkable as the stronghold (1656) of Sivaji—founder of the Mahratta Empire. A charming drive of about 9 m. down the Fitzgerald Ghat on the road to Mahad leads to the village of Ambenali (primitive but beautifully situated R.H.) at the foot of the hill. There a branch road goes up hill to the foot of the fort whence about 500 steps take you into the fort itself.

Sivaji, having provoked hostilities with Bijapur, whose army he could not meet in the open, determined to parley with its General, Afzal Khan, at a personal interview, on condition that the two commanders should meet unarmed, in the midst, between the two armies, with only one armed attendant. They accordingly met in white robes, apparently muslin; but Sivaji wore defensive mail under his robe and turban, and carried concealed in his left hand a weapon called a Wághnakh, "the tiger's claws", consisting of four sharp steel claws attached by rings to his fingers. The Khan seized and stabbed him, but Sivaji drove these claws into him, tore out his vitals, and despatched him with a hidden dagger. His head was struck off and buried under the Afzal Burj in the fort. Meanwhile the Mahrattas, concealed in ambush in the jungle, rushed out upon the Bijapur forces and cut them to pieces, taking great booty.

From Wathar station the main line proceeds to

78 m. **Satara Road** station. From here it is a 10 m. drive to **Satara** (2203 ft. high; motor-cars available; D.B.K.), in a hollow between two ranges of hills, which rise above it on the E. and W. and partly overlap it on the S. The hill on the W. is the termination of a spur from the Mahabaleshwar Hills. From this hill to the city, water is conveyed 4 m. in pipes; and there are also two fine tanks. The city has many historic recollections, and the station is one of the most salubrious and pleasant in the Deccan.

The ruling family of Satara was descended from Sahu (the grandson of Sivaji), who was brought up at the Mughal court.

The Old Palace is the Judge's Court. The New Palace, near the centre of the city, was built for Appa Sahib (Raja Shahaji) between 1838 and 1844 by a British engineer, who also built the bridges over the Verna and Kistna rivers. On the façade are several mythological pictures, much defaced by the weather. On the W. side of the court is a hall (83 ft. long, 45 ft. broad). The roof is supported by sixty-four teak pillars, with four more in front.

About 200 yd. beyond in a villa may be seen the crown jewels of the Satara family, Jai Bhawani, the famous sword of Sivaji, and his other arms. The sword is 3 ft. 9 in. long in the blade and the handle is 8 in. long, but so small that a European can hardly get his hand into it.[1] Like most of the famous blades in India, it is of Euro-

[1] There are other weapons at Kolhapur and elsewhere which claim to be the original Bhawani sword. The balance of probability favours the Satara sword. A number of other relics of Sivaji are in the Bombay Museum (p. 96).

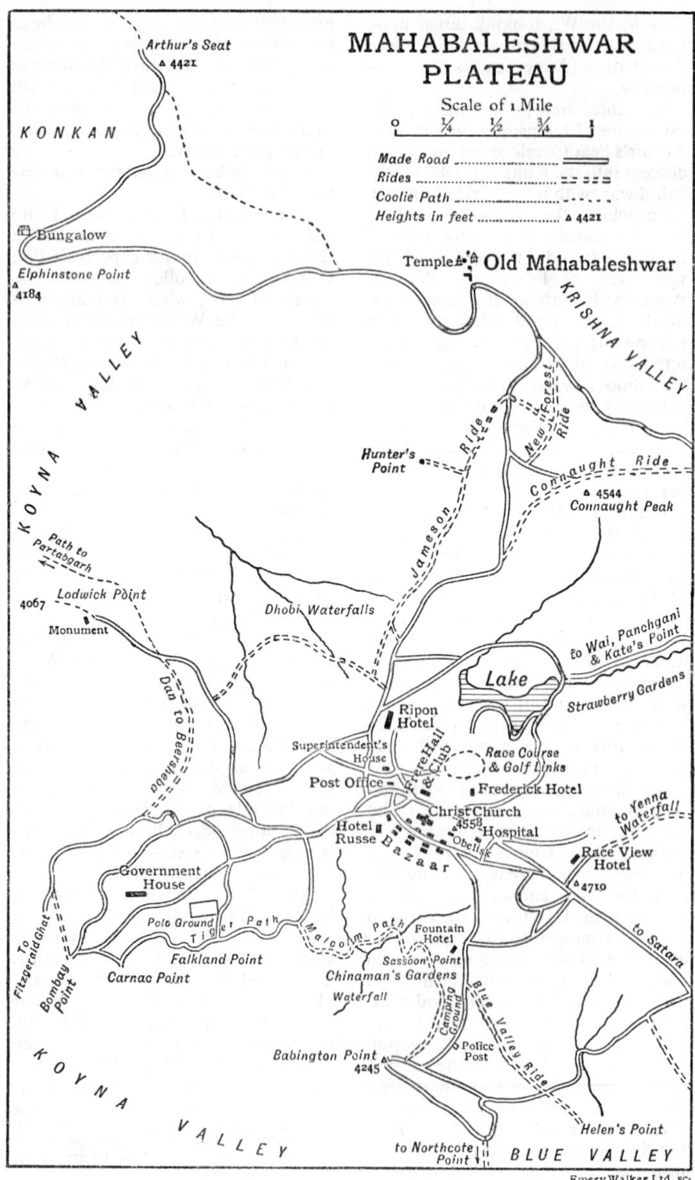
MAHABALESHWAR
PLATEAU
Scale of 1 Mile
0 1/4 1/2 3/4 1
Made Road
Rides
Coolie Path
Heights in feet 4421
Arthur's Seat
4421
KONKAN
Bungalow
Elphinstone Point
4184
Temple
Old Mahabaleshwar
KRISHNA VALLEY
KOYNA VALLEY
New Forest Ride
Jameson Ride
Hunter's Point
Connaught Ride
4544
Connaught Peak
Path to Partabgarh
4067
Lodwick Point
Monument
Dhobi Waterfalls
to Wai, Panchgani & Kate's Point
Lake
Strawberry Gardens
Dan to Beersheba
Ripon Hotel
Superintendent's House
Frere Hall & Club
Race Course & Golf Links
Post Office
Frederick Hotel
Christ Church
4558
Hospital
to Yenna Waterfall
Hotel Russe
Bazaar
Obelisk
Race View Hotel
4710
Government House
Polo Ground
Tiger Path
Malcolm Path
Fountain Hotel
to Satara
To Fitzgerald Ghat
Bombay Point
Carnac Point
Falkland Point
Sassoon Point
Chinaman's Gardens
Waterfall
Camping Ground
Blue Valley Ride
Police Post
Babington Point
4245
KOYNA VALLEY
Helen's Point
to Northcote Point
BLUE VALLEY
Emery Walker Ltd. sc.

pean make, and has the stamp of Genoa. The Wághnakh, or "tiger's claws", described on p. 443, has rings which pass over the first and fourth fingers, but are too small for a European hand. The shield is of rhinoceros hide, and has four stars or bosses of diamonds. The gold casket for holding Sivaji's seal is ornamented with diamonds, rubies, pearls and emeralds, and there is an inkstand and pen-holder of gold and gems. The quilted coat which Sivaji is said to have worn when he killed Afzal Khan may also be seen. It is only a cloak of thick quilted silk, which is inconsistent with the appearance of muslin. It is lined with red silk, is richly embroidered with gold, and is very heavy. The dagger is very handsome, and is 18 in. long. In the handle are fine diamonds, emerald and rubies.

The **Shri Chhatrapati Sivaji Maharaj Museum,** by the bus station, contains a collection of documents invaluable for research, and other relics of the Mahratta Empire which was made by the late Rao Bahadur B. D. Parasnis. There are three rooms open to the public containing an interesting collection of weaponry, saddlery and clothing; pictures and coins.

The **Fort of Wasota** on the S. side of the town is accessible by a path. The stone gate is very strongly built, with buttresses 40 ft. high. The interior contains a bungalow, one small temple, and the remains of the Raja's palace. The fort, taken by the British on 10th February 1818, is stated in a copper-plate record to have been built by a Raja of Panhala who reigned in 1192.[1] By him, too, were erected the forts of Wairatgad and Pandavgad, near Wai, and Chandan-Wandan, near Satara.

History.—Long before the time of the Adil Shahi dynasty at Bijapur the Fort of Satara was used as a State prison, and Sivaji, who captured it in 1673, after a siege of several months, unwittingly furnished for his descendants a prison in which they were confined by the Peshwas from 1752. In 1698 Satara was made the capital by Raja Ram, son of Sivaji and Regent. Aurangzeb, with a great army, in 1699 pitched his tents on the N. side.[1] His son, Prince Azam Shah, was on the W. side, at a village since called Shahpur; Shirzi Khan invested the S., and Tarbiyat Khan occupied the E. quarter. Chains of posts between the different camps effectually secured the blockade. The fort was defended by Pryagji Prabhu, hawaldar, who rolled down huge stones from the rock above, which did great execution. The blockade, however, was complete, and the besieged must have been compelled to surrender had not Parshuram Trimbak, who had thrown himself into the Fort of Parali, purchased the connivance of Azam Shah, and replenished stores. The grand attack was directed against the N.E. angle, the rock being 42 ft. high, with a bastion on the top of 25 ft. of masonry. Tarbiyat Khan undertook to mine this angle and at the end of four and a half months had completed two mines. The storming party, confident of success, was formed under the brow of the hill. The Emperor moved out in grand procession to view the attack, and the garrison crowded to the rampart. The first mine burst several fissures in the rock, and caused a great part of the masonry to fall inwards and crush many of the garrison; but the second and larger mine burst outwards and destroyed upwards of 2000 of the besiegers. Pryagji was buried by the first explosion close to a temple to Bhavani, but was dug out alive. This was regarded by the Mahrattas as a happy omen, but provisions fell

[1] *Grant Duff*, 1, 26 (edition of 1921). The prince was Bhoj II (1178-93); he is said to have built fourteen other forts, including Pawangarh and Panhala (p. 447).

[1] A pillar on the W. of the village of Karanja, about 2½ m. N.E. of Satara fort, and N. of the Poona-Satara Road, marks the site of the Emperor's camp.

short, and Azam Shah would no longer connive at their introduction. Proposals of surrender were therefore made through him, and the honour of the capture, which he so ill-merited, was not only assigned to him, but the very name was changed by the Emperor to 'Azamtara.

In 1705 the fort was retaken by the Mahrattas, through the artifice of a Brahmin named Anaji Pant. He ingratiated himself with the Mughals under the character of a mendicant devotee, amusing them with stories and songs, and, being allowed to reside in the fort, introduced a body of Mawalis, and put every man of the garrison to the sword.

In 1818 Pratap Singh, eldest son of Shahu II, was released and installed as Raja. He held the principality twenty-one years, but, being found guilty of conspiring to establish the dynasty, was sent prisoner to Varanasi in 1839, being succeeded by his brother, Appa Sahib (Shahaji) on whose death without issue, in 1848, the territory was annexed.

Mahuli.—This place, at the confluence of the Kistna and Venna (Yena) rivers, is about 3 m. E. of Satara. It is considered a place of great sanctity. Kshetra Mahuli is the name of the village on the opposite (left) bank downstream, built in 1825, and dedicated to Radha Shankar.

On the same bank is the temple of Bholeswar Mahadev, built in 1742. The next temple is on the same bank, dedicated to Rameswar, and was built in 1700, with a flight of steps leading up to it. On the W. bank of the Kistna and the N. of the Venna, is the Temple of Sangameswar Mahadev, built in 1679. Below it and at the junction of the rivers is a triangular plot of ground, with the *tombs* of a Gosain named Banshapuri and his disciples. That of the Gosain is an octagonal building of grey basalt, with open sides surmounted by a low dome. The largest temple on the S. side of the Venna, at its confluence with the Kistna, is sacred to Visheswar Mahadev, and was built in 1735. A shivlinga marks the cremation of Shahu, when his widow committed *sati*, and there is a monument to his dog.

The fine bridge over the Kistna river below the confluence of the rivers was opened in 1915.

84 m. **Koregaon,** not to be confused with Corygaum (see p. 435).

160 m. **Miraj** Junction station (R., D.B.). Terminus of the Barsi Light Ry. from Kurduwadi and Pandharpur (p. 437). Miraj is the centre of two former small Mahratta States. A short line of 6 m. connects Miraj with Sangli, the capital till 1947 of another Mahratta State (1136 sq. m.). With the coming of independence these states lost their separate identities, and were absorbed in Bombay.

A branch line runs W. to

30 m. **Kolhapur*** station (alt. 1849 ft.) (pop. 259,000 in 1971), capital (1731) of what was formerly the leading Mahratta State, with an area of about 3117 sq. m., now, however, merged with the rest in Maharashtra. It is celebrated on account of the antiquity of its temples, and is distinguished for its fine modern buildings.

The former Ruling Family traced their descent from Sivaji through Raja Ram, the younger son and their title of Chhatrapati (lord of the umbrella or paramount sovereign) was one of those which were assumed by Sivaji at his coronation (1674).

Among the leading buildings are the New Palace and the Albert Edward Hospital. Opposite the hospital is the Town Hall, situated in the Public Gardens. The Rajaram College is near the Old Palace in the centre of the town, and fronting it is the Kolhapur General Library. The former Residency is close to the New Palace, and All Saints' Church. The Irwin Agricultural Museum contains Andhra coins. A Nakkar Khana, or music gallery, forms the entrance to the Palace Square. To the right on entering is the Rajwada, or Old Palace, with a stone gateway in the centre and wooden pillars. On the second storey is a Darbar-room, in which there is a picture of the cenotaph at Florence, erected over the spot where the body was cremated of Maharaja Rajaram I, who died there in 1870, while returning from England. In the third storey is an Armoury, in which are many curious swords, one of which may have belonged to Auranangzeb, for it has in Persian the name Alamgir but has the date 1012 A.H. (A.D. 1604). There is also a Persian sword given by Sir John Malcolm to Pratap Singh.

Adjoining the Treasury, in the S. face of the square, are other Government Offices, and behind them the shrine of Amba Bai, the tutelary deity of Kolhapur. The old great bell of the temple, now in the Irwin Museum, is inscribed: "Ave Maria Gratiæ Plena Dominus Tecum", and may have been captured from the Portuguese at Bassein (1739). It was replaced by one brought by H.H. Shri Shaju Maharaj from England after attending the Coronation in 1902.

N. of the town is a sacred spot—the Brahmapuri Hill—where the Brahmins undergo cremation. About 100 yd. N. of this, close to the Panchanganga river, is what is called the Rani's Garden, where the bodies of the ruling family were cremated. From this spot is seen a bridge over the river, with five arches (1878). Beyond Rani's Garden is a massive stone gateway, 20 ft. high, which leads to the Cenotaph of Raja Sambhaji (d. 1760) just opposite the door, to that of Sivaji (d. 1721), and, more to the left, that of his mother, Tara-Bai, widow of Raja Ram.

Ratnagiri (D.B.) is 82 m. from Kolhapur *via* the Ambaghat (1822). Thibaw, last King of Burma, was interned here (1886) until his death in 1916. This was the birthplace of Gangadhar Tilak and G. K. Gokhale.

Hill Forts of **Panhala** *and* **Pawangarh.**—Panhala lies 12 m. N.W. of the capital, up a steep ascent. There is an excellent road up the 1000 ft. into the fort.

Jotiba's Hill, close to the road, and also about 1000 ft. high above the plain, is covered with temples (none of great age). Near the hill are the Pawala Caves (of Buddhistic origin; one large hall with fourteen pillars and an irregular *chaitya* cave). The road passes under the scarp of Pawangarh fort, which is about 1500 yd. from the E. gate of Panhala. The two main entrances were taken down when the fort was demolished in 1844.

The fortress of **Panhala,** 2992 ft. above sea-level, is one of the most interesting in the W. of India. It was the stronghold of a Raja Bhoj II in 1192, who reigned over the territory from the Mahadeo Hills, N. of Satara, to the River Hiranyakeshi in Kolhapur State. It was taken by the Sultans of Bijapur, who restored it in 1549; was captured in 1659 by Sivaji, who made some of his most successful expeditions from it; and surrendered to the Mughals in 1690, but recovered 1707. In a rebellion of 1844 it was stormed and taken by the British.

At the Char Darwaza (quadruple gate) is a temple of Maruti; passing on, there is a Muslim tomb of granite on the left, and a temple of *Sambhaji*, also on the left. The Sivaji Tower, or Sujja Kothi (1600), is a building of two storeys, facing E. and standing at the brink of a precipice. About ¼ m. S.W. of the tower are stone granaries which enabled Sivaji to stand a siege of five months. They are 30 ft. high, 57 ft. broad, and 130 ft. long. At the W. side of the fort is the Tin Darwaza, a triple gate handsomely sculptured. To the right at about 40 yd. distance, is the breach made by the British when they stormed the fort in 1844.

180 m. The Kistna (or Krishna) river is crossed.

213 m. **Gokak Road** station (R.) (conveyances available). 3½ m. from here are the falls of the Ghataprabha river, known as the **Gokak Falls.** In the rainy season they are very fine. The height of the falls is 176 ft., and

the pool below is very deep. Near the falls, on both banks, are groups of old temples. The Gokak cotton-mills overlook the falls, and are worked by turbines supplied with water from the falls. They are on the right bank of the river, which is crossed at this point by a suspension-bridge. There are the remains of many dolmens S.E. of the village of Konur, 1 m. from the falls. The Gokak Canal is fed by a reservoir formed by a dam at Dhupdal across the Ghataprabha river, and irrigates 30 sq. m.

246 m. **Belgaum** station (H.R., D.B.), called Shahpur Belgaum (pop. 213,000 in 1971) from the neighbouring town of Shahpur, which lies to the S. It is situated in a plain 2520 ft. above the sea, on the Bombay, Poona, Bangalore air-line. The fort stands to the E. of the town. It is built of stone and oval in shape. It was taken by Khwaja Mahmud Gawan, Minister of Humayun the Cruel, of the Bahmani dynasty, in 1473. Sir T. Munro, captured it on the 10th of April 1818, attacking from the North.

At 120 yd. distance is the ruined Nakkar Khana, or music gallery. There used to be a fort church, but it has been demolished.

Beyond the Nakkar Khana to the E. is a neat, plain mosque, known as the Masjid-i-Sata. Over the entrance is an inscription in Persian with a date equivalent to 1519, the year in which it was built by Azad Khan, a famous Bijapur captain and governor of Belgaum. Farther S. is a Jain Temple, built of laterite. There is a low wall at the entrance, along which are carved figures of musicians. The façade has four pillars and two pilasters, all of a very complicated character. An inscription in the old Kanara language, beautifully cut on a slab of black porphyry, in the Bombay Museum of the Royal Asiatic Society, states that Malikarjuna, whose descent for three generations is given, built the temple.

The second Jain Temple is within the Commissariat Store Yard. The roof is a most complicated piece of carving, rising in tiers, with cornices about 2 ft. broad, which rest on bar-like corbels from the pillars. The principal entrance faces the N.W., and has one elephant remaining at the side, much mutilated; there is a quadruple pendant in the centre. The niches are shell-shaped. There are four porches, 7 ft. square each, and each with four black basalt pillars. There is no image. Dr Burgess says: "The pillars of the temple are square and massive, but relieved by having all the principal facets, the triangles on the base and neck carved with floral ornamentations. The door leading from the mandapam to the temple has been carved with uncommon care. On the centre of the lintel is a Tirthankar, and above the cornice are four squat human figures. On the neat colonnettes of the jambs are five bands with human groups, in some of which the figures are little more than an inch high, yet in high relief; inside this is a band of rampant *sinhas* (lions), with a sort of high frill round their necks. Outside the colonnettes is a band of *chakwas*, or sacred geese, another of *sinhas*, and then one of human figures, mostly on bended knees."

Shooting passes can be had from the Conservator of Forests, S.C., Dharwar, for the jungles in the S. of Belgaum District and in the neighbouring District of N. Kanara.

The Bombay-Bangalore road leads to Dharwar (47 m.).

277 m. **Londa** Junction (R.). The railway to Goa proceeds W. To the E. a line runs to Hubli Junction and Bezwada, at the head of the delta of the Kistna river. A third line goes S.E. to Bangalore (Route 28).

On the line to Goa is

293 m. **Castle Rock** station (R.), (1907 ft.). This was, until the end of 1961, the frontier of the former Portuguese India, but there are now no formalities since Goa passed into Indian hands. In the first 10 m. the line passes through a dozen tunnels, and magnificent scenery. Taxis are also available.

307 m. **Dudh Sagar** station, or the "sea of milk", where there is a very fine waterfall.

325 m. **Collem.**

336 m. **Margao** (Hotel dos Alliados); important town. Motor-bus to Panjim, 25 m.; or launch for Panjim from Marmagoa harbour to Dona Paula.

360 m. **Vasco da Gama.** The old port and an important commercial centre.

363 m. The terminus of the railway is on the quay at the **Port of Marmagao,** which is now to be developed as an Indian naval base; the airport of Dabolim is serviced by only one flight a day, from Bombay. There is no good accommodation at Marmagao. Over the bay is Panjim, once capital of Portuguese India. Alternative routes to Panjim are (1) by launch (½ hr.) from Rachol to Dona Paula (timings must be checked locally as the service is intermittent). A motor-bus runs (taxis also) from Dona Paula to Panjim. (2) The Chowgula Steamship Coy. service between Bombay and Panjim, and between Bombay and Marmagao is again operating. Time 21hr. But the quickest way is to fly (2 hours) by I.A.C. Coaches run from the airfield, crossing the estuary to Panjim by ferry. Goa is now connected by road with the major places in India. Buses run from Poona, Bombay and Mysore. An alternative to the Bombay-Bangalore road is the very picturesque coastal road through the Konkan which branches off the Bombay-Poona road after Panvel.

Panjim, capital of Goa proper (best hotel the Mandovi: Government Tourist Hotel). More than half the Indian population are Christian descendants of Hindus converted by the Jesuits and other religious orders. With Vasco da Gama (1524) there came to Goa members of the Portuguese nobility, some of whose descendants by mixed marriages are still living in Goa. Panjim stands on the S. bank of the Mandovi, which is navigable by steam launches as far as Sanvordem. The streets are broad and the squares are ornamented by statues. There is a Tourist Information Bureau which operates conducted tours, and provides guides (Rua Afonso do Albuquerque) and indicates places of interest.

A row of handsome buildings lines the quay, including the Old Fort, now the Secretariat and formerly the residence of the Governor-General, who removed hither from Old Goa about 1760, and in 1843 by Royal Decree made this the seat of government. Portraits of the Viceroys since 1520, once in Government House, are now in the Museum at Old Goa, as are the statues of Albuquerque and Vasco da Gama. To the S.W. is the Palace of the Archbishop, who is Primate of the Roman Catholic Church in India. It contains some life-sized portraits of the Archbishops.

To the W. are the Barracks of the Indian garrison.

A good road leads from New to Old Goa about 7 m. higher up the valley. (Motors available; 3 hours should be allowed; lunch at restaurant opposite Bom Jesus.) The road first crosses a causeway thrown over the swamp to *Ribandar* village. From here coconut plantations and dwelling-houses line the way, which commands a fine view N. across the river to the hilly, wooded country beyond, and includes a hill, crowned by the Church of Our Lady of Pity and conventual buildings, upon the river-island of Divar. *En route* are passed the later Archepiscopal Palace and the Fountain of Banguinim, which used to supply water to Old Goa.

Old Goa (Velha Goa, "Senhora de todo o Oriente", Camoens, 2, 51) owes its origin to Afonso do Albuquerque, who carried by storm a small coast-town of the Bijapur State in 1510, founded by horse-dealers from Bhatkal. It rose rapidly into prosperity and importance, and by 1565 became a very wealthy city

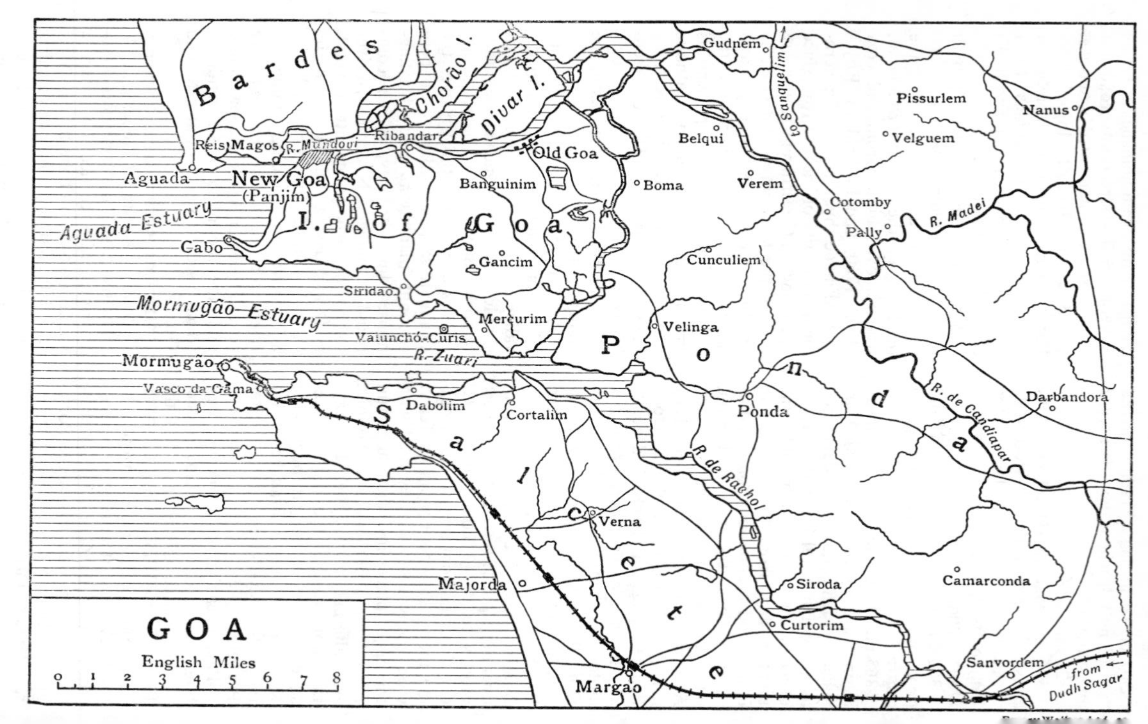
GOA
English Miles
0 1 2 3 4 5 6 7 8
Bardes
Chorão I.
Divar I.
Reis Magos
R. Mundovi
Ribandar
Old Goa
Aguada
New Goa
(Panjim)
Aguada Estuary
I. of Goa
Cabo
Banguinim
Gancim
Siridao
Mormugão Estuary
Mercurim
Valunchó Curis
R. Zuari
Mormugão
Vasco da Gama
Dabolim
Cortalim
Salcete
Verna
Majorda
Margao
Gudnem
to Sanquelim
Belqui
Boma
Verem
Pissurlem
Velguem
Nanus
Cotomby
Pally
R. Madei
Cunculiem
Velinga
Ponda
R. de Candiapar
Darbandora
R. de Rachol
Siroda
Curtorim
Camarconda
Sanvordem
from Dudh Sagar

(Goa dourada,) the capital[1] and seat of Government of the then vast Portuguese territory, with a population of 200,000—"ilha illustrissima de Goa" (Camoens). Moreover, it was the first Christian colony in the Indies and the scene of the labours of St Francis Xavier in 1542-52. But decay followed rapidly on the fall of Vijayanagar, with which a very profitable trade in horses was carried on. Its site proved pestilential, and it was deserted by its inhabitants. It is now literally a city of ruins. Goa nevertheless remains a city of magnificent churches and convents, four or five ranking as first class and in perfect preservation.

The road from Panjim leads past the Arsenal on the left and the hill of the Church of the Rosary on the right into a large central square, named the Pelourinho from the stocks in it, and surrounded by churches and convents. The most important of these and the holiest, because it contains the body of St Francis Xavier, is the Basilica of **Bom** (the Good) **Jesus,** on the right (S.) side, erected in 1594. Its handsome façade runs on into that of another great building with lofty halls and lengthy corridors, all empty, the Professed House of the Jesuits, which was finished in 1589, thirty-eight years after the death of St Francis, whence devoted missionaries went out across the world. Now used as priests quarters and for retreats. The order was suppressed here in 1759, the other monastic orders in 1835, when their property was confiscated by the State. The endowments of the Churches are now negligible.

The **Church of Bom Jesus** may be entered by the main portal or by a side door from the Jesuits' College, passing the Sacristy. Near it hangs a portrait of St Francis Xavier at the age of 44—a dark face of sweet expression.

[1] See V. T. Gune: *Ancient Shrines of Goa*: a pictorial survey (1965). F. X. Gomes Catao, *Old Goa* (1964). P. Rayanna, *St Francis Xavier* (1964). J. N. da Fonseca, *Historical and Archaeological Sketch of the City of Goa* (Bombay, 1878—best but rare).

The Tomb and Shrine of St Francis Xavier (1696) occupy a side chapel, richly adorned; the walls are lined with pictures illustrating some of the acts of his life. He was in India (1542-47), went to Japan and died (1552), and was canonised (1622) by Pope Gregory XV.

The monument consists of three tiers of sarcophagi, of jasper and marble, the gift of a Grand Duke of Tuscany. The upper tier is ornamented with panels curiously wrought in bronze so as to represent scenes in the life of the saint; the whole is surmounted by an outer coffin adorned with reliefs also in silver, and with figures of angels in the same metal supporting a cross. The inner coffin weighing 600 marks of silver which was frequently opened to disclose the body, long in a wonderful state of preservation but now shrunk to a mummy, is discarded and the body is now in a glass casket.

In the body of the church is a solid silver statue of the saint. W. from Bom Jesus runs the road to Monte Santo and an important group of buildings including the only Nunnery in Goa and the Priory of Our Lady of the Rosary.

250 yd. distant, on the opposite side (N.) of the square, stands the **Cathedral** of St Catherine,[1] built in 1562-1623, the church next in sacred importance to the Bom Jesus, and known as the Se Primaçial. It is 250 ft. long, 180 ft. wide, with façade 116 ft. high, with a high altar at the W. end. It alone of all the churches retains a dwindling staff of ancient canons who chant the hours on Sundays. From the terraced roof of the cathedral solemn and terrible sights were seen in the square below, when the great bell of this church tolled to announce the celebration of an *auto-da-fé*.

S.E. of the cathedral stood the Palace of the Inquisition, with its dungeons and prisons, established in 1560 and suppressed in 1812 which has now completely disappeared.

[1] Goa was recaptured on St Catherine's Day; 25th November.

N.W. of the cathedral is the Archbishop's Palace, a magnificent residence, still occupied occasionally.

W. of the cathedral is the once gorgeous Convent of **San Francisco d'Assisi,** the oldest here. It now houses the Museum under the Archaeological Survey.

S. of the Inquisition were the buildings of the **Misericordia,** enclosing the Church of Nossa Senhora de Serra, built by Albuquerque in fulfilment of a vow at sea, and in which he was originally buried. From these the Rua Direita led to the river front and the Viceroy's Palace. The **Arch of the Viceroys** stands over the principal landing-place known as the Ribeira dos Vicereys, which extended W. to the Quai of the Galleys (Ribeira dos Galés) and E. to the Customs House (Alfandega) and the Great Bazar. On the Arch is sculptured the figure of St Catherine subjugating Yusuf Adil Shah, from whom Albuquerque took Goa. Of the Palace of the Viceroys, only a portal of Bijapur style remains.

E. of the Palace and the bazar and about ¼ m. N. of the Church of Bom Jesus is the *Church of St Cajetan*, perhaps the best preserved, built 1665, and surmounted by a dome and by two low towers; the façade is of red laterite, whitewashed. The convent is now a seminary. Beyond lay the convent of the Dominicans, with that of the Carmelites on a hill, and the famous missionary **College of Saint Paul,** or Santa Fé, which is about ½ m. E. from the Bom Jesus. The *autos-da-fé* used to take place in the Campo San Lazaro, near this. At the W. end of the town, near the Arsenal, was the famous **Royal Hospital,** founded by Albuquerque, the first established by Europeans in the East.

Goa Administrative Area.—The territory of Goa has a coast-line of about 65 m., and an area of 1350 sq. m. including the small island of Anjediva, near Karwar. It was once divided into two tracts, known as the Old and New Conquests (Velhas e Novas Conquistas), and in turn subdivided into four and seven subdistrict charges respectively, at the head of each of which was an Administrator and a Municipal Council. Damão (p. 240) is now under a Collector and Diu under an Administrator, both responsible to the Lieutenant Governor. There is a High Court (Tribunal de Relacão) of second instance at Goa, consisting of five judges, and a subordinate judge in each "comarca" (judicial sub-district). Panjim has a Lyceum, a normal school, and a medical school; and primary schools exist in the Goa country.

The scenery in the districts is often very fine, and some delightful excursions by car or rail may be made, e.g. to

(1) The waterfalls at Arvalem (17 m.) and Dudhsagar (44 m.).

(2) Chandranate Hill, which affords a wonderful view (33 m.).

(3) Aguada Fort (5 m.).

(4) Arecais de Ponda, with splendid views and walks (18 m.).

(5) Bathing: Dona Paula Bay. Calangute Beach (Tourist accommodation) **Colva Beach** (very good Tourist Bungalows).

River and sea trips may also be made in launches provided by the Port Authorities through the many waterways. Good shooting is available in the forests of Sanguem and Canacona, and on the Island of Morcego excellent sea-fishing is to be had.

Afonso do Albuquerque, the conqueror and founder of Goa, was born in 1453, and was therefore fifty years old when he visited Cochin and Quilon on his first journey to India in 1503. In 1506 he occupied Socotra on behalf of the Portuguese Crown, and in November 1509 he became Governor of the Eastern possessions. Panjim was taken from and retaken by Bijapur in 1510, but was recovered on 25th November following. During the next two years Albuquerque was occupied with the affairs of Malacca; in 1513 he attempted to capture Aden, but failed; and in 1514 he caused a fort to be erected at Calicut after the Zamorin had been poisoned. In February 1515 he proceeded to Ormuz and obtained possession oi the fort there, and died on his way back from that place to Goa on 18th December 1515. His body was finally transferred to Lisbon, and now rests there in the Church of Nossa Senhora da Graça.

From 1580 to 1640 Portugal was absorbed into Spain and in 1639 the Dutch tried to capture Goa.

By a Treaty of 1800 Goa was occupied by British troops, and again in 1808 on the invasion of Portugal by the French.

Since 1962, Goa has been administered as part of India, but with respect for the ancient rights and institutions to which its inhabitants are accustomed.

There is now a popularly elected Assembly and a Chief Minister. In 1967 an "opinion poll" confirmed the Territory's wish to remain distinct from Maharashtra. As there is no prohibition, there are many week-end visitors from Bombay. The unspoiled and extensive beaches are a great attraction to tourists, and the National Tourism Board are planning a new air terminal building at Dabolim (Panaji) as well as further moderate-priced accommodation.

The new bridge across the Mandovi at Panjim allows direct motor connections with the beaches to the north. The Zuari river bridge at Cortalim which is now (1980) in an advanced stage of construction will permit vehicles to drive directly from Panjim to Margao without taking the longer route via Ponda.

ROUTE 25

WADI JUNCTION to **Bidar, HYDERABAD, Golconda, Secunderabad, Kazipet** Junction, **Warangal,** and **Bezwada (Vijayawada).**

On the Central Ry. main line from Poona to Madras (Route 23) *is*

376 m. from Bombay, **Wadi** Junction station (R.) (see p. 438); the western terminus of the broad-gauge section of the former Nizam's State Ry., which runs to (115 m.) Hyderabad and thence to (338 m.) Bezwada, where it connects with the main line of the Southern Ry. from Calcutta to Madras (Route 22).

10 m. from Wadi, **Chittapur** station. About 1 m. to the S. is **Nagai,** a deserted town, with ruined temples dating from A.D. 1050. In one of them is a life-size bull cut out of a solid block of basalt.

16 m. **Malkher Road** station for the old Rashtrakuta capital of Malkhed (2½ m.). Yatagiri (30 m. S.) was a Chalukhya capital until A.D. 1050.

24 m. **Seram** station. A richly carved temple, of 1200, dedicated to Siva.

44 m. **Tandur** station (R.). Duck and snipe shooting in the cold weather.

57 m. **Dharur.** Railway bungalow, which may be made available on application to the Station-master, Secunderabad. The jungle to the S. of the line is a forest reserve.

70 m. **Vikarabad** (R.; alt. 2057 ft.); named after Nawab Vikar-ul-Umara (Minister 1893 to 1901) in whose jagir it was. 3 m. from the station, on the summit of one of the Ananthagiri hills, is a shrine with an image of Vishnu.

Branch line (57 m.) *to* **Mohamadabad Bidar,** (108 m.) Udgir, (168 m.) Purli Vaijnath (p. 154) and Parbhani.

Bidar (R.H. and P.W.D.G.H., apply Executive Engineer, Bidar),

Vidarba, has a striking situation on a level plateau, alt. 2208 ft., and was an Air Force station during the last war. It was the capital, after 1428, of Bahmani Kings and then of the Barid Shahi dynasty (1492-1609). It was taken (1656) by Amir Jumla, wazir of Shah Jahan. The fort (plan on sale), 6 m. in perimeter, was built in 1428 by Ahmad Shah Wali, the ninth Bahmani King, who moved here from Gulbarga (p. 437).

The *madrasa* of Khwaja Mahmud Gawán,[1] the famous Wazir of the Bahmani King, Muhammad Shah III, has been partially restored. The many-coloured encaustic tiles on the façade deserve notice. The grave of Salabat Jang is in the enclosure of the tomb of Multani Pasha. The tombs of twelve Bahmani Kings are in the village of Ashtur to the N.E. of the town, including that of Humayun the Cruel, known as the Khuni ("bloody") Sultan (1458-61). The tombs of the Barid Sultans are W. of the town. They were well preserved by the Archaeological Dept. of the former Hyderabad State.

The industry of Bidar, Bidri work, or Tutanaig, of silver and gold inlaid on iron, has been revived at the Industrial School, and attractive pieces are now available.

The Chalukyan capital of Kalyani from 1050 is 36 m. N.W. of Bidar. Hazar Khotri caves.

81 m. Bhalki. Fort and temple of Khandi Rao.

108 m. **Udgir.** Fort taken by Shahjahan, 1636. Battle and Treaty with the Mahrattas, 1760.

48 m. from Udgir and 25 m. from Nander (p. 154), **Fort of Khandar Sharif** (2143 ft.).

145 m. **Pangaon.** Temple.

On the main line.

80 m. **Gollaguda.** Buddhist remains. (2 m.).

[1] This Minister, who long upheld the Bahmani dynasty, was unjustly put to death in 1481 by Muhammad Shah III. This caused a revolt and the break-up of the Kingdom. The date was commemorated in the chronogram *Qatl-i-nahaq* (the Unjust Execution).

88 m. **Shankarapalli**; waiting-rooms at the station. 2 m. to the W. is the Rajampet State Stud Farm.

100 m. **Lingampalli** station (D.B.). Groups of underground temples are to be seen in the neighbourhood. Small game shooting in the jungle; also duck and snipe in the tanks. (Permits from the Conservator of Forests at Hyderabad.) Soon after this the country is dotted with outcrops, extending to Bhongir, 28 m. E. of Hyderabad.

5 m. to the N.W. of Lingampalli, on the road from Hyderabad to Bidar, is **Patancheru,** an important centre of Jain worship from the 7th to the 10th centuries A.D. The temples have disappeared, but colossal statues of Mahavira have been found under mounds or below the Brahmanical constructions. A Rural Reconstruction Centre operates here with great success.

112 m. **Begampet** station (see p. 462). The airfield on the Bombay-Madras and Delhi-Madras runs is here, with quick connections by jet airliners from Bombay, Madras (*via* Bangalore), Delhi and intermediate places.

115 m. **HYDERABAD** station* (broad gauge) 1¾ m. from the nearest city gate (Afzalganj). The metre-gauge station (p. 455) is 4 m. distant. There are several good hotels; also many Clubs, some of which admit visitors. There is no Prohibition.

The city of Hyderabad (pop. 1,798,000 in 1971) is now the capital of Andhra Pradesh. It was founded (as Bhagnagar) in 1589 by Muhammad Kuli, the fifth Kutb Shahi King of Golconda. In 1687 Golconda (5 m. to the W., see p. 460) was taken by Aurangzeb, and a subadar governed the Deccan until the Nizam-ul-Mulk, Asaf Jah, defeated the Mughal Governor of Khandesh in 1724.

The Nizam succeeded his grandfather in 1967. The title of "Exalted Highness" was conferred in 1918, and in 1936 Berar was added to the title, the heir-apparent being styled Prince of Berar. The Nizam was the eighth (three not being recognised)

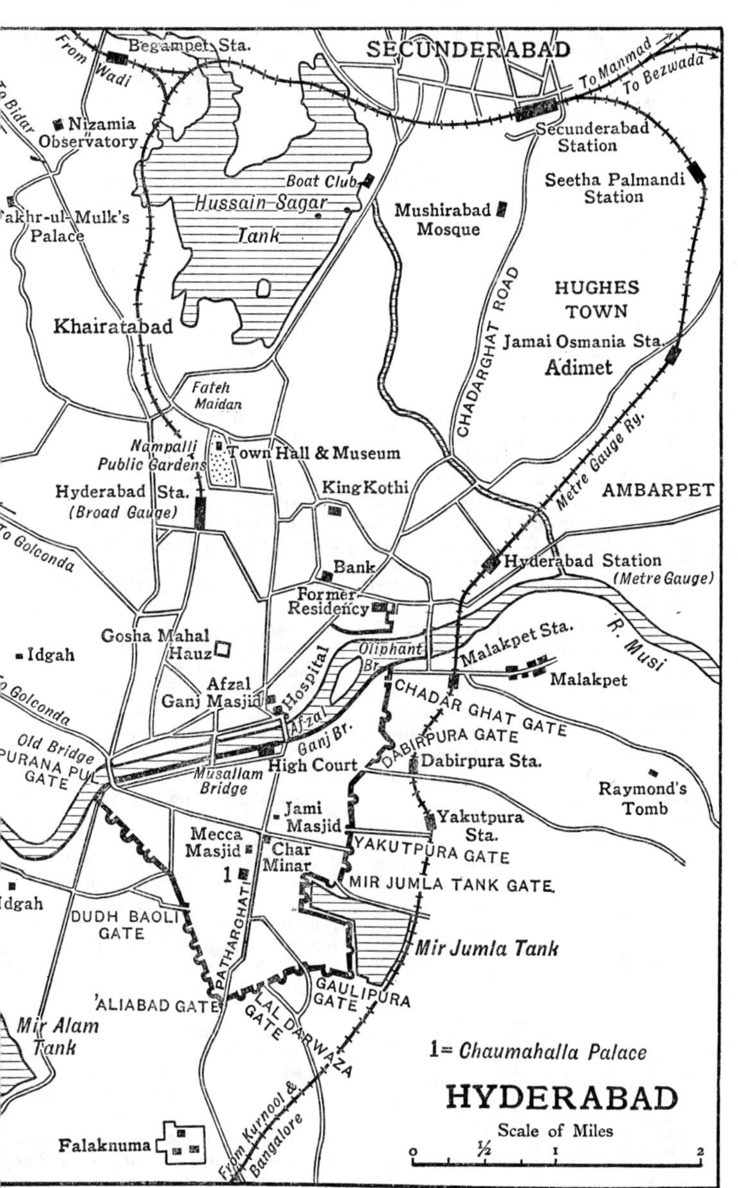

Emery Walker Ltd. sc.

since the independent dynasty was founded in 1724 by Asaf Jah Nizam-ul-Mulk (Subadar in 1712). The family are directly descended from Nizam Ali (1762-1803), who was the fourth son of Asaf Jah.[1] Other sons of Asaf Jah played a part in the rivalry of the French and English East India Companies in S. India.[2] Hyderabad State was forcibly incorporated in the Indian Union in 1948, and has since been divided up between Maharashra, Karnataka, and Andhra Pradesh, of which Hyderabad City is the seat of Government.

Hyderabad maintains a considerable manufacture of textile fabrics, carpets, velvets for horse-trappings, and a material composed of cotton and silk. Hyderabad is famous for pearl dealers. Gold and Silver thread-work. Filigree work, Bidri work, ivory inlay. Kondapalli (p. 426) toys are extensively made here. Glass, sugar and paper factories have also been established. The Government Handicrafts Emporium (Gun-foundry) is worth a visit.

In shape the **City** is a trapezoid, and is surrounded by a stone wall, which was commenced by Mubariz Khan, the last Mughal governor, and completed by the Nizam-ul-Mulk. It has some remarkable buildings, which it owes principally to Sultan Muhammad Kuli, its founder (1581-1612). The *bazars* are thronged with representatives of all parts of India. A City Improvement Board has been at work for some years, and wide avenues in the City and towards Khairatabad and Secunderabad mark the scene of their labours. There is a Tourist Information Bureau in Mukarramjahi Rd. with luxury coaches and guides to places of interest, including the Salar Jung Museum, two Archaeological museums, the Nehru Zoological Gardens, and several Parks.

On the N.W. side are four *Gateways*—viz., on the extreme E. the Chadarghat Gate; next, to the W., the Delhi or Afzalganj Gate; then follow the Char Mahal, and the Old Bridge (Purana Pul) Gates in succession. In the S.W. side there is, first, the Dudh Baoli Gate, then the Fateh Darwaza and the Aliabad Gate, which is in the S.W. corner. On the S. side are the Lal Darwaza and the Gaulipura Gate; and on the E. are the Mir Jumla, Yakutpura and Dabirpura Gates.

The Musi river, on the N. side, is crossed by four Bridges. Farthest to the E. is the Oliphant Bridge, which was erected in 1831 by Colonel James Oliphant, of the Madras Engineers, afterwards (1844-56) a Director of the East India Company and Chairman of the Court in 1854. The next bridge to the W. is the Afzalganj Bridge, which leads to the broad-gauge railway station. Upstream the Musallam (also called the Muslim Jang) Bridge, built in 1898 by the late Nawab Laik-ud-daula, and the Old Bridge (Saak in 1777) were the only ones which withstood a terrible flood of 1908. The Char Mahal Gate is slightly to the N. of the Musallam Bridge.

The road from the broad-gauge railway station crosses the river by the Afzalganj Bridge, W. of which is the High Court. The site of the Champa Gate, demolished in 1918, is marked by a few steps near the High Court. Facing these buildings, and on the N. bank of the Musi, are the River Gardens and the Osmania General Hospital, built in the Indo-Saracenic style. Adjoining the hospital on the N. is the Afzalganj Masjid (Mosque), a fine building with four lofty minarets. On the other side

[1] Nasir Jang (d. 1750), Muzaffar Jang, grandson (d. 1751), Salabat Jang (deposed 1761 and died at Bidar 1763), Nizam Ali (d. 1803), Sikandar Jah (d. 1829), Nasir-ud-daula (d. 1857) and Afzal-ud-daula (d. 1869). The late Nizam succeeded in 1869 at the age of three. Asaf Jah was the son of the first Ghazi-ud-din (p. 326), Subadar of Berar, and the real conqueror of Golconda: he died 1748 and is buried at Rauza (p. 144).

[2] The second Nizam owed his throne to the East India Company, and the third and fourth were French nominees. Nizam Ali, the fifth, sided alternately with Haidar Ali and the English, but ultimately aided Lord Cornwallis in the first siege of Seringapatam in 1792.

of the road is the Victoria Zenana Hospital for women, the foundation-stone of which was laid by H.M. Queen Mary, then Princess of Wales, in 1906. The establishment can be inspected by ladies only.

The Osmania University, formerly near the Afzal Gate, is now at Adikmet, about 6 m. from the City. It covers an area of 1500 acres. The University, founded September 1918, is named after the late Nizam, who was its Patron. There are faculties in Arts, Science, Law, Theology, Medicine and Engineering.

A broad street, known as Patharghati, or the Stone Causeway, runs through the city from the Afzalganj Gate to the Aliabad Gate. At the junction of four roads, and about ½ m. from the Afzalganj Gate, is a stately rectangular building with four minarets, hence called the **Char Minar,** 186 ft. high and 100 ft. wide on each side; it was built in 1591 and is a masterpiece of the Kutb Shahi period. There is a small fee for admission; the views over the City are impressive. Just before reaching it the road passes under an arch called the Machhli Kaman, or "Arch of the Fish"—an emblem of high distinction in the Mughal hierarchy. There are four arches (Char Kaman) 50 ft. high across the streets, one to each quarter of the compass, with a fountain in the centre. W. of the Char Minar is the Mecca Masjid, the principal mosque in the city; the gateway was completed by Aurangzeb in 1692. It has four minars and five arches in front, occupying one side of the paved quadrangle 360 ft. square—date 1614. In the quadrangle are the graves of all the Nizams from the time of Nizam Ali (d. 1803). On the E. of the main road, a narrow lane leads to the Jami Masjid, erected in 1598 by Sultan Muhammad Kuli, and the oldest in Hyderabad.

The **Chaumahalla Palace** lies to the S. of the Char Minar; from the Chauk a fine gateway leads to a large quadrangle. At the S.W. corner of this a narrow road leads into a second quadrangle; a passage from the S.W. corner of this leads into a third quadrangle, beyond which are the ladies' apartments (*zenana*). The buildings on each side resemble the Shah's Palace at Teheran.

In a side street 200 yd. beyond the Palace is the baradari, in which the well-known Maharaja Chandu Lal, who was Peshkar (Minister) from 1806 to 1843, died in 1843. It is a highly ornamented Hindu house.

Near the W. wall of the city is the vast palace or baradari built by Nawab Tegh Jang, the first Shams-ul-umara, who died in 1786. It covers a large space, is handsomely furnished and contains a gigantic suit of armour and sword belonging to Tegh Jang, whose stature is said to have been 6 ft. 6 in.

The Jahannuma, also built by the Shams-ul-umara, in a suburb of the same name outside the Aliabad Gate, is reached by a good road. This is the old Portuguese quarter of the city; services are still held in a chapel which dates from about 1800.

Near the Afzal Gate and a few hundred yards on the left is the Palace of the famous Sir Salar Jang, whose able administration of the State lasted from 1853 to his death in 1883. His priceless collection of Victoriana, paintings, china, armour and other antiques, Indian and foreign, is now housed in a new Museum building next door, and is one of the three National Museums of India. It is open from 10 a.m. to 5 p.m.; closed Fridays. Admission Rs. 1 which does not include the marvellous Jade Room (50 paise). The Chini Khana, about 14 ft. square and 12 ft. high, is covered with china cemented to the walls. Within the same enclosure are Sir Salar Jang's baradari and Lakkar Kot (wooden palace). Across the road is the Badshahi Ashur Khana, which is well worth a visit. The original part of the building, which consists of a hall, was built by Muhammad Kuli Kutb Shah in 1597. The walls are adorned with Persian enamels, which are extremely rich in colour.

In the N.E. quarter of the city, between the Yakutpura Gate and the Dabirpura Gate, is the **Purani Haveli,** or old Palace, which was built by Asaf Jah, Nizam-ul-Mulk. On the road leading from the Chadar Ghat Gate to the Gaulipura Gate, about 200 yd. to the N.W. is the *Darus-Shafa* or hospital, which was built by Sultan Kuli Kutb Shah, and consists of a paved quadrangular courtyard surrounded by chambers; it is no longer used as a hospital. Opposite the entrance is a mosque, which was erected at the same time.

The former **British Residency** can be approached from the city through the Chadar Ghat Gate and across the Oliphant Bridge. It stands about 1¾ m. S.W. of the broad-gauge station, and N.E. of the city, in the suburb of Chadarghat, and is surrounded by the Sultan Bazar. The grounds are spacious and full of grand old trees, and are enclosed by a wall, which was strengthened by Colonel Davidson after an attack upon the Residency on the morning of 17th July 1857. That attack was made by a band of Rohillas and others, and was repelled by the troops at the Residency under Major Briggs, Military Secretary. The bastions commanding the approaches were erected then.

On the site of the Residency there was formerly a villa belonging to a favourite of Nizam Ali, and in it Sir John Kennaway, who was appointed Resident in 1788, was received. The present structure was built 1803-08. The design was planned by Lieut. S. Russell, of the Madras Engineers, a son of John Russell, R.A., the artist (1744-1806).

The N. front (Grand Entrance) looks away from the Musi river. A flight of 22 wide granite steps, flanked on either side by a colossal lion, leads up to a portico, 60 ft. long and 26 ft. broad. Six Corinthian columns support the roof. The Darbar Hall measures 60 ft. in length and 33 ft. in breadth, and is 50 ft. high; some of the furniture came from the Pavilion at Brighton. To the W. and E. are the private apartments. Among the trees are some enormous specimens of the *Ficus Indica*, the trunk of one measuring 30 ft. round. There is also a gigantic tamarind-tree and even larger mahogany-tree. The park (which is sometimes open to the public) contains an obelisk raised to the memory of Lieut. William John Darby, who was killed in 1815 within the city of Hyderabad, while gallantly leading the Grenadiers in a charge against some rebels. In a small cemetery behind the Residency are the graves of four Residents and also of two members of the notorious firm of Palmer & Co., financiers of the State (1814-23). Subsequent to the departure of the British Resident in 1947, the buildings have been occupied by a Women's College.

Within the Sultan Bazar is the **Pestonji Kothi** (also known as the Kothi of Raja Narsingh Gir), a large building erected on a high stone basement by the famous Parsi bankers Pestonji & Co., who farmed the revenues of Berar from 1839-45. Close to this is St George's School and Church.

King Kothi, the former residence of the Nizam, is also in the vicinity, but it is not open to the public. To the S.E. of King Kothi is an old building, known as Rumbold's Kothi. On the roadside, not far from the Bank, is the remarkable tomb (built in Muslim style) of William Palmer (1867), who was styled "King" Palmer, and was the head of the banking firm bearing his name.[1] N. of the church are the Nizam's College, and the Roman Catholic Church, a two-storeyed building standing on the summit of a hill. Near the chapel is one of the old French gun-foundries

[1] He was a son of General William Palmer, who was military secretary to Warren Hastings, and Bibi Faiz Bakhsh, Begum of Oudh. His daughter married Col. Philip Meadows Taylor, C.S.I., the author of *The Confessions of a Thug*, who was in the Nizam's service.

erected by M. Raymond (p. 460). It is not unlike an immense racket court.

The metre-gauge railway station (for Bangalore) lies to the E. of the Residency near the river. It links up with the Chadarghat Road from the Residency to Secunderabad station. On the W. of this main road and about 1 m. S. of Secunderabad station is the Mushirabad mosque, a typical building of the Kutb Shahi style, with slender minarets and decorated with cut-plaster work.

To the S.W. of the city, standing on a hill, is the **Falaknuma Palace** of the Nizam. It was built as a private residence by the late Minister, Sir Vikar-ul-umara, and was purchased in 1897 by the then Nizam. Many distinguished visitors have been housed there since that date. The approach is by a hill road.

The Palace stands on a terrace, the front of which is artistically laid out in flower-beds in the English style. The façade is Grecian, the cornice resting on a double row of Corinthian columns. The handsome vestibule, the walls of which are beautifully painted, is fitted with marble seats surrounding a marble fountain. The vestibule leads into the waiting-room, adjoining which are the Library and Council Chamber. The staircase to the upper floor is of marble, with beautifully carved balustrades, supporting at intervals marble figures with candelabra. On the walls are oil paintings of His Exalted Highness the Nizam and past Residents and other notable personages of the State. The Reception-room is decorated and furnished in Louis XIV style. The Ballroom, the Dining-room, the Smoking-room, and bedrooms are all artistically furnished. From the upper floor a fine view can be obtained of the city, the Mir Alam Tank, and the surrounding country.

Between the Purana and Dudh Baoli Gates is a road leading W. out of the city, through the Khirki-i-Bawahir (a postern) to the Mir Alam Tank, a lake 8 m. round. The dam is formed of twenty-one arches, convex upstream. It is 1120 yd. long, and was built by French engineers. It was commenced by Mir Alam, the great Minister of the Nizam, who led his master's forces during the war with Tipu Sultan in 1799, the prize-money which fell to his share after the fall of Seringapatam being used for the construction. The embankment was completed in 1811 by his son-in-law, Munir-ul-Mulk (1809-1832), the father of the first Sir Salar Jang. At the extreme W. end of the lake, on a wooded hill about 80 ft. high, is the Dargah, or shrine, of Mir Mahmud. This is a beautiful structure and well placed, looking down on the waters of the lake. It is symmetrical, and was once covered with blue tiles.

The Gosha Mahal Hauz, 1 m. to the N. of the city, is now dry and used for football matches and parades; the palace, completed (1685) by Abul Hasan, the last King of Golconda, and once residence of de Bussy, is used by the Masonic Foundation.

To the N. of the broad-gauge railway station are the Nampalli Public Gardens, covering an extensive area, and surrounded by a high wall castellated with two lofty gateways. In addition to rare plants the *Gardens* contain an **Archaeological Museum** (1931) with prehistoric objects from Paithan; also Celadon ware. The Jubilee Hall commemorates the fortieth birthday (1906) of the late Nizam.

Outside the gardens to the N. is a picturesque Black Rock—the Naubat Pahar or "Drum Rock"—so called because all communications of Mughal Emperors to subadars were proclaimed from this rock to the sound of music. On an adjacent hill-top stands the Sri Venkateshwara Temple erected by the Birla Foundation. N. of the gardens is the Saifabad Cantonment, once inhabited by the Nizam's regular troops. On the Fateh Maidan are a race-course and a polo-ground. The quarters of the Nizam's former African Cavalry Guards are to the S.W. on the Golconda Road.

EXCURSIONS FROM HYDERABAD

(1) The **Tomb of M. Raymond** (1755-98) is in Sarur Nagar (Pleasure Town), just 500 yards to the S. of the new TV tower, and stands at the end of a terrace 180 ft. long by 85 ft. broad, on an eminence known as Myseram Tekri, or Monsieur Raymond's Hill. The tomb consists of an obelisk of grey stone, 25 ft. high, with the letters "J. R." on each side. In front of the tomb is a small flat-roofed building, supported on a number of small pillars, and open at the sides. He died on 25th March 1798.

He had raised, since 1786, 15,000 good troops, and possessed more power than the British Resident. On 20th October 1798, the whole force was disbanded as the result of a treaty concluded with the Nizam by the British Resident, Col. James Achilles Kirkpatrick. The tomb and platform are illuminated on the anniversary of Raymond's death, and a large fair is held.

(2) **GOLCONDA.** The **Fort** and **Tombs** lie 5 m. W. of the city. No permission is now necessary for entry, for visitors wishing to inspect the Fort. The road from Hyderabad leaves the city by the Purana Pul Gate and crosses the Old Bridge.

Golconda, once famous as a cutting-place and market for the diamonds from neighbouring mines (p. 465)—the Koh-i-Noor diamond came from here—was the capital of the Kutb Shahi kingdom[1] (1507-1687), overthrown by the Emperor Aurangzeb. The **Fort**[2] is surrounded by a strongly built crenellated stone wall or curtain, a little over 3 m. in circumference, with eighty-seven bastions at the angles, on which there are still some of the old Kutb Shahi guns. The walls and bastions are built of solid blocks of granite, many of which weigh considerably over a ton. There is a remarkable echo from the entry gate; a handclap from this point can be heard at the very top of the Fort. The moat is filled up in many places. Of the original eight gates, only the Banjara and Fateh, the Mecca and Jamali are now in use. It was besieged (1650) by Sultan Muhammad, eldest son of Aurangzeb, Viceroy of the Deccan, in treacherous concert with the Minister Mir Jumla, and was taken by the Emperor in 1687, after a desperate defence of nine months by the last King, Abul Hasan, Abdur Razzak Khan Lari being the hero of the siege. When the Nizam-ul-Mulk took possession (1724) he added a new wall to the fortifications on the E., so as to include a small hill formerly situated outside the fort. The large sheet of water in front of this portion of the fort is styled the *Langar Talao.*

Aurangzeb entered in 1687 by the *Banjara Gate*, a massive structure of granite, some 50 ft. high, with platforms and chambers on either side for the guards, and a pair of high teakwood gates studded with iron wrought into various fanciful devices and huge sharp-pointed iron spikes, intended to prevent elephants from battering them in. The road passes straight through the fort to the gate on the N.W. side. A short distance from the gate is a large stone cistern, said to have been built by Ibrahim Kutb Shah, which is connected with a tank some distance off by a line of underground pipes. The old buildings inside the Fort were used as the headquarters of the Golconda Brigade. The Nau Mahal, built by Nizam Ali, stands in a garden of fruit trees.

Beyond the Nau Mahal there is a lofty granite structure, said to have been used as a Nakkar Khana (Music Gallery), which forms the entrance to the first line of the Bala Hissar or citadel fortification. A little to the right of this is the Jami Masjid. An Arabic inscription over the gateway states that it was erected by Sultan Kuli Kutb Shah (1512-43).

[1] This kingdom included all the country from Golconda in the west to the east sea-coast from Orissa to the Kistna. For a detailed account of it, see Haig's *Historic Landmarks of the Deccan.*

[2] Literature and Guides from the Tourist Information Bureau.

The Bala Hissar, 350 ft. high, at the summit has several tiers of fortifications. Inside the gateway, on the left side, are the remains of the Sila-Khana **(Armoury)** and the Zenana palaces. Parts of the old hydraulic machinery for lifting water from ground level to the roof gardens and pavilions for irrigation and cooling purposes are still visible. A series of roughly paved steps leads to the summit. Half-way up is a large well and nearby the ruins of the Ambar Khana, or King's Stores. A slab of black basalt, which has fallen from its position over the entrance, contains a Persian inscription to the effect that the Ambar Khana was built during the reign of Abdullah Kutb Shah (1626-72). The N. portion of the ground was at one time most thickly populated; the ground inside the walls is said to have been so valuable that it used to sell for one ashrafi (Rs. 20) per square yard. The E. and S. portions are strewn with ruins.

Inside the Fateh Gate are two French arsenals. Farther on are the Qiladar's (Commandant's) House and the Mubariz-ud-daula Palace, and to the S. of these two large enclosures with underground galleries. In front of the citadel is a triumphal arch. The paved path leads up through various gateways to the summit of the citadel, on which are the remains of a lofty palace, the two-storeyed Baradari, affording a splendid view of all the country round; on the roof is a stone throne. The upper storey has a spacious hall with side rooms and a large courtyard in front.

The Kings' Tombs. About 600 yd. to the N.W. of the fort stand on the plain the tombs of the Kutb Shahi Kings, reached by turning N. from the entrance to the citadel and passing a stone tank to the N.W. corner of the fort. The tombs were repaired at the instance of the first Sir Salar Jang, when the gardens which had formerly existed around some of them were replanted and the whole enclosed by a substantial stone wall. The tombs standing are those of: (1) Sultan Kuli Kutb Shah, 1512-43; (2) Jamshaid Kutb Shah, 1543-50; (3) Ibrahim Kutb Shah, 1550-80; (4) Princess Hayat Bakhsh Begam, daughter of (3), 1617; (5) Muhammad Kuli Kutb Shah, 1580-1612; and (6) Muhammad Kutb Shah, 1612-26, with minor tombs and mosques.

The finest tomb is that of Muhammad Kuli Kutb Shah, who founded the city of Hyderabad and erected many public edifices and Palaces. It is 168 ft. high from the basement to the summit of the dome. Beyond this is the tomb of Ibrahim Kuli Kutb Shah, the fourth King, who died in 1580. To the S. of it is the tomb of Sultan Muhammad Amin, King Ibrahim's youngest son, who died in 1595. A short distance from here in a N. direction is the tomb of Kulsam Begam, and close to it is that of the first of the Kutb Shahi Kings, Sultan Kuli Kutb, murdered at the instigation of his son Jamshaid in 1543 at the age of ninety. Between the walled enclosure and the fort walls is the tomb of Abdulla Kutb Shah, who died in 1672, after a reign of forty-eight years, enriched with very fine carvings and minarets at each corner of the platform.

The last of the Kutb Shahi Kings, Abul Hasan, ended his days in the fortress of Daulatabad, 1704, and is the only one not interred here.

The general plan of the tombs is a dome standing upon a square base, which is surrounded by an arcade of pointed arches. The arcade is single-storeyed in the case of the smaller tombs; in the larger tombs it is doubled. The prevailing colour is white, in some cases picked out with green. Each large tomb has its mosque or musalla (chapel), usually a hall or a hall-porch opening eastward, with a mihrab to the W., and flanked by minarets on either side. The interiors are laid out with intersecting arches of great variety. Flights of stairs lead to the unbalconied galleries above, and down to the graves contained in the arches and alcoved basements. The tombs are of black basalt or greenstone. The shape is oblong and stepped with six or eight slabs diminishing above. The top is either *bombé* or flat, and the sides bear inscriptions in Naskh and Nasta 'alik characters (wrongly called Kufic). At one time the walls and cupolas of the principal tombs were decorated with glazed tiles; fragments of these can be traced.[1]

The return to Hyderabad may be made by the N. road, passing at 1 m. to the N.W. the Baradari and Masjid of Bhagmati (after whom Hyderabad was first called Bhagnagar), a favourite mistress of the Kutb Shahi King, Muhammad Kuli. On all sides rise outcrops of granite, gneiss and low hills, which have weathered into the most fantastic shapes. The popular legend is that the Creator, after finishing the construction of the world, threw away the surplus material here.

The Osman Sagar (16 m. W., Upper and Lower Income Guest Houses, picnic spots), protects the city from floods, such as occurred in 1908, and supplies water. The Himayat Sagar (4 m. S. from the Osman Sagar) supplements the supply. There is a large dairy farm here. Another beauty spot 6 m. further on is Himayat Sagar, where there are R.Hs., bungalows and picnic spots. Further afield, in the Nizamabad District, nearly 100 m. away, but accessible by a good road is the Nizam Sagar, on the Manjra river, irrigating land under sugar cane. Near it there is a large sugar factory.

On leaving Hyderabad (broad-gauge) station, the train returns to Hussain Sagar Junction (p. 455) and, turning to the E. past the N. edge of the Hussain Sagar tank, enters

121 m. from Wadi Junction, **Secunderabad** Junction (R.),* 5½ m. N. of the Hyderabad Residency. Secunderabad is named after the Nizam Sikandar Jah (1803-29). It is one of the largest Cantonments in India and stands 1830 ft. above sea-level. Excellent roads connect Hyderabad, Secunderabad and Bolarum.

The main road from Hyderabad to Secunderabad passes along the E. edge of the Husain Sagar, a fine lake about 11 m. in circumference, said to have been constructed by Ibrahim Kutb Shah (1550-80). The principal feeder is a channel 36 m. long, which runs from the Musi river above Hyderabad. The view across the Husain Sagar from this main road, which is built on the bund (1 m. long), is most picturesque. At the N. or Secunderabad end of the bund is a Boat Club.

On the S. bank is the Saifabad Palace, till recently used as the Mint, where some of the Government offices are located. This building opens on the Saifabad Road by an elaborate and imposing iron gateway. S. of this is the Fateh Maidan (p. 455).

Another road, running along the W. bank of the Husain Sagar Lake, passes through the popular suburb of Khairatabad, where most of the State officials reside, and, leaving the Bidar Road just past the palace built by the late Nawab Fakhr-ul-mulk on a hill, skirts the W. bank of the lake some 20 ft. above the water. The Observatory, astronomical and meteorological, is on the W.

At the point where the road crosses the Hyderabad Wadi line of railway, is situated the station of Begampet. On a road from Hyderabad Public School in Begampet to the Secunderabad race course is a group of buildings where Sir Ronald Ross made his famous discovery of the connection between mosquitoes and malaria when he was stationed here with his Regiment at the end of the last century. "Ronald Ross Road" is named in his honour. The main road then enters the Secunderabad Cantonment, which comprises the areas of Chilkalguda, Bowenpalli, Begampet, Trimalgiri, North Trimalgiri and Bolarum. To the E. of the junction station is Lallaguda, the railway colony.

[1] For a full description, see the *Annual Report* for 1926-27 of Mr G. Yazdani (at that time) Director or Archaeology, Hyderabad State.

The Brigade Parade-ground at Secunderabad is used almost entirely for ceremonial purposes. Alongside is the Race Course. There are several fine buildings in the Cantonment, including the King Edward VII Memorial Hospital (with 225 beds); the United Service Club stands out as a landmark for miles around. The two hotels are on the Maidan, close to the railway station.

At **Trimalgiri** (Trimulgherry), 3 m. N.E. of Secunderabad, is an entrenched camp surrounded by a stone ditch. The Military Prison, which stands due W. of the S.W. bastion of the entrenchment, is popularly called Windsor Castle, from its high tower and castellated look. The Station Hospital is due S. of the S.E. bastion. Several large base hospitals were erected in this vicinity during the last war.

Bolarum, 6 m. N. of Secunderabad, and now incorporated with it, was formerly the principal Cantonment of the Hyderabad Contingent Force, which was absorbed in 1903 into the Indian Army. Here also is the former country abode of the British Resident, now one of the official residences of the President of India during the rainy season. To the East lies the golf-course, and military exercise ground. There is a frequent bus service.

From Secunderabad a metre-gauge line runs to Aurangabad and Manmad (Route 4). Bolarum is a station on this line. Another metre-gauge line runs S. and connects with the Southern Rly. at Kurnool (Route 27, p. 481); there is a direct train service between Secunderabad and Bangalore by this line, which passes through Hyderabad station (metre gauge).

From Secunderabad the line to Bezwada (Vijayawada) runs E.

149 m. from Wadi Junction is **Bhangir** (Bhongir) (R.), celebrated for its pottery. Prehistoric remains have been found at the foot of a fortified rock, on which are the ruins of a palace.

153 m. At **Raigir** there are prehistoric cairns.

202 m. **Kazipet** Junction (R.) for the railway to Chanda (p. 194). 4 m. from this station is **Hanamkonda,** with a remarkable temple (*c.* 1163) built by King Rudra Deva. Never finished and ruined by an earthquake, it is still a fine specimen of the Kakatiya style. In front of the triapsidal temple was a splendid Hall of Columns; both of these are placed on high basements, and both contain numbers of elaborately decorated pillars of very hard dark stone, with pierced screens between those in the outer rows. It is dedicated to Siva, Vishnu and Surya. Note particularly the massive monolithic figure of Siva's bull-mount, Nandi, in front of the pavilion.

A road to Chanda runs 16 m. past the Jail (worth a visit for its carpet-weaving) to **Warangal** (below). There is a motor-bus service. The station-master at Kazipet, if advised in advance, will arrange for a car; provisions must be taken.

At **Palampet,** on the shores of Ramappa Lake, dating from Kakatiya times, 8 sq. m. in extent, is an impressive example of ancient Turk civilisation. Two other lakes, **Pakhal** and **Laknavaram** can be reached by road from Hanamkonda. 40 m. N.E. of Hanamkonda, are some temples which have been described[1] as "the brightest stars in the galaxy of mediaeval Deccan temples". The Ramappa Temple (13th century) has pillars and ceilings carved with scenes from the Epics: the figures outside, carved from black basalt with a high polish, are most beautiful. The road is suitable for motors. There is a P.W.D. bungalow (permit from Divisional Engineer, Warangal) at Mulag (motor-bus service, 33 m. from Kazipet), 12 m. from Ramappa, a noted centre for big game.

B.G. line from Kazipet to Belharshah

A broad-gauge line of railway, crossing the Godavari river at 63 m.

[1] *The Temples of Palampet*, by G. Yazdani, Dir. of Archaeology, Hyderabad State (No. 6, *Memoirs, Arch. Survey of India*, Calcutta, 1922).

by a bridge 3820 ft. long (1927), the Painganga, and the Wardha river at 142 m., runs from Kazipet to (146 m.) Balharshah (p. 194), where it connects with the Central Ry. line to Chanda and Nagpur. The Grand Trunk Express runs daily between Madras (p. 500) and Delhi. But it is quicker and more comfortable to travel by air.

8 m. Hasanparthi Road has a temple of Venkateshwar Swami. A religious fair is held annually. Iron ore is found in the vicinity and small quantities of iron and steel which are manufactured here are employed for agricultural implements.

23 m. **Jumekoonta.** In the centre of a village is a pillar bearing an inscription in Ooriya which has not been deciphered. At Ellondasoonta, 2½ m. E., there is a temple dedicated to Rama, where an annual fair is held.

47 m. **Pedapalli** (D.B.). A Jagir. There is a motor-bus service from Pedapalli station to **Karimnagar,** (47 m.) noted for its silver filigree work. During solar and lunar eclipses pilgrims visit the bathing-ghats of the Godavari river, which is 6 m. distant. There is a quarry in Ramayana where good stone is available.

79 m. **Belampalli.** A coalfield has been opened in the vicinity of this station.

94 m. **Asifabad Road.** 12 m. from the town of Asifabad (D.B.). There is a famous Hindu temple nearby with a frieze containing some sex symbolism.

114 m. **Sirpur.** The first Gond King, Bhima Ballal Singh, made Sirpur his capital about 1240. In the reign of the seventh Gond King, Dirken Singh, Sirpur flourished as a great literary centre.

140 m. **Manickgarh.** The ancient fort of Manickgarh was a principal fortress of the Gond Kings.

Main Line

208 m. **Warangal** (pop. 207,000 in 1971) station (D.B.K.). ½ m. from the station, visible thence only as a long line of earthworks, stands the noted Hindu fort city of Warangal (Orakka "solitary rock"). It was the ancie capital of the Kakatiya, or Ganpa dynasty, which was attacked by Mal Kafur in 1309 and captured b Muhammad Tughlaq in 1323, fro Pratapa Rudradeva II, the last Raj Bukka Raya of Vijayanagar retook i The Bahmani King, Ahmad Wali conquered it in 1424. Trial excavation within the Fort have revealed remai of a large Chalukya-style templ whose boundaries are marked by fou Kirthi Stambhas which (like th Sanchi gateways) reproduce woode forms, the side struts being speciall remarkable. There is also a small hal ruined temple with some capit figures of bulls in front of it. The fin hall and other buildings belong to th Muslim period. There is a large col lection of images, carvings and slab Warangal has been famous fo centuries for carpet and cotto weaving. Marco Polo praised the hig quality of the fabrics made in his time

The line to Bezwada (Vijayawada turns sharply S.E. to

216 m. Chintapali. 26 m. E. on th dam of the Pakhal Tank is a pillar.

261 m. **Dornakal** Junction statio (R.). See of the first Indian Anglica Bishop Azariah, who died in 1946 The Cathedral was built by India Christians in their own style.

Branch to Singareni Collieries (16 *m.*)

From (10 m.) Karepalli Junctio on the Singareni branch, a line run (30 m.) to **Bhadrachalam Road,** whic is the station for the famous Templ of **Bhadrachalam** (D.B.), 20 m. Publi motor-bus service to Borgham Paha on the S. bank of the Godavari, wher the river is crossed; the ferry-boat land visitors within a few yards of th temple. Rama is said to have crosse the Godavari near this spot on hi journey to Lanka (Ceylon) in searc of his wife, Sita; and his house i shown to Hindus. The wealth of th temple, which is surrounded b twenty-four smaller shrines, is ver great.

Main Line

275 m. Khammameth (D.B.); fort ccessible by motor-bus from Hyder-bad.

303 m. Madhra. In this taluk, ormerly the S. taluk of Warangal, he Koh-i-Nur diamond was found 1623) near Kollur, on a hillside near he Krishna river. At Partial the Regent diamond was found, bought y Thomas Pitt, President of Madras 1701) and sold to the Duc d'Orléans, Regent of France, for a great sum. t was cut from 410 carats to 137 arats.

328 m. **Kondapalli** station. Ruins f a once celebrated fortress, built n 1360. It was taken by the Bahmani ing, Humayun the Cruel, in 1458, nd changed hands several times. The old palace of the Kutb Shahi ings stands on an elevation above he valley; part of it has been adapted s a R.H. It was taken by the Emperor Aurangzeb in 1687, and by the British nder General Caillaud, in 1766. Panthers formerly abounded in the eighbouring hills. Kondapalli is oted for its manufacture of wooden oy models of bungalows, with furni-ure and crockery complete.

338 m. **Bezwada,** or Kistna, tation (R., D.B.) (see p. 426), on he main line between Madras and Calcutta (Route 22).

ROUTE 26

HOTGI JUNCTION to BIJAPUR, Caves and Temples of Badami, and Gadag Junction.

292 m. from Bombay, on the Central Ry. main line from Bombay to Madras (Route 23), and 10 m. S.E. of Sholapur Junction (p. 437) is

Hotgi (Hudgi) Junction (R.). A metre-gauge line runs S. (174 m.) to Gadag, where it connects with the line from Hubli to Guntakal Junction (Route 27).

At 16 m. the Bhima river is crossed. From **Minchnal** (47 m.) the domes and minarets of Bijapur are plainly seen to the S.

*58 m. **BIJAPUR** station, other-wise Vijayapura, "City of Victory". There is a Tourist Bungalow and a more expensive Tourist Lodge run by the Indian Tourist Corp. The railway station is E. of the city (pop. 103,000 in 1971) and close to the Gol Gumbaz, the great tomb of Muhammad Adil Shah.

Yusaf Khan, the first King of Bijapur on the decay of the Bahmani dynasty, was a son of Amurath II, of Anatolia, and a Turk of pure blood, whose mother was forced to send him from Constantinople to Alexandria as an infant. He reached India (1459), was purchased for the bodyguard at Bidar (p. 453) by Mahmud Gawan, became governor of Bijapur, and in 1489 was enabled to proclaim inde-pendence and to found the Adil Shahi dynasty of Bijapur. The follow-ing is the order of their accession:

		A.D.
Yusaf Khan, Adil Shah		1490
Ismail	,,	1510
Mallu	,,	1534
Ibrahim I	,,	1535
Ali I	,,	1557
Ibrahim II	,,	1580
Muhammad	,,	1626
Ali II	,,	1656
Sikandar	,, 1659 to	1686

in which year the city was taken by Aurangzeb.

A great architectural outburst—there are more than 50 mosques and numerous tombs and palaces—followed on the capture and spoil of Vijayanagar (p. 477) after the Battle of Talikota in 1565. The kingdom extended to the west coast, including Goa.

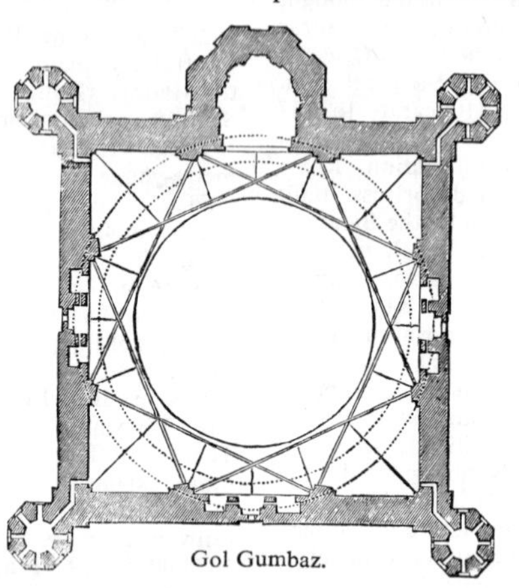

Gol Gumbaz.

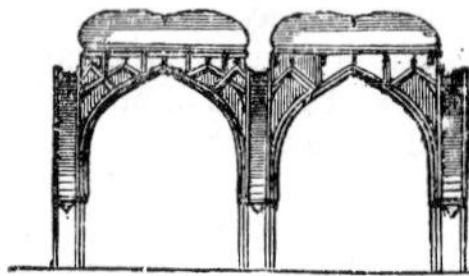

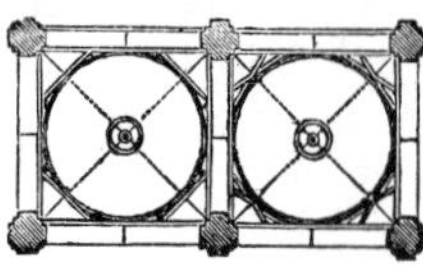

Section of Domes, Jami Masjid.

The Kaladgi District was re-named Bijapur in 1883, when the British Government re-occupied the old capital as administrative headquarters. A number of the buildings at Bijapur have been taken into official use, thereby saving them from destruction.

Torweh, or **Nauraspur,** about 1610 was a great suburb; but by 1686 it was depopulated. This suburb, then, whose walls extended 3 m. from the W. gate of the fort, and probably other suburbs, must have been included in the 30 m. circuit which tradition ascribes to Bijapur. What is called the city now is the fort only, of which Grant Duff says it was 6 m. in circumference. Within the circuit is the citadel, with walls extending 1650 ft. from N. to S. and 1900 ft. from W. to E. The buildings give proof of the former riches and magnificence of this old capital. Two days for the principal buildings alone will not be too much. There is a Travellers' Lodge and 2 Inspection Bungalows; reservation from the Chief Officer, Bijapur Municipality.

The **Gates** of the fort or city are:

The Fateh Gate, in the centre of the S. wall of the city, by which Aurangzeb is said to have entered. The Shahpur Gate, on the N.W. The doors are furnished with long iron spikes on the outside, to protect them from being battered in by elephants. This was a common device in India. W. of the city, is the Zohrapur = Jorapur Gate; and 600 ft. to the S. of that is the Makka Gate, with representations on either side of lions trampling on an elephant. This gate is closed and converted into a school. A minor road a few hundred yards farther N., serves its purpose. Almost opposite to it, on the E. side of the city, is the Alipur Gate, or High Gate, wrongly called in maps and elsewhere the Allahpur Gate. N. of it is the Padshahpur Gate, near the railway station. In the centre of the N. wall is the Bahmani Gate.

The Mausoleum of Muhammad Adil Shah, seventh King (1626-1656), is called Gol Gumbaz, or "Round Dome" (1).[1] It is built on a platform 600 ft. square and 2 ft. high. In front is a great gateway, 94 ft. by 88 ft., with a Nakkar Khana (music gallery), now a museum, in which there are some of the famous Bijapur carpets and Chinese porcelain.

The tomb is square, with sides of 196 ft. (exterior), and at each corner is a tower, seven storeys high. In the centre is the great dome, 124 ft. in diameter, while that of St Peter's at Rome is 139 ft., and that of St Paul's in London 108 ft. Over the entrance are three inscriptions—"Sultan Muhammad, inhabitant of Paradise"; "Muhammad whose end was commendable"; "Muhammad became a particle of heaven (lit. House of Salvation), 1067". The derived date, thus three times repeated, is 1659.

The surface for the most part is covered with plaster. Three façades have a wide, lofty arch in the centre, pierced with small windows and a blind one on either side, and above each is a cornice of grey basalt and a row of small arches supporting a second line of plain work, surmounted by a balustrade 6 ft. high.

[1] The numbers refer to the corresponding numbers on the plan of Bijapur (p. 473).

The corner towers are entered from winding staircases in the walls of the main building, and terminate in cupolas. Each storey has seven small arched windows opening into the court below. From the eighth storey there is an entrance to a broad gallery inside the dome, which is so wide that a carriage might pass round it. Here there is a most remarkable echo; a soft whisper at one point of the gallery can be heard most distinctly at the opposite point.

The great hall, over which the dome is raised, is the largest domed space in the world. The internal area is 18,225 sq. ft., while that of the Pantheon at Rome is only 15,833. "At the height of 57 ft. from the floor-line," says Fergusson (*Hist. of Ind. Arch.*, 2, 274), "the hall begins to contract by a series of pendentives as ingenious as they are beautiful,[1] to a circular opening 97 ft. in diameter. On the platform of these pendentives, at a height of 109 ft. 6 in., the dome is erected, 124 ft. 5 in. in diameter, thus leaving a gallery more than 12 ft. wide all round the interior. Internally the dome is 178 ft. above the floor, and externally 198 ft. from the outside platform; its thickness at the springing is about 10 ft., and at the crown 9 ft." From the gallery outside a view shows, on the E., 'Alipur; on the W. are seen the Ibrahim Rauza, the Upari Burj, the Sherza Burj, or Lion Bastion; to the N.W. is the unfinished tomb of Ali Adil Shah II; about 1 m. towards the N. the ruins of the villages of the masons and painters employed on the Gol Gumbaz; and on the S.W. is the dome of the Jami Masjid.

A small annexe to the mausoleum on the N. was built by Sultan Muham-

[1] "The most ingenious and novel part of the construction is the mode in which its lateral and outward thrust is counteracted. This was accomplished by forming the pendentives so that they not only cut off the angles, but that, as shown in the plan, their arches intersect one another and form a very considerable mass of masonry perfectly stable in itself; and, by its weight acting inwards, counteracting any thrust that can possibly be brought to bear upon it by the pressure of the dome."—Fergusson, *Ind. Arch.*, 2, 274.

mad as a tomb, it is supposed, for his mother, Zohra Sahiba, from whom one of the suburbs was called Zohrapur, now called Jorapur. It was never finished or occupied.

Below the dome is the cenotaph of Sultan Muhammad in the centre. On the E. side are the graves of his youngest wife and of the son of Ali Adil Shah II; on the W. are those of his favourite Hindu mistress, a dancing-girl Rambha, his daughter, and his eldest wife, mentioned by Bernier.

On the edge of the platform W. is the mosque attached to the mausoleum, a building of no mean size and of considerable beauty of design, but quite eclipsed by the size of the Gol Gumbaz.

The road to the dak bungalow (over a mile) passes the Mahal of Khawas Khan and Mosque of Mustafa Khan, a lofty building with a façade of three arches and a central dome supported on pendentives. Behind the mosque W. are the ruins of the Khan's Palace. Mustafa Khan Ardistani was a distinguished nobleman at the court of Ali Adil Shah I, and was murdered in 1581 by Kishwar Khan, who usurped the regency in the time of Ibrahim Adil Shah II.

The **Jami Masjid**, nearly ½ m. S.W. of the Gol Gumbaz, is entered by a gateway on the E. side. The arcades on the N. and S. sides are 31 ft. broad. In the centre of the quadrangle is the *hauz* or tank for ablutions, now dry.

It was commenced by Ali Adil Shah I (1557-79), and, though continued by his successors, was not finished by 1686. The mosque proper has a façade of nine bays, and is five bays in depth. Each square has a domed roof, beautiful, but flat and invisible externally. The centre, a space 70 ft. square, corresponding to twelve of these squares, is roofed over by the great dome, which is 57 ft. in diameter. It is supported on pendentives in the same manner as the Gol Gumbaz. The pavement below the dome is of chunam, divided by black lines into numerous squares called musallahs, or compartments for persons to pray on, imitating the musallah, or prayer-carpet, which the faithful carry with them to the mosques. These were made by order of Aurangzeb when he carried away the velvet carpets, the large golden chain and other valuables.

The mihrab, which marks the place on the W. to which the people turn in prayer, is gilded and ornamented with much Arabic writing. There is also a Persian chronogram. The derived date is 1636.

The **Mihtari Mahal** (2) is the name given to the entrance gateway to the Mihtari Mosque which stands between the Jami Masjid and the citadel, on the S. of the road. It is a small but elegant structure, three storeys high, with minarets at the corners and ornamental carving in soft stone about its balconied and projecting windows. Fergusson says (2, 278) of this structure: "One of the most remarkable edifices is a little gateway, known as the Mihtari Mahal. It is in the Hindu-Saracenic style, every part and every detail covered with ornament, but always equally appropriate and elegant."

The Palace of the **Asár-i-Sharif** (3), "illustrious relics", which are hairs of the Prophet's beard, is a large building of brick and lime, standing outside the moat of the inner citadel and the centre of its E. rampart. The E. side is entirely open from the ground to the ceiling, which is supported by four massive teak pillars, 60 ft. high. This forms a deep portico 36 ft. broad, and looks upon a tank 250 ft. square. The ceiling is panelled in wood and has been very handsomely painted. The whole of the W. side is occupied by rooms in two storeys. A flight of stairs ascends to a hall 81 ft. long and 27 ft. broad, where some of the old carpets and brocades of the Palace are shown under glass. Opening right from this hall is an upper veranda or antechamber which looks down into the portico (already described) below.

Its ceilings and walls have been gilded; the doors are inlaid with ivory, and in the palmy days of Bijapur the effect must have been very striking. The Asár-i-Sharíf formerly communicated with the citadel (W.) by a bridge. Originally built as a court of justice by Muhammad Shah about 1646, it succeeded to the honour of holding the precious relics of the Prophet after a similar building within the citadel had been burned down.

The Arkilla or Citadel

The only gateway that remains is at the extreme S., facing E.; here the walls are full of ancient pillars and sculptured stones, taken from Jain temples, and others were utilised in the two "old mosques" within the citadel.

The **Old Mosque** (4), just N.W. of the gate, is a converted Jain temple. The central mandapam, or hall, two storeys high, serves as the porch. The inner doorway, with perforated screens, is Muslim, but the mosque proper is made up of Hindu or Jain pillars of various patterns and heights. At the N. side, near the centre row, is a carved black pillar, and to the N.E. of it an ancient Kanarese inscription. On several of the pillars around are inscriptions, some in Sanskrit and some in Kanarese. One bears the date 1320.

The **Anand Mahal** (5), or "Palace of Delight", where the ladies of the seraglio lived, is in the centre of the citadel. It was built by Ibrahim II in 1589, and intended partly for his own use, but the façade was never finished. It contains a very fine hall, and is used as an official residence.

The **Gagan Mahal** (6), or "Sky (Heavenly)" Palace, supposed to have been built by Ali Adil Shah I, is on the W. of the citadel close to the moat, and faces N. It has three magnificent arches. The span of the central one is 61 ft., and that of each of the side arches 18 ft. The height of all three is the same—about 50 ft. It was used as a darbar hall, and on the roof was a gallery, from which the ladies looked down on to the open space in front. It is said that here the Emperor Aurangzeb received the submission of the King and the nobles on the fall of Bijapur.

An old gateway of the Palace to the S.E. of the Gagan Mahal was at one time a church but is now closed and derelict (7).

About 150 yd. to the N.E. of the Gagan Mahal is another old mosque (8), built with the stones of a Jain temple. It has ten rows of pillars seven deep.

E. of this is the **Adalat Mahal,** with a small mosque on the N. side, and an extremely pretty pavilion or pleasure house E. of it, on a corner of the citadel wall. A little to the N. of this is Yakut Dabuli's Tomb and Mosque. The tomb is square, with stone lattice-work screens. He decorated the mihrab of the Jami Masjid.

On the extreme W. of the citadel is the **Sat-Manzili** (9), or "Seven Storeys", Rambha's pleasure Palace from the top of which the whole city could be overlooked. Of this only five storeys now remain. A peculiarity of the building is the number of water-pipes and cisterns round about it. It formed the N.W. corner of a vast structure wrongly called the **Granary** (10), at the S. end of which is a large building, which was the public Palace of the Sultans where their public audiences were held.

This Palace is called the **Chini Mahal** (11), from the quantity of broken china found there, and possesses a fine hall 128 ft. long.

In front of the Sat-Manzili (9), in the centre of the road, stands a beautifully ornamented little pavilion known as **Jal Mandir** (12), signifying that jets of water played in it. From this the moat of the citadel is crossed by a causeway 140 ft. long. At the far end is the **Nalika Jahan** or **Jhanjiri Mosque,** one of the most effective buildings in Bijapur.

N.E. of the gateway and the Old Mosque is the **Makka Masjid** (13), a miniature mosque of beautiful proportions and great simplicity of design The massive minarets at the corners of the high walls which surround it in all probability belonged to an earlier building. The façade of the mosque proper has five bays of arches about 8 ft. high, is two bays deep, and is surmounted by a dome.

Immediately to the W. is a huge walled space, known as the Háthikhana (18) (elephant stable), and adjoining it S. is a tower which was probably used for the storage of grain. Close by on the E. wall of the citadel is the picturesquely situated high-standing Chinch Diddi Mosque.

The unfinished **Tomb of Ali Adil Shah II** lies W. of the dak bungalow. It is a noble ruin, a square with seven large Gothic-looking arches on each side, constructed on a terrace 15 ft. high and 215 ft. square. The death of the Sultan (1659) prevented its completion. The cenotaph is in the centre enclosure, which is 78 ft. square, and should have been crowned by a dome.

Close to this tomb on the S.W. is the pretty **Bukhara Masjid,** and just N. of this is the beautiful mosque and tomb of Mirza Sandal. To the W. again, half-way to the Haidar Burj, is the **Sikandar Rauza,** the plain grave of the last Sultan (1659-86).

South-Western Quarter

The **Andu Masjid** (1608) stands on the E. side of the road, which runs S. from the citadel. It is a two-storeyed building, the lower part forming a hall, and the upper part the mosque proper and its small court. The façade has three bays; it is surmounted by a fluted dome and four small minarets, and the masonry and workmanship are finer than those of any other building in Bijapur.

On the **Landa Kasab** bastion, W. of the Fateh Gate and near the road from the Andu Masjid leading through the S. wall, is a fine cannon measuring 21 ft. 7 in. long, with a diameter at the breech of 4 ft. 4 in., and at the muzzle of 4 ft. 5 in., which must weigh nearly 50 tons. A road W. from Andu Masjid leads to the tomb of the Begam Sahiba, a wife of the Emperor Aurangzeb, who died of plague, and to the Nau Bagh. Another road to the W. from 300 yd. S. of the Andu Mosque leads to the Jami Masjid of Ibrahim I, and to the traditional tomb of Ali I, a simple building with an arcade all round. In front, on a high platform, is a fine tombstone of dark green stone.

The old execution tree (14), an *Adamsonia* or "Gorah Imli", is passed on the way from the citadel to the "Two Sisters", in the compound of the Judge's bungalow. Near the Makka Gate two domed tombs very much alike are known as the Jor Gumbaz and to Europeans as the **"Two Sisters"** (15). The octagonal one contains the remains of Khan Muhammud, assassinated at the instigation of Sultan Muhammad for his treacherous dealings with Aurangzeb, and of his son Khawas Khan, Wazir to Sikandar. The dome is nearly complete, and springs from a band of lozenge-shaped leaves. The space within forms a beautiful room. The square building is the mausoleum of Abdul Razzak, the religious tutor of Khawas Khan. It is a large building, now much decayed. Near it (S.) is the Tomb, with its unfinished brick dome, of Kishwar Khan, whose father, Asad Khan, is repeatedly mentioned by Portuguese writers. He founded the fort of Dharur in the time of Ali Adil Shah I, and was taken and put to death by one of the Nizam Shahi Kings.

Western Quarter

The **Taj Bauri,** named after Taj Sultana, principal wife of Ibrahim II, is inside the Makka Gate. The E. wing of the façade of the tank is partly ruined. Two flights of steps lead down to the water beneath an arch of 34 ft. span and about the same height, flanked by two octagonal towers. The tank at the water's edge is 231 ft. square. The water comes partly from springs and partly from drainage, and is 30 ft. deep in the dry weather.

Outside the W. wall of the city, 400 yd. from the Makka Gate, is the **Ibrahim Rauza** (also called Roza), a group of buildings which includes the tombs of Ibrahim II, Taj Sultana, and four other members of his family. It is said to have been erected by a Persian architect. It is enclosed by a strong wall with a lofty gateway. The courtyard within was once a garden; in the centre of an oblong platform, is the tomb, and to the W. of it a mosque, with a fountain and reservoir between them. The five arches which form the E. façade of the Mosque are very graceful; above them, under the rich cornice, hang heavy chains cut out of stone.

An arcade of seven arches forms a veranda 15 ft. broad round the *Tomb*, and its ceiling is exquisitely carved with verses of the Koran, enclosed in compartments and interspersed with wreaths of flowers. The letters were originally gilded, and the ground is still a most brilliant azure. The border of every compartment is different from that of the one adjoining. The windows are formed of lattice-work of Arabic sentences, cut out of stone slabs, with a space between each letter to admit the light. This work is admirably executed. Above the double arcade outside the building is a magnificent cornice with a minaret four storeys high at each corner and eight smaller ones between them. From an inner cornice, with four minarets on each side, rises the dome.

In plan the building resembles the tombs at Golconda. The principal apartment is 40 ft. square, with a stone-slab roof, perfectly flat in the centre, and supported only by a cove projecting 10 ft. from the walls on every side and depending on the tensile strength of shell lime. "How the roof is supported is a mystery which can only be understood by those who are familiar with the use the Indians make of masses of concrete, and with exceedingly good mortar, which seems capable of infinite applications. Above this apartment is another in the dome as ornamental as the one below it, though its only object is to obtain externally the height required for architectural effect, and access to its interior can only be obtained by a dark, narrow staircase in the thickness of the wall."[1] Over the N. door is an inscription in Persian extolling the building in very exaggerated terms. The last line is a chronogram, which gives the date 1036 A.H. = A.D. 1626 Over the S. door is another inscription in praise of the monarch, with the date 1633. Over the same door is inscribed:

(*Translation*)

The work of beautifying this Mausoleum was completed by Malik Sandal.[2]
Taj-i-Sultan issued orders for the construction of this Roza.
At the beauty of which Paradise stood amazed.
He expended over 1½ lakhs of huns,
And 900 more.

The hun being Rs. 3½, the total expense was about £50,000. When Aurangzeb besieged Bijapur in 1686 he took up his quarters in the Ibrahim Rauza, which received some damage from the Bijapur gun, now repaired.

Guns and Bastions.—The **Burj-i-Sherza,** or "Lion Bastion" (16), so called from being ornamented by two lions' heads in stone, is 300 yd. N. of the Zohrapur Gate. In the W. wall on the right-hand side on ascending the steps of the bastion is an inscription stating that it was built in five months, and giving the date 1671. On the top of this bastion

[1] *History of Indian Architecture*, 2, 273. Fergusson also says that Ibrahim commenced his tomb "on so small a plan, 116 ft. sq., that it was only by ornament that he could render it worthy of himself, his favourite wife, and other members of his family".

[2] The tomb of this personage is W. of the incomplete tomb of Ali Adil Shah II. See p. 470.

is a huge cannon, called the **Malik-i-Maidan,** "Lord of the Battle Plain". At the sides of the muzzle the representation of the mouth of a monster swallowing an elephant is wrought in relief. It was cast at Ahmadnagar in a bell metal which takes a very high polish. It is 14 ft. long, the circumference is about 13 ft. 6 in., and the diameter of the bore is 2 ft. 4 in. Just above the touch-hole is the following inscription:

The work of Muhammad Bin Husain Rumi.

At the muzzle is the following:

The servant of the family of the Prophet of God, Abu'l Ghazi Nisam Shah, 956 A.H. (=1551).
In the 30th year of the exalted reign, 1097 A.H., Shah Alamgir, conqueror of infidels, King, Defender of the Faith,
Conquered Bijapur, and for the date of his triumph,
He fulfilled what justice required, and annexed the territory of the Shahs,
Success showed itself, and he took the Malik-i-Maidan.

About 150 yd. E. of the Sherza Burj, and near the heavy Idgah, is a strange building, called the **Upari Burj,** or "Upper Bastion", also called the Haidar Burj (17), after a General of Ali I and Ibrahim II. It is a tower 61 ft. high, oval in plan, with an outside staircase. On the way up a Persian inscription recording the building of the tower in 1583 will be noticed. On the top are two guns made of longitudinal bars held together with iron bands. The larger, called the Lamcharri, "far flier", is 30 ft. 8 in. long, and has a diameter of 2 ft. 5 in. at the muzzle and 3 ft. at the breech; the bore is 12 in. in diameter. The other gun is 19 ft. 10 in. long, with 1 ft. diameter at the muzzle and 1 ft. 6 in. in diameter at breech.

North-Western Quarter

The **Chánd Bauri**—named after Chánd Bibi, central figure of Meadows Taylor's "A Noble Queen", was built in 1579, on the model of the Taj Bauri, and also has a fine arch over the steps leading down to it. The gaol, N.W., the way to which passes between lines of mausolea, big and small, is located in an old musafarkhana or caravanserai of remarkable proportions. Close to it, the *Amin Dargah*, of considerable importance, has a collection of old pictures.

1½ m. to the S.W. of the Shahapur suburb, situated to the N.W. of the city, is the Palace of Afzal Khan (p. 445). Adjoining is a mosque of two storeys, and on a platform to the S.W. are eleven rows of tombs of women, which have given rise to the tale that they were the wives of Afzal Khan put to death by him.

Waterworks.—Bijapur was supplied with abundant water by underground ducts. One source of supply, was a spring beyond the suburb of Torweh, 5 m. W. of the citadel; another was the Begam Tank, 3 m. to the S. Along the line of the water supply occur towers for the purpose of relieving the pressure in the pipes. Traces of innumerable baths and cisterns are found in every direction. The water from the reservoirs, for instance, in the ruined Palace of Mustafa Khan, ran into a tank, from which it brimmed over into narrow stone channels which passed in circuitous courses through the gardens, running over uneven surfaces to give it a sparkling and rippling effect.

The modern waterworks are at Bhutnal, about 4½ m. N.W.

From Bijapur the line continues and at 98 m. crosses the Kistna river by a bridge 3392 ft. long.

115 m. **Bagalkot.** Some 25 m. E. at a bend of the river, near the village of Tondihal, not easily accessible, was fought the famous Battle of Talikota on 23rd January 1565, which caused the downfall of the Vijayanagar kingdom (p. 477). The small town of Talikota lies 30 m. N. of the field of battle.

Structural temples show development of the Dravidian style, and the early Chalukyan (Indo-Aryan) style,

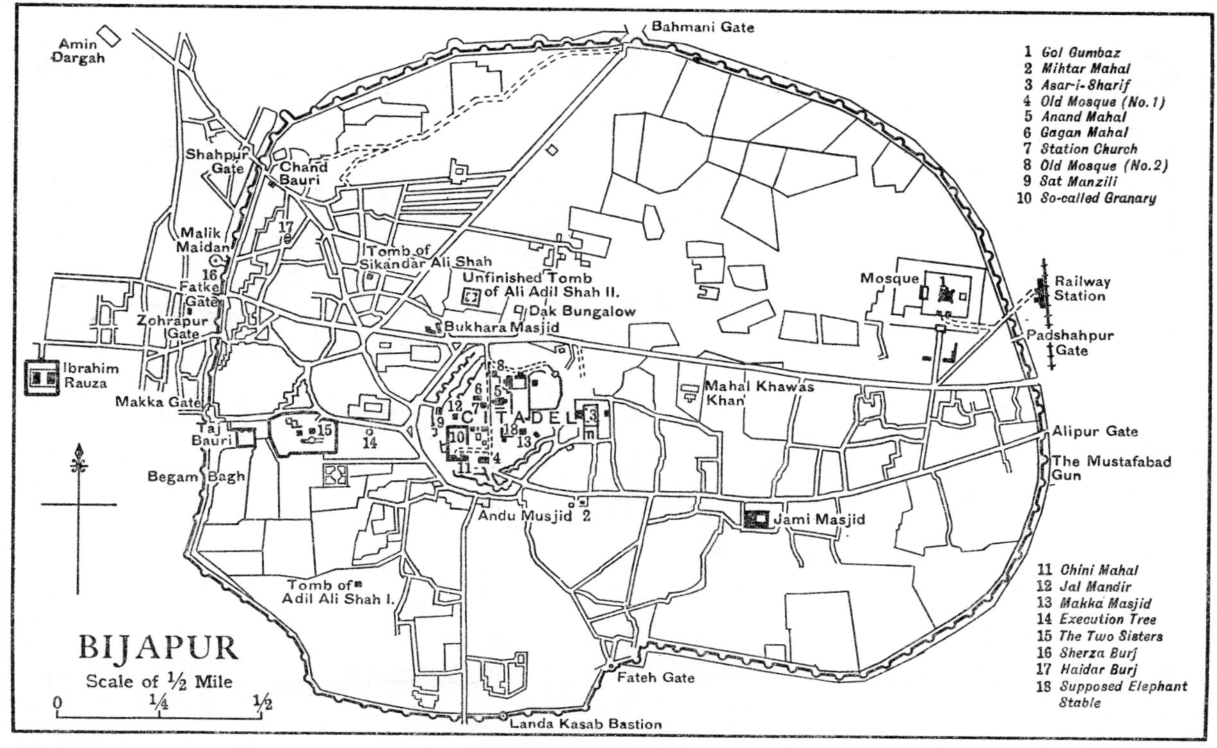

BIJAPUR
Scale of ½ Mile
0 ¼ ½
1 Gol Gumbaz
2 Mihtar Mahal
3 Asar-i-Sharif
4 Old Mosque (No.1)
5 Anand Mahal
6 Gagan Mahal
7 Station Church
8 Old Mosque (No.2)
9 Sat Manzili
10 So-called Granary
11 Chini Mahal
12 Jal Mandir
13 Makka Masjid
14 Execution Tree
15 The Two Sisters
16 Sherza Burj
17 Haidar Burj
18 Supposed Elephant Stable
Amin Dargah
Bahmani Gate
Shahpur Gate
Chand Bauri
Malik Maidan
Fatke Gate
Zohrapur Gate
Ibrahim Rauza
Makka Gate
Taj Bauri
Begam Bagh
Tomb of Sikandar Ali Shah
Unfinished Tomb of Ali Adil Shah II.
Dak Bungalow
Bukhara Masjid
CITADEL
Mosque
Railway Station
Padshahpur Gate
Mahal Khawas Khan
Alipur Gate
The Mustafabad Gun
Andu Musjid
Jami Masjid
Tomb of Adil Ali Shah I.
Fateh Gate
Landa Kasab Bastion

while the caves (Hindu) are earlier than the Brahman caves at Ellora. Visitors should take torches with them.[1]

131 m. **Badami** station for Badami (3 m.) Tourist B. and I.B. in the same compound in outskirts of town. Tongas and buses from the station. The caves and temples lie 74 m. W., P.W.D. There is a good new road from Hospet (p. 477) *via* Gadag to Badami and then Bijapur.

The quickest way to visit the temples of Badami, Aiholi and Pattadakal is to take a taxi and a packed lunch from Bijapur or Bagalkot. However, they are some of the most outstanding examples of Hindu architecture and merit a longer visit, now possible thanks to the good Tourist Bungalows at Badami and Aiholi. Written permission must be obtained from the Archaelogical Dept.Aurangabad to photograph these temples with tripod or flash.

Badami (Vatapipura) was once the capital of the Chalukyan Pulakesin I (A.D. 550-566). Narsinhavarman, a Pahlava, took it in 640 from

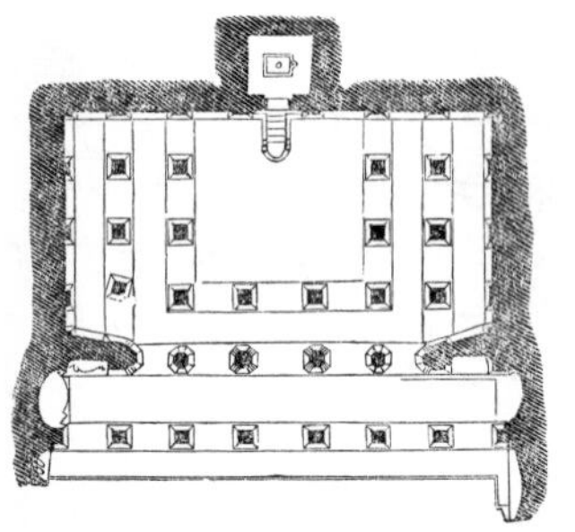

Third Cave, from a plan by Dr Burgess.

Pulakesin II (609-40) and destroyed it. Vengi became the capital until Vikramaditya I came back in 653. The Rashtrakutas occupied it in 753.

The fort of Badami is to the N.E. of the town, 3 m. E. from the railway station, and on the heights above are some picturesque temples. One (Dravidian) resembles the Dharmaraja Rath at Mahabalipuram (p. 515), another the Orissan style. To the S. is another rocky, fort-crowned hill, in the face of which are four cave temples. The two hills (about 400 ft. high) approach so close to each other as to leave only a gorge, into which the town extends. E. of this is a fine tank.

Sir Thomas Munro took Badami from the Mahrattas (1818) and the fort appears in his coat of arms as a Baronet.

Three of the **Cave Temples** are Brahmanical, and date from A.D. 550 to A.D. 580; the fourth is Jain, and probably dates from A.D. 650. The First Cave, excavated about 50 ft. up in the face of the rock, is consecrated to Siva. The pillars are slightly carved in relief to about halfway from the top. The veranda rests on a plinth, along the front of which are Ganas (dwarf attendants of Siva) in all sorts of attitudes. On the left of the veranda is a dwarpal with a Nandi over him. Opposite this dwarapal is a figure of Siva, 5 ft. high, with eighteen arms, dancing the tandava.[1] Behind the veranda is a chapel, and beyond an antechamber in which, on the left, is Vishnu, or Harihara, with four hands, holding the usual symbols, and on the right the Arddhanariswar, or combined male and female figure, attended by a Nandi bull and the skeleton Bringi. A figure of Mahesheshwari, or Durga, destroying the buffalo-demon Mahesheshwar is on the back wall, on the right wall Ganpati, and on the left Skanda. Between the antechamber and the hall are two pillars only. The hall has eight columns of the Elephanta type, and measures 42 ft. by 24½ ft. The ceiling and that of the antechamber are divided into compartments by carved beams. In the centre of the antechamber roof is a relief of the Great Snake's head. At the back of the hall is a small

[1] A good description of the Caves is given in the *Bas Reliefs of Badami*, by R. D. Banerjee, published by the Archaeological Society of India.

[1] See descriptions on pp. 107-108.

chapel with a lingam. The Second Cave Temple is rather higher. At the ends of the forecourt in front of it are two dwarapals with a female attendant. Four square columns, finely carved, separate the platform from the veranda, on the left of which is the Vahara Avatar, or Vishnu in the form of a boar, and on the right the Dwarf Avatar of Vishnu, dilated to an immense size, putting one foot on the earth and lifting the other over the heavens. On the ceiling in front of this is Vishnu with four arms, riding on Garuda, and in the central square of the ceiling is a lotus with sixteen fishes round it. On the top of the wall in a frieze are the figures of Vishnu as Krishna. The roof of the inner chamber, 33 ft. by 23½ ft., is supported by eight pillars; and the corbels are lions, human figures, vampires, elephants, etc. The adytum has only a square *Chavaranga*, or altar. A sloping ascent and more flights of steps lead up to a platform, and to a doorway; on the right of it is an inscription in old Kanarese (A.D. 786), a charter from Sita Mahadevi, wife of Dhruva Rashtrakuta (775-815). At the top of yet another flight of steps is the platform in front of the Third Cave, below a scarp of 100 ft. of perpendicular rock, which is, says Dr Burgess, "one of the most interesting Brahmanical works in India". The façade is 70 ft. from N. to S. Eleven steps lead up to the cave, and on the plinth Ganas are represented. The brackets of the pillars represent male and female figures, Arddhanariswar, Siva, and Parvati, and on the columns themselves are carved elaborate festoons, and below medallions with groups of figures. Traces of painting are visible on the under-side of the eaves and the roof of the veranda. At the W. end of the veranda is a statue of Narsingh, the fourth avatar of Vishnu, a very spirited figure, 11 ft. high. On the S. wall is Harihara, of the same height, and beyond the veranda at the side of the first is the Dwarf or Vamana Avatar. At the E. end is Narayan, seated under Sheshnag. On the outer side of this is Vishnu reclining on a great snake, and on the inner wall is the Varaha, or Boar, incarnation; to the right is an inscription in Kanarese of Mangalesvara, dated Saka 500 = A.D. 578. The hall measures 65 ft. by 37 ft. Eight pillars form a space in front of the shrine, and on each side a recess. The ceilings are divided into compartments, with carved panels.

The Fourth, or Jain Cave, lies E. of the other three. The platform beyond the wall overlooks the lake or tank, and commands a fine view. A broad overhanging eave has been cut out of the rock in front of this cave. On the left of the veranda, 31 ft. by 6 ft., is the Jain divinity Parasnath, with bands round his thighs and cobras coming out below his feet. On the right of the veranda is a Gautama Swami attended by snakes. The hall behind is 25 ft. by 6 ft.; in the shrine is a seated statue of Mahavira.

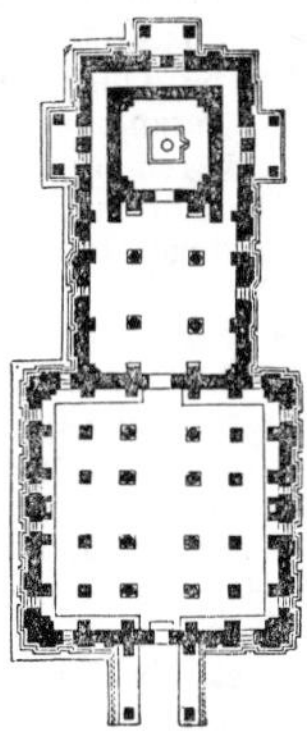

Temple of Papnath, Pattadakal.

At **Pattadakal,** 10 m. N.E. of Badami, on the left bank of the Malprabha river (bus services to and from Badami), are several temples, both Brahmanical and Jain, dating from the 7th or 8th century. They "are very pure examples of the Dravidian style of architecture; they are all square pyramids divided into distinct storeys, and each storey ornamented with cells alternately oblong and square. Their style of ornamentation is also very much coarser than that of the Chalukyan style, and differs very much in character. The domical termination of the spires is also different, and much less graceful, and the overhanging cornices of double curvature are much more prominent and important" (Burgess).

The main group is very interesting because it exhibits the Dravidian and Chalukyan styles in absolute juxtaposition (see *Architecture of Dharwar and Mysore*, pp. 63, 64). The Temple of Papnath is of the Chalukyan style, another, rather later, of Virupaksha, dates from about A.D. 800. The Temple of Papnath, 90 ft. long, including the porch, and 40 ft. broad, may have inspired Kailasa at Ellora.

At **Aihole**, (Govt. T.B.) (1970), 8 m. to the N.E. of Pattadakal, there is a very numerous collection of archaic temples. The Meguti Temple (early Chalukyan) bears an inscription (A.D. 634) of Pulikasin II; some pillars are carved. The Durga Temple is apsidal with a veranda all round and has some very remarkable carving. The Ravan Pahadi cave temple also has good carvings. There are many dolmens at this site.

Aihoe can be reached from Katgeri station (123 m.), at a distance of about 12 m. from the railway; the Malprabha river must be crossed.

143 m. (from Hotgi) the Malprabha river is crossed. 173 m. from Hotgi is **Gadag** Junction (R., D.B., ½ m.).

Gadag (anciently Kratuka) is a centre of cotton trade. The cotton and the Maconochie Markets are of excellent design. In its N.W. corner is a Vaishnavite Temple. The entrance is under a high gateway or gopuram, with four storeys, and 50 ft. high. The door is handsomely carved with sixteen rows of figures in relief on either side. The Someswara Temple, now a school, is richly decorated throughout.

In the fort is a Saivite Temple of **Trimbakeswar** or Trikuteswar, the "Lord of the Three Peaks". The outside is one mass of most elaborate carving. Two rows of figures run along the entire front and back; those of the lower row are 2 ft. 9 in. high, including their canopy, and are 156 in number. In the upper row are 104 figures, 13 in. high, 52 in the front, and the same in the back. Between the four pillars on the E. is a colossal bull. Immediately behind the main portion of the temple, to the right of the enclosure, is a *Temple to Saraswati*. The porch is the finest part of it; it contains eighteen pillars, some of them exquisitely carved, and six pilasters. The three first of the two centre rows of pillars deserve particular notice for their elegance of design and exquisite carving.[1] There are numerous inscriptions at the temples, one of which has the date Saka 790 = A.D. 868.

Lakkandi (anciently Lokkikandi) is about 8 m. S.E. of Gadag. The place is full of ancient temples.

The façade of the Kashi Vishwanath Temple has been supported by four pillars, of which that to the N. has gone. The doorways are elaborately carved, and though the roof is ruined, the temple is by far the handsomest here; but, being built of coarse granite, the carving is not clear and sharply defined.

To the W., on the opposite side of the road, is a Temple to Nandeswar, or "Siva, Lord of the Bull Nandi". There is a Kanarese inscription on

[1] Meadows Taylor says: "It is impossible to describe the exquisite finish of the pillars of the interior of this temple, which are of black hornblende, or to estimate how they were completed in their present condition, unless they were turned in a lathe; yet there can be little doubt that they were set up originally as rough masses of rock, and afterwards carved into their present forms. The carving on some of the pillars and of the lintels and architraves of the doors is quite beyond description. No chased work in silver or gold could possibly be finer, and the patterns to this day are copied by goldsmiths, who take casts and moulds from them, but fail in representing the sharpness and finish of the original."

the ledge of the W. division of the roof, between the four pillars. It stands on the N. side of a tank.

The Temple of Iswara, the roof of which has fallen in, is very old; the exterior is handsomely carved, and is said to be the work of Janak Acharya, the great sculptor and architect of the Hoysala Ballala kings, who executed the carvings at Halebid (p. 487).

A narrow path thickly shaded for about 100 yd., leads from it to a Baoli, or well, the sides of which are faced with stone. There are flights of steps to the water on three sides, and on either side of the first step is an elephant, so well carved that it is popularly attributed to Janak Acharya.

200 yd. from this is a Temple to Manikeswar, a name of Krishna, so called because every day he gave to Radha a ruby (manik). A very pretty small tank adjoins the temple. It is faced with stone, and has several buttresses projecting into the water, said to be carved by Janak Acharya. On either side of the entrance into the temple are four pillars of black basalt. This temple is surrounded by beautiful trees of great size.[1]

From Gadag the railway runs E. to Guntakal Junction (Route 27) and W. to Hubli Junction (for Bangalore and Mysore), to Dharwar, and Londa Junction (Route 28).

[1] See *Architectural Antiquities of Western India*, by H. Cousens, p. 27.

ROUTE 27

GADAG JUNCTION to **HOSPET** (for **HAMPI** or **Vijayanagar**), **Bellary**, and **Guntakal Junction**.

GUNTAKAL JUNCTION to

(*a*) **Dronachellam** for **Kurnool** and **Secunderabad, Nandyal, Guntur,** and **Vijayawada**; and

(*b*) **Dharmavaram** and **Bangalore.**

Gadag Junction (R., D.B.) (p. 476) on the Hubli-Guntakal Section of the Southern Ry.

35 m. from Gadag, **Koppal.** This area was formerly part of the Salar Jung jagir in the Hyderabad State. There are two forts at Koppal; the upper, which is on the summit of a hill, 400 ft. above the plain, was described by Sir John Malcolm as the strongest place he had seen in India. The lower fort was rebuilt in 1786 by Tipu's French engineers, and was taken in 1790, after two months' siege, by the British and the Nizam's forces. It was taken by Brig.-Gen. Pritzler in 1819.

49 m. Munirabad. 3 m. to Mallapuram (dam for irrigation and electric supply).

52 m. the Tungabhadra river used to be the boundary between Madras and Hyderabad.

53 m. **Hospet** Junction (R., D.B.). A n.g. branch runs 43 m. S., to Kotturu, and another to Ramandrug, 18 m., and Samehalli, 37 m. The Ramandrug plateau (3500 ft.) which lies within the former Sandur State (p. 481), was the sanatorium of Bellary when troops were stationed there.

Hampi (9 m.) (Restaurant) or Vijayanagar can be visited from Hospet. Transport available. But Bellary (p. 480) is only 34 m. away by car, and Tungabadra 10 m. (p. 480).

Vijayanagar (City of Victory) and Hampi.—Hampi is the site of the ancient capital of the Vijayanagar Kings, who dominated S. India from 1336 to 1565, the date of the Battle of Talikota; even after 1565 they continued to rule elsewhere in S. India. The 600th anniversary of the founding was celebrated in December 1936.

The ruins cover 9 sq. m., including Kamalapur (I.B.) on the S. and Anagundi, the earliest seat of the dynasty, N. of the Tungabhadra. Mr R. Sewell's *A Forgotten Empire* (George Allen, 1924) is still the best book on the subject.

The Kamalapur I.B. is 7 m. N.E. from Hospet; it is a converted temple.

No cook. There is a good I.B. at Hampi Camp (permission from District Engineer, Tungabhadra Hydro-electric Scheme, Hampi). There is a fair road (buses, jeeps and taxis available) through the area between Kamalapur and Hampi, described as "virtually a vast open-air museum of Hindu monuments in the Dravidian style of architecture".

Vijayanagar was founded on the fall of the Hoysala Ballala dynasty (p. 487), about 1336, by two brothers, Bukka and Harihara, who had been driven out of Warangal. Their descendants flourished here till the Battle of Talikota (1565), and afterwards at Penukonda, Vellore, Chandragiri, and (as some writers say) Chingleput, for another century, until finally overwhelmed by Bijapur and Golconda. The Rajas of Anagundi, an old village on the northern bank of the Tungabhadra river claim to be the surviving representatives of the dynasty. During the two and a quarter centuries that the Vijayanagar Rajas held the city of Hampi they extended it and beautified it. The Venetian traveller Caesar Frederick, who saw "Bezenagar" in 1567 soon after its fall, describes it as being 24 m. round, enclosing several hills. There were ordinary dwellings with earthen walls, but the three palaces and the pagodas were all built of fine marble. The rout of the Hindu forces at Talikota was so complete, and the dismay caused by the death of the old King Rama Raya was so great, that no attempt was made to defend the city, which was completely gutted. Colonel Briggs stated that for two centuries afterwards the head of the Hindu Prince used to be annually exhibited at Ahmadnagar. The main portion of the city was enclosed by walls forming a semicircle on the S. bank of the river; in the middle of this was the inner walled citadel and palace, and on the N. bank of the river was another large fortified area occupying the suburb of Anagundi; further outer lines of fortifications enclosed the city on the S. side.

Proceeding N. for ¼ m. from the D.B., the first remarkable building is the **King's or Ladies' Bath,** forming a portion of the King's Palace. It is a rectangular structure, with a *hauz*, or reservoir, in the centre, 50 ft. square and 6 ft. deep, in which fountains played. N.W. of the entrance are remains of the granite aqueduct which was carried from near the throne to the bath. The corridor of the bath, supported by twenty pillars, is decorated with incised plasterwork in floral patterns.

Slightly to the N. of the bath is a fine tank, and N. of this is the structure called the Arena, or the *Singhasan*, the King's Throne. It consists of a succession of granite platforms 31 ft. high, the outer walls of which are carved in relief with representations of elephants, dancing-girls, hunting scenes from the *Ramayana*, and camels, well executed. W. of the throne is an underground labyrinth, and N. are a remarkable stone trough and the ruins of a fine bazar. The stone forming the trough measures about 4½ ft. by 3 ft. by 2½ ft., and the supports are 5 ft. 8 in. high.

N. is the temple of Ramachandraswami (1513), with pillars handsomely carved in relief with figures. The quadrangle inside measurement is 110 ft. from N. to S. and 200 ft. from E. to W. The temple has a vestibule carried on twelve pillars. The shrine is supported by black pillars most elaborately carved. On the plinth of the left gateway is a very long inscription in Old Kanarese. The blocks of which this temple is built average 7 ft. 7 in. long and 2 ft. 6 in. deep.

To the E. of this group of buildings, and across the road leading through the citadel to the N., are the ruins of three temples, one situated on the top of a small hill; while at a distance of ½ m. to the N.W. of it are situated the **Zenana.** The Elephant Stables and the Riding School lie N.E.

In an enclosure of walls 40 ft. high is the building called the Zenana Palace in the N.W. corner, and a pavilion, figured in Fergusson's

Indian Architecture (1, 417), and commonly called the Lotus Mahal (Diwan Khana) towards the S.E. corner. At various corners of the walls are similar small pavilions; in the N. wall is a large tower, and in the W. wall is a fine gateway closed over by corbelled stones. The pavilions are too heavy to be really effective, but are picturesque in their present state of ruin; the painted decoration of the upper rooms of the main pavilion is still visible.

To the E. of the Zenana enclosure is a smaller singhasan, or throne, and the range of **Elephant Stables** divided into eleven domed compartments, some of which were elaborately decorated inside. Along the front of the building is a broad drip-stone carried by brackets. The so-called Riding School or Concert Hall stands at right angles to the stables on the N. S.W. is another temple, Yallamna, and between it and the three temples on the hill is an interesting rock excavation, one of the chambers of which has a drip-stone carved on it.

Turning ½ m. W., and passing outside the citadel through a gateway, and crossing the remains of a fine bazar, the next group of buildings of interest is reached on the S. side of the hill which dominates the village of Hampi.

The first object, on the left of the road, is a gigantic image of the **Narsingh Avatar** (1528), carved out of a block of granite, in an enclosure of ponderous granite blocks. The figure is that of a colossal lion-headed man with enormous projecting circular eyes and a huge mouth; it is seated, and has its legs and arms broken. A spirited carving of the Shesh Nag forms the canopy of the idol. The monolithic uprights at the door are 18 ft. 8 in. high out of the ground. Just outside the gate is an upright stone with a Kanarese inscription on both sides. A few yards N. of this enclosure is a small temple containing a huge Lingam and Yoni.

N.E. is a **temple to Krishnaswami** (1513), enclosed by a granite wall. The breadth of the chief court is 200 ft. from N. to S., and the length 320 ft. from E. to W. At the gopuram which forms the entrance is a stone 8 ft. high, with a Kanarese inscription on both sides. There is also on the columns of the gopuram an inscription in Nagri and Kanarese. The carving of the various portions of the temple is noticeable.

N. of this temple, 50 yd. off the road, is a temple with a **Ganesh** 10 ft. high; and a few yards farther another, built of granite, also dedicated to Ganesh, in which the idol is 18 ft. high. The size of the enormous granite slabs which form the roof is remarkable.

The precincts of what is now called Hampi are entered, and Langur monkeys may be seen in considerable numbers. A roadway, at a steep incline, has been substituted for the old steps. After passing on the left a square building, which may have been a *math*, the **great temple of Hampi,** which is sacred to Siva, under the name of Pampapati Swami, is reached. The gopuram at the N. entrance is truly gigantic (being over 165 ft. high). The length of the first quadrangle from E. to W. is 208 ft., and its breadth from N. to S. 134 ft. The second quadrangle is smaller, and has arcades all round built of granite. The great mandapa (pillared hall) in front of the sanctuary has a ceiling completely covered with paintings of mythological scenes in the Vijayanagara style comprising the best preserved series of paintings of the period in existence.

At the E. end of the grassy avenue in front of the temple is another large temple, on a ridge approached by a long flight of steps with pavilions. The road now follows the river, which bends at this point, and after passing a temple of Ramaswami (Ramchandra), with a stone lamp-stand in front and the ruins of an old bridge, reaches at a distance of ¾ m. the Vaishnavite temple (1521) of **Vitthala.** In front of this is a stone-weighing frame, and at the S. end of it is a stone rath (car), 26 ft. high, with wheels which revolve.

There are three temples in the enclosure, which has four Dravidian gopurams. The second temple, on the left of the entrance, is much the largest and finest. The ceiling was formed of slabs of granite 35 ft. long, but all the slabs have been thrown down except two in the centre. There are fourteen columns, which supported the roof. Most of them are carved into representations of horsemen mounted on *yali* lions. One represents the Narsingh Avatar. In some cases the yali is supported by elephants. Within is a court 100 ft. long from E. to W. and 62 ft. broad from N. to S. On the S. side are numerous Kanarese inscriptions. S. of the temple is a large dharmsala with sixty-two pillars, on which are curious reliefs of female monkeys and dwarfs. On the right of the entrance is a platform with thirty-nine shorter pillars. These are also carved with curious representations of monkeys, their heads crowned with two small figures of gods. The third temple is some 20 yd. N. of the car.

Anyone who may wish to ascend the hills above Anagundi, on the left bank of the river, for the sake of a general view over Vijayanagar, can cross the Tungabhadra in a circular basket-boat such as has been used on the Tigris and Euphrates for 2500 years, but the Matanga Temple affords a general view.

For fuller details of the ruins, see Tourist Information Bureau literature and Archaeological Department Reports.

10 m. to the W. of Hampi is the noteworthy Tungabhadra Irrigation Project, with its great masonry Dam, the largest in S. India. There is a P.W.D. I.B.

93 m. from Gadag Junction, **Bellary** (pop. 125,000 in 1971) (R., D.B.; alt. 1619 ft.) junction for Rayadrug (34 m. S.). Formerly an important military station on the Madras-Bombay Trunk Road. A spur from the Sandur range runs along the S. side of the Cantonment, and extends E. to Budihal, 8 m. distant, where it abruptly terminates. On the N. and Peacock hills neoliths were found in 1872. A high point in this range opposite the fort is called the Copper Mountain, the height being 1800 ft. above the plain and 3285 ft. above the sea. Excavations are still to be seen, said to be the remains of mines worked by order of Haidar Ali, but abandoned. Hematitic iron ore is found in large quantities, some possessing magnetic properties.

The Fort is built on a bare granite rock of semi-elliptical form, rising abruptly from the plain to the height of 450 ft., and defended by two distinct lines of works, constituting the lower and upper forts, both built of granite. In the upper one stands the citadel, which is reputed to be of great antiquity. Several tanks or cisterns, partly artificial, exist in the rock, and hold rain-water.

Under the wall at the E. gate is a tomb, built in the Muslim style, but said to cover the grave of a French engineer. The tradition is that when Haidar Ali took possession of Bellary in 1768, he employed this man to build the upper and lower forts, and then hanged him. A similar story is told of the Hosur fort in the Salem District, but with Tipu Sultan and a British officer, who was his prisoner, as the persons concerned.

Bellary came into British possession in 1800, when the Nizam made over to the East India Company the districts of Anantapur, Cuddapah, and Bellary (ceded to him after the fall of Seringapatam in 1799) in lieu of arrears of payment for the subsidiary force maintained at Hyderabad. Moplah (p. 527) prisoners captured after the rising in Malabar in 1921 were interned here.

The hill fortress of **Rayadrug** has Jain antiquities (rock-cut bas-relief sculptures) and three cells. Other sights are the Temple of Bhimeswara at Nilagunda, 8 m. S.W. of Harpanahalli (excellent road for 7 m.); the ruined Harpanahalli Fort; the Kalleswara Temple at Bagali, 4 m. N. of Harpanahalli; a prehistoric mound at Budi-Canive, representing the remains either of those slain in battle or of great sacrificial holocausts; the Kappagallu, known as "Peacock Hill"; and a very fine well at Tambarahalli.

16 m. W. of Bellary there was formerly **Sandur,** a small Mahratta State (p. 477). The first chief (family name, Hindu Rao Ghorpade) settled here in 1715.

Ramandrug (p. 477) can be reached by a road which winds along the face of the hill and is just wide enough for a motor.

101 m. the Hagari river is crossed.

123 m. **Guntakal** station. Junction for the broad-gauge line from Bombay *via* Raichur to Madras (Route 23). A metre-gauge branch line runs S. to Bangalore (see (*b*) below). Another metre-gauge line proceeds N.E. to Dronachellam (Jn. for Kurnool and Secunderabad) and thence to Vijayawada.

(*a*) Guntakal to Dronachellam and Vijayawada (Bezwada) (p. 426)

17 m. from Guntakal, **Tuggali** station. Pattikonda (D.B.) is 7 m. by road to the N. of Tuggali. Sir Thomas Munro, Governor of Madras, died here on 6th July 1827 of cholera, when on tour in the District. To his memory Government constructed a fine cut-stone well with a mandapam, or porch, and planted a grove o tamarind-trees around it. A new town called Munro's Square was built on this occasion, with a rampart wall all round. Munro was known in the "Ceded Districts" of Bellary, Kurnool and Cuddapah as the "Father of the People", and local ballads, which are still sung, were composed in his honour.

43 m. from Guntakal, **Dronachellam** or **Dhone** (R., D.B.).

Pyapalli (D.B.) is 15 m. from Dhone, on the Gooty road, and 11 m. from Gooty station on the Madras-Raichur line. It is situated at the foot of a granite hill, and is 1750 ft. above the sea-level; it serves as a sanatorium for the Kurnool District.

Dronachellam (Dhone) to Kurnool and Secunderabad

A metre-gauge line runs N. from Dhone to Kurnool and Secunderabad.

12 m. from Dhone, **Veldurti** (D.B.). 5 m. to the N.E. of Veldurti is a village called Ramallakota, where there are indications of alluvial washings and rock-working for diamonds.

34 m. from Dhone, **Kurnool** (pop. 136,000 in 1971; D.B.) is situated at the junction of the Hindri and the Tungabhandra. The old fort was dismantled in 1862, but the wall along the River Tungabhadra and some of the bastions are still intact. There are two gates leading to the river. The ruined Palace of the Nawabs stands on a bluff.

There are mosques and a fine mausoleum of Abdul Wahab, Subadar of Bijapur and the first Nawab, to whom the place was given in jagir by the Emperor Aurangzeb.

Alampur, 6 m. from Kurnool on the banks of the Tungabhadra, a large village with the ruins of an old fort and a group of early Chalukyan temples of the 7th and early 8th centuries called the Nave Brahma temples. Though named for the nine mind-born sons of Brahma, who mostly became sages (rishis), they are all dedicated to Shiva. Most have curvilinear spires and flat-roofed halls and are decorated with elaborate blind windows and the figures of flying gandharvas, heavenly musicians. The carving is exquisite and in very good condition, and there is an excellent small museum nearby. Alampur has been threatened by the back flooding of the river due to the Krishna dam at Srisailam and has recently been protected by tremendous walls.

Srisailam, 112 m. east of Kurnool by bus through Dornala. It stands on a ridge of jungle-clad hills above a gorge of the Krishna River. Below, a modern dam has just been completed. This is a popular and very old Shaivite pilgrimage place. Until recently it meant 30 miles of bridle-path and harassment by primitive Chenchu tribals to get there. The temple complex itself has been repeatedly damaged and rebuilt. It is enclosed by a most astounding wall about 15 ft. high and 300 yds. long. Almost every one of its huge blocks is either carved in light relief or incised with stories from the Skanda Purana, Shaivite legends, or heavenly figures. As at Mahaballipuram there are scenes of sacrifice by self-beheading. The history of Srisailam is obscure, it seems in its day to have been held by several deviant sects, self-mutilating, tantro-erotic, and fanatic. It is now in Lingayat hands, the austere proto-protestants of Hindu India.

From Kurnool the line runs N. (151 m.) to Hyderabad and **Secunderabad,** p. 462 (Route 25): there is a direct service of trains between Secunderabad and Bangalore city (403 m.) *via* Dronachellam, Guntakal and Dharmavaram.

The Tungabhadra river is crossed by a bridge 2950 ft. long, and at 33 m. the Kistna river bridge is 2958 ft. long.

34 m. from Kurnool on this line is **Gadwal,** with a palace and old Hindu temples. The walls of the fort, which are well preserved, are of mud. Under the Hindu Empire of Vijayanagar (1336-1565) the Poligars of Gadwal were important barons.

80 m. **Mahbubnagar** (alt. 1636 ft.) is a commercial centre.

91 m. **Jadcharla.** The station is surrounded by rocky hills. Motor-bus service, 25 m., to Nagar Kurnool; the road continues to Amrabad, where big game is found. Arrangements for transport can be made at Jadcharla with the Railway motor-bus service: State R.H. at Manamora. E. of Jadcharla is the Hindu fort of Devarakonda.

114 m. **Shadnagar** (D.B.), 2102 ft. above sea-level, on the watershed of the Kistna and Godavari rivers, is the highest station on this line.

151 m. Hyderabad (metre-gauge) station; thence 5 m. to **Secunderabad** Junction (p. 462) for the Godavery Valley line to Aurangabad (for Ellora) and Manmad (Route 4).

Dronachellam to Vijayawada

51 m. from Guntakal **Malkapuram.** 7 m. to the S. of this there is a village called Alliabad, a hamlet of Munimaduga, where diamonds used to be mined.

66 m. from Guntakal, **Betamcherla.** Ruins of a rock fortress. Barytes and steatite are found in the neighbouring villages of Muddavaram, Ambapuram, and Balapalapalli.

81 m. from Guntakal, **Panyam** (D.B.). A road connects it with Banganapalle, the chief town of a former Muslim State, now part of Andhra Pradesh. There are diamond mines near Banganapalle. Black-buck shooting is sometimes available in the vicinity.

91 m. from Guntakal is **Nandyal** (alt. 675 ft.), in the basin of the Penner river. There is a R.H. which is often available on previous application to the Superintendent, Agricultural Department, Bellary. The Government Agricultural Farm is close by. There is also a canal bungalow. The place takes its name from Nandi, the bull of Siva, to whom a temple is dedicated. A hoard of Roman coins was found in 1932. There are several mission buildings.

Before reaching Nandyal the line passes through the Yerramalai Hills, and after passing it, through the Nallamalai Hills, by many picturesque curves.

100 m. from Guntakal, **Gazulapalli.** Big-game shooting can be obtained in the Nallamalais on licence granted by application to the District Forest Officer, South Kurnool. Mahanandi, a place of pilgrimage with a temple and a perennial spring, is 5 m. distant.

115 m. the Dorabhavi Viaduct, 670 ft. long, is 153 ft. high.

133 m. from Guntakal, **Giddalur.** A P.W.D. R.H. and forest R.H. The road from Nandyal to Giddalur runs

through the Nallamalai Forest, which covers some thousands of miles and in some parts is almost impenetrable. During the First World War, hay was pressed and baled for despatch to other parts of India and Mesopotamia.

154 m. from Guntakal, **Cumbum.** Varadarajamma, wife of Krishna Devarayadu of Vijayanagar (1509-1530), is said to have constructed the beautiful tank here, by damming by a bund 57 ft. high a gorge between two hills. It irrigates 6000 acres. There is a P.W.D. R.H. on the tank bund.

209 m. from Guntakal is **Vinukonda** (D.B.), celebrated in Hindu mythology as the place where Rama heard of the abduction of his wife Sita: it has a striking hill with twin peaks.

260 m. from Guntakal is **Guntur** (pop. 269,000 in 1971) Junction (R.; D.B.). A metre-gauge line and road run 80 m. W. to Macherla, near the River Kistna. At **Nagarjunakonda** (15 m.) is a Buddhist stupa (discovered 1925), and a Museum. The ruins are more impressive than those at Amaravati (427) with remarkable sculptures. They have been rescued from the waters of a great modern irrigation project, centred on a new township of **Vijayapuri** with rest houses for tourists.

The principal Telugu-speaking districts are Nellore, Guntur, Godavari (Rajahmundry) and Kistna (Masulipatam). Guntur was important in the 18th century as a capital of the 4 N. Circars (Sirkars). Under the treaty of 1766 the Murtazanagar or Guntur circar was given to Basalat Jang, the brother of Salabat Jang and Nizam Ali. He took over French troops in 1759, and was never without a French officer in his service. There are many old French tombs in the cemetery.

Guntur is an American Mission centre. Kondavid (1674 ft.) to the W. was a much-contested fortress in the times of the Golconda kingdom. The Buddhist remains at Amaravati (p. 427) are 22 m. by road from Guntur. The railway crosses the Kistna (p. 427) before entering

279 m. **Vijayawada** (R., D.B.) on the main line between Madras and Calcutta (Route 22, p. 426). Except during the monsoon months, motorists can cross the river by the *anicut* dam.

(*b*) Guntakal to Bangalore

Passengers for Bangalore by the Bombay-Madras mail (Route 23) change at Guntakal. From Secunderabad there is a direct service to Bangalore (see p. 488). Bangalore is easily reached by air from Madras, Hyderabad and Bombay.

24 m. the Penner river is crossed.

43 m. **Anantapur** (D.B.K.). There are interesting antiquities at Penukonda ("Big Hill"), a residence of the Vijayanagar Rajas as early as 1354. Tirumal Raya moved there after the disastrous Battle of Talikota, 1565. The remains of the citadel of the fort are on the top of the hill, 3058 ft. high. In the compound of the Sub-Collector's office is a fine stambha or stone pillar, some 40 ft. high. When the "Ceded Districts" (Bellary, Kurnool and Cuddapah) were made over to the East India Company by the Nizam in 1800 (p. 481), Thomas Munro was appointed First Principal Collector. Anantapur contains several buildings associated with his name. A tablet on the Collector's guest-house records that he lived there; and the Court House, in which there is an engraving of Shee's portrait, is known as Munro Hall.

Near Kalyandrug, 36 m. W.S.W. of Anantapur and 22 m. E. of Rayadrug, there are innumerable prehistoric remains, cairns and ruined cell-tombs.

Bus services to Tadpatri, N.E.

63 m. from Guntakal is **Dharmavaram** Junction (R.; alt. 1182 ft.); famous for silk saris. From here there is a branch line to Pakala Junction (142 m.) on the Renigunta-Katpadi line (Route 23, p. 428). 3½ m. from the Mulakalacheruvu station (65 m.) on the Pakala line is the picturesque

Sompalle Temple, with a stone car and beautiful monolithic flagstaff 50 ft. high.

113 m. from Guntakal, **Hindupur** (R.). At Lepakshi, 9 m. E. of Hindupur, is a large temple to Virabhadra (a form of Siva), with a colossal stone bull about 15 ft. high and 27 ft. in length standing near it. The temple is in the Vijayanagar style of architecture, and has an inscription ascribing to its building the date 1538.

Karnataka State is now entered.

152 m. **Dodballapur.** 12 m. to the E. of this station rises

Nandidrug, a strong hill fort 4851 ft. above sea-level, 30 m. from Bangalore by the Bellary road. It was thought impregnable by Tipu Sultan, being inaccessible except from the W., and there strongly fortified, but it was captured by the British on the 19th October 1791, with only thirty casualties. Tipu's Drop, or Rock of Death, projecting from the fortress, has a precipice of 1000 ft. clear below it.

From the foot of the hill to the top there is a flight of 1175 steps, for which chairs and coolies may be obtained; but the journey may also now be made by car, as a motor-road has been constructed. There is a perennial spring of pure water (Amrita Sarovar or "Lake of Nectar") at the summit. Five furnished bungalows and an hotel with electric light are available for travellers. The place is under State management; and the Superintendent, Government Gardens, Lal Bagh, Bangalore, will, on application arrange for accommodation and food. There are sheds for motors.

174 m. from Guntakal is **Bangalore** Junction (Route 28, p. 488).

ROUTE 28

POONA by **Londa** Junction to **Dharwar, Hubli** Junction, **Harihar, Birur** (for **Shimoga** and the **Gersoppa Falls**), **Banavar** (for expedition to the temples at **Halebid** and **Belur,** also to the Hill of **Indrabetta,** near **Sravana Belgola**), **Arsikere, Tumkur** and BANGALORE.

The Poona-Bangalore mail proceeds as in Route 24 to (277 m.) **Londa** Junction (p. 448). From Londa the line runs E. to **Dharwar** (R.D.B., 1½ m.), 321 m. from Poona and 305 m. from Bangalore. This was once the headquarters of the Southern Mahratta Ry., before amalgamation with the Madras Ry. Dharwar is a large town on the watershed, but 20 m. inland from the edge of the ghats, with an altitude of 2384 ft. It was formerly a Cantonment, but the last regular troops left in 1884, and the site of the old Cantonment is now occupied by the Police Lines.

On the N. is the Fort, which was taken from the Mahrattas by Haidar Ali in 1778, and stood a siege in 1790 from a British force co-operating with the Mahratta army under Parshuram Bhao. One of Tipu's Generals, Badr-ul-zaman, defended it with great spirit, and surrendered on condition of being allowed to march out with all the honours of war. The allies took possession of the fort on 4th April 1791, and the Mahrattas attacked Badr-ul-zaman as he was marching away, wounded him, made him prisoner, and dispersed his force. Little remains of the fort, which is occupied by the Civil Hospital and a number of bungalows.

Dharwar is the site of the University of Karnataka which covers about 20 colleges including Training Colleges for teachers. There is a University G.H. and an I.B. 47 m. by road is the **Dandeli Wild Life Sanctuary,** not accessible during the monsoon. Big game, including elephants, bisons, tigers and panthers can be viewed from watchtowers. There are 4 Forest Bs. (Apply to Forest Dept., Dandeli.)

60 yd. from the D.B. is an obelisk to the memory of Mr St John Thackeray, Principal Collector and Political Agent, Southern Mahratta Doab, an uncle of the novelist, who was killed in an insurrection at Kittur on the 23rd October 1824.

Dharwar is connected by a metalled road through densely-wooded terrain (105 m.) with **Karwar** (D.B.K.) on the sea-coast, headquarters of the North Kanara district. There is a pleasant beach: good fishing and some shooting in the season. *Grand* Hotel: D.B. and I.B. There are four D.Bs. on the road, which crosses the Sahyadri range (Western Ghats) by the Arbail pass, 12 m. S. of Yellapur (D.B.), 55 m. from Karwar. The road runs through Hubli (12 m.).

44 m. S. of Dharwar was the fortress of **Bankapur** (Shahabazar), commanding the road from Bhatkal and Honawar to Vijayanagar. The Bahmani minister, Mahmud Gawan, took it in 1471. There is a Jain Temple of Rangaswami here.

Nargund is not easily accessible, but its compact hill-fort rising straight out of the plain is a conspicuous object on clear days from Dharwar to the N.E. and from the Gadag-Hotgi Railway (Route 26) to the W.

334 m. **Hubli** (pop. 379,000 in 1971) Junction (R., Dist. B. and D.B.), a centre of the cotton trade, contains the work-shops for the metre-gauge rolling stock of the former M. and S.M. portion of the Southern Ry. A line runs E. to (37 m.) Gadag Junction, for Hospet, Bellary and Guntakal Junction (Route 27).

400 m. **Ranibennur** was taken by Colonel Arthur Wellesley in 1800, in punishment for his troops having been sniped there. 2 m. S. is the Chol Marali or Scorpion Hill.

415 m. from Poona is **Harihar** station (R.), on the right bank of the Tungabhadra. Good D.B. The railway bridge was constructed in 1886, the road bridge in 1868. An inscription on copper has been found here of the 7th century, and there are several of the 12th. The temple of Shri Harihareswara was erected in 1223. In 1268 additions were made by Soma, the founder of Somnathpur in the Mysore District (p. 491). At Harihar General Wellesley concentrated his troops to restore the Peshwa in 1803. A Machine Tool Factory was started in 1942.

424 m. **Davangere.** A centre for cotton, grain and ground-nuts.

453 m. **Chik Jajur** Junction. Branch, 21 m. N.E., to Chitaldrug (D.B.K.; alt. 2648 ft.), which is a cotton trade centre and possesses a fortified hill, taken by Haidar Ali in 1776. Chandravalli nearby is an ancient place.

471 m. **Hosdurga Road** station. From here (32 m.) may be visited the great Marikanave Lake, formed by a dam, 1330 ft. long and 142 ft. high, across the Vedavali river, and covering 35 sq. m. There is a penstock with a fall of 60 ft. by the dam, close to which is a D.B. This work was inaugurated by Sir K. Seshadri Iyer, Diwan of Mysore (1885-1900).

495 m. **Birur** Junction, branch to **Tarikere** Junction, 16 m. (n.g. railway to Narasimharajapura, 27 m.), **Shimoga** (pop. 102,000 in 1971), 38 m. (R., D.B.; alt. 1898 ft.), and Anandapuram (74 m.). Motor services run from Shimoga, N.E. to Harihar (see above), and S.W. through forests to Agumbi and Mangalore (see p. 530).

28 m. At **Bhadravati** (pop. 101,000 in 1971) station, on the banks of the Bhadra river, 12 m. from Shimoga, the Mysore Iron and Steel Works produce iron castings and pipes, steel ingots, acetate, tar products and refined alcohol. The wood distillation plant is unique in India. The works were started in 1923 with power from Sivasamudram.

Shimoga is the most convenient

starting-point for the **Gersoppa** or **Jog Falls** of the Shiravati, distant 62 m., buses run (62 m.) from Shimoga, where cars also can be hired. The road passes through much fine bamboo and tree forest. Some miles above the falls, the road to the Mysore bungalow on the left bank (permit obtainable from the Dy. Com., Shimoga), turns down to the Shiravati ferry across a broad, deep stream flowing between high wooded banks, while the main Honavar road continues, branching off to the Bombay, or Jog, bungalow (permit obtainable from the Ex. Eng., Kanara Dist., Karwar) at Kodkani, on the right bank close to the Raja Fall.

There are in all four falls, which have been called the Raja or Horseshoe, the Roarer, the Rocket, and La Dame Blanche. In the Horseshoe the water in considerable volume leaps sheer down a height of 829 ft., measured by line, and falls into a pool 132 ft. deep. The spectator can look right down into this abyss. In the next, the Roarer, the water rushes foaming down a tortuous channel into a cavern or cup, which turns it into the rift of the Raja below. The name given to the third fall, at a little distance to the S., the Rocket, is very appropriate. It continually shoots out in jets of foam, which burst like fire-rockets into showers of glittering drops. The Dame Blanche, nearest the S. end of the cliff, streams in a succession of lace-like cascades over the sloping surfaces of the rock wall underneath it. The finest view of all four falls is that from the Karnataka side, as from it the black chasm into which the Raja and Roarer leap and pour is fully seen, as well as the curving face of the cliff down which the Rocket and Dame Blanche shoot and stream. A particularly fine view is that from Lady Curzon's seat and Watkin's platform to the W. of the Mysore bungalow; and no one should fail to make the expedition to the foot of the falls, though the paths are steep for returning. The whole of the deep recess into which the waters are hurled is covered with fine trees and dense undergrowth (full of leeches!), and the river disappears to the W. between the dark walls of a gorge. In the dry season the amount of water in the falls becomes very small, and in the rains the whole of the recess may be shrouded in thick impenetrable mist. The best time for a visit is early in the cold weather, as soon as the rains have ceased.

The Mahatma Gandhi Hydro-electric Works at Jog and the Sharavati Valley Project H.Q. can be visited by application to the Superintendent (R.Hs. and I.B.).

The Queen of Gersoppa, called by the Portuguese the Rainha da Pimenta, or Pepper Queen, was a great dignitary in the 17th century. Her subjects were chiefly Jains, by whom the nearest village to the falls is at present almost entirely inhabited. Among the ruins of the city of Bednur are two ordinary Jain temples.

Main Line

513 m. from Poona, **Banava** station.

The renowned ruins of Halebi (below) lie 18 m. S.W. from thi point by motor-bus, past *Jyavaga* (12 m.). 10 m. beyond in the sam direction is *Belur*. The circuit may b continued to Hassan (24 m.) an Chennarayapatnam (18 m.), fo Sravana Belgola (8 m.), and fron Chennarayapatnam to Arsikere rai way station (32 m.). **Hassan** is on th branch line from Arsikere (pp. 488 495) to Mysore City. Motor-bus ser vices ply between Belur and Hassar and between Hassan and Sakleshpu Hassan (Travellers' Lodge) is a con venient centre for visiting Belur an Jog Falls as well as Halebid, Sarvana Belgola and Sringeri (Pilgrims centr temple and *math*). An Indian Touris Corp. motel has been opened there.

At **Jyavagal** there is a temple ded cated to Narsingh, and built entirel of balapam or pot-stone. "It highly ornamented after the Hind fashion, and on the outside eve part of its walls is covered with small images in full relief."

Halebid (R.H.), named from the Kanarese words hale, "old", bidu, "capital", is on the site of Dwarasamudra, the capital of the Hoysala Ballala Kings, a dynasty traditionally founded by Sala in 1006. Vishnuvardhana (1111-41) was ardently religious, a conqueror, architect and builder of Halebid. The dynasty seems to have ended with Ballala IV in 1343. Halebid was rebuilt in the middle ot the 13th century by Vira Someswara, and some inscriptions represent him to be the founder. Attacked by leprosy, he withdrew to the neighbouring Hill of Pushpagiri ("Mountain of Flowers"), where he was instructed to erect temples to Siva to obtain a cure. The Muslims under Malik Kafur from Delhi took the city in 1310, and plundered it. In 1326 another army of Muslims destroyed the city. The Raja next removed to Tonnur, then a flourishing place (3 m. N. of French Rocks station, p. 492).

There are two most remarkable temples remaining. The **Kedaresvara,** is the smaller of the two. A tree took root in the vimana, or tower, over the sanctuary, and, dislodging the stones, rendered much of the temple a heap of ruins. The temple was star-shaped, with sixteen points, and had a porch that from base to top "was covered with sculptures of the very best Indian art".

The second temple, the **Hoysaleswara** ("Lord of the Hoysalas"), stands on a terrace, 5 ft. 6 in. in height, paved with large slabs. The temple itself is 160 ft. from N. to S. by 122 ft. from E. to W., and beyond its walls there is a clear margin of platform all round of about 20 ft. The height from the terrace to the cornice is 25 ft. It is a double temple, one half being sacred to Siva, and the other to his wife. Each half has a pavilion in front containing the Basava[1] Nandi, or bull. The larger of the two is 16 ft. long by 7 ft. broad and 10 ft. high, the animal being represented kneeling.

Some of the pillars in the inner part of the temple are of black hornblende, and have a dazzling polish. Fergusson says: "Some of these friezes are carved with a minute elaboration of detail which can only be reproduced by photography, and may probably be considered as one of the most marvellous exhibitions of human labour to be found even in the patient East". He adds: "Here the artistic combination of horizontal with vertical lines, and the play of outline and of light and shade, far surpass anything in Gothic art". Fergusson places Halebid Temple and the Parthenon as the two extremes of architectural art. There is a group of extremely beautiful **Jain Bastis** at the farther end of the village.

Belur (or Baillur) (R.H., Tourist B.), 10 m. from Halebid and 24 m. from Hassan (cars available), stands on the right bank of the Yagachi. In the Puranas and old inscriptions it is called Velapura. The famous temple of Chenna Kesava was erected and endowed by the Hoysala King, Vishnu Vardhana (whose capital it was), on exchanging the Jain faith for that of Vishnu about 1133. The carving rivals that of Halebid, and is the work of the same artist, Jakan Acharya.

The image of the god is said to have been brought from the Baba Budan Hills (N.W., rising to a peak 6317 ft.), known in Puranic times as **Chandradrona,** or Crater of the Moon, and a place of pilgrimage for both Hindus and Muslims. The hills lie 10 m. from Chickmagalur (Travellers' B.; bus service) and there are coffee estates. The image of his goddess Mahishashura-mardin was left behind, which obliges him to pay her visits.

The Great Temple is justly famous for the beauty of its bracket capitals in the form of Apsaras (celestial nymphs) and Yakshis (tree nymphs). It is set within a high wall which surrounds a court 440 ft. by 360 ft., and

[1] Basava was founder in the 12th century of the Lingayat Saivite sect in S. and W. India. The members, who are vegetarians, admit the equality of women with men, allow widow marriage, and disregard Brahman sanctity.

has on the E. front two fine gopurams. In this court are smaller shrines. "The Great Temple", said Fergusson (*Ind. Arch.*, 1, 439), "consists of a very solid vimana, with an antarala, or porch; and in front of this a porch, or mahamantapam, of the usual star-like form, measuring 90 ft. across. . . ." The windows to the porch are twenty-eight, all different. Some are pierced with star-shaped conventional patterns, and with foliaged patterns between. Others are interspersed with mythological figures as the Varaha Avatar. The base is very richly carved, and is supported on a frieze of elephants. "The amount of labour which each facet of this porch displays is such as never was bestowed on any surface of equal extent in any building in the world".

523 m. from Poona, **Arsikere** Junction (R.). There is a beautiful temple here, built by Ballala II (end of the 12th century A.D.). Branch line to Hassan (R.), 29 m. and to Mysore City, 103 m. (p. 494). From Hassan (alt. 3094 ft.) there is a motor service to Belur.

32 m. S. from Arsikere is the ancient town of Chennarayapatnam. From here

8 m. S.E. again is **Sravana Belgola** (white lake), a centre of Digambara Jains. Bhadra Bahu, a sage who died here in the 4th century B.C., was a Sruta kevala, or immediate "hearer", of the six disciples of Mahavira, founder of the Jain sect. His attendant is said to have been the famous Mauryan Emperor Chandragupta, or Sandracottus, who abdicated to live the life of a recluse with him. This is confirmed by inscriptions on the rock of very great antiquity. Asoka, the grandson of Chandragupta, is said to have visited the spot with an army.

Near the town are two hills—Indrabetta or Vindhyagiri or Doddabetta and Chandragiri or Chikkabetta.

On Indrabetta, reached by a steep flight of steps going straight up the rock (470 ft.) is a colossal[1] statue (*c.* A.D. 983) of Gomata Raya (or Gomateswara), 57 ft. It is nude, and faces the N. The face has the calm look usual in Buddhist statues. The hair is curled in short spiral ringlets all over the head. From the knees downwards the legs carved in relief on the rock are unnaturally short; the feet rest on a lotus. Ant-hills rise on either side, with a creeping plant springing from them which twines round the thighs and arms. These symbolise the deep abstraction of the sage. The stone looks as fresh as if newly quarried, owing to its being profusely anointed at intervals of 25 years. Within the enclosure are 72 small statues, of like appearance, in compartments. An inscription on the front of the colossus states that it was erected by Chamunda Raya. The most interesting inscriptions (see *Epigraphia-Karnataka*, by Rao Bahadur R. Narasimhacharya) are cut in the face of the rock at Indrabetta in ancient characters 1 ft. high.

On Chandagiri (220 ft. high) there are fifteen Jain temples in clusters (Bastis) and a number of stone lamp shafts. The monastery (W.) contains many mural paintings.

583 m. from Poona, **Tumkur** station (R.). 10 m. N.E. is a health resort on the Devarayadurga hills. At Kunigal, 24 m. S., connected by motor-bus, is a Government stud farm.

626 m. **BANGALORE City*** Junction station (alt. 3000 ft.) both for air and rail services. Railways run S.W. to Mysore City (Route 29 (*a*)); N. to Guntakal and Secunderabad (Route 27), and E. to Bowringpet and Jalarpet for Madras (Route 29 (*b*)). Rapid air services link Bangalore to Madras, Hyderabad, Bombay, Belgaum, Cochin and Trivandrum. The name is literally "the town of bengalu", a kind of bean. Bangalore became the administration centre of Mysore State, which became independent after the fall of Vijayanagar, and remained under its own rulers until 1759, when the Hindu ruler Chikka Krishna Raj Wadiyar was dispossessed by one of his captains,

[1] There are similar colossal images at Karkal and Venur near Mangalore (p. 530).

the famous Haidar Ali. The Wadiyar family was restored by Lord Wellesley after the fall of Seringapatam in 1799, in the person of the grandson of the deposed Raja, a child of five. The later conduct of the Maharaja, and a rising in Bednur (1830), led to the resumption of the administration by a British Commissioner. Maharaja Krishna Raja Wadiyar died in 1868, and in 1881 the "rendition" of the State to Maharaja Chama Rajendra Wadiyar was carried out, the Cantonment area of 13½ sq. m. being assigned to the British Government for military purposes.

The State acceded to the Indian Union in 1947, and the then Maharaja, Sir Jaya Chamaraja Wadiyar, nephew of his predecessor, became Rajapramukh (died 1975).

As a result of the States Reorganisation Act of 1956, the boundaries of the State were greatly extended to the N. and W. on a linguistic basis, so that it now includes Coorg, and portions of the old Bombay and Madras Presidencies, as well as a large slice of the former Hyderabad State. The Maharaja, universally popular, remained Governor for a further period. Bangalore is the capital of the State of Karnataka as Mysore State is now called and has well planned and laid out modern surburbs. One of its most pleasing features are the beautiful gardens; and there are some impressive new buildings, such as Vidhan Soudha, which houses the Secretariat and the Legislature.

The **Cantonment**[1] and **City** of Bangalore (combined pop. 1,648,000 in 1971) stretch from the Maharaja's Palace on the N., 6500 yd., to the Koramangala Tank on the S., and an equal distance from the Petta on the W. to the Sappers' Practice-ground on the E. Bangalore proper lies S. of the Dharmambudhi and Sampangi Tanks which lie in the N.W. and E. corners of the *Petta*, or town.

In the Cantonment, from N.W. to S.E., the first building is the **Maharaja's** handsome **Palace.** 2 m. N. of the Palace is the **Indian Institute of Science** for post-graduate research (founded by the liberality of the well-known Parsi **Tata** family) which has attained a world-wide reputation. S.E. of this is one railway station, and S. again is Miller's Tank, which communicates with the much larger Ulsoor Tank on the E. edge of the Cantonment (boating available).

N.E. are the suburbs of Cleveland Town, Fraser Town and Richards Town (a modern extension) with a large factory of the Peninsular Tobacco Co. St Xavier's (Roman Catholic) Church, a Wesleyan Church and the (Anglican) Church of St John, are in Cleveland Town. In St John's cemetery is the grave of General J. W. Cleveland, who died in 1883 in his 92nd year, after a service of 75 years in the Madras Army. The Regimental Centre of the famous Madras Sappers and Miners adjoins the suburb and large tank of Ulsoor.

S. of the Sapper lines are the Infantry Barracks, and then in order along the N. side of the great Parade-ground, the old St Andrew's Kirk, the Main Guard, the Y.M.C.A., the Bowring Civil Hospital, and the Lady Curzon Women's Hospital. Directly S. of Ulsoor are the Artillery Barracks and S. again of them the Cavalry Barracks, the old Cemetery, the Mounted Parade, the Artillery Practice - grounds and Y.M.C.A. buildings.

Trinity Church (*Anglican*) contains some interesting memorials. W. of Trinity Church are the Wesleyan Chapel, the Public Offices, Mayo Hall, which contains the municipal office, and the Gymkhana, standing in the General Parade-ground, which is more than 1 m. long from E. to W. A little S. of its centre is St Joseph's College, and S.E. the Roman Catholic Cathedral and All Saints' Church.

At the W. end of the Grand Parade-ground is *St Mark's Church*. To the W. of this is the *Cubbon Park*. In this are the Museum (1865) and the Sir Seshadri Memorial Hall, where

[1] Morris's Guide to Bangalore, locally obtainable, can be recommended.

the Public Library and the new Legislature Building are located.

In the vestibule of the Museum is a slab with twelve Persian distiches, brought from Tipu's Palace in the fort, also a relief of Seringapatam in 1800. In the large room adjoining there is a collection of geological specimens. Upstairs are stuffed animals, butterflies, Indian ornaments and dresses, and a most remarkable collection of fishes.

N.E. is a Memorial Statue of Queen Victoria, and farther N. is a statue of King Edward VII. To the W. is a building which contains the Karnataka High Court. In front is a statue of Sir Mark Cubbon, Commissioner from 1834 to 1861. He died at Suez after a service of 62 years in India. The former **Residency,** now a State Guest House, is about ¼ m. N. of the Public Offices.

The city of Bangalore proper has an area of 11·8 sq. m. The **Petta,** as it is called, was until 1898 surrounded by a deep ditch and thorn hedge. There is an excellent market between the Fort and Mysore Gates. The grain-market, Taragu-petta, and cotton market, Arale-petta, present busy scenes. Fruit and vegetables are sent to Madras and Bombay.

The **Fort** is due S. of the Petta. Rebuilt in stone in 1761, it is 2400 ft. from N. to S. and 1800 ft. from E. to W., of an oval shape, with one gateway remaining—the Delhi Gate, built of cut granite, on the N. face opposite the Petta. It was captured by Lord Cornwallis, on the 21st March 1791, after a determined resistance, in spite of the presence of Tipu with a large army, a few miles away.

In the centre of the fort is the arsenal, and some remains of Tipu's Palace. There is a small temple near the Mysore Gate. The ramparts of the walls deserve a visit. Outside the N.W. corner of the fort is the Victoria Hospital, maintained by the State. To the W. is the Minto Ophthalmic Hospital and a hospital for women and children.

There are large cotton, woollen, carpet, silk, leather and soap industries, as well as the cigarette factory referred to above. The Telephone Factory, a Machine Tools Factory, Bharat Electronics, the Silk Weaving Factory and the Sandalwood Oil Factory and the Hindustan Aircraft Factory are among India's biggest industrial enterprises.

In consequence of the former prevalence of plague in Bangalore many modern extensions have been built S.W., S.E. and N.W.

The State was fortunate in having had for many years a succession of good Diwans, and to one of those, the late Sir Mirza Ismail, who devoted himself to town planning and improvement, both Bangalore and Mysore owe much of their attraction. There are no more pleasant places in India for the European or American tourist. Among the beauty-spots of Bangalore the Lal Bagh, a botanical garden laid out originally by Haidar Ali and Tipu Sultan, ranks high. It is 1½ m. to the E. of the Petta and fort. The Pleasure Gardens called Brindavan at Krishnaraja Sagar are well worth visiting from Mysore (p. 494) 12 m.—one of the biggest dams in S. India. There is a good modern Hotel. On the way, the **Ranganthittoo Bird Sanctuary** (p. 494) can be visited.

ROUTE 29

BANGALORE to

(*a*) **Falls of the Cauvery, Seringapatam,** and **Mysore City**, and

(*b*) **Bowringpet** (for **Kolar Gold Fields**), **Jalarpet** Junction **Vellore, Arcot** and **Arkonam** Junction (for **Madras**).

(*a*) The Falls of the Cauvery, Seringapatam, and Mysore City.

A metre-gauge railway runs S.W. from Bangalore to (86 m.) Mysore City.

28 m. **Closepet** (D.B.K., to Indians Kalispet) is named after Sir Barry Close, the first British Resident in Mysore from 1799 to 1801. It was founded in 1800 by the Diwan Purnaiya (p. 494) to secure the road which passed through dense jungle. The place is also known as Ramgiri from the neighbouring hill.

36 m. **Channapatna** station, noted for lacquer ware and steel strings for musical instruments. Two large Muslim tombs N. of the town, one of the religious preceptor of Tipu.

46 m. **Maddur** station (R., D.B.), once headquarters of a Vijayanagar Viceroy, suffered heavily during the wars with Tipu Sultan. There are two large Vaishnava temples here, sacred to Narasimha Swami and Varada Raja, the "Man-Lion" and the "Boon-giving King". A brick bridge with seven arches, built in 1850, spans the Shimsha, on the right bank of which the town is built. A road runs 150 m. to Coimbatore.

Regular bus services run to Sivasamudram (30 m., see below) from Maddur station.

By road 14 m. S. is **Malvalli** (D.B.). The Mysore-Bangalore and Maddur-Sivasamudram roads cross at this place. On the 27th of March 1799 General Harris defeated the army of Tipu Sultan here. The left wing of the British was commanded by Colonel Arthur Wellesley, afterwards Duke of Wellington.

12 m. S.W. of Malvalli is the village of **Somnathpur,**[1] famous for its star-shaped temple, attributed to Janak Acharya, the famous sculptor and architect of the Hoysala Kings. The three pyramidal towers or vimanas over the triple shrine are completely finished. The central shrine is that of Prasanna Channa Kesava, that on the S. is sacred to Gopala, and that on the N. to Janardhana. Round the outer base are carved with dexterity incidents from the Hindu Epics. The end of each scene is indicated by a closed door. Around lie seventy-four mutilated statues, which once stood on the basement. There is a fine inscription at the entrance, which declares that the building was completed in 1270 by Soma, a high officer of the Hoysala State and a member of the royal family. Ruins of a large Saiva temple bear inscriptions, deciphered in *Epigraphia Karnataka*.

From Malvalli the road leads S. 12½ m. to

Sivasamudram (R.H., C.H., I.B.). 3 m. N. of the Cauvery the road turns off to the E., and conducts to the **Cauvery Falls** Electric Power Station. The river divides into two branches, embracing the Sivasamudram Island, about ¾ m. above the point where the main road reaches it. This island was connected with the left shore by a bridge (destroyed and rebuilt upstream), at the farther end of which is situated a R.H. (permit from the Supt., Power Station). From a curved regulator the channel leading to the penstock chamber takes off on the left. The main road crosses to the island, and turns to the S. point, where a similar stone bridge, the Kollegal Bridge, makes connection with the right shore in the Coimbatore District. At this point also is a regulator, by which the whole water of the stream

[1] See Fergusson's *Ind. Arch.*, 1, 437.

can, if necessary, be diverted into the Western channel.

The river turns sharply above the head of the island, and flows from S. to N. past it, turning again to the E. at the junction below the Falls. These are known as the Barachukki Fall, on the right arm, and the Gaganchukki, on the left arm; the former is 1¾ m. from the R.H., and the latter 2¼ m.

The height of the Falls is 320 ft., but hardly any one of the many shoots has such a clear leap. They are spread over a considerable face of rock, and in the case of the Gaganchukki (Western branch) and its Falls, curve round considerably to the left front. The foot of the Barachukki Fall can be reached by a long flight of slippery stone steps. The descent to the Gaganchukki is possible on the W. bank only. On the E. bank, in front of it, are some Muslim buildings. A cloud of spray constantly rises from the pools below them, and at a distance may be observed overhanging the head of the Falls. The ordinary monsoon discharge is 18,000 cubic ft. per second, but the discharge of a high flood has been known to be 200,000 cubic ft. On the left bank, in front of the Gaganchukki, steel pipes, or penstocks, carry the water down a vertical height of 400 ft. to the generators, which deliver power as far as the Kolar Gold Field, 93 m. distant. The scheme was initiated by Diwan Sir Seshadri Iyer, and carried out by Colonel Joly de Lotbiniere, R.E. (in 1900-02), for 6000 kW. It is still being enlarged.

56 m. **Mandya** station. The Mysore Sugar Coy. manufactures sugar and denatured spirit since 1933.

75 m. **French Rocks** station, the place where French officers in the service of Haidar Ali and Tipu Sultan were stationed from about 1780. The name is properly Hirode. The fort, 2882 ft. above sea-level, is 3 m. N. of the railway station.

77 m. from Bangalore and 9 m. from Mysore is SRIRANGAPATNAM (**SERINGAPATAM**) station (R.H., Travellers' B., D.B.K.), inside the fort, which is built at the W. end of an island 3 m. long in the Cauvery river, 2412 ft. above sea-level; the suburb of Ganjam is on the E. The name is derived from a temple of Vishnu Sri Rangam, which is of much higher antiquity than the city.[1]

In 1133 Ramanujachari, the Vaishnava reformer, fled to Mysore from the Chola Raja, and converted from the Jain faith Vishnu Vardhana of the Hoysala Ballala dynasty. The royal convert gave him the province of Ashtagrama, including Seringapatam, over which he appointed officers called Prabhus and Hebbars. In 1454 the Hebbar Timmana obtained from Sri Krishna Devaraya of Vijayanagar the government of Seringapatam, with leave to build a fort there. His descendants governed till Sri Rangaraya of Vijayanagar appointed viceroys, the last of whom, Tirumala Raja, in 1610 surrendered his power to Raja Wadiyar; Seringapatam then became the capital of the Mysore Rajas, and of Haidar Ali and Tipu, till the fort was stormed by a British army. After its capture from Tipu, Seringapatam became British territory, and troops were stationed there, but it was very feverish and was subsequently exchanged for land at Bangalore.

The **Fort** had double ramparts, the northern, the longest, face being just a mile in extent. The breach by which it was stormed on 4th May 1799 lies only a short distance to the S.W. of the railway station, beyond a ruined mosque, and is marked by an obelisk erected by the Mysore Government in 1907 in commemoration. On the S. shore two cannons, buried upright, mark the line from which the assaulting column advanced across the stream.

Just across the railway line on the N. side is the dungeon in which the captives from Pollilore (see p. 513), including David Baird, were im-

[1] An excellent account of the place was written by the Rev. E. W. Thompson, Mysore.

prisoned for four years. A marble tablet indicates the spot, which is reached by descending a flight of steep and narrow steps. S. of this is the Sri Ranganatha Swami Temple, and considerably to the E., across the open space which was once the Parade-ground, is the Gangadhareswara Temple, with a store-house of State Sandalwood (monopoly) to the S. of it, occupying the site of Tipu Sultan's Palace.

N.E. of this is the Water Gate, outside of which is a very picturesque enclosed space between walls with many stone idols and reliefs of serpents under banyan-trees. On the right of this space is the spot where Tipu Sultan fell, and outside it upon the river-bank is a bridge over the fort ditch and a ghat built in memory of Maharaja Krishna Raja Wadijar.

S.E., and facing the Ganjam Gate, is the Masjid-i-Ala, with two lofty minarets. Outside, to the N.E. of the Ganjam Gate, is the Darya Daulat Palace, and E. of it, at a distance of nearly 2 m., is the Lalbagh, with the mausoleum of Haidar Ali and Tipu Sultan. Just outside the Fort is the Scott Bungalow (now private property). Its furniture has been preserved by the Mysore Art Gallery from the time of an (unsubstantiated) tragedy in 1817, when Colonel Scott (Commandant of Seringapatam) drowned himself on returning to find his wife and daughter dead from cholera.

The first **Siege of Seringapatam** was in 1792. Lord Cornwallis had appeared before the place on 13th May 1791, after the capture of Bangalore, but was compelled by loss of transport to fall back, destroying his battering train. In February 1792 the attack was made from the N.W. side of the fort from French Rocks, where an army of 19,000 European and 29,000 Indian troops, with 400 guns and a large force of Mahratta and Hyderabad Cavalry had been assembled under Lord Cornwallis.

Outside the fort on the N. of the Cauvery a "bound hedge" of cactus and thorn enclosed a large space. That on the N. was 1 m. to 1½ m. deep by 3 m. long along the river, and was defended by six redoubts. In a night attack on 6th February the British carried these and got a footing on the island. Trenches were then opened, and, General Abercrombie having arrived with 9000 additional troops from Bombay, Tipu Sultan decided to submit, on 23rd April, surrendering half his territories to the three allies. The handing over of two of his sons, aged 10 and 8, as hostages, one condition of peace, supplied a subject for several pictures by English contemporary artists.

The second siege commenced on 17th April and ended on the 4th of May 1799. The forces under General Harris arrived S.W. of the fort on 5th April, and were joined by the Bombay troops under General Stuart on the 14th. By the 27th April the enemy had been driven out of the whole outer zone of defence. By the 3rd May a practicable breach had been made in the walls, and this was stormed next day. The defenders were taken by surprise, and the troops, having surmounted the outer wall within seven minutes, turned right and left along the deep inner ditch. Tipu Sultan, awakened, who had hurriedly proceeded to the point of the breach, found himself cut off, and therefore fell back along the N. wall, seeking to regain the Palace from that side. In front of the inner wicket gate there he was severely wounded and placed inside a palanquin, but meanwhile the wicket had been seized by the besiegers. As he lay disabled outside it a European soldier attempted to snatch off his jewelled sword-belt, and, being wounded by the Sultan, shot him through the head.

His two sons, formerly hostages, then surrendered, and next day the eldest son, Fateh Haidar, who was commanding a force outside the fort, surrendered also. The reserve on the occasion of the assault was commanded by Colonel Wellesley, who became Commandant of the place and the troops left in it. The evening after the assault was ushered in by a storm of extraordinary violence. Tipu Sultan was buried next day in the Lalbagh Mausoleum with military honours. His sword is in the Victoria and Albert Museum.

The island is connected with the N. bank of the Cauvery by the Wellesley Bridge, and with the S. bank by the Periapatnam Bridge, on stone piers. An inscription on the Wellesley Bridge records that it was built between the years 1802 and 1804 and dedicated to Richard, Marquess Wellesley by the Diwan Purnaiya, the Prime Minister, who served with equal loyalty Haidar Ali, Tipu Sultan, the British and the restored ruler, from 1799-1811, and who died at Seringapatam in 1812.

Beyond the Periapatnam Bridge is a canal, and following the left bank to the W. the visitor passes along the outer zone occupied by the defenders in the siege of 1799. Close to the bridge was Wallace's Post, captured on 26th April. Half a mile from it are the guns opposite the breach, and beyond these again is MacDonald's Post. Just S. of the canal is a very sacred Hindu temple at a Sangam or junction of rivers. The island was evacuated on account of its unhealthiness in 1811.

The **Darya Daulat Bagh** (museum), a Summer Palace of Tipu Sultan just outside the E. side of the fort, is distinguished for the arabesque work in rich colours which covers it. The W. wall is painted with a representation of the victory of Haidar Ali over Colonel Baillie at Pollilore, near Conjeeveram (see p. 513). It had been defaced prior to the siege of 1790, but Colonel Arthur Wellesley, who made this garden his residence, had it restored. It was afterwards whitewashed, but Lord Dalhousie, visiting the spot, had it repainted by an Indian artist who remembered the original. The perspective is bad and the effect grotesque, but the painter has succeeded in capturing the expression and attitude of the stolid clean-shaven British soldiers, and the excited moustachioed Frenchman which are very lifelike.

The **Lalbagh** is a garden 2 m. E. of the fort on the other side of the Ganjam suburb (which has a church of Abbé Dubois founded in 1800). It contains the mausoleum of Haidar Ali and Tipu Sultan, a square building surmounted by a dome, with minarets at the angles, and surrounded by a corridor which is supported by pillars of black hornblende, remarkable for its beautiful polish. The double doors of rosewood, inlaid with ivory, were given by Lord Dalhousie. Each of the tombs is covered with a crimson pall. The tablet on Tipu's tomb is in verse to this effect—"The light of Islam and the faith left the world: Tipu became a martyr for the faith of Muhammad: The sword was lost and the son of Haidar fell a noble martyr". The chronogram gives the date 1213 A.H. = A.D. 1799.

In front of the Lalbagh is a memorial (1816) by Colonel John Baillie, then Resident at Lucknow, to his uncle, Colonel William Baillie, who died in 1782 a prisoner of Tipu Sultan, and the graves of many British soldiers.

In the garrison cemetery are graves of officers of the Regiment de Meuron, a Swiss proprietary regiment, first in Dutch service and then in that of the East India Company, which took part in the second siege of Seringapatam and was afterwards quartered on the island.

A remarkable arch, near the railway line, in brick and mortar, built in 1801 by de Haviland, with a very flat span of 112 ft., was broken in 1937, having lasted more than a century. 1 m. from the city is the **Ranganthittoo Bird Sanctuary,** famous as a heron-breeding spot.

Mysore (pop. 356,000 in 1971) (R.H., G.H., University), the old capital of the State, is 86 m. distant from Bangalore by a fine motor road and 2493 ft. above sea-level. The city is built in a valley formed by two

ʼdges running N. and S. The streets re broad and regular, and there are ıany substantial houses two or three toreys high, with terraced roofs. The own has a neat and thriving look, and ıuch attention has been paid to the menities by the municipality. The Iary Holdsworth Hospital (1906) is a ıemorial to a Wesleyan missionary vho lived in and for Mysore.

To the E. are the Summer Palace, he Lalitha Mahal which is now luxury hotel, and a striking new ..C. cathedral. To the W. are he Public Offices, the Maharaja's College, University buildings (1916), nd the Maharani's College. S. f the town is the fort, a quadangular, moated enclosure of some 50 yd.; in front of it lie the Curzon 'ark, the Gordon Park, Nishat agh and the Hardinge Circle. In he centre of the town are the Sri Crishnarajendra Hospital, the Chaıarajendra Technical Institute, the ubilee Clock Tower (1927), and the ,ansdowne Bazar. The British Residency until 1884, known as Governıent House, contains a very large oom, without pillars, with a Madras erraced roof.

The Maharaja's Palace (1897) in he fort faces due E. and replaces one artly burnt down. The general ppearance and the outline are Indoaracenic; but the details of decoraion are distinctly "Hoysala". The entral tower is the dominating eature. The carvings and colour ombinations are highly artistic. In he Sajje or Dasahra Hall the Mahaaja formerly showed himself to the eople, seated on his throne, at the Navaratri festival in September.

The throne, only exhibited during he Dasahra Festival, is remarkable. According to one account, it was resented to the ambassadors of Chikka Deva Raja of Mysore in 1699 y the Emperor Aurangzeb. The 'alace legend at Mysore is that it was riginally the throne of the Pandus, nd was found buried at Penukonda y the founders of the Vijayanagar Empire, who were told where it was by an ascetic. It was found in a lumber room when Seringapatam was taken by the British, and was employed at the installation of the Wadiyar Raja. It was originally of figwood overlaid with ivory, but the ivory has been plated with gold and silver carved with Hindu mythological figures.

The magnificent new Palace Offices were constructed in 1925. A Zoo to the E. of the city on the way to the race-course contains a varied collection of wild animals and birds among the best in India.

Chamundi, the hill which overlooks Mysore, is 2 m. S.E. of the fort. It is precipitous, and rises to 3489 ft. above sea-level; an excellent road, suitable for motors, $5\frac{1}{2}$ m. long, leads to the top, on which is a temple. Two-thirds of the way up is a colossal figure of Nandi, the sacred bull of Siva, 16 ft. high, hewn out of the solid rock—a well-executed work of the date of 1659. Chamundi, family goddess of the Wadiyars, is a title of the goddess Kali (see p. 20) who killed two demons, Chanda and Mundi, on the hill. On the top is the Hotel Rajendra Vilas Imperial.

48 m. from Mysore on the road to Ootacamund (p. 521) is the **Bandipur** Wild Life Sanctuary famous throughout India; it can be visited at any season. Formerly a game preserve of the Maharaja, it abounds in elephants, bison, tiger, leopard and many kinds of deer. Many motorable roads: elephants can be hired; observation towers. There are 3 Forest Lodges (apply Divisional Forest Officer, Mysore) and a P.W.D. I.B.

Branch Line

A metre-gauge line runs from Mysore City to Hassan (74 m.) and (103 m.) **Arsikere** Junction (p. 488), where it connects with the line from Hubli Junction to Bangalore (Route 28). The first station on this line after leaving Mysore City is Belagula, which is 3 m. from the **Krishnaraja Sagar,** a reservoir

(49½ sq. m.) with a dam (1¾ m. long and 130 ft. high) across the Cauvery constructed to store water for irrigation purposes, and to maintain a continuous flow of water at Sivasamudram for generating electric power. The place is 12 m. by road from Mysore City. There is a fine hotel, and terraced gardens (Brindavan) below the dam with fountains, floodlit by night, and a "fairy land", which is a very popular resort for families, particularly at the week-end. The Irwin Canal passes through a tunnel 3200 ft. long.

Main Line

102 m. from Bangalore, **Nanjangud** (D.B.), has a temple 385 ft. long by 160 ft. broad, supported by 147 columns. It is one of the most sacred in Karnataka, and enjoys a Government grant. There is a car-festival here in March, which lasts three days.

124 m. **Chamarajnagar** (alt. 2805 ft.). From the railway terminus here a motor-road runs through interesting jungle country, E. of the Nilgiris, to Coimbatore.

Coorg

Coorg (anglicised form of "Kodagu"), of which the chief town, **Mercara**, G.H., R.H. (Mahadeopet), 75 m. W. of Mysore, is reached by bus service.

At Hunsur (Gadipotra) on the Lakshman Tirth river (27 m., R.H., permit from the Amildar), are the headquarters of the breeding establishment of the famous Mysore bullocks (Hallikar and Amrit Mahal). With them Haidar Ali marched 100 m. in 3½ days to the relief of Chidambaram (p. 535) in 1781. Near **Khushalnagar** (formerly Fraserpet, named after Col. Fraser, the first British Political Agent. 1834) the Cauvery is crossed. Haidar Ali heard here of the birth of Tipu and called it Khushalnagar.

The capital of Coorg was moved from Haleri to Mercara by Muddu Raja in 1681. Mercara has an ol fort, which was besieged by Vir Raja of Coorg in 1791, but he le Tipu's relief column in. Coorg wa overrun by Haidar Ali in 1773 an ravaged by Tipu in 1782-1783. I the old fort are various offices; th Church in the compound is now museum. The draft treaty of Sering apatam barred Tipu from Coorg an the West Coast. He was unwilling t accept the clause, and preparation were made to resume the siege, bu he consented and signed on 19t March 1792. The subjects of Vir Raja were maltreated and man wished to come under British rul in 1834. The Raja surrendered th country to Colonel Fraser, and be came a political pensioner. Th Kodagus are a sturdy, much inter married race. Since 1956, Coorg ha been part of Mysore (now Karnataka State.

Mercara is now a prosperous town (pop. 19,500 in 1971) with thre hotels—*Capitol*, *Tourist*, *East End* Tourist and I.Bs. (not recommend ed). There are coffee plantations rice fields and orange groves. Th region is well-wooded and the scener beautiful—it has been compare to that of Wales. 61 m. fron Mercara is the **Nagarhole** Wil Life Sanctuary, with wild elephants panthers, deer and occasional tiger For arrangements, Forest Office Mercara should be contacted. Muc of the country lies at an altitude o 4000 ft. or over, and the climate i excellent except during the rains when 100 in. fall at the top, and muc more on the slopes of the Ghats.

Two roads divide at Kushalnaga where there is a large, Governmen sponsored Tibetan settlement and a bridge over the Cauvery, which rise in Coorg, near the peak of Brahma giri, 5272 ft. One road runs to Mercara, headquarters of the District The other runs, with a branch to Pollibetta and the Planters' Club through Virarajendrapet (named after the uncle of the last Raja) down to Mattanur, where it branches to Can ınore and Tellicherry. The scenery ı *route* is lovely. Many rare butter-.es are found in this area. There is a ·.B. at Wattekuli and mahseer-fishing : the bottom of the ghat.

·) **Bangalore City** to **Bowringpet, Jalarpet Junction,** and **Arkonam Junction** (for **Madras**).

Rail communication between Ban-ılore and Madras City is made y a broad-gauge line (222 m.); but ıe air service (I.A.C.) takes only 1¼ ours.

35 m. from Bangalore, **Nandi,** on ıe narrow-gauge loop to Bowringpet ation for Nandidrug (see Route 27, . 484).

28 m. **Faykal** station. There are vo outcrops with Puranic inscrip-ons. From quarries here, granite is xported.

44 m. from Bangalore city is **owringpet** (called after a former 'hief Commissioner of Mysore), ınction for the broad-gauge Kolar ;old Field Ry. to Ooregaum and Iarikuppam (10 m.), and for the ;olar District Ry., loop (102 m.) to ·angalore city. The Gold Field ·op. 76,000 in 1971) is 8 m. distant. he mines were nationalised in 1956. ince mining on modern principles 'as begun on the Field in 1882, the ıines have yielded gold to the value f hundreds of millions sterling. The ıines are supplied with electricity for ll purposes by the Cauvery Falls ower Works (p. 492). Two of the ıines are over 9000 ft. deep.

89 m. **Jalarpet**; junction with the ıain broad-gauge line of the Southern ty.

109 m. **Ambur,** with a barrier ɔrt. Headquarters of the Apostolic 'hurch of the Indies (Syrian and)rthodox).

141 m. from Bangalore is **Katpadi** unction (R.).

From here (1) a metre-gauge line uns past Vellore (7 m.) to (100 m.) 'illupuram Junction for Pondicherry p. 533, Route 33); and (2) another uns N. to (21 m.) Chittoor, Pakala, Tirupati (64 m.), and (71 m.) Reni-gunta (Route 23, p. 440).

Vellore Town (pop. 138,000 in 1971; alt. 689 ft.), headquarters of the N. Arcot District, is 5 m. S. of Katpadi station on the opposite bank of the Palar river, which is spanned by a brick road bridge and a railway bridge.

The **Fort** of Vellore was occupied by Narsingh Raja of Vijayanagar about 1500. It is a perfect specimen of military architecture. The design suggests the work of Italian engineers; but local tradition ascribes it to Bommi Reddi, who came from the Kurnool district. A main rampart is broken by round towers and rect-angular projections, and is surrounded by a moat. The old entrance was by a winding roadway with massive gates across a drawbridge. On the S. is a sally-port approached by a footpath which crosses the ditch by a stone causeway. Within the fort is a parade-ground fringed by buildings. Noticeable among these are the great mahals or double-storeyed lines of rooms built round large courtyards. The Madras Europeans were besieged by Haidar Ali from 1780-82.

The **Temple,** which is likewise in the Fort, contains no image and may be entered freely by Europeans. The gateway is surmounted by a seven-storeyed gopuram of blue granite, 100 ft. high, and flanked by two dwarpals. The door is of wood studded with bosses of iron like lotus flowers. The passage under the gopuram is lined with pilasters orna-mented with circular medallions containing groups of figures. On the left in the courtyard is a stone pavilion, called the Kaliana-manda-pam (marriage of the gods), ex-quisitely carved. On either side of the steps ascending to the mandapam are monolith pillars, carved to repre-sent various animals and monsters, one above another. In the portico or ante-chamber is a carved ceiling, with a centre-piece representing a fruit, round which parrots are clustered in a circle, hanging by their claws with their heads down towards the fruit; the several richly carved pillars of the interior are all different from each other.

The Sepoy **Mutiny** at Vellore in 1806 was due primarily to injudicious orders of Sir John Cradock (afterwards Lord Howden), the Commander-in-Chief in Madras, which prohibited the wearing of beards and sect-marks by the sepoys. The garrison consisted of 380 British soldiers of the 69th Regiment and 1500 sepoys. On the morning of the 10th July the sepoys, led by the Indian officers, shot down the British officers and penned the men of the 69th in their barracks, where 82 were killed and 91 wounded. Escaping, the soldiers made their way to the rampart, and there, under the command of two young surgeons, Jones and Dean, held their own. The flag of Tipu Sultan was raised by the insurgents.

An officer who lived outside had ridden post-haste to Ranipet Cantonment, 14 m. away. Colonel Rollo Gillespie turned out at once with a squadron of his own regiment, H.M. 19th Dragoons and a troop of the 7th Madras Cavalry, ordering the galloper guns to follow. Gillespie swarmed up the ramparts by a rope and took command of the defenders. The guns came up, and blew open the gates. The cavalry dashed in, and the mutiny was soon quelled. In the old cemetery to the right of the entrance to the fort is a walled-in enclosure with a low sarcophagus inscribed to the memory of the officers and men of the 69th who fell during the mutiny.

¾ m. to the W. of the fort are the Tombs of Tipu Sultan's Family in a well-kept enclosure. Right of the entrance is the tomb of Padshah Begam, wife of Tipu Sultan, who died in 1834. The second tomb on the right is that of Aftab Khan, who was second instructor to the ladies. Then comes a handsome tank, with stone embankment and steps. Next are two plain tombs of female attendants, and then a handsome granite pavilion with a massive roof supported by four pillars; inside is a black marb tomb to Mirza Raza, who marrie one of Tipu Sultan's daughters. A the end of these is the largest buildin of all—a domed mausoleum, 20 f square, to the memory of Bakhs Begam (the widow of Haidar Ali who died in 1806. Left of this is mosque without any inscription.

As the family of Tipu Sultan, wh were State prisoners in the fort wer suspected of complicity in the mutiny they were removed to Calcutta.

The last King of Kandy was in terned in Vellore from 1816 until h death in 1832.

157 m. from Bangalore is **Walaja Road** Junction for Ranipet (3 m.) an Arcot (no station). The Palar rive flows between these two, and i crossed by a stone causeway. **Ranip** was for many years a large cavalr Cantonment. It was built in 1771 b the Nawab of Arcot in honour of Rani of Gingee (p. 532), who pe formed *sati* on her husband's grav There are many European tombs i the cemetery.

Near **Arcot** (Arkát) a small pagod is reached and portions of the tow wall, which was of red brick. It wa blown up by Tipu, but the founda tions remain. ¼ m. farther S.E., alon the bank of the Palar, is the Delh Gate, which is the only one tha remains so far uninjured that it i possible to form an idea of what th fortification was. Above the gate i Clive's Room. A road from here lead S. into the heart of the old town and in ¼ m. to the Taluk Cutcherry After passing this building and turn ing E., the broad moat, which sur rounded the citadel and is now dr with trees growing in it, is passed Here are two small tanks, which onc had fountains in the centre, and near by is the Makbara, or Tomb of Sa' adatullah Khan. In the same enclosur is the *Jami Masjid*. The tomb has stone inserted over the door with a inscription, which says that the Nawa died in 1733.

W. of the Jami Masjid is the ruine Palace of the Nawabs of the Carnatic on a mound overlooking the large lake called the Nawab's Tank. The walls of the darbar-room are still standing. Opposite is the Kala Masjid, or Black Mosque, and near the Palace is the tomb of a Muslim ascetic. To the W. is the mosque of Fakir Muhammad. Near it is a tomb, apparently unfinished, in which was laid the body of the Subadar Nasir Jang, murdered in camp W. of Gingi on 5th December 1750, till its removal to Rauza (p. 144). Just across the road is the tomb of Tipu Auliya, of brick whitewashed. In the W. wall is a stone with an inscription, which says that Sa'adatullah Khan erected this tomb for Tipu, who was a man of God. After this saint Tipu Sultan received his name.

History

After Zulfikar Khan, Aurangzeb's General, took the Mahratta frontier fortress of Gingi in 1698, he made Daud Khan Governor of the Carnatic, and this officer colonised the place with Muslims. In 1712 Sa'adatullah Khan, who first took the title of **Nawab of the Carnatic,**[1] made Arcot his capital. Arcot, however, is chiefly known for its remarkable capture and defence by Captain Robert Clive, who here laid the foundation of his fame.

About the year 1736 Chanda Sahib the minister of Ali Dost Khan, nephew and successor of Sa'adatullah, obtained possession of the Hindu kingdom of Trichinopoly. The Mahrattas in 1739 invaded the Carnatic and took Chanda a prisoner to Satara. Ali Dost was killed in battle and his son Safdar Ali was murdered by his brother-in-law, Murtaza Ali. Two years later (1742) Safdar Ali's son was murdered at Arcot. Muhammad Anwar-ud-din, who was appointed Nawab of the Carnatic by Nizam-ul-Mulk (1744), was defeated and killed by Chanda Sahib at the battle of Ambus in 1749. The Council at Madras set up his son Muhammad Ali as Nawab; and Chanda Sahib, with aid from the French, besieged him in Trichinopoly.

Clive led an expedition against Arcot in 1751 in order to divert a part of the enemy from the siege.[1] Clive had with him only 200 British, with eight officers, six of whom had never before been in action, 300 sepoys and three field-pieces. He left Madras on the 26th of August, and arrived at Conjeeveram on the 29th. Here he learned that the garrison of Arcot amounted to 1100 men. On the 31st he arrived within 10 m. of Arcot, and marched on through a tremendous storm. The enemy's spies reported the coolness with which the English advanced in these circumstances, and this made such an impression on the garrison that they abandoned the fort.

On 4th September Clive marched out against the garrison, which had taken up a position at Timeri, a fort 6 m. S. of Arcot. The enemy retreated to the hills, and the English marched out again on the 6th, and drove the enemy from a tank near Timeri. After ten days the enemy, who by reinforcements had grown to 3000 men, encamped within 3 m. of Arcot, where they were attacked at 2 a.m. on the 14th of September by Clive, and utterly routed. Two 18-pounders despatched from Madras had now nearly reached Clive, who sent out all the men he had, except 30 Europeans and 50 sepoys, to bring them in. During this emergency the enemy attacked the fort, but were signally repulsed.

Chanda Sahib thereupon sent 4000 men from Trichinopoly under his son Raja Sahib, who entered the town of Arcot on the 23rd of September. On the 24th Clive sallied from the citadel and fought a desperate battle with

1 The Carnatic extended from the Kistna river to the Coleroon, and was bounded on the W. by the present administrative districts of Cuddapah, Salem and Dindigal, which once formed part of the State of Vijayanagar.

1 "Mr Clive, a volunteer, had the command given to him to attack a place named Arcourt".—*Contemporary Newsletter* (1751).

Raja Sahib's force. On the 25th Murtaza Ali brought 2000 more men from Vellore to join Raja Sahib.

Clive's situation appeared desperate: as the fort was of enormous extent and the walls were in ruinous condition, but the small garrison held out against overwhelming odds, the sepoys displaying unsurpassed devotion for 50 days.

The gallantry of Clive's defence so impressed the Mahratta leader, Murari Rao, who was at the head of 6000 men, that he determined to help them, and put his troops in motion. This alarmed Raja Sahib, and he determined to storm Arcot before succour could arrive. He chose the great day of the Muharram, and Clive, who was exhausted with fatigue, was roused by the shouts of the enemy rushing to the attack, and was instantly at his post. The struggle lasted about an hour and the assault was driven off, about 400 of the assailants being killed. Next morning the enemy abandoned their camp, into which the garrison marched and brought off four guns, four mortars, and a large quantity of ammunition. Thus ended on the 15th November this famous siege, and Clive, being reinforced by Captain Kilpatrick, marched out on the 19th and took the Fort of Timeri. A few days later, he defeated a force of 300 French, 2000 horse, and 2500 sepoys, with four guns, and took Arni, with Raja Sahib's treasure and baggage.

In 1758 Lally seized the Fort of Arcot by bribing the Indian commandant; but in 1760 it was recaptured from the French by Colonel Coote. In 1780 Haidar Ali, after his victory at Pollilore over Colonel Baillie, made himself master of Arcot, and strengthened the fortifications, but Tipu Sultan abandoned it in 1783.

Muhammad Ali, who had received the title of Walajah from Shah Alam in 1765, removed in 1767 from Arcot to Chepak in Madras, and died there in 1795. In 1801, on the death of his son, Umdat-ul Umara, the Carnatic was annexed by the East India Company, and the districts of N. and S. Arcot, Nellore, Trichinopoly and Tinnevelly, were thus added to their territories.

166 m. from Bangalore, **Sholinghur.** Near here, on a rocky ridge, Sir Eyre Coote defeated Haidar Ali and young Lally on the 27th September 1781.

179 m. from Bangalore is **Arkonam** Junction (R.), 43 m. from Madras (p. 441). A metre-gauge line runs S. to Conjeeveram and Chingleput.

222 m. from Bangalore, **Madras** Central Station (Route 31).

ROUTE 30

MADRAS CITY AND ENVIRONS

CONTENTS

MADRAS.*—Capital of the former Presidency of Fort Saint George, and now of Tamil Nadu State. Lat. 13° 4′, long. 80° 14′ 54″ E. Population (1971), 2,470,000. Distances by rail: 794 m. from Bombay (Route 23); 1032 m. from Calcutta (Route 22): 1318 m. from Delhi (Route 9); 737 m. to Colombo (Route 33); 357 m. to Ootacamund (Route 32). Indian Airlines services daily from Delhi, Bombay, Calcutta, Bangalore, Nagpur, Colombo. Also served by Air India and services and excursions from Govt. of India Tourist Office and State Information Centre, 34-5 Mount Road.

History

Madras[1] was the site of the earliest important settlement of the first East India Company, and was founded from the station of Armagaum (which lay N. of Pulicat, itself 25 m. N. of Madras), in 1639 by Francis Day, on territory given by the deputy of the Raja of Chandragiri, the last representative of the Vijayanagar Royal family, and confirmed by the Raja six years later by a grant inscribed on a plate of gold. The Nawab of Arcot confirmed the tenure (in jaghir) in 1762.

A small fort was erected in the settlement in 1644, which was known as Chennapatnam, and a town named the Black Town, now George Town, arose N. of it. In 1683 the settlement was made independent of that of Bantam in Java (founded in 1602), and Mr Aaron Baker was appointed its first President. The Municipal Corporation is the oldest in India. It was constituted on 29th September 1688 by a charter issued under the

[1] For the history of Madras see references in *Oxford History of India*, also pamphlets and other literature obtainable in the Govt. of India Tourist Office, 35 Mount Road, and State Information Centre, Govt. Estate, Madras 2.

orders of His Majesty James II, under the East India Company's seal on 30th December 1687. The charter constituted the "Town of Fort St George, and all the Territories thereunto belonging, not exceeding the distance of 10 m. from Fort St George to be a Corporation by the name and title of the Mayor, Aldermen, and Burgesses of the Town of Fort St George and City of Madrassapatam". A new charter was given in 1726.

The most notable Governors of Fort St George were Elihu Yale (1687-91), Thomas Pitt (1730-35), the grandfather of Lord Chatham, Lord W. Bentinck, and Sir Thomas Munro (1820-27). Warren Hastings was second member of Council from 1769 to 1772.

The Chamber of Commerce was constituted in 1836. Besides cotton mills and other factories of long standing, Madras now possesses an area of great industrial expansion in the outskirts of the city: including a number of all-India industrial enterprises, motor-assembly plants, railway-coach (Perambur), cycle, and motor-cycle factories, engineering plants, cigarette factories, cinema studios, etc. The increasing importance of Madras is shown by the new institutions opened in the last few years, e.g. the Vivekananda College, the Madras Institute of Technology, and the Leather Research Laboratory.

Arrival at Madras.—The mail trains from Calcutta, Delhi, Bombay, and Bangalore terminate at the **Central Station.** But the speed and ease of air-travel bring increasing numbers by I.A.C. service. The **Egmore Station** is the starting-point of the trains to Colombo *via* Dhanushkodi, and the South of India generally (Route 33). Those visitors who prefer the sea route from Calcutta or Colombo, will be rewarded by a magnificent view of the city, especially from the S., the first object being the spire of the Roman Catholic Cathedral at San Thomé. The seaside Marina, some 4 m. in length, runs from San Thomé to the Napier Bridge over the River Cooum. Next comes Fort St George, and N. of this is the High Court and the Harbour.

The centre of Madras is **Mount Road,** on or near which the principal hotels and shops are situated.

Between Old Government House, situated at the N.E. end of the road, and the fort is the Island embraced by two branches of the Cooum. The Gymkana Club is in the S.W. corner. On the road to the fort is a bronze equestrian Statue of Sir T. Munro, by Chantrey, erected by public subscription in 1839. The S. branch of the river is spanned by the Willingdon Bridge, the N. branch by Wallajah Bridge.

Old **Government House,** now used for public offices, contains a most interesting collection of pictures. In the lower hall is a picture of the installation of the last titular Nawab of Arcot, Ghulam Muhammad Ghaus Khan, under the Governorship of Lord Elphinstone, with the date 1842. In the drawing-room, amongst others, is a full-length portrait of Lady Munro (the beautiful Jane Campbell), by Sir Thomas Lawrence, also a remarkable portrait group, attributed to Chinnery, of Major Stringer Lawrence and the Nawab of the Carnatic.

The Banqueting (or Rajaji) Hall detached, is 80 ft. long and 60 ft. broad. The principal entrance is on the N., and is approached by a broad flight of stone steps. Round the walls there are many portraits of notables of the British régime.

On the sea-front, East of Old Government House, are the **Chepauk Park and Buildings,** once the property of the Nawabs of the Carnatic. On the death of the last in 1855, the property was acquired by the Government. The entrance, by the Wallajah Road is through an ornamental gateway with representations in porcelain of the various incarnations of Vishnu, executed by the Madras School of Art. The palace was divided into the Kalsa Mahal, a two-storeyed building with a small dome, and the Humayun Mahal and Diwan Khana. Beyond these are the Public Works'

Secretariat and the Presidency College, originally organised in 1855, with the Students' Hostel behind it.

On the sea-shore almost opposite the Presidency College is a fine public swimming-pool, with a restaurant attached. The Caste and Gosha (purdah) Hospital lies to the W. hidden amongst trees, and beyond the Madras Cricket Club ground. N. of the old Palace is the Senate House of the University (1857), begun in 1874 and completed in 1879.

S.W. of the Chepauk Palace and S. of Government House is Triplicane, containing the Palace of the Prince of Arcot, a title conferred in 1867, the representative of the family of the Nawabs of the Carnatic.

The **Marina** is a fine esplanade which extends nearly 4 m. from the Napier Bridge on the N. almost to the Roman Catholic Cathedral of San Thomé. The *Aquarium* (open 14.00-20.00 except Mondays—admission 20p) should not be missed. From the S. end of the Marina, Edward Elliot's Road and Cathedral Road runs nearly due W. about 2 m. to St George's Cathedral, the South Beach (Marina) Road then turning inland to "the Adyar", from the river of that name. At Adyar are the headquarters of the Theosophical Society, with a famous Library (open 9.00-10.00 and 14.00-16.00), beautiful grounds and residential accommodation. Adyar is also the home of the Kalakshetra School of Indian classical dancing. The Adyar Club has a white cupola; a broad terrace on the S. overlooks the Adyar river, on which excellent sailing and boating is to be had. In the 60-acre grounds there is room for a riding-track and a golf-course. The name of the original owner of the estate, Robert Moubray, who came to Madras in 1771, survives in the inland road to the main entrance.

San Thomé was first Portuguese, then fell to Golconda (1669). The French captured it (1672), but were expelled by the Dutch (1674). It then had seven churches. The British occupied it in 1749.

The **Roman Catholic Cathedral** (1504, but rebuilt in 1893) is reputed to cover the remains of St Thomas. His tomb is pointed out in a subterraneous recess covered by an altar. On the E. side of the Cathedral is an Anglican church situated on a sand-dune. This tract and that stretching to the W. of it is also known as Mylapore (p. 508), where stands the famous Kapaleswara Temple. Good seabathing can be had at Elliot's Beach (drive from end of Marina through San Thomé and over the Elphinstone Bridge across the Adyar). But occasional heavy waves must be watched for.

After crossing the Cooum river by the Napier Bridge, the (Marina) South Beach Road runs past **Fort St George,** situated on the seafront N. of the island, containing the Arsenal and St Mary's Church. The E. face of the fort, which is straight, is now separated from the sea by the road and a sandy foreshore. In the centre is the old **Sea-Gate**. The W. face landward is in the form of a crescent, surrounded by a deep fosse, crossed by drawbridges. There are two gates on this side, the Wallajah and St George's Gates. On the N. are the Choultry Gate, now bricked up, and the North Gate. The San Thomé Gate is in the S. wall.

The original fort was founded in 1644. Designs for remodelling were prepared by Bartholomew Robins, once mathematical professor at Woolwich, in 1750. It had been unsuccessfully attacked by Daud Khan, General of Aurangzeb, in 1702, and by the Mahrattas in 1741; but in 1746 La Bourdonnais held the town to ransom for £400,000, and received in the name of the French King the surrendered keys, which were restored (21st August 1749) by the Treaty of Aix-la-Chapelle to Admiral Edward Boscawen.

On 14th December 1758 the French again arrived before the fort, under the command of Count Lally. The defence was conducted by Governor Pigot and Colonel Stringer Lawrence.

Upon the arrival of a British fleet of six men-of-war, the French, however, retreated after a siege of two months, leaving behind them fifty-two cannon and many of their wounded.

In April 1769 Haidar Ali appeared, and dictated terms of a treaty. Again on 10th August 1780, and once more in January 1792, the garrison were alarmed by the appearance of the Mysore cavalry. It was from the fort that Clive marched to Arcot.

If the fort is entered from the E. by the Sea Gate, the Secretariat buildings will be seen in the centre, with St Mary's Church to the S. and Cornwallis Square to the W. of them. The Legislative Council Chamber lies behind the Secretariat.

St Mary's Church,[1] built 1678-80 by Streynsham Master, was the first English church in India, but was entirely rebuilt in 1759. Robert Clive was married here in 1753 to Margaret Maskelyne, and many distinguished persons are buried here. One piece of the Church plate was given in 1687 by Governor Elihu Yale, afterwards the benefactor of Yale University, U.S.A. The most remarkable monument is one erected by the East India Company to the famous missionary Schwartz, at one time the intermediary between the British and Haidar Ali. He is represented dying on his bed surrounded by a group of friends, with an angel appearing above. In the Church hung the old colours of the Madras Fusiliers, the first European regiment of the East India Company. Lord Clive, Sir John Malcolm, and Sir Barry Close served in it.

On the W. side of Charles Street, leading to the gate of San Thomé (the S. gate of the fort), are pointed out quarters which, according to tradition, were once occupied by Col. Arthur Wellesley (later the Duke of Wellington). The office of the Accountant-General, which is close to the Church, was at one time the Government House.

[1] *Fort St George, Madras,* by Mrs F. Penny, and the *Vicissitudes of Fort St George*, by Mr D. Leighton, will be found to contain many interesting details regarding this church.

The **Arsenal** forms a long parallelogram. In the *Museum* on the first floor are four cornets, or flags, belonging to the 1st and 2nd Regiments of Madras Cavalry; old flags taken from the Dutch and French, sewn up in corners, to protect them from the squirrels, and many other battle trophies.

N. of the fort and at the S.E. corner of the city, is the old **Lighthouse** (1844) on the Esplanade, superseded by a tower on the **High Court.** The Lighthouse tower is 160 ft. high and commands panoramic views but is closed. Its light was visible 20 m. off at sea. The High Court building, designed in the Hindu-Saracenic style, was opened in 1892.

A tomb in the shape of a pyramid stands in the compound outside, the solitary survivor of the many which stood here in the old cemetery of the Settlement. Lally made use of the monuments as cover in 1758, and they were removed after the siege. There are two inscriptions on the tomb: one to the only son of Elihu Yale (28th January 1682) and the other to Joseph Hynmers, second in Council (28th May 1680), whose widow married Yale.

Opposite the High Court is the Y.M.C.A., of red sandstone, presented by the Hon. W. Wanamaker, formerly Postmaster-General of the United States. W. of the High Court is the **Law College,** in similar style. The former **Madras Christian College Buildings** are situated opposite the High Court and to the E. of the Y.M.C.A. buildings. The College was moved, however (1937) to Tambaram, where a World Christian Conference was held in 1938.

First Line Beach, the most important commercial thoroughfare, begins N. of the Esplanade from Parry's Corner. It represents the old line of the sea-wall, but the Harbour has caused the accretion of sand. Here are the **Beach Ry. Station,** the **Port** and **Customs Offices,** and various houses of business. W. of it is Second Line Beach and the thickly inhabited bazar area, formerly known as Black Town and re-named **George Town,** in 1905, in honour of the visit of King George V as Prince of Wales. A broad modern highway has now been driven through the heart of George Town, emerging about six miles N. of the old city boundary at Ennore, where visitors can enjoy boating, bathing, and fishing.

Armenian Street, parallel to the sea-front, contains the Mosque of Nawab Muhammad Ali, an Armenian church, and a Roman Catholic cathedral, dating from the beginning of the 18th century; farther to the W. of Armenian Street lies Popham's Broadway. N. of the city are the Monegar Choultry, a Poorhouse for destitute Indians, and the Leper Asylum; and at the N.W. corner in Wall Tax Street are some remains of the old town walls. The name of this street commemorates a tax imposed in order to defray the cost of a rampart, an assessment being made on "every house and garden within the walls", and a Collector of the Town Wall Tax was duly appointed. But legal opinion was received from Bengal that the East India Company had no power to tax the inhabitants.[1] Other streets running N. and S. are Godown Street and Mint Street, at the N. end of which was the Mint in the present Government Press building. From E. to W. runs Old Jail Road, and at its junction with Mint Street are seven wells from which the fort drew its water-supply.

The **Harbour.** The foundation-stone of the harbour works was laid by H.R.H. the Prince of Wales, in 1875, but in October 1881 the works completed up to that time were much damaged by a cyclone. These violent storms have visited Madras from time to time. Such occurred in October 1746, in 1782, 1807, and 1811. On 2nd May 1872, in another great storm, the "Hotspur" and eight European vessels and twenty Indian vessels of altogether 4133 tons were lost. In December 1901, 11 in. of rain fell in about 8 hours. The cyclone of November 1927 passed over the city and spent its fury on Nellore (p. 427). The sand beach shelves out to a depth of 10 fathoms at a distance of a couple of miles from the shore. The harbour, therefore, has had to be an entirely artificial one: "a challenge flaunted in the face of nature". It was formed of break-waters extending out from the shore 3000 ft. apart, now closed at their seaward end by another work which extends to a distance of 1500 ft. N. of the northern of the two breakwaters, forming a shelter for a new entrance, 400 ft. wide and 35 ft. deep at low water, which has been formed near the eastern or seaward end of the N. breakwater. The western or shoreward side of the enclosed 200 acres has been furnished with a deep-water quay. Steamers call at the port regularly, embarking and landing passengers direct at the quays, where trains come direct to ship's side. Shore accommodation has been provided, facing the South Quay; and customs examination and the medical inspection of emigrants take place here. Both the broad and the metre-gauge railways enter the harbour premises, where they are handled by the Port Trust.

Madras has assumed great and growing industrial importance in the New India. In addition to the developments described on p. 502, it is now an important centre of the Indian cinema industry.

W. of the fort is a group of buildings, consisting of the Memorial Hall, the Medical College, the General Hospital, the offices of the Southern Ry., and the Central Ry. Station.

The **Memorial Hall** was erected by public subscription in gratitude for Madras having escaped the Mutiny of 1857. It is used for public meetings.

The **General Hospital** is opposite the Central Ry. Station. The records go back to 1829. Dr Mortimer published an account of it in 1838. The Medical

[1] Molony, *A Book of South India*, p. 21.

School is accommodated in a detached building to the E. side. The **Central Ry. Station** has a clock tower 136 ft. high.

Across the Buckingham Canal is the Choultry (R.H.) of Sir Ramaswami Mudaliar. The Moore Market is at the entrance to the People's Park; to the E. is the Evening Bazar building. Alongside the Market is the **Victoria Public Hall,** erected during 1883-88. This serves for a theatre as well as an "assembly room".

W. of the Victoria Public Hall, in the People's Park, the "Ripon Building", after the Viceroy, Lord Ripon, the founder of local self-government in India, is occupied by the Corporation of Madras. It has a clock tower higher than that of the Central Ry. Station. In the centre of the eastern portion of the park, the S. Indian Athletic Association occupy a large piece of land where athletic sports and annual fairs are held. Moore Pavilion is at the northern end. To the N. of this is a Swimming Bath. The **People's Park** originated with Sir Charles Trevelyan while Governor of Madras, and was opened in 1859. It embraces 116 acres of land. It has eleven artificial lakes, an athletic ground, a fine zoological collection, tennis-courts, and a bandstand.

The Poonamalle Road skirts the S. of the quarter of Vepery and leading to the quarter of Egmore, passes the School of Arts and St Andrew's Church. Vepery is largely occupied by Anglo-Indians, whose Association, founded in 1879, is the leading society of its class in India. The Church of St Matthias was given by Admiral Boscawen in place of one destroyed during the 1746 War with the French. W. of the church is the Doveton Protestant College, founded in 1855.

The **School of Arts** was established as a private institution by Dr Alexander Hunter in 1850. Besides drawing, painting, engraving and modelling, the crafts of cabinet-making and carpet-weaving, pottery, and lacquer, metal and jewellers' work, are taught.

St Andrew's Church was built in 1818-20. The stucco, or *chunam,* in the interior gives to the pillars all the whiteness and polish of the finest marble. The steeple rises to the height of 166 ft., and, after the lighthouse tower of the High Court, is the principal landmark in Madras; the building is remarkable for the complete absence of timber, which might be destroyed by white ants.

In the **Egmore** quarter are the M.G. **Station,** the Maternity and Ophthalmic Hospitals, and the Museum.

Pantheon Road leads S.W. to the **Central Museum** (1854), nucleus of a group including the Victoria Technical Institute (1902), the Connemara Library, the New Theatre and the National Art Gallery. To these has been added the **Empress Victoria Memorial Hall,** a graceful building, which was opened in 1909. The collection was formed in 1846, and owes its present development to Dr Balfour. In the various Departments of Natural History, Botany, Geology and Industrial Arts are many objects of great interest. The Department of Antiquities and Archaeology contains some very beautiful remains of the Buddhist tope at Amaravati (p. 427), excavated by Mr R. Sewell, M.C.S. Indian bronze images of Krishna and the dancing Siva are superb; the collection of South India bronzes is the best in the world. Objects of interest formerly in the Arsenal are:—iron helmets captured at Manila; a gun captured from Holkar in 1804; a victim-post surmounted by an elephant's head, at which human sacrifices were made (ground-floor); the cage in which Captain Philip Anstruther was confined in China.[1] The Connemara Library has a reading-room, in which in addition to works on S. India the books of the Madras

[1] Capt. Anstruther of the Madras Artillery (1807-84) was captured by a Chinese mob in September 1840, and carried about the country in this cage until the following January. He was over 6 ft. high. A lady, Mrs Noble, was kept in a similar cage.

Branch of the Royal Asiatic Society are kept. Archaeological remains are arranged in the grounds in front of the Museum. The statue of Lord Cornwallis, which once stood in the Fort Square (p. 503), has been placed in the reading-room. On the pedestal is sculptured the surrender of Tipu Sultan's sons in 1792.

From near the Museum the Commander-in-Chief's Road leads to the bridge so named, and to Mount Road. A road to the N. crossing the Cooum river by Anderson's Bridge leads to the old **Observatory** in Nungambakkam, past the **Old College,** corresponding to Writers' Buildings in Calcutta (p. 184), and Doveton House, now Government Training College for Girls.

The Observatory originated in a small private station started in 1787 by Mr W. Petrie, a scientific member of Council. The present building was erected in 1793 under orders from the Directors of the East India Company. It is now used as a meteorological station only, the Observatory having been moved in 1899 to Kodaikanal (p. 545).

From the Observatory a thoroughfare runs S. to the **Horticultural Gardens** and **St George's Cathedral.** The gardens, which occupy an area of 22 acres, are laid out in a highly ornamental manner, one of the great attractions being the splendid *Victoria Regia,* in a couple of small ponds. The Society possesses a valuable Library, containing many rare works. The gardens were brought into existence mainly through the efforts of Dr Wright about the year 1836.

The **Cathedral** of St George stands on the W. side of the gardens. The exterior is not handsome, but the dazzling white *chunam,* the decorated roof, the tablets and tombs, and the lofty and massive pillars in the interior, produce a very pleasing impression. The Church was consecrated in 1816, and became the Cathedral Church when the Diocese of Madras was constituted in 1835.

From the Cathedral the road to Guindy and the southern suburbs runs for nearly 3 m. to the modern Maraimalai Adihal Bridge, spanning the Adyar river. This replaces the former **Marmalong Bridge** (said to be *Mamillanna,* "Our Lady of the Mangoes"), which had twenty-nine arches, and was erected in 1726 by Petrus Uscan, an Armenian, *pro bono publico;* hence its former name, the "Armenian Bridge". To the left of the road before crossing the river will be observed the *Teachers' Training College.* At Saidapet (5 m. S. from Egmore station) are the headquarters of the Chingleput District.

The **Little Mount,** a curious spot on a rocky eminence on the left of the road after crossing Marmalong Bridge, is famous in connection with the tradition of the martyrdom of the Apostle St Thomas. It was formerly called Antenodur, but the Portuguese named it Little Mount to distinguish it from St Thomas's Mount, which they called Big Mount. The Apostle St Thomas (so runs the tradition) used to live here periodically and pray on the top of the hill (Little Mount) according to the Jewish custom. When praying in the cave he was, it is said, mortally wounded by a lance. In that state he ran to St Thomas's Mount, where he was killed. His body was carried by his converts to San Thomé, where it was buried, and his tomb is in the Cathedral of San Thomé.

A flight of steps leads to the Church. On the left of the entrance is a portrait of St Thomas with an old Portuguese inscription. The Church was built by one Antonia Gonsalves De Taide, 1612 (who appears to have been a Goanese), and was endowed with 32 acres by the Nawab of Arcot. It is dedicated to Our Lady of Health.

Some steps on the left from the Church lead down to a *cavern* hewn out of the rock. The entrance is low and narrow; there is nothing to see but an altar with the image of St Thomas. Daylight is admitted by a narrow aperture, through which, it is said, St Thomas escaped. In the vestry-room is a Missal with the date 1793. A dark cell full of bats is reputed to be the oldest part of the Church, where St Thomas himself worshipped.

At the N. of the Church there is a **Masonry Cross** on the top of a rock, from which St Thomas is said to have preached.

To the W. of the Church there is a cleft in the rock, which, it is said, was miraculously made by St Thomas to provide himself with water. The small Greek cross and foundation of a building are relics of St Thomas's prayer-house. At the foot of this rock, at the S., there is St Thomas's **Fountain,** which has water throughout the year. To the E. of the Church there are some rocks believed to be marked with the prints of the feet, hands, and knees of St Thomas, where he lay prostrate on them when he was wounded. The ancient tradition that St Thomas was martyred on 21st December A.D. 68 at Mylapore, which H. H. Wilson (*Roy. As. Soc. Trans.*, 1, 161) identified with Mihilaropye, or Mihilapur, now St Thomé, is not confirmed by modern historical research.

At the top of the parochial house, about 90 ft. high, there is a visitors' room furnished; a panorama of Madras, St Thomas's Mount, the Governor's House, Guindy, the King's Institute, Teachers' College, and the surrounding hills and country may be obtained from here. Visitors are welcomed, and a guide is available.

Beyond the Little Mount is Guindy Park, the former **Country House** of the Governor, now his official residence, RAJ BHAVAN, standing in a large park with many deer. It is faced with the beautiful white *chunam* for which Madras is famous; the centre hall contains a bust of the Duke of Wellington. There is an attractive Gandhi memorial pavilion and a Snake Park operated by the World Wildlife Fund. The flower-garden lies to the S.

The **Race-Course** in Guindy is beautifully situated and laid out on modern lines with an electric Totalisator and a fine grandstand and other buildings. The track is 1½ m. round. There is a golf-course.

St Thomas's Mount, or the **Great Mount,** 8 m. S.W. of Madras, lies S. of Guindy railway station (7 m. from Egmore). At the base are the old *Cantonment* and a building which used to be the headquarters of the Madras Artillery. It was the home of Warren Hastings while a member of Council (1769-72). The hill is about 250-300 ft. above sea-level, and has a flight of 132 steps, built by an Armenian.

Mention of St Thomas's Mount, which is known to Indians as *Faranghi Mahal* ("The Hill of the Franks"), is made by Marco Polo as early as the 13th century. As already mentioned (p. 507) St Thomas is said to have been killed, after being wounded on the Little Mount, whilst kneeling on a stone which is now on the central altar of the Church. The stone has an inscription in Pahlavi (a dialect spoken in those days in the suburbs of Madras), which alludes to the martyrdom. Relics of the lance with which a Brahmin is said to have attacked the Apostle are kept in the Cathedral of San Thomé at Mylapore. The Church was built by the Portuguese in 1547. Over an archway is the date 1726, and within are several slabs with epitaphs. The main gate and portico were built by one C. Zacharias in 1707. Behind the altar and above it is a remarkable cross with a Nestorian inscription in Sassanian Pahlavi of about A.D. 800. The inscription begins to the right of the top of the arch. Dr Burnell translated it: "Ever pure . . . is in favour with Him who bore the cross". Besides the stone, the Church contains a picture of the Virgin Mary, said to have been painted by St Luke, and brought by St Thomas to this place.

In the 15th century the Nestorian Church in India fell into decline, until in most places it totally disappeared, but this hill continued to be the resort of Nestorian monks till the beginning of the 16th century, when the Portuguese built the Church dedicated to Our Lady of Expectation, now under the care of the R.C. priest at St Thomas's Mount.

Next to the Church there is a Convent of Franciscan Missionary Nuns of Mary, who are in charge of an Indian girls' orphanage and industrial school.

The **Anglican Church,** a few hundred yards from the old mess-house, is a handsome building, with a well-proportioned steeple. There are monuments here to several distinguished officers.

The Madras airport (Meenambakkam) lies about a mile South of St Thomas's Mount.

Pallavaram (12 m. from Egmore) is the next station to St Thomas's Mount. It was ceded by Muhammad Ali in 1750 and became a Cantonment (1777). The hill is about 500 ft. high, with a long, low range extending for 3 m. S. 2 m. from the station is the site of old Pallavaram, where there are three rock-cut shrines ascribed to the 7th century A.D. One of these is now in the possession of Muslims, who have placed in it the *panja*, or hand symbol.

Pleasant excursions can be made by car from Madras to **Yedanthangal Bird Sanctuary**—one of the two in India—(53 m.) where between November and January many migrants can be observed; also to (34 m.) Chingleput, and (19 m.) farther on is **Mahabalipuram,** or the **Seven Pagodas** (Route 31). Between Chingleput and Mahabalipuram is **Tirukkalikkundram** with a Siva temple and a shrine where two sacred kites come to feed daily, shortly before noon. The climb is steep and visitors should start early, as large crowds assemble.

ROUTE 31

MADRAS to **KANCHIPURAM,** then to **Chingleput,** for **MAHABALIPURAM** (the **Seven Pagodas**), and back to Madras.

This excursion embraces both Kanchipuram, "The Benares of the South", and the wonderful remains at Mahabalipuram, known as the Seven Pagodas. The entire trip can be accomplished by car; Kanchipuram is 24 m. by road from Chingleput; the Seven Pagodas 19 m. from Chingleput; Chingleput is 34 m. from Madras. For the journey by rail *via* Chingleput to Kanchipuram the train should be taken at the **Beach** or **Egmore Stations.** Certain passenger trains run through.

22 m. from Chingleput is **Kanchipuram** (Conjeeveram) (pop 110,000 in 1971) (the Golden City), one of the oldest towns of India, and one of its seven sacred places.[1] There is a Travellers' Lodge with restaurant, and a Municipal Rest House, where accommodation can be reserved, but food is not available. Guide services are obtainable from the Municipal Commissioner's Office. Inscriptions show the town to have occupied a position of influence before the Christian era. In the 5th century B.C. Gautama Buddha is said to have converted the people of Kanchipuram, and in the 3rd century B.C. Asoka is said to have built many Buddhist topes in the neighbourhood though none now remain. In the 7th century A.D. the Pallava Kings ruled in the Southern Deccan until defeated by the W. Chalukyans, who were defeated in turn by Cholas from the Cauvery Valley. They carried on

[1] Of the other six (see p. 155), three are sacred to Siva and three to Vishnu. Kanchipuram is sacred to both.

an extensive commerce both with West and East, and were renowned for their skill in war, and for their achievements in architecture and the Arts. Their capital, Kanchi, is famous in ancient Indian history. The larger Dravidian temples (of comparatively recent date) are at the present time the most conspicuous objects; but the special attractions are the Pallava temples, which are among the oldest known examples of Hindu architecture in S. India.

Great Kanchipuram is W. of the railway, **Little Kanchipuram** about 2 m. S.E. The route between the two towns is studded with a number of important temples—a few dedicated to Vishnu and a large number to Siva. In and around Kanchipuram there are said to be a thousand temples and ten thousand lingams.

The Vaikunta Perumal Temple, one of the eighteen important Vishnu temples of Kanchipuram where worship is still conducted, is S.W. of the station. The vimana tower has tiers of three shrines one over the other, with figures of Vishnu in each shrine. The sculptures on the different sides of the vimana represent scenes from the Puranas.

There are two covered Prakaras of the shrine, and the courtyard has a colonnade on the four sides. As usual, the shrine is entered from the E. and through an ardhamandapam with its eight yali piers and four pilasters and sculptured panels. On the E. side of the courtyard the mahamandapam is entirely roofed up to the unfinished gopuram built by the later Vijayanagar Kings.

There are figures on the right and left side of the entrance gopuram, exhibiting an abundance of detail and sculpture. The design has been well thought out.

S.W. from this temple, and at a little distance, stands the Matangeswara Temple. Its plan is simple—a small shrine with massive walls and entrance through a pillared porch; there is a similarity between this and the Kailasanath tower (below).

The tower over the shrine is hollow. It is square and built in three storeys. The pillars at the porch are distinctly of the Pallava type. Each has a lion base, the tail of the lion being curved up the back of the pillar. Over the lion is an ornamental band with polygonal-sided necking, large projecting capital, and a square abacus over.

The back of the porch has pilasters responding to detached piers with figured panels on each side. The pilasters at the corners have yalis and riders. The N. and the E. walls have Saivite figures and sculptured panels between the pilasters.

The most important of the group of Pallava structures is the Kailasanath Temple, more than 1000 years old, some distance to the W. Its plan is unusual, a single surrounding wall with a cross-wall dividing the enclosure into a large and a small courtyard, with a group of shrines in the large one.

In the small court on the interior side of the outer wall the sculptures are all figures of Siva in different postures. The most noticeable is that on the large panel to the right. It has a group of twelve sages, evidently listening to the exhortations of Siva, who is seated under a banyan-tree in a panel on the S. side wall. On another large panel eleven seated sages are similarly listening to Siva, armed with different symbolical weapons, and seeming to preach war.

Built into the cross-wall is a small temple, and on either side there are doors from one court to the other. Ranged along the E. face of the small court are eight small shrines, each with a tower over it. They closely resemble in design the raths of Mahabalipuram. The spaces between all but one are now filled with rubble work, hiding the sculptured panels on the sides.

Each of these is called a rath. That on the extreme left stands completely detached from the rest. It is in shape a square, and has carved figures of Siva and Parvati in a sitting posture on the back. On the exterior wall are the yalis, partly carved, each yali supporting a pilaster with moulded caps over. On the back and sides are rough blocks and panels. Between these panel spaces and the corner *yalis* are small pilasters.

The small platform in front has yali piers, whose capitals only are complete; there are traces of carved floral ornaments on the cornices, and a series of small mouldings with carved projections at intervals; the octagonal-domed sikhara has carved pedimental ornaments on each side.

The next rath has yalis on the piers and the dwarapals on each side of the door panels are all carved. Siva is seated under a tree with long, matted hair and a naga, or serpent, on his left.

The other connected raths are of the same type, but the yalis differ, some having tusks and twisted trunks. The inscriptions on the granite plinths —some in Pallava grantha character —also deserve careful study. The panel on the northern side of the last rath has a standing figure of Siva with matted hair, two hands, and a serpent over his shoulder. Over the panelled niche in which the figures stand is a floral pedimental ornament only partly carved.

The sculpture on the back of the successive raths should be noticed. Behind the back of the rath on the extreme N. is Siva on an elephant, with the death-noose in his left, the trident in his lower right hand, and a naga in the lower left, and his right foot uplifted on the elephant's head. He is represented as stripping the elephant's skin, which he waves aloft in his two upper hands.

There is a group of posed female figures on some of the small panels, and on the back of the sixth rath is a chariot drawn by two horses, with the figure of Siva in a boon-conferring attitude.

The small shrine in the centre of the wall dividing the lesser and larger courts is at present known as the Narada Linga Shrine. The plinth has two courses of granite, over them a freestone course on which gandharvas are sculptured. They have their hands raised over their heads with the palms of their hands flattened against the moulding above, as if supporting the building.

On the exterior of the porch on the right side is a row of hansa, or sacred swans. A panel on the inner side of the porch has a large finely carved figure of Siva, with matted hair and his right knee bent; he has a richly carved crown, and ornaments on the neck, arm and leg. Over his left shoulder is a garland of (apparently) bones. Another has alternate square and round ornaments, on each of which is a sculptured skull.

The exterior of this shrine is again full of sculptures—all representations of Siva. The features of all these figures have a marked form of countenance. The noses are pointed and flat, and give a curious expression to the face, and it is believed that they represent Kurumbars, one of the early tribes in this country.

The doorways into the W. court have yalis at the corners, pilasters on the angles of the doors, and a cornice over. Above the cornice is an upright portion of wall rising above the court walls on either side. In the centre of this is a panel with Siva and Parvati and attendants. Brahma and Vishnu are shown worshipping them.

On each side of the large court (W.) is a continuous series of cells, each with a small tower and sikhara over it. This has given rise to a belief that this must originally have been a Jain temple; but in the sculpture there is not a single figure which could be called Jain. These cells were occupied by lingas, each with a separate name and representing a different manifestation of Siva. The inscriptions on the face of each are mostly in an early palaeographical form of grantha character. A notable peculiarity is the scrolled foliation attached to letters of these inscriptions, which either give the names of the different lingas or the titles of kings who erected the building. The sikharas (towers) originally projected above the wall of the court, with elephants and nandis placed alternately on the wall-head between them. But the modern owners have blocked up the spaces between, so that the outside of the court forms a continuous line of dead wall. The weight of this masonry has caused large cracks in parts of the walls. The cell towers show on the inside of the courtyard wall. On the N. and S. sides of this court the cells directly opposite the central vimanas are larger than the others, and have higher towers over them.

To the E. of the temple stands the nandi mandapam. The basement only remains. There are four yali piers at each corner. It must have had a roof, but now there are no traces of it.

Then comes the mahamandapam, originally detached, but now joined to the shrine by the ardhamandapam. The piers in the ardhamandapam are widely spaced, slender columns, and are of a later structure, evidently built in the time of the later Vijayanagar Kings.

The mahamandapam, however, has massive stone piers, with heavy square capitals and inscriptions on them of a later date. One says that King Vikramaditya made a grant to the temple. The piers are without bases. The capitals are of one design throughout—square with great projection. Several have circular lotus discs carved on the faces of the lower and upper square portions. These were evidently intended to support some great overhead weight. The perforated window which leads into the mahamandapam is much older, and is of black stone. The perforated work is a series of twisting boughs with openings between partly filled by cross-buds. Over the opening is a triple cornice with horseshoe-shaped panel; in it is a figure of Siva with eight arms. On the circumference of the panel is a leaf ornament springing from yalis at the foot.

The sculptures at different elevations of the mandapam are mostly figures of Parvati. In the lower right panel of the S. elevation is the figure of Lakshmi seated on a lotus flower, holding lotus buds, conch, and chakra. In the pier of the minor panels on each side are chauris, elephants, gandharvas and attendants. Some of the walls are quite plain, without ornaments of any kind.

The central shrine is surmounted by a lofty pyramidal tower. The entrances to the central vimana are from the E. and N. At each corner, and on the N., S. and W. sides, is a shrine. All shrines and the porch have seven smaller towers, which rise up to and are grouped alongside the greater one. Near the base, at each corner and face, between the projecting shrines, a large nandi (sacred bull) lies on the ground. The figures sculptured on the exterior ground storey of the vimana are again representations of Siva, Brahma and Vishnu worshipping him, and of Parvati. The sikharas over the corner shrines are square, and over those on the façades are semi-barrel shaped.

On the main tower is a storey with a series of two weather-worn sculptured panels on each face of the central projection, and one at each corner. Over this is a double cornice with small sikharas; the storeys above are successively stepped back, forming a slight platform between each. The tower is capped by an octagonal sikhara with small medallions on each front. The whole tower is plastered over, and the plaster faithfully represents the underlying stonework, but is much coarser in execution.

On the W. is another entrance, a gateway with a small tower. An elephant and gandharva are seated on the wall-head, and an upper central panel has Siva seated with his hand across his knees. On this façade of the court wall there are five yali pilasters on either side of the central doorway. The S. exterior side is spaced by similar pilasters. Sikharas, elephants and Nandis are exposed to view here.

The chief street of Great Kanchipuram leads to Ekambareswara (Siva) Temple, which has a sixteen-pillar mandapam in front of it. It is 188 ft. high, divided into ten storeys, and was built by Krishna Devaraja of Vijayanagar in 1509. From the topmost storey a grand view is obtainable of the whole town and its surroundings. No two towers of the temple are opposite each other, no two walls of the temple are parallel, and there is hardly a right angle in the place. Through the gateway a large open space is entered, to the left of which is the "Hall of a Thousand Pillars" (really 540); most of the columns are beautifully carved and support richly decorated friezes. In the centre of the hall are a number of grotesque wooden figures, which are taken out on occasions of processions. The interior of the temple is now open to visitors and in the courtyard behind the shrine there is a prodigious mango tree. It is said to be two thousand years old and to bear on each of its five branches a different kind of mango.

This temple served as a fort during the Carnatic Wars, and was attacked by Haidar Ali. From this building Sir Hector Munro retreated to Chingleput on learning that Col. William Baillie's force had been cut to pieces by Haidar Ali at Pollilore (see below), a few miles away. It had been ordered down from Guntur, but was unable to effect a connection. To the S. of this temple is the Sarvatirtham Tank, into which Munro threw his guns and baggage. Its four sides are studded with little pagodas.

About five furlongs from this tank is the temple dedicated to Kamakshi, the "Loving-eyed" Parvati. The consort of Siva is worshipped in Kasi (Varanasi) by the name of the "Broad-eyes", in Madura as the "Fish-eyed", and at Kanchipuram by the name of Kamakshi. This ancient temple is believed to contain the samadh (burial-place) of Sri Sankara Acharya.

About 2 m. from the borders of the town is a famous Jain temple of the Chola era (907-1310) in the village on the bank of the Palar.

At Pullalur (Pollilore) 10 m. N. of Kanchipuram, which was the scene of Baillie's disaster in 1780, are two lofty obelisks commemorating the death of two officers in the engagement. Another battle was fought on the same ground by Sir Eyre Coote, on 27th August 1781; Haidar Ali claimed this as a drawn battle, but left the field.

Of the latter Dravidian temples, the most important is that of Varadaraja Swami, a form of Vishnu, at **Little Kanchipuram.** One of the most ancient, it has been renovated within the last four hundred years. The tower is about 100 ft. high, and has seven storeys. It contains no figures or representations of Hindu deities. The original builders apparently intended to build it higher than it is. The tower at the E. extremity of the temple, just opposite the one at the main entrance, is the higher, and evidently more ancient. Until a few centuries ago the E. tower was the front one, and the idol in the temple faced E. There are two tanks adjoining the towers. These are fine structures nearly squared, with sides sloping to the bottom in gradual rows of cut granite steps. The tank at the E. tower is much the older.

Within the first courtyard are singularly beautiful pavilions, with painted roofs resting on four tall, slender pillars. These are situated in front of the flag-staff and a monolith column of granite intended as a lamp-holder. The remarkable Hall of Pillars, to the N. of the mandapams, is one of the beauties of S. India.

The mandapam has often felt the shock of wars, and hence the figures are slightly mutilated, apparently by shot and sword. The sacrilege is ascribed to Muslim invaders, and to Haidar Ali in particular. The hall has ninety-six pillars, carved at the base into horsemen and hippogriffs. The carvings on the pillars are mainly illustrations of the Avatars of Vishnu and incidents mentioned in the Ramayana and Mahabharata. There are a few lay-figures of great interest. In the fourth pillar from the W., at the N. extremity, facing the tank, there is a figure of a Rajput warrior with a gun in his hand. At the top of this pillar there is a grotesque figure of the god of death. Each of the corner stones on the roof of the hall is a monolith of great size. Not only are parrots, snakes, etc., sculptured on the top, but chains of stone originally hung down nine feet. The story is told that Haidar Ali wanted to try the strength of his sword and cut them to pieces. The chains are now connected together by iron rings.

Into the second court non-Hindus are not permitted to enter. The colossal cars, or vahanams, on which the idol is carried in procession on the occasion of the Brahma Uthsavam festival in May of every year are of great beauty. This temple is also famous for its umbrellas. A pair of the largest and the best of these cost Rs. 750. The jewels of this temple are not so valuable as those in Tirupati or Sri Rangam, but the workmanship is of a very superior order. They will be shown by the trustee, if desired. Among them is a necklace, which is said to have been given by Clive. At this temple there is a periodical recitation of the Vedas by the Aiyangar Brahmans of this place. As many as 1000 congregate for its recitation.

About 1 m. from the Vishnu Kanchipuram is the magnificently carved wooden car, very high, with massive wooden wheels. In Hodgsonpet the cloth bazars have the silk-bordered cloths and saris for which Kanchipuram has always been famous. There is a Weavers' Service Centre in Railway Station Road, interesting to visitors.

Chingleput Junction (R.) is 35 m. from Madras (Route 33).

Chengalpat (Singhala petta) means "the town of the lotus".

The **Fort** stands on the margin of an irrigation reservoir or tank. It is of Vijayanagar origin. A slab embedded upside down in one of the ramparts evidently relates some deed or Narasimha (1486), the founder of the second Vijayanagar dynasty. Tradition states that the fort was built by Timmu Raya after his flight S. in 1565. It is certainly a typical Hindu structure, built after the model of Gingi, "the modern Troy". The walls are formed of roughly dressed stone, hewn for the purpose by families of workmen, who affixed their marks to the stones. It is nearly a parallelogram, 400 yd. by 320 yd.

About 1646 territory up to the Palar was occupied by Mir Jumla, the General of the King of Golconda and, on the fall of Golconda in 1687, it passed with the rest of the Carnatic into the hands of the Mughal Emperor. The French acquired possession of the fort in 1751, and it was taken by Clive in 1752. During the struggle for supremacy in the Carnatic it was used by the English as a base for keeping stores, as a place of confinement for French prisoners, and for harassing the rear of Lally's army, which was investing Madras in 1758-59. It was granted to the British as part of a jagir in 1750 by Muhammad Ali, Nawab of Arcot, for services rendered, and the grant was confirmed by Shah Alam in 1765.

During the wars with Haidar Ali, it was once taken and twice unsuccessfully besieged. On the last occasion it was relieved by Sir Eyre Coote in January 1781. The fort is in ruins and the railway runs through it. The royal apartments, the granary, the barracks and armoury, have all been razed to the ground; but two old buildings exist.

The Raja Mahal is also known as Ther Mahal (Ther = car), on account of its shape. Timmu Raya built this "Ther Mahal" exactly in the form of the Kanchipuram car of Varadaraja Swami (p. 513). It originally consisted of five storeys; one was subsequently pulled down. The unusual height of the structure was due to the fact that the Ranis of the Palace desired to worship daily at 12 o'clock, in sight of the temple of Kanchipuram. A series of arcades of Moorish arches surrounds a small inner dome-shaped room without a single piece of wood in its entire construction. The roof of the dome-shaped room in the first storey is decorated with plaster-work, and was evidently used as a mandapam for the habitation of the household deities. The staircases were straight, were all located inside, and ran parallel to and above each other from one storey to another. The steps are extremely narrow.

The lower storey of the residence of the Deputy-Superintendent of the Reformatory School was a Hindu temple, built for the use of the Prime Minister of the Raja. When the fort was taken by the Muslims, this was partly converted into a mosque, and the Saracenic arch and the Hindu pillar exist side by side. From the veranda of the upper storey a picturesque view is obtained, with the tank in front and a background of hills.

In the town is a temple dedicated to the monkey-god of Anjaneya, who was a devotee to Kothandaramaswami (Rama with a bow). This was once within the fort and was transferred (1813) with the permission of the East India Company. 1 m. from Chingleput are the Pallava Caves of Vallam, with archaic inscriptions.

From Chingleput it is 19 m. by motor-car or motor-bus to **Mamallapuram** (Mahabalipuram), or the **Seven Pagodas,** one of the most remarkable places in India.[1] There is a good road through Tirukalikunram (p. 509). There is a Hotel (H. *Silver Sands*; reservations and free transport from 123 Mount Road Madras); a Travellers' Lodge and Restaurant; and Tourist Guest House.

The official name of the Seven Pagodas is **Mahabalipuram,** believed to connect the place with the demon Mahabali, overpowered by god Vishnu in his vamana-avatara, or dwarf-incarnation. It has been suggested that the village owes its existence to the Banas, who claim their descent from the demon Mahabali, or Mahabali-chakravartin. There is, however, no evidence to show that the Banas extended their dominions so far. But in ancient Chola inscriptions found at the Seven Pagodas the name of the place is Mamallapuram; this is evidently a corruption of Mahamallapuram, meaning the "city or town of Mahamalla" ("the great wrestler"), which occurs as a surname of the Pallava King Narasimhavarman I (A.D. 625-645) in a mutilated record at Badami (p. 474) which he claims to have captured.

The earliest inscriptions on the Raths, in the opinion of Professor Hultzsch, are birudas of a King named Narasimha. It is thus not unlikely that Mahallapuram, or Mavalavaram, was the original name of the village, and that it was founded and named after himself by Narasimhavarman.

3 m. N. of Balipitham, the landing-place, is Saluvan Kuppan, with two cave temples. One of these is usually filled with drift-sand. The other is carved with nine lions' (or tigers') heads round the cells, and has two elephants' heads under miniature cells to the right of it.

Running S., and between the canal and the sea, distant nearly 1½ m., is a low granite ridge rising about 120 ft. above the plain in its highest part. Upon this ridge are various excavations and carvings; on the E. face of it is a famous relief of the Penance of Arjuna (p. 517), and 700 yd. beyond the S. extremity of it are the five monolithic temples called the *Raths*, all works, it is believed, of the Pallavas (p. 509), and dating from the 7th century A.D. The modern village lies E. of the great relief, and the old temple lies beyond it again on the seashore.

The visitor can go by boat to opposite the Raths, or by foot from

[1] A full description of the excavations and carvings at Mamallapuram will be found in the *Cave Temples of India*, by Fergusson and Burgess, and in the brochures and literature obtainable from Tourist Bureaux.

Balipitham along the top of the ridge, or below its eastern side, as he may feel disposed. Everyone will probably prefer to visit the Raths first before working back to the N., as they are embryos of the Dravidian style, and of the great Kailasa Temple at Ellora, absolutely unique in the whole of India.

The monoliths known as **Raths** are associated with the Pallavas. The Dharmaraja Rath, the Ganesa Temple, the Dharmaraja-mandapa and the Ramanuja-mandapa bear inscriptions which prove beyond doubt that they were all shaped by Pallava Kings. The Ganesa Temple and the Dharmarajamandapa are called Atyantakama Pallavesvara-griha. The same name is engraved on the outside of the third storey of the Dharmaraja Rath.

The Saluvan Kuppan Cave (above), N. of Mahabalipuram, was excavated by Atiranachanda-Pallava, and was accordingly called Atiranachanda-Pallavesvara-griha. The identity of Atyantakama and Atiranachanda with any of the Kings known from the copper-plate grants remains to be established.

Chola inscriptions in the Shore Temple of the Seven Pagodas mention three shrines at Mamallapuram—viz. Kshatriyasimha-Pallava-Isvara, Rajasimha-Pallava-Isvara and Pallikondaruliyadevar, which were apparently situated in the temple called Jalasayana—i.e. the Shore Temple. Kshatriyasimha-Pallava-Isvara was in all probability the ancient name of the principal shrine in the Shore Temple. Rajasimha-Pallava-Isvara might be the name of the smaller shrine in the same temple, while Pallikondaruliya probably denotes the shrine connected with the larger temple, where a large mutilated statue of the god Vishnu is lying.

The most northerly of the Raths is called after Draupadi, the wife of the five Pandavas (see p. 21, Introd.). It is the smallest of all, measuring only 11 ft. square, has three storeys and a pointed roof, like a thatched Toda hut in the Nilgiris, rising 18 ft. from the ground, and once crowned by a stone finial. The image of a goddess inside is popularly explained as Draupadi, but more probably represents Durga. At her feet are two kneeling figures, one of which is shown in the act of making an offering of his hair.

W. of the Draupadi Rath are an elephant and a lion carved out of single blocks of stone, and E. of it is a nandi bull. These animals are the vehicles (váhanas) of the thunder-god Indra, the goddess Durga, and Siva, and were presumably intended to be placed in front of the respective shrines.

The next Rath, named after Arjan, was probably a temple dedicated to Indra, whose effigy is shown in a niche in the back wall. It is a copy of a terraced Buddhist Vihara. It measures nearly 27 ft. by 29 ft., and is 35 ft. high; it has four storeys, three with simulated cells round them, and the fourth of a dome-shape. In each round window decorating the cells is a head as of a monk looking out of it. The basement storey has round it columns of the Elephanta type (p. 106), with lions at their base.

The Bhima Rath comes next, and W. of this, outside the line of the other four, the Rath of Sahadeva and Nakula. The Bhima is the largest of all, measuring 48 ft. by 25 ft., and rising 26 ft. from the ground. Only part of the hall has been excavated, the pillars having cushion capitals and lion bases (see above). The carved roof of the upper storey closely simulates the wooden form of a free structure of the kind.

The Sahadeva Nakula Rath is smaller again, 18 ft. by 11 ft. by 16 ft. high; it has an apsidal end on the N. side, and is intended to represent a Chaitya or Buddhist chapel. At the S. end is a porch with two pillars in front of a cell. Simulated cells are represented on the terraces.

The last Rath in the line of Dharmaraja (or Yudhistir), resembles the Arjan Rath, but is a Siva Temple of the Pallava Narasim havarman (A.D. 625-645). It measures 27 ft. by 29 ft. by 35 ft. high, and has four storeys, the fourth a sort of dome or stupa. The columns have lion bases. The Atya kanta inscription is on the third storey.

Each work is carved out of a single mass of stone, and probably from a continuous outcrop.

At the southern extremity of the ridge there will be found on the isolated rocks near the E. corner a representation of a Penance of Arjuna and on the W. side the Varáhaswami Temple, used for Hindu worship and not accessible to tourists.

The **Great Bas-relief** of the **Penance of Arjuna,** 96 ft. long and 43 ft. high, dates from the 7th century. The N. half of the relief is occupied below by two large elephants (one 17 ft. long) and four small ones, and above by a crowd of figures hurrying to the centre. In a cleft is a statue of the Nag Raja, overshadowed by a seven-hooded serpent, and of his wife below him, with other serpent-crowned figures and animals. On the southern part is Siva with an ascetic, from whom the relief is named the Penance of Arjuna, on his left, and a large number of dwarfs, flying figures, human beings, and animals, including lions, monkeys, hares, deer and birds, round him. The lower part has been blocked out for more carving.

S. of the relief is a large unfinished cave, known as the mandapam of the Páncha Pandavas, with two rows of pillars and models of cells on the façade; and farther again and not far above the S.E. corner of the ridge is the Krishna mandapam of later date than any of the other excavations, supported by twelve columns in four rows, and containing at the back a sculptured relief of Krishna holding up the mountain of Gobardhan (p. 296). The central figure of a cow being milked is very natural.

A little S. of the Lighthouse is the Yamapuri or Mahishamardini mandapam, a cave 33 ft. long and 15 ft. deep, with representations of the combat between Durga, wife of Siva, and the buffalo-headed demon, and of Vishnu reclining on the Shesh Snake; at the back of the cave are three cells.

N. again, beyond some excavations and the Ramanuja mandapam, a cave 18 ft. by 10 ft., with two pillars resting on lions' heads, are the excavations known as the Lion throne or couch of the Dharmaraja, and the bath or vat of Draupadi, nearly opposite the gateway of the Vishnu Temple, known as the Rayula Gopuram, which was begun about the 12th century, on the E. side of the ridge above the great bas-relief, but was abandoned.

To the N. of the gopuram is a monolithic temple, called after Ganesha, measuring 19 ft. by 11 ft., and rising 28 ft. from the rock. It has three storeys, the two lower with simulated cells, and the carved roof of the topmost carrying a row of finials; the pillars of the base are of very slender and wooden form.

S. of this, facing W., is a cave, 19½ ft. by 9½ ft., with bold representations of (1) the Varaha, or Boar incarnation[1] of Vishnu; (2) elephants pouring water over

[1] The representation of the *Varaha* incarnation is fairly well done, but unfinished. The central figure is the four-armed Vishnu with a huge boar's head, who lifts up the Earth Goddess and places his right leg on the head of a snake-hooded figure issuing from the waves. The latter is the giant Hiranyáksha, "Golden eye", who had carried off the earth into the infinite abyss. Vishnu with the head of a boar "pursued and slew him and saved the Earth". The representation of the *vamana-avatara*, or dwarf-incarnation, is very spirited. Vishnu, dilated to an immense size, places one foot on the earth, and lifts another to the sky. The god has eight arms, with which he holds a sword, a quoit, a shield, a bow, and a lotus, and with one he points. The other two are indistinct. Worshippers or attendants are at his feet, and other figures appear in the skies. One to the W. has the head of a dog. The legend is that when Bali became Ruler over the whole earth Vishnu approached him in the shape of a dwarf and asked for so much space as he could cover in three steps. Bali granted this modest request, whereupon Vishnu dilated to immense proportions and planted one foot on earth, one on the sky, and with a third thrust Bali down to Hell.

Lakshmi; (3) Durga; (4) Mahabali and the Dwarf (Vamana) incarnation. Farther N. again is a cave on the W. side with another on the E. side known as the Isvara mandapam, containing three shrines with statues of the Hindu Triad; there is a large stone bowl in front of the cave, and at the back of it a relief of elephants, and a monkey and a peacock. Just beyond the N. end of the ridge, and near the hamlet of Pillaiyan Kovil, is a life-like sculpture of three monkeys in the round.

A path leads from the bas-relief past a Lotus tank to the seashore temple, dating from the 8th century. It is five-storeyed, a pyramid 60 ft. high and 50 ft. each way at the base. In front is a small temple, the original porch. Inside is a fallen lingam, and inside a vestibule on the W. of it is a recumbent figure of Vishnu, 11 ft. long; 75 ft. distant, in the sea, are the remains of a dipa stambha, or lamp pillar. S. of the temple are two rocks with recesses surrounded by lions' heads excavated on their W. side. In front of these is a stone lion, and at the back an elephant's head and a horse. All have to be protected from the sea air. Excellent sea-bathing may be had, but care must be taken not to venture out too far.

On the way back to Chingleput, a halt may be made at **Tirukalikundram** (7 m.), where the road branches S. to Sadras. There are two very fine temples—one on the hill and one in the village—a spacious and beautiful tank with steps all round, and a rock-cut temple, on whose pillars are many Dutch and some English signatures, ranging in date from 1664 to 1687. The temple in the village is full of ancient inscriptions.

For the feeding of the Sacred Kites, from which the place is named, see p. 509.

Sadras (D.B. fairly good), an old Dutch settlement (founded in 1647) lies on the Buckingham Canal 7 m. S. of Mamallapuram. The place was once famous for its printed cottons. The ruined Dutch fort and the old Dutch cemetery are the principal objects of interest. Sadras was taken by the British in 1781, and again in 1795, and restored to the Dutch in 1818; six years later it was made over to the British by a treaty, together with the rest of the Dutch settlements in India, in exchange for Fort Marlborough and other places in Sumatra. During the siege of Madras by Count Lally (1758-59) the ladies were sheltered here.

Covelong (Kovilam) or Saadat Bundar, 15 m. S. of Sadras on the N. of the Palar river, was a port built by Saadat Ali, Nawab of the Carnatic. Labourdonnais landed troops here in 1746. It was taken from the French by Clive in 1752 and destroyed.

ROUTE 32

MADRAS to MANGALORE by way of **Salem** (for **Yercaud** and the **Shevaroy Hills**), **Erode, Podanur** (for **Coimbatore** and the **Nilgiris**), **Olavakkot, Shoranur** (for **Cochin**), **Calicut, Tellicherry,** and **Cannamore**; and from **Mangalore** to **Bombay** by sea.

The broad-gauge line of the Southern Ry. to the Nilgiris and Mangalore by way of Arkonam (Route 23, p. 441) covers routes previously described as far as Jalarpet (Route 29, p. 497).

From Jalarpet Junction (R.) the stations are shown with their mileage from Madras.

138 m. **Tirupattur** (D.B.K.) Junction N.G. railway to **Krishnagiri,** 26 m., one of Tipu Sultan's key forts, in what was known as the Baramahal.

167 m. **Morappur** Junction. N.G. railway by the Palahodu Pass, to **Hosur,** 73 m., from which a large Cattle Farm is 2½ m. distant, close to the Mysore border.

207 m. **Salem** Junction (R., I.B., Hotel *Dwarka*). Salem town (pop. 308,000 in 1971), the headquarters of the District formed out of the Balaghat, Baramahal and Talaghat in 1792, is 3½ m. on a metre-gauge branch to (87 m.) Vriddhachalam (p. 532).

Another branch, broad-gauge, opened 1929, runs W. 25 m. to the Mettur Dam (1934) of the Cauvery river; the dam, a mile long and 214 ft. high, has three times the volume of the Assuan Dam; the lake is 60 sq. m. in extent, and there is a hydro-electric plant (1937) feeding a large area.

Motor-bus services run to Rasipur, Namakkal and Attur; also to Tiruchengodu, Mettur and Bangalore.

Tiruchengodu (3 m. S.W.) temple is on a large hill with another at the base. A hooded snake, 80 ft. long, is carved half-way up.

The Shevaroyan Hills. Motor omnibuses run from Salem Junction to **Yercaud** (21 m.) by the ghat road. The scenery along the whole length of the road is magnificent. The road has nineteen hairpin corners, which are not easy for a car with a long wheel base.

Yercaud (I.B., R.H.), a small town, the height of which varies from 4000 ft. (at the lake) to about 4800 ft. above sea-level, is essentially a place for a quiet holiday—smaller and less expensive than Ootacamund or Kodaikanal.

A few view-points are given below, with their approximate distances from Yercaud Church (gate):

	Miles
Ladies' Seat	1½
Prospect Point	1½
Bear's Hill	1½
Pagoda Point	2
Kiliyur Falls (after rain) . .	2½
Shevaroyan (5314 ft.) . . .	3½
Honey Rock	6½
Shengalvaray Precipices (2 m. of difficult walking) . . .	14

The Shevaroyan Hills cover an area of about 100 sq. m., the elevation ranging from about 3500 ft. to about 5300 ft. There are excellent roads; the gradient is steep in places but negotiable. The district consists mainly of coffee and orange estates, broken up by picturesque villages and "greens", inhabited by hill-folk (Malayalis). Only the highest points (especially the Shevaroyan and the Green Hills) are cultivated and covered with short grass, varied by *shola* (evergreen hill-trees). Botanists and entomologists will find a visit to these hills worthy of their interest.

242 m. The Cauvery river is crossed.

245 m. **Erode** (pop. 103,000 in 1971) Junction (R. and D.B.). Motor service to Bhavani, 9 m. A broad-gauge branch runs to (88 m.) **Trichinopoly** (Tiruchirapalli) Junction (Route 33, p. 540).

Tiruchirapalli Branch Line

On this branch at 21 m. **Unjalur** station. In an enclosure, several huge terra-cotta figures of horses and other animals can be seen from the train.

41 m. **Karur** station (D.B.), on the Amaravati river. This was the capital of the ancient kingdom of Chera, conquered by the Cholas in A.D. 990. The fort was constantly besieged both in ancient times and during the wars with Tipu Sultan. In 1801 it was abandoned as a military station. The ruins of the fort and an old temple are interesting.

85 m. from Erode is **Tiruchirapalli Fort.**

Main Line

303 m. from Madras, **Podanur** Junction (R.).

To the Anamalais and Dindigal

A branch metre-gauge line runs to Pollachi, 25 m., for the Anamalai Hills 14 m. distant. From Pollachi the line proceeds to Dindigal (p. 544). There is a motor service from Pollachi to Valparai on the Anamalai Hills; and a motorable road from Udhampet Ry. Station (D.B.K.) to Munnar (54 m.) **Munnar** (D.B.K.), 4500 ft. above sea-level, near Anaimudi Peak (8841 ft.), is the centre of the **High Range** district of the Travancore hills. There is a motor-road from Munnar to Alwaye.

To Coimbatore and the Nilgiris

For the most up-to-date information about tourist facilities and accommodation in the Nilgiris, apply to the Government Tourist Office, Mount Road, Madras.

From Singanallur, an avoiding line (1939) for Mettupalaiyam and the hill railway to the Nilgiris, turns N., and passes to

307 m. **Coimbatore** (D.B.K.), airport, 1398 ft. above sea-level (pop. 353,000 in 1971). This city has developed greatly as an industrial centre during the past decade owing to the availability of electric power, and long stapled cotton. There are many mills and factories as well as technical and other colleges. Coimbatore is also the centre of a tea and coffee plantation area. I.A.C. services connect it to Madras, Bangalore, Hyderabad, Cochin and Trivandrum.

The great sight of Coimbatore (3 m.) is the **Temple of Perur.** Fergusson says: "The date of the porch at Perur is ascertained within narrow limits by the figure of a sepoy loading a musket being carved on the base of one of its pillars, and his costume and the shape of his arm are exactly those we find in contemporary pictures of the wars of Aurangzeb or the early Mahrattas in the beginning of the 18th century". (The inscriptions copied at Perur refer themselves to the 12th century and later.) The bracket shafts are attached to the piers, as in Tirumal Nayak's buildings at Madura.

In front of the small temple is a **Dwaja Stambha** (stone flag-staff), 35 ft. high. The central shrine, desecrated by Tipu, is dedicated to Goshthisvara. The shrine of Sabhapati, a name of Siva, occupies a subordinate position. There is a smaller temple to Patteswar. They were both built in Tirumal's time (1623-59). There is one gopuram, with five storeys, about 55 ft. high. In the corridor leading to the vimana there are eight very richly carved pillars on either side of the Kanchipuram or Madura type. From the ceiling hang stone chains, perhaps an imitation of the chains with bells which hang from the Dwaja Stambha. The pillars represent Siva dancing the Tandava; Siva killing Gajasur, the elephant-headed demon, treading on his head and waving the skin, appropriate in a locality where wild elephants used to do such mischief; Vira Bhadra slaying his foes; and the Sinha, or lion of the south.

A road runs to Satyamangalam (44 m.) and thence either to Kollegal (112 m.), or to Chamarajnagar (90 m.) (see p. 496), Nanjangud and Mysore. There is also a road *via* Palghat to **Malampuzha** (Tourist B.) where there is a fine lake and illuminated gardens.

328 m. **Mettupalaiyam** station (R.). From here the metre-gauge Nilgiri Ry. ascends 4000 ft. to (17 m.) Coonoor, and to Ootacamund, 12 m. farther on. The Nilgiri Express leaves Madras in the evening, arrives on the following morning, and Ootacamund is reached in time for lunch. On the mountain gradient the railway is furnished for 12 m. with a central Abt rack rail, enabling it to ascend 1 in 12½, the extension being on a grade of 1 in 23·81. Care must be taken to guard against the drop of 20 to 30 degrees in temperature. On the road to Ootacamund (32 m.) there are 13 hairpin bends in 19 m.

Coonoor is 6100 ft. above sea-level (Travellers' B., I.B.). The climate is warmer than that of Ootacamund. A Pasteur Institute for S. India has been established here. The mildness of the climate has made Coonoor a favourite resort for persons of delicate health. There are several hotels (*Hampton* and *Ritz*) and board-houses; also good tennis courts at the Wellington Gymkhana race-course, and an excellent golf-course. Lady Canning visited Coonoor in April 1858 and compared the view over the plains with that over the Mediterranean from the Corniche at Monte Carlo.[1]

Sim's Park contains an excellent collection of plants. One shady dell is full of splendid tree-ferns and other ferns of large size, and is overshadowed by large trees of scarlet rhododendron. Below the park is the Wellington Race-course. A ride of 7 m. brings the traveller opposite to the St Catherine's Waterfall, which is N.E. of Coonoor. The road leads for 3 m. along the skirts of pretty copses (*sholas*), and then, turning off into a valley, reaches (4 m.) a rocky bluff called Lady Canning's Seat. Below, to the S. and E., lie extensive coffee plantations. The path then descends considerably, and turns S.E. to a bluff overlooking the chasm into which the stream takes a leap of 250 ft. into a very deep ravine.

[1] See *Charlotte Canning* by Virginia Surtees (John Murray, 1975)

S.W. of Coonoor there is another waterfall near Karteri, which has been harnessed to supply electric power for the Government Cordite Factory at Aruvankadu, near Wellington—a huge enclosure with a high wall running round it for miles.

An Excursion may be made to the **Hulikal Drug**, or Tiger-rock Fort, which is on the summit of a hill that towers up to the left of the pass in ascending from Mettupalaiyam. It is half an hours' drive from Coonoor through the Nonsuch Estate, and then a pleasant 1 m. walk. A rough bridle-path along the ridge leads to it. The peak is about 6294 ft. high, and in clear weather commands a splendid view. The Fort is 16th century.

From the Post Office at Coonoor it is about 3 m. to the barracks at **Wellington.** At a fountain the road to the barracks turns off sharply to the left. The original buildings lie half-way up a very steep hill, on which is the Commandant's house, with a fine public garden.

Motor-bus service, 13 m. from Coonoor to Kotagiri (p. 524).

Ootacamund[1] (alt. 7440 ft.), 9 m. from Wellington, formerly summer headquarters of the Government of Madras, has been called the "Queen of Hill Stations". It can be reached by bus from Mysore, by train (changing at Mettupalayam), and by bus or taxi from the airport at Coimbatore. The astonishing charm of its scenery seems likely to survive modern developments, which include extensive hydro-electric projects at Paikara, a vast new Government factory for the manufacture of cinema film and a population that now tops 60,000. Its climate has long been famous. As early as 1821, Europeans began to build their homes there.

Ootacamund (mund = "village of huts") is surrounded by lofty hills. Of these Dodabetta on the E. is the highest, being 8640 ft. above sea-level. The Lake, with boats for hire,

[1] Consult *Ooty Preserved: A Victorian Hill Station in India* by Mollie Panter-Downes (1967).

is about 2 m. long from E. to W., but narrow. The principal Church, St Stephen's, is near the Club, the Post Office, the Public Library, and the principal shops. The market is a busy centre worth visiting. St Thomas's Church is on the E. side of the lake, with Hobart Park and the Race-course. The railway passes the E. end of the lake to the terminus station, outside which is the main bus station for the Nilgiris, with over 70 routes. Fernhill, Palace of the Maharaja of Mysore, lies to the S. Now a hotel.

The Botanical Gardens, through which Government House (1880) is approached, were established in 1840 by public subscription, and are beautifully laid out in broad terraces one above another at the foot of Dodabetta, 1206 ft. above the gardens.

Ootacamund was once a centre for the manufacture of quinine from the bark of Cinchona, introduced *via* Kew Gardens in 1862. The plantation lay 3 m. N.E. from St Stephen's Church. A Government quinine factory was situated in later plantations at Naduvattam; but little is grown now.

From Dodabetta ridge a most superb panorama is seen. To the S.E. is Elk Hill (8090 ft.), behind which Lawrence Memorial School still flourishes (7330 ft.). Farther to the S. of the lake is Chinna Dodabetta, or Little Dodabetta (7849 ft.), and in the far W. Cairn Hill (7583 ft.), and St Stephen's Church Hill (7429 ft.). Beyond, to the N. of the lake, are still higher hills, as Snowdon (8299 ft.), and Club Hill (8030 ft.). The finest view, however, is to the E. Here is Orange Valley, where oranges once used to grow. To the N. is the Moyar Valley, termed the "Mysore Ditch", not artificial. To the E. are seen dimly the Gajalhatti Pass and N. Coimbatore mountains, covered with dense forests abounding with game.

The St George's Homes at Ketti, 5 m. S.E., once a refuge for orphan and destitute children of European descent, has now become a boarding school.

The house occupied by the **Club** was built in 1831-32 by Sir William Rumbold, and it was rented by Lord William Bentinck, the Governor-General, who received Macaulay here as Member of the Bengal Council. Stonehouse, on the site of the first house built at Ootacamund is occupied by the Government Arts College, a branch of Madras University, where liberal arts and sciences are taught to several hundred undergraduates. The grounds possess many beautiful shrubs, with heliotrope and verbena attaining astonishing size. The eucalyptus was introduced from Australia and has spread extensively.

N.W. of the lake are the downs, with the golf-course. The Wenlock downs, named after a former Governor of Madras, were once dear to the Ootacamund Hunt (p. 524). Large dams have created beautiful lakes; views from many vantage points.

The **Mukurti Peak** (or Taigannam) is 16 m. due W. of Ootacamund, among the mountains of the Kundas. 5½ m. can be driven; the remaining 10½ m. must be done on horseback; or, by another route, 21 m. can be driven, leaving 5 m. only. Refreshments must be taken. This peak is 8380 ft. high, while Avalanche Hill is 8497 ft., and Kunda Peak 8304 ft. "It is a spot held sacred by the Todas as the residence of a personage whom they believe to be the keeper of the gates of heaven." The religion of this tribe once dying out but now numbering more than 1000 is classed as Animist. Excellent embroidery is done in their villages. They are a handsome and dignified people.

The road passes along the ridges of the Governor Shola range of hills, crosses the Parsons Valley and Krurmund streams, and for some distance follows the windings of the Mukurti stream, which is the head of the Paikara river.

An easy ascent of 1½ m. leads to the summit of the peak. Towards the S. the N. termination of the Kunda range may be seen rising in abrupt escarpments and precipices. The N.

side of the mountain is a precipice of at least 1500 ft., and it seems to have been cut sheer through the centre.

On the W. side are the paddy flats of the Wynaad, and the plains of Malabar as far as the Arabian Sea.

The Mukurti Dam, 100 ft. high, at an altitude of 6795 ft., is reached by the Gudalur road (14 m.) and then 6 m. S. This hydro-electric project (opened 1938) supplies power as far south as Ramnad and links with the Mettur generators near Salem.

Other sights on the Nilgiris are the Waterfalls at Kalhatti, and the Paikara Falls (utilised since 1932 for purposes of electric power) at the N.W. corner of the plateau. In the heart of the Kundas the Bhavani Falls, 400 ft. or 500 ft. high, are surrounded by scenery of the most savage grandeur. In this area are extensive hydro-electric projects built with the help of the Canadian Government. The Rangaswami Peak may also be visited.

Stone circles, which the Todas call Phins, are found in many parts of the hills; but the most accessible locality is the Hill of Karoni, 3 m. to the S. The circles are built of rough unhewn stones, some of them of large size, which must have been brought from a considerable distance.

The tea industry flourishes. Sport is varied and interesting. Elephants and bison can still be seen in the **Mudumalai Game Reserve,** which can be reached by road *via* Gudalur or Mysore. There are regular bus services. There is a good hotel in which visitors are made comfortable. Elephants can be hired, from the back of which the visitor can watch many big and small animals, birds and snakes. A small fee is charged for private cars.

Panthers are numerous, and the black variety, so rare in most parts of India, is less uncommon here. Owing to the exertions of the Nilgiri Game Association, which was founded in 1877, the game is strictly preserved.

The Nilgiri "ibex", a unique genus of the goat tribe, whose habitat is confined to the Madras Presidency, is found along the precipitous sides of the plateau. Owing to the extreme wariness of the ibex and to the dangerous nature of the ground, the sport of ibex-stalking calls for a steady nerve. On the plateau, too, occurs the little barking deer or Munt-jac, locally known as the "jungle sheep", although less common than formerly.

The chital, or spotted deer, the most beautiful of all the deer family, frequents the lower slopes of the plateau and the valleys of the Moyar and the Bhavani rivers, and here, too, are found the mouse-deer and the four-horned antelope.

To the list of large game may be added the sloth bear, the hyena, and the wild boar, an enemy to the potato crops of the peasantry.

The Common, the rare Lion-tailed, Macaque monkey and the grey langur may be seen below the Gudalur Ghat, and the black Nilgiri monkey on the Nilgiri Plateau and sometimes near Ootacamund.

From September to March snipe may be found, and small bags are compensated for by the pleasure of being able to use spaniels and other English sporting dogs to put up the birds. The woodcock, the solitary and the wood-snipe are all found during these months. The only indigenous game-bird is the "jungle fowl". They are carefully protected and encouraged by the Game Association, which has also been at considerable trouble to introduce other sporting birds.

Below the plateau there are quail, the common brown partridge, the spur-fowl, and pigeons, two species of which, the Nilgiri wood-pigeon and the Imperial pigeon are found on the plateau also.

For the fisherman the Nilgiris have also special attractions. The Moyar and the Bhavani and their tributaries are the home of mahseer and the Carnatic carp. The rivers are under strict conservancy. On the plateau streams have been stocked with trout since 1863, and sport can be obtained at a very moderate cost.

The once famous Ootacamund Hunt was started in 1847. It is now only a memory; but riding is still popular.

The racing season is May and June: accommodation should be booked well in advance.

Kotagiri (Travellers' B.), the oldest station on the Nilgiris, is 13 m. from Coonoor and 18 m. from Ootacamund. A motor-bus service runs from Coonoor railway station and there are buses from Ootacamund and Mettupalaiyam. Kotagiri is 6511 ft. above sea-level. Magnificent views on the road to Ootacamund and also on the road to Kodanad, 6 m. N. by E. The temperature of Kotagiri is halfway between that of Coonoor and Ootacamund; the average for the year may be put at 62 degrees. The rainfall is approximately the same. The first English cottage, built in 1819, still stands in the hamlet of Dimhatti, 1 m. N. of Kotagiri.

Good fishing is available in the various trout-streams and lakes.

Podanur Junction to Cochin

From Podanur (alt. 843 ft.) the railway runs through a gap in the ghats, 20 m. broad, known as the Palghat gap, the only real break in the 600 m. stretch of the W. Ghats. All this portion of the line runs through dense forest, with views of the bare mountain-side close at hand on the N. The mountains on the S. side of the pass are only visible in the distance.

333 m. **Olavakkot** Junction, for a short line (3 m.) to Palghat (D.B.K.), the second town of the Palni District. The fort, built by Haidar Ali in 1766, was captured in 1784, and again in 1790. The glacis, moat and walls are in good preservation.

360 m. **Shoranur** Junction (R.). Across the Ponnani river is a D.B. A branch line was opened in 1927 to Nilambur (42 m. N.) through the Moplah country; Nilambur is famous for its teak forests.

S. of Shoranur the railway crosses the Ponnani river and enters the former Cochin State, now part of Kerala, running (21 m.) to Trichur and (65 m.) to Ernakulam.

At **Trichur** (21 m.; comfortable Tourist B.) there is an ancient temple of Vadakkunnathan, possibly a Buddhist shrine, also a Museum and a Zoological Garden. In Hannington Gardens is the Town Hall and Public Library. The celebration of the **Pooram** festival (April-May) is unique with its elephant procession, fireworks and sumptuous extravagance. On the road between Trichur and Alwaye is **Kaladi,** birthplace of Shri Shankaracharya (8th century) Saint and philosopher (Ashram). Another interesting place accessible by road from Trichur is **Cheruthuruti,** where there is the Kalamandalam Arts Academy, the home of Kerala's music, drama, and dance, especially the Kathakali. There is a R.H. for visitors. Between Trichur and Cochin is a most picturesque backwater.

At **Chowera,** on a road to Munnar, there was formerly an aerodrome.

Alwaye (54 m.), an important industrial complex, Tourist B. and Tourist Home (nearest accommodation to Kaladi), where the railway crosses the Periyar river, has a pleasant climate from March to May with good bathing when adequate water. It is the seat of an important Government "rare earths" plant, which processes the monazite sands of Kerala —a source of radioactive thorium. There are also chemical, glass, aluminium, rayon, tyres and fertiliser factories. The Alwaye Palace on the banks of the river is now a Class I Tourist Bungalow.

Ernakulam (65 m.) (airport served by I.A.C.), capital of the former Cochin State (D.B.K.) (pop. 117,253 in 1971), now part of Kerala. There are excellent hotels in both Western and Indian styles, G.H. Across the lagoon, on Bolghatty Island (Tourist

B. in Old Palace—apply Ernakulam G.H., Marine Drive, for ferry service and for reservations), is the former British Residency, built by the Dutch in 1744, with a beautiful garden.

3 m. across the lagoon, at the N. end of a long, sandy spit, is the town of Kuchi Bandar (1 sq. m.) or **Cochin,** At the N.W. end are the remains of the old Portuguese fort of St Emanuel. An old tombstone, with a Portuguese inscription and the date 1524, is in the Post office compound in Parade Road. The S. of the town is known as Mattancheri.

Between Vypin Island on the N. and Cochin town on the S. is the harbour mouth (1932) with the famous Chinese-style fishing nets. A channel 16,000 ft. long and 450 ft. wide has been cut through the bar and deepened to 37 ft. at low water, and this connects the deep sea with backwaters and canals extending some 100 miles. An island, named after the former Viceroy, Lord Willingdon, has been reclaimed E. of Cochin. Cargo and passenger liners call regularly at the port. A few buildings of modern type, but founded on the old Dutch models, such as the Harbour House and the Malabar Hotel (swimming-bath), have sprung up on Willingdon Island. There is a Government of India Tourist office and a Guide Service. It is well worth while to take a tour of the harbour, run by the Tourist Office, as the views are beautiful. The port is equipped with deep-water wharves, transit sheds, warehouses, and through railway connections with the broad-gauge system of India, as well as with air connections to Bombay, Madras, Colombo and Bangalore.

At the S. end of the long main street, in Mattancheri, is the Jews' quarter, with two synagogues. That of the white Jews is floored with Chinese 18th-century tiles. The Jews are divided into two sections—the Black, who claim to have settled in 587 B.C., and the White, who are believed to have arrived here at a much later date. Black Jews possess a copper grant from the Prince of Malabar, which is dated A.D. 388, or, according to Buchanan-Hamilton, A.D. 490. The oldest tombstone in the Beth-haim ("House of Life"), or Jewish cemetery, at the back of the Jews' quarter, is dated 1666.

The old Mattancheri Palace containing some frescoes from the Hindu epics, was built by the Portuguese in 1515 for the Ruler. Elephantiasis (alternatively known as "Cochin leg") is unhappily common in Cochin.

Cochin (pop. 438,000 in 1971) is of special interest as the earliest European settlement in India. A friar, Jordanus, visited it in 1324, Ibn Batuta in 1347, a Chinese in 1409, and a Persian in 1442. In 1500 the Portuguese adventurer Cabral landed at Cochin and met with a friendly reception, returning to Portugal with a cargo of pepper. He was followed by Juan da Nova Castelho. In 1502 Vasco da Gama, on his second voyage, came to Cochin, and established a factory.

Albuquerque, the Portuguese admiral, arrived (1503) in time to succour the Cochin Raja, besieged by the Zamorin of Calicut. He built a wooden fort, "Manuel Kolati", or Fort St Emanuel, on Cochin Island. Franciscan friars, who accompanied him, erected a chapel where the Church of St Francis stands. (The 20th-century Santa Cruz Cathedral should also be visited.)

Upon Albuquerque's return the Zamorin invaded Cochin; but Duarte Pacheco resisted all attacks and forced him to retreat to Calicut. In 1505 Francisco Almeyda, the first Portuguese Viceroy (without territory), came with a large fleet and was in 1510 succeeded by Albuquerque. On Christmas Day 1524 da Gama died here, and was buried in the principal chapel of the Franciscan monastery, then dedicated to St Anthony. His body was afterwards (1538) removed to Portugal and rests in the Belem Convent at Lisbon, but his tombstone is in the church.

In 1544 St Francis Xavier, the

apostle of the Indies, made many converts. In 1557 the Church of Santa Cruz was consecrated as the cathedral of a Bishop. In 1577 the Society of Jesus published at Cochin the first book printed in India. In 1585 Cochin was visited by the English traveller Ralph Fitch in the course of a voyage from Sri Lanka to Goa.

In 1616 the English (Keeling) engaged to assist the Zamorin in attacking Cochin, on an understanding that an English factory was to be established there. This, however, was not founded until 1635. In 1663 the town and fort were captured from the Portuguese by the Dutch, and the English retired to Ponnani. The Dutch greatly improved the place and its trade, but the Franciscan Church, which still survives, with interesting Portuguese and Dutch monuments on each side, was converted into a Protestant chapel, and the cathedral was turned into a warehouse.

In 1773, the north part of Cochin was subjugated by Haidar Ali up to a strip taken by Travancore (1757) across which the Vypin lines were made (1764). Tipu Sultan attacked the lines (1789) and war with the British resulted. By treaty, protection was secured for an annual subsidy. In 1795 Cochin town was taken by the British from the Dutch.

The **Malabar Backwaters.**[1]—By a network of lagoons and canals the entire journey from Kotatyyam to Quilon (p. 551) can be made by water. Delightful leisurely trips can be arranged, passing through beautiful scenery. Particulars from Tourist Information Bureaux. A short trip from Alleppey to Kottayyam (p. 527) takes under 3 hrs. There is a regular ferry service.

Alleppey (pop. 160,000 in 1971) (Govt. R.H., new R.H.), the chief port of Travancore, is built on either side of the main waterway, with occasional bridges over wide canals. There is an extensive industry in coir matting and a good beach. The snake-boat race, held annually in August, is one of the great sights of "Tourist India". The chief event is "The Prime Minister's Trophy", which Jowaharlal Nehru presented for competition. Some of the snake-boats carry 100 oarsmen. There are special viewing facilities for tourists.

[1] See Gopalan, A. J., *Kerala Past and Present* (London, 1959).

Christians in Malabar. In both Cochin and the former State of Travancore Christians, known as Nazaráni (i.e. Nazarenes), are numerous. Tradition ascribes the first conversions to the Apostle Thomas, at Cranganur (A.D. 52). After the condemnation of the Nestorian heresy by the Council of Ephesus in A.D. 431 colonisation by Syrian refugees and conversions among high-caste Hindus followed.

When the Portuguese landed, they found a flourishing Christian community, chiefly Nestorian, and governed either by bishops sent by one or other of the Eastern patriarchs or under Metrans (Metropolitans) of their own. Their prosperity and influence is a striking tribute to the tolerance of the Hindu rulers of the surrounding country. At first the Portuguese made no attempt to interfere with the doctrines or ritual; but, after the Inquisition had been set up at Goa in 1560, proselytism began, accompanied by in the main successful efforts to cut off the Syrian Christian Maronites from communication with the Patriarchs by interception of their correspondence and by seizure and imprisonment of several Bishops on their way from Asia Minor to take charge of Malabar sees.

The first fissure in the Christian Church in Malabar dates from 1663. Mar Gregory the Bishop, who was sent by the Patriarch of Antioch in 1665, being a Jacobite, the majority henceforward became known as the Jacobite Syrians, while the minority who adhered to the Church of Rome, are called Romo-Syrians. In 1663 the Dutch captured Cochin and an era of tolerance followed, but internal dissensions and disputes in the matter of doctrine and liturgy continued.

Of Roman Catholics, some use the Latin rite under the Archbishop of Verapoly (Cochin) and the Bishop of Quilon, chiefly recent converts from the lower castes, and Romo-Syrians under Indian Vicars-Apostolic, owing allegiance to and appointed by the Pope of Rome. Then there is the so-called Nestorian Church under a Bishop from Mardin appointed by the Patriarch of Nineveh, and the Mar Thoma Christians under Metrans appointed by the Patriarch of Antioch, who are Romish in doctrinal beliefs, but do not acknowledge the Papal supremacy. The Reformed and Jacobite Churches divided (1896) under separate Metropolitans. Among the Protestants the formation of the Church of South India has led to extensive reorganisation.

Kottayam (D.B.K., Tourist B.), 45 m. S.E. of Ernakulam, is the chief Christian centre in Travancore and the see (1879) of the Bishop in Travancore and Cochin. There is a regular ferry service through the lagoons to Allepey (2½ hr.).

Periyar is S.E. of Cochin about 120 m. *via* Kottayam, and about 70 m. S. of Kodaikanal (p. 545, Route 33); alt. 2000 ft. The dam of the Periyar river irrigation scheme is 1240 ft. by 173 ft. high. Water which flowed to the Indian Ocean has been turned through a tunnel 5940 ft. long so as to flow into the Bay of Bengal by the Vaigai river, irrigating the country.

A **Wild Life Sanctuary**, unique in India, 300 m. in extent, centering on **Thekkady** was created round the lake by the former Travancore State authorities, and there are now numerous wild elephant, bison and a few tigers in the vicinity. There is a State Guest House on the lake, and motor launches are available from which elephant and bison can sometimes be seen especially in the early morning. **Thekkady** is 170 m. by road from Cochin and 90 m. from Madurai. The drive up from Kottayam to Periyar is very beautiful. There is a Tourist B. at Peermade (46 m.) also an Hotel (*Aranya Nivas*) at Thekkady. Tourist Bs. and Dormitories available at Thekkady and nearby places. Guides available from the Game Department, also fishing permits. Launches arranged by Hotel or by Wild Life Reservation Officer.

Main Line to Calicut and Mangalore

The main line proceeds from Shoranur Junction (p. 524) to

388 m. from Madras, **Tirur** (D.B.). Roads for Ponnani and Malappuram meet here. On the backwaters motor-boats ply, in connection with the trains, to

Ponnani (D.B.); a religious centre of the Moplahs (Mappillas), a strict Muslim sect peculiar to the W. coast; and the place of residence of the Makhdum Tangal, their spiritual head. The religious college over which he presides is attended by Mullas from all parts of Malabar. His office is hereditary in the female line, in conformity with the custom among Malabar Hindus. Malappuram, 14 m. from Tirur, is the centre of a country in which there have been many Moplah risings.

393 m. **Tanur** (D.B.). The Government Fisheries Department has a fish-curing and canning factory here. A fine mosque. Visited by St Francis Xavier, 1546.

407 m. the Ferok river is crossed to Ferok station, for the port of Beypore.

414 m. **Calicut** (Kozhikode) station (D.B., fine Tourist B., G.Hs., *Sea Queen* hotel and others), pop. 333,000 in 1971. Anchorage 2 m. from shore. Golf course. Motor-bus services to Manjeri (30 m.) and to Vayittiri (59 m.), on the ghat road from Calicut to (131 m.) Mysore City (p. 494) through the Wynaad (see p. 529), also to Ootacamund.

Buchanan - Hamilton[1] wrote: "When Cheruman Perumal had divided Malabar, and had no principality remaining to bestow on the ancestors of the Tamuri, he gave that

[1] *Journey through Mysore, Canara and Malabar* (1807), vol. 2, p. 474.

chief his sword, with all the territory in which a cock crowing at a small temple here could be heard. This formed the original dominions of the Tamuri, and was called Colicudu, or the Cock-crowing." Others have held that the name of the place is Kallikot, the fort on the Kallayi river. The term Tamuri is a corruption of Samatiri, or sea-lord, and was, before 1500, transformed into Zamorin. It is still the title of the Raja (a personal title) of Calicut, who enjoys a pension.

To the S. the Moplah quarter has several mosques. To the N. at West Hill railway station, 3 m. from Calicut railway station, there are barracks. In the centre is the Anglo-Indian quarter, with R.C. and Anglican Churches, and near the Judge's Court are the remains of the old palace and a new palace.

Facing the sea there are some better-class residences, the Custom House, and the Club. There is a temple in Talli, the Brahmin quarter. Cotton cloth, originally exported from this town, derives from it its name of calico. The Basel Mission once started a large textile factory here, now State-owned. There is a flourishing timber industry and boat-building yard.

At Calicut, on 20th May 1498, arrived Vasco da Gama, after a voyage of ten months and two days from Lisbon, recorded in the "Os Lusiades" of Camoens. Calicut and the adjoining coast were, at that time, under the suzerainty of Vijayanagar (p. 426); and the town contained a Brahmin temple. A memorial tablet swept away by the sea was restored in 1939. In 1509 the Maréchal of Portugal, Don Fernando Coutinho, made an attack, but was slain and his forces repulsed with great loss. In 1510 Albuquerque landed, burnt the town, and plundered the palace, but was eventually obliged to sail away with great loss. In 1513 the Zamorin made peace with the Portuguese, and permitted them to build a fortified factory.

English factors came (1616) to a factory. In 1695 Captain Kidd the pirate ravaged the port. In 1766 Haidar Ali invaded the country, and the Zamorin, finding that offers of submission would be in vain, barricaded himself in his palace, and, setting fire to it, perished. Haidar Ali soon left, and the territory revolted, but was reconquered in 1773. In 1781 the victors were expelled by the British, from Tellicherry, but in 1789 Tipu Sultan overran the country and laid it waste. Coconut and sandal trees were cut down, and plantations of pepper were torn up by the roots. The town was almost entirely demolished, and the materials carried 6 m. to the S.E., to build a fort and town called Farrukhabad, "Fortunate City". The next year Tipu Sultan's general, Martab Khan, was totally defeated and taken prisoner by Col. Hartley at Tirurangadi, 15 m. S. of Feroke, who captured the so-called "Fortunate City"; and in 1792 the whole territory was ceded to the British by the Treaty of Seringapatam.

It is said that two pillars of the old palace in which da Gama was received still remain. The Portuguese leader knelt down on his way to some Hindu idols, taking them for distorted images of Catholic saints. "Perhaps they may be devils", said one of the sailors. "No matter", said da Gama, "I kneel before them and worship the true God."

451 m. **Mahé** (named after M. Mahé de Labourdonnais when he captured it in 1725—originally called Mayyazhi) was a dependent territory of 2½ sq. m., belonging to the French —their only possession on the W. coast, under an Administrator. It was made over to the Indian Government along with the other French settlements.

It is finely situated on high ground overlooking the river, the entrance of which is closed by rocks. None but small craft can pass the bar in safety, and that only in fair weather; but the river is navigable for boats to a considerable distance inland. On a high hill some way off is seen the Mission House built by the Basel missionaries. From this hill there is a beautiful view of the wooded mountains of Wynaad.

Mahé was taken by the British under Hector Munro in 1761, but after several vicissitudes it was restored to the French in 1817.

There is excellent fishing.

456 m. **Tellicherry** (D.B.K.). Anchorage 1¼ m. from shore. Motor service to Iritti, 32 m., at the bottom of the Periambadi Ghat good mahseer fishing. There is a reef of rocks which forms a natural breakwater and provides good bathing. In 1783 H.M. ship "Superb", of seventy-four guns, was lost here. The fort is built close to the sea, about 40 ft. above its level. The whole of the N.W. side of the citadel is occupied by an old lofty building. The town contains good examples of the better Moplah houses. The main bazar street is one of the most fascinating in Malabar, and the coast scenery and bathing are delightful.

The English factory at Tellicherry, which was established chiefly for the purchase of pepper and cardamoms, was first opened in 1683, under orders from the Presidency of Surat. It was the first regular English factory on the Malabar coast. In 1708 the East India Company obtained from the Cherikal Raja a grant of the fort. In 1781 Haidar Ali attacked the place, but was compelled by a vigorous sally of the garrison to raise the siege.

The cardamoms and coffee of the Wynaad and S. Coorg are exported from Tellicherry. The **Wynaad** is a plateau about 3000 ft. above sea-level in the E. of the Malabar District, containing many tea, coffee, and pepper estates.

Two main roads lead into the Wynaad; both are practicable for motors. The Calicut-Mysore road (p. 495) passes through the planting centres of (39 m.) **Vayittiri** (small R.H., Club) and (65 m.) **Manantoddy** (2558 ft. above sea-level; D.B.). About 2 m. from Manantoddy on the banks of the river is the Vallurkavu or Fish Pagoda, dedicated to the goddess Durga. The carp are sacred and merit is acquired by feeding them. At Kalpatta (6 m. from Vayittiri) a branch road (motorable) runs through (14 m.) Sultan's Battery (Ganapathivattam) to (48 m.) Gundlupet in Karnataka State, and thence (36 m.) to Mysore City.

The other road runs from Tellicherry to (48 m.) Manantoddy, with a good bus service.

Sultan's Battery (Tourist B.) is a fort built by Tipu Sultan on the site of the police station. 4 m. E. of Sultan's Battery is a natural fissure in the rock; the walls are covered with crude drawings and there are four inscriptions (see *Indian Antiquary*, vol. 30).

469 m. **Cannanore** (D.B.K., and Tourist B.; two H.; also a Club, golf-course, and good sea-bathing, not from Hs. but from beach (2 m.)). Anchorage 2 m. from shore. The old Cantonment is on a jutting portion of land, which forms the N.W. side of the bay. Near the end of this is a promontory, on which stands Fort St Angelo, built by the Portuguese (1505) at the edge of cliffs from 30 ft. to 50 ft. high. The bungalows of officials are most of them built on these cliffs, and enjoy a cool sea-breeze. Farther inland, and in the centre of the Cantonment, are the Church and burial-ground, contiguous to one another. The Portuguese Church, once the Portuguese factory, is close to the sea. The old Moplah town, with some picturesque mosques, the Raja's palace and narrow crooked lanes, lie round the Bay to the S. of the Fort. The Portuguese were expelled by the Dutch, who subsequently sold the place to a Moplah family, the head of which is called the Ali Raja (sea-lord), or Bibi if a woman. His territory consisted of the town and a little of the adjacent country on the S., and he also claimed sovereignty over the Laccadive islands. These islands were sequestrated for mismanagement, and were administered for over thirty years by the Collector of Mala-

bar. Eventually in 1911 they were finally ceded, and the Raja was given a pension.

In 1768 Ali Raja, then ruling Chief, readily submitted to Haidar Ali, and joined him on his invading Malabar. In the war with Tipu Sultan, in 1784, Cannanore was occupied by the British; but on the conclusion of peace next year it was restored to the Bibi. She again dallied with Tipu Sultan, and Cannanore was finally stormed and captured by General Abercromby in 1790.

473 m. **Azhikkal** or Baliapatam (Valarpattanam), on a river crossed by a bridge 1288 ft. long (1906). Close by is the bold bluff eminence of **Mount Deli** (720 ft.) on the coast, a well-known landmark. It was the first land in India sighted by Vasco da Gama on 18th May 1498, on his way S. to Calicut.

521 m. the Payasavali river.

543 m. the Netravati river.

550 m. **Mangalore** headquarters of the S. Kanara District (D.B.K. and P.W.D. (pop. 214,000 in 1971). Reached by air from Bombay, Belgaum, Bangalore, Cochin and Madras. Inspection Bungalow at Kadri). The place is separated from the sea by a backwater round two sides of a peninsula. The great bazar stretches N. on the edge of the back water about ½ m. From the hill on which the old lighthouse stands a remarkable view of the coast and the hills can be had.

In ancient times Mangalore was a place of very great commerce. Ibn Batuta, in the middle of the 14th century, mentions 4000 Muslim merchants as resident there. Forbes speaks of it, in 1772, as the principal seaport in the dominions of Haidar Ali, whose ships were built at Mangalore of the fine teak produced on the slopes of the Western Ghats. Coffee is exported from Coorg and Mysore, but this is the principal cashew nut port in the world.

Mangalore, captured by the British in 1768, was gallantly defended by Colonel John Campbell, of H.M. 42nd Foot, from 6th May 1783 to 23rd January 1784, with a garrison of 1850 men, against Tipu Sultan's whole army, but in the end had to surrender with all the honours of war.

In 1918 the Swiss Mission resigned its commercial activities—printing, book-binding, carpentry, tile manufacture. There are two colleges affiliated to the Madras University—the Government College and the Jesuit College of St Aloysius (Museum).

There are three places containing interesting Jain buildings. At Mudbidri, in a stone temple with pitched roof called the Shreeh Candranath Swamy Tribhuvana Tilaka, are remarkable Jain carvings: at Karkal and Venur are two colossal images, the third—there are only three in the world—being at Sravana Belgola. Mudbrdii is 22 m. N.E. by a good road, and Karkal is 12 m. farther N.; Venur is 16 m. farther E., and not easily accessible. Motor-bus services are run to Karkal, Mudbidri, Udipi, Kandapur; to Bantval, Beltangadi, Puttur; to Mercara in Coorg; to Shimoga in Mysore; and to Goa *via* Karwar (see p. 531).

From Mangalore to Bombay by Sea

Mangalore is the terminus of the West Coast Section of the Southern Ry.; it is also the ultimate port of call from the middle of September until the middle of May for a service of steamers, twice a week, to Bombay (412 m.), The steamers leave Mangalore every Saturday and Tuesday morning and arrive at Bombay (Alexandra Dock, Ferry Wharf) in two days, calling *en route* as below.

Malpé (35 m. from Mangalore by sea) is the best natural port in S. Kanara; the roadstead is sheltered by the island of Darya Bahadurgarh. 3 m. to S.W. are St Mary's Isles, where Vasco da Gama landed in 1498 and set up a cross.

Kandapur (19 m. from Malpé), S. of an estuary into which three rivers flow; an ancient port which dates back to the time of the Bednur Kings (16th century). The ruined city of **Bednur** (Hydernagar), in Karnataka

State, lies about 30 m. inland on a high plateau, about 4000 ft. above sea-level.

Bhatkal (19 m. from Kandapur) is the first port in Karnataka and lies 3 m. from the mouth of the river. It was the port for Vijayanagar, *via* Honawar, higher up the coast.

Kumpta (31 m. from Bhatkal) is on a tidal creek to S. of Tadri river; vessels anchor ½ m. off the mouth.

Tadri (7 m.) is a small port at the mouth of the river; vessels anchor off the bar.

Karwar (D.B., 22 m. farther N.) is the headquarters of the district of N. Kanara and an attractive sea resort; anchorage 500 yd. from the shore; on the Kalinadi river. From 1638 to 1752 an English factory was established here and carried on a trade in pepper. The N. fort was taken by the Portuguese in 1752, and by 1801 old Karwar (3 m. E.) was in ruins. There is a lighthouse on the Oyster Rocks, and 5 m. to the S.E. is the island of Anjediva, formerly Portuguese, where many English soldiers died, awaiting the transfer to Bombay. For Mormugão (Goa), which is 45 m. from Karwar (see p. 449, Route 24).

Vengurla (29 m. from Mormugão and 196 m. from Bombay). It was ceded to the British in 1812 by the Rani of Sawantwari, and was once on the border of that State. In former times it was notorious as a haunt of pirates. The public offices are in the old Dutch factory (1638); a British factory was established here in 1772. From Vengurla the steamers proceed direct to Bombay.

At **Ratnagiri** (84 m. N. of Vengurla) King Thibaw of Burma was interned (1886).

ROUTE 33

MADRAS to COLOMBO by the Southern Ry., by way of **Chingleput, Tindivanam** (for **Gingee**), **Villupuram** (for **Pondicherry**), **Cuddalore** (for **Fort St David**), **Porto Novo, Chidambaram, Mayavaram** (for **Tiruvarur** and **Tranquebar**), **Kumbakonam, TANJORE** (for **Negapatam**), **Tiruchirapalli, Dindigal, Kodaikanal, MADURAI** (for **Tuticorin, Tinnevelly, Kuttalam, Cape Comorin, Quilon** and **Trivandrum**), **Rameswaram** (for **Talaimannar** in **Sri Lanka**).

The Ceylon Boat Mail train runs from Madras to Dhanushkhodi (456 m.). There is a ferry to Talaimannar and a railway runs to Colombo. Travellers commonly go by air.

Madras. Egmore station (p. 506).

35 m. from Madras is **Chingleput** Junction (R., D.B. ¼ m.) for Kanchipuram (Conjeeveram) (Route 31) and Arkonam, junction (R.), on the railway to Poona and Bombay (Route 23).

45 m. The Palar river is crossed by a bridge and a road causeway.

76 m. **Tindivanam** station (R., D.B.).

(1) 24 m. N.W. of this station is **Wandiwash** (Vandivasu). Here may be seen a ruined fort and, 2 m. to the N., a rocky hill. Between the hill and the fort was fought, on 21st January 1760, the battle which broke the French power in S. India. Count Lally had been holding Wandiwash, but was obliged by a mutiny of his troops to withdraw to Pondicherry. Coote[1] occupied Wandiwash in November 1759, and left a garrison which Lally continued to besiege against the advice of Bussy, while Coote was returning. Lally was defeated with heavy loss and the capture of all his guns, ammunition and

[1] See note on p. 534.

stores. The battle was fought by the Europeans only; the sepoys looked on, Bussy being taken prisoner. The fort was abandoned and blown up in February 1783.

(2) 18 m. W. of the Tindivanam station by road is **Gingee** (Chenji), the most famous fort in the Carnatic. (Motor-bus service; R.H.: food to be taken.) The fortress comprises three strongly fortified hills connected by walls 3 m. in perimeter, with seven gates. The highest and most important hill, Rajagiri, about 500 ft. high, consists of a ridge terminating in an overhanging bluff, facing the S., and falling with a precipitous sweep to the plain on the N. On the summit of this bluff stands the citadel. On the S.W., where the crest of the ridge meets the base of the bluff, across a narrow and steep ravine, three walls, each about 20 ft. or 25 ft. high, rise one behind the other. On the N. side the Fort is defended by a narrow chasm, artificially prolonged and deepened, a wooden bridge over it being the only means of ingress into the citadel through a narrow stone gateway facing the bridge.

Of the ruined buildings inside the most remarkable are the two temples and the Kaliyana Mahal, a square court surrounded by rooms for the ladies of the Governor's household. In the middle is a square tower of eight storeys, with a pyramidal roof.

Other objects of interest are—the great gun on the top of Rajagiri, which has the figures 7560 stamped on it; the Raja's bathing-stone, a large smooth slab of granite; and the Prisoners' Well, a very singular boulder about 15 ft. to 20 ft. high, with a natural hollow passing through it, poised on a rock near the Chakrakulam, and surmounted by a low, circular, brick wall.

Gingee was a stronghold of the Vijayanagar power, built 1442. In 1638 it fell to Bijapur. In 1677 Sivaji took it by stratagem, and it remained in Mahratta hands for twenty-one years. In 1690 the armies of the Delhi Emperor, under Zulfikar Khan were despatched against Raja Ram, son of Sivaji, at Gingee: the fort fell in 1698, and became the headquarters of the standing army in Arcot. In 1750 the French, under d'Auteuil and M. Bussy, captured it by night and held it for eleven years, surrendering after night attack, in 1762.

99 m. **Villupuram** Junction (R., D.B.). Sleeping room at station; ticket to be purchased at the Booking-office. There are locomotive workshops here.

Branch lines N.W. to Katpadi (p. 497), passing through Tiruvannamalai (which stood in the way of Haidar Ali's invasions) on the Penner river, and E. to Pondicherry and Cuddalore (p. 504). **Tiruvannamalai** (Ramana Ashram, R.R.). Pilgrimage centre at base of Arunachala Hill (trad. home of Siva and Parbati and renowned for the great Tamil Saint Ramana Maharishi, who lived and died there). There are over 100 temples, one of them, the Arunachaleswar, dedicated to Siva and Parbati, is said to be the largest in S. India and is contemporary with Madurai. Length 1480 ft.: breadth 680 ft. The E. Gopuram is 216 ft. high with 13 stories. Overseas visitors are welcome at the Ashram. 2 m. from R.S.

A chord from Villupuram S. to (33 m.) Vriddhachalam Junction and (110 m.) Tiruchirapalli Junction (p. 540). On this line, 7 m. from Villupuram, is the Ponniar river.

From Vriddhachalam (R.) branch lines run E. to (38 m.) Cuddalore, and W. to (87 m.) Salem (p. 519).

Close by is the hill fort of Thiagar, which changed hands often during the Seven Years War.

46 m. the Vellar river.

102 m. the Coleroon river, near Srirangam.

104 m. the Cauvery river.

Pondicherry Branch

16 m. E. from Villupuram the Gingee river is crossed, and the

Pondicherry railway terminates at 24 m. from Villupuram. 104 m. by road from Madras is **Pondicherry** (Puducheri), which was the capital of the French settlements in India[1] until the 1st November 1954, on which date they were handed over to Indian administration after 250 years of French rule.

The town, founded 1674 by François Martin, and rebuilt by M. Jean Law between 1756-77, is divided by a canal into White (La Ville Blanche, next the sea) and Black Towns. The main streets run N. and S. from the Place Charles de Gaulle, parallel to the sea. In the public garden there is a statue of Joan of Arc and a Memorial of the First World War, unveiled 1938.

There is a large trade in groundnuts, oil-seeds, and cotton cloth.

Pondicherry is not a very "live" town and is best known to foreign visitors today as the place where the philosopher Aurobindo Ghose lived and worked for many years. His memory is preserved by an Ashram which attracts visitors from all over the world, an International Centre of Education and a new city, **Auroville**, designed as a focus of international culture, with a growing student population. The leader of the community was a French woman known as The Mother, who died in 1974, aged 97. She is the chief disciple of Sri Aurobindo. The buildings at Auroville already completed are of great interest and should not be missed.

The Hôtel de l'Europe occupies the mansion of Camille Guerre, a famous local *avocat*. The Government House, a handsome building, is situated at the N. side of the *Place* within 300 yd. of the sea. The church, built 1855, of Notre Dame des Anges, has two square towers. The tomb of Bussy, whom Orme described as "the only man of distinction who served under Dupleix", is in the cemetery (apply to the Curé) opposite the church; he died at Pondicherry in 1785, aged 67, when holding the office of Governor.

At the site of the former *Pier*, is a semicircle of eight pillars, 38 ft. high, of a greyish-blue stone, brought from Gingee (p. 532), which is 40 m. distant. On the third pillar on the left side, looking towards the sea, is an astronomical plan by some savants who were charged with fixing the longitude of Pondicherry. There is a French Institute and in the Public Library are some valuable records. At the S. end of the promenade is the Hôtel de Ville. There is also a Lighthouse, with a light 89 ft. above the sea. European cemeteries S. of the railway station are worth a visit.

In 1672 Pondicherry, then a small village, was purchased by the French from the King of Bijapur. In 1693 the Dutch took Pondicherry, but restored it in 1697 at the Peace of Ryswick. Under Dupleix it increased wonderfully. On the 26th of August 1748 Admiral Boscawen besieged it with a large force, but was compelled to raise the siege on the 6th of October.

During the Seven Years War, on the 29th of April 1758 Lally landed with his own regiment and that of Lorraine and commenced a war, which ended ruinously for the French. In the beginning of July 1760 Colonel Coote began to blockade Pondicherry. On the 2nd of September the British carried the bound-hedge of cactus and two of four redoubts which defended it. Hopes of deliverance in the minds of the French were dispelled by the arrival of fresh British men-of-war from Ceylon and Madras. On 16th January 1761, the town surrendered and was razed except for two temples.

In 1765 Pondicherry was restored by the Treaty of Paris of 1763. In the War for American Independence, on 9th August 1778, Sir Hector Munro again laid siege to it. On the 10th Sir E. Vernon, with four ships, fought an indecisive battle in the roads with five French ships under M. Tronjoly, who some days after sailed off at

[1] See *History of the French in India*, by G. B. Malleson (Grant, Edinburgh, 1893).

night and left the town to its fate. Pondicherry, after an obstinate defence, was surrendered in the middle of October by M. Bellecombe, the Governor; and shortly after, the fortifications were destroyed. In 1783 it was retransferred to the French, and on the 23rd of August 1793 retaken by the British.

The Treaty of Amiens (1802) restored it to its original masters, whereupon Napoleon sent thither General de Caen, with seven other generals and 1400 regulars. He found the British still in possession and sailed at once for Mauritius. The place was then included in S. Arcot (Cuddalore). When restored to the French in 1817 the population was only 25,000. The place declared for de Gaulle and the Free French in 1940, so that occupation was unnecessary.

The former **French India.**—The French possessions in India, on the date of handing over to the Indian Republic in 1962, consisted of the four establishments of Pondicherry and Karikal on the Coromandel coast, Yanaon on the Orissa coast, and Mahé on the Malabar coast. Pondicherry, in particular, still retains its typically French appearance and culture, and is well worth a visit. It is represented in the Lok Sabha by a nominated member.

The total area of French India at the time of handing over was 185 sq. m. with a population of 369,000.

Former Main Line

107 m. from Madras the Ponniar river.

126 m. the Gadilam river.

126 m. is **Cuddalore** (total pop. 101,000 in 1971) New Town station (D.B.).

Fort St David, 1½ m. from New Town, is interesting only for its history. From 1690, after purchase from the Mahratta, Sambhaji, son of Sivaji, by the East India Company, it remained in the hands of the British until 1758 (Clive being Deputy Governor in 1756), when it was taken by Lally and destroyed, after many attempts from 1747 onwards, but restored by the Peace of 1783.[1] All that now remains of the fort are the ditch, the foundations of the ramparts, and some masses of the fallen walls.

128 m. **Cuddalore** (Old Town) Junction for a line W. to Vriddichellam Junction (R.) and Salem.

From New Town station Fort St David can most conveniently be visited; it is also nearest to the D.B.

145 m. **Porto Novo** station. The town stands on the N. bank of the River Vellar, close to the sea, and is called by the inhabitants Mahmud Bandar and Farangipettai. The Portuguese settled here about 1575, being the first Europeans who landed on the Coromandel coast. They lost it to the Dutch in 1660, who, however, abandoned their factory in 1678 and went to Pulicat (p. 427). In 1690 the English began trading. Iron ore from Salem was smelted, 1833-38.

Within 3 m. to the N., close to the seashore, a very important Indian battle was fought. Sir Eyre Coote[2] had returned to Porto Novo on the 19th of June 1781, after having been repelled the day before in an attack on the fortified pagoda of Chidambaram.

Haidar Ali marched from the W., took up and fortified an advantageous position on the only road by which the British could advance to Cuddalore. The British force consisted of 2000 Europeans, 6000 sepoys and 41 guns, Haidar Ali's forces of 40,000 Indians (some French-trained) and 100 guns. Sir J. Malcolm said: "If a moment was to be named when the existence of the British power de-

[1] That Bernadotte, afterwards Marshal of France and King of Sweden, was captured in a sortie during the siege of 1783, is not authenticated.

[2] Sir Eyre Coote was with the 39th Foot at Plassey; won the great victory of Wandiwash on 21st January 1760; took Pondicherry on 16th January 1761; was made K.C.B. in 1771; was Commander-in-Chief in Bengal, 1779; defeated Haidar Ali at Arni (74 m. S.W. of Madras) on 2nd June 1782; and was sent again in 1783 to check Haidar Ali, but died at Madras, worn out by his campaigns, on 27th April 1783.

pended upon its native troops, we should fix upon the Battle of Porto Novo. Driven to the seashore, attacked by an enemy exulting in recent success, confident in his numbers, and strong in the terror of his name, every circumstance combined that could dishearten the small body of men on whom the fate of the war depended. Not a heart shrank from the trial." The victory was won on 1st July 1781. Coote especially praised the steadiness of the 73rd Highlanders and presented them with a sum of money to purchase silver-mounted pipes in honour of the day.

151 m. **Chidambaram** (Chillumbrum) station, a capital of the Cholas (907-1310), on the Coleroon river. (I.B., Municipal B.). Renowned as the home of many S. Indian saints and poets.

The Temples at Chidambaram are the oldest in the S. of India, and portions of them are gems of Dravidian art. The principal temple (Nabaraja) is sacred to Siva, and is affirmed to have been erected, or at least embellished, by Hiranya Varna Chakravarti, the "golden-coloured Emperor", said to have originally borne the name of Swetavarma, the "white-coloured", on account of his leprosy, and to have come S. on a pilgrimage from Kashmir (*c.* A.D. 500). He miraculously recovered at Chidambaram after taking a bath in the tank in the centre of the temple, and thereupon rebuilt or enlarged the temples. He is said to have brought 3000 Brahmans from the N.

By tradition, Vira Chola Raja (A.D. 927-997) saw the Sabhapati (Siva) dancing on the seashore with his wife, Parvati, and erected the Kanak Sabha, or golden shrine, in memory of the god, who is here called *Natesa* or Nateswar, "God of Dancing".

The whole area, thirty-two acres, is surrounded by two high walls. The outer wall of all is 1800 ft. long on the E. and 1480 ft. from E. to W. At the four points of the compass are four vast gopurams, those on the N. and S. being about 160 ft. high. The 108 classical postures relating to Natya Sastra, the Science of Dancing, are depicted. E. of the temple is a tank, 315 ft. by 180 ft., S. of which is the Hall of 1000 Pillars, which is 340 ft. long and 190 ft. broad.

The Temple of Parvati (N.E.) or Sivakami Amman (14th century), the wife of Siva, is remarkable for its porch. The roof is supported by cantilever brackets with transverse purlins till a space of only 9 ft. is left to be spanned. The partly projecting enclosure is elaborate, with two storeys of pillars.

Adjoining this Temple of Parvati is one to Subrahmanya, the enclosure of which is 250 ft. by 305 ft. The images of a peacock and two elephants stand before it, then a portico with four pillars in front, with an inner court. Fergusson assigned 1700 as the date. Other shrines to Subrahmanya, and to Ganesh (the effigy is said to be the largest in India), are in the corner of the great enclosure.

The enclosure of this principal temple is W. of the tank. In the S.W. corner of this enclosure is a temple to Parvati, and in the centre of the S. side an idol of Nateswar. The sanctuary consists of two parts. In this is the most sacred image of the dancing Siva, which is that of a naked giant with four arms, his right leg planted on the ground and his left lifted sideways. The roof of this building is covered with plates of gilt copper.

There is also a tiny shrine, of which Fergusson wrote: "The oldest thing now existing here. . . . A porch of fifty-six pillars about 8 ft. high, and most delicately carved, resting on a stylobate, ornamented with dancing figures, more graceful and more elegantly executed than any others of their class, so far as I know, in S. India. At the sides are wheels and horses, the whole being intended to represent a car. . . ."

At **Anamalainagar** is the residential University, named after its founder, Raja Sir Anamalai Chettia. The library is well worth a visit.

158 m. The Coleroon river. Devikotta is at the mouth.

174 m. from Madras is **Mayavaram** Junction (D.B.K.) from which a branch line takes off for Tranquebar. The town, 3 m. distant, is a place of pilgrimage in November, the Siva Pagoda has one large gopuram and one small one. To the W. of the Great Gopuram is a Teppa Kulam Tank, in which the god is rowed on a raft.

Arantangi Branch

From Mayavaram a line runs S. to 10 m. Peralam, junction for a short line of 14 m. to the former French settlement of **Karikal,** situated on a branch of the Cauvery, 12 m. N. of Negapatam (p. 540).

The line then continues to (24 m.) **Tiruvarur** (on the Southern Ry. line from Tanjore to Negapatam).

At Tiruturaipundi Junction (40 m.) there is a branch (29 m.) S.E. to Point Calimere (Kalimettu, "Hill of the Euphorbia"). On the beach at the Point is a column, 90 ft. high, which bears an inscription on the S.W. face, recording its erection by Sarfoji, the Raja of Tanjore, in 1814, in commemoration of "the downfall of Bonaparte"; it was used at one time as a lighthouse.

The temple at **Tiruvarur** (Tanjore District) should not be confused with the Vishnu temple of Viraraghava at Tiruvallur (p. 441). Fergusson writes of it (*Ind. Arch.*, 1, 367[1]):

"The nucleus here was a small village temple. It is a double shrine, dedicated to Valmikeswara, or Siva, and his consort, standing in a cloistered court which measures 191 ft. by 156 ft. over all, and has one gopuram in front."

The deity is said to have been made from an ant-hill (Valmika).

". . . At some subsequent period a second or outer court was added, measuring 470 ft. each way, with two gopurams, higher than the original one, and containing within its walls numberless little shrines and porches. Additions were again made at some subsequent date, the whole being enclosed in a court 957 ft. by 726 ft. this time with five gopurams, irregular in height and spacing . . . and several important shrines."

One shrine is dedicated to Sri Tyagaraja-Swami, who performed 364 miracles (lilas) here. It was intended to endow the temple with one of those great halls which were considered indispensable in temples of the first class, and generally intended to have 1000 columns. This has only 807, and almost one-half of these mere posts, not fitted to carry a roof of any sort. A wooden model of this temple is in the Madras Museum, and a drawing on p. 538.

Tranquebar Branch

18 m. from Mayavaraj Tranquebar (93 sq. m.), was a Danish settlement from 1616 (bought from the Nayakka ruler of Tanjore) to 1845, when it was acquired by the British Government along with Serampore. The Tamil name Tarangambadi means "the village by the sound of the wave".

The fort, known as the Dansborg ("Danish Castle") was built by Ovo Gedde on behalf of the Danish East India Company in 1620. It is now a travellers' bungalow (not good). A wooden tablet, bearing a curious monogram of Christian V of Denmark, dated 1677, which was formerly fixed in a room in the Dansborg, has been removed to the Museum at Madras.

The first Protestant mission in India was founded at Tranquebar in 1706. There are several very old churches in Tranquebar, and some interesting relics of earlier Christianity survive, including no fewer than five cemeteries, the tombs in which bear inscriptions in nine languages: Armenian, Danish, Dutch, English, French, German, Latin, Portuguese and Swedish.

[1] See also *South Indian Shrines,* by P. V. Jagadisa Aiyar, Madras, 1929.

The road enters by a gateway, bearing the date 1792 and the monogram of the King of Denmark. The principal thoroughfares retain their names of King and Queen Street. on the E. of King Street is the Lutheran Mission Church ("New Jerusalem"), and opposite is the English Church ("Zion"). The spire of the latter is shaped like a spiked helmet, and the bell is dated 1752; in the vestry is a painting of the Last Supper, coloured in relief upon wood, in the manner of Albrecht Dürer.

Catherine Nöel Werleé (1762-1835), the wife of G. F. Grand, a Bengal civilian, whose escapade with Philip Francis cost the latter Rs. 50,000, was born here. She subsequently married Talleyrand (1802) and became Princess of Benevento (1806).

Main Line

The line continues from Mayavaram to

194 m. **Kumbakonam** (pop. 112,000 in 1971) station (R., D.B.), in the Tanjore District. The city is of great antiquity, with 18 shrines and a **Math** (monastic institution), and a College. It is famous for gold and silver jewellery, for textiles and for brass ware. The betel grown here is famous for its quality. The temples, near the centre of the town, are about 1 m. from the station. The largest temple is dedicated to Vishnu (Sarangapani) and the Great Gopuram here has eleven storeys. The total height is 147 ft. A street arched over leads to the Temple of Kumbeshwara with a slender-pillared pavilion in front. The Ramaswami Temple has excellent carvings in its Hall of Pillars.

To the E. side of the road from the station to the temples is the Mahamakham Tank—into which, it is supposed, the Ganges flows once in twelve years. So vast a concourse of people enter the water to bathe that the surface rises some inches.

A motorable road leads 22 miles to *Gangaikondacholapuram*, once the capital of King Rajendra Chola (1002-1044). The Shiva temple, although little known, is impressive and ranks next to the great Tanjore temple among the best examples of Chola architecture. Well worth a visit.

218 m. **TANJORE** (Thanjavar) Junction (R., D.B., I.B. Tourist B., Travellers' Lodge 2 R.Hs.) (pop. 140,000 in 1971) stands near the head of the Cauvery river delta which is considered the garden of Southern India. It carries a dense population, and is highly irrigated. With its 74 temples, Tanjore is among the great cultural centres of the S.

The Tanjore country was under the Cholas during the whole of their supremacy (907-1310); *c.* 1510 Krishna Raya of Vijayanagar annexed it. Vyankoji, the brother of Sivaji, moved here from Bangalore (1674), proclaimed himself independent, and established a Mahratta dynasty. The British first came into touch with the place, by an expedition in 1749, and later in the year the Raja was besieged by Chanda Sahib, the French candidate for the Nawabship of the Carnatic. In 1758 it was attacked by the French Count Lally. A treaty was made with Madras in 1762, Colonel Joseph Smith captured the fort for Muhammad Ali in 1773, and in 1776 it was restored.

Raja Sarfoji, by a treaty in 1779, ceded the dependent territory to the British, retaining only the capital and a small tract. Sarfoji was succeeded in 1832 by his son Sivaji, who died in 1853 without legitimate male issue, when the State lapsed to the British Government, but a pension is continued. "For ages Tanjore has been one of the chief political, literary and religious centres of the South."

The Little Fort, containing the Great Temple of Brihadiswara, Schwartz's Church, the Sivaganga Tank and the People's Park, adjoins the Great Fort, with the Palace of the Raja. On a rampart there is a huge cannon called Raja Gopal, 24 ft. in length, 10 ft. in its outer circumference, and 2 ft. in its bore, which has been fired only once.

The **Great Temple** of Brihadiswara has been called "the grandest temple in India".—The entrance from the E. is under a gopuram 90 ft. high. Then a passage 170 ft. long between two enclosures, desecrated by French occupation in 1777, according to an inscription on the gateway, leads to a second gopuram of smaller dimensions. There is a long inscription in Tamil characters on either side of the passage under the second gopuram. From this the outer enclosure of the temple is entered. It is 415 ft. by 800 ft., and is surrounded by cloister-chapels, each containing a large lingam, whereas the sculptures on the gopurams are Vishnuvite. Visitors may walk everywhere in the enclosure, but cannot enter the Great Temple or the halls of approach to it.

On the right is the Yajnasala, where sacrifices are offered, and the Sabhapati Kovil, or Shrine of Siva, as the presiding god of an assembly. There are two Balipidams, or altars, close to the E. wall, one inside and one outside; and at about 40 ft. from the E. wall is a gigantic nandi (bull) in black granite, a monolith 12 ft. 10 in. high and 16 ft. long, sculptured out of a solid block of rock, said to have been brought a distance of 400 m. It is daily anointed with oil, which makes it shine like the finest bronze.

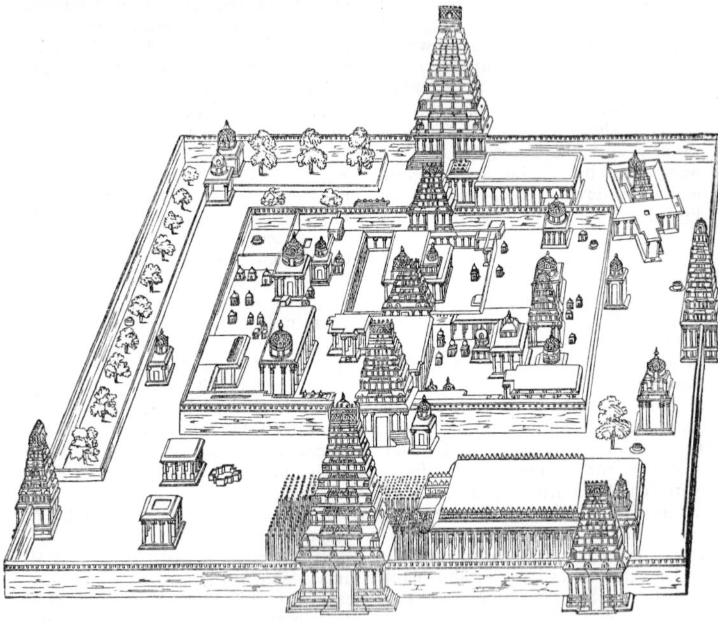

Bird's-eye View, Temple of Tiruvarur.
(see p. 536)

A portico leads to two halls; beyond these is the shrine, 56 ft. by 54 ft., over which rises the vast tower of the vimana, 216 ft. high, including the great monolithic dome-shaped top and the Stupi or ornament.

N.E. of the Great Tower is the Chandikasan Kovil, or shrine of the god who reports to the chief god the arrival of worshippers. W. of this, at the N.W. corner of the outer enclosure, is the Subrahmanya Kovil, Shrine of Kartikkeya, the son of Siva and deity of war, who is called Subrahmanya (from su, good, brahman, a Brahman) because he is the especial protector of Brahmans. Fergusson wrote that it "is as exquisite a piece of decorative architecture as is to be found in the S. of India" (*Ind. Arch.*, 1, 365). It is probably of the 16th or 17th century. Its carving seems to be in imitation of wood.

In the mandapam (48 ft. by 45 ft.) a museum was opened in 1935, on the birthday of the Chola King, Rajaraja the Great (985-1014), the founder of the temple. It contains objects of the Chola and Nayak periods and some paintings of the Maratha Rajas. The temple jewels are displayed on great occasions. The library contains 20,000 Sanskrit manuscripts.

The base of the grand temple—i.e. the vimana and halls leading to it—is covered with Tamil inscriptions, which would give the date as approximately A.D. 1009. The pyramidal tower over the shrine has evidently often been repaired in its upper part, where the images are now only of cement. This tower is only 38 ft. lower than the Qutb Minar at Delhi.

Dr Burnell says in *The Great Temple of Tanjore*[1]: "This style arose under the Chola Kings in the 11th century A.D., when nearly all the great temples to Siva in S. India were built, and it continued in use in the 12th and 13th centuries, during which the great temples to Vishnu were erected. Up to the beginning of the 16th century these temples remained almost unchanged, but at that time all S. India became subject to the Kings of Vijayanagar, and one of these, named Krishnaraya (1509-30), rebuilt or added to most of the great temples of the S. The chief feature of the architecture of this later period is the construction of enormous gopurams so built by Krishnaraya; they do not form part of the original style, but were intended as fortifications to protect the shrines from foreign invaders, and certain plunder and desecration, as the Hindus first discovered on the Muhammadan invasion of 1310."

Vijay Rajendra Chola (1054-60) made grants for the annual performance of a play in April-May. The text was forgotten and Raja Sarfoji instituted a ceremonial dance (Kuruvanchik-Kottu) performed at this season.

The **Palace.**—This building is in the Great Fort, lying E. of the Little Fort. Some portions of it are occupied by the representatives of the Palace family, and the remainder is used for Government offices. It is a vast building of masonry, and stands on the left of the street, which runs northward through the fort; it was built partly by the Nayakkas about 1550, partly by the Mahrattas. After passing through two quadrangles a third is entered, on the S. side of which is a building like a gopuram, 190 ft. high, with eight storeys. It was once an armoury.

E. of the quadrangle is the Telugu Darbar-room of the Nayakkar Kings. On the sides of a platform of black granite are sculptured in alto-relievo Surs and Asurs fighting. On this platform stands a white marble statue, by Flaxman, of Sarfoji, pupil of Schwartz. He is standing with the palms of his hands joined as if in prayer. This room forms the core of the Tanjore Art Gallery with a splendid collection of bronzes.

On one side of the quadrangle is the Saraswati Mahal Library, in which is a remarkable collection of more than 18,000 MSS. in Sanskrit, Tamil and other Indian languages, as well as printed books. This library (which has been converted into a public trust) dates from about 1700. In the Mahratta Darbar, in another quadrangle, is a large picture of Sivaji, the last Raja of Tanjore with his chief secretary and his Diwan.

[1] See also a book with the same title by M. Somasundram Pillai.

E. again lies Schwartz's Church close to the Sivaganga Tank. Over the gate is the date 1777, and over the façade of the church is 1779. In the centre, opposite the communion table, is a group of figures in white marble, by Flaxman, representing the death of Schwartz in 1798. The aged missionary is extended on his bed, and on his left stands the Raja Sarfoji, his pupil (whom he helped to regain the throne), with two attendants, while on his right is the missionary Kohlmer, and near the bottom of the bed are four boys. The inscription contains a summary of his career. The small house N.W. of the church, and close to it, is said to have been Schwartz's habitation.

Next to the Sivaganga Tank is the People's Park. Other buildings are the Sangita Mahal ("Mansion of Music" —now restored), a miniature of the surviving Court of Tirumala Nayak's Palace in Madurai; the Arsenal or Armoury; and the Clock-tower, so called on account of a former device for marking the time, now removed.

The Tanjore District was the scene of the earliest labours of Protestant missionaries in India. In 1706 two German missionaries established a Lutheran mission in the Danish settlement of Tranquebar, under the patronage of the King of Denmark; and in 1841 their establishments were taken over by the Leipzig Evangelical Lutheran Mission, which subsequently extended its operations into the District. The mission at Tanjore was founded in 1778 by the Rev. C. F. Schwartz, of the Tranquebar Mission, who some time previously had transferred his services to the Society for Promoting Christian Knowledge.

Roman Catholic missions in Tanjore date from the first half of the 17th century. Their principal seats are Negapatam, Velanganni (on the coast, 6 m. S. of Negapatam), Tanjore, Vallam, and Kunbakonam.

Tanjore is famous for its silk, carpets, jewellery, repoussé work, copper ware, Indian musical instruments, and models in pith. The repoussé work, and the copper work are inlaid with brass and silver *swámi* (or god) figures.

Vallam, 7 m. S.W. of Tanjore, is the headquarters of the Collector of the District.

Motor-bus service (36 m.) from Tanjore to **Pudukkottai** (museum; colleges); capital of the former State of that name, merged in Madras (1948) with some fine public buildings and a collection of pictures in the palace. (Access by rail also from Trichinopoly, below.) The ruling family, known as the Tondiman Rajas, founded by Raghunatha Raya Tondiman in 1686, played a leading part in S. Indian history, and were old allies of the British in wars with the French, Haidar Ali, Tipu Sultan, and the Poligars. The town stands on the ancient pilgrim route to Rameswaram.

Negapatam Branch Line

A branch railway runs from Tanjore, 48 m. E. *via* Tiruvarur Junction (p. 536) to

Negapatam, or Nagai (R., D.B.), an old port doing a brisk trade with the Straits Settlements and Coast Ports. According to Colonel Yule, it is the "Malefattan" of Arab geographers. It was one of the earliest settlements of the Portuguese, was taken by the Dutch in 1660 and by the British in 1781. The Dutch Church and the old graves in the Karicop cemetery are interesting.

The branch runs on to **Nagore,** 53 m. A centre of Muslim S. India. Interesting 16th-century mosque, enclosing the tomb of a Muslim saint: the inner doors are plated with silver, a somewhat unusual adornment, which recalls a Hindu temple rather than an orthodox Muslim place of worship. Nagore was received by the Dutch from the Tanjore Raja.

Main Line

249 m. from Madras, **Tiruchirapalli** (Trichinopoly) Junction (R.) *(D.B.;

Travellers' B.; Hotels; pop. 306,000 in 1971; alt. 256 ft.). Air service from Madras and Bangalore. The name is properly Tiruchirapalli, or the "City of the Three-headed Demon". The famous **Rock** dominates the landscape for some miles before reaching the station. A broad-gauge railway runs (88 m. W.) to Erode (p. 519), the junction for the line from Madras to the West Coast (Route 32). A chord line runs through Pudukkottai (p. 540) to Manamadurai on the main line, avoiding Madurai (p. 545) but shortening the Indo-Ceylon route to Rameswaram by about 70 m.

St John's Church, in which Bishop Heber is buried, is close to the station; the grave in the chancel is marked by a fine brass. The bath in which he died in 1826 is near the house and court of the Judge of Tiruchirapalli. There is a marble slab monument on the spot.

Two historic masses of granite, the Golden Rock and the Fakir's Rock, are in the plain to the S. Near the Golden Rock the French were defeated in two engagements in the second siege of 1753, which followed on the demand of the Mysore General that the town should be made over to him. Golden coins were found here, but a syndicate endeavoured without success to discover further buried treasure. There are Boys' and Girls' Schools and a Convent. Near the Gymkhana is the Cathedral House of the Roman Catholic Bishop of Tiruchirapalli. There is also a tomb of Nathar (or Nadir) Shah, a saint (969-1039).

S. of the Junction station are the Race-course and aerodrome.

3 m. S.W. of Tiruchirapalli is a fortified temple which was occupied by the French in 1753, and recaptured by the British under Colonel Stringer Lawrence.

Tiruchirapalli Fort station is 3 m. on the broad-gauge *Erode Branch.* The Fort has been dismantled, but this part of the town is still known as "the fort".

Muhammad Ali, the candidate supported by the British for the Nawabship of Arcot, was beleaguered by Chanda Sahib and the French. During the siege (1753-54), in November 1753, the French made a night attack on the Fort, and succeeded in entering the outer line of fortifications at *Dalton's Battery* at the N.W. angle. Here there was a pit 30 ft. deep, into which many of the assailants fell. Their screams alarmed the garrison, who repelled them and made 360 of the French prisoners. This portion of the old fort is all that has been left standing. The moat that surrounded it has been filled in and planted as a boulevard.

On the N. side of the city is the **Rock,** 236 ft. high (best reached from Trichi Town Station on the metre-gauge line to Madras). An early morning visit is advisable. At the foot of the W. side is a handsome *Teppa Kulam* or sacred tank, with stone steps and a *mandapam,* or pavilion, in the centre. E. of the tank is a house, which bears a medallion with an inscription stating that Robert (afterwards Lord) Clive occupied it *c.* 1752. There is, however, little evidence to corroborate this story.

The most striking buildings are St Joseph's College and Bishop Heber's College. The former is situated in the N.W. corner of the fort, near the Main Guard Gate. It was founded by the Jesuit Mission in 1844 at Negapatam, and was transferred to Tiruchirapalli in 1883. St Joseph's College includes the College Church and the Lawley Hall.

Bishop Heber's College was developed from schools founded by the Rev. C. F. Schwartz of the S.P.C.K. It is situated E. of the Main Guard Gate, and just opposite the Teppa Kulam. In 1762 Schwartz visited Tiruchirapalli and founded the first English Church in 1765-66. This stands opposite to the Caldwell Hostel on the way to Sri Rangam. Schwartz remained for many years in Tiruchirapalli and died in Tanjore in 1798, aged 72. The National College, close by, was founded by the late G. Shesha Iyengar.

The ascent of the Rock is by a covered passage from the S.; on the sides are stone elephants and pillars about 18 ft. high, which bear the stamp of Jain architecture. The pillars have carved capitals representing the lion of the S. and various figures of men and women. The frieze above is ornamented with carvings of animals. Flights of very steep steps, 290 in number, lead through this passage to the vestibule of a Saiva temple on the left, whence on certain days the images of the gods—viz. of Siva, Parvati, Ganesh, and Subrahmanya or Skanda—are carried in procession. The temple and the original fort were built by a Madurai Nayakka in 1660-70. The cave temples, cut into the rock on the left side of the steps, are worth visiting. The pillars in these temples bear archaic inscriptions in Pallava characters. Half-way up, the stairs emerge into the open at a small shrine dedicated to Ganesh (here called Pillayar, "the Son"): it is lighted up every evening by three lamps. The steps of the ascent were the scene of a terrible disaster in 1849, when in a panic 500 people were killed.

From the temple the stairs turn E. and lead out on to the surface of the Rock, up which a rough approach has been cut to the *mandapam*, or pavilion, crowning the top, from which there is one of the finest panoramic views to be seen in the plains of India. On all sides the eye traverses the plain for 20 m. or 30 m. The height of the Rock is only 236 ft., but the plain is so flat that this height is sufficient. There is a beautiful Pallava Love Temple at the S.W. foot of the rock.

On the S. is the *Golden Rock*, about 100 ft. high. S.E. of this, a patch of low, rocky ground is seen about 40 ft. high. This is *French Rocks*, about 2 m. from the fort. Within the town, distant only a few hundred yards, is the *Nawab's Palace*, which is now used for courts and public offices.

N. of the Fort Rock is the broad shallow bed of the Cauvery, in which, except in the rains, there is but a narrow streak of water. Beyond is the *Island of Sri Rangam*, very sacred to Vaishnavites, with the two great temples, that of *Sri Rangam* to the W., and that of Jambukeswar to the E. Srirangam station is on the metre-gauge line to Madras. Beyond to the N. in the far distance rises a long line of hills. To the N.W. is the Tale Malai range, the greatest height of which is 1800 ft.; while due N. of the Fort Rock are the Kale Malai (Kollimalai) Hills, which attain 4000 ft.; and E. of these are the Pachaī Malais (Green Hills), which in some parts rise to 2300 ft.

The old Cantonment of Warriore (Uraiyur), on the site of a Chola capital, lies to the W. of the city. It consists of a square fringed by European bungalows; and was used as the headquarters of the former South Indian Ry., whose locomotive carriage and wagon works are near Golden Rock. A custom prevails in Tiruchirapalli whereby the *Kavalgaran*, or watchman, whom every householder employs, is taken from the thief caste.[1]

The most important local *Industries* are weaving, wooden and clay toys, glass bangles, artificial gems, and tobacco and cigar making, but the best Tiruchirapalli cheroots come for the most part from Dindigul. The local gold- and silver-smiths are very successful in their filigree work.

About 2 m. N. from the Rock, on an island, 17 m. long and 1¼ m. broad, formed by a bifurcation of the River **Cauvery**, is the town of *Sri Rangam*, a place of Hindu pilgrimage to be ranked with Benares and Rameswaram. A bridge of thirty-two arches joins the mainland to the island on the S. An inscription on a slab let into the parapet commemorates the defence of Tiruchirapalli by Stringer Lawrence and the two actions fought by him on 26th June and 21st September 1753, "which mainly contributed to lay the foundations of the British Empire in India".

[1] J. C. Molony, *A Book of South India* (Methuen, 1926, p. 38).

The **Great Temple of Raghunathaswami at Sri Rangam,** built by the Nayakkas of Madurai, is 1 m. N.W. of the bridge. The entrance is by a grand S. gateway, 48 ft. high, which appears to have been built as the base of a great gopuram. The sides of the passage are lines with pilasters and ornamented. The passage is about 100 ft. long, and the inner height, exclusive of the roof, is 43 ft. Vast monoliths have been used as uprights in the construction, some of them over 40 ft. high. The stones on the roof, laid horizontally, are also huge. The stone on the inside of the arch is 29 ft. 7 in. long, 4 ft. 5 in. broad, and about 8 ft. thick.

From the terrace at the top of the gateway is seen the vast outer wall which encloses the gardens as well as the buildings. The temple is composed of seven rectangular enclosures; the outermost, which measures 2475 ft. by 2880 ft., contains a bazar. Within this is a second wall 20 ft. high enclosing the dwellings of the Brahmins in the service of the temple. The buildings diminish from the exterior to the innermost enclosure. "If its principle of design could be reversed, it would be one of the finest temples in the S. of India."[1] Others take the opposite view. There are two great gopurams on the E. side, two smaller on the W., and three of a medium height on the S.

Beyond the still incomplete gopuram the road passes under a small mandapam, and then through a gopuram about 60 ft. high. The decoration of the gopurams is all painted, and the ceiling of this one represents the Varaha, or Boar Incarnation, of Vishnu, as well as other Avataras with multitudes of human beings adoring them. A second mandapam is then passed, and a second and third gopuram.

Another enclosing wall surrounds the more sacred part, or real temple, beyond which is the vimana, or adytum, which none but Hindus are allowed to enter. At a third mandapam the jewels of the temple may be examined.

In the court round the central enclosure is the so-called Hall of 1000 Pillars. The actual number is about 940, granite monoliths 18 ft. high, with pediments, slightly carved to the height of 3 ft., and they all have the plantain bracket at the top. To the S., separated by a large court, is a mandapam the N. side of which has the famous rearing-horse pillars. These represent men on rearing horses spearing tigers, the horses' feet being supported by the shields of men on foot beside them. The carved horses spring out from the pillars, all being carved from one block. It is here that the Vaikunta-Ekadasi festival, which attracts thousands of pilgrims is celebrated in December. The great gopuram on the N. is 152 ft. high. In the floor of the passage under this gopuram leading to the Coleroon river is a stone with a Kanarese inscription.

Temple of Jambukeswar.—In the S. of India temples are often found in pairs. If there is one dedicated to Vishnu, there will be one dedicated to Siva. So here, at about 1¼ m. E. of the Great Temple, is a smaller one sacred to Jambukeswar, or Siva, from jambuka, "rose-apple", and iswar, "lord", or Lord of India, Jambu being a division of the world = "India".

The Jambukeswar Temple has been restored. It has five courts, and is very much smaller than the other. The plan of the building is more artistic, and the main corridor and proportions are fine. On the right of the entrance is an upright stone 4 ft. high, with a long Tamil inscription. The first gopuram is also the gateway of entrance. The ceiling is painted with flowers of the lotus. Within the inner court is a remarkable Teppa Kulam, or tank, fed by spring water, with a pavilion in the centre. Round the S., the E. and the N. sides run corridors of two storeys supported by pillars. Beyond this is a second

[1] See 1, 368 of Fergusson's *Ind. Arch.* where an illustration and a description of the temples will be found.

gopuram, and a third which forms part of the wall enclosing the shrine. Thence a broad corridor leads to the *vimana*. This temple is probably older than that of Sri Rangam.

The **Anikuts**, or dams.—about 9 m. to the W. of Tiruchirapalli the Cauvery separates into two branches, which enclose the island, the N. branch being called the Coleroon or Kolidun, and the S. the Cauvery. These anikuts are in several cases modern improvements on very ancient irrigation works constructed by the Chola Kings. A dam was constructed across the Coleroon in 1836 to prevent the river deserting the S. arm, from which a number of branches irrigate Tanjore, the chief one being called the Vennar, which falls into the sea 20 m. S. of the mouth of the Coleroon.

This anikut, designed by Sir Arthur Cotton, R.E., in 1843, but since altered, consists of three parts, being broken by two islands. It is a brick wall 7 ft. high and 6 ft. thick, capped with stone, and is founded on two rows of wells. It is defended by an apron of cut stone from 21 ft. to 40 ft. broad, and has twenty-four sluices, which help to scour the bed.

About 9 m. E. of Tiruchirapalli is the Grand Anikut, an ancient work dating perhaps from the 11th century, and below that is the Lower Anikut, also built in 1836, joining the tail of Sri Rangam island to the bank.

An interesting irrigation feature is the Korambu system. Above the anikuts, channels take off flush with the river. They get a supply while the river is full. When the river goes down, Korambus are built—i.e. temporary dams of brushwood, piles, earth, etc.—to catch up some water and divert it into the channels. If a freshet comes they are swept away and have to be put up again.

307 m. from Madras (Egmore), **Dindigal** (pop. 127,000 in 1971) Junction (R.; alt. 943 ft.). It has well-known tobacco factories, tanneries, and a large cotton factory.

The great rock on which the fort is built forms a conspicuous object; its summit is 1223 ft. above sea-level, 280 ft. above the plain. Its inaccessible sides were strongly fortified under the first Nayakka Kings of Madurai, and for a long time it was the W. key of the Province of Madurai. It was taken by Mysore in 1745.

Haidar Ali was appointed Governor in 1755, and used it as a base for the invasion of Madurai, disposing of his prisoners by throwing them from the top of the rock. The place was taken by the British from Tipu Sultan in 1781, restored to him in 1784, retaken in 1790, and finally ceded in 1792 by the Treaty of Seringapatam.

The Dindigul Kottayam road passes close to the Periyar Lake (p. 527).

Dindigul to Podanur

A branch line runs from Dindigul to (76 m.) **Pollachi**, where it connects with the line to (25 m.) **Podanur** Junction (p. 520).

37 m. from Dindigal is the famous hill shrine at **Palni** (D.B.K., alt. 1057 ft.), dedicated to Subrahmanya, an aspect of Siva, which stands on a picturesque hill, a continuation of the Kodaikanal range; the image, known as Palni Andavar, represents the god as an infant. The two hillocks, Sakti and Siva, are said to have been given to the Sage Agastya to be placed in the south of India; Idambasura, a demon, to whom the sage entrusted the task, carried them on his shoulders in a Kavadi, or pair of baskets, and they dropped at this spot. Many of the devotees, who throng the road and who mostly perform the pilgrimage under a vow either of silence or of fasting, may be seen with *Kavadis* slung on a pole across their shoulders; these are filled with milk or sugar and taken round the temple on arrival. The women who visit Palni invariably sacrifice their hair; and the quantity left at the temple is sold annually to a contractor for several thousand rupees.

There is a motor service from Palni to Dharapuram (22 m. N.), and from the next station, **Udamalpet,** to

Munnar (54 m.) in the Travancore High Range. Between Udamalpet and Pollachi, the line skirts a black cotton tract. To the S. are extensive sugar-cane plantations. On the lower slopes of the Palni hills, tea, coffee and cardamoms are grown. Here may be the Regis Pandionis of Ptolemy.

Pollachi (76 m.) is situated opposite the **Palghat** Gap (p. 524).

Branch line (33½ m.) to Palghat.

A new road links Palni directly to Kodaikanal (bus service).

Main Line

320 m. **Ammayanayakkanur** station, or Kodaikanal Road (D.B.K.). The distance to **Kodaikanal** (alt. 7375 ft.) is 50 m. by road. Motor services run. This station (hotels and boarding-houses) enjoys great popularity, and many Missions make it their summer retreat. There are places where the views of the low country and the Anaimalai Hills to the W. are beautiful past description. There is a lovely lake with a 3 m. road round it and numerous beautiful waterfalls, along with vantage points giving views over the countryside. Nutmeg, cinnamon, and pepper-vine grow wild. Orange-trees, lime-trees, citron, and sago are cultivated. The Observatory, removed from Madras in 1899, stands 7700 ft. above sea-level.

Kodaikanal Road is also the station for the Travancore hills, and for the Periyar lake, 80 m. The chief places in the Travancore hills are Vandiperiyar, and Peermade; which can be reached by way of Thekkady (Periyar Lake). A motor-bus service runs between Kodaikanal Road and (62 m.) Cumbum; and from Cumbum to (14 m.) Kumili, there is another bus service (inquiry should be made whether this is in operation). From Kumili to Thekkady, the distance is 3 m., and from Thekkady to Kottayam 71 m. For **Kottayam** and **Periyar,** see p. 527, Route 32.

345 m. **MADURAI** (MADURA) "City of Festivals" station (R., D.B., Travellers' Lodge, HOTEL: *Pandyan*; pop. 548,000 in 1971; alt. 442 ft.), upon the *Vaigai* river. Air services from Madras, Bangalore and Cochin. Caverns and rock-cut Jain figures at Anaimalai and Alagarmalai are interesting. Motor services run to Tirupattur (38 m.), Devacottah (60 m. and Karaikudi (52 m.). A branch railway runs (56 m.) to Bodinayakkanur, where the produce of the tea, coffee and cardamom estates on the Kanam Devan hills in Travancore passes. Madurai was the capital of the Pandya Kings, one of whom sacked Anuradhapura, A.D. 1001 (p. 731). A Jesuit mission under the famous Robert de Nobili settled here in 1606 and made many converts by professing to accept the Hindu conception of caste. The city is famous as a home of the arts; it has been both a centre of commerce and the seat of many academies under the patronage of Tamil Kings.

The **Great Temple**[1] at Madurai (about ½ m. E. of the railway station) forms a parallelogram about 847 ft. by 729 ft., surrounded by nine gopurams, of which the largest is 152 ft. high. All the most beautiful portions of the temple as it now stands were built by Tirumala Nayak (1623-60). It is a twin temple—on the S. a temple to Minákshi, "the fish-eyed goddess", the consort of Siva; and on the N. one to Siva, here called Sundareswar, the legend being that the god under this form married the daughter of the local Pandya Chief, an event celebrated by the annual car festival and procession. The colourful festivities last for three days in the month of Chaitra (April-May). Plan on p. 548.

Facilities, accorded for visiting all the outer courts and corridors up to the doors of the two adyta, make this temple the most interesting to visit of all the Hindu shrines of India, giving the most complete idea of Hindu ritual.

The only entrance is by the gate of

[1] Recent extensive exterior and interior painting rather diminish the original splendour.

Minákshi's Temple, through a painted corridor about 30 ft. long, which is called the Hall of the Eight Saktis, from eight statues of that goddess which form the supports of the roof on either side; in it various dealers ply their trade. On the right of the gate at the end of the hall is an image of Subrahmanya, or Kartikkeya, the Hindu Mars. On the left is an image of Ganesh.

A second stone corridor follows, with rows of pillars on either side, called the Minákshi Nayaka Mandapam, built by Minakshi Nayak, Diwan of the predecessor of Tirumala. Here elephants are kept. Some of the pillars have for capitals the curved plantain-flower bracket, but much of the detail is hidden by the stall shops. At the end of the second corridor, 166 ft. long, is a large door of brass, which has stands to hold many lamps that are lighted at night.

A very dark corridor, under a small gopuram, ends in one broader, which has three figures on either side, carved with spirit, and leads to a quadrangle with a Teppa Kulam. This tank is called Swarnapushpakarini, or Pottamarai, "Tank of the Golden Lilies". All round it runs an arcade.

On the N. and E. sides the walls of this are painted with the representations of the most famous temples in India; from the S. side a very good view is obtained of the gopurams and gilded spires of the shrines. On the N.W. side is the belfry, with an American bell of fine tone.

The corridor beyond the entrance to the temple has twelve very spirited figures, which form pillars on either side, six of them being the Yali, a name given to a strange monster which is the conventional lion of S. India, sometimes represented with a long snout or proboscis. Between every two Yalis is a figure of one of the five Pandava brothers (p. 21 of the Introduction). First on the right is Yudhishthir, and opposite to him on the left is Arjun with his famous bow. Then comes Sahadeva on the right, and Nakula on the left. Then follows Bhima on the right with his club, and opposite, on the left, is the shrine of the goddess and the figure of a Dwarapalagam (doorkeeper).

A gopuram leads from the Minákshí Temple into that of Sundareswar, surrounded by a fine corridor. On the S. side of it is a Nandi hall, and eight steps lead into the Aruvati Muvar, the Temple of the Saivite Saints, in which are a very large number of Statues of Hindu saints and gods. N.E. of the groups are chambers where gold-plated Vahanas, or vehicles, of Minákshí and Sundareswar are kept. The jewel-house adjoining will be opened for a fee. There are two palkis (litters), and two with rods for canopies; also vehicles plated with silver, such as a Hamsa, or goose, a Nandi, or bull. Among other treasures is a pair of golden stirrups presented by Mr Rous Peter, who was Collector of Madurai from 1812 to 1828, and lived on a scale of regal magnificence.

In the N.E. corner is the most striking feature of the temple—the Sahasrasthambha Mandapam, or **Hall of 1000 Pillars.** There are in fact 997, but many are hid from view, as the intervals between them have been bricked up. "There is a small shrine dedicated to the god Sabhapati, which occupies the space of fifteen columns, but it is not their number but their marvellous elaboration that makes it the wonder of the place" (Fergusson, *Ind. Arch.*, 1, 392). Nearly all are different. This hall was built *c.* 1560 by Arianayakam Mudali, Minister of Vishvanath Nayakka, founder of the dynasty. He is represented on the left of the entrance sitting gracefully on a rearing horse. In the row behind him are some spirited figures of men and women, or male and female deities dancing. The recent conversion of the Hall into a museum with show-cases has diminished the impression of size. In the outer corridor, there are pillars which give a musical note when tapped.

The Great Raya Gopuram is on the E. side of the Pudh Mandapam; had it been completed in accordance with its foundations (174 ft. by 107 ft.) it would have been by far the loftiest gopuram in all S. India.

The Pudhu Mandapam, or New Gallery, is known as **Tirulama's Choultry,** and was built by him for the presiding deity of the place, Sundareswar, who paid him a visit of ten days annually on a pedestal provided at the end. It is also called the Vasanta Mandapam, as the visit was in the spring. If this building had been finished, it would have surpassed in magnificence all the other buildings of this monarch; and as the date of its construction is known (1623-45), it forms a fixed point in the chronology of the style.

The hall, 333 ft. long and 105 ft. broad over the plinth, has four rows of pillars supporting a flat roof, and on either side of the centre corridor five pillars represent ten life-size Nayakkas. Tirumala is distinguished by having a canopy over him and two figures at his back; the figure on the left is his wife, the Princess of Tanjore, with a gash on the left thigh where he stabbed her for some rude remark. On the left of the doorway a singular group represents one of the Nayaks shooting a wild boar and sows, according to the legend, which says that Siva commiserated the litter of little pigs, took them up in his arms, and, assuming the shape of the sow, suckled them. A portly figure, either that of Siva or the Nayak is seen holding up the dozen little pigs. Zodiacal signs are on the ceiling.

¾ m. from the temple to the S.E. is the **Palace of Tirumala Nayak.** The building, showing Saracenic influence, has pillars of rough granite cased with beautiful chunam or cement supporting scalloped arches, and is now utilised as a museum. The main entrance—a granite portico built in honour of Lord Napier and Ettrick (Governor of Madras, 1866-1872), who ordered the restoration—on the E. side gives access to a quadrangle 252 ft. by 151 ft. On the E., N. and S. sides of this quadrangle is a corridor, the roof supported by arches resting on granite pillars 40 ft. high with carved backings. On the W. and opposite the main entrance stands the "Swarga Vilasam", or Celestial Pavilion, formerly the throne-room of the Palace. It is an arcaded octagon, covered by a dome 60 ft. in diameter and 70 ft. high.

N. of this is another hall, the two corresponding with the Diwan-i-Khas and Diwan-i-Am of Mughal Palaces. The hall is 140 ft. long by 70 ft. wide, and its height to the centre of the roof is 70 ft., and it is not unlike a Cathedral in the Gothic style (see Fergusson's *Ind. Arch.*, 1, 412-14), although his illustration, taken from Daniell's drawing (made in 1792) exaggerates the proportions.

The Anglican Cathedral stands in an open space in the middle of the town S.W. of the Great Temple. The Fort had a perimeter of 4 m.

On the N. side of the River Vaigai, N. of the city, and about 1 m. from the road bridge to Dindigul, is a curious building called the *Tumkum,* built by Tirumala for exhibiting fights between wild beasts and gladiators. N. again is the Civil Station.

3 m. E. is the Vandiyur Teppa Kulam, enclosed by a granite parapet (1000 ft. square), and with a pretty temple in the middle. On the way is passed a garden with a very fine specimen of the *Ficus indica.* In *Tumkum,* 3 m. from the R.S. is the Gandhi Memorial Museum in the Rani Mangammal Palace (open 9-12 and 4-8 except Wednesdays). At *Alagar Koil* (11 m.; good road), there is a temple (exquisite carvings) dedicated to Alagar, brother of the Golden Minakshi.

Madurai to Tuticorin, Tinnevelly, Quilon and Trivandrum

From Madurai a branch line, the old main line to Tinnevelly, runs S. to Maniyachi Junction. Direct road to Tinnevelly.

401 m. from Madras **Koilpatti** station. The beautiful rock-cut Jain

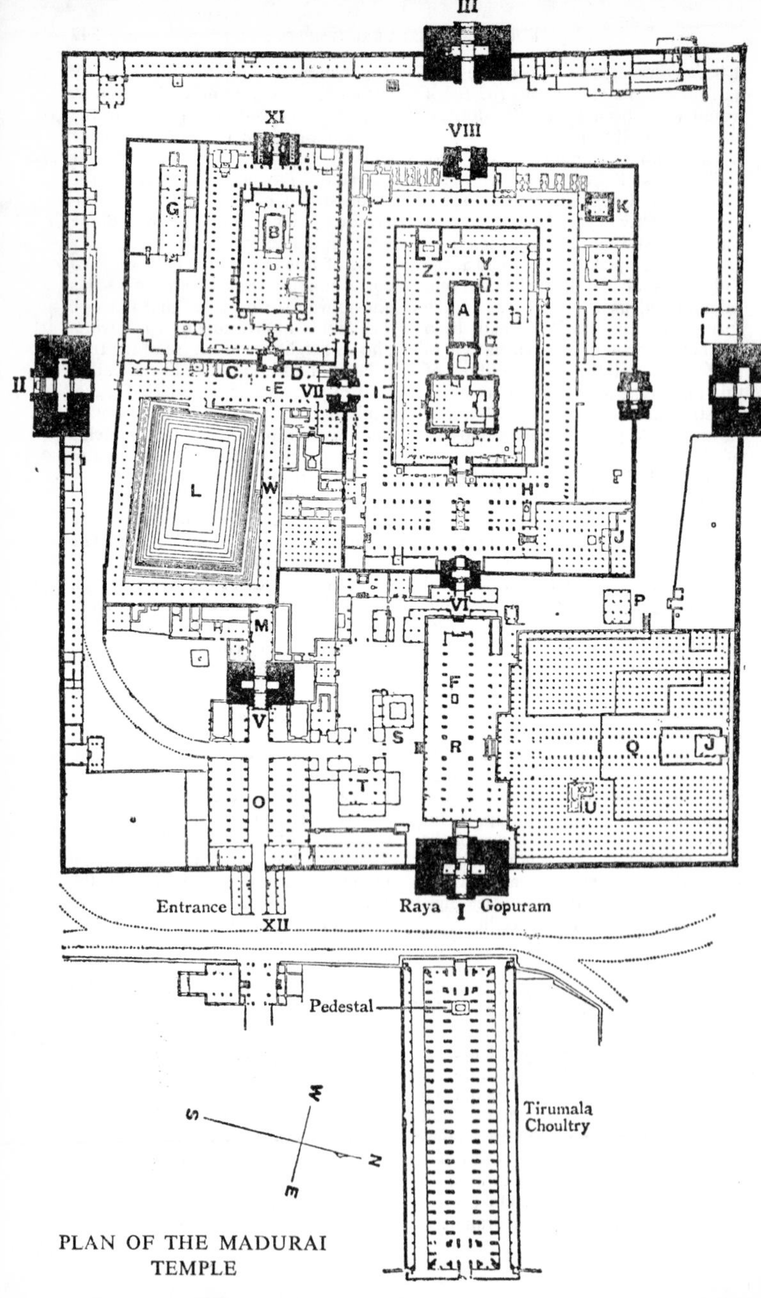

PLAN OF THE MADURAI TEMPLE

PLAN OF THE MADURAI TEMPLE

Key to the Plan

A Shrine of God Sundareswar.
AA Pudu mandápam (Tirumala's Choultry).
B Shrine of Goddess Minákshí-deví.
C Small shrine of Ganesa.
D Small shrine of Subrahmánva
E Vedi or Altar.
F Nandi Pavilion.
G Javandísvara mandápam.
H Navagraha or nine planets.
I Large Ganesa.
JJ Shrines of Nátesvar.
K Poet's College.
L Tank of Golden Lilies. (Teppakulam.)
M Mudali Pillai mandápam.
O Ashta-Sakti hall.
P Sixteen-pillar mandápam.
Q Thousand-pillar mandápam.
R Viravasantaráya mandápam.
S Katyána Sundara mandápam.
T Servaikaran mandápam.
U Lingam.
W Chitra mandápam.
Y Ellamvatta-siddha.
Z Madurai Náyaka temple.
I-IV Four outer Gopurams.
V Tiruvachi Gopuram.
VI, VIII, IX Three Gopurams of the second Prákará.
X, XI Gates to the Minákshí prakárám.
VII Gate between the temples.
XII Ashta-Sakti mandápam.

figures and a monolithic temple (unfinished), dating about A.D. 950, with turtle-backed roofs, at Kalugumalai, 13 m. from Koilpatti, are worth visiting.

425 m. **Maniyachi** Junction for Tuticorin (for line to Tinnevelly (Tirunelveli), Quilon and Trivandrum, *see below*).

444 m. **Tuticorin** (pop. 154,000 in 1971) station (Tuttukudi) (R., D.B.). Steamers leave regularly for Colombo (14 hours). The anchorage is 6 m. to 7 m. from the shore. Passengers are conveyed to and from the steamers by launches, but the journey from Madras to Colombo is better made by way of Dhanushkodi and Talaimanaar (p. 552), or by air.

Tuticorin was originally a Portuguese settlement, founded about 1540. In 1658 it was captured by the Dutch, and in 1782 by the British. It was restored to the Dutch in 1785, and reoccupied by the British in 1795. During the Poligar War of 1801 it was held for a short time by the Poligar of Panchalamkurichi. It was returned to the Dutch in 1818, and finally taken in exchange in 1825. It has a flourishing trade with Sri Lanka and is famous for the industries of salt, fishing and pearl-diving.

The old Dutch cemetery contains tombstones on which are carved armorial bearings and raised inscriptions. "Our Lady of the Snows", the principal Roman Catholic Church was built by the Portuguese.

Maniyachi to Tinnevelly, Quilon and Trivandrum

18 m. from Maniyachi Junction is **Tinnevelly Bridge** and 2 m. farther **Tinnevelly Town,** or Tirunelveli (pop. 108,000 in 1971) (D.B.), on the left bank of the Tambrapurni river, and 1½ m. from it. On the other side is Palamcotta.

Tinnevelly is the most Christianised District in India, with an Anglican Diocese, founded 1896. The S.P.G. and the C.M.S., established 1820, have important stations at the headquarters and at Palamcotta, as have also the Jesuits. It was here that St Francis Xavier (1506-52) began his preaching in India. The town is famous for finely-woven mats and articles made from palmyra leaf.

The Temple at Tinnevelly is divided into two equal parts, of which the S. is dedicated to Parvati, the consort of Siva, and the N. to Siva himself, each 508 ft. by 378 ft. There are three gateways, or gopurams, to either half, one being common to both temples, those on the E. being the principal, and having porches outside them. On entering the Parvati temple is a porch, on the right of which is a Teppa Kulam, and on the left a thousand-pillared hall, which runs nearly the whole breadth of the enclosure, and is 63 ft. broad.

Palamcotta (D.B. furnished), is 3½ m. E. of Tinnevelly. The old fort has been demolished.

Between the bridge over the Tambrapurni and the fort stands the Church of the C.M.S., the spire of which is 110 ft. high. St John's College was built in 1878.

From Palamcotta to Cape Comorin (D.B.) is a distance of about 50 m. along a metalled road. There is a regular motor service to Nagarcoil (pop. 141,000 in 1971), 8 m. from Cape Comorin, with Jain images (9th century), and thence on to Trivandrum.

Cape Comorin (D.B.K., Tourist Bs.), "*κομαρια ακρον*" of Ptolemy and "Comori" of Marco Polo, is named from the greatly venerated temple of Kumari (the Virgin, an attribute of Durga) built at the southernmost point of the Indian peninsula. Monazite and ilmenite sands are deposited by the tide on the seashore. The temple and village stand on rocks. There are considerable remains of fortifications a few miles N. of the temple, built by a Dutch officer, de Lannoy, in Travancore service. The old Residency has been made into a guest-house. Spectacular sunrises and sunsets over the Bay of Bengal, the Arabian Sea and the Indian Ocean.

Branch Lines

To the E. from Tinnevelly a line (38 m.) connects with **Tiruchendur** (D.B.), which lies 20 m. S. of Tuticorin on the coast. Here there is a large and important temple dedicated to Subrahmanya, the god of war, and second son of Siva. The temple contains some excellent sculpture and several inscriptions. There is also a cave with rock-cut sculptures (on the list of preserved monuments).

From Tiruchendur a N.G. railway runs to Kulasekharapatnam and Tissianvillai. S. of Kulasekharapatnam is the prosperous Roman Catholic village of Manapad, lying under the shelter of a headland. The Church stands in a well-kept square. St Francis Xavier is said to have lived in a cave on the headland. Close to Tissianvillai (D.B.K.) is the Protestant settlement of Idayangudi, founded by Bishop Caldwell, who is buried there; also de Lannoy (above).

The railway to Travancore turns W. from Tinnevelley, and runs to (22 m.) **Ambasamudram**; the nearest station for **Papanasham** (papa, "sin", nasham, "effacing"), 29 m. by road from Palamcotta. Near the Agastia temple the Tambrapurni river takes its last fall from the hills, operating spinning mills. The height is only 80 ft., but the body of water is greater than at Kuttalam, with fine hydro-electric potential.

45 m. **Tenkasi** Junction; 3 m. from **Kuttalam** (Courtallam, D.B.), which is 38 m. N.W. of Tinnevelly by road, motors available; resorted to by Indians of position. The S.W. winds blowing through a gap in the W. ghats, bring with them coolness particularly enjoyable in June, July and August. There are R.Hs. for short stays and comfortable bungalows may be rented (visitors should address the Collector at Tinnevelly regarding accommodation).

There are three falls in the Chittar river, the lowest having a plunge of 200 ft., but broken midway. The average temperature of the water is from 72° to 75° F., and invalids derive great benefit. The bathing-place is under a fine shelving rock, which affords a shower-bath. The scenery is strikingly picturesque, with a mixture of bold rocks and woods.

A line from Tenkasi Junction connects with Virudhunager on the Madurai-Maniyachi section.

50 m. from Tinnevelly, **Shencottah** (D.B.). The line passes through a gap in the Western Ghats to Punalur (D.B.) (81 m.), and so to

109 m. **Quilon** (pop. 124,000 in 1971) (D.B.K., Tourist B.—very attractive, formerly a Palace—Hotel *Neela*. Bus services from Trivandrum and Cochin)—the Koilum of Marco Polo—on the W. coast of the former Travancore State. Now a prosperous commercial city it has a long history as a seaport used by Phoenician, Persian, Arab, Greek, Roman and Chinese shipping—there was a Chinese trade settlement here. Motor launch trips can be arranged on Lake Ashtamudi and through the famous Kerala backwaters to Alleppey and Kotayyam. Quilon has a growing industrial reputation for ceramics, coir tiles and aluminium. Its cashew nuts are world famous.

2 m. from Quilon is **Tangasseri** (Changana-Cheri), formerly an outlying British possession, 96 acres in extent. There are two cemeteries on the headland near the lighthouse. A ruined belfry stands in the centre of the Protestant graveyard. Fort Thomas, of which the greater part has fallen into the sea, was built by the Portuguese in 1503. Between Quilon and Trivandrum **Attingal** was the capital of the Tamburettis, who reigned over Travancore until 1758.

Near 129 m. **Kadakavur** station. On the sea-coast, close by, is the old English factory (1684) of **Anjengo**, the birthplace (1744) of Mrs Draper, Laurence Sterne's "Eliza", and of Robert Orme, the historian (1728). There is a Portuguese church, a massive laterite fort, and an English cemetery, in which the earliest tomb dates back to 1704. The factory was abandoned in 1810.

149 m. from Tinnevelly, **Trivandrum** (pop. 409,000 in 1971; R., R.R., D.B.). Air services from Madras, Bangalore, etc., capital formerly of Travancore and now of Kerala State, 44 m. by road S.E. of Quilon.

Travancore and Cochin were combined in 1956 to form the State of Kerala, thus reviving the old name for this area. The ancient custom of descent from Chera rulers through the female line still prevails in the Nair (Malayali Sudra) community.[1]

Trivandrum, originally Thiru-Vananta—Puram (Abode of the Sacred Serpent) became the capital in 1750, when Raja Marthanda Varma transferred thither from Padmanabhapuram and dedicated the whole State of Travancore to Vishna under the title of Padmanabha. The Padmanabhaswamy Temple, with its seven-storey gopuram, is the main landmark of the city. Non-Hindus have no access, but can view the tower and the tank from outside. There are two annual festivals—March-April and October-November, with impressive processions to the sea shore. The temple stands in the Fort, with several other ancient shrines.

There are impressive modern buildings, standing in groves and parks. Among them are several Palaces, the Observatory, the Secretariat, the Legislative Building and the Colleges of the University—all in the attractive indigenous style. The Napier Museum has a notable collection of bronzes, sculptures and ancient musical instruments. Near it is the Chitralaya (Art Gallery) with a large collection of ancient and modern paintings of all the principal Indian Schools as well as those of China, Japan, Java and Bali. The Zoo is close by. The Oriental MSS Library is worth visiting, as is the Aquarium on the beach. There are facilities for boating, golf, swimming and cricket. (Guides and information from the Kerala Govt. Tourist Officer, Govt. Press Road.) Some notable excursions help to make Trivandrum one of the pleasantest places for the tourist in S. India. 8 m. away is **Kovalam** Beach, a famous bathing bay and angling resort, with a Tourist H. and Board and Lodging in the Palace, once the home of the Rani of Travancore. There is a bus service from Trivandrum. Farther off (37 m.) is **Ponmudi,** a health resort 3000 ft. up in the hills, with accommodation for visitors. 33 m. on the road to Cape Comorin (550) is the old **Padmanabhapuram Palace,** a gem of Kerala architecture with many relics of antiquity. There are numerous fine murals (17th and 18th centuries) depicting scenes from the Epics. At **Aruvikara** (10 m.) there are delightful picnic spots.

Kanniyakumari is now linked to Trivandrum by a 55 m. broad gauge railway.

Madurai to Rameswaram

From Madurai the route[1] proceeds S.E. to Manamadurai Junction, **Ramnad** (Ramanatha-puram) and **Mandapam** (R., R.H.). A Scherzer lifting railway bridge of 214 ft. span and a viaduct across the Pamban channel (total length 6739 ft.) carry the line to

Pamban on the island of Rameswaram (18 m. long). The line runs from Pamban to Rameswaram where it now terminates. A steamer in about 2 hours crosses in the lee of Adam's Bridge (seven islands) to **Talaimanaar** in Sri Lanka, 22 m. distant. Boats leave only on Mondays, Wednesdays and Fridays at 10.00 hr. The Customs' and passport examination is held on the steamer.

Rameswaram (R.R., R.Hs. Dharamsala) is also called Saithoo. Near the railway station is a building containing two long tombs, placed side by

[1] For full information regarding this and other interesting customs which prevail in Malabar, Mr J. A. Thorne's notes to the second volume of *The Book of Duarte Barbosa* (Hakluyt Society, 1921) may be consulted.

[1] The Indo-Sri Lanka route from Tiruchirapalli Junction to Manamadurai avoids Madurai.

side, which are said to be those of Cain and Abel. They are in the care of the Muslim community.

The Temple of **Rameswaram** is a deeply venerated Siva shrine founded, according to tradition, by Rama himself, and therefore associated with Rama's journey to Sri Lanka in search of Sita, as related in the *Ramayana.* It shares with Varanasi the fame of an All India Hindu religious centre. An old vimana (on the right of the entrance corridor) contains Nandi bulls.

By control of the passage from India to Sri Lanka the Rajas of Ramnad derive their hereditary title of Setupati, "Lord of the Causeway". Statutes of the Rajas are sculptured on pillars of the mandapams and courtyards (prakarams).

The island is to a great extent covered with babúl (*Acacia arabica*) coconut and umbrella-trees. It is inhabited principally by Brahmans.

The great **Temple** stands on rising ground above a fresh-water lake, about 3 m. in circumference, in the N. part of the island. It is built in a quadrangular enclosure 657 ft. broad by about 1000 ft. long, entered by a gateway 100 ft. high. It is a grand example of the Dravidian style which, in the opinion of competent judges, it displays in the greatest perfection. It possesses a priceless collection of antique jewellery.

The oldest portion is built of a dark, hard limestone. Local tradition asserts that this part was erected by the Vara Raja Sekkarar, of Kandy, with stone cut and polished in Sri Lanka, and that its cost was defrayed by the seaport dues of all the coast towns during the year it was building. The massiveness of the workmanship (slabs 40 ft. long being used in the doorways and ceilings) and the wonderful pillared halls which surround the inner shrine are noticeable.

The temple consists of three prakáráms (courts). Excepting the mulasthanam, or the innermost shrine, inner portions of the first and second prakáráms have been renovated with black granite. The corridors (not symmetrical) of the outer or third prakárám remain untouched.

Fergusson wrote: "The glory of this temple resides in its corridors. These extend to nearly 4000 ft. in length. The breadth varies from 17 ft. to 21 ft. of free floor space, and their height is apparently about 30 ft. from the floor to the centre of the roof. Each pillar or pier is compound, 12 ft. in height, standing on a platform 5 ft. from the floor, and richer and more elaborate in design than those of the Parvati porch at Chidambaram (p. 535), and are certainly more modern in date."

The paintings on the ceilings and the colonnades have faded badly. The lingam, supposed to have been placed here by Rama, is daily washed with Ganges water, which is afterwards sold to pilgrims. Only the outer corridor of the Temple is open to non-Hindus.

There is a good new T.T.D.C. (Tamilnadu Tourist Development Corporation) Bungalow next to the beach. However, accommodation in both Rameswaram and Talaimamaan is a problem because a lot of Sri Lankan pilgrims come to Rameswaram.

THE ISLAMIC REPUBLIC OF PAKISTAN

Area: 310,403 sq. m.
Population: (est.) 73,400,000
Head of State: Major-General Mohammed Zia-Ul-Haq

The partition of Indian territory in 1947 between two independent countries, India and Pakistan, arose primarily from Muslim fears lest the massive Hindu majority in an undivided India should reduce Muslims to the status of a mere minority community in a country in which, prior to the arrival of the British, they had exercised imperial rule for some eight centuries. The common aim of achieving a National Home for Muslims united the Muslim majority in East Bengal with the ethnically and culturally very different peoples of the Punjab, the North West Frontier, Sind and Baluchistan; and under the leadership of M. A. Jinnah, reverenced as Quaid-i-Azam ("Supreme Leader") this aim was realised with the reluctant agreement of the Indian National Congress and in spite of British hopes that the administrative unity of the subcontinent might be maintained. Pakistan now consists of four Provinces, Punjab: North-West Frontier: Sind: and Baluchistan.

From the beginning, the new State faced grave difficulties; it had inherited no well-tried machinery of central administration and its component parts were economically under-developed except for the production of raw material for factories then located in India on the other side of the new international frontier. With the exception of the Punjab, all the component units were comparatively poor. This complicated the problem—also faced by India—of resettling the millions of refugees who flocked to the new National Home. Jinnah helped by able colleagues, made heroic efforts to deal with all these difficulties; and by the time that he died towards the end of 1948 the survival of Pakistan was assured. With the assistance of foreign aid and by tireless work, both heavy and light industries were set up and a number of State Corporations were formed—Water and Power, Development, Finance, Small Industries, and the like—to implement successive Five Year Plans. The economic development of Pakistan, its high growth rate in Gross National Product, and the prudent management of its finances, represent an achievement of no mean order. In the political and constitutional fields, Pakistan suffered from a lack of the continuity of direction which Jawaharlal Nehru's long tenure of power conferred upon India. The death of Jinnah left Pakistan without a charismatic figure around which sentiment could rally and this was the more serious because differences in aims and outlook between the two "wings" of Pakistan—divided as they were by some 1000 miles of Indian territory—inevitably grew. West Pakistan was greatly influenced by resentment against India over such matters as the partition of the Indus Valley waters for irrigation and the position of Kashmir. East Pakistan felt that its point of view, which centred on greater control of local affairs and a more effective voice in national policy—especially since East Pakistan commanded a majority of the people of Pakistan—was insufficiently regarded at the Centre.

Great difficulties were encountered by the Constituent Assembly—which also functioned as a legislature—in framing a constitution which would at the same time adhere to Islamic principles and meet the needs of a modern State. When

Jinnah died, he was followed as Governor-General by Nazimuddin, a distinguished East Pakistani, with Liaquat Ali as Prime Minister. Unluckily for the country, Liaquat Ali, a practical statesman of great ability, was assassinated in 1951, whereupon Nazimuddin stepped into his place as Prime Minister and Ghulam Muhommed became Governor-General. During his time the original Constituent Assembly was dissolved because of his differences with it; and the four Provinces of West Pakistan were combined into a single unit to "balance" the great block of East Pakistan, with its unity of culture and language (see Bangladesh below, p. 694). After much labour, a constitution was prepared in 1956, by which time Ghulam Muhommed had resigned because of ill-health and had been succeeded by Major-General Iskander Mirza—the first of the three soldiers to rule Pakistan between 1955 and 1972. The constitution of 1956 made Pakistan an Islamic Republic, still within the Commonwealth, and Iskander Mirza became the first President. In 1958 he abrogated the constitution as unworkable, dissolved the National and Provincial Assemblies and declared martial law. He quickly lost power to General (later Field Marshal) Ayub Khan, who instituted many administrative and social reforms and in 1962 promulgated a new constitution based on village self-government ("Basic Democracies") and indirect election for the legislatures. The intelligentsia and the students grew restless; East Pakistan resented the concentration of power in the West Wing, and in spite of Ayub Khan's efforts to give East Pakistanis a liberal share in the administrative and other Services, discontent grew to a pitch which obliged him to resign and hand over power to the Commander-in-Chief, Yahya Khan in 1969. The new President announced his aim to be the restoration of democratic institutions; he restored autonomy to the four Provinces merged in 1955; and at the end of 1970 held elections based on adult suffrage. As a result, Zulfikar Ali Bhutto's Pakistan People's Party won the majority of seats in the West, while in the East Shaikh Mujibur Rahman's Awami League swept the board, and thanks to the East's population-majority, was also in a position to dominate the new National Assembly. Yahya Khan, in an endeavour to hold Pakistan together, tried to arrange some accommodation between the two leaders. When these efforts failed, disorders broke out which challenged the authority of the Central Government. With Indian assistance, this rising triumphed, and the territory of East Pakistan became an independent nation under the name of Bangladesh. At the end of 1971, Yahya Khan resigned in favour of Zulfikar Ali Bhutto; and the uphill task of reconstructing a truncated Pakistan was set in hand. Steady progress was made: a new democratic constitution based on adult suffrage came into force in 1973: several outstanding causes of disagreement with India were adjusted: and the independence of Bangladesh was formally recognised in February 1974. In 1977 Zulfikar Ali Bhutto met much opposition stemming from accusations of electoral malpractices and after considerable rioting he was removed from power by the military and eventually executed in 1979.

In Pakistan's early years, there were strong links with the Western democracies, exemplified by a defence agreement with Washington. This policy changed, under Ayub Khan's direction, into one of friendship with Communist and non-Communist alike, without any "entangling alliances". But strong links, economic as well as political, were established with Iran and Turkey under a scheme known as the "Regional Cooperation for Development", with a common policy for cultural exchanges, banking, insurance, tourism and the like. Mr Bhutto continued these ties, but left the Commonwealth in 1972. The aim has been to maintain good relations with Russia as well as China, and to strengthen the links between Pakistan and other Muslim countries. Since 1973 the "Northern Areas" with the picturesque valleys and magnificent mountains of Hunza, Gilgit and Chitral have been opened to tourists.

KARACHI

Karachi (pop. over 3 million) (International Airport; Hotels) was the first capital of Pakistan. and remains the capital of the Province of Sind. It has expanded from being a comparatively small provincial town into a large city. Since 1960, it has ceased to be the capital, which is now located at Islamabad, a new city well laid out on the Potwar plateau near Rawalpindi. But some Government offices still remain in Karachi, which is the principal commercial centre of Pakistan.

It is strung round a natural rock-bound haven formed by the S. extremity of the Khirthar Mountains. It existed as a mere fort from 1725 to 1838, when it was taken by the British from the Talpur Amirs. Sir Charles Napier first discerned the advantages of this natural harbour over the old capital of the Amirs at Hyderabad. It is a large seaport, and is served by several British, Indian and foreign shipping lines.

With the development of domestic and international air communications, Karachi has assumed new importance as a junction for air services between the eastern and the western world. The international airport on Drigh Road, which is constantly being enlarged, is a calling-point for all the important airlines. It is also the hub of frequent domestic services in Pakistan and of services to all the main cities of India.

N. are the old golf-course, now occupied by refugee camps, but in process of rapid evacuation as the inhabitants are resettled in new towns such as Korangi (p. 557); the Napier Barracks (now Government Offices and the Jinnah and Military Hospitals); and a block of buildings extending over the maidan. N. of the **Lines** is the **R.C. Cathedral** (St **Patrick**). A vast new town is springing up between here and Drigh Road Airport. The new golf-course is near Drigh Road Ry. Station. A little farther on is the Imperial War Graves Cemetery for British Officers and O.Rs.

W. of Frere Street, leading from the City ry. station, is the former **Frere Hall,** now Bagh-i-Jinnah. The building contains a museum, the Pakistan Institute of International Affairs and the Karachi General Library. In the grounds are fine statues of Queen Victoria and of King Edward VII; close by stands the Baluch Regiment Memorial, erected in 1922. Near by are the Sind Club, Karachi Gymkana, etc.

Old **Government House,** built by Sir C. Napier; the present house, built in 1940, is a residence of the President. E. is **Trinity Church** with its square campanile. N. is the Y.M.C.A.; farther N. is St Andrew's Church, and near by is the Empress Market. The graves of the Quaid-i-Azam, Mohammed Ali Jinnah and the late Prime Minister, Mr Liaquat Ali Khan, are situated in the old Exhibition ground on Bunder Road extension. Near the President's house is the Legislative Assembly building and the Secretariat of some Government Departments.

The **Law Courts** were moved from McLeod Road to the Old Artillery Maidan.

McLeod Road leads to the **General Post Office** and the **D. J. Sind College.** On the left is the Karachi **City** Railway Station. The Chamber of Commerce, Banks and Steamship Agencies are in this road. The bazar part of the city lies to the N. of McLeod Road, between it and the Layari river, and is traversed by Bunder Road, which joins McLeod Road near the memorial clock-tower of Sir William Merewether. Just off it is an office of the U.K. Ambassador.

The Bunder Road runs N.E. to S.E. across the Chinna Creek to the Napier Mole fronting the Karachi Harbour. Along or near it are the following buildings: U.S. Embassy, Y.W.C.A., Civil Hospital, C.M.S. Mission and Church, G. H. Khalikdina Hall, Municipal offices, Max Denso Hall and the Port Trust offices. Housing schemes have populated the Eastern end of the road, and the Sind Textile Mills are situated here.

2 m. along the Napier Mole is **Keamari** (4 m. from the centre of Karachi), a busy shipping port, with its long line of wharves, connected with Karachi by rail and tram. Once this was an island. At Keamari the **Karachi Harbour** commences. It is a first-class harbour, and additional railway facilities have constantly been added. There is very good sea-fishing to be had in the harbour, which is famed for its fish and oysters. The Karachi Yacht Club holds races thrice weekly throughout the year.

Near the Napier Mole, on the Chinna Creek, is the **Karachi Boat Club.** On the *Manora* headland, at the entrance to the harbour on the West, the **lighthouse** shows a fixed light 148 ft. above sea-level, visible 17 m. in clear weather. On the meridian of Karachi there is no land between Manora and the South Pole. There are bathing resorts at Sandspit, Hawkes Bay, Baleji and Two Mile Beach farther W., but the most important recent development has been the basing here of the Pakistan Navy, which started in 1947 from very small beginnings. It is already of considerable sea-going strength and has numerous shore establishments. The most interesting of these is the P.N. Boys' Training establishment on Manora Island, but many are worth a visit if permission can be obtained. A large dry-dock lies on the West Wharf.

Racing has become more frequent on the race-course.

Clifton, 3 m. S. of Karachi proper, a favourite afternoon ride and drive, stands on the sea. Since 1947, an important residential suburb has grown up here, which formerly included most of the foreign embassies and legations, many of which have now moved to Islamabad. The Ministry of External Affairs has an office here, but Clifton has lost some of the characteristics of a Diplomatic *enclave*. There is a fine sandy beach here, extending S.E. for miles, on which turtles in August, September and October come up at night to lay their eggs, and turtle-turning is a pastime. During the cold weather the tanks and jhils about Karachi swarm with small game birds, while in the Baluch Mountains, 25 m. W. of Manora, ibex, urial, panther, and bear are occasionally to be found. In the Hab River, the boundary between Sind and Baluchistan (20 m. from Karachi) mahseer fishing can be had during spates.

Mungho Pir, 11 m. N. of Karachi, on a good motor road, can be seen in an evening. A Leper Asylum has been established here. From the roots of a clump of date-trees a stream of hot water gushes out, the temperature of which is 133°. On the W. side of the valley is a temple surrounded by a thick grove and close to a swamp caused by the superfluous waters of the spring. A tank surrounded by a 5-ft. mud wall contains crocodiles. The Muslims in charge of the Pir's Tomb will kill goats for visitors who wish to see the crocodiles fed. They are of the dangerous snub-nosed species, different from the long-snouted *gharial* of the Indus.

Korangi. Visitors should make a point of seeing the new city of Korangi, first designed to accommodate refugees, but now developing into a well-planned urban unit, with its own light industries, residential areas, markets, schools and hospitals.

The University of Karachi contains a number of colleges and has a rapidly increasing student population.

Note

There is still good small-game shooting to be had in many parts of Sind, particularly duck, quail, snipe, black and grey partridge. But the extension of perennial irrigation canals is altering local conditions so rapidly that visitors planning a shooting holiday should consult the Government Tourist Bureau at the Hotel Intercontinental or in Club Road, Karachi. During the winter months, touring by car is very pleasant: and good highway maps can be obtained from the Government Tourist Bureau and from the "Shell" Agencies. A variant of this procedure is to travel by air to the more important centres (p. 76) and hire a car for excursions on arrival.

As already noted in the Introductory Information (pp. 12-14) Pakistan is linked to Europe *via* Afghanistan, Iran and Turkey by roads running through Torkham and the Khyber: through Chaman to Quetta and through Mirdjaveh to Quetta. Inside Pakistan there is a good network of motorable and jeepable roads, of which details are available from the A.A. of Karachi and the A.A. of Lahore, as well as from Tourist Information Offices. Among the main routes for motorists the following may be mentioned, particulars of servicing facilities, petrol supplies, hotels and rest houses can be ascertained in advance.

1. Karachi-Lahore *via* Sukkur and Multan (811 m).
2. Sukkur-Quetta *via* Jacobabad (262 m.).
3. Quetta-Zahidan *via* Qila Safed (447 m.).
4. Quetta-Chaman (80 m.) (for Kandahar).
5. Quetta-Fort Sandeman (206 m.).
6. Panjnad-Multan *via* Bahawalpur (117 m.). Boat bridge or Ferry.
7. Multan-Quetta *via* Loralai (355 m.).
8. Multan-Peshawar *via* Khushab (384 m.).
9. Multan-Mianwali (196 m.).
10. Lahore-Peshawar-Torkham (310 m.).
11. Lahore-Bannu (343 m.).
12. Rawalpindi-Murree-Muzaffarabad (86 m.).
13. Rawalpindi-Abbottabad (73 m.).
14. Abbottabad-Babusar *via* Kaghan (140 m.).
15. Peshawar-Saidu Sharif (108 m.).
16. Saidu-Sharif-Kalam (63 m.).
17. Peshawar-Parachinar *via* Kohat (157 m.).

For those who prefer to base their travels on the railways, the itinerary is as follows.

ROUTE 1

(*a*) KARACHI to LAHORE (*via* Indus. E. Bank) by Jangshahi (for **Thatta**), **Kotri, Hyderabad, Khairpur, Rohri, Samasata, Bahawalpur, Sher Shah** Junction, **Multan, Montgomery** (for **Harappa**).

(*b*) KOTRI-ROHRI loop-line (*via* Indus W. bank) by **Sehwan**, Bubak Road, Dadu, Sita Road, Dokri (**Mohenjodaro**), Larkana, Ruk Junction, **Sukkur.**

(*c*) RUK JUNCTION to CHAMAN and QUETTA by **Shikarpur, Jacobabad, Sibi**, and **Quetta**, also branch to Harnai.

13 m. Malir is a garden suburb of Karachi, accessible by bus or train. There is a good hotel with a swimming-pool. The Malir river bridge is endangered occasionally by floods after cyclonic rains. Between Karachi and Thatta (by road) at **Banbhore** (R.H.) are the newly excavated remains ascribed to **Debal,** the port where the Muslims first landed in Sind in the 8th century A.D. The **Haleji Lake** (54 m. from Karachi, D.Bs.) provides excellent fishing. **Kalri Lake** (70 m.) is a picnic resort with tourist accommodation and much small game. **Jherruck** (D.B.) 33 m. from Thatta is a favourite health resort with shooting and fishing.

54 m. **Jangshahi** station (R.). A good road runs 13 m. S.E. to Thatta on the Indus, and on the Karachi-Khyber Highway. On the Makli Hill (11 m.) (I.B., R.H.) there are many monuments of Samma, Arghun, Turkhan and Mughal rulers. There is also a T.B. Sanatorium. Partridge, grouse and snipe are found around Thatta; the lesser Indian bustard (Houbara) on the plains; hog and deer in the Thatta forests.

Thatta, pop. 12,786, but as late as 1739 a great city of 60,000 inhabitants, first comes into notice as the place where Alexander the Great bade farewell to his Admiral Nearchus before despatching him to explore the sea-route westwards. Later it was the seat of the Samma rulers of Lower Sind (1351-1517), who rebelled against Delhi and reached the zenith of their power in the reign of Nizam-uddin (1461-1509). The Jam Nindo is still remembered by the people as the prince-hero of the Golden Age of Sind. The Samma rulers gave place to Arghuns (1519-54) and Turkhans (1554-1625), invaders from the N. In 1555 a Portuguese fleet of 28 ships, under Pedro Baretto Rolim, arrived at Thatta, and, in the absence of the ruler in Upper Sind, sacked and burned the city and carried off much booty. The last Turkhan died in 1625, and Jahangir annexed Lower Sind. In 1739 the Empire collapsed beneath the onslaught of Nadir Shah, after whose death (1747) new Sindi dynasties arose with capitals farther N. at Khudabad (near Dadu) and Hyderabad; thus Thatta declined. A British factory was allowed by Jehangir in 1631, and again for a few years by Mohammed Kalhora in 1758.

The most remarkable sight in Thatta is the great mosque, 600 ft. by 90 ft. with 100 domes, begun by Shah Jahan in 1647 and finished by Aurangzeb, recently restored, 1980. The glory of ancient Thatta is on the Makli Hill, 2 m. N.W. This vast necropolis, covering an area of 6 sq. m., is said to contain 1,000,000 graves. A few mausolea still survive.

Immediately N. of the steep incline which carries the road down the Eastern scarp of the hill is the tomb of Mirza Jani Beg, the last of the Turkhan rulers. It was built in 1599 and is of brick, the faces of which are glazed blue and blue-green.

Farther N. rises the splendid mausoleum of Nawab Isa Khan, Mughal Governor of Sind, who died in 1644. It is built entirely of stone in the Fatehpur-Sikri style, richly decorated throughout with surface tracery. It stands on a raised platform in the middle of a court, surrounded by a colonnade on carved pillars, with an upper storey. Stairs on the E. lead up to the roof.

A little distance to the E., on the very edge of the hill, is a low building of stone in the same style, containing the tombs of the ladies of the zenana of Nawab Isa Khan. The walls inside are covered with carving in low relief. The view from the Eastern doorway, across the intervening lake to the present town of Tatta, is beautiful.

Near the N.W. corner of Nawab Isa Khan's tomb is that of Diwan Shurfa Khan, in whose lifetime it was built (1638). It is a massive square structure with heavy round towers at the corners and is constructed of fine brickwork, pointed in the joints with strips of dark blue tiling. The dome was covered with blue glazed tiles, a portion only of which remains.

1½ m. farther N. along the crest of the hill is the tomb of the famous Nizam-ud-din (Jam Nindo). This is a square stone structure, which some have thought was built from the remains of a Hindu temple. The W. façade is magnificently carved in a purely Hindu style. Inside, the springing of the great arches to support a dome, which was never built, affords an excellent example of the early attempts of Hindu craftsmen to arrive at the Saracenic arch by their own method of corbelling flat stones. The noble simplicity of the interior is in striking contrast with the Hindu richness of the W. façade.

105 m. **Kotri** (D.B.) (loop-line along the W. bank of the Indus to Rohri, p. 542), H.Q. of the great lower Sind Barrage, 4½ m. N. of Kotri, named after the late Governor-General, Mr Ghulam Mohammed. The railway quits the Indus for Karachi, which lies some 50 m. N.N.W. of its mouths. Kotri is connected with Karachi by a trunk road 120 m. long.

The main line now crosses the Indus by a bridge of five spans of 350 ft. (1900), carrying a road also, to 111 m. **Hyderabad** (Haidarabad) (Hotels) (seat of Sind University), with a pop. of about 300,000. It is situated (alt. 84 ft.) 2 m. N. of the Ganja hills, from which it is separated by an old course of the Indus. This river now flows to the W. of the city. On the E. is the Fuleli Canal, which used to leave the main stream 12 m. above the town, but is now supplied by a new cut which encircles Hyderabad hill on the N. From the earliest times the hill seems to have been occupied in part by a fort called "Neran", but no trace exists. The modern city was laid out by Sarfaraz Khan, son of Ghulam Shah Kalhora, in 1782. A strong S.W. wind blowing at the end of April for forty days (Chalika) is caught by wind scoops which are a prominent feature of the town, and help to mitigate the heat.

The **Fort,** built 1782, is of a very irregular form, and about ¾ m. in circumference; in the centre is a large "burj", or a keep, with a water-tank, and a revolving beacon for aircraft. The ditch has been filled in. It was crossed by a bridge leading to one of these intricate gateways which have so often yielded to a "coup de main". The residences of the Talpur Mirs (1783-1843) have now almost disappeared. In fact, since an explosion in the fort in 1906, very little remains but the tower. Portions of Mir Nasir Khan's palace are kept up. He became head of the Baluchis on the death of his brother, Mir Nur Mahomed Khan, in 1840, but was sent to Calcutta in 1843 and died 1846. The painted Chamber is a protected monument. In the recesses various historical subjects connected with the Kalhora family are delineated. A picture in one recess represents an interview between one of the Amirs and an English officer in political uniform, intended either for Colonel Henry Pottinger or Sir James Outram. An ascent to the circular tower gives a view of the surrounding country, with the Fuleli on one side, winding through the dusty plain, and the Kotri side of the Indus, with a buttress of rock, an offshoot of the Khirthar range, in the background.

The Kutchery (1912) consists of Revenue and Judicial offices. Just S. of it, and overlooking the railway, is the tomb of Shah Makkai, a saint from Mecca, said to have come here in 1260. The battlemented mud wall round the tomb was built by Ghulam Shah Kalhora. The main bazar runs for over a mile in a straight line from the fort gate to the new market.

The tombs of the Kalhoras and Talpurs cover the N. portion of the hill on which Hyderabad is built. The tombs of the Talpurs are very beautiful, but not quite in such exquisite taste as that of **Ghulam Shah Kalhora,** deputy of the King of Kabul from 1762-72, the description of which may serve for all.

On entering the enclosure by a small but richly carved door the visitor is impressed by the beautiful symmetry of the mausoleum and the religious feeling displayed in the decorations, marble tomb, rich fresco paintings on the walls. The dome fell and has been replaced by a flat roof. The beautiful marble railing surrounding the tomb was shattered by the fall, and only the fragments of it remain. Over one of the archways is an inscription in Persian, written by the order of his son Sarfaraz, whose tomb is in a burial-ground below the hill, and was built in 1785.

There are four tombs of the Talpurs —that of Mir Karam Ali (1811-28), a domed rectangular building, with a turret at each corner, built in 1812, with marble fretwork and roofed with coloured tiles; those of Mirs Murad Ali (1828-33), Nur Muhammad (1833-40), Nasir Khan, with white marble tombs inside; that of Mir Ghulam Shah and Fazl Ali, erected in 1855; and that of Mir Muhammad, built in 1857.

The **Cantonment** lies on a low ridge N.W. of the town. Not far off is the church of St Thomas. On the N. side of the communion-table is a brass showing the number of officers and men who fell at Miani and Dabo (1843).

Hyderabad is famous for its embroideries, especially "Nats", the leather covers for the saddles of riding camels, in silk and gold—only a few Baluchi Sirdars still use them—and its silver tissues.

In the Mirs' time there was a great demand for enamelling of their swords, matchlocks and horse-trappings, which were profusely decorated with enamelled ornaments. In enamelling on gold the colours red and crimson are chiefly used, and blue and green on silver.

At the close of the 18th century Sind owed only a nominal allegiance to Afghanistan, and was coveted both by the Sikhs and by the East India Company, which had held commercial interests there for a long time; but the First Afghan War broke out in 1838, and as Sind was then the only corridor to Afghanistan available, Ranjit Singh being in control of the Punjab, the East India Company became more concerned in its future, and eventually in spite of local opposition took Sind under their protection in 1839. The Amirs resented this high-handed action and resorted to arms.

On 15th February 1843, Major Outram was attacked in the Residency at Hyderabad, and two days later Sir C. Napier defeated the Amirs at Miani.

A memorial pillar has been erected in the old Cantonment near the river just S. of One Tree Bunder, 3 m. from Hyderabad, to commemorate the site of the Residency.

A visit can be made to the famous battlefields of **Miani** and **Dabo,** on which, in 1843, was decided the fate of Sind. The three places form a triangle, Miani being on the Fuleli 6 m. to the N.W. of Hyderabad and Dabo 5½ m. to the E. (near the railway), where Napier defeated Mir Sher Mahomed Khan of Mirpur Khas.

On the E. side of the monument at Miani are the names of the officers who fell.

A branch line (broad-gauge) and

a motor road run S. to (62 m.) *Badin*, on the edge of the Tharparkar Desert of which a portion is now irrigated.

From Hyderabad the metre-gauge line (previously part of the Jodhpur Rly.) runs to Khokrapar, and formerly continued thence to Luni Junction (309 m.) (p. 259), Jodhpur and Ahmedabad, with a branch to Khudro (N). and a loop on the S. It is now interrupted at the Indian frontier between Khokrapar and Munabao. At Mirpur Khas, 42 m. E. (by road also), is a stupa, 50 ft. each way, with terra-cotta figures of Buddha.

At Chhor (89 m. E.) a road runs to Umarkot (12 m. S.), a mediaeval Rajput fort, celebrated as the birthplace of Akbar. In 1540 the Emperor Humayun, after defeat by Sher Khan Sur of Ghor, obtained succour at Umarkot from the Rana. The child who afterwards became the Emperor Akbar was born (23rd November 1542) by tradition under an "ak" bush (whence his name), and a stone today indicates the supposed site. On the main road lies Diji, a fort of the Talpur Amirs: nearby is the pre-Mohenjo Daro site of Kot Diji (*see* pamphlet of Pakistan Archaeology Dept.).

280 m. **Khairpur,** built 1783, seat of a branch of the Sind Amirs, the Talpurs, and capital of the former Khairpur State. Khairpur is celebrated for its fine pottery and enamelled woodwork. S. of Nawabshah, at Chauhu Daro, a Chalcolithic site was excavated in 1935.

296 m. **Rohri,** or Lohri, station (District Bungalow for Government Officers), alt. 228 ft., is on the E. bank of the Indus, on limestone, interspersed with flints much quarried for railway ballast. The houses, two and three storeys high, have flat roofs surrounded by balustrades. It is said to have been founded by Saiyad Rukn-ud-din Shah in 1297, more than 300 years after the Indus deserted a former bed at Alor for the Bhakkar Pass. The rocky site ends in a precipice 40 ft. high, rising from the river-bank. The Sukkur Barrage keeps the level high for 6 m. upstream. Excellent dates are grown.

The *Jami Masjid* is decorated with glazed porcelain tiles. A Persian inscription records that it was built by Fateh Khan, an officer of the Emperor Akbar, about 1583. One of the relics is the *Mui Mubarak*, or "a hair of the Prophet", in amber, and preserved in a gold tube adorned with rubies in the War Mubarak (War, in Sindi = mui, Persian for hair), a building 25 ft. sq. on the N. of the town, said to have been erected about 1545 by Mir Muhammad. The hair was brought from Constantinople by one Abdul Baki, whose descendants have still the keeping of it. The present building, with its striking green dome and painted walls, was built by the Pir (Muslim saint) of Kingri. The *Idgah* was erected in 1593 by Mir Muhammad Ma'sum. Near Rohri are forests, covering 90 sq. m., which were planted in 1820 by the Talpur Amirs, now under the Sind Forest Department. The wood is of little use except as fuel and is no longer used in railway engines.

The **E. Nara Canal,** built by J. G. Fife (1858), used to run from Rohri due S. through Khairpur, into the Tharparkar District.

It is now 525 m. long, fed by the Lloyd Barrage lower down. The pala fish which used to run up the river are now stopped by the barrage.

Excursion to Arore (Aror)—formerly the very ancient Alor[1]—is only 5 m. distant to the E. Alor was visited about 640 by the Chinese pilgrim Hiuen Tsang, who gave the picture of a Sind stretching from Kashmir to the sea with a capital at Alor under a Sudra monarch. Thereafter a Brahmin, Chach, usurped the throne; and in 711 his son and successor, Dahir, was defeated by the invading Arabs under Muhammad bin Kasim. At that time the Indus washed the walls of the city, but was diverted into its present channel by an earthquake in 962.

[1] Alor, Uch, and Hyderabad are believed to have been the sites of three of many Alexandrias.

Once the road from Rohri crossed, by a bridge over 600 ft. long, the ancient channel of the Indus, but only a few stones show where the bridge once stood. The modern metalled road from Rohri does not pass through the village of Arore, which is on an elevation, but skirts its base. A ridge of ruins runs N.E. One ruin bears the name of Alamgir's Mosque. Two of them are shrines, one to Shakarganj Shah, and the other to Kutb-ud-din Shah. To the first tomb people of the neighbouring villages still make pilgrimages. It has no dome or building over it, but is a plain, white, neat tombstone, with a border of carved flowers. Half a mile away is a Hindu shrine of Kalika Devi, where a light is kept burning day and night.

367 m. **Reti** station (R. and railway R.H.). 4 m. S. are the vast ruins of *Vijnot*, a leading city before the Muslim conquest: there is nothing to be seen but debris. The country now is subject to spills from the Sutlej and there are swarms of black partridge.

Following the course of the Indus, through a very dusty tract, the railway, now in the former Bahawalpur State, reaches

504 m. **Samasata,** junction for the branch line (not connected at present however beyond the Indian frontier) to Bhatinda (p. 363) and Delhi: also for a loop S. to Bahawalnagar *via* Fort Abbas (68 m.). By the canals flowing from the headworks at Islam (near Bakshan Khan station on this line) and Sulemanki (p. 565) water is supplied to the desert tracts of the Bahawalpur district.

512 m. **Bahawalpur** (D.B.), was the chief town (called Baghdad-ul-Jadid), and capital of the State of that name before it was absorbed in W. Pakistan.

The former Rulers, were by race Daudputras (sons of David), a descendant of Daud Khan of Shikarpur, Sind. Their ancestors assumed independence of Afghan rule after the first expulsion of Shah Shuja from Kabul.

The town was built (*c.* 1780) by Bhawal Khan on an old site. The Palace of the Amirs is to the E. At the side are underground rooms, where the thermometer remains at 70°, while it rises from 100° to 110° in the upper rooms. An extensive view E. can be obtained from the roof towards the Desert of Bikaner, which stretches for 100 m. In Rahimyar Khan, nearby, great developments have taken place. Lever Bros. have erected a huge soap factory, while cotton and other factories are also springing up. Bahawalpur has a large hospital and various school buildings, all worth a visit. It is famous also for its light-weight pottery and delicate embroidery.

516 m. the **Adamwahan Bridge,** carries the N.W. railway and road across the Sutlej river.

521 m. from Karachi *via* Chord line is **Lodhran** Junction for the Sutlej Valley line from Kasur to Lodhran *via* Pakpattan (p. 565).

566 m. **Sher Shah** junction (D.B.), whence the Sind-Sagar Railway (p. 586) branches off W. and N., and crosses the Chenab, by a bridge of seventeen 200-ft. girders carrying the road also.

575 m. **Multan Cantonment** (R., D.B.) station (alt. 401 ft.) and

576 m. **Multan city** (D.B. in Cantonment, 1 m. from Cantonment stn. Hotels: Tourist B.) has a pop. of more than 200,000. It is 4 m. from the left bank of the Chenab and not far from the old bed of the Ravi. It is a place of great antiquity, and supposed to be the capital of the Malli mentioned in Alexander's time.

The first mention of Multan by name is by Hiuen Tsang in 641. Istakhri, who wrote in 950, describes the temple of the idol of Multan as a strong edifice between the bazars of ivory dealers and the shops of the coppersmiths. The idol was of a human shape, with eyes of jewels and the head covered with a crown of gold. Soon after 950 Multan was taken by the Karmatian[1] Chief,

[1] A short-lived sect in Iraq founded A.D. 891. Karmat took Mecca from the Kaliph, A.D. 930.

Jelem, son of Shiban, who killed the priests and broke the idol in pieces. It was restored in 1138. In 1666 Thévenot describes the temple of the Sun God as still standing, and the idol as clothed in red leather and having two pearls for eyes. This idol was destroyed by the orders of Aurangzeb.

Muhammad bin Kasim from Arabia conquered Multan for the Khalifs (712), and it was taken by Mahmud of Ghazni in 1005, and by Timur in October 1398. Subsequently it formed part of the Mughal Empire, later (1739) of Nadir Shah's dominions and (1752) of the Durani kingdom under Ahmad Shah. In 1779 the Governor was Muzaffar Khan, a Sadozai Afghan. He was killed with his five sons when Ranjit Singh stormed the place in 1818.

In 1829 Sawan Mal was appointed Sikh governor. He was shot in 1844, and was succeeded by his son Mulraj. Upon his omission to pay revenue to the Sikh Council of Regency after the First Sikh War, Mr Vans-Agnew and Lieut. Anderson, who were sent to instal a new governor under the Regency, were murdered at the Idgah on 20th April 1848, whereupon Mulraj went into rebellion. His forces were twice defeated by Lieut. Herbert Edwardes from the Derajat, and he was shut up in the fort; but Sikh forces sent from Lahore under the command of Maharaja Sher Singh, also went into rebellion, and this led to the Second Sikh War. On 22nd January 1849 the city was stormed by General Whish, and the fort was surrendered by Mulraj.

The heat of Multan is notorious, and the annual rainfall, from occasional thunderstorms, is little above 7 in. The saying goes:

> Dust, heat, beggars and tombs
> Are the four specialities of Multan.

The *Cantonment* lies to the W. of the town.

The **old Fort** is on the N. of the city. The entrance is by the Deo (Dewal = temple) Gate, so called because it leads to the famous temple of the Narsingh (Lion Man) form of Siva or Prahladpuri. The original temple stood in the middle of the fort and was destroyed by Aurangzeb, while the mosque built upon its site was totally blown up in the siege of 1848.

Inside the enclosure is a modern temple, and, farther on, the **Shrine** of **Rukn-ud-din,** grandson of Bahawal Haq (below), commonly known as Rukn-ul-Alam ("Pillar of the World"). This is an octagon of red brick, bonded with beams of Shisham wood, and supported by sloping towers at the angles. Over this is a smaller octagon, leaving a narrow passage all round for the muezzin to call the faithful to prayers. Above this is a hemispherical dome. The total height is 100 ft., but as the tomb stands on high ground it is visible for 30 m. round. One of the towers was thrown down when the powder magazine blew up in the siege of 1848, and was rebuilt in faithful imitation of the old one, including the timber bonds. The whole outside is ornamented with glazed tile patterns and string courses and battlements. The colours used are dark blue, azure and white, contrasted with the deep red of the finely polished bricks. The mosaics are not like those of later days, mere plain surfaces, but the patterns are raised from half an inch to two inches. The tomb was built by the Emperor Tughlaq Shah (1340-50) for himself, but given by his son Muhammad Tughlaq as a mausoleum for Rukn-ud-din.

Farther on, to the right, is an *obelisk* about 50 ft. high, erected in memory of Vans-Agnew and Anderson.

About ¾ m. to the N.W. of the fort is the Idgah, erected by Nawab Abdus Samad Khan in 1770 (1148 A.H.). It was restored to the Muslims in 1863.

The **Tomb of Baha-ud-din Zakharia** ("The Ornament of the Faith"), commonly called Baha-ul-Haq, or Bahawal Haq, is as old as the reign of the Emperor Balban (1264-86). It was almost completely ruined during the siege of 1848. Some glazed tiles remain outside. The lower part is a square; above this is an octagon half the height of the square, and above that a hemi-spherical dome. The son of Bahawal Haq, whose name was Sadr-ud-din, is buried in the same tomb. His cenotaph is adorned with green tiles. Opposite, in the corner of the vestibule, is the tomb of Nawab Muzaffar Khan, the last Muslim governor under the Duranis (d. 1818).

The **Tomb of Shams-i-Tabriz,** a celebrated Sufi martyr, murdered in 1247, stands ½ m. to the E. of the fort on the high bank of the old bed of the Ravi. The tomb, rebuilt 1780, is a square surrounded by a veranda, with seven openings in each side. Above is an octagon, surmounted by a hemispherical dome covered with glazed sky-blue tiles. The whole height is 62 ft. To the left of the entrance is a small square building, dignified as the Imambara. There are other shrines of martyrs in 1270.

The Medical College of great reputation is worth seeing. Multan is noted for its handcrafts, and cottage industries like tile-work, enamelling, silk and carpet weaving, fine light-weight pottery and parchment work.

578 m. **Khanewal** Junction. The lines serving the Chenab-Jhelum Canal Colonies, *via* Lyallpur and Shorkot Road, join the main line (Lahore to Karachi) here. A chord line, Khanewal to Lodhran, saves 26 m. Multan is on the original, now a loop, line.

652 m. **Montgomery** station (R., D.B.). This place is the headquarters of a District formerly known as Gugaira, and received its present name from Sir Robert Montgomery, Lieutenant-Governor of the Punjab (1859-65). It is an attractive town surrounded by fruit farms.

Pakpattan, 30 m. S., near the Sutlej river, is an ancient place, first known in history as *Ajudhan*, and identified with one of the towns belonging to the Sudrakoi or Oxudrakoi of Alexander's historians. Motors and tongas ply on a metalled road between Montgomery and Pakpattan. Trains from Lahore and back allow of four hours for a visit.

Originally a Hindu shrine, it was converted to Muslim worship by Baba Farid-ud-din Ganj Shakkar (1173-1265), of the Chishti family (pp. 265, 311). A great pilgrimage takes place here at the *Muharram*.

Pakpattan is a stn. on the Sutlej Valley line which runs between Kasur and Lodhran (p. 563). About 10 m. E. are the Sulemanki headworks of the Sutlej Valley Irrigation Project (p. 562).

15 m. from Montgomery station (motors available) by a canal road (with permission) or service road without restriction, are the remains of the prehistoric city of **Harappa,** situated beside the former bed of the River Ravi (116 m. S.W. of Lahore). Harappa Road, the next station but one, is 4 m. distant; intending visitors should make arrangements through a Tourist Information Bureau at Karachi or Lahore.

The mounds which cover the site of Harappa have a height of some 60 ft. above the plains and a present circuit of nearly 3 m., but much of the ancient city probably lies buried. Their exploration was begun by the Archaeological Department in 1920-1921. Owing to prolonged quarrying for bricks the site has been much damaged, and most of the buildings exposed are in a very fragmentary condition.

The largest mound was the Citadel, which was strongly defended by walls of baked and unbaked brick, with rectangular towers at close intervals. Below and to the N. of the Citadel is the Great Granary block, consisting of a double series of narrow halls with a broad aisle down the centre. The halls are about 52 ft. in length. Nearby are barracks for workmen and lines of circular working-platforms. To the S. of the Citadel are the cemeteries both of the townsfolk and of another people who came later upon the scene, perhaps after 1500 B.C.

Like those of Mohenjodaro (p. 567), the remains belong to several successive cities, one on the ruins of another. They appertain to the Chalcolithic Age when, with copper and bronze, stone was still being used for implements of everyday use. The inclusive dates may be about 2500-1500 B.C.

All the buildings brought to light are constructed of well-burnt bricks; the bonding material is usually mud, but occasionally gypsum. So far as can be judged the dwelling-houses and streets of Harappa closely resembled those of Mohenjodaro, and the social customs, religion and daily life in the two cities were generally similar.

There is a well-stocked Museum on the site. "Finds" include numerous seals of soap-stone, faience, shell, etc., engraved with legends in a pictographic script and with devices which generally take the form of real or fabulous animals. The copper objects include weapons and implements, double axes, daggers, lance-heads, mace-heads, celts and chisels. A model of a two-wheeled cart with gabled roof and driver seated in front is one of the oldest examples of a wheeled vehicle yet discovered. Other objects deserving notice are faience bangles with cogged edge and numerous rings of stone, terra-cotta, and other materials—some plain, others undulating—which appear to have been objects of cult worship.

The site of Harappa was partially reoccupied during the early centuries of the Christian era, but the only remains of a later date are a *Naugaza* grave (27 ft. long) of a Muslim saint and a ruined mosque.

730 m. **Raiwind** Junction station (R.) for Kasur, an old Pathan stronghold.

751 m. **Lahore Cantonment**, W.

754 m. **Lahore** Junction station (R. good). Lines run N. to Rawalpindi and Peshawar (Route 4).

(*b*) Kotri-Rohri loop-line (*via* Indus W. bank)

75 m. from Kotri is **Tirath Laki** station (R.), good quail, duck and snipe shooting in the neighbourhood. The railway runs through the Laki Pass, at an elevation of 200 ft., the Indus lying below. This range of hills contains several hot springs, and shows many signs of volcanic action. There are also lead, antimony and copper in them.

87 m. **Sehwan** station (D.B. in the old fort), 117 ft. above sea-level. Sehwan, a city of great antiquity, has been hallowed since 1272 by the memory of the very famous Persian Saint Sheikh Usman Merwandi, also called Kalandar Lal Shahbaz, who died here. His tomb, surmounted by a dome and lantern, is adorned with beautiful encaustic tiles and Arabic inscriptions. Mirza Jani Beg, of the Turkhan dynasty, built a still larger tomb to this saint, which was completed in 1639 by Nawab Dindar Khan. The gate and balustrade are of wood, encased in hammered silver, the gift of Rais Karam Ali Talpur, who also crowned the domes with silver spires. A great fair is held in Sehwan annually on the 18th *Shaaban*, when Hindus and Muslims join in paying reverence at the shrine. Sehwan was the capital of the Buddhist ascetic, Bhartari Hari, brother of Vikramaditya Chandragupta II, the 3rd Gupta Emperor (A.D. 375-413).

The town of Sehwan rises on a conical hill. A deep valley separates it from a fort so old that it has been ascribed to Alexander the Great, and is said to have surrendered to Muhammad bin Kasim about 711.

The **Manchhar Lake** is not very far from Sehwan to the W.; Bubak Road (8 m.) is the nearest rly. station. It is a large natural depression, supplied with water by hill torrents and by Indus water, which reaches it by way of the W. Nara outfall and the Aral Canal. In the cold weather there is abundance of water-fowl shooting, and excellent snipe, quail and partridge shooting round the edge of the lake, and an extraordinary number of fine fish.

The fish, formerly caught with spears, are now taken by an ingenious circular enclosure of nets, supported by poles. A flotilla of boats containing men with drums and noisy instruments surrounds the enclosure. The fish, frightened by the din, press nearer to the net flinging themselves into the air to jump over the lower net, but striking against the upper ones to fall into the bag below. Divers then go inside the net and examine it carefully under water, securing more fish.

113 m. Dadu station. 4 m. S. is an old capital, Khudabad of Khudayar Khan Kalhora.

128 m. **Sita Road** station. Road, 7 m., to Pat, where in 1541-42 the Emperor Humayun was married to Hamida Begam, from which union the Emperor Akbar sprang.

166 m. **Dokri.** 8½ m. E. by motor road from this station is **Mohenjodaro** (66 m. S.W. from Sukkur in the Larkana district). There are P.I.A. tourist flights from Karachi to a landing-ground near the Museum; taxis are available at **Sukkur** and **Larkana.** The Museum and Site can be visited in a day; but there is an Archaeological Dept. D.B. where meals can be had. An excellent brochure can be had from the Dept. of Tourism. Tongas available on application to the station-master at Dokri.

Mohenjodaro (the "Mound of the Dead") is a site of the Chalcolithic Age, and like Harappa (p. 565), representative of the "Indus" Civilisation. It covers the accumulated remains of a large city rebuilt on many occasions during the thousand years of its existence (about 2500-1500 B.C.). The visible ruins cover about 250 acres, but the outlying parts of the ancient cities are hidden deep beneath alluvium, and water is near the surface.

Near the N.W. corner and surmounting the highest mound is a **Buddhist Stupa** of the time of the Kushan king Vasudeva I (A.D. 182-220). It was in excavating this stupa that the ruins of Mohenjodaro were first discovered in 1922. With this exception all the buildings exposed belong to the prehistoric era.

The high mound which carries the Stupa was the citadel of the ancient city. Remains of its fortifications can be seen at the S.E. corner, and on the summit W. of the Stupa, is the **Great Tank or Bath,** which probably served for ablution purposes in connection with religious rites. It was 39 ft. long by 23 ft. wide, enclosed on three sides by a number of halls and chambers. A flight of steps, once paved with wood, led down into it at either end. In order to render the tank waterproof its brickwork was laid in gypsum mortar and further protected by a backing of bitumen. Near the S.W. corner is a drain for emptying or filling it. After passing through an inspection chamber provided with a manhole, this drain flows into a 6-ft.-high culvert furnished with a corbelled roof. To the N. of the tank and separated from it by a narrow lane is a double row of well-paved bathrooms ranged alongside a passage, down which runs an open drain. Each room has its own staircase leading to the top, and is so planned as to secure complete privacy for its inmate. Immediately W. of the tank is the massive brick substructure of the **Great Granary,** formerly surmounted by a timber superstructure, the floor of which was ventilated by air-passages visible in the brickwork. On the N. side of the building is a loading-platform, with an alcove for vehicles.

The remains excavated at Mohenjodaro are mainly residences and shops, the best examples of which are to be seen on the mounds to the E. and S.E. of the Buddhist Stupa N. of the road to Dokri. There are exposed a broad street and blocks of well-built houses, with stairways ascending to the upper floors, bathrooms, wells and underground drains. In this part of the city are two square sewage tanks in the main street, one of which is provided with steps inside to facilitate cleaning. In the area to the S. of the Dokri road, the visitor should notice in particular the corbelled doorways and drain culverts, as well as the inclined water-chutes connecting with the street drains. It is evident that the inhabitants of the place in the 3rd and 2nd millennia B.C. had advanced ideas both of town-planning and of municipal administration. Their commodious and well-planned houses bespeak a degree of luxury that was unknown at many later periods. It seems that the city was sacked, and its inhabitants ruthlessly murdered, by a sudden attack of invading Aryan hordes from the N.

In the **Museum** (1925) is an interesting collection of antiquities from this site, including engraved seals, jewellery, personal ornaments, implements, weapons, domestic utensils, sculptures, figurines, children's toys and painted pottery. Others are in the museum at Karachi.

171 m. **Larkana** Junction (D.B.). The country surrounding it is fertile and populous, and watered by the Sukkur Barrage. Branch line, N.W. to Jacobabad.

212 m. **Habib Kot** Junction (R.). From here the Quetta railway branches N. (see p. 569). The loop, once the main line, continues to

225 m. **Sukkur** station (R., D.B.; Circuit House, Canal Bungalow, available, if not occupied, and railway R.H.), headquarters of the Sukkur District, standing on the right bank of the Indus. The heat is great, but a breeze at night follows the river in the hottest season. There used to be carriage and wagon shops of the North-Western Railway here. Low, bare limestone ridges slope down to the Indus, and on them is the official quarter, called **New Sukkur,** a cantonment built by Sir C. Napier (1842).

There are tombs of Shah Khair-ud-din, a saint, built 1760, and Muhammad Ma'sum Shah Bakhri, Nawab of Sukkur, at the foot of a tower 90 ft. high, which he erected, and which overlooks the country for many miles. The town was ceded to the Khairpur Amirs between 1809 and 1824. In 1833 Shah Shuja defeated the Talpurs here with a force raised at Shikarpur (p. 569) in an attempt to recover Afghanistan, but he was himself defeated by Dost Muhammad near Kandahar, and returned to Ludhiana.

The **Sukkur Barrage,** 4725 ft. long, originally called after the late Lord Lloyd, then Governor of Bombay, who initiated this great enterprise, is 2 m. W. of New Sukkur. It was begun in 1923 and completed in January 1932. The barrage, 46 spans of 60 ft. across the Indus, feeds seven main canals with a total length of 400 m. One canal is wider than the Suez or Panama Canals and much longer. It irrigates approximately 6 million acres, much of which was virgin land, and is the largest irrigation work of its kind in the world. At the N. end is a memorial to General J. G. Fife, who first suggested its possibility.

On an island rock in the Indus, commanding a good view of the Lansdowne Bridge, is the picturesque temple of Shri Sadbella, with a monastery of Udiasin Sannyasis founded in 1823.

228 m. from Kotri is Rohri Junction (R.R.).

Opposite to Rohri, in the Indus, is the small *Island of Khwaja Khizr.* Here is a mosque with an inscription, the last words of which, "Dargah-i-Ali", give the date 952. The shrine of Khizr, who was also called Zinda Pir, or "the living saint", is venerated by Hindus and Muslims alike.

A little to the S. of the Isle of Khizr is the larger **Island of Bukkur.** It is a limestone rock of oval shape, 800 yd. long, 300 yd. wide, and about 25 ft. high, commanding the river. The fortress has two gateways, one facing Rohri on the E., the other Sukkur on the W. As early as 1025 Abdur Razzak, Minister of Mahmud of Ghazni, expelled an Arab Governor from Bukkur. In the beginning of the 13th century it was an important fortress of Nasir-ud-din Kabachas.

In 1327 Bukkur must have been

a place of note, for Muhammad Tughlaq of Delhi sent persons of importance to command there. Under the Samma Princes (p. 559) the fort changed hands, being sometimes under their rule and sometimes under that of Delhi. During the reign of Shah Beg Arghun the fortifications were rebuilt, the fort of Alor, 6 m. away, being destroyed to supply material. In 1574 it was delivered up to Keshu Khan, an official of the Emperor Akbar. In 1736 it fell into the hands of the Kalhoras, and subsequently into those of the Afghans, who retained it till it was taken by Mir Rustam of Khairpur. The Amirs attached much importance to this fort. But during the Afghan War of 1838 it was placed on demand at the disposal of the British, and was used first as an arsenal, and then, until 1876, as a prison for Baluchi robbers.

The Indus is crossed by the *Lansdowne Bridge*, connecting Rohri with the Island of Bukkur; the line then crosses the island to Sukkur by another bridge of 290 ft. span. The great span between Rohri and Bukkur is 840 ft. from centre to centre of the cantilevers; each cantilever is 320 ft. long, and the central girder connecting them is 200 ft. long. Since 1962 rail traffic has crossed the Indus by the **Ayub Arch**, the first bridge to have the railway deck slung on coiled wire rope suspenders. **Sukkur,** pop. 77,000, was formerly famous for its pearl trade and gold embroidery. It now has modern industries, including a biscuit factory.

From Sukkur a main road runs to Quetta, Chaman and thence to Afghanistan, Iran, Turkey and Europe. There is an alternative route from Quetta to Zahedan (Iran).

On the W. bank of the Indus a road runs *via* Kandkot to **Sui,** from which natural gas is widely distributed to Karachi and other cities.

(*c*) **Ruk Junction** to **Quetta** and **Chaman**

Habib Kot Junction (R., D.B.), 15 m. on the Karachi side of Sukkur (see p. 568). The first station of importance on the Sind-Pishin Railway, is

11 m. **Shikarpur** station (D.B., Circuit House, Inspection Bungalow, and railway R.H.), a municipal town, founded 1617. The old road (16 marches to Dadur across a desert) to Kandahar and Central Asia passes through Shikarpur, which was long a great trade depot. Shikarpuri traders used to be found all over Sinkiang, but since 1947 most have been driven out by the Chinese.

The bazar is covered in on account of the heat in summer. A branch of the Church Missionary Society at Quetta maintains a hospital for eye diseases, made famous by Sir Henry Holland, whose name is still legendary in Pakistan.

There is a drainage system, which is unusual. Shikarpur is connected with Sukkur by the trunk road, which continues towards

37 m. **Jacobabad** Junction, for the new line on the W. bank of the Indus via Kashmor and Dera Ghazi Khan, over the Taunsa Barrage to junction with Sind Sagar railway at Kot Adu (p. 588).

The town was planned and laid out on the site of the village of Khangarh by General John Jacob, the distinguished Political Superintendent and Commandant, Upper Sind Frontier (1847-58), who built the Residency. The main porch contains a commemorative tablet. A wonderful clock made by Jacob is still working, and he made a rifle (shown). He is buried here under a massive tomb. When he arrived in Upper Sind the whole country about Khangarh was in a state of anarchy; bodies of mounted robbers—Bugtis, Dombkis, Burdis or Marris—swept the plains and robbed and murdered those they encountered. General Jacob's rule put an end to all these troubles. Jacobabad is the headquarters of a civil district. The temperatures at Jacobabad are often the highest recorded in the Indian sub-continent, with an occasional reading of 127° F. in the shade in the months of May and June. It is 190 ft. above sea-level.

134 m. **Sibi** Junction station (R., D.B.); alt. 433 ft. Headquarters of the Sibi Agency. Each February, there is a very picturesque gathering of tribesmen, with a horse and cattle show and races. This place is in the valley of the River Nari, near the entrance of the Bolan Pass.

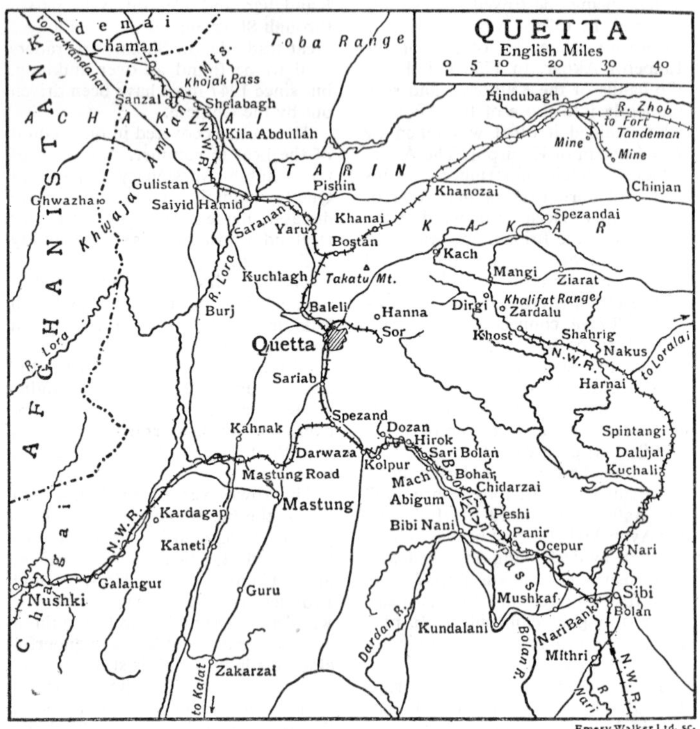

From *Sibi* there are two lines—the Northern, to *Harnai* and Khost, with gradients of 1 in 40; and the Southern, Mushkaf-Bolan line to *Quetta*. In the winter 22° to 23° of frost is not at all uncommon on the higher parts of the line, whilst in summer 120° inside the house is not an unfrequent temperature at Nari. The thickest clothing is necessary during a cold-weather tour.

Sibi to Bostan and Chaman by the Mushkaf-Bolan Route

The original alignment of this railway along the Bolan bed was afterwards abandoned in favour of the present line. It rises 5440 ft. to Kolpur and falls 375 ft. to Quetta. Bolan is said to mean "entrance" of the Mundas (prehistoric).

From **Mushkaf** (144 m.) the line runs for 28 m. up the Mushkaf Valley with easy gradients. It then passes by the Panir Tunnel, 3000 ft. long, into the upper Bolan. There is a road also. For 6 m. beyond the tunnel the gradients are exceptionally heavy, but from there up to **Mach** (181 m., 3250 ft.—engine changing station) they are lighter. From **Hirok** (189 m.) they become very heavy again, and the Bolan is crossed nine times. Three engines are usually attached to a train from Abigum (173 m.).

206 m. **Spezand,** junction for a railway over 83 m. of desert to Nushki (see below). The line extends to Duzdap, now known as Zahidan, 510 m. from Quetta.

222 m. **Quetta** (Shalkot) station (R.R., D.B., C.H., Hotels). The Tourist Information Office has recently moved to Jinnah Road. **Quetta** (Pushtu: *Kwatta* — Fort) (pop. over 100,000) is the headquarters of the Commissioner in charge of the Quetta division. It is connected by air with Karachi, Lahore, Multan and Rawalpindi. It is the home of the Staff College and its elevation (5500 ft.) makes it a favourite resort for southern Pakistan during the hot weather. It is an ancient place, its history goes back to the kingdom of Ghazni under Sultan Mahmud (A.D. 977-1030). It is still famous for embroidery and brass work, to be seen at the Pakistan Arts and Crafts Centre and in the bazars. It is situated at the N. end of the Shal Valley, 100¼ m. N. of Kalat, and is a place of great strategic importance, commanding with its outpost of Baleli both the Khojak and Bolan passes. Almost all the buildings in the Civil Station and City, including the Residency, the Club, the Sandeman Hall (in the City), the Sandeman Library, McMahon Museum, Town Hall and the Memorial Sarai were destroyed in the great earthquake of 31st May 1935. It happened at 3 minutes past 3 a.m., with its epicentre near Mach, and the casualties were enormous. Altogether 23,000 were killed in Quetta and the surrounding villages, including Mastung. Since then the place has been entirely rebuilt: there are three public parks, a broadcasting station, a geophysical observatory, three hotels and two sanatoria, and a number of cinemas and restaurants. E. of the City is the McMahon Park. To the N., on the farther side of the Habib Nulla, are the Cantonments. To the N.W. stands the *miri*, or fort, a former residence of the officials of His Highness the Wali of Kalat. The Staff College is on the road to *Hanna* (R.H., tea house and snack-bar), a favourite tourist resort famous for its fruit and natural lake. Two motorable roads link Quetta to Ziarat (below).

In winter the cold is very severe. The summer climate, however, is delightful. Fruit of every sort is abundant.

Quetta was occupied by British troops in the first expedition in 1838-1842 to Kabul. By the Treaty of Jacobabad (1876) a British political officer was again posted at Quetta (which was taken in lease in 1883), when the famous Sir Robert Sandeman was appointed Agent to the Governor-General for Baluchistan. He was buried at Las Bela.

The line now proceeds up the Quetta Valley by Baleli and Kuchlagh to

242 m. **Bostan** Junction for Khanai (see p. 572).

About 20 m. beyond Bostan Junction the Lora river is passed, the first stream on the Central Asian watershed.

250 m. **Yaru Karez,** the station for **Pishin,** on the trunk road to Chaman (76 m.). The Pishin valley is surrounded by 12,000 acres of vineyards and orchards: the town itself has a High School. There is good duck-shooting nearby.

272 m. **Gulistan** station. The main line turns due N. to

281 m. **Kila Abdullah** (R.).

291 m. (from Ruk), **Shelabagh** is at the foot of the *Khojak Pass*, and near the S.E. end of the tunnel passing under the Khwaja Amran Mountains. To the N. is the Tabina plateau, attained by the Zaraband Pass. This tunnel is about 2½ m. long, on a heavy grade, and the atmosphere sometimes

is bad. Passing through it, we reach Sanzalla (R.) and then, by a winding descent, the terminus at

310 m. **Chaman** station, alt. 4817 ft. is the last before the Afghan frontier is crossed. The trunk road runs on across Afghanistan and Iran to Turkey and Europe (see p. 12).

The Khojak Pass is surmounted by a military road also, and those who have the opportunity should ascend it (7200 ft.) to see the view W. over the Kadanai Plain and N. to beyond Kandahar, which is hidden by intervening hills.

The distance to Kandahar, the Gandhára of ancient India and the Arachosia of Alexander, is about 65 m.

Quetta-Nushki Railway

The Quetta-Nushki B.G. branch from Spezand, 16 m. from Quetta, enters the Chagi District at Galangur, 61 m. from Spezand, and runs in a Westerly direction to Nushki, 83 m.; thence to Dalbandin and Nok Kundi (219 m. from Nushki). The distance is 221 m. from Nok Kundi to Zahidan (Duzdap), in Persian territory, *via* Qila Safed on the border.

Trade converges at Nushki from Kharan and Shorawak; at Dalbandin from (*a*) Jalk and Mashkel; (*b*) Garmsel and the Eastern Helmand.

Bostan to Kach

The scenery of this route should be seen by daylight. Leaving **Bostan** (R.) the line, skirting the northern slopes of the Takatu Mountain on a gradually rising gradient, in one place forming a complete circle and passing over itself, runs to

Khanai Junction, N.G. line for Hindubagh (46 m., chrome mines), and opened in 1929 to Fort Sandeman or Apozai (174 m.), in the Upper Zhob valley, headquarters of a Political Agency; alt. 4778 ft. The **Zhob** Valley is little known to tourists but it contains some of the most beautiful scenery in Pakistan. Situated on one of the ancient caravan routes, it shows traces of an ancient civilisation akin to that of the Indus Valley. It is a paradise of wild flowers in the spring and of fruit in the autumn but the winter climate is severe. There are D.Bs. and R.Hs. at Hindubagh, Qilla, Sargullah and Fort Sandeman from which it can be explored. There is very good small game shooting.

A section of the former loop railway to Sibi, *via* Kach, Mangi, Khost and Harnai has been replaced by a motor road, as it was badly damaged by floods in July 1942.

Kach, 60 m. from Quetta, 6357 ft. The motor road carries on 33 m. farther to **Ziarat** (D.B. Rondavels: apply Deputy Commissioner giving a week's notice), a favourite retreat of the Quaid-i-Azam, a valley 8000 ft. above the sea, set amongst hills clothed in juniper forests. Ziarat is entirely shut up in the winter, as it is subject to heavy snowfalls. It enjoys an excellent climate, but lack of water—a reservoir on the hills collects water from natural springs in the rocks—has limited its development as a hill station. Fishing is available in the Kahan Tangi (10 m.), and there is much game in the locality.

Mangi, 13 m. From here a riding road goes to Ziarat (21 m. E.), traversing the narrow, deep defile of Mir Kasim Tangi.

4 m. below Mangi the **Chappar Rift** is traversed. The shoulder of a mountain has cracked from top to bottom through the solid mass of limestone, a common feature on the N.W. Frontier. The Rift (93-94 m.) was crossed by a bridge nearly 300 ft. above the bed of the stream. The line near the Rift ran through tunnels and across high bridges. A magnificent view is obtained of the Khalifat Range (11,440 ft.) rising sheer out of the valley on the N.W.

Branch Line from Sibi to Khost

This was formerly part of a through route to Bostan and Quetta, but is now a dead-end line.

Harnai (R.), 58 m. from Sibi; motor road to Loralai: not recommended (Bori; alt. 4700 ft.) and Fort Sandeman (Apozai).

Khost, 82 m. from Sibi, is the present terminus. Travellers by rail should enquire about the services here, which do not run daily.

ROUTE 2

LAHORE

(*Map faces p.* 580)

LAHORE[1] (alt. 705 ft.) is the capital of the West Punjab, the seat of two Episcopal Sees, Anglican and R.C., the principal social, cultural and academic centre of Pakistan (pop. 2 million). The annual Horse and Cattle Show, held in late February or early March, accompanied by polo, tent pegging, camel fights and other attractions, is a national event. Numerous excellent hotels.

Guide services and conducted tours are available through the Tourist Office in Egerton Road. There is much to see, as Lahore is full of historic relics. The most famous of these are perhaps the Lahore Fort, the Badshahi Masjid, the Mosque of Wazir Khan, Jehangir's Tomb and the Shalimar Gardens. Lahore, with important modern institutions, is also a great centre of learning focused on the famous Punjab University and its Colleges. Local amenities include golf, racing, clubs and restaurants. If only a short time can be devoted to sight-seeing, a good deal can be covered in the course of a drive along the Mall to the Fort and back through the City. Drive to Faisal Square, formerly Charing Cross, where five roads meet, and E. along the **Mall,** passing (in this order), right, the **Masonic Lodge,** a fine edifice at the entrance to the **Jinnah** (formerly **Lawrence) Gardens;** left, the **Lahore Hilton Hotel;** right, the combined

[1] Maps and Handbooks (historical and other) are obtainable from the Tourist Office and from many booksellers.

Lawrence and **Montgomery Halls;** left, **Government House,** the residence of the Governor of the Punjab; **Aitchison College;** 3 m. farther on is Mian Mir (Lahore Cantonment), beyond the Upper Bari Doab Canal (1859) which irrigates 27,000 sq. m.

The route along the Mall to the W. from Charing Cross, near which is Faletti's Hotel, passes on the right the Anglican Cathedral and on the left the **High Court** which the Federal Court of Pakistan also shares when sitting; several **Banks,** and then on the right, the **Telegraph Office**; and on the left, the **Post Office.** Near a slight turn in the road, on the left, are the **Tollinton Market,** the **Lahore Museum** (with "Kim's Gun" outside), the **National College of Arts** and the **Town Hall,** and beyond, the entrance to the **Anarkali Gardens;** the tomb of Anarkali and the principal Government offices lie to the S.W. of these, the rest of the offices and the **University** being opposite to the Museum. Turning N. along the Lower Mall the **Government College** is passed, right; left, **Deputy-Commissioner's Court** and **Government Model School.** Farther E. is the **King Edward Memorial Medical College** and **Hospital.** Proceeding round the W. side of the city the **Cemetery** is passed left, and, farther on, the road divides—that left leading to **Shahdara** (p. 583) across the Ravi river bridge, and that right passing the Badshahi Mosque, and the **Fort,** by a circular road round the N. of the city, to the railway station.

In the Public Buildings of Lahore an attempt has been made to adapt Hindu and Muslim styles to modern requirements.

History.—In 1013 Lahore, then called Panchalnagar, was in the hands of a Brahmin King of Kabul, from whom it was wrested by Mahmud of Ghazni, whose famous slave, Malik Ayaz, was Governor here. It was conquered by Shahab-ud-din Ghori in 1184, but did not, however, attain to magnificence till the rule of the Mughals. Akbar held his court here at times (1594-98), enlarged the fort and surrounded the town with a wall (which has been demolished). Jahangir often resided at Lahore, and during his reign Arjan Dev, Guru of the Sikhs, compiler of the *Adi Granth*, died in prison here. Shah Jahan built the palace of Lahore, and Aurangzeb built the great Badshahi Mosque, but in his time the city began to decline, and was much ruined from 1749 onwards by Ahmad Shah Abdali. Of its glory in its prime the proverb ran: "Isfahan and Shiraz united would not equal the half of Lahore". Vigorous Muslim governors, Abdul Samand Khan, Zakaria Khan (1717-1738), Yahia Khan (1738-48), the son of the latter, and nephew of the Delhi Wazir Kamar-ud-din Khan, and Mir Mannu, son of Yahia (1748-1752), maintained themselves in the Punjab, and fought with the Sikhs, but submitted to the Persians under Nadir Shah, and to the Afghans under Ahmad Shah. When the widow of Mir Mannu, Murad Begam, governing for her son, was entrapped by the Wazir of Delhi, Ghazi-ud-din, Adina Beg (1755-58) was made Governor of the Province; and it was his rebellion and the summoning of the Mahrattas to protect him against the Sikhs that led in 1761 to the Battle of Panipat. From 1775 the Sikhs were the real rulers. Under Ranjit Singh, Lahore grew greatly in importance, and under British rule from 1849 to 1947 its growth was intensified.

The Circular road runs round the city, to which it gives access by a number of gates.

In the N.W. corner is the Citadel. The city moat has been filled in and has been partly converted into lawns. The **Ravi** river, flowing W., once washed the walls of the city, and in 1662 made such encroachments as to necessitate the construction of a massive embankment 4 m. long, but it now passes at about 1 m. W. of the city.

At Charing Cross a Parliament Chamber forms part of a Government centre.

The Upper Mall—E. of Charing Cross

The **Jinnah Gardens** contain varieties of trees and shrubs such as the *Pinus longifolia*, the Australian gum-tree, and the carob-tree of Syria; also a zoo, a cricket ground, on which the M.C.C. sometimes play one of their Test Matches against Pakistan, and an open-air theatre.

At the N. side fronting the **Mall** is the **Lawrence Hall,** built in memory of Sir John Lawrence in 1862. The **Montgomery Hall,** built in 1866 in memory of Sir Robert Montgomery (Lawrence's successor as Lieutenant-Governor), faces the central avenue of the gardens.

Government House stands on the opposite side of the Mall, N. of the Jinnah Gardens. It was the tomb of Muhammad Kasim Khan, cousin of the Emperor Akbar. He was a great patron of wrestlers, and his tomb used to be called *Kushtiwala Gumbaz*, or Wrestler's Dome. E. of this is the **Gymkhana Club,** and E. again the **Aitchison College.**

The Mall—W. of Charing Cross

The **R.C. Cathedral** is a very fine building; the **Anglican Cathedral,** designed by Sir Gilbert Scott, was erected 1884-87. The **High Court** building is in the late Pathan style of the 14th century. The Telegraph Office, the Post Office and the State Bank are all handsome buildings. Adjoining the last is the original building of the **Forman Christian College,** now situated on the Canal bank.

The **Lahore Museum,** opened in 1894, contains antique sculptures, coins, Kangra and Mughal paintings, the arts and crafts of the Province, textile manufactures and some raw products. The Graeco-Buddhist sculptures were excavated from sites in the Peshawar district and surrounding territories, the ancient Gandhára country. These were largely the work of Graeco-Bactrian sculptors, and show a very strong Hellenistic influence, for example, in Corinthian capitals from Jamalgiri. The subjects are purely Indian, the bas-reliefs illustrating scenes of Buddha's life. The Buddha image itself is, in all probability, a creation of the artists of Gandhára. The flourishing period of the Graeco-Buddhist school is believed by the best authorities to fall in the 1st century A.D., though the most classical specimens are probably earlier. A stupa drum of Sikri occupies the centre of the archaeological gallery. It is carved all round with various scenes of Buddha's life, including that of his being fed by a monkey. The statue of Gautama Buddha, emaciated after his long fast, is striking. Among inscriptions may be seen that of Takht-i-Bahai, dated in the reign of King Gondophares, at whose court St Thomas, the Apostle of India, is believed to have lived (A.D. 40), and, according to local tradition, to have suffered martyrdom.

In the archaeological department the bases of two pillars brought by General Cunningham from Taxila; numerous Buddhist sculptures from the Yusafzai country and elsewhere, in which the classical influence is plainly discerned; a Buddhist pillar about 9 ft. high, with a huge head projecting on one side, dug up near Jhelum. Two relics of the prehistoric age—finely finished celts of porphyritic greenstone—were found in Swat.

The collection of jewellery, both antique and modern, includes specimens from the Trans-Indus territory. A collection of huqqas of all periods and in all materials is contained in another interesting case. There is also a comprehensive collection of musical instruments made by the late Lockwood Kipling, and a good collection of Indian arms and armour, among which a dagger fancifully decorated with pearls running in grooves in the blade, and a sword, the hilt and scabbard of which are decorated with Niello work, are particularly noticeable. Other cases contain specimens of pottery and Punjab glass, and of the *Koftgari* work of Gujarat and Sialkot; cups and ornaments of vitreous enamel from Bahawalpur; silver inlaid in pewter and perforated metalwork from Delhi.

There are specimens of the silk manufactures of Bahawalpur and Multan, and satinettes. The embroideries called *shishadar phulkaris*, of soft floss silk on cotton, interspersed among which are small bits of glass, are special to the Punjab; the rude painted idols were worshipped by the ladies of the Sikh Court. There are choice examples of Kashmir shawls, both woven and hand-embroidered, and some in which the two processes are combined, and specimens of that interesting process called "tie-dyeing", showing the method of manufacture. Miniature model groups show workers engaged in making pottery, glass, metal ware, lacquer work, turning, etc. There are also collections of the leathern ware of the Punjab; of ethnographical heads by Messrs Schlagentweit; lay figures habited in the costumes of the people of Lahaul, Spiti and Ladakh; and Tibetan curiosities, such as prayer-wheels.

In the mineral section will be seen a model of the *Koh-i-Nur* made for the London Exhibition of 1851. According to the Hindus, this diamond belonged to Karna, King of Anga, and according to the Persians, it and its sister diamond, the Darya-i-Nur, or "Sea of Light", were worn by Afrasiab.

Among the specimens of the mineral resources of the country will be seen iron ore from Bajaur. It is a magnetic oxide of singular purity. Antimony and lead are also shown, and gold found in the sands of the Punjab rivers in small quantities, with specimens of rock-salt of two kinds—one from the Salt Range between the Jhelum and the Indus, and the other from the hills beyond the Indus.

The numismatic section, which is almost unique for the period of the Greek rule in Bactria and the Punjab, and contains also Mughal and Indian coins of great interest, can be seen on application to the Curator. Illustrated catalogues of the Museum collections are on sale.

The Tibetan collection includes some remarkable specimens of Lamaistic temple banners. Finest among them is the embroidered banner, showing Padma-Sambhava (Lotus-born), who converted Tibet to Buddhism. One of the painted banners depicts the "Wheel of Existence" and other scenes of Buddha's life from his conception and birth till his Nirvana and the worship of his relics.

Among minor antiquities should be noted a Buddha statuette of brass inlaid with silver and copper from Fatehpur, in the Kangra District. It belongs to the 6th century A.D.

Opposite the Museum is the University Hall and University Laboratory, and in front of the latter is the famous "Kim's" gun, called the Zamzama, "Hummer", or Lion's Roar. The Sikhs called it the Bhangianwali Top—that is, the cannon of the Bhangi confederacy. The gun was made for Shah Wali Khan, Wazir of Ahmad Shah Abdali, and was used by him at the Battle of Panipat. After Ahmad Shah left India it came into the hands of the Bhangi Misl, and Maharaja Ranjit Singh eventually got possession of it, and used it at the siege of Multan in 1818, when it was damaged, after firing only two rounds. It was then placed at the Delhi Gate of Lahore until 1860, when it was removed to its present site. Persian inscriptions give the date of casting 1760. Beside the Museum is an ordinary sign-post indicating the distance and direction not of a nearby place, but of London.

The **National College of Arts** attained considerable eminence under Lockwood, Kipling, Percy Brown, and Sardar Bahadur Ram Singh. The school has always been a centre of craftwork in the Punjab. Lionel Heath expanded the school by direct dealing with small craftsmen. Tourists interested in local handicrafts should also visit APWA Cottage Industries; Pakistan Handicrafts; Cooperative Handicrafts—all located in The Mall.

W. of the Museum is the **Town Hall,** and to the S. is the **Punjab Public Library,** said by some to have been built by Wazir Khan, by others by Ilahi Bakhsh. It has four white cupolas, and contains many valuable books. One wing is a memorial to Sir Muhammad Iqbal, the famous Urdu poet and philosopher, whose memory is venerated in Pakistan as second only to that of the Quaid-i-Azam, because he advocated with such fervour and devotion the creation of a Muslim state to take its place beside independent India.

Not far off, on the E. outskirts of the Anarkali Bazar, is the Nila Gumbaz, or Blue Dome, the tomb of Abdul Razak, a saint of the time of Humayun. Farther S., near the Presbyterian church, is the shrine of another Muslim saint. Over the door is a Persian inscription which says it is the tomb of Syed Muhammad Shah Mauj-i-Darya, son of Nurullah, who was a spiritual guide in the time of Akbar.

The **Tomb of Anarkali,** Pomegranate Blossom (a name given to a favourite lady in the harem of Akbar, who was also called Nadira Begam, or Sharfunnissa), is an octagon cased in plaster and surmounted by a dome. It was once occupied by Kharak Singh, the heir-apparent of Ranjit Singh: later it was given to General Ventura, an Italian of Jewish extraction in the Sikh army, who removed later on to the adjoining house, now the Secretariat, and used the tomb as his zenana. After the annexation of the Punjab by the British in 1849 the tomb was converted into the church of the Civil Station (St James), but it is now used as the Historical Record Room. This is a model of its kind and should be visited (apply to the Keeper of the Records). Many interesting documents are on view.

The cenotaph, now at the E. end of the central chamber, is of white marble, and the ninety-nine names of God are exquisitely carved. On the side, below the names, is written *Majnun Salim-i-Akbar* (the enamoured Salim, son of Akbar), Salim being the name of Jahangir. On the W. side is a date, above the words "In Lahore", corresponding to 1615, which is probably the date of the building of the tomb. The story is that Anarkali was beloved by Salim, and was seen by Akbar, his father, to smile when the Prince entered the harem. As a punishment for this it is said that she was buried alive, and the pathetic distich engraved on her sarcophagus certainly indicates that Salim was her lover:

"Ah gar man baz binam rue yar-i-khwesh ra.
Ta kiamat shukar goyam Kardagari, khwesh ra."

"Ah, if I could again see the face of my beloved,
To the day of judgment I would give thanks to my Creator."

The grave of the French General Allard's daughter is in the Kuri Bagh, formerly a garden of the Maharaja of Kapurthala.

The **Government College** is opposite the District Courts, on the right of the Lower Mall. It has a high reputation for sport as well as learning. Farther back to the W. from here is the noted shrine of **Data Ganj Bakhsh,** a saint of the time of Mahmud of Ghazni. Next, a view is obtained of the great mosque, and the fort rising above it. The **Badshahi Masjid** (which contains relics, including a hair of the Prophet) was built by Aurangzeb well worth a visit.

N. of the mosque are Sikh shrines. The first is that of **Guru Arjan,** the fifth Guru, and compiler of the *Adi* (original) *Granth.* The *Granth* is read here daily in a huge volume over which attendants reverently wave *chauris.* According to Sikh legend, he disappeared in the Ravi on this spot, upon which Maharaja Ranjit Singh accordingly built this memorial.

The **Samadh** covers the ashes of Maharajas Ranjit Singh, Kharak

Singh and Nau Nihal Singh, grandson of Ranjit Singh. It faces the E. wall of the fort, and is a square stucco building, restored in part in 1840, on a high platform of marble. The ceilings are decorated with traceries in stucco inlaid with mirrors. The arches of the interior are of marble, strengthened with brick and *chunam*, and clamped with iron. In the centre is a raised platform of marble, on which is a lotus flower carved in marble, surrounded by eleven smaller flowers. The central flower covers the ashes of Ranjit Singh (d. 1839); the others those of four wives and seven concubines who became *satis*.

In the centre of the **Hazuribagh** is the **Baradari,** a marble pavilion built by Ranjit Singh from the spoils of Mughal edifices. Its historical associations render it of special interest. It is frequently mentioned by European travellers who visited Lahore during the Sikh period. William Moorcroft, the explorer, was lodged here in May 1820, in the reign of Ranjit Singh, and Captain Leopold von Orlich was received in audience by Sher Singh in January 1843.

The **Hazuribagh Darwaza** of the Lahore Fort,[1] is sometimes called the Akbari Darwaza, the Gate of Akbar, but the present gate is a later structure, apparently built at the same time as the Badshahi Masjid, and renewed by the Sikhs.

The Hazuribagh Darwaza and the Masti Darwaza (the other main gate which gave access to the fort from the side of the city) have long been closed.[2] The fort is now entered through a modern postern dating from the year 1853, where a register of visitors is kept. Behind it rises the Hathi Pol, or Elephant Gate, which once formed the private entrance to the apartments occupied by the Emperor and his ladies.

[1] The best account of the Lahore Fort is still Dr Vogel's *Historical Notes on the Lahore Fort* (*Journal Punjab Historical Society*, 1911, 1, 38-55).

[2] The old elephant route into the fort is also closed. It originally gave access directly to the Shish Mahal Court.

The gate is decorated with *Kashi* tile mosaics, continued all along the W. and N. faces of the fort wall.[1] Though this tile-work has suffered irreparable damage owing to neglect and the repeated bombardments during the Sikh period, it still retains its brilliancy of colour. This *Kashi* work was a favourite mode of decorating brick buildings in the days of Shah Jahan, and is common in the buildings of his reign at Lahore. But the decoration of the fort wall is unique in that in several of the panels figures of living beings have been introduced. Many panels depict elephant fights, the favourite recreation of the Mughal Court. The elephants are full of vigour. The spandrels are decorated with winged figures of Persian fairies (*paris*) in floating robes, carrying a fan or a lamb or holding a horned demon with horns tied in front.

On the wall of the Saman Burj two panels depict a camel fight, and one, much damaged, shows four Mughal horsemen playing polo, the goal-posts consisting of two upright slabs. Polo, or *chaugan* as it is called in Persian, was a favourite sport at the Court of the Great Mughals.

On the N. wall beneath the Khwabgah of Jahangir may be seen a pair of fine blue dragons (the dragon, or *azhdaha*, was one of the emblems carried in front of the Emperor), while another panel shows the familiar scene of the goat and monkey-man.

The enamelled tile-work on the N. wall belongs, perhaps, to the reign of Jahangir, but that on the Saman Burj and on the W. wall may be safely ascribed to the beginning of Shah Jahan's reign.[2] A Persian inscription over the Hathi Pol records that Shah Jahan built a Royal Tower (*Shah Burj*) in 1631-32, which is now known as *Saman Burj*.

Three distinct building periods are noticeable in the palace proper—the

[1] On these tile mosaics, see *Journal of Indian Art and Industry*, vol. 14, Nos. 113-17.

[2] See the *Mosaics of the Lahore Fort*, by Dr J. Vogel.

early Mughal palace, completed by Jahangir in 1617-18; Shah Jahan's palace, completed in 1631-32; and the additions due to the Sikhs, who restored the palace after a period of neglect.

From the *Hathi Pol* two roads lead up to the palace buildings. The ancient road, now closed to the public, starts to the N. (left) of the gate, and by a twisted flight of steps leads up to a courtyard which, by a marble gate, communicates with another court adjoining the square of the *Saman Burj*. It was once the private entrance to the imperial palace. The modern road is a ramp of military construction which takes the visitor to the W. end of what was once the quadrangle of the Diwan-i-Am. The cloistered row of buildings forming this square was demolished after the military occupation, except a block in front of the Pearl Mosque, or *Moti Masjid*. This will convey some idea of the original cloister. Over the gate there is a marble slab with a Persian inscription which records the completion of the early Mughal palace by Ma'mur Khan in the twelfth regnal year of Jahangir—1027 of the Hijra (1617-18).

This gate and the little courtyard behind give access to the Pearl Mosque, or **Moti Masjid,** apparently the earliest of four buildings of the name.[1] It is of white marble, with a court in front. The Sikhs converted it into a treasury, and it continued to be used as such until it was rescued by Lord Curzon, who ordered its restoration in 1903-04. The variety of ceiling construction in the various compartments of the prayer chamber should be noticed.

The **Diwan-i-Am,** in the centre of the fort, consists of two distinct buildings. The smaller at the back (N. side), which consists of rows of small apartments, is the older portion which existed in the reign of Jahangir. The open hall in front, supported on four rows of ten sandstone pillars, was added by Shah Jahan in 1626, the first year of his reign, so that his courtiers, when attending the daily audience, might be sheltered. The entire superstructure is modern, and the buildings appear to have been reconstructed, perhaps during the Sikh period. The most interesting part is the throne balcony, or *jharoka,* in which the Emperor used to make his daily appearance. Between the front row of columns may be observed remnants of a white marble railing, whilst along the platform in front of the hall a red sandstone railing is partly preserved. These railings separated the nobles, according to their rank and dignity.

The historical associations of the *Diwan-i-Am* are many. It was probably here that Manucci rejoined Dara Shikoh after his defeat at Samugarh.[1] In the days of Ranjit Singh the *Diwan-i-Am* was known as *Takht*—i.e. the Throne. It was here that after Ranjit Singh's death his body lay in state. Dr Martin Honigberger, his court physician, gives a graphic description of how he met in the great courtyard one of the four Queens who were to be burnt with the remains of their husband.[2]

At the back (N.) of the *Diwan-i-Am* is the oldest portion of the Lahore palace. It is usually designated as the Quadrangle of Jahangir, although it is possible that these edifices go back to the reign of Akbar. They consist of two rows of buildings facing each other, with sandstone porches characterised as early Mughal by eaves supported on ancient brackets. The carved work on the two slightly projecting edifices at the ends of both rows is particularly fine.

In the centre of the N. side of the quadrangle the *Bari Khwabgah,* ascribed to Jahangir but evidently modernised, has been converted into

[1] The Pearl Mosque in the Agra Fort was built by Shah Jahan, that in the Delhi Fort by Aurangzeb, and that at Mahrauli, or Old Delhi (Kutb), by Bahadur Shah I.

[1] Nicolao Manucci, *Storia do Mogor,* translated by William Irvine (Murray, 1907), vol. 1, pp. 158, 309.

[2] Honigberger, *Früchte aus dem Morgenlande,* p. 111 (English translation, p. 97).

a museum (1928) with a collection of Sikh weapons and old plans of the Fort. The central portion of the quadrangle was once occupied by a square tank and ornamental garden.

The smaller square adjoining Jahangir's Quadrangle on the W. has preserved more of its original character. It is occupied by a formal garden, with a platform and fountain in the centre. The open pavilion on the N. side of this garden is the *Chhoti Khwabgah*, or Lesser Bedchamber. It is a pavilion of white marble supported on five rows of five pillars carrying scalloped arches. The archways on the N. are closed with pierced screens. An eave, supported on brackets, runs along the four sides of the building. The roof has a parapet with marble facing decorated with a border of *pietra dura*. The interior is paved with variegated marbles, and the centre is occupied by a fountain basin scalloped out and inlaid with semi-precious stones, most of which have disappeared. The marble ceiling is modern.

Below the *Khwabgah* a ruined structure will be seen at the foot of the fort wall. It is the *Arzgah*—i.e. the place where in the morning the nobles assembled to pay their respects to the Emperor. Note the panels mentioned on p. 578.

The next court is called *Khilat Khana*. In the N.W. corner of the adjoining square there is an open pavilion which dates from the reign of Ranjit Singh, and was used by him as a *Kutchery*, or Court of Justice. Its Sikh origin is clearly indicated by the combination of white marble and red sandstone brackets, and the juxtaposition of marble trellis screens with red sandstone posts in the ornamental railing on the roof of the building. The curious frescoes on the N. wall, relating to the legend of Krishna, are evidently the work of one of Ranjit Singh's court painters.

The court in the N.W. corner of the palace is *Saman Burj*[1] (p. 578), formerly the *Shah Burj*, or Royal Tower.

A large hall, now known as *Shish Mahal*, or Palace of Mirrors, occupies the N. side of the square. It was here that in March 1849 the sovereignty of the Punjab was assumed by the British Government, as is recorded on a marble tablet let into the wall, and the Koh-i-Nur diamond was handed to Sir John Lawrence. The *Shish Mahal* is built on a semi-octagonal plan. Its largest side, facing the square, has a row of double pillars of inlaid white marble, forming five archways surmounted by an eave of red sandstone. Within, the spandrels over the arches are decorated with *pietra dura*. The graceful vine pattern over the two outer arches deserves special notice. The main room, a rectangular hall of noble dimensions, has a dado of white marble, while the upper portion of the walls and the ceiling are decorated with mosaic of glass laid in gypsum, which accounts for the name of Palace of Mirrors. This decoration belongs to two different epochs. The ceiling, with its prevailing aspect of subdued gilt, formed undoubtedly part of the original edifice. The wall decoration is inferior, with sherds of blue and white china. It is typical Sikh work. The central hall is surrounded by a row of nine smaller rooms decorated in the same fashion. In the largest of these rooms, at the back of the main hall, is a marble screen of trellis-work. The roof of the *Shish Mahal* is encumbered with structures dating from the Sikh period.

The ornamental marble pavilion, with "Bengali" roof, which stands on the W. side of the square, is called *Naulakha*—a modern name which is explained from its having cost nine lakhs of rupees to build. In one of the dado panels there appears a "Chinese" cloud converted by the Sikhs into a bird. The painting and mirror work of the wooden ceiling is also certainly due to the Sikhs. The roof must once have been covered with sheet copper and pinnacles of the same metal.

[1] The word *saman* is an abbreviation of Arabic *musamman*, meaning "octagonal".

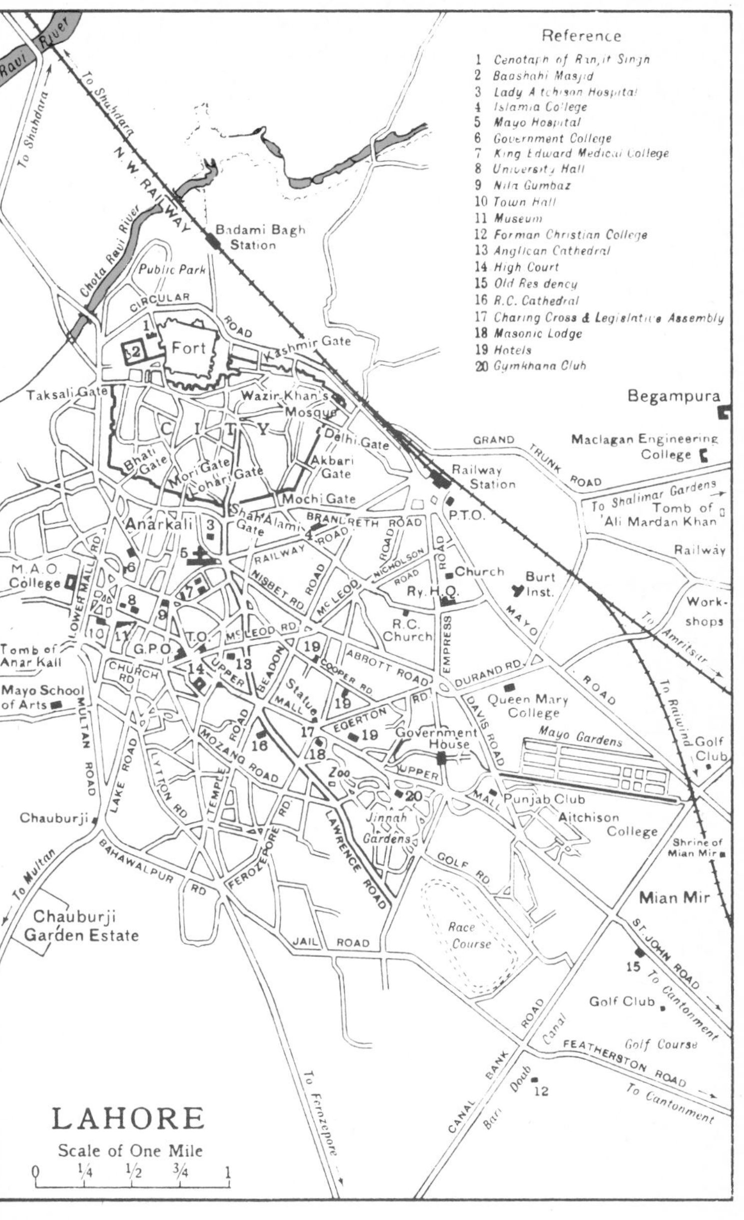
Reference
1 Cenotaph of Ranjit Singh
2 Badshahi Masjid
3 Lady Aitchison Hospital
4 Islamia College
5 Mayo Hospital
6 Government College
7 King Edward Medical College
8 University Hall
9 Nila Gumbaz
10 Town Hall
11 Museum
12 Forman Christian College
13 Anglican Cathedral
14 High Court
15 Old Residency
16 R.C. Cathedral
17 Charing Cross & Legislative Assembly
18 Masonic Lodge
19 Hotels
20 Gymkhana Club
Ravi River
To Shahdara
To Shahdara
N.W. RAILWAY
Chota Ravi River
Badami Bagh Station
Public Park
CIRCULAR
ROAD
Fort
Kashmir Gate
Taksali Gate
Wazir Khan's Mosque
CITY
Delhi Gate
Bhati Gate
Mori Gate
Lohari Gate
Akbari Gate
Mochi Gate
Shah Alami Gate
Anarkali
BRANDRETH ROAD
RAILWAY ROAD
NISBET RD.
McLEOD ROAD
NICHOLSON ROAD
M.A.O. College
LOWER MALL RD
T.O.
McLEOD RD
G.P.O.
Tomb of Anar Kali
CHURCH RD
UPPER
Mayo School of Arts
MULTAN ROAD
BEADON
Statue
MALL
ABBOTT ROAD
COOPER RD.
EGERTON RD.
MOZANG ROAD
LAKE ROAD
LYTTON RD
TEMPLE ROAD
FEROZEPORE RD.
LAWRENCE ROAD
Zoo
Jinnah Gardens
UPPER MALL
Chauburji
To Multan
BAHAWALPUR RD
Chauburji Garden Estate
JAIL ROAD
To Ferozepore
Railway Station
P.T.O.
Church
Ry. H.Q.
R.C. Church
EMPRESS ROAD
DURAND RD.
Burt Inst.
MAYO ROAD
Queen Mary College
DAVIS ROAD
Government House
Mayo Gardens
Punjab Club
Aitchison College
GOLF RD
Race Course
GRAND TRUNK ROAD
Begampura
Maclagan Engineering College
To Shalimar Gardens
Tomb of 'Ali Mardan Khan
Railway
Workshops
To Amritsar
To Raiwind
Golf Club
Shrine of Mian Mir
Mian Mir
ST. JOHN ROAD
To Cantonment
Golf Club
Canal
CANAL BANK ROAD
Bari Doab
FEATHERSTON ROAD
Golf Course
To Cantonment
LAHORE
Scale of One Mile
0 1/4 1/2 3/4 1

The remaining buildings of the *Shah Burj* are not remarkable. The courtyard is paved with grey and variegated marble, and the centre is occupied by a reservoir. In the N.W. corner of the court there is a stone floor, measuring 9 ft. 6 in. square, which does not belong to the original pavement. It belonged originally to a mansion in the city, and was purchased by Ranjit Singh. An apartment in the N.E. corner of the square is indicated as Sher Singh's bathroom.

N.W. of the Fort is the public park, much used for training the various volunteer forces that have been raised for the defence of Pakistan, in particular the Pakistan National Guard.

Leaving the Hazuribagh by the S. gate, and turning E. into the crowded city streets, the **Sonehri Masjid,** or Golden Mosque, is reached. This has three gilt domes, and was built in 1753 by Bokhari Khan, a favourite of the widow of Mir Mannu, who governed Lahore for her son under Ahmed Shah Durani. He is said to have displeased the lady, whose female attendants beat him to death with their shoes.

In a courtyard behind the mosque is a large well, with steps descending to the water. It is said to have been dug by Arjan, the fifth Guru.

A street with some fine balconies leads E. again from here to a *chauk*, or square, where is the very beautiful **Mosque of Wazir Khan.** It was built in 1634 by Hakim Ala-ud-din of Chiniot, Governor of the Punjab under Shah Jahan. The brick walls are faced inside with Nakkashi, glazed tiles, with a yellow ground. Over the entrance is written in Persian: "Remove thy heart from the gardens of the world, and know that this building is the true abode of man". In the centre front of the mosque is the Muslim credo, and in panels along the façade are beautifully written verses from the Koran. The structure and its decoration are notably Persian in character. From the gallery round the minarets, about 3 ft. broad, there is a view over the city.

Beyond the *chauk* and the Delhi Gate of the city, the Landa Bazar leads to the railway station. The palace of Dara Shikoh and the great Tripulia Bazar lay between the city and the station; and the houses and gardens and tombs of the nobles extended along the Ravi as far E. as Shalimar. The ruined tomb of Mir Mannu adjoins the open space W. of the railway station; the mosque of Dai Anga, E. of the station, was built by a foster-mother of Shah Jahan in 1635.

In the old town the balconies and projecting oriel windows of the irregular brick houses, together with the variety and colour of the costumes of the people, form a striking picture. The most effective corners will be found at the N. ends of the streets leading from the Mochi and Lohari Gates. S. of the latter the Anarkali Bazar runs for $\frac{3}{4}$ m. to near the Punjab Museum. To the E. of it are situated the Female Hospitals. A college for girls commemorates the visit of Queen Mary in 1912.

At the Multan and Bahawalpur road junction is the ruined Chauburji (Four Towers). This led to the garden of Zebunnissa Begam, a daughter of the Emperor Aurangzeb, and is faced with blue and green encaustic tiles. This lady, who died in 1669, long before her father, and who was a poetess under the name of Makhfi (Hidden), is said to have been buried at Nawan Kot, 1 m. S. from this garden.

Excursions from Lahore

(1) The Maclagan Engineering College is on the left of the Grand Trunk Road to the **Shalimar Gardens,** 5 m. E. on the Amritsar Road from the main railway station. About half-way to them is the gateway to the **Gulabi Bagh,** or Rose Garden, laid out in 1655 by Sultan Beg, Admiral of the Fleet to Shah Jahan. The Nakkashi work of coloured tiles on the gate is hardly inferior to that on Wazir Khan's Mosque. On the gateway is inscribed in Persian:

"Sweet is this garden; through envy of it,
the tulip is spotted,
The rose of the sun and moon forms its
beautiful lamp."

Close to this is the tomb of Sharf-unnissa Begam, sister of Zakaria Khan, Governor 1717-38, which is decorated with representations of cypress-trees in enamelled plaster.

N.E. of Maclagan College is the village of Begampur. The ruined octagonal tomb to the E., known as the Bagga Gumbaz, or White Dome, is the tomb of Yahia Khan (d. 1748). Nearby are the mosque and grave of Zakaria Khan and his father, in a garden. Nearer the river again is the garden tomb of Shah Bilawal, a saint honoured by Shah Jahan, where Maharaja Sher Singh was murdered in 1843.

Opposite to the Gulabi Bagh, and within a railway enclosure to the S. of the road, is the **Tomb of Ali Mardan Khan,** the Mughal engineer, who created the Shalimar Gardens. Its lofty archway retains traces of exquisitely coloured tiles. 50 yd. S. of this is the octagonal tomb built of brick, now much ruined, in Mughalpura, where the railway workshops are.

The **Shalimar Gardens** were laid out in 1637 by order of Shah Jahan. They are divided into three parts, in tiers of different levels; the highest was known as the Farhat Bakhsh, and the two lower as Faiz Bakhsh. The whole extent is about 80 acres, surrounded by a wall, with a large gateway and pavilions at each corner. The original pavilions were of white marble. Canals traverse the garden, and there is a tank in the centre with an island and a passage across to it. There are one hundred small fountains in the first garden, and double that number in the tank.

On the opposite side of the road are two other gardens, the **Sindhanwala** and **Misr Brijlal's**; to the E. is the fine garden of **Jamadar Khushhal Singh,** and across the road to the N.E. that of **Lehna Singh.**

(2) 4 m. from Lahore on the line to Raiwind (Route 2, p. 566) is **Lahore Cantonment** station. At Mian Mir, Jowahir Singh, uncle and minister of the infant Maharaja Dhulip Singh, was executed by the Sikh army in 1845.

After crossing the Bari Doab Canal by the road from the station to the Cantonment, is the *Shrine of* **Mian Mir,** a saint from whom the Cantonment derived its former name, and who was honoured by the Emperors Jahangir and Shah Jahan, his real name being Muhammad Mir. It stands in the centre of a quadrangle 200ft. square, on a marble platform. Over the entrance is an inscription in Persian giving the date = 1635. The left side of the enclosure is occupied by a mosque.

Near the former Garrison Church (still filled on Sundays by the many devout Pakistani Christians) are memorials to Sir Charles Napier and Sir Michael O'Dwyer, the latter being a fine building used as a Clubhouse for Junior Commissioned Officers (the equivalent of the V.C.Os. of the British Raj).

Returning towards the railway station, on the right is the village of **Shahu-ki-Ghari,** where are a number of large tombs, all more or less ruined. At the corner of Nicholson Road is Kila Gujar Singh, fort of a Bhangi Sardar and upon Macleod Road is the venerated **Tomb of Bibi Pakdaman** (the chaste lady). According to tradi-

Changes in Street Names on Map

Brandreth Rd	Bo Ali Sina Rd
McLeod Rd	Shahrah-e-Liaquat Ali Khan
Abbott Rd	Imtiaz Ali Taj Rd
Egerton Rd	Suharwardy Rd
Davis Rd	Mamdott Rd
Upper Mall	Shara-e-Quaid-e-Azam
Lytton Rd	Salahuddin Rd
Temple Rd	Allama Abdul Karim Rd
Lawrence Rd	Mian Muzadfin Rd
Ferozepore Rd	Fatima Jinnah Rd
Beadon Rd	Jauhar Rd
Mayo Rd	Allama Iqbal Rd

tion, this saint was the daughter of the younger brother of Ali by a different mother. Her real name was Ruqayya Khanum, and she was the eldest of six sisters, all buried here, who fled with her from Baghdad after the battle at Karbala in 680; she died in 728, at the age of ninety. Visitors are expected to take off their shoes. There are five enclosures, and the tomb of Ruqayya is in the fifth. It is of brick, whitewashed.

(3) **Shahdara** is situated on the W. bank of the Ravi, N. of the railway and road bridges, from which the **Tomb of the Emperor Jahangir** is 1¼ m. It is convenient to go by motor (about 5½ m. drive).

Before crossing the railway is seen (right) the tomb of **Nurjahan,** wife of Jahangir, a plain building of one storey. After crossing the railway a domed building is passed on the right. This is the tomb of Asaf Khan (see below).

Immediately E. of it is the *sarai* or outer court. An archway of white marble, and 50 ft. high, leads into the garden court of Jahangir's mausoleum, once the Dilkusha garden of the Empress Nurjahan (Mihr-un-nissa). The low building on a terraced platform has four minarets, 95 ft. high, at the corners and a small pavilion over the tomb chamber in the centre,[1] the passage into which is paved with beautifully streaked marble. The cenotaph is of white marble, inlaid with *pietra dura* work. On the E. and W. sides are the ninety-nine names of God, most beautifully carved, and on the S. side is inscribed, "The Glorious Tomb of His High Majesty, Asylum of Pardon, Nur-ud-din Muhammad, the Emperor Jahangir", 1627. On the four sides are screens of lattice-work. The lamp over the tomb was presented by the Maharao of Kotah.

A staircase in one minaret leads up to the flat roof of the terrace, covered with a marble tessellated pavement. The marble balustrade was taken away by Maharaja Ranjit Singh to Amritsar. The minarets are four storeys high, and are built of magnificent blocks of stone 8 ft. long. From the top there is a view over the Ravi to the city of Lahore.

The **Tomb of Asaf Khan,** brother of the Empress Nurjahan, is an octagon surmounted by a dome. It shows marked Persian influence. It has been almost entirely stripped of the *kashi* work. The cenotaph is of white marble. The Tughra writing on it resembles that on the tomb of Jahangir. Before marrying Jahangir, Nurjahan was married to an Afghan, Ali Kuli Khan, who lived at Burhanpur. Jahangir compassed his death, and carried Nurjahan away to Delhi; as she refused to marry him, he imprisoned her in a small palace, and made her an allowance of 14 annas a day. Eventually Asaf Khan persuaded her to marry Jahangir. On his death Nurjahan wished a younger son of the Emperor married to her daughter by her Afghan husband to succeed him: but Asaf Khan stood by Shah Jahan, and the ex-Queen retired into private life. Asaf Khan died in 1611, having attained to the rank of Khan-i-Khanan and Governor of Lahore, under Shah Jehan, who erected the tomb. Nurjahan survived her brother for four years.

(4) 26 m. W. of Lahore is **Sheikhupura** once Jahangirabad, the hunting-seat of Jahangir and of Dara Shikoh, the eldest brother of Aurangzeb. There is an imposing hunting lodge, once Jahangir's residence, known locally as the Kila. Now empty, its crumbling walls are supported by long pole braces. The road crosses the bridge over the Ravi. The Upper Chenab Canal is crossed at mile 18. On the way the Deg, a famous local stream, is crossed.

On the left, at Sheikhupura, is a garden-house built by Rani Nakayan, wife of Ranjit Singh. At the S.W. corner of the garden is her Samadh, an octagonal building. Over the door is a picture of the ten Gurus, with an inscription.

[1] The tomb was modelled on that of Itimad-ud-daula at Agra.

On leaving Sheikhupura by the Sargodha road, a track, now metalled leads to the Harin Minar, a tower and drinking-tank for animals built by Jahangir in memory of a pet deer. An underground passage is said to lead to the hunting-lodge at Sheikhupura.

(5) Accessible by car from Lahore is the **Changa Manga** Wild Life Sanctuary, where many species of deer can be seen. Restaurant. Boating.

ROUTE 3

LAHORE to **PESHAWAR** and the **KHYBER PASS** by **Gujranwala, Wazirabad** Junction (for **Sialkot,** also for **Lyallpur** and **Khanewal**), **Gujrat, Lala Musa** Junction, **Jhelum, Rohtas, Manikyala, Rawalpindi, Golra** (for **Khushalgarh** and **Kohat**), **Taxila, Hassan Abdal** (for **Abbottabad** and parts of **Kashmir** under Pakistan), **Attock** and **Naushahra** (for **Hoti Mardan** and **Malakand**).

This route is better followed by road, which affords a fine view of the country. For those who prefer rail-travel, the sequence of places is as follows.

Lahore to Peshawar Cantonment is 288 m. by the North-Western Railway.

4 m. The bridge over the Ravi river carries a road also.

5 m. from Lahore, **Shahdara** station. The tomb of the Emperor Jahangir, 1¼ m. off, is described on p. 583 (Excursion 3). From here a branch line runs (57 m.) to Sangla Hill (p. 585) and Lyallpur (85 m.).

38 m. Here the main Upper Chenab Canal (opened 1913) is crossed.

43 m. **Gujranwala** station (R., three R.H., Canal Dept., P.W.D., and Municipal Committee), the birthplace of Ranjit Singh in 1780. At the S.E. corner of the town is the *Samadh of Mahan Singh*, his father, an octagonal building, 81 ft. high to the top of the gilt ornament on the summit. Within are the sculptured rosettes or knobs which mark where the ashes are deposited. The large rosette surrounded by twelve smaller ones is inscribed "Sarkar Ranjit Singh". That nearest the entrance is in memory of a blue pigeon that fell down into the flames in which Ranjit Singh and his concubines were being

consumed at Lahore in 1839. Other rosettes mark the ashes of Mohan Singh Padshah, Maharaja Sher Singh and Kaur Nau Nihal Singhji. There is a narrow but lofty pavilion, covered with mythological pictures, among which is one of Duryodhana ordering Draupadi (p. 21) to be stripped. As fast as the clothes were pulled off her she was supernaturally reclothed. At 100 yd. to the E. is the pavilion of Mahan Singh. Close to the market-place is the house where Ranjit Singh was born, with a frieze of geese round the courtyard.

In the Fort N.E. of the town is the *Baradari*, or pavilion, of the famous Sikh General Hari Singh Nalwa, who was killed in 1837 at Jamrud (p. 600) in action against the Afghans. It stands in 40 acres of garden and grounds. To the E. is a pavilion 12 ft. high, full of small niches for lamps. At 70 yd. to the N. of the house is the Samadh of Hari Singh. The place where the ashes (brought from Peshawar) lie is marked by a knob shaped like a budding flower. There are no *sati* memorials. A picture on the wall inside is a portrait of Hari Singh hawking, with a string of ducks passing over his head. The gardens round Gujranwala are famous for Malta oranges. Gujranwala is known for its iron safes, which are exported in large numbers.

62 m. **Wazirabad** Junction station (R., D.B. with four suites). This place, founded by Wazir Khan in the reign of Shah Jahan, became under Ranjit Singh the headquarters of Avitabile, his Italian general, who built a completely new town on the plan of a parallelogram surrounded by a wall. A broad bazar runs from end to end. Wazirabad is famous for its cutlery and sword-sticks.

N. is the great *Alexandra Bridge* over the Chenab, opened in 1876. The Chenab is subject to sudden furious floods. 20 m. S. is the ford and battlefield of Ramnagar (1848).

From Wazirabad a branch line runs E. to Sialkot.

27 m. **Sialkot** station (D.B.K.; alt. 880 ft.). Seat of a large sports industry with important export trade. Tennis rackets and hockey sticks are made of mulberry. Perhaps, however, its most important industry now is surgical instrument and equipment making. There is also a large new Government Ordnance factory.

Sialkot is identified with the ancient Sagala, the capital *c.* 160 B.C. of the Indo-Greek Menander (the Milinda of the Buddhists) and of Mihiragula the Hun. The *Church* is a striking edifice, having a steeple 150 ft. high. Near the railway station and the city is a lofty old fort, in which the British residents took refuge on the mutiny of the 46th Bengal Infantry and a wing of the 9th Light Cavalry on 9th July 1857. A number were killed. After these outrages, the mutinous cavalry-men invited two of the surviving field officers to command them with higher pay and a guarantee of furlough to the hills every hot weather!

At **Marala** (N. of Sialkot) are head-works of the Upper Chenab Canal, which runs to the Balloki barrage on the Ravi river and feeds the Lower Bari Doab Canal.

The railway line extends to Jammu, and there is a branch from Sialkot S.E. to Narowal (39 m.), junction on the Amritsar line (both now out of use pending settlement of the Kashmir dispute).

Lyallpur Branch Line

Another branch line S.W. from Wazirabad runs through the Rechna Doab by Sangla, 68 m., and **Lyallpur,** 96 m. (D.B.K.), named after Sir James Lyall, to Shorkot Road Junction, 163 m., and Khanewal to Multan, 201 m. There is a network of lines required to convey grain to Karachi.

The District of **Lyallpur,** area 3511 sq. m., is the largest wheat-exporting District in Pakistan, and grows high-grade cotton. Its existence depends on the irrigation afforded by the Lower Chenab Canal, but constant efforts are needed to keep salination in check because of the high water level. The Government Agricultural College is famous—well worth a visit. There are several large new Cotton Mills.

Main Line

71 m. from Lahore **Gujrat** station is the headquarters of a district. The town (D.B.K.; alt. 780 ft.) stands on the ancient site of two earlier cities. The second, according to General Cunningham, was destroyed in 1303. Two centuries later Sher Shah Sur was in possession of the country, and either he or Akbar founded the present town. Akbar's fort stands in the centre of the city. It was first garrisoned by Gujars, and took the name of Gujarat Akbarabad. Akbar's administrative records are still preserved in the families of the hereditary registrars. During the reign of Shah Jahan, Gujrat became the residence of a famous saint, Pir Shah Daula, who adorned it with numerous buildings. In 1741 the Ghakkars established themselves, and in 1765 the Manjhai Sikhs acquired the country. The **Civil Station,** in which is the D.B. lies to the N. In it is a Church of Scotland Mission.

The Battlefield. — The decisive Battle of Gujrat, which ended the Second Sikh War, was fought on 21st February 1849. The two villages of Kalra, 2½ m. S. of the D.B., were the key of the Sikh position, in a flat plain. From Shadiwal at 7 a.m. on the morning of 21st February the British army started the battle with a heavy artillery bombardment. By 11.30 a.m. most of the Sikh guns had been withdrawn, dismounted or abandoned. The British infantry then advanced, deployed and drove the Sikhs from their position in Kalra.

Next day General Gilbert, with 12,000 men, started in pursuit of the enemy, and at Manihyala received the submission of the entire Sikh army on 14th March.

In the cemetery at *Shah Jahangir*, called after a fakir of that name, are the tombs of those who fell in the battle. Beyond, to the E., are two mosques, one of which is rather remarkable. Gujrat is a starting-point for one of the old routes into Kashmir.

83 m. **Lala Musa** Junction station (R.).

Loop Line to Multan

The Sind-Sagar line runs W. to the Indus, and then S. 345 m. to Sher Shah Junction, S. of Multan (p. 563).

At 21 m. **Chilianwala** was fought, in the Second Sikh War, on 13th January 1849, the most desperate of all the battles between the British and the Sikhs. The Sikhs advanced from their position on high ground between Rasul on the N. (soon to be well known as the site of a great hydro-electric scheme) to Moong on the S., and opened a heavy fire on the British troops, and Lord Gough ordered a general attack on them, though only a very short time of daylight remained. Their advance was checked, but finally the British troops were recalled with the loss of some of their guns.

Alexander the Great crossed the Jhelum somewhere in the neighbourhood of Tasul (on a branch from Mandi Baha-ud-din jn.), and defeated Porus in 326 B.C., not very far from the field of Chilianwala. At Rasul there is an Engineering College.

At 45 m. **Malakwal** Junction, a short line runs to Bhera (18 m.), where archaeological finds have been made, and to Kheura; a second branch runs S.W. to Sargodha Junction (for Khushab) and Hundewali Junction (for Chak Jumra), in the Rechna Doab, crossing two channels of the Chenab river and continuing to **Shorkot Road,** where it crosses the Chenab river by the Rivaz bridge, 2314 ft. long. At Trimmu (14 m. S.W. of Jhang) is the Emerson Barrage, at the junction of the Jhelum and Chenab rivers.

At Shorkot Road lines from Wazirabad and Lahore (Shahdara) running through the Lyallpur District converge. Crossing the Ravi river by the Abdul Hakim bridge, near the Sidhnai dam, this branch continues to Khanewal and Lodhran on the Sutlej river.

49 m. from **Lala Musa** Junction the Victoria bridge over the Jhelum river is 2720 ft. long (1887).

Mayo Mine.—A famous salt mine at **Khewra,** in the Pind Dadan Khan tehsil: can be visited by permission of the Superintendent. There are three R.Hs. for the accommodation of travellers. When the salt was first worked is not known, but excavations existed on the spot as far back as the time of Akbar, and the miners have a tradition that their first settlement dates from the 6th century of the Muhammadan era. The existing mine was named after Lord Mayo in 1870.

57 m. **Pind Dadan Khan,** a centre for several excursions:—

Katas.—A pool sacred to Hindus in the centre of the Salt Range, 15 m. N. of Pind Dadan Khan, at an elevation of over 2000 ft. The story is that, Siva being inconsolable at the death of his wife, Sati ("The True One"), tears rained from his eyes and formed the two pools of Katas, or Kataksha ("Raining Eyes"), and Pushkar, near Ajmer. At the foot of Kotera, the W. hill, are the remains of temples in the Kashmir style clustered in a corner of an old fort. These *Sat Ghara,* or seven temples, are popularly attributed to the Pandavas, who are said to have lived at Katas during a portion of their seven years' wanderings. At Amb, S.W., is a temple in the Kashmiri style. The village of **Choa Saidan Shah** (good R.H.) is noted for roses and attar (perfume).

Nandana.—A place 14 m. W. of Choa Saidan Shah, in a remarkable dip in the outer Salt Range. Nearby are extensive remains of a temple, a fort, and a large village. The temple is in the Kashmiri style, but faces W. instead of E., as temples of that style usually do. Of the fort two bastions of large well-cut sandstone blocks still remain. Nandana is mentioned as the objective of one of Mahmud of Ghazni's expeditions in 1014. Early in the 13th century it was held by Kamruddin Karmani, who was dispossessed by a general of Jalaluddin Sultan of Khwarizm. The latter was defeated on the Indus in 1221 by Chingiz Khan, one of whose officers —Turti, the Mongol—took Nandana and put its inhabitants to the sword. It appears in the list of places conquered by Altamish, who entrusted it to one of his nobles.

Jalalpur.—An ancient site on the N. bank of the Jhelum river, possibly the site of the ancient Bucephala, built by Alexander the Great in memory of his famous charger, which was killed in the battle with Porus at the crossing of the Jhelum; Sir Aurel Stein accepted the identification. Jalalpur is now the seat of one of the leading Muslim "Pirs" of the Punjab, and is annually visited by a large number of disciples at the time of the *Urs* (anniversary of the death of the founder).

Malot.—A fort and temple on a precipitous spur projecting from the Southern edge of the Salt Range, about 9 m. from Katas. The fort is said to have been built five or six centuries ago by Raja Mal, a Janjua Chief, whose descendants still hold the village. The temple, with its gateway, stands on the extreme end of the cliff. They are in the earlier Kashmiri style, built of coarse red stone, much injured by the action of the weather. The temple is 18 ft. square inside, with remarkable fluted pilasters and capitals, on each of which is a kneeling figure.

Siv Ganga, 3 m. N.E. of Malot. In it stands a small temple in the later Kashmiri style, and near Warala, a hamlet on the adjacent spur, a broken Buddhist sculpture was found some years ago and set up by Hindus in a small temple at Siv Ganga, but having been rendered useless for purpose of worship, the Hindus allowed its fragments to be sent to the Lahore Museum, where it was restored. The relief originally contained eighteen or nineteen figures, the central one, a Bodhisattwa, carved in a somewhat late stage of Gandhara art.

105 m. **Khushab** Junction, on the right bank of the Jhelum river, a place of great antiquity. Branch crossing the river by the Montmorency bridge to Shahpur City and Sargodha Junction (29 m.; alt. 614 ft.)

158 m. **Kundian,** junction for the line running N. to Campbellpur (p. 594). The Sind Sagar railway now turns S. through a desolate and salty tract on the E. bank of the Indus.

209 m. **Darya Khan** for **Dera Ismail Khan** (D.B.K.), formerly Akalgarh, 12 m. distant, W. of the Indus, in the N.W.F. Province. There is a bridge of boats in the low-water season and a steamer ferry at times, otherwise special arrangements for crossing the river must be made. Sir Mortimer Durand, who fixed the boundary ("the Durand line") between India and Afghanistan, lost his life at Tank by an accident and is buried in the churchyard here. Roads run to Bannu, Tank (42 m.), and to Fort Sandeman in the valley of the Zhob, *via* Chaudhwan. Near Pezu on the Bannu road is Sheikh Budin (now vacated) on a hill (4516 ft.) which is devoid of water, but a few officials used to spend the summer here.

N. of Dera Ismail Khan are two forts of **Kafir Kot,** close to Bilot, situated on small hills attached to the lower spurs of the Khasor range, and overlooking the Indus. The main features of these forts are an outer defensive wall, and groups of buildings. These forts could have held a good-sized garrison. Traces can be seen of the arrangements for raising water from the Kachi below. Legends connect them with the last of the Hindu Rajas, Tel and Bil, and they indicate that in times before the Muslim invasion, a Hindu Raj possessed considerable resources and architectural skill.

221 m. **Bhakkar** (D.B.). The table rock of the Takht-i-Suleman ("Throne of Solomon", 11,672 ft.) can be seen to the west on clear days.

300 m. **Kot Adu,** junction for new line over Taunsa Barrage along W. bank of Indus to Jacobabad *via* **Dera Ghazi Khan** (alt. 398 ft.), a district of the Punjab, also accessible by motor car or bus *via* the motor road over the **Taunsa** barrage. Here the irrigation works are amoog the most impressive in Pakistan and are well worth a visit. The road to Fort Munro (alt. 6307 ft.) 51 m. W. lies through Saki Sawar, picturesque shrine of a Muslim Saint. It is possible to motor to Afghanistan, Iran and Europe by the road from Fort Munro to Loralai and Quetta; but the longer route *via* Sukkur and the Bolan Pass is much better and less hazardous.

336 m. **Muzaffargarh,** where the one-time well-known novelist Flora Annie Steel was Inspectress of Schools. From Muzaffargarh there is a road to Ghazi Ghat for Dera Ghazi Khan.

346 m. after crossing the Chenab river (p. 583) **Sher Shah,** junction with the Karachi-Lahore line (Route 2).

Main Line

Beyond **Kharian** (92 m. from Lahore on the main line to Peshawar) the ry. traverses a tract called the Pabbi, crosses the Upper Jhelum Canal, and then the Jhelum river by a bridge, affording a view of the snows of the Pir Panjal and of the town on the N. bank. The bridge, 4892 ft. long, carries the Grand Trunk Road, on the same piers, down-stream. The canal runs to the Khanki Barrage on the Chenab river, feeding the Lower Chenab Canal.

103 m. **Jhelum** station (R., D.B.K.), on the right bank of the Jhelum river, is headquarters of a district. The Civil Lines and Cantonment lie 1 m. E. and W. of the town respectively. Many ancient pillars have been dug up near the railway station, and amongst them one with a human face in the Greek style, which is now in Lahore Museum. Another is to be seen in the railway engineer's compound.

Till the political changes of 1947 Jhelum was an important timber-depot. The timber cut in the Kashmir forests was floated down the river and collected. The American Presbyterian Mission maintains a hospital for women, while R.C. nuns from England and Ireland have, since Partition, been given facilities for starting a school which is already very popular amongst better-class Pakistanis. The Regimental Centre of the 1st Punjab Regiment has also been built here since Partition, the main feature being an impressive mosque which was formally brought into use in 1951. North of Jhelum by a good road is **Mangla**, one of Pakistan's greatest irrigation works (well worth visiting). There is a R.H., Tourist Bs. and an Information Centre.

Tangrot, some 28 m. from Jhelum (in Kashmir), is a well-known place for *mahseer* fishing.

Rohtas is 12 m. N.W. of Jhelum. Road to the Kahan river 8 m., and after that a cart-track along the river, and then a bridle-path below barren hills 200 ft. high. This famous fort, which is partly visible from the railway, stands on a hill overlooking the gorge of the Kahan river. Its wall extends for 3 m. in places from 30 ft. to 40 ft. thick, and encloses about 260 acres. It was built by Sher Shah in 1542 as a check on the Ghakkar tribes. There are 68 towers and 12 gateways. The entrance, up a steep path, is by the Khawas Khan Gate, on the N.E. of the hill. The Sohal Gate (where is the R.H.) is on the S.W. It is a fine specimen of the Pathan style, over 70 ft. in height, with balconies on the outer walls, and is reached through the town, with a deep fissure on the left, and on the right an inner wall with a lofty gateway, called after Shah Chand Wali. Within this, in ruins, is the palace of Man Singh of Jodhpur, built after he occupied Kabul (1585). The S.W. corner is a lofty baradari, with a stone finely carved with figures of birds, etc. In the S.E. corner is a smaller baradari, about 25 ft. high. The wall between the two is gone. There were twelve gates to the fort. but they are now nearly all in ruins. The Shisha Gate (an inner gate) was so called from the harim's Hall of Mirrors, which adjoined it.

The gradient between Jhelum and (135 m.) **Sohawa** is still steep, although reduced from 1 in 50 to 1 in 100 by a winding realignment. The scenery of the East extremity of the Salt Range, through which the line passes, is very wild in parts.

Tilla, an Eastward continuation of the Salt Range, 3242 ft. above the sea. The hill is sometimes used as a summer resort by officers of Jhelum District. A famous monastery of Jogi fakirs, one of the oldest religious institutions in the North, is situated here.

155 m. on the main line from Lahore to Peshawar **Mandra Junction,** branch line to Bhaun, 47 m.

164 m. **Mankiala** station is the nearest point to Manikyala Tope, which is 1 m. distant.

Manikyala was first noticed by Mountstuart Elphinstone in 1809, on a mission to Shah Shuja of Kabul, and thoroughly explored by General Ventura in 1830. In 1834 the stupa was explored by General Court,[1] and thirty years after by General Cunningham. There are coins taken from it, at different levels, of Kanishka and Huvishka which date from the beginning of the Christian era, but with them was found a gold coin of Yaso Varma of Kanauj, who reigned not earlier than 720, and many silver Sassano-Arabian coins of the same period. It is thought that the stupa might have been originally built by Huvishka, who deposited coins of his own reign and of his predecessor Kanishka, and that the stupa, having become ruinous, was rebuilt in its present massive form by Yaso Varma of Kanauj (after 720), who re-deposited the relic-caskets with the addition of a gold coin of himself and several contemporary coins of Arab governors.

[1] Ventura and Court were European officers in the service of Ranjit Singh.

The dome of the stupa, which was probably about 100 ft. high, is an exact hemisphere, 127 ft. in diameter. The outer circle measures 500 ft. in circumference, and is ascended by four flights of steps, one in each face, leading to a procession path 16 ft. in width, ornamented both above and below by a range of dwarf pilasters. The tee has gone.

At 2 m. to the N. of Ventura's Tope is **Court's Tope.** Here the earth is of a bright red colour, and General Cunningham identified this stupa with that mentioned by Hiuen Tsang as "the stupa of the body-offering" while at 1000 ft. to the S. of it is Hiuen Tsang's "stupa of the blood-offering", attributed to its being stained with the blood of Buddha, who, according to a curious legend, is said (in a previous existence) to have offered his body to appease the hunger of seven tiger cubs. The stupa of the body-offering was opened by General Court, who found in a stone niche, covered by a large inscribed slab, three cylindrical caskets of copper, silver and gold, each containing coins of the same metal; four gold coins of Kanishka were found in the gold box; in the silver box were seven silver Roman denarii of the last years of the Republic, the latest being M. Antonius Triumvir, and therefore not earlier than 43 B.C. The eight copper coins in the box belonged to Kanishka and his predecessors. The inscription has been studied by M. Senart and Professor Luders.

General Cunningham ran trenches across another mound, and brought to light the outer wall and cells of the monks, forming a square of 160 ft.

176 m. Sohan river.

180 m. **Rawalpindi,*** alt. 1687 ft. (D.B., Hotels, C.H. Tourist H. Information Centre). It is the headquarters of the Pakistan Army. There are air-services not only to Lahore, Karachi and Peshawar but also to Chitral, Gilgit and Skardu in Baltistan (permits needed). It shares Government institutions with the adjacent new capital, **Islamabad**, now in the later stages of construction and very impressive. It was laid out by a famous Greek town-planner (Mr Doxiadis) who took full advantage of the great natural beauty of the site to provide vistas, avenues, and panoramas of the fine modern buildings against the background of the foothills. The majority of the foreign Embassies are located here, although some are to be found on the road from Rawalpindi which has now become extensively built up along most of its length. Rawalpindi itself has a population of more than half a million; it still houses the President of Pakistan and many civil and military establishments including the Staff College. It is an ancient place, with a history extending back to the kingdom of Ghazni under Sultan Mahmud (977-1030 A.D.). It is still famous for embroidery and brass work, to be seen at the Pakistan Arts and Crafts Centre.

The Mall runs for 4 m. through the station, forming part of the Grand Trunk Road. On it is situated Flashman's Hotel and the Inter-Continental. Behind the latter and to the right is the Army Museum. The *Anglican Church* is about 1 m. from the railway station, and nearby are the *Scottish* and *R.C. Churches.* About ½ m. S. of that again is Ayub National Park covering some 2,300 acres, with a low forest well preserved, and close by is the *Golf-Course* (18 holes). Opposite is the great Ordnance Depot. The American Missionary hospital, built since Partition, is one of the best hospitals in Pakistan and visitors are cordially welcomed.

Rawalpindi is the starting-place of the motor road which passes Islamabad on the way to **Murree**, 37 m.; alt. 7527 ft. (Many hotels and B.Hs.) Taxi and Bus services from Rawalpindi. Information Centre near G.P.O. It is now being used as a summer resort by the Pakistan Government, and the Diplomatic Corps. The houses in Murree are built on the summit and sides of an irregular ridge and enjoy magnificent views over forest-clad hills into deep valleys, studded with villages and cultivated fields, with the snow-covered peaks of Kashmir in the background. On the S.E. is the former Lawrence School for the children of British soldiers, which still carries on as a school, but with many different types of boys. The peaks behind the sanatorium attain a height of over 9000 ft. The climate is temperate, the lowest recorded temperature being 21°, the highest 96°.

The small stations in the hills N.W. of Murree, known as the **Galis** (Barian, Ghora Dacca, Khanspur, Dunga, Changlagali, Khairagali and Nathiagali) are conveniently reached from Murree (p. 590) as well as from Abbottabad (p. 594). Four of them, Ghora Dhaka, Khanspur, Changlagali and Khairagali are now known as "Ayubia" with very spectacular views and much small game: the area is being developed into a tourist centre with facilities for winter and summer sports. The most Northerly of them, Nathiagali (Hotels: G.H., R.Hs., Tourist Information Centre) is an occasional residence of the President of Pakistan. The walks through the Galis are lovely in spring—nothing in the whole Himalayas is more beautiful. A regular bus service connects Abbottabad with Murree and the Galis, but it is liable to interruption from snow in the cold weather.

16 m. beyond Rawalpindi, on an eminence above the Margala Pass, a cutting made in Akbar's time, is the monument of General John Nicholson, with the following inscription:

> "Erected by friends, British and Native, to the memory of Brigadier-General John Nicholson, C.B., who, after taking a hero's part in four great wars, fell mortally wounded, in leading to victory the main Column of assault at the great siege of Delhi, and died 22nd September 1857, age 34."

189 m. **Golra** Junction for the line to Basal Junction, where it meets the line from Campbellpur (p. 594).

200 m. **Taxila (Saraikala)** Junction (R.R., R.H., D.B., Youth Hostel). Bus and Taxi services from Rawalpindi 20 m. for the line (35 m.) to Havelian (9½ m. from Abbottabad, see p. 594), and station for the ruins of Taxila (ancient *Takshasila*). conveniently visited by car from Rawalpindi (21 m.) along the Grand Trunk Road, off which motor roads run close to the principal objects of interest. To visit all the remains, one day is required. For a prolonged visit there is a small Archaeological Dept. R.H., permission to occupy which may be obtained from the Director of Archaeology, Rawalpindi. But it is easy to stay in Rawalpindi and journey to and from a comfortable hotel. Near the station is the Archaeological Museum, where permits can be had to view the excavations. (See Tourist Dept. brochures, obtainable at the Office.)

The remains (discovered 1852), E. and N.E., are spread over an area of some 25 sq. m. They comprise three distinct cities. The earliest of these is situated on the Bhir mound (at the N. end of which stand the Archaeological Museum and bungalow), and was in occupation for some centuries before about 180 B.C. The second city, known as Sirkap, N.E. of the mound on the farther side of the Tamra Nala (*Tibero-nalo* or *Tibero-potamos* of the Greek historians), a tributary of the Haro river, appears to have been built by the Bactrian Greeks and to have been occupied successively by the Scythians, the Parthians and the early Kushans. The third city, now called Sirsukh, about 1 m. N.E. of Sirkap, was probably founded, as shown by the "diaper" masonry, by the great Kushan Emperor Kanishka (*c.* A.D. 120) and flourished for some five or six centuries. In this city the Chinese pilgrim, Fa Hian, stayed at the beginning of the 5th century and described it as a very flourishing place. But when Hiuen Tsang saw it in the 7th century, it had somewhat decayed, although it was still sufficiently important to serve as a point from which the distances and directions to the various monuments described by him are calculated. Little of this city is visible. Besides these three cities, to each of which the name of Taxila (Takshasila) was transferred in succession, other outlying monuments have been excavated, the most important among them being the Dharmarajika Stupa near the village of Shahpur, on the S. side of the Hathial spur, a massive temple with Ionic pillars at Jandial, N. of Sirkap, and two groups of Buddhist buildings, one in a defile in the hills near the village of Mohra Moradu, about 1 m. S.E. of Sirsukh, and the other on a hill near the village of Jaulian. There is a less accessible fortress of Giri, dating from A.D. 400, possibly a refuge from the White Huns who destroyed Sirsukh *c.* A.D. 500.

A good plan is to drive to the **Chir Tope** (Dharmarajika Stupa), walk (about 1¼ m. N.W.) through a defile in the hills to the stupa of Kunala, and descend into the city of Sirkap. The car can go round to the N. side of Sirkap, and the visitor can drive to the Temple of Jandial, and thence E. to Mohra Moradu and Jaulian. The **Museum** (opened in April 1928) contains ten thousand coins collected since 1913.

The remains at the **Chir Tope**, so called because it has been "split" by earlier excavators, comprise a large number of Buddhist stupas, chapels and monastic dwellings near Shahpur and the Hathial spur. In the centre is the Main Stupa, erected possibly in the time of Asoka, but subsequently enlarged. The decorative stone facing on the E. side dates from about the 4th century. Around the main edifice there originally stood a circle of small stupas, but a series of chapels was constructed on their ruins, and numerous other stupas and chapels were erected round about, with a monastery to the N. The buildings on this site are constructed in various styles of masonry, and as their relative ages have been ascertained they offer reliable data for fixing the age of other monuments in this part of India. Among them the visitor should notice in particular the chapel in the N.E. corner with the feet of a colossal figure of the Buddha, once about 35 ft. in height, a small apsidal Chaitya on the W. side of the Main Stupa, and a chapel not far from it, where relics of the Buddha, accompanied by a Kharosthi inscription on a silver scroll (of the year 136 of Azes = A.D. 78) were discovered.

The **Stupa of Kunala,** at the S. end of Sirkap, is said to commemorate the spot where Kunala, the son of the Emperor Asoka and Viceroy of Taxila, had his eyes put out through the guile of his stepmother Tishyarakshita. The story, which resembles that of Phaedra and Hippolytus, is told by Hiuen Tsang.

The original stupa, only about 10 ft. in height, can be seen emerging from the core of the larger structure on its W. side. It was erected probably by Scytho-Parthians; the larger structure was built around it about A.D. 300 and extended over the ruins of an ancient city wall. An exceptional feature of this later stupa is the concave curvature of the plinth—an idea which was perhaps borrowed from the Greeks. Immediately to the W. of the stupa is a spacious monastery.

From the Kunala Stupa a view can be obtained of the city of Sirkap below and the broad Haro Valley beyond. The monument about 5 m. distant on the last spur of the hills bounding the valley on the N., is the **Stupa of the Head-gift,** now known as the Bhallar Stupa, in the monastery belonging to which Kumaralabda composed his Buddhist treatise.

The remains excavated in **Sirkap** comprise the main street running N. and S., with the fortifications at its N. end and a variety of buildings separated by lanes laid out with considerable regularity. The buildings visible on the surface belong mainly to the Parthian and early Kushan period. Beneath are two layers of buildings of the Scythian period and below these two more layers of the

Greek period (190-85 B.C.). In the upper layers are a number of houses, several small shrines, believed to be Jain, a large Buddhist apsidal temple, and a palace closely resembling in plan the palaces of Assyria.

The houses were two- or three-storeyed with chambers around open courts. They were occupied either by several families or by professors with their numerous pupils, for Taxila was the most famous seat of learning in ancient India and attracted students from far and near. A feature of the houses, which is noticed also by Philostratus in his *Life of Apollonius*, is that there are underground rooms (*taikhanas*), access to which was provided by trap-doors from the chambers above. Large numbers of antiquities, including domestic utensils, have been found. Noteworthy among them are an Aramaic inscription of about 400 B.C., a head in silver repoussé of the Greek god Dionysus, a bronze statuette of Harpocrates, the Egyptian child-god of silence, and gold jewellery of Greek workmanship.

The **Temple of Jandial,** N. of Sirkap dates from about the Christian era, and is planned like a Greek temple, with the addition of a solid tower or *ziggurat* between the *naos* (sanctuary) and *opisthodomos* (back porch), from which the rising and setting sun could be observed. This and other considerations (notably the absence of images) suggest that it was a temple of Zoroastrian fire-worshippers during the Scytho-Parthian period. It is possible that this is the temple described by Philostratus where Apollonius waited before entering the city of Taxila.

The Buddhist stupas and monasteries at **Mohra Moradu, Kalawan,** S.E. of Sirsukh, and **Jaulian** are well preserved. Those at Mohra Moradu were first erected about A.D. 200; two or three centuries later images and reliefs, which adorn the walls, were added. The monastery was two-storeyed and consisted of a court surrounded by 27 cells, with several additional chambers, on its E. side, one probably a bathroom and another a refectory. In one cell of the larger court was a perfect stupa, with all its umbrellas complete (in the Museum), and in the same court are several interesting groups of stucco figures. The main stupa, W. of the monastery, is chiefly remarkable for the masterly stucco reliefs of the Buddha and his attendants which are now in the Museum. From it a charming view is obtained of the Mohra Moradu gorge and valley of the Haro below.

The remains at Jaulian (E. of Mohra Moradu and on a hill) are of the same character, probably slightly earlier. The stupa is enclosed by courts surrounded by a series of chapels, and there are numerous smaller stupas adorned with unique stucco and clay reliefs. In one of the smaller stupas (to the S. of the main edifice) a remarkable relic-casket of lime plaster was discovered, painted and studded with gems. In the burnt monastery a half-charred manuscript of birch bark in Brahmi of the Gupta period was also found.

209 m. by rail from Lahore is **Hassan Abdal** station (D.B.), famous for the so-called *Lalla Rookh's*[1] tomb, which is close by; also on account of the spring of *Baba Wali*, or, as the Sikhs call it, Panja Sahib. Baba Wali was a Musalman saint, and one version of the local legend is that Guru Nanak, the founder and Guru of the Sikhs, caught a rock thrown at him by Baba Wali, who had refused him water, and commanded water to flow from it. (The impression of Guru Nanak's hand is said to have remained ever since, and at one end of the tank there is a rude representation of a hand in relief on a rock, from underneath which the water flows into the tank.) This place has been appropriated in turn by Buddhist, Brahman, Muslim and Sikh. The shrine of the saint Pir Wali Kandahari is on the peak of a

[1] The last poem in *Lalla Rookh*, that of the "Fair Nurmahal", was recited by the disguised Prince at Hassan Abdal.

lofty and precipitous hill best climbed from the S.

The Panja Sahib Sikh Gurdwara is at the E. entrance to the town, on the right. The road to it through the town leads down to a brook, crossed by stepping-stones. A Sikh temple has been constructed at the tank, which is a beautiful pool of water canopied with mulberry and pipal-trees, and full of mahseer, some of them as big as a 15-lb salmon. The walk leads some 250 yd. along the stream, past some historic architectural remains of Jahangir, and past another pool, to Lalla Rookh's tomb, which is very plain, and stands in a garden surrounded by a wall, with four slim towers, one at each corner; the enclosure is well filled with trees, amongst which is a cypress more than 50 ft. high.

At Wah, a mile from Hassan Abdal there is a Mughal garden, said to have been built by Akbar, who exclaimed, "Wah! Wah!" at the beauty of the view. It is a protected monument, in the charge of the family of Sardar Muhammad Hayat, to whom it was given after the Mutiny.

At Haripur, 20 m. from Hassan Abdal, is a memorial to "Colonel Canora", who was killed defending his guns against the Sikh insurgents in 1848. "Canora" is a corruption of Kennedy, an American deserter from the Navy who became a colonel in the Sikh service, and with Holmes (at Bannu), Foulkes and other European officers, lost his life by refusing to take part in the Sikh War of 1848 against the British. The road from Haripur to Tarbela has been submerged under the artificial lake of the **Tarbela Dam** which is reached from Hatia on the Grand Trunk Road near Lawrencepur. The town of Ghazi is about 10 m. from the panoramic viewpoint overlooking the dam and surrounding area. A road runs across the top of the dam to the right bank of the Indus.

From Hassan Abdal to **Abbottabad** (D.B., hotels, Tourist Office), 44 m. by metalled road, *via* Havelian. A branch line of the N.W.R. runs from Taxila Junction on the main line to Havelian, 9½ m. from Abbottabad, but it is quicker to go by taxi from the junction. Abbottabad is a pretty hill station (alt. 4010 ft.) popular for its quietness and the comfort of its hotels. The name is derived from Major Abbott (1849-1853), who demarcated the station and pacified the district after the British annexation.

Nearby at Kakul is the Pakistan Military Academy, the Sandhurst of Pakistan, while in Abbottabad various regimental centres and other military institutions may be seen, including the Piffer Mess still maintained as well as ever it was before Partition.

The "Galis" (p. 591) are easily reached from Abbottabad.

There is a metalled motor road from the Grand Trunk Road through Abottabad to Muzuffarabad, and to the tourist resorts on the Pakistan side of the cease-fire line in Kashmir (see pp. 604 ff.) (SEE *The Tourist's Kashmir* p. 603 *below*.)

231 m. from Lahore, on the main line to Peshawar, is **Campbellpur,** headquarters of the Attock District. This is the junction for an important strategic railway which runs *via* Mianwali to Kundian Junction, with branch lines across the Indus into the former N.W.F.P.

Branch Lines to Kohat, Bannu and Tank

20 m. from Campbellpur, Basal Junction connects with a direct line (1881) from Golra Junction near Rawalpindi.

36 m. Jand Junction for a branch to **Kohat** Cantonment (37 m.), crossing the Indus at **Khushalgarh** by a cantilever bridge, with a roadway. N. of the road are the hills of the Jowaki Afridis. From Kohat (alt. 1710 ft.) a N.G. line continues to Thal, running under the Samana range of the Orakzai. On this range is Fort **Saragarhi** (p. 356). Thal (62 m.) is at the mouth of the Kurram Valley, detached from Afghanistan in 1879. The tribesmen are Shias. A road leads

to **Parachinar** (a delightful spot with D.B. and Tourist Cottages, accessible by road from Peshawar *via* Kohat) and to the Peiwar Kotal, crossed by Lord Roberts in the Second Afghan War in 1879. The Safed Koh range, with a high peak, Sika Ram, runs along the N. side of the valley. In 1919 the Afghans invaded and marched down the valley to Thal, where they were met and decisively defeated by Brigadier-General Dyer.

Between Thal and Bannu is the Ahmadzai salient of tribal territory, with Kafir Kot (alt. 4000 ft.) in the Juni Ghar range.

From Kohat a road runs to Peshawar (40 m.) through territory of the Adam Khel Afridis, with a rifle factory quite close to the road. The area was once dangerous for foreigners; but since Pakistan displaced the British *raj*, strangers are welcome and many tourists visit it, to buy hand-made copies of modern firearms as souvenirs.

92 m. from Campbellpur, at Daud Khel Junction there are two cement factories. A branch crosses the Indus at Mari-Indus below the gorges by a bridge 3057 ft. long to Kalabagh, where the new Jinnah Barrage is located and a narrow-gauge railway runs to Laki Marwat Junction (52 m.). Here a branch runs to **Bannu,** at the mouth of the Tochi Valley, which leads to Datta Khel *via* Miranshah (2982 ft.). A circular road takes off leading to the disused Cantonment of **Razmak**[1] (7000 ft.) in the Mahsud country, with a branch road to Wana, in the Waziri country N. of the Gumal river. The N.G. railway continues to Pezu (26 m.) and Tank (46 m.) and meets the circular road near Manzai (68 m. from Laki Marwat). Murtaza, near Tank, is on the Gumal river, by which route the Powindahs used to come down from Afghanistan with their flocks and herds. This migration is now strictly controlled in the interests of public health and animal husbandry.

[1] Abandoned by Pakistan in 1948 from (justified) confidence in the friendship of the Mahsuds.

122 m. from Campbellpur Junction Kundian, junction with the Sind Sagar railway (p. 563).

Main Line

241 m. by rail from Lahore is **Attock Bridge** station (D.B.), 1 m. below the town and fort. There is a R.H. at **Kund** which is a favourite picnic spot. The railway crosses the Indus by a bridge, on steel trestles encased in piers, has two spans of 308 ft. and three of 257 ft., and is 100 ft. high above low water. The rails are on the top of the girders, and there is a road below, closed from sunset to dawn, otherwise open to motor traffic. Each end is protected by a fortified gate. The river has been known to rise 90 ft. in flood near the fort, where the channel becomes very narrow. An endeavour to tunnel under the bed failed.

The **Fort,** situated on a commanding height, overhanging the E. bank of the Indus, and a little S. of the confluence with the Kabul river on the W. bank, is very extensive, and has a most imposing appearance. It was built by the Emperor Akbar in 1586, who also established the ferry which it commands. Maharaja Ranjit Singh occupied the place in 1813, and it remained in the hands of the Sikhs till the British conquest of 1849.

The views extend N. and W. as far as the distant peaks of the Safed Koh.

To the N. of the fort is an old sarai, now in ruins, divided from the higher hill on which the fort stands by a ravine. S. of the fort is another ravine, which separates it from the village of Mullahi Tola, the ferrymen's quarter.

The hills that line the river have old round towers and ruined forts, and the Attock Fort resembles an ancient baronial castle. Close to the bridge is a R.H. on a hill overlooking the junction of the Indus and Kabul rivers.

Outside the fort, to the W., is the tomb of a Diwan of the saint Abdul

Kadir Gilani. It stands in a small enclosure on the edge of a cliff.

Local arrangements can sometimes be made for a trip by boat down the Indus to Khushalgarh, or to Kalabagh and Mari, which will afford picturesque views of the deep, dark gorges of the Indus.

The Frontier

244 m. **Khairabad** station (R.), fine retrospect of the bridge and Attock Fort.

261 m. **Nowshera** Junction (D.B.), is the headquarters of a subdivision of the same name in Peshawar District, on the S. of the Kabul river. The Cantonment is on both banks. About 2 m. distant on the Grand Trunk Road is a ruined fort built by the Sikhs.

Branch Line

From Nowshera a branch crosses the Kabul river and runs past the Cantonment of Risalpur and (15 m.) Mardan to Dargai (41 m.), at the foot of the **Malakand Pass.** Good motor road. Splendid scenery. There are bus and taxi and excellent transport services from Nowshera and Peshawar and the Tourist Bureau in Peshawar will assist visitors.

The Benton Tunnel (2 m. long) utilises water from the Swat river for irrigation and a hydro-electric grid.

10 m. beyond the Malakand crest, on the farther bank of the Swat river, is the Fort of Chakdarra. Beyond is a good motor road to Saidu Sharif, capital of the former **Swat** State, (Tourist Bureau). There are comfortable hotels at Saidu Sharif, Mingora, Madyan and Kalam: the entire area is now among the most popular tourist resorts of Pakistan. Excellent walking, golf, and shooting. The streams of Swat provide some of the best fishing anywhere. English Brown Trout have been introduced, and flourish side by side with indigenous species. There are comfortable R.H.s at all the best fishing spots. A skiing resort is being developed at Malam Jabha. A road is being built to Gilgit (p. 611 *below*) across the mountains, which will link the Karakoram area with Peshawar and Rawalpindi *via* the Malakand Pass. There are good roads and an extensive system of R.H.s linked by telephone throughout Swat.

The country is full of Buddhist remains and sculptures, fine specimens of which can be seen in the Saidu Shaief Museum. At Udegram and Mingora, impressive Buddhist sites have been exposed, and should be visited.

Mardan was the headquarters of Queen Victoria's Own *Corps of Guides* (1846). The little Guides' Cemetery nearby is still beautifully maintained. The largest sugar mill in Asia is in Mardan.

7 m. N.E. of Mardan is the famous rock of Shahbazgarhi, 24 ft. by 10 ft., situated about 80 ft. up a slope, with one of the great Asoka inscriptions. As at Mansehra (p. 610), the script is Kharoshthi, a form of Aramaic character, introduced from Persia about 500 B.C.

At 24 m. from Nowshera, at Takht-i-Bahai, an isolated hill rising 650 ft., are remains of a Buddhist monastery or convent (2nd-3rd century), and another at Shahr-i-Bahlol at its foot. Buddhist carvings, images and sculptures from both sites are in the Peshawar Museum.

The entire Malakand Agency area as well as Swat, Dir and Chitral are well worth a visit. Much is being done in both areas for the convenience of tourists. The scenery is splendid and the surroundings unspoiled. For certain areas permits may be necessary—enquire from the Tourist Bureau at Peshawar. Air services connect Peshawar with **Chitral.** There is a jeepable (summer only) road from the head of the Malakand Pass through Dir to Chitral. The stages are: Peshawar to Dir 134 m., Dir to Lowari Pass 12 m., Lowari Pass to

Drosh 21 m., Dhrosh to Chitral 24 m., Total 191 m. The town of Chitral with its shopping centre notable for embroidery, dagger belts, swords and handloom products, is overshadowed by the great peak of

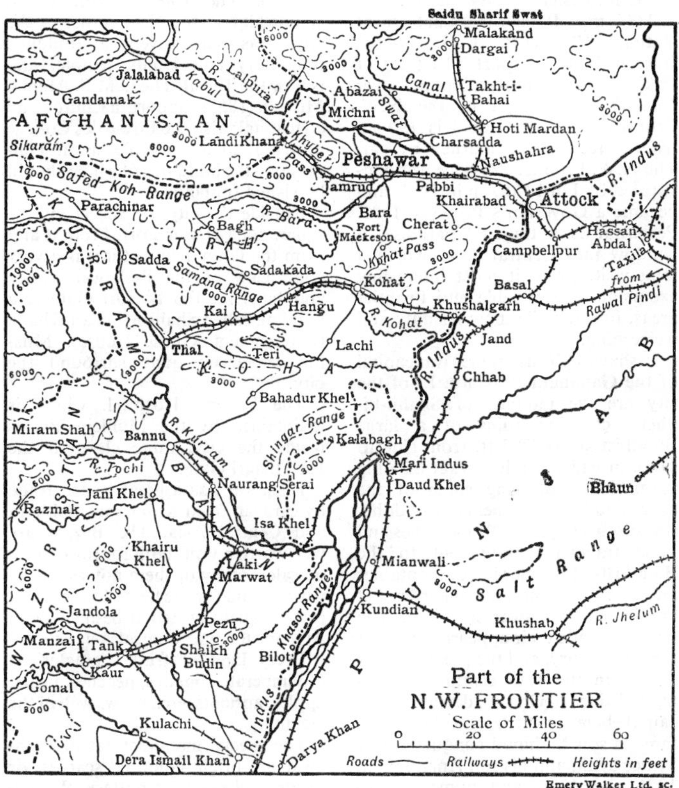

Tirichmir; there is a R.H. and a motel and the Palace is earmarked for the tourist trade. The surrounding valleys are very fertile, and include Brior and Bombret (with rest houses) in which the picturesque and peaceful communities of "Black Kafirs" carry on a life unchanged for centuries. Their ceremonial dances are well worth seeing (enquire from the authorities in Chitral). There are many other worthwhile excursions from Chitral, including Lutcoh valley (34 m.) with its hot springs, excellent trout-fishing and comfortable R.H.

Main Line

274 m. **Pabbi** station. 23 m. from here is **Cherat** (D.B.), a hill Cantonment and sanatorium for Peshawar, 4500 ft. above sea-level, where the badges of units of the British and Indian armies may be seen cut into the rock faces. These are well main-

tained, having recently been re-coloured. A mail and passenger lorry service runs between Pabbi and Cherat. There is a Government Fruit Farm 4 m. from Pabbi towards Peshawar. After crossing the Bara river, which drains Afridi Tirah.

285 m. **Peshawar City** station.

288 m. **Peshawar Cantonment** station* (R., D.B., C.H. Tourist Bureau, hotels, airport TL) (HQ of Pakistan Air Force), pop. over 250,000; the capital of the N.W. Frontier Province. Kabul is 190 m. from here, a day's journey by car. The N.W. Frontier Province was constituted by Lord Curzon in 1901, and became a Governor's Province 1931. Peshawar is a tourists' paradise, a window into Central Asia, worth a long visit. From it most interesting excursions are possible into Frontier areas, once hostile, now friendly and welcoming.

Peshawar (Purushapura) was capital of the Gandhara Province. E. of the city are the mounds of Shahji-ki-dheri, covering ruins of a large Buddhist stupa (285 ft. from side to side), in which a relic-casket of King Kanishka, containing some of the ashes and bone fragments of Buddha, was discovered in 1909. The ashes and bone fragments were sent to the Buddhists of Burma; but the container and the surrounding copper casket are in the Peshawar Museum. The Pathans made their appearance about the 8th century, and the present tribes settled in the 15th century. Sabaktagin, Prince of Ghazni, defeated Raja Jaipal here in 978, and his more famous son Mahmud conquered this Prince again and his son Anandpal in 1001 and 1008, and numerous invaders including Babur passed through it later. The old name was changed by Akbar to the present name meaning "Frontier Town", Pesh Awar. Nadir Shah of Persia took it in 1739. It was taken by the Sikhs in 1833, and occupied by General Gilbert on 21st March 1849.

The **City,** once surrounded by a wall built by General Avitabile, has twenty gates. The streets are irregular and tortuous but the bazaars, and the separate trade-quarters for sword-smiths, tinsmiths and the like are among the most picturesque in all Asia. The Kabul Gate leads to the main Kissa Kahani ("Story-tellers' street"). The *Ghor Khatri,* which stands high in the N.E. corner of the city, was successively a Buddhist monastery and Hindu temple, and is now the Tehsil. The C.M.S. Afghan Mission (1853) supports a Church and a Hospital; also the Edwardes College now part of the new Peshawar University—the buildings of which should be visited (p. 600).

Outside the city, on the N., is the square Bala Hissar Fort. From it and from the Ghor Khatri there is a very good view of the Peshawar Valley and hills. At the Bajauri Gate is a building called Shahi Mihman Khana (Government Guest House). Muslim cemeteries quite surround the city.

The Zenana Hospital, which is maintained by the Municipality, is inside the city, quite close to the Hashtnagri Gate.

Peshawar has a great transit trade by caravan from Kabul and Bokhara and Central Asia. The **Bazars** are well worth a visit, both for the objects on sale—many of them not seen elsewhere—and for the fierce-looking and picturesquely armed tribesmen from Afghanistan and Central Asia.

Every kind of fruit characteristic of temperate climates, peaches, pears, apples, apricots, etc., grows well in the vicinity.

The special manufactures of Peshawar are bright-coloured scarves, or *lungis*, and excellent pottery. Waxed-cloth work and ornamental needle-work are also made here, also knives; a special form of wood-carving flourishes.

The **Cantonments,** 2 m. W. of the city, and 3½ m. long by 1¼ m. broad, are situated on higher ground. In them are Government House and the Provincial Legislative Assembly building; also the Victoria Memorial building, now a **Museum** with a very fine collection of grave-images from Kafiristan and Graeco-Buddhist sculptures. Many were excavated at Shahr-i-Bahlol and Takht-i-Bahai (p. 596), by Dr D. B. Spooner, who also arranged them on scientific lines. Illustrated handbooks can be bought at the Museum.

During the winter it is often very cold, and warm clothing is essential. In the spring, when the roses and fruit-trees are in bloom and the fresh winter snows stand up grandly to the N. and W., the place is extremely beautiful. The Club, Roman Catholic and Anglican Churches lie about two-thirds of the way along the Mall, which extends from the Saddar road, near the railway station, to the Bara Gate. On a side road is the grave of a *naugaza* (nine-yard) saint. Since the creation of Pakistan, there has been great development in and around Peshawar. Visitors should not miss the impressive Warsak Dam on the Kabul River. This is 18 m. N. of Peshawar and lies in the heart of tribal territory. It was built by Canadian engineers using largely tribal labour, and is widely regarded as a symbol of the peaceful economic development which is transforming once turbulent tribal areas. Visitors need a Tourist Introduction Card to enter the site. The University Quarter is magnificently laid out and contains Faculties of Arts and of Science. The sons of many influential tribal Chiefs attend it preparatory to entering the armed forces and civil cadres of Pakistan (pp. 590, 594).

For British visitors, Peshawar has many associations with 1857. On the outbreak of the Mutiny, a movable column was formed, which restored order in the Punjab and after many exploits took part in the recapture of Delhi.

From Bara (7 m., D.B.), famous throughout the subcontinent for the exceptional quality of its rice, which fetches high prices among gourmets, roads run N. to Kachagarhi and S.E. to Matanni on the Kohat road, while others run to forts and posts commanding the two plains.

Abazai protects the headworks of the canal (1875) from the junction of the Swat and Kabul rivers at Nisatha, 15 m. N.E. of Peshawar. The headworks can be visited by car.

A first-class motor road runs 37 m. from Peshawar to Kohat through the Kohat Pass, to the rifle factory (p. 595). A monument to Handyside, of the Frontier Constabulary, spans the road.

Fort Mackeson lies on the left of the road, N. of Aimal Chabutra, 20 m. from Peshawar.

Charsadda, 16 m. N.E. of Peshawar, with imposing mounds, has been identified with Pushkalavati (Penkeleos), the pre-Kushan capital of Gandhara. Alexander the Great besieged and captured it in 324 B.C., receiving the surrender in person.

THE KHYBER PASS AND RAILWAY

The Khyber Pass.—No one should leave Peshawar without visiting the Pass. The trip is best done by car, as the train service at present runs on Fridays only as far as Landi Kotal, but if the timings fit in, it is interesting to do the return journey by rail. The Government Transport service runs a weekly excursion bus *via* Warsak to Torkham on the Afghan frontier; the micro-buses of the Tourism Department follow the same route. But many visitors prefer to use private taxis. The Pass is closed at sunset, and the official regulations should be carefully observed regarding the limits within which the visitor must keep.

The Pakistan Government, however, are keen to encourage tourism and impose no restrictions other than those necessary in the interests of visitors' safety. Visitors can take picnics or can get refreshments at the new Tourist Centre at Turkham.

The railway through the Pass (1920-1925) is 26½ m. long and cost over two millions sterling, having 34 tunnels aggregating 3 m. in length, with 92 bridges and culverts, besides many road diversions and heavy work. It has excited the admiration of foreign engineers, and was considered an impossible undertaking.

The Khyber Pass is not merely a valley between hills, but rises to over 3500 ft. in height and falls steeply afterwards. It has brought many invaders to India: its long story is inscribed on stone at its entrance for tourists to read. It has been for centuries the trade route from Central Asia, followed by caravans (*kafilas*) two miles long, of heavily loaded Bactrian camels with double humps, bullocks and asses, with attendant drivers and their families. The *kafilas* do not use the motor road, but at one or two points the two roads merge, and some congestion may arise.

The railway leaves Peshawar Cantonment station and circles round the perimeter on the west. On the left is the airport, with daily services to Rawalpindi, Lahore and Karachi, on the right a broad space with Flagstaff House and the golf-course. The land is occupied up to Islamia College (3 m.), opened in 1915 for the sons of notables; expanded in 1950 into Peshawar University with many students from Tribal areas in impressive buildings forming a University Quarter with the Village AID Academy (p. 555). Farther on is a mud fort, Hari Singh Burj, where this Sikh "Warden of the Marches" was cremated in 1837. Then comes a causeway over the Narai Khwar, bridged by the railway. Kacha Garhi is then reached. A road to the left leads to Bara (p. 594). To the S. is a fort guarding waterworks, from which water gravitates here to be pumped to Jamrud.

The railway and road run on over rising ground, which in spring is carpeted with wild flowers but in summer is arid, crossing the administrative boundary of tribal territory, marked by pillars. A bridge over the Jam Nala flowing from the Khyber is crossed and both railway and road curve to the left, to diverge on either side of the caravanserai, where the *kafilas* assemble and shelter for the night.

Jamrud Fort (1500 ft.) from a distance resembles a battleship. It was built in 1823 by Sirdar Hari Singh Nalwa, who was killed in action here by troops of the Amir Dost Muhammad in January 1837. The walls are more than ten feet thick, with bastions and double gates, with several hornworks. The road then divides into three, passing villages of the Kuki Khel (clan) on the way to an opening in the hills defined by a peak on each side. This is not the course taken by the Khyber stream, which emerges 2 m. S. of Jamrud.

In the First Afghan War the main line of attack proceeded by the Khyber stream, but a subsidiary attack was made in the Bagiari basin, through which both roads and railway approach the Khyber valley. There was some stiff fighting, but the Afghans were driven out of the Pass and a shorter way to Kabul was opened. Lieut. Mackeson, afterwards Commissioner of Peshawar, then made the first road up to Ali Masjid, and down from Landi Kotal. In 1842, after the disaster at Kabul, General Pollock forced the Pass by flanking methods, and inflicted a decisive defeat on the Afghans at the Jagdalak Pass. In 1878 during the Second Afghan War, General Sir Sam Browne with his army again followed the line of 1839, but effected a turning movement by a night march through the Mullagori country to the N. of the Pass, coming out at Katakushta, above the Ali Masjid gorge, just too late to intercept the Afghan cavalry, while the other defenders of Ali Masjid fort dispersed.

The Pass was held after 1890 by the Khyber Rifles, a militia mainly recruited from the Afridis. In 1897 and again in 1908 they would not fight against their relatives, and the Pass was occupied by regular troops, while expeditions were sent to punish the turbulent Zakka Khel in the Bazar Valley S. of the Pass. Restored again to their trust, the Khyber Rifles deserted in the Third Afghan War of 1919, and harassed the First Division, which advanced from Peshawar. A battle took place with the Afghans on the heights W. of Landi Kotal, and a second near Dakka on the Kabul river. Aeroplanes bombed Kabul and an armistice was granted, followed by peace. After this for a number of years the Pass was held by regular troops, but since Partition the Khyber Rifles have been revived. They are raised from the surrounding Tribal Areas, and officered by regular officers of the Pakistan Army, in whose Mess are retained and cherished with pride the old treasures of their predecessors, including Visitors' Books dating back to the last century.

West of Jamrud, the roads are crossed on the level by the railway, but the next level-crossing is 10 m. farther on, a rather remarkable fact. Close to the peaks which form the jaws of the Bagiari basin, after crossing a bridge, the car should be halted. The railway is on the left, but circles round the Bagiari fort, and crosses the valley on a viaduct, above which can be seen the Changai spur, crowned by a fortified station building, which marks the upper reversing station, the lower being marked by a scar on the spur. The railway alignment here takes the shape of a *w* to make distance and to gain height, 390 ft. in less than a mile as the crow flies, from the viaduct. The roads fork, the left one being the caravan road, while the motor road continues under the viaduct, to turn left and ascend the Bagiari spur, up which, like Mackeson's first road, both roads ascend. The railway gradient is now 1 in 33, while the roads rise at 1 in 13, and the railway is nowhere a quarter of a mile S. of the road.

Proceeding by the road, the Changai spur should be watched, and

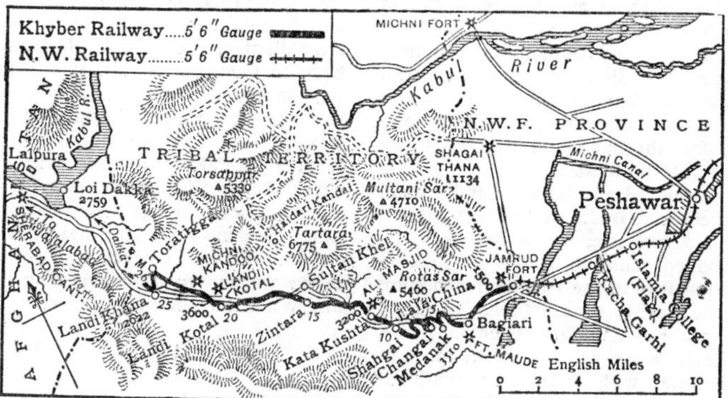

the railway will be seen emerging from a tunnel through the spur, between the two reversing stations, and above the tunnel mouth, running to bend round the head of the valley. Near Fort Maude a railway bridge spans the roads, and beyond Mackeson, or Barley, Ridge, the roads diverge to enclose the Shagai plateau. The railway station is 2688 ft. above sea-level, nearly 1200 ft. above Jamrud. Farther on both roads and the railway are carried on the same bank at different levels across a ravine, and the caravan road runs to the left to the bed of the Khyber valley.

Coming round a spur, a view is obtained of the limestone gorge, named from a small green building, Ali Masjid. The car may be stopped here. The cliffs on the N. side are precipitous, rising to the Tartarra peak (6800 ft.), but both roads and the railway, much higher up, are carried along the cliffs. Only fleeting glimpses of the gorge can be obtained from the railway, which is in tunnel most of the way. Ali Masjid Fort stands on a pinnacle (2453 ft.) above the right bank of the stream. The head of the gorge is at Katakushta, after which the valley opens out gradually. Fortified towers and villages are numerous near Zintara. Up to Katakushta the territory belongs, with no very clear demarcations, to the Kuki, Malikdin, Kambar and other clans, but beyond and almost up to Landi Kotal the Zakka Khel live, and round the Cantonment are many Shinwari villages. A road past the Shinwari villages leads into the Shilman country, and by a long detour through the Mullagori country back to Peshawar.

About 3 m. before Landi Kotal there is a Buddhist "Shpola Stupa" on a pinnacle, but it has been despoiled, and an image of Buddha from it is in the Peshawar Museum. The road to the right leads to Landi Kotal Fort and Cantonment (3518 ft.). Landi Kotal is now a thriving emporium, with a large international trade and modern houses built by rich tribal *maliks*. It is a favourite spot for Sunday excursions from Peshawar, and a large variety of articles, coming from Japan, West Germany and other foreign countries are available at astonishingly reasonable prices.

The roads and the railway now begin the descent to Landi Khana, past a caravanserai. The railway gradient for 5 m. is now 1 in 25. A ravine is followed with several waterfalls, which must have been obstacles to invading armies, and the railway in avoiding the roads has several tunnels. It is best to follow the caravan road to appreciate the difficulty. At Michni Kandao a panorama opens out in a steeply sloped basin, down which it seems impossible for a railway to go, and in fact only one or two walls can be seen, for it tunnels into the Tora Tigga valley beyond the basin to the N., and there a reversing station brings it back to Landi Khana (2500 ft.). The roads wind round the northern slopes of the basin.

Beyond Landi Khana a black cliff on the left of the stream bed is Torkham, marking the Frontier, which on the right-hand bank of the stream trends forward, as indicated by a fort on a spur. There is a pleasant rest house at Torkham, from which the road to Jalalabad can be seen. The railway formation has been completed to the frontier here. The valley bed carries the road to Dakka, Jalalabad and Kabul. Above Torkham are the red walls of Kafir Kot, probably dating back to Gandhara times. It was in Afghan territory until 1919. Left of this are the springs of Bagh which supply water to both sides of the frontier: the Pakistan authorities never cut off the supply to Afghanistan even when relations are strained, as sometimes happen. N.W. are high black ranges, their tops covered with snow in the winter. On the S., running E. and W., is the Safed Koh range.

THE TOURIST'S KASHMIR

General—The *Valley* of Kashmir is an oval plain, some 84 m. in length and 20 m. to 25 m. in breadth, at an average height of about 5200 ft., and entirely surrounded by high mountain ranges. Up to the end of May, and sometimes by the beginning of October, there is a continuous ring of snowy peaks around the valley, the principal being—N. of the Wular Lake, Nanga Parbat, 26,620 ft.; E., Haramukh, 16,900 ft., and Amarnath, 17,320 ft.; S., the Pir Panjal range, with peaks of 15,000 ft.; and W., Kazi Nag, 12,125 ft. These are all visible from the valley. Farther distant, but still in the territory of Kashmir, are many peaks of over 20,000 ft., the highest of which is Mount Godwin Austen or K2, 28,278 ft. In the Chitral State, about 200 m. N.W. of Srinagar, is the peak Agram, 25,426 ft., in the Hindu Kush range.

The Valley of Kashmir is drained by the Jhelum and its tributaries, which find an outlet in the gorge at Baramula to the Punjab. The soil is fertile. Rice and maize are the chief crops. The saffron (*Crocus sativus*) is famous for its yellow dye, and its cultivation is an ancient industry. The floating gardens of the Dal Lake are made of long strips of the lake reed, laid criss-cross, which are moored at the four corners by poles driven into the lake bed, heaps of weed and mud being then formed into small cones on the reeds. Melons, tomatoes and cucumbers grow upon these cones with astonishing vigour. The *singhara*, or water chestnut, grows wild in the Wular and Dal lakes; the kernel, which is white and mealy, is either ground into flour or parched, and so eaten. All the fruits and vegetables of temperate climes grow well in the valley. The mulberry, cherry, plum, apple, pear, grape, walnut and pomegranate are indigenous; the apricot and peach have spread all over the valley, also strawberries and raspberries. The forest trees grow to a great size. The principal among them are the deodar, the blue pine, spruce, horse-chestnut and plane (or *chenar*), which is the special glory of the valley. Willow is grown for cricket bats. The main roads are lined by poplars.

The climate is delightful in the early summer, and autumn, but in July and August the stillness of the air causes the heat to be oppressive in the valley, and the mosquitoes are troublesome. At this period visitors are glad to ascend to the upland plateaux—Gulmarg, Sonamarg (in the Sind Valley), Nagmarg, Pahalgam (at the head of the Liddar Valley) and Gurais. The spring months are showery, and the snows set in about Christmas time. In some severe winters there has been skating all over the Dal Lake, and Khilanmarg, accessible from Gulmarg, has become a winter-sports centre which attracts many visitors (p. 609). Very heavy falls of snow are experienced on occasion, temporarily rendering the valley inaccessible. Mild earthquakes are frequent.

Antiquities.—The chief ruins of Kashmir are those at Patan, Parihasapura, Pandrethan, Payer, Avantipur, Martand, Harwan and Wangat. They exhibit traces of Greek influence, and are of great archaeological interest.

History.—For many centuries Kashmir was ruled by Scythian Hindu Princes, who were succeeded by Tatars. A Muslim, Shams-ud-din, gained possession of it in 1341, and in 1588 the country was conquered by Akbar, who built the fort on Hari Parbat Hill. His successor, Jahangir, made many expeditions (1605-27) to Kashmir, where he planted chenar-trees and constructed lovely pleasure-gardens. Aurangzeb visited it once in 1664. In 1739 Nadir Shah the Persian annexed Kashmir and it passed into the hands of Ahmad Shah Abdali, the first Durani Chief, in 1748. In 1819, on his third attempt, Ranjit Singh's general, Misr Chand, defeated the Pathan Governor, Jabbar Khan, at Sherpayan, and annexed the country. In 1846, on the close of the First Sikh War, Kashmir was assigned by treaty to Maharaja Gulab Singh of Jammu, who founded a dynasty of Dogra Rajputs ruling a mainly Muslim population.

In 1947 protracted agitation, constitutional and otherwise, by the Muslim population against Dogra rule culminated in open revolt in Poonch, Mirpur and Muzaffarabad. Maharaja Hari Singh sought military aid from India, and, being told that to get it he must join the Indian Union, hurriedly did so. Indian troops were flown into Srinagar. But the Poonch-Mirpur-Muzaffarabad rebellion intensified; Gilgit and Baltistan revolted. The Security Council sent a Commission out, which, fearing open war between India and Pakistan, suggested a cease-fire, which was ultimately arranged by the military on each side. A line was demarcated, which has ever since been under the eye of U.N. observers. The area not under Indian control consists partly of what is known as Azad (free) Kashmir; which includes the Muzaffarabad and Mirpur *ilaqas* and tracts of Poonch; and partly of the "Northern Territories"—the former Gilgit Agency, with Hunza and Nagar: and most of Baltistan. The result of this, from the point of view of the intending visitor, is that he must make up his mind what parts of the former State of Jammu and Kashmir he wishes to visit. For the famous Vale of Kashmir, with Srinagar and the delightful tourist resorts of Gulmarg, Pahalgam, Achabal, Kokarnag, beloved by so many generations of visitors, he enters from India. For Murree, Muzaffarabad, Gilgit, Hunza, Nagar, and Skardu in Baltistan, he enters from Pakistan (see below pp. 609-614).

Facilities for tourists have been much improved. Both India and Pakistan have devoted money and energy to developing the portions of Kashmir which fall under their respective influences; and the economic position of the peasantry on both sides of the political frontier is rapidly improving.

PLACES ACCESSIBLE FROM INDIA

Travel and Accommodation.—The terminal for travellers by rail as already mentioned is now Jammu (p. 359) reached direct from Delhi or Calcutta. There is also a bus and taxi service from Pathankot to Jammu whence buses and taxis run to Srinagar (p. 605). For travellers who like to go by road the whole way, there are passenger coaches from Delhi *via* Jammu, which leave Delhi in the early morning and reach Jammu that same evening. Details from the Tourist Information Offices. But many people now prefer to go by air; there is a daily flight (70 minutes) between Delhi and Srinagar direct or *via* Chandigarh, Amritsar and Jammu, which is both quick and comfortable. Jammu to Srinagar by road is 182 m. For road travellers, the stages are these:

Kud (66 m.) Tourist B. Summer Resort. Dormitories for large parties.

Batote (78 m.) Tourist B. Dormitories for large parties.

Ramban. Tourist B. Crossing R. Chenab. Beautiful scenery.

Banihal. This is where the all-weather "double-barrel" tunnel dives under the Banihal Pass (9763 ft.). Tourist Bs. and large dormitories for parties. Passengers by motor coach from Pathankot may have an overnight stop. Between Ramban and Banihal the scenery is bleak, but after the tunnel it is again beautiful. Other Tourist Bs. *en route* are Qazigund and Khanibal, where tourists can break journey and get meals.

For those who take their own car, there are petrol pumps at Pathankot, Lakhampur, Samba, Jammu Udhampur, Kud, Ramban, Banihal, Khanabal and Srinagar. There is a toll tax on passage through the Banihal tunnel.

Taxis and cars, running at a regular tariff, can be hired at Pathankot and at Jammu for the journey to Srinagar.

Communications inside the Vale are good. There are now 6000 miles of practicable roads; the old leisurely system of travelling from place to place in the Vale along the canals and lakes by boat has now been superseded for most tourists by rapid journeys in cars, buses and sightseeing coaches. Typical of the "round trips" regularly made are: Srinagar-Mughal Gardens (26 m.); Srinagar-Achibal-Kokarnag-Pahalgam (152 m.); Srinagar-Tangmarg (for Gulmarg) (24 m.); Srinagar-Wular Lake—including Pattan, Manasbal Lake and Gandarbal (100 m.); Srinagar-Sonamarg (51 m.); and Srinagar-Yusmarg (30 m.).

On reaching Srinagar, the visitor is advised to make an early call at the Government of India Information Centre in Residency Road; and upon the Directorate of Tourism, Jammu and Kashmir Govt., at the impressive Tourist Reception Centre. Here he will be given copies of the rules for the stay and comfort of visitors, and of the tariffs governing the hiring of houseboats, huts, tents, camping equipment, along with details of the tours and excursions which are available. In addition to these facilities, the tourist will find the offices of Indian Airlines and of the Transport Services in the same building. The best centre from which to explore the surrounding country is Srinagar itself. There are at least half a dozen good hotels; but many tourists, in accordance with long tradition, feel that no holiday in Kashmir is complete unless they hire a houseboat as a residence. There are four classes, reckoned under categories A, B, C, according to the luxury of the accommodation, and a fourth class, D (Doonga Class), simpler and cheaper. Attached to each boat is a separate kitchen-boat and a small, light craft called *shikara*, which is used for water transport and short trips. Standards of accommodation and charges are carefully fixed by the authorities. Many houseboats are tied up to their own small gardens, but can be shifted from place to place—for example, from the Jhelum River to the Dal Lake, and from the Dal Lake to the Nagin Lake, at fixed charges. They are completely furnished, including glass, linen and crockery; most have electricity and radios. From a houseboat, the canals and lakes round Srinagar City can be explored by shikara, and longer excursions by road can be made by car or sightseeing coach. In July and August, the Vale gets very hot and humid, and visitors then mostly leave Srinagar and go to one of the several hill-stations, which are readily accessible.

Both in Srinagar and in the hill stations, there is provision for accommodation at very reasonable rates for students and other visitors whose means are limited. Particulars are available from the Tourist Reception Centre.

Srinagar* (erroneously derived from Suryanagar; air-field at Damodar Karawa; alt. 5227 ft.) is the summer capital of the former Kashmir State. is beautifully situated, has good hotels, a pop. (1971 census) 403,000, and is divided into two parts by the River *Jhelum*, along the banks of which it stretches for nearly 2 m. The river is crossed by quaint wooden bridges, but the uppermost, or Amira Kadal, has been rebuilt on modern lines. Parts of the embankment are of masonry in which carved stones from demolished temples may frequently be noticed.

The city, traversed also by canals, was built by Raja Pravarasen in the 6th century, and consists chiefly of wooden houses, some of them several storeys high, surmounted by sloping roofs covered with earth. Within the *Sher Garhi*, formerly surrounded by massive walls of the city fort, is the former *residence* of the Maharajas. The **Jami Masjid**, near the Mar Nalla (*c.* 1393-1416), but often burnt was founded by Sikandar Butshikan ("idol-smasher"). The existing one dates from 1674. It was restored to the Muslims by Maharaja Sher Singh in 1841. Its principal features are the massive enclosure-wall built of brick and the immense deodar pine pillars turned from whole trees 50 ft. high.

Another wooden mosque in the city, the **Shah Hamadan,** with pagoda-like lines, is picturesquely situated on the river bank. Not far from it, on the opposite (left) bank of the river, is a stone mosque built by Nurjahan, wife of the Emperor Jahangir.

Below the fourth bridge is the tomb of the widow of Sikandar Butshikan, on the plinth of a 9th-century Hindu stone shrine, converted into a mausoleum by the addition of domes of brick.

A fine view of the city and its neighbourhood is obtained from the hill formerly known as the **Takht-i-Sulaiman** ("Throne of Solomon"), 6210 ft., where there is a stone **temple,** founded in the 8th century by the great Hindu sage, Shankar Acharya, after whom the hill is now called the **Shankar Acharya Hill. Hari Parbat** (5671 ft.), an isolated hill on the N. outskirts of the city, should also be ascended. It is surrounded by an extensive wall, and surmounted by the **Fort,** built by Akbar at the end of the 16th century. At the foot is Nagin Bagh (swimming) and an annexe of the Club.

Many good subjects for the artist may be found in Srinagar.

The chief **industries** are those of the carpet and silk factories, woollen goods, woodcarvers, embroidery-makers, gold, silver and copper smiths, papier-mâché makers, leather workers, and dealers in precious stones. The Kashmir Govt. Art Emporium, the Silk and Carpet Factories, and the Gandhi Ashram should be visited, as also the Government Museum: the Sri Prata Singh Museum at Lal Mundi.

The former British Residency, which lay above the city, has been converted into the J. & K. Government Emporium, but its lovely grounds are still used for Receptions. In the centre of the Residency quarter there was a polo and cricket ground where Radio Kashmir is now located; on the N. side of this are Nedou's Hotel and a golf-course; and at the N.E. corner is the Shankar Acharya Hill, with the entrance to the Dal Lake at its foot.

Main Roads in and round the Vale o Kashmir (Buses, taxis, and sight-seeing coaches ply along many of these routes. Details from the Tourist Centre.)

1. Srinagar to Baramula and Uri (p. 609).
2. Srinagar N. *via* Anchar to Gandarbal and the Sind Valley (p. 607).
3. Srinagar *via* the Boulevard, Nishat Bagh, Shalimar Bagh to Harwan (p. 606).
4. Srinagar S.E. to Khanabal and Islamabad (Anantnag) (p. 608).
5. Islamabad to Achibal, and N. up Liddar Valley to Pahalgam (p. 608).
6. Khanabal *via* Qazigund and Banihal to Jammu (p. 609).
7. Islamabad to Verinag (p. 608).
8. Srinagar to Sonamarg (bus service). The Srinagar-Sonamarg road continues to Leh in Ladakh (3 days by bus).

Excursions from Srinagar

(1) The ideal way to visit the **Dal Lake** and the Mughal Gardens is by boat; but if time is short, the journey by road is quicker. Skirting the W. and N. sides of the Shankar Acharya Hill from the Dal Gate, and passing through a stretch of floating gardens, the **Nishat Bagh,** on the shore of the Bod Dal, will be first reached on the E. side of the lake. The ten terraces and the water falling down them from fountains (on Sundays) are extremely beautiful, and the top terrace affords glimpses of the lake.

2 m. farther on is the **Shalimar Bagh,** on the shore of the lake, built

gh

m

shat
agh

zi
h

hma
ahi
al

by Jahangir, who lived there in the summer months with Nurjahan, "The Light of the World".

In crossing the lake to the W. a view is obtained of the mountains behind these two gardens. Beyond a small island called "Char Chinar", or Four Plane trees, lies the **Nasim Bagh,** 6 m. by road from Srinagar, closely planted with magnificent chenar-trees. Well raised above the lake, it catches the breeze, whence its name is derived.

On the way back along the W. shore, is a village with a large mosque, called Hazrat Bal. The name is derived from a hair of the Prophet Muhammad, the greatest treasure of the mosque. Farther on is a view of picturesque Hari Parbat, from which the Nasim Bagh Canal leads to the Dal Gate.

The Eastern shores of the lake may also be reached on foot. Starting from the Munshi Bagh, the road leads S. of the Takht-i-Sulaiman to the edge of the lake. A romantic building, high up the mountain-side farther on, is the Pari Mahal, built by Dara Shikoh, containing numerous fountains and tanks, now restored which indicate that it was originally a water-palace. Beyond are vineyards, and then, higher up, the Chashma Shahi, 5½ m., a small formal garden with a strong spring. The Nishat Bagh is 2 m. N., 5 m. in all from the Munshi Bagh, and Shalimar 2 m. beyond that.

(2) Starting again from the Dal Gate, and turning to the left, the Mar Nulla leads through the Northern part of the city to the W. of Hari Parbat and the Anchar Lake, across which a boat can proceed to Gandarbal, 14 m. from Srinagar. Beyond the Dilawar Khan Bagh the canal passes under a series of bridges and balconied houses, and affords some of the most picturesque views in the whole city. Near the end of it is the Idgah. From outside the Dal sluicegate the Tsont-i-Kul, or Apple Canal, leads past the Chenarbagh (a great resort for house-boats) to the river opposite the Sher Garhi, presenting varied and beautiful views all the way. The excursion can also be done by road.

(3) The **Temple of Pandrethan** lies about 3 m. E. of the Residency by road in the military cantonment area. It is about 18 ft. square and 30 ft. high and appears to have been built in the centre of a small stone tank. The beauty of the temple lies in its proportions, in the excellent sculptures of the interior, and in the trefoil-headed arches and the roof which form the chief characteristics of the Kashmir style, unknown elsewhere except in a few out-of-the-way places in the Punjab. The temple was built about A.D. 900, and dedicated to Siva.

(4) **Islamabad, Martand, Verinag** and the **Liddar Valley.** These places can be reached by the motor-road up the valley from Srinagar, which forms part of the route into Kashmir from Jammu. At 17 m. is **Avantipur** (D.B.); at 31 m. is **Khanabal** (D.B.), where the Jammu road branches off; and at 33½ m. is **Islamabad** (alternative name, Anantnag). If the visitor proceeds by boat up the river, he passes at 8 m. *Pampur*, and 6 m. farther reaches *Kakapur*, for the **Temple of Payer,** 1 m. distant. The inner temple (only 8 ft. square) is constructed of eight stones only, and is dedicated to Siva. Its date is about the 9th century A.D. In the interior is a large stone *lingam.*

About 6 m. above Kakapur is **Avantipur,** once a famous city and the capital of King Avantivarman, who reigned 855 to 883. Two of the temples built by him are still extant, a smaller and more ornate one of Vishnu-Avantisvami near the village of Avantipur, and a larger one of Siva-Avantisvara about ½ m. along the road to Srinagar. The former has a sculptured plinth, a handsome gateway, and well-preserved peristyle.

At *Bijbehara* (10 m. on the main road to Khanabal) there is a good camping-ground above the town and bridge; fair fishing may be obtained.

From here it is 4 m. to Khanabal: and then 2 m. by road to **Islamabad** (Anantnag), originally the capital of the valley. The springs in the town are exceedingly picturesque.

From Islamabad one can proceed 26 m. by car to Pahalgam (7200 ft.), the road passing within a mile of the **Ruins of Martand,** which are 5½ m. N.E., and stand on an elevated plateau above the valley. The roofless temple, the largest in Kashmir—63 ft. long and equally high—is also the finest example of the ancient Kashmiri style, which is remarkable for its quasi-classical features, derived, no doubt, from the earlier Indo-Hellenistic art of Gandhara and the North-West. There are reasons for ascribing its date to the reign of Lalitaditya (724-760). It was probably built for the worship of the sun-god, a phase of Hinduism which prevailed in Kashmir and parts of the Punjab during that period. It was largely destroyed by Sikandar Butshikan (1393-1416), sixth descendant of Shah Mirza, first Muslim King of Kashmir.

A road leads to **Achabal** (7 m. from Islamabad), with a strong spring and cascades, groves of chenar-trees, and the old pleasure-garden of Jahangir. There is an extensive trout-hatchery, where brown and rainbow trout, originally imported from Britain are bred and then introduced into the lakes and streams which make the Vale of Kashmir an angler's paradise. There is a bungalow and an excellent camping-ground.

From Achabal a path leads *via Shahabad* to (13 m.) **Verinag** (6100 ft.), also accessible by a circuitous route from the Banihal Road. Here is the source of the River Jhelum, which rises in an octagonal tank in a garden near the foot of the Banihal Pass (9763 ft.). One of the recesses of the enclosure round the tank bears an inscription by Jahangir. This spot was a favourite haunt of his empress Nur Jahan. The tank is full of sacred fish (fishing is prohibited). Tourist huts are available on hire.

On the Pahalgam Road is **Bawan,** with celebrated chenars and tanks and excellent camping-grounds. From here it is 9¼ m. up the Liddar Valley to *Ishmakam,* where there is an old ziarat. **Pahalgam** (Pailgam), a favourite summer resort, is 13 m. farther on, and 62 m. by motor-bus from Srinagar. Pahalgam has been extensively developed in recent years. There are a number of hotels, large and small (reservations must be made with the Directorate of Tourism at least 2 months ahead); also Government Tourist Huts of varying types: and tents, large and small. Rents and charges for camping furniture are fixed by Government, as are the rates for hiring ponies, porters and dandies (carrying chairs) for excursions.

From Pahalgam an expedition may be made farther up the valley to (7 m.) *Thanin,* or *Chandanwari* (10,500 ft.), whence it is a stiff climb to (6 m.) *Shisha Nag* (12,000 ft.), a fine sheet of water covered with ice till the month of June. From Shisha Nag it is 11 m. to *Amarnath Cave* (12,729 ft.), a famous resort of pilgrims. The expedition to the *Kolahoi Glacier* (24 m.) at the head of the Liddar valley is easy.

From Pahalgam another route leads N. through Aru (6 m.) and Liddarwat (16 m.) into the Sind Valley. This route is not an easy one, and as it ascends over 14,000 ft., it is often under snow till July. The usual descent into the Sind Valley is *via* Sekiwas to Kulan.

(5) There are now tour buses and taxis which drive from Srinagar right up to **Gulmarg**, passing Magam (D.B.) at 14 m. and Tangmarg at 24 m. Gulmarg (or "Meadow of Flowers") is a lovely but somewhat rainy spot at an elevation of 8500 ft. Above it is the ridge of the Firozepur Pass and the Apharwat Mountain, 14,500 ft. The snowy peak of Nanga Parbat, nearly 26,600 ft., is in full view.

2000 feet above Gulmarg lies Khillanmarg which is now being developed as a ski-ing resort. The only building there is the Ski-Club hut, but refreshment tents are pitched in the season.

There is a pony track from Gulmarg to **Baramula**, where the river emerges from the gorges into the Vale of Kashmir. The road from Baramula to Srinagar was a welcome sight, with its beautiful avenues, to visitors who entered Kashmir by the Jhelum Valley Road from Rawalpindi before the cease-fire line came into being, but now, as already indicated, the approach to Kashmir is by the Banihal route. The Srinagar-Baramula road continues to Rampur and Uri before being interrupted by the cease-fire line at Chakothi: but this area is under military control. S.E. of Baramula (16 m.) is Patan, with the ruins of two 9th-century temples: nearer Srinagar lies Parihasapura, with 8th-century temples of Vishnu and a Buddhist monastery built by Laladitya (724-760) 3 m. off road.

Like Pahalgam, Gulmarg has become a very popular tourist resort. There are three hotels, residential huts in the Golf Club (temporary membership for visitors—said to be the world's highest golf course) and Government Tourist Huts providing different classes of accommodation at reasonable rates. There are fixed tariffs for the hire of ponies and dandies for excursions to Khilanmarg (tobogganing and bob-sleighing), Lien Marg, Ningal Nullah, Ferozepur Nullah, Alapathir (mountain lake), Baba Rishi, and other picnic and beauty spots.

Another beautiful expedition may be made from Srinagar up the **Sind Valley.** The first stage is (14 m.) *Gandarbal*, a village at the mouth of the valley. From Gandarbal the stages up the valley are—to *Kangan* (11 m.), to *Gund* (13 m.), to *Gagangair* (7 m.), and **Sonamarg** (7 m. Telegraph Office; 6 m. camping-ground at Tajiwaz), now connected with Srinagar by a bus service.

8 m. N. from Wangan are the temples of **Wangal,** or Naghal, placed above the stream, and now the most picturesque of all the ruined temples of Kashmir. The route from Gund onwards is extremely beautiful, and the torrent pass, in which small snow glaciers will have to be crossed early in the season, leading up to Sonamarg, is extraordinarily fine. Sonamarg (8750 ft.) in the Glacier Valley was once the chief sanatorium of Kashmir. The next stage, *Baltal* (9¼ m. from camping-ground 9282 ft.) is at the foot of the Zojila Pass (11,300 ft.). From Baltal the Cave of Amarnath (p. 608) may be reached in the spring or early summer before the snow bridges have melted.

Since 1975, the **Ladakh** area has been opened up for tourists and many thousands come for a taste of Tibetan Buddhism. During the summer (June-Oct.) it is possible to go by bus in two days from Srinagar, over the Zojila Pass and the Zaskar Range to the capital Leh in the Indus Valley (270 m.). The alternative is to fly in.

After the Zojila Pass the green wooded valleys of Kashmir change to the barren hills of Central Asia. The night stop is at Kargil, mostly Shia Muslim, but at Mulbeck there is an 18-foot Maitreya Buddha carved from a boulder right by the road. At Lamayuru, further on, there is an old gompa (monastery) overlooking an incredible landscape.

Leh, a vast military base, is already showing the impact of tourism. Most Ladakhis are Buddhists with Mongoloid features who still wear the traditional dress of long coats belted at the waist and high top hats. Ladakhi religious art can be considered as a provincial school of Tibetan art. On the hillside above Leh is the crumbling 8-storey old palace. Near the palace is a gompa with a large prayer hall decorated with frescoes and tankas (paintings on cloth scrolls) and an adjoining building contains an enormous Maitreya Buddha. In a field 1 m. N of Leh is Samkar Gompa: many gilded images at the back of the chapel. Open only in the early morning and late afternoon. 5 m. from Leh near the lower end of the airstrip by the Indus is Spituk Gompa.

The road to Manali runs up the Indus Valley S.E. from Leh but visitors without a permit can only go as far as Upsih. 10 m. out of Leh on this road is Shey with its ruined palace. There is a giant copper Buddha in the chapel. Several m. beyond Shey is Thiksey with perhaps the largest and most impressive of all Ladakhi gompas, situated on a hilltop overlooking the Indus Valley. There are a number of chapels to be visited here, each with rich collections of tankas, statues, etc. The admission ticket allows entry to all.

Hemis, 27 m. from Leh, is the oldest and most important of the gompas but it is also more difficult to reach. It contains several large chapels with silver jewelled stupas, tankas, and a large golden Buddha. At many points along the road from Leh the weathered stupas and larger decorated chortens with their connecting mani walls set against the desert mountains create an evocative sight. (See pp. 630-631.)

PLACES ACCESSIBLE FROM PAKISTAN

The areas of the former State of Kashmir which tourists can enter from Pakistan contain some very impressive scenery, which is all the more attractive to visitors because the surroundings remain so largely unspoiled by commercial exploitation. Moreover there is the finest fishing and big and small game shooting in the entire Subcontinent, including urial, markhor, ibex, and snow leopard. The season is from mid-September until March. Licenses are inexpensive but the regulations are strongly enforced.

The southern part of this tourist country, the Kaghan Valley, lies to the east of Swat (p. 596) and is separated from the northern part, the Gilgit Agency, by the Babusar Pass. The Gilgit Agency, in addition, includes the fabulously beautiful areas of Hunza and Nagar, on the southern slopes of the Karakoram Range and is one of the gateways to Skardu in Baltistan.

The Kaghan Valley can be reached from Murree (p. 590) along the Indus Valley Road—the old route to Kashmir before India was partitioned—to Muzaffarabad, now the capital of Azad Kashmir. Azad ("Free") Kashmir consists of the former districts of Muzaffarabad, Mirpur, and part of Poonch. The inhabitants revolted against the Jammu and Kashmir authorities when the Maharaja of that State acceded to India in 1947. Azad Kashmir is not a part of Pakistan, having its own administration under Pakistan's protection. The territory stretches along the old Indus Valley road as far as Chakothi, after which the road enters the territory of Kashmir State, the border being guarded by Indian troops. No transit is possible for the ordinary visitor. Azad Kashmir is famous for its big and small game; apply to the Azad Kashmir Forest Dept., Muzaffarabad. From Muzaffarabad a road via Garhi Habibullah strikes the Valley just south of Balakot, where a Government jeep service and a bus service to Naran start.

But the easiest and pleasantest approach to the Kaghan Valley is by Abbottabad (p. 594) which can be reached by road from Rawalpindi, Islamabad and Peshawar, from all of which places there are half-hourly bus services. Special transport can also be arranged through the Tourist Offices, which also help with reservations and advice.

The Valley really begins at **Balakot**, but before this is reached (45 m. from Abbottabad) the excellent road running through well-wooded and watered country passes Mansehra after 16 miles. The first stop is usually made at **Kawai**, 15 m. farther on where there is a PWD Rest House, and the traveller begins to get his foretaste of the terraced fields, forested slopes, and snowy peaks which are typical of Kaghan Valley scenery. Both at Balakot and Kawai there is tourist accommodation; and Kawai is the branching-off point for a five-mile forest road leading to a vantage point on the slopes of **Shogran** with views of Musa-ka-Musalla (the Praying-mat of Moses) 14,000 ft., Makra 14,000 ft. and Mailika Parbat 17,000 ft. There is tourist accommodation at Shogran. From Kawai the main road goes on to **Paras**, the turning-off point to **Shinu**, with its trout hatcheries and also for the plateau of Sharan.

Mahandri, 13 m. from Kawai, is an important centre of the timber trade. There is Tourist accommodation. 11 m. on from Mahandri is the little town of **Kaghan**, from which the Valley takes its name. There is a PWD R.H., hospital, police post and Post Office. Near Kaghan there is very good fishing. Beats can be reserved during the fishing season. Licences and conditions from the offices of the Fisheries Directorate at Shinu and **Naran**. The Tourist Office at Abbottabad can also make prior arrangements. Licences are inexpensive, while the excellence of the sport and the beauty of the surroundings make the Kaghan Valley something like an angler's paradise.

15 m. beyond Kaghan is **Naran**, now developing into a very popular —but still uncrowded—tourist resort, There are chalets and rest houses, and adequate accommodation at a wide variety of prices. The River Kunhar winds its way over a rocky bed; on the slopes are cypress, cedar and poplar, with snow capped peaks behind. A favourite excursion by jeep or on foot is the **Saiful Muluk Lake** at 10,000 ft. surrounded by high mountains. The trout run very large here; there is boating on the lake and accommodation for travellers. (Prior reservation essential.) Legend has it that in the lake is imprisoned a handsome Prince named Saiful Mulk, kept there by a wicked fairy who loves him.

10 m. along the main road from Naran is **Battakundi**. From here a side road leads 2½ m. to the 10,500 ft. high plateau of **Lalusar**, well-wooded with pines and firs, and with a comfortable rest house.

About 30 m. beyond Naran at the northern end of the Kaghan Valley lies **Lulusar Lake** which is the source of the River Kunhar itself. The Lake area is famous for its wild flowers.

By the time that the jeep road reaches the Babusar Pass, 34 m. from Naran, it has become narrow and winding, as well as steep. The Pass itself is 13,684 ft. and is snow-bound for most of the year. Travellers are advised not to attempt to cross it except with a guide and after careful enquiries; but the view from the summit is breath-taking, including as it does (on a clear day before noon) the magnificent peak of **Nanga Parbat** (26,660 ft.). There is a Rest House 9910 ft. at Babusar. If conditions are favourable, the jeep track affords entry to the Gilgit Agency by road. It descends to Gonar (2500 ft.). The last 30 m. before Gilgit run along the banks of the River Indus. Nowadays most visitors go to the Gilgit area by air from Rawalpindi.

Gilgit (4770 ft.) is the headquarters of a scattered district which stretches up into Central Asia and contains some of the finest mountain scenery in the world. Within a radius of 65 miles there are eleven peaks ranging from 18,000 to 20,000 ft., six from 22,000 to 24,000 ft. and eight from 24,000 to 26,000 ft. The area is of great strategic importance; to the north-west lie the Wakhan and Badakhshan districts of Afghanistan bordering on the Oxus in Soviet territory; to the north is the Chinese province of Sinkiang; in the east are Baltistan and Ladakh; to the west lie Chitral and adjoining tribal areas. Through Gilgit district ran the ancient "Silk Road"—Marco Polo's trail—

along which the caravans from Central Asia went to the bazars of the sub-continent. The Chinese pilgrims Fa Hien and Hieun Tsang both used this route; the latter has left a hair-raising description of the perilous track clinging to the mountain-side above terrifying gorges. From the new Karakoram Highway, built in part by Pakistani and in part by Chinese engineers, visitors can catch glimpses of the old trail as they travel comfortably in jeeps and even lorries, between Gilgit Town and Baltit, in the former State of Hunza, on the frontier of Sinkiang.

History. Until the ninth century A.D. Gilgit was ruled by Hindu kings and there was a numerous Buddhist population. Islam seems to have been brought by Turkish tribes, who made Gilgit their base for raiding Kashmir proper at the time when Alberuni was making his travel notes. The whole area has until recently lacked real political unity; rulers of Gilgit exercised some kind of nominal authority over the feudal lords of Punial, Gupis, Yasin, Ishkoman and other areas while themselves owing allegiance to the Kashmir authorities who eventually displaced them by imposing the rule of the Jammu Dynasty. The Mirs of Hunza and Nagar in the N., who between them controlled the Marco Polo trail, took very little notice of their nominal overlords, the Kashmir Durbar. At the end of the nineteenth century, growing Russian influence in Sinkiang aroused the British Raj to the strategic importance of Gilgit; and by arrangement with the Kashmir Durbar, a British Political Agent was established in Gilgit to keep an eye on Frontier events. For a short time British troops were in occupation of Baltit to enforce the cooperation of Hunza and Nagar in securing the safety of traffic along the Marco Polo trail. The British Agent had no administrative authority outside his own little enclave, where a school, a hospital, and other amenities were set up. The rule of distant Jammu and Srinagar was unpopular with the people of Gilgit. In 1947 when India was partitioned, the territories of what is now the Gilgit Agency, along with Hunza, Nagar and Baltistan, revolted against the Kashmir Government and joined Pakistan. The Pakistan Government then sent its representative with the title Resident, Gilgit and Baltistan, with coordinating authority over these territories. More lately, the former smaller chiefs as well as the Mirs of Hunza and Nagar have surrendered their powers, and the entire area is now administered like any other part of Pakistan, but with an overall eye to its local conditions and strategic importance. Social and economic amenities have greatly increased.

Facilities for Tourists. It is only since 1973 that the Gilgit Agency has been open to tourists. Previously, access was confined to Pakistani nationals and even in their case, movement was restricted. At the present time, it is much easier to visit these areas; but save in the case of exceptionally privileged persons, such as accredited diplomats, tourists travel in parties arranged by Pakistan International Airlines in cooperation with the Tourist Development Corporation.

Visitors wishing to tour this area, which also includes the former Hunza State, would be well advised to allow for an elastic time table. Access to Gilgit is by daily air service from Rawalpindi; but everything depends upon the weather. The plane will not start unless the airport at Gilgit reports conditions suitable for landing with good prospects of these conditions holding for the 1½ hour air journey. Similar uncertainty controls the return flights from Gilgit; a traveller may experience considerable delay before the conditions for take-off are right. But any frustration is far outweighed by the rewards of the trip. The outward flight is itself a remarkable experience—high above the smaller peaks, with the great pinnacle of Nanga

Parbat towering higher still, and the ice-wall of the Karakoram Range like a backdrop to the scene.

Now that the new Karakoram Highway promises to increase trade with Sinkiang, the opening up of a new land route between Gilgit and the rest of Pakistan has become a matter of urgency. Work has been going on now for some years and when the last few miles of this considerable feat of road engineering are completed, all-the-year-round communication between Gilgit and Karora in Swat will be established. From Swat there are excellent roads to the Malakand and thence to Rawalpindi and Peshawar; so that it will soon be possible for cars and tourist coaches from the two cities to reach Gilgit.

At Gilgit there is a comfortable Tourist Rest House, a PWD Rest House, and an Information Office, which will arrange excursions and supply particulars of places of interest. A 40-room PIA motel is now under construction.

There are a number of picturesque places to visit round Gilgit where tourists are welcomed. There is a rock-carving of Buddha on the Gilgit-Gupis road 3 m. from Gilgit Town; at Gupis 68 m. there is a Rest House at 7070 ft. Kargah Nullah, near Gilgit, is a Game Reserve, where there is excellent fishing. Naltar, where there is good skiing (Rest House) is 28 m. from Gilgit amid scenery which recalls Switzerland. There is good partridge (Chikor) and other small game shooting, good fishing, and big game such as ibex and snow leopard in the Astore Valley, 69 m. to the S. of Gilgit. Particulars of licences, etc. from the Game Secretary, HQ Corps of Gilgit Scouts. The conditions of big game shooting are tough but rewarding. It is often possible to bag a markhor in one day. There is tourist accommodation at Astore. 94 m. from Gilgit is the fertile Yasin Valley, divided into the three districts (formerly small baronies) of Gupis, Ishkoman and Yasin. There are hot springs at Darkut and Rest Houses at Yasin and Gupis. The largest village in Ishkoman is Chator Khun (6850 ft.) where there is a PWD Rest House, a Cooperative Shop and a dispensary. Gupis is barely 15 m. from the Chinese border, and as a rule only scientific expeditions studying wild life, glaciology, or plant life can obtain permission to visit the area. Near Gupis there are primitive rock carvings of men hunting ibex, markhor, lynx and snow leopard.

The entire Gilgit Agency territory, including Baltistan (see below) abounds in wild life, but some of the species represented are already rare. The Pakistan Government take their responsibilities for preservation very seriously; and a number of species are strictly protected.[1]

No visitor should leave Gilgit without attending a polo match. Polo is the national game of the entire area; each village has its team, and the competition for trophies presented by Presidents of Pakistan and others is very keen. The game strikes western visitors as a free for all; the rough-coated village ponies are not changed; the mallets are home-made. Throughout the game, a band plays traditional tunes, which vary according to the social status of the players; and the end of the match is marked by a dance performed by the defeated team.

As has been mentioned, excursions from Gilgit are now available to **Hunza**, which because of its proximity to the Chinese frontier has until recently been closed to tourists. The Pakistan Tourist Development Corporation has its own fleet of jeeps at Gilgit available at fixed rates. There are rest-houses at Chalt, Karimabad, Gulmit, and Khunjerab. Travellers should take their own bedding. The road mainly follows the course of the Hunza River, and the scenery is extremely impressive with

[1] On the wild life of the Gilgit Agency, Guy Mountfort, *The Vanishing Jungle* (Collins, London, 1969) may be consulted.

views of Rakaposhi and some of the highest peaks of the Karakorams. As the tourist approaches **Baltit** (8000 ft.) after a 70 mile journey, the country becomes very fertile; crops of every kind are grown on terraces skilfully cut out of the mountain sides and irrigated from the glaciers above them. The inhabitants of Hunza, like those of the sister-state Nagar across the gorge, claim to have developed a technique for creating artificial glaciers where they are needed for irrigation; they will show a visitor some examples if he does not mind a climb. During the season, Hunza, with its flowers and fruit, and its hardy, fair-complexioned, friendly people who are prosperous, long-lived, and remarkably free from ailments, makes a great impression upon visitors. The former Ruling Family are very hospitable; but there are now modern motels and other amenities for tourists.

To the south-east of Hunza lies the ancient land of **Baltistan,** whose history is closely linked with that of Gilgit by dynastic alliances and dynastic feuds. Like Gilgit, it was subject to the rule of the former Kashmir Durbar; like Gilgit, it revolted against Dogra rule in 1947. In Durbar times it was readily accessible from Srinagar, a road to the capital, **Skardu**, taking off at Kargil from the main Srinagar–Leh highway. The road between Kargil and Skardu is now cut by the control-line between the Pakistan and the Indian spheres, so that for some time now the main connection between Skardu and the outside world has been by air from Rawalpindi. Everything that the people of Baltistan need beyond what they grow themselves, from kerosene to parts of tractors and lighting plants has to come by air along one of the most difficult and dangerous flying routes in the world, but this has not prevented considerable local development and the establishment of schools, dispensaries and a good hospital.

Like the Gilgit Agency, Baltistan abuts on the Chinese frontiers and is an area of strategic importance. Visitors require a permit to enter it. The air service from Rawalpindi, like that from Rawalpindi to Gilgit, is subject to weather conditions; and it is not uncommon for a visitor to Skardu to be weather-bound for a considerable period before communications are restored. There is a difficult mule-track from the Gilgit area, but it is usually snow-bound.

In Skardu itself the visitor should not fail to see the old castle of Queen Mindok ("flower" in Tibetan) 1595-1633; and the great contemporary acqueduct at Sadpar. The country around is very picturesque and there are pleasant excursions by jeep up the side valleys which branch off. About 20 m. from Skardu is Katsura (or Kachura Lake), where there is a camping ground and excellent trout fishing. The apples grown nearby are locally famous.

The whole of Baltistan teems with game; but the preservation of some rare species like musk deer is strictly enforced. Shooting licences are required and the number of animals that may be killed is restricted. Snow leopard are often exempted from this restriction, as they are a nuisance to cultivators. Baltistan is a highly picturesque, individual, and largely "unspoiled" country, and those visitors who are able to stay there usually enjoy the experience greatly. The Baltis are cheerful, hospitable and delighted to see strangers, while the locally posted Pakistan officers, civil and military are helpful and welcoming. The depot of the Northern Scouts at Skardu is very kind to visitors.

THE KINGDOM OF NEPAL

ELIZABETH VON FÜRER HAIMENDORF

Area: 55,000 square miles
Population: (est.) 13,000,000
Sovereign: KING BIRENDRA BIR BIKRAM SHAH DEVA

INTRODUCTION

Visas.—Visas are required by all foreign visitors entering Nepal; application should be made to Royal Nepalese Embassies and Consulates abroad. Indian nationals must carry an identity card issued by the magistrate of their home district. Visas are issued in the first instance for a stay of 30 days and are valid for the Kathmandu Valley, Pokhara and Chitawan. Extensions of visas may be had on application to the Ministry of Home and Panchayat, Ram Shah Path Kathmandu, who also issue the travel permits required by those wishing to travel to areas other than those specified above. Visitors are advised to carry 4 extra passport photographs for official use.

International inoculation certificates (small-pox and cholera) must be produced at places of entry.

Means of Access.—The most convenient way to enter Nepal is by air to the capital, Kathmandu. Royal Nepalese Airlines Corporation (RNAC) and Indian Airlines Corporation operate daily services from New Delhi, Calcutta, Patna, Varanasi and Bagdogra. Burma Airways fly from Rangoon once and Thai International from Bangkok four times a week.

From the south Kathmandu may be reached by the mountain highway Tribhuvan Rajpath (opened 1965) which connects the Indian town of Raxaul with Birgunj–Hitaura–Kathmandu (129 mi.; 207 km.)[1] Asphalted roads link Jayanagar (India) with Janakpur (18 mi.; 29 km.) and Jogbani (India) with Biratnagar–Dharan (34 mi.; 54 km.). Some towns and railheads in the Indian States of Bihar, West Bengal and Uttar Pradesh are connected by dirt roads with Nepalese border townships, whence a network of major trails leads into the interior: the principal places of entry are Philibit–Tanakpur, Gauri Phanta–Dhangarhi, Nepalganj Road–Nepalganj, Nautanwa–Bhairawa, Galgalia–Bhadrapur. From the north the Arniko Rajmarga (opened 1967) connects Kodari on the Nepal–China–Tibet border with Kathmandu (66 mi.; 106 km.); it links up with the Lhasa-Peking highway. Fourteen major passes, negotiable on foot and with pack animals cross the Himalayas into Nepal from the Tibet Region of the People's Republic of China; travel permits on these routes are only issued to Nepalese and Chinese nationals.

A narrow-gauge Nepal Government railway operates in the Nepalese Terai from Jayangar (India) to the pilgrimage centre of Janakpur (18 mi.; 29 km.). Freight is transported to Kathmandu by the Hitaura ropeway (built in 1964 to replace the earlier ropeway constructed during the premiership of Maharaja Chandra Shumshere).

Inland Travel.—Within Nepal the Royal Nepalese Airlines Corporation operates scheduled services to and from 19 of the 32 airfields; the remaining 13 are used for special and charter flights. In addition there are several S.T.O.L. airstrips in mountainous areas. For scheduled services and charter flights see Kathmandu, pp. 643-644.

[1] Distances and heights in the Nepalese section of the Handbook are given in miles (mi.) and kilometres (km.), feet (ft.) and metres (me.).

Motorable roads inside Nepal are few; completed to date are: Hitaura–Narayangarh, Rapti Valley road (53 mi.; 85 km.); Sunauli–Pokhara, Siddhartha Rajmarga (128 mi.; 206 km.); Jogbani–Biratnagar–Dharan (34 mi.; 54 km.); Kathmandu–Trisuli (40 mi.; 64 km.) and Kathmandu–Pokhara, Prithivi Rajpath (109 mi.; 176 km.). The Mahendra Rajpath, the East–West road (639 mi.; 1028 km.), planned as part of the Asia Highway, is under construction; when completed it will carry motorised traffic from Sattighat, Mechi Zone in the East to Banbasa, Mahakali Zone in the West.

The major towns and villages of the Kathmandu Valley and some parts of the Terai are served by a system of regional and feeder roads, which are dirt surfaced but motorable in fair weather. Outside these areas travel is on foot; in some localities ponies or yak may be hired but baggage is transported by back-carrying porters or on pack animals.

General Information.—The Kingdom of Nepal lies in the centre of the great arc of the Himalayas at 80°·4'-88°·2' East longitude and 26°·22'-30°·27' North latitude. An elongated territory with an average length of 500 mi. (800 km.), an average breadth of 100 mi. (160 km.) and an area of 55,000 sq. mi. (142,000 sq. km.), it stretches southwards from the Great Himalayan range to the fringe of the Indo–Gangetic Plain. The 1971 Census recorded 11,555,983[1] inhabitants. Officially Nepal is a Hindu State, ruled by the only Hindu monarch in the world; the population consists of 10,330,009 Hindus, 866,411 Buddhists, 351,186 Muslims, 2541 Jains and 3975 of other religions.

Nepal is a land of villages. 93 per cent. of the population is engaged primarily in agriculture; 72 per cent. of cultivators own their own land and 27·8 per cent. till land on various categories of tenancy. In 1969–70 rice (2,321,611 tons), maize (899,564 tons) and wheat (226,998 tons) were the chief crops. Seven towns have a population of over 10,000; three (Kathmandu, Lalitpur, and Bhadgaon) are situated in the Kathmandu Valley and four (Nepalganj, Birgunj, Biratnagar and Dharan) lie in the Terai and Inner Terai.

Between 1955 and 1970 Nepal's economic development followed the programmes laid down in the 1st 5-Year Plan 1956-61, the 2nd Plan 1962-65, and the 2nd 5-Year Plan 1965-70. In 1970 the National Planning Commission, H.M.G./Nepal introduced new guide lines for a 4th Plan, based on a regional development strategy, it envisaged "a series of north-south growth axis of development corridors linking the diverse regions . . .".[2] with regional development headquarters at Dhankuta, Pokhara, Surket and Kathmandu.

The annual budget in million rupees has risen from 52·5 in 1951-52 to 841 in 1969-70 and Foreign Aid to Nepal from 0·02 in 1951-52 to 329·28 in 1969-70.

The Nepalese calendar, Bikram Samvat (B.S.), dates from 57 B.C.; New Year's day is the 14th April. The Gregorian calendar is in use only in government offices. Historical documents are dated according to Nepali Samvat (N.S.), introduced during the reign of King Raghudeva Varma in A.D. 1879-1880, or Saka Era (S.E.), which commences in A.D. 78. The Newars use their own calendar for all business transactions, religious festivals and traditional ceremonial, and the Tibetan-speaking peoples of the northern regions employ the Tibetan system of twelve-year cycles. The days of the week correspond to European usage. Saturday is a government and bank holiday; western embassies operate on Saturdays and are closed on Sundays. Many religious festivals are reckoned as state and bank holidays, as are the birthdays of the late kings Prithivi Narayan Shah, Tribhuvan Bir Bikram Shah, Mahendra Bir Bikram Shah and of the ruling monarch Birendra Bikram Shah Deva (see p. 640).

[1] H.M.G./Nepal, *Census of Nepal* 1971. Kathmandu. National Planning Secretariat, Department of Statistics, Vol. 1, Table 3.

[2] H.M.G./Nepal, *The Fourth Plan* 1970-1975. Kathmandu. National Planning Commission, 1970.

Nepalese time is 5½ hours in advance of Greenwich Mean Time and 10 minutes in advance of Indian Standard Time.

Administrative Divisions.—A re-organisation of administrative units was carried out in 1961. The country is now divided into 14 Zones (*anchal*), 75 Development Districts (*zilla*), 3,916 village and 16 town panchayats.

The present administrative Zones with their headquarters are: Mahakali (Mahendranagar), Seti (Dhangarhi), Karnali (Jumla), Bheri (Nepalganj), Rapti (Tulsipur), Dhaulagiri (Baglung), Gandaki (Pokhara), Lumbini (Bhairawa), Narayani (Birganj), Bagmati (Kathmandu), Janakpur (Jaleswar), Sagarmatha (Rajbiraj), Kosi (Biratnagar), Mechi (Ilam).

Banking and Currency.—The currency of Nepal is the Nepalese Rupee (100 *paisa*). Banking and exchange facilities are available at the Nepal Bank, Juddha Sadak, Kathmandu; branches at Asan Tol and Tribhuvan (Gauchar) Airport. In some Zonal Headquarters there are banking establishments, but advance arrangements for the cashing of letters of credit should be made in Kathmandu before departure from the capital. Nepalese currency can be bought at places of entry and from authorised dealers on presentation of a passport; the larger hotels will change resident's travellers' cheques. Foreign visitors, other than those of Indian nationality, are not permitted to buy Nepali rupees with Indian currency.

Post and Telephones.—Nepal belongs to the International Postal Union, and letters and telegrams are accepted for all parts of the world. Postal services operate throughout the Kathmandu Valley; postal facilities are available at Zonal and district headquarters and in some areas of local importance there are post-boxes, but in outlying areas deliveries are slow and stamps are not always available.

The towns and some villages of the Kathmandu Valley are linked by telephone, and T.E.L.E. communication is maintained between the capital and Zonal headquarters. Trunk and telegraph lines connect Nepal with India, Pakistan and Bangladesh.

Motoring.—International driving licences are valid for Nepal. Driving is on the left of the road. Cars imported for personal use are subject to duty, refundable on export. Vehicles sold in Nepal forfeit the rebate. Drivers should note that travelling is often delayed by bad weather and landslides on mountain highways, and that on fair-weather roads passage is seldom possible in the monsoon months. All enquiries should be addressed to the Automobile Association of Nepal, Ram Shah Path (opposite Singha Darbar, H.M. Government Secretariat).

Sport.—Tourists bringing sporting guns and ammunition into Nepal should be covered by a licence obtained from H.M.G. Nepal. Tiger, rhinoceros, elephant, leopard, crocodile, *gaur* (wild ox), wild boar and buffalo inhabiting the forests of the Bhabar and Churia Hills in the south of Nepal and snow leopard and musk deer in high Himalayan regions are protected animals and may not be shot. Application for hunting permits to shoot the lesser game and the current regulations relating to the protection of specified animals are obtainable from the Chief Conservator of Forests, Kathmandu, and local Forest Divisional Officers.[1]

Good fishing is available. Information on localities leased to private individuals and therefore not open to tourist sport can be supplied by the Fisheries Department, H.M.G./Nepal, Kathmandu or local Fishing Development Offices. Mahseer (*barbus puttitora*) are plentiful in the larger rivers lying south of the Great Himalayan ranges and Asla (*orinus richersonii*), the snow trout, abound in the rivers and streams lying between 2000 and 9800 ft. (600 me. and

[1] At the present time (1975), all big-game hunting is forbidden in Nepal.

3000 me.). Over 12,000 ft. (9000 me.) the water is too cold and the winters too long to support fish-life.

Nine areas have been designated national parks and wild life reserves: Chitawan, Sagarmartha, Langtang, Lake Rara, Sukla Phanta, Karnali, Shey, Koshi Tappu, Narayani. Forests in Jhapa, Kosi Janakpur, Kosi Nawalpur, Bardiya and Kanchanpur have recently been declared Royal Forests. Enquiries regarding new notifications should be made in Kathmandu.

18-hole golf courses are laid out at Gauchar, Kathmandu and Dharan, Kosi Zone; there is a miniature golf course at Kakani. The Olympic-size swimming pool at Balaju is open to the public and at the Soaltee hotel, Kathmandu, visitors may use the hotel pool. Bathing in the rivers of the Great Himalayan Region and the Middle Ranges is hazardous on account of strong currents and ice-cold water, but the many hot springs offer a pleasant, if somewhat public pleasure.

Trekking.[1]—A permit for travel outside the areas specified on Nepal visas (Kathmandu Valley, Pokhara and Chitawan) is obtainable from the Ministry of Home and Panchayat, Ram Shah Path, Kathmandu (2 photographs). Travel permits are readily issued except for areas designated restricted; they relate to a clearly stated itinerary and must be produced on demand at military and police check posts encountered *en route*. In general, October to May is considered the best trekking season. Clear skies and the best views are to be obtained in the autumn. December, January and February bring cold weather, with heavy snow blocking passes in northern regions; the warmer weather of March, April and May spreads haze over the landscape, but these are the best months for viewing the flowering rhododendrons, magnolia, iris and primula of the Middle Ranges.

Recent improvements in road and air transport now offer a wide choice of trekking bases. Timely reservation on outgoing transport from Kathmandu is necessary as most scheduled flights, charter planes and hired and public vehicular transport are heavily overbooked. District trails are well trodden and the major rivers bridged at intervals; though ascents and descents are often long and steep, they are, up to 12,000 ft. (4000 me.), negotiable by the average trekker. Altitude sickness can be experienced at heights as low as 8000 ft. (2666 me.) and with the first symptoms (shortness of breath, headache, nausea, dizziness, loss of appetite) the sufferer should descend. Those flying direct to high altitude destinations are more vulnerable than those who make the gradual ascent on foot.

Basically, three modes of trekking are open to the traveller in Nepal: professional trekking, under the auspices of an agency, whose inclusive fees relate to a selected itinerary for a stated number of days and include the arrangement of travel permits, English-speaking sirdar (guide), camp servants, cook, load-carrying porters, camp equipment, messing, and route and map sheets; free-lance trekking, the party being responsible for all arrangements, recruitment of personnel, supply of camp equipment and messing; and back-pack trekking, in which the trekker depends on shelter and food procured against payment in villages *en route*.

The most luxurious professional service is operated by Mountain Travel, Maharajganj, P.O. Box 170, Tel. 12808. Annapurna Trekking and Mountaineering Private Ltd., Seto Darbar, Darbar Marg, Himalayan Trekking Private Ltd., Putali Sadak, Ram Shah Path and Sherpa Trekking Service, Lal Darbar, P.O. Box 500, all with headquarters in Kathmandu, organise comprehensive treks on a more modest scale.

[1] Bezruchka Stephen, *A Guide to Trekking in Nepal* (Kathmandu, n.d.).

Trekking schedules are available on application from these agencies; bookings should be made 3-6 months in advance.

Sirdars, Camp Servants and Load-carrying Porters.—Sherpas are the experienced Sirdars and camp servants of Nepal. Their services may be recruited through Trekking Agencies, the Himalayan Society, Ram Shah Path, or by private recommendation. Recognised rates of remuneration are reckoned according to terms and length of service required. English-speaking sirdars and cooks command the highest pay.

With the increase in the number of trekkers in Nepal, communities such as Tamang, Bhotiya, Rai, Limbu, Gurung, and Tibetans of the refugee camps are being drawn into the touring business; for high-altitude mountaineering their experience does not equal that of trained Sherpas, but they provide a more than satisfactory alternative for trekking and their local knowledge is invaluable to the tourist.

Sirdars will organise load-carrying porters or pack animals. The standard load is 60 lb for porters and 2 loads of 60 lb for pack animals. Rates per day or by round trip vary according to area and enquiries should be made of responsible persons in the locality. It should be noted that during the pressure months of the agricultural season and in northern districts, after the winter exodus, it is difficult to recruit local porters at a reasonable rate.

Equipment.—All equipment should be transported by air to Kathmandu. The minimum requirements for personal gear are sleeping sack and mattress, anorak, long trousers, boots, socks, sweater and shirt; for high altitudes, a down jacket, gloves and sun glasses are essentials. A limited amount of camping and personal equipment may be hired from the Himalayan Society and some trekking agencies. Various items left over from mountaineering expeditions may be purchased in Kathmandu at high cost.

Provisions.—Tinned supplies and medicines of Indian manufacture are available in the shops in Juddha Sadak and Sukra Path, Kathmandu. Cereals, sugar and spices may be bought in market centres in the capital and in district and zonal headquarters. An ample supply of cooking fat and kerosene, often in short supply in the districts, should be purchased in Kathmandu and transported in sealed containers. Day-to-day supplies of locally-grown vegetables and fruit in season, chickens and eggs can be bought in villages and country markets.

Accommodation en route.—Outside Kathmandu hotels providing board and lodging are only found in the larger Terai towns (country style), and in Pokhara, Daman, Kakani, Nagarkot, Hitaura, Meghauli and Shyamboche. Elsewhere "hotel" denotes tea-shop, food-stall or liquor stand serving the porter traffic. *Patti* and *dharmasala* situated in or near villages on main trails offer a night's shelter. Hospitality is offered against payment in private houses by Buddhist populations, but caste restrictions inhibit the entertainment of strangers in Hindu houses. It should be noted that trekking in high altitude areas frequently entails journeys in uninhabited country: *goth*, herdsmen's huts may be utilised as over-night cover and dried dung collected in the vicinity produces a satisfactory fire; nevertheless some form of shelter and a minimum of fuel should be carried.

Amenities available at Administrative Headquarters.—Zonal (Anchal) headquarters in charge of a Zonal Commissioner (Anchaladi) are equipped with T.E.L.E. communication centres linked with Kathmandu, a hospital, an airstrip, a post-office, a branch of one of the Kathmandu banks, a bazaar and a complement of government establishments (police, judiciary, military, agricultural, educational, etc.). District (Zilla) headquarters, under a Chief District Officer, are linked by T.E.L.E.-communication with zonal headquarters. Contact with panchayat officers can prove rewarding to the traveller.

Mountaineering.[1]—Mountain climbing in Nepal requires the permission of H.M. Government; a royalty is payable on each peak attempted. Application should be made on special forms available from Nepalese embassies abroad or the Ministry of Foreign Affairs, H.M. Government, Kathmandu. A list of peaks free in the desired season is supplied on request. Mountain Travel, P.O.B. 170, Kathmandu, Tel. 12808, and the Himalayan Society, Ram Shah Path, Kathmandu, are two organisations who undertake arrangements for mountaineering expeditions. Expedition equipment and high-altitude rations should be imported by air. Duty is payable on all items brought into the country, but refunds are made on re-exported equipment.

Scholars and Scientific Teams engaged in Research.—For permits and general arrangements see *Trekking*. Liaison should be established with the Dean of the Institute of Nepal and Asian Studies, Tribhuvan University.

Geography.[2]—Nepal is a land of great diversity. 25 per cent. of the country's land surface, including nearly 1160 sq. mi. (3000 sq.km.) under ice and snow, exceeds 10,000 ft. (3000 me.) in altitude; 20 per cent. has an elevation of less than 1000 ft. above sea-level. The main topographical features are the three latitudinal mountain chains which extend across the country from west to east. In the south the Churia and Siwalik ranges with a general elevation of 2460–6000 ft. (750–1800 me.) rise steeply from the Gangetic Plain. In the north the Great Himalayan range forms a rugged barrier of perpetual snow and ice and contains some of the highest peaks in the world: Mount Everest (Sagarmatha) 29,023 ft. (8848 me.), Kanchenjunga 28,216 ft. (8598 me.), Makalu 27,824 ft. (8481 me.), Annapurna 26,604 ft. (8091 me.), Dhaulagiri 26,975 ft. (8167 me.), Lhotse 27,824 ft. (8511 me.), Manaslu 26,658 ft. (8156 me.), and Cho-Oyu 26,867 ft. (8153 me.). The Middle Ranges, the Mahabharat, are an intricate complex of mountains with elevations rising to between 5000 ft. (1500 me.) and 8850 ft. (2700 me.). Separating these three ranges are low-lying areas: the Terai (Madesh), a 15-24 mi. (25-40 km.) broad plain of gently sloping country lies south of the Siwalik and Churia, on the fringe of the Gangetic plain; the Dun or Inner Terai (Bhitre Madesh) is enclosed by the Churia and Siwalik and the Mahabharat ranges, and the Pahar, a 35-50 mi. (60-80 km.) broad belt of hills and valleys, divides the Mahabharat from the Great Himalayan Range. The trans-Himalayan Bhot Valleys of western and central Nepal include large areas lying north of the main Himalayan Range.

Vertically, the country is dissected by the three great river systems of Karnali, Gandaki and Kosi. Rising from or beyond the main range of the Himalaya they flow in a general north-south direction and debouch finally into the Ganges. The Mahakali River forms Nepal's western and the Mechi River her eastern border. The four rivers Kamala, Bagmati, Rapti and Babai, rising in the Mahabharat and Churia ranges, water extensive valleys in the Middle Ranges and the Terai.

Flora.—See appendix by J. D. A. Stainton, pp. 632-635.

Climate.—Nepal's climate is ruled by the south-west monsoon which sweeps up from the Bay of Bengal in the first or second week of June and lasts until the first week in October. The majority of the annual rain falls in June, July, August and September; light showers occur in January and February, and thunderstorms can be experienced in April and May. The climatic extremes in Nepal are exemplified by the humid, tropical Terai summer and the tundra-like High Himalayan winter; the climate in the Middle Ranges is temperate. The cold season lasts from December to January, the hot season from June to

[1] Gurung, Harka B., *Annapurna to Dhaulagiri. A Decade of Mountaineering in Nepal*: 1950-1960, Vol. I, 1968 (Kathmandu). (Vol. II in the press.)

[2] Karan, P. P., *Nepal. A Physical and Cultural Geography* (Lexington, U.S.A., 1960).

August, and, relative to altitude, the months of September–October and February–April are mild.

People and Language[1].—The population of Nepal is composed of caucasoid and mongoloid racial elements, which dovetail and intermingle to form in many areas a complex racial pattern. Dominant in all except the northernmost lands are the "twice-born" Hindu castes of Brahmin, Thakuri and Chetri. Together with several service castes of lower status they speak Nepali (khaskhura), an Indo-Aryan language written in the Devanagri script; they constitute a hierarchically organised society which extends from the western border, across the greater part of the Middle Ranges and the Terai to the eastern frontier. The members of the Thakuri caste are reputedly the descendants of ruling houses of northern and central India, who at the time of the Muslim conquest moved into the Nepalese hills and there carved out positions of political power.

The people of the Nepalese Terai (Madesh) are akin to the population of the adjacent Indian Terai. Orthodox Hindus and Muslims, they live in large villages or small towns, raise rice, jute, sugar, tobacco, etc., and speak Maithili, Bhojpuri and Awadi. It is here close to the Indian communication network that Nepal's early industrial enterprises were established and where Nepalese will derive the most benefit from the establishment of multi-purpose irrigation projects on Nepal's great rivers.

In the low forested hills of the Churia and the Dun areas live such cultivating tribal groups as Tharu, Santal, Dhani, Mechi, Koch and Rajbansi; they speak their own dialects and though influenced to a great extent by Hindu ritual and belief, adhere to their traditional patterns of worship. In the last two decades land reclamation, development and settlement schemes and the commercial exploitation of the forests have modified the isolation of these groups and drawn them into the wider arena of Nepal's national life.

The Middle Ranges, the Mahabharat and the Pahar are the traditional home of mongoloid, tribally-organised populations; in certain areas they live in homogeneous blocks, but today the majority share their habitat with members of other ethnic groups. In the west are Magar and Gurung, in the centre and east Tamang, and in the east Sunwar, Rai and Limbu. All these groups are hill farmers, cultivating on terraced hill-fields and in valley bottoms, irrigating their crops where water is available and combining agricultural pursuits with animal husbandry and seasonal trading. The Gurung and Magar dwell in compact well-built villages, while the Tamang, Sunwar, Rai and Limbu favour a scattered settlement pattern. These groups speak Tibeto-Burman dialects and adhere to indigenous cults, overlaid to a varying degree by Hinduism and Buddhism. Since the end of the 19th century recruitment for service in the British and, since 1952, in the British and Indian Gurkha regiments[2] has resulted in considerable economic benefit to the Middle Range peoples and provided Nepal with a most welcome source of foreign exchange in the shape of salaries and pensions.

The high-altitude alpine zone of the Great and Inner Himalaya is inhabited by peoples of mongoloid racial type, who speak dialects of Tibetan. Known in Nepal as Bhotiya, they include the famous Sherpas of the Solu-Khumbu District, and the inhabitants of Yelmu, Langtang, Manang, Mustang, Walungchung, the upper Arun River, Dolpo and the valleys of the Upper Karnali. They profess Mahayana Buddhism, and their religious institutions, including a large number of monasteries, conform to the lamaistic system evolved in Tibet.

[1] Bista, Dor Bahadur, *People of Nepal*, 2nd edition (Kathmandu, 1967); Furer-Haimendorf, Christoph von, *Caste and Kin in Nepal, India and Ceylon* (London, 1966)
[2] Tuker, Francis, *Gorkha. The Story of the Gurkhas* (London, 1957).

The Bhotiya transhumance economy is based on a five-month agricultural season, the breeding and herding of yak, and winter trading expeditions. Before the extension of Chinese control in Tibet in 1959, the border people derived large profits from trans-Himalayan trade, bartering Nepalese grain for Tibetan salt and wool, and the purchase and sale of commodities of Indian, Tibetan and Chinese origin in such widely separated areas as Lhasa and Calcutta.

Distinct from all these populations are the Newars, who in medieval times created a highly developed urban civilisation in the Kathmandu Valley. Expert agriculturists and craftsmen, their artistic achievements surpass those of all other populations in Nepal, and their business acumen and trading skills have been largely responsible for Nepal's pre-eminence in historical times. Their language, Newari, belongs to the Tibeto–Burman family; written in its own script it possesses a large literature. The Newars subscribe to both the Hindu and the Buddhist faiths, the population being divided into two parallel caste hierarchies, the Shiva *margi* and the Buddha *margi*.

Muslims appeared first in Nepal in the 17th century and, except for small communities of artisans and cultivators in rural areas, are mainly to be found in Kathmandu, Pokhara and parts of the Terai. There are only a few Christians. Although in the 18th century Capuchin and Jesuit missionaries passed through the Kathmandu Valley on the India–China route, some even residing for a time in the kingdoms of Kathmandu, Bhadgaon, Palpa and Kaski, the few converts made were expelled together with the Capuchin fathers in 1852. Since 1952 educational and medical missionaries engaged in nation-building projects in various parts of Nepal have been forbidden to proselytise.

Tibetans have always exercised a measure of socio-economic and religious influence in certain parts of Nepal. Annually they have crossed the Himalayan passes to visit the great Buddhist shrines of the Kathmandu Valley. They have come as pilgrims, as traders, as craftsmen and as seasonal labourers. Since the advent of Chinese rule in Tibet, large numbers of refugees have been settled by the International Red Cross in camps at Jawalakhel, near Lalitpur, in Pokhara and Dhorpatan in the west and in Chalsa in the east. There are also loose groups of traders and herders, as well as several religiously based communities who have taken root in congenial areas of the Middle Ranges and the valleys of the High Himalaya.

During the last hundred years the west-east population drift in Nepal, which followed Prithivi Narayan Shah's unification of the lands lying between the Mechi and Mahakali Rivers, has been extended to countries adjacent to Nepal. In India there are over 6 million domiciled Nepalese distributed over the states of Assam, West Bengal and Bihar, and in Bhutan, Sikkim and Malaysia Nepalese form a significant proportion of the population. More recently malaria eradication has resulted in a north-south movement of land-hungry hillmen to the newly opened lands of the Terai and Inner Terai.

History[1].—Siddhartha Gautama Buddha, the Enlightened One, was born in Lumbini in the Nepalese Terai in 624 B.C., and it is popularly believed that together with his disciple Ananda he visited the Kathmandu Valley. The visit of the Emperor Ashoka to Buddha's birthplace and the marriage of his daughter Charumati to the Kshatriya Devapala, whose capital Deo Patan lay close to the Bagmati River, establishes the Kathmandu Valley, then known as Nepal, within the framework of the ancient civilisations dating from 3rd century B.C.

From inscriptions and references in Indian Hindu and Buddhist literature it would seem that during the last centuries before and the first centuries after the birth of Christ, centres of political power, other than those centred on the Kathmandu Valley, were established in the Himalayas. Little is known of the

[1] Regmi, D. R., *Ancient, Medieval and Modern Nepal*, 3 Vols. (Calcutta, 1960-1965).

principalities which at that time stretched from Kashmir to Assam, the dynastic names of many of whose rulers are synonymous with those well known to Indian historians. But for the Valley of Kathmandu, there is the evidence of the *vamśāvali*, the Nepalese Chronicles written in the 14th and 18th centuries A.D., which speak first of Gopala rulers and then of their successors the Kiranti. About the 3rd century A.D. the Kiranti gave way to the Lichhavis, a Vaishnavaite dynasty. Coins commemorate the marriage of Chandragupta II to a Lichhavi princess in the 4th century and a pillar-inscription of his son Samundragupta lists Nepal as a tributary of the Gupta Empire.

With the decline of the Imperial Guptas, King Manadeva (462-505) established the autonomy of his kingdom in the Kathmandu Valley, extending his domain as far as the Gandaki River in the west, the Kosi River in the east and the high passes of the Himalaya in the north. His deeds are recorded on a pillar still standing at Changu Narayan, not far from the site of his capital Deopatan. This pillar constitutes the first authentic historical document in Nepal. Rivalries of ambitious feudatories troubled the reigns of subsequent Lichhavi kings, but in 609 the Buddhist Amsuvarna, a Thakuri feudal lord, married the king's daughter and, ascending the throne, inaugurated one of the most remarkable periods in Nepalese history. In 643 the Chinese traveller Hsuan Tsang remarked in his memoirs on the excellence of Amsuvarma's administration, and noted the close commercial and cultural relations existing between India and Nepal.

In 679 Nanyadeva, a scion of the earlier Lichhavis, regained the throne and strengthened Nepal's relations with the rising empire of Tibet; Brikuti, a Nepalese princess, was married to the Tibetan King Srong-tsen-gompa and she, together with her Chinese co-wife, introduced Buddhism to Tibet and opened the way to commercial and artistic intercourse between the two countries. Chinese chronicles tell of the many eminent Chinese and Nepalese travellers who crossed the high Himalayan passes at this time and it appears that from the beginning of the 7th century, the Tibet-Nepal route from China to India gained in importance, establishing Nepal's position as a staging post on the trade route between Central Asia and the Gangetic Plain. Chinese documents also record the arrival of the first official Chinese envoy to Nepal in 644 and the return visit of a Nepalese delegation to Peking in 647.

Tibetan cultural and political influence in Nepal endured for a hundred and fifty years, when following serious disturbances in Tibet, it was replaced by that of the Palas of Bengal (770-942), and later by their one-time vassals the Senas of Bihar.

The 9th century is important in Nepalese history for Raghadeva's initiation of the Nepalese era in 879-880 A.D., and the defeat in 880 of the invasions of King Jayapita of Kashmir. There followed two centuries of internecine strife, and a succession of short-lived dynasties, but by the 11th century civil conditions were stable enough to permit the great sage Atisa to travel through the country on his way from Bengal to Ladakh (A.D. 1044).

In 1200 Ari Malla, said to have been connected with the Mallas of Kusinagara and Pava, introduced a new dynastic line to the throne of Nepal. His strong rule was followed by the reigns of five Malla and four kings of a successor, probably a Thakuri dynasty, but the unity of the kingdom was undermined by the use of collegial rule and the rise of powerful feudatories. Nevertheless, Nepal withstood the invasions of Ramasimha of Mithala (1244), Mukudsena of Palpa (1258), the King of Tirhut (1280) and the four raids o the Khasa kings of the Karnali Basin (1287-88, 1293, 1313 and 1328), none of whom succeeded in establishing himself in the Kathmandu Valley. But in 1336 Jayarajadeva failed to repulse Sultan Shams-ud-din of Bengal, who for seven days pillaged towns and villages destroyed temples and shrines and mutilated many sacred images.

The period of lawlessness that followed the Muslim onslaught ended when Jayasthiti Malla of Bhadgaon established his suzerainity over a realm which his descendants were to rule for four hundred years. According to the Chronicles Jayasthiti Malla (1380-1422) instituted economic and social reforms, codified the law and, with Brahmin advisers from India, regulated the system of caste according to the four *varna*.

Jayasthiti Malla was one of the most remarkable kings of Nepal. During the fifty-three years of his rule the country prospered: the intricate economic and commercial patterns which led to Nepal's dominance in the Himalaya were established and the control of the trade routes over the Central Himalayan passes secured. Yaksha Malla (1428-1482), the grandson of Jayasthiti Malla, was the last king to rule the valley kingdom. On his death the country was divided between his heirs: the kingdoms of Kathmandu, Bhadgaon and Banepa to his three sons and Lalitpur to his daughter.

The era of the four, subsequently three, kingdoms, the later Mallas (1482-1767), was despite or perhaps because of intense inter-state rivalry, a period of great cultural activity. The numerous documents and inscriptions preserved in the Kathmandu Valley belonging to this period relate to ambitious building projects, the endowment of irrigation channels, of secular and religious institutions, and the continuous feuding of the Valley kings.

By the 18th century the political supremacy of the rulers of the Kathmandu Valley and their monopoly of the lucrative trade that flowed over the Central Himalayan passes was challenged by the rising power of Ksatriya princes. Several confederacies extended to the east and west of the Kathmandu Valley; the Lepchas and Limbus under the Raja of Sikkim, the Kiranti chiefs and the Raja of Vijayapur, the Terai chiefs and the Raja of Palpa, the Chaubaisi (24 rajas) of the Kali Gandaki and the Baisi (22 rajas) of the Karnali basin; the overlord of most of the western principalities was the Raja of Jumla, a descendant of the Khasa Nagadeva Malla, who in the 12th century had conquered a collateral branch of the Ladakh dynasty then ruling from Sinja.

In 1559 the Rajput Druvya Shah of the Chittoor royal line had established his rule in Gorkha in west-central Nepal. By the middle of the 18th century Gorkha had extended its dominion and its frontiers marched with those of the ruler of Kathmandu. In 1757 Druvya Shah's grandson, Prithivi Narayan Shah captured Nawakot and secured for himself equal rights with the kingdom of Kathmandu in the trade over the Kyirong pass. He attacked the Kathmandu Valley, capturing at the third attempt the town of Kirtipur, and accepted the surrender of the kingdoms of Lalitpur, Bhadgaon and Kathmandu. In 1767 Prithivi Narayan Shah became the first Gorkha ruler of the Kathmandu Valley and established the Shah dynasty on the throne of Nepal.

Determined on the control of the lucrative trade routes from China and Tibet to India, Prithivi Narayan embarked on campaigns which would bring all the passes under his control. He subdued the Kiranti, and his successors, continuing his policy, extended Nepal's territories beyond the Mechi River in the east, including Sikkim, Darjeeling and a large part of the eastern Terai; in the west they annexed or rendered tributary the Chaubaisi and Baisi Rajas, defeated the Raja of Jumla and the rulers of Kumaon and Garhwal. These military campaigns were followed by the exclusion of all foreign interests in the trans-Himalayan trade and the setting up of trade marts at strategic places along the northern and southern borders where taxes and customs were levied.

Uneasy relations with Tibet resulting from disputes over the value of the Nepalese minted coinage used in Tibet, the quality of Tibetan salt imported into Nepal, Tibet's treatment of the Nepali commercial community in Lhasa and the operation of the trade marts were aggravated by the presence in Kathmandu of the fourth Karmapa Lama. In 1768 the Regent Bahadur Shah invaded

Tibet and seized four Tibetan districts. Under the 1789 treaty Nepal agreed to withdraw from the occupied districts and Tibet contracted to pay an annual tribute of 300 *dotsed* of silver (Rs. 57,600). In 1791 the Nepalese, on the plea that the Tibetans had not honoured the treaty, seized the trade marts of Kuti and Tingri, the monastic centres of Sakya and Shigatse and plundered Tashi-lumpo; after some procrastination, a combined Tibetan-Chinese force pursued the Nepalese to the fringe of the Kathmandu Valley; the treaty of Nawakot (1792) defined the local Nepal-Tibet border and provided for 5-yearly visits of a Nepalese delegation to China.

In 1767 the British East India Company, who had replaced the Muslims as the paramount power in North India, had recognised Prithivi Narayan Shah as sovereign of Nepal; but by the end of the century they were viewing with some apprehension the Regent Bhimsen Thapa's expansionist policies and the Nepal Darbar's claims to large stretches of the British-controlled Terai. The non-ratification of the Anglo-Nepal treaty of Commerce drawn up and signed in Sugauli in 1792 and the advance of the Nepalese forces to the banks of the Sutlej, determined the British on the invasion of Nepal. In 1814 four columns advanced into the hills; two were defeated by the terrain, one was repulsed by the Nepalese and the fourth, under General Ochterlony, persuaded the Nepalese commander, General Amar Sing Thapa to relinquish the conquered territories lying between the Mahakali and Sutlej rivers. In 1816, after further delays in ratifying the treaty General Ochterlony led a second force into the hills and, out-flanking the Nepalese defences at Mackwanpur, opened the way to Kathmandu. The ratification of the treaty which followed the second Anglo-Nepal war provided for the establishment of a British residency in Kathmandu, the surrender of the hill territories east of the Mechi River, the disputed Terai lands, and the area lying between the Singalite Range and the Tista River which was restored to Sikkim.

Following these reverses, Bhimsen Thapa's political authority declined and with the accession of King Girhan Juddha's infant son, Rajendra Bikram Shah, the Queen Mother and her supporters succeeded in ousting the Regent. The subsequent period of internal instability ended in the summer of 1846 when Jang Bahadur Kunwar survived his political rivals at the time of the Kot Massacre. Appointed Mukhtyar, he exiled first the Queen Mother and later King Rajendra Bikram Shah, and installed Prince Surendra (1830-1881) on the throne.

Unrest in Ch'ing China and a period of internal weakness in Tibet, encouraged Jang Bahadur to revenge the treaty of Nawakot. In 1855 when various demands were not met, Nepalese forces attacked across all the major Himalayan passes. Before the Tibetans sued for peace Kyirong, Kuti and Dzong Ka had fallen. After protracted negotiations and further military engagements during which key positions changed hands several times, the Tibetans signed a treaty in which they agreed to pay Nepal 10,000 Rupees annually, not to levy duty on goods brought into Tibet by Nepalis and to allow the installation of a Nepali "Baradar" (envoy) and a trading establishment in Lhasa.

In 1856 Jang Bahadur obtained the King's *lal mohar* conferring on him and his agnatic heirs the hereditary right to the offices of Prime Minister and Commander-in-Chief; later he was granted the title of Maharaja of Lamjung and Kaski. An astute politician, Jang Bahadur decided to safeguard the independence of Nepal, by then the only remaining Hindu sovereign state in Asia, through friendship with the British. He visited England and France, and at the time of the Mutiny he personally led 8000 Nepali troops to the relief of Lucknow. For this service the disputed Terai territories in the west were returned to Nepal.

The autocratic rule of Jang Bahadur's descendants, popularly known as

Ranas, endured from 1856 to 1951. During nearly a century the King served as little more than a figurehead while the *de facto* power rested with the Rana Prime Ministers. Internal stability was maintained by a rigid system of law and a hierarchically organised administration which denied entry to the country to outsiders and restricted foreign travel to Nepalese citizens. Of the eight incumbents, three are best remembered for their cultural and socio-economic innovations. Bir Shumshere (1885-1901) founded the Bir Library of ancient manuscripts, the Darbar School, the Bir Hospital and the Bir Dhara Waterworks. His successor Chandra Shumshere (1901-1929) established Tri Chandra College and built the Chandra Canal, the Pharping Power House, the narrow gauge railway from Raxaul to Amlekhganj and the Darsing–Kisipidi–Kathmandu ropeway. During Juddha Shumshere's term of office (1932-1945) the India-Nepal Treaty (1934) recognising Nepal's independent sovereign status was signed and a Nepalese embassy was established in London. But by the middle of the 20th century considerable opposition to the Rana regime had developed. In 1947 non-violent demonstrations pressurised Prime Minister Padma Shumshere (1945-1948) into promulgating the Government of Nepal Act.

This provided for a council of ministers, a bicameral legislature and an independent judiciary. The party leaders considered the Act unsatisfactory because it sought to maintain the supremacy of the Ranas; Padma Shumshere resigned and was succeeded by Mohan Shumshere (1945-1951). In 1950 India and Nepal signed a treaty of friendship and in the following year the Nepali Congress launched armed anti-Rana attacks in eastern, western and southern Nepal, and in the Bagmati Valley.

Negotiations between King Tribhuvan (1906-1955) who had sought refuge in India, the Rana Prime Minister Mohan Shumshere and the Nepali Congress resulted in the "Delhi Compromise". This "middle way" solution which prescribed a ten-man cabinet made up of five Nepali Congressmen and five Ranas under the Prime Ministership of Mohan Shumshere was short lived. A few months later King Tribhavan returned from Delhi, abolished the hereditary rule of the Rana Prime Ministers and proclaimed a consitutional monarchy. The leader of the Nepali Congress, M. P. Koirala, became Prime Minister and set up a 61-man Advisory Council from which all members of the Rana family were excluded.

In the last years of Rana rule Nepal had entered into diplomatic relations with the U.S.A. and France and in 1951 the first Point 4 Programme and the Kathmandu based U.S. Technical Co-operation Missions were established. Indian Advisory missions assisted in setting up the new machinery for a democratic state and over the next decades contributed considerable sums in Indian Aid to improving communications, notably the airport at Gauchar, the Raxaul–Kathmandu road and the construction of multi-purpose irrigation projects on the Kosi, Gandaki and Trisuli Rivers.

King Tribhuvan died in 1955 and was succeeded by his son Mahendra Bikram Shah Deva (1955-1972). In this year Nepal became a member of the United Nations. King Mahendra's government embarked on a policy of diversification in foreign relations and of non-alignment in international affairs. A treaty of friendship was concluded with China who, in the following years, contributed cash and machinery for the construction of several factories and the Kathmandu–Kodari and Kathmandu–Pokhara roads. The boundary demarcation agreements between Nepal and China were signed in 1961.

The first general election was held in 1959 but after 19 months King Mahendra abrogated the 1959 Constitution and set up a partyless form of administration based on panchayat democracy.

The Panchayat Constitution proclaimed in 1962 is based on a two-tiered system of administration: "At the national level, governmental authorities include H.M. the King, the Palace Secretariat, the Council of Ministers, the Ministerial Secretariat, the National Panchayat and the thirteen Ministeries and their departments".[1] The elected councils at ward, village, town, district, and zonal level share responsibility with government officers for the implementation of development and administrative policy.

In 1972 King Mahendra died and was succeeded by his son H.M. King Birendra Bikram Shah Deva.

THE SHAH DYNASTY OF NEPAL

Prithiwi Narayan Shah	1742-1774
Singha Pratap Sing	1774-1777
Rana Bahadur Shah	1777-1799
Girvan Judha Bikram Shah	1799-1816
Rajendra Bir Bikram Shah	1816-1847
Surendra Bir Bikram Shah	1847-1881
Prithivi Bir Bikram Shah	1881-1911
Tribuvan Bir Bikram Shah	1911-1955
Mahendra Bir Bikram Shah Deva	1955-1972
Birendra Bir Bikram Shah Deva	1972-

Art and Religion.[2]—The art of Nepal, fundamentally a religious art, may be conveniently divided into six stylistic periods, named after the principal Nepalese dynasties. Pre-Lichhavi (before A.D. 400), Lichhavi (5th-8th centuries), Transitional (6th-10th centuries), Early Malla (11th-14th centuries), Late Malla (15th-18th centuries), and Shah or Gorkha (from mid-18th century).

Of prehistoric times little is known. A few neolithic-type stone axes have recently come to light in the Kathmandu Valley and a collection of surface finds have been assembled from the vicinity of the Narayani river, Chitawan District. But no prehistoric artefacts have been uncovered *in situ* within the borders of Nepal.

The 1962-64 excations at Tiraulakot, Banjarahi and Paisi in the Central Terai yielded numerous small terra-cotta animal figures and a terra-cotta head, attributable to the 3rd century B.C. and comparable to Mauryan and Sunga artefacts of adjoining areas of North India. To the same period belong the oldest stone-carved monuments on Nepalese soil: the pillars at Nigalisagar and Kudan and Ashoka's inscribed pillar set up to commemorate his pilgramage to Lumbini, Buddha's birthplace. The early type, low-domed *chaitya*, four in Lalitpur and one in Kirtipur erected under the influence of Ashokan missionaries, suggest that the teachings of Buddha had penetrated the Kathmandu Valley in Kiranti times. During the five centuries, two before and three after the Christian era, Buddhism dominated Central Nepal, gradually absorbing the indigenous folk cults, and transforming the stone-carvers' clumsy, heavy figures of *yaksha* and *yakshi*, spirits of trees, mountain and river, into graceful Buddhist dryads. By the 5th century A.D. Buddhism had forsaken the ascetic path of Hinayana and the ideal of a preaching Buddha for the Mahayana doctrine and the concept of a transcendental Buddha standing at the centre of existence. From the emanative principle evolved a formalised structure first of three and later of five Buddha-families made up of Manusi (earthly) Buddhas and Maitreya, the Buddha to come, the Dhyani (Celestial Buddhas),

1 H.M.G./Nepal, Ministry of Public Works, Transport and Communications: *Physical Development Plan for the Kathmandu Valley*, p. 99 (Kathmandu, 1969).

2 Gordon, Annett, *Tibetan Religious Art* (New York, 1952); Kramrisch, Stella, *The Art of Nepal* (New York, 1964). See also the relevant passages on the art and religion of the Kathmandu Valley below, pp. 637-640.

sometimes called meditating Buddhas, and Bodhisattvas. Although several early statues of Sakya Muni survive, the favourite motives of Mahayana art were the 5 Celestial Buddhas and the Bodhisattvas. The construction of the two great *chaitya*, Svayambunath and Bodhnath stem from this period of Buddhist efflorescence. Both have retained their character as shrines of great sanctity and centres of pilgrimage.

The ascendancy of the Vaishnavite Lichhavi kings in the 5th century, ushered in the classical age of Nepalese art, with the reign of Amsuvarma (A.D. 609-621) making "the most creative of Nepalese contributions to the classical arts". The artists and scholars from the declining Imperial Gupta empire, who followed the Lichhavis to the Kathmandu Valley, merged their talents with the skills of indigenous craftsmen and produced a vigourous and vital art style. Little remains of this period except for some remarkable examples of the plastic arts, whose subjects, conceived in a theatrical idiom, were derived from Hindu mythological themes: stone carvings in relief and in the round depict Vishnu in his ten incarnated forms, his consort Lakshmi, his mount the sun-eagle Garuda; Shiva appears in his fierce form Bhairava, his consort Devi as Devi Mahishasuramardini, and their sons as the six-headed Karttikeya and the elephant-headed Ganesh. To these were later added the man-animal configurations and the anthropomorphic themes of the Yogi of the Himalaya, the *mithuna*, loving couples, and the popular representation *uma-maheśvara*. The persistence of the clearly defined ideal of Gupta beauty, richly clad and bejewelled figures with tightly curled hair-styles, is an outstanding characteristic, particularly of the Buddha figures, of Lichhavi art.

The Chinese pilgrims Yuan Chwang and I Tsing referred to Nepal of the 7th century as a country with two thousand monks of the Hinayana and Mahayana persuasions and to Buddhist monasteries and Hindu temples standing side by side. The pagoda temple, the first reference to which occurs in the T'ang Annals of the 7th century, was already an established architectural form.

Diverse trends appear in Lichhavi sculptural works after the end of the 7th century. Tibetan influence introduced two new deities Harit (green) and Sveta (white) Tara, whose icons in stone, bronze and paint have retained their popularity in Nepal and in the lands of the Mahayana. The predilection of the Rashtrakuta Governors of North India for monumental works in stone, presaged the creation of such massive sculptures in Nepal as the huge sleeping Vishnu at Buddha Nilkanta. In the 9th century a shift in cult affiliation and the influence of the Hindu reformer Sankacharya raised Shiva, and his phallus or *lingam* representation to a position of pre-eminence. Narrative style compositions of Shaivite themes show early eastern influences, a slenderising of form and a certain ornateness obscuring the earlier clarity of line.

By the 10th century Tantric influences stemming from the east dominated both the religion and art of the Kathmandu Valley. The emphasis on the mystic, the esoteric and the exaltation of the female principle introduced a new class of deities. The mother goddesses, the Ashta Matrikas, the female partners of the traditional male divinities and the ritual importance of blood sacrifice were incorporated into both Tantric Hindu and Vajrayana Buddhist practice; the two religions, sharing common beliefs in the efficacy of magical spells and secret rituals became inextricably intertwined.

In the early Malla period (11th-14th centuries), art styles perfected in the monastic centres of Bodh Gaya, Nalanda, Odantapuri and Vikramasala superseded the Gupta mannerisms of the Lichhavi period. The slender, narrow-waisted figures modelled on Pala bronzes, which later assumed elongated and sensuous forms, evince a this worldly orientation in sharp contrast to the ascetic concepts of early Buddhism.

The late Malla period (14th-18th centuries), which followed the Muslim extermination of the cultural centures of Buddhist and Hindu art in North India, saw the development of a style unmistakably Nepalese. Figures become shorter and stockier, faces assume a Mongolian caste and decorative elements, richly modelled and elaborately carved form an integral part of compositions in stone, wood and bronze. Hindu and Buddhist divinities appear with a multiplicity of attributes, emblems, heads, arms and hands, and in configurated dual, and man-animal form. The eternal divine couples, Shiva-Parvati, Vishnu-Laxmi and the father-mother *yab-yum* couples of Buddhist persuasions were motives which in late Malla times assumed enormous ritual importance. The art traditions of the Kathmandu Valley, assessed in the early period, largely in relation to carving in stone, encompassed, from the 13th century onwards, skillful craftsmanship in the carving of wood, the casting, hammering and embossing of bronze, copper and brass and the painting of scrolls, frescoes and, in the 19th century, paper based pictures. The reputation of excellence which prompted the employment of the Newari master bronze-caster Arniko at the courts of Qublai Khan and of Peking persisted throughout subsequent centuries. Tibetan, Chinese and Central Asian influences, discernible in decorative motives and the flowing robes of Buddha figures, appear on objects of domestic use and in painted scrolls (*tanka*, *papa* or *paubha*). The temples and secular buildings standing today in the Kathmandu Valley, few of which pre-date the 14th century, testify to the remarkable talents of Newari craftsmen and artists.

In contrast to the architectural magnificence concentrated within the narrow confines of the Kathmandu Valley, the eastern and western hills are poor in noteworthy buildings. The palaces and sanctuaries of royal tutelary deities that still stand in such erstwhile capitals of the medieval princes as Gorkha and Jajarkot, and the small pagodas situated at centres of Hindu pilgrimage demonstrate the extension of Valley tradition. But in general the rural nature of shrines dedicated to domestic and localised cults serve to emphasize the simple character of the religious systems of the hill communities.

Monuments that fall outside Newari tradition are the ruined forts of the Middle Range peoples and the commemorative monuments of Rai, Limbu, Gurung, Magar and Tamang. The stone walls, flights of steps, tanks, seats and pillars are designed not as vehicles of religious art but as memorials honouring the dead.

In the extreme west the stone ruins of Sinja and Dullu indicate the persistence of Indo-Buddhist influences in early medieval times. The domed temples of Jumla and Bharahachhetra and the famous Indo-Persian sanctuary of Sita at Janakpur owe their structural forms to the inspiration of models introduced during the Shah period.

The Buddhism of the Tibetan-speaking peoples of the high-altitude regions is related to the lamaistic system which prevailed in Tibet. Most of the Red Hat, or unreformed sects are represented among the Bhotiya populations and in areas such as Dolpo, there are lamas and temples of the old pre-Buddhist religion of Tibet, Bon. While from the 8th century Tibet received Buddhist teaching through Nepalese intermediaries, in more recent times cultural influences infiltrating from the north have provided constant reaffirmation of the precepts of Tibetan Buddhism. Monasteries and nunneries modelled on Tibetan monastic institutions provide a focus for the life-style of the high altitude peoples and are the pivots of an artistic tradition which has elsewhere been obliterated. The *chorten* and *mani*, the magnificent frescoes, the bronze, copper and brass temple furniture and the carved-wood decoration belong to a tradition distinct from that developed in the Kathmandu Valley.

The 19th and 20th centuries witnessed a hardening of Hindu caste ideas both at the centre and throughout the country. Brahmin, Thakuri, Chetri and

Newar settlers infiltrating the remotest hills and villages brought with them Brahmanical concepts; the "Gurkhas" returning after years of cultural exposure in India introduced Hindu religious attitudes into their homeland; the influx of settlers into the Nepalese Terai strengthened religious and cultural ties with the Hindus and Muslims of adjacent North Indian territories. By the late nineteen-sixties the strengthening of centrally administered controls and the extension of communications were operating as instruments of religious and cultural as well as political integration; the stark forms imposed by the use of cement as a building material dominated the wholly secular architecture.

BRIEF BIBLIOGRAPHY

BOULNOIS, L. and MILLOT, H. 1967. *Bibliographie du Nepal.* Paris

HAGEN, TONI. 1961. *Nepal. The Kingdom of the Himalayas.* Berne

HOSKEN, FRAN P. 1974. *The Kathmandu Valley Towns. A Record of Life and Change in Nepal.* New York/Tokyo

PETECH, L. 1959. *Medieval History of Nepal,* 2 Vols. Rome

RANA, PASHUPATI SHUMSHERE J. B. and MALLA, KAMAL P. 1973. *Nepal in Perspective.* Kathmandu (CEDA)

SINGH, MADANJETT. 1968. *Himalayan Art.* London (Paperback)

STILLER, LUDWIG F. 1973. *The Rise of the House of Gorkha. A Study in the Unification of Nepal* 1768-1816. New Delhi

WADDELL, L. A. 1934. *The Buddhism of Tibet, or Lamaism.* Cambridge, U.K.

WALDSCHMIDT, ERNST and ROSE. 1969. *Nepal, Art Treasures of the Himalayas.* London

GLOSSARY OF THE PRINCIPAL VERNACULAR TERMS USED IN NEPAL

(N) signifies Nepali; (S) Sanskrit; (Tib) Tibetan.

ANCHAL, (N) Administrative Zone.

BAHAL, BAHI, (N) units of Newar urban settlement, smaller than Tol.

BATTI, (N) country inn.

BHOTIYA, (N) generic term used for speakers of Tibetan dialects, Buddhist faith and inhabitants of Northern border areas.

BODHISATTVA, (S) future Buddha.

BON-PO, (Tib) ancient religion of Tibet, predating Buddhism.

CHAITYA, (S) originally a relic mound; commemorative or dedicatory monument, equivalent to Indian stupa.

CHAKRA, The wheel of law.

CHATTRA, (S) parasol, symbol of royalty.

CHAUTARA, (N) stone-built resting place.

CHORTEN, (Tib) monument, equivalent to chaitya and stupa, but of varied form.

CHOWK, (N) open place of assembly; inner court of palace; piazza.

DHARA, (N) stone-lined watering place.

DHARMASALA, (N) resthouse for pilgrims or travellers.

DHARMA, (S) the Buddhist Law.

DHYANI BUDDHA, (S) Celestial Buddha.

GOMPA, (Tib) Buddhist temple.

GORKHA, capital of the medieval kingdom whose king became the first Shah ruler of a unified Nepal.

GOTH, (N) herdsmen's hut.

GURKHA, Nepalese recruits to the British and Indian armies.

GURKHALI, (N) synonymous with Khas-khura, the language of the Khas; popularly used to denote soldiers of Nepal or the Nepali recruits to the British and Indian armies.

HARMIKA, steeple mounted on a chaitya torana, often composed of thirteen rungs symbolising the thirteen stages of enlightenment leading to nirvana.
HINAYANA, (S) early ascetic form of Buddhism; the lesser vehicle.
JATRA, (N) ritual festivities that include idol decoration and processions.
KALASHA, KALASH, (S) literally water vessel, vase; symbol of a deity, generally a female deity.
KATH, (N) ritual litter in which idol is carried in procession.
KHAS, (N) Hindu hill peoples; generally applied to Chetris of the western hills, the original speakers of Khas khura.
KHAS-KHURA, (N) language spoken by the Khas, i.e. Nepali.
KIRANTI, generic term for Limbu and Rai peoples; the dynastic power which controlled the Kathmandu Valley before the Lichavis.
LAMA, (Tib) priests of Lamaism.
LAMAISM, (Tib) popular name for Vajrayana Buddhism.
LHA-KANG, (Tib) Buddhist chapel.
LIMBUAN, eastern districts of Nepal, traditionally the homeland of the Limbus.
MAHAYANA, (S) late form of Buddhism; the great vehicle.
MAKARA, (S) mythical water monster; architectural ornament, often employed as water spout.
MANDALA, (S) magical religious diagram.
MANI, (Tib) religious formula engraved on rock, or inscribed on stone tablets aligned in walls.
MANI-RIMDU, (Tib) dance-drama relating the triumph of Buddhism over alien gods and spirits.
MANTRA, (S) magical religious formula.
MANUSI BUDDHA, (S) earthly Buddha.
MARGA, (N) highway, main road.
MELA, (N) Fair.
MITHUNA, (S) couple, usually portrayed in erotic postures.
MUKHA LINGAM, (S) phallus form of Shiva carved with four faces.
NAGA, (S) mythical semi-divine being with human face and serpent tail; snake.
NIRVANA, (S) extinction of worldly desires and escape from re-birth; ultimate goal in the practice of Buddhism.
NYINGMA-PA, (Tib) members of the red-hat sect, or unreformed sect of Mahayana Buddhism.
OM MANI PADME HUM, (S) sacred formula repeated by Buddhists to avoid re-birth. "Hail! Jewel in the Lotus".
PADMASAMBHAVA, (S) Buddhist saint, patron of the Nyingma-pa sect.
PATTI, (N) resthouse, equivalent of dharmasala.
PRAJNA, (S) female counterpart of Buddhist male divinities.
PRANALI, (S) stone water fount.
RAJPATH, (N) highway, road; literally king's road.
RATH, (S) ritual chariot in which idol is drawn in procession.
SAKYA MUNI, the Sakya Sage, i.e. Gautama Buddha.
SAMGHA, (S) Buddhist congregation.
SHAKTI, (S) female counterpart of Hindu male divinities.
SHANKHA, (S) conch shell.
SHIKHARA, decorated tower, often curvilinear in form, surmounting a temple sanctum.
SIRDAR, (N) leader, or controller of porter gang.
STUPA, (S) originally a relic mound; commemorative or dedicatory monument called in Nepal chaitya.
TANKA, (Tib) Buddhist scroll painting.
TAMAPATRA, (S) copper plate inscription.
TANTRAS, (S) religious treatise relating to magical formula.

TANTRICISM, system of magical ceremonies based on the Tantras.
TOL, (N) town quarter.
TORAṆA, squared top-piece surmounting a chaitya dome.
TRI RATNA, (S) Buddhist triad: Buddha-Dharma-Samgha (Buddha-the-Law-the congregation). "The Three Jewels".
TRISULA, (S) trident, emblem of Shiva.
VAHANA, (S) vehicle; animal-god mount of a divinity.
VAJRA, (S) thunderbolt; symbol of magical power in Vajrayana Buddhism.
VAJRA DHATU-MANDALA, (S) mandala with Vairocana as central Lord.
VAJRAYANA, (S) late branch of Buddhism, laying stress on magical spells; literally vehicle of the thunderbolt, vajra.
VAMŚĀVALI, (S) (VAMSHAVALI) genealogical rolls of kings; chronicles.
VIHARA, (S) monasteries inhabited by celibate monks; term retained to denote an urban dwelling pattern in the Kathmandu Valley.
YAB-YUM, (Tib) literally father-mother; male and female divinities, represented in art as couples.
YOGACHARYA, (S) Mahayana Buddhism.
ZILLA, (N) administrative district.

ETYMOLOGY OF SOME PLACE-NAMES IN NEPAL

Bhanjyang, (N) Pass.
Chaur, (N) Flat land.
Chowk, (N) Open place of assembly; inner court of palace.
Danda, (N) Hill.
Deorali, (N) Pass, or peak with shrine.
Dhara, (N) Stone-lined watering place.
Dhobham, (N) Confluence of rivers
Himal, (N) Snow mountains.
Khani, (N) Mine.
Khola, (N) River.
Kot, (N) Fort.
La, (Tib) Pass.
Lekh, (N) Mountain ridge with winter snow.
Nadi, (N) Stream.
Pahar, (N) Hill.
Parbat, (N) Hill, mountain.
Pokhari, (N) Pond, tank.
Sanghu, (N) Bridge.
Tal, (N) Lake.

THE FLORA OF NEPAL

By J. D. A. STAINTON

Bibliography

Although Nepal was the scene of the earliest Himalayan botanical exploration by Buchanan Hamilton and Nathaniel Wallich at the beginning of the last century, the flora of the country remained largely unknown until 1949. Since that date many botanists have collected in Nepal, but no full list of the plants of the whole country has yet been published, nor is there any comprehensive illustrated guide to the flora.

The flora of limited parts of Nepal has been described in a number of publications, which are listed by Dobremez, J. F., Vigny, F., and Williams, L. H. J. (1972) in *Bibliographie du Nepal*, Centre de la Recherche Scientifique.

The following works contain illustrations which may be useful in making identifications:

Hara, H. (1963), *Spring Flora of Sikkim Himalaya*. Hoikusha, Japan.
Hara, H. (1966), *The Flora of Eastern Himalaya*. University of Tokyo.
Hara, H. (1968), *Photo-album of Plants of Eastern Himalaya*. Inoue Book Co., Tokyo.
Nakao, S. (1964), *Living Himalayan Flowers*. Mainichi Newspapers, Tokyo.
Stainton, J. D. A. (1972), *Forests of Nepal*. John Murray.

The latter work also contains a description of the forest vegetation of the whole country.

An ecological map of Nepal, of which to date three sheets have been published, is in course of preparation by Dobremez, J. F., at Grenoble University.

The Terai and outer foothills

Those parts of Nepal which lie below 3000 ft. were until recently very malarious, and the hillmen have been reluctant to settle there. As a result much forest survives uncut on the outer foothills and in the waterless "bahbar" country at their base. In contrast most of the Terai, the flat land along the Indian border, has been cleared for agriculture.

February to May is the principal flowering season of the tropical trees and shrubs, though some plants can be seen in flower at any time of year. It is too hot to travel on foot in comfort after the middle of March.

Many of the trees are deciduous, losing their leaves at the beginning of the hot weather. "Sal" (*Shorea robusta*) predominates over wide areas, but along river-sides there is often a mixed type of deciduous forest in which big trees of *Bombax malabaricum* are prominent, and on recent alluvium there may be pure stands of *Acacia catechu* or *Dalbergia sissoo*. On hot dry hillsides *Anogeissus latifolia*, *Terminalia tomentosa* and *Engelhardtia spicata* are common.

These deciduous forests are light and open, but some dark evergreen forest occurs in damp shady sites. Its component species have an Assam–Burma–Malaya distribution, and include species of *Cinnamomum*, *Cryptocaria*, *Machilus*, *Phoebe*, *Cycas*, *Dysoxylum*, *Michelia*, *Ostodes*, *Pandanus* and *Turpinia*.

The midlands

The country which lies between the outer foothills and the main snow ranges is densely populated. Most hillsides have long since been cleared for grazing or terraced for agriculture. The main crops are rice, maize, wheat, barley, millet and potatoes.

Little forest survives uncut. Some "sal" grows on the red laterite soil of the lower valleys, and between 4000 and 8000 ft. there is often some *Quercus lanuginosa*, or in West Nepal *Q. incana*. These evergreen oaks are lopped for cattle fodder, and the spread of their branches is much reduced. In East Nepal *Castanopsis indica*, *C. tribuloides* and *Schima wallichii* are also common.

The cactus-like *Euphorbia royleana* is used with *Agave mexicana* and species of *Opuntia* to hedge the tracks around the villages. Clumps of bamboo are planted, and wayside resting places are shaded with *Ficus benghalensis* and *F. religiosa*. In shrubberies where the cattle graze are *Rhododendron arboreum*, *Lyonia ovalifolia*, *Rosa brunonii*, *Pyrus pashia*, *Pyracantha crenulata*, *Deutzia staminea*, *Philadelphus tomentosus*, *Jasminum humile*, *Colquounia coccinea*. *Luculia gratissima* and *Berberis asiatica*.

The southern sides of the main snow ranges

Temperate forest. From June to September altitudes above 8000 ft. are almost constantly enveloped in monsoon rainclouds. Crops will not ripen under these conditions, and villages cease at this height. The higher ridges are therefore still covered with much uncut forest, which is one of the outstanding sights of Nepal in April and May when the rhododendrons are in flower. Many of the component species of this forest are Sino-Himalayan in distribution, and since this eastern element is much more strongly represented in East Nepal than in West Nepal it will be convenient to describe the two parts separately, taking the valley of the Kali Gandaki as the dividing line.

West Nepal. The spiny-leaved oak, *Quercus semecarpifolia*, in some places predominates from 8000 ft. up to the treeline (12,000-13,000 ft.) More often *Abies spectabilis* succeeds at about 10,000 ft. with *Betula utilis* forming a belt at the treeline. Between 8,000 and 10,000 ft. a mixed broadleaved forest of *Aesculus indica, Juglans regia, Quercus dilatata* and *Acer* species may occur. *Tsuga dumosa* and *Pinus wallichiana* are common.

The shrub flora includes *Rhododendron arboreum, R. barbatum, R. campanulatum, Lyonia ovalifolia, Viburnum cotinifolium, V. grandiflorum, Lonicera webbiana, L. quinquelocularis, Cornus capitata* and *Staphylea emodi.*

East Nepal. *Quercus semecarpifolia* remains common, except in the wettest places where it is replaced by *Quercus lamellosa* and *Q. oxyodon.* These two evergreen oaks often form a distinct belt between 8000 and 9000 ft. with a dense dark understory composed of species of *Symplocos* and of the family *Lauraceae.* A mixed broadleaved forest with *Magnolia campbellii, Michelia doltsopa, Acer campbellii, Osmanthus suavis, Scheffera impressa* and other East Himalayan species also occurs, and forest of *Tsuga dumosa* is common.

Rhododendron species are much more numerous than in the west. Including alpines about thirty species have been recorded from East Nepal, whereas in the west the number drops to about five. Some of the larger species are up to forty feet tall (*R. grande, R. falconeri, R. hodgsonii, R. arboreum*). Others are epiphytic (*R. dalhousiae, R. lindleyi, R. pendulum*). Species of *Gaultheria, Vaccinium, Pieris, Lyonia* and *Enkianthus* are abundant.

Abies spectabilis usually predominates above 10,000 ft., with a belt of *Betula utilis* adjoining the alphine slopes, but in the wettest parts of the upper forest may consist almost entirely of *Rhododendron.*

The alpine zone. The slopes to the south of the main ranges receive the full force of the monsoon rains. The main flowering time in the alpine zone coincides with the rains, and travelling conditions are not easy then. Few plants flower before June, and by October almost all except the gentians are over.

During the summer these slopes are grazed by sheep, goats and cattle brought up from the villages below. The big *Meconopsis* species thrive in heavily grazed places (*M. grandis, M. regia, M. paniculata, M. nepalensis*), and so do some of the bigger *Primula* species (*P. sikkimensis, P. stuartii, P. obliqua*). Species of *Ranunculus, Caltha, Anemone, Geum* and *Potentilla* are also common. Alpine shrubs ascend to about 15,000 ft.

At about 16,000 ft. a high-altitude flora begins. Many plants form mats or cushions (*Saxifraga, Androsace*), or are covered with woolly hairs (*Saussurea*). Cliffs and rock ledges have a distinct flora, including the beautiful *Paraquilegia grandiflora.*

Humla-Jumla

Humla-Jumla in N. W. Nepal lies to the south of the main Himalayan chain, but is sheltered from much of the monsoon rain by a subsidiary chain of mountains lying to the south with a crestline of about 15,000 ft. The main flowering season begins later than in other parts of Nepal, and little is in flower until June. Even during the monsoon months rainfall is not often heavy enough seriously to inconvenience the traveller. The houses have flat roofs, and groves of walnut and almond surround the villages. Cultivation is carried on up to 10,500 ft., the main crops being wheat, barley, buckwheat and potatoes.

The forests are of a West Himalayan mixed coniferous type. *Pinus walli-*

chiana or *Picea smithiana* predominate to 10,000 ft., and *Abies spectabilis* above, with *Betula utilis* at the treeline. *Quercus semecarpifolia* is also common, and in gulleys there is broadleaved forest of *Aesculus indica, Juglans regia, Populus ciliata, Ulmus wallichiana* and *Acer cappadocicum*. Other indicators of the West Himalayan nature of the flora are *Cedrus deodara, Cupressus torulosa, Abies pindrow* and shrubs such as *Corylus jacquemontii, Rhus cotinus, Morus serrata, Syringa emodi* and *Rosa webbiana*.

Inner valleys

Rainfall in the valleys which lie deep within the main snow ranges is much lower than on the southern sides of these ranges.

East Nepal. This diminution in rainfall is not very great at lower altitudes, but in the valley heads at and above the treeline the rainfall is much reduced. Fields and villages are found up to 14,500 ft., and here on the glacial U-shaped valley floors *Spiraea arcuata, Lonicera myrtillus, Hippophae thibetana, Primula sikkimensis, Iris kumaonensis, Myricaria rosea, Ephedra gerardiana* and the species of *Artemisia, Berberis* and *Caragana* are well adapted to withstand the heavy grazing of yak and sheep. The black juniper of the dry country, *Juniperus wallichiana*, replaces the juniper of the wet country, *J. recurva*, above about 14,000 ft. Other species occurring here which are more typical of transhimalayan country than of monsoon Nepal are *Lancea tibetica, Arisaema jacquemontii, Waldheimia glabra, Phlomis rotata, Oreosolen wattii*. The alpine flora is at its best in late July.

West Nepal. Rainfall diminishes at altitudes low enough to affect the forest composition. Conifers predominate except at the treeline, where usually there is much *Betula utilis*. *Pinus wallichiana* is much the most abundant of the conifers, and in some places it ascends to 14,500 ft., but certain of the West Himalayan conifers also occur in the drier conditions prevailing here. *Cedrus deodara* extends as far east as the upper Bheri valley near Tarakot, *Cupressus torulosa* as far east as Tukucha, and *Picea smithiana* as far east as the Buri Gandaki valley, where it overlaps with the East Himalayan *Larix griffithiana*.

Many of the slopes between 10,000 and 15,000 ft. are covered with dry alpine scrub consisting of *Juniperus wallichiana, J. recurva, Lonicera myrtillus, Spiraea arcuata, Hippophae thibetana, Ephedra gerardiana, Rosa sericea* and *Caragana* species.

The arid zone

North of Dhaulagiri and Annapurna lies an almost treeless country with a climate and flora which are Tibetan in character. Villages are found up to 14,500 ft., and all fields are irrigated. The main crops are barley and buckwheat. A few willow trees grow along the irrigation channels, *Clematis vernayi* rambles on stone walls, *Stellara chamaejasme* and species of *Artemisia* are common on wasteland, and there is much *Rosa sericea*. A number of plants are in flower by early June.

The alpine slopes are sparsely covered with low spiny bushes of *Lonicera spinosa* and *Caragana* species. Along streams there are thickets of willow or of *Myricaria wardii*, and on boggy ground grow *Primula tibetica, Gentianella paludosa* and *Pedicularis longiflora* var. *tubiformis*. On rocks and sandy screes are *Incarvillea arguta, Dicranostigma lactucoides, Silene moorcroftiana* and *Morina polyphylla*. In this dry country the few species with big leaves tend to carry them flush with the ground, such as *Phlomis rotata, Oreosolen wattii, Incarvillea grandiflora* and *Rheum spiciforme*.

The shrub flora ceases about 16,000 ft., and above this the stony slopes grow increasingly bare of vegetation. At 18,000 ft. there are only scattered cushion plants (*Thylacospermum rupifragum, Arenaria polytrichioides, Potentilla biflora*) or woolly plants (*Eriophyton wallichianum, Tanacetum nubigenum, Saussurea* species). The high-altitude flora is seen at its best in late July or August.

THE KATHMANDU VALLEY

The Valley of Kathmandu, popularly known as the "Nepal Valley", is situated in the Lesser Himalaya at 85° 20′ E. longitude, 27° 40′ N. latitude. The valley, approximately 15 mi. (25 km.) long, 12 mi. (19 km.) broad and with an area of 250 sq. mi. (467 sq. km.), lies at an altitude of 4150 ft. (1350 me.) above sea-level. Roughly oval in shape, it is encircled by mountains which rise to an average height of 1800-3750 ft. (600-1350 me.) above the valley floor; the highest peaks are Sheopuri (8943 ft. 2732 me.) in the north, Phulchoki (9050 ft. 2750 me.) in the south-east and Chandragiri (8520 ft. 2550 me.) in the south-west. Spur and ridge extensions protrude from the encircling mountain wall and the irregularity of outline is further enhanced by raised plateau-like terraces, *tar*, and low-lying alluvial *dol* which seam the valley floor.

The main river is the Bagmati which, rising on Mount Sheopuri, passes through the three gorge areas of Gokarna, Pashupati and Chobar. The main tributaries, the Vishnumati, Hanumante, Dhobi and Manohara, and many smaller streams, flow off the encircling mountains and converge on the Bagmati within the confines of the valley. To the south, the combined waters of the Bagmati and its tributaries, passing between the Chandragiri and Phulchoki massifs, flow through the Katwaldaha gorge to the Terai and the plains of India.

Beyond the mountains ringing the Nepal valley there are minor valleys comparable in topography and climate: in the south-west the valley of Chitlang, a subordinate valley of the Pannauti river; in the north-west the valleys of Duna and Kalpu watered by tributaries of the Trisuli river; in the north the valley of Nawakot watered by the Trisuli river and the subsidiary valleys of Tadi, Likhu and Sindara; and in the east the valley of Banepa watered by a tributary of the Sun Kosi. Sometimes known as "Little Nepals", their inhabitants share a common heritage with those of the Kathmandu Valley with whom they have been politically and culturally linked throughout historic times.

The climate of the Valley is temperate: the mean monthly maximum in June, the hottest month, being 24°C. and in January, the coldest month, 7°C. 80 per cent. of the annual rain falls in the monsoon, the monthy means recorded in Kathmandu in millimetres being: 105·7 (May); 228·1 (June), 361·0 (July), 355·5 (August), 152·5 (September); 29·5, 46·3 and 46·2 in March, April and October respectively; 40·5 in the months of January, February and November. The least rain, 2·6, falls in December.

The population of the Valley[1] is 515,000, which amounts to 5 per cent of the total for Nepal and represents an overall density of 2000 per sq. km. It includes representatives of most of Nepal's ethnic groups. The 1961 breakdown by mother-tongue was given as 52 per cent. Newari speakers, 41 per cent. Nepali speakers, 5·1 per cent. Tamang speakers, with smaller linguistic groups accounting for the remainder.

The three cities, Kathmandu, Lalitpur and Bhadgaon, with populations of 122,507, 46,713 and 33,880, respectively account for 60·3 per cent. of the Valley's population; the average population of villages is about 2000 inhabitants.

Newar civilisation, developed in ancient and medieval times, dominates the Kathmandu Valley; the unique flavour of the Newars socio-religious heritage[2] persists, despite diverse influences introduced over the last 250 years, into the modern age. From the air the ethnic basis of the traditional settlement pattern is

[1] 1971 figures not available. 1961 demographic statistics have been taken from H.M.G./Nepal, *The Physical Development Plan for the Kathmandu Valley*, (Kathmandu, 1969).

[2] Nepali, Gopal Singh, *The Newars* (Bombay, 1965).

still discernible. In Kathmandu, and to a lesser degree in Lalitpur, modern developments have tended to blurr distinctions; but in the rest of the Valley the compact conurbations of the Newars situated on raised *tar* above irrigated rice-lands stand out from the dispersed hamlets of Brahmin, Thakuri, Chetri and Tamang built high on hill-sides terraced for dry crops.

Numerically, rural and urban dwellers are fairly evenly balanced, but in spite of a large urban-based population 65 per cent. of the inhabitants are primarily agriculturists. Rice is the main crop, with maize and wheat standing next in importance. Traditionally, regional specialisation on the production of vegetables, oilseed, milk products, fruit, tiles, bricks and handloom textiles provided a basis for a self-sufficient economy with surplusses with which to finance trade, regarded as an important and gainful activity. The influx of foreign, largely Indian, commodities during the last two decades has encouraged a demand for imported consumer goods and a corresponding emphasis on cash-producing enterprises.

Though the medieval walls of the old city capitals have vanished, Newar towns and villages have retained their traditional characteristics. Tightly organised on narrow sites, the urban style complexes of wall-to-wall, two- and three-storey houses are arranged in *bahal, vihara* and *tol* configurations. The ancient Buddhist *vihara* with temple and dwellings for a monastic community enclosing a rectangular court has, despite the disappearance of celibate monks, persisted as a popular dwelling pattern. Membership of joint family, agnatic lineage, caste and sub-caste are residential criteria dictating the localisation of social groups who share temple, water source or piazza (*chowk*). In the capitals of the medieval city states the royal palace (*darbar*) occupied a central position at the junction of major thoroughfares; the great quadrangles fronting the principal façade served as places of public assembly.

The religious affiliation of the inhabitants of the Kathmandu Valley was given in the 1961 Census as Hindus 371,243, Buddhists 86,276, Muslims 1127, and others 1344.

Few of the 3500 temples and 2,500,000 shrines popularly believed to exist today in the Kathmandu Valley predate the 14th century. The majority were erected in the time of the Malla dynasties, particularly in the centuries following the division of the kingdom into city states in A.D. 1482. During the subsequent 250 years of continual feuding, the rival kings of Kathmandu, Lalitpur and Bhadgaon beautified their capitals, patronised the arts and endowed the religious institutions of both Hindus and Buddhists. Their temples are set on hilltops, in groves of trees, on the banks of streams, in towns and villages, and are grouped in incomparable array in the quadrangles fronting the royal palaces.

Architecture.—The main types of religious buildings[1] fall into distinct categories. The *chaitya*, the Indian stupa, originally a Buddhist relic mound, developed from the simple Mauryan low-dome type of the four directional *chaitya* in Lalitpur into the massive hemispherical, brick-built, white-plastered structures of Svayambunath and Bodhnath. The dome, surrounded by circumambulatory passages, rows of prayer wheels and diverse images, is surmounted by a squared *torana*, painted on four sides with the "all-seeing eyes of supreme buddhahood" and a thirteen-stepped *harmika*, symbolising the stages of enlightenment leading to *nirvana*. Smaller dedicatory and funerary *chaitya*, ranging from the 6th-century *ashok* type, and the later bell-shaped and composite forms are found in the precincts of great *chaitya* and in temple, monastery and residential courtyards.

[1] Snellgrove, D. L., Shrines and Temples of Nepal. In *Arts Asiatiques*, 1961, Vol. VIII, Fasc. 1 and 2.

The characteristic temple form is that termed by Westerners "pagoda", after the tapering, multi-tiered roof surmounting the square brick-built sanctum. Pagoda temples are free-standing as exemplified by the Taleju Temple at Hanuman Dhoka, Kathmandu, the Shiva Temple, Pashupatinath, and the Nyatapola Temple, Bhadgaon, or enclosed on one side of a "monastic" courtyard as in the Hiranayana Mahavihara, Lalitpur. Temple complexes, often centres of pilgrimage, stand generally in locations removed from residential areas and are associated with subsidiary temples, shrines, tanks and pilgrim rest-houses (*dharmasala*).

Shikhara temples date from the medieval period, the most famous being Krishna Mandir standing in the Darbar Square, Lalitpur. The square stone entablement over the sanctum carries a series of carved stone porticos and a pyramidal, curvilinear steeple. Domed temples, influenced by Moghul architectural forms gained popularity in the 19th century under the Shah dynasty. The style is best represented by the Satya Narayan Temple in Kalomochan, Kathmandu.

The uniform use of locally manufactured brick and tile as a building medium emphasises the overall sense of harmony and order pervading Newar settlements. Architectural diversity is represented by the varying height of podium and pedestal, memorial pillars surmounted by copper-gilt figures of kings, divinities and sacred emblems, by gateways and flights of steps flanked by stone and copper-gilt "guardians", by elegant pavilions sheltering the seat of kings, ceremonial bells, drums and giant prayer wheels and by tanks and watering places (*pranali*, *hitti*) furnished with *makara*-headed waterspouts. A wealth of carved wood enhances both sacred and secular buildings. The visitor's attention is directed to the workmanship of window and door frames with their characteristically extended lintels, lattice screens, arched tympanums and to the roof-struts, many of which bear some of the most remarkable examples of wood-carving. Decorative elements in hammered, embossed and cast metal enrich architectural compositions in brick and wood; the abundant use of gilt on roofs, finials, banners and images produces scenes of unparelleled splendour.

Religious Practice.—The divinities of the Kathmandu Valley, Brahmanical, Buddhist, Tantric, and those of the Vajrayana pantheon command the reverence of a deeply religious population. A uniform system of rituals, the tendency to equate the gods and goddesses of sister religions and to worship at shrines and temples irrespective of caste and sectarian affiliation has achieved a syncretisation of religious practice.

Shiva, the national deity of Nepal, is worshipped in his benign aspect as Pashupatinath, Lord of the Animals, Bhupati, Lord of all Creatures, as Maheśvara, Great Lord, as Virabhadra, He who carries the trident, and Natyesvara, Lord of the Dance. His symbol is the *lingam*, the organ of reproductive and creative power. In his terrible aspect he appears as Bhairava of the sixty-four forms, wearing in both Buddhist and Hindu images a garland of human skulls. Shiva's consort is Parvati, the gentle mountain daughter of the Himalaya, Uma the light, Gauri, the Brilliant, Devi, the benevolent Universal Mother. She is also worshipped as Durga, the blood-thirsty Kali, Chandi, Bhairavi, Guhyeśvari, the "secret Goddess", and Taleju, the tutelary deity of the Malla kings. Their sons are the warrior Kārttikeya, also known as Kumar, and the elephant-headed Ganesh, the remover of obstacles and bestower of success.

Vishnu is worshipped as Narayan and Mahadev, as Hari, called also Hari-Har, and in his incarnated forms, the most popular of which are the flute-playing Krishna, Rama, the hero of the Ramayana and, according to popular belief, Lord Buddha himself; as Ananta Shayin he sleeps on the coiled snake of eternity and is equated by Buddhists with Nilakantha Lokeśvara. The kings of the Shah dynasty are looked on as incarnations of Vishnu. Vishnu's partner is Lakshmi, goddess of beauty and good fortune, propitiated in villages as Mahalakshmi, the harvest goddess. Associated with the Vaishnavite cult is Garuda, the sun-eagle mount of Vishnu; in bird or half-human form he is often found in positions of humility before temples dedicated to Vishnu-Narayan-Mahadev.

The role of the monkey-god Hanuman is guardian of the door; Bhimsen, the second of the five Pāṇḍavas, is worshipped in several large temples and is the tutelary deity of Newar traders. Of the Vedic gods, Surya, the sun god, and Indra, the god of victory, whose annual festival is celebrated with great pomp and ceremony, are the most important. The Brahmanical goddess of learning, Saraswati, is greatly revered, and is popularly regarded as the consort of the Bodhisattva Manjuśri.

The patron deity of the Kathmandu Valley, Machhendranath, is worshipped as the bringer of rain and bountiful harvests, and his annual festival is a national event. Known also as Karunamaya, the compassionate one, and as Bunga Deo, after the village in which the idol resides for six months of the year, Machhendranath is said to have appeared in the Kathmandu Valley to avert a drought. He is associated with Gorakhnath, a Siddhi of the Natha sect and equated by Buddhists with Lokeśvara, Lord of the Universe. The relation of red Machhendranath of Lalitpur and Bungamati with White Machhendranath of Kathmandu, whose ritual attendants are Green Tara and White Tara, is far from clear, but Minnath of Lalitpur, known as Chakwa Deo, is considered Machhendranath's offspring.

Adi Buddha, the centre of Buddhist reverence, is symbolised by the ever-burning flame. To the highest of all celestial beings are dedicated Svayambunath and innumerable temples and *chaitya*. The Tri Ratna, Buddha, Samgha and Dharma, and Dipankara —a forerunner of the Manusi Buddhas, whose cult forms the centre of 5- and 12-yearly rites, occupy places of honour in *chaitya, vihara* and temple. Images of the Dhyani Buddhas, the celestial Buddhas, are set in characteristic poses at the cardinal directions in temples and on *chaitya*: Aksobhya to the east, Ratnasambhava to the south, Amitabha to the west, Amoghasiddhi to the north and Vairocana in the centre.

Sakya Muni, the most important of the Manusi or earthly Buddhas, is represented in human form or by footprints in black stone; his birthday is the occasion of an annual festival. The Bodhisattvas Manjuśri, the glorious gentle one, to whom legend ascribes the draining of the lake which once covered the Kathmandu Valley, and Avalokiteśvara, the compassionate one, identified with Machhendranath and Lokeśvara, stand high in popular esteem and receive the homage of both Hindus and Buddhists.

The worship of female goddesses is an important element in the popular religion of the Kathmandu Valley. The female principle *shakti*, the active partner of the male Hindu deities, appears under countless names. Propitiated with blood sacrifice and often referred to as mother or grandmother, the female divinities are worshipped as the averters of evil and in their role as guardian deities are often named for the locality over which they preside. The Vajrayana female counterpart, *prajna*, is the passive partner; despite textual descriptions which tend to polarise *sakti* and *prajna*, the role of the consorts of the fierce and tranquil Buddhas and Bodhisattvas is, in common usage, comparable to that played by Hindu *sakti*.

Rites and Festivals.—In the Kathmandu Valley religious rites are regulated according to the lunar calendar, the month being divided into two fortnights, the 15 days of the waning and the 15 days of the waxing moon. Ekadasi, the 11th, and Chaturdasi the 14th day of each lunar fortnight, Aunsi the 15th day of the waning moon and Purnima, full moon day, are days of special ritual significance.

Mes Sankranti, or Baisakh Sankranti, the beginning of the official Nepalese New Year in April-May (Baisakh) and Magh Sankranti falling six months later are reckoned according to the Solar calendar. The Buddhist New Year falls on the 2nd day of the waxing moon of October-November (Kartik).

State holidays, attended by military parades and government officials at Tundikhel in Kathmandu are Constitution day, or Democracy Day, coinciding with the birthday of the late King Mahendra Bir Bikram Shah Deva, the birthday of H.M. King Birendra Bir Bikram Shah Deva, and the birthday of King Prithivi Narayan Shah, founder of the Shah dynasty. These are held in December-January (Pus).

Mela (fairs), *jatra* (idol decoration ceremonies), and *kath* (litter) and *rath* (chariot) processions associated with specific religious rites occur throughout the year. The visitor will find these colourful occasions, which are accompanied by dancers, musicians and dramatic representations, rewarding to attend. For details as to time and place reference may be made to Anderson, M., *The Festivals of Nepal* (New York, 1969).

KATHMANDU

History.—Kathmandu, said to have been founded by the Lichhavi king, Gunakarna Deva, in the 8th century A.D., was known until the 17th century as Kantipur, "City of Glory" (Newari: Yem or Yambu). Situated at the junction of the Raswua Garhi (Tibet), Bodnath–Pashupathinath–Kodari (Tibet) and the Chandragiri (India) trade routes it was ruled until the 15th century by feudatories under the overlordship of Lalitpur-Bhadgaon. In 1482 it became the capital of Yaksha Malla's second son, Ratna Malla. The kings of this new line of the Malla dynasty reigned for 285 years; the extent of their influence and the area of their dominions fluctuated with the fortunes of war, including at times the kingdoms of Lalitpur and Banepa, and the territories lying between the Indravati and the Trisuli Rivers.

To the Malla dynasty, Kathmandu owes a large proportion of her medieval buildings. The most notable of the builder-kings were: Ratna Malla (1482-1528), Mahendra Malla (1560-1574), Sadasiva Malla (1574-1583), Sivasimha Malla (1578-1620), Pratap Malla (1641-1674), Bhaskara Malla (1687-1714), Jagatjaya Malla (1722-1736), and Jayaprakasa Malla (1736-1768).

In 1767 King Prithivi Narayan Shah made Kathmandu the capital of an enlarged and unified Nepal. He added extra courts and several towers and terraces to the royal palace and subsequent Shah kings embellished the town with temples, statuary and public buildings. The development of Kathmandu from a medieval town to a modern state capital dates from the second half of the 19th century. It followed the introduction of a new architectural dimension, the erection of numerous noblemen's palaces on the outskirts of the old town which provided a focus for the extension of the residential area and the alignment of a new road system. Built by successive Maharajas and their kin these palaces (Bhavan, Mahal, Darbar) were of grandiose proportions, their façades drawn from models of 17th-, 18th- and 19th-century European palace architecture; their interiors were lavishly furnished in Western style and their walled gardens laid out with formal flower beds, fountains and decorative statuary. Today the majority are no longer private residences but are utilised as offices of government, headquarters of foreign missions and as libraries, colleges and training centres; they serve as reminders of the past glories of Rana times and of the ingenuity of builders who transported all foreign goods over the Chandragiri pass on porters' backs.

The most remarkable of the Kathmandu palaces were: **Thapathali**,[1] built by Maharaja Jang Bahadur, and **Narayanhitti Seto Darbar**,[2] built by Maharaja Bir Shumshere, in whose extensive grounds the Royal Palace **Narayanhitti** now stands. **Singha Darbar**, situated east of Tundikhel in Ram Shah Path, was erected in 1903 by Maharaja Chandra Shumshere, who employed a French architect to build a "little Versailles"; it contained 7 inner courts and 1600 rooms and served for twenty years as H.M. Government Secretariat; in the summer of 1973 it was unhappily gutted by fire. During the 1930's the Nepalese architects Kishor Narsingh Rana and Kumar Narsingh Rana designed **Sital Nivas**, now the State Guest House, **Bahadur Bhavan**,[3] now to be demolished to make room for the new Inter-continental Hotel and **Kaiser Mahal**, the residence of General Kaiser Shumshere, whose remarkable library and beautiful garden are now open to the public.

The devastation caused by the 1934 earthquake allowed for such planning innovations as the development of a new commercial centre south-east of the old city and the erection of the gateway at the entrance of Juddah Sadak. Since 1951 the growth in the number of Kathmandu's residents, the needs of a modern administration and the ever-increasing influx of tourists has led to the opening up of the city and its suburbs to housing, hotel development, and a network of motorable roads recently linked with a ring road encircling Kathmandu and Lalitpur.

Kathmandu (pop. 121,019), the capital of Nepal, is the administrative headquarters of Bagmati Zone and Kathmandu District. Situated on high ground between the Bagmati and Vishnumati Rivers, it is the largest city in Nepal, with a net population density of 45,000 persons per square kilometre; in Ward 7, the heart of Kathmandu, 75,000 persons inhabit 1 square kilometre. The population includes the largest number of foreigners and the most extra-zonal migrants of any city in Nepal. Nepali-speakers outweigh Newari-speakers and Hindus outnumber Buddhists. Despite the continuing importance of agriculture as a source of income, a large proportion of the inhabitants is engaged in commerce and wage and salaried occupations.

The core of the old city falls within the area enclosed by the Vishnumati–Bagmati Rivers and the Tundikhel, the 18th-century parade ground. Constructed during the premiership of Bhimsen Thapa it is now bounded by two broad asphalt roads, on the west by Kanti Path and on the east by Darbar Marg. Most government offices, public buildings, foreign embassies, cultural institutions, travel agents and the larger hotels are situated east, north and south of the old city core.

Hotels (Service charge 10 per cent.; Hotel tax 10 per cent.). Below are listed the main hotels existing at present; others are under construction. Other establishments offer simple accommodation at modest cost and there are motels providing parking facilities for vehicles.

*****Soaltee-Oberoi. 206 beds with bath. Swimming Pool. Himalayan Heights, Kalimati. Tel. 11211, 11106, 11724, 11736.

[1] Damaged in the 1934 earthquake; subsequent restoration and rebuilding work has largely eclipsed the original building.

[2] Seto Darbar now houses the Yak and Yeti Restaurant.

[3] Leased to Boris Lissanowitz during 1950-1966, it operated as the world-famous Royal Hotel.

*****de l'Annapurna (Hilton International). 180 beds with bath. Darbar Marg. Tel. 11711, 11531, 11552.

*** Shanker. 20 beds. Lazimpet. Tel. 11973.

*** Snow View. 28 beds. Lazimpet. Tel. 11195.

** Crystal. 58 beds. Sukra Path. Tel. 12630, 13611, 13397.

** Mt. Makalu. 36 beds. Juddha Sadak. Tel. 11252.

** Leo. 26 beds. Bagh Bazaar. Tel. 11252.

* Paras. 30 beds. Dharma Path. Tel. 11233.

* Green. 24 beds. Juddha Sadak. Tel. 11961.

* Blue Star. 30 beds. Thapathali. Tel. 12318, 13218.

* Panorama. Kichapokhari. Tel. 11502.

* Samjana. 20 beds. Kanti Path. Tel. 13569.

* Hotel Kt. Indra Chowk. Tel. 14417.

* Camp. Maruhity. Tel. 13145.

Restaurants

*****Yak and Yeti, Lal Darbar, Kamal Pokhari.

*** Tokyo. Darbar Marg

** Min-Ming. Darbar Marg

* Nook. Behind U.S. Embassy.

* Park (Indian specialities; 'Tandoori' Chicken). Rani Pokhari.

* Indira (Indian specialities). Juddah Sadak.

* Kwality (Indian specialities). Juddah Sadak.

* Utse (Tibetan-Chinese specialities). Lainchaur.

* Unity (American management). Behind Juddha Sadak.

Learned Societies, Libraries, Reading Rooms, Museums, Art Galleries, etc.

American Library, Juddha Sadak, Kathmandu. Tel. 11078.

Archaeological Garden, Darbar Square, Lalitpur.

Arniko Art Gallery, Ghato Kulo, Dilli Bazaar, Kathmandu.

Bhadgaon National Art Gallery, Darbar Square, Bhadgaon.

Bir Library, National Archives, Ram Shah Path, Kathmandu.

British Council Library, Kanti Path, Kathmandu. Tel. 11305.

Central Library, Lal Darbar, Kathmandu.

French Cultural Centre, Bagh Bazaar, Kathmandu.

Indian Reading Room, Kanti Path, Kathmandu.

Kaiser Mahal Library, Kanti Path, Kathmandu.

Nepal Art Gallery, Kwalakhu, Kathmandu. Tel. 21477.

Nepal Association of Fine Arts.

Nepal-Bharat Cultural Centre, Juddha Sadak, Kathmandu. Tel. 11497.

Nepal-Bharat Sanskritik Kendra Pustakalay, Ganga Path, Kathmandu.

Nepal China Maitri Pustakalya, Shukra Path, Kathmandu.

Nepal Maitri Sangh, Basantapur, Kathmandu.

National Museum, Chhaoni, Kathmandu. Tel. 11504, 11478.

National Numismatic Museum, Hanuman Dhoka, Kathmandu. Tel. 13638.

Nepal Research Centre Library, Thyssen House, Chhaoni, Kathmandu P.O.B. 180. Tel. 12263.

Nepal National Library, Hari Har Bhavan, Lalitpur. Tel. 21132.

Royal Nepal Academy, Kamaladi, Ganeshan, Kathmandu. Tel. 11283.

Science Education Centre, Hari Har Bhavan, Kathmandu.

Tribhuvan University, Kirtipur. Information: Tel. 11071, 11040, 11270, 11283, 11487.

Hospitals and Sanatorium

Bir Hospital, Kanti Path, Kathmandu. Tel. 11119.

Indra Rajya Laxmi Prasuti Griha (Maternity Hospital), Thapathli, Kathmandu. Tel. 11243.

Kanti Children's Hospital, Maharajganj, Kathmandu. Tel. 11550.

Military Hospital, Kanti Path, Kathmandu.

Tokha Sanatorium, Tokha Hill, Kathmandu.

United Mission Hospital, Shanta Bhavan, Jhamsikhel, Lalitpur. Tel. 21304.

Parks and Public Gardens

Balaju Pleasure Park and Swimming Pool, Balaju, (2 mi.; 3 km. north of Kathmandu).

Chidiyakhana (Zoo), Jawalakhel, Patan.

Botanical Gardens, Godavari (14½ mi.; 22 km. south of Kathmandu).

Kanti Park, Kanti Path, Kathmandu.

Royal Forest and Game Sanctuary, Gokarna (2 mi.; 3 km. east of Kathmandu).

Tourist Information Centres, Travel Agents

Department of Tourism, Ram Shah Path. Tel. 11293, 14519.

Tourist Information Centre, H.M. Government of Nepal, Basantapur. Tel. 11293.

Tourist Information Centre, Tribhuvan Airport (Gauchar). Tel. 11814.

Everest Travel Service, Ganga Path. Tel. 11216.

Gorkha Travels, Darbar Marg. Tel. 11234.

Himalayan Travel & Tours, Darbar Marg. Tel. 11682.

Kathmandu Travels & Tours, Ganga Path. Tel 1446.

Mountain Travel, Maharajgunj. Tel. 12808.

Nataraj Travels & Tours, Ghanta Ghar. Tel. 12014.

Rhino Bus Service, Directorate of Tourism, Basantapur. Tel. 11293.

Sherpa Trekking Service, Lal Darbar, P.O.B. 500, Kathmandu.

Shanker Tours and Travels, Hotel Shanker, Lazimpet. Tel. 11973.

Air Line Offices

Air France, Darbar Marg. Tel. 11339.

Air India International, Kanti Path. Tel. 12335.

British Airways, Kanti Path. Tel. 12508.

Burma Airways, Darbar Marg. Tel. 12716.

Indian Airlines, Ratna Park. Tel. 11198.

Lufthansa, Darbar Marg. Tel. 13052.

P.I.A., Darbar Marg. Tel. 12107.

Pan American World Airways, Hotel Soaltee-Oberoi, Kalimati Tel. 11211.

Thai Airways International, Darbar Marg. Tel. 13565.

Royal Nepal Airlines Corporation, Kanti Path. Booking Office: Tel. 11055, 11368.

Tribhuvan Airport, Gauchar. Tel. 11043, 11059.

Hired Transport

Taxis, and cycle rickshaws are available for hire. Arrangements may be made through hotels, or at the hire stands (taxis: junction of Juddha Sadak and Dharma Path; cycle rickshaws: junction of Kanti Path and Kamaladi). Tiger taxis, so called because of the stripes with which they are painted, are metered; visitors are advised to settle fares and waiting charges in advance when engaging unmetered vehicles.

Bicycles may be hired by the day or week from the stand in Kanti Path, near the U.S. Embassy.

Taxis, jeeps and cars may be rented for journeys outside Kathmandu on fixed charge.

Guided sightseeing tours are arranged by most travel agents and the management of some of the larger hotels.

Bus Services operate to and from Kathmandu on the following routes (timely booking of seats on longer journeys is advisable): Birgunj (Raxaul), 126 mi. (203 km.); Bhadgaon 10 mi. (16 km.); Gausala (Pashupatinath), 2½ mi. (4 km.); Bansbari (Maharajganj), 4 mi. (6 km.); Trisuli, 43 mi. (70 km.); Barabise, 54 mi. (87 km.); Dolalghat, 35 mi. (57 km.); Balaju Pleasure Park, 2½ mi. (4 km.); Dhulikhel, 18½ mi. (30 km.); Lalitpur, 3 mi. (5 km.); Thankot, 5 mi. (8 km.); Pokhara, 93 mi. (150 km.); Kodari, 71 mi. (114 km.); Siliguri, via Janakpur.

Air Services (Internal)

The Royal Nepal Airlines Corporation (RNAC) operate scheduled services between Kathmandu and the following air-fields. Flights are liable to cancellation during the monsoon months.

East Nepal—Bhadrapur, Biratnagar, Rajbiraj, Janakpur, Rumjatar (Okhaldhunga), Tumlingtar, Lamidanda.

Central Nepal—Simra, Bharatpur, Gorkha, Pokhara, Bhairawa, Rukumkot.

West Nepal—Dang, Surket, Nepalganj, Dhangarhi, Silgarhi-Dhoti, Mahendranagar, Jumla.

Charter flights by S.T.O.L. Avro, Pilatus Porter or Twin Otter aircraft may be arranged by Royal Nepal Airlines Corporation to the above airfields and a few other localities with suitable landing facilities. Charges are reckoned per flight kilometre. The helicopter wing of RNAC, managed by Helicopter Services Private Ltd., Singapore, operates Bell 206-B Jet Ranger and Helicopter charter services for set or personalised itineraries. Minimum 3, maximum 4 passengers.

All details of bus and air services should be checked locally; travel is subject to weather conditions.

ROUTE 1

KATHMANDU CENTRE OF OLD CITY

Note that only modern roads in Kathmandu are named. In all urban areas in the Kathmandu Valley thoroughfares are identified with reference to adjacent *tol*, *bahal* or *vihara* and are described variously in Nepali, Sanskrit or Newari.

Rani Pokhari lies to the north of Ratna Park and is a convenient and easily identifiable starting point from which to set out on a tour of old Kathmandu. The stone-lined tank was built by Pratap Malla in 1676/67 to console his queen for the death of their son Chakravertendra Malla. At the end of a causeway leading from the western pavement to the middle of the tank is a small, white, domed temple dedicated to Shiva; it replaces the original temple destroyed by earthquake in 1934. On the southern pavement stands a sculptured elephant, carrying in royal manner three riders, reputedly the king, his queen and their deceased son. Looking across the waters of Rani Pokhari, Tri Chandra College built in 1918 by Maharaja Chandra Shumshere and the Clock Tower set up in 1895 by Maharaja Bir Shumshere may be seen in the east.

Leave the north-west corner of Rani Pokhari; cross Kanti Path and turn left into Kamalachhi, an ancient thoroughfare lined with old houses and open fronted shops. Proceed to **Asan Tol**, a piazza situated at the junction of Bhotanhity, Tendha Tol and Nhendan Tol, where an important grain market operates. To the right is the shrine of Ganesh and to the left stands the pagoda temple dedicated to the Mother Goddess Annapurna.

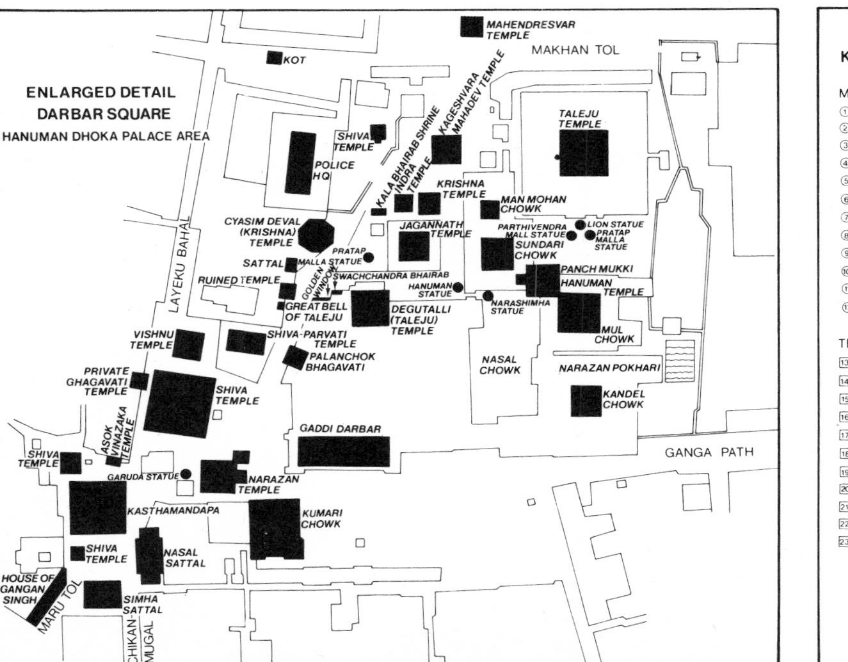

KEY TO NUMBERS ON MAIN MAP

MEMORIALS

① King Prithivi Bir Bikram Shah Dev (1881-1911)
② Maharajah Chandra Shumshere (1901-1929)
③ Maharajah Juddha Shumshere (1932-1945)
④ Maharajah Rana Udip (1877-1885)
⑤ Maharajah Jang Bahadur Rana (1856-1879)
⑥ General Dir Shumshere (1884)
⑦ Maharajah Bir Shumshere (1885-1901)
⑧ Maharajah Juddha Shumshere (1932-1945)
⑨ Desemadaj Jha (window)
⑩ Buddha sculpture
⑪ Kumarasambharan bas relief
⑫ Padmapani Lokesvara statue (Dharma Kirti Vihara)

TEMPLES

13 Seto Machhendra Nath Temple
14 Mahendresvara Temple
15 Atak Narayan Temple
16 Kankesvari Temple
17 Itum Bahal
18 Vishnu Temple
19 Ganesh Temple
20 House of the Elephant
21 Shriga Chaitya (Singha Vihara)
22 Nagha Vihara
23 Chusya Bahal

Continue up Kamalachhi, passing on the right the temple of Krishna. To the right of the junction with Kel Tol is the 3-storied pagoda temple dedicated to Luchu Bhalu, and the ornate, dragon-flanked entrance to Jana Bahal. The 2-storied pagoda temple dedicated to Seto Machhendra stands in a paved court set with many small *chaitya* and various sculptured forms of Avalokiteśvara, with whom Machhendra is identified. The gilt-roofed temple is lavishly decorated with copper-gilt; rows of prayer wheels are ranged on three sides of the sanctum. The figures carved on pillars, roof-struts and railings represent Hindu and Buddhist divinities. The enshrined image is the white-faced, Buddha-like Seto Machhendra, whose original temple formed the centre of a *vihara* in Jamal.

In **Indra Chowk**, a piazza at the junction of Chokhachen Galli, Knun Bahal, Makhan Tol and Sukra Path, is a picturesque street market frequented by hill people, where woollen rugs, blankets and shawls of Nepalese manufacture are displayed for sale. To the west of Indra Chowk stands the pagoda temple of Akash Bhairab, the guardian deity of the locality. Follow the road through Makhan Tol; on the right, shortly after the road bears right, is the kneeling figure of a fine 10th-century Garuda. 30 yds. (30 me.) further on there stands, on the right, the gilt-roofed, pagoda temple dedicated to Mahendresvar (Pashupati). Raised on a stepped plinth, it was erected in the 16th century by Mahendra Malla, who also installed the *lingam* in the sanctum. The lane running due west leads to the **Kot**, the old armoury, the scene of the 1846 massacre from which Jang Bahadur emerged all powerful, and of the great buffalo sacrifices performed during Dasain.

The stepped podium of the Mahendresvar temple provides a good vantage point from which to view the northern wing of the royal palace, the temple of Taleju rising behind its enclosing walls, and the temple precinct fronting the palace known as **Hanuman Dhoka**. Of the monuments standing in the paved quadrangle, all of which belong to the Malla period, the most important are: the 2-storied pagoda temple dedicated to Indra; the 3-storied *shikhara* temple dedicated to Krishna; the 3-storied **Jagannath** temple dedicated to **Vishnu,** remarkable for the erotic carvings on the roof-struts and Pratap Malla's 1657 inscription on the eastern side of the plinth recording, in fifteen languages, a prayer to the goddess Kalika; the shrine of **Kala Bhairab** (Shiva in terrifying aspect), represented by a 17th century black stone image, six armed, of ferocious countenance and mounted on a goblin (before Kala Bhairab government officers of medieval times took the oath of office and criminals protested their innocence); **Memorial Pillar,** surmounted by the gilded figures of Pratap Malla, his two queens and their five sons.

Hanuman Dhoka Darbar[1] the Royal Palace, the residence of the Malla kings of Kantipur, and subsequently of the Shah dynasty of Nepal comprises several complexes of interlinking courts. Its foundation is popularly attributed to Ratna Malla, but the Pashupati inscriptions of Parthivendra Malla record that the palace was built in the 16th century during the reign of Mahendra Malla. In the 17th century Pratap Malla enlarged the original building, adding many of the temples which stand today in the courts associated with the Darbar. The southern wing was erected by King Prithivi Narayan Shah. Completed, according to an inscription on the southern façade, on the 5th day of the bright half of the month of Chait 1771, it was named Basanta, spring, after the season in which it was completed. King Pratap Singh Shah built the southern gate and set up the inscription which

[1] Anonymous, *The Hanumandhoka Royal Palace. A Brief Introduction* (Kathmandu, Ramgham Office, Royal Palace, 1972).

states that Prithivi Narayan Shah built Vilas Mandir. In 1908 King Prithivi Bikram Shah and Maharaja Chandra Shumshere added the south-western wing, Gaddi Darbar. Subsequent Shah monarchs embellished the palace with interior and external furnishings and the late Kings Tribhuvan and Mahendra and the reigning sovereign H.M. King Birendra Bikram Shah Deva have sponsored considerable restoration work. The royal residence is now Narayan Hitti palace, but the old Darbar retains its ritual and ceremonial importance; within its precincts the Kings of Nepal are crowned and many ritually prescribed ceremonies enacted.

Access to the Darbar is by **Suvarnaduar,** the gilded doorway set up according to the inscription in gold letters during the "glorious reign of the noblest of Gorkha rulers", the cost being met out of income derived from grants recorded on copper (tamapatra). To the left of the palace entrance Pratap Malla installed in the 17th century the statue of Hanuman, after whom the northern wing of the Darbar and the precincts fronting it are known as **Hanuman Dhoka.** To the right is an open verandah, and above it a 3-storied **Degutalli** (Taleju) Temple; embedded in the west wall of the palace is the 12 ft. (360 cm.) grill-protected mask of **Swachchandra Bhairab** (White Bhairab), set up by King Rana Bahadur Shah in the 18th century; once a year during Indra Jatra the wooden grill is removed and *thon,* a local fermented liquor, pours through the mask's mouth and is caught by the assembled crowd. At the gilded window embracing the north-west corner at first floor level the sovereign used to make public appearances; the central figure of the tympanum is a seven-headed snake, the emblem of Vishnu, of whom the kings of Nepal are incarnations.

A 3-storied temple dedicated to **Taleju** rises above the entrance to the Malla palace; on the left of the lobby is the famous black stone statue, inlaid with silver of **Narashimha** and the demon Hiranyakashipur; it was set up, according to the pedestal inscription by Pratap Malla in 1672. In 1869 King Surendra Bikram Shah provided a gilt canopy for the statue and in the same year Crown Prince Trilokya Bikram Shah and the Crown Princess donated a silver standard and gilding for the shrine roof.

The central court, **Nasal Chowk,** was built by Pratap Malla in the 17th century. Said to accommodate 10,000 people, it provides a forum for ritual dances and public assembly on ceremonial occasions. The chowk is named after the god **Nasal** (Natyesvara), whose image stands in the eastern side. To the north-east is the 5-storied, circular temple dedicated to the 5-faced god Hanuman. The **Coronation Platform** on which the kings of Nepal are crowned in accordance with Vedic rites occupies the centre of the court; the royal apartments form the western wall. In a nearby verandah is the 17th-century statue of Maha Vishnu and Lakshmi, installed after the earthquake of 1834; in the vicinity is the **Nishan Ghar** and the **Maulo,** "sacrificial pillar". King Rajendra Bikram Shah paved Nasal Chowk and the coronation platform in the 19th century; the court has recently been renovated by H.M. King Birendra Bikram Shah Deva.

North of Nasal Chowk is **Sundari Chowk** built by Pratap Malla in 1648/49-1650/51. Of the sculptural works displayed in the court, the most notable is the Kaliyadaman image dating from the Lichhavi period, which Pratap Malla caused to be transported from an unknown site. A *lingam* standing in the court receives daily worship from palace Brahmins. The court was extensively renovated by King Rajendra Bikram Shah in the 19th century. Lying to the north of Sundari Chowk is **Man Mohan Chowk,** popularly known as **Mohan Chowk**; it was built, according to the gold-lettered inscription on a pillar of the northern verandah, by Pratap Malla, who in 1630 also installed the gold water-spout and stone bath carved with 34 images of gods and goddesses. Mohan Chowk contains a number of interesting statues of Mohankali and the Nau Durga, the terra-cotta figures of Bhairava, Natyesvara and the characters of the Shiva-Bhasmasur legend; in the northern verandah are stone images of Vishnu in his incarnated forms, personages of the Krishna life-story and, on a golden canopy, the image of Shesasai Vishnu. In one corner stands a carved wooden seat on which the Malla kings sat to receive foreign delegations or preside over important meetings. To the east is the image of Balgopal and two *mukha lingam.* Large wooden images of Vakasur Vadh, Kaliyadaman, Putana Vadh and other characters of the Krishna life-story are on the side-walks. The exterior beams of the *chowk* are carved with figures drawn from the Krishna and Ram Chandra legend.

Paintings representing the Goddess Mohankali adorn the western wall, and above are frescoes depicting the divinities Mohankali, Vishnu, Shiva, Ganesh, Karttikeya and episodes illustrating the legends of Chandi, the Devasura battle and Durga slaying the buffalo demon Mahisāsura. The court was extensively renovated by King Rajendra Bikram Shah in the 19th century.

Mul Chowk, built by Pratap Malla in 1649/50-1651/52 and situated to the east of Nasal Chowk, contains wood-carvings of exceptional workmanship and those depicting Durga slaying the buffalo demon Mahisāsura should be particularly noted; the intricately designed gilt tympanum over the door is one of the most remarkable of its kind. Extensive renovation work was carried out in Mul Chowk during the reign of the late King Mahendra Bir Bikram Shah Deva.

Trisuli Chowk, accessible from Mul Chowk, is an open paved court in which stands the temple dedicated to Taleju, the family deity of the Malla kings. Though it is believed that Ratna Malla installed his tutelary deity in his new capital, the present structure was erected by Mahendra Malla in the 16th century; the cost, according to inscriptions, being defrayed by the rulers of Lalitpur, Bhaktapur and Kirtipur. The three-storied temple, projected in the form of a mystic *yantra*, is one of the finest examples of the Nepalese pagoda style. Elevated on a high-stepped podium on which stand ten small 2-storied pagodas, it is decorated with a profusion of elaborately carved wood, stone and bronze images and gilded ornament. The gilded temple door, tympanum and hanging banner were donated by Pratap Malla in the 17th century. Opposite the entrance are pillars surmounted by the gilded statues of Pratap Malla, Parthivendra Malla and a lion. The court takes its name from the tall gilt trident (*trisula*), the emblem of Shiva, set up on the steps of the temple. The late King Mahendra Bir Bikram Shah Deva initiated large-scale renovations in 1970. Trisuli Chowk is only open to Hindus.

South-east of Trisuli Chowk is **Dasain Chowk.** It contains the Dasain ghar of the Shah dynasty to which the sacred *kalash* is brought from Gorkha during the annual Dasain rites; close by is **Narayan Pokhari**, a large stone-lined tank in which an image of Vishnu reclines on the coils of a snake.

The complex of courts known as Basantapur Darbar and built by the Shah kings lies to the south of Pratap Malla's palace. **Lohan Chowk,** or **Tejarath Chowk,** is separated from Nasal Chowk by a huge wooden portal carved with floral motifs and the figures of the Ashta Matrikas, the eight mother goddesses. The terraces enclosing the court on three sides are **Bangala** in the north-west, **Lakshmi Vilas Mandir** in the north-east and **Vilas Mandir** in the south-east.

Kandel Chowk, a square inner court, contains a ruined temple dedicated to Natyesvara and a temple sacred to Kandel Bhagwati. The 4-storied structure enclosing the court is surmounted on the north by a 2-storied and on the west by a 7-storied tower, similar to that which King Prithivi Narayan constructed at Nawakot.

The most recent of the palace courts is **Gaddi Darbar**, the Throne Room, lying west of and adjoining Basantapur Darbar. Built in neo-classical style in 1908, it was designed by Maharaja Chandra Shumshere as a reception room for visiting foreign delegates; it contains the silver throne and numerous portraits of the Shah Kings.

The western façade of the Darbar extends from Hanuman Dhoka to Ganga Path; the temple of Palanchok Bagavati marks the limits of the Malla Palace; the neo-classical entrance to Gaddi Darbar, used on ceremonial occasions, is now only opened during Kumari Jatra.

The temples standing in the quadrangle west of Gaddi Darbar are: to the north, the 2-storied pagoda temple dedicated to Shiva and Parvati (18th century), whose painted wooden images appear at a first floor window, and the 3-storied pagoda temple dedicated to Vishnu (17th century); in the centre, the 3-storied pagoda temple dedicated to Shiva, erected by Riddi Lakshmi, the mother of Bhupalendra Malla (1691/92); to the south, the 3-storied pagoda dedicated to Narayan (1668/69), with, to the west the statue of Garuda (1689/90), erected by Bhupalendra Malla and his chief minister Lakshmi Narayan Joshi; further west are several smaller temples, the most important being that dedicated to Ashok Vinayak, popularly known as Kathmandu Ganesh, whose large bell was donated by the Queen Mother, Lalita Tripura Sundari Devi 1831/32.

From the steps of Shiva's temple a good view is obtained of Basantapur Darbar, the cupola roofs, the towers and terraces erected by the kings of the Shah dynasty.

Kasthamandapa, the largest and one of the oldest standing temples in Kathmandu, is situated at the head of Maru Tol, at the north-west exit of Basantapur quadrangle. The popular belief that it was built by Siddhi Luipi, a mendicant from Gāur, during the reign of Laxmi Narsingha Malla in the 16th century has now been disproved. References to Kasthamandapa occur in the *nana sangiti* manuscript (11th century) and in the *paramartha namsangiti* manuscript (12th century), where it is described as a Buddhist temple. That Kasthamandapa lent its name to Kathmandu is a fact corroborated by a passage in the *sragdharastotra* manuscript (1473-74) which describes the town as Kasthamandapa Mahanagara. One copper plate inscription preserved in the building is dated 1303-1304 and another dated 1484-85 records the enrichment of Kasthamandapa with gold during the reign of Yaksha Malla. The building, said to have been fashioned from the wood of a single tree, stands on a 4½ ft. (1·26 me.) high podium, measuring 70 sq. ft. (19·78 sq. me.). Four massive squared posts support a wooden superstructure with an overall height of 65 ft. (19·60 me.). The tiled, three-tiered pagoda roof has low hanging eaves and is surmounted by a finial. Interior wooden stairs ascend from the ground floor to the two upper storeys; the corner terraces at ground and the balconies at first and second floor level are enclosed by elegantly carved railings. Deities enshrined within the building include Shiva, Parvati, Ganesh, Bhairava, Mahakal, Tara, Sarasvati, Natyesvara and Sakhya Muni; the principal shrine on the ground floor contains a carved stone statue of the presiding deity, Goraknath; the building is regarded as a foundation of the Natha sect and now serves as a *sattal*, resthouse for travellers and the homeless. Kasthamandapa was extensively restored in 1966 by H.M.G./Nepal's

Department of Archaeology with funds supplied by the Kasthamandapa Guthi Samasthan.

The small piazza south of Kasthamandapa, is enclosed by three ancient buildings: **Nasa Sattal**, containing a shrine of Natyeśvara (1672-73), **Simha Sattal** and a pagoda temple dedicated to Shiva. Maru tol leads from Kastamandapa to the bridge over the Vishnumati. On the right is the erstwhile house of General Gangan Singh. Bhimsen Than occupies the lower part of Maru Tol; on the right stands the 3-storied pagoda temple dedicated to Bhimsen, the first documentary mention of which was in 1545-46.

East of the Narayan temple, on the south side of Ganga path, opposite Gaddi Darbar, is **Kumari Chowk**, the temple-residence of Kumari, the virgin goddess, regarded by Hindus as the incarnation of Parvati and by Buddhists as the incarnation of Tara. Often referred to as the "living goddess", she is a maiden selected by esoteric rites from a group of three- to five-year old Buddhist Newar girls of Guwaju caste. Her divinity endures until puberty, when she returns to secular life and is entitled to marry. During her term of office she lives in seclusion and carries out prescribed ritual duties, sanctifying with her presence such ceremonial occasions as Indra Jatra and Bhottu Jatra.

The Kumari's dwelling is an imposing red-brick building, erected by Jaya Prakash Malla who initiated the cult of the virgin goddess. The entrance, flanked by stone lions, leads into a square sunken court surrounded by apartments; in the centre is a stone fountain. Visitors are permitted to enter the courtyard from where the Kumari may sometimes be seen at a first-floor window. A small donation is expected, but no photographs may be taken.

From Kumari Chowk a return to Rani Pokhari may be made by turning right down Ganga Path; cross the junction of Sukra Path and Juddha Sadak, where there is a statue of Maharaja Juddha Shumshere; the Nepal Bank is on the right. Continue down Juddha Sadak, pass under the modern archway and turn left into Kanti Path; Rani Pokhari lies approximately 500 metres to the north.

ROUTE 2

KATHMANDU. Southern Quarter of the Old City

From Kasthamandapa pass between Simha Sattal and Nasa Sattal and proceed on the ancient south-running thoroughfare known as Chikanmugal. To the left are two 2-storied temples both dedicated to Vishnu; an enshrined image of Manjuśri, standing a little back from the road is considered the oldest representation of the deity in the Kathmandu Valley. At the first major cross-roads is a 2-storied pagoda temple dedicated to Vishnu; the west-running road leads to Maru Tol and Bhimsen Temple; the east-running road passes between Tama and Buddha Bahals to Om Bahal and the sanctuary of **Jor Ganesh**; the path continuing east passes Bhaku Bahal, turns right, skirts the rear of the Nepal Bank and Kicha Pokhari and arrives in the vicinity of the delapidated palace of the 19th-century Prime minister Bhimsen Thapa. To the right is **Dhara Hara**, a watch tower erected in 1825 by Queen Tripurasundari; damaged by earthquake in 1834 and 1934, it has twice been rebuilt.

Return to the Vishnu Temple in Chikanmugal, turn left and continue south. At the next major cross-roads is **Jaisi Deval**, a pagoda temple built in 1687/88 and dedicated to Kumar;

turn left and proceed eastwards through Kila, Iku and Onta Bahals to Lagan Bahal, where there is a *chaitya* of unknown date dedicated to **Adinath**; restored in 1297 by Bandhava Singha, it stands on a stone-faced, 2-terraced basement with small *chaitya* set at the four corners of the upper terrace. Shrines of the Dhyani Buddhas decorate the base of the dome; the spire is crowned with a gilt *chattra*. Nearby is a temple dedicated to Vishnu.

East of Lagan Bahal is the **Arsenal**. Pass Taa Bahal and turn sharp right. To rejoin Chikanmugal proceed westwards through No, Bara Barse, Innar and Musum Bahals. At the shrine of **Humata Narayan**, turn left and descend to the main Tripureswar–Kalimati highway. The east-running highway leads to the Bagmati Bridge at the southern end of Ram Shah Path; it passes the pagoda temple of **Machali Ajima** and crosses the Tukucha river. In Kalomachan, south of the road, stands the temple dedicated to **Satya Narayan**, the largest domed temple in the Kathmandu Valley. The building, commenced by Bhimsen Thapa, was completed by Maharaja Jang Bahadur Rana in 1873 on the site, so it is said, of the mass graves of the victims of the Kot massacre.

The square sanctum, raised on a 3-stepped podium, has doors carved with the figures of Vishnu and Lakshmi. The four corners of the entablement carry gilt dragons at first and octagonal turrets at second storey level. The dome is surmounted by a gilt finial. In the courtyard are four, octagonal domed chapels; the enshrined images are Vishnu in his incarnated forms and his consort Lakshmi. Before the temple entrance a large bronze **Garuda** is mounted on a pedestal, and small stone garudas are set before the four domed chapels. The central monument in the temple courtyard is a gilt statue of Maharaja Jang Bahadur in full court dress; the pedestal bears a laudatory inscription recounting his exploits.

To return to Rani Pokhari, turn left outside the Satya Narayan temple, and follow the main highway through Tripureswar; bear right at the road junction, pass the National Stadium and proceed north along Kanti Path to Rani Pokhari.

ROUTE 3

KATHMANDU. Northern quarter of the Old City.

From Kasthamandapa proceed north, passing to the east of the Ashok Vinayak Temple, and further on, to the west of the Kot. Continue to the junction of the north-running road and the east-running road, Chochachen Galli. On the left is **Yetkha Bahal**, where to the west of a "monastic" square, is the oldest standing temple in the Kathmandu Valley. Three gilt finials surmount the single-tier roof; four of the original roof-struts survive and are carved with representations of *yaksi*. Opposite Yetkha Bahal is Taram Bahal and the sanctuary of **Kankeswari**.

At the next major cross-roads, where the north-running road meets Kilaghar and Nacho Pacho stands a pagoda temple dedicated to Shiva and a shrine of **Sveta Kali**. Adjacent to the Shiva temple, in a dilapidated courtyard, is the window known as **Desemadaj Jha**, one of the most remarkable examples of Newari wood carving in the Kathmandu Valley.

On the left of the north-running thoroughfare is the pagoda temple of **Nara Devi**, a landmark on the medieval trade route entering Kathmandu from Rasuwa Garhi and the Tibetan frontier.

Turn right (east) down Kilaghar. On the right is the entrance to **Itum Bahal**, where many *chaitya* stand in an unpaved courtyard. Enter **Parvate Keshchandra Krit Mahavihara,** "Great monastery built by Keshchandra of the Pigeons", considered one of the oldest monastic complexes in Kathmandu. It is dated, according to the record of images donated to the monastery, 1382/83. The single-roofed pagoda temple forms one side of a "monastic" square which encloses a *chaitya*. The tympanum over the main entrance displays Mara's temptation of Buddha, with Surya and Chandra in their sky chariots appearing in two medallions below; above is Buddha preaching to devotees. Of the many carved roof-struts to either side of the eastern entrance one to the left and two to the right bear carvings of early-type *yakshi*. On the tympanum over the sanctum door is a multi-headed Maha Vajradhara; six of the struts flanking the door bear carvings of the Dhyani Buddhas, four of whom are paired with Lokapala, guardians of the four quarters. Set in the north-east wall of the courtyard is a painted mask of Guru Mapha, whom the Chronicles credit with the building of Itum Bahal. Four large repoussé-work plaques set on the northern façade illustrate episodes of the Guru Mapha legend, which provides sanction for the folk rite performed at Tundikhel during the Pachare celebrations.

Return to Kilaghar and proceed east; two, 2-storied temples dedicated to Vishnu and Ganesh, and the **House of the White Elephant** stand on the north and a 2-storied pagoda temple dedicated to Shiva on the south side of the thoroughfare. At the ruined Shiva Temple standing at the junction of Kilaghar and Kel Tol turn left. Proceed to the locality known as **Bangemuda,** situated at the junction of Nhenkan Tol and Nyakha Bahal. Here in a small piazza is a 2-storied pagoda temple dedicated to Narayan, which has several finely carved 15th-century roof-struts; close-by is a remarkable early stone bas-relief of Buddha with devotees grouped at the master's feet. Continue on the north-running road passing an ancient *sattal* and **Kumara-Sambhavan,** a Lichhavi-period stone relief. A little further on, to the left, is **Singha Vihara,** an ancient site containing several stone inscriptions and sculptures of the Lichhavi period. The large, elliptical-shaped *chaitya,* known as **Shriga Chaitya** (Kathe Simbhu), is dedicated to Adi Buddha and stands in the centre of a paved courtyard. The building was commenced by Narendra Malla, son of Umar Malla in the 15th century; Pratap Malla took over the construction in 1647/49, but died shortly after and the work was never completed. The *chaitya* is encircled by shrines dedicated to the Dhyani Buddhas, and carved and perforated stone tablets, symbolising the Buddha consorts. Stone slabs on the third terrace enclosing the *chaitya* are carved in relief with figures of Bodhisattvas, Lamas, Siddhas and Buddhist symbols. To the right of Shriga Chaitya is a fine 8th-century stone relief of Avalokiteśvara, behind which, in a narrow alley, is a small stone wall-plaque of early date carved in relief with the figures of Shiva, Parvati and their first-born son Karttikeya. Set in the wall, near the entrance to **Dharma Kirti Vihara** is an ancient stone relief of Padmapani Lokeśvara.

East of Singha Vihara is the lion-guarded entrance of **Nagha Vihara.** Inside on the right stands a stone *pranali,* incorporating decorative panels of the Lichhavi period; the 8 ft. (2·5 me.) long stone slabs display carvings of divinities, animals and trees set against a stylised mountain background; there is a remarkable 8-9th-century *uma-maheśvara* bas-relief set up to the left of the *pranali.*

From Nagha Vihara continue north to **Thahity Tol.** A small *chaitya* erected, according to an inscription leaning against the dome, in 1523/24, is believed to mark the site of a dried-out spring from which gold, not water, once flowed. To the south, in a small square, four bronze monkeys support a bronze canopy over a bell-shaped *chaitya.* **Kwa Bahal,** with a vihara containing a cupola-roofed temple is situated north of Thahity Tol; the images of Manjuśri and Tara set in the porch walls are inscribed with the dates 1676 and 1668.

Follow the south-east-running road from Thahity Tol (that would lead the visitor to Asan Tol). On the right is the 3-storied pagoda temple dedicated to **Indrayani** and opposite, the low entrance to **Dhvaka Bahal,** a complex of buildings and courts characteristic of the dwelling pattern of later non-celibate Buddhist communities. In an open court a stone *pranali* stands in association with a small Lichhavi-type *chaitya*; inset in the wall of the dome are the figures of the Dhyani Buddhas, and on the tiered base are found standing images of Sakhya Muni and Avalokiteśvara, each flanked by devotees. The undated, largely defaced inscription round the base of the dome is in Gupta characters.

To visit **Musya Bahal** and **Chusya Bahal** it is convenient to return from Dhvaka Bahal to Thahity Tol and take the east-running lane. Musya Bahal lies on the right. The pagoda temple dates from the 17th century. The central figure of the tympanum is Vairocana and some of the roof-struts are carved with representations of the Dhyani Buddhas, their appropriate mounts and weapons. Eighteen other struts carry figures of Bodhisattva on the upper, and benefactors on the lower sections. Further east lies Chusya Bahal. The tympanum over the temple door is dated 1673. In construction and decoration the temples of Musya Bahal and Chusya Bahal are similar, but the carvings on the roof-struts of the latter show greater variation; the five feminine Buddha partners, all named, appear on the struts to the right of those carved with the figures of the Dhyani Buddhas; twelve of the exterior struts carry on the upper sections the figures of the twelve defenders and on the lower the twelve lunar mansions; a further sixteen lunar mansions are carved on the lower sections of sixteen of the eighteen interior struts.

A return to Kanti Path may be made by following the narrow lane eastwards; at the junction with Kanti Path turn right; Rani Pokhari lies approximately 150 yd. (150 me.) to the south.

EXCURSIONS FROM KATHMANDU

Kathmandu is the pivot of Nepal's communication system. Tourists dependent on air and motorised transport should note that many excursions from Kathmandu require a return to the capital. Those planning round trips combining one or more excursions should be prepared for cross-country journeying on foot. In the absence of an official survey, distances given must be taken as approximate.

ROUTE 4

KATHMANDU—LALITPUR

Lalitpur, Lalita Patan—"Beautiful City", now often called Patan, was known in medieval times as Lalitabrunna (Newari: Yella; Tibetan: Ye-ran). Tradition relates that Gautama Buddha visited the area in the 6th century B.C. and to the 3rd century B.C. Ashokan missionary influence are ascribed the directional *chaitya* still standing on the northern, southern, western and eastern outskirts of the town.

According to the Chronicles, however, Lalitpur was founded by King Veera Deva in A.D. 299. The capital of the Lichhavi, Thakuri and early Malla dynasties, it was an intermediary in the Indo-Tibetan Trade and, renowned as a seat of culture and learning, it attracted scholars and artists from both north and south of the Himalayas. Remaining the nominal seat of government after Jayasthiti Malla (1380-1395) transferred the royal residence to Bhadgaon, it became on Yaksha Malla's death (1482) the capital of the realm apportioned to his daughter.

The 16th century brought domination by Kathmandu, from whose royal line subsequent kings of Lalitpur were descended. In the 17th and 18th centuries, Lalitpur, using the feudatories of Kirtipur in the west and Pharping in the south as intermediaries, engaged in commercial relationships with the neighbouring Tanahu, Gorkha, and Palpa, states in which her coinage was current. The most notable of the kings who in the 17th and early 18th centuries augmented the earlier fame of Lalitpur were Sidhhinarasimha Malla (1620-1661), Srinivasa Malla (1681-1684), Yogendra Malla (1684-1705), Vishnu Malla (1729-1745) Rajyaprakasa Malla (1745-1758) and Visvajita Malla (1758-1760).

The decline in prosperity, which followed the establishment of Kathmandu as Prithivi Narayan's capital, was arrested in 1951 when the opening up of the Kathmandu Valley began to offer increased opportunities to the craftsmen and artisans forming a substantial part of Lalitpur's population. During the last two decades the goldsmiths, silversmiths, woodcarvers and workers in bronze, brass and copper have profited from the expanded demand for art-wares both for sale to tourists and for export overseas.

Leave Kathmandu at the southern end of Ram Shah Path, cross the Bagmati Bridge. Bear right at the Nepal Engineering Institute, and continue through Phulchok to the **Western Ashok Chaitya**. Turn left, entering the town through Na, Sēbal, Gawal and Māhapal Tols and proceed to Mangal Bazaar, the quadrangle fronting the royal palace.

3 mi. (5 km.) **Lalitpur** (pop. 147,323), the oldest existing city in the Kathmandu Valley, is situated on a low plateau lying south of Kathmandu. The Bagmati River runs along the northern and eastern borders of the town, and to the west and south are the 20th-century residential suburbs of Phulchok, Kopundol, Jhamsikhel and Jawalakhel. The ancient city is centred on an east-west, north-south axis at the junction of the trade routes which in medieval times brought prosperity to the town. Today the population is composed largely of Newari-speaking Buddhists, who support the largest number of *vihara* (149 *vihara* and 18 *maha*, or great *vihara*) of any city in the Kathmandu Valley.

Deotalli Darbar, the palace of the Malla kings, encloses Mangal Bazaar on the east. It was built by Siddhinarasimha Malla (1620-1661), and enlarged by Srinivasa Malla (1661-1684) and Vishnu Malla (1729-1745). Behind the red brick façade only four of the numerous courts traditionally believed to have comprised the Darbar remain.

Sundari Chowk, lying to the south, was built by Srinivasa Malla in the 17th century. The entrance is flanked by the figures of Hanuman, Ganesh and Varaha, the boar incarnation of Vishnu. The interior court is surrounded on three sides by the storied royal apartments, the windows and overhanging balconies supported by struts carved with figures in erotic poses. A fine oval, stone-bath decorated with a frieze of puranic deities and with a coiled-snake surround stands in the centre of the court; the *makara*-headed water-spout is set with the copper-gilt figures of Vishnu and his consort Lakshmi. Elsewhere in the court are stone figures of Ganesh, Hanuman, an eight-headed Shiva and a pair of lion-guardians. The tympanums over the doors are of fine workmanship. Especially remarkable is the representation of Surya, the Sun-god, riding in a seven-horse chariot driven by Arjuna.

The court has recently been restored and is now open to the public.

Mul Chowk, built by Siddhinarasimha Malla, lies to the north of Sundari Chowk. Before the entrance stands the great bell dedicated to Taleju; erected in 1736/37 it replaced the original 1703/04 bell now hanging in the temple of Machhendra. The *chowk* was re-constructed by Srinivasa Malla in 1665/66 after it had been severely damaged by fire. To the north of the court is the circular 5-storied **Degutalle** temple tower; and to the south the 4-storied temple dedicated to **Taleju Bhavani**, before whose portals stand the statues of Sri and Lakshmi. The main sanctuary of **Taleju** is situated at first-floor level to the north of Mul Chowk. It was built by Siddhinarasimha Malla; destroyed, once by fire in 1662/63 and again by earthquake in 1934, it has twice been rebuilt. A **Memorial Pillar** surmounted by the gilded, kneeling figure of Yogendra Malla stands in Mangal Bazaar opposite the entrance of the Taleju sanctuary.

Mani Chowk, the most northerly of the palace courts, was erected by Vishnu Malla in 1733/34. Access is by **Sundokha**, a richly gilded entrance with doors faced with embossed copper-gilt panels; the figures of the gilded tympanum are Parvati and Shiva, Ganesh and Kumar. Above Sundhoka at first-floor level is the gilded window at which the sovereign made public appearances; the *chowk* houses a shrine containing a 13th-century image of Lakshmi Narayan and a small museum.

Nathe, or **Natyeśvara Chowk** is approached through a vestibule lying between Mani Chowk and the temple of Taleju. In Malla times the open court was used as an auditorium for ritual dances and dramatic performances. The west wall carries a frieze of figures in erotic poses.

The **Royal Garden**, situated to the east of the palace, is approached through Mul Chowk. Within the walled enclosure is **Kamal Pokhari**, a large, brick-lined tank constructed by Siddhinarasimha Malla in the 17th century.

Mangal Bazaar, the quadrangle facing the royal palace, is the economic and cultural centre of Lalitpur and, reputedly, the Managriha whose magnificence was noted by medieval Chinese travellers. A visit to Mangal Bazaar on festival days, when devotees worship at the many shrines, or at the time of the morning market which operates between the monuments is rewarding. Of the many temples disposed in the court the most important are as follows. The octagonal *sikhara* temple dedicated to **Chasing Deval** (Krishna) was erected by the Queen Mother Yogamati in 1722/23. The 2-storied pagoda temple dedicated to **Hari Shanker** (Vishnu/Shiva) was erected in 1704/05 by Rudramati, the daughter of Yoganarendra Malla; the pillars of the ambulatory are surmounted by a running *torana* and the stone plinth is carved with mythological scenes. The 2-storied pagoda temple dedicated to **Jagannarayan** was erected in 1565/66 by Purandara Simha; the pillars supporting the roof are carved with the divinities of the Vaishnavite pantheon and the roof-struts bear images of the incarnated forms of Vishnu on the upper, and of characters drawn from the Prahlada life-story on the lower sections. The *shikara* temple, known as **Krishna Mandir**, dedicated to Krishna and his consort Radha, was erected in the mode of the Pancha Mahal at Fatepur Sikri by Siddhinarasimha Malla in 1636/37. Considered the finest example of the *shikhara* style in Nepal, it stands 5 storeys high, with a series of carved stone porticos and a curvilinear steeple mounted on a square entablement; the walls of the sanctum carry friezes illustrating the Ramayana and Mahabharata. In front of the temple stands a pillar, 3 ft. (1 me.) high and 3 ft. (1 me.) in circumference, surmounted by an image of Garuda. The 2-storied pagoda temple dedicated to **Visvanatha** (Bhai Devala), was erected by Siddinarasimha Malla in 1625/26; the lion guardians on the northern steps were set up by Chief Minister Bhagirath Bhaiya in 1676/77. The pagoda temple dedicated to **Bhimsen** was converted from a single to a 3-storied building by Srinivasa Malla in 1680/81; the sanctuary lies on the first floor behind a seven-winged, gilded window; the black stone lion-guardians are dated 1706/07 and the gilded lions 1656/57; the carvings on the roof-struts represent male and female personages of the Mahabharata and are dated 1679/1680.

Across the quadrangle, opposite the Visvanatha temple, and situated north of Mani Chowk, is a small piazza in which stand a watering place, a rest house and **Mani Mandap**, a tiled roof pavilion with a black stone seat. Installed in 1700/01 for use at royal gatherings and the crowning of monarchs, it is decorated with a gilded 7-headed serpent, the emblem of Vishnu.

The **Archaeological Garden** lies to the east of the Darbar and may most conveniently be approached through Mul Chowk. It contains some remarkable stone sculptures of the early and medieval periods.

The major sites of architectural interest in Lalitpur are to be found grouped to either side of the east-west and north-south thoroughfares which lead from Mangal Bazaar to and beyond the great **Ashok Chaitya** standing on the northern, southern, eastern and western outskirts of the town; these monuments, of varying size and height, are presumed to date from Lichhavi or even earlier times, but centuries of neglect have reduced their artistic interest; the central *chaitya* which completed the classical *mandala* formation is no longer identifiable.

The road leading to the Eastern Ashok Chaitya leaves the south-east corner of Mangal Bazaar and, passing in front of the Land Office, continues through Haurkha Tol to Saugal Tol, where in a piazza are temples dedicated to Mahadev, Shiva and Vishnu; to the left, a statue of Surya, dated 1082/83 stands before a 2-storied temple dedicated to Lakshmi Narayan.

From Saugal Tol an east-running road leads to Chyasal Tol and temples dedicated to Ganesh, Durga, Mahadev and a shrine of Ganesh; an early *uma-maheśvara* bas-relief is set in the stone lined watering-place.

Return to Saugal Tol and continue southwards to Sundhara Tol, passing on the right a pagoda temple dedicated to Krishna. Temples dedicated to Krishna and Uma-Maheśvara (ruined) stand in the piazza; to the east is an early *uma-maheśvara* bas-relief, and, in Hena Bahal, a statue of Bhimsen.

From Sundhara Tol a side trip may by made to Mahaboudha Vihara and Rudra Varna Mahavihara. Turn right and, in *c.* 100 yd. (100 me.), turn right again. **Mahaboudha Vihara** stands at the end of a narrow lane in a "monastic" courtyard. The *shikhara* temple was erected, according to Regmi, in the 13th century by the Buddhist priest Abbaye Vajracharya. Dedicated to Maya Devi, the mother of Sakya Muni, it is said to be a copy of the Bodh Gaya shrine which marks the place of Buddha's enlightenment. The temple stands *c.* 75 ft. (22·50 me.) high, and is constructed entirely of moulded terracotta and bricks, each of which bears a buddha-imprint. The tapering steeple has decorated apertures at spaced intervals and is surmounted by *chakra* and *chattra*. Small replicas of the steeple are mounted at the four corners of the entablature, and rows of buddha-images are set in niches at first floor level. The enshrined divinity is **Sakya Muni**, approached through an east-facing porch; above, shrine-chambers in the steeple, placed one above the other, contain images of Amitabha, a stone *chaitya*, a *dharma dhatu-mandala* and a *vajra dhatu-mandala*. The temple was destroyed by earthquake in 1934 and rebuilt according to the specifications of a model preserved in another Lalitpur *vihara*.

At the entrance to Mahaboudha Vihara turn right and proceed to U-Bahal and **Rudra Varna Mahavihara**, a monastic foundation with an enclosed pagoda temple. The *vihara* is a foundation of the Lichhavi king, Sivadeva (*c.* 590-604); it was restored by Rudra Deva II (*c.* 1167-1174). A fine figure of Buddha and many interesting works in stone and bronze are disposed in the courtyard.

Return to Sundhara Tol, continue through Dhālchē to Thyagal Tol where there are two temples dedicated to Ganesh, the House of the **White Elephant** and, on the left of the piazza, a stone *uma-maheśvara* relief dated 1011/12. In *c.* 400 yd. (400 me.) the **Eastern Ashok Chaitya** can be seen on the left of the road.

A side trip from Thyagal Tol may be made to Bhinche Bahal and **Mayur Varna Mahavihara**, one of the few *vihara* founded in Lichhavi times which can still be identified by name. Behind the pagoda temple is an ancient enshrined image of Avalok-Iteśvara and next to it a statue of Buddha.

To visit the temples of Rato Machhendranath and Minnath return to Mangal Bazaar and turning sharp left into Taungal Tol take the south-running road that leads to the Southern Ashok Chaitya. Pass three temples dedicated to Narayan and an ancient *sattal*. At the junction of an east-running road are temples of Narayan and Shiva-Parvati. **Minnath Temple** is situated on the left of the road in Thepat Tol. The entrance lies behind an ancient stone-lined watering place, inset with buddha- and *uma-maheśvara* images. The free-standing pagoda temple dedicated to Minnath, known locally as Chakwa Deo, stands in a walled courtyard. The two-tiered roof is surmounted by a bell-shaped finial mounted on a metal superstructure. The gilded shrine door and tympanum are set in walls covered, some 20 years ago, with green, white and floral porcelain tiles. The enshrined image, between whose eyes is set a precious jewel, is associated with ceremonial traditions dating from the 3rd century A.D.

Cross Taungal Tol and continue westwards.

Rato Machhendranath Temple stands in a walled court, surrounded by a small park. The original temple, believed to date from the 5th century, still stands on one side of the *vihara* courtyard, its roof-struts carved with different forms of Lokeśvara. The present pagoda temple, surmounted by a bell-shaped finial and *chattra* mounted on the heads of four standing serpents, was erected in the 13th century. In 1664/65 Srinivas Malla repaired the building and gilded two of the roofs, the third being gilded by Jayaprakash Malla in 1726/27. The three-storey building has three chambers placed one above the other. In the ground-floor sanctum, enclosed by silver plated doors, is the enshrined image of the red-painted Rato Machhendra, so admired in the 13th century by Chos-rje-dral (Dharmasvamin). According to the newly published treatise on his biography, he noted the miraculous image of Avalokiteśvara made of sandalwood, of red colour, in the aspect of a five-year-old boy. The image was then in the *vihara* of Bukham (Bungamati), the temple to which the divinity repairs for six months of the year. The ceremonies recorded in the biography tally with those enacted today.

In front of the temple are finely moulded animal bronzes, the symbols of the Tibetan calendrical year, mounted on 3 ft. (1 me.) high pillars. The **Southern Ashok Chaitya** stands to the left of the road, *c.* 500 yd. (500 me.) due south.

Return to Mangal Bazaar; from the Bhimsen Temple follow the road leading north to the Northern Ashok Chaitya. At the first cross-roads a temple dedicated to Krishna stands in Sotha Tol. (See below for Hiranayana Mahavihara and Kumbeśvara Temple lying north, and Pim Bahal lying south of the west-running road.) Continue northwards, passing between a 3-storied Krishna temple and a Narayan temple. Beyond a **Joshi** family temple, turn right into Kilimi Tol where, in a small temple there is an *uma-maheśvara* bas-relief dated 986/987. Continue on the north-running road through Kubal Tol; pass a 2-storied Uma-Maheśvara and a Krishna Temple; at the bend of the road is a statue of Padmapani. In *c.* 100 yd. (100 me.) the **Northern Ashok Chaitya** is to be seen on the left of the road. Continue through Sik Bahi to the 3-storied temple dedicated to **Chaumunda.** The north-running road leads to the Bagmati River, the Sakamul bridge and the Baneswor locality of Kathmandu; the east-running road terminates at the **Jagannath Temple.**

To visit Hiranayana Mahavihara return to the 3-storied Krishna temple standing in Sotha Tol; at the junction of Kva Bahal, Kwalaku Tol and Dhalache Tol turn north. **Hiranayana Mahavihara** stands on the left of the road in Kva Bahal. Founded in the 11th century by Bhaskara Varma as a monastery for celibate monks, it is one of the most ancient and today one of the richest monastic foundations in Lalitpur. The decorated doorway of the main entrance leads through a small fore-court; a black stone portal, surmounted by a 1759/60 gilded *torana* whose central figure is Buddha opens on to the main court; the guardians of the steps are gilded stone elephants mounted on tortoises and carrying riders attired in Malla costume.

In the centre of a sunken court stands a 3-storied, gilt-roofed pagoda temple enshrining a silver-plated *chaitya* dating from the 17th century. The dwellings of those who serve the shrine are situated to the right and left of the court and are separated from it by a railed-off pavement. Copper-gilt griffins decorate the four corners of the shrine-roof and from the eaves hang rows of copper-gilt repoussé-work plaques. In front of the shrine is a copper-gilt *vajra dhatu-mandala*. The doors of the sanctum, faced with copper-gilt repoussé-work panels, are set in a double pilaster frame and surmounted by an elaborately worked tympanum, whose central figure is Padmapani Avalokiteśvara.

The north side of the court is occupied by a 3-storied gilt-roofed temple, enshrining the gilded image of a seated Lokeśvara. The gilt and silver embellishments, dating largely from the 17th century, are of great ornateness. The guardians of the steps are elephants and griffins.

Raised on pedestals in the four corners of the *vihara* court are statues of **Padmapani Lokeśvara.** The famous 14th-century statue of **Avalokiteśvara**, represented standing, the right hand outstretched, the left holding the stem of a lotus is now housed inside the *vihara.* Ascent to the first floor prayer hall is by a narrow stair at the north-east corner of the courtyard. The walls are painted with frescoes of Mahayana divinities, executed by a Tibetan painter from Kyirong. At one end of the room is an altar and rows of seats for lamas and lay folk. Arranged on shelves is a library of wood-bound, block-printed volumes of the Mahayana scriptures.

The doorway at the western corner of the *vihara* courtyard gives on to a series of large, dwelling-enclosed courts in which there are numerous *chaitya*, temples and other monuments.

Leave Hiranayana Mahavihara by the eastern door, turn left and proceed some 170 yd. (170 me.). On the left is an extensive stone-lined watering place associated with a Ganesh shrine.

Kumbeśvara Temple, situated on the right of the road, is a complex of temples, shrines and stone-lined tanks surrounded by a brick wall. The great pagoda temple dedicated to Shiva was built by Jayasthiti Malla in the 15th century, the finial being added, according to an inscription in 1492/93. The 5-tiered roof stands 75 ft. (22·50 me.) high; the 4 ft. (1·20 me.) high plinth measures 27 ft. (8·10 me.) by 25 ft. (7·50 me.). The idols in the sanctum are two, 3 ft. (1 me.) high *lingam*, one of copper-gilt carved with the faces of Shiva, the other of gold, the body encircled by a coiled snake.

The rectangular stone-lined tank situated to the north-west of the courtyard is fed by a natural spring said to be connected with the waters of the sacred Gosainkund Lake in the Langtang Himal. The images of Ganesh, Narayan, Sitala, Basuki, Buari, Kirtimukhi and Agama Devata associated with the tank were erected by Jayasthiti Malla in the 15th century.

To the south of the courtyard stands the temple of **Unmatesvar Bhairab**, whose life-sized wooden statue is set in a latticed niche; at times of festival his erect penis is draped with flowers offered by barren women.

Return to the junction of Kva Bahal, Kwalaku Tol and Dhalache Tol. Proceed on the north-west-running road, the old Lalitpur-Kathmandu highway, which passes through an ancient Lalitpur gateway. In *c.* 600 yd. (600 me.) a 2-storied temple dedicated to Ganesh stands on the right of the road; opposite, a south-running road leads past a 2-storied Shiva Temple and a private sanctuary of the Joshi family, to Pim Bahal. A large rectangular tank lies in the centre of the *chowk* with, on the northern pavement, a 3-storied temple dedicated to Chandresvari. To the west stands the beautifully situated *chaitya* identified by some authorities as the **Central Ashok Chaitya**, the fifth of the directional *chaitya* of Lalitpur, to which old documents refer.

ROUTE 5

KATHMANDU—BHADGAON

Bhadgaon, known also as Bhaktagrama and as Bhaktapur, the "City of Devotees" (Newari: Khwapa) appears in the 14th-century *vamśāvali* as Khopa or Koawa. Although it is clear from the inscriptions translated by Gnoli, that Bhadgaon was already established in the 6th century, the 18th-century Chronicles ascribe the foundation of the town to Ananda Malla, who erected a royal palace and peopled the villages of Banepa, Pannauti, Nala, Dhulikhel, Khadpur, Choukot and Sanga.

In the 14th century Jayasthiti Malla transferred the royal residence from Lalitpur to Bhadgaon. Here the kings of Nepal continued to reside until the division of the kingdom in 1482, when Bhadgaon became the capital of Yaksha Malla's eldest son Raya Malla. The 16th-century king, Ekshah Mal Malla, enlarged his realm; at varying periods during the next 250 years Bhadgaon dominated not only the traditional territories of Changu Narayan, Thimi, Bode, Sankhu and Nakadeśa, but also Banepa, Dolalghat, Dhulikhel, parts of Kabre Palanchok and Pannauti; at the height of her power she controlled the Dudh Kosi basin up to the frontiers of Limbuan. Direct contact with the Tibetan border, often challenged by the kings of Kathmandu, resulted in profitable trade, particularly in the exchange of gold and silver bullion and the minting of coins for use in Tibet.

Of the three major towns in the Kathmandu Valley Bhadgaon has been least affected by modern developments. The medieval town plan has remained intact and agriculture and cottage industries have remained economically important. Predominantly a Hindu city, with a Newar population, speaking a distinctive dialect of Newari, it has 24 Buddhist *vihara* and a great many beautiful free-standing pagoda temples dedicated to Hindu divinities.

The architectural glory of Bhadgaon is largely due to Yaksha Malla (1428-1482), to his eldest son Raya Malla (1482-1505) and the successor kings Eksha Mal Malla (1505-1568), Jagat Prakash Malla (1644-1673), Jitramitra Malla (1673-1696), Bupatindra Malla 1696-1722) and Ranajit Malla (1722-1769). The special relationship existing between Prithivi Narayan Shah of Gorkha and Ranajit Malla of Bhadgaon at the time of the Gorkha incursions, saved the town from destruction, and prompted the defeated kings of Lalitpur and Kathmandu to choose it as a place of refuge.

Two routes lead to Bhadgaon. That via Thimi leaves Kathmandou by the Bagh Bazaar–Dilli Bazaar road, crosses the Dhobi Khola and Bagmati bridges and turns sharp right at the road junction; bear left at the next fork for **Thimi** (pop. 7500), an ancient settlement specialising in the growing of vegetables. The four pagoda temples in the village are dedicated to Narayan (Inaya Tol, 16th century), Bhairava (Degu Tol, built by Narasimha Duwar, 16th century), Mahadeo (15th century) and Bal Kumari, the protectress of ailing children. A footpath leads from Thimi across the Hanumante river to the important pagoda temple of **Dakshin Varahi.** Follow the road from Thimi, eastwards to Bhadgaon.

The alternative route leaves Kathmandu at the southern end of Ram Shah Path, passes through Thapathali and crosses the Dhobi Khola, Bagmati and Hanumante bridges. At the bifurcation take the left-hand fork, sign-posted Tribhuvan Airport. Turn sharp right and ascend through pine woodland to the top of the hill. Pass the Tundikhel and Military Barracks. On the left is **Siddha Pokhari** (Nau Pokhari), a stone-lined tank over 300 yds. (275 me.) long and 100 yds. (92 me.) broad. Constructed in the 15th century by Yaksha Malla it was, in 1674/75, linked by Jitramitra Malla with Nag Pokhari in the Bhadgaon Royal Palace by the channel known as Thanthu Rajakula. Siddhi Pokhari was damaged by Pratap Malla of Kantipur in 1662/63 and repaired by Jitamitra Malla in 1677/78; restoration work was carried out in the 19th century during the premiership of Bhimsen Thapa, when it was stocked with fish imported from China.

To the right of the road is **Bhaju Pokhari,** also constructed by Yaksha Malla. At the next road junction bear left, and passing **Guhe Pokhari** follow Etachhey Tol.

10 mi. (16 km.). **Bhadgaon** (pop. 33,877) is situated on high ground above the right bank of the Hanumante river, which flows on its eastern and southern flanks.

At the western approach to Bhadgaon stands the **Lion Gate,** erected by Bhupatindra Malla, who also installed the stone statues of Ugra Chandi and Bhairava on either side of the entrance. In front of the gate is a complex of temples dedicated to Jagannath, Bhadri (Vishnu), Rameshwar (Shiva) and Krishna which were badly damaged in the 1934 earthquake. Beyond is **Tripura Darbar,** the royal palace situated on the north side of a great quadrangle. Considered the most splendid of the medieval palaces of Nepal, it was founded by Yaksha Malla (1428-1482) and embellished by successive kings: Jagat Prakash Malla (1644-1673), Jitamitra Malla (1673-1696) and Bhupatindra Malla (1696-1722). The brick façade is broken at ground and first-floor level by symetrically placed triple and single windows and doorways of varying height and width. Of the reputed ninety-nine original courts seven remain. The entrance to **Malati Chowk,** situated in the western wing, is guarded by statues of Narasimha and Hanuman erected in 1697/98. The first floor of the 3-

storied building now houses the Bhadgaon National Art Gallery which contains a fine collection of Hindu and Buddhist scroll paintings of Tantric schools, palm leaf manuscripts and perhaps the best assembly of sculptured wood, stone, and bronze images in Nepal. North of Malati Chowk is **Kumari Chowk. Mul Chowk** lies to the east of Malati Chowk. It is entered through the golden gate, **Sundhoka**, erected by Ranajit Malla in 1729 and described by Percy Brown as "the richest piece of art work in the whole kingdom". It is set in an elegant single-storey porch whose gilded roof is decorated with mythical beasts, bell-shaped finials, triangular standards and an embossed metal arch; the two-fold door, faced with embossed copper-gilt panels is framed by pilasters decorated with *kalash* and figures of the mother goddesses; the central figure of the elaborate trifoil tympanum is the many-armed Goddess Taleju, flanked by Sri and Lakshmi. Before the entrance stands a **Memorial Pillar** set up by Ranajit Malla in memory of his father, Bhupatindra Malla, whose kneeling figure in devotional pose surmounts a lotus capital.

Beside the pillar hangs a large, decorated bronze bell installed by Ranajit Malla in 1737/38. Dedicated to Taleju, it is rung daily at the time of worship. Pass through Sundhoka and then into **Bhairav Chowk** which was built by Naresa Malla and refurnished by Bhupatindra Malla in the 17th century. To the left stands a late 17th-century stone *mukha lingam* carved on the north, east and west faces with elaborately crowned Shivas, and on the southern face with a Bodhisattva wearing a mitred head-dress.

The west side of Bhairava Chowk is occupied by the entrance to the temple dedicated to **Taleju**, the tutelary deity of the Malla kings. Gilded decorative elements set in symmetrical precision against the red brick wall, furnish a façade of unique splendour. In the centre, the two-fold gilded door is set in a five-fold pilaster frame; it is surmounted by a tympanum dated 1694/95, whose central figure is the sixteen-armed, four-headed Taleju Bhavani. Above is a five-fold gilded window, flanked by two smaller windows erected and gilded by Naresa Malla in 1636/37. Gilded statues of female divinities spaced at regular intervals at ground and first floor level, rows of embossed medallions, and plaques bearing *kalash* designs and dedicatory inscriptions are additional embellishments. The gilded pagoda roof was repaired by Bhupatindra Malla in the 18th century.

The interior of the temple, which only Hindus may enter, contains some interesting 15th-, 17th- and 18th-century wall paintings. Those ascribed to the 15th century are 5 × 10 inch (12 × 25 cm.) miniatures of *shakti* manifestations, arranged in three rows on the north-facing wall. The 17th- and 18th-century frescoes in the main courtyard depict divinities of the Hindu pantheon: Sumbha, Nisuma and Devi Bhairavi of the Markandeya Purana, dancing Vishnu and his consort Lakshmi, flute-playing Krishna and his cymbal-playing wife Radha and Garuda devouring his enemy the serpent; of particular interest is a series of tantric configurated figures: a dancing woman-elephant Ganapathihardaya, a human-elephant Lokapala, a human-bird Unmati, a human-serpent Kakot Naga with his consort Nagini and a man-animal Bhairava in *tandava* dance pose.

The 3-storied eastern wing of the Darbar is known as the **Palace of the 55 Windows**, named for the row of lattice-windows spanning the third-floor façade. The palace was erected by Yaksha Malla in the 16th century, restored by Bhupatindra Malla in the 18th century and rebuilt after the severe damage wrought by the 1934 earthquake. The royal bedroom, with interesting wall frescoes, is situated on the second floor and is open to the public. **Nag Pokhari** lies to the north of the Palace of the 55 Windows; it contains the royal bath, which was connected by the channel Tanthu Rajakula with the waters of Siddha Pokhari in 1687/88. In the course of recent repairs the palace's Newari roof-tiles have been replaced with the large, light-coloured products of the Chinese-sponsored factory in the vicinity.

The east-west aligned quadrangle fronting the palace is enclosed on the south by 2-storied buildings which were utilised by the officers of the palace administration. Many of the temples standing in the quadrangle suffered damage in the 1934 earthquake and some have never been repaired. Of the standing temples, four are important. The *shikhara* temple dedicated to **Maya Dyoga** (Shiva), erected during the reign of Jitamitra Malla in 1674/5 stands at the western end. To the east is the 40 ft. (12 me.) high *shikhara* temple dedicated to **Vatsala Devi** (goddess of dance); it was erected in 1671/72 during the reign of Jagatprakash Malla; the large bronze bell standing on the terrace was set up by Bhupatindra Malla in 1720/21. South of the Vatsala Devi temple is the 2-storied pagoda temple dedicated to **Shiva,** in his aspect Pashupati; built in the likeness of the great temple of Pashupatinath by Sumati Jayajitra Malla in 1628, it possesses a wealth of good wood carving. Adjoining the eastern wing of the palace is a group of largely ruined shrines and temples, the most important of which is the pagoda temple dedicated to **Siddhi Lakshmi.** It was erected in 1671/72 by Jagat Prakash Malla and restored by Ranajit Malla in the 18th century; the steps ascending to the sanctum are flanked on six levels by guardians in the form of horses, rhinoceros, man-lions, camels and, on the bottom step, female and male attendants carrying a child and a dog.

Leave the Darbar Square at the eastern corner, pass through **Laso Dhoka** gateway and enter Taomādi Tol. The temple called **Nyatapola,** dedicated to Siddhi Lakshmi, stands to the north of a large public square. Built by Bhupatindra Malla in 1700/02, it was consecrated in 1701/02. The 5-tiered pagoda roof, supported on carved struts projecting at an angle of 45°, stands on a 5-tiered podium. The steps ascending to the sanctum are flanked by paired stone figures, each pair representative of ten times the strength and power of the pair below; the mythical wrestlers Jayamel and Phaṭtu, elephants, lions, griffins and 2 ft. (75 cm.) high statues of Bhagini and Singhini.

Bhairava Temple is situated on the east of the square; in 1716/17 Bhupatindra Malla added a second storey to the original single storied building, and after the 1934 earthquake it was enlarged to a 3-tiered structure with gilt finials surmounting the roof. A brass mask of Bhairava is set on the façade at first floor level.

In a 2-storied shrine dedicated to Narayan which lies south of Bhairava's temple is a statue of Mahadev, known as Tila Mahadev, dated according to the pedestal inscription 1169/70.

To visit Chatur Varma Vihara and other temple sites lying to the north and north-east of Bhadgaon, it is convenient to return to the Darbar Square. Take the north-east running road, bear left and pass the Nagar Panchāyat building; on the right of the road is the low ornamented door of **Chatur Varma Vihara**, an ancient Buddhist monastic foundation with a fine enshrined silver image of Lokeśvara. The carvings in wood that ornament pillars, doors and windows are among the most beautiful in the Kathmandu Valley; the roof-struts carry representations of the Dhyani Buddhas, of Vairocana standing on two lions, Vajrsattva on two men and various manifestations of Lokeśvara. An inscription at the base of one of the struts records the date 1655.

Continue north-east, passing through Tolache Tol, Sukul Dhoka and Gomadi Tol to Inna Chowk. The thoroughfare ascends gently until it reaches Tapacha Tol, a large open piazza lined with *math*, two on the north and four on the south side. At the western end is a pagoda temple erected in 1645/55 and dedicated to Bhimsen. At the eastern end stands the **Dattaraya** (Dhattatreya) **Temple**; erected by Yaksha Malla in the 15th century, it was later restored by Viśva Malla. The 3-tiered pagoda temple is raised on a 5-stepped podium with the wrestlers, Jayamel and Phaṭtu, at the entrance. Dedicated to Brahma, Vishnu and Maheśwar, it is a foundation of the same sect of Yogins as Kasthamandapa of Kathmandu, which in its architectural proportions it resembles. On a pillar standing in front of the temple is a gilt-bronze Garuda.

To the south of the Dattareya temple is **Pujari Math**, a monastery of the Gorakhnath Yogins, also built in the reign of Yaksha Malla and restored by Viśva Malla. The building is remarkable for the high standard of the carving carried on wooden beams, pillars, lattice screens, doors and niches; particular attention may be given to the skilfully executed design of the sandalwood "peacock" window set in the east wall.

The Dattaraya temple and Pujari Math were sympathetically restored under the supervision of German experts in the winters of 1971 and 1972.

Visitors who feel inclined to view the artisan quarter of Bhadgaon should take the south-running lane that passes behind Pujari Math and descend gently through Talache Tole to Surya Mādhi Tol, where there is a pagoda temple dedicated to Garuda Narayan, dated, according to a pillar inscription, 1408/09.

The low-lying area north of the Hanumante River is inhabited by weaver and potter castes who ply their traditional crafts in the public thoroughfares.

ROUTE 6

KATHMANDU—NATIONAL MUSEUM—SVAYAMBUNATH

Leave Hanuman Dhoka, pass Kasthamandapa, and descend through Maru Tol to the Vishnumati Bridge. Proceed uphill through Tahachal and Chhaoni. On the left of the road is the **National Museum**; it contains sculptures in stone, bronze and copper-gilt and a few scroll paintings; displayed in a neighbouring building is a notable collection of arms and weapons, including a sword of Louis Napoleon (III) presented to Jang Bahadur Rana and a Tibetan leather cannon captured in the war of 1855/56. Admittance 10 a.m. to 5 p.m. Closed on Tuesdays.

On leaving the Museum continue westwards. Turn right and follow the road that skirts the base of Padmachala Hill, called in Newari Sri-yem-gum, "glorious hill of Yem". The stairway which ascends to Svayambunath Chaitya is on the left. 2 mi. (3 km.) **Svayambunath**, also known as Sengyu or Simbu is the most important centre of Buddhist worship in Nepal. The eastern approach is by a broad flight of c. 385 steps. At the foot of the climb are three large **Tri Ratna** images erected by Lachmindhar Singh Malla and his son Pratap Malla in 1637/38; to either side of the stairway are Buddha figures and the stone carved mounts of Buddhist deities: sun eagles, peacocks, horses, elephants and lions. A stone-paved terrace lying at a height of 500 ft. (175 me.) above the valley, crowns Padmachala Hill. It is enclosed by the ancient and modern storied dwellings of those who serve the site and *dharmasala*, shops, a museum, and a Buddhist library.

In the centre of the terrace stands **Svayambunath Chaitya**, the Self-existent One, said to have risen from the lotus flowering on the surface of the primaeval lake, Nagarahad, which once covered the Kathmandu Valley. Popularly believed to be over 2000 years old the *chaitya* is dedicated to Adi Buddha. The white plastered herispherical dome, 60 ft. (20 me.) in diameter and 30 ft. (10 me.) high, is surrounded by a wrought-iron balustrade and groupings of iron lamps and prayer wheels, inscribed with the sacred formula *om mani padme hum.* The gilded *torana*, painted on four sides with the "all-seeing" eyes of supreme Buddhahood, is decorated with flanges carrying the figures of the Dhyani Buddhas; at the four corners are 4 ft. (1·35 me.) high prayer wheels donated in the 17th century by Pratap Malla. The thirteen gilt-ring *harmika* is surmounted by a framework supporting two *chattra*, the upper donated by a Tibetan lama, who in 1639/40 also re-gilded the *torana* and the *harmika.* The central beam repaired by two visiting lamas from Lhasa in 1750/51 was, following storm damage, replaced in 1825/26, the costs being met by public subscription.

The dome of the *chaitya* shows signs of frequent riveting. An inset inscription dated 1372/73, addressing the *chaitya* as *dharma dhatu*, "the delighter of the world and all merciful", is said to relate to restorations carried out after the destruction wrought by the 14th-century Muslim invaders. Three other inscriptions record subsequent repairs by Siva Singh Malla in 1593/94, by Shiyah Mah, a Lama from Lhasa, in 1639/40 and by Pratap Malla in 1640-50.

The five brick and plaster chapels spaced round the dome were erected by Pratap Malla. Each contains a life-size image of a Dhyani Buddha, who with consort and attendants appear as the central figures of the gilt-repoussé tympanums and on the stone pedestals. The chapel entrances are protected by chain curtains, raised by devotees when making offerings; between the five chapels are five shrines dedicated to the Buddha consorts, each containing a stone tablet carved with the triangular emblem of female divinities, floral designs and representations of *kalash.* Stone and copper-gilt figures of female attendants and Newar donors appear inside the shrines and on the pedestals. Separating chapels and shrines are stone slabs decorated with Buddhist figures, symbols and emblems.

To the east of the *chaitya*, at the head of the eastern stair-way is a large copper-gilt *dharma dhatu-mandala* set up by Pratap Malla. The 6 ft. (2 me.) long *varja* rests on a copper-gilt disc engraved with 22 Buddhist symbols and a circular base decorated with the twelve symbols of the Tibetan calendrical year; the guardian lions associated with the *mandal* were also donated by Pratap Malla.

Two temples, **Partabpur** and **Anantapur,** donated by Pratap Malla, stand north and south of the eastern stairway; copper-gilt, bell-shaped finials and the drawn sword emblem of female divinities surmount the *shikhara* steeples. The enshrined images are Tantric female divinities and their spouses; flanking the entrances are woman-bird configured images.

Behind the southern Partabpur temple is a shrine dedicated to **Basundhara,** a consort of Manjuśri. The enshrined image, Basundhara flanked by Padmapani and Viswapani, is believed to be the oldest standing monument in the locality. The figures of the tympanum are Basundhara, flanked by Vajradhara and attendants and two Bodhisattvas and their consorts. The guardians of the entrance may be viewed in the Svayambu Museum.

Associated with the chapels of the Svayambunath Chaitya are several monuments of interest. In front of the northern chapel of Amoghasiddha is a square sunken water place, said once to have been the abode of mythical serpents. A small brass *vajra dhatu-mandala* is set before the south-east chapel of Vairocana; the guardian dragons were donated by Pratap Malla in the 17th century. Opposite the western chapel of Amitabha is a tall pillar surmounted by a copper-gilt peacock, Amitabha's emblem, and a two-tiered pagoda temple sacred to **Sitala Devi**, the small-pox goddess.

In the western precincts is a 9th century, 5 ft. 4 in. (1·80 me.) high relief of Sakya Muni wearing monk's robes with right hand outstretched and left hand touching the right armpit. To the north of the great Svayambunath Chaitya is a monastery, with before it, a temple housing a modern, life-size Buddha-image and the tall, bronze cauldron containing the sacred, everlasting fire, the symbol of Adi Buddha. To the west of the Sitala temple, close to the statue of Sakya Muni, is a *vihara* centred on an ancient *chaitya* and surrounded by 2-storied monks' dwellings.

Disposed over the terrace of Svayambunath Chaitya, particularly in the areas to the north and west, are stone and gilded images of divinities, and funerary and dedicatory *chaitya* of varying design. In particular the small 6th-century ashok-style *chaitya* and the *lingam-yoni-chaitya* configurated types should be noted.

North-west of Svayambunath, on a hillock known as Manju Parbat, is the *chaitya* dedicated to **Manjuśri**, the Bodhisattva believed to have hewn a passage through the Chobar Gorge and thus drained the lake which once covered the Kathmandu Valley. It stands in a small courtyard with a bronze canopy sheltering the *chaitya*. The courtyard and rest-house have recently been rebuilt and the images formerly associated with the *chaitya* have been cemented into the surrounding wall. The Dhyani Buddhas appear on the square plinth of *chaitya* in their directional positions. On the west face is a small shrine sacred to **Saraswati Devi** who, as the goddess of learning, receives the worship of both Hindus and Buddhists; before the shrine are the black stone footprints of her consort Manjusri.

North of the Sitala temple, a path descends to a terrace occupied by dwelling-houses, *chaitya*, shrines and monuments. A large tiled building, closed to the public, contains images of Tantric divinities. The guardians of the door are the six-handed, animal-headed Singhini and Baghini, and in front is a reputedly 18th-century figure of a seated Sayka Muni, flanked by mendicant monks. Near by is an enshrined image of an elaborately sculptured Tri Ratna.

The flagged stone path descending the wooded western shoulder of Padmachal Hill passes several buildings devoted to the teaching of Buddhism and joins the main road from Kathmandu below the Gelugpa monastery.

To visit **Ichangu**, a small settlement situated at the base of Mount Nagarjun, turn right and continue for *c.* 2 mi. (3 km.). The pagoda temple in the village is dedicated to Narayan, one of the four principal Vishnu shrines in the Kathmandu Valley. Standing on a site consecrated by Vijayakama Deva in 1199/1200, it was erected by Svarna Malla, son of Raya Malla after the famine of 1512/13. The enshrined image, said to have been dug out of the bed of the Bagmati River where it had been buried by Bhotiya, was installed by the Brahmin Saharsa Sivananda. Associated with the temple is an early classical stone sculpture and an inscription dated 1200/01. On a grassy hill above Ichangu a small pagoda temple dedicated to Bhagwati commands a magnificent view across the Kathmandu Valley.

The Ring Road can be used to proceed directly from the vicinity of Svayambunath to the Balaju Water Garden (route 9).

ROUTE 7

KATHMANDU—DEO PATAN—PASHUPATINATH—GUHYEŚVARI—CHABAHIL—BODHNATH—GOKARNA—CHANGU NARAYAN—SANKHU—KADGA JOGINI

Leave Kathmandu by the Bagh Bazaar–Dilli Bazaar road. Cross the bridge over the Dhobi Khola. At the next road-junction bear right and take the second major turning to the left.

3 mi. (4·5 km.) **Deo Patan–Devapatnam**, an ancient settlement with a long historical tradition. Known from inscriptions and from references in the Chronicles as Pasupata Ksetra, "City of Gods", and Navagriha; in the 3rd century B.C. it was the capital of Devapal, who married Emperor Ashoka's daughter Charumati. In the 6th century A.D. Sivadeva, whose capital was Vageśvari, is reported to have built a 9-storied palace called Kailasakuta in Deo Patan; he founded nine *tol* in the vicinity and in each set up an image of Ganesh. Kailasakuta palace was described in the Chinese Annals at the time of Sivadeva's son Narendradeva as being more than 400 ft. (130 me.) in circumference with three 7-storied terraces, accommodation for more than 10,000 men and four pavilions containing sculptures decorated with stones and pearls. The palace no longer stands, but the name Kailasakuta is associated with a large ruin-strewn mound in the vicinity.

The present village is inhabited largely by the families of the priests and attendants serving the Pashupatinath temple. In the street near the pagoda temple dedicated to Bhavaneśvara, an ancient *lingam*, carved with the four faces of Shiva is enshrined in a stone temple of later date. Other stone sculptures of note are a 12th-century stele carved with a composite image of Vishnu, Lakshmi and Garuda, and an 11th-century Vishnu riding Garuda, flanked by his consorts Sri and Lakshmi. The earliest of the numerous inscriptions in the village is engraved on a slate slab standing near a small Ganesh Temple; set up by Amsuvarma in the 7th century, it records in Gupta characters the erection of three *lingam* by members of his family and makes provision for their maintenance.

1·5 mi. (2·5 km.). **Pashupatinath** (pop. 2300), a temple complex sacred to Shiva, in his aspect Pashupati, Lord of the Animals. The temples, paved courts, tanks and *dharmasala* associated with the temple of Shiva extend along both banks of the Bagmati gorge; the west bank being known as Kailas and the east as Mrigasthalli. Vehicles must be left at the entrance to Kailas. Hindus only are permitted to enter the temples and descend to the banks of the Bagmati River, but other visitors may cross the main footbridge to a terrace on Mrigasthalli where a good view is obtained.

Shiva is the national deity of Nepal, and Pashupatinath, the national shrine, attracts pilgrims from all over Nepal and the Hindu lands south of the Himalaya; at Shivaratri more than 10,000 devotees assemble to celebrate the rites.

Though the site is undoubtedly an ancient centre of Shiva worship, the present temple of Shiva, situated to the left of the entrance to Kailas, was built by Jaisingh Ramadeva in the 13th century. The 16th-century Queen Ganga carried out extensive restoration work, re-gilded the roof and consecrated a subterranean passage linking her residence in Kathmandu with the temple precincts. After storm damage in 1687/88 Prithivendra Malla and his subjects are believed to have repaired the temple in twenty-four hours.

The 3-tiered pagoda temple dedicated to Shiva stands in a paved court, enclosed by the dwellings of priests and temple servants and *dharmasala*; access is by doorways placed to the north, south, west and east. The sanctum and cloistered ambulatory are decorated with elaborately carved and gilded woodwork. The gilt hanging banner and the roof finials were donated by Pratap Malla in the 17th century. In the 18th century King Rajendra Bikram Shah re-gilded the roof.

D. R. Regmi lists a 2nd-3rd century ruined *lingam* as lying outside the temple. The present *mukha lingam*, installed by Minister Jayasimharaman is of sandstone; it stands 3½ ft. (1·15 me.) high on a silver plated base 18 in. (50 cm.) high and 4 ft. (1·25 me.) in diameter. Over the *lingam* is suspended a silver lotus in a square frame. Inside the sanctum are several interesting images; a copper-cast Parvati set up in 1447/48 in the name of Sansara Devi, the mother of Yaksha Malla, stone figures of an 8th-century Lakshmi, a 1660/61 Vajramahakala, a 7th-century relief of Bachhaleśvari and the right-hand panel of a blueish-black limestone 9th-century frieze depicting the Heavenly Court of Vishnu.

Of the numerous images, *lingam*, shrines and temples which occupy the temple precints the following are the most noteworthy. A five-times life-size gilt **Nandi**, the bull-mount of Shiva which stands before the west temple door. Behind it is a 4 ft. 4 in. (1·35 me.) by 3 ft. 4 in. (1·10 me.) black slate slab recording Jayadeva's 8th-century donation of a golden lotus to the temple. To the left of the west door stands a sandstone slab inscribed in Newari characters that records the gift of a golden *kalash* to the temple of Pashupatinath. Opposite the northern temple door stands a 20 ft. (6·66 me.) high Trisula, the gilt trident emblem of Shiva, donated, according to the Chronicles, by Sankaradeva, the grandfather of Manadeva; associated with the trident is an inscribed stone which was originally the base of a *lingam* erected by Jayavarman during the reign of Manadeva in the 7th century. The donations of the kings of Kantipur to the shrines and statues standing within the temple precincts are: a stone image of Unmata Bhairava, the patron of ailing children set up by Sivasimha Malla in the 16th century; the shrine of Vasuki, and the images of Narashima and Kala Bhairab, erected by Pratap Malla in the 17th century and the image of Dakshin Kali, installed by Ratna Malla in the 16th century. Other notable monuments are an enshrined image of Raghunatha, an image of Chandeśvara, the shrine of Basant Naga and the 2-tiered temple dedicated to Bachhaleśvari. Of the many inscriptions on stone and copper two deserve mention: the inscribed stone, decorated with a trident and two *nandi*, recording Pratap Malla's gift of *tulapurusha* (the royal weight in gold, silver, and pearls) and one hundred horses to the temple of Pashupatinath in the 17th century; and an inscribed stone standing outside the southern gate of the temple, recording Sivadeva's 8th-century grant of a village to a fraternity of Buddhist monks residing in Sivadeva *vihara*.

Steps lead down from the temple courtyard to the Bagmati River, where for a distance of a quarter of a mile stone-paved terraces and numerous shrines line the banks on both sides of the gorge. On the Kailas bank rows of *dharmasala* provide shelter for the aged and the dying whose wish is to die with their feet in the sacred river; close to the water, clearly differentiated stone slabs serve as cremation platforms for kings, nobles and commoners whose ashes are scattered in the river.

Raised on a paved terrace above the Mrigasthalli bank are rows of *samadhi*, massive squared stone memorial shrines commemorating deceased members of the royal family and the nobility. The tallest was erected in the name of Maharaja Chandra Shumshere in 1829/30.

On the banks of the Bagmati are several remarkable stone sculptures which are unhappily accessible only to Hindus: a 6th-century *lingam* carved with the "lovely face" of Parvati, a 5th-6th-century "nobleman", and at the confluence of Tilganga and Bagmati a *vishnu vikranta* frieze fashioned from black limestone.

A stone stairway climbs the pleasantly wooded Mgristalli hill, where long ago Shiva is believed to have appeared in the form of a deer. Shrines and temples stand among the trees and on the top of the hill is a *math* of the Gorakhnath Yoginis with *dharmasala* to provide shelter for pilgrims.

Leave Kailas, turn right and proceed eastwards. Cross the Bagmati bridge at Gauri Ghat. 400 yd. (375 me.) **Guhyeśvari Temple** stands in the Islamantak grove, on the site where legend decrees a portion of the goddess' corpse fell as Mahadeo carried it southwards and where in her name the Bodhisattva Manjuśri is believed to have built a temple in the form of a three-leafed lotus. The present structure was erected by Pratap Malla in the 17th century. He installed the images of the Nau Durga on the walls of the sanctum, the shrines of Bhairava, Narasimha and Ganesh in the courtyard, the pillar topped with a gilded lion in front of the temple entrance, and he surrounded the precincts with a high wall, which denies entrance to all but Hindus.

The temple, designed after the tantric *yantra*, stands in a paved court surrounded by *dharmasala*. The flat roof is open in the centre and is surmounted by a copper-gilt construction terminating in four snakes who support a bell-shaped finial. The enshrined image is the *kalash* emblem of the goddess. Blood sacrifices offered in her name three times a year are made before the shrine of Bhairab in the temple courtyard.

2 mi. (3·6 km.). **Chabahil**, a small village with an architecturally insignificant but ritually important pagoda temple sacred to Ganesh. On the outskirts of the village is **Dhanju Chaitya**, known also as **Ca-Bahi**. Dedicated to Adi Nath, it is said to have been built by King Dharma Datta. The present structure probably dates from the 6th-7th centuries, but the site is associated with the name of Charumati, the daughter of Ashoka, who in the 2nd century B.C. married the Kshatriya Devapal. The earliest inscription on the site is of 1661/1662 and relates to repairs carried out by the Darbar of Deo Patan. The hemispherical dome is set on a circular plinth and surrounded by a pavement set with stones engraved with *mandala*. The *torana* is painted with the "all-seeing eyes of supreme buddhahood"; the solid pyramidal *harmika*, whose original gilt-copper plating was used to defray the expenses of the Malla King's defence against the Gorkha invasion of 1767/68 is of solid brick; it is surmounted by a bell-shaped finial.

During repairs to the central beam carried out in 1845/46 at the expense of Newars of Deo Patan, the dome was found to contain images of Buddhas and their consorts and a collection of coins.

Shrines of the Dhyani Buddhas are set at the four cardinal points on the base of the dome, with Vairocana, guarded by stone lions, placed to the right of Aksobhya; four stone slabs carved with images of their consorts stand between the shrines. Leaning against the base of the dome are stone slabs carved with the images of Bodhisattvas, Siddhas, divinities and *chaitya*; the most notable is the relief of a Naga king and a female devotee set into the revetment of the dome below the northern shrine of Amoghasiddhi. A 6th-7th-century standing cloaked Buddha figure is among the numerous images and small *chaitya* disposed over the paved courtyard. To the west of the Dhanju Chaitya stands a small *vihara* and to the north a tiled-roof building shelters a 16th-century seated image of Sakya Muni.

2½ mi. (4 km.). **Bauddha**, a small village, with dwelling-houses and shops situated to both sides of the road. 53 per cent. of the inhabitants are speakers of languages other than Nepali and Newari, many being northern hill peoples, religious specialists, and commercial and industrial entrepreneurs engaged in the tourist and pilgrim traffic.

On the left of the road is the entrance to **Bodhnath**, the largest *chaitya* and, after Svayambhu, the most important Buddhist shrine in Nepal. Called in Newari Khāsti and in Tibetan Bya-run-Ka'sor, it has been throughout historical times a pilgrimage centre for the Buddhists of Nepal, India, Tibet, China and Central Asia. The Nepalese Chronicles ascribe the building of the *chaitya* to Manadeva in 500 A.D.

The white-washed, brick and masonry hemispherical dome, 100 yd. (100 me.) in circumference, is surmounted by a squared *torana*, painted on four sides with the "all-seeing eyes of supreme buddhahood". The pyramidal *harmika*, plated with copper-gilt carries a gilded *chattra* and a bell-shaped finial. The height of the *chaitya* is 125 ft. (38 me.). Superimposed on the dome is a complicated series of terraces, accessible by a flight of steps. The entrance is flanked by prayer flags and the steps guarded by man-carrying elephants.

The base of the dome is enclosed by an outer wall in which a continuous row of prayer wheels in series of five are set in niches painted with the figures of the five Dhyani Buddhas. The circular paved court surrounding the *chaitya* is ringed by dwelling-houses offering lodging to pilgrims, or curios, religious artifacts and tibetan style clothing for sale. Visitors may watch the manufacture of silverware by the *cire perdue* process in ground-floor workshops. To the west of the *chaitya* is the chapel where religious rites are conducted; the stucco-faced building with green painted woodwork is the abode of the custodian of Bodhnath; known as the Chini Lama, he is the fourth generation of his family to hold this office. Monks of a Kagdyu sect occupy **Da-pdu Gompa** which stands to the left.

North of the *chaitya*, a sharp left turn leads down a lane where in a house on the left is kept the sacred flame, the symbol of Adi Nath. On the right is **Sopa Gompa**, a Gelugpa foundation, built by refugee monks from Mongolia. It stands in its own compound with the dwellings of monks to either side of the entrance. The temple is built in Tibetan style. On the ground floor is a large assembly hall, and on the first floor a number of chambers of specified ritual purpose. The interior is painted with frescoes of Mahayana deities and the woodwork decorated with gesso-work. *Gompa* of the Gelugpa, Kagdyupa and Ningmapa sects have recently been built in the vicinity of Bodnath.

1 m. (1·8 km.). **Gokarna Royal Forest and Game Sanctuary**, a wooded area of 7 square miles (1813 hectares) enclosed by a brick wall. Species of native deer, peacocks and monkeys may be observed in natural surroundings and may be photographed from purpose-built elevated terraces. Information on visiting the sanctuary is obtainable from the gamekeeper at the entrance. To the north is **Gokarna**, a small village which, according to the Chronicles, was once the fortified capital of a Kiranti king. In the gorge area below the village stands the temple of Gokarneshwar dedicated to Mahadev, Shiva. According to legend it marks the site on which lies buried a section of the horn captured by Brahma, Indra and Vishnu from the golden-deer impersonation of Shiva. The temple situated in a bend of the Bagmati river was built by Ganga Rani, wife of Siva Simha; it was renovated and endowed by King Jayasthiti

Malla in the 14th century. Pagoda-styled, it is enclosed by long lattice casements; the roof has recently been repaired with corrugated-iron sheeting, but the original struts, carved with figures in erotic poses, remain. The enshrined *lingam* is one of the most revered in the valley and the temple is a place of pilgrimage for those offering prayers for living and deceased fathers.

Proceed north-east; turn right onto a dirt road leading to Changu Narayan. Vehicles should be left at Nayapati and one hour allowed for the ascent of Doladri (Dolarvata) Hill.

3½ mi. (6 km.). **Changu Narayan,** a temple complex of great art-historical importance, is situated on a spur of a west-running ridge 600 ft. (200 me.) above the valley floor. The 2-tiered pagoda temple, erected by Queen Lakshmi in 1694/95, is one of the four important related sites sacred to Vishnu in the Kathmandu Valley. The gilded and painted woodwork is elaborately carved and the roof-struts are decorated with figures of the Vaishnavite pantheon. The triple-framed doorways of the sanctum have doors, three of which are blind, decorated with floral designs. The entrance door is plated with embossed brass panels; the central figures of the tympanum are Vishnu and his consorts Lakshmi and Sri. The enshrined image is a gilt 4-tiered, composite statue of Lokeśvara mounted on Vishnu, who stands on Garuda perched on a griffin.

Pillars before the entrance are surmounted by gilt *chakra* and *shankha*; the left-hand pillar is the lower part of the 20 ft. (6½ me.) memorial pillar bearing the famous inscription of Manadeva. Dated 464/65, it records his victories in the east and west and is the earliest historical document in Nepal. The pillar was re-erected in the 19th century by a devotee, who had made for it and its companion the gilt lotus capitals surmounted by *chakra* and *shankha*.

In the temple precincts are several famous stone sculptures of the Lichhavi and Malla periods: the original Garuda statue which surmounted the Manadeva pillar, a 5th-6th-century Vishnu Vishvarupa, and the 12th-13th-century Narasimha and Vaikunthnatha.

Changu Narayan is a centre of pilgrimage for Hindus and Buddhists, who worship the image as Hari-Har, Avalokiteśvara. At the *mila punhi* festival held at the full moon of Magh the silver *kalash* emblem of the deity is carried in procession to the Taleju Temple in Kathmandu where it is greeted by the Virgin Goddess, Kumari.

8½ mi. (14 km.). **Sankhu** (pop. 4385), is an important town situated on the banks of the Salinadi, a tributary of the Sun Kosi River. Its population is 95 per cent. Newari-speaking, and predominantly Hindu. Established in Lichhavi times, it is one of the oldest settlements in the Valley and occupied an important position on the Tibet-Nepal trade route. The great Hindu reformer Sankaracharya is said to have visited Sankhu in the 8th century, and there to have abandoned his mission to stamp out Buddhism. Falling in medieval times within the feudal territories of Kantipur, it enjoyed great prosperity; in recent years the opening of the Arniko highway, which bypasses Sankhu, has resulted in a decline in commercial activity.

On the hillside above the west bank of the Salinadi is the pagoda temple dedicated to **Mahadev-Narayan,** whose deity is a late-period, configurated image. At the pilgrimage site on the top of the hill above the temple are many sculptured images, among which are some notable *lingam*, idols of Vishnu Bhagavan, Sita-Rama and Saraswati, the goddess of learning. Other sacred sites are the low ten foot boulder at the river's edge, representing **Mahadev-Narayan,** known also as Hari-Har, and the three rocks approached by stepping stones across the river, believed to represent Chandravati and her two litter bearers, who according to the texts of the *swastani purana* perished in the sacred Salinadi River.

Kadga Jogini Temple lies to the north of Sankhu. Leave the town by a cobbled street, and climb the pine covered hill-side. Half way up the stone stairway is a shelter where shoes should be left; good views of Sankhu and the eastern end of the Kathmandu Valley may be obtained. Near by is **Bhairab Than**, where a natural rock represents the terrible aspect of Shiva and a stone-carved image depicts Ganesh.

On the crown of the hill is the temple complex sacred to **Kadga (Vajra) Jogini**. The paved, split-level courtyards are formally laid out with rest houses for pilgrims, shrines, *chaitya* of early and late date and three temples.

The central temple is dedicated to **Blue Tara**, known also as Ugra the ferocious one, and as Vajra or Khadga (sword) Jogini. According to an inscription in the courtyard the present structure was erected in 1655/56 by Pratap Malla of Kathmandu, but the site has certainly older Buddhist associations. The pagoda temple stands on a low plinth with a 3-tiered roof of sheet copper, the uppermost gilded and bearing an elaborate gold finial; a copper-gilt banner hangs above the entrance door. The eaves are decorated with rows of repoussé-work copper-gilt plaques; the wooden roof-struts are carved—the corner ones with protective animals and the remainder with deities of the Mahayana pantheon. The southern façade and doorway are plated with repoussé-work copper-gilt panels. The figures of the tympanum are Blue Tara, wreathed in skulls, carrying tantric weapons and symbols in her eight hands; to the right and left are four-armed Blue Taras, flanked by Baghini and Singhini.

The enshrined image is the red-painted Blue Tara, and her attendants Singhini and Baghini. The three idols are richly clothed and bejewelled. The deities are served by Buddhist Vajracharya priests who reside in Sankhu.

To the west of Blue Tara's temple is a standing, Lichhavi-style Buddha; to the east is a large pagoda temple, enshrining a *chaitya*, dating reputedly from the 16th century. The uppermost of the double-tiered roof is gilded and the roof-struts bear carvings of *yakshi*. The upper storey of the temple is decorated with carved wooden beasts and dancing, four-armed Tantric deities. The wood-carving of lintels and doors at the four entrances is of particularly fine quality; the western door is plated with copper-gilt repoussé-work panels of a later date. The central figure of the tympanum is Maha Mayuri mounted on a peacock.

A rock, protected by a low railing, stands in front of the temple and represents the King of Serpents. Large bronze bells, late-style *chaitya* and a gilt lion mounted on a pillar are disposed at various points in the courtyard.

North of Blue Tara's courtyard is a second courtyard which is surrounded by pilgrim rest houses and priests' dwellings. Permission must be sought to enter the building on the left. In a small first-floor room is a 12 ft. (3·50 me.) high copper-gilt *chaitya*, and buried in the floor a huge, cast-copper Buddha-head. Above is a shrine-room containing several bronze images: the copper-gilt figures of Jogini, Singhini and Baghini, a caste-bronze standing Pala-style Buddha and a standing 13th-14th-century Lokeśvara.

West of Blue Tara's courtyard lies a cave used, reputedly, for Tantric practices. Over the entrance is an inscription in large Tibetan characters and in a small chamber leading off the cave is a stone image of Nil Saraswati, equated with Nil Tara (Blue Tara), carrying sword, lotus, axe and human skull cap. The chamber is lit by a small aperture, through which it is believed only the virtuous may pass.

Manichu Than, a hermit's cave, is situated on a hill to the west. Three hours should be allowed for the climb. A pool in front of the cave drains over a waterfall, and there is a small stone image of Raja Manichuda, who on this site is believed to have split open his own skull to secure a precious jewel offering for Kadga Yogini.

ROUTE 8

KATHMANDU—JAWALAKHEL—KHOKANA—BUNGAMATI

Leave Kathmandu at the south end of Ram Shah Path, cross the Bagmati Bridge. Bear right at the Nepal Engineering Institute and continue through Pulchok, passing the Western Ashok Chaitya. Turn sharp right at the Fire Brigade and continue through Jawalakhel. On the right is the Zoo. Open 10 a.m.–5 p.m.

To the south of Jawalakhel is Ekantakuna Bhavan, the headquarters of SATO (Swiss Association for Technical Assistance). Inside the gate on the right is the sales depot for the products of the Tibetan Refugee camp which offers carpets of traditional design, handwoven woollen jackets, Tibetan style aprons, felt boots and a variety of toys both from stock and on order. Bear right for the Tibetan Refugee camp and left for the Khokana-Bungamati road.

4 mi. (7 km.). **Khokana** (pop. 2042), a Newar village with a predominantly Buddhist population. Situated in the valley of the Naku River, its chief industry is the production and sale of oil. Visitors may view the large traditional oil-presses in operation in private houses.

The pagoda temple in the village, and the associated shrine in the fields to the north of the residential area are dedicated to Shekkal Devi, a deity propitiated in times of epidemic.

5½ mi. (9 km.). **Bungamati** (pop. 2042), a village situated on high ground above the valley of the Naku River, is inhabited by 65 per cent. Newari-speaking Buddhists. Visitors travelling by car should continue to the end of the village, where in Jawalakhel there is the only parking space. Return on foot to the road junction at the entrance to the village. Turn right, pass a large tank and turn sharp left. The *shikhara* temple dedicated to Machhendranath, known as Bunga Deo and equated with Avalokiteśvara, stands in a raised quadrangle at the end of a flight of steps. The tall steeple is richly ornamented and the woodwork of pillars and windows of excellent craftsmanship; the carving on one of the roof-struts is comparable to the strut carvings in Pannauti temples. The door plated with embossed brass panels, and the brass tympanum enclosing three images of Lokeśvara were, according to an inscription on the lintel dated 1671/72, donated by Srinivasa Malla.

The gilded shrine of Machhendranath, in which the image reposes during its six months annual residence in Bungamati, has finely modelled pilasters and a tympanum embossed with the figures of Avalokiteśvara, attendants and coiled serpents. The base is supported on four elephants and the plinth on four lions.

Buried in a field east of the village is a sandstone slab engraved in Gupta characters. It bears the Buddha-symbols of the wheel of the law between two deer and a 7th-century inscription of Amsuvarman which, addressing the villagers of Bungamati "according to their rank", orders them to preserve the life of animals. The stone is unearthed at the time of the twelve yearly *jatra*.

ROUTE 9

KATHMANDU—BALAJU WATER GARDEN—KAULI—KAKANI

Leave Kathmandu by the suburb of Lainchaur, turn right into Naya Bazaar. Cross the Vishnumati bridge and proceed north-west on the Kathmandu-Nawakot road.

2½ mi. (4 km.). **Balaju Water Garden and Pleasure Park** lies at the foot of a well-wooded spur of Nagarjun Hill. Pleasantly planted with trees and flowers, it contains an Olympic-sized swimming-pool open to the public. To the right of the park entrance is a rectangular, stone-lined tank, in which a 10 ft. (3 me.) long black stone image of Vishnu Narayan lies sleeping on a bed of coiled snakes. The image, a replica of the 7th-century Buddha Nilkantha, on whom the Kings of Nepal as incarnations of Vishnu may not look, is known as Bala Nilkantha; it was installed by Pratap Malla in 1650/51.

Balaju Baisedhara, built by King Rana Bahadur Shah in *c.* 1860, is a castellated wall set with 22 *makara* headed spouts; above it the waters of several springs fall into pools stocked with fish.

The park contains a small 18th-century, 2-tiered pagoda-style temple dedicated to Balaji; the roof-struts are carved with figures in erotic poses.

To the north of Balaju is Nagarjun royal forest and game sanctuary. On the hill-top, **Jamacho**, is a small Buddhist *chaitya*. It marks the mythical dwelling-place of the first human Buddha Bipaswi, who on the full moon of Chait sowed the lotus seed from which sprang the holy fire, the symbol of Adi Nath. The numerous miniature *chaitya* in the vicinity have been erected by Buddhists in memory of deceased relatives.

Continue on the Kathmandu-Nawakot road to Kauli; at the bifurcation turn right and ascend Kakani Hill.

16 mi. (26 km.). **Kakani** (alt. 6482 ft. 1976 me.), is a small dispersed settlement inhabited by Tamangs. The top of Kakani Hill, and the small bungalow on a north-west saddle, which in the 19th century was put at the disposal of the British Ambassador by the Rana Prime Minister, command very fine panoramic views of the Great Himalayas from Dhaulagiri in the west to Kariolung in the east; particularly arresting is the view of the fluted flank of Himachuli. Attached to the British Embassy bungalow is a miniature golf course.

Simple accommodation at modest cost is offered by the Hotel Kakani; reservations may be made through the Samjhana Hotel, Kanti Path, Kathmandu.

Trekkers from Kathmandu to Kakani should allow three days: Kathmandu – Balaju – Jitpur – Basant Pawa-Kakani. One may follow the Ring Road from Balaju N. then E. to the Bansbari turn-off to combine routes 9 and 10, reaching Buddha Nilkantha without having to return to Kathmandu.

ROUTE 10

KATHMANDU—BUDDHA NILKANTHA

Leave Kathmandu via the suburb of Maharajgunj; proceed on metalled road in a north-easterly direction.

5 mi. (8 km.). **Buddha Nilkantha**, situated in the vicinity of Shivapuri village, is a shrine sacred to Vishnu in his aspect Ananta Shayin Narayana. The 13 ft. (4 me.) long black basalt, monolithic image is represented sleeping in water on the coils of the serpent of eternity; the tank is 43 ft. (13 me.) long and is fed by the river Rudramati. Known as Buddha Nilkantha, Old Blue Throat, it is wor-

shipped not only by Vaishnavites, but by followers of Shiva, to whom the epithet Nilkantha properly belongs, and by Buddhists who regard the idol as a manifestation of Lokeśvara.

A 7th-century inscription records the acquisition of the huge stone from which the image was carved, the construction of the shrine by Koli artisans and its installation by King Bhimajuna Deva and his regent Vishnugupta. An undated broken stone slab fixed in a wall near by bears King Siva Deva's 6th-century Sanskrit inscription in Gupta characters praising his minister Amsuvarma; Buddha Nilkantha appears in another 7th-century inscription as one of the shrines benefiting from Amsuvarma's donations.

The site, originally named Jalasayan "lying in water", is believed to have been more than once buried by landslides from Mount Sheopuri and to have been miraculously rediscovered. The image's broken nose is attributed to the despoilation of the 14th-century Muslim invaders. An image of Ganesh and bronze bells hung on wooden arches stand on the rim of the tank. Unfortunately, the simplicity of the shrine has been marred by recent cement restoration work.

ROUTE 11

KATHMANDU—BANEPA—DHULIKHEL—DOLALGHAT—BARABISE BAZAAR—KODARI (via the ARNIKO RAJMARGA)

Leave Kathmandu at the southern end of Ram Shah Path. Turn left through Thapathali, cross the bridges over the Dhobi Khola, the Bagmati, Manohara and Hanumante Rivers; continue eastwards to the bifurcation below Bhadgaon. Bear right on to the Arniko Rajmarga, named for the famous Newar bronze-caster who in the 13th century worked in Tibet and at the court of Peking.

The Arniko Rajmarga, now carrying by motorised transport most of the China - Tibet - Nepal trade, traverses the eastern portion of the Bagmati Zone. At the toll-gate on Sangha Bhanjgang, the pass that marks the end of the Kathmandu Valley, the road enters the District of Kabre Palanchok and continues through the District of Sunduli Palanchok.

16 mi. (26 km.). **Banepa**, an ancient Newar town, was the medieval capital of powerful feudatories, the most important of whom were the 13th-14th-century Ramavardhnas. Dominating the area of Palanchok and Chautara, a territory known as Bhottarajya, Banepa controlled an important trade route to Tibet and enjoyed a considerable prosperity. In the accounts of Chinese travellers of the period the Banepa feudatory, known as the Bhotta Raja, is mistakenly referred to as the ruler of Nepal. In 1482 the youngest of Yaksha Malla's sons inherited Banepa together with seven villages, but he died without issue and the rich principality fell first under the dominion of Bhadgaon and later under the overlordship of Kathmandu.

To the right of the road stands a pagoda temple dedicated to **Chandresvari**, an important pilgrimage centre attracting devotees from all parts of the Valley. In Baku Tol is a pagoda temple erected in 1708/09 and dedicated to Jagesvara (Shiva); in the vicinity are the extensive remains of the buildings of the old capital.

Ten minutes walk north-east of Banepa is **Nala**, a Newar village with a 4-tiered pagoda temple dedicated to Bhagwati. On the outskirts of the settlement stands the Buddhist pagoda temple acred to Karunamaya, an important centre of Avalokiteśvara worship. The milk collection centre for the Dairy in Lainchaur, Kathmandu is situated north of Nala; it was founded with Swiss and New Zealand Aid.

c. 3 mi. (5 km.) south of Banepa, the Newar town of **Pannauti** lies to the west of the Sun Kosi River, at the confluence of the Rudramati and Bhokhusi tributaries. Appearing in the Chronicles as Pananti or Purnamatideśa, Pannauti is listed in the Rani Pokhari inscription as one of the fifty-one important places of pilgrimage in India and Nepal. In medieval times Pannauti was linked with Banepa and it is to the beneficence of the Banepa feudatories that it owes many of its ancient buildings. The most famous of the early period monuments is the 3-tiered pagoda temple dedicated to **Indreśvara**. Erected, according to the Chronicles by the crown princess of Banepa, Viramadevi in 1294/95, it contains the stone *lingam*, Indreśvar which was gilded, according to a copper-plate inscription, in memory of Jayasimha in the 15th century. The remarkable 13th-century carvings on the roof-struts are of great art-historical importance. They depict characters of the Mahabharata and Ramayana epics, the Ashta Matrikas and *yaksha* and *yakshi*. A pagoda temple dedicated to Krishna Narayan possesses wood-carvings comparable in date and style to those of the Indreśvara temple as well as some fine stone sculptures. A pagoda temple standing on the river bank dedicated to Brahmayani displays some interesting wall frescoes. Close by, in the village of Sathighar is a pagoda temple of Lichhavi foundation; it is dedicated to Vijaya Bhagwati and contains an inscription dated 1304/05.

2½ mi. (4 km.). **Dhulikhel** (alt. 4500 ft. 1372 me.) is an ancient Newar town. Once a fortified outpost of the Malla kings, whose ruined fort may still be seen, it is now the district headquarters of Kabre Palanchok. A plateau lying north of the town affords the only viewpoint on the Arniko Rajmarga.

Descend the winding road from which the fields of the village of Panchkhal in the valley of the Jhiku are visible.

5 mi. (8 km.). **Dolalghat**, a market centre where there is a toll gate. Cross the modern bridge spanning the Indravati River above its confluence with the Sun Kosi. From here a trail leads eastwards via Chyaubas to Solu Khumbu. The Arniko Rajmarga follows the course of the Sun Kosi, at an average height of 5000 ft. (1700 me.). The mountainous country is sparsely forested, and the dispersed-type settlements which lie out of sight of the road on hillslopes and ridges require a minimum two hours to reach. After crossing the Balephi Khola, the Bhote Kosi above its junction with the Sun Kosi and passing the market centre of Balephidobham, the road continues along the west bank of the Bhote Kosi.

31 mi. (50 km.). **Barabise Bazaar** (alt. *c.* 4000 ft. 1220 me.) is a market centre with a small bazaar, shops dispensing tea and a toll gate. South of Barabise Bazaar is **Longusangu** with a pumping station and electricity generators built with Chinese aid.

Continue northwards; the road winds over barren north-south running ridges and re-crosses the Bhote Kosi, the only river of the Indrawati–Sun Kosi system to break through the Great Himalayan watershed. On the west bank is the market centre of Tatopani, so-called for the hot springs in the vicinity.

12 mi. (20 km.). **Kodari**, situated on the frontier of the Tibet Region of the Peoples Republic of China. A barricade before the bridge and Chinese guards deny to those without passes access to the historic Kuti pass and the Lhasa–Peking road. Foreigners are allowed to take the daily mail bus right up to the border itself without having to obtain any special permission for a look into China.

ROUTE 12

KATHMANDU—TRIBHUVAN UNIVERSITY—KIRTIPUR—MACHCHEGAON

Leave Kathmandu by the Tripureswar–Kalimati road; turn left at the National Trading Company, cross the bridge at the confluence of Vishnumati and Bagmati Rivers and proceed southwards on the Pharping–Dakshinkali road. 4 mi. (6 km.) south-west of Kathmandu, turn right. Pass **Tribhuvan University**, founded by Maharaja Mohan Shumshere and opened to classes in 1957. Proceed south-west and ascend Kirtipur Hill on foot.

5 mi. (8 km.). **Kirtipur** (pop. 4880), the "City of Fame", is situated on a plateau, part of a low ridge that traverses the south-western quarter of the Kathmandu Valley. Standing 328 ft. (100 me.) above the level of the plain, the town occupies a natural strategic position and is protected by precipitous slopes on all sides.

Founded by Sada Sivadeva in the 7th century, it is one of the oldest settlements in the valley. Once the capital of an independent principality, it became a feudatory of Lalitpur in the 12th century. Between 1765 and 1767 it withstood three sieges by the invading armies of Prithivi Narayan Shah; finally, having lost a part of the town through treachery, Kirtipur's leader Danuventa agreed to surrender. The promised amnesty was not honoured, the principal citizens were murdered and the noses and lips of all male citizens except those of babes at the breast and musicians were cut off. The name of the town was changed by decree to Naskatpur, "City of Cut Noses".

Kirtipur recovered slowly from this misfortune. The shift of power and the centralisation of administration directed from Kathmandu cut across the trading monopolies which the community, straddling one of the main trade routes to the south, had previously enjoyed; the recent appropriation of much irrigated rice-land to accommodate Tribhuvan University Campus has resulted in a further narrowing of economic activity. The population is 100 per cent. Newari-speaking and predominantly Buddhist. 46 per cent. of families are primarily engaged in agriculture, a low percentage compared with other Valley settlements. Crafts and cottage industries play an important economic role, with handloom textiles and stone masonry enjoying a high reputation.

Enter the town by the north-east gate; proceed along the perimeter street to the ruined Darbar. A flight of stone steps flanked by carved stone elephants, each carrying a headless warrior and trampling a man underfoot, lead up to the former throne-room and stronghold; overlooking the town are the overgrown ruins of several temples, the most remarkable being that dedicated to Mahadeo and Parvati which was built in 1555/56.

At the northern edge of the town, at the top of one of the footpaths by which the hill may be ascended from the east, is a small Ganesh shrine erected in 1665/66 by a Shresta Newar of Jaisi caste. The carvings on the stone gateway depict Ganesh and the Ashta Matrikas on their traditional mounts: on the right Kumari on a peacock, Varahi on a buffalo, Kali on a demon; on the left Vishnavi on a sun-eagle, Indriani on an elephant, Maha Laxmi on a lion; over the entrance Bhairab is flanked by Brahmani on a goose and Rudraini on a bull.

The *chaitya* of **Cilandrya** (Chillandeo, Chitubihar) stands in the south-eastern quarter of the town; comparable in style to the four directional *chaitya* of Lalitpur and classed with them as a foundation of the Lichhavi period, it has a low, flat dome, squared torana and gilded harmika. An inscription set in the dome relates to the year 1677/78. Notable are the associated *pranali* and a group of ashok-type *chaitya*. To the east is a *dharma dhatu-mandala* carved with the eight jewels and the eight signs of good fortune; it was constructed in 1669/70 by two Newar brothers. Situated to the north-west is the *shikhara* temple erected in 1680/81 and dedicated to Adi Nath. The enshrined Tri Ratna image was installed by Vajra Acharya in 1673/74. The entrance is flanked by Karak Bir and Vajra Bir.

Leave Kirtipur and proceed on dirt road southwards.

1½ mi. (2·3 km.). **Machchegaon,** a small village situated in hilly country, 6 mi. (9·5 km.) south-west of the capital; it commands an attractive view of the Kirtipur skyline against the northern rim of the Valley and the snow peaks of the Great Himalaya. Two pools, fed by streams flowing off the Chandragiri massif, and a small island shrine are centres of pilgrimage where *sraddha* offerings are made in the name of deceased mothers.

ROUTE 13

KATHMANDU—HARISIDDHI—THAIBO—BANDEGAON—GODAVARI

Leave Kathmandu at the southern end of Ram Shah Path, cross the Bagmati Bridge, bear right at the Nepal Engineering Institute and continue through Pulchok. At the Western Ashok Chaitya turn left and proceed through Lalitpur via Na Tol and Go Bahal. Turn sharp right at the south-east corner of Mangal Bazaar; pass through Tangal to the Southern Ashok Chaitya; turn left and proceed south-east.

6½ mi. (10 km.). **Harisiddhi** (pop. 3500), a Newar village with a 4-tiered pagoda temple dedicated to Harisiddhi Bhavani.

1 mi. (2 km.). **Thaibo** (pop. 1400), a Newar village situated east of the Naku River. A natural rock shrine dedicated to Santaneswar Mahadeo, to whom worshippers pray for fertility, lies on a nearby hill.

1 mi. (2 km.). **Bandegaon.** Bear left at the entrance to the village for the cave sanctuary of **Bisankhu Narayan,** one of the four most important Vishnu shrines in the Kathmandu Valley. Return to the main road on a cross-country track, passing the dispersed Chetri and Brahmin settlements of **Bistachap, Godamchaur** and **Bisankhu.**

5 mi. (8 km.). **Godavari** (14 mi. 22 km. south-east of Kathmandu) lies at the foot of Mount Phulchoki (alt. 7274 ft. 2758 me.), the highest of the hills ringing the Kathmandu Valley. Surrounded by luxuriant forest, the area is noted for the beauty of the spring-flowering rhododendrons, the excellence of the small game shooting and the wide choice of picnic places.

The **Royal Botanical Gardens,** lying on the left of the road, contain an interesting collection of orchids and plants native to Nepal. The ground is laid out in rock gardens, lotus ponds and hot-house nurseries. Situated below the Gardens are St Xavier's boarding school for boys, marble quarries opened in 1840 and installed with modern equipment in 1934, an agricultural extension farm and a fish hatchery.

Phulchok Mai Nau Dhara, the nine water spouts of Phulchok Mai, stand in the courtyard of a pagoda temple dedicated to Mai-Bhagwati. The *makara*-shaped spouts are fed by the waters of nine streams, which flow off Mount Phulchoki and fall into a natural rock basin. The temple possesses an interesting collection of masks and images of numerous deities including those of Vishnu, Shiva and Buddha.

A motorable road ascends half-way

up Mount Phulchoki. The summit, reached on foot in one hour, is sacred to Lord Shiva, whose three great tridents, together with a small image of Bhagwati, Shiva's partner, are stuck in the rocks. Nearby, on the heights is a Buddhist shrine, from which a good view of the valley and the snow ranges may be obtained.

ROUTE 14

KATHMANDU—CHOBAR—PHARPING—DAKSHINKALI

Leave Kathmandu by the Tripureswar–Kalimati road. Turn left at the National Trading Company, cross the bridge over the Vishnumati. Follow the road running south on the west bank of the Bagmati River.

5 mi. (8 km.). **Chobar**, a small Newar village situated at the foot of the Chandragiri massif. The pagoda temple dedicated to **Jal Vinayak** (Ganesh), stands on the banks of the Bagmati River. Close by is the Chobar Gorge, which legend relates is the outlet hewn by the Bodhisattva Manjuśri to drain the lake which once covered the Valley. A steel suspension bridge spans the river in the gorge area, and a paved stairway leads to the top of Chobar Hill (alt. 4727 ft.; 1441 me.). The complex of religious buildings centred on the pagoda temple dedicated to Adi Nath, popularly known as Ananda Lokeśwara, lies just below the summit. Stone steps give access to the top of the hill, from where there is a good view of the Kathmandu Valley and the distant snows.

At the foot of Hattiban Hill, close to Chobar, is **Lake Tondaha**, the legendary habitat of Kartotak Naga, who dwelt in the primaeval lake.

7½ mi. (10 km.). **Pharping**, an ancient town and, in Malla times, the capital of feudatory chiefs calling themselves Maharabutta. Situated in the valley of the Bagmati, on the eastern flank of the Chandragiri massif it contains many interesting buildings and inscriptions. To the north lies the pagoda temple dedicated to **Shekhu Narayan**. Constructed by Pratap Malla in the 17th century, it is excavated from the perpendicular stalactite rock cliff. Associated with this important Vishnu shrine are clear pools fed by streams running off the surrounding hills and two stone statues of the Lichhavi period, one of which is a *vishnu vikranta* bas-relief set up in 467/68.

To the west of Pharping, half-way up a wooded hill stands a pagoda temple dedicated to Vajra Yogini; above it lies a cave sacred to Gorakhnath, a Siddhi of the Natha sect.

The temple complex of **Dakshin Kali** is situated at the confluence of the Bagmati River and a tributary stream. The enshrined image is a black stone representation of Kali, the fierce aspect of Shiva's consort. Rest houses line the banks of the rivers, which are linked by bridges giving access to the surrounding forested hills.

The annual festival is held on Kala Ratri (Dassain). Throughout the year sacrificial rites are held every Tuesday and Saturday.

ROUTE 15

KATHMANDU—NAGARKOT

Leave Kathmandu at the southern end of Ram Shah Path. Turn left through Thapathali, cross the bridges over the Dhobi Khola, Bagmati, Manohara and Hanumante Rivers. At the bifurcation below Bhadgaon turn left. Take the second turning right and, passing through Methibari and Byansi localities, turn sharp right (road to left leads to Changu

Narayan), then left; proceed in a north-easterly direction.

15 mi. (20 km.). **Nagarkot** (alt. 7111 ft. 2168 me.), a village situated in the hills dividing the Indravati–Sunkosi and Bagmati basins, and commanding magnificent views of the Great Himalayan Ranges to the north, east and west: the Dhaulagiri, Annapurna, Ganesh, Langtang, Jugal, Rolwaling and Khumbu Himals. The forested hills and alpine meadows in the vicinity provide varied opportunities for trekking, walking and small game shooting. A four-hour climb to **Mahadeo Pokhari** (alt. 7133 ft. 2175 me.), a small lake with a Mahadeo shrine, is rewarded by views of Mount Everest, Gosainthan, Dorje Lakba and Gauri Shanker.

Accommodation at a modest charge is provided by Mount Everest Lodge. Reservations may be made in Kathmandu through the Tourist Department, Hotel Kakani, Juddha Sadak or the Everest Travel Service, Basantapur.

Trekkers from Kathmandu to Nagarkot should allow 4 days: Kathmandu – Bhadgaon – Kharepati – Gadgade – Nagarkot.

ROUTE 16

KATHMANDU—BALAMBU—DAMAN (via TRIBHUVAN RAJPATH)

Leave Kathmandu via Tripureswar –Kalimati road; cross the Vishnumati bridge in Teku. In 7½ mi. (12 km.) join the Tribhuvan Rajpath.

10 mi. (16 km.). **Balambu**, a Newar village situated on the edge of the Kathmandu Valley. To the north, across a small stream, lies the ruined fort of Dahachok, believed to have been a one-time capital of the Kiranti chief Maradeva.

Continue past Thankot; at Naubisi bear left and continue on the Tribhuvan Rajpath.

50 mi. (80 km.). **Daman** (alt. 6960 ft. 2320 me.), a viewing station, situated below the highest point on the Tribhuvan Rajpath. It commands one of the best sweeping views of the Great Himalaya. On clear days the whole of the main range from Kariolung in the east to Dhaulagiri in the west is visible. The Department of Tourism has installed a view tower for public use. Everest Point Motel and Restaurant provides meals and accommodation (running hot and cold water, modern toilets). Trekking in the forested hills surrounding Daman provides fine vistas of varied landscape and, in the months of March, April and May, a wealth of flowering rhododendrons.

Reservations through Yeti Travels, Seto Darbar, Kathmandu.

ROUTE 17

KATHMANDU—POKHARA

Pokhara (Kaski District, Gandaki Zone) lies north of the Mahabharat. Situated at a height of 2160 ft. (720 me.), in the valley of the Seti River it commands the most spectacular view of snow mountains in Nepal. No major range intervenes between the Pokhara Valley and the main range of the Himalaya and the great peaks of the Ganesh Himal, the Dhaulagiri Himal, the Kanjiroba Himal and the Annapurna Himal, tower above the northern rim of the valley. Due north of Pokhara is the elegant form of Mt. Machhapuchhare (Fish Tail Mountain) whose base is only 16 mi. (25 km.) from the town.

Pokhara is most conveniently reached by RNAC scheduled flight from Kathmandu, and is connected by air with Bhairawa, Dang, Nepalganj, Surkhet, Dhangarhi, Gorkha, Meghauli and Bharatpur. Motorised transport can use the Prithivi Rajmarga 110 mi. (176·4 km.) from Kathmandu to Pokhara and the Sidhartha Rajmarga, 114 mi. (184 km.) from Sunauli to Pokhara. 6-7 days should be allowed for the trek Kathmandu–Pokhara.

110 mi. (176·4 km.). **Pokhara** (35 minutes by air from Kathmandu. Nagdhunga Airport ½ hour from town; hired motorised transport available) is the District, Zonal and Western Development Region headquarters. T.E.L.E. communications. P.O., banks, bazaar, hospitals, and tourist and country-style hotels.

As an old trading centre Pokhara has a large bazaar, with well-built 2- and 3-storey houses; the population is predominantly Newar, Thakali, Brahmin and Chetri, with considerable numbers of Gurung and Magar. Pagoda temples dedicated to Bhagwati (Bindu Basini temple near Moharia Tol), to Bhadrakali (near Kunahar) stand in Pokhara town, and in the campus of Prithivi Narayan College is a large boulder sacred to Bhimsen. Within the last decade the people of the Manang Valley have built a *gompa* to the north of the town.

A feature of the Pokhara Valley are the lakes: to the south of the town, west of the airport is the 3 mi. (5 km.) long Phewa Tal; canoes may be hired to visit the island temple dedicated to **Varahi**. To the east of the town approximately 9 mi. (14 km.) distant are the spring-fed lakes of Begnas Tal (1·2 sq. mi. 3·1 sq. km.) and Rupa Tal (1·2 sq. mi. 3·1 sq. km.) At the foot of Arghaun Lekh lie the three small lakes Khaste Tal, Deepang Tal and Maidi Tal.

Fadke waterfall, 10 minutes walking distance from the airport, the gorge of the Seti River, with a canyon of 108 ft. (33 me.) to 216 ft. (66 me.) deep at Ram Ghat, and Mahendra Gupha, a stalactite cave situated near the village of Batalachaur, are sights worth the tourist's attention. There is good fishing for mahseer in Phewa Tal and the Seti River and for *alsa* in streams, rivers and lakes.

Small game is comparatively plentiful in the forests of the nearby hills and there are opportunities for duck shooting on the lakes at the eastern end of the valley. Pokhara is a convenient base for short or long treks into the hills.

Reservations for the four-star Fish Tail Lodge and Hotel Phewa to the north and south of Phewa Tal, should be made through the management, or through travel agents in Kathmandu. In Pokhara town are a number of hotels and lodging houses, and near the airport are the Snow View, New Crystal and Mount Annapurna Hotels and several Tibetan-style restaurants offering board and lodging.

Arrangements for tours and excursions from Pokhara may be made through Pokhara Tours and Travels, the Managers of the Tibetan Himalaya Hotel, and the Fish Tail Lodge, all of whom maintain representatives at Pokhara Airport.

ROUTE 18

KATHMANDU—JANAKPUR

Janakpur (Mahottari District, Janakpur Zone) lies in the eastern Terai. Famed as the capital of the legendary King Janak, whose daughter Sita married Rama, the hero of the Ramayana, it is a place of pilgrimage for all Hindus.

Janakpur is most conveniently reached from Kathmandu by RNAC Scheduled flight; it is also linked by air with Rajbiraj, Biratnagar and Bhadrapur. Motorable roads serve traffic between Janakpur and Jaleswar, the zonal headquarters, and a feeder road links up with the nearly completed section (Dhalkebar–Ahdar) of the Mahendra Rajpath (East-West Highway). The Nepal Government Railway runs between Jayanagar (Indian rail-head, branch line of the North-East Railway) to Janakpur.

Janakpur (pop. 8928). Airport, T.E.L.E. communications, P.O., bank, shops, bazaar, country-style hotels and rest houses.

Places of importance to visit are the palace of the medieval kings of Mithila, the temple of Rama and the white marble, Indo-Persian-style temple dedicated to Janaki (Sita).

ROUTE 19

KATHMANDU—MEGHAULI—NATIONAL PARK and WILD GAME SANCTUARY—TIGER TOPS HOTEL

Leave Kathmandu by RNAC charter flight (45 minutes).

94 mi. (120 km.). **Meghauli Airfield** (Chitawan District, Narayani Zone). Proceed by elephant or Landrover to the National Park and Wild Game Sanctuary which covers over 519 sq. mi. (1500 sq. km.) of tall-grass jungle in the Nepalese Terai. The wild game inhabiting the area includes tiger, the rare one-horned rhinoceros, leopard, crocodile, bear, antelope, wild boar, *gaur* or wild ox, peafowl, jungle fowl, partridge, pheasant and a host of tropical bird species as well as monkeys. Accommodation is provided by Tiger Tops Jungle Lodge, a comfortable hotel built on 20 ft. high stilts inside the Game Sanctuary. The American management undertakes all-in arrangements: provides veteran guides for excursions by Landrover or elephant to view and photograph wild life, canoes or motor launches for sightseeing tours on the Rapti River and facilities for mahseer fishing (fishing tackle can be hired). Reservations may be made through Tiger Tops Jungle Lodge, P.O. Box 242, Kathmandu, or recognised Travel Agents. *Note:* the section Kathmandu-Tiger Tops (Meghauli) may be included as part of an international air ticket and included free in the mileage allowance.

ROUTE 20

KATHMANDU—BHARATPUR—GOVERNMENT ELEPHANT CAMP

Leave Kathmandu by RNAC scheduled flight (40 minutes).

70 mi. (110 km.). **Bharatpur Airfield** (Chitawan District, Narayani Zone). Proceed by Landrover to Chitawan Valley. Continue by elephant to the Government Elephant Camp situated on the banks of the Rapti River. Excursions are arranged to view the wild game in natural surroundings: tiger, the rare one-horned rhinoceros, crocodile, leopard, bear, antelope, wild boar, *gaur* or wild ox, peafowl, jungle fowl, partridge, pheasant and a host of tropical bird species.

Visitors may return to Kathmandu direct, or to Kathmandu via Pokhara. Reservations may be made through Sherpa Trekking Service, Lal Darbar, P.O. Box 500, Kathmandu, or their foreign representative, Cultural Tours Ltd., 29 rue Cambon, Paris 1, France.

ROUTE 21

KATHMANDU—BHAIRAWA—LUMBINI—KAPILAVASTU

Lumbini (Rupandehi District, Lumbini Zone), the birthplace of Gautama Buddha, lies in the central

Terai, 158 mi. (225 km.) south-west of Kathmandu. Visitors from Nepal may approach via Bhairawa, whence a 16 mi. (25·6 km.) road leads to Lumbini. RNAC scheduled flights to Bhairawa operate from Kathmandu, Bharatpur, Dang, Nepalganj and Dhangarhi; by road from Pokhara on the Siddhartha Rajmarga it is 124 mi. (200 km.). Approached from the Indian rail-head (branch line of the North East Railway) Nautanwa/Naugarh, Lumbini is 14 mi. (22·5 km.) on a direct road. Bus services and hired transport are available both in Bhairawa and Nautanwa/Naugarh.

Bhairawa (pop. 1804). Zonal and district headquarters. Airport, Government Offices, T.E.L.E. communications, P.O., bank, hospital, country-style hotels.

16 mi. (25·6 km.). **Lumbini Grove** was laid out as a pilgrim centre (U.N. Development Aid Funds) in 1956 for the 2500 anniversary celebrations of Buddha's death. Government rest house. *Dharmasala.* Monastery. Modern Nepalese temple, and shrines erected by Buddhist communities of foreign lands.

The vaulted cell sheltering the spot where Buddha was born (624 B.C.) is surrounded by recently constructed terraces and extended flights of steps. Within, is a Mathura-style 2nd-3rd century A.D. sandstone bas-relief depicting a standing Maya Devi grasping the branch of a *sal* tree, and giving birth to the Buddha; Indra, attended by Brahma and a serving woman, is receiving the child. Beside the largely defaced stele stands a modern replica in Burman marble and Burman style. In front of the birth-shrine is a polished stone column enclosed by an iron railing. The Pali inscription records that the column was erected by Emperor Ashoka in 492 B.C. to commemorate his visit to the place where "the Exalted One was born". The column, buried in the ground with the shaft split down the middle, was discovered by the archaeologist Dr Fürer in 1896; it was subsequently re-erected.

Only fragments of the horse capital noted by the Chinese pilgrim Hsuan-Tsang in the 7th century have been recovered. Near by is a pool in which, according to the 5th-century Chinese traveller Fa-hsien, the mother of Buddha bathed before the birth.

A modern obelisk standing within the pilgrimage centre is inscribed with the achievements of the late King Mahendra Bikram Shah Deva (1955-1972).

At **Tiraulakot** (Kapilavastu District, Lumbini Zone), *c.* 12 mi. (20 km.) west of the Lumbini Grove, are the extensive ruins of Kapilavastu, the ancient capital of the Sakyas. Close to a pool, said to mark the site of the palace of King Suddhodana, the father of Buddha, stands a small red-brick building of uncertain date. The shrine and statue of the king mentioned in 636 by Hsuan-Tsang have disappeared.

The most notable finds of the 1962/63 and 1964/65 excavations carried out by the Archaeological Department of H.M.G./Nepal in the area are baked clay and terracotta reliefs and figurines from Taulihawa District attributable to the 2nd century B.C.—1st century A.D., and a terracotta female head from Banjarahi (Rupandehi District) dating from the 3rd century B.C. These, together with the moulded bricks excavated from a medieval temple site at Lori Kudan (Taulihawa District), are displayed in the Department of Archaeology, Kathmandu. In the vicinity of Kudan and at Nigali Sagar are stone carved memorial pillars set up by Emperor Ashoka in the 3rd century B.C.

ROUTE 22

KATHMANDU—BIRATNAGAR—DHARAN

Biratnagar (Morang District, Kosi Zone), the industrial heart of

Nepal, is situated in the eastern Terai, 194 mi. (312 km.) south-east of Kathmandu. Scheduled RNAC flights operate to Biratnagar from Kathmandu, Bhadrapur, Rajbiraj and Janakpur. Access by road is via Jogbani, Bihar State (Indian railhead, branch line of the North East Railway), 9 mi. (14 km.). The now-under-construction Sattighat-Dhalkebar section of the Mahendra Rajpath (East-West Highway) runs north of Biratnagar and is linked to it by the Biratnagar–Dharan road.

Biratnagar (pop. 35,355). Zonal and district headquarters. Airport. T.E.L.E. communications, P.O., banks, shops, bazaar, Government Offices, electricity (Letang-Kosi generator). Country style hotels. Well-organised industrial and commercial centre with a large import-export trade.

The fertile alluvial plain of the eastern Terai in which Biratnagar is situated was ruled in the 18th century by the eastern Senas, whose capital was at Vijayapur; it was incorporated into Prithivi Narayan's unified Nepal, but was subsequently annexed by the British. The area was returned to Nepal in the mid-19th century. During the period of the Rana oligarchy the encouragement of land-hungry Maithili-speaking emigrants (1890-1930), the enlargement of the cultivable area following large-scale felling of forest for the Indian timber-market (1914 onwards) and the extension of the Indian road and rail network to the borders of Nepal, created a favourable environment for the development of Biratnagar. Since 1951 the eradication of malaria, the irrigation potential afforded by the newly constructed Chattra canal and, following the erection of the first factory in 1930, the steady growth of industrial enterprise has led to a phenomenal increase in the population. It is now the third largest city in Nepal. *c.* 25 mi. (40 km.) north of Biratnagar lies **Dharan,** the fifth largest town in Nepal and the site of the Eastern Recruiting and Pension Paying Depot of the British Brigade of Gurkhas. Landing facilities for charter planes. A metalled road, crossing the now-under-construction Sattighat–Dhalkebar section of the Mahendra Rajpath (East-West Highway) connects Dharan with Biratnagar. Fair weather roads link Dharan with Dhankuta, district and Eastern Development Region headquarters, and with Ilam district headquarters (Mechi Zone).

Dharan (pop. 13,988) lies in the Tamur Valley, at the foot of Vijayapur Hill (alt. *c.* 11,480 ft. 3500 me.). T.E.L.E. communications. P.O., banks, hospitals, shops, bazaar, golf course.

Situated in the heart of Limbuan, the traditional homeland of the Limbus, whose ruined forts may still be seen at places such as Hedanga and Chainpur, Dharan commands good views of the snows. It is an excellent base for pheasant shooting, mahseer and *alsa* fishing and for long and short treks.

The complex of buildings that comprise the Recruiting and Pension Paying Depot of the British Brigade of Gurkhas was completed in 1960 on a site surveyed in 1953/54. Its establishment followed the post-Independence division of the Gurkha regiments of the British Army between India and Britain, and resulted from Indian Government representations calling for the removal of all British Gurkha depots from Indian soil. The 1955 agreement between H.M. Government of Nepal and the British Government provided for the setting up of Depots within the borders of Nepal: Goom Depot (Darjeeling District, West Bengal) was transferred to Dharan and the Gorakpur Depot (Basti District, Uttar Pradesh) to Pauklihawa (Narayani Zone). North of Dharan is Hille, one of the hill-based agricultural training centres for ex-service men and their families maintained by the Gurkha Welfare Board.

West of Dharan, at the confluence

of the Sapta Kosi, lies **Bharahachhetra,** a temple complex with a domed shrine containing an image of Varaha, the boar incarnation of Vishnu.

ROUTE 23

KATHMANDU—SHYAMBOCHE —HOTEL EVEREST VIEW

Leave Kathmandu by charter aircraft (45 minutes).

Shyamboche Airfield (Solu-Khumbu District, Sagarmatha Zone; alt. 12,280 ft. 4026 me.). Proceed on foot or on horse-back for half an hour to Hotel Everest View, a modern Japanese-managed establishment (electricity, hot and cold water, air conditioning, oxygen masks for those feeling the height, good restaurant). Situated on a ledge overlooking the Dudh Kosi Valley, 980 ft. (300 me.) above the Sherpa Village of Namche Bazaar, it commands panoramic views of the great snow peaks of the Khumbu Himal; Amadablam (22,494 ft. 6856 me.), Thamserku (21,730 ft. 6623 me.), Lhotse (27,890 ft.; 8501 me.), Nuptse (25,850 ft. 7879 me.), and Everest (29,028 ft. 8848 me.). The management undertakes the arrangement of tours on foot from the hotel and the supply of tents, camping equipment and guides: Everest base-camp (*c.* 5 days), Gokyo glacier lake (*c.* 4 days), Tengboche Monastery (*c.* 2 days) (*see* Trekking to Khumbu and Everest base-camp, pp. 688-689 for particulars of the area). Reservations may be made through Trans-Himalayan Tours Ltd, Bungalow No. 1, Seto Darbar, Kathmandu. Tel. 13854; or The Tokyo Office, Himala Kando K. Co, Ltd, 3-10 Kauda-ogawacho, Chiyoda-ku, Tokyo, Japan.

TREKKING

The itineraries are described in relation to villages encountered en route; a mid-day break of 1-1½ hours is included in travel times. Wherever possible overnight stops are scheduled in inhabited localities. Enclosed in square brackets, at points of departure from the main trails, are side trips offering special interest. Distance in miles and kilometres and heights in feet and metres are as recorded by travellers in Nepal. In the absence of official surveys they are as accurate as present circumstances permit.

KATHMANDU—HELMU—LANGTANG

The regions of high altitude most easily accessible from Kathmandu are Helmu (known also as Yelambu) and Langtang. Tourists lacking the time for the more extensive treks in western and eastern Nepal can gain an impression of Buddhist culture and alpine landscapes in areas close to the main Himalayan range. The approach to these regions leads through villages inhabited by Hindu castes and Tamangs, but as height is gained Hindu influence recedes and the country, growing more rugged, is inhabited by mongoloid people professing Lamaist Buddhism. In Helmu Sherpas constitute the majority of the population. They are distant kinsmen of the Sherpas of Solu-Khumbu; their women dress in Bhotiya style, but the men have adopted Nepali dress. Langtang is inhabited by Bhotiya who call themselves "Tamang", but conform in speech and culture to other Nepalese Bhotiya populations. They are yak-breeders and farmers and the tourist can observe in Langtang the pastoral life of a high-altitude people akin to the inhabitants of the adjoining parts of the Tibetan Region of the Peoples Republic of China. A side trip to the sacred lakes of Gosainkund which lie in the Langtang Himal may be included in either the Helmu or Langtang treks.

KATHMANDU—HELMU

The Kathmandu–Helmu trek begins at Sundarijal hydro-electric generating station situated 9 mi. (14 km.) north-east of Kathmandu. Motorised transport can reach the water pipe from which the ascent begins. Bus services operate between Kathmandu and Bodhnath and it is then 2-3 hours walk to Sundarijal.

1st day. 6 hours. Keeping on the left of the water pipe, climb the stone stairway to the schoolhouse; turn left and cross the water reservoir (5200 ft. 1768 me.). Continue climbing past Mulkharka (5800 ft. 1768 me.) and Chaubas (7324 ft. 2233 me.). In 2 hours reach Burlang Bhanjyang (8000 ft. 2438 me.). Descend through forest and camp at Chisapani (7200 ft. 2194 me.). Good views of the snows.

2nd day. 8 hours. Descend through farmlands to Pati Bhanjyang (5800 ft. 1768 me.). Police Check Post. Climb the north slope of the hill and take the right-hand fork to the Tamang village of Kakani. Descend to Basilari, and follow the Tarang Marang Khola to its junction with the Malenchi Khola. [From Tarang Marang Khola to Panchkhal on the Arniko Rajmarga. 1 day.] Camp beside river.

3rd day. 8 hours. Cross the Malenchi Khola. Climb steeply up hills lying east of the valley; after passing Palchok, proceed along ridge-crest dividing Malenchi and Indravati valleys, keeping at an average height of 8800 ft. (2,680 me.). Pass the Sherpa village and monastery of Raithaneghyang and camp in Sherpa village of Smarthang (8100 ft. 2770 me.). [From Smarthang to Panch Pokhari + the descent to Balephi on the Arniko Rajmarga. 6 days.]

4th day. 6 hours. Descend 330 ft. (100 me.); follow contour path at a height of 8200 ft. (2500 me.) northwards to Tarke Ghyang (8400 ft. 2560 me.), the largest Sherpa village in Helmu. Monastery and *gompa*. Behind Tarke Ghyang is Yangri Danda and a path leading to many yak pastures from where good views of the snow ranges may be obtained.

5th day. 6 hours. Descend steeply to the Malenchi Khola (6560 ft. 2000 me.); cross the river and ascend the opposite hill. Malenchigaon, the summer seat of the Chini Lama, Abbot of Bodhnath, is situated at a height of 8400 ft. (2560 me.). Camp on ledge above the village.

6th day. 8 hours. Climb steeply through rhododendron forest to reach the crest of a bare ridge dividing the Trisuli and Malenchi Valleys. Tharepati Pass lies at a height of 11,766 ft. (3587 me.). Camp near herdsmen's huts. [From Tharepati Pass to Gosainkund Lakes 2 days+ return.]

7th day. 6 hours. Descend the south-running ridge; pass a *chorten* and after descending further, cross to the west flank of the hill and reach Panghu Danda. Steep descent through rhododendron forest to small village of Kutumsang (8100 ft. 2468 me.).

8th day. 7 hours. Follow the ridge trail, dropping occasionally to west slope. Negotiate Thodang Danda and descend to Gul Bhanjyang (7025 ft. 2350 me.). Make the steep descent to Pati Bhanjyang. Good camp site on grass below water point.

9th day. 7 hours. Climb to ridge-crest and return to Sundarijal via Chisapani, Burlang Bhanjyang and Mulkharka.

KATHMANDU—LANGTANG

The starting point for the Kathmandu–Langtang trek is Trisuli Bazaar, a small town lying on the west bank of the Trisuli River, 45 mi. (72½ km.) north-west of Kathmandu. It may be reached by motorised transport from Kathmandu in 4-5 hours. Bus service from Pakanjol, Kathmandu to Trisuli Bazaar.

1st day. 5 hours. Leave Trisuli Bazaar on the north-running road; keep to the east of the canal. Pass the reservoir and in 1 hour from Trisuli Bazaar cross the Trisuli River. Continue on the east bank to Betrawati (2100 ft. 641 me.), situated above the junction of the Phalangu Khola and the Trisuli River. Cross the suspension bridge over the Phalangu Khola and proceed on the old Rasuwa Garhi trade route. After a short climb to Bogata (2350 ft. 783 me.) continue through deciduous forest and stretches of open country. It is 2½ hours from Bogata to Manigaon (3923 ft. 1196 me.).

2nd day. 8½ hours. Follow trail northwards to Ramche (5875 ft. 1791 me.) and then to the villages of Grang (6200 ft 1890 me.) and Thare (6525 ft. 1989 me.). Good views of Langtang I and II from the trail. Camp beyond Thare beside stream.

3rd day. 7 hours. Continue 1 hour on forest trail to Bokajhung (6200 ft. 1890 me.) and climb 1½ hours to Dhunche (6450 ft. 1966 me.), situated at the junction of the Trisuli Khola and the Bhote Kosi. Police Check Post. Shops. [From Dhunche to Gosainkund Lakes 1½ days; the climb to Tharepati Pass from Gosainkund Lakes requires 1 day; for descent from Tharepati to Helmu see: Kathmandu-Helmu trek.] Leave Dhunche at the north end of the town, bear left and descend steeply to the river. Cross and climb steeply up the north bank (6498 ft. 1981 me.). Pass Bharku village. Descend to the Bhote Kosi, and camp in Syabrubensi (4800 ft. 1463 me.), at the junction of the Bhote Kosi and the Langtang Khola.

4th day. 8 hours. Follow trail up east side of the Bhote Kosi Valley. Climb steeply and in 3 hours pass Khangjung. Continue climbing to 10,168 ft. (3100 me.). Descend to Syarpagaon (*c.* 8495 ft. 2590 me.). View of the Langtang Valley.

5th day. 7 hours. Descend gently to Langtang rapids; proceed eastwards keeping to the north bank of the river. Good camp site on yak pastures at Ghora Tabela (10,824 ft. 3300 me.).

6th day. 6½ hours. Traverse valley floor to Langtang village (11,523 ft. 3523 me.). In 3½ hours arrive at Kyangin *gompa* (12,700 ft. 3871 me.), and the summer settlement of Langtang Bhotiya. Spectacular mountain scenery. S.T.O.L. airfield lies *c.* 200 ft. (60 me.) below the *gompa.* [From Kyangin *gompa* to Langsisa pastures and Langtang Glacier, 1 day + return. From Kyangin *gompa* to H.M. Government's Yala Cheese Factory, established with Swiss Aid, ½ day + return].

A return to Kathmandu from Kyangin *gompa* may be made by chartered S.T.O.L. aircraft, by the approach route, or by the route Kyangin *gompa* to Gosainkund lakes, 2 days, and thence to Tharepati Pass and Helmu. *See* Kathmandu–Helmu trek. The direct route Kyangin *gompa* to Tarke Ghyang in Helmu via the Ganja La (15,803 ft. 5123 me.) should only be attempted by mountaineers with adequate equipment.

KATHMANDU—NAMCHE BAZAAR—TENGBOCHE MONASTERY—EVEREST BASE CAMP

For those prepared to spend several weeks on one trek, a visit to Khumbu[1] is the most rewarding experience Nepal has to offer. The route leads for about 8 days through mixed Hindu, Tamang, Sunwar and Jirel villages. It then traverses for 2 days the region known as Solu[2], an extensive valley where substantial Sherpa villages and several monasteries are enclosed by hills clothed in pine and rhododendron forest.

[1] Fürer-Haimendorf, C. von, *The Sherpas of Nepal. Buddhist highlanders* (London, 1964); Hillary, Edmund, *Schoolhouse in the Clouds* (London, 1968).

[2] Snellgrove, D. L. *Buddhist Himalaya* Oxford, 1957).

Across the ridge to the north-east of Solu, the trail leads to Pharak, the gateway to Khumbu, with Sherpa villages set high above the bed of the Dudh Kosi River. North of the confluence of the Dudh Kosi and the Bhote Kosi is Khumbu, the region lying at the foot of some of the highest mountains in the world. Here the villages are situated at altitudes of 11,480-12,464 ft. (3500-3800 me.) and many summer settlements lie well above the 13,120 ft. (4000 me.) line. The population consists of Sherpas, a Buddhist people of Tibetan language and culture believed to have immigrated to Nepal 300-400 years ago, and some more recent immigrants from Tibet. Farming and the breeding of yak, of which large numbers can be seen on the high pastures, constitute the basis of the economy; until some ten years ago extensive trading with Tibet contributed to the region's prosperity but engagement in the tourist traffic has now replaced trade as a source of income. The attraction of Khumbu to the tourist lies in the magnificent Himalayan landscape and in contact with the homeland of the Sherpas whose mountaineering exploits have so often been recorded.

Namche Bazaar (Solu-Khumbu District, Sagarmatha Zone), the first village in Khumbu may be reached by a combination of air journeys (chartered) and walking days: by air to Lukla in the Pharak region + 2 walking days; by air to Salleri in the Solu Valley + 5 walking days; by air to Jiri in Ramechap District, Janakpur Zone + 10 walking days. Guests of the Everest View Hotel, situated above Namche Bazaar can fly to Shyangboche S.T.O.L. Airfield + 1½ hour's walk.

A minimum of 15 walking days is required for the trek from Dolalghat, on the Arniko Rajmarga to Namche Bazaar. The journey Kathmandu to Dolalghat 35 mi. (56 km.) can be made by bus or other motorised transport.

1st day. Dolalghat. Check Post. Shops. Cross suspension bridge over Sunkosi River. Make the long steep climb to the Hindu village of Dumre (4000 ft. 1250 me.). Continue climbing the whole day and camp on grassy slope near the Tamang village of Chyaubas (6890 ft. 2100 me.).

2nd day. 5 hours. Short climb, then follow trail along the crest of an east-west running ridge; descend to and cross small stream. A gentle ascent leads to Risingo, a mixed Brahmin, Newar and Tamang village with a Buddhist *gompa*, decorated in Tibetan style; camping is permitted in the *gompa* courtyard.

3rd day. 6 hours. Steep descent to river; after crossing, continue for 3 hours through terraced rice-fields to Phedi; climb steeply through sub-tropical forest to the Newar village of Chitre (7700 ft. 2350 me.). Camp on grassy slope.

4th day. 5 hours. Climb for 1 hour to Manga Deorali Pass (8266 ft. 2520 me.). Good views of Mts. Gaurishanker and Meluntse. Pleasant descent through pine forest to Charnawati Khola. In about 3 hours cross river by chain bridge, and climb to the Hindu village of Kiran-tichap (4330 ft. 1320 me.). Camp under shady trees.

5th day. 6½ hours. Descend for one hour through pine and deciduous forest into the valley of the Bhote Kosi (2800 ft. 853 me.); cross the river by a good bridge. Climb the east bank, reaching in about 2½ hours Namdu (4900 ft. 1493 me.). Keeping on the south side of the ridge, continue through terraced fields; pass a small pagoda temple dedicated to Mahadeo and arrive at Kabre (6023 ft. 1836 me.). After a short descent to the Yarsa Khola, climb to the Hindu village of Yarsa (6475 ft. 1974 me.).

6th day. 6½ hours. Steep ascent of 2-3 hours through forest to pass (8276 ft. 2523 me.). Good views of Rolwaling Himal and the rocky spire of Mt. Chobo Bhamare (19,546 ft. 5959 me.). Below the pass is a small Sherpa settlement. Follow trail eastwards. A long pleasant descent leads to the valley of the Sikri Khola (6250 ft. 1905 me.). [From Sikri Khola to Jiri (6250 ft. 1905 me.) 1½ hours. Government Offices, Weekly Saturday Market. H.M. Government Agricultural and Veterinary Development Centre. Hospital. Sherpa restaurant. Rest rooms for hire. S.T.O.L. airfield. From Jiri to Those 3 hours + 1 hour to rejoin main trail at Kattike on the Khimti Khola.] Cross to the east bank of the river and climb to the opposite ridge. Pass a group of *chorten* (6796 ft. 2072 me.) and descend past the settlement of Kattike to the Khimti Khola. Cross by suspension bridge and camp by the river.

7th day. 6½ hours. Follow east bank of Khimti Khola upstream and after 1½ hours reach the Newar settlement of Shivalaya (5800 ft. 1769 me.). Climb steeply to Sangbadanda schoolhouse. Bear right for main trail. [From Schoolhouse bear left for Thodang Cheese Factory (10,140 ft. 3091 me.), founded with Swiss Aid and now administered by H.M. Government. 3 hours + 1 hour to rejoin main trail on pass. From Thodang Cheese Factory to Thodang *gompa* ½ hour + 1½ hours to rejoin main trail on pass]. Ascend the forest trail on north side of the Mohabir Khola Valley that leads to the pass lying at 8900 ft. (2713 me.), marked by a large collection of *mani* walls; there is a water point just below the pass. Descend to Bandar-Changma (7196 ft. 2194 me.), a fertile valley inhabited mainly by Sherpas, but with some recent Newar and Brahmin settlers. Pass groups of *chorten* and camp on grass slopes below Changma, or crave the hospitality of a Sherpa house.

8th day. 5½ hours. Make the long descent to and across two streams; continue through forest and terraced fields to the Surma Khola (5100 ft. 1555 me.). Cross to the north bank and continue descent to Likhu Khola. Cross suspension bridge and proceed upstream. On the east bank of the Kenja Khola is the Hindu settlement of Kenja. An arduous 3-hour climb up the south side of the west-lying ridge leads to Seti (8446 ft. 2575 me.), a Sherpa settlement with a *gompa* in which a night's shelter may be sought.

9th day. 7 hours. Long steep ascent through mixed rhododendron forest; at 11,149 ft. (3399 me.), bear left and reach in 3-4 hours Lamjura Pass (11,572 ft. 3530 me.). Good views from the peak north of the pass. Descend through pine forest interspersed with rhododendrons into the valley of the Solu River. Pass forest clearings used as yak and horse pastures and reach Thakto (9381 ft. 2860 me.) in 1½ hours. Continue on trail skirting north side of the valley. In 1 hour reach Junbesi, a large and prosperous Sherpa village, with two- and three-storey houses, 2 *gompa* and many *chorten*. Camp below the village close to pine grove and water, or accept hospitality in a Sherpa house. [From Junbesi to Thubtencholing Gompa ½ hour. From Junbesi to Chalsa International Red Cross Tibetan Refugee Centre and Carpet Factory, via Chiong Gompa, Phaphlu, Salleri District headquarters and Dorphu weekly market: 5 hours + return.]

10th day. 6½ hours. Cross log bridge over Junbesi Khola. Proceed on upper trail. Round Sallung Ridge (10,000 ft. 3048 me.) and continue northwards, keeping high above the valley of the Ringmo Khola. In Sallung (8525 ft. 2599 me.), basic supplies may be purchased. The path descends gradually along the hillside, dropping suddenly to a small stream. On the opposite bank climb to the Sherpa village of Ringmo. Proceed eastwards, pass *mani* walls and ascend to Trakshindu Pass (10,122 ft. 3086 me.), with *chorten*, *mani* walls and prayer flags marking the summit. Descend 530 ft. (162 me.) to the monastery of Trakshindu, founded by a monk from Tengboche. Guest house and English-speaking Abbot.

Fine frescoes painted by a Solu Sherpa. Continue descent through forest for 2 hours and camp on grass below the small Sherpa village of Manidingma (7196 ft. 2194 me.).

11th day. 5 hours. Continue descent, passing terraces and the scattered settlements of Chorco (7000 ft. 2134 me.) and Phuleli (6494 ft. 1980 me.). After 1½-2 hours through mixed forest cross the Swiss-built suspension bridge over the Dudh Kosi River. Climb steeply to the Rai village of Jubing (5500 ft. 1676 me.). Scale the cliff path behind the village and follow a contour path to the mixed Magar-Sherpa-Rai village of Khari Khola. Camp in village. Sherpa "hotel".

12th day. 6 hours. Cross the bridge over the Karikhola river. A long steep climb leads to the Sherpa settlement of Karte. Good water point. Continue climbing through mixed forest, with a wealth of rhododendron and magnolia, to Khari Pass (10,197 ft. 3109 me.), where there is an "hotel". Descend 1150 ft. (350 me.) to stream cascading through narrow valley and camp.

13th day. 7 hours. Climb up north side of valley to Phuiyan (7823 ft. 2385 me.) and continue along crest of ridge. Good views of the Pharak Region, and the Dudh Kosi Valley with Sherpa villages situated on ledges high above the bed of the river. Long descent to Surkya (7672 ft. 2339 me.) situated at the bridge-crossing of a Dudh Kosi tributary. Climb out of the valley and proceed north, passing on the left, the path leading in 1 hour to Lukla airfield (8213 ft. 2827 me.). Descend into a deep gorge with a high waterfall and ascend to Chaurikarkha (8500 ft. 2530 me.), a village with three massive *chorten* and a *gompa*. Shop. The trail passes through terraced fields and climbs to a ridge (8850 ft. 2698 me.). Continue over gently undulating country and then gradually descend to the Dudh Kosi bridge leading to Ghat (8348 ft. 2545 me.). Follow path along east bank through Chhutrawa (8500 ft. 2591 me.) to Phakding (8700 ft. 2652 me.) and camp on the west bank of the Dudh Kosi.

14th day. 5 hours. Follow trail running beside Dudh Kosi River, crossing and re-crossing good bridges and ascending and descending short steep inclines. The scenery in the narrow valley offers pine forest and a profusion of flowers in the spring. After 1 hour pass Benkar bridge (9530 ft. 2905 me.); continue to Jorsale, situated on the west bank, with a hermitage built against the rock face above the village. Beyond Jorsale the valley narrows; the junction of the Bhote Kosi, flowing from the north, and the Dudh Kosi flowing from the north-east marks the borders of the Khumbu region. Follow the Bhote Kosi. Cross the two bridges built by Sir Edmund Hillary in 1964, which have given the name "Bridges Camp" (9296 ft. 2834 me.) to the locality. Climb steeply out of the gorge; after about 1650 ft. (500 me.) Mt. Everest behind the Lhotse-Nuptse ridge can be seen through the Dudh Kosi Gorge. 2½-3 hours from Bridges Camp is Namche Bazaar (11,300 ft. 3446 me.), an important Sherpa village and traditionally the entrepot station on the Nepal–Tibet trade route over the Nangpa La. Military and Police Check Posts. Government Offices. Shops. T.E.L.E. communications. Weekly Saturday market. Tibetan-run restaurant. *gompa*. [From Namche Bazaar to Thami *gompa*[1] (12,497 ft. 3810 me.) via the Gong La (11,402 ft. 3476 me.), and then to Thomde village, *gompa* and Check Post (11,497 ft. 3505 me.). 1 day + return].

15th day. 5 hours. Climb to the saddle east of Namche Bazaar. Follow contour path running high above the Dudh Kosi Gorge and

[1] No permits are issued for routes north of Thami. The route eastwards from Thami to the Rolwaling Valley, via the Teshi Laptsha Pass (18,877 ft. 5755 me.) is for mountaineers only.

continue to the head of the descent to the Dudh Kosi River, where the path from Namche and that from Khumjung meet. [From Namche-Khumjung cross-roads to Everest View Hotel. ½ an hour.] Descend through forest, passing below the winter settlement of Teshinga to the Dudh Kosi River (10,650 ft. 3247 me.), where there is a bridge, water mills, tea and liquor stalls and the small village of Phuki. Climb 2 hours to Tengboche monastery (12,714 ft. 3876 me.). Monastery and *gompa*, founded in 1934 by Gulu Lama, a Sherpa of Khumbu. Good frescoes in the interior. Guest House. Lama-run restaurant. Mani-rimdu dance drama performed in November/December[1]. Visitors are welcome and respects can be paid to the abbot; donations are appreciated.

16th day. 4 hours. Descend in a north-easterly direction through pleasant woodland, where blood pheasant and deer are protected; pass Devuche nunnery and *gompa*, proceed to Milingbo (12,399 ft. 3780 me.) and continue to the Imja Khola. Cross to the left bank and climb past *mani* walls to Pangboche (12,796 ft. 3901 me.), a village with the oldest *gompa* in Khumbu. Follow path on west bank of the Imja Khola climbing gradually past the summer settlements of Shomare, Orsho and Og to the Khumbu Khola near its junction with the Imja Khola (13,648 ft. 1461 me.). Camp on yak pastures. [From the junction of the Khumbu Khola and Imja Khola to Chukung yak pastures, via the summer settlement of Dingboche, and the Imja Glacier. 5 hours + return.]

17th day. 6 hours. Proceed north over grass-flats; pass the summer settlement of Phalang Karpo. Turn north-east and climb the lateral moraine of the Khumbu Glacier. After gaining the crest, descend and cross two glacial streams. Continue north-east to the stone-built huts and yak pastures of Lobuche summer settlement (16,171 ft. 4930 me.). Good view from ridge west of Loboche.

18th day. 2½-3 hours. Follow trail running through a trough adjacent to the Khumbu glacier and crossing the terminal moraines flowing in from the north-west. Continue over rough ground to the glacier lake and follow contour path round the lake to Gorak Shep. Memorials to Jake Breitenback, killed on the 1963 American Everest Expedition and to a former Indian Ambassador, H. Dayal, who died here in 1964. 1½ hours north of Gorak Shep is Kalar Pattar, a rounded, rubble-covered hill standing to the south of Mt. Pumo Ri. Good view of the South Col of Everest from cairn at the north end of Kalar Pattar (18,444 ft. 5623 me.).

19th day. 6 hours. Proceed over rough ground to the foot of the Khumbu Glacier and the base-camps of the expeditions climbing Everest (17,400 ft. 5304 me.). Good view of Khumbu Icefall. Return to Pheriche and camp on yak pastures.

20th day. 5 hours. Return to Tengboche.

21st day. 4 hours. Descend through woods to the bridge over the Dudh Kosi and ascend to the plateau lying below Khumbi Yulha mountain. Proceed to Khumjung village and *gompa*. Sir Edmund Hillary's school is situated to the south of the great *mani* wall, on the left of the path that leads to Shyamboche S.T.O.L. Airfield and Namche Bazaar. [From Khumjung to Gokyo Glacier Lake (15,715 ft. 4791 me.), via summer settlements and yak pastures of Lhaparma (14,196 ft. 4328 me.), Lusa (14,399 ft. 4390 me.), and Machherma (14,646 ft. 4465 me.) 1½ days + return.] Continue westwards to Khunde where there is a Hillary Hospital staffed with New Zealand doctors. Leave Khunde by path leading south; after a short ascent, descend to Namche Bazaar.

The return to Kathmandu can be made by any of the combinations of air journeys and walking days listed on p. 686.

[1] Jerstad, L. G., *Mani-rimdu. Sherpa Dance Drama* (Seattle, U.S.A., 1969).

POKHARA—KALI GANDAKI VALLEY—JOMOSOM[1]

This trek provides a variety of landscape and many spectacular views. From the broad sub-tropical valley of Pokhara, the trail rises to the Ghorapani Pass, then drops into the Kali Gandaki River, which here flows in a deep gorge between the Dhaulagiri and Annapurna massifs. The villages en route are inhabited by a mixed population of Hindu castes and several tribal groups; the hills to the east are the traditional homeland of Gurungs and those to the west of Magars.[2] Above the gorge the valley opens out and the Kali Gandaki, flowing through a broad bed, becomes fordable. To either side of the river is the area known as Thak Khola and the 13 villages of the Thakali, a mongoloid people speaking a Tibeto-Burman language. In the mid-19th and early 20th century they controlled the important trade in Tibetan salt and wool on the north-south route from Tibet, via Mustang to the central highlands of Nepal; today the Thakali élite have deserted Thak Khola and entered the wider field of the country's economic development and their commercial undertakings extend over large areas of Central and Southern Nepal. Beyond Tukche, the main entrepôt in the salt-trade, lie the 5 villages of Panchgaon, whose inhabitants are closely related to the Thakali. To the north of Panchgaon extends an arid region known as Baragaon. Here Tibetan cultural influence prevails and the population resembles the Bhotiya of other border areas. Muktinath, an important centre of pilgrimage for both Hindus and Buddhists, lies at the foot of the Annapurna Himal. Between Baragaon and the frontier is Mustang, once an autonomous principality, whose rulers were of Tibetan stock. In a barren landscape similar to that of the Tibetan plateau villages and monasteries are situated close to the source of water, and cultivation is confined to small areas of irrigated land in the vicinity of settlements. Lo M'angthang, the capital of Mustang is a rectangular walled town whose gates are closed at nightfall.

The most convenient base for the Kali Gandaki Valley trek is Pokhara, which can be reached by air or road from Kathmandu (*see* Excursions from Kathmandu: Pokhara). In the dry season direct charter flights by S.T.O.L. aircraft can be arranged between Kathmandu and Jomosom. A minimum of 7 walking days + return should be allowed for the trek from Pokhara to Jomosom.

1st day. 5 hours. Trekkers should leave Pokhara town at the north-west end, passing the British Mission Hospital (Shining Hospital) and crossing the Yangadi Khola. Continue for 1½ hours to the Tibetan Refugee Camp at Hyangja (3500 ft. 1067 me.). Accommodation and messing available at the camp.

2nd day. 7 hours. Proceed westwards over the rice fields of the upper Yangadi Khola Valley to Suikhet (3598 ft. 1097 me.); continue along stony stream-bed to ford below Naudanda Hill. Climb zig-zag path to summit (4783 ft. 1458 me.). Good views of Phewa Tal to the south and Mt. Machhapuchhre and the Annapurna Himal to the north-east.

3rd day. 6½ hours. Descend to Lumle and the Agricultural Training Centre maintained by the Gurkha Welfare Board. Continue to Chandrakot at the west end of the ridge. Drop steeply to the Modi Khola and cross suspension bridge to Birethanti (3401 ft. 1037 me.). Shops and bazaar. [From Birethanti to Annapurna Sanctuary (11,697 ft. 3566 me.), via the Modi Khola Valley and the Gurung village of Ghandrung. 6 days + return.] Follow the east bank of Bhurungdi Khola westwards, pass

[1] Snellgrove, D. L., *Himalayan Pilgrimage* (Oxford, 1961).
[2] Hitchcock, John T., *The Magars of Banyan Hill* (New York, 1966).

Hille and camp at Tirkedhunga (4720 ft. 1439 me.).

4th day. 6-7 hours. Cross log bridges over the Bhurungdi Khola and a tributary stream. Climb steeply to Ulleri (6800 ft. 2073 me.) and continue climbing through luxuriant rhododendron forest to Thanti. After 5 hours cross Ghorapani Pass (9300 ft. 2835 me.). Below the pass is a small settlement and a good camp site. Views of Dhaulagiri and Tukche peak may be obtained from a clearing east of the pass.

5th day. 7 hours. Descend through farmland. Pass villages of Chitre (7698 ft. 2347 me.), Phalate (7400 ft. 2256 me.) and Sikha (6599 ft. 2012 me.), where there is a dispensary, shop and good food stall. Continue descent to Ghara, and then more steeply to the Kali Gandaki River, flowing here through the gorge separating the Annapurna and Dhaulagiri massifs. Cross good suspension bridge to west bank. 2 hours from Ghara is Tatopani. Shops. "Hotels". Hot springs. [From Tatopani to Dhorpatan, via Ching Khola, Kainhe Khani, Lumsum and Gurja Khani. 10 days + return. From Tatopani to Pokhara via Baglung: 3 days.]

6th day. 7 hours. Follow track on west bank of gorge. Cross to east bank, and return to west bank. In 2 hours reach the large village of Dana (4750 ft. 1448 me.). Police Check Post; Government Offices. Continue upstream, crossing the Kali Gandaki River below Rukse Khola waterfall. Good view of the Kali Gandaki cataracts. Re-cross the river and follow rock-cut trail on west bank, which runs high above the gorge, to Kabre (5901 ft. 1799 me.). Descend to river-bank and climb again to Ghasa (6599 ft. 2012 me.), the first Thakali village.

7th day. 7 hours. Follow mule trail northwards. Cross the Kaidu Khola and the Lete Khola, and climb through forests to the dispersed Thakali village of Lete. Continue 1½ hours to Kalo Pani (8397 ft. 2560 me.). [From Kalo Pani to Miristi Khola (12,996 ft. 3962 me.) and the mountain cirque of Annapurna, Tilicho and the Nilgiri mountains. 4 days + return.] Good views of Annapurna I to the east and Dhaulagiri and Tukche Peak to the west. Cross the Kali Gandaki River at Dhumpu; proceed through pine forest on the west bank to Sirkung (8499 ft. 2591 me.) and continue to the delta of the Ghatte Khola, which is crossed by a series of log bridges. The Kali Gandaki Valley now opens out; Dhaulagiri is seen vertically above the trail. Cross the Larjung Khola, pass the Thakali village of Larjung (8397 ft. 2560 me.) and camp in Khobang (8397 ft. 2560 me.); Devi Than Gompa stands on a knoll east of the village.

8th day. 6 hours. Follow trail along west bank of the Kali Gandaki River for 1 hour to Tukche, an ancient trading post and the old seat of the Subba (Government contractor) administration. The centre of Thakali commercial enterprise, it has many storied-houses enclosing courtyards. Two *gompa* and several *manī* walls. Post-box. Basic stores available. Continue along river-bank, passing the bridge leading to Tserok village and *gompa*. 1 hour from Tukche is H.M. Government's fruit and vegetable farm which offers produce for sale. ½ hour to the north is the Panchgaon town of Marpha; the *gompa* on the hill has good wall-paintings and temple furniture; the monks perform the *mani-rimdu* dance drama in October. [From Marpha to Tukche via the high altitude areas of Marpha Fields, lower Tukche yak pasture, Dampus Pass (17,004 ft. 5184 me.) and the "Hidden" Valley. 5-6 days.] Cross the Pongkyu Khola; visible to the west is Syang village and *gompa* and to the east Thimigaon village and *gompa* (9496 ft. 2895 me.). [From Thimigaon to Tilicho Pass (16,728 ft. 5100 me.) and Tilicho Glacier Lake. 3 days + return.] Continue on the west bank of the Kali Gandaki. 4 hours from Tukche is Jomosom (8899 ft. 2713 me.). Military and Police Check Posts.

T.E.L.E. communications, S.T.O.L. Airfield, inn, shops. A good bridge leads to Jomosom village situated on the east bank of the Kali Gandaki River. [Routes for permit holders only: From Jomosom to Tsarka, Dolpa District, via Dangarjong. 5 days + return. From Jomosom to Muktinath pilgrimage centre, via Kagbeni. 2 days + return. From Jomosom to Lo M'angthang. 4 days + return.]

KATHMANDU—JUMLA—RARA LAKE (Mahendra Tal)

Western Nepal has only recently been opened to tourists, and in the remoter valleys, there are still those who are shy of strangers. However, the scenic beauty of the Jumla region, which is richer in forests than any other part of Nepal, merits a visit by those prepared to trek and camp in country providing as yet few facilities for travellers.

The easiest approach is by RNAC scheduled flight (not operational during the monsoon, June-September) from Kathmandu to Jumla, the headquarters of the Karnali Zone and of Jumla District. Combined air and walking journeys to Jumla may be undertaken as follows: RNAC scheduled flight to Pokhara + 16 walking days via Dhorpatan; RNAC scheduled flight to Surkhet + 9 walking days via Dailekh; RNAC scheduled flight to Nepalganj + 11 walking days via Surkhet. Chartered planes can land on the flats at the south end of Rara Lake.

Jumla, locally known as Khalanga (8036 ft. 2450 me.), once the capital of the overlords of the medieval Baisi and Chaubisi Rajas of Western Nepal, is situated in the valley of the Tila River. Ruined forts of the Jumla rajas stand in outlying parts of the Jumla kingdom, but in the vicinity of Jumla town only a shrine to the royal tutelary deity marks the site of the old palace. The Jumla kingdom was incorporated into Nepal at the end of the 18th century. Until recently a small town, it is now rapidly developing into an important administrative centre. Military and Police Check Posts, T.E.L.E. communications, airfield, Post Office, shops. Temples dedicated to Bhairab and Chandranath are centres of pilgrimage. The town's population consists mainly of high Hindu castes (Brahmin, Thakuri, Chetri and some Newar); Thakuri, Brahmin and Chetri dominate the major valleys of Jumla District, but the interior hills are inhabited by Matwali Chetri and the most northerly regions by Bhotiya. Scattered over the Jumla region are the architectural remains of the ancient Malla[1] kingdom which from the 13th-14th centuries ruled large parts of Western Nepal, as well as the Tibetan regions of Purang and Guge from the capital, Sinja. Easily accessible from Jumla is the complex of temples, stele and *chaitya* in Michagaon village (1 hour's walk west of Jumla). Most of the monuments combine Buddhist and Hindu features and bear Sanskrit inscriptions.

Rara lake, 4 days' journey from Jumla, is the largest expanse of water in Nepal. It is surrounded by low wooded hills and on the western shore are two villages inhabited by Thakuri and Chetri. The inhabitants own no boats and fish with harpoons, standing knee high in water. In the winter season the lake attracts a large number of water birds migrating from Central Asia.

For the trek to Rara Lake a minimum of 4 walking days is required. The return to Jumla may be made either on the approach route or via the Chuchimara Lekh and Sinja, the ruined capital of the 12th-14th-century Malla kings. The round trip Jumla–Rara–Sinja–Jumla requires a minimum of 8 walking days.

1st day. 6 hours. Proceed north from Jumla town and ascend first through cultivated fields and then over grassland to an easy pass (9840

[1] Tucci, Guiseppe, *Nepal. The Discovery of the Malla* (New York, 1962).

ft. 3280 me.). Descend to Padmara and camp on the outskirts of the village.

2nd day. 6 hours. Ascend through pine forest to high grazing grounds and continue for 1 hour over grassland. Descend steeply to the Neura Khola. Cross to the right bank. Climb to a trail, which running high above the gorge, rises steadily to Bumra village. Drop to the valley of the Kabre Khola and camp in forest on the fringe of a small settlement of Matwali Chetri.

3rd day. 7-8 hours. Climb to and follow west-running contour path high above the river; proceed to Boda village; descend steeply to Chauta. "Hotel". Turn right and climb through forest and patches of cultivated land; continue long ascent of rolling grassland to cairn marking the pass. Descend steeply on stony path for 3 hours. Good views from the trail of the basin of the Mugu Karnali. Camp in Pina, a small village above the large village of Gum where there is a District Commissioner's Office, T.E.L.E. communications and a P.O.; basic stores available. [From Pina to Mugu 5 days + return. From Pina to the Nara La via Simikot 16 days + return.]

4th day. 7 hours. Proceed westwards, passing several villages inhabited by Thakuri and Chetri. Climb to the crest of a hill overlooking Rara Lake. Descend to the lakeside and follow trail encircling the south and west of Rara Lake to Rara village. Camp near the shore below the houses. A good view of Rara lake may be obtained by climbing the hill to the west of Rara village.

5th day. 7 hours. Return to the south west corner of Rara Lake. Follow the stream flowing south and continue to the foot of Chuchimara Lekh. Bear west and climb through forest, and then more steeply up a barren ridge (*c.* 13,120 ft. 4000 me.). Magnificent view of the Saipal Range to the west and of Rara Lake to the north. Negotiate a second ridge; descend into a south-running valley and camp in stream bed where water is available.

6th day. 7 hours. Climb and descend several sharp inclines and cross several west-east running streams, maintaining a general southwards direction. At the head of the last steep climb a ridge is gained from which there is a view of a wide valley. Descend to Luma village; continue descending, following the path running parallel with the stream that flows into the Sinja Khola. Turn left before the confluence and proceed upstream; camp in Hat Sinja, a large and prosperous village situated on the west bank of the Sinja Khola, inhabited mainly by Thakuri.

7th day. 7 hours. Leave the village at the north end, cross the Sinja Khola and climb to the ruined fort of the 12th-14th-century Sinja kings. No structures of historical significance now stand, but several carved stone lions testify to the former importance of Indo-Buddhist influence. The temple dedicated to Kanakasundari is of relatively recent date. Leave the fort area, and ascend through forest to an altitude of *c.* 10,496 ft. (3200 me.); camp near the stream in any one of the many forest clearings.

8th day. 8 hours. Follow trail first through forest and then over rolling meadow-land. Descend steeply on a good path and enter Jumla (Khalanga) at the north-west end of town.

THE PEOPLE'S REPUBLIC OF BANGLADESH

Area 55,126 sq.m.

Population 81,000,000.

President: Major-General Ziaur Rahman.

History. In Mughal and British times the territory of Bangladesh was known as East Bengal, with a highly individual culture of its own. In 1947, strongly supporting Mr Jinnah's campaign for a Muslim National Home, it became part of the new State under the name of East Pakistan.

Eventually aspirations for separate statehood led to an armed rising against the authority of the Central Government of Pakistan; and with the help of Indian troops a Government of Bangladesh was set up in Dacca under Sheikh Mujibur Rahman in December 1971 and independence was declared. The new State quickly secured general international recognition and Pakistan followed suit in February 1974 in which month Sheikh Mujibur Rahman attended the Islamic Conference in Lahore. From its inception Bangladesh became a prey to economic disasters. After the failure of Sheikh Mujibur Rahman's efforts to improve matters by assuming autocratic powers early in 1975, he and his family perished in a military *coup d'etat* in the following August. The current ruler is Major-General Ziaur Rahman.

Before the partition of the subcontinent, in 1947, the usual route followed by travellers to the country which is now Bangladesh was via Calcutta and thence either by steamer or by railway plus steamer. So long as the country was part of Pakistan access by these means largely ceased; with the independence of Bangladesh, the former links have been restored, and have again become popular with visitors who have the time and inclination to tour through this very beautiful, very fertile and almost waterlogged country. Relations between India and Bangladesh being close and cordial, customs formalities at the frontier present few difficulties. Steamer traffic on the Brahmaputra R. between Assam and West Bengal via the harbours of Bangladesh is functioning again. **Visitors should note that with few exceptions—India is one—travellers coming from other countries need a visa of entry.** This applies to almost all countries of the Commonwealth, although Bangladesh herself is a member.

The majority of tourists now prefer to travel to Dacca by air. The flight from Calcutta to Dacca, where there is a fine international airport, takes only 1½ hours. Dacca itself is linked to all the principal places in Bangladesh by the national airline, Bangladesh Biman, so that rapid tours of the country are easy for visitors with little time to spend. There is a good road from West Bengal which links up with the road networks of Bangladesh, and touring by car is very pleasant. Particulars can be had from Automobile Association offices in Calcutta and Dacca.

For travellers by train from West Bengal the routes are as follows:

ROUTE 1

(1.) (*a*) Calcutta *via* Goalundo to Narainganj and Dacca.

5 m. Dumdum Junction for Khulna.

46 m. **Ranaghat Junction** (D.B.). Branch E. to Bongaon, connecting with the Jessore and Khulna line and branch N.W. to Murshidabad.

Just before Darsana (75 m.) between Ranaghat and Chuadanga the frontier is crossed, and passport and customs examination takes place there. A railway connection has also been made from Darsana to Jessore, *via* Kotchandpur.

84 m. Chuadanga, indigo-growing centre until 1880.

103 m. Poradaha Junction. Here the through route to Dacca and Chittagong *via* Goalundo Ghat turns East.

111 m. Kushtia (D.B.K.).

114 m., near Kumarkhali, the Gorai river, a spill of the Ganges, is crossed.

136 m. Kalukhali. Branch line to **Faridpur** (30 m.) and Bhatiapara (47 m.).

155 m. **Goalundo Ghat** is near the junction of the Ganges and Brahmaputra rivers, which below this point is called the Padma. Later, when it is joined by the Meghna from the N., it forms a body of water so wide across that in the centre the low shores are scarcely visible. Above the confluence the Brahmaputra is locally called the Jamuna.

There is a regular daily service by steamer to *Narainganj* for *Dacca*: and to *Chandpur* for *Chittagong*, *Comilla* and *Sylhet* by railway. There are also frequent launches from Narainganj to Munshiganj and from there to Dacca.

Narainganj (D.B.), situated at the junction of the Lakhya with the Dhaleswari, an arm of the Meghna, is the river-port of Dacca, and has a large trade, particularly in jute. Near it there are some old forts of Mir Jumla's, and opposite the town, on the E. bank of the Lakhya, a celebrated shrine of Kadam Rasul. There is a good club.

The great Adamji jute mills, the largest in the world, are well worth visiting: and many other new industries have sprung up at Narainganj.

Near Munshiganj, across the Dhaleswari, Idrakpur Fort built by Mir Jumla (1660), is still in good condition, and the Sub-divisional officer's residence has been built over the former magazine.

From Narainganj the railway runs 11 m. to

Dacca (23° 43′ N. and 90° 24′ E.) now the capital of Bangladesh and the seat of Parliament, is pleasant in the winter and has hotels which cater for European and American visitors. The Intercontinental Hotel has every amenity. Accommodation may also be available at the Dacca Club on adequate notice being given. The city, with a population of over half a million, lies on the N. bank of the Buriganga river, along which it extends for nearly 4 m. from beyond the Lal Bagh on the W. to the suspension bridge over the Dholai Khal (Creek) on the E., presenting an imposing river frontage. The Brahmaputra once ran E. of the city.

Along the central portion of the river front runs a fine promenade called the Buckland Bund, Behind it is the Ahsan Manzil palace of the Nawabs of Dacca, where the French factory stood. Here, too, within a short distance, are many important buildings, various Banks, the Collegiate School (formerly Dacca College), on the site of the English factory, the Courts and Government Kutcheries, the English Church, the Baptist Mission buildings and the Roman Catholic Cathedral. A Church of the Austin Friars is recorded in 1666. There are two interesting museums: the Archaeological (sculpture, paintings, coins) and the Dacca Museum (Mughal arms, jewellery, muslins).

Opposite the Gulistan Cinema near the stadium stands an ancient cannon, by tradition a male gun, "Kale Jham Jham", whose mate, Bibi Mariam, lies at the bottom of the river, and calls to him every night, and thus causes the mysterious booming noises known as the "Barisal guns". A broad road runs due N. from the Sadar Ghat to the Civil Station of Ramna.

Above the Bund the Bara (great) Katra faces the bank of the river. It was built in 1644 by the Dewan Mir Abdul Kasim, and seems to have been intended for a royal residence. From the roof a good view of the city and river is to be had. About 100 yd. E. of this is the Chhota (little) Katra, built by Shaista Khan in 1664.

S.E. is the Salimullah Medical College Hospital, on the site of the Dutch factory. A short distance to the N.W. is the Lal Bagh fort, built by Muhammad Azam, third son of Aurangzeb, when Viceroy of Bengal, in 1678, but left unfinished. Aurangzeb afterwards gave it as a *Jagir* to Shaista Khan, whose daughter, Pari Bibi, lies buried in a tomb within the fort.

Amongst many other interesting monuments at Dacca are: the *Husani Dalan*, built by Mir Murad in 1642, where the Muharram is celebrated annually with intense fervour; the *Temple of Dhakeswari*, the most famous Hindu shrine in these parts; the *Sat Gumbad* (seven domes) mosque, some 6 m. W. of Dacca, said to have been built by Shaista Khan, with the Sat Gumbad Mausoleum 100 yd. E. of it, containing two tombs, where two of his daughters are said to be buried.

When the Generals of Akbar conquered Eastern Bengal in 1575, the capital of the province was at Sonargaon, some 20 m. E. of Dacca, where there are still many interesting ruins. These include the tomb of Sultan Ghiasuddin (1399-1409), the Shrines of Panjpirs and Shah Abdul Ali, and a notable mosque in Goaldi village. In the reign of Jahangir the capital was transferred to Dacca by the Governor, Islam Khan, grandson of Shaikh Salim Chishti. The English factors settled here first in 1666, and not long afterwards were subjected to great oppression by the Governor, Shaista Khan, uncle of the Emperor Aurangzeb. In 1704 the Governor moved to Murshidabad, and the glory of Dacca grew dim, until (1905-1911) it revived while Dacca was capital of the new province of Eastern Bengal and Assam. Government officials mostly left the old town for the new residential area of Ramna, where the Secretariat and Government House were located. Dacca was made capital of the new province of East Pakistan and the legislative capital of the Federation, by the Pakistan Government.

At Ramna there is the Atomic Energy Centre. The Club is to the N.; the Dacca University area lie mainly to the S. and W. The University of Dacca was opened in 1921. It inherited the old Dacca College (1842) and has been greatly extended since 1947 with many new buildings, science laboratories, and halls of residence. The Museum (1913) and Library of old Sanskrit and Persian MSS. are well worth a visit.

During the period when Bangladesh was part of Pakistan, Dacca as the second capital was endowed with fine new extensions and many modern buildings in the Motijheel commercial area, a stadium, a technical college, broadcasting studios, and a go-ahead Development Board. It forged ahead both industrially and economically, although much damage was done during the fighting of 1971-72. It is proving very difficult to get the economy moving once more.

At Kurmitola, 10 m. distant by road, where the new Cantonments are located, a forest begins, which stretches N. for over 100 m. to Tangail, but big game has now been driven farther afield. Duck are plentiful in places, but snipe are scarce.

In the Rains much of Dacca District is deep under water.

The railway from Dacca proceeds N. to

14 m. Tangi, junction for **Bhairab Bazar,** an important communications centre. From Bhairab Bazar there is a direct line *via* Kishoreganj, a subdivisional headquarters, to Mymensingh. The line *via* Brahmanbaria, a big trading centre, to Akhaura, links up with the line between Chittagong and Sylhet (see p. 701).

76 m. Mymensingh (see 3 below).

109 m. Singhjani Junction (see 3 below).

(1.) (*b*) **Calcutta** *via* **Goalundo** to **Chandpur** and **Chittagong.**

The route as far as Goalundo is the same as that for Dacca. From Goalundo there is a regular service of steamers to **Chandpur** (D.B.), a thriving river-port and jute centre, from which there is rail connection with

32 m. **Laksam** Junction station, whence the railway runs S.E. to **Chittagong,** 81 m. A branch line also runs S. to Noakhali, and the main line runs on to Comilla, Akhaura and Sylhet.

(2.) From **Calcutta** to **N. Bengal** *via* the **Hardinge Bridge** and **Parbatipur.**

(For the journey from Calcutta to Poradaha (103 m.) see p. 696.)

125 m. **Ishurdi** Junction, after crossing the Ganges by the Hardinge Bridge, N.E. to Siraganj. Motor-bus to Pabna, 18 m.

132 m. **Gopalpur,** branch to Rajshahi (29 m.) and Amnura. **Rajshahi** has a museum ("Barendra" called after the ancient kingdom of that name) and is an important University centre, second in repute only to Dacca itself. It is the main centre of the sericulture and silk industry, with 1500 acres of mulberry for rearing silkworms. The Rajshahi area contains some of the most notable antiquities in Bangladesh. **Mahasthan Garh** shows three periods of rule—Buddhist, Hindu and Muslim.

173 m. **Santahar** Junction. Branch line (M.G.) to Bogra and Teesta Junction.

At **Paharpur,** 2 m. from Jamalganj station (208 m.), are the ruins of the largest Buddhist buildings south of the Himalayas. The central shrine, with terracotta plaques, is so lofty that it has given its name ("Pahar" = Hill) to the whole locality. There have been many valuable finds—coins, images, inscribed plaques in the ruins of the monastery, which is said to have been founded by King Dharma Aal (700 A.D.).

233 m. **Parbatipur** (R.), from this junction railways branch N. to Haldibari, W. to Dinajpur (formerly this line linked up with Katihar Junction) and E. past **Rangpur** (D.B.) to **Kaunia** (D.B.), where it joins a line from Santahar.

272 m. **Teesta** Junction, crossing the Teesta by a bridge 2100 ft. long (1901) to

280 m. **Lalmanirhat** (R. and D.B.), whence, *via* Golakganj Junction and Fakiragram, it is possible to join the Assam Railway running between Siliguri and Pandu. Lalmanirhat is also the junction for the Branch railway *via* Gaibanda and Bogra for Santahar.

(3.) From **Calcutta** to **Mymensingh** *via* the **Hardinge Bridge** and **Sirajganj.**

(For the journey from Calcutta to Ishurdi Junction (143 m.) see p. 698.)

194 m. **Sirajganj** is a big jute centre. A steamer normally leaves twice daily for Jagannathganj, an important riverside market and railway junction, but the service is temporarily suspended. From **Jagannathganj** there is an alternate day steamer service to **Goalundo.**

17 m. from **Jagannathganj** at **Singhjani** Junction the line from Bahadurabad to Narainganj is joined. From Bahadurabad Ghat there is a railway steamer and wagon ferry to Tistamukh Ghat, enabling connection to be made with Santahar or Lalmanirhat.

50 m. **Mymensingh** (D.B.K.). The headquarters of what was the most populous district in undivided India and the centre of a great jute-growing area. Good snipe and duck-shooting possibly available in the country round. Along the N. frontier of the district are aboriginal tribes—Garos, Hajangs, Kochis and others—with their own cultures. There is a wealth of folk art.

126 m. **Dacca** (see p. 696).

136 m. **Narainganj** (see p. 696).

(4.) **Calcutta** to **Chandpur** and **Narainganj** *via* **Khulna.**

If combined with a return journey *via* the Goalundo route above, this will make an interesting round trip, which may fill in a few days at a very small cost—less than hotel charges—and the scenery is unusual and often beautiful. There is considerable traffic on this route, steamers, or launches towing flats usually loaded with jute and country boats also.

An interesting sight is the water hyacinth, floating on the creeks, especially when it is in flower. This is said to have been introduced from California as a pot plant in the Calcutta market. Like the rabbit in Australia, or the Lantana in Coorg, it has spread like wildfire, choking the smaller channels, filling the railway borrowpits and creeping over the fields. Its roots enable it to flourish in water or on land, and it presents a serious problem.

The railway to Khulna, after passing through Dumdum Junction (5 m.) and Bongaon Junction (48 m.), crosses the West Bengal-Bangladesh frontier midway between Bongaon and Jessore (75 m.). **Jessore** (D.B.K.) is now linked, *via* Kotchandpur and Darsana, with the Goalundo line. A century ago it was a leading centre of the Indigo industry. From Jessore the railway goes on to **Khulna** (108 m). (HOTELS), which is now developing rapidly as an important river-port and headquarters of a district. From Khulna the **Sunderbans**—dense forest with many tigers—can be visited by boat. There is an extensive Wild Life Sanctuary and varied animal life teems everywhere. As well as tiger, waterfowl and deer, python, crocodiles and wild boar abound, along with many species of monkey. The flora is also notable, with mangroves, climbers, and herbaceous plants. 18 m. S. of Khulna, a new port called **Chalna** for ocean-going steamers is being developed (8 moorings). There is a river passenger service from Khulna to Chalna, and travellers can go there and return the same day, as there is not any hotel accommodation at Chalna. At the present time Chalna has no shore establishments or warehouse facilities; goods and passengers being transhipped midstream between river-craft and ocean vessels.

Daulatpur, just N. of Khulna, is being developed as an industrial centre, and several jute-mills and presses are being erected there. It is likely to increase in importance rapidly.

Note.—Cargo steamers, which do not run to an exact time-table, ply almost daily to Bangladesh, Assam, Cachar and Bihar, calling at places like Goalundo, Narainganj, Chandpur, Chittagong, Karimganj, Silchar, Sirajganj, Madaripur, Barisal, Khepupara and Barguna. These almost all have cabins, and special arrangements may be made through Tourist Information Centres to travel on them. The first station of call outside Calcutta is Khulna, where the passengers can either entrain for Calcutta, or transfer to a regular passenger service.

ROUTE 2

Chittagong to **Sylhet,** the **Surma Valley,** and **Assam**

Among the places to be visited from Dacca, Chittagong is a "must". By air, the journey takes only 70 minutes. It can also be reached by the twice-weekly steamer service from Barisa.

Chittagong (est. pop. 363,000), formerly Islamabad (Circuit House, D.B.K., Hotels. The Club, takes in recommended visitors), was once part of the Kingdom of Tripura. There are several important historic buildings, among them the Juma mosque and the shrine of Sultan Bayazid Bustani. It was visited by the Chinese traveller Hiuen Tsang in the 7th century, who described it as "a sleeping beauty emerging from mists and waters". It was burnt by the Portuguese in 1538, and recaptured by the Mughals from the Raja of Arakan in 1668. Inroads by the Burmese caused the First Burmese War. The town is most picturesque, many houses being perched on separate little hillocks. It is the headquarters of the Chittagong District, home of the Maghs, once pirates, now famous as cooks, and has been developed rapidly as the chief port of Bangladesh for ocean-going steamers. It is also an industrial centre for jute, cotton, engineering, chemicals, cigarettes, plywood, with the only steel plant in Bangladesh. There is a Tourist Information Office. At Chandragona, 30 m. above Chittagong, is a paper-mill, said to be the biggest in Asia. Slightly higher up there is Kaptai, H.Q. of the Karnaphuli hydro-electric project. Both should be visited, by launch if possible. The Karnaphuli project with its glorious lake is among the most impressive in the country. There is excellent fishing and boating, Tourist R.Hs. and V.I.P. Rest Houses.

The port, 12 m. up the Karnaphuli river, has now berths or anchorage for up to 15 vessels. Steamer service up the river to **Rangamati** (Hotel), headquarters of the Chittagong Hill Tracts, has been discontinued but it is connected with Chittagong by road. From Rangamati, with excellent roads and many amenities, it is pleasant to explore the Chittagong Hill Tracts. The area is some 5000 sq. m. and the tribal inhabitants, mostly Buddhists, friendly and hospitable, include Chakmas, Tripuras, Maghs, Kukis, Morangs and Tenchangyas. There is a Tribal Museum on the main road; and at Tabalchuri a handicraft centre. The textiles, bamboo work, ivory and silver jewellery are notable. At Alikhyong, 27 m. S. of Rangamati there is excellent big-game shooting in great variety and a Tourist B. There is a Wild Life National Park at Pablakhali, 80 m. from Rangamati, while in the Kassalong Forest Reserves, rather closer (50 m.), there is another Game Sanctuary, with Forest Bs. for visitors. South of Rangamati and Kaptai is Bandarban, home of the Murangs and Maghs. There is a comfortable Tourist B. **Cox's Bazar** (founded by Capt. Cox, Madras Army), where there is excellent sea-bathing, lies farther S. It is connected with Chittagong by a good road, and by air. It is a popular tourist resort, with 2 R.Hs., 3 Motels, 2 Hotels and many miles of golden sands. There is a Tourist Information Office. At Rama to the E. there is a famous Buddhist temple.

56 m. **Feni** Junction, branch to Belonia.

81 m. **Laksam** Junction. From Laksam branch lines run W. to Chandpur, and S. to **Noakhali** (31 m.), the headquarters of the district of that name, which has had to be more or less abandoned because of river erosion. From Chandpur there is a frequent launch service to Narainganj. Chandpur railway station adjoins the steamer ghat.

96 m. **Comilla** (D.B.K.), headquarters of the Tippera District, and on to **Akhaura,** 125 m. Comilla is distinguished by the number and size of its tanks, and its remarkable freedom from malaria. There is excellent snipe- and duck-shooting in the country round. The village AID Academy which is also the main development authority for the surrounding district should be visited. A road 32 m. long, with a first-class surface, has been constructed from Comilla to Daudkandi and on to Dacca. Buses ply on this road. **Mainamati** 5 m. W. of Comilla, was the seat of an extensive nexus of Buddhist culture. Recent excavations have revealed stupas, shrines, images, coins, pottery and utensils. An important *vihara* has been excavated at Salbon; there are 11 sq. m. of hillocks studded with Buddhist sites. The Mainamati Museum (closed Thursdays) adjoins Salbon Vihara.

125 m. **Akhaura.** From Akhaura a branch runs N.W. to Ashuganj Ghat, on the Meghna river, and Bhairab Bazar, whence it bifurcates to Dacca and Mymensingh (see p. 698).

221 m. **Kalaura** Junction, with branch line to Karimganj, 35 m., where it meets the local line of the Assam Railway from Silchar. At Badarpur on this local line, just after the Assam[1] Bangladesh frontier is crossed, connection is made with the hill section of the Assam Railway to Lumding (see p. 408).

251 m. **Sylhet** (D.B.K., Tourist B. and Circuit House) is the headquarters of the District of that name. It used to be part of Assam, but is now in Bangladesh. There are numerous tea gardens in the Surma Valley, with many Bengali planters. Oil and gas have recently been found there. The district suffers from frequent earthquakes. The scenery is delightful, particularly in the neighbourhood of the Kasi and Jhaintia Hills, where the border with India has been demarcated.

Sylhet was among the earliest of Muslim settlements in the country now known as Bangladesh. The town itself has many mosques and tombs, the most famous of which are those of Shah Jalal and his followers, who came from Turkestan in 1303 A.D. to spread the Faith. West of Sylhet town is Chatak, an important trading centre; south lies Fenchuganj, with its great fertiliser factory based on natural gas. There is a guest house for visitors. Sylhet district provides excellent shooting, with both big and small game. 40 m. from Sylhet town is Maulvi Bazar, with a rest house and with hunting lodges at Akbarpur and Laiyani. Conducted hunting trips can be arranged.

[1] Visitors should enquire if through traffic to Assam is practicable.

REPUBLIC OF SRI LANKA (CEYLON)

Area: 25,332 sq. miles
Population: 14·5 m.
Head of State: J. R. Jayawardene

INTRODUCTION

(*Map faces p.* 724)

Sri Lanka is a Republic within the Commonwealth. The population, 14·5 million, consists of Sinhalese (70%), Tamils (21%) with minority groups of Moors (of Arab descent), Burghers (Dutch and Portuguese stock), Eurasians, Malays, Europeans and Veddhas (aboriginals). Power vests in a unicameral National State Assembly (p. 706). The President is Mr J. R. Jayawardene and the Prime Minister Mrs Bandaranaike.

General Information.—The scenery of Sri Lanka is magnificent, and its climate attracts an increasing number of visitors. It is very easy to reach Sri Lanka by steamer from a European port to Colombo or by air; and there is direct railway communication with Madras and S. India by the mail route *via* Talaimanaar (p. 729). Visitors, not only from the East generally, but also from England, spend months in Nuwara Eliya, where there is an 18 hole golf-course, one of the best in the East. In addition to hunting and fishing (p. 739 ff.) many other sports are available to the tourist. The Fort Tennis Club and the Sri Lanka Lawn Tennis Association (both in Colombo) offer full facilities. There are a number of swimming clubs. Bathing is excellent, so is water skiing. There is scuba diving at Hikkaduwa (p. 723). There is a first-rate golf course at the Royal Colombo Golf Club. Canoe enthusiasts find travel by the canals fascinating.

In Sri Lanka the visitor, whether tourist, naturalist, archaeologist, sportsman, or even gourmet, will be enchanted by what he experiences. The climate, like the scenery, is rich in variations, but never too oppressive. The people are friendly and hospitable, and English is widely spoken and understood. There are many colourful festivals in the life of the country—Buddhist, Hindu, Muslim and Christian—of which particulars are set out in a leaflet available from the Tourist Board. Visitors should not miss them.

The most suitable time for a visit to Sri Lanka is between the months of November and March; but Nuwara Eliya (season February to May) is enjoyable also from August to January. The Sri Lanka High Commission, 13 Hyde Park Gardens, London, W.2, or The Government Tourist Bureau, Colombo, may be consulted, and anyone proposing to tour in the interior by car should get in touch with the Automobile Association of Ceylon, 40 Sir Macan Markar Mawatha, Galle Face, Colombo 3, and purchase their Handbook. The Government attaches great importance to tourists: the Tourist Bureau publishes a useful handbook for them: a Tourist Board and an Hotel Corporation exist to serve their interests. Visitors should not fail to make contact with the Board office (25 Galle Face Centre Rd., Colombo) for advice and help in planning tours. A number of excellent pamphlets and guidebooks are obtainable, also Tourist Introduction Cards which open up many facilities.

Travelling in Sri Lanka is easy and there are special Tourist Concessions. The **Railway** has always been a Government system. There are now luxury trains with air-conditioned coaches and observation saloons for the benefit of tourists. Advance booking is advisable. On the main lines good sleeping accommodation is provided for a small supplement.[1] Refreshment cars are attached to the express trains from Colombo to Talaimanaar and to Kandy. Air Sri Lanka operates domestic services from Colombo to most important places, and special charter flights for tourists. Booking and information from Air Sri Lanka at Lower Chatham Street or 63 Queen Street.

Roads are mostly excellent. The rule of the road for traffic is to keep to the left, and overtake on the right. The **Rest houses,** which are controlled by Government and are situated throughout Sri Lanka, are far more comfortable places of abode than the corresponding institutions in India. In the larger towns they are hotels; but the traveller is not allowed to remain in them more than three days without permission, which, however, is easily procured. On all the principal roads they are provided with bed- and table-linen, baths, tea and dinner services, etc.

Motor-omnibuses, generally comfortable, run on nearly every main road with seating accommodation for 42 to 68 persons; light luggage may be taken, free of charge. A list of services will be found in Ferguson's *Sri Lanka Directory.* Taxis and chauffeur-driven cars can be hired. Private mini-bus services too.

Good **maps** may be procured at the Surveyor-General's office, including a motor map, HIND/CLN. 6, also from the Automobile Association. There are some *air* landing-grounds.

There is now no horse-racing in Sri Lanka. The track at Colombo is occupied by Trade Fair buildings and the University of Ceylon; that at Nuwara Eliya is overgrown.

Among the great attractions of Sri Lanka are the excellent Wild Life sanctuaries. There are no fewer than 24 of them. Among the most important are three National Parks: **Ruhuna** (S.E. coast 175 m. from Colombo: admission office at Palutupana); **Wilpattu** (120 m. from Colombo) and **Gal Oya** (air strip). In addition there are a number of sanctuaries: **Wirawila Tissa** (160 m. from Colombo); **Kumana** (near Potuvil on the E. coast); **Mihintale** (possibly the world's oldest) near Anuradhapura; **Lahngala-Kitulana** near Gal Oya. Particulars of accommodation, conducted tours, and precautions to be observed by visitors are obtainable from the Wild Life Department Office, Echelon Square, Colombo. Small fees are charged for admission of visitors and their cars to the sanctuaries.

The public debt has been incurred for harbour works, railways, irrigation canals, water-works, drainage and other development works. The old kings constructed irrigation works by which a great part of Sri Lanka was made cultivable. The principal exports are tea, rubber, coconut. Cinnamon, gems, handicrafts, shoes, and cut flowers are among minor exports, Research Institutes for which are at Talawakela, Madampe and Matugama respectively. For home consumption the staple crop is rice.

The Currency of the island is on a decimal basis, and the rupee is divided into cents. The coins are cupro-nickel (1 cent, 2 cent pieces), nickel (5 cent, 10 cent, 25 cent and 50 cent and R. 1·00 pieces). Sri Lanka Government currency notes of Rs. 1000 down to Rs. 2·00 are in circulation.

Capitals.—The capital of Sri Lanka, now Colombo, has changed from time to time, and various dates have been assigned to the moves. Anuradhapura,

[1] Sleeping berths should be booked well in advance. See the *Time and Fare Tables* of the Government Railway.

founded in the 4th century B.C., was the capital till A.D. 729; according to other statements from 500 B.C. to mid-9th century. Within the above period Sigiriya was the capital for 18 years from A.D. 477, during the reign of Kasyapa I. Polonnaruwa, as a capital, has been dated from A.D. 781 to A.D. 1288; also, variously to A.D. 1013, and, with breaks, up to A.D. 1314. Yapahuwa was the capital for less than 20 years in the 13th century, *c.* A.D. 1277. The capital was at Kandy from A.D. 1592 to A.D. 1815. Before Kandy, Kotte near Colombo, and (for a short time) Gampola, S. of Kandy, were capitals.

Buddhism in Sri Lanka.—The census has shown the Buddhists to be more numerous in Sri Lanka than the followers of all other religions. The whole subject of Buddhism in Sri Lanka (belonging to what is called the Southern School) has been exhaustively treated in Bishop Copleston's work, *Buddhism, Primitive and Present, in Magadha and Ceylon*, from which a few facts have, with permission, been taken.

When Mahendra introduced Buddhism into Sri Lanka from India about 236 B.C., he met the reigning king Tissa at the place now known as Mihintale (Mahindatale). He brought with him (in memory, for none of the books were yet written) the collection of Buddhist "Canonical Books", known by the name of the Three Pitakas, and the Commentaries upon them all in Pali. He translated them into Sinhalese (a language which was closely allied to Pali), and they are believed to have been preserved in Sri Lanka by oral tradition, till they were committed to writing about 80 B.C.

From Mahendra's time, Buddhism may be said to have been the national religion, and was officially patronised; shrines were built, viharas constructed as dwellings for the monks, and many inscriptions are still to be seen in which such donations are recorded. A very fine specimen of such an inscription, on the living rock, in "Asoka" characters, is to be seen close to the high road from Kurunegala to Puttalam, about 18 m. from the latter. It is in one line, over 100 ft. long.

Frequent invasions of Tamils from Southern India, and the usurpation of the throne by Pandyan dynasties, repeatedly led to the expulsion of the monks and the destruction of their buildings. About A.D. 400 Buddhaghosa, the chief commentator, is said to have come from Magadha to inquire into these Commentaries. He translated into Pali what he found and composed more. His works have left their impress on the Sri Lanka school of Buddhism, and have been considered as absolute authorities on the interpretation of the sacred text. During the succeeding centuries the religion underwent many vicissitudes; but the victories of King Parakrama Bahu I, A.D. 1153-92 or A.D. 1153-86, "established him in undisputed power, which he used for the reformation and promotion of Buddhism and for the erection of innumerable buildings for its service". This period of prosperity was followed again by troublous times, and Buddhism had little vitality at the time of the British occupation in A.D. 1796. In the period A.D. 1875-1900, however, there was a remarkable revival.

To the Muslim, Sri Lanka is the abode of Adam and Eve after expulsion from Eden.

History.—The Mahavansa is the chief national chronicle, written in Pali, on talipot palm-leaves in the 5th century A.D. by Mahanama, a priest of the royal line. This has been translated by Turnour (of the Ceylon Civil Service, 1837), Wijesinha and Geiger (Pali Text Society, Colombo, 1912). The Dipavansa, an older chronicle, is the history of the Island. The Culuvansa is the chronicle which continues the history of the monarchy from the end of the Mahavansa.

Wijaya (543 or 483 B.C.) is said to have come over from India on a raiding expedition and established himself in Sri Lanka. Though the Mahavansa describes a visit of Gautama Buddha there is no historical evidence for it.

During the reign of Dewanampiya Tissa (307-267 B.C.), Buddhism, however was introduced by Mahendra (Mahinda), reputed to be a son of the great Asoka, King of Magadha in India.

The Tamils (= damilos in the Mahavansa), i.e. the Cholyans and Pandyans of S. India, constantly raided the island. Elara was a Cholyan king (205-161 B.C.); his cenotaph is at Anuradhapura. Another Tamil invasion was in 104 B.C.; another in the middle of the 9th century. Sena II crossed to India to help a Pandyan prince. The Indians looted Anuradhapura and carried Mahinda V (1001) captive.

Wijaya Bahu I, a poet (1065), recovered Polonnaruwa from the Tamils. This was the seat of Parakrama Bahu I, the great king and poet (1153 or 1164). for 33 years.

The Portuguese appeared on the scene in 1505, and from 1592 the native kings ruled from Kandy. "The Dutch dispossessed the Portuguese in 1658, but gave way in turn to the British, who have held the Maritime Provinces since 1796, and the whole Island, including the interior and Kandyan Kingdom, which neither the Portuguese nor the Dutch ever occupied, since 1815."—(*The Ceylon Manual*, by H. White.)

Under British rule the island was a Crown Colony. On the 4th February 1948 Ceylon became a self-governing dominion in the British Commonwealth. The new constitution provided for a Governor-General, a Cabinet headed by a Prime Minister and a legislature of two houses (a Senate and House of Representatives) to which the Cabinet is responsible. Sir Henry Monck-Mason Moore, was the first Governor-General, and he was succeeded in 1949 by Lord Soulbury. Sir Oliver Goonetilleke succeeded Lord Soulbury in July 1954 and was followed by Mr William Gopallawa in 1962. The Rt. Hon. D. S. Senanayake, who was the first Prime Minister, died in 1952, and was succeeded in office by his son, Mr Dudley Senanayake, the Minister of Agriculture and Lands in the previous Government. The latter resigned in 1953, and was succeeded by the Rt. Hon. Sir John Kotelawala, the former Minister of Communications and Works.

Soon after independence, differences arose between the advocates of Sinhalese as the sole official language and those who wished for both Sinhalese and Tamil. In 1955 there was an upsurge of communalism between the Sinhalese and Tamil races, and the demand for Sinhalese as the exclusive official language gained ground. The Kotelawala Government's policy of toleration for Tamil, with English as a third language, lost support: and at the general election in 1956 the Government party of Sir John Kotelawala, although it had a sweeping victory in 1952, suffered a heavy defeat, and the leader of the opposition, Mr S. W. R. D. Bandaranaike, became Prime Minister, and pledged his Government to the goal of a neutralist republic, a democratic and socialist policy, and to greater efficiency. On the 15th June 1956 the new government of Mr Bandaranaike made Sinhalese the only official language. In pursuance of its policy of neutralism moreover, it pressed for the eviction of the British from the naval base at Trincomalee and from the air-base at Katunayahe; and at the time of the Commonwealth Prime Ministers' Conference in July, Britain agreed to hand over the bases. He retained office until 1959 (September) when he was assassinated: and Mr Dahanyake succeeded him as Prime Minister and leader of the Sri Lanka Freedom party—United Front coalition. Elections held in March 1960 returned Mr Dudley Senanyake to power without a working majority. Fresh elections in July 1960 brought back the late Mr Bandaranaike's Sri Lanka Freedom party: and his widow became the first woman Prime Minister in the world. She visited London in that capacity when she attended the meeting of Commonwealth Prime Ministers in 1960. Toward the end of 1962, she called a conference of six non-aligned Asian and African countries to make proposals for a settlement of the dispute between India and China; and herself visited Peking and Delhi to discuss the proposals. In 1965, her party lost the elections to the United National Party, and Mr Dudley Senanayake became Prime Minister. In May 1970, the United Front Sri Lanka Freedom party led by Mrs Bandaranaike was returned to power, with a mandate to produce a new constitution. A Constituent Assembly sat from July 1970 to May 1972 and the new constitution terminated a century and a half link with the British Crown by setting up a Republic under the ancient name of Sri Lanka, but still within the Commonwealth. Supreme power is vested in the unicameral National State Assembly, and the first President is J. R. Jayawardene.

Sri Lanka is committed to social democracy, with Government taking a share in economic development. Some sectors of the economy have been nationalised: other sectors are shaped by regulations. But private enterprise continues side by side encouraged by concessions and incentives. Some foreign-owned industries have been "Ceylonised", but development has been rapid, and foreign aid and investment are now encouraged.

COLOMBO

(*Map faces p.* 708)

COLOMBO* (lat. 6° 55′ N., long. 79° 50′ E., pop. 430,000 in 1953). Whether the visitor crosses over to Ceylon from India by the mail route from Madras (p. 552), or whether he makes his entry by sea or air, Colombo the "Charing Cross of the East", will be his first port of call. The international aerodrome is at Katanayake and is linked to all the principal countries of the world, 20 m. N., while Ratmalana, 8 m. S. is used for internal and regional traffic. From Ratmalana the tourist passes "Temple Trees", the official residence of Sri Lanka's Prime Minister.

The Passenger Landing Jetty and Custom House lie at the S. end of the harbour, and receive the protection of four magnificent breakwaters, of which the S.W. was completed in 1885. It is 4212 ft. long, and terminates in a circular head, 62 ft. in diameter, on which stands the Pilot Station and a small lighthouse showing a red light.

The N.E. Breakwater is a rubble embankment 1100 ft. long, completed in 1902. The N.W. Breakwater is an island work 2670 ft. in length, leaving a S. entrance of 800 ft. and a N. entrance of 700 ft. It was completed in 1907.

The area protected by these breakwaters is 643 acres, or 1 sq. m., three-fourths of which have water more than 27 ft. deep, and afford shelter during the S.W. monsoon.

There are two jetties for bunkering oil-fuel, and one jetty for the discharge of oil-tankers. There are warehouses on reclaimed ground on the S.E. margin of the harbour. A canal connects the harbour with the Lake.

Motor launches can convey passengers from steamers moored in the inner harbour to the jetty. For these and rowing-boats there tariffs are fixed, higher by night. On the landing-jetty, is the Sri Lanka Travel Centre, where all information relating to travel is available and Tourist Introduction Cards are obtainable which carry considerable advantages. Many liners now moor in fifteen along-side berths constructed under the £6 million Harbour Development Scheme. The first of these was inaugurated by H.M. the Queen during her visit to Ceylon in April 1954.

The Hotel Taprobane stands near to and overlooking the Harbour, and close by are the Bristol Hotel, "President's House" (the President's residence), the Barracks and some remains of the old Dutch Fort.

Between the Taprobane and the Senate Building, and facing the harbour, is **St Peter's Church,** the old residence of the Dutch Governors. It contains many interesting monuments, one to William Tolfray (1778-1817), a retired officer who served under Wellesley (1803-4) and translated books of the Bible into Pali and Sinhalese.

Half a mile away is the Galle Face Hotel. The visitor will pass by the Senate Building, looking out on the Gordon Gardens, and, proceeding between President's House on his right, and the General Post Office on the left, he will, after passing the Clock Tower, the Barracks, the National State Assembly and Secretariat, find himself on the fine open space called the Galle Face. A good view of the city may be had from the top of the **Clock Tower.**

Towards the S. of the Galle Face Esplanade is what was once the Colombo Club and is now the Tourist Board and Samudra—the Tourist Reception Centre. About the middle of the Promenade is a stone like a milestone, with an inscription in which Sir Henry Ward, who made it, recommends the walk to his successors in the interest of ladies and children of Colombo.

The City of Colombo extends from the Kelani river on the N. to the fourth mile on the Galle Road on the S., and has a breadth of 3½ m. from the sea to the E. outskirts.

Drives.—Colombo affords many charming and picturesque drives. The first given below is recommended to those who have not yet seen anything of the East, and will afford a pleasing introduction to the distinguishing characteristics of Oriental life and scenery.

(1) Commence at the Galle Face Hotel, and take the road N. past the Barracks, until the statue of Sir E. Barnes is reached. He was Governor between 1824 and 1831. Then turn to the right down Princes Street into the Pettah, formerly the residential quarter of the Dutch burghers and now a typical Eastern bazar; and continue past an old Dutch belfry, beyond which are the old *Town Hall* (replaced by a fine new building overlooking Viharanaha Devi Park) and *Public Market-place.*

Here two streets diverge—to one the left, Sea Street, where dwell the dealers in rice and cotton, and where are two *Hindu Temples* of no great size or importance; the other, Wolfendahl Street, to the right, conducts to **Wolfendhal Church,** a massive cruciform building on high ground, built by the Dutch in 1749, on the site of an old Portuguese church called *Aqua de Lupo*, and commanding a fine view of the city and harbour. Here are monuments and hatchments recording the decease of Dutch officials. It is the most interesting as well as the most complete of the few remaining relics of the Dutch occupation, which ended in 1796.

The drive may be continued in a N.E. direction to the R.C. *Cathedral of Santa Lucia*, the finest ecclesiastical edifice in the Island. Adjoining it is a college for Roman Catholic boys and a convent. Then N. and a little W. the Anglican *Cathedral of Christ Church* (known as the "Stone Church") is reached. It stands in a park, given by Dr Chapman, the first Bishop. The Diocese was formed in 1845. About 1 m. to the N. is *St James's Roman Catholic Church* in Modara.

The suburb of **Mutwal** is chiefly inhabited by fishermen, mostly Roman Catholics, as the numerous large and imposing R.C. Churches testify. In Mutwal are the new **Graving-dock,** the Elie House Reservoir in connection with the town water-supply and the cold-storage and fish-processing plant of the Canadian-Colombo Plan Fisheries Project.

At the **Kelani river** at the end of Mutwal, turn to the right, and, crossing a tongue of land till the river is again reached, follow its bank to the **Victoria Bridge** and the new Kelaniya Bridge), which carries the great road to Kandy. This part of the drive shows to perfection the way in which the tiny houses and small churches are nestled under the shelter of the trees.

Turning to the right at the bridge, follow the road into Grandpass and Prince of Wales Avenue. Turn to the left at Skinner's Road until Maradana Railway Station is reached. Thence proceed along the Lake to Union Place and to Galle Face.

(2) The second drive commences by crossing the bridge from Galle Face, not far from the hotel, to Slave Island, and then driving along the edge of a beautiful fresh-water lake to **Viharamaha Devi Park,** which occupies the site of the old **Cinnamon Gardens,** and is well laid out with ornamental grounds. A **Museum** (closed on Fridays) was built in 1877. It is exclusively devoted to the exhibition of Ceylon products, antiquities and natural history. A famous tortoise, said to have been over two hundred years old at his death, is preserved here. On the ground floor are some interesting stone fragments (the colossal stone lion, once here, has now been restored to Polonnaruwa (p. 736)), one of the unique windows from the ruins of Yapahuwa (p. 728), the cast

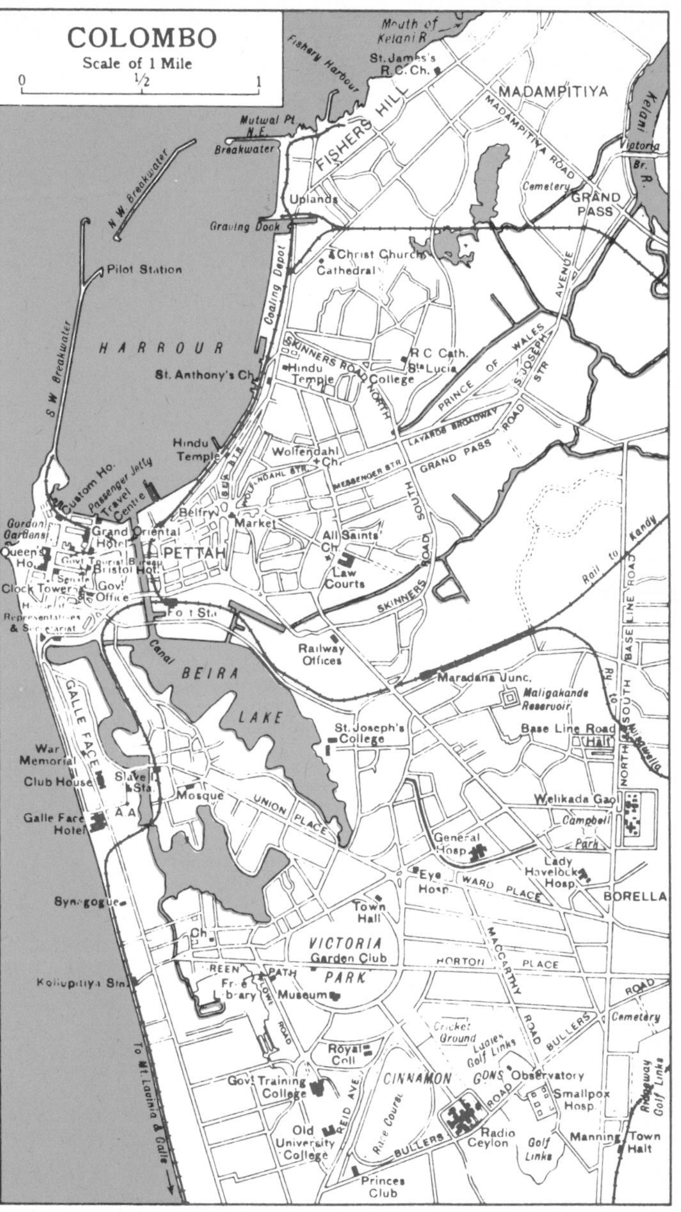

COLOMBO
Scale of 1 Mile
0
½
1
Mouth of Kelani R.
Fishery Harbour
St. James's R.C. Ch.
MADAMPITIYA
MADAMPITIYA ROAD
Kelani R.
Victoria Br.
Mutwal Pt.
N.E. Breakwater
FISHERS HILL
N.W. Breakwater
Cemetery
GRAND PASS
Uplands
Graving Dock
Christ Church Cathedral
Pilot Station
Coaling Depot
AVENUE
HARBOUR
SKINNERS ROAD NORTH
R C Cath. Sta Lucia
PRINCE OF WALES
ST. JOSEPH STR
Hindu Temple
College
St. Anthony's Ch.
S W Breakwater
LAYARDS BROADWAY
ROAD
Hindu Temple
Wolfendahl Ch.
GRAND PASS
Custom Ho.
Passenger Jetty
Travel Centre
SEA STR
WOLFENDAHL STR
MESSENGER STR
SOUTH
Belfry
Market
Gordon Gardens
Grand Oriental Hotel
PETTAH
All Saints' Ch.
Queen's Ho.
Bristol Hot.
Law Courts
Rail to Kandy
Clock Tower
Govt. Office
SKINNERS ROAD
BASE LINE ROAD
Fort Sta.
Canal
Railway Offices
BEIRA
Maradana Junc.
Maligakande Reservoir
GALLE FACE
LAKE
St. Joseph's College
Base Line Road Halt
War Memorial
NORTH SOUTH
Club House
Slave Is. Sta.
Mosque
UNION PLACE
Welikada Gaol
Campbell Park
Galle Face Hotel
General Hosp.
Lady Havelock Hosp.
Eye Hosp.
WARD PLACE
BORELLA
Synagogue
Town Hall
MACCARTHY ROAD
Ch.
VICTORIA PARK
Garden Club
HORTON PLACE
GREEN PATH
Kollupitiya Stn.
Free Library
Museum
FLOWER ROAD
ROAD
Cemetery
Cricket Ground
Ladies Golf Links
BULLERS
Royal Coll.
To Mt. Lavinia & Galle
Govt. Training College
CINNAMON GDNS.
Observatory
REID AVE.
ROAD
Smallpox Hosp.
Race Course
Ridgeway Golf Links
Old University College
Radio Ceylon
Golf Links
Manning Town Halt
BULLERS ROAD
Princes Club

of a colossal portrait statue of King Parakrama Bahu, 1153, some bronze statues from Polonnaruwa, also a stone Buddha from Toluvila.

Copies of the frescoes at Sigiriya (p. 730) are on the walls of the staircase; also a Portuguese cannon dredged from the harbour. The crown, throne and footstool of the ast King of Kandy were restored n 1934 by King George V. There is a aluable library. The Garden Club overlooks Victoria Park.

(3) A drive may be taken from York St., near the Passenger Jetty, o Borella (S.E.). The interest of this rive is the bright picture it gives of e life of the people.

(4) Another drive would follow nion Place (avenue of Peltophorum-ees), past the Eye Hospital in Ward ace; thence on Alexandra Road st the new Town Hall, Victoria ark, and branching left into Reid venue with the former Race-course, w occupied by University buildings, the left, and the Royal College on e right. The visitor can return by ller's Road, past Prince's Club, to llupitiya (Colpetty) and Galle Face go on to the Zoo, farther S. This ve would cover the residential area led the Cinnamon Gardens.

xcursions.—One of the pleasantest hat to a Buddhist temple at the age of **Kelani,** on the bank of the r. Pass through the hot and dusty **tah,** the Outer Town (which is trading centre) for about 4 m., ar as the river, which is crossed he massive steel **Victoria Bridge** p. 708). After crossing the bridge road passes through coconut es and houses for another 2 m., n the temple itself is reached.

e *Mahavansa Chronicle* refers to niya as a sacred place visited by Buddha. The Dagoba, built by Yatalatissa in the 3rd century is believed to enshrine a gem-set e on which the Buddha is said to sat.

ne of the exclusiveness which guishes Hindu and Muslim s is to be found in the Buddhist temples, to every part of which a stranger is freely welcomed by the yellow-robed monks. This, however, does not apply to the devalas, which are, strictly speaking, Hindu shrines.

A favourite excursion especially on Sundays for lunch, is to **Mount Lavinia,** 7 m. from Colombo. The Hotel, which was built by Sir E. Barnes, when Governor, as his Marine Villa, stands on a rocky eminence close to the station. It has a special fish cuisine, swimming pool, and facilities for sea-bathing. A fine view of Colombo can be had from the terrace. The Colombo Fort station is the most convenient starting-place for the journey by train which runs along the sea; but taxis are always available or a car.

Motor-omnibuses run from Colombo E. to **Kaduwela** (p. 719) and from Borella S.E. to **Kotte,** the latter linking up with the Colombo Borella trolley-bus service.

ROUTE 1

COLOMBO to **KANDY**

By rail 75 m.

Those who are newcomers to the tropics will see for the first time vast stretches of paddy land of the most vivid green, the unfamiliar but soon recognised forms of the cashew, the breadfruit, the jack, the frangipani and the various forms of palm—coconut, areca, kitul, and above all the talipot, a specimen of whose gigantic white flower is generally visible at some point on the journey.

From 1 m. **Maradana Junction,** a N.G. line runs to Avisawella and Ratnapura (p. 720).

4 m. **Kelaniya** stn. Bridge over the Kelani river.

At 9 m. **Ragama** stn. The buildings of the former Boer prisoners' camp are now used as a Hospital. There is a branch line from here to Negombo, Chilaw and Puttalam (see Route 6, p. 727).

Mahara (10½ m.). The R.H., 8½ m. by road from Colombo, is a delightful resort for travellers.

Gampaha Station (16½ m.). (R.H. good.) Here is one of the most beautiful model garden towns in Ceylon. ¾ m. from the station is a Government Botanic and Experiment Garden, opened in 1876 for the cultivation of the first Para rubber plants introduced into Ceylon. Seeds of the *Hevea brasiliensis* were brought from the Upper Amazon and germinated at Kew. The original trees, as well as the succeeding generations, may be seen here. Here may be seen Gambier (*Uncaria gambier*), also a caoutchouc-yielding shrub of Malaya, which thrives and produces seed here, though not at Peradeniya; also species of rubber-producing lianas (*Landolphia*); the valuable drug ipecacuanha, which thrives in the moist tropical heat here to an extent not known at higher elevations. A female specimen of the "Double Coconut" (Coco-de-mer), planted in 1884, flowered and bore fruit here in 1915 for the first time in Ceylon. A portio of the original jungle of the lo country of Ceylon has been preserve in the Garden.

3 m. from the next station, *Veyangoda* (23½ m.), is the Rock Templ of Warana, to the E. of the Kand Road.

35 m. **Ambepussa** station (goo R.H.). The line here enters the low hills. The soil is very suitable f coconuts.

46 m. **Polgahawela Junction** statio R. (R.H. commodious), altitude 2 ft. above sea-level. 2 m. from he are a large Buddhist monastery a temple at Denagomuwa. Polgahawe is the junction for the N. of the Islar

8 m. S. of Polgahawela is **Kega** (R.H.), a small town encompass by the most delightful scenery. It the headquarters of the Kega District.

53 m. **Rambukkana** station (R.I Here the ascent of the "Incline" co mences at an elevation of 313 and continues 12 m. with a grad of 1 in 45 to an elevation of 1698 The vegetation is here of great r ness and beauty.

65 m. **Kadugannawa** station is the top of the pass. A precipic called "Sensation Point". Two tun (one of them a very long one) se immunity from rock-falls, wh during the monsoons, formerly in rupted through-communication. the top of the incline a road is see the right, winding up the hill. The roads reach the summit of the at the same spot, and there a co (a copy in brick of the Duk York's Column in London) has erected to the memory of Ca Dawson, the engineer of the

road. Just over the station is the Hill of Belungala (the Watcher's Rock), 2543 ft. above sea-level, from which, in the troubled days of old, a watch was kept to report an enemy advancing from the plains.

71 m. **Peradeniya Junction** station (R.H. good). This place is 136 ft. lower than the top of the pass. The main line continues S., whilst the branch line to Kandy and Matale strikes N. Half a mile from the junction is New Peradeniya station (R.H., ½ m.), where, if the visitor is pressed for time, he should arrange to have a taxi waiting for him, drive round the Botanic Gardens, and proceed to Kandy. The new home of the Sri Lanka University has been located at Peradeniya. The site and buildings were planned by Sir Patrick Abercrombie and are acknowledged to be amongst the most beautiful of any university.

New Peradeniya Station. The Royal Botanic Gardens at Peradeniya are one of the modern Seven Wonders of the World, 3½ m. from Kandy. Their chief features are the enormous clumps of giant bamboo, the extensive and well-kept lawns surrounded by magnificent specimens of trees, the avenues of palms (Talipot, Palmyra, Royal palm and Cabbage palm) and the specimens of *Ficus elastica*, with its enormous buttressed roots. Approaching the Gardens, on the right is a row of the beautiful tree *Amherstia nobilis*, the most beautiful of flowering trees. Opposite, on the left approach, there was for upwards of seventy years a striking landmark in a row of Rambong rubber trees (*Ficus elastica*), which, dying from old age, were replaced by a row of young plants of the same species in 1914.

On entering, is an oval lawn studded with beds of cannas of new varieties. To the right is the Spice Collection, including very fine nutmeg trees over eighty years old, also cloves, cinnamon, allspice, vanilla, cardamom, ginger, etc. The Main Central Drive is bordered on either side by a sloping bank of mixed tropical foliage and flowering shrubs, etc., and shaded by tall trees in the background. Branching off to the left at right angles is the Monument drive, leading to the Gardner Monument, and passing through a young avenue of the interesting "Double Coconut" palm (Coco-de-mer). Opposite to this, on the right, is the short but shady Liana drive, along which are to be seen fine specimens of tropical climbers, including the climbing rattan palm (*Calamus*) and the curious chain-like stems of *Bauhinia anguina* and the *Monstera deliciosa* of Mexico with perforated leaves and edible fruit.

At a circle with a tank in the centre containing interesting water plants, the visitor should stop to visit the Floricultural section, Orchid House, Octagon Conservatory, Fernery, the pergolas of the curious flowered *Aristolochia* (Fly-catchers) and other flowering climbers.

Returning to the central drive and continuing, a collection of tropical fruit trees is passed on the left, also close to the drive a row of young Talipots—the Majestic palm. On turning the loop of the drive, note on the left some very large specimens of the *Inga Saman* or Rain-tree of tropical South America. These were introduced about 1850, and are the parents of trees along the roadsides throughout the Island. Next to these, close to the drive, is a row of the Cannon-ball tree, also of South America, bearing along the stem a profusion of curiously shaped flowers in March and April, followed by large brown fruits resembling cannon-balls.

Behind are the Nurseries, and a row of the buttressed tree known as Java Almond (*Canarium commune*). Farther on, on the left, is a straight avenue of Palmyra palm, which is indigenous to the dry region of Northern Sri Lanka, where the Palmyra palm is equal in usefulness to the coconut in the wetter areas.

The drive now passes through an avenue of the Cabbage Palm (*Oreodoxa oleracea*) planted 1905, skirts the

Arboretum and follows the river bank. Glimpses may be obtained across the river of Gannoruwa hill and valley.

The Great Circle is a lawn with a group of palms in the centre. Here the first Rubber Exhibition ever held took place in 1906. Extending to the N. is a straight avenue of the Royal palm (*Oreodoxa regia*), planted 1898. Round the circle are many fine trees, some planted by Royalties, including one each by King Edward VII, King George V, Prince of Wales (later Duke of Windsor), and Queen Elizabeth in 1954.

On the way back the Central Drive may be followed to where two roads diverge off on the right. These lead to the Office of the Botanist of the Department of Agriculture, herbarium, economic museum and laboratory. The museum is open to the public and contains botanical exhibits as well as agricultural products.

Returning, the Great Lawn is passed on the right, the Fernery and Floricultural section on the left. Turning to the right on the Monument Road and turning to the right again, a row of the fine foliaged and flowering tree (*Jacaranda ovalifolia*) is passed on the hillside to the left. Reaching the River Drive by the short loop to the left, a good view of the river and the bamboos fringing its banks is obtained. On the right an avenue of the golden *Cassia multijuga* of Guiana, planted 1932, is at its best in August-September. The small lake now reached contains interesting water plants, including the Egyptian Papyrus and the Giant Water-lily (*Victoria regia*).

The main drive enters the new Palmetum, planted in 1916. Here is a young avenue of the Talipot palm, the giant of the palm tribe, planted in 1930, to replace some famous specimens. Behind the avenue is a collection of medicinal herbs of value to the Vederala and Ayurdevic Institutions. The Pinetum, enlarged in 1919 and again in 1930, is one of the best conifer collections in the tropics. At the end of the Talipot avenue is the New Students' collection of herbaceous plants formed in 1935. Beyond the crescent is a collection of Bamboos and screw-pines (*Pandanus*). Here a glimpse may be obtained of the three-spanned iron and concrete bridge which displaced in 1906 the famous one-spanned Satinwood Bridge.

The tour ends by returning to the Main Entrance along the Lake drive bordered by the Shoe Flower (*Hibiscus rosa-sinensis*) on the right, and on the left by the Okari (edible) nut of New Guinea, the deadly Upas-tree and the Cadjuput, oil from the bark of which is used for rheumatism.

Crossing the river by the suspension bridge to the Experiment Station and the School of Tropical Agriculture at Gannoruwa, areas of tea, coffee, cacao, rubber, coconuts, rice and vanilla may be seen, and smaller plots of various fodder grasses and other plants of economic importance in the tropics.

Tapping and manurial experiments with Para rubber are of importance to the rubber industry of Sri Lanka while the advantages of growing leguminous shrubs between the tea has been clearly demonstrated. Experiments with cacao and coconuts are conducted, and comparative trials of rice and other economic plants carried out. The remains of an old Portuguese Fort are maintained in good condition.

The collections in the laboratories of the Dept. of Agriculture may be inspected by arrangement.

The links of the Kandy Golf Club are near the gates.

75 m. **KANDY** station* (Junction for Matale, p. 729). The capital of the former kingdom of Kandy, 1602 ft. above sea-level.

History.—The first authentic mention of Kandy as a city is in the Sagama inscription of the 14th century. In 1542, according to the *Mahavansa Chronicle*, it became the seat of Vira Vikrama, king of the up-country, but it became the capital of the island under Vimala Dharma Suriya I after the destruction of Kotte and the defeat of Raja Sinha I of Sitawaka in 1592. During the wars with the Portuguese and Dutch, Kandy was so often burned that scarcely any of the ancient buildings, except the temples and the royal residence, were remaining when the British took it in 1815.

The old *Palace* consisted of a number of buildings scattered over the area behind the Temple of the Tooth and along Malabar Street, so called from the dwellings of the "Malabar" or Tamil relatives of the later kings. The improvement of the city was undertaken subsequent to 1803 by the last king, Sri Vikrama Raja Sinha, by whom the Octagon, the main Portico of the Palace (now leading to the Maligawa Temple), and the lake, were either completed or commenced. In the Temple, the sacred tooth is deposited. Kandy was headquarters of the South East Asia Command during the last war.

Description.—Kandy is on the banks of a small artificial lake, overhung on all sides by hills. A road called Lady Horton's Walk winds round one of those hills, and on the E. side, which is almost precipitous, looks down on the valley of Dumbara, through which the Mahaweliganga rolls over a channel of rocks, "presenting a scene that in majestic beauty can scarcely be surpassed". In a park at the foot of this acclivity is the Pavilion of the Governor, erected *c.* 1835.

The **Dalada Maligawa,** or "Temple of the Tooth", stands with its back against a wooded hill; at its feet lies the long moat or tank, alive with tortoises, and crossed by a small bridge, flanked by two carved stone elephants. Above, an enclosing battlemented wall looks over the greenest grass dotted with trees.

In the centre of the courtyard is the sacred building. On a lotus flower of pure gold, hidden under seven concentric bell-shaped gold caskets, increasing in richness as they diminish in size, and containing jewels of much beauty, reposes the sacred relic. Annually in July-August a great pageant, Esala Perahera, one of the most magnificent religious spectacles in the world, is held in honour of the Sacred Relic. Some sixty elephants take part.

The "sacred tooth" is said to have been brought to Sri Lanka in the reign of Sri Meghavanna, A.D. 304-332 (according to Geiger, A.D. 352-379), in charge of a Princess of Kalinga, who concealed it in the folds of her hair. It was taken by the Pandyans about 1283, and again carried to India, but was recovered by Parakrama Bahu III. Later on the Relic was at Kotte. The Portuguese assert that they took the relic to Goa and burnt it. The Buddhists say that what was removed was an imitation of the Sacred Relic, and believe that the one in Kandy is the genuine Relic. There are many other jewels and ornaments of interest in the shrine, the brazen doors of which merit observation. The eaves of the projecting roof, the massive supporting pillars, corbels and ceilings are profusely decorated in bright colours with painted figures, grotesque monsters and floral patterns. Adjacent to the Temple, the Octagon contains the Oriental library.

The old Kachcheri, the District Court, and the Supreme Court form three sides of a rectangle. The audience hall of the Kandyan Kings (erected 1784-1820) now serves as a Supreme Court House; the carving of the wooden pillars is notable. Near by is the **Kandy Museum,** located in an ancient building. At the Kandyan Art Association, in Victoria Drive, ancient Kandyan arts are practised, and articles in silver, copper, brass, ivory, etc., are for sale at reasonable prices. An imposing new Kachcheri in Brownrigg Street was opened in 1957. ¾ m. W. of the town in lovely surroundings, is Asgiriya Temple with a large recumbent Buddha in the main shrine room. Large stone slabs with inscriptions are imbedded in the back wall of the temple.

An interesting excursion may be made to two Buddhist temples. **Lankatilaka Vihare** (4 m. from Peradeniya) was built in 1344: it looks like a Norwegian wooden church. **Gadaladeniya Vihare,** of the same date, is ¼ m. off the Peradeniya-Kadugannuwa road, at a turning 2 m. from Peradeniya on the left. Cars can proceed up to both temples.

There are many pleasant drives and rides to be taken in the neighbourhood of Kandy; the Upper Lake (or Gregory's) road; Lady Blake's drive; Lady M'Callum drive; the extensive plantations of cacao on the banks of the Mahaweli-ganga, a few miles below Kandy, deserve a visit.

Excursions

(1) To **Kurunegala** (N.W.) *via* the (16 m.) **Galagedera** (R.H.) **Pass,** where there is good snipe-shooting in season.

(2) To (15 m.) E. **Teldeniya** (R.H.). 6 m. from here is the **Medamaha Nuwara Peak,** on which is an old Sinhalese Fort and City of Refuge. Near the 20th mile is visible a pillar on the right, marking where the last King of Kandy was captured by the British troops. The road leads on

(3) To **Madugoda** (R.H.), thence by a road to **Weragamtota** (R.H.), in the Central Province. After this the view Eastwards is one of the finest in the Island. The Mahaweli-ganga is crossed by a bridge to **Alutnuwara** (see p. 717), in the Uva Province. The traveller is now in the Bintenna country. The straight course due N. taken by river is remarkable.

Burrows' *Visitors' Guide to Kandy and Nuwara Eliya*, also Dr Willis's guide-book, may be consulted with advantage.

ROUTE 2

COLOMBO to NUWARA ELIYA, BANDARAWELA, BADULLA, and BATTICALOA.

(Rail to Nuwara Eliya and Badulla; motor-omnibus service and air service to Batticaloa and Gal Oya (p. 718).

This route to Peradeniya Junction is the same as Route 1.

(There is a sleeping-car on the night mails between Colombo and Nanu-oya.)

From Peradeniya the line continues S. to 79 m. **Gampola** (1573 ft.) (good Rest House). From here a road runs S.E. to Nuwara Eliya (see p. 715).

88 m. **Nawalapitiya** (1913 ft.), whence a road leads to (22 m.) Talawakelle (see below).

From that point the stations are on a constantly rising level to

109 m. **Hatton** station,* 4141 ft. above the sea.

At Hatton roads from Nawalapitiya Dickoya (including Maskeliya and Bogawantalawa) and Talawakele meet.

The drive (12 m.) to **Talawakele** (3932 ft.) is very pleasant (see p. 715). Good views of the very pretty *Devon Falls* and the magnificent *St Clair Falls*. Motor-lorry leaves Talawakele for Diyagama (17 m.) both morning and evening. (see Horton Plains, p. 715).

From Hatton the **ascent of Adam's Peak** (7420 ft.), the most celebrated, though not the highest, mountain in Ceylon, is most easily made. The wonderful shadow cast by the peak at sunrise is a sight which will repay the trouble and fatigue. Camoens, the Portuguese, mentions it in his *Lusiad.* The manager of the Adam's Peak

Hotel at Hatton makes all arrangements for the visitor. A moonlight night is generally chosen. It is a very beautiful drive of 12 m. to Maskeliya (4200 ft.) and 14 m. to **Laxapana** (Raksapana). From here it is 8 m. to the top, though the climb now starts at **Dalhousie,** and steps have been cut to a point near the summit. Chains of old date facilitate the scramble up the last portion to the actual summit. Stout boots and warm clothing are needed for the trip, and blankets should be taken up from the hotel—also means of making tea on the summit, which is only 150 ft. square, where a few Buddhist monks live. Under a wooden canopy is the sacred object of the pilgrimage—an impression of the foot of Buddha on the natural rock. The foot is covered by a stone slab on which a foot 5½ ft. by 2½ ft. broad and 3-5 in. in depth has been incised.

Hatton is also the point from which the great tea-districts of **Dikoya** and **Dimbula** may be most conveniently visited. These valleys were celebrated for their production of coffee, but are now entirely devoted to tea cultivation. About the year 1870 the coffee plantations were attacked by a new fungus, *Hemileia vastatrix,* which in ten years' time reduced the planting community to a state of ruin, but they set to work to remedy the disaster, and by the substitution of tea and rubber for coffee have thoroughly succeeded in doing so. In 1875 only 282 lb. of tea were exported from Ceylon, now over 458,000,000 lb. (1970).

The **Dikoya** Valley (Kandy District) is the site of a hydro-electric scheme which involved damming the River Kehelgamu-oya at Norton, and erecting a power-house at Horowalatenna on the E. bank of the Maskeliya-oya.

Dikoya is on the motor-bus route from Hatton to Norwood; and there is another service from Norwood to Maskeliya.

The valley of **Maskeliya** is separated by a ridge from that of Dikoya, to which it is parallel. The Dimbula valley is traversed by a road from Nawalapitiya to Nuwara Eliya, into which a branch road from Hatton leads.

On leaving Hatton the train passes through the longest tunnel on the railway. Just after the 114th mile the very fine *St Clair Falls* are seen on the left (see p. 714).

117 m. **Talawakele** station (R.H.). Motor-bus service, 14 m., from Agrapatna. The Tea Research Institute is open on the second and last Wednesdays of each month.

The Horton Plains (see p. 716) may be reached by this route, but motor-coach to **Diyagama** (17 m.), thence on foot or horseback (8 m.).

From Talawakele the line again rises steadily to

129 m. **Nanuoya** Junction[1] (5291 ft.). There is (4½ m.) a good road, and a motor-car to meet the train at Nanuoya can be obtained from the Grand Hotel or the Public Stand at Nuwara Eliya.

4½ m. **NUWARA ELIYA,*** the sanatorium of Sri Lanka, is 6199 ft. above the sea-level. The summer residence of the Governor-General (Queen's Cottage) the Hill Club and Hotels are to the N.W. of the lake. Much of the ground about Nuwara Eliya is open and moor-like, and is thickly dotted with bushes of crimson rhododendron. The cypress and the golden wattle have been largely planted about Nuwara Eliya, and the landscape has a somewhat Italian air imparted to it by the numerous *Kina*-trees (*Calophyllum tomentosum*), resembling a stone-pine.

Nuwara Eliya has a beautiful park and one of the finest golf-courses in the East. The Lawn Tennis Championship at the Hail Club Courts was revived in 1946. It is also the headquarters of the Sri Lanka Fishing Club. The streams are well stocked with rainbow trout, which afford

[1] Travellers are recommended to have warm clothes with them, as the temperature here is very much lower than that of the plains, or even of Kandy.

good sport in the open season, May-October.

Of expeditions of all sorts,[1] the finest are:

(1) Round the *Moon Plains,* 5 m.

(2) To the top of *Ramboda Pass* and back, 30 m.

(3) Round the *Lake,* 6 m. To Hakgala (see below), 6 m. *Pidurutalagala,* the highest mountain in Ceylon (8820 ft.), may be easily ascended from Nuwara Eliya. There is a bridle-path to the top, whence the view is extensive.

(4) A longer excursion is that to the **Horton Plains,** 18 m. from Nuwara Eliya (see also under Talawakele, p. 715), *via* Blackpool and the Elk Plains. The easier route is by train to Pattipola, and thence by foot or on horseback: distance 6½ m.

This excursion will take a day, and can be made on horseback. A bridle-path terminates at a large R.H., in the neighbourhood of which are tremendous precipices, which descend to the great plain of the Kalu Ganga. At the "World's End", ¾ m. easy walk from the R.H., along a charming jungle path, there is a very striking view. The mountains, **Totapala** (7741 ft.) and **Kirigalpotta** (7857 ft.), may be ascended from here. The path to the summit of the latter (about 2 hr. from R.H.) is somewhat difficult; a guide should be taken. The view is magnificent.

(5) A drive out to **Kandapola** (6½ m.) is very agreeable on a fine day.

(6) The **Botanic Gardens** at **Hakgala,** 6 m. (see below on road to Badulla).

From Nuwara Eliya the traveller may return to (35 m.) Gampola (p. 714) by the Ramboda Pass (motor-bus from Gampola to Nuwara Eliya). The pass is negotiated by a series of zigzags. Several pretty waterfalls are seen at (15 m.) **Ramboda** (R.H.).

Just before entering Gampola the Mahaweli-ganga is crossed by a bridge.

The drive from Nuwara Eliya to Badulla is extremely picturesque. There is a motor-bus service to Hakgala and Welimada (see below).

On leaving Nuwara Eliya the road to Badulla rises after quitting the lake, and then commences a very steep descent of several thousand feet. At 6 m. from Nuwara Eliya we reach the *Botanic Gardens* at **Hakgala** (which derives its name from the resemblance the bare rock above has to a human jaw), a visit to which ought on no account to be omitted by anyone making a stay, however short, at Nuwara Eliya. The visitor is equally repaid by the beauty of the views from the gardens, and by the beauty of the gardens themselves, in which all the flowers and plants of temperate climates flourish freely, combined with much beautiful natural vegetation. Behind the Hakgala gardens rises the precipitous wall of bare rock which forms the face of the Hakgala mountain, whilst in front the ground sinks abruptly to valleys and low hills far below, and backed in the distance by the mountains of Uva.

The road descends to (13 m.) *Wilson's Bungalow* and to **Welimada** (R.H.), from which a public road branches off to the right to Bandarawella (13 m.).

26 m. **Ettampitiya** (Atampitiya), on the same level as Wilson's Bungalow. Terrace-cultivation is practised, the steepest hillsides being fashioned into a series of narrow terraces, carefully irrigated, on which abundant crops of paddy are grown. From Ettampitiya the road again falls continuously, until, after passing **Dikwella,** where it is joined by the road from Bandarawela, it reaches (37 m.) Badulla (see below).

Nanuoya to Badulla by Rail

The main railway from Nanuoya continues to

140 m. (R.H.) **Pattipola** station. A bridle-path (6 m.) leads to the Horton Plains (see p. 714). Shortly after the train reaches the summit level (6224 ft.). It then enters a tunnel, and

[1] Burrows' *Visitors' Guide to Kandy and Nuwara Eliya* is a useful handbook.

emerging, a most magnificent view of the Uva country is disclosed with dramatic suddenness to the left.

154 m. **Haputale** station (4583 ft.) (R.H.) (see p. 721).

158 m. **Diyatalawa** station (5024 ft.). Below, to the left, there was a Boer P.O.W. Camp, during the South African War. It was subsequently used by the Royal Navy as a sanatorium for sailors on the East India Station.

161 m. **Bandarawela** station (4036 ft.) (Hotel).

5¼ m. out of Bandarawela, on the way to Badulla, a road breaks off to the right to (7½ m.) **Ella,** where there is a small but beautifully situated Rest house. The traveller may continue by this road to (18 m.) Passara through very fine scenery.

182 m. **BADULLA** station, alt. 2225 ft. (good Rest house), the capital of the Province of Uva, one of the oldest, most cheerful, and most attractive towns in Ceylon. It is situated in a hollow entirely surrounded by green paddy-fields, and in the immediate vicinity of a fine river, while on all sides the background is formed by mountains of very beautiful outline.

Fine avenues of *Inga samon* and other trees adorn the town. The racecourse is overgrown and not in use. It is in the centre of a very flourishing group of tea-estates. The church, the nave of which was built by subscriptions from Kandyan chiefs to the memory of Major Rogers, administrator and sportsman, and the old garrison burial-ground, containing a tomb of 1817, uplifted by a Bo-Tree, merit a visit. The fine **Dunhinda Waterfall** is only 3½ m. away, but is rather difficult of access.

Of the ancient city not a vestige is to be seen of the palace of the kings, and scarcely any indication of any buildings of considerable antiquity. There are, however, two large and wealthy temples, one Buddhist, the *Mutiyangane Vihare* and one Hindu, the *Kataragama Dewali*. They occupy ancient sites, and the dagoba at the Mutiyangane Vihare is undoubtedly of very early origin.

A very interesting excursion may be made from Badulla to **Alutnuwara,** 30 m. N., on the Mahaweli-ganga, where there is an ancient dagoba in the midst of fine scenery. Alutnuwara is better reached from Kandy, and one of the views on that route at the head of the sudden descent to the great eastern plain is among the finest in Sri Lanka (p. 703).

Badulla to Batticaloa by road

Batticaloa is accessible by rail *via* Maho Junction on the line to Jaffna (Route 7), but the motor-coach route from Badulla will probably be preferred. The distance is 103½ m.

Leaving the railway at Badulla, the road, which passes chiefly through tea-estates, rises rapidly to Debedda Gap (3800 ft.) and then falls to

12 m. **Passara,** 2900 ft. (R.H.), with Namunakula Hill (6679 ft.) on the W. A short road to Bandarawela by Ella leads through beautiful scenery.

Proceeding, the road continues through some of the finest scenery in Sri Lanka to

25 m. **Lunugala,** 2450 ft. (R.H.). Nothing can exceed the beauty of the drive between this place and

36 m. **Bibile,** 800 ft. (R.H.), a good starting-point for excursions into the wild country to the E. and S. (see p. 739). There are some springs of warm water near here. Either here or at the next following rest houses,

47¼ m. from Badulla iron bridge **Ekiriyankumbara,** 500 ft., or

57 m. **Galodai** (Kallodai), 320 ft., the traveller is likely to meet Veddas. They are a remnant of the aboriginal inhabitants of Sri Lanka, and are divided into two classes—the Rock and the Village Veddas. The Rock Veddas are absolute primitives, who remain concealed in the forests: the type is fast becoming extinct. The Village Veddas, though often indulging their migratory instincts, live in collections of mud and bark huts, in the vicinity of which they carry on

some rude cultivation (see *Wild Ceylon: the Present-day Veddas*, by R. L. Spittel (Colombo, 1924)).

67 m. **Maha Oya,** 200 ft. (R.H., on the borders of a tank, with excellent shooting in season). At Unuwatura Bubula, 3 m. off, is a spring of *hot* water.

80 m. **Tumpalancholai,** 100 ft.

83 m. a road to left leads to **Rukam Tank,** about 1½ m., restored by Sir H. Ward, and now irrigating a large tract of country.

From Bibile to Kumburuwella the traveller passes through what is known as the Bintenna country, where good shooting may be had in season.

93½ m. **Chenkaladi** (R.H.). We have now entered a country almost wholly inhabited by Tamils and "Moors", Sri Lanka Muslims. The Buddhist dagoba is no longer seen in the villages, and its place is taken by the Hindu temple or the mosque. From Rukam onwards the country is highly cultivated and populous.

At Chenkaladi the road from Badulla joins the North Coast road; distance to Trincomalee, about 74 m. (eight ferries to be crossed).

Muttur (small Rest house), on the S. of Kottiyar Bay, about 57 m. from Chenkaladi, is famous as the scene of the capture of Robert Knox, the author of *An Historical Relation of the Island Ceylon, by Robert Knox, a captive there near twenty years* (1660-1679), published in 1681 (reprints, Maclehose, 1911 and *Ceylon Historical Journal*, 1958).

From Chankaladi the road turns sharply to S.E. to

103½ m. **Batticaloa** (good Rest house) is on an island in a remarkable salt-water lake, which extends for over 30 m. in length by from 5 m. to 2 m. in breadth, and is separated from the sea by a broad sandy belt now rich with coconut groves and swarming with Tamil and Moorish villages. The approach to the town by a causeway across the lake is picturesque. The walls of the small old Dutch fort are well preserved.

Batticaloa is famous for the "singing-fish". On calm nights, especially about the time of the full moon, musical sounds are to be heard proceeding from the bottom of the lagoon. They resemble those which are produced by rubbing the rim of a glass vessel with a moistened finger. As a rule not more than two distinct musical notes are heard, one much higher than the other, but credible witnesses, such as Sir E. Tennent, asserted that they had heard a multitude of sounds, "each clear and distinct in itself, the sweetest treble mingling with the lowest bass". The people attribute the production of the sound to the shell-fish *Cerithium palustre*. This may be doubtful, but it is unquestionable that the sounds come from the bottom of the lagoon, and may be distinctly heard rising to the surface on all sides of a boat floating on the lake. If a pole be inserted in the water and its upper end applied to the ear, much louder and stronger sounds are heard.

The edible oyster is good and plentiful here.

The Tamils call Batticaloa "Tamarind Island", from the graceful tamarind-tree which is frequently seen.

Motor-buses run daily between Batticaloa and Badulla. There is another service from Batticaloa to Trincomalee.

From Batticaloa there is a good road for some 77 m. to Panama, thence by track to **Palutupana** (p. 726), through the *Yala Game Sanctuary*.

The railroad from Batticaloa to Gal Oya Junction, on the branch line from Maho Junction to Trincomalee (Route 7), passes through Polonnaruwa and Minneriya (p. 736).

25 m. S. of Batticaloa, on the coast, is Kalmunai. 2 m. S. of this town is the road leading to the Gal Oya Valley Scheme, the largest land development project in Sri Lanka. The waters of the 67-mile-long Gal Oya river have been impounded in a 30-square-mile hill-girt lake and are used for irrigating some of the richest rice-fields in the basin,

generating power for industrial development, and flood protection.

A little over one-half of the Scheme has been completed with the reclamation of 120,000 acres of jungle land now utilised for agriculture and industry, on which have been developed 40 new villages and 7 small towns, with schools, co-operatives, medical centres and other amenities necessary for rural life.

To preserve wild life driven from the reclaimed jungle land, the entire area surrounding the lake has been made a National Park and Sanctuary. The tourist town of Inginiyagala nestles at the entrance to it right below the dam of the lake (¾ mile long, 150 ft. high and 800 ft. broad at the base). It has a modern R.H. (22 rooms) with hot and cold water, drainage, a Palm Lounge with a Bar and even a Juke Box. The Gal Oya National Park is the only one in the country accessible by air. There are daily flights (except Tuesdays)—flying time from Colombo, 1 hr. The planes leave early in the morning and return late in the evening. The main attractions are (1) Mechanised land-development and settlement of peasant farming families, (2) Industrial enterprises, (3) Launch rides on the main reservoir to see wild life, including elephants and aquatic birds, (4) Fishing in the 50,000 acres of fresh water available, (5) Bird-watching and hiking in the jungles.

ROUTE 3

COLOMBO to **RATNAPURA** and **BANDARAWELA**

Rail to Avisawella, Ratnapura and Opanake; thence by motor-omnibus to Haputale (p. 721), and thence rail to Bandarawela; or, *alternatively*, by motor-omnibus the whole way. As the drive is a beautiful one, the road to Avisawella is described in place of the railway (narrow-gauge).

For convenience of arrangement this route has been described from Colombo to Bandarawela. The long ascent, however, takes time, and the traveller who has not much leisure is recommended to go to Bandarawela by railway (Route 2), and to return to Colombo by this route.

No excursion could show more of the characteristic features of Sri Lanka scenery and life than this. It is one strongly recommended to those having time to perform it. The journey to Bandarawela will occupy about three days—one day by train. Those with less time should go as far as Ratnapura, returning to Colombo by the alternative route (No. 4) mentioned on p. 722. To Ratnapura and back by alternative route will occupy more than a day. At **Colombo Fort** the narrow-gauge Kelani Valley railway (87 m. to Opanake) begins.

Leaving Colombo by the narrow and crowded streets of the "Pettah", a very pretty road along the S. bank of the Kelani river may be followed, or a more direct but less picturesque road across the plain to

10 m. **Kaduwela,** a R.H. charmingly situated on a bluff of red rocks above the river at a point where it makes a sharp turn. The R.H. veranda all but overhangs the river, and commands a delightful

view, enlivened by the constant passage of leaf-thatched barges and sailing-boats, and by the picturesque groups all day crossing the river at the ferry close by. A short distance off is an ancient Buddhist temple of some size. There is also the Irrigation Tank of Mulleriyawa. The road continues near the river, through a rapid succession of villages and groves, to

21 m. **Hanwella** (R.H.), a large village with a R.H., commanding a beautiful view up and down the river and situated on the site of a Portuguese fort. 9 m. S. of Hanwella is the tank of Labugama, which supplies Colombo with water. It is picturesquely situated among wooded hills.

The road leaves the Kelani river and passes through country in which rubber alternates with coconut, whilst here and there are patches of tea, to Puwakpittya and

30 m. **Avisawella Junction** station (good Rest house) is surrounded by country of great natural beauty, and is the centre of the rubber industry. The ruins of a royal palace and a temple destroyed by the Portuguese in the 16th century are still to be seen on the opposite bank of the river, reached by an iron bridge.

A road N. from Avisawella crosses the Sitawaka and Kelani rivers by fine iron bridges, both commanding lovely views, and passes, by **Ruwanwella** (where there is an old Dutch fort converted into a very charming R.H.), through a lovely wooded and undulating country to **Kegalla** (p. 710).

44 m. **Pussellawa** (good R.H.). The road crosses the Kuruwita river near the village of Ekneligoda—in which is situated the *walauwa* (residence) of the late Ekneligoda Dissawe, a great Sinhalese chief and landholder—and reaches

56 m. **Ratnapura** (R.H.), the capital of the province of Sabaragamuwa, with an average rainfall of 155 in. Ratnapura is situated in the midst of the most exquisite scenery, and the views from the summit of the fort, the bridge and the circular road are especially recommended. A ride or drive of a few miles up the road leading from the bridge to Gilimale will amply repay the trouble, revealing as it does the magnificent mountain-wall which rises all but perpendicularly to the N. From Ratnapura the finest views of Adam's Peak are to be obtained. There is a specially good one within a few minutes' walk of the R.H.

Ratnapura (City of gems) is surrounded by pits from which gems are extracted. Sapphires, rubies, topazes and cat's-eyes are those most commonly found. The mining operation is simple. A pit is dug, and when the *illan*, a peculiar gravel in which the gems are usually found, is reached, all that is dug up is carefully washed and sifted, and the good stones set aside. *Genuine* stones are found in large quantities, but stones of marketable value are more rare, the greater number having only a faint shade of colour, and being disfigured by flaws. There is now a State Gem Corporation (409 Banddhaloka, Mawata, Colombo 7) which Tourists are advised to consult before purchasing gems. It regulates the industry.

A mile or two W. from Ratnapura is the *Maha Saman Dewale*, one of the richest Buddhist temples in Ceylon, and possessed of considerable estates. Some interesting relics are preserved there, but the building itself, though picturesque, has no architectural interest. In the outer court, built into the wall, stands one of the very few monuments of the Portuguese domination remaining in Sri Lanka—a slab representing the full-length figure of a Portuguese knight in armour killing and trampling upon a prostrate Sinhalese. There is also a round-arched gateway, supposed to be Portuguese.

The **ascent of Adam's Peak** (23 m.) can be made by the following route, but is more easily made from Hatton (p. 714):

5 m. from Ratnapura is **Malwala**, on the River *Kalu Ganga*.

2 m. farther up the river is **Gilimale**, a large village.

5 m. **Palabaddala,** 1200 ft., halting-station of pilgrims. Motorable roads run from Malwala *via* Carney Estate to Palebbada only 3 m. from here. The path becomes very steep and rugged.

8 m. **Heramitipana,** 4400 ft., halting-station at the base of the peak.

3 m. farther is the summit of the mountain (7420 ft.), where is the much venerated imprint of the foot of Gautama Buddha.

Leaving Ratnapura by the bridge, and not forgetting to notice the beautiful views obtainable from it, the road passes through paddy-fields fertilised by the Batugedara irrigation works, and after a drive of 12 m. reaches

68 m. **Pelmadulla** (R.H.), whence a road S.E. leads to **Rakwana** (R.H.), the chief village of a tea-district. The views on this road are some of the most beautiful in Sri Lanka. Between Pelmadulla and Rakwana is Madampe, whence there is a motor-bus service to Tissamaharama (p. 725) on the S. coast through forests.

The woods about Pelmadulla, at the proper season, are bright with the splendid blooms of the *Dendrodium maccarthii.*

From Rakwana an interesting trip may be made Southwards on another road to Hambantota in the Southern province. It is a riding-road only, though practicable for bullock-carts in most places. As far as Maduwanwela the scenery is very pretty.

At Maduwanwela is one of the best-known of the ancient *walauwas* of the Kandyan Chiefs. It consists of several small courts built on a sort of Pompeian plan, the small rooms looking into the court, which, as at Pompeii, is in every case furnished with an impluvium. There is a small private chapel (Buddhist), and the massive outer door, made of one huge piece of wood, is marked by bullets and other traces of resistance to assailants in older times. Within is displayed the silver staff, shaped like a crozier, the badge of office of one of the ancestors of the family, who was chief Adigar or Prime Minister of the King of Kandy.

Beyond, the track leads chiefly through thick forest, a great resort for elephants and deer. After passing the irrigation works on the Walawe river, the main road between Galle and Hambantota is joined at Ambalantota (see p. 725).

84 m. **Balangoda** (R.H.). Nothing can exceed the beauty and variety of the scenery along the whole road from Ratnapura to this place. It is entirely free from monotony.

94 m. **Belihuloya,** 1900 ft. (R.H. overlooking the stream from the Horton Plains), to which spot an ascent can be made. The road leads into tea-estates, whence the forest has been cleared, and the bare hill-sides now lack all trace of their original beauty.

From Pelmadulla the road, varied by occasional descents, has been rising, and by the time it has reached

105 m. **Haldummulla,** 3350 ft. (R.H.), a magnificent view is obtained over all the country lying between Haldummulla and the sea to the S.

From Haldummulla the traveller may proceed E. to **Koslande** (R.H), thence, passing the very fine **Diyaluma Waterfall,** nearly 560 ft. high *en route* to **Wellawaya** (R.H.). Tellula (R.H.), some 10 m. to the S. on the Hambantota road, is the nearest point possible for a shooting head-quarters. From Wellawaya the road runs E. to Pottuvil.

Another steep road of about 8 m. ascends to the top of the pass at **Haputale** (R.H.), on the railway line, at an elevation of 4583 ft. The view hence is even grander than that from Haldummulla. By road (or rail) the traveller proceeds to

120 m. **Bandarawela** (Hotels) (p. 717), which is said to enjoy the best and most equable climate in Sri Lanka. A road through Welimada leads 30 m. to Nuwara Eliya.

ROUTE 4

COLOMBO to RATNAPURA *via* Panadura and Nambapane.

(Rail and road.)

This is an alternative route to Ratnapura, but somewhat longer. It passes through very pretty country, and those who go no farther than Ratnapura are strongly recommended to go by one and return by the other of these routes. The traveller proceeds to *Panadura* by rail (see Route 5), and completes the journey to Ratnapura by motor-bus (3¾ hr.).

A few miles after quitting Panadura the Bolgoda lake, headquarters of the Colombo Motor Yacht Club, is crossed by a bridge, and at

10 m. **Horana** is reached. The R.H. here is built among the remains of an ancient Buddhist monastery, and on the opposite side of the road is a large and handsome Buddhist temple. It contains a bronze candlestick worthy of notice. It is about 8 ft. high, and of remarkably fine workmanship.

28 m. **Nambapane.** The road here follows the Kalu Ganga river as far as the Kuruwita river, which it crosses. The road now keeps at a greater distance from the river, though it follows its general course till it reaches

42 m. **Ratnapura** (R.H.) (see p. 720). Shortly before arriving at Ratnapura the Maha Saman Dewale temple is passed. The whole road is extremely beautiful. Fine views of Adam's Peak and the other principal points of the Central Mountains are to be obtained on this route.

Another route to Ratnapura, by far the best for motorists, is that by the new high-level road *via* Homagama. This route is free of floods.

Leaving Colombo, the route described in Excursion 4, p. 722, should be followed to Reid Avenue and thence through Havelock Road, passing the Police Headquarters on the left and farther the Wellawatte Spinning and Weaving Mills on the right, bearing left at the fork to reach the high-level road on crossing the bridge over the canal. The road then leads to

Nugegoda (5 m.), a suburb which is fast developing into a residential quarter of the city of Colombo. **Kotte,** the capital of Sri Lanka during the 14th, 15th and 16th centuries, is 1½ m. from here. The road then runs almost parallel to the Kelani Valley Railway line through a very pleasant countryside to

Homagama (15¼ m.). R.H. ¼ m. from road, up to date and very pleasantly situated. At the junction the road bears left—the road on the right leads to Padukka—(22½ m.) railway station. R.H. good—to Mipe (22 m.), where the turn to the right should be taken; the straight road leads to (3¾ m.) Hanwella (p. 720). Thence the road leads through Bope (25¼ m.) and Malagala (28¾ m.) to

Ingiriya (33½ m.), where it joins route No. 3 (p. 720) to Ratnapura (56½ m.).

ROUTE 5

COLOMBO to **GALLE, MATARA, Hambantota,** and **Tissamaharama.**

(Rail to Matara. From Matara to Hambantota, motor-bus service daily; also from Hambantota to Tissamaharama.)

The journey is worth making, at all events as far as Galle or Matara, for the sake of the coast scenery. The first five stations—namely, the Fort, Companna Vidiya (the drive from Galle Face Hotel to this station is about ¼ m.), Kollupitiya (Colpetty), Bambalapitya and Wellawatte—are all in the city of Colombo.

At 7 m. is **Mount Lavinia** station (hotel) (see p. 709).

11½ m. **Moratuwa** station is a very flourishing place with an important College. It is justly celebrated for its furniture.

16 m. **Panadura** station (R.H.) (motor-omnibus to Ratnapura; see Route 4).

26 m. **Kalutara** station (R.H.) is approached by a fine steel bridge over the Kalu Ganga. It is over 1200 ft. long, being composed of twelve spans of 100 ft. each. On the site of the former residence of the Govt. Agent stood in turn a Buddhist temple, a Portuguese fort, and a Dutch fort. It is now once more a Buddhist shrine. The R.H. is a good starting-point for the excursions which may be made over excellent roads into the very pretty country to the E., which is the premier rubber-growing area of the island. Snipe and whistling teal are plentiful from November to February. The hog-deer (*Cervus porcinus*), not found anywhere else in Ceylon, is said to have been introduced into the Kalutara District by the Dutch from its home in the Ganges Delta.

The Mangosteen grows well in Kalutara. Its fruit is delicious.

Plumbago, or graphite, is largely mined in the Kalutara District. Ornamental basket-, mat- and hat-weaving with the leaf of the "Indi" palm has been developed. There is a Government model distillery.

37 m. **Alutgama** station for Bentota (R.H. very good) on the other side of the river; celebrated for its oysters and a favourite week-end resort. The drive to Galle from here, generally within sight of the sea, passes under an uninterrupted grove of coconut and other trees. The district is extremely populous.

51 m. **Ambalangoda** station. The R.H. (good) is close to the sea, and has a good bathing-place among the rocks below it.

59 m. **Hikkaduwa** station (Hotel; good R.H.); good sea-bathing and scuba diving. Tropical fish can be easily observed through a snorkel mask.

At (7 m.) **Baddegama** is an old English church consecrated by Bishop Heber in 1825. The first sugar factory in the island was established here in 1853.

63 m. **Dodanduwa** station. There is a fine Buddhist temple here in a somewhat unusual position, approached by a long narrow and steep flight of stone stairs.

72 m. **GALLE** (Portuguese) was the principal port of call for vessels between Aden and the Far East before the completion of the breakwater at Colombo. The harbour is difficult to make in rough weather. The narrow entrance is visible only when very near. *The Lighthouse* is about 60 ft. high. To the E. there is a hill 2170 ft. high called the Haycock, known in Sinhalese as "Hinidum Kanda". It is about 1½ m. from the Rest house at Hiniduma. *All Saints' Church* is about a furlong from the landing-place. It is an ugly stone building of pointed architecture. Adjoining is a fine old Dutch church

(1752-54), containing interesting monuments. The ramparts of the old fort form a charming promenade towards the sea.

The place is supposed to be Tarshish, but is hardly mentioned in the native chronicles before 1267. Ibn Batuta, in the middle of the 14th century, calls it a small town. After the Portuguese occupation (1507) it rose to importance. When the Dutch succeeded the Portuguese they greatly strengthened the fortifications, which had been vigorously defended against their Admiral, Kosten. The magnificent old Dutch fort, which encloses the older part of the town, is in almost perfect preservation. In the marriage treaty of the Infanta of Portugal with Charles II of England it was agreed that if the Portuguese recovered Sri Lanka they were to hand over Galle to the English, but they never did manage to recover it.

The name of Galle is from the Sinhalese *gala*, a rock; but the Portuguese and Dutch settlers derived it from the Latin *gallus*, a cock, and carved an image of a cock on the front of the old Government House, which dated from 1687. The present Government House is the "Residency", which is about ¾ m. from the fort. The Post Office stands on the former "Kerkhof" or Dutch burial-ground. In the environs there are many old and interesting Buddhist monasteries to be explored.

The **Pettah** is a busy centre of native traders about ¾ m. from the fort. There is an orphanage for girls known as "Buona Vista" at Unawatuna, in Talpe Pattu.

There is a large Catholic cathedral, St Mary, on Mount Calvary Hill at Kaluwella.

Akmimana is about 5¼ m. from the fort. It is known as the "Gabadagama" (granary) of the Galle Four Gravets. Paddy-growing is very systematically carried on. At one time there was a sitting Magistrate here; he is said to have held Court at the old R.H. premises. There is at present a Gansabhawa or Village Tribunal. The headworks of the Galle water-supply are about 2¾ m. from the Gansabhawa. They are known as "Hiyare Waterworks".

Wakwella is about 5 m. from the fort. There is a fair R.H. on the banks of the Ginganga. Angling and snipe shooting.

88 m. **Weligama** station (R.H.), a populous and thriving village, beautifully situated on the lovely little bay of the same name. A tiny island opposite the R.H. was once owned by a Frenchman, Count de Mauny, who built a beautiful house and garden there. Half a mile before entering the village, on the right-hand side of the high road from Galle, is a remarkable rock-cut colossal statue of a Sinhalese king in perfect preservation. The statue is popularly styled that of the "Leper King", but the legends attached to it are obscure and contradictory.

The road continues along the seashore, through an almost uninterrupted grove of coconut trees. The whole district is densely populated. The journey is worth making for the sake of the coast scenery, especially in the vicinity of Tangalla. As far as Matara it can be performed by rail. The best way to see the country is to travel by motor along the coast road.

97 m. **Matara** station, the railway terminus, the birthplace of Sir Henry Lawrence (1806) and of Sir George Lawrence (1805). The Nilwala Ganga is here crossed by a fine bridge. Matara is the residence of many of the old and rich Sinhalese lowland families. In the fort there is a Rest House and a handsome clock tower.

At Matara there is a Buddhist hermitage called Chula Lanka. It is an islet connected with the mainland by a causeway, and founded as a Buddhist seminary by a Siamese Prince Priest.

Motor-bus services along the coast to (51 m.) Hambantota; N.E. to Hakmana; and N. to (43 m.) Deniyaya, a planting district in the hill-country.

4 m. from Matara **Dondra,** a fishing

village situated on the southernmost point of Sri Lanka. There was here a stately temple, destroyed by the Portuguese, of which few fragments now remain. There is, however, in the modern vihara a fine gateway elaborately sculptured, and about ½ m. to the N. is a stone cell in perfect preservation. On the headland about 1 m. to the S. of the road is a magnificent lighthouse, erected in 1899.

12½ m. **Dikwella.** About 1 m. inland is the Wewrukannala temple with remarkable statues and tableaux. The temple is very interesting as showing the modern tendency of popular Buddhist religious art.

22½ m. **Tangalla** with a good R.H. close to the sea; a great place for catching turtles.

N. of Tangalla are the extensive irrigation works of the Kirama valley and the large tank of Udukiriwila, a few miles to the S. of which is situated one of the oldest and most remarkable Buddhist monasteries in Sri Lanka—Mulkirigala, an isolated rock rising abruptly from the plain, and honeycombed with caves and temples.

30 m. **Ranna.** About a mile before reaching it we see on the S. a picturesque Buddhist temple on the summit of a high, wooded rock.

The population now becomes far more sparse, and the country is covered with scrub jungle containing peacocks.

40 m. **Ambalantota** (R.H.), a small river, a noble stream here, crossed by a long iron bridge.

10 m. N. of Ambalantota are the headworks of the Walawe Irrigation Scheme. A stone dam diverts the stream into a system of canals and channels.

The road now passes through a desolate country to

48 m. **Hambantota** (R.H.), on a small bay (good bathing). Here are the headquarters of the District, the Government Agent's residence, the Kachcheri, Court-house, etc. Here, too, is one of the two chief salt manufactories in Sri Lanka. A great part of the population are Moors. In the immediate vicinity of the town are sand-hills which long threatened the town. Their onward progress is now checked by the growth of a peculiar grass, and by plantations of the palmyra palm. Motor-bus service to Tissamaharama, *via* Wirawila (see below).

About 20 m. N.E. of Hambantota, off the road to Wellawaya, is **Tissamaharama** (R.H.), one of the oldest of the abandoned royal cities of Sri Lanka. Except as a place of pilgrimage, the site had been wholly abandoned till the restoration of three tanks by the Government. The ruins are of great antiquity. One of the oldest and largest of the dagobas, over 150 ft. high, which was in a very ruinous condition, has been entirely restored by the unassisted labour of the Buddhist population. There are several other very large dagobas, mostly in ruins, and some smaller ones in fair condition. The remains of large buildings are numerous, and the ruins of what is styled the King's palace, but is more probably the lower storey of a many-storeyed monastery like the *Brazen Palace* at Anuradhapura (p. 731), are worthy of notice. They consist of rows of huge monolithic columns, much larger than any at Anuradhapura or Polonnaruwa. Ruins are everywhere scattered through the dense forest.

There are two ways of reaching Tissamaharama from Hambantota:

(1) The easiest route is that by the high road to Badulla. On leaving Hambantota the great *lewayas*, or natural salt-pans, whence great amounts of salt, a Government monopoly, are annually taken, are passed. They present the appearance of frozen lakes.

(2) A more interesting, but from Bundala (12 m.) onwards a difficult, route is along the coast 21 m. to **Kirinda,** a small port. The road thence to Tissamaharama, about 8 m. in length, passes many remains of antiquity.

6 m. beyond Kirinda, along the

coast, is **Palutupana,** close to the border of the Ruhuna National Park. In the jungle is an old British fort, erected in 1813 and called Fort Brownrigg after the Governor who laid the foundation-stone.

From Palutupana there is a track, good for a rough bullock-cart, to Batticaloa (130 m.) (see p. 718).

ROUTE 6

COLOMBO up the W. coast to **Negombo,** thence, by rail or road, **Chilaw** and **Puttalam**; and by road to **Anuradhapura** and **Trincomalee** on the E. coast.

Railway to Puttalam: thence by motor-omnibus. Both Anuradhapura (p. 731) and Trincomalee (p. 738) are accessible by rail from Colombo. (See Routes 7 and 8) as well as by air.

9 m. from Colombo, **Ragama** (p. 710).

13 m. **Ja-ela** (R.H.).

24 m. **Negombo** (two R.H.; accommodation can be booked by telephone from Colombo), a true Dutch settlement situated among lagoons and canals; a Dutch canal runs to Colombo and Chilaw. There is a picturesque Dutch gateway (dated 1672), and a banyan tree of magnificent dimensions. The District Judge's residence is an old Dutch house, dated 1682. The brass-work of Negombo is celebrated; also its crabs and prawns. Bathing is not safe in the S.W. monsoon. The whole District between Colombo and Negombo is densely inhabited. The innumerable villages are scattered through coconut groves, cinnamon gardens, and groves of jack-fruit. The artist and the photographer can find many pictures.

The road then crosses the Maha Oya by a fine bridge, about 400 ft. in length, and proceeds through luxuriant coconut groves and tobacco plantations to

36 m. **Marawila,** 2½ m. from Nattandiya station. Near it is an enormous Roman Catholic church. One of the most striking features on this route is the number and size of the

Roman Catholic churches, erected for the most part by the people of the fishing villages along the coast, who almost all profess that religion.

44 m. **Madampe** (Coconut Research Institute; open third Wednesday in the month); road to Kurunegala (p. 728) passing Dandagamuwa, where there is a picturesque temple.

51 m. **Chilaw** (R.H.). Here is another huge Roman Catholic church. A large Hindu temple at Munneseram is worth a visit.

4 m. beyond Chilaw the River Deduru Oya is passed by an iron bridge. A good road, through a flat, jungle country, interspersed with coconut plantations, leads to

63 m. **Battulu Oya** stn., where another large river is crossed by an iron bridge. The road continues through extensive coconut plantations to

84 m. **Puttalam** (R.H.), a terminus. The island is supplied with salt either from this place or Hambantota. The right season to visit is June to September. On the tongue of land which lies between Puttalam Lake and the sea is St Anne's Roman Catholic Church. On the Saint's festival, 26th July, enormous crowds go thither on pilgrimage—mostly Roman Catholics and other Christians, with a sprinkling of Buddhists.

A canal connects Puttalam with Negombo and Colombo, used for the transport of salt and copra. Roads lead from Puttalam to Kurunegala (motor-bus service, 4¼ hr.) and along the coast to Manaar; the latter runs through very wild country, and is not much used. The road to Anuradhapura (motor-bus service, 3½ hr.) strikes inland through a jungle district. There are no Rest Houses but the road is good and often used by motors.

At 103 m. **Kala Oya,** there is a Circuit Bungalow of the P.W.D. (permit from Dist. Engr., Puttalam). The *Kala Oya river* is crossed by a bridge, with a span of 165 ft., 55 ft. above the ordinary level of the stream, which, nevertheless, carried away the bridge in 1885.

127 m. **Anuradhapura** (Hotel) (see p. 731). Railway station. Motor-bus services to (65¼ m.) Trincomalee in about 4 hr.

The road from Anuradhapura to Trincomalee passes through the old capital.

135 m. **Mihintale** (see p. 734); road to Kandy (p. 712).

160 m. **Horowupotana** (R.H.). A large tank and village.

177 m. **Pankulam.** At Kanniya, 9 m. from Pankulam, and 6 m. from Trincomalee, there are seven hot springs. They are considered equally sacred by Buddhists, Hindus and Muslims; the ruins of a dagoba, a temple of Vishnu and a mosque stand together.

192 m. **Trincomalee** (see p. 738).

ROUTE 7

COLOMBO to TALAIMANAAR (for **Rameswaram** and **South India**) *via* **Polgahawela, Kurunegala, Maho** Junction (for **Trincomalee, Polonnaruwa** and **Batticaloa), Anuradhapura** and **Madawachchiya** (for **Jaffna** and **Kankesanturai).**

Colombo Fort to Talaimanaar. 209½ m. by rail. Sea-passage to Rameswaram, about 2 hr. The Customs and passport examination is held on board the steamer. Currency notes can also be changed on board. Travellers to and from India by the mail route can visit Anuradhapura by breaking the journey.

The route taken by the Sri Lanka-India Boat Mail train from Colombo to

46 m. **Polgahawela,** R. (R.H.), junction for Kandy (Route 1).

59 m. **Kurunegala** (R.H.) in the North-Western Province is situated at the back of a chain of rocks, which from their fancied resemblance to animal forms bear such names as **Etagala,** or **Elephant Rock, Ibbagala,** or **Tortoise Rock, Andagala,** or **Eel Rock,** etc. Kurunegala town itself is situated at the foot of **Etagala**—an enormous black boulder over 1000 ft. in height, resembling the head and shoulders of an elephant. From the top of this rock a noble view is obtained. At its foot is an artificial lake. 12 m. N.E. of Kurunegala is the **Ridi** (or silver) **Vihare,** a very ancient Buddhist monastery, most picturesquely situated at a considerable elevation. (Good motoring road to the foot of the 200 steps.) It contains a large and rare collection of ancient ola (palm-leaf) volumes of the Buddhist Scriptures. Some of the doors of the temple are carved and inlaid in ivory.

From Kurunegala there are good roads S.W. to Negombo and N.W. to Puttalam (see Route 6). The road from Kurunegala to Negombo, passing through **Narammale** (R.H.), Dambadeniya, Giriulla (R.H.) and Welihinda is very pleasing from its varying character and constant succession of woodlands, paddy-fields and coconut groves.

At Dambadeniya, 19 m., is a large and famous temple, close to which is a high, apparently inaccessible isolated rock, on which, according to tradition, prisoners were confined. The steps cut in the rock are, according to tradition, the work of a prisoner who attempted to escape.

12 m. from Kurunegala, on the road to Puttalam is **Wariyapola.** 3 m. beyond this the road branches off to Anuradhapura. 10 m. beyond the junction, after crossing the Deduru Oya by a causeway (not fordable by motor in wet weather, and avoidable by making a short detour *via* Nikaweratiya, where there is a R.H.).

86 m. from Colombo, **Maho** (R.H.); junction for the line to **Trincomalee.**

2½ m. from Maho is **Yapahuwa** (=the excellent mountain), picturesque and curious. It was at one time the abode of the sacred tooth in a *Dalada Maligawa* (tooth-temple); hence the tooth-relic was carried off to India, and recovered by Parakrama Bahu III in 1288. The ruins, possibly of a royal palace, standing at the head of a great flight of steps, are quite unique; the decorative sculptures of animals and human figures are particularly fine. Its traceried windows, one of which is in the Museum at Colombo, are especially curious.

99½ m. from Colombo, **Galgamuwa** station (R.H.). 5 m. from Galgamuwa on the Anuradhapura road, and thence 2 m. along a village road, are the ancient ruins of Rajangane.

126½ m. **Anuradhapura** station, R. (Hotels) (see pp. 731-4).

142½ m. **Madawachchiya** (R.H. 2½ m.). Junction for the line running N. to Jaffna and Kankesanturai (see Route 8).

192½ m. **Mannar** station (R.H.).

Mannar is a dreary spot, commanded by a picturesque old Dutch fort, remarkable for the number of the African *Baobabs*, probably imported by Arabs in the Middle Ages, and for a breed of black cattle. The church in the Fort contains some 16th-century Portuguese tombstones.

Due S. of Mannar, and half-way between it and Puttalam, is *Marichchukaddi*, the former Pearl Fishing centre. The Pearl Banks were leased to a London Company for 20 years, but in 1912 the Company went into liquidation and the Government resumed possession. Fishing has only recently been resumed. The "Banks" lie mostly in the Gulf of Mannar at a depth of about 7 fathoms. They have excited the cupidity of the nations of all ages from the Phoenicians onwards. There is a large literature on the subject. A monograph by Mr James Hornell (formerly the marine biologist to the Ceylon Govt.), propounded a theory as to the true causation of the Orient pearl in the body of the oyster.

207½ m. **Talaimanaar,** at the N.W. point of the island. 2 m. farther on is **Talaimanaar Pier,** whence passengers for Madras and S. India cross to (22 m.) Rameswaram by a steamer of the S. Indian Railway (see p. 552, Route 33) in 90 minutes, on Tuesdays, Thursdays and Saturdays.

Those proceeding from Mannar to Jaffna can follow a direct road N. to Sangupiddy (bus service) from where there is a ferry across to the Jaffna side.

ROUTE 8

KANDY to **Matale**; thence by road *via* Dambulla and **Sigiriya** to **ANURADHAPURA, Mihintale** and **Jaffna.**

The railway on leaving Kandy (p. 712) crosses the *Mahaweliganga* by a fine bridge and continues to

16 m. **Matale** terminus station (R.H.), a great cattle centre. On the hill above Saxton Park are remains of Fort Macdowall, called after the General Commanding in the Kandyan War of 1803.

About 2 m. out of Matale is the remarkable Buddhist temple of *Alu Vihare*. Huge masses of granite rock have, at some remote period, fallen from the mountains overhanging the valley. In the fissures of these boulders, at a considerable height above the road, the monastery has been constructed. It is difficult to imagine a site more picturesque or more theatrical.

From Matale a motor-bus runs to Anuradhapura *via* Dambulla.

30 m. from Kandy, **Nalanda.** The R.H. is situated under fine trees. A steep descent leads to a bridge, a path from which, of about ½ m. to the E., conducts to the ruins of a *Hindu temple* beautifully situated. Nalanda was at one time the residence, not the capital, of Parakrama the Great (p. 704), who built a fortress.

The scenery for 5 m. after leaving Nalanda is very pleasing. At **Naula** a road to the E. leads to *Elahera*, the headworks of an ancient irrigation system of colossal dimensions.

45 m. **Dambulla** (Dambool) (R.H.),

a large village immediately under the huge black rock in which is situated the **Cave Temple** that makes this place famous. There is a fine view from the top of the rock, Sigiriya can be seen above the trees. The temple has large landed possessions in the neighbourhood. The five cave-temples display a mixture of Hinduism and Buddhism: one has a recumbent statue of Buddha, 47 ft. long.

1 m. after leaving Dambulla the *Mirisgoni Oya* is crossed by a very high bridge. Immediately after passing it the road divides. The road straight on leads N.E. to Trincomalee (see Route 9); 4 m. along this road, on the right, just opposite to a Public Works barracks, or "lines", is the turn off to

11 m. from Dambulla **Sigiriya** (R.H.). Irregular bus service. A guide of the Archaeological Dept. is available. It is best to go overnight to Sigiriya and ascend the Lion rock early, returning to Dambulla.

To Sigiriya fortress the King Kasyapa retired (to avoid his brother Moggallana's vengeance) after the murder by him of his father, Dhatu Sena. Here he built his palace and reigned 18 years about A.D. 500. This extraordinary natural stronghold is situated in the heart of the great central forest, above which it rises abruptly. Remains of the old stairway can be seen on the road to the summit. Iron railings and ladders ease the ascent, and niches are cut in the rock and protecting walls are provided. Some frescoes, considered superior to those at Ajanta, high up in a cavity may be seen via a spiral staircase (made in Cornwall).

The Palace, just traceable on the N.W., and the rock itself, are supposed to have been surrounded by a fosse; a tank still exists on the S.W. side. The Lion Staircase House, the granite throne, the Audience Hall, and the dagoba (¾ m. from the rock, but close to the road) should also be seen. Cave's *Ruined Cities of Ceylon*, Burrows' *Buried Cities of Ceylon*, Mitton's *The Lost Cities of Ceylon*, chap. xi, and Bell's *Archaeological Reports* may be consulted.

The branch turning to the left, N., at the *Mirisgoni Oya* bridge is that for Anuradhapura and Jaffna, and passes over an undulating park-like country, and past many newly restored irrigation works to

58 m. **Kekirawa** (R.H.). Station on the branch line from Maho Junction (p. 728) to Trincomalee.

From Kekirawa an expedition should be made, 8 m. W. by a good motor-road, to the **Kalawewa Tank** (also reached by rail from Maho Junction on the line to Trincomalee). This magnificent sheet of water, with an area of about 7 sq. m., was originally formed by King Dhatu Sena about A.D. 460, who built a bund 6 m. long, 50 ft. high and 20 ft. broad on the top. This bund retains the waters of two rivers, and forms a lake which even now, when the spill only reaches a height of 25 ft., has a contour of nearly 40 m. The Yoda Ela canal from one of the sluices carries water to Anuradhapura, a distance of 54 m., and supplies over 100 village tanks in its course. A few miles of the canal at the end nearest Anuradhapura were restored about 50 years ago, but the tank itself and the remainder of the canal remained in ruin, as they had been for many centuries, till 1884, when the Ceylon Government decided to restore them. The work was completed at the end of 1887. The bungalow of the engineer in charge commands a fine view over the lake. The ancient spill, 260 ft. long, 200 ft. wide and 40 ft. high, is still in perfect preservation, the tank having been destroyed, not by any failure of the spill but by an enormous breach on one side of it—now covered by the new spill wall, a fine structure over 1000 ft. in length. At the foot of the bund are ruins of the very ancient city of **Vijitapura,** sometimes, but doubtfully, identified with Wijito.

2 m. W. of Kalawewa is the **Aukana Vihara,** an ancient monastery in a wild and secluded situation where

is an enormous rock-cut standing statue of Buddha, 39 ft. high. The statue has a thin support to the rock from which it is carved, and the right arm is raised and free from the body of the statue.

The road from Kekirawa passes for the most part through monotonous and uninteresting forest to

72 m. **Tirapane.** 4 m. farther, at Galkulama, there is a division in the road. The branch leading due N. is the direct road to Jaffna through Mihintale; the other proceeds N.W. to

86 m. **ANURADHAPURA** (Hotel and R.H.) (126½ m. from Colombo by rail, see p. 727); "The buried city of Ceylon", famous throughout the East for its ancient and extremely interesting ruins—the relics of a civilisation that existed more than 2000 years ago, when the city was the capital of a succession of ancient kings. The city is said to have measured 256 sq. m., i.e. 16 m. in each direction: rather it comprised two cities, one within the other. A motor-car to visit the ruins can be arranged by the manager of the hotel; also the services of licensed guides. For a thorough examination of the ruins all necessary information and assistance will be given at the Kachcheri. Cave's *Ruined Cities of Ceylon*, Burrows' *Buried Cities of Ceylon*, Still's *Guide to the Ancient Capitals of Ceylon*, Mitton's *The Lost Cities of Ceylon*, chaps. iii-ix, and vol. iii of the Archaeological Survey of Ceylon may be studied. The headquarters of the Survey are at Anuradhapura. A certain number of the ruins lie within 1½ m. of the cross-roads, the Brazen Palace and the Bo-Tree being close on the E., and the Thuparama (the oldest stupa in Ceylon, dating from the 3rd century B.C.) and Ruanwelli dagobas on the N. The larger Jetawanarama and Abhayagiriya dagobas lie N.

Anuradhapura was founded by King Pandukabhaya, who made it his capital in 377 B.C., and called it after the constellation Anuradha. It attained its highest magnificence about the commencement of the Christian era. It suffered much during the earlier Tamil invasions and was finally deserted as a royal residence in the 9th century A.D. A small village has always remained on the site, but it was only after the constitution of the North Central Province in 1872, by Sir W. Gregory, that any revival took place in this much-neglected District. Village tanks have been restored; famine and the dreadful disease called *parangi* (produced by the use of bad water and food) have been driven away. Sisal hemp and food products are grown. The Archaeological Survey also is now busy with the restoration of the ruins.

The main objects of interest at Anuradhapura may be divided into *Dagobas*, *Monastic Buildings* and *Pokunas* or *Tanks*. The **Moonstones** of Sri Lanka have been described as unique: these are not the "milky-blue" jewels of Sri Lanka, but are semi-circular granite stones, placed at the foot of a flight of entrance steps, and wonderfully carved in concentric rings, containing processions of animals and floral scrolls of artistic design. Fine specimens are to be seen at a building near the Thuparama stupa and at Polonnaruwa (p. 736). The eight **Sacred Places** held by the Buddhist Community at Anuradhapura are—The Bo-Tree, Brazen Palace, Abhayagiriya, Jetawanarama, Lankarama, Miriswetiya, Ruanweli, Thuparama dagobas. Permits (priced according to camera-sizes) to photograph these places may be obtained from the Archaeological Dept., or the Tourist Bureau.

I. **Dagobas.**—A dagoba is a bell-shaped construction erected over some relic of Buddha or a disciple (see p. 30). It is always solid, and is surmounted by a cubical structure called the *hataras kotuwa* (Burmese *hti*), which again is surmounted by a lofty spire. The number is countless, varying in size from the four great dagobas to tiny objects. There are signs of what may be serpent worship in some of the sculptures.

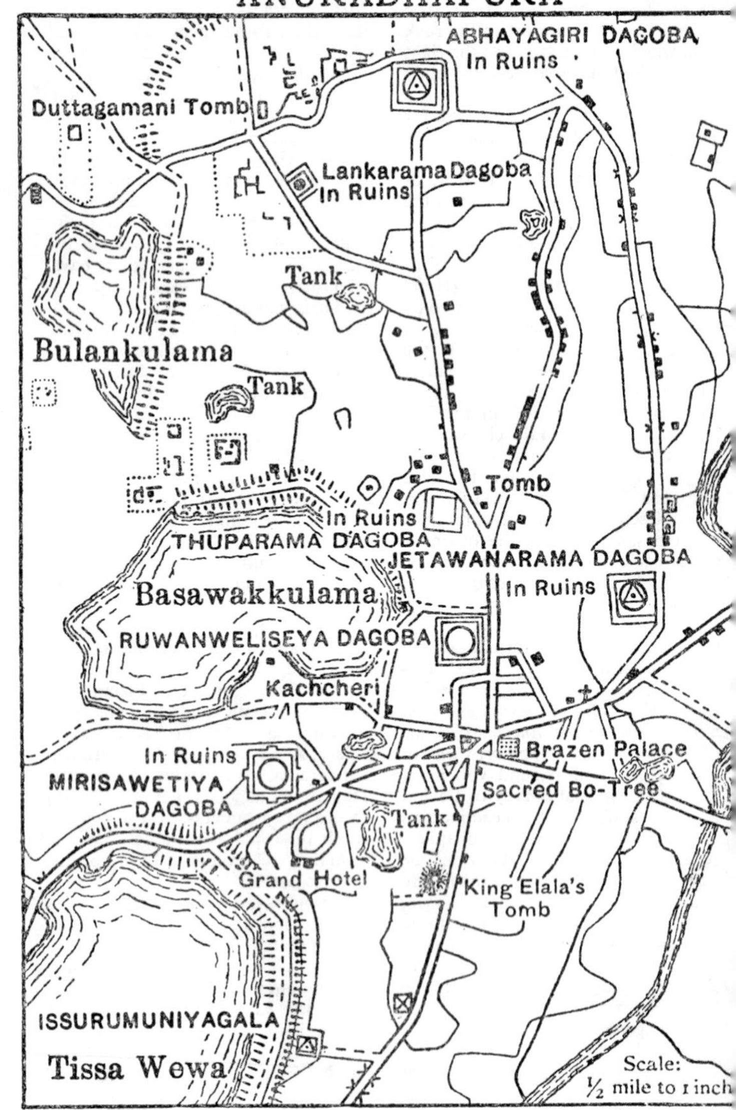
ANURADHAPURA
ABHAYAGIRI DAGOBA
In Ruins
Duttagamani Tomb
Lankarama Dagoba
In Ruins
Tank
Bulankulama
Tank
Tomb
In Ruins
THUPARAMA DAGOBA
JETAWANARAMA DAGOBA
In Ruins
Basawakkulama
RUWANWELISEYA DAGOBA
Kachcheri
Brazen Palace
In Ruins
MIRISAWETIYA
DAGOBA
Sacred Bo-Tree
Tank
Grand Hotel
King Elala's
Tomb
ISSURUMUNIYAGALA
Tissa Wewa
Scale:
½ mile to 1 inch

The four chief dagobas are:

1. The *Ruanweli Dagoba* was a real dagoba, i.e. relic storehouse, commenced by King Dutugemunu, completed about 90 B.C. Its diameter is 252 ft., but having been much injured by the Tamils in different invasions, it is now only 180 ft. in height. The lower part of the structure and the platform on which it stands were cleared about the year 1873, and the various fragments of the so-called four "chapels" facing the cardinal points were put together. This dagoba has been restored by the Buddhists. In shape it is a solid inverted bowl, with a small passage leading to the relic-chamber.

2. The *Jetawanarama* (Mount of Safety) the largest dagoba, was begun by King Mahasena, A.D. 275-292. Its diameter is 327 ft., and its height when perfect was about 270 ft., but is now only about 249 ft. It stands on a grand paved platform, eight acres in extent, raised some feet above the surrounding enclosure. It has been calculated that the bricks are sufficient to build a wall 10 ft. high from London to Edinburgh. The *Hataras kotuwa* on the summit having shown symptoms of falling, it and the stump of the spire above it have been made safe, but the lower part remains untouched. The summit, easily reached, commands a magnificent view.

3. The *Abhayagiriya*, built in the 4th century A.D., was of about the same dimensions as the Jetawanarama. It has been suggested, with some probability, that the names of these two dagobas have been transposed, possibly from the 12th century. Supposing that Jetawanarama is the ancient Abhayagiriya, its foundation is dated 88 B.C., and its enlargement A.D. 113-125.

4. The *Miriswetiya* was built by King Dutugemunu in the 2nd century B.C., and rebuilt by Kasyapa V (929-939). It is surrounded by monastery ruins on three sides. Though smaller than the Jetawanarama, it is remarkable for the unusually fine sculpture of its "chapels", or shrines, of the Dhyani Buddhas. It has been partly restored at the expense of a late King of Siam.

Among the minor dagobas, the Thuparama (the oldest in Sri Lanka) and Lankarama, or Pokarama surrounded by three or four circles of carved columns, are among the most remarkable and most elegant. These columns are a special feature of Sri Lanka dagobas.

The ruined *Dalada Maligawa*, or Temple of the Tooth, is identified by an inscription. The tooth-relic is enshrined (p. 713) at the Dalada Maligawa at Kandy. N. of this temple, in the Citadel, a brick building was unearthed in 1932-33. Near the Mahapali or Alms-hall a stone well, with galleries and flights of steps, was found at the same time.

II. The remains of **Monastic Buildings** are to be found in every direction in the shape of raised stone platforms, foundations and stone pillars. The walls themselves between the pillars, being of brick, have disappeared.

One of the most remarkable consists of 1600 stone pillars about 12 ft. high and only a few feet distant from each other, arranged in forty parallel rows. These formed the lowest storey of the famous **"Brazen Palace"**, or monastery, erected by King Dutugemunu 161 B.C., nine storeys high (reduced to seven) as described in the Mahavamsa. It may have been the nucleus of the Mahavihara, or Chief Monastery of the town; the upper storeys were of wood.

Buildings of this type in every direction for 10 m. are innumerable. Among the most remarkable is one called the Queen's Pavilion, the semicircular doorstep of which is carved with a double procession of animals and studies of flowers. Another, excavated 1932-35, is close to the Thuparama stupa.

III. The **Pokunas** are bathing-tanks, or tanks for the supply of drinking-water, being wholly constructed of masonry or of cement. These are to be found everywhere through the jungle. The finest is the double (Kuttam) tank in the outer circular road, and to the E. of the Abhayagiri Dagoba, into which elaborately carved staircases descend.

Another object of interest is the **sacred Pipal** or **Bo-Tree** (*Ficus religiosa*), originally brought from Buddh Gaya (p. 130). Though only a fragment now remains this is probably the oldest historical tree existing. It was originally brought by the sister of Mahinda, the Princess Sanghamitta, as a branch of the bo-tree under which Buddha sat at Buddh Gaya, and planted after 236 B.C. when Buddhism was first introduced. From that time to this it has been watched over by an uninterrupted succession of guardians. It stands on a small terraced mound, and is surrounded by a number of descendants. The adjacent buildings are all modern, but the entrance to the enclosure possesses a fine semicircular doorstep or "moonstone".

Some fine bronze statues found at Anuradhapura in 1908 are now in the Colombo Museum.

Another object of interest is the **Rock Temple** at **Isurumuniya** (S. of the hotel), carved in the solid rock, with a large seated Buddha inside and sculptures in low relief on the terraces.

Other objects of interest at Anuradhapura and in the neighbourhood are—the stone canoes (purpose uncertain) the Peacock Palace, a vihara W. of Ruanweli, the Selachaitiya dagoba, rock-dwellings (galgé, etc.), the so-called Elephant Stables (with the guardstone), the King's Palace, the Pankuliya monastery, Vijayarama, Yantragalas (square stones with holes), Elala's tomb, Vessagiriya monastery (a town in itself), groups of buildings on the Arippu Road, the Kiribath Dagoba, the Mullegalla and Puliyankulam monasteries. A colossal Buddha has recently been brought here from Puravasankulam in the district.

8 m. E. of Anuradhapura is **Mihintale,** a centre of Buddhist pilgrimage. (A motor-coach from Anuradhapura to Trincomallee passes Mihintale, or a conveyance can be obtained at the Hotel.) It is a rocky hill crowned with a large dagoba, and literally covered with the remains of temples and hermitages. Ancient and picturesque stairs of many hundred steps lead to the summit, whence there is a very fine view over the forest plain, from which the great dagobas of Anuradhapura stand up like the pyramids or natural hills.

A mound on a spur of the hill, excavated 1932-35, has proved to be a stupa, the Kantaka Cetiya, 425 ft. in circumference at its base, and probably once 100 ft. high. It has "frontispieces" (at the four cardinal points), the sculptures on which deserve careful study. It is mentioned in the Mahavamsa and is very old.

The centre of attraction at Mihintale is *Mahinda's Bed*, the undoubted cell occupied by Mahinda the apostle of Buddhism in Sri Lanka and containing the stone couch on which he lay. The outlook is enhanced by the position from which it is obtained between the rocks which overhang the "bed". Beside the cell is the Ambasthala Dagoba, erected on the traditional spot where King Dewanampia Tissa met the missionary Mahinda.

Mihintale has various other objects to be visited, such as the Alms Hall, the Half-way House, the open-air Lion bath, the stone boat, Giribandha Dagoba Naga Pokuna, Kaludiya Pokuna, the Elephant Calf Hill, and on the summit the Mahaseya Dagoba, containing a hair of Gautama Buddha.

Travellers for the North can either go direct by rail to Jaffna (p. 735, Route 7) and Kankesanturai or by road. The stages are as follows:

95 m. from Kandy (by direct road through Mihintale) **Madawachchiya** (R.H.) (see p. 728).

From here a road leads N.W. to (52 m.) Mannar (R.H.) (p. 728), passing the *Giant's Tank* and the magnificent masonry dam which diverts the *Aruvi Avu* to fill it, and a railway, 65 m. long, runs to Talaimanaar (see p. 729).

111 m. from Kandy. **Vavuniya** (R.H.), a small town on the edge of a restored tank.

126 m. **Puliyankulam** (P.W.D. bungalow).

139 m. **Mankulam** (R.H.). From here there is a good metalled road, 30 m., to **Mullaittivu,** on N.E. coast (motor-bus service), the headquarters of the District, under an Asst. Govt. Agent.

154 m. **Iranaimadu.** Here are large irrigation works.

166 m. **Elephant Pass** (R.H.), so named because here the herds of elephants were in the habit of coming from the mainland through the shallow water to the peninsula of Jaffna. This is now entered by a long causeway crossing the arm of the sea which all but cuts off the Jaffna District from the remainder of Sri Lanka. There is fishing on the lagoon, November to January.

174 m. **Pallai.** The region now attained is totally different from that between Anuradhapura and Elephant Pass. The peninsula of Jaffna is the home of a busy, industrious and closely packed population. Every cultivable acre is cultivated, and the garden-culture is of beautiful neatness. Great quantities of tobacco of a very coarse description are grown, a portion of which is exported to S. India. The fine road passes through a succession of large villages as it proceeds.

187 m. **Chavakachcheri** (R.H.), a large village surrounded by groves of the palmyra palm, which takes the place occupied by the coconut palm in the south.

201 m. **Jaffna** or Jaffnapatam (R.H.) is the see of a Roman Catholic bishop.

The old *Dutch Fort* is in perfect preservation, and is a good specimen of fortification (1680). Within it are the *King's House* (the Governor-General's residence when he visits Jaffna), and old *Dutch Church* containing curious tombstones (one dated 1621), the residences of certain officials, and the prison. On the esplanade between the fort and the city stands a graceful *Clock Tower*, built in 1882. The Dutch expelled the Portuguese from Jaffna, their last station in Ceylon, in 1658.

The following excursions may be made:

1. To the Mission Stations at Uduvil, Vaddu Koddai and Kopay, where thousands of children are educated. American Mission Hospitals at Inuvil and Manipay. The Rosarion Monastery at Tholacutty.

2. To Puttur, where is a very remarkable well of great depth, which is apparently inexhaustible, and ebbs and flows slightly daily.

3. To Point Pedro, the Northernmost port of Jaffna; motor-bus service, 21 m., *via* Valvettiturai.

4. **Kankesanturai** (R.H.) (11½ m. from Jaffna). The terminus of the Northern Railway. Sea-bathing.

5. By coast road and ferry to the island of **Kayts,** where the old Dutch fort is a miniature Château d'If. It is called the Hammenhiel Fort and is on a tiny island of its own. Motor-bus service, 14 m. from Jaffna *via* **Karaitivu** reached by a 2-m. causeway with 10 bridges.

6. Keerimalai tank, a fresh-water bathing tank almost on the sea-shore.

7. The Nallur Kanaswamy Kovil, one of the oldest Hindu temples.

8. Excavations at Kandarodari near Chumakam have revealed 48 small Buddhist dagobas to date.

Jaffna is celebrated for its mangoes, esteemed by some as superior even to the far-famed Bombay Alfonzos. Grapes are also grown. Turtles are caught, and *bêche-de-mer*, or *trepang*, a species of sea slug, is fished for, and exported to China, where it is considered a great delicacy. *Chanks* (the shells of a mollusc) are also fished for and exported to N. India, where they are highly esteemed for jewellery. In the little Island of Delft, S.W. of the Jaffna Peninsula, ponies used to be bred.

ROUTE 9

KANDY to **TRINCOMALEE** (with excursion to **Polonnaruwa**).

Bus service from Kandy to Trincomalee; from Matale, *via* Dambulla, to Habarane; and from Trincomalee to Anuradhapura. Rail from Habarane to Polonnaruwa *via* Gal Oya Junction.

Trincomalee can be most conveniently reached by rail from Colombo (184 m.) *via* Maho Junction. For those who prefer the road journey, Matale (p. 729, 113 m. from Trincomalee) is recommended as a starting-point. From Matale to **Dambulla** the route is the same as Route 8.

On crossing the bridge over the *Mirisgoni Oya*, instead of turning left to Anuradhapura and Jaffna (Route 8), the road proceeds straight on and passing at 50 m. the road to Sigiriya (p. 730), continues to (60 m. from Kandy) Habarane (R.H.).

Habarane (130 m. from Colombo) (R.H.) is a station on the railway from Maho Junction to Trincomalee. There is a picturesque *Buddhist Temple* of considerable antiquity to be seen here; the paintings are of better design and execution than are usual in such places. From the lofty rock by the tank a remarkable view is obtained over the great sea of forest to the N. and E., out of which rises with startling abruptness the rock pillar of Sigiriya (see Route 8).

From Habarane an extremely interesting excursion may be made to **Polonnaruwa** (27 m., R.H.), one of the ancient and deserted capitals of Sri Lanka. In the Mahavamsa Polonnaruwa is called Pulatthi or Pulastipura; its real name is Toparé, from the adjacent Topawewa (below). Rail to Gal Oya Junction (p. 718). There is a motor-bus service, and motoring roads lead to all the ruins.

After passing 12 m. through dense forest up to a few yards on either side of the path, **Minneriya** is reached. This magnificent tank, built by King Maha Sena in A.D. 275, was restored in 1903. The reservoir is upwards of 20 m. in circumference, and no point in its margin commands a view of its entire expanse. The scenery of this lake is enchanting, and nothing can exceed the beauty both in form and colour of the mountain ranges to the S. At 20 m. is the small lake of **Giritale.**

The **Polonnaruwa** Rest house is situated on a promontory in the Topawewa Lake (rooms should be engaged beforehand). The view is very similar to that from Minneriya, and is of great beauty.

Polonnaruwa first became a royal residence in A.D. 368, when the lake of **Topawewa** was formed, but it did not take rank as the capital till the middle of the 8th century. The principal ruins, however, are of a later date, being chiefly of the time of Parakrama Bahu, 1153-86, the epic hero and chief name at Polonnaruwa; the Mahavamsa is full of his prowess. It seems to have been abandoned about 1288 owing to a breach in the dam, but has recently been recolonised. The ancient sites are all in the care of the Government and the ruins are being restored.

Close to the R.H. and to the E. of it are the **Audience Hall** and the **Council Chamber**; in which is the colossal stone lion, 6 ft. from the sole of the foot to the crown, brought back from the Colombo Museum (p. 708); it served as a support for the throne. To the E. again is the **Citadel,** some 25 acres in extent, containing a massive building which has been identified with the Royal Palace. Hard by is the beautiful **Elephant Pavilion,** which rises on three platforms; elephants are carved in the panels on the lowest stage, and lions and dwarfs on the other two. Just outside the Citadel, a stone bathing pool (Kumara Pokuna) has been restored (1933-35). It was constructed by Parakrama Bahu I (p. 737).

About 1 m. S. of the R.H. is the colossal rock-cut figure, 11 ft. 6 in. in height, believed to be the statue of **Parakrama Bahu I.** In the Ceylon Arch. Survey Report for 1909 it was pronounced to be "a rock-hewn portrait of a revered religious teacher from the Indian Continent", but this view has now been abandoned. Straight in front of the statue, and about 200 yards away, is the **Potgul Vehera,** or Library Dagoba, a circular building with remarkably thick walls (nearly 15 ft. at the ground). There is a tradition that it once contained the sacred books; hence the name. To the W. of the R.H. lie the ruins of what appears to have been a strong tower, the probably wooden interior of which is wholly gone; and a little farther in the same direction are the royal pavilions and bathing-tank, ornamented by much elegant sculpture.

About 1 m. to the N. is a remarkable group of buildings—the popularly named **Dalada Maligawa,** or tooth-shrine, officially called **Siva Devale,** No. 1. (It is really a Hindu temple of about 1200, a fine granite building having much elegant ornament of quasi-Hindu design, where the Tooth relic may have received temporary shelter.) The **Thuparama,** a large, massive brick temple, of the 12th century, Hindu in design—containing images of Buddha—the front and Eastern roof have fallen, while the inner chamber preserves its vault and a tower; the **Wata Dage** (= circular relic-house), a curious circular edifice, 58 ft. in diameter, on a raised mound, with four carved staircases and a low stone terrace with an ornamental parapet, once 14 ft. high, of unique design; and to the N. of this the **Ata** (or **Hata) Dage** (= house of eight relics) a large ruined temple. Lying to the E. of the Ata Dage is the massive **Galpota,** or Stone Book, a slab weighing nearly 25 tons, in the shape of a palm-leaf book. In the same vicinity are the **Satmahal Prasada,** a tower of seven storeys of diminishing size; the **Nissanka-latamanda-paya,** called the Floral Altar, and sometimes, perhaps wrongly, regarded as a **Buddhist "post and rail" enclosure** (see p. 30); and a little farther to the N. the **Vishnu Dewale,** a very ornamental structure of Hindu design, in good preservation. Due N. from the Satmal Prasada are also the **Pabulu Vehera,** the third largest at Polonnaruwa, and the **Siva Devale,** No. 2.

1 m. farther N. is the **Rankot Dagoba,** built in the 12th century. It is 200 ft. in height, with a diameter of 180 ft. The spire is very perfect, even the statues surrounding the drum being clearly discernible. Near it, but to the N., is the **Jetawanarama,** a mass of ruins, of which the principal ruin is called **Buddha-sima-prasada,** the "House of the Elder", a temple 170 ft. long, 70 ft. wide and 70 ft. high, at the end of which is a statue of Buddha once nearly 45 ft. high, now headless. The **Kiri** (= milk-white) **Dagoba** about 100 ft. high, the chunam coating of which is still very perfect, adjoins this building.

Another 1 m. of jungle has to be traversed S. to reach the **Gal** (= Kalugal, or the Black-rock) **Vehera,** a spot where are a rock-cut figure of Buddha sitting, a colossal statue, 23 ft. high, of Ananda, Buddha's favourite disciple, in a pose of deep sorrow, and a reclining figure of the unconscious Buddha, 46 ft. long, cut out of the solid rock.

1 m. farther N. again is the **Demala Maha Seya,** containing an upright Buddha, once over 40 ft. high; a very large building, highly ornamented, of which the roof and upper part of the walls have fallen in. The *debris* was partially cleared away in 1886, when many interesting frescoes were found on the walls, but these have since to a great extent perished from exposure.

2 m. to the N. beyond this (4 m. from the R.H.) is the famous **Lotus**

Bath, which is thus described in the Ceylon Arch. Survey Report for 1909: "Imagine a gigantic lotus flower of granite, full blown, 24 ft. 9 in. in diameter, with five concentric lamina of eight petals, gradually diminishing to a stamen. Then decide to reverse nature's order, and instead of a convex shape, depress the petal rings into a concavity . . . and we have the granite bath as it exists in all its shapeliness to this day." Not very far to the S. is the **Unagala Vehera,** now a shapeless mass, but once the largest of the dagobas.

The dagobas of Polonnaruwa will not compare with those of Anuradhapura, but the buildings are in far better preservation. A huge red lotus grows in great profusion in the lake, probably the descendant of those cultivated for use in the temples and palaces of the city.

Varied sport can be obtained from Polonnaruwa under the Government Regulations: there is a close season for certain animals.

140 m. from Colombo is **Gal Oya** Junction, for a branch line (77 m.) to Batticaloa (p. 718). 7 m. from Gal Oya on this line is **Minneriya** (p. 736) and 14 m. farther on is **Polonnaruwa** (p. 736).

On the road to Trincomalee is (76 m. from Kandy)

Alutoya (P.W.D. Bungalow, permit from Dist. Engr., Maradan Kadawela) in the midst of the thick forest. Monkeys are certain to be seen crossing the road in large troops during this portion of the journey.

159 m. **Kantalai** station (R.H.), on the bund of the great tank of Kantalai.

170 m. **Tampalakamam** (Tamblegam). Irrigation Circuit Bungalow, permit from Divl. Engr., Batticaloa.

In *Tampalakamam Bay*, the *window-pane* oyster (*Placuna placenta*) is found—so called from the use to which the Chinese sometimes put the flat translucent shells. The Placuna pearls, valueless as gems, are used by the wealthy classes in India to make lime to chew with "betel".

184 m. by rail, also 3 flights weekly, from Colombo, **Trincomalee** (R.H.) 65 m. from Anuradhapura, to which there are daily bus services (also daily between Trincomalee and Colombo, Kandy, Matale, Jaffna and Batticaloa). It is a town with a magnificent natural harbour, very important in the days of sail. It is built on the N. side of the bay, on the neck of a bold peninsula, separating the outer from the inner harbour, about 4 sq. m. in extent, with very deep water.

The Tamils built a great temple where Fort Frederick now stands. The building was destroyed by the Portuguese when they took the place in 1622, and the materials were employed to build the fort; but the site is still held in great veneration, and every week a Brahman priest, in the presence of a large crowd, throws offerings into the sea from a ledge near the summit of a huge precipice, named Swami Rock or Lovers' Leap, of black rock—a most picturesque scene.

A monument on the summit bears an inscription in Dutch, which purports to commemorate the death of a young Dutch lady, who, according to tradition, in 1687, being disappointed in a love affair, committed suicide at the spot. But the prosaic fact is that the lady long survived the erection of the monument (*Rept. on Dutch Records*, by R. G. Anthonisz, Govt. Archivist, p. 39).

After the Portuguese, European nations have held the place in the following order: Dutch, 1639; French, 1673; Dutch, 1674; English, 1782 (Jan.); French (Suffren), 1782 (Aug.); restored by French to Dutch, 1783; English, 1795. It was formally ceded to Great Britain at the Peace of Amiens in 1802 and is now the main naval base of independent Sri Lanka.

The entrance is marked by a lighthouse at Foul Point, and another light is placed farther in on Round Island. The Mahaweliganga, the largest river in the island, disembogues here.

About 6 m. N.W., at Kanniyai, there are seven *hot* springs. Ravana is said to have struck his spear in a rage.

Good shooting (principally snipe) is to be had in season in the neighbourhood of Trincomalee.

In *Kottiyar Bay*, S. of Trincomalee, the ship *Ann* was refitting in 1660, when Captain Knox, his son Robert and his crew were captured. A white stone at the foot of an old tree is inscribed: "This is the White Man's Tree under which Robert Knox, Captain of the ship *Ann*, was captured, A.D. 1660. Knox was held captive by the Kandyam king for 19 years. This stone was placed here in 1893." (See p. 718.)

On the hill between the bays is the reputed grave of Ravana, the demon of the Ramayana Epic.

There is a regular boat service from Trincomalee across the harbour to Mutur.

ROUTE 10

Sporting Tours

The open season for game (including pea-fowl) is from 1st November to 29th April. Shooting is strictly regulated by law. No game may be shot without a licence. No licences are issued to shoot elephants or buffaloes for sport. A permit to enter any intermediate zone is needed. Separate licences are required to shoot deer, sambhur, and pea-fowl there. Permits, licences, and any further information may be obtained from the Warden, Department of Wild Life, Echelon Square, Colombo. Any further information required may be obtained from the latter. See "Sporting Districts" in the *Times of Ceylon Green Book*. Sportsmen should also consult the Tourist Bureau for full information about rest houses and other facilities. Food may have to be carried; but the rest house staff can cook suitable meals.

In the *Southern Province* all R.H.s are well furnished and provided with beds and bed linen, crockery, cooking utensils, etc. Supplies, except fowl, eggs, rice, etc., are not usually found except in the principal R.Hs.

1. The South Eastern Area. It is not likely that any sportsman would make the *whole* of this tour, but it indicates a line of country any part of which would make a good centre for sport. Peacock abound in the forests, and the tanks and marshes are full of wild-fowl; they also swarm with crocodile.

Starting from **Badulla** (R.H.) by car, the road to Bibile (R.H.) is described in Route 2.

6 hrs. **Nilgara.** A small village with a little patch of paddy cultivation, situated most picturesquely on a river at the entrance to a wild and narrow pass.

4 hrs. **Dambagalla** (Circuit Bungalow, permit from Govt. Agent,

Badulla). A small village N. of the road to Puttovil.

Medagama, in very pretty jungle country abounding with elephants, can be reached by a road liable to floods at causeways 10 m. S. from Bibile.

The road runs on to

20 m. **Nakkala.** There is a picturesque Buddhist temple on the side of a mountain in the neighbourhood.

25 m. **Hulandawa,** junction with the Rutnapura road. Turning to the right, after 10 m. at

Buttala. An oasis of cultivation in the jungle, due to the restoration of its ancient irrigation works of which everywhere through the forests ruins are to be found. Excellent snipe-shooting during October to January.

4 hr. S. from Buttala **Galge.** A group of bare rocks rising from the jungle.

3 hr. **Kataragama.** Dedicated to the Hindu war-god Skanda Kumara. A famous place of Hindu pilgrimage, to which worshippers resort annually from all parts of India. The temple itself is but an insignificant building, and a single gilt-metal tile forms the only relic of the golden roof for which it was once celebrated. There is a festival and fire-walking ceremony in August.

6 hr. **Palutupana** (see p. 726), on the coast situated near the entrance to the Ruhuna National Park. There is a track to Panama, motorable except in very wet weather.

2 hr. **Menik Ganga** (Yala Park Bungalow). From here on wild buffalo are found. On both banks of the Menik Ganga large tracts of country have been proclaimed by Government, in which *shooting or hunting of any sort* is prohibited. The Yala Strict Natural Reserve is bounded by the Menik Ganga on the S., the Kumbukkan river on the N. and for most of the seaward side by Block No. 2 of the **Ruhunu National Park.** This is well worth a visit. There are many wild elephant. The Park Bungalow has beds, but no sheets. Mosquito nets are provided. It is essential to make a reservation ahead, and to bring food. The bungalow keeper can cook it. In this part of the island many inscriptions were found in the year 1934.

3 hr. **Uda Potana.** No R.H. About 2 hr. from Uda Potana is the ford crossing the Kumbukkan Aru, the boundary between the Southern and Eastern Province and about ½ hr. farther is **Kumuna** (P.W.D. Bungalow), near a small village. Part of this route however now falls within the Yala Natural Reserve, entry into which is strictly prohibited except for scientific purposes.

6 hr. **Okanda** at the foot of a bare rock rising out of the sea of jungle. Peafowl are to be found in great abundance in the neighbourhood.

3 hr. **Panawa** or Panama (Irrigation Bungalow, permit from Divl. Inspector, Batticaloa). Fair weather Road to Pottuvil.

6 hr. **Lahugalawewa** (Mahawewa). A restored tank, the haunt of many wild-fowl. There is an Irrigation Bungalow at the tank, permit from Divl. Inspector, Batticaloa. Many elephants live in the neighbourhood.

From this point an excursion of some days may be made through the country on the border of Uva and the Eastern Province. There are hardly any villages, and the only accommodation, not specially provided for, would have to be found in the meagre hospitality of some secluded Buddhist monastery, of which a few are scattered through the forests. Any further route would certainly depend upon the reports received as to the haunts of wild animals at the time.

It may, however, be assumed that a return to inhabited country will be made at Irrakaman, a restored tank, where there is an Irrigation Bungalow (permit from Divl. Irrigation Engineer, Batticaloa). In its vicinity are the scanty ruins of what was once an enormous dagoba, and a road leads hence to **Kalmunai** (R.H.) on the coast, and thence to (25 m.) **Batticaloa** (see Route 2). The sportsman will probably prefer to proceed to **Chadaiyantalawa** and **Amparai** tanks, both of which are swarming with crocodile; and from the latter to

6 hr. the River **Namal Aru** (Namal Oya), the boundary of the Eastern Province, on crossing which the traveller finds himself again in Uva.

A 5 hr. ride along a good track will bring him back to **Nilgala,** from whence he may either return to Badulla the way he came or 10 m. to **Madagama** and 4 hr. Alupota, rejoining the main road to Badulla at (2 hr.) **Passara.** (See Route 2.) Sir Samuel Baker's *Rifle and Hound in Ceylon,* published 1854, relates to the shooting in this area.

2. The **Horton Plains** (see Route 2). There is also excellent trout and carp fishing in season. Full particulars may be obtained at *The Hill Club*, Nuwara Eliya, or from the Government Agent at that place. There is a good Rest house in Horton Plains.

3. **The Trincomalee District** (see Route 9).

4. **The Puttalam District** (see Route 6).

The Wilpattu Sanctuary. This Sanctuary of 150 sq. m. was formed in 1903 on the lines of that of Yala.

5. **The Hambantota District** (see pp. 721, 725).

6. **Minneriya and Polonnaruwa** (Route 9).

Fishing is good in Sri Lanka. The Angling Club, Chaitya Road, Colombo, provides facilities for inshore fishing. Game fishing is also available there and at Trincomalee (Sea Anglers' Club). Then, as mentioned above, there is trout fishing in the streams of Nuwara Eliya and Horton Plains. Facilities are available through the Fishing Club, Tangakelle Estate, Lindula.

SELECTION OF BOOKS ON CEYLON

Times of Sri Lanka Green Book; a Directory of Ceylon. (Annual.)
Ceylon Dictionary. (Ferguson's Annual.)
Automobile Association of Sri Lanka Handbook.
H. A. J. Hulugalle, *Ceylon*. (Oxford, 1949.)
E. F. C. Ludowyk, *The Story of Ceylon* (1962). *The Modern History of Ceylon* (1966).
History of Ceylon: University of Ceylon publication.
G. E. Mitton, *The Lost Cities of Ceylon*. (Murray, 1951.)
G. C. Mendis, *Early History of Ceylon* (1940).
H. Williams, *Ceylon, Pearl of the East* (1952).
E. K. Cook, *Geography of Ceylon* (1939).
A. J. Tresidder, *Ceylon—Resplendent Isle* (1962).
W. Rahule, *History of Buddhism in Ceylon* (1959).
E. W. Adikaram, *Early History of Buddhism in Ceylon* (1946).
Sir John Kotelawala, *An Asian Prime Minister's Story* (1956).
Ceylon. A Tourist Guide (1951).
Arthur Clark, *Off the Reefs of Taprobane* (1957).
Sri Lanka Year Book.

Names of Places.—The names of places in Sri Lanka have a formidable appearance; but acquaintance with the language explains them. Many of them end in *-pura*, or in the Tamil districts *-puram*, which means "town" (Sanskrit, *pura*), or in *-nuwara*, "city" (Sanskrit, *nagara*); many in *-gama* (Sanskrit, *grāma*) "village"; others in *-gala* (Sanskrit, *giri*), "rock" or "hill"; *-kanda* is a "mountain"; *-ganga*, a river; *-oya*, a large stream.

Others, again, are formed with *-tara* (Sanskrit, *tāra*) or its equivalent, *-tota*, meaning a ford, or if on the coast, a port; thus *Kalutara* or *Kalutota* = Black Port or Ford. To these *-turai* corresponds in Tamil Districts.

Others are named after the artificial lakes, or "tanks", which are called in Sinhalese *tale* (Pali, *talāka*), or *wewa* (Sanskrit, *vāpī*), and in Tamil *kulam*; while smaller ponds give the termination *-vila* (Tamil, *-vilei*). Other common endings are *-deniya*, "a strip of rice-field running into hilly ground"; *-pitiya*, "park"; *-watte*, "garden".

Among prefixes are *maha*, "great"; *duwa*, "an island"; *ela*, "a stream"; *gaha*, "tree". The earlier part of the name is very frequently the name of a tree; just as in England we have Ashdown and Beech Hill. The word *ārāma*, a "monastery" or "park", explains Tissamaharama, "King Tissa's Great Monastery", and Thuparama, the park of the oldest "stupa" or "dagoba" in the Island.

The visitor may thus recognise in Nuwara Eliya the "plain" in the territory of "the city" (Kandy); in Anuradhapura the "city" of the constellation Anuradha; Hambantota is the "port" of the Malay boats, called "hambans" or "sampans". Even Kahatagasdigiliwewa becomes intelligible as the "lake of the kahata-tree branch", and Urugasmanhandiya as the "junction of roads by the uru-tree".

DIRECTORY
(Index of Places)

Travellers are advised to consult the local Tourist Information Offices and Automobile Association Offices for current conditions of routes, accommodation, petrol supplies, banking facilities, etc. As noted on p. 6, Guest Houses, Circuit Houses, and Inspection Bungalows ordinarily cannot be occupied without the previous permission of the appropriate local authority.

The Publishers have used their discrimination and excluded a number of places, about which information is given in the text. JOHN MURRAY will be greatly obliged to travellers who may be kind enough to send corrections and additions.

R = Refreshment Room; RR = Railway Retiring Rooms; DB = Dak Bungalow; K = presence of a khansamah or messman; CH = Circuit House; RH = Rest House; IB = Inspection Bungalow; GH = Guest House; H = Hotel; TL = Travellers' Lodge; TB = Tourist Bungalow; L = Lodge.

A

AAREY (Milk Colony), 109.
ABBOTTABAD, 594 (by car 9 m. from Havelian); DB, 3 RH; Hotels: Palm, Palace, Bokhara, Springfield; Tourist Information Centre.
ABU ROAD, 255; R, DB; For Mount Abu; Temples; Excursions from Jaipur by car and bus.
ACHABAL (Kashmir), 608; DB; garden of Jahangir.
ACHALGARH (Mt. Abu), 258; temples.
ACHNERA, 292; R.
ADAM'S PEAK, 714; scenery.
ADAMWAHAN, 563; Sutlej Bridge.
ADONI, 439; DB; fort.
ADRA, 200; R, D.B.
AGARTALA, 411; Airport; CH, DB; Ritz Hotel; Information Centre.
AGRA, 299-311; R, DBK, RH; Hotels: Clark's, Shiraz, Laurie's, Imperial, Agra, Grand, Mughal, Holiday Inn; Tourist B; Tourist Information Office, the Mall; U.P. Tourist Bureau, Mahatma Gandhi Rd.
AHMADABAD (AHMEDABAD), 247-254; Airport; R, RR, CH, RH (Shahibag); Hotels: Cama, Ritz, Capital, Capri.
AHMADNAGAR, 436; R, DBK (4), RH; fort.
AIHOLE, 476; temples.
AJAIGARH, 231; RH; fort.
AJANTA, 138-143; GH, IB, Travellers' Restaurant; by car from Jalgaon (38½ m.), or Aurangabad (60 m.); DBK at Fardapur, 3 m. from the caves.
AJMER, 263-6; R, RR, CH, DBK, IB, TB; Mosque, Dargah, Pushkar.
AJODHYA, 372 (near Fyzabad); temples.
AKHAURA, 700; railway junction.
AKOLA, 193; DBK.
AKOT, 193; RHK.
ALAMPUR, 481; temples.
ALIGARH, 377; R, RR, DBK, RH; fort.
ALI MASJID, 602; fort in Khyber Pass.
ALIPUR (Duars), 405; DB.
ALIWAL, 355; battlefield.
ALLAHABAD, 123-7; Airport; R, DBK, RR, Tourist B., YMCA, Tourist Office, Hotels: Royal, South Road; Barnett's, in Canning Road.
ALLEPPEY, 526; 2 DBK, RH; port.
ALMORA, 371; Deodar Hotel; Tourist Home; DBS.
ALUTNUWARA, 717.
ALWAR, 270; CH, Tourist RH; State Hotel; Palaces; Art Gallery (closed Fridays); Wild Life Sanctuary at Sariska (Tourist RH).
ALWAYE, 524; RH; Tourist B (old palace); Tourist H; Important industrial complex (nearest accommodation for Kaladi).
AMALNER, 118.
AMARAVATI, 427; old capital; Tourist B; Southern centre of Mahayana Buddhism; Remarkable sculptures and ruins; Museum.
AMARKANTAK, plateau, 198.
AMARNATH, 608; cave; pilgrimage centre.
AMBALA, 347; R, DB; Hotels: Cecil, Parry's.
AMBARNATH, 428; Temple.
AMBASAMUDRAM, 551; waterfalls.
AMBER, 269; fortress, deserted city.
AMGAON, 197; R, DB.
AMMAYANAYAKKANUR, or Kodai Kanal Road, 545; R, DBK.
AMRAOTI, 193; DBK.
AMRITSAR, 355-8; Airport; R, RR, DBK, H; Tourist B; A.A. of Upper India; Academy of Fine Arts; Golden Temple, fort; Hotels: Ritz; Guest House: Mrs Bhandari, 10 Cantonment; Information Bureau, 8 Grand Trunk Road.
ANAKAPALLI, 425; Buddhist remains.

ANAND, 246; RH.
ANANTAPUR, 483; DB; Penukonda fort.
ANANTNAJ (Islamabad, Kashmir), 607.
ANHILWARA (Patan), 255; old city.
ANJENGO, 551: fort.
ANURADHAPURA, 731-4; R, H; old city.
ARCOT, 498-500; DB; fort.
ARKONAM, 441; R, RR.
AROR, 562; ancient city.
ARRAH, 133; DBK; Mutiny Monument.
ARSIKERE, 488 (for Sravana Belgola); R, DB; 12 c temple.
ASANSOL, 136, 200; R, DBK.
ASIRGARH, 119; RH; fortress.
ASSAM, 406.
ASSAYE, 153; battlefield.
ATGAON (for Tansa Lake), 114; DB.
ATTOCK, 595; DBK, RH; fortress.
AUNDHA, 154; temple; Museum paintings.
AURANGABAD, 151; Airport; R, DBK, 2 RH, fort; Buddhist caves; for Ellora 13 m. and Ajanta 60 m.; Aurangabad Hotel; Tourist B.; Welcom Hotel Rama; Tourist Information Office, Nehru Chowk Road.
AUROVILLE, 533; new city.
AVANTIPUR (Kashmir), 607; old capital; temples.
AVISAWELLA, 720, ruins
AZAMGARH, 393; DBK, RH.
AZHIKKAL, 530.
AZIMGANJ, 390; DBK.

B

BABA BUDAN HILLS, 487; planting.
BADAMI, 474; DB, 2 RH; old capital; caves; for Pattadakal 10 m.; Tourist B.
BADARPUR, 340; R.
BADLI-KI-SARAI, 321; battle.
BADNERA, 193; R, DBK.
BADRINATH, 366; DB, IB; Shrine and Pilgrimage Centre.
BADULLA, 717; RH; waterfall.
BAGDOGRA, 312; Airport for Kalimpong, Darjeeling and Gangtok.
BAGH, 205; 2 RH; Buddhist caves, paintings.
BAHAWALPUR, 563; DBK.
BAHRAICH, 372; DBK, RH.
BAHURIBAND, 122 (see Sihora Road); ancient city.
BAIDYANATH, 128; old capital.
BAKHTYARPUR, 136; DB; for Nalanda.
BALAJU, 672; Water Garden; Nagarjung Royal Forest and Game Sanctuary; Baisedhara.
BALASORE, 412; R, DBK; old settlement.
BALHARSHAH, 194; DBK; Gond fortress.
BALRAMPUR, 372; DB; for Saheth Maheth.
BALSAR (Bulsar), 240; RH.
BALTISTAN, 613.
BALUGAN (for Chilka Lake), 423; RH.
BAMRAULI, 123; Airport, for Allahabad.
BANAVAR, for Halebid, 486; DB.
BANBHORE (near Karachi), 469; Excavations of Ancient Seaport.
BANBASSA, 369; Sarda barrage.
BANDA, 230; R, DBK, RH; fort.
BANDARAWELA, 717; hunting; Hotels: Bandarawela, Grand.
BANDEL, 137, 190; bridge.
BANDIKUI, 270; R.
BANDIPUR, 495; Wild Life Sanctuary; 3 Forest L., I.B.
BANDRA, 109; for Juhu; bathing.
BANEPA, 673-4; Chandresvari Temple; Jagesvari Temple.
BANGALORE, 488-90; Airport; R, RR, LGH; Hotels, Bangalore International, Palace, West End, Tourist, Madras Woodland, Shilton.
BANIHAL, 604; route to Vale of Kashmir; DBK.
BANJARAHI, 627, 681.
BANKAPUR, 485; RH; fort.
BANKI, 414; RH.
BANKIPORE, 133; DB; old Civil Station of Patna.
BANNU, 595; DB.
BARABANKI, 372; R, DBK, RH.
BARABAR CAVES, 129 (Asoka).
BARAHACHHETRA, 629, 683; Varaha Temple.
BARAKAR, 132; DB (3), K.
BARAMULA, 609; DB.
BAREILLY, 369; R, RR; Hotels: Royal, Civil-Military; DBK.
BARETH, 222; temple.
BARGAON, 122; temple.
BARODA, 245; Airport; R, RR, DBK, RH, CH; Utsav Hotel.
BAROGH, 348; R, RH.
BARRACKPORE, 186.
BARSANA, 296.
BARWASAGAR, 225; DB; lake.
BASSEIN, 111; RH; Portuguese settlement.
BASTI, 393; R, DBK, RH.
BATTICALOA, 718; RH; Dutch fort singing fish.
BAUDDHA, 668; *see* Bodhnath.
BAYANA, 290; R; battle.
BEAWAR, 263; DB.
BEDNUR (Nagar), 530.
BEGAMPET, 454; R; airport for Hyderabad.
BELATAL, 226; RH; lake.
BELGAUM, 448; R, DB (3) K; Jain temples; fort; Green's Hotel.
BELLARY, 480; R, RR, DBK.
BELUR (Mysore), 487; RH; ancient city; temples.
BENARES (Varanasi), 155-68; Tourist B; R, DBK, RH, Tourist L; Hotels: Clark's, Hotel de Paris; Tourist Information Office, 5 The Mall.
BERAR, 192; cotton and grain.
BERHAMPUR, 424; R, DB.
BESNAGAR, 221; ancient city.
BETTIAH, 392; DBK.
BETUL, 120; DBK, RH.
BEZWADA, Vijayawada, 426.
BHABUA, 128; DBK; ancient city.
BHADGAON, 636, 658-62; Siddhi Pokhari; Tripura Darbar; Nytapola Temple; Bhairava Temple; Chatur Varma Vihara; Dattaraya Temple; Pujari Math.
BHADRACHALAM, 464; DB; temple.
BHADRAK, 412; DB.
BHADRAVATI, 485; Mysore Iron Works.
BHAGALPUR, 391; DBK.
BHAIRAB BAZAR, 697; river port.
BHAJA AND BEDZA, 431; caves.
BHAKRA NANGAL (dam), 64; Tourist B; Hostels.

BHAKTAGRAMMA, *see* Bhadgaon.
BHAKTAPUR, *see* Bhadgaon.
BHANDARA, 196; DBK.
BHANGIR (Bhongir), 463; R; fort.
BHARATPUR, 291; R, DB; Motel; fortress; Ghana Bird Sanctuary Forest RH.
BHARATPUR, (Nepal) 690; Chitawan National Park and Wild Life Reserve; Elephant Camp.
BHARHUT, 122; near Satna, stupa.
BHATINDA, 363; R, DB; fort.
BHATKAL, 531; port.
BHAVNAGAR, 276; Airport; RR, CH; Hotel Topmost (Indian Style); DBK; GH.
BHAYNDAR, 111; scenery.
BHILAI (Iron and Steel), 198.
BHILSA, 221; DB; ancient city.
BHITA, 126; ancient cities.
BHOPAL, 216; Airport; R, CH, DB; Hotels: Imperial Sabre, Pagoda.
BHOR GHAT, 112, 429.
BHUBANESWAR, 416; Airport; R, CH, GH, DB, RH, Tourist BS; Travellers' L; Youth Hostel; temples.
BHUJ, 272; CH.
BHUSAWAL, 118; R, DB, RH.
BHUTAN, 405.
BIDAR, 453; fort.
BIJAPUR, 465-72; R, DB, CH, RH, GH, IB; Tourist BS; Travellers' L; old capital; museum.
BIJNOR, 368; DBK.
BIKANER, 261; DB, CH.
BILASPUR, 198; R, DB.
BINA, 222; R, DBK; ruins at Eran.
BISHNUPUR, 188; temples.
BIRUR, 485; R; for Shimoga.
BITHUR, 380; RH; legends.
BITRAGUNTA, 427; R.
BOBBILI, 424; DB; battle.
BODH-GAYA, 130; RH, IB, Travellers L, Tourist B; Tourist Information Centre; very ancient city; temples.
BODHNATH, 637, 668; Kasti Chaitya; Gelugpa, Kagdyupa and Ningmapa *gompa*.
BOLAN PASS, 570.
BOLARUM, 463.
BOLPUR, 390; R, RR.
BOMBAY, 86-105; R at Ballard Pier, Victoria Terminus, Bombay Central; Bed-, Dressing-, Bathrooms at the Victoria Terminus; Hotels: Taj Mahal, Green's (near the Apollo Bunder), Nataraj, Ambassador, Shalimar, West End, Oberoi Sheraton, Sun 'n Sand (Juhu); Tourist Information Office, 123 Queen's Rd., Church Gate (Tel. 32446).
BORIVLI station, for caves, 109.
BOSTAN, 571; R.
BOWRINGPET (for goldfields), 497; R, DB.
BRINDABAN (Vrindaban), 297; Jaipuria Bhawan; GH; temples.
BROACH, 243; R, DB; ancient city.
BUDAON, 369; R, DBK, RH.
BUDDH GAYA, 130; *see* Bodh Gaya.
BUDDHA NILKANTHA, 672; Ananta Shayin Narayana shrine.
BULDANA, 193; DBK.
BUNDELKHAND, 223.
BUNDI, 215; CH, DBK; old Rajput town.
BURDWAN, 137; R, DBK.
BURHANPUR, 119; DB.
BUXAR, 132; R, DBK; battlefield.

C

CACHAR, 411; DBK.
CALCUTTA, 169-92; R at Howrah and Sealdah Termini; Hotels: Oberoi Grand, Continental (J. L. Nehru Rd.), Hindustan International (Jagadish Bose Rd.), Carlton, Great Eastern (Old Court House St.), Spence's (Wellesley Pl.), Majestic (Madan St.), and others; International Students' Home (New Park St.); YMCA; YWCA; there are also many Boarding Houses; G. of India Tourist Office, 4, Shakespeare Sarani; G. of West Bengal Tourist Bureau, 3/2 Dalhousie Square; Calcutta Information Centre, 1/1 Jagdish Bose Rd.; A.A. of Eastern India, 13 Ballygunj Circular Rd.
CALICUT (Kozikhode), 527; Tourist B; Sea Queen Hotel; Guest Houses.
CAMBAY, 246; ancient port.
CAMPBELLPUR, 594; R, DB.
CANNANORE, 529; R, DBK; Government Tourist B.
CAPE COMORIN, 550; DB, CH, Cape Hotel; Tourist B; Kerala House.
CASTLE ROCK, 448; R; scenery.
CAUVERY FALLS, 491; DBK; Motor-buses from Maddur, 30 m; Hydro-electric station.
CAWNPORE, *see* Kanpur.
CEYLON, 702-42.
CHABAHIL, 667-8; Dhanju Chaitya.
CHAIBASA, 199; DBK.
CHAINPUR, 128; fort.
CHAKRADHARPUR, 199; R, DBK.
CHAKRATA, 367; DBK; Snow View Hotel.
CHALISGAON, 118; DB.
CHALNA, 699; new anchorage in Ganges delta S. of Khulna.
CHALSA, 687; International Red Cross Tibetan Refugee Centre.
CHAMAN, 572.
CHAMBA, 360; DB.
CHAMPANER, 289; fortress.
CHANDA, 194; DB, RH; ancient city (Bhadravati); Gond capital.
CHANDAUSI, 377; R, DB; Railway College.
CHANDERI, 222; RH; old city.
CHANDERNAGORE, 188; H.
CHANDIGARH, 348; DBK, RH; Union and State GHs, Holiday Home, YMCA; new capital of Punjab; Shared by Haryana; Mount View Hotel.
CHANDNI (for Asirgarh), 119.
CHANDOR, 118; fort; Chandravati.
CHANDPUR, 698; R, RH.
CHANDRAGIRI, 440; fort.
CHANGA MANGA (Lahore), 584; Wild Life Sanctuary.
CHANGU NARAYAN, 623, 669; Vaishnavite Temple; Manadeva Pillar; 5th-6th and 12th-13th century stone sculptures.
CHANNAPATNA, 491; Muslim tombs.
CHAPRA, 393; DBK.
CHARSADDA, 599; DBK.
CHATRAPUR, 424; DB.
CHATTISGARH, 197.

CHAUL, 108; RH; Portuguese forts.
CHERAT, 598; DB.
CHERRAPUNJI, 408; DBK; scenery.
CHERUTHURUTI, 524; RH; Kerala Arts Academy.
CHHATARPUR (for Khajuraho), 226; CH.
CHHINDWARA, 197; DBK, CH; coal-field.
CHICACOLE, 424; DB, RH.
CHIDAMBARAM, 535; DB; temples; Anamalai University; battle.
CHILIANWALA, 586; DB; battlefield.
CHILKA LAKE, 423; IB; Wildfowling; Fishing.
CHINGLEPUT, 514; R, DB; fort.
CHINSURA, 190; DB; Dutch settlement.
CHITALDRUG (Chitradurga), 485; DBK; fort.
CHITAWAN, 618, 627; Chitawan National Park and Wild Life Reserve.
CHITORGARH, 209-12; RR, DBK, IB; Rajput fortress, Jain towers; Taxis and buses from Udaipur.
CHITRAL, 597; DB; State Guest House; accessible by air, permit required.
CHITTAGONG, 699; Airport; R, CH; Hotels: Agrabad, Shah Jahan; Major seaport.
CHITTAGONG HILL TRACTS, 700.
CHITTAPUR, 453 (for Nagai, old city).
CHITTARANJAN (Locomotive Factory) 137.
CHITTOOR (Madras), 441; R, DBK; Haidar Ali monument.
CHOBAR, 636, 664, 677; Gorge; Jal Vinayak Temple; Adinath Temple.
CHONDI, 154; RH; Aundha temple.
CHOTA NAGPUR, 201.
CHUNAR, 127; RH; fort.
CLOSEPET, 491; DBK.
COCANADA, 425; RH; port.
COCHIN, 525; GH, Tourist B, Travellers B; Hotels: Casino, Malabar and many others; YMCA; YWCA; *see* also Ernakulam (524); Tourist Information Office, Willingdon Island.
COIMBATORE, 520; Airport; DB; Alankar Hotel.
COLOMBO, 707-9; Airport; Hotels: Grand Oriental (usually known as the G.O.H.); Bristol, York St.; Metropole, Queen St.; Galle Face, close to the sea, 1¼ m. from the landing place. Swimming-bath attached; the Grand at Mount Lavinia, 7 m. distant by rail from Colombo, is situated on a promontory overlooking the sea. Excellent fish tiffins on Sundays; sea bathing.
COLVA BEACH, 452; Goa resort.
COMILLA, 700; DBK.
COMORIN, CAPE, 463; Tourist B.
CONJEEVERAM *see* Kanchipuram, 509-514.
COOCH BEHAR, 405; R, DBK.
COONOOR, 521; R, DBK; scenery; Hotels: Ritz, Hampton; Boarding Houses: Belmont, Hanson Lodge, Clovelly, Fairway, Bakeleigh.
COORG, 496.
CORBETT NATIONAL PARK, 370; RH; Wild Life Sanctuary.
CORYGAUM, 435; battle.
COURTALLAM (Kuttalam), 551; RHS; Waterfalls; Health Resort.
COX'S BAZAR, 700; 2 RH, 3 motels; Coxy Hotel; Holiday resort with sea bathing.
CUDDALORE, 534; R, DB; Fort St David.
CUDDAPAH, 440; R, DBK.
CUMBUM, 483; DB, RH; lake.
CUTCH, *see* Kutch 272, 273.
CUTTACK, 413; R, DBK, CH.

D

DABHOI, 244; fort.
DABO, 561; battle.
DACCA, 696; Airport: Tejgaon; R; Hotels: Intercontinental, Purbani.
DAGSHAI, 349.
DALHOUSIE, 359; CH, RH, Tourist H; Hotels: Claire's, Grand View, Mount View, Dalhousie Club.
DAL LAKE (Kashmir), 606.
DALTONGANJ, 129, 201; DBK.
DAMAN (Portuguese), 240; 2 RH.
DAMAN, 619, 678; hill resort.
DAMBULLA, 729; cave temple.
DAMODAR VALLEY AUTHORITY, 64, 131, 137.
DAMOH, 222; DBK.
DANDELI, 485; Forest BS; Wild life sanctuary.
DARA (Kotah), 290; game sanctuary.
DARBHANGA, 392; DBK.
DARJEELING, 401; DB; Luxury Tourist L; Youth Hostels; Information Centres, Nehru Rd. and Robertson Rd.; Hotels: Mount Everest, with fine views; Windermere, Central.
DARYA KHAN, 588; R, DB.
DATIA, 231; RH.
DAULATABAD, 143; DB; old fortress (Deogiri).
DAURALA, 352; for Sardhana.
DEESA, 255; DB.
DEHRA DUN, 366; R, RR, DBK, CH; Railhead for Mussoorie (q.v.); White House Hotel.
DEHRI-ON-SON, 128; DBK, 2 RH.
DELHI, 317-44; Airport: Palam; R, RR; Hotels: Old Delhi: Maiden's, Grand, Swiss and Cecil; New Delhi: Airlines, Ashoka, Imperial, Intercontinental, Janpath, Claridge's, Ambassador, Marina, Ranjit. Tourist Information Office, 88 Janpath, New Delhi, (Tel. 48649).
DEOGARH (*via* Jakhlaun), 222; ancient temples.
DEOLALI, 115; Hotels: Coronation, Rugby.
DEOLI, 215; DBK.
DEO PATAN, 622, 623, 665; Bhavanesvara Temple.
DERA GHAZI KHAN, 588; DBK.
DERA ISMAIL KHAN, 588; DBK, 2 RH.
DEVA PATNAM, *see* Deo Patan.
DHANBAD, 132; R, DBK; coalfield.
DHANJU CHAITYA, *see* Chabahil.
DHAR, 204; DBK; old capital, 151.
DHARAMTAR, 442.
DHARAN, 615, 682; recruiting and pension paying depot of the British Brigade of Gurkhas.
DHARMAVARAM, 483; R.
DHARMPUR, 348; RH.

E

F

G

GUHYEŚVARI TEMPLE, 667.
GUJRANWALA, 584; R, DBK, 3 RH; birthplace of Ranjit Singh.
GUJRAT, 586; DBK; battlefield.
GULBARGA, 437; DB; fort.
GULMARG (Kashmir), 609; DB, Tourist Huts; Hotels: Nedous, Golf View, Highlands Park; Boarding houses; camping grounds.
GUNTAKAL, 439, 481; R.
GUNTUR, 483; R, DBK; capital Northern Circars.
GURDASPUR, 359; DBK; Trimmu Ghat battlefield.
GURGAON, 272; DBK, RH.
GWALIOR, 231-8; Airport; R; The rly. sta. is about 1½ m. from Lashkar (New Town); Hotels: Gujri Mahal; Usha Kiran Palace.
GYARASPUR, 221; caves, colossus.

H

HAFLONG, 411; H.
HALEBID, 487; Travellers' B; old capital; temples; Jain Bastis.
HALEJI, 559; DB; Lake near Karachi.
HAMBANTOTA, 425; RH; for Tissamaharama, old city.
HAMIRPUR, 226; DBK, RH.
HAMPI (Vijayanagar), 478-80; Restaurant; DBK at Kamalapuram; old capital.
HANAMKONDA, 463; DB; temple.
HANNA, (Quetta), 571; 2RHS; Tourist Resort, Lake
HANSI, 363; DB; fort.
HARAPPA (*via* Montgomery), 565; prehistoric city; Museum.
HARDA, 120; DB.
HARDOI, 371; R, DB.
HARDWAR, 365; RR, DBK; pilgrimages.
HARYANA, (state) 348, (cattle) 363.
HARIHAR, 485; R, DB; temple.
HARIPUR, 594; DBK; monument.
HARISIDDHI, 676.
HARNAI, 573; R, DB, RH; for Loralai.
HARPALPUR, 225; R; for Nowgong and Khajuraho.
HASSAN ABDAL, 593; DBK; Tourist B; Lalla Rookh's tomb.
HATHRAS, 378; R, RH; fort.
HAT SINJA, *see* Sinja.
HATTON, 714; R; Peak Hotel (for Adam's Peak).
HAVELIAN, 594; R; for Abbottabad.
HAZARIBAGH, 131; RH, Tourist L, DBK; National Park, Wild Life Sanctuary.
HELAMBU, *see* Helmu.
HINDUBAGH (Zhob Valley), 572; chrome.
HINDUPUR, 484; R; old temple at Lepakshi.
HINGOLI, 154; R.
HIRAKUD, 199; RH, CH, IB; Lake.
HISSAR, 363; R, DB; cattle ranch.
HITAURA, 615.
HOOGHLY, 189; early European settlements.
HOSDURGA ROAD, 485; for Marikanave Lake.
HOSHANGABAD, 216; DBK.
HOSPET (for Vijayanagar), 477; R, DB, RHS (air conditioned).
HOTGI, 437; R.
HOTI MARDAN (for Shahbazgarhi), 596; RH.
HOWRAH, 187.
HUBLI, 485; R, DB (3) K, RH.
HUNZA, 613.
HYANGJA, 690; International Red Cross Tibetan Refugee Centre.
HYDERABAD (Capital of Andra Pradesh), 454-63; Airport; RR, GH; YMCA; Tourist Information Bureau; Hotels: Blue Moon, Rock Castle, Aashiana, Percy's, Nagarjuna, Ritz.
HYDERABAD (Sind), 560; R, DBK; fort, battlefields; Hotels: Orient, Indus.

I

ICHANGU, 664; Narayan Temple; Bhagawati Temple.
IDAR, 254; DB.
IGAPTURI, 115; R, DB.
IMPHAL (Capital of Manipur State), 408; Airport; RH, CH, Tourist H.
INDORE, 206; R, DB; Hotels: Central, Lantern.
ISHURDI, 698; R, DB; for Pabna; Hardinge Bridge over Ganges.
ISLAMABAD (Kashmir), 607.
ISLAMABAD (capital of Pakistan), 590; Shahrazad Hotel.
ITARSI, 120, 216; R, DBK.

J

JABALPUR, 121; R, CH, DBS; Jackson's Hotel.
JACOBABAD, 569; DBK; old frontier post.
JAFFNA, 735; RH; Dutch fort.
JAGINDARNAGAR, 361; hydro-electric station.
JAIPUR, 266-70; Airport; CH, DBK; Hotels: Rambagh Palace, Jaimahal Palace, Rajasthan State, Kaiser-i-Hind, L.M.B; Tourist B; Tourist Information Office, Rajasthan State Hotel; Jaipur City Palace, Close to Amber, Purana Ghat, Galta, etc.
JAISALMER, 259; RH, DB.
JAITPUR, 226; RH; fort.
JAJPUR, 412; DBK; old capital of Orissa.
JAKHAL, 363.
JAKKO, 349.
JAKHLAUN, 222; RH; for Deogarh, temples.
JALALPUR, 587; probable Bucephala.
JALAMB, 193; DB.
JALARPET, 497; R.
JALGAON, 118; RR, DB (2) K; for Ajanta Caves, 38; Hotel Morako; Tourist Information Office, near Ry. Station.
JALNA, 153; DB (for Assaye, 30 m.); old city.
JALPAIGURI, 401; R, 2 DBK.
JAMALPUR, 391; R, RR.
JAMMU TAWI, 359; Airport; DBK, CH; Cosmo Hotel; Tourist Reception Centre; Art Gallery.
JAMNAGAR, 287; Airport; RR; Ashoka Hotel; Guest House.
JAMRUD, 600; Sikh border fort.

JAMSHEDPUR (Tatanagar), 200; Airport; steel works; GH, CH, IB, RR; Hotels: Tisco, Boulevard, Natraj.
JANAKPUR, 615, 629, 679-80; Mithala Royal Palace; Rama Temple; Janaki Temple.
JANGSHAHI, 559; R, DB; for Tatta.
JAORA, 208; DB.
JAUNPUR, 373; R, DBK, RH.
JAWALAKHEL, 671; Zoo; International Red Cross Tibetan Refugee Centre.
JESSORE, 699; DBK.
JETALSAR, 276; R.
JHALRAPATAN, 289; CH, DBK.
JHANSI, 223; R; DBK, 2 RH; hotel.
JHARSAGUDA, 199; R, RH.
JHELUM, 588; R, DBK, RH.
JHERRUCK (Thatta), 559; DB; Health Resort.
JHUSI, 127; ancient capital.
JIND, 354; DB.
JIRI, 687.
JODPHUR, 259-60; Airport; RR, CH, Tourist H; Rajasthan State Hotel; Umaid Bhawan Palace.
JOGESHWAR, 109; Brahman Caves.
JOG FALLS, 486.
JORHAT, 320; Airport.
JUBBULPORE *see* Jabalpur, 121.
JULLUNDUR, 355; R; DBK, RH; Jubilee Hotel; ancient city.
JUMLA, 634, 692, 693; Chandranath-Bhadranath Temples.
JUNAGADH, 276-8; Airport; CH, Tourist GH, RR, IB, DBK; Gir Forest Wild Life Sanctuary; Girnar Mountain, Asoka stone.
JUNBESI, 687; *gompa*; Thubtencholing Gompa.
JUTOGH, 349.
JWALAMUKHI, 361; Temple.

K

KACH (for Ziarat), 572; DBK (May to October.)
KADGA JOGINI TEMPLE, 670-1.
KAGHAN, 610; DBK; Naran Park Hotel; Tourist Information Office; Tourist Resort.
KAIRA, 247; RH.
KAITHAL, 347; RH; fort by lake.
KAKANI HILL RESORT, 619, 672.
KALABAGH, 595; R; Indus Bridge.
KALADI, 524; Birthplace and Ashram of Shri Shankaracharya.
KALANAUR, 359; RH; Akbar monument.
KALAR PATTAR, 689.
KALAWEWA, 730; great tank. Accommodation at Government Bungalow on the Bund by arrangement beforehand with the Divisional Irrigation Engineer.
KALGHAT (Narbada), 118; DBK, RH.
KALIMPONG, 400; DBK, Tourist LS, IB; Himalaya Hotel.
KALINJAR, 230; RH; fort.
KALKA, 348; R, DB; Lowrie's Hotel.
KALPI (Bundelkhand), 224; RH; old city and battlefield.
KALRI LAKE, 559; Tourist BS, Fishing.
KALSI, 366; DB; Asoka Rock edict.
KALUTARA, 723.
KALYAN, 114; R.
KAMPTI, 195; DBK.
KAMRUP (Assam), 407; Manas Wild Life Sanctuary.
KANARAK *see* Konarak.
KANAUJ, 378; DB; old capital, battle.
KANCHIPURAM, 509-14; DB, IB, Tourist B and Restaurant; Temples
KANDAPUR, 530; ancient port.
KANDLA, 255, 273; new seaport in Kutch.
KANDY, 712-14; old capital, Temple of the Tooth, beautiful surroundings; Hotels: Queen's, Suisse, facing the lake.
KANGRA, 360; DBK.
KANHA, 197; RHS, Cabins; National Park; Wild Life Sanctuary.
KANHERI, 109; Buddhist Caves.
KANPUR, 379; Airport; R, RR, DBK, 2 RH; Meghdoot Hotel.
KANTIPUR, *see* Kathmandu City.
KANYA KUMARI, 550; Cape Comorin.
KAPILAVASTU, *see* Tiraulakot.
KAPTAI, 700; Tourist BS; Lake.
KAPURTHALA, 355; DBK.
KARA (Currah), 380.
KARACHI, 556-7; Airport; R, DBK; Hotels: Intercontinental, Beach Luxury, Jabees, Metropole, Central, Palace, Midway (in airport), Tourist Inn and others.
KAREPALLI, 464; for Bhadrachellam Temple.
KARIKAL, 536.
KARJAT, 429; RR (2).
KARKAL, 530; colossus.
KARLI (Buddhist Cave), 113, 429; RH.
KARNAL, 346; DBK, RH; battle.
KARNALI, 618; National Park and Wild Life Reserve.
KARNAPHULI, 700; hydroelectric site with beautiful lake.
KARUR, 520; DB; fort, old Chera capital.
KARWAR, 485, 531; DB (3), K; Grand Hotel.
KARWITARAHWAN, 231; DB; temples.
KASARA, 114; R.
KASAULI, 348; DBK, RH; Alasia Hotel.
KASHMIR, 603-14.
KASIA, 393, *see* Kushinagar.
KASIMBAZAR, 395; DB at Berhampore.
KASUR, 566; RH; fort.
KATAS, 587; sacred pool.
KATHGODAM, 370; R, RR, DBK; Railway Hotel.
KATHIAWAR, 272.
KATHMANDU CITY, 392, 616, 636, 640-52.
KATIHAR, 391; R.
KATNI, 122; R, DBK, RH.
KATPADI, 497; R, for Vellore.
KAUNIA, 698; DB.
KAUSHAMBI (Kosam), 125; DB; ancient city; Pabhosa (2 m.), rock inscriptions.
KAZIPET (for Hanamkonda), 463; R, DB.
KAZIRANGA, 409; Wild Life Sanctuary; Tourist L.
KEAMARI, 557; port of Karachi.
KEDARNATH, 366; DB, IB; famous shrine.
KELANI VALLEY, 720.
KHAIRPUR, RH; 562.
KHAJUHA, 380; RH; battle.
KHAJURAHO, 227; CH, RH, Tourist BS; Chandela Hotel; temples and Museum.
KHALANGA, *see* Jumla
KHAMGAON, 193; DB.

KHANDAGIRI, 416; RH; Buddhist and Jain caves.
KHANDALA, 429; RH; scenery; Khandala Hotel.
KHANDWA, 119, 202; R, DBK.
KHANEWAL, 565; R, DB, RH.
KHARAGODA, 273; salt works.
KHARAGPUR, 411; R, DB.
KHEWRA (salt mines), 587; 3 RH.
KHOJAK PASS, 572
KHOKANA, 671.
KHOR, 209; old temples.
KHULNA, 699; Hotels: Shahin, Salim; River Port; Centre for the Sunderbans.
KHUMJUNG, 689; Sir Edmund Hillary School.
KHURDA ROAD, 419; R, DBK; for Bhubaneshwar.
KHUSHAB, 588; R, DB; ancient city.
KHUSHALGARH, 594; RH; Indus bridge.
KHUSHALNAGAR, 496; formerly Frozerpet.
KHYBER PASS, 599-602.
KINCHINJANGA PEAK, 402.
KIRKEE, 431; battle.
KIRTIPUR, 627, 653, 675-6; Darbar; Ganesh shrine; Cilandrya Chaitya.
KOBANG, 691; Devi Than Gompa.
KODAIKANAL, 545; CH, Travellers' B, RHS; Hotels: Carlton, Holiday Home.
KODARI, 615, 674.
KODARMA, 131; DB; for Hazaribagh.
KOHAT, 594; R, DBK, 3 RH; Tribal rifle factory.
KOHIMA, 408; War cemetery.
KOILPATTI, 547; DB; Jain statues.
KOLAR GOLDFIELDS, 492, 497; CH, DBK, Govt. GH, Oorgaum.
KOLHAPUR, 446; DBK, RH; Guest House; forts, Irwin Museum.
KONARAK, 422; Travellers' L, Tourist B, DB; Sun Temple; Museum.
KONDAPALLI, 465; RH; fortress.
KONKAN, 429.
KOPPAL, 477; forts.
KOSI RIVER SCHEME, 64.
KOSI TAPPU, 618; National Park and Wild Life Reserve.
KOT ADU, 569, 588.
KOTAGIRI, 524; DB, Travellers B.
KOTAH, 215, 290; R, CH, DBK; Navrang Hotel; Chambal gorge.
KOTDWARA (for Lansdowne), 368; DBK.
KOTRI, 560; R, DB.
KOTTAYAM, 527; DB; Tourist B; Ambassador Hotel.
KOVALAM-ON-SEA, 552; RH.
KOZHIKODE, *see* Calicut, 527.
KRISHNAGAR, 394; DB.
KRISHNAGIRI, 519; DB; fort.
KRISHNARAJA SAGAR, 495; Hotel.
KUCHI BANDAR (Cochin), 525.
KUDRA, 128; DB; for Shergarh fort, 16 m.
KULTI, 132; industrial centre.
KULU, 361; Travellers' L (Tourist Corporation); Hotels: Riverview, GH (Govt. operated, Katrain), Sunshine Orchards, GH; Govt. Tourist B, Log Huts, Tourist L, John Barnes GH (all in Manali); Reservations from Tourist Office, Kulu and Manali.
KUMBAKONAM, 537; R, DB; temple.
KUNDE, 689; Sir Edmund Hillary Hospital.
KUNDIAN, 588; R.
KURDUWADI, 437; R, DB.
KURNOOL, 481; DB; fortress on Tungabhadra R.
KURSEONG, 401; R, DB; Ravi Prasad Hotel.
KUSHINAGAR, 393; RH, IB, Travellers L; Buddhist pilgrimage centre and Relics.
KURUKSHETRA, 347; RH; Holy Places; University.
KUTCH, 272-3; CH.
KUTTALAM, 551, *see* Courtallam.

L

LADAKH, 609.
LAHAUL, 362.
LAHORE, 573-84; Airport; R; Hotels: Faletti's, Intercontinental, International, Waldorf, Ambassador, Park Luxury and others; YMCA, YWCA; Youth Hostel; A.A. Guest House; Information Centres: at Airport and in Egerton Road.
LAKKANDI, 476; temples.
LAKSAM, 698, 700; R, DB.
LALA MUSA, 586; R, DB, RH.
LALGOLA GHAT, 396; DB.
LALITA PATAN (Lalitpur), 652.
LALITPUR, 222; DBK, RH.
LALMANIRHAT, 698; R.
LANDI KOTAL, 602.
LANGTANG, 618, 683, 684-5; National Park and Wild Life Reserve; Kyangin Gompa; Yala Government Cheese Factory.
LANSDOWNE, 368; DBK, RH.
LARKANA, 568; DB.
LASALGAON, 118, for Chandor hill fort; 14 m.
LASHKAR (Gwalior), 237; Usha Kiran Palace Hotel.
LASWARI, 271; battle.
LAURIYA NANDANGARH, 392; Asoka lat.
LEH (Ladakh), 609.
LHAKSAR, 365; R.
LIMBDI, 274.
LINGAMPALLI, 454; RH; cave temples for Patancheru, 5 m. N.W.
LODHRAN, 563; R.
LO M'ANGTANG, 690, 692.
LONAVLA, 429; R; for Karli Cave; Hotels, Lonavla, Woodlands, Hamilton.
LONDA, 448; R.
LORALAI, 573; DBK.
LORI KUDAN, 681; Medieval Temple Site; Ashokan Stone Pillar.
LOTHAL, 251; Indus Civilisation Seaport.
LUCKNOW, 381-389; Airport; R, RR, Tourist B; YMCA; A.A. of Upper India Information Centre (Hazratgang); Hotels: Carlton, Gulmarg.
LUDHIANA, 355; R, DBK; Gulmar Hotel; battlefields.
LUMBINI, 393, 622, 627, 681; Buddha's birth shrine; Ashokan Pillar; Mahendra Pillar, Government RH; Information Centre.
LUMDING, 408; R, DB.
LYALLPUR, 585; R, DBK.

M

MACHCHEGAON, 676.
MADAMPE, 727; Coco-nut Research.

MADAN MAHAL, 121; remarkable Gond fort and temple (17 m. from Jabalpur).
MADDUR, 491; R; for Cauvery Falls, 30 m., temples.
MADRAS, 500-509; Central Station R; Egmore R, RR (10); Airport: Meenambakam; Hotels: Airlines, Claridges, Asoka, Connemara, Ambassador, in Mount Rd.; Oceanic, in san Thomé High Rd.; Victoria, Imperial, in Egmore; Queens, Romana, Dasaprakash (Indian style); Tourist H; YMCAs (3); Tourist Information Office: Govt. of India, 35 Mount Rd.; U.S.A., 158 Mount Rd.; U.K., Catholic Centre, Armenian St; A.A. of Southern India, 38A Mount Rd.
MADURA (Madurai), 545-7; R, RR (11), DBK, CH; Tourist B; Pandyan Hotel; temples; Jain caves; Periyar Wild Life Sanctuary.
MAHABALESHWAR, 442; Hotels: Frederick's, Race View, and others; By car from Poona in 4½ hrs.
MAHABALIPURAM, RH, IB, Travellers' L; (Seven Pagodas), 515-18; Pallava monolithic sculptures and cave temples.
MAHABAN, 294; ancient city.
MAHASU, 350.
MAHBUBNAGAR, 482; R, DBK, RH.
MAHÉ, 528.
MAHENDRAGIRI HILL, 424; temples, pillar.
MAHENDRA TAL, *see* Rara Lake.
MAHENDRUGHAT, 392; Ganges ferry.
MAHESHWAR, 203; prehistoric site.
MAHOBA, 226; DBK, 2 RH; ancient city.
MAHULI, 446; temples.
MAINAMATI, 700; Buddhist site.
MALABAR, 526.
MALAMPUZHA, 520; Tourist B; Lake.
MALAPPURAM (Moplah centre), 527.
MALAVLI, 429; RH; for Karli and Bhaja Caves.
MALDA, 398 (for English Bazar, Gaur and Pandua); Museum.
MALENCHIGAON, 684.
MALER KOTLA, 355; DB.
MALKAPUR, 193; DBK; for Buldana, 28 m.
MALKHER ROAD, 453; for Malkhed, Chalukyan capital.
MALOT, 587; fort, 20 m. from Pind Dadan Khan.
MALPÉ, 530.
MALVALLI, 491; DB; battle.
MAMALLAPURAM, 515; Mahabalipuram.
MANAAR, 728; RH; Dutch fort.
MANALI, 361; *see* Kulu.
MANAMADURAI, 552.
MANANTODDY (Wynaad), 529; DB.
MANAS, 407; Forest B; Camping Sites; Wild Life Sanctuary.
MANCHHAR LAKE, 566, *via* Bubak Rd.
MANDAPAM, 552; R, RH.
MANDASOR, 208; DB; ancient city, pillars.
MANDHATA (Omkarji), 202; ancient temples, *via* Mortakka, 6 m.
MANDI, 361; DBK.
MANDLA, 196; DBK; old Gond capital.
MANDOR, 261; old capital of Jodphur.
MANDU, 204; 2 RH; Modern Tourist Bungalows; old capital of Malwa.
MANDVI, 272; port of Kutch.
MANGALORE, 530; R, RR, DBK, RH; Moti Mahal Hotel.
MANGI, 572.
MANGLA, 589; RH, TBS; Dam and Lake.
MANICKGARH, 464; Gond fortress.
MANIKPUR, 122; RH.
MANIPUR ROAD (for Imphal), 408, R, RH.
MANKIALA, 589; stupas.
MANIYACHI, 550; R.
MANMAD, 118, 143; R, RR, DB (2) K; for Ankai fort (3200 feet) and caves.
MARDAN, 596; DB.
MARGHERITA, 409; DB; colliery.
MARIANI, 409; R, DB.
MARI INDUS, 595; R; Indus Bridge.
MARMAGAO, 449; Mormugao.
MARPHA, 691.
MARTAND (Kashmir), 608; old city and temple.
MARWAR JUNCTION, 258; R, DB.
MASHOBRA, 350.
MASKI, *see* Raichur, 438.
MASULIPATAM, 427; DB; English settlement.
MATALE, 729; cattle centre.
MATHERAN, 113, 428; resort from Bombay; Hotels: Central, Lord's.
MATHURA, *see* Muttra, 290.
MAU-RANIPUR, 225; DB, RH; fort.
MAYAVARAM, 536; R, DBK.
MEERUT, 351-2; RH; large military station.
MEGHALAYA, 406; Hill state within Assam.
MEGHAULI, 680.
MERCARA, 496; CH; GH, DB; fort.
MERTA, 261; battle.
METTUR, 519; Cauvery barrage.
METTUPALAIYAM, 521; R, RR, DB; Nilgiri Mountain Railway.
MHOW, 203; R, DBK; for Mandu and Bagh caves.
MIAN MIR, 582; DBK.
MIANI (Sind), 561; battle.
MICHNI KANDAO (Khyber Pass), 602; view over Afghanistan.
MIDNAPORE, 412; DBK.
MIHINTALE, 734; RH; stupas.
MINNERIYA, 736; ancient reservoir, also *via* Habarane.
MIRAJ, 446; R, DB.
MIRANPUR KATRA, 371; battle in Rohilla War.
MIRPUR KHAS, 561; R; stupa.
MIRZAPUR, 127; DBK, RH.
MOGHUL-SARAI, 127; R, DB (4), RH.
MOHANBARI, 409; Airport for Dibrugarh.
MOHENJODARO, 567; RH; prehistoric city, stupa, Museum.
MOKAMEH, 136; R, DB.
MOMINABAD, 154; *via* Purli Vainjath, 14 m.; Brahman and Jain caves.
MONGHYR, 391; DB; fort.
MONTGOMERY, 565; R, DBK, for Harappa.
MONTPEZIR CAVES (Brahman), 110; *via* Borivli.
MORADABAD, 368; R, RR, DBK, RH.
MORMUGAO, 449; Airport, Dabolim, *see* Goa.
MORTAKKA, 202; RH; for Omkarji.

MORVI, 288.
MOUNT ABU, 255; CH, DB, Tourist B; Temples, Golf; Museums; Gardens; Hotels: Mount, Palace, Jaipur Lake House.
MOUNT LAVINIA, 709; seaside; Grand Hotel.
MUDBIDRI, 530; Jain temple.
MUDKI, 364; DB; battle.
MUDUMALAI, 523; game reserve.
MUKTAGIRI, 193; Jain temples, 7 m. N. of Ellichpur.
MULTAN, 563; R, DB; fort; Shrines.
MUMBRA, 112; scenery.
MUNNAR, 520; DB; Tourist B; scenery.
MURI, 201; aluminium factory.
MURREE, 590; DBK, RH; Hotels: Cecil, Brightlands, Lockwood, Ritz, also Tourist Flats; Tourist Information Centre near GPO.
MURSHIDABAD, 395; DB at Berhampore, palace, gun.
MUSSOORIE, 367; RH; YMCA; Hotels: Savoy, Hakman's Grand, Roan Oke, Library Club and others.
MUTTRA (Mathura), 290-4; R, RR, DB, RH, IBS, Forest RH; ancient city sacred to Hindus; Kwality Hotel and others.
MUZAFFARABAD, 610; DBK; The headquarters of the Azad Kashmir Government.
MUZAFFARGARH, 588; DBK.
MUZAFFARPUR, 392; DBK.
MYMENSINGH, 698; R, DB; jute centre.
MYSORE CITY, 494; R, RR, RH, GH, DBK; Hotels: Metropole, Dasaprakash, Krishnarajasagar, Lalith Mahal.

N

NABADWIP, 394; place of pilgrimage.
NABHA, 354.
NADIA, 394; old city (Nabadwip).
NADIAD, 246; RH.
NAGAR, 613.
NAGARCOIL, 550; DBK; 8 m. from Cape Comorin.
NAGARJUNG, 664, 672; Royal Forest and Game Sanctuary.
NAGARJUNAKONDA, 483; Buddhist Relics; Museum; Dam Project.
NAGARKOT, 619, 677-8; Hill Resort.
NAGDA, 289; on Chambal river.
NAGINA, 368; DBK; ebony work.
NAGORE, 540; old Dutch settlement.
NAGPUR, 194; R, RR, DB; Hotels: Mount, Palace, Empire.
NAINI JUNCTION, 123; R; for Allahabad.
NAINI TAL, 370; RH; Hotels: Belvedere, Swiss, Grand, Royal, Waldorf, etc.
NAINPUR, 196; R, DBK.
NAJIBABAD, 368; R, DBK.
NALA, 673-4; Bagawati Temple; Avalokiteśvara Temple.
NALANDA (Bihar), 136; RH; ancient monastery, Museum (late Gupta).
NALANDA (Ceylon), 729; RH; fortress.
NALATIGIRI, 413; RH; *via* Jagatpur Junction, Buddhist caves.
NAMCHE BAZAAR, 685, 688, 689.
NANDANA, 587; old city.
NANDER, 154; R, DB; Sikh Gurudwara.
NANDIDRUG, 484; fortress; Cubbon Bungalow Hotel.
NANDYAL, 482; 2 RH.
NANGAL *see* Bhakra-Nangal.
NANJANGUD, 496; temple.
NARAN (Kaghan Valley), 610; Navah Hotel; Information Office.
NARAYANGANJ, 696; DB; jute centre.
NARAYANI, 618; National Park and Wild Life Reserve.
NARNAUL, 272; battle in 1857.
NARORA, 369; Ganges barrage.
NARWAR, 238; fortress.
NASIK ROAD (5 m. to Nasik), 115-16; R, DB; (for Pandu Lena caves); Tramway to City; Greenview Hotel.
NASIRABAD, 215; DB.
NATHDWARA, 215.
NATHIAGALI, 591; GH, 3 RHS; Hotels: Pines, Valley View, New Green's.
NASIRABAD, 215; DB.
NAVSARI, 240; RH; Old Parsi Settlement.
NAWAKOT, 636.
NAYAKOT, *see* Nawakot.
NEGAPATAM, 540; R, RR (2); port.
NEGOMBO, 726; 2 RH; Old Dutch Settlements.
NELLORE, 427; DBK; fortress.
NERAL (for Matheran), 428; R.
NETARHAT, 201; DB, IB, RH; Youth Hostel.
NIGALI SAGAR, 627, 681; Ashokan Pillar.
NILGIRI HILLS, 522-23.
NIMACH, 208; R, DBK, for Khor Temples, 15 m.
NIRA, 441; for Lloyd Dam.
NOAKHALI, 700; DBK.
NOWGONG (Assam); 408, DB.
NOWGONG (Bundelkhand), 225; DBK, RH; 19 m. from Harpalpur, former British Cantonment; Dubela Palace, Lake, museum.
NOWSHERA, 596; DBK, RH; The George Hotel.
NUL SAROVAR, 274; bird sanctuary.
NUWARA ELIYA, 715; Hotels: The Grand, St Andrew's, Grosvenor, and others. Also Carlton, Torrington, and other Boarding Houses.

O

OLAVAKKOT, 524; DB; fort.
ONGOLE, 427; R, DB.
OOTACAMUND, 521-4; R, RR (3); Tourist B; Hotels: Savoy, Cecil, Modern Lodge, Dasaprakash, Fernhill, also several Boarding Houses.
ORAI, 224; R, DBK, RH.
ORCHHA, 225; fortress.
ORISSA, 412.
OSIAN, 261.
OSMANABAD, 437; Jain and Brahman caves.

P

PABBI, 598; RH; for Cherat, 23 m.
PACHMARHI, 120; CH, VIPGH, IB; Tourist Information Centre; Pachmarhi Block Hotel; Boarding Houses.
PADMANABHAPURAM, 552, palace.

PAHALGAM, 608; DB, Tourist huts Camping Ground; Hotels: Kashmir Khalsa, Pahalgam, Mount View and others.
PAHARPUR, 698; Buddhist remains.
PAHUR, 138; 2 RH; on Ajanta route.
PAISI, 687; 3rd century B.C. archaeological site.
PAITHAN, 153; DB; Andhra capital.
PAK PATTAN, 565; DB; for Suleimanke barrage, 10 m.
PALAMCOTTA, 550; DB; Mission centre.
PALAMPET, 463; lake, temples.
PALAMPUR (Kangra), 361; DBK; Brahman temples.
PALANPUR (Rajputana), 255; R, DB.
PALEZAGHAT, Ganges ferry to Dighagat.
PALGHAT, 524; DBK.
PALITANA, 275; Guest Houses; for Satrunjaya Mountain, Jain temples.
PALNI, 544 DBK; temple.
PALWAL, 298.
PAMBAN, 552; viaduct to Rameswaram Island.
PANCHET, 137; Dam.
PANCHGANI, 442; Hotels; Boarding houses.
PANDHARPUR, 437; DB; temple.
PANDU, 407; R; Brahmaputra Ferry, Motor Service to Shillong.
PANDU LENA, 116; Hinayana Buddhist caves.
PANDUA (Hooghly), 137; battle, monument.
PANDUA (Malda), 399; IB; old city.
PANHALA, 447; old fortress.
PANIPAT, 345; DBK, 2 RH; three battles.
PANJIM, *see* Goa.
PANNAUTI, 636, 674; Indrésvara Temple; Brahmani Temple.
PANTNAGAR, 370; Airport (seasonal) for Naini Tal; Agricultural University.
PANYAM, 482; DB; for Banganapalle.
PARACHINAR (Kurram Valley), 595; DB, Tourist Cottages.
PARASNATH, 131; RH; Jain temples.
PARBATIPUR, 698; R, DB.
PARTABGARH, 371; R, DBK, RH.
PASHUPATINATH, 636, 638, 665-7; Shiva Temple.
PATAN, *see* Lalitpur.
PATAN (Anhilwara), 255; ancient capital.
PATAN SOMNATH, 283; RH; ancient temple.
PATANCHERU, 454; DB; colossal Jain statues.
PATHANKOT, 359; R, RR, DBK, RH, Tourist B; fort.
PATIALA, 353; DBK; Baradari Guest House; Greens Hotel.
PATNA, 133-6; R, DB, CH; ancient Pataliputra, Museum; Hotels: Republic, Natraj, Palace.
PATTADAKAL, 475; *via* Badami, 10 m.; Brahman and Jain temples.
PENUKONDA, 483-4; DB; near Anantapur, fort.
PERADENIYA, 711; small RH; botanical garden and University.
PERAMBUR, Carriage Factory, 502.
PERIYAR, 527; GH; Wild Life Sanctuary, lake, scenery; Hotels: Aranya, Nivas.
PESHAWAR, 598; R, DBK; Hotels: Dean's International, Habib.
PHARPING, 653, 677; Shekhu Narayan Temple; Vajra Yogini Temple; Dakshin Kali Temple.
PHILLAUR, 355; RH; fort.
PHULERA, 266; R.
PILIBHIT, 369; R, DBK, RH.
PIND DADAN KHAN, 587; DB.
PIPARIYA, 120; DB; for Pachmarhi.
PIPRAWA, 393; stupa.
PLASSEY, 394; RH; battle monument.
PODANUR, 544; R, RR (2).
POKHARA, 616, 617, 678-9, 690; Phewa Tal; Varahi Temple; Fadke Waterfall, Mahendra Gupha; Lake District.
POLLACHI, 544; DB; for Anamalai Hills.
POLLIBETTA, 496.
POLLILORE, 513; battle.
POLONNARURAWA, 736; RH; ancient city, dagobas.
PONDICHERRY, 533; DB; Former capital of French India; Ashram of of Aurobindo Ghose; Grand Hôtel de l'Europe, Rue Suffren.
PONMUDI, 552; Hill Station.
PONNANI, 527; Moplahs.
PONNERI, 427; for Pulicat, Dutch Settlement, 10 m.
POONA, 113, 432-6; R; Hotels: Wellesley, Poona, Amir, Gulmohr, Ritz.
PORBANDAR, 286; DBK; Guest House; port, ancient city.
PORTO NOVO, 534; battle.
PUDUKOTTAI, 540; DBK; Museum.
PURI (Jagannath), 419; DB, CH, Tourist B; Brahman temples; S.E. Rly. Hotel.
PURLI VAIJNATH, 453; temple.
PURNA, 154; R; for Aundha temple.
PURNEA, 400; DBK.
PURULIA, 200; R, DBK.
PUSA, 392; botanical research.
PUSHKAR, 266; Tourist B; sacred lake, *see* Ajmer.

Q

QUETTA, 571; Airport; R, RR, CH; Tourist Information Centre, Room 30, Secretariat; Hotels: Chiltan, Lourdes, Grand.
QUILON, 551; R, DBK, GH; Tourist B; Neela Hotel; ancient city.

R

RAE BARELI, 371; R, DBK, RH; fort.
RAICHUR, 438; R, DB; fort, for Maski, 65 m. S.W.
RAIPUR, 198; R, DB.
RAIWIND, 566; R.
RAJAGRIHA (Rajgir), 136; CH, IBS, RR, Tourist B, Youth Hostel; ancient capital; Museum.
RAJAMUNDRY, 425; R; Godavari barrage.
RAJKOT, 287; DBK; Guest House.
RAJMAHAL, 390; DBK; old capital.
RAJPUR, 367; Hotels: Chapman's, Denis Dale, Ellenborough, Imperial, Carlton.
RAJPURA, 353; R, DB.
RAJSHAHI, 698; CH, DBK; University.
RAKWANA, 721; views.
RAMBODA, 716; RH; waterfalls.

RAMESWARAM, 552; fire temple.
RAMPUR (Rohilkhand), 368; Guest House; Aiwan-i-Shahi Hotel; Library.
RAMTEK, 196; DB; fort, temples.
RANAGHAT, 394, 695; R, DB.
RANAKPUR, 215; Jain temple.
RANCHI, 201; DBK, CH, IB; Tourist Information Centre; Hotels: Yavraj, Mount, Railway, Grand, etc.
ANGAMATI, 700; CH; Wilderness Hotel.
RANGANTHITTOO, 494; Wild Life Sanctuary; Heronry.
RANGIYA, 406; R.
RANGPUR, 698; DB.
RANIBENNUR, 485; RH.
RANIGANJ, 137; 3 DBK, RH; coalfields.
RANIKHET, 371; DBK, RH; Hotels: Norton, Moon, West View, and Boarding Houses.
RANIPET, 498; DB; for Arcot.
RARA LAKE, 692-3.
RARA, 618; National Park and Wild Life Reserve.
RATANPUR, 198; DB; fort, for Pali Temple, 13 m.
RATLAM, 208, 289; R, DB.
RATNAGIRI, 447.
RATNAPURA, 720; RH; scenery, gems.
RAUZA (Khuldabad), 144; DB, 2 RH; tomb of Aurangzeb, near Ellora, 2 m.
RAWALPINDI, 590; Airport; R, DBK, RH; Hotels: Intercontinental, Flashman's, Gaitmells, New Kamran; Information Centre, Club Annexe, The Mall.
RAXAUL, 392; (for Kathmandu).
RAYADRUG, 481; hill fort.
RAZMAK, 595.
RENIGUNTA, 440; R.
RETI, 563; R, RH (railway).
REWA, 122; DB; 31 m. from Satna; Highway Hotel.
REWARI, 271; R, DB; fort.
RISINGO, 686.
ROHILKHAND (Rohillas), 369.
ROHRI, 562; R, RH; near Sukkur, for Aror, 5 m. (ancient city).
ROHTAK, 363; DBK, RH.
ROHTAS (on Son R.), 128; ancient fort; RH on plateau.
ROHTAS (Jhelum), 589; DBK, RH; fortress.
ROORKEE, 365; DBK, RH; Polaris Motel; Engineering University.
ROURKELA, 199; Airport; GH, IB; Hindustan Steel Plant.
RUK, 569; R, DB.
RUMMIN DEI (Nepal), 393; stupa, Asoka lat; birthplace of Buddha.
RUPAR, 355; RH; Sutlej barrage.
RUPNATH, 122; Asoka Edict.
RUWANWELLA, 720; RH; fort.

S

SABARMATI (Gandhi's Ashram), 247.
SADRAS, 518; DB; Dutch fort.
SADRI, 258; Jain temple.
SAGAR ISLAND, 192; mouth of Hooghly.
SAGARMATHA, *see* Everest.
SAGARMATHA, 618; National Park and Wild Life Reserve.
SAHARANPUR, 353; R, DBK, RH.
SAHETH MAHETH, 372, *via* Balrampur; GH, RH, IB; ancient Sravasti.
SAHIBGANJ, 391; R, DB.
SAIDU SHARIF, *see* Swat, 596.
SAKRIGALI, 391; Ganges ferry.
SALEM JUNCTION, 519; R, RR (3); for Shevaroy Hills; Salem 3 m; Dwaraka Hotel.
SAMALKOT, 425; R, DB; for Cocanada.
SAMASATA, 563; R, RH.
SAMASTIPUR, 392; DBK.
SAMBALPUR, 199; DBK, CH, Dam.
SAMBHAR LAKE, 263; salt works.
SANCHI, 217-21; CH, DBK, RH, GH, Travellers' L; Buddhist monuments; Information Centre at Museum.
SANDAKPHU, 403; DB; Himalayan panorama.
SANGANER, 270; old city; Jain temples.
SANGRUR, 355; DB; Jind State.
SANKASYA, 378; IB; Stupas; Buddhist site.
SANTA CRUZ (Airport), 91, 109.
SANTAHAR, 698; R, DB.
SANTINIKETAN, 390, 397; Tagore University (Viswa Bharati), GH.
SARAGARHI POST, 595.
SARDHANA, 352; RH.
SARGODHA, 586; R, DBK.
SARISKA, 271; Wild Life Sanctuary.
SARNATH, 165; RH; stupas, Museum.
SASARAM, 128; DBK; tomb of Sher Shah.
SATARA, 443; DB (2), K; Hotel de Luxe; fort.
SATNA, 122; R, DB; for Rewah, 31 m.
SAUGOR, 222; DBK; fort.
SAWAI MADHUPUR, 290; R, RR, DB.
SECUNDERABAD, 462; R, RR; Hotels: Percy's, Ritz.
SEHORE, 217; DB.
SEHWAN, 566; DB.
SEONI, 197; DBK.
SERAMPORE, 187; former Danish Settlement; famous old Baptist Missionary Centre.
SERINGAPATAM (Sriranga Patnam); 492-4; DB (2) K, RH, Travellers B; fortress.
SEVAGRAM (Gandhi's Ashram), 194.
SHAHABAD, 438; R.
SHAHDARA (Lahore), 583; tomb of Jahangir.
SHAHJAHANPUR, 371; DBK, RH.
SHAHR-I-BAHLOL, 596; Buddhist monastery.
SHENCOTTAH, 551; R, DB; scenery.
SHERSHAH, 563; R, DB, Chenab bridge.
SHEVAROY HILLS, 519; scenery.
SHIKARPUR (Sind), 569; DB, 2 RH; covered bazar.
SHIKOHABAD, 378; R, DBK, RH.
SHILLONG, 407; DBK, Tourist B; Hotels: Pinewood, Peak.
SHIMOGA, 485; R, DBK; for Gersoppa Falls, 65 m.
SHIVPURI (Sipri), 238; CH, RH, DB; National Park; Wild Life Sanctuary; Shivpuri Hotel.
SHOLAPUR, 437; DB (4) K; fort, battle.
SHOLINGHUR, 500; battle.
SHORANUR, 524; R, DB.
SHORKOT ROAD, 586; R.
SIALKOT, 585; DBK; Mount View Hotel.
SIBI, 570; R, DB.

SIDHPUR, 255; DB; ancient temple.
SIGIRIYA, 730; RH; old capital fortress.
SIHOR, 275; DB; old capital.
SIHORA ROAD, 122 (for Rupnath and Bahuriband): Asoka Edict, Jain statue.
SIKANDRA, 310; Mausoleum of Akbar.
SIKKIM (Tours), 404-5.
SILCHAR (Surma Valley), 411; Airport; DB; Tea-garden centre.
SILGHAT, 408; DB; on Brahmaputra R.
SILIGURI, 400; R, DBK; for Darjeeling Railway.
SIMLA, 349; CH, RH; Capital of Himachal Pradesh; Hotels: Oberoi Cecil, Oberoi Clarkes, Samrat, Lord's Grey; YMCA Holiday Home.
SIND, 556.
SIND VALLEY (Kashmir), 608
SINGARENI, 464; 2 RH; coal-mines.
SINJA, 692, 693; Medieval fort; Tripura Sundari Temple.
SIRAJGANJ, 698; DB; Brahmaputra ferry.
SIRHIND, 354; ancient city.
SIRPUR, 464; Gond capital.
SIRSA, 363; R, DBK; ancient city.
SIRUR, 435; DB; former cantonment.
SITAPUR, 370; DBK; sugar industry.
SIVASAMUDRAM, 491; RH, IB; Falls.
SKARDU (Baltistan), 613; Airport; GHS.
SOHNA, 272; hot spring.
SOLON, 349; DBK; Hotel.
SOMNATH (see Veraval), 284; GH; ancient temple.
SOMNATHPUR (Mysore), 491; old temples.
SONEPAT, 344; ancient site.
SONEPORE, 392.
SONGADH, 275; for Valabhipur, 12 m.
SOPARA, 112; *via* Bassein Rd., ancient port.
SPEZAND (for Nushki), 571
SRAVANA BELGOLA, 488; ancient town, Jain colossus.
SRAVASTI (*see* Saheth-Maheth), 372.
SRINAGAR (Kashmir), 605; Airport; Hotels: Oberoi Palace, Nedous, Badshah, Park, Mazda, Lala Rookh; The Govt. of India and Kashmir State Tourist Offices are on the Bund, close to the Srinagar Club.
SRINGERI, 486; Chenna Kesava Temple, Math, Pilgrimage Centre.
SRIRANGA PATNAM, 492, *see* Seringapatam.
SRISAILAM, 482; temple.
SUKKUR, 568; R, DB, 2 RH; Indus bridge, barrage.
SUKLA PHANTA, 618; National Park and Wild Life Reserve.
SULEMANKE, 565; Sutlej barrage.
SULTANPUR (Kulu), 361.
SULTANPUR (Oudh), 371; DBK, RH.
SULTAN'S BATTERY (Wynaad), 529; Tourist B.
SUNDERBANS, 699; tidal forest, Wild Life Sanctuary.
SURAT, 241-3; R, DB (4) K; at Nanpura on Tapti.
SURIVAYA, 223; fortress and ruined temples.
SURMA VALLEY, 701.
SVAYAMBUNATH, 637, 662-3.
SWAT (N.-W.F.P.), 596; capital Siadu Sharif; Hotels: Park (Mingora), Madyan and Pines (Madyan), Falaksar (Kalam), State (Saidu Shaarf).
SYLHET, 701; DB.

T

TADPATRI, 439; R, DB; Brahman temples.
TAKHT-I-BAHAI, 596; Buddhist monastery.
TALAIMANAR, 729; Ceylon terminus of ferry to India, 22 m.
TALAWAKELE, 715; RH; waterfalls; Tea Research.
TALBAHAT, 223; RH; for lake.
TALIKOTA, 472; battlefield near Tondihal village.
TAMLUK, 191; ancient port.
TANDUR, 453; R, RH; sport.
TANGASSERI, 551.
TANJORE (Thanjavar), 537-40; R, RR (6); DB; IB, 2RHS, Tourist B; temple, Museum.
TANK, 595; 3 RH.
TANSA LAKE, 112.
TANUR, 527; DB; old mosque.
TARAKESWAR, 188; temple.
TARBELA, 594; GH; Dam Site.
TARKE GHYANG, 684.
TARN TARAN, 358; DB; Sikh shrine.
TATANAGAR, 200; R, RR, GH, DB; steel works.
TATTA, *see* Thatta.
TATOPANI, 691.
TAUNSA, 588; Barrage and extensive irrigation works.
TAXILA, 591; RR, RH, DB, Youth Hostel; world-famous ancient cities, Museum.
TELLICHERRY, 529; DBK; coffee export.
TENGBOCHE MONASTERY, 689.
TENKASI, 551; for Kuttalam.
TEZPUR, 408; Airport; DB, CH, RH; tea plantations.
THAIBO, 676.
THAL GHAT, 112; scenery.
THANA, 113; DB; early Portuguese Settlement; Diamond Jubilee Hotel.
THANESAR, 347; DB; for Kurukshetra.
THANJAVUR, *see* Tanjore, 537.
THATTA, 539; Tourist Cottages at Kotri; Ancient and famous Port; Mosques and tombs.
THEKKADY, 527; Wild Life Sanctuary.
TINDHARIA, 401; R, RH.
TINDIVANAM, 531; R, DBK; for Wandiwash, battle and Gingee fort.
TINNEVELLY, 550; R, DBK; temple.
TINSUKIA, 409; DB.
TIRAULAKOT, 627, 681; Ruined Sakya capital.
TIRHUT, 392.
TIRTH LAKI, 556; R; sport.
TIRUCHENDUR, 551; DB; temple.
TIRUCHIRAPALLI, 540-4; R, RR (12), DBK, Tourist B, Travellers' L; Hotels: Aristo, Ashby, Ashok Bhawan, Sangam; fort, temples.
TIRUKALIKUNDRAM, 518; temples.
TIRUPATI, 440; DB; temple; Sri Venkateswara University.
TIRUVANNAMALAI, 532; town of pilgrimage.

TIRUVARUR (Tanjore), 536; DB; temple.
TISSAMAHARAMA, 725; RH; old city.
TISTAMUKH GHAT, 698; ferry across Brahmaputra.
TITHAL, 240; seaside resort.
TONK, 290.
TOSHAM, 364; DB; ancient inscriptions.
TRAKSHINDU MONASTERY, 687.
TRANQUEBAR, 563; DB in Danish fort.
TRAVANCORE, 552.
TRIBHUVAN UNIVERSITY, 675.
TRICHINOPOLY, see Tiruchirapalli.
TRICHUR, 524; DBK, Tourist B; temple; Museum (reptiles).
TRIMALGIRI, 463.
TRIMBAK, 117; *via* Nasik, 18 m.; fort, temple, source of Godavari.
TRINCOMALEE, 738; RH; naval base.
TRIVANDRUM, 552; Airport; R, RR (9); DB; Hotels: Mascot, Magnet; Guest Houses.
TRIVELLORE, 441; DB; fort, Vishnu temple.
TUCHE, 690.
TUMKUR, 488; R, DBK.
TUNDLA, 378; R.
TUNGA BADRA, 480; Dam and Irrigation Works.
TUTICORIN, 550; R, RR, (1) DB; port; Metropolitan Hotel.

U

UDAIPUR, 212-15; Airport; CH, Tourist B, Travellers' L; Hotels: Lakshmi Vilas Palace, Lake Palace, Alka, State; Museum.
UDAYGIRI (Orissa), 414; RH at Khandagiri; caves and carvings.
UDAYAPUR, 222; Remarkable Temple (1059 A.D.).
UDGIR, 453; fort.
UDUMALPET, 544.
UJJAIN, 207; R, RR, DB; Grand Hotel; ancient capital, observatory.
UMARIA, 198; coal-field.
UMARKOT, 562; fort, birthplace of Akbar.
UNAO, 381; DBK, RH.
USKA BAZAR, 393 (for Piprawa); DB
UTKAL, 416; University.

V

VADGAON (Wargaon), 431; RH; battlefield.
VADNAGAR, 254; ancient city.
VADODARA (*see* Baroda), 245.
VAISALI, 392; RH, Tourist H, Youth Hostel; Ancient capital.
VAJRA YOGINI, *see* Kadga Jogini.
VALABHIPUR, 275; ancient city; Museum.
VARANASI, 155-68; see Benares.
VAYITTIRI (Wynaad), 529; RH (small).
VELDURTI, 481; DB; temple, 2 m.
VELLORE, 497; DBK; Carnatic capital, fort, old temple.
VENGURLA, 531; DB (3); Old Dutch and British Settlements.
VENUR, 530; colossus.
VERAVAL, 282; RH (Junagadh); ancient port and temples.
VIJAYADRUG, 109; Angria pirate stronghold.
VIJAYANAGAR, *see* Hampi, 477-80; DB; Hindu capital, temples.
VIJAYAPURI, 483; RH; Irrigation Project; Museum.
VIJAYAWADA (formerly Bezwada), 426; Airport; RR, R, GH, IB; Buddhist Shrines; Hotels: Durga Bhawan, Manorama, Welcome.
VIKARABAD, 453; R; resort.
VILLUPURAM, 532; R, RR (1), DB.
VIRAJENDRAPET, 496.
VIRAMGAM, 273; DB; sport.
VISAKHAPATNAM, 425; Airport; DB; port; University; Hindustan Shipyard; Hotels: Marina, Apsara, Sun n' Sand.
VIZAGAPATAM, *see* Visakhapatnam.
VIZIANAGRAM, 424; R; fort, for Ramatirtham (Buddhist site).
VRINDABAN, *see* Brindaban, 297.
VYASSOROVAR (Jaipur Road), 413.

W

WADHWAN, 274; R, DBK.
WADI, 438, 453; R.
WAH, 591, 594; Akbar's Garden.
WAI, 442; DB; temples, on Krishna R.
WALTAIR, 425; R, DB, CH; Andhra University.
WANDIWASH, 531; DB; fort and battlefield.
WARANGAL, 464; DBK; ancient capital, fortress.
WARDHA, 193; R, RR, DB; for Sevagram Ashram.
WARSAK, 599; dam and hydel scheme.
WATHAR, 441; R; for Mahableshwar.
WAZIRABAD, 585; R, DB (4) K, RH; Chenab bridge.
WELIGAMA, 724; RH; colossus.
WELLINGTON, 521.
WYNAAD, 529

Y

YALA, 740; game sanctuary.
YAPAHUWA, 728; ancient capital.
YEDANTHANGAL, 509; bird sanctuary.
YELAMBU, *see* Helmu.
YERCAUD, 519; scenery; By motor-bus from Salem; Hotels: Tipperary, Fair Lawns, also a boarding house.

Z

ZAFARABAD, 373; DB; (civil station of Jaunpur).
ZHOB VALLEY (from Quetta) 572; unspoiled beauty spots.
ZIARAT, 572; DBK; Tourist Rondavels, Youth Hostel; *via* Quetta.

INDEX

This is supplementary to the historical matter in the Introduction. It deals mainly with persons, while the Directory deals with places. The dates may show discrepancies, due partly to differences between authorities or Gazetteers, sometimes because of differences in calendars. It is thought better to give an approximate date rather than leave the reader to guess within the compass of a century.

Books on the Subcontinent from John Murray

Into India
John Keay

"A perceptive introduction to the country and its people."
The Times

Where Men and Mountains Meet
John Keay

The explorers of the Western Himalayas 1820-1875.

The Gilgit Game
John Keay

The explorers of the Western Himalayas 1865-1895.

The Road to India
John Prendergast

A guide to the overland routes to the East.

Family Web
Sarah Hobson

Life in a south Indian village.

On a Shoestring to Coorg
Dervla Murphy

An unconventional journey through southern India.

Where the Indus is Young
Dervla Murphy

A winter in Baltistan. "Altogether the most appallingly fascinating travel book I have ever read." Jan Morris, *The Times*

Return to the Naked Nagas
Christoph von Fürer-Haimendorf

A delightful mixture of personal experience and anthropological observation.

Books on the Subcontinent from John Murray (cont.)

Himalayan Traders
Christoph von Fürer-Haimendorf

Life among the Sherpas and other peoples of Highland Nepal.

Krishnamurti
Mary Lutyens

The years of awakening (1895-1929). "One of the strangest tales of the century." *The Spectator*

Agents in India: Allied Publishers Private Ltd; offices in New Delhi, Bombay, Calcutta, Madras.

Delhi 317

Darjeeling 401

Nepal 615

Jaipur 266

Agra 299